VERIFICATION AND VALIDATION IN SCIENTIFIC COMPUTING

Advances in scientific computing have made modeling and simulation an important part of the decision-making process in engineering, science, and public policy. This book provides a comprehensive and systematic development of the basic concepts, principles, and procedures for verification and validation of models and simulations. The emphasis is placed on models that are described by partial differential and integral equations and the simulations that result from their numerical solution. The methods described can be applied to a wide range of technical fields, such as the physical sciences, engineering, and technology, as well as to a wide range of applications in industry, environmental regulations and safety, product and plant safety, financial investing, and governmental regulations.

This book will be genuinely welcomed by researchers, practitioners, and decision-makers in a broad range of fields who seek to improve the credibility and reliability of simulation results. It will also be appropriate for either university courses or independent study.

WILLIAM L. OBERKAMPF has 39 years of experience in research and development in fluid dynamics, heat transfer, flight dynamics, and solid mechanics. He has worked in both computational and experimental areas, and taught 30 short courses in the field of verification and validation. He recently retired as a Distinguished Member of the Technical Staff at Sandia National Laboratories.

CHRISTOPHER J. ROY is an Associate Professor in the Aerospace and Ocean Engineering Department at Virginia Tech. After receiving his PhD from North Carolina State University in 1998, he spent five years working as a Senior Member of the Technical Staff at Sandia National Laboratories. He has published numerous articles on verification and validation in the area of computational fluid dynamics. In 2006, he received a Presidential Early Career Award for Scientists and Engineers for his work on verification and validation in computational science and engineering.

VERIFICATION AND VALIDATION IN SCIENTIFIC COMPUTING

WILLIAM L. OBERKAMPF
CHRISTOPHER J. ROY

CAMBRIDGE
UNIVERSITY PRESS

CAMBRIDGE
UNIVERSITY PRESS

University Printing House, Cambridge CB2 8BS, United Kingdom

Published in the United States of America by Cambridge University Press, New York

Cambridge University Press is part of the University of Cambridge.

It furthers the University's mission by disseminating knowledge in the pursuit of education, learning and research at the highest international levels of excellence.

www.cambridge.org
Information on this title: www.cambridge.org/9780521113601

First published 2010
Reprinted 2012

A catalogue record for this publication is available from the British Library

Library of Congress Cataloguing in Publication data
Oberkampf, William L., 1944–
Verification and validation in scientific computing / William L. Oberkampf, Christopher J. Roy.
p.   cm.
Includes index.
ISBN 978-0-521-11360-1 (hardback)
1. Science – Data processing.   2. Numerical calculations – Verification.   3. Computer programs – Validation.
4. Decision making – Mathematical models.   I. Roy, Christopher J.   II. Title.
Q183.9.O24   2010
502.85 – dc22   2010021488

ISBN 978-0-521-11360-1 Hardback

To our wives, Sandra and Rachel

Contents

         The color plates will be found between pages 370 and 371.

Preface

Modeling and simulation are used in a myriad of ways in business and government. The range covers science, engineering and technology, industry, environmental regulations and safety, product and plant safety, financial investing, design of military systems, governmental planning, and many more. In all of these activities models are built that are mental constructs of how we believe the activity functions and how it is influenced by events or surroundings. All models are abstractions of the real activity that are based on many different types of approximation. These models are then programmed for execution on a digital computer, and the computer produces a simulation result. The simulation result may have high fidelity to the actual activity of interest, or it may be complete nonsense. The question is: how can we tell which is which? This book deals with various technical and procedural tools that can be used to assess the fidelity of modeling and simulation aspects of scientific computing. Our focus is on physical processes and systems in a broad range of the natural sciences and engineering.

The tools discussed here are primarily focused on mathematical models that are represented by differential and/or integral equations. Many of these mathematical models occur in physics, chemistry, astronomy, Earth sciences, and engineering, but they also occur in other fields of modeling and simulation. The topics addressed in this book are all related to the principles involved in assessing the credibility of the models and the simulation results. We do not deal with the specific details of modeling the physical process or system of interest, but with assessment procedures relating to the fidelity of the models and simulations. These procedures are typically described by the terms *verification* and *validation*.

We present the state of the art in verification and validation of mathematical models and scientific computing simulations. Although we will discuss the terminology in detail, *verification* can simply be described as "solving the equations right" and *validation* as "solving the right equations." Verification and validation (V&V) are built on the concept of quantitative accuracy assessment. V&V do not answer the entire question of simulation credibility, but they are key contributors. V&V could be described as the processes that provide evidence of the correctness and/or accuracy of computational results. To measure correctness, one must have accurate benchmarks or reference values with which to compare. However, the majority of simulations of complex processes do not have a computable or measurable reference value. For these situations we must rely on numerical error estimation and estimation of the effects of all of the contributors to uncertainty in system responses. In verification, the primary benchmarks are highly accurate solutions to specific, although limited, mathematical models. In validation, the benchmarks are high-quality experimental measurements of system response quantities of interest. These experimental measurements, and the detailed information of the system being tested, should also have carefully estimated uncertainty in all of the quantities that are needed to perform a simulation of the experiment.

Mathematical models are built and programmed into software for the purpose of making predictions of system responses for cases where we do not have experimental data. We refer to this step as *prediction*. Since prediction is the usual goal of modeling and simulation, we discuss how accuracy assessment results from V&V activities enter into prediction uncertainty. We discuss methods for including the estimated numerical errors from the solution of the differential and/or integral equations into the prediction result. We review methods dealing with model input uncertainty and we present one approach for including estimated model uncertainty into the prediction result. The topic of how to incorporate the outcomes of V&V processes into prediction uncertainty is an active area of current research.

Because the field of V&V for models and simulations is in the early development stage, this book does not simply provide a prescriptive list of steps to be followed. The procedures and techniques presented will apply in the majority of cases, but there remain many open research issues. For example, there are times where we point out that some procedures may not be reliable, may simply not work, or may yield misleading results.

As the impact of modeling and simulation has rapidly increased during the last two decades, the interest in V&V has also increased. Although various techniques and procedures have been developed in V&V, the philosophical foundation of the field is *skepticism*. Stated differently, if the evidence for computer code correctness, numerical error estimation, and model accuracy assessment are not presented as part of a prediction, then the V&V perspective presumes these activities were not done and the results should be questioned. We feel this is the appropriate counter balance to commonly unsubstantiated claims of accuracy made by modeling and simulation. As humankind steadily moves from decision making primarily based on system testing to decision making based more heavily on modeling and simulation, increased prudence and caution are in order.

Acknowledgments

Although only two names appear on the cover of this book, we recognize that if other people had not been there for us, and many others had not helped, this book would have never been written. These people provided training and guidance, created opportunities, gave advice and encouragement, corrected us when we were wrong, and showed the way to improved understanding of the subject. Although there were many pivotal individuals early in our lives, here we only mention those who have contributed during the last decade when the idea for this book first came to mind.

Timothy Trucano, Frederic Blottner, Patrick Roache, Dominique Pelletier, Daniel Aeschlimam, and Luís Eça have been critical in generously providing technical insights for many years. We have benefited from their deep knowledge of verification and validation, as well as a number of other fields. Jon Helton and Scott Ferson have guided our way to an understanding of uncertainty quantification and how it is used in risk-informed decision making. They have also provided key ideas concerning how to connect quantitative validation results with uncertainty estimates in model predictions. Without these people entering our technical lives, we would not be where we are today in our understanding of the field.

Martin Pilch created opportunities and provided long-term funding support at Sandia National Laboratories, without which we would not have been able to help advance the state of the art in V&V. He, along with Paul Hommert, Walter Rutledge, and Basil Hassan at Sandia, understood that V&V and uncertainty quantification were critical to building credibility and confidence in modeling and simulation. They all recognized that both technical advancements and changes in the culture of people and organizations were needed so that more reliable and understandable information could be provided to project managers and decision makers.

Many colleagues provided technical and conceptual ideas, as well as help in working through analyses. Although we cannot list them all, we must mention Mathew Barone, Robert Croll, Sharon DeLand, Kathleen Diegert, Ravi Duggirala, John Henfling, Harold Iuzzolino, Jay Johnson, Cliff Joslyn, David Larson, Mary McWherter-Payne, Brian Rutherford, Gary Don Seidel, Kari Sentz, James Stewart, Laura Swiler, and Roger Tate. We have benefited from the outstanding technical editing support through the years from Rhonda Reinert and Cynthia Gruver. Help from students Dylan Wood, S. Pavan Veluri, and John Janeski in computations for examples and/or presentation of graphical results was vital.

Reviewers of the manuscript have provided invaluable constructive criticism, corrections, and suggestions for improvements. Edward Allen, Ryan Bond, James Carpenter, Anthony Giunta, Matthew Hopkins, Edward Luke, Chris Nelson, Martin Pilch, William Rider, and William Wood reviewed one or more chapters and helped immeasurably in improving the quality and correctness of the material. Special recognition must be given to Tim Trucano, Rob Easterling, Luís Eça, Patrick Knupp, and Frederick Blottner for commenting on and correcting several draft chapters, or in some cases, the entire manuscript. We take full responsibility for any errors or misconceptions still remaining.

We were blessed with encouragement and patience from our wives, Sandra and Rachel. They tolerated our long hours of work on this book for longer than we deserved.

1

Introduction

This chapter briefly sketches the historical beginnings of modeling and simulation (M&S). Although claiming the beginning of anything is simply a matter of convenience, we will start with the stunning invention of calculus. We then discuss how the steadily increasing performance and decreasing costs of computing have been another critical driver in advancing M&S. Contributors to the credibility of M&S are discussed, and the preliminary concepts of verification and validation are mentioned. We close the chapter with an outline of the book and suggest how the book might be used by students and professionals.

1.1 Historical and modern role of modeling and simulation

1.1.1 Historical role of modeling and simulation

For centuries, the primary method for designing an engineered system has been to improve the successful design of an existing system incrementally. During and after the system was built, it would be gradually tested in a number of ways. The first tests would usually be done during the building process in order to begin to understand the characteristics and responses of the new system. This new system was commonly a change in the old system's geometrical character, materials, fastening techniques, or assembly techniques, or a combination of all of these changes. If the system was intended to be used in some new environment such as a longer bridge span, a taller structure, or propelled at higher speeds, the system was always tested first in environments where the experience base already existed. Often, during the building and testing process, design or assembly weaknesses and flaws were discovered and modifications to the system were made. Sometimes a catastrophic failure of a monumental project would occur and the process would start over: occasionally after attending the funeral of the previous chief designer and his apprentices (DeCamp, 1995). In ancient times, chief designers understood the consequences of a major design failure; they had skin in the game.

After the invention of calculus by Newton and Leibniz around 1700, the mathematical modeling of physics slowly began to have an impact on concepts for the understanding of nature and the design of engineered systems. The second key ingredient to have an impact on mathematical physics was the invention of logarithms by John Napier about 1594 (Kirby *et al.*, 1956). A mathematical model is of little practical use until it is exercised, which today is referred to as obtaining a *simulation result*. Until the existence and use of logarithms, it was not practical to conduct simulations on a routine basis. Then, not long after the invention of logarithms, the slide rule was invented by William Oughtred. This device provided a mechanical method for adding and subtracting logarithms and enabling rapid multiplication and division of numbers. The slide rule and mechanical calculators revolutionized not only simulation, but also such fields as surveying, navigation, and astronomy. Even though by today's standards the combination of mathematical theory and computing machines would be called "Before Computers," it provided the opportunity for the beginning of massive changes in science, engineering, and technology.

Starting with the Industrial Revolution, roughly around 1800 in England, the impact of modeling and simulation on engineering and design began to grow rapidly. However, during the Industrial Revolution, M&S was always an adjunct to experimentation and testing of engineered systems, always playing a minor support role. The primary reason for this was that computations were typically done by hand on a slide rule or mechanical calculator. By the early 1960s, programmable digital computers began to appear in a wide number of industrial, academic, and governmental organizations. During this time period, the number of arithmetic calculations commonly done for a simulation grew from hundreds or thousands to millions of calculations. It would be reasonable to identify the 1960s as the beginning of widespread scientific computing. In this book, we restrict the term *scientific computing* to the numerical solution of models given by partial differential equations (PDEs) or integro-differential equations. During the 1960s, computer power reached the level where scientific computing began to have a significant effect on the design and decision making of engineered systems, particularly aerospace and military systems. It is appropriate to view scientific computing as a field within the broader topic of M&S, which today includes systems that would have, for example, fundamental involvement with human behavior, such as economic and investment modeling, and individual and social modeling.

There were a few important exceptions, such as nuclear weapons design in the US, where scientific computing began to significantly influence designs in the 1940s and 1950s. The initial impetus for building much faster computers was the Cold War between the US and the Soviet Union. (See Edwards, 1997 for a perspective of the early history of electronic computing and their influence.) M&S activities were primarily modeling activities in the sense that models were simplified until it was realistic to obtain simulation results in an acceptable time period so as to have an impact on the design of a system or research activity. Relative to today's standards, these were extremely simplified models because there was relatively minimal computing power. This in no way denigrates the M&S conducted during the 1940s or the century before. Indeed, one could convincingly argue that the M&S conducted before the 1960s was more creative and insightful than present day scientific computing because the modeler had to sort carefully through what was physically and mathematically important to decide what could be ignored. This took great understanding, skill, and experience regarding the physics involved in the system of interest.

One of the most stunning scientific computing articles to appear during the 1960s was "Computer Experiments in Fluid Dynamics" by Harlow and Fromm (1965). This article, probably more than any other, planted the seed that scientific computing should be thought of as the third pillar of science, along with theory and experiment. During the 1970s and 80s, many traditionalists strongly resisted this suggestion, but that resistance faded as the power of scientific computing became dominant in advancing science and engineering. It is now widely accepted that scientific computing does indeed provide the third pillar of science and engineering and that it has its own unique strengths and weaknesses.

From a historical perspective, it should be recognized that we are *only beginning* to build this third pillar. One could argue that the pillar of experiment and measurement has been built, tested, and continually refined since the beginning of the Italian Renaissance in the 1400s. One could also argue that this pillar has much earlier historical roots with the Mesopotamian, Egyptian, Babylonian, and Indus Valley civilizations. The pillar of theory, i.e., theoretical physics, has been built, tested, and refined since the late 1700s. Understanding the strengths and weaknesses of each of these pillars has not come without major controversies. For example, the importance of uncertainty estimation in experimental measurements, particularly the importance of using different measurement techniques, is well understood and documented. History has shown, even in modern times, the bitter and sometimes destructive debates that occur when there is a paradigm shift, e.g., the shift from Newtonian mechanics to relativistic mechanics. In a century or so, when present day human egos and organizational and national agendas have faded, science and engineering will admit that the pillar of scientific computing is just now beginning to be constructed. By this we mean that the weaknesses and failings of all the elements contributing to scientific computing are beginning to be better understood. More importantly, the weaknesses and failings are often simply ignored in the quest for publicity and grabbing media headlines. However, we must learn to balance this youthful enthusiasm and naiveté with the centuries of experience and errors encountered during the building of the pillars of experiment and theory.

1.1.2 Changing role of scientific computing in engineering

1.1.2.1 Changing role of scientific computing in design, performance and safety of engineering systems

The capability and impact of scientific computing has increased at an astounding pace. For example, scientific simulations that were published in research journals in the 1990s are now given as homework problems in graduate courses. In a similar vein, what was at the competitive leading edge in scientific computing applied to engineering system design in the 1990s is now common design practice in industry. The impact of scientific computing has also increased with regard to helping designers and project managers improve their decision making, as well as in the assessment of the safety and reliability of manufactured products and public works projects. During most of this scientific computing revolution, system design and development were based primarily on testing and experience in the operating environment of the system, while scientific computing was commonly a secondary contributor in both preliminary and final design. For example, if there was some type of system failure, malfunction, or manufacturing issue that could not be solved quickly by testing, scientific computing was frequently called on for assistance and insight. Another common mode for the use of scientific computing was to reduce the number of design-then-test-then-redesign iterations that were needed for a product to perform better than competing products or to meet reliability or safety requirements. Specialized mathematical models for components or features of components were commonly constructed to better understand specific performance issues, flaws, or sensitivities of the components. For example, models were made to study the effect of joint stiffness and damping on structural response modes. Similarly, specialized mathematical models were built so that certain impractical, expensive, or restricted tests could be eliminated. Some examples were tests of high-speed entry of a space probe into the atmosphere of another planet or the structural failure of a full-scale containment vessel of a nuclear power plant.

As scientific computing steadily moves from a supporting role to a leading role in engineering system design and evaluation, new terminology has been introduced. Terminology such as *virtual prototyping* and *virtual testing* is now being used in engineering development to describe scientific computing used in the evaluation and "testing" of new components and subsystems, and even entire systems. As is common in the marketing of anything new, there is a modicum of truth to this terminology. For relatively simple components, manufacturing processes, or low-consequence systems, such as many consumer products, virtual prototyping can greatly reduce the time to market of new products. However, for complex, high-performance systems, such as gas turbine engines, commercial and military aircraft, and rocket engines, these systems continue to go through a long and careful development process based on testing, modification, and retesting. For these complex systems it would be fair to say that scientific computing plays a supporting role.

The trend toward using scientific computing more substantially in engineering systems is driven by increased competition in many markets, particularly aircraft, automobiles, propulsion systems, military systems, and systems for the exploration for oil and gas deposits. The need to decrease the time and cost of bringing products to market is intense. For example, scientific computing is relied on to reduce the high cost and time required to test components, subsystems, and complete systems. In addition, scientific computing is used in the highly industrialized nations of the world, e.g., the US, European Union, and Japan, to improve automated manufacturing processes. The industrialized nations increasingly rely on scientific computing to improve their competitiveness against nations that have much lower labor costs.

The safety aspects of products or systems also represent an important, sometimes dominant, element of both scientific computing and testing. The potential legal and liability costs of hardware failures can be staggering to a company, the environment, or the public.

This is especially true in the litigious culture of the US. The engineering systems of interest are both existing or proposed systems that operate, for example, at design conditions, off-design conditions, misuse conditions, and failure-mode conditions in accident scenarios. In addition, after the terrorist attacks on September 11, 2001, scientific computing is now being used to analyze and improve the safety of a wide range of civil systems that may need to function in hostile environments.

Scientific computing is used in assessing the reliability, robustness, and safety systems in two rather different situations. The first situation, which is by far the most common, is to *supplement* test-based engineering; for example, to supplement crash worthiness testing of automobiles to meet federal safety regulations. In fact, crash worthiness has become so important to some customers that automobile manufactures now use this feature in marketing their products. The second situation is to depend almost entirely on scientific computing for reliability, robustness, and safety assessment of high-consequence systems that cannot be tested in fully representative environments and scenarios; for example, failure of a large-scale dam due to an earthquake, explosive failure of the containment building of a nuclear power plant, underground storage of nuclear waste, and a nuclear weapon in a transportation accident. These types of high-consequence system analyses attempt to predict events that very rarely, if ever, occur subject to the design and intent of the system. That is, scientific computing is used to assess the reliability, robustness, and safety of systems where little or no direct experimental data exists.

For these types of situation, the burden of credibility and confidence that is required of scientific computing is dramatically higher than when scientific computing supplements test-based engineering. However, at this relatively early stage in the development of scientific computing, the methodologies and techniques for attaining this high level of credibility are not well developed, nor well implemented in engineering and risk assessment practice. Major improvements need to be made in the transparency, understandability, and maturity of all of the elements of scientific computing so that risk-informed decision making can be improved. Stated differently, decision makers and stakeholders need to be informed of the limitations, weaknesses, and uncertainties of M&S, as well as the strengths. The needed improvements are not just technical, but also cultural.

1.1.2.2 Interaction of scientific computing and experimental investigations

Interactions of scientific computing and experimental investigations have traditionally been very much one-way; from experiments to scientific computing. For example, experimental measurements were made and then mathematical models of physics were formulated, or experimental measurements were used to assess the accuracy of a simulation result. Given the limited capabilities of scientific computing until recently, this was an appropriate relationship. With the dramatic improvements in computing capabilities, however, the relationship between scientific computing and experiment is in the midst of change, although the changes have been slow and sometimes painful. When viewed from a historical as well as human perspective, the slow rate of change is perhaps understandable. Building the third pillar of science and engineering is viewed by some with vested interests in the established pillars of theory and experiment as a competitor, or sometimes a threat for resources and prestige. Sometimes the building of the scientific computing pillar is simply ignored by those who believe in the validity and preeminence of the established pillars. This view could be summarized as "Stay out of my way and don't expect me to change the way that I have been conducting my research activities." This attitude seriously undermines and retards the growth of scientific computing and its positive impact on science, engineering, and technology.

The fields of computational fluid dynamics (CFD) and computational solid mechanics (CSM) have pioneered many of the theoretical, practical, and methodological developments in scientific computing. The relationship between experiment and scientific computing in each of these fields, however, has been quite different. In CSM, there has been a long term and consistent tradition of a constructive and symbiotic relationship. Because of the nature of the physics modeled, CSM is fundamentally and critically dependent on experimental results for the construction of the physics models being used. To give a simple example, suppose one is interested in predicting the linear elastic modes of a built-up structure, e.g., a structure that is constructed from a number of individual beams that are fastened together by bolts. A mathematical model is formulated for the elastic beams in the structure and the joints between the beams are simply modeled as torsional springs and dampers. The stiffness and damping of the joints are treated as calibrated model parameters, along with the fluid dynamic and internal damping of the structure. The physical structure is built and then tested by excitation of many of the modes of the structure. Using the results of the experimental measurements, the stiffness and damping parameters in the mathematical model are optimized (calibrated) so that the results of the model best match the measurements of the experiment. It is seen in this example that the computational model could not be completed, in a practical way, without the experimental testing.

The relationship between experiment and CFD has not always been as collegial. Very early in the development of CFD, an article was published entitled "Computers vs. Wind Tunnels" (Chapman *et al.*, 1975). This article by influential leaders in CFD set a very negative and competitive tone early on in the relationship. One could certainly argue that the authors of this article simply gave voice to the brash claims of some CFD practitioners in the 1970s and 80s, such as "Wind tunnels will be used to store the output from CFD simulations." These attitudes often set a competitive and frequently adversarial relationship between experimentalists and CFD practitioners, which has led to a lack of cooperation between the two groups. Where cooperation has occurred, it seems as often as not to have been due to small research teams forming voluntarily or in industrial settings where engineering project needs were paramount. There were several early researchers and technology leaders who properly recognized that such competition does not best serve the interests of either CFD practitioners or experimentalists (Bradley, 1988; Marvin, 1988; Neumann, 1990; Mehta, 1991; Dwoyer, 1992; Oberkampf and Aeschliman, 1992; Ashill, 1993; Lynch *et al.*, 1993; Cosner, 1994; Oberkampf, 1994).

As will be discussed at length in this book, the most efficient and rapid progress in scientific computing and experiment is obtained through a synergistic and cooperative environment. Although this may seem obvious to proponents in this viewpoint, there have been, and will remain, human and organizational attitudes that will work against this type of environment. There will also be practical issues that will hinder progress in both simulation and experiment. Here, we mention two examples of practical difficulties: one related to simulation and one related to experiment.

It is a commonly held view among scientific computing practitioners that comparison of computational results and experimental results, commonly referred to as the *validation* step, can be accomplished through comparison to existing data. These data are normally documented in corporate or institute reports, conference papers, and archival journal articles. Our experience, and that of many others, has shown that this approach is commonly less quantitative and precise than desired. Almost invariably, critical details are missing from published data, particularly for journal articles where discussion is limited in the interest of reducing article length. When important details, such as precise boundary conditions and initial conditions, are missing, the scientific computing practitioner commonly uses this lack of knowledge as freedom to adjust unknown quantities to obtain the best agreement with experimental data. That is, the comparison of computational results with experimental data begins to take on the character of a *calibration* of a model, as opposed to the evaluation of the predictive accuracy of the model. Many scientific computing practitioners will argue that this is unavoidable. We disagree. Although this calibration mentality is prevalent, an alternative methodology can be used which directly addresses the uncertainties in the simulation.

An important practical difficulty for experimentalists, particularly in the US, is that, with the rapid increase in the visibility and importance of simulation, many funding sources for experimental activities have evaporated. In addition, the attitude of many funding sources, both governmental and industrial, is that simulation will provide all of the important breakthroughs in research and technology, *not* experimental activities. This attitude over the last two decades has produced a decrease in the number of experimental research projects, including funding for graduate students, and a dramatic decrease in the number of experimental facilities. Also, with restricted funding for experimental activities, there is less research into the development of new experimental diagnostic techniques. We believe this has had an unintended detrimental effect on the growth of simulation. That is, with less high-quality experimental data available for validation activities, the ability to critically assess our computational results will decrease, or worse, we will have a false sense of confidence in our simulations. For example, major efforts are being initiated in multi-scale and multi-physics modeling. This type of modeling commonly bridges at least two spatial scales. Spatial scales are usually divided into the macro-scale (e.g., meter scale), the meso-scale (e.g., millimeter scale), the micro-scale (e.g., the micrometer scale), and the nano-scale (e.g., nanometer scale). The question that arises in mathematical model building or validation is: what new diagnostic techniques must be developed to obtain experimental data at multiple scales, particularly the micro- and nano-scales?

1.1.3 Changing role of scientific computing in various fields of science

Beginning around the 1960s, scientific computing has had an ever-increasing impact on a wide number of fields in science. The first that should be mentioned is computational physics. Although there is significant overlap between computational physics and computational engineering, there are certain areas of physics that are now dominated by simulation. Some examples are nuclear physics, solid state physics, quantum mechanics, high energy/particle physics, condensed matter physics, and astrophysics.

A second major area where simulation has become a major factor is environmental science. Some of the environmental areas where simulation is having a dominant impact are atmospheric science, ecology, oceanography, hydrology, and environmental assessment. Atmospheric science has received worldwide attention with the debate over global warming. Environmental assessment, particularly when it deals with long-term, underground storage of nuclear waste, has also achieved very high visibility. The predictions in fields such as global warming and underground storage of nuclear waste are extremely challenging because large uncertainties are present, and because the prediction time scales are on the order of tens of centuries. The accuracy of these predictions cannot be confirmed or falsified for many generations. Because of the widespread, potentially catastrophic effects studied in environmental science, the credibility of computational results is being scrutinized far more closely than in the past. Computational results can affect public policy, the well-being of entire industries, and the determination of legal liability in the event of loss of life or environmental damage. With this major level of impact of computational results, the credibility and uncertainty quantification in these areas must be greatly improved and standardized. If this is not done, hubris and the political and personal agendas of the participants will take precedence.

1.2 Credibility of scientific computing

1.2.1 Computer speed and maturity of scientific computing

The speed of computers over the last 50 years has consistently increased at a rate that can only be described as *stunning*. Figure 1.1 shows the increase in computing speed of the fastest computer in the world, the 500th fastest computer, and the sum of computing speed of the 500 fastest computers in the world as of November 2008. As can be seen, the speed of the fastest computer has consistently increased by roughly a factor of 10 every four years. Over the last few decades, many predicted that this rate of increase could not be maintained because of physics and technology constraints. However, the computer industry has creatively and consistently found ways around these hurdles and the steady increase in computing speed has been the real engine behind the increasing impact of computational simulation in science and engineering.

Measuring computer speed on the highest performance computers is done with a very carefully crafted set of rules, benchmark calculations, and performance measurements. Many people, particularly non-technically trained individuals, feel that computer speed

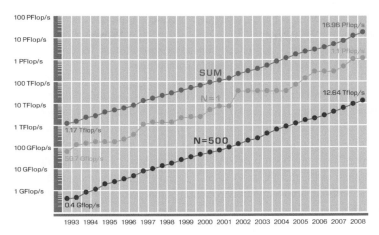

Figure 1.1 Computing speed of the 500 fastest computers in the world (Top500, 2008). See color plate section.

is directly related to maturity and impact of scientific computing. There is a relationship between computer speed and maturity and impact, but it is far from direct. Maturity of scientific computing clearly relates to issues such as credibility, trust, and reliability of the computational results. Impact of scientific computing relies directly on its trustworthiness, in addition to many other issues that depend on how the computational results are used. In industry, for example, some of the key perspectives are how scientific computing can reduce costs of product development, its ability to bring new products to market more quickly and improve profitability or market share, and the usability of results to improve decision making. In government, impact might be measured more in terms of how scientific computing improves risk assessment and the understanding of possible alternatives and unintended consequences. In academia, impact is measured in terms of new understanding and knowledge created from computational results.

In 1986, the US National Aeronautics and Space Administration (NASA) requested and funded a study conducted by the National Research Council to study the maturity and potential impact of CFD (NaRC, 1986). This study, chaired by Richard Bradley, was one of the first to examine broadly the field of CFD from a business and economic competitiveness perspective. They sent questionnaires to a wide range of individuals in industry and government to evaluate the maturity of CFD. Although they specifically examined CFD, we believe their high-level analysis is equally applicable to *any* field in scientific computing. In this study, the committee identified five stages of maturity of predictive capability. These stages, along with their descriptive characteristics, are:

- Stage 1: Developing enabling technology – scientific papers published, know-how developed.
- Stage 2: Demonstration and confidence building – limited pioneering applications, subject to surprise.
- Stage 3: Putting it all together – major commitment made, gradual evolution of capability.

- Stage 4: Learning to use effectively – changes the engineering process, value exceeds expectations, skilled user groups exist.
- Stage 5: Mature capability – dependable capability, cost effective for design applications, most analyses done without supporting experimental comparisons.

Using these descriptors for the various stages, the individuals ranked the maturity according to a matrix of elements. The matrix was formed on one side by increasing levels of complexity of the modeling approach to CFD, and on the other by increasing levels of complexity of engineering systems that would be of interest. A score of 0 meant that scientific papers have not been published and know-how has not been developed for that particular element in the matrix. A score of 5 meant that a mature capability existed – most analyses done without supporting experimental comparisons. What they found was, rather surprisingly, that depending on the model complexity and on the system complexity, the scores ranged from 0 to 5 over the matrix.

One would imagine that if the survey were conducted today, 20 years after the original survey, the maturity levels would be higher for essentially all of the elements in the matrix. However, there would still be a very wide range of scores in the matrix. Our point is that even within a well-developed field of scientific computing, such as CFD, the range of maturity varies greatly, depending on the modeling approach and the application of interest. Claims of high maturity in CFD for complex systems, whether from commercial software companies or any other organization, are, we believe, unfounded. Companies and agencies that sell programs primarily based on colorful graphics and flashy video animations have no skin in the game. We also claim that this is the case in essentially all fields of scientific computing.

1.2.2 Perspectives on credibility of scientific computing

People tend to think that their perspective on what is required for credibility or believability of an event or situation is similar to most other individuals. Broader experience, however, shows that this view is fundamentally mistaken. With regard to the present topic of scientific computing, there exists a wide range of perspectives regarding what is required for various individuals to say, "I believe this simulation is credible and I am comfortable making the needed decision." In human nature, a key factor in decision making is the heavier weighting on downside risk as opposed to upside gain (Tversky and Kahneman, 1992; Kahneman and Tversky, 2000); that is, a person's loss, pain, or embarrassment from a decision is weighed much more heavily than the expected gain. For example, when a decision must be made based on the results from a simulation, the individual's perspective is weighted more heavily toward "What are the personal consequences of a poor decision because of a deficient or misleading simulation?" as opposed to "What are the personal gains that may result from a successful simulation?" If there is little downside risk, however, individuals and organizations can more easily convince themselves of the strengths of a simulation than its weaknesses. When an analyst is conducting the simulation, they will normally work toward attaining *their* required level of confidence in the simulation, given the time and resources available. If they are working in a team environment, each member of the team will have to make their own value judgment concerning their contribution to the combined result.

If the computational results are to be submitted to an archival journal for publication, the individual(s) authoring the work will ask themselves a slightly more demanding question: "Will other people (editor, reviewers, readers) believe the results?" This is usually a more demanding test of credibility of the work than the judgment of most individuals. Within the group of editor, reviewers, and readers, there will certainly be a wide range of perspectives toward the credibility of the work presented. However, the final decision maker concerning credibility and whether the article is published is the editor. In this regard, several well-known journals, such as the ASME Journal of Fluids Engineering, and all of the AIAA journals, have been increasing the requirements for credibility of computational results.

If the computational results are to be used as an important element in the decision making regarding some type of engineering project, then the issue of credibility of the computational results becomes more important. For this situation, presume that the individual computational analysts have satisfied themselves as to the credibility of their results. The engineering project manager must assess the credibility of the computational results based on their own personal requirements for credibility. This judgment will involve not only the computational results themselves, but also any knowledge he/she might have concerning the individuals involved in the analysis. Personal knowledge of the individuals involved is a great advantage to the project manager. However, for large-scale projects, or projects that have contributions from individuals or teams from around the country or around the world, this type of information is very rare. To judge the credibility of the computational results, some of the questions the project manager might ask are: "Am I willing to bet the success of my project (my career or my company) on these results?" These kinds of perspectives of the project manager are rarely appreciated by all of the contributors to the project.

Certain projects are of such magnitude that the effects of the success or failure of the project, or decisions made on the project, have major consequences beyond the project itself. For this type of situation, we refer to these as *high-consequence systems*. Two examples of these situations and the types of decisions made are the following.

- NASA uses scientific computing as part of it day-to-day activities in preparation for each of its Space Shuttle launches, as well as the safety assessment of major systems during each Space Shuttle flight. Individual analysts through high-level managers commonly ask themselves: "Am I willing the bet the lives of the flight crew on the results of this analysis?"
- The US Nuclear Regulatory Commission and the Environmental Protection Agency use scientific computing for analyzing the safety of nuclear power reactors and the underground storage of nuclear waste. These analyses commonly deal with the immediate effects of a possible accident, as well as the effects on the environment for thousands of years. For these situations, analysts and managers commonly ask themselves: "Am I willing to bet the public's safety and catastrophic damage to the environment for possibly centuries to come based on the results of this analysis?"

High-consequence systems are not mentioned to dramatize the importance of scientific computing in decision making, but to point out that there is a very wide range of impact of scientific computing. Typically, scientists and engineers work in one or two technical fields, e.g., research or system design. Rarely do individuals, especially those involved in academic research, consider the wide range of impact that scientific computing is having on real systems.

1.2.3 How is credibility built in scientific computing?

By *credibility* of computational results we mean that the results of an analysis are worthy of belief or confidence. The fundamental elements that build credibility in computational results are (a) quality of the analysts conducting the work, (b) quality of the physics modeling, (c) verification and validation activities, and (d) uncertainty quantification and sensitivity analyses. We believe that all of these elements are necessary for credibility, and more importantly accuracy, but none is sufficient in itself. Our perspective in discussing these elements is that *scientific computing is a tool for generating information about some physical situation, process, or system.* This information could be used in a wide variety of ways, some of which were discussed in the previous section. The quality of the information depends on how it was developed, but the quality of the decisions made based on the information depends on many other factors. Two key factors are the user's depth of understanding of the information produced and the appropriateness of the information for its intended use. Although it is beyond the scope of this book to discuss how the information might be used, methods for clarifying how the information should be used and methods to reduce the possible misuse of the information will be discussed later in the text.

1.2.3.1 Quality of the analysts conducting the scientific computing

When we refer to *analysts*, we mean the group of individuals that: (a) construct the conceptual model for the problem of interest, (b) formulate the mathematical model, (c) choose the discretization and numerical solution algorithms, (d) program the software to compute the numerical solution, (e) compute the simulation on a digital computer, and (f) analyze and prepare the results from the simulation. On small-scale analyses of subsystems or components, or on research projects, a single individual may conduct all of these tasks. On any significantly sized effort, a team of individuals conducts all of these tasks.

The quality of the analysts encompasses their training, experience, sound technical judgment, and understanding of the needs of the customer of the computational information. Some have expressed the view that the quality of a computational effort should be entirely centered on the quality of the analysts involved. For example, it has been said, "I have such confidence in this analyst that whatever simulation he/she produces, I'll believe it." No one would argue against the extraordinary value added by the quality and experience of the analysts involved. However, many large projects and organizations have learned, often painfully, that they cannot completely depend on a few extraordinarily talented individuals for long-term success. Large organizations must develop and put into place business, technology, training, and management processes for all the elements that contribute to the quality and on-time delivery of their product. In addition, many modern large-scale projects will typically involve groups that are physically and culturally separated, often around the nation or around the world. For these situations, users of the computational information will have minimal personal knowledge of the individual contributors, their backgrounds, or value systems.

1.2.3.2 Quality of the physics modeling

By *quality of the physics modeling*, we mean the fidelity and comprehensiveness of physical detail embodied in the mathematical model representing the relevant physics taking place in the system of interest. These modeling decisions are made in the formulation of the conceptual and mathematical model of the system of interest. Two contrasting levels of physics model fidelity are (a) at the low end, fully empirical models that are entirely built on statistical fits of experimental data with no fundamental relationship to physics-based principles; and (b) at the high end, physics-based models that are reliant on PDEs or integro-differential equations that represent conservation of mass, momentum, and energy in the system. Comprehensiveness of the modeling refers to the number of different types of physics modeled in the system, the level of coupling of the various physical processes, and the extent of possible environments and scenarios that are considered for the system.

We are *not* saying that the highest possible level of quality of physics modeling should be used for every computational activity. Efficiency, cost effectiveness, and schedule should dictate the appropriate level of physics modeling to meet the information needs of the scientific computing customer. Stated differently, the analysts should understand the needs of the scientific computing customer and then decide on the simplest level of physics modeling fidelity that is needed to meet those needs. To accomplish this requires significant experience on the part of the analysts for the specific problem at hand, very clear communication with the customer of what they think they need, and how they intend to use the results of the computational effort. Quality of the physics modeling is a very problem-specific judgment. It is *not* one size fits all.

1.2.3.3 Verification and validation activities

Verification is the process of assessing software correctness and numerical accuracy of the solution to a given mathematical model. *Validation* is the process of assessing the physical accuracy of a mathematical model based on comparisons between computational results and experimental data. Verification and validation (V&V) are the primary processes for assessing and quantifying the accuracy of computational results. The perspective of V&V is distinctly on the side of skepticism, sometimes to the degree of being radical (Tetlock, 2005). In verification, the association or relationship of the simulation to the real world is *not* an issue. In validation, the relationship between the mathematical model and the real world (experimental data) *is* the issue. Blottner (1990) captured the essence of each in the compact expressions: "Verification is solving the equations right;" "Validation is solving the right equations." These expressions follow the similar definitions of Boehm (1981).

The pragmatic philosophy of V&V is fundamentally built on the concept of *accuracy assessment*. This may sound obvious, but in Chapter 2, Fundamental Concepts and Terminology, it will become clear that there are wide variations on the fundamental concepts of V&V. In our present context, it is clear how accuracy assessment is a necessary building block of "How is credibility built in scientific computing?" V&V do not answer the entire question of simulation credibility, but they are the key contributors. V&V could be described as processes that develop and present evidence of the accuracy of computational results. To measure accuracy, one must have accurate benchmarks or reference values. In verification, the primary benchmarks are highly accurate solutions to specific mathematical models. In validation, the benchmarks are high-quality experimental measurements. Given this perspective of V&V, it should be pointed out that a critical additional element is needed: estimation of accuracy when no benchmark is available.

The pivotal importance of V&V in the credibility of scientific computing was captured by Roache (2004) when he said

In an age of spreading pseudoscience and anti-rationalism, it behooves those of us who believe in the good of science and engineering to be above reproach whenever possible. Public confidence is further eroded with every error we make. Although many of society's problems can be solved with a simple change of values, major issues such as radioactive waste disposal and environmental modeling require technological solutions that necessarily involve computational physics. As Robert Laughlin noted in this magazine, "there is a serious danger of this power [of simulations] being misused, either by accident or through deliberate deception." Our intellectual and moral traditions will be served well by conscientious attention to verification of codes, verification of calculations, and validation, including the attention given to building new codes or modifying existing codes with specific features that enable these activities.

1.2.3.4 Uncertainty quantification and sensitivity analyses

Uncertainty quantification is the process of identifying, characterizing, and quantifying those factors in an analysis that could affect the accuracy of the computational results. Uncertainties can arise from many sources, but they are commonly addressed in three steps of the modeling and simulation process: (a) construction of the conceptual model, (b) formulation of the mathematical model, and (c) computation of the simulation results. Some common sources of uncertainty are in the assumptions or mathematical form of either the conceptual or mathematical model, the initial conditions or boundary conditions for the PDEs, and the parameters occurring in the mathematical model chosen. Using the computational model, these sources of uncertainty are propagated to uncertainties in the simulation results. By *propagated* we mean that the sources of uncertainty, wherever they originate, are mathematically mapped to the uncertainties in the simulation results. The primary responsibility for identifying, characterizing and quantifying the uncertainties in a simulation is the team of analysts involved in conjunction with the customer for the simulation results.

Sensitivity analysis is the process of determining how the simulation results, i.e., the outputs, depend on all of the factors that make up the model. These are usually referred to as *inputs* to the simulation, but one must recognize that sensitivity analysis also deals with the question of how outputs depend on assumptions, or mathematical models, in the analysis. Uncertainties due to assumptions or choice of mathematical models in an analysis are typically referred to as model form, or model structure, uncertainties. Uncertainty quantification and sensitivity analysis critically contribute to credibility by informing the user of the simulation results how uncertain the results are and what factors are the most important in uncertain results.

1.3 Outline and use of the book

1.3.1 Structure of the book

The book is structured into five parts. Part I: Fundamental concepts (Chapters 1–3) deals with the development of the foundational concepts of verification and validation (V&V), the meaning of V&V that has been used by different communities, fundamentals of modeling and simulation, and the six phases of computational simulation. Part II: Code verification (Chapters 4–6) deals with how code verification is closely related to software quality assurance, different methodological approaches to code verification, traditional methods of code verification, and the method of manufactured solutions. Part III: Solution verification (Chapters 7–9) covers fundamental concepts of solution verification, iterative convergence error, finite-element-based error estimation procedures, extrapolation-based error estimation procedures, and practical aspects of mesh refinement. Part IV: Model validation and prediction (Chapters 10–13) addresses the fundamental concepts of model validation, the design and execution of validation experiments, quantitative assessment of model accuracy using experimental data, and discusses the six steps of a nondeterministic model prediction. Part V: Planning, management, and implementation issues (Chapters 14–16) discusses planning and prioritization of modeling activities and V&V, maturity assessment of modeling and simulation, and finally, development and responsibilities of V&V and uncertainty quantification.

The book covers the fundamental issues of V&V as well as their practical aspects. The theoretical issues are discussed only in as far as they are needed to implement the practical procedures. V&V commonly deals with quality control concepts, procedures, and best practices, as opposed to mathematics and physics issues. Our emphasis is on how V&V activities can improve the quality of simulations and, as a result, the decisions based on those simulations. Since V&V is still a relatively new field of formal technology and practice, there are commonly various methods and divergent opinions on many of the topics discussed. This book does not cover every approach to a topic, but attempts to mention and reference most approaches. Typically, one or two approaches are discussed that have proven to be effective in certain situations. One of our goals is to provide readers with enough detail on a few methods so they can be used in practical applications of scientific computing. Strengths and weaknesses of methods are pointed out and cautions are given where methods should not be used. Most chapters discuss an example application of the principles discussed in the chapter. Some of the examples are continually developed throughout different chapters of the book as new concepts are introduced.

The field of V&V is not associated with specific application areas, such as physics, chemistry, or mechanical engineering. It can be applied to essentially any application domain where M&S is used, including modeling of human behavior and financial modeling. V&V is a fascinating mixture of computer science, numerical solution of PDEs, probability, statistics, and uncertainty estimation. Knowledge of the application domain clearly influences what V&V procedures might be used on a particular problem, but the application domain is not considered part of the field of V&V. It is presumed that the practitioners of the application domain bring the needed technical knowledge with them.

The book is written so that it can be used either as a textbook in a university semester course, or by professionals working in their discipline. The emphasis of the book is directed toward models that are represented by partial differential equations or integro-differential equations. Readers who are only interested in models that are represented by ordinary differential equations (ODEs) can use all of the fundamental principles discussed in the book, but many of the methods, particularly in code and solution verification, will not be applicable. Most parts of the book require some knowledge of probability and statistics. The book does not require that any particular computer software or programming language be used. To complete some of the examples, however, it is beneficial to have general purpose software packages, such as MATLAB or Mathematica. In addition, general-purpose software packages that solve PDEs would also be helpful for either completing some of the examples or for the reader to generate his/her own example problems in their application domain.

1.3.2 Use of the book in undergraduate and graduate courses

For senior-level undergraduates to get the most out of the book, they should have completed courses in introduction to numerical methods, probability and statistics, and analytical solution methods for PDEs. Chapters of interest, at least in part, are Chapters 1–4 and 10–13. Depending on the background of the students, these chapters could be supplemented with the needed background material. Although some elements of these chapters may not be covered in depth, the students would learn many of the fundamentals of V&V, and, more generally, what the primary issues are in assessing the credibility of computational results. Ideally, homework problems or semester projects could be given to teams of individuals working together in some application area, e.g., fluid mechanics or solid mechanics. Instead of working with PDEs, simulations can be assigned that only require solution of ODEs.

For a graduate course, all the chapters in the book could be covered. In addition to the courses just mentioned, it is recommended that students have completed a graduate course in the numerical solution of PDEs. If the students have not had a course in probability and statistics, they may need supplementary material in this area. Assigned homework problems or semester projects are, again, ideally suited to teams of individuals. A more flexible alternative is for each team to pick the application area for their project, with the approval of the instructor. Our view is that teams of individuals are very beneficial because other team members experienced in one area can assist any individual lacking in knowledge in those areas. Also, learning to work in a team environment is exceptionally important in any science or engineering field. The semester projects could be defined such that each element of the project builds on the previous elements completed. Each element of the project could deal with specific topics in various chapters of the book, and each could be graded separately. This approach would be similar in structure to that commonly used in engineering fields for the senior design project.

1.3.3 Use of the book by professionals

Use of the book by professionals working in their particular application area would be quite different than a classroom environment. Professionals typically scan through an entire book, and then concentrate on particular topics of interest at the moment. In the following list, five groups of professionals are identified and chapters that may be of particular interest are suggested:

- code builders and software developers: Chapters 1–9;
- builders of mathematical models of physical processes: Chapters 1–3 and 10–13;
- computational analysts: Chapters 1–16;
- experimentalists: Chapters 1–3 and 10–13;
- project managers and decision makers: Chapters 1–3, 5, 7, 10, and 13–16.

1.4 References

Ashill, P. R. (1993). Boundary flow measurement methods for wall interference assessment and correction: classification and review. *Fluid Dynamics Panel Symposium: Wall Interference, Support Interference, and Flow Field Measurements, AGARD-CP-535*, Brussels, Belgium, AGARD, 12.1–12.21.

Blottner, F. G. (1990). Accurate Navier–Stokes results for the hypersonic flow over a spherical nosetip. *Journal of Spacecraft and Rockets*. **27**(2), 113–122.

Boehm, B. W. (1981). *Software Engineering Economics*, Saddle River, NJ, Prentice-Hall.

Bradley, R. G. (1988). CFD validation philosophy. *Fluid Dynamics Panel Symposium: Validation of Computational Fluid Dynamics, AGARD-CP-437*, Lisbon, Portugal, North Atlantic Treaty Organization.

Chapman, D. R., H. Mark, and M. W. Pirtle (1975). Computer vs. wind tunnels. *Astronautics & Aeronautics*. **13**(4), 22–30.

Cosner, R. R. (1994). Issues in aerospace application of CFD analysis. *32nd Aerospace Sciences Meeting & Exhibit, AIAA Paper 94–0464*, Reno, NV, American Institute of Aeronautics and Astronautics.

DeCamp, L. S. (1995). *The Ancient Engineers*, New York, Ballantine Books.

Dwoyer, D. (1992). The relation between computational fluid dynamics and experiment. *AIAA 17th Ground Testing Conference*, Nashville, TN, American Institute of Aeronautics and Astronautics.

Edwards, P. N. (1997). *The Closed World: Computers and the Politics of Discourse in Cold War America*, Cambridge, MA, The MIT Press.

Harlow, F. H. and J. E. Fromm (1965). Computer experiments in fluid dynamics. *Scientific American*. **212**(3), 104–110.

Kahneman, D. and A. Tversky, Eds. (2000). *Choices, Values, and Frames*. Cambridge, UK, Cambridge University Press.

Kirby, R. S., S. Withington, A. B. Darling, and F. G. Kilgour (1956). *Engineering in History*, New York, NY, McGraw-Hill.

Lynch, F. T., R. C. Crites, and F. W. Spaid (1993). The crucial role of wall interference, support interference, and flow field measurements in the development of advanced aircraft configurations. *Fluid Dynamics Panel Symposium: Wall Interference, Support Interference, and Flow Field Measurements, AGARD-CP-535*, Brussels, Belgium, AGARD, 1.1–1.38.

Marvin, J. G. (1988). Accuracy requirements and benchmark experiments for CFD validation. *Fluid Dynamics Panel Symposium: Validation of Computational Fluid Dynamics, AGARD-CP-437*, Lisbon, Portugal, AGARD.

Mehta, U. B. (1991). Some aspects of uncertainty in computational fluid dynamics results. *Journal of Fluids Engineering*. **113**(4), 538–543.

NaRC (1986). *Current Capabilities and Future Directions in Computational Fluid Dynamics*, Washington, DC, National Research Council.

Neumann, R. D. (1990). CFD validation – the interaction of experimental capabilities and numerical computations, *16th Aerodynamic Ground Testing Conference, AIAA Paper 90–3030*, Portland, OR, American Institute of Aeronautics and Astronautics.

Oberkampf, W. L. (1994). A proposed framework for computational fluid dynamics code calibration/validation. *18th AIAA Aerospace Ground Testing Conference, AIAA Paper 94–2540*, Colorado Springs, CO, American Institute of Aeronautics and Astronautics.

Oberkampf, W. L. and D. P. Aeschliman (1992). Joint computational/experimental aerodynamics research on a hypersonic vehicle: Part 1, experimental results. *AIAA Journal*. **30**(8), 2000–2009.

Roache, P. J. (2004). Building PDE codes to be verifiable and validatable. *Computing in Science and Engineering*. **6**(5), 30–38.

Tetlock, P. E. (2005). *Expert Political Judgment: How good is it? How can we know?*, Princeton, NJ, Princeton University Press.

Top500 (2008). *32nd Edition of TOP500 Supercomputers*. www.top500.org/.

Tversky, A. and D. Kahneman (1992). Advances in prospect theory: cumulative representation of uncertainty. *Journal of Risk and Uncertainty*. **5**(4), 297–323.

Part I

Fundamental concepts

Chapter 2, *Fundamental Concepts and Terminology* and Chapter 3, *Modeling and Computational Simulation* form the foundation of the book. These chapters are recommended reading for individuals interested in any aspect of verification and validation (V&V) of mathematical models and scientific computing simulations. In Chapter 2, all of the key terms are defined and discussed. The chapter is much more than a glossary because it describes the development of the terminology and the underlying philosophical principles of each concept. The reader may be surprised that this chapter is devoted to fundamental concepts and terminology; however, understanding the underlying concepts is critical because many of the terms (e.g., verification, validation, predictive capability, calibration, uncertainty, and error) have a common language meaning that is imprecise and some terms are even contradictory from one technical field to another. One of the exciting aspects of the new field of V&V is that all of the principles developed must be applicable to *any* field of scientific computing, and even beyond. This is also challenging, and at times frustrating, because the terminology from various technical fields can be at odds with the terminology that is developing in the field of V&V. The discussion presents clear arguments why the concepts and terminology are logical and useable in real applications of scientific computing. Chapter 2 closes with an in-depth discussion of a framework of how all of the aspects of V&V and predictive capability are related and sequentially accomplished.

Chapter 3 discusses the basic concepts in modeling and simulation (M&S) with the emphasis on the physical sciences and engineering. We formally define the terms *system*, *surroundings*, *environments*, and *scenarios*. Although the latter two terms are not used in many areas of the physical sciences, the two terms are very useful for the analysis of engineered systems. We discuss the concept of nondeterministic simulations and why the concept is important in the analysis of most systems. Some fields have conducted nondeterministic simulations for decades, while some have only conducted deterministic simulations. The key goal of nondeterministic simulations is to carefully and unambiguously characterize the various sources of uncertainties, as they are understood at a given point in the analysis, and determine how they impact the predicted response of the system of interest. It is pointed out that there are two fundamentally different types of uncertainty. First, uncertainty due to inherent randomness in the system, surrounding, environments, and scenarios, which is referred to as *aleatory uncertainty*. Second, uncertainty due to our lack of knowledge of the system, surroundings, environments, and scenarios, which is referred to as *epistemic uncertainty*. The second half of Chapter 3 combines these concepts with a conceptual framework for the six formal phases in computational simulation.

2

Fundamental concepts and terminology

This chapter discusses the fundamental concepts and terminology associated with verification and validation (V&V) of models and simulations. We begin with a brief history of the philosophical foundations so that the reader can better understand why there are a wide variety of views toward V&V principles and procedures. Various perspectives of V&V have also generated different formal definitions of the terms *verification* and *validation* in important communities. Although the terminology is moving toward convergence within some communities, there are still significant differences. The reader needs to be aware of these differences in terminology to help minimize confusion and unnecessary disagreements, as well as to anticipate possible difficulties in contractual obligations in business and government. We also discuss a number of important and closely related terms in modeling and simulation (M&S). Examples are predictive capability, calibration, certification, uncertainty, and error. We end the chapter with a discussion of a conceptual framework for integrating verification, validation, and predictive capability. Although there are different frameworks for integrating these concepts, the framework discussed here has proven very helpful in understanding how the various activities in scientific computing are related.

2.1 Development of concepts and terminology

Philosophers of science have been struggling with the fundamental concepts underlying verification and validation (V&V) for at least two millennia. During the twentieth century, key philosophical concepts of epistemology were fundamentally altered (Popper, 1959; Kuhn, 1962; Carnap, 1963; Popper, 1969). These changes were heavily influenced by the experiments and theories associated with quantum mechanics and the theory of relativity. Usurping the throne of Newtonian mechanics, which had reigned for 300 years, did not come easily or painlessly to modern physics. Some researchers in engineering and the applied sciences have used several of the modern concepts in the philosophy of science to develop the fundamental principles and terminology of V&V. See Kleindorfer *et al.* (1998) for an excellent historical review of the philosophy of science viewpoint of validation. When this viewpoint is carried to the extreme (Oreskes *et al.*, 1994), one is left with the following position: one can only *disprove* or *fail to disprove* theories and laws of nature. Stated differently, theories and laws cannot be proved; they can only be falsified (Popper, 1969). This position is valuable for philosophy of science, but it is nearly useless for assessing the credibility of computational results in engineering and technology. Engineering and technology must deal with practical decision making that is usually focused on requirements, schedule, and cost. During the last two decades a workable and constructive approach to the concepts, terminology, and methodology of V&V has been developed, but it was based on practical realities in business and government, *not* the issue of absolute truth in the philosophy of nature.

2.1.1 Early efforts of the operations research community

The first applied technical discipline that began to struggle with the methodology and terminology of V&V was the operations research (OR) community, also referred to as systems analysis or modeling and simulation (M&S) community. Some of the key early contributors in the OR field in the 1960s and 1970s were Naylor and Finger (1967); Churchman (1968); Klir (1969); Shannon (1975); Zeigler (1976); Oren and Zeigler (1979); and Sargent (1979). See Sheng *et al.* (1993) for a historical review of the development of V&V concepts from the OR viewpoint. For a conceptual and theoretical discussion of V&V in modern texts on M&S, see Bossel (1994); Zeigler *et al.* (2000); Roza (2004); Law (2006); Raczynski (2006). In the OR activities, the systems analyzed could be extraordinarily complex, e.g., industrial production models, business or governmental organizations, marketing models, national and world economic models, and military conflict models. These complex models commonly involve a strong coupling of complex physical processes, human behavior in a wide variety of conditions, and computer-controlled systems that adapt to changing system characteristics and environments. For such complex systems and processes, fundamental conceptual issues immediately arise with regard to (a) defining the system as opposed to its external influences, (b) issues of causality, (c) human behavior, (d) measuring system responses, and (e) assessing the accuracy of the model.

A key milestone in the early work by the OR community was the publication of the first definitions of V&V by the Society for Computer Simulation (SCS) in 1979 (Schlesinger, 1979).

Model verification: substantiation that a computerized model represents a conceptual model within specified limits of accuracy.

Model validation: substantiation that a computerized model within its domain of applicability possesses a satisfactory range of accuracy consistent with the intended application of the model.

The SCS definition of verification, although brief, is quite informative. The main implication is that the computerized model, i.e., the computer code, must accurately mimic the model that was originally conceptualized. The SCS definition of validation, although instructive, appears somewhat vague. Both definitions, however, contain a critical concept: *substantiation* or evidence of correctness.

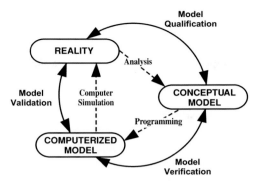

Figure 2.1 Phases of M&S and the role of V&V (Schlesinger, 1979 © 1979 by Simulation Councils, Inc.).

Along with these definitions, the SCS published the first useful diagram depicting the role of V&V within M&S (Figure 2.1).

Figure 2.1 identifies two types of model: a conceptual model and a computerized model. The *conceptual model* comprises all relevant information, modeling assumptions, and mathematical equations that describe the physical system or process of interest. The conceptual model is produced by analyzing and observing the system of interest. The SCS defined *qualification* as "Determination of adequacy of the conceptual model to provide an acceptable level of agreement for the domain of intended application." The *computerized model* is an operational computer program that implements a conceptual model using computer programming. Modern terminology typically refers to the computerized model as the computer model or code. Figure 2.1 emphasizes that *verification* deals with the relationship between the conceptual model and the computerized model and that *validation* deals with the relationship between the computerized model and reality. These relationships are not always recognized in other definitions of V&V, as will be discussed shortly.

The OR community clearly recognized, as it still does today, that V&V are tools for assessing the accuracy of the conceptual and computerized models. For much of the OR work, the assessment was so difficult, if not impossible, that V&V became more associated with the issue of credibility, i.e., whether the model is worthy of belief, or a model's power to elicit belief. In science and engineering, however, quantitative assessment of accuracy for important physical cases related to the intended application *is* mandatory. In certain situations, accuracy assessment can only be conducted using subscale physical models, a subset of the dominant physical processes occurring in the system, or a subsystem of the complete system. As will be discussed later in this chapter, the issue of extrapolation of models is more directly addressed in recent developments.

2.1.2 IEEE and related communities

During the 1970s, computer-controlled systems started to become important and widespread in commercial and public systems, particularly automatic flight-control systems for aircraft and high-consequence systems, such as nuclear power reactors. In response to this interest, the Institute of Electrical and Electronics Engineers (IEEE) defined verification as follows (IEEE, 1984; IEEE, 1991):

Verification: the process of evaluating the products of a software development phase to provide assurance that they meet the requirements defined for them by the previous phase.

This IEEE definition is quite general, but it is also strongly referential in the sense that the value of the definition directly depends on the specification of "requirements defined for them by the previous phase." Because those requirements are not stated in the definition, the definition does not contribute much to the intuitive understanding of verification or to the development of specific methods for verification. While the definition clearly includes a requirement for the consistency of products (e.g., computer programming) from one phase to another, the definition does not contain any indication of what the requirement for correctness or accuracy might be.

At the same time, IEEE defined validation as follows (IEEE, 1984; IEEE, 1991):

Validation: the process of testing a computer program and evaluating the results to ensure compliance with specific requirements.

Both IEEE definitions emphasize that both V&V are processes, that is, ongoing activities. The definition of validation is also referential because of the phrase "compliance with specific requirements." Because specific requirements are not defined (to make the definition as generally applicable as possible), the definition of validation is not particularly useful by itself. The substance of the meaning must be provided in the specification of additional information.

One may ask why the IEEE definitions are included, as they seem to provide less understanding and utility than the earlier definitions of the SCS. First, these definitions provide a distinctly different perspective toward the entire issue of V&V than what is needed in scientific computing. The IEEE perspective asserts that because of the extreme variety of requirements for M&S, the requirements should be defined in a separate document for each application, not in the definitions of V&V. For example, the requirement of model accuracy as measured by comparisons with experimental data could be placed in a requirements document. Second, the IEEE definitions are the more prevalent definitions used in engineering as a whole. As a result, one must be aware of the potential confusion when other definitions are used in conversations, publications, government regulations, and contract specifications. The IEEE definitions are dominant because of the worldwide influence of this organization and the prevalence of electrical and electronics engineers. It should also be noted that the computer science community, the software quality assurance community, and the International Organization for Standardization (ISO) (ISO, 1991) use the IEEE definitions.

In addition, and more importantly for scientific computing, the IEEE definitions of V&V have been used by the American Nuclear Society (ANS) (ANS, 1987). However, in 2006 the ANS formed a new committee to reconsider their use of the IEEE definitions for V&V.

2.1.3 US Department of Defense community

In the early 1990s, the US Department of Defense (DoD) began to recognize the importance of putting into place terminology and procedures for V&V that would serve their very broad range of needs in M&S (Davis, 1992; Hodges and Dewar, 1992). The DoD tasked the Defense Modeling and Simulation Office (DMSO) to study the terminology put into place by the IEEE and to determine if the IEEE definitions would serve their needs. The DMSO obtained the expertise of researchers in the fields of OR, operational testing of combined hardware and software systems, man-in-the-loop training simulators, and warfare simulation. They concluded that the IEEE definitions were too restricted to software V&V instead of their need for much broader range of M&S. In 1994, the DoD/DMSO published their basic concepts and definitions of V&V (DoD, 1994).

Verification: the process of determining that a model implementation accurately represents the developer's conceptual description of the model.

Validation: the process of determining the degree to which a model is an accurate representation of the real world from the perspective of the intended uses of the model.

From a comparison of these definitions with those codified by the IEEE, it is clear there was a major break in conceptualization of V&V by the DoD. The DoD definitions could be referred to as *model V&V*, as opposed to the IEEE definitions of *software V&V*. The DoD definitions are actually similar to those formed by the SCS in 1979.

As noted in the discussion of the IEEE definitions, the DoD definitions also stress that both V&V are "process[es] of determining." V&V are ongoing activities that do not have a clearly defined completion point, unless additional specifications are given in terms of intended uses of the model and adequacy. The definitions include the ongoing nature of the process because of an unavoidable but distressing fact: the veracity, correctness, and accuracy of a computational model cannot be demonstrated for all possible conditions and applications, except for trivial models. For example, one cannot prove that even a moderately complex computer code has no errors. Likewise, models of physics cannot be proven correct; they can only be proven incorrect.

The key feature of the DoD definitions, which is not mentioned in the IEEE definitions, is the emphasis on *accuracy*. This feature assumes that a measure of accuracy can be determined. Accuracy can be measured relative to any accepted referent. In verification, the referent could be either well-accepted solutions to simplified model problems or expert opinions as to the reasonableness of the solution. In validation, the referent could be either experimentally measured data or expert opinions as to what is a reasonable or credible result of the model.

2.1.4 AIAA and ASME communities

Most science and engineering communities focus on their particular types of application, as opposed to the very broad range of DoD systems. Specifically, scientific computing

concentrates on modeling physical systems that have limited aspects of human interaction
with the system. Typically, the mathematical model of the system of interest is dominated
by physical processes that are described by partial differential equations (PDEs) or integro-
differential equations. Human interaction with the system, as well as the effect of computer
control systems, is explicitly given by way of the boundary conditions, initial conditions,
system excitation, or other auxiliary submodels. The effect of this narrow focus of the
science and engineering communities will be apparent in the further development of V&V
terminology, concepts, and methods.

The computational fluid dynamics (CFD) community, primarily through the American
Institute of Aeronautics and Astronautics (AIAA), was the first engineering community to
seriously begin developing concepts and procedures for V&V methodology. Some of the
key early contributors were Bradley (1988); Marvin (1988); Blottner (1990); Mehta (1990);
Roache (1990); and Oberkampf and Aeschliman (1992). For a more complete history of
the development of V&V concepts in CFD, see Oberkampf and Trucano (2002).

2.1.4.1 AIAA Guide

In 1992, the AIAA Committee on Standards for Computational Fluid Dynamics (AIAA
COS) began a project to formulate and standardize the basic terminology and methodology in V&V for CFD simulations. The committee was composed of representatives from
academia, industry, and government, with representation from the US, Canada, Japan, Belgium, Australia, and Italy. After six years of discussion and debate, the committee's project
culminated in the publication of *Guide for the Verification and Validation of Computational Fluid Dynamics Simulations* (AIAA, 1998), referred to herein as the *AIAA Guide*.
The AIAA Guide defines a number of key terms, discusses fundamental concepts, and
specifies general procedures for conducting V&V in CFD.

The AIAA Guide (AIAA, 1998) modified slightly the DoD definition for verification,
giving the following definition:

Verification: the process of determining that a model implementation accurately represents the
developer's conceptual description of the model and the solution to the model.

The DoD definition of verification did not make it clear that the accuracy of the numerical solution to the conceptual model should be included in the definition. Science and
engineering communities, however, are keenly interested in the accuracy of the numerical
solution – a concern that is common to essentially all of the fields in scientific computing.

Although the AIAA Guide adopted verbatim the DoD definition of *validation*, there are
important differences in interpretation. These will be discussed in the next section, as well
as in Section 2.2.3.

The fundamental strategy of verification is the identification, quantification, and reduction of errors in the computer code and the numerical solution. Verification provides
evidence or substantiation that the conceptual (continuum mathematics) model is solved
accurately by the discrete mathematics model embodied in the computer code. To quantify
computer coding errors, a highly accurate, reliable benchmark solution must be available.

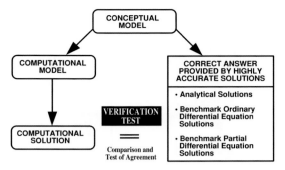

Figure 2.2 Verification process (AIAA, 1998).

Highly accurate solutions, unfortunately, are only available for simplified model problems. Verification does *not* deal with the relationship of the conceptual model to the real world. As Roache (1998) lucidly points out: "Verification is a mathematics issue; not a physics issue." *Validation* is a physical science issue. Figure 2.2 depicts the verification process of comparing the numerical solution from the code in question with various types of highly accurate solutions.

In the AIAA Guide, a significant break was made from the DoD perspective on validation in terms of the types of comparison allowed for accuracy assessment with respect to "the real world." The AIAA Guide specifically required that assessment of the accuracy of computational results be *only* allowed using experimental measurements. The fundamental strategy of validation involves identification and quantification of the error and uncertainty in the conceptual and mathematical models. This involves the quantification of the numerical error in the computational solution, estimation of the experimental uncertainty, and comparison between the computational results and the experimental data. That is, accuracy is measured in relation to experimental data, our best measure of reality. This strategy *does not* assume that the experimental measurements are more accurate than the computational results; it only asserts that experimental measurements are the most faithful reflections of reality for the purposes of validation. Figure 2.3 depicts the validation process of comparing the computational results with experimental data from various sources.

Because of the infeasibility and impracticality of conducting true validation experiments on most complex systems, the recommended method is to use a building block, or system complexity hierarchy, approach. This approach was originally developed by Sindir and his colleagues (Lin *et al.*, 1992; Sindir *et al.*, 1996), as well as Cosner (1995); and Marvin (1995). It divides the complex engineering system of interest into multiple, progressively simpler tiers; e.g., subsystem cases, benchmark cases, and unit problems. The strategy in the tiered approach is to assess how accurately the computational results compare with the experimental data (with quantified uncertainty estimates) at multiple degrees of physics coupling and geometric complexity (Figure 2.4). The approach is clearly constructive in that it (a) recognizes a hierarchy of complexity in systems and simulations, (b) recognizes that the quantity and accuracy of information obtained from experiments varies radically

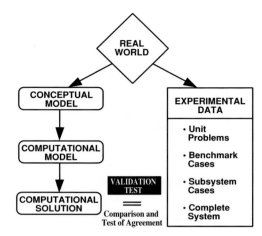

Figure 2.3 Validation process (AIAA, 1998).

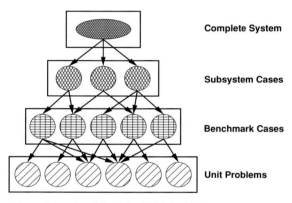

Figure 2.4 Validation tiers of a system hierarchy (AIAA, 1998).

over the range of tiers, and (c) guides the accumulation of validation evidence with the focus always being on the complete system. It should also be noted that additional building-block tiers beyond the four discussed here could be defined; however, additional tiers would not fundamentally alter the recommended methodology.

In the AIAA Guide's discussion of validation (depicted in Figure 2.3) is the concept that validation is the comparison of computational results with experimental measurements for the purpose of model accuracy assessment. Thinking of validation in this way requires one to then deal with the issue of *prediction*. The AIAA Guide gives the following definition:

Prediction: use of a computational model to foretell the state of a physical system under conditions for which the computational model has not been validated.

A prediction refers to the computational simulation of a specific case of interest that is *different* in some way from cases that have been validated. This definition differs from the common-language meaning of prediction and refers only to *pre*diction, not *post*diction (replication of previously obtained results). If this restriction is not made, then one is only demonstrating previous agreement with experimental data in the validation database. The results of the validation process should be viewed as historical statements of model comparisons with experimental data. Stated differently, the validation database represents reproducible evidence that a model has achieved a given level of accuracy in the solution of specified problems. From this perspective, it becomes clear that validation comparisons do not directly make claims about the accuracy of predictions generally; rather, they allow inferences from the model concerning responses of similar systems. The issue of segregating validation (in the sense of model accuracy assessment) and inferred accuracy in prediction is a major conceptual issue that will resurface in several chapters.

2.1.4.2 ASME Guide

In the late 1990s, members of the solid mechanics community became interested in the concepts and methodology of V&V. The first V&V committee within the Codes and Standards branch of the American Society of Mechanical Engineers (ASME) was formed in 2001 and designated Performance Test Codes 60, Committee on Verification and Validation in Computational Solid Mechanics. Under the leadership of the committee chair, Leonard Schwer, the committee painstakingly debated and struggled with the subtleties of the terminology and appropriate methodology for V&V. Late in 2006, the *ASME Guide for Verification and Validation in Computational Solid Mechanics*, herein referred to as the *ASME Guide*, was completed (ASME, 2006).

The ASME Guide slightly modified the definition of verification as formulated by the AIAA Guide:

Verification: the process of determining that a computational model accurately represents the under-
    lying mathematical model and its solution.

The ASME Guide adopted the definition of *validation* as formulated by the DoD and used by the AIAA Guide. Key issues of interpretation will be given below and in Section 2.2.3. Building on many of the concepts described in the AIAA Guide, in addition to newly published methods in V&V, the ASME Guide significantly extended the engineering standards literature in V&V.

Instead of graphically showing V&V as separate entities, as in the AIAA Guide, the AMSE Guide constructed a comprehensive diagram showing both activities, along with other complementary activities (Figure 2.5). It is important to recognize that the diagram and all of the activities shown can be applied to any tier of a system hierarchy. The analogous activities in both the mathematical modeling and the physical modeling are clearly shown, along with their interactions. The conceptual model, the mathematical model, and the computational model are all shown in the figure, as well as being defined in the ASME Guide. The separation of the concepts and activities in each of these three types of models significantly improved the understanding of not only the V&V process, but also the M&S process. Two elements of verification are identified: code verification and

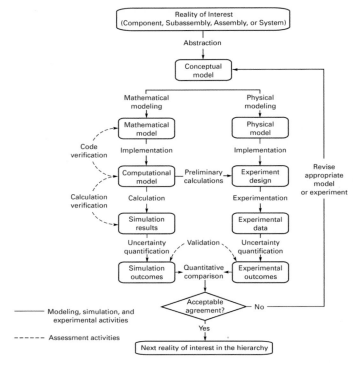

Figure 2.5 Verification and validation activities and products (ASME, 2006).

calculation verification. This separation of verification activities followed the pioneering work of Blottner (1990) and Roache (1995). With this separation of verification activities, a much clearer set of techniques could be discussed to improve coding reliability and numerical accuracy assessment of the computational model.

As shown at the bottom of Figure 2.5, an important decision point in the V&V activities is the answer to the question: Is there acceptable agreement between the computational results and the experimental measurements? The ASME Guide discusses how this decision should be made, specifically with regard to the key phrase in the definition of validation: "intended uses of the model." In some communities the phrase that is used is "fit for purpose," instead of "intended uses of the model." In the formulation of the conceptual model, several tasks are defined, among them: (a) identify which physical processes in the reality of interest are anticipated to have significant effects on the responses of interest and which processes are not expected to be important, (b) determine requirements for demonstrating the accuracy and predictive capability of the model, and (c) specify the model's domain of intended use. The specification of accuracy requirements for responses of interest predicted by the model allows the "acceptable agreement" question to be answered. Only with accuracy requirements can the decision be made whether to accept or revise a model. Without accuracy requirements, the question: "How good is good enough?" cannot be answered.

The emphasis in the specification of the model's domain of intended use deals with the operating conditions under which the model is to be used, e.g., range of boundary conditions, initial conditions, external system excitation, materials, and geometries. The ASME Guide, as well as the DoD community, recognizes the importance, and difficulty, of specifying the model's domain of intended use.

2.1.5 Hydrology community

The hydrology community, particularly surface and subsurface transport, has also been actively developing concepts and methods concerning V&V. Most of this work, however, has been essentially developed independently of many of the activities discussed earlier in this chapter. Some of the early key contributors to this work were Beck (1987); Tsang (1989); LeGore (1990); Davis *et al.* (1991); and Konikow and Bredehoeft (1992). The work of the hydrology community is significant for two reasons. First, it addresses validation for complex processes in the physical sciences where validation of models is extremely difficult, if not impossible. One reason for this difficulty is remarkably limited knowledge of the specific underground transport characteristics and material properties associated with the validation database. For such situations, one must deal more explicitly with calibration or parameter estimation in models instead of the concepts of validation developed by the AIAA and ASME. This critical issue of validation versus calibration of models will be dealt with in several chapters in this book. Second, because of the limited knowledge about the physical characteristics of the system under consideration, the hydrology field has strongly adopted statistical methods of calibration and validation assessment. In hydrology, it is not just calibration of scalar parameters, but also scalar and tensor fields. For a good review of the state of the art in hydrology V&V, see Anderson and Bates (2001).

In more recent work, the hydrology community in Europe (Rykiel, 1996; Beven, 2002; Refsgaard and Henriksen, 2004) has independently developed ideas about V&V that are very similar to those being developed in the United States. Rykiel (1996) makes an important practical point, especially to analysts and decision makers, about the difference between the philosophy-of-science viewpoint and the practitioner's view of validation: "Validation is not a procedure for testing scientific theory or for certifying the 'truth' of current scientific understanding. . . . Validation means that a model is acceptable for its intended use because it meets specified performance requirements." Refsgaard and Henriksen (2004) recommended terminology and fundamental procedures for V&V that are very similar to the AIAA Guide and ASME Guide. They define model validation as "Substantiation that a model within its domain of applicability possesses a satisfactory range of accuracy consistent with the intended application of the model." Refsgaard and Henriksen (2004) also stressed another crucial issue that is corroborated by the AIAA Guide and the ASME Guide: "Validation tests against independent data that have not also been used for calibration are necessary in order to be able to document the predictive capability of a model." In other words, the major challenge in validation is to perform an assessment of the model in a blind-test with experimental data, whereas the key issue in calibration is to adjust the physical modeling parameters to improve agreement with experimental data. It is difficult, and sometimes impossible, to make blind-test comparisons; e.g., when well-known benchmark validation data are available for comparison. As a result, one must be very cautious in making conclusions about the predictive accuracy of models when the computational analyst has seen the data. Knowing the correct answer beforehand is extremely seductive, even to a saint.

2.2 Primary terms and concepts

This section will discuss in more detail the concepts and underlying principles behind the formal definitions of V&V. This book will use the definitions of V&V as given by the ASME Guide. Also defined and discussed in this section are the terms code verification, solution verification, predictive capability, calibration, certification, and accreditation. Definitions for these terms will be primarily drawn from ASME, AIAA, IEEE, and DoD.

The modern scientific method is very much aligned with the philosophy of nature approach referred to as deductivism. Deductivism is the method of drawing conclusions by logically combining new ideas with facts that have been accepted as true. Deductivism argues from the general to the particular, or reasons from known general principles to deduce previously unobserved or unknown phenomena. This perspective can be most clearly seen in the manner in which scientists and engineers are trained, as well as in mathematical modeling of physical processes. V&V, however, is aligned with inductive reasoning processes, i.e., processes that present the correctness of individual pieces of evidence to support the conclusion of correctness of the generalization. The philosophical perspective of V&V is one of *fundamental skepticism*: if any claim cannot be demonstrated or proven, then it is not accepted as true. The dichotomy of perspectives between the training of scientists and engineers, as opposed to the philosophy of V&V, is sometimes at the root of the lack of interest, or open resistance, to many V&V activities by some scientists and engineers.

2.2.1 Code verification

The ASME Guide (ASME, 2006) defines *code verification* as:

Code verification: the process of determining that the numerical algorithms are correctly implemented in the computer code and of identifying errors in the software.

Code verification can be segregated into two activities: numerical algorithm verification and software quality assurance (SQA), as shown in Figure 2.6. Numerical algorithm verification addresses the mathematical correctness in the software implementation of all the numerical algorithms that affect the numerical accuracy of the computational results. The major goal of numerical algorithm verification is to accumulate evidence that demonstrates that the numerical algorithms in the code are implemented correctly and that they are functioning as intended. As an example, numerical algorithm verification would demonstrate that a spatial discretization method would produce the expected convergence rate, as the mesh is refined for the specific PDE being tested. The emphasis in SQA is on determining whether

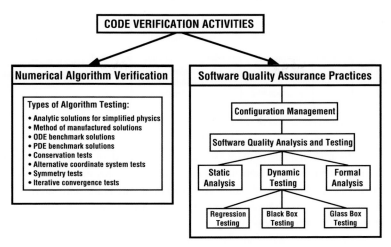

Figure 2.6 Integrated view of code verification in M&S (Oberkampf *et al.*, 2004).

or not the code, as part of a software system, is implemented correctly and that it produces repeatable results on specified computer hardware and in a specified software environment. Such environments include computer operating systems, compilers, function libraries, etc. Although there are many software system elements in modern computer simulations, such as pre- and post-processor codes, focus in this book will be on SQA practices applied to the source code associated with scientific computing.

Numerical algorithm verification is fundamentally empirical. Specifically, it is based on testing, observations, comparisons, and analyses of code results for individual executions of the code. It focuses on careful investigations of numerical aspects, such as spatial and temporal convergence rates, spatial convergence in the presence of discontinuities, independence of solutions to coordinate transformations, and symmetry tests related to various types of boundary conditions (BCs). Analytical or formal error analysis is inadequate in numerical algorithm verification because the code itself must *demonstrate* the analytical and formal results of the numerical analysis. Numerical algorithm verification is usually conducted by comparing computational solutions with highly accurate solutions, which are commonly referred to as verification benchmarks. Oberkampf and Trucano (2007) divided the types of highly accurate solution into four categories (listed from highest to lowest in accuracy): manufactured solutions, analytical solutions, numerical solutions to ordinary differential equations, and numerical solutions to PDEs. Methods for numerical algorithm verification will be discussed in detail in Chapters 5 and 6.

SQA activities consist of practices, procedures, and processes that are primarily developed by researchers and practitioners in the computer science and software engineering communities. Conventional SQA emphasizes processes (i.e., management, planning, design, acquisition, supply, development, operation, and maintenance), as well as reporting, administrative, and documentation requirements. A key element or process of SQA

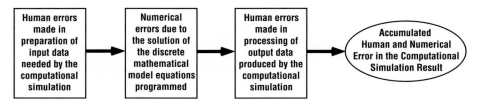

Figure 2.7 Error sources addressed in solution verification.

is software configuration management, which is composed of configuration identification, configuration and change control, and configuration status accounting. As shown in
Figure 2.6, software quality analysis and testing can be divided into static analysis, dynamic
testing, and formal analysis. Dynamic testing can be further divided into such elements
of common practice as regression testing, black box testing, and glass box testing. From
an SQA perspective, Figure 2.6 could be reorganized so that all types of algorithm testing
categorized under numerical algorithm verification could be moved to dynamic testing.
Although this perspective is useful, it fails to stress the importance of numerical algorithm
verification that is critical in the numerical solution of PDEs. We stress that SQA is a necessary element of code verification. SQA methods will be discussed in Chapter 4, Software
engineering for scientific computing.

2.2.2 *Solution verification*

Solution verification, also called calculation verification, is defined as:

Solution verification: the process of determining the correctness of the input data, the numerical accuracy of the solution obtained, and the correctness of the output data for a particular
simulation.

Solution verification attempts to identify and quantify three sources of errors that can occur
in the exercise of the computer simulation code (Figure 2.7). First, errors, blunders, or
mistakes made by the computational analysts in preparation of the input for the computer
simulation code. Second, numerical errors resulting from computing the discretized solution
of the mathematical model on a digital computer. Third, errors, blunders or mistakes made
by the computational analysts in any processing of the output data that is produced by
the simulation code. The first and third sources of errors are of a very different type than
the second. The first error source does *not* refer to errors or approximations made in the
formulation or construction of the mathematical model. The first and third sources refer to
human errors exclusive of any other sources. Human errors can be very difficult to detect
in large-scale computational analyses of complex systems. Even in relatively small-scale
analyses, human errors can go undetected if procedural or data-checking methods are not
employed to detect possible errors. For example, if a solid mechanics analysis contains tens
of CAD/CAM files, perhaps hundreds of different materials, and thousands of Monte Carlo

simulation samples, human errors, even by the most experienced and careful practitioners, commonly occur.

The second source, numerical solution errors, is primarily concerned with (a) spatial and temporal discretization errors in the numerical solution of PDEs, and (b) iterative solution errors usually resulting from a chosen solution approach to a set of nonlinear equations. There are other sources of numerical solution errors and these will be discussed in Chapter 3, Modeling and computational simulation. The importance and difficulty of numerical error estimation has increased as the complexity of the physics and mathematical models has increased, e.g., mathematical models given by nonlinear PDEs with singularities and discontinuities. It should be noted that the ASME Guide definition of calculation verification is not used in this book because it only refers to the second source of error, as opposed to all three sources.

The two basic approaches for estimating the error in the numerical solution of a PDE are *a priori* and *a posteriori* error estimation techniques. An *a priori* technique only uses information about the numerical algorithm that approximates the given PDE and the given initial conditions (ICs) and BCs. *A priori* error estimation is a significant element of classical numerical analysis for linear PDEs, especially in analyzing finite element methods. An *a posteriori* approach can use all the *a priori* information as well as the computational results from previous numerical solutions, e.g., solutions using different mesh resolutions or solutions using different order-of-accuracy methods. During the last decade it has become clear that the only way to achieve a useful quantitative estimate of numerical error in practical cases for nonlinear PDEs is by using *a posteriori* error estimates. Estimation of numerical solution errors will be discussed in detail in Chapters 8 and 9.

2.2.3 Model validation

Even though the DoD, the AIAA Guide, and the ASME Guide use the same formal definition for validation, our discussion in Section 2.1 hinted at differences in the interpretation and implications of the term. For example, it was pointed out that the AIAA Guide and the ASME Guide require *experimental measured data* when comparisons are made with simulations, whereas in the DoD interpretation this is not required. The recent paper of Oberkampf and Trucano (2008) clearly addressed the three aspects of validation and how different communities view each. Figure 2.8 depicts these three aspects as follows.

- Quantification of the accuracy of the computational model results by comparing the computed system response quantities (SRQs) of interest with experimentally measured SRQs.
- Use of the computational model to make predictions, in the sense of interpolation or extrapolation of the model, for conditions corresponding to the model's domain of intended use.
- Determination of whether the estimated accuracy of the computational model results satisfies the accuracy requirements specified for the SRQs of interest.

As depicted in Figure 2.8, Aspect 1 deals with assessing the accuracy of results from the model by comparisons with available experimental data. The assessment could be conducted

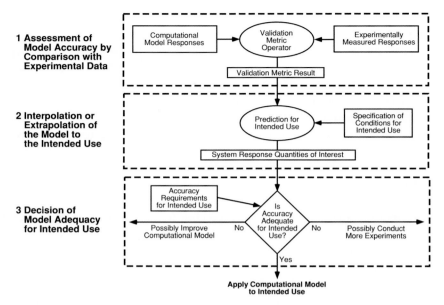

Figure 2.8 Three aspects of model validation (Oberkampf and Trucano, 2008).

for the actual system of interest or *any* related system. Some examples are (a) the actual system at operational conditions for the intended use of the system, (b) the actual system operating at lower than anticipated or less demanding conditions, or (c) subsystems or components of the actual system that have been identified in the system hierarchy. Model accuracy is quantitatively estimated using a *validation metric operator*. This operator computes a difference between the computational results and the experimental results for individual SRQs as a function of the input or control parameters in the validation domain. The operator can also be referred to as a *mismatch* operator between the computational results and the experimental results over the multidimensional space of all input parameters. In general, it is a statistical operator because the computational results and the experimental results are not single numbers but distributions of numbers (e.g., a cumulative distribution function) or quantities that are interval valued. This topic will be discussed in detail in Chapter 13, Model accuracy assessment.

Aspect 2 deals with a fundamentally and conceptually different topic: use of the model to make a prediction. As noted earlier, the AIAA Guide defined *prediction* (AIAA, 1998) as "foretelling the response of a system under conditions for which the model has not been validated." Prediction can also be thought of as interpolating or extrapolating the model beyond the specific conditions tested in the validation domain to the conditions of the intended use of the model. Several other authors have stressed the important aspect of extrapolation of the model and the attendant increase in uncertainty, which is usually referred to as *model form uncertainty*. See, for example, Cullen and Frey (1999) or Suter (2007). The important issue here is the estimated total uncertainty in the SRQs of interest as a function of (a) the (in)accuracy in the model that was observed over the validation domain, and (b) the estimated model input parameters; both of these at the specified conditions of the intended use of the model. Stated differently, Aspect 2 does *not* deal with aspects of adequacy or accuracy requirements on the prediction, but focuses on the uncertainty in the SRQs of interest for the applications conditions of interest. The estimated total uncertainty is due to a wide variety of sources, such as inherent uncertainty in the system, lack of knowledge concerning the conditions of the intended use of the system, and model form uncertainty. The basic concepts in the topic of predictive uncertainty estimation will be summarized in Chapter 13, Predictive capability. See, for example, Morgan and Henrion (1990); Kumamoto and Henley (1996); Cullen and Frey (1999); Ayyub and Klir (2006); and Suter (2007).

Aspect 3 deals with (a) the comparison of the estimated accuracy of the model relative to the accuracy requirements of the model for the domain of the model's intended use, and (b) the decision of adequacy or inadequacy of the model over the domain of the model's intended use. The more general assessment of model adequacy or inadequacy typically depends on many factors, such as computer resource requirements, speed with which re-meshing can be done for a new geometry, and ease of use of the software for the given experience level of the analysts involved. The validation decision in Aspect 3 *only* refers to whether the model satisfies or does not satisfy the accuracy requirements specified. An accuracy requirement may be stated as: the estimated maximum allowable model form uncertainty for specified SRQs cannot exceed a fixed value over the domain of the model's intended use. The model form uncertainty will be a function of the input parameters describing the model's intended use, but model accuracy can also depend on uncertainty in the parameters themselves. The maximum allowable uncertainty over the parameter range of the intended use of the model would typically be an absolute-value quantity (i.e., the uncertainty cannot exceed a specified value) or a relative-uncertainty quantity (i.e., the uncertainty is scaled by the magnitude of the quantity). There are two types of *yes* decision that could occur in Aspect 3: (a) the estimated uncertainty is less than the maximum allowable uncertainty over the parameter range of the model's intended use, or (b) the parameter range of the model's intended use must be modified, e.g., restricted, such that the estimated uncertainty does not exceed the maximum allowable uncertainty.

A final important conceptual point should be mentioned in regard to Aspect 3. The decision governed by model adequacy assessment is only concerned with the adequacy of the computational model, *not* the performance of the engineering system being analyzed. Whether the system of interest, e.g., a gas turbine engine or a flight vehicle, meets its performance, safety, or reliability requirements is, of course, a completely separate topic from the aspects discussed relative to Figure 2.8. Simply put, a computational model of a system could be accurate, but the system itself could be lacking in performance, safety, or reliability because of inadequate design.

Understanding that there are three aspects to the term *validation* presented in Figure 2.8, there are two viewpoints underlying interpretation of the term. One interpretation is what is called the *encompassing view of validation*. When employing this perspective, one means *all three aspects* discussed above. The DoD community usually takes the encompassing view of validation, although there is commonly confusion on this issue. The *restricted view of validation* considers each aspect of validation separately. That is, Aspect 1 is referred to as validation assessment, model accuracy assessment, or model validation. Aspect 2 is referred to as model prediction, predictive capability, or model extrapolation. Aspect 3 is referred to as model adequacy assessment or adequacy assessment for intended use. The AIAA Guide takes the restricted view of validation. The ASME Guide generally takes the encompassing view of validation, but in a few sections of this Guide, the concepts can only be understood using the restricted view of validation.

Either interpretation can be used in validation activities related to scientific computing. However, it is our view, and the experience of many, that an encompassing view of validation commonly leads to misunderstandings and confusion in discussions and in communication of computational results. The primary reason for this confusion is the dissimilarity between each of the three aspects discussed above. Misunderstandings and confusion can be particularly risky and damaging, for example, in communication of computational results to system designers, project managers, decision makers, and individuals not trained in science or engineering. As a result, *this book will use the restricted view of validation*. For this restricted view of validation, the terms *model validation*, *validation assessment*, and *model accuracy assessment* will also be used; all referring only to Aspect 1.

One term that has been used extensively is *model*, although this term has not yet been carefully defined. As is well known, there are many types of model used in scientific computing. The three major types of model are conceptual, mathematical, and computational. A *conceptual model* specifies (a) the physical system, the system surroundings, and the phenomena of interest, (b) the operating environment of the system and its domain of intended use, (c) the physical assumptions that simplify the system and the phenomena of interest, (d) the SRQs of interest, and (e) the accuracy requirements for the SRQs of interest. A *mathematical model* is derived from the conceptual model, and it is a set of mathematical and logical relations that represent the physical system of interest and its responses to the environment and the ICs of the system. The mathematical model is commonly given by a set of PDEs, integral equations, BCs and ICs, material properties, and excitation equations. A *computational model* is derived from the numerical implementation of the mathematical model, a process that results in a set of discretized equations and solution algorithms, and then these equations and algorithms are programmed into a computer. Another way to describe the computational model is that it is a mapping of the mathematical model into a software package that, when combined with the proper input, produces simulation results. Commonly the computational model is simply referred to as the *code*. The different types of model will be discussed in detail in Chapter 3.

When the term *model validation* is used, one is actually referring to validation of the mathematical model, even though the computational model results are compared with experimental data. The essence of what is being assessed in validation and the essence of what is making a prediction is embodied in the mathematical model. Viewing model

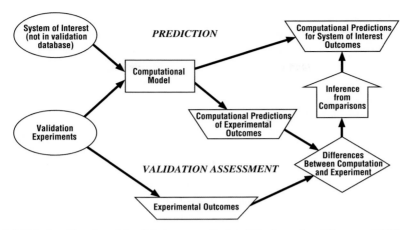

Figure 2.9 Relationship of model validation to prediction (Oberkampf and Trucano, 2002).

validation as *mathematical model validation* fundamentally relies on the following assumptions: (a) that the numerical algorithms are reliable and accurate, (b) the computer program is correct, (c) no human procedural errors have been made in the input or output for the simulation, and (d) the numerical solution error is small. Evidence for the veracity of these assumptions must be demonstrated by the activities conducted in code verification and solution verification.

2.2.4 Predictive capability

This book will use the definition of the term *prediction* as given by the AIAA Guide (AIAA, 1998):

Prediction: use of a computational model to foretell the state of a physical system under conditions for which the computational model has not been validated.

As discussed earlier, this definition is very specific and restrictive compared to common-language usage. The meaning of predictive capability is depicted as Aspect 2 of Figure 2.8, i.e., extrapolation or interpolation of the model to specific conditions defined by the intended use of the model. The results of the model validation process, Aspect 1, should be viewed as reproducible evidence that a model has achieved a given level of accuracy in the solution of specified problems. The evidence compiled allows inferences to be made concerning similar systems exposed to similar conditions. The strength of the inference depends on the explanatory power of the model as opposed to the descriptive power of the model. The suggested relationship between model validation and prediction is shown in Figure 2.9.

Figure 2.9 attempts to capture the distinction between model validation and prediction. The bottom portion of the figure represents the model validation process. Although it is not readily apparent, the validation process shown in Figure 2.9 is fundamentally the same as that shown in Figure 2.3. In Figure 2.9, the block Validation Experiments produces one or more physical realizations of the "real world." The Experimental Outcomes are the experimental data measured in the experiment. The physical conditions from the actual validation experiments, i.e., model input parameters, initial conditions, and boundary conditions, are input to the Computational Model, which produces the Computational Results of Experimental Outcomes. These results are then compared with the experimentally determined outcomes in the block Differences Between Computation and Experiment. This block was referred to as Validation Metric Operator in Figure 2.8. Based on the magnitude of these differences in quantities of interest and on the depth of understanding of the physical process, an Inference from Comparisons is made.

The upper portion of Figure 2.9 represents the prediction process. The System of Interest should drive the entire scientific computing process, but some of the realizations of interest, i.e., predictions, are commonly not in the validation database. That is, when a physical realization is conducted as part of the validation database, regardless of the validation tier as discussed in Section 2.1.4 above, the realization becomes part of the Validation Experiments. Predictions for conditions of interest are made using the Computational Model, resulting in Computational Predictions of System of Interest Outcomes. The confidence in these predictions is determined by (a) the strength of the Inference from Comparisons, (b) the similarity of the complex system of interest to the existing validation experiments, and (c) the depth of understanding of the physical processes involved, i.e., the explanatory power of the mathematical model.

The process of logical and mathematical inference of accuracy of a computational model stemming from its associated validation database is analogous to similar processes and conclusions for classical scientific theories. However, the strength or confidence in the inference from scientific computing is, and should be, much weaker than traditional scientific theories. Computational simulation relies on the same logic as science theories, but it also relies on many additional issues that are not present in traditional scientific theories, such as, code verification, solution verification, and extrapolation of models that have varying degrees of calibrated parameters. One of the key theoretical issues is the state of knowledge of the process being modeled. Bossel (1994); Zeigler *et al.* (2000); and Roza (2004) give a discussion of hierarchical levels of knowledge of a system. For physical processes that are well understood both physically and mathematically, the inference can be quite strong. For complex physical processes, the inference can be quite weak. A general mathematical method for determining how the inference degrades as the physical process becomes more complex and less well understood has not been formulated. For example, in a complex physical process how do you determine *how nearby* the prediction case is from cases in the validation database? This could be viewed as a topological question in some type of high-dimensional space composed of both model form uncertainty and parameter uncertainty. Struggling with the rigorous specification of the strength or quantification of the inference in a prediction is, and will remain, an important topic of research (Bossel, 1994; Chiles and Delfiner, 1999; Zeigler *et al.*, 2000; Anderson and Bates, 2001).

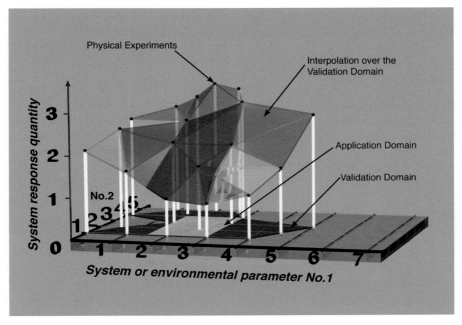

Figure 2.10 Possible relationships of the validation domain to the application domain. See color plate section. (a) Complete overlap of the application domain and the validation domain.

To better explain the important relationship of prediction to model validation, consider Figure 2.10. The two horizontal axes of the figure are labeled *system or environmental parameters No. 1 and No. 2*. These are parameters in the model of a physical system that typically come from the system itself, the surroundings, or the environment in which the system is operating. Examples of these parameters are (a) initial speed and angle of impact of an automobile in a crash environment, (b) Mach number and Reynolds number in a gas dynamics problem, (c) amplitude and frequency of vibrational excitation of a structure, and (d) damaged state of a system exposed to an accident or hostile environment. The vertical axis is the SRQ of interest. In most computational analyses, there is typically a group of SRQs of interest, each depending on several system or environmental parameters.

The values of the system or environmental parameters in the physical experiments are shown in Figure 2.10 as points, at the bottom of the white pillars, in the two dimensional space of the system response and system/environmental parameters. The validation domain is defined by the boundary of the physical experiments that have been conducted (the maroon colored region, including the interior region noted by the tan color). The tan-colored rectangular region indicates the application domain. The experimental measurements of the SRQ are shown as the black dots at the top of each white pillar. The SRQ over the validation domain is indicated as a response surface constructed using a piecewise linear interpolation (the light-blue colored surface). The SRQ over the application domain is indicated as the response surface colored either purple or green. For the purpose of discussion here,

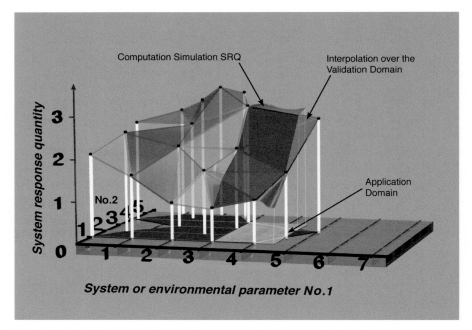

Figure 2.10(b) Partial overlap of the application domain and the validation domain.

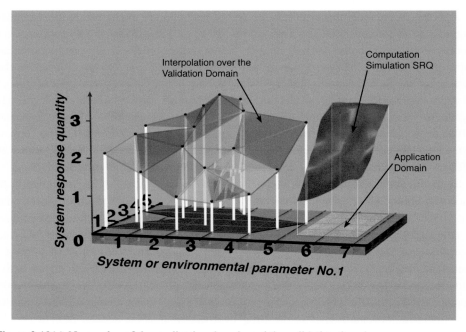

Figure 2.10(c) No overlap of the application domain and the validation domain.

we presume the following three features concerning the experimental and computational results obtained over the validation domain. First, in this region there is high confidence that the relevant physics is understood and modeled at a level that is commensurate with the needs of the application. Second, this confidence has been quantitatively demonstrated by satisfactory agreement between computations and experiments over the validation domain. Third, outside the validation domain there are physical and statistical reasons to expect degradation in confidence in the quantitative predictive capability of the model. Stated differently, if the model is physics-based, then the model has some credibility outside the validation domain. However, its quantitative predictive capability has not been assessed and, therefore, can only be estimated by extrapolation.

Figure 2.10a depicts the prevalent and desirable situation in engineering; that is, the complete overlap of the validation domain with the application domain. In this region the SRQ can be computed from interpolation of either the experimental measurements or the computational results, whichever is judged to be more accurate and/or reliable. The vast majority of modern engineering system design is represented in Figure 2.10a. Stated differently, engineering systems over the centuries have been predominately designed, and their performance determined, based on experimental testing.

Figure 2.10b represents the common engineering situation where there is significant overlap between the validation domain and the application domain. There are, however, portions of the application domain outside the validation domain, shown in green in Figure 2.10b. These regions primarily rely on extrapolation of the model to predict the SRQs of interest. Here we are *not* dealing with the question of whether the validation domain can or cannot be extended to include the application domain shown in green. Keep in mind that the number of the system or environmental parameters in a real engineering system commonly numbers ten to hundreds. For this high dimensional space, it is very common for portions of the application domain to be outside the validation domain in at least some of the parameter dimensions. In fact, in high dimensional spaces, it becomes very difficult to even determine if one is within a hyper-volume or not. Some examples of significant overlap of the validation domain and the application domain are: prediction of the crash response of automobile structures and occupants at conditions slightly different from the test database, prediction of aerodynamic drag on a vehicle design that is somewhat different than the test database on existing vehicles, and prediction of the performance of a gas turbine engine for flight conditions that are similar to, but not exactly attainable, using existing test facilities.

Figure 2.10c depicts the situation where there is not only no overlap between the validation domain and the application domain, but the application domain is *far* from the validation domain. This situation necessitates model extrapolation well beyond the demonstrated physical understanding and the statistical knowledge gained from the experimental data. Some examples are: entry of a spacecraft probe into the atmosphere of another planet; prediction of the fracture dynamics of an aircraft engine fan cowling made of new materials under operational conditions, such as the loss of a fan blade; and prediction of steam explosions in a severe accident environment of a nuclear power plant. For many high-consequence systems, predictions are in this realm because experiments cannot be performed for closely related conditions. For the case suggested in Figure 2.10c, the strength of inference from the validation domain must rely primarily on the fidelity of the physics embodied in the model. The need to perform this extrapolation reinforces our need for models to be critically judged on the basis of achieving the right answers for the right reasons in the validation regime.

A detailed discussion of the procedural steps used in developing a predictive capability is given in Chapter 13.

2.2.5 Calibration

The ASME Guide (ASME, 2006) gives the definition of model *calibration* as:

Calibration: the process of adjusting physical modeling parameters in the computational model to improve agreement with experimental data.

Calibration is primarily directed toward improving the agreement of computational results with existing experimental data, *not* determining the accuracy of the results. Model calibration is also referred to as model updating or model tuning. Because of technical issues (such as limited experimental data or poor understanding of the physics), or practical issues (such as constraints in program schedules, fiscal budgets, and computer resources), calibration is a more appropriate process than is validation. If one were to concentrate on experiments and simulations for only one component or unit problem, then the distinction between calibration and validation would usually be clear. However, if one examines a complete system, it is found that some elements of the validation hierarchy involved calibration and some are focused on validation. As a result, both model calibration and validation commonly occur during different phases of the computational analysis of a complete system. Attempts should be made to recognize when calibration is done simply for expediency because it directly impacts the confidence in predictions from the model. Calibration of model parameters typically confounds a variety of weaknesses in a model, thereby resulting in decreased predictive capability of the model. *How* model calibration impacts the confidence in predictive capability is very difficult to determine and is presently an active research topic.

Model calibration can be considered as part of the broader field of parameter estimation. Parameter estimation refers to procedures for estimating any type of parameter in a model using supplied data, e.g., experimentally measured data or computationally generated data. The estimated parameter can be either a deterministic value, such as a single value determined by some optimization process, or a nondeterministic value, such as a random variable.

Calibration is generally needed in the modeling of complex physical processes, when one must deal with incomplete or imprecise measurements in the experiments, or when physical parameters cannot be directly measured in an experiment. Examples of technical fields that commonly use model calibration are multi-phase fluid flow, structural dynamics, fracture

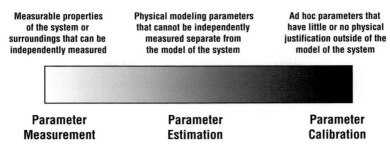

Measurable properties of the system or surroundings that can be independently measured	Physical modeling parameters that cannot be independently measured separate from the model of the system	Ad hoc parameters that have little or no physical justification outside of the model of the system
Parameter Measurement	**Parameter Estimation**	**Parameter Calibration**

Figure 2.11 Spectrum of parameter measurement, estimation, and calibration.

mechanics, meteorology, hydrology, and reservoir engineering. Sometimes the parameters requiring calibration result from a phenomenological model or approximations made in mathematical modeling, e.g., effective quantities. Phenomenological models are those that express mathematically the results of observed phenomena without paying detailed attention to the physical causes. These types of model are commonly used as submodels in describing complex physical processes. Quite often the parameters that need calibration are not independently or physically measurable at all, but only exist as adjustable parameters in a mathematical model. Although the definition of calibration refers to a parameter, the parameter can be a scalar, a scalar field, a vector, or a tensor field.

Because of the wide range in which calibration and parameter estimation can enter a simulation, these procedures should be considered as a spectrum of activities. Figure 2.11 shows a three-level spectrum that can constructively segregate these different activities. At the left, more confident, end of the spectrum one has *parameter measurement*. By this we mean the determination of physically meaningful parameters that can be measured, in principle, using simple, independent models. There are many physical parameters in this category, for example: mechanical properties, such as Young's modulus, tensile strength, hardness, mass density, viscosity, and porosity; electrical properties, such as electrical conductivity, dielectric constant, and piezoelectric constants; thermal properties, such as thermal conductivity, specific heat, vapor pressure, and melting point; and chemical properties, such as pH, surface energy, and reactivity. In the middle of the spectrum one has *parameter estimation*. By this we mean the determination of physically meaningful parameters that can only, in practice, be determined using a complex model. Some examples are (a) internal dynamic damping in a material, (b) aerodynamic damping of a structure, (c) damping and stiffness of assembled joints in a multi-element structure, (d) effective reaction rate in turbulent reacting flow, and (e) effective surface area of droplets in multiphase flow. At the right end of the spectrum one has *parameter calibration*. By this we mean adjustment of a parameter that has little or no physical meaning outside of the model in which it is used. Some examples are (a) most parameters in fluid dynamic turbulence models, (b) parameters obtained by regression fits of experimental data, and (c) ad hoc parameters that are added to a model to simply obtain agreement with experimental data.

The spectrum shown in Figure 2.11 can aid in judging the physical soundness and trust-worthiness of how parameters are determined. As one moves to the right in this spectrum, the confidence in extrapolating the model decreases significantly. Stated differently, the uncertainty in a prediction increases rapidly as one extrapolates a model that has heavily relied on parameter estimation and especially calibration. Concerning parameter adjustment in models versus blind prediction of models, Lipton made a graphic comparison:

Accommodation [calibration] is like drawing the bull's-eye afterwards, whereas in prediction the target is there in advance (Lipton, 2005).

There are situations where the spectrum shown in Figure 2.11 is distorted because of the procedure that is used to determine a parameter. That is, when certain parameter adjustment procedures are used that are normally considered as parameter measurement or parameter estimation, one can cause a fundamental shift toward the parameter calibration category. Some examples are:

- well-known, physically meaningful parameters are changed simply to obtain agreement with newly obtained system-level experimental measurements;
- parameters are readjusted when unrelated submodels are changed;
- parameters are readjusted when spatial mesh refinement or discretization time step are changed;
- parameters are readjusted when numerical algorithms are changed;
- parameters are readjusted when a code bug is eliminated, and the code bug had nothing to do with the parameters being adjusted.

Such things as convenience, expediency, excessive experimental and simulation costs, and project schedule requirements commonly induce the above listed examples.

Consider the following three examples to help clarify the issues involved in parameter measurement, parameter estimation, and calibration. First, suppose one is interested in determining Young's modulus, also known as the modulus of elasticity of a material, in solid mechanics. Young's modulus, E, is defined as

$$E = \frac{\text{tensile stress}}{\text{tensile strain}} . \tag{2.1}$$

An experiment is conducted in which the tensile stress and tensile strain are measured over the linear elastic range of the material and then a value for E is computed. Although a mathematical model is used to define E, it would be inappropriate to say that E is calibrated because the physics of the process is very well understood. The appropriate term for this activity would be *measurement* of E. If a large number of material samples were drawn from some production batch of material, then parameter estimation methods could be used to characterize the variability of the production batch. The result would then be given as a probability distribution to describe the variability in E.

Second, suppose that a structural dynamics simulation is conducted on a structure that is constructed from several structural members and all of these members are bolted together. All of the structural members are made from the same batch of material as the previous experiment to measure E, which is needed in the simulation. A finite element model is made for the structure and an experiment is conducted in which the structure is excited over the linear range. Various vibration modes of the structure are measured and a parameter optimization procedure is used to determine the joint stiffness and damping in the mathematical model that results in the best match of the experimental data. Assume that all of the attachment joints are of the same design and the pre-load torque on all of the bolts is the same. This procedure to determine the stiffness and damping in the bolted joints is referred to as *parameter estimation*. It is obvious that these two parameters, joint stiffness and damping, cannot be measured independently from the model for the vibration of the structure, i.e., the structural members must be bolted together before the structure exists. As a result, the term *parameter estimation* would properly characterize this procedure in the spectrum shown in Figure 2.11.

Third, consider a similar structural dynamics simulation to before, but now the geometry of the structure is more complex with many structural members of varying thicknesses and cross-sections, all bolted together. All of the structural members, however, are made from the same batch of material as the above experimental measurement of E. If the value of E in the simulation of the vibration of this structure were allowed to be an adjustable parameter, then E would be considered as a *calibrated* parameter. That is, the parameter is allowed to change simply due to expediency in the simulation. For this simple example, there is no physical reason to claim that E has changed. Confidence in the predictive capability of the calibrated model could be seriously questioned and the uncertainty in the predictions for similar structures would be difficult to estimate.

A more detailed discussion of the more common calibration procedures is given in Chapters 12 and 13.

2.2.6 *Certification and accreditation*

The IEEE (IEEE, 1991) defines *certification* as:

Certification: a written guarantee that a system or component complies with its specified requirements and is acceptable for operational use.

For our purposes, the "system or component" will be considered either a model, a code, or a simulation. For simplicity, all of these will be referred to as an *entity*. In certification of an entity, the written guarantee of acceptable performance can be generated by anyone who is willing to accept the responsibility or legal liability associated with the guarantee. Model developers, code developers, code assessors, or organizations could provide the written guarantee required for certification. For example, a national laboratory, a governmental organization, or a commercial code company could certify their own codes. The documentation for certification is normally done in a more formal manner than is the documentation for model validation. Thus, the team or organization conducting the certification would provide the detailed documentation for the simulations conducted, the experimental data used in the test cases, and the results from comparing simulations with highly-accurate solutions and experiments.

The DoD (DoD, 1994; DoD, 1996; DoD, 1997) defines *accreditation* as:

Accreditation: the official certification that a model or simulation is acceptable for use for a specific
  purpose.

The definition of accreditation uses the phrase "model or simulation," whereas the definition
of certification uses the phrase "system or component." This, however, is not the crux of the
difference between these two terms. The fundamental difference between the terms certification and accreditation is the phrase "written guarantee" versus "official certification" in
certification and accreditation, respectively. As one might suspect, these terms suggest that
the focus is changing from technical issues to legal, control authority, and liability issues
when moving from certification to accreditation. Note that the DoD does not formally use
the term *certification*, and the IEEE does not formally use the term *accreditation*.

   In accreditation, *only* officially designated individuals or organizations can provide the
guarantee of "acceptable for use for a specific purpose." Typically, the customer (or potential customer) or a separate legal representative has the authority to select the individual or
organization that can accredit the entity. The accrediting authority is *never* the entity developers, anyone from the developers' organization, or anyone else who might have a vested
interest in the performance, accuracy, or sale of the entity. Considering high-consequence
public safety risks and environmental impact, one can make a convincing argument that
accreditation of entities is plainly needed. The fundamental difference between accreditation and certification is the level of authority, independence, and responsibility to guarantee
the performance or accuracy of the entity. In addition, when compared to certification, the
accreditation of an entity is generally more formal, involves more in-depth entity testing,
and requires more extensive documentation. Note that commercial software companies
never make any statement of certification or accreditation. In fact, the *Conditions of Use*
statement that one must agree to specifically states, "No warranty is expressed or implied
with this product." It is doubtful, however, this would absolve the software company of
complete legal liability.

   Certification and accreditation can also be viewed as increasing levels of independence
of assessment in V&V activities. A number of researchers and practitioners over a wide
range of fields of scientific computing have pointed out the importance and value of independent V&V (see, e.g., Lewis, 1992; Gass, 1993; Arthur and Nance, 1996). The levels
of independence in the V&V assessment of scientific computing entities can be viewed
as a continuum (Figure 2.12). The least independent evaluation, i.e., no independence,
occurs when the entity developer conducts assessment activities. Essentially all research
activities are conducted at this first level of assessment. Some observers may question the
adequacy of the first-level assessment, except possibly the developer. Only with some level
of independence and objectivity of the assessors can one have the proper perspective for
critical appraisal. For example, it is common that the developer's ego, his/her professional
esteem or reputation, or the public image or future business opportunities of the sponsoring organization are intertwined with the entity. Evaluation only by developers is *never*

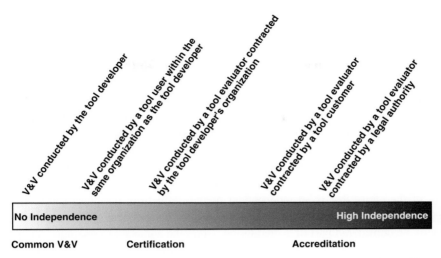

Figure 2.12 Spectrum of independence of V&V levels applied to scientific computing entities.

recommended for any production or commercial entity, or any computational results that can have significant organizational, safety, or security impact.

At the second level, the V&V evaluation is conducted by a user of the entity who is in the same or a closely related organization as the developer of the entity. Thus, a user can also be an entity evaluator, but the user *cannot* be one of the developers. This level of independence in evaluation is a major step commonly not appreciated by the management of research organizations that develop scientific computing entities. The entity evaluator at this second level can have various degrees of independence from the entity developer. If the entity evaluator is in the same group or team, e.g., the lowest-level organizational unit, then the independence of the entity evaluator is marginal. If the entity evaluator is in a group separated laterally by two or three lines of management from the entity developer's management, then the evaluation has much improved independence. For example, the entity evaluator could be a potential user of the entity in a design group that conducts computational analyses for product design or manufacturing processes. It is suggested that the minimum level of evaluation independence that should be considered for certification is separation of the entity developer and the entity evaluator by two to three lines of management.

At the third level, the V&V evaluation is conducted by an entity evaluator who is contracted by the entity developer's organization. This level of evaluation typically provides considerable independence for the entity evaluator because an external contractor is commonly hired for the task. At this level, and the higher levels to be discussed, information concerning the credentials of the contractor should be obtained to ensure that the contractor is objective in the evaluation and has the proper expertise for the evaluation. Occasionally, a monetary bonus is paid to the contractor if the contractor demonstrates exceptional thoroughness and vigor in evaluating the entity. For example, the contractor may be paid a bonus for each coding error, data input error, or failure to meet a specification. If national security classification or extraordinary proprietary issues are a concern, the evaluator could be employed from a subsidiary or sister organization. For this case, the evaluator would not have any organizational connection to the entity developer's organization or to the anticipated users of the entity. This level of independent V&V provides fresh perspectives on the entity's performance, robustness, applicability, and reliability. In addition, this level of independent V&V commonly provides helpful and constructive ideas for significant improvements in the entity's performance or documentation. This level of independence could be viewed as strong certification, but not accreditation because the entity developer's organization is still in control of all of the information obtained in the assessment.

At the fourth level, the V&V evaluation is conducted by an entity evaluator who is contracted by the customer or potential customer of the entity. By *customer* we mean a user of the entity that is an independent organization from the developer's organization. This shift is a significant increase in the level of independent assessment and would normally be considered part of accreditation. Here, the authority to guarantee the performance, accuracy, or quality of the entity has moved from the entity developer's organization to a customer-oriented organization. This amount of insulation between the entity developer and the entity evaluator is appropriate for certain situations, such as those mentioned previously, but can also cause technical and practical problems. These problems are discussed as part of the next level of independence. The interpretation of accreditation commonly assumes that the assessment authority moves from the developer to the customer of the entity. If the developer and customer of the entity are essentially the same, then our assumption of independence does not apply. For example, in many DoD simulation activities the developer and the customer are essentially the same, or very closely related. As a result, this arrangement would not adhere to our interpretation of accreditation independence.

At the fifth level of independence, the V&V evaluation is conducted by an entity evaluator who is contracted by an *independent legal authority* or *governmental organization*. The evaluation authority has now moved not only further from the entity developer, but also moved from the entity customer, i.e., the user. The amount of insulation between the entity developer and the entity evaluator at the fifth level can be quite beneficial to the independent legal authority or governmental organization responsible for performance assessment of high-consequence systems. However, this insulation can have a detrimental effect on the quality of the computational analysis desired by the scientific and engineering community. Weakening the scientific quality of the entity is clearly not the intent of accreditation, but it can be a by-product. For example, any changes to the entity, even those intended to improve accuracy, efficiency, or robustness, cannot be made unless the entity is re-accredited. As a result, modifying an entity becomes a very time-consuming and expensive process. The degree to which the accreditation procedure can weaken the quality of computational analyses is illustrated, in our view, by the history of the safety assessment of nuclear power reactors in the United States. Currently, it is not clear how to achieve a better balance between the need for improving the quality of entities and the need for adequate assurance of public safety.

2.3 Types and sources of uncertainties

Computational simulation attempts to bring together what is known in terms of certainty and what is uncertain in the analysis of a system. Science and engineering has strongly tended to emphasize what we know, or think we know, instead of what is uncertain. There can be many different types of uncertainties that occur in computational analyses. A large number of researchers and practitioners in risk assessment (Morgan and Henrion, 1990; Kumamoto and Henley, 1996; Cullen and Frey, 1999; Suter, 2007; Vose, 2008; Haimes, 2009), engineering reliability (Melchers, 1999; Modarres *et al.*, 1999; Ayyub and Klir, 2006), information theory (Krause and Clark, 1993; Klir *et al.*, 1997; Cox, 1999), and philosophy of science (Smithson, 1989) have dealt with categorizing types of uncertainty. Many of the categorizations that have been constructed tend to mix the nature or essence of a type of uncertainty with how or where it might occur in computational analysis. For example, some taxonomies would have randomness as one type and model-form uncertainty as another type. A sound taxonomy would *only* categorize uncertainty types according to their fundamental essence, and then discuss how that essence could be embodied in different aspects of a simulation. For types of uncertainty that can be identified and characterized in some way, the computational analysis that incorporates these uncertainties will result in nondeterministic outcomes. By *nondeterministic* outcomes we mean those that explicitly acknowledge uncertainty in some way. Although these outcomes may be more difficult to interpret and deal with than deterministic outcomes, the goal of nondeterministic simulations is to improve the understanding of the processes in complex systems, as well as to improve the design and decision making related to these systems.

During the last 25 years, the risk assessment community, primarily the nuclear reactor safety community, has developed the most workable and effective categorization of uncertainties: aleatory and epistemic uncertainties. Some of the key developers of this categorization were Kaplan and Garrick (1981); Parry and Winter (1981); Bogen and Spear (1987); Parry (1988); Apostolakis (1990); Morgan and Henrion (1990); Hoffman and Hammonds (1994); Ferson and Ginzburg (1996); and Paté-Cornell (1996). See the following texts for a detailed discussion of aleatory and epistemic uncertainties: Casti (1990); Morgan and Henrion (1990); Cullen and Frey (1999); Ayyub and Klir (2006); Vose (2008); and Haimes (2009). The benefits of distinguishing between aleatory and epistemic uncertainty include improved interpretation of simulation results by analysts and decision makers, and improved strategies on how to decrease system response uncertainty when both are present. As will be discussed, the fundamental nature of each is different. As a result, different approaches are required to characterize and reduce each type of uncertainty.

2.3.1 Aleatory uncertainty

Consistent with the references just given, *aleatory uncertainty* is defined as:

Aleatory uncertainty: uncertainty due to inherent randomness.

Aleatory uncertainty is also referred to as stochastic uncertainty, variability, inherent uncertainty, uncertainty due to chance, and Type A uncertainty. The fundamental nature of aleatory uncertainty is randomness, e.g., from a stochastic process. Randomness can, in principle, be reduced, e.g., by improved control of a random process, but if it is removed, for example, by assumption, then you have fundamentally changed the nature of the analysis. Aleatory uncertainty can exist due to inter-individual differences, such as random heterogeneity in a population, and it can exist spatially or temporally. Sources of aleatory uncertainty can commonly be singled out from other contributors to uncertainty by their representation as randomly distributed quantities that may take on values in a known range, but for which the exact value will vary by chance from unit to unit, point to point in space, or time to time. The mathematical representation, or characterization, most commonly used for aleatory uncertainty is a probability distribution.

Aleatory uncertainty can be embodied in two ways in computational analyses: in the model form itself and in parameters of the model. If the model is given by a differential operator, then aleatory uncertainty in the model form can be expressed as a stochastic differential operator. Although there have been some applications of stochastic differential operators to actual engineering systems, this type of modeling is in its very early stages (Taylor and Karlin, 1998; Kloeden and Platen, 2000; Serrano, 2001; Oksendal, 2003). Aleatory uncertainty in parameters is, by far, a much more common situation in computational analyses. Aleatory uncertainty in parameters can occur in the mathematical description of the system and its characteristics, initial conditions, boundary conditions, or excitation function. Typically, aleatory uncertainty occurs in a scalar quantity appearing in the PDE, but it can also appear as a vector or a field quantity. Some examples of scalar parameters having random variability are: variability in geometric dimensions of manufactured parts; variability of the gross takeoff weight of a commercial airliner; and variability of the atmospheric temperature on a given day, at a given location on earth.

Consider a simple example of a scalar variability in a heat conduction analysis. Suppose one were interested in heat conduction through a homogenous material whose thermal conductivity varied from unit to unit due to a manufacturing process. Assume that a large number of samples have been drawn from the material population produced by the manufacturing process and the thermal conductivity has been measured on each of these samples. Figure 2.13 shows both the probability density function (PDF) and the cumulative distribution function (CDF) representing the thermal conductivity as a continuous random variable. The PDF and the CDF both represent the variability of the thermal conductivity of the population, but each show it in a different way. The variability of the population could also be shown as a histogram. The PDF (Figure 2.13a) shows the probability density of any chosen value of conductivity x. Stated differently, it shows the probability per unit variation in conductivity for any value x. The CDF (Figure 2.13b) shows the fraction of the population that would have a conductivity less than or equal to the particular value of conductivity chosen x. For example, the probability is 0.87 that all possible thermal conductivity values will be 0.7 or lower.

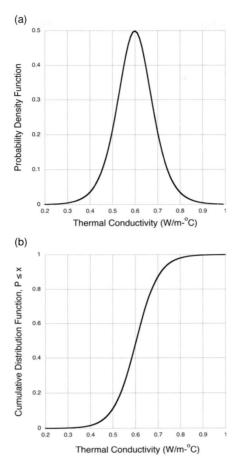

Figure 2.13 Examples of PDF and CDF for variability of thermal conductivity: (a) probability density function and (b) cumulative distribution function.

2.3.2 Epistemic uncertainty

Consistent with references cited above, *epistemic uncertainty* is defined as:

Epistemic uncertainty: uncertainty due to lack of knowledge.

Epistemic uncertainty is also referred to as reducible uncertainty, knowledge uncertainty, and subjective uncertainty. In the risk assessment community, it is common to refer to epistemic uncertainty simply as *uncertainty* and aleatory uncertainty as *variability*. The fundamental source of epistemic uncertainty is incomplete information or incomplete knowledge of any type that is related to the system of interest or its simulation. Epistemic uncertainty is a property of the modeler or observer, whereas aleatory uncertainty is a property of the system being modeled or observed. The lack of knowledge can be related to modeling issues for

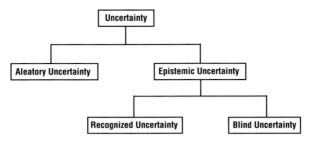

Figure 2.14 Classification of uncertainties.

the system, computational issues of the model, or experimental data needed for validation. Modeling issues include lack of knowledge of characteristics or processes in the system, the initial state of the system, or the surroundings or environment of the system. Computational issues include programming mistakes, estimation of numerical solution errors, and numerical approximations in algorithms. Experimental data issues include incomplete knowledge of experimental information that is needed for simulation of the experiment and approximations or corrections that are made in the processing of the experimental data. An increase in knowledge or information can lead to a reduction in epistemic uncertainty and thereby a reduction in the uncertainty of the response of the system, given that no other changes are made.

Taking a complementary perspective, it is seen that the fundamental characteristic of epistemic uncertainty is ignorance; specifically ignorance by an individual, or group of individuals, conducting a computational analysis. Smithson (1989) points out that ignorance is a social construction, analogous to the creation of knowledge. Ignorance can only be discussed by referring to the viewpoint of one individual (or group) with respect to another. Smithson gives the following working definition of ignorance:

A is *ignorant* from B's viewpoint if A fails to agree with or show awareness of ideas which B defines as actually or potentially valid.

This definition avoids the absolutist problem by placing the onus on B to define what he/she means by ignorance. It also permits self-attributed ignorance, since A and B can be the same person.

Ayyub (2001), following Smithson, divides ignorance into two types: conscious ignorance and blind ignorance. Conscious ignorance is defined as a self-ignorance recognized through reflection. Conscious ignorance would include, for example, any assumptions or approximations made in modeling, the use of expert opinion, and numerical solution errors. For conscious ignorance, we will use the term *recognized uncertainty* to mean any epistemic uncertainty that has been recognized in some way. Blind ignorance is defined as ignorance of self-ignorance or unknown unknowns. For blind ignorance, we will use the term *blind uncertainty* to mean any epistemic uncertainty that has *not* been recognized in some way. Figure 2.14 shows the categorization of uncertainty that will be used. Recognized uncertainty and blind uncertainty will now be discussed in detail, along with where and how they occur in computational analyses.

2.3.2.1 Recognized uncertainty

Although introduced above, we define *recognized uncertainty* more formally as:

Recognized uncertainty: an epistemic uncertainty for which a conscious decision has been made to either characterize or deal with it in some way, or to ignore it for practical reasons.

For example, in making decisions concerning the modeling of a system, one makes assumptions concerning what physics will be included in the model and what will be ignored. Whether a certain type of physical phenomenon is included or ignored, or a specific type of conceptual model is chosen, these are recognized uncertainties. Assumptions such as these are usually referred to as model form uncertainties, i.e., uncertainties due to the assumptions made in the modeling of the physics. Depending on the complexity of the physics involved, a modeler could, in concept, change the assumptions or the model and possibly estimate the magnitude of the effect on system response quantities of interest. Regardless of what level of physics modeling fidelity is chosen there are *always* spatial and temporal scales of physics, as well as coupled physics, that are ignored. A balance must be decided between what physics should be included in the modeling and the time and effort (both computational and experimental resources) needed to simulate the desired system responses. Whether the magnitude of the effect of an assumption or approximation is estimated or not, it is still a recognized uncertainty.

Another example of a recognized uncertainty is obtaining opinions from experts when experimental data is not available. For example, suppose an expert is asked to provide an opinion on his/her belief of a scalar parameter in the system that is a fixed quantity, but the value of the quantity is not known. The expert may provide an opinion in the form of a single number, but more likely the opinion would be given as an interval in which the true value is believed to be. Similarly, suppose an expert is asked to provide an opinion on a parameter that is characterized by a random variable. They would probably provide a named family of distributions for the characterization, along with estimated fixed values for the parameters of the family. Alternately, they could also provide interval values for the parameters of the family. In either case, the scalar parameter in the system would be a mixture of aleatory and epistemic uncertainty, because it represents expert opinion for a random variable.

Since the root cause of a recognized uncertainty is incomplete knowledge, increasing the knowledge base can reduce the epistemic uncertainty. Epistemic uncertainty can be reduced by an action that generates relevant information, such as allowing for a stronger level of physics coupling in a model, accounting for a newly recognized failure mode of a system, changing a calculation from single precision to double precision arithmetic, and performing an experiment to obtain knowledge of system parameters or boundary conditions imposed on the system. Epistemic uncertainty can also be reduced by eliminating the possibility of the existence of certain states, conditions, or values of a quantity. By reducing the collection (or sample space) of possible events, one is reducing the magnitude of uncertainty due to ignorance. For example, suppose a system failure mode or dangerous system state has been identified such that it could occur if the system is incorrectly assembled. If the system is redesigned such that the system cannot be improperly assembled, then the epistemic uncertainty in the system response has been reduced.

The amount of information produced by an action could be measured by the resulting reduction in the uncertainty of either an input or output quantity. Treating uncertainty as an aspect of information theory or considering more general representations of uncertainty has led to the development of a number of new, or expanded, mathematical theories during the last three decades. Examples of the newer theories are (a) fuzzy set theory (Klir *et al.*, 1997; Cox, 1999; Dubois and Prade, 2000); (b) interval analysis (Moore, 1979; Kearfott and Kreinovich, 1996); (c) probability bounds analysis, which is closely related to second order probability, two-dimensional Monte Carlo sampling, and nested Monte Carlo sampling (Bogen and Spear, 1987; Helton, 1994; Hoffman and Hammonds, 1994; Ferson and Ginzburg, 1996; Helton, 1997; Cullen and Frey, 1999; Ferson and Hajagos, 2004; Suter, 2007; Vose, 2008); (d) evidence theory, also called Dempster–Shafer theory (Guan and Bell, 1991; Krause and Clark, 1993; Almond, 1995; Kohlas and Monney, 1995; Klir and Wierman, 1998; Fetz *et al.*, 2000; Helton *et al.*, 2005; Oberkampf and Helton, 2005; Bae *et al.*, 2006); (e) possibility theory (Dubois and Prade, 1988; de Cooman *et al.*, 1995); and (f) theory of upper and lower previsions (Walley, 1991; Kozine, 1999). Some of these theories only deal with epistemic uncertainty, but most deal with both epistemic and aleatory uncertainty. In addition, some deal with other varieties of uncertainty, e.g., nonclassical logics appropriate for artificial intelligence and vagueness due to language (Klir and Yuan, 1995).

2.3.2.2 Blind Uncertainty

Our formal definition of *blind uncertainty* is:

Blind uncertainty: an epistemic uncertainty for which it is not recognized that the knowledge is incomplete and that the knowledge is relevant to modeling the system of interest.

Adding knowledge can reduce blind uncertainty, just as with recognized uncertainty. However, the approach and the procedures are quite different because one is attempting to identify unknown unknowns. The most common causes of blind uncertainty are human errors, blunders, or mistakes in judgment. Some examples are: programming errors made in software used in the simulation, mistakes made in the preparation of input data or post-processing of output data, blunders made in recording or processing experimental data used for validation, and not recognizing how a system could be easily misused or damaged so that the system could be very dangerous to operate. Blind uncertainty can also be caused by inadequate communication between individuals contributing to the M&S, for example: (a) between those providing expert opinion and those interpreting and characterizing the information for input to the modeling, and (b) between computational analysts and experimentalists working on validation activities. In experimental activities, some additional examples of blind uncertainty are unrecognized bias errors in diagnostic techniques or experimental facilities and improper procedures in using a reference standard in the calibration of experimental equipment.

There are *no* reliable methods for estimating or bounding the magnitude of blind uncertainties, their impact on a model, its simulation, or on the system's response. As a result, the primary approach for dealing with blind uncertainties is to try to identify them through such techniques as: (a) redundant procedures and protocols for operations or analyses, (b) various software and hardware testing procedures, (c) use of different experimental facilities, (d) use of a variety of expert opinions, and (e) use of broader sampling procedures to try to detect a blind uncertainty. Once blind uncertainties are identified or a hint of their existence is recognized, then they can be pursued or dealt with in some way or the impact of their effect could possibly be estimated or removed. For example, as discussed earlier in code verification, testing of numerical algorithms and SQA practices have proven effective in finding algorithm deficiencies and code bugs. Methods have been developed to estimate the frequency of coding errors, e.g., average number of static or dynamic faults per hundred lines of code. However, these measures do not address the possible *impact* of undetected coding errors. Human mistakes made in input preparation for simulations and mistakes in processing of output data are most commonly detected by having separate individuals check the data or by having completely separate teams conduct the same simulation, using the same modeling assumptions, and possibly even the same computer code, to detect any differences in results. For centuries, experimental science has been built on the crucial importance of independent reproducibility of experimental results and measurements. Scientific computing has a great deal to learn from this venerable tradition.

To stress the personal or social aspect of blind uncertainty, (Ayyub, 2001) gives several thought-provoking examples of root causes of blind uncertainty: knowledge that is dismissed as irrelevant (yet it is relevant); knowledge or experience that is ignored (yet it should not be ignored); and knowledge or questioning that is avoided or shunned because it is socially, culturally, or politically considered taboo. This personal aspect of blind uncertainty, and some of those mentioned earlier, can be countered, to some extent, by independent and/or external peer reviews of a computational effort. The effectiveness of an external review depends to a great extent on the independence, creativeness, expertise, and authority of the external reviewers. If an external review is focused on finding weaknesses, errors, or deficiencies, they are commonly referred to as *Red Team* reviews. Sometimes Red Teams have such high enthusiasm and zeal, one wonders if they are friends or enemies.

2.4 Error in a quantity

There are many situations in scientific computing and in experimental measurements where the concept of *error* proves to be quite useful. We will use the common dictionary definition of error.

Error in a quantity: a deviation from the true value of the quantity.

This definition is also used in a number of metrology texts (Grabe, 2005; Rabinovich, 2005; Drosg, 2007). To be more specific, let y_T be the true value of the quantity y, and let

$y_{obtained}$ be the obtained value of the quantity *y*. *Obtained value* means that the result can be derived from any source, e.g., numerical solution, computational simulation, experimental measurement, or expert opinion. It is assumed that y_T and $y_{obtained}$ are fixed numbers, as opposed to random quantities, i.e., realizations of a random variable. Then the error in $y_{obtained}$ is defined as

$$\varepsilon_{obtained} = y_{obtained} - y_T. \tag{2.2}$$

Many texts and technical articles use the terms *error* and *uncertainty* interchangeably. We believe, however, that this produces a great deal of confusion and misinterpretation of the fundamental concepts. In addition, interchangeable use of the terms error and uncertainty can lead to a misrepresentation of results, causing misguided efforts directed at reduction or elimination of the source of the error or uncertainty.

As was discussed in Section 2.3, the concept of uncertainty fundamentally deals with whether the source is either stochastic in nature or its nature is lack of knowledge. The concept of error *does not* address the nature of the source, but concentrates on the identification of the true value. The true value can be defined in a number of different ways. For example, the true value of a physical constant, such as the gravitational constant or the speed of light in a vacuum, can be defined in multiple ways depending on the accuracy needed for the situation. The true value can also be defined as a reference standard, for example, the reference standards for length, mass, and time are set by the International System of Units. In scientific computing, it is sometimes convenient to define a true value as a floating-point number with specified precision in a computer. However, in most simulations the true value in not known or is not representable with finite precision, and in experimental measurements of engineering and scientific quantities the true value is *never* known.

As a result, the usefulness of the concept of error in practical applications depends on the definition and accuracy of the true value. If the accuracy of the true value is known, or the true value is given by an appropriate definition, and the accuracy of the true value is much higher than the $y_{obtained}$ value, then the concept of error is quite useful, both conceptually and practically. For example, consider the case in code verification where an analytical solution to the PDEs can be computed with high accuracy, e.g., known to the double precision accuracy of the computer being used. One could define the error as the difference between the particular solution obtained by a code and the highly accurate analytical solution. If, however, the accuracy of the analytical solution is not computed very accurately, e.g., using an insufficient number of terms in an infinite series expansion, then the concepts and terminology associated with uncertainties are more useful in practice.

For example, consider the case of two computer codes solving the same physics models, but using different numerical solution procedures. Suppose that one of the codes has been traditionally accepted as producing the "correct" result and the other code is relatively new. One could define the error as the difference between the new code result and the traditional code result. Unless the traditional code result has been thoroughly investigated and the accuracy carefully documented over the range of input parameters, it would be foolish to consider it as producing the true value. A more appropriate

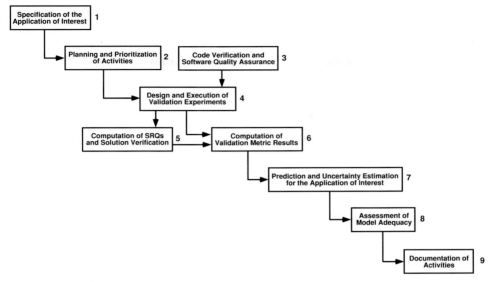

Figure 2.15 Integrated view of the elements of verification, validation, and prediction (adapted from Trucano *et al.*, 2002).

approach would be to characterize the accuracy of the result from each code as epistemically uncertain.

2.5 Integration of verification, validation, and prediction

As suggested earlier in this chapter, V&V are contributing elements in the development of a computational predictive capability. Researchers and code developers in M&S often stress the generality and capability of their models and codes. In some applications of M&S, however, the focus is on (a) quantitative assessment of confidence in the predictions made for a particular application of interest, and (b) how the predictions can be effectively used in a risk-informed decision-making process. By *risk-informed decision-making* we mean decision making that is guided and aided by both the estimated uncertainty in possible future outcomes, as well as the risk associated with those outcomes. Since uncertainty and risk can be very difficult to quantify, in addition to the issue of personal or organizational tolerance for risk, we use the term risk-informed decision-making. Many chapters will discuss uncertainty, and Chapter 3 will define and discuss risk in more detail.

Figure 2.15 depicts an integrated view of the nine elements of the verification, validation, and prediction process we discuss in detail in this book. This integrated view is similar to the ASME Guide diagram (Figure 2.5), but Figure 2.15 stresses the sequential nature of all of the elements of the M&S process. Each of these elements will be discussed in detail in various chapters of this book; however, a brief description of each element will be given here. Many of the concepts described in each element are based on Trucano *et al.* (2002).

Note that although the activities in Figure 2.15 are shown sequentially, the process is commonly an iterative one in practice. For example, when the computational results are compared with the experimental measurements in Element 6, it may be found that the computational results are not as good as expected. One may have several options for iterative adjustment of previously completed elements: (a) alteration of the modeling assumptions made in Element 1; (b) alteration of the application domain specified in Element 1; (c) reprioritization of certain V&V activities in Element 2 so as to better address the cause of the problem; (d) performance of additional code verification activities in Element 3 if the coding is suspect; (e) conducting additional experimental measurements in Element 4 if experimental measurements are suspect; and (f) computing solutions on finer mesh resolutions in Element 5 if the solution error is suspected of causing a problem.

2.5.1 Specification of the application of interest

The first element of the M&S process describes what physical process, engineering system, or event is of interest. One should define in some detail the specific purpose for which the M&S process is being undertaken. If different environments are of interest, such as accident and hostile environments, then it is appropriate to construct completely separate diagrams such as Figure 2.15; one for each environment. (System environments and scenarios will be discussed in detail in Chapter 3.) V&V can be accomplished without the focus on a specific application of interest, such as in software development and research into physical processes. Throughout this text, however, the discussion will usually focus on an application-driven V&V processes. In this first element, the customer for the computational results should be specified, along with how the customer intends to use the results, such as design, optimization, or policy making.

It may seem obvious that the specifications are given for the application of interest at the beginning of a M&S process. However, in both large and small-scale M&S activities there is commonly inadequate communication concerning the primary and secondary goals of the complete activity. The key participants in this discussion are the ultimate users of the computational information generated (referred to as customers of the M&S effort), the stakeholders in the activities, and the computational analysts conducting the work. Each group usually has similar ideas concerning the goals of the effort, but each group always brings a different perspective, priorities, and agenda to the activities. It is common that only after significant effort has been expended, or there are difficulties with the M&S activity, that these groups discover that each has surprisingly different goals for the activities. These types of miscommunication, or lack of communication, are particularly likely if the funding source of the M&S activity is *not* the user of the resulting capability, but some third party. For example, suppose the funding source is a governmental agency that is interested in developing a M&S capability in some application area under their regulatory control. Suppose the intended user of the capability is a contractor to the governmental agency, and the developer of the capability is a different contractor. This triad is especially susceptible to failure due to miscommunication.

As part of the first element, a description should be given for the application domain for the intended use of the model. This would include, for example, specification of the environments and scenarios that the system could be exposed to and which the M&S is suppose to address. This could also include general specification of all of the initial conditions, boundary conditions, and excitation conditions that the system might be exposed to. The anticipated validation domain needed for the application domain should also be described in general terms. At this early stage, the validation domain may only be vaguely anticipated because either the system is in the early design phase or the predictive capability of the model is poorly understood. However, unless the application domain is extremely different from the experience base on similar systems, some existing experimental data will be pertinent to the application domain. Note that an application domain and a validation domain can be specified at multiple tiers of the validation hierarchy discussed earlier in Figure 2.4.

An important part of the first element is the specification of all of the SRQs that are needed from the computational analysis. Some examples of SRQs that may be of interest are (a) temperature distribution inside or on the surface of a solid, (b) maximum stress level within a component or group of components, (c) maximum acceleration as a function of time at any point in or on a structural system, and (d) concentration level of a contaminant or toxic waste along a specified boundary. Closely associated with specification of the SRQs of interest is the specification of the predictive accuracy requirements that are needed from the M&S effort. It is the customer of the effort who should define the predictive accuracy requirements. Sometimes, however, the customer either (a) fails to do this, or (b) is overly demanding of the accuracy requirements. This results in a constructive dialogue and negotiation between the customer and the analysts concerning the cost and schedule required for certain levels of predictive accuracy. Although estimates for costs and schedule, as well as estimated predictive accuracy, are often very poorly known early in an effort, these discussions are critical early on so that all parties, including stakeholders and experimentalists that may need to provide additional validation data, have some feel for the trade-offs involved. Too often, understanding of trade-offs between cost, schedule, and achieved predictive accuracy occur very late in the effort after significant resources, time, and modeling effort have been expended or wasted.

Many of the activities in this element are discussed in Chapters 3, 10, and 14.

2.5.2 *Planning and prioritization of activities*

Formal planning and prioritization of M&S, V&V, and prediction activities are conducted in the second element. The planning and prioritization should attempt to address all of the activities that are conducted in the remaining seven elements shown in Figure 2.15, given the specifications made in Element 1. On a large M&S project, this requires significant resources and effort from a wide variety of individuals and, sometimes, a variety of organizations. On a large project, the effort should also include documentation of the planning and prioritization in a V&V Plan. Preparation of a V&V Plan is also discussed and recommended in the ASME

Guide (ASME, 2006). The Plan should be appropriate to the magnitude of the project and to the consequences of the decisions made based on the computational results.

The focus of the planning and prioritization effort should always be:

Given the resources available (people, time, money, computational facilities, experimental facilities, etc), what is the appropriate level of effort in each activity needed to achieve the goals of the M&S effort identified in Element 1?

Some examples of the types of question addressed in the planning and prioritization element are the following.

- What physical phenomena are important and what level of coupling of the various phenomena are appropriate for the goals of the analysis?
- What are the anticipated application domains and validation domains?
- What are the SRQs of interest and what are the prediction accuracy requirements expected by the customer?
- What code verification and SQA activities are appropriate for the application of interest?
- Are existing numerical error estimation techniques adequate?
- Are new mesh generation capabilities needed for the analysis?
- Are new experimental diagnostics or facilities needed for validation activities?
- Do new validation metric operators need to be developed?
- Are adequate methods available for propagating input uncertainties through the model to obtain output uncertainties?
- If model accuracy or experimental measurements are found to be lacking, what alternatives or contingency plans should be considered?

In our experience, the most commonly used approach for planning and prioritization is the Phenomena Identification and Ranking Table (PIRT) (Boyack *et al.*, 1990; Wilson *et al.*, 1990; Wulff *et al.*, 1990; Wilson and Boyack, 1998; Zuber *et al.*, 1998). PIRT was originally developed to identify physical phenomena, and the coupling of physical phenomena, that could affect nuclear power plant safety in accident scenarios. PIRT should be viewed as a process as well as a collection of information. As stressed by Boyack *et al.* (1990), the PIRT is most certainly not set in stone once it is formulated and documented. While a given formulation of a PIRT guides M&S activities, it must also adapt to reflect the information gathered during the conduct of those activities.

An additional planning and prioritization process was developed by Pilch *et al.*, (2001); Tieszen *et al.* (2002); Trucano *et al.* (2002); and Boughton *et al.* (2003). This process, referred to as a gap analysis, begins with the results of the PIRT process and attempts to answer the question:

Where does the M&S effort presently stand relative to the phenomena and SRQs that have been identified as important?

In the gap analysis portion of the process, the emphasis shifts from improving the understanding of the environments, scenarios, system, and physical phenomena, to an understanding the possible gap between the *present* capabilities and required capabilities of M&S tools.

Answers to this question with regard to modeling, computer codes, verification, validation, and uncertainty quantification can directly aid in planning and prioritization.

The PIRT and gap analysis processes are discussed in detail in Chapter 14, Planning and prioritization in modeling and simulation.

2.5.3 Code verification and software quality assurance activities

Code verification and software quality assurance (SQA) activities are conducted in the third element. Both of these activities can be viewed as the accumulation of evidence to support the belief that: (a) the numerical algorithms are functioning as intended, (b) the source code is implemented correctly and it is functioning as intended, and (c) the computer system hardware and software environment is functioning as intended. It is well known, although rarely stated, that these three essentials (source code, hardware, and system software) *cannot* be proven to be correct and functioning as intended. In fact, experience on any computer system shows that application source codes have programming errors, and hardware and system software have limitations and flaws (sometimes known, i.e., recognized uncertainties, and sometimes unknown, i.e., blind uncertainties). As a result, computer users tend to develop the mind set that the potential for software and hardware errors is ignored up to some level. Individual tolerance levels primarily depend on two very different factors. First, how averse is the individual to the severity and frequency of errors and unreliability in the software and hardware? Second, what are the individual's options for using other software and hardware to accomplish their job? For example, if a user has a low tolerance for software bugs, *and* they have the option to change software, then they may be motivated to make a change. On the other hand, a user: (a) may tolerate buggy, unreliable, software if they have no options, e.g., if there is near monopoly in the software market, or (b) may be forced to use certain system or application software because of corporate or organizational mandates (Platt, 2007).

Given the perspective of the balance between individual tolerance of errors and unreliability on the one hand, and the availability of software options on the other, it is our observation that computer users of computational software show a high tolerance for errors and lack of robustness, as long as the features and capabilities they need for their simulations are perceived to be met. Stated differently, computational software users place little value on the accumulation of evidence for code verification and SQA, as opposed to the value they place on the software having the features and capabilities they need to do their job. This commonly held value-system is, we believe, at the root of why Element 3 in the M&S process receives considerable lip service, but minimal effort when it competes for code development resources. Code development groups, whether they are in-house groups or commercial software companies, understand this value system and they respond accordingly.

The integrated view of V&V and prediction shown in Figure 2.15 does not solve the problem of the competition of resources between code verification and SQA activities versus implementation of features and capabilities needed to complete the M&S goals at hand.

However, Figure 2.15 does call attention to the critical foundation that code verification and SQA activities play in assessing the credibility of a computational result. For example, if a code bug is found later on in the M&S process, say in Element 7, all of the effort devoted to Elements 5 through 7 must be rechecked to see if the bug affected the previous work. If the bug did have an effect on the earlier results, then much of the work is wasted and most has to be redone. The far more dangerous situation is if a relevant code bug was *not found* and trust was placed in the computational results. For example, if good agreement was found between computational and experimental results in Element 6, little interest, energy, and resources may be found to conduct code verification and SQA activities. By using misleading computational results, decision makers may then have unknowingly made erroneous decisions on system safety, performance, or reliability.

Code verification and SQA will be discussed in detail in Chapters 4–6.

2.5.4 Design and execution of validation experiments

Element 4 deals with the design and execution of validation experiments, as well as the more common situation of using existing experimental data in validation activities. Before briefly discussing the design and execution of validation experiments, a few comments should be made concerning how a validation experiment is different from traditional types of experiments. Traditional experiments can generally be grouped into three broad categories (Oberkampf *et al.*, 1995; Aeschliman and Oberkampf, 1998; Oberkampf and Blottner, 1998; Oberkampf and Trucano, 2002). The first category comprises experiments that are conducted primarily for the purpose of improving the fundamental understanding of some physical process. Sometimes these are referred to as physical-discovery or phenomena-discovery experiments. Examples are experiments that investigate (a) turbulent reacting flow, (b) decomposition of materials as they decompose, (c) micromechanics processes underlying crack growth in solids, and (d) properties of materials undergoing phase change at extreme pressure and temperature.

The second category of traditional experiments consists of those conducted primarily for constructing or improving mathematical models of fairly well-understood physical processes. Sometimes these are called model development or model calibration experiments. For these types of experiment, the range of applicability of the model or the level of detail of the physics in the model is not usually important. Examples are experiments to (a) measure the reaction-rate parameters in a model for reacting flows, (b) determine the joint-attachment damping and the aerodynamic damping parameters in the vibration of a built-up structure, (c) determine the parameters in a model for crack propagation in a certain class of composite materials, and (d) calibrate the constitutive parameters in a material model for reinforced concrete.

The third category of traditional experiments includes those that determine the reliability, performance, or safety of components or subsystems, as well as complete engineering systems. Sometimes these are called reliability tests, performance tests, safety tests, certification tests, or qualification tests. Examples are (a) tests of a new compressor or combustor design in a gas turbine engine, (b) tests of a new propellant formulation for a solid rocket motor, (c) tests of the crash worthiness of a new automobile design, and (d) qualification tests of a modified submarine design submerging to maximum operational depth.

A validation experiment, on the other hand, is conducted for the primary purpose of assessing the accuracy of a mathematical model. In other words, a validation experiment is designed, executed, and analyzed for the purpose of quantitatively determining the ability of a mathematical model expressed in computer software to simulate a well-characterized physical process. Thus, in a validation experiment one could state that *the computational analyst is the customer* or *the code is the customer* for the experiment as opposed to, for example, a physical phenomena researcher, a model builder, or a system project manager. Only during the last few decades has M&S matured to the point where it could even be considered as a viable customer. As modern technology increasingly moves toward engineering systems that are designed, certified, and possibly even fielded, based on M&S, then M&S itself will increasingly become the customer of validation experiments.

Since a validation experiment, as defined here, is a relatively new concept, most experimental data generated in Element 4 will be from different types of traditional experiment. Use of experimental data from traditional experiments when used for validation assessment must, as a result, deal with a number of technical and practical difficulties. These difficulties are discussed in Chapter 10, Model validation fundamentals. Here a brief discussion will be given of some of the important aspects of the design and execution of validation experiments. A more detailed discussion will be given in Chapter 11, Design and execution of validation experiments.

Validation experiments in the present context should be designed specifically for the purpose of evaluating the computational predictive capability that is directed toward the application of interest identified in Element 1. Validation experiments can, of course, be designed and executed without a specific application of interest in mind. However, our focus here is on validation experiments directed toward a specific application driver. The planning and prioritization of validation experiments should be a product of Element 2, not only for experimental activities, but also across the entire M&S project. For example, referring back to Figure 2.10c, the issue should be raised in Element 2 concerning resources required for conducting a new validation experiment within the application domain, versus resources expended on additional modeling activities. The approach to these trade-off studies should be: for a given quantity of resources expended, which option most reduces the estimated uncertainty in the predicted SRQs of interest? Even though it is constructive to frame the question as an optimization problem, it must be realized that it is still a very difficult question to answer. Some of these reasons are (a) the resources needed to achieve a certain goal or capability are poorly known; (b) it is only vaguely known what is needed to decrease the uncertainty in an input parameter in order to achieve a decrease in uncertainty in SRQs of interest; (c) the number of parameters in the trade-off space is extremely high; and (d) there are commonly unknown dependencies between some of the parameters in trade-off space, i.e., all of the coordinates in the space are not orthogonal. These issues will be discussed in Chapter 14.

The primary guidelines for the design and execution of validation experiments have been formulated by Aeschliman and Oberkampf (1998); Oberkampf and Blottner (1998); and Oberkampf and Trucano (2002). These six guidelines are:

1 A validation experiment should be jointly designed by experimentalists, model developers, code developers, and code users working closely together throughout the program, from inception to documentation, with complete candor about the strengths and weaknesses of each approach.
2 A validation experiment should be designed to capture the essential physics of interest, and measure all relevant physical modeling data, initial and boundary conditions, and system excitation information required by the model.
3 A validation experiment should strive to emphasize the inherent synergism attainable between computational and experimental approaches.
4 Although the experimental design should be developed cooperatively, independence must be maintained in obtaining the computational and experimental system response results.
5 Experimental measurements should be made of a hierarchy of system response quantities; for example, from globally integrated quantities to local quantities.
6 The experimental design should be constructed to analyze and estimate the components of random (precision) and systematic (bias) experimental uncertainties.

These guidelines will be discussed in detail in Chapter 11, along with a high quality validation experiment example that demonstrates each guideline.

2.5.5 Computation of the system response quantities and solution verification

Element 5 deals with obtaining simulations for the validation experiments conducted, as well as assessing the numerical accuracy of those solutions. In Figure 2.15, the arrow drawn from Element 4 to Element 5 indicates that information from the validation experiment must be provided to the analyst to compute the SRQs that were measured in the validation experiment. Examples of the information needed for the simulation are the boundary conditions, initial conditions, geometric details, material properties, and system excitation. The information provided by the experimentalist should be accompanied by uncertainty estimates for each quantity provided. Here we stress estimates of uncertainties for both the SRQs, as well as the input quantities needed for the simulation. This is one of the important characteristics of high quality validation experiments. The uncertainty estimates provided could be characterized in several different ways, e.g., either probability density functions (PDFs) or equivalently cumulative distribution functions (CDFs), or simply interval-valued quantities with no likelihood information provided. However the uncertainty is characterized, this same characterization should be used when these uncertainties are propagated through the model to obtain SRQs with similarly characterized uncertainty.

As pointed out earlier in this chapter, and by several authors in the literature, the SRQs measured in the experiment should *not* be provided to the computational analysts before the simulations are completed. The optimum situation is for the analysts to make a blind prediction of the validation experiment results, provided only with the input quantities needed for their simulation. For well-known experiments in the validation database, however, this is not possible. There are varying opinions on how damaging it is to the value or credibility of the comparisons of computational and experimental results if the analysts know the measured SRQs. We are of the belief that it is *very* damaging to the usefulness of validation and the credibility of predictive capability. Stated differently, it has been our experience, and the experience of many others, that when the analysts know the measured responses they are influenced in many ways, some obvious and some not so obvious. Some examples of influence are (a) modification in modeling assumptions, (b) choice of numerical algorithm parameters, (c) mesh or temporal convergence resolution, and (d) adjustment of free parameters in the model or poorly known physical parameters from the experiment.

Solution verification activities are conducted on the solutions that are used to compare results with experimental data. Two very different types of verification are conducted: verification of the input and output processing and verification of the numerical solution accuracy. Most of the formal solution verification effort is typically directed toward estimating numerical convergence errors (space, time, and iterative). *A posteriori* methods are, generally, the most accurate and effective approach for estimating numerical solution error in the SRQs of interest. If the SRQs of interest are field quantities, such as local pressure and temperature over the domain of the PDE, then numerical error must be estimated directly in terms of these quantities. It is well known that error estimation in local or field quantities is much more demanding in term of discretization and iterative convergence than error estimation of norms of quantities over the entire domain of the PDE.

If a relatively large number of validation experiments are to be simulated, then numerical solution error estimates are usually computed for representative conditions of various classes or groups of similar conditions. This procedure, if it can be properly justified, can greatly reduce the computational effort needed compared to estimating the numerical solution error for each experiment simulated. For example, a solution class could be defined for conditions that have similar geometries, similar nondimensional parameters occurring in the PDEs, similar interactions of physical processes, and similar material properties. After a solution class is defined, then one should choose either a representative condition from the entire class or, if it can be physically justified, the most computationally demanding condition from the class. For example, the most demanding in terms of mesh resolution and iterative convergence may be one that has the highest gradient solutions, the highest sensitivity to certain physical characteristics occurring in the field, or the highest interaction of coupled physics.

Computation of SRQs will be discussed in detail in Chapters 3 and 13, and solution verification will be discussed in Chapters 7 and 8.

2.5.6 Computation of validation metric results

Element 6 of Figure 2.15 deals with the quantitative comparison of computational and experimental results by using validation metric operators. It is common practice in all fields of engineering and science to compare computational results and experimental data using graphs. Graphical comparisons are usually made by plotting a computational SRQ along with the experimentally measured SRQ over a range of some parameter. Common practice has been that if the computational results generally agree with the experimental data over the range of measurements, the model is commonly declared "validated." Comparing computational results and experimental data on a graph, however, is only incrementally better than making a subjective comparison. In a graphical comparison, one rarely sees quantification of numerical solution error or quantification of uncertainties in the experiment or the simulation. Uncertainties arise from experimental measurement uncertainty, uncertainty due to variability in experimental conditions, initial conditions or boundary conditions not reported by the experimentalist, or poorly known boundary conditions in the experiment. The experimental condition uncertainties, or those that are unreported from the experiment, are commonly considered as free parameters in the computational analysis and, as a result, they are adjusted to obtain better agreement with the experimental measurements.

The topic of validation metrics has received a great deal of attention during the last decade, primarily by researchers associated with Sandia National Laboratories. For some of the early work in this field, see Coleman and Stern (1997); Hills and Trucano (1999); Oberkampf and Trucano (2000); Dowding (2001); Easterling (2001a), (2001b); Hills and Trucano (2001); Paez and Urbina (2001); Stern *et al.* (2001); Trucano *et al.* (2001); Urbina and Paez (2001); Hills and Trucano (2002); and Oberkampf and Trucano (2002). A validation metric operator can be viewed as a difference operator between computational and experimental results for the same SRQ. The validation metric operator could also be referred to as a mismatch operator. The output from the difference operator is called the *validation metric result* and it is a measure of the model-form bias error for the specific conditions of the validation experiment. The validation metric result is a *quantitative* statement of the difference between the model predictions and the experimental measurements. The validation metric result is of significant practical value because it is an objective measure, as opposed to subjective personal opinions as to "good" or "bad" agreement. If the validation domain encompasses the application domain, as shown in Figure 2.10a, then the validation metric result can be directly compared with the model accuracy requirements specified in Element 1. In addition, the aggregation of validation metric results over the entire validation domain can be used to form the basis for characterization of model-form uncertainty for extrapolations outside of the validation domain. Stated differently, validation metric results are based on *observed* performance of the model that can be used to estimate model-form uncertainty for extrapolations to other conditions of interest.

The construction of validation metric operators is relatively new and there are different opinions as to what they should include, and exclude, and how they should be constructed. The following recommendations give one perspective on a constructive approach to formulation of validation metrics (Oberkampf and Trucano, 2002; Oberkampf and Barone, 2004, 2006; Oberkampf and Ferson, 2007).

1 A metric should either: (a) explicitly include an estimate of the numerical error in the SRQ of interest resulting from the computational simulation or (b) exclude the numerical error in the SRQ of interest, but only if the numerical error was previously estimated, by some reasonable means, to be small.
2 A metric should be a quantitative evaluation of predictive accuracy of the SRQ of interest, including all of the combined modeling assumptions, physics approximations, and previously obtained physical parameters embodied in the model.
3 A metric should include, either implicitly or explicitly, an estimate of the error resulting from post-processing of the experimental data to obtain the same SRQ that results from the model.
4 A metric should incorporate, or include in some explicit way, an estimate of the measurement errors in the experimental data for the SRQ that is compared with the model.
5 A metric should generalize, in a mathematically rigorous way, the concept of a difference between scalar quantities that have no uncertainty and quantities that can have both aleatory and epistemic uncertainty.
6 A metric should exclude any indications, either explicit or implicit, of the level of adequacy in agreement, or satisfaction of accuracy requirements, between computational and experimental results.
7 A validation metric should be a true metric in the mathematical sense, i.e., retaining essential features of a true distance measure.

A detailed discussion of the construction and use of validation metrics will be given in Chapter 12.

2.5.7 Prediction and uncertainty estimation for the application of interest

In the analysis of the performance, safety, and reliability of many systems, predictions are viewed strictly as deterministic, i.e., uncertainties in the modeling of the physical process or system are considered small or they are simply ignored. To account for any uncertainties that exist, a safety factor is then added to the various design features of the system (Elishakoff, 2004). A second approach that is sometimes used is to try and identify the worst condition, or most demanding operational condition, under which the system might be required to operate. The system is then designed to operate successfully and safely under those conditions. Depending on the needs of the analysis and the systems involved, either approach can be appropriate and cost effective.

During the last three decades, the fields of nuclear reactor safety (Morgan and Henrion, 1990; NRC, 1990; Modarres, 1993; Kafka, 1994; Kumamoto and Henley, 1996) and underground storage of toxic and radioactive materials (LeGore, 1990; Helton, 1993; 1999; Stockman *et al.*, 2000) have pioneered modern approaches to risk assessment. The performance and risk analysis of high-consequence systems such as these required the development of new and more credible nondeterministic methods. The mathematical model of the system, which includes the influence of the surroundings on the system, is considered nondeterministic in the sense that: (a) the model can produce nonunique system responses because of the existence of uncertainty in the input data for the model, (b) the analysis may consider multiple possible environments and scenarios that the system may experience, and

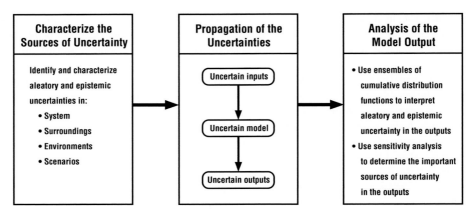

Figure 2.16 Basic steps in an uncertainty analysis.

(c) there may be multiple alternative mathematical models for the same system of interest. The term *nondeterministic* is used instead of *stochastic* because the nondeterminism can be due to either aleatory or epistemic uncertainty or, more commonly, a combination of both. The mathematical models, however, are assumed to be deterministic in the sense that when all necessary input data for a designated model are specified, the model produces only one value for every output quantity. That is, there is a one-to-one correspondence from input to output of the model. To predict the nondeterministic response of the system, it is necessary to evaluate the mathematical model, or alternative mathematical models, of the system multiple times using different input data and under possibly different environments and scenarios.

Element 7 deals with the nondeterministic prediction of the SRQs for the application of interest by incorporating into the mathematical model any uncertainties that have been identified. The most common strategy for incorporating uncertainty directly into the computational analysis involves three basic steps (Figure 2.16). The first step is called *characterizing the sources of uncertainty*. The uncertainties can be characterized as either an aleatory uncertainty or as a recognized epistemic uncertainty (Figure 2.13). If an uncertainty is purely aleatory, then it is characterized as a PDF or a CDF. If it is characterized as purely epistemic, then it is characterized as an interval-valued quantity with no likelihood information specified. An uncertainty can also be characterized as mixture of aleatory and epistemic uncertainty, i.e., some portions of the characterization are probability distributions and some are given as intervals.

In the second step, called *propagation of the uncertainty*, values from the uncertain input quantities specified in the previous step are propagated through the model to obtain uncertain output quantities. There are a number of propagation methods available to compute the mapping of input to output quantities. (For a detailed discussion of propagation methods, see the following texts: Morgan and Henrion, 1990; Cullen and Frey, 1999; Melchers, 1999; Haldar and Mahadevan, 2000; Ang and Tang, 2007; Choi *et al.*, 2007; Suter, 2007;

Rubinstein and Kroese, 2008; Vose, 2008.) In this text, we will concentrate on using statistical sampling procedures, such as Monte Carlo or Latin Hypercube Sampling, for two primary reasons. First, sampling methods are conceptually straightforward to understand and apply in practice. They can be used as a pre- and post-processor to any type of mathematical model, in the sense that they can be used as an *outer loop* or *wrapper* to the simulation code. Second, sampling methods can easily accommodate aleatory and epistemic uncertainties. Samples are taken from both the aleatory and epistemic uncertainties, but each type of uncertainty is treated separately and kept segregated in the analysis and in the interpretation of the results (Helton, 1994; Hoffman and Hammonds, 1994; Ferson and Ginzburg, 1996; Cullen and Frey, 1999; Ferson *et al.*, 2004; Suter, 2007; Vose, 2008). Samples from aleatory uncertainties represent stochastic uncertainty or variability and, as a result, these samples represent aleatory uncertainty in the SRQs. Samples from the epistemic uncertainties represent lack of knowledge uncertainty and, therefore, these samples represent *possible* realizations in the SRQs. That is, no probability or likelihood is associated with any samples taken from epistemically uncertain input quantities. Note that if alternative mathematical models are used to estimate the model form uncertainty, then the results from each model are also considered as epistemic uncertainties. The complete set of all samples for the SRQs is sometimes called an *ensemble of calculations*. Where once one might have performed a single calculation for a deterministic result, now one must perform a potentially large number of calculations for a nondeterministic simulation.

After the set of calculations has been generated, the third step, *analysis of the model output*, is performed. This step involves interpretation of the ensemble of calculations produced by sampling for the SRQs of interest. The general form of the ensemble of calculations is a family of CDFs or, equivalently, a family of complementary cumulative distribution functions. Multiple probability distributions are produced because of the existence of epistemic uncertainty. Each probability distribution represents the results from sampling all of the aleatory uncertainties, from *one* sample from all of the epistemically uncertainty quantities. Each one of the probability distributions represents a *possible* probability distribution of the SRQs.

The analysis of the output should also include a sensitivity analysis of the results (Cacuci, 2003; Saltelli *et al.*, 2004, 2008). Sensitivity analysis is the study of how the variation in the model outputs can be apportioned to different sources of variation in the model inputs (Saltelli *et al.*, 2008). Sensitivity analyses are commonly grouped into local and global analyses. Local sensitivity analyses deal with the question: how do uncertain outputs change as a function of uncertainty inputs? Global sensitivity analyses deal with the broader question: how does the uncertainty structure of the inputs, including multiple models, map to the uncertainty structure of the outputs? Answering these types of question can be extremely important from a design optimization, project management, or decision-making perspective because one can begin to focus on the causes of large uncertainties in system performance, safety, and reliability.

Each of the activities discussed in this element will be discussed in detail in Chapter 13.

2.5.8 Assessment of model adequacy

The assessment of model adequacy conducted in Element 8 primarily deals with assessment of estimated model accuracy as compared to required model accuracy specified in Element 1. As mentioned earlier, many other practical and programmatic issues enter into the decision of model adequacy for an intended application. In validation activities, we are only concerned with the estimate of model accuracy relative to the required accuracy. If the model accuracy requirements are not specified, the underlying philosophy of validation is put at risk. Accuracy requirements should be given over the entire application domain for all of the SRQs of interest. Since there is commonly a broad range in SRQs of interest in an analysis, and their importance to the system performance varies widely, the accuracy requirements can vary from one SRQ to another. In addition, the accuracy requirements for a given SRQ typically vary considerably over the application domain. For example, in regions of the application domain that are unimportant from a system performance or risk perspective, the accuracy requirements may be relatively low.

If there is sufficient validation data, the estimate of model accuracy can be built directly on the validation metric results obtained in Element 6. As mentioned earlier, the validation metric result is a direct measure of the model-form bias error over the validation domain. A validation metric result can be computed using a multi-dimensional interpolation procedure to compute the difference (mismatch) between the computational results and experimental measurements. If the application domain is completely enclosed by the validation domain (Figure 2.10a), the interpolated mismatch can then be compared with the model accuracy requirements to determine the adequacy of the model. If the model accuracy is adequate, then the model, along with the mismatch represented as an epistemic uncertainty, can be used in predictions for the system of interest. If the model accuracy is inadequate, then improvements to the model can be made in two ways. First, adjustable parameters in the model can be calibrated to obtain better agreement with the experimental data. Second, assumptions made in the conceptual model can be updated so as to improve the model form. In this latter case, however, one may need to repeat many of the elements in the entire process shown in Figure 2.15. Alternatively, the computational approach may be abandoned, such as the case shown in Figure 2.10a, and the system performance estimated using only the available experimental data and the judgment of the decision makers.

If any portion of the application domain is outside of the validation domain (Figure 2.10b), then the validation metric results must be extrapolated to the conditions of the application of interest. If the application domain is far from the validation domain (Figure 2.10c), then the extrapolation procedure can introduce large uncertainty in the estimated model-form bias error. In an attempt to try and address this issue, various extrapolation procedures could be used to estimate the uncertainty due to the extrapolation. The results of each of these extrapolation procedures could be compared to the model accuracy requirements to determine the adequacy of the model. Note that this extrapolation is completely separate from the model prediction that relies on the physics-based assumptions in the model and the conditions at the application of interest. With model-form uncertainty we are dealing with an extrapolation of the estimated error in the model.

Conceptually, the model adequacy assessment approach outlined is logically well founded and, most importantly, it directly ties model accuracy assessment to the application-specific requirements. However, there are severe technical and practical difficulties that can arise in using the procedure when large extrapolation of the validation metric result is required (Figure 2.10c). Here we mention one, but a more complete discussion is given in Chapters 12 and 13. Suppose one is dealing with a situation where there is a system or environmental parameter that cannot be considered as a continuous variable. For example, suppose that experimental facilities can only produce relevant physical conditions on components or subsystems, but the complete system *cannot* be tested. As a result, all of the validation domain data exists at lower tiers in the validation hierarchy (Figure 2.4). Then one is dealing with the vague concept of increasing system complexity and its impact on the credibility of the model predictions. One could simply ignore the additional uncertainty in the model that is due to coupling of the models from the tested level of the hierarchy to the untested level of the hierarchy. This is certainly not appealing. Another approach is to use alternative plausible models at the tested and untested levels of the hierarchy so as to obtain multiple model predictions at the untested level. Considering the difference between each model prediction as an epistemic uncertainty, one could begin to estimate the uncertainty due to coupling of the models. This approach will not necessarily bound the prediction uncertainty, but it will give the decision maker a rough indication of the magnitude of the uncertainty.

2.5.9 Documentation of M&S activities

Although the topic of documentation in M&S usually generates little enthusiasm (at best) among analysts, some level of documentation is always needed. The magnitude of the documentation effort usually depends on the size and goals of the M&S project, as well as the consequences of the risk-informed decision-making that is based on the simulation results. For example, at the minimal end of the documentation spectrum would be quick response in-house studies or informal questions asked by a design group. In the middle part of the spectrum would be documentation requirements for a corporate product that had either performance guaranties associated with the product, or some aspect of legal liability. At the extreme end of the spectrum would be documentation requirements for high-consequence systems that could affect large portions of the population or the environment if a failure occurred. Our comments here are directed at the middle to high end of the documentation spectrum.

The goals of documentation are usually discussed in terms of the need for reproducibility, traceability, and transparency of the M&S activity. By *transparency* we mean that all aspects of the M&S activity can be examined and probed by technically qualified individuals. When proprietary models or software are used, however, transparency suffers greatly. These documentation goals are important in any simulation effort, particularly those that support certification or regulatory approval of the safety and reliability of high-consequence systems. Some examples are the performance and risk assessment for nuclear reactor safety, large scale public structures such skyscrapers and dams, and long-term underground storage of nuclear or toxic wastes, such as the Waste Isolation Pilot Plant (WIPP) and the Yucca Mountain Project. The US DoD has stressed documentation in all of its V&V and accreditation activities and their recommendations for the structure and information content are given in DoD (2008).

Since the documentation goals of reproducibility, traceability, and transparency seem rather aloof and uninteresting to most personnel involved in M&S activities, we give the following examples that may be more motivational to various individual perspectives. These examples are listed in the order of the elements shown in Figure 2.15.

- Clear documentation of the application of interest (including system environments and scenarios), assumptions made in the modeling, and the prediction requirements expected of the M&S capability.
- Documented justification for the planning and prioritization of the M&S and V&V activities, not only at the beginning of the project, but also any changes that are needed during the project.
- Documentation of code verification and SQA activities that have (and have not) been conducted, as well as the ability to reproduce the activities during the project.
- Documentation of the design and execution of validation experiments not only for use in the present project, but also for use in future projects.
- Detailed documentation of simulations computed and numerical methods used so that the results can be explained and justified to the customer of the effort, delivered as part of a contractual agreement, or reproduced for training new staff members, an investigation board, or a regulatory or legal authority.
- Documentation of the validation domain, particularly its relationship to the application domain, as well as model accuracy assessment for various SRQs over the validation domain.
- Documentation of when and how model calibration was conducted so that changing model predictions can be traceable to specific calibration activities.
- Documentation of the predicted SRQs and their uncertainties for the conditions of the application of interest.
- Documentation of model adequacy (and any identified inadequacies) relative to the prediction accuracy requirements, for the application of interest.

Whatever the level or type of documentation generated, an electronic records management system (RMS) should be used. Some commercial RMS software is available, but on large-scale projects it is common to construct a tailor-made system. The RMS could be organized in a tree or folder/subfolder structure so that at the base level would be the particular M&S project, then it would divide into the eight elements shown in Figure 2.15, and then any further appropriate subdivisions. The RMS should be searchable by key words within any portion of any information element. The search engine could operate much like that found in Google or Wikipedia. Functionality could be expanded to include a relevancy-ranking feature that would further improve the search-and-retrieval capability. The overall system design could include searchable elements such as design configuration, computer code, experimental facility, system safety features, and personnel involved. After the results were retrieved, they could be sorted according to their relevance to the words input to the search. The high-level results retrieved should be embedded with hyperlinks. One could then select the hyperlinks to pursue more detailed information of interest, including photographic images and audio/video records of experiments.

2.6 References

Aeschliman, D. P. and W. L. Oberkampf (1998). Experimental methodology for computational fluid dynamics code validation. *AIAA Journal*. **36**(5), 733–741.

AIAA (1998). Guide for the verification and validation of computational fluid dynamics simulations. *American Institute of Aeronautics and Astronautics*, AIAA-G-077–1998, Reston, VA.

Almond, R. G. (1995). *Graphical Belief Modeling*. 1st edn., London, Chapman & Hall.

Anderson, M. G. and P. D. Bates, eds. (2001). *Model Validation: Perspectives in Hydrological Science*. New York, NY, John Wiley & Sons Ltd.

Ang, A. H.-S. and W. H. Tang (2007). *Probability Concepts in Engineering: Emphasis on Applications to Civil and Environmental Engineering*. 2nd edn., New York, Wiley.

ANS (1987). Guidelines for the verification and validation of scientific and engineering computer programs for the nuclear industry. *American Nuclear Society, ANSI/ANS-10.4–1987*, La Grange Park, IL.

Apostolakis, G. (1990). The concept of probability in safety assessments of technological systems. *Science*. **250**(4986), 1359–1364.

Arthur, J. D. and R. E. Nance (1996). Independent verification and validation: a missing link in simulation methodology? 1996 *Winter Simulation Conference*, Coronado, CA, 229–236.

ASME (2006). Guide for verification and validation in computational solid mechanics. *American Society of Mechanical Engineers*, ASME Standard V&V 10–2006, New York, NY.

Ayyub, B. M. (2001). *Elicitation of Expert Opinions for Uncertainty and Risks*, Boca Raton, FL, CRC Press.

Ayyub, B. M. and G. J. Klir (2006). *Uncertainty Modeling and Analysis in Engineering and the Sciences*, Boca Raton, FL, Chapman & Hall.

Bae, H.-R., R. V. Grandhi, and R. A. Canfield (2006). Sensitivity analysis of structural response uncertainty propagation using evidence theory. *Structural and Multidisciplinary Optimization*. **31**(4), 270–279.

Beck, M. B. (1987). Water quality modeling: a review of the analysis of uncertainty. *Water Resources Research*. **23**(8), 1393–1442.

Beven, K. (2002). Towards a coherent philosophy of modelling the environment. *Proceedings of the Royal Society of London, Series A*. **458**(2026), 2465–2484.

Blottner, F. G. (1990). Accurate Navier–Stokes results for the hypersonic flow over a spherical nosetip. *Journal of Spacecraft and Rockets*. **27**(2), 113–122.

Bogen, K. T. and R. C. Spear (1987). Integrating uncertainty and interindividual variability in environmental risk assessment. *Risk Analysis*. **7**(4), 427–436.

Bossel, H. (1994). *Modeling and Simulation*. 1st edn., Wellesley, MA, A. K. Peters.

Boughton, B., V. J. Romero, S. R. Tieszen, and K. B. Sobolik (2003). Integrated modeling and simulation validation plan for W80–3 abnormal thermal environment qualification – Version 1.0 (OUO). *Sandia National Laboratories, SAND2003–4152 (OUO)*, Albuquerque, NM.

Boyack, B. E., I. Catton, R. B. Duffey, P. Griffith, K. R. Katsma, G. S. Lellouche, S. Levy, U. S. Rohatgi, G. E. Wilson, W. Wulff, and N. Zuber (1990). Quantifying reactor safety margins, Part 1: An overview of the code scaling, applicability, and uncertainty evaluation methodology. *Nuclear Engineering and Design.* **119**, 1–15.

Bradley, R. G. (1988). CFD validation philosophy. *Fluid Dynamics Panel Symposium: Validation of Computational Fluid Dynamics, AGARD-CP-437*, Lisbon, Portugal, North Atlantic Treaty Organization.

Cacuci, D. G. (2003). *Sensitivity and Uncertainty Analysis: Theory*, Boca Raton, FL, Chapman & Hall/CRC.

Carnap, R. (1963). Testability and meaning. *Philosophy of Science.* **3**(4), 419–471.

Casti, J. L. (1990). *Searching for Certainty: What Scientists Can Know About the Future*, New York, William Morrow.

Chiles, J.-P. and P. Delfiner (1999). *Geostatistics: Modeling Spatial Uncertainty*, New York, John Wiley.

Choi, S.-K., R. V. Grandhi, and R. A. Canfield (2007). *Reliability-based Structural Design*, London, Springer-Verlag.

Churchman, C. W. (1968). *The Systems Approach*, New York, Dell.

Coleman, H. W. and F. Stern (1997). Uncertainties and CFD code validation. *Journal of Fluids Engineering.* **119**, 795–803.

Cosner, R. R. (1995). CFD validation requirements for technology transition. *26th AIAA Fluid Dynamics Conference, AIAA Paper 95–2227*, San Diego, CA, American Institute of Aeronautics and Astronautics.

Cox, E. (1999). *The Fuzzy Systems Handbook: a Practitioner's Guide to Building, Using, and Maintaining Fuzzy Systems.* 2nd edn., San Diego, CA, AP Professional.

Cullen, A. C. and H. C. Frey (1999). *Probabilistic Techniques in Exposure Assessment: a Handbook for Dealing with Variability and Uncertainty in Models and Inputs*, New York, Plenum Press.

Davis, P. A., N. E. Olague, and M. T. Goodrich (1991). Approaches for the validation of models used for performance assessment of high-level nuclear waste repositories. *Sandia National Laboratories, NUREG/CR-5537; SAND90–0575*, Albuquerque, NM.

Davis, P. K. (1992). Generalizing concepts and methods of verification, validation, and accreditation (VV&A) for military simulations. *RAND, R-4249-ACQ*, Santa Monica, CA.

de Cooman, G., D. Ruan, and E. E. Kerre, eds. (1995). *Foundations and Applications of Possibility Theory.* Singapore, World Scientific Publishing Co.

DoD (1994). *DoD Directive No. 5000.59: Modeling and Simulation (M&S) Management.* from www.msco.mil.

DoD (1996). *DoD Instruction 5000.61: Modeling and Simulation (M&S) Verification, Validation, and Accreditation (VV&A)*, Defense Modeling and Simulation Office, Office of the Director of Defense Research and Engineering.

DoD (1997). *DoD Modeling and Simulation Glossary.* from www.msco.mil.

DoD (2008). *Department of Defense Standard Practice: Documentation of Verification, Validation, and Accreditation (VV&A) for Models and Simulations.* US Washington, DC, Department of Defense.

Dowding, K. (2001). Quantitative validation of mathematical models. *ASME International Mechanical Engineering Congress Exposition*, New York, American Society of Mechanical Engineers.

Drosg, M. (2007). *Dealing with Uncertainties: a Guide to Error Analysis*, Berlin, Springer.

Dubois, D. and H. Prade (1988). *Possibility Theory: an Approach to Computerized Processing of Uncertainty*, New York, Plenum Press.

Dubois, D. and H. Prade, eds. (2000). *Fundamentals of Fuzzy Sets*. Boston, MA, Kluwer Academic Publishers.

Easterling, R. G. (2001a). Measuring the predictive capability of computational models: principles and methods, issues and illustrations. *Sandia National Laboratories, SAND2001–0243*, Albuquerque, NM.

Easterling, R. G. (2001b). "Quantifying the Uncertainty of Computational Predictions." *Sandia National Laboratories, SAND2001–0919C*, Albuquerque, NM.

Elishakoff, I. (2004). *Safety Factors and Reliability: Friends or Foes?*, Norwell, MA, Kluwer Academic Publishers.

Ferson, S. and L. R. Ginzburg (1996). Different methods are needed to propagate ignorance and variability. *Reliability Engineering and System Safety*. **54**, 133–144.

Ferson, S. and J. G. Hajagos (2004). Arithmetic with uncertain numbers: rigorous and (often) best possible answers. *Reliability Engineering and System Safety*. **85**(1–3), 135–152.

Ferson, S., R. B. Nelsen, J. Hajagos, D. J. Berleant, J. Zhang, W. T. Tucker, L. R. Ginzburg, and W. L. Oberkampf (2004). Dependence in probabilistic modeling, Dempster – Shafer theory, and probability bounds analysis. *Sandia National Laboratories, SAND2004–3072*, Albuquerque, NM.

Fetz, T., M. Oberguggenberger, and S. Pittschmann (2000). Applications of possibility and evidence theory in civil engineering. *International Journal of Uncertainty*. **8**(3), 295–309.

Gass, S. I. (1993). Model accreditation: a rationale and process for determining a numerical rating. *European Journal of Operational Research*. **66**, 250–258.

Grabe, M. (2005). *Measurement Uncertainties in Science and Technology*, Berlin, Springer.

Guan, J. and D. A. Bell (1991). *Evidence Theory and Its Applications*, Amsterdam, North Holland.

Haimes, Y. Y. (2009). *Risk Modeling, Assessment, and Management*. 3rd edn., New York, John Wiley.

Haldar, A. and S. Mahadevan (2000). *Probability, Reliability, and Statistical Methods in Engineering Design*, New York, John Wiley.

Helton, J. C. (1993). Uncertainty and sensitivity analysis techniques for use in performance assessment for radioactive waste disposal. *Reliability Engineering and System Safety*. **42**(2–3), 327–367.

Helton, J. C. (1994). Treatment of uncertainty in performance assessments for complex systems. *Risk Analysis*. **14**(4), 483–511.

Helton, J. C. (1997). Uncertainty and sensitivity analysis in the presence of stochastic and subjective uncertainty. *Journal of Statistical Computation and Simulation*. **57**, 3–76.

Helton, J. C. (1999). Uncertainty and sensitivity analysis in performance assessment for the waste isolation pilot plant. *Computer Physics Communications*. **117**(1–2), 156–180.

Helton, J. C., W. L. Oberkampf, and J. D. Johnson (2005). Competing failure risk analysis using evidence theory. *Risk Analysis*. **25**(4), 973–995.

Hills, R. G. and T. G. Trucano (1999). Statistical validation of engineering and scientific models: background. *Sandia National Laboratories, SAND99–1256*, Albuquerque, NM.

Hills, R. G. and T. G. Trucano (2001). Statistical validation of engineering and scientific models with application to CTH. *Sandia National Laboratories, SAND2001–0312*, Albuquerque, NM.

Hills, R. G. and T. G. Trucano (2002). Statistical validation of engineering and scientific models: a maximum likelihood based metric. *Sandia National Laboratories, SAND2001–1783*, Albuquerque, NM.

Hodges, J. S. and J. A. Dewar (1992). Is it you or your model talking? A framework for model validation. *RAND, R-4114-AF/A/OSD*, Santa Monica, CA.

Hoffman, F. O. and J. S. Hammonds (1994). Propagation of uncertainty in risk assessments: the need to distinguish between uncertainty due to lack of knowledge and uncertainty due to variability. *Risk Analysis.* **14**(5), 707–712.

IEEE (1984). *IEEE Standard Dictionary of Electrical and Electronics Terms.* ANSI/IEEE Std 100–1984, New York.

IEEE (1991). *IEEE Standard Glossary of Software Engineering Terminology.* IEEE Std 610.12–1990, New York.

ISO (1991). *ISO 9000–3: Quality Management and Quality Assurance Standards – Part 3: Guidelines for the Application of ISO 9001 to the Development, Supply and Maintenance of Software.* Geneva, Switzerland, International Organization for Standardization.

Kafka, P. (1994). Important issues using PSA technology for design of new systems and plants. *Reliability Engineering and System Safety.* **45**(1–2), 205–213.

Kaplan, S. and B. J. Garrick (1981). On the quantitative definition of risk. *Risk Analysis.* **1**(1), 11–27.

Kearfott, R. B. and V. Kreinovich, eds. (1996). *Applications of Interval Computations.* Boston, MA, Kluwer Academic Publishers.

Kleindorfer, G. B., L. O'Neill, and R. Ganeshan (1998). Validation in simulation: various positions in the philosophy of science. *Management Science.* **44**(8), 1087–1099.

Klir, G. J. (1969). *An Approach to General Systems Theory*, New York, NY, Van Nostrand Reinhold.

Klir, G. J. and M. J. Wierman (1998). *Uncertainty-Based Information: Elements of Generalized Information Theory*, Heidelberg, Physica-Verlag.

Klir, G. J. and B. Yuan (1995). *Fuzzy Sets and Fuzzy Logic*, Saddle River, NJ, Prentice Hall.

Klir, G. J., U. St. Clair, and B. Yuan (1997). *Fuzzy Set Theory: Foundations and Applications*, Upper Saddle River, NJ, Prentice Hall PTR.

Kloeden, P. E. and E. Platen (2000). *Numerical Solution of Stochastic Differential Equations*, New York, Springer.

Kohlas, J. and P.-A. Monney (1995). *A Mathematical Theory of Hints – an Approach to the Dempster – Shafer Theory of Evidence*, Berlin, Springer.

Konikow, L. F. and J. D. Bredehoeft (1992). Ground-water models cannot be validated. *Advances in Water Resources.* **15**, 75–83.

Kozine, I. (1999). Imprecise probabilities relating to prior reliability assessments. *1st International Symposium on Imprecise Probabilities and Their Applications*, Ghent, Belgium.

Krause, P. and D. Clark (1993). *Representing Uncertain Knowledge: an Artificial Intelligence Approach*, Dordrecht, The Netherlands, Kluwer Academic Publishers.

Kuhn, T. S. (1962). *The Structure of Scientific Revolutions.* 3rd edn., Chicago and London, University of Chicago Press.

Kumamoto, H. and E. J. Henley (1996). *Probabilistic Risk Assessment and Management for Engineers and Scientists.* 2nd edn., New York, IEEE Press.

Law, A. M. (2006). *Simulation Modeling and Analysis.* 4th edn., New York, McGraw-Hill.

LeGore, T. (1990). Predictive software validation methodology for use with experiments having limited replicability. In *Benchmark Test Cases for Computational Fluid Dynamics.* I. Celik and C. J. Freitas (eds.). New York, American Society of Mechanical Engineers. FED-Vol. 93: 21–27.

Lewis, R. O. (1992). *Independent Verification and Validation.* 1st edn., New York, John Wiley.

Lin, S. J., S. L. Barson, and M. M. Sindir (1992). Development of evaluation criteria and a procedure for assessing predictive capability and code performance. *Advanced Earth-to-Orbit Propulsion Technology Conference*, Huntsville, AL, Marshall Space Flight Center.

Lipton, P. (2005). Testing hypotheses: prediction and prejudice. *Science.* **307**, 219–221.

Marvin, J. G. (1988). Accuracy requirements and benchmark experiments for CFD validation. *Fluid Dynamics Panel Symposium: Validation of Computational Fluid Dynamics, AGARD-CP-437*, Lisbon, Portugal, AGARD.

Marvin, J. G. (1995). Perspective on computational fluid dynamics validation. *AIAA Journal.* **33**(10), 1778–1787.

Mehta, U. B. (1990). The aerospace plane design challenge: credible computational fluid dynamics results. Moffett Field, NASA, TM 102887.

Melchers, R. E. (1999). *Structural Reliability Analysis and Prediction.* 2nd Edn., New York, John Wiley.

Modarres, M. (1993). *What Every Engineer Should Know about Reliability and Risk Analysis*, New York, Marcel Dekker.

Modarres, M., M. Kaminskiy, and V. Krivtsov (1999). *Reliability Engineering and Risk Analysis; a Practical Guide*, Boca Raton, FL, CRC Press.

Moore, R. E. (1979). *Methods and Applications of Interval Analysis*, Philadelphia, PA, SIAM.

Morgan, M. G. and M. Henrion (1990). *Uncertainty: a Guide to Dealing with Uncertainty in Quantitative Risk and Policy Analysis.* 1st edn., Cambridge, UK, Cambridge University Press.

Naylor, T. H. and J. M. Finger (1967). Verification of computer simulation models. *Management Science.* **14**(2), 92–101.

NRC (1990). *Severe Accident Risks: An Assessment for Five U.S. Nuclear Power Plants.* U.S. Nuclear Regulatory Commission, Office of Nuclear Regulatory Research, Division of Systems Research, NUREG-1150, Washington, DC.

Oberkampf, W. L. and D. P. Aeschliman (1992). Joint computational/experimental aerodynamics research on a hypersonic vehicle: Part 1, experimental results. *AIAA Journal.* **30**(8), 2000–2009.

Oberkampf, W. L. and M. F. Barone (2004). Measures of agreement between computation and experiment: validation metrics. *34th AIAA Fluid Dynamics Conference, AIAA Paper 2004–2626*, Portland, OR, American Institute of Aeronautics and Astronautics.

Oberkampf, W. L. and M. F. Barone (2006). Measures of agreement between computation and experiment: validation metrics. *Journal of Computational Physics.* **217**(1), 5–36.

Oberkampf, W. L. and F. G. Blottner (1998). Issues in computational fluid dynamics code verification and validation. *AIAA Journal.* **36**(5), 687–695.

Oberkampf, W. L. and S. Ferson (2007). Model validation under both aleatory and epistemic uncertainty. *NATO/RTO Symposium on Computational Uncertainty in Military Vehicle Design, AVT-147/RSY-022*, Athens, Greece, NATO.

Oberkampf, W. L. and J. C. Helton (2005). Evidence theory for engineering applications. In *Engineering Design Reliability Handbook*. E. Nikolaidis, D. M. Ghiocel, and S. Singhal, eds. New York, NY, CRC Press: 29.

Oberkampf, W. L. and T. G. Trucano (2000). Validation methodology in computational fluid dynamics. *Fluids 2000 Conference, AIAA Paper 2000–2549*, Denver, CO, American Institute of Aeronautics and Astronautics.

Oberkampf, W. L. and T. G. Trucano (2002). Verification and validation in computational fluid dynamics. *Progress in Aerospace Sciences*. **38**(3), 209–272.

Oberkampf, W. L. and T. G. Trucano (2007). *Verification and Validation Benchmarks*. Albuquerque, NM, Sandia National Laboratories, SAND2007–0853.

Oberkampf, W. L. and T. G. Trucano (2008). Verification and validation benchmarks. *Nuclear Engineering and Design*. **238**(3), 716–743.

Oberkampf, W. L., F. G. Blottner, and D. P. Aeschliman (1995). Methodology for computational fluid dynamics code verification/validation. *26th AIAA Fluid Dynamics Conference, AIAA Paper 95–2226*, San Diego, CA, American Institute of Aeronautics and Astronautics.

Oberkampf, W. L., T. G. Trucano, and C. Hirsch (2004). Verification, validation, and predictive capability in computational engineering and physics. *Applied Mechanics Reviews*. **57**(5), 345–384.

Oksendal, B. (2003). *Stochastic Differential Equations: an Introduction with Applications*. 6th edn., Berlin, Springer.

Oren, T. I. and B. P. Zeigler (1979). Concepts for advanced simulation methodologies. *Simulation*, 69–82.

Oreskes, N., K. Shrader-Frechette, and K. Belitz (1994). Verification, validation, and confirmation of numerical models in the Earth Sciences. *Science*. **263**, 641–646.

Paez, T. and A. Urbina (2001). Validation of structural dynamics models via hypothesis testing. *Society of Experimental Mechanics Annual Conference*, Portland, OR, Society of Experimental Mechanics.

Parry, G. W. (1988). On the meaning of probability in probabilistic safety assessment. *Reliability Engineering and System Safety*. **23**, 309–314.

Parry, G. W. and P. W. Winter (1981). Characterization and evaluation of uncertainty in probabilistic risk analysis. *Nuclear Safety*. **22**(1), 28–41.

Paté-Cornell, M. E. (1996). Uncertainties in risk analysis: six levels of treatment. *Reliability Engineering and System Safety*. **54**, 95–111.

Pilch, M., T. G. Trucano, J. L. Moya, G. K. Froehlich, A. L. Hodges, and D. E. Peercy (2001). *Guidelines for Sandia ASCI Verification and Validation Plans – Content and Format: Version 2*. Albuquerque, NM, Sandia National Laboratories, SAND2000–3101.

Platt, D. S. (2007). *Why Software Sucks . . . and what you can do about it*, Upper Saddle River, NJ, Addison-Wesley.

Popper, K. R. (1959). *The Logic of Scientific Discovery*, New York, Basic Books.

Popper, K. R. (1969). *Conjectures and Refutations: the Growth of Scientific Knowledge*, London, Routledge and Kegan.

Rabinovich, S. G. (2005). *Measurement Errors and Uncertainties: Theory and Practice*. 3rd edn., New York, Springer-Verlag.

Raczynski, S. (2006). *Modeling and Simulation: the Computer Science of Illusion*, New York, Wiley.

Refsgaard, J. C. and H. J. Henriksen (2004). Modelling guidelines – terminology and guiding principles. *Advances in Water Resources*. **27**, 71–82.

Roache, P. J. (1990). Need for control of numerical accuracy. *Journal of Spacecraft and Rockets*. **27**(2), 98–102.

Roache, P. J. (1995). Verification of codes and calculations. *26th AIAA Fluid Dynamics Conference, AIAA Paper 95–2224*, San Diego, CA, American Institute of Aeronautics and Astronautics.

Roache, P. J. (1998). *Verification and Validation in Computational Science and Engineering*, Albuquerque, NM, Hermosa Publishers.

Roza, Z. C. (2004). *Simulation Fidelity, Theory and Practice: a Unified Approach to Defining, Specifying and Measuring the Realism of Simulations*, Delft, The Netherlands, Delft University Press.

Rubinstein, R. Y. and D. P. Kroese (2008). *Simulation and the Monte Carlo Method*. 2nd edn., Hoboken, NJ, John Wiley.

Rykiel, E. J. (1996). Testing ecological models: the meaning of validation. *Ecological Modelling*. **90**(3), 229–244.

Saltelli, A., S. Tarantola, F. Campolongo, and M. Ratto (2004). *Sensitivity Analysis in Practice: a Guide to Assessing Scientific Models*, Chichester, England, John Wiley & Sons, Ltd.

Saltelli, A., M. Ratto, T. Andres, F. Campolongo, J. Cariboni, D. Gatelli, M. Saisana, and S. Tarantola (2008). *Global Sensitivity Analysis: the Primer*, Hoboken, NJ, Wiley.

Sargent, R. G. (1979). Validation of simulation models. *1979 Winter Simulation Conference*, San Diego, CA, 497–503.

Schlesinger, S. (1979). Terminology for model credibility. *Simulation*. **32**(3), 103–104.

Serrano, S. E. (2001). *Engineering Uncertainty and Risk Analysis: a Balanced Approach to Probability, Statistics, Stochastic Modeling, and Stochastic Differential Equations*, Lexington, KY, HydroScience Inc.

Shannon, R. E. (1975). *Systems Simulation: the Art and Science*, Englewood Cliffs, NJ, Prentice-Hall.

Sheng, G., M. S. Elzas, T. I. Oren, and B. T. Cronhjort (1993). Model validation: a systemic and systematic approach. *Reliability Engineering and System Safety*. **42**, 247–259.

Sindir, M. M., S. L. Barson, D. C. Chan, and W. H. Lin (1996). On the development and demonstration of a code validation process for industrial applications. *27th AIAA Fluid Dynamics Conference, AIAA Paper 96–2032*, New Orleans, LA, American Institute of Aeronautics and Astronautics.

Smithson, M. (1989). *Ignorance and Uncertainty: Emerging Paradigms*, New York, Springer-Verlag.

Stern, F., R. V. Wilson, H. W. Coleman, and E. G. Paterson (2001). Comprehensive approach to verification and validation of CFD simulations – Part 1: Methodology and procedures. *Journal of Fluids Engineering*. **123**(4), 793–802.

Stockman, C. T., J. W. Garner, J. C. Helton, J. D. Johnson, A. Shinta, and L. N. Smith (2000). Radionuclide transport in the vicinity of the repository and associated complementary cumulative distribution functions in the 1996 performance assessment for the Waste Isolation Pilot Plant. *Reliability Engineering and System Safety*. **69**(1–3), 369–396.

Suter, G. W. (2007). *Ecological Risk Assessment*. 2nd edn., Boca Raton, FL, CRC Press.

Taylor, H. M. and S. Karlin (1998). *An Introduction to Stochastic Modeling*. 3rd edn., Boston, Academic Press.

Tieszen, S. R., T. Y. Chu, D. Dobranich, V. J. Romero, T. G. Trucano, J. T. Nakos, W. C. Moffatt, T. F. Hendrickson, K. B. Sobolik, S. N. Kempka, and M. Pilch (2002).

Integrated Modeling and Simulation Validation Plan for W76–1 Abnormal Thermal Environment Qualification – Version 1.0 (OUO). Sandia National Laboratories, SAND2002–1740 (OUO), Albuquerque.

Trucano, T. G., R. G. Easterling, K. J. Dowding, T. L. Paez, A. Urbina, V. J. Romero, R. M. Rutherford, and R. G. Hills (2001). *Description of the Sandia Validation Metrics Project*. Albuquerque, NM, Sandia National Laboratories, SAND2001–1339.

Trucano, T. G., M. Pilch, and W. L. Oberkampf (2002). *General Concepts for Experimental Validation of ASCI Code Applications*. Albuquerque, NM, Sandia National Laboratories, SAND2002–0341.

Tsang, C.-F. (1989). A broad view of model validation. *Proceedings of the Symposium on Safety Assessment of Radioactive Waste Repositories, Paris, France*, Paris, France, OECD, 707–716.

Urbina, A. and T. L. Paez (2001). Statistical validation of structural dynamics models. *Annual Technical Meeting & Exposition of the Institute of Environmental Sciences and Technology*, Phoenix, AZ.

Vose, D. (2008). *Risk Analysis: a Quantitative Guide*. 3rd edn., New York, Wiley.

Walley, P. (1991). *Statistical Reasoning with Imprecise Probabilities*, London, Chapman & Hall.

Wilson, G. E. and B. E. Boyack (1998). The role of the PIRT in experiments, code development and code applications associated with reactor safety assessment. *Nuclear Engineering and Design*. **186**, 23–37.

Wilson, G. E., B. E. Boyack, I. Catton, R. B. Duffey, P. Griffith, K. R. Katsma, G. S. Lellouche, S. Levy, U. S. Rohatgi, W. Wulff, and N. Zuber (1990). Quantifying reactor safety margins, Part 2: Characterization of important contributors to uncertainty. *Nuclear Engineering and Design*. **119**, 17–31.

Wulff, W., B. E. Boyack, I. Catton, R. B. Duffey, P. Griffith, K. R. Katsma, G. S. Lellouche, S. Levy, U. S. Rohatgi, G. E. Wilson, and N. Zuber (1990). Quantifying reactor safety margins, Part 3: Assessment and ranging of parameters. *Nuclear Engineering and Design*. **119**, 33–65.

Zeigler, B. P. (1976). *Theory of Modelling and Simulation*. 1st edn., New York, John Wiley.

Zeigler, B. P., H. Praehofer, and T. G. Kim (2000). *Theory of Modeling and Simulation: Integrating Discrete Event and Continuous Complex Dynamic Systems*. 2nd edn., San Diego, CA, Academic Press.

Zuber, N., G. E. Wilson, M. Ishii, W. Wulff, B. E. Boyack, A. E. Dukler, P. Griffith, J. M. Healzer, R. E. Henry, J. R. Lehner, S. Levy, and F. J. Moody (1998). An integrated structure and scaling methodology for severe accident technical issue resolution: development of methodology. *Nuclear Engineering and Design*. **186**(1–2), 1–21.

3

Modeling and computational simulation

The phrases *modeling and simulation* and *computational simulation* are becoming prevalent in a wide variety of technical, economic, governmental, and business activities (Schrage, 1999). Indeed, the phrases are becoming so common that one is even beginning to see them in the mass media. What do they mean? These phrases can have a wide variety of meanings depending on the field and the context. Here, we are concerned with the fields of the physical sciences and engineering. By examining the fundamentals of modeling and simulation (M&S) and scientific computing, our goal is to see the similarities in model formulation and computational issues across a wide range of physical systems. Our approach to scientific computing emphasizes the similarities that exist in mathematical form and structure of models in many technical disciplines. Then a framework, an overarching structure, is constructed for either attacking more detailed features of the system or for attacking more complex systems. Commonly, more complex systems involve coupling different types of physical phenomena, incorporation of additional elements from the system or the surroundings, and effects of human intervention in the system. Similarities in model formulation issues exist because many of the model properties are not determined by their physical nature, but by their mathematical structure, the interaction of the system with the surroundings, and the similarity in the nature of the system responses.

Many of the difficult issues that must be dealt with in verification, validation, and uncertainty quantification (VV&UQ) can be traced back to ambiguities and inconsistencies in the model formulation, the mapping of continuum mathematics models to discrete mathematics models, and vague or improper characterizations of uncertainties. This chapter deals with many of those issues by examining the fundamentals of M&S.

We begin by carefully defining and discussing the terms system, surroundings, environments, and scenarios. We discuss the importance of constructing models such that they can produce nondeterministic simulations. To help clarify this concept, we discuss an example for the nondeterministic oscillation of a simple mechanical system. We then discuss the six phases of computational simulation: conceptual modeling, discretization and algorithm selection, computer programming, numerical solution, and solution representation. We close the chapter with a detailed example of the flight dynamics of a missile that demonstrates each of these six phases.

3.1 Fundamentals of system specifications

3.1.1 Systems and surroundings

The concept and understanding of the meaning of a system is probably the most important element in modeling. The definition of a system that is most useful for modeling physical systems is:

System: a set of physical entities that interact and are observable, where the entities can be a specified quantity of matter or a volume in space.

For those with some background in thermodynamics, this definition is similar to that given for a system in thermodynamics. The stress in this definition is on physical entities that can interact and are observable. As in thermodynamics, this definition allows for the system to be closed or open. A closed system means there is no exchange of mass with the surroundings of the system. An open system can have mass flow into and out of the system. A system can have forces acting on it, work done on it, and energy exchanged with the surroundings. Also, a system can be time-invariant (static) or time-variant (dynamic).

Our definition of a system, although very broad, is actually more restrictive than that used in many fields, for example, Operations Research (Neelamkavil, 1987). Our definition excludes human organizations, governments, societies, economies, and human mental processes. However, these are valid topics of modeling in many fields. All of these types of entity can be considered as living or sentient entities and are, by almost any measure, much more complex entities than physical systems of interest here. In using the present definition of a system, however, the physical body of a person, or any part or organ of the body, could be considered as a system. For example, the physiological, mechanical, and chemical changes of an organ exposed to various wavelengths of the electromagnetic spectrum could be considered within our definition of a system.

The state of a system can be influenced as a result of (a) processes internal to the system, i.e., endogenous processes, and (b) processes or activities external to the system, i.e., exogenous effects. Influences or activities not considered as part of the system are considered as part of the surroundings of the system. Since the complement to the system is the surroundings, it is important that a precise definition be given:

Surroundings: all entities and influences that are physically or conceptually separate from the system.

A system is influenced by the surroundings, but the surroundings are *not* modeled as part of the system (Neelamkavil, 1987). In most models, the system *responds* to the surroundings, but the surroundings are *not* influenced by the system. In rare modeling situations, the surroundings can be influenced by the system. When this occurs, one of two possible modeling changes must occur.

- A separate mathematical model is constructed for the surroundings. Then the surroundings become another system that interacts with the first system.

- A weak coupling is constructed between the system and the surroundings. The surroundings are not considered another system, but they can respond in very simple, specific ways. That is, the weak coupling is dependent on the response of the system, typically as a result of some type of experimentally observed correlation function that represents how the surroundings respond to specific processes modeled within the system.

The distinction between the system and the surroundings should not be simply thought of as a physical boundary, or location outside the physical system. The distinction between the system and the surroundings can be entirely conceptual. The decision of what physical elements and features should be considered as part of the system, and what should be considered part of the surroundings, depends on the purpose of the analysis. System-surroundings specifications are not always well thought out and, as a result, they can cause modeling errors or conceptual inconsistencies in the formulation of a mathematical model. Finally, humans can be a conceptual part of a system. When a human is part of the system, they are referred to as an *actor* (Bossel, 1994). By *actor* we mean an element of a system that can influence the system in some physical way, or respond to events or activities occurring in the system in a conscious manner. *Conscious manner* usually means with a goal or purpose in mind, but it does not necessarily mean what would normally be considered rational or logical. The actor can also be unpredictable, unreliable, or acting with an unknown value system or some malicious agenda. Actors can become important elements in many complex physical systems; for example, systems that are human controlled or controlled by a combination of a human and a computer, such as a safety control system. Another example is accidental or unanticipated human involvement in a system that is normally thought of as isolated from humans or under computer control.

A few examples of systems and surroundings are in order to help clarify these concepts:

Example 1: Orbiting spacecraft

Consider a spacecraft in orbit around the Earth as a system. Assume the system behavior of interest is the three-degree-of-freedom orbital dynamics of the spacecraft. The spacecraft would be considered as the system and the primary characteristics of the system would be the mass and velocity of the craft. The surroundings would be represented by the forces acting on the craft: (a) the gravitational force of the Earth, Moon, Sun, and other planets; (b) the aerodynamic or molecular drag on the craft; and (c) the solar wind and electrostatic forces on the vehicle. If the spacecraft has a thrust control system onboard to change its orbital parameters, then the force exerted by the thrusters on the spacecraft would be part of the *surroundings*. However, the mass of the thrusters and their propellants are part of the system. As the thrusters are fired, the mass of the system would change due to consumption of propellants. As a result, the system is actually an open system since mass is leaving the system.

Example 2: Beam deflection

Consider the deflection of a beam clamped on one end and free on the other. Assume the system behavior of interest is the static deflection of the beam under a specified loading. The mass, material, and geometric properties of the beam would be considered as the system. The surroundings would be the static load distribution and how the clamped end affects the deflection of the beam. For example, the clamped end may be assumed to be perfectly rigid, i.e., no deflection or rotation occurs at the clamped end. Alternatively, the clamped end could be considered to have no translational deflection, but rotational deflection occurs around three orthogonal axes. For example, three rotational spring stiffnesses could be used to represent the clamped end as part of the surroundings. The system is influenced by the surroundings, but the surroundings are not influenced by the system. One could add fidelity and complexity to the model by including a first order approximation concerning how the clamped end could lose some of its rotational stiffness as a function of the number of deflection cycles of the beam. If this complexity were added to the model, it would be based on a combination of the predicted motion of the beam, and on a correlation of data from observed experiments of how the clamped end lost stiffness as a function of the number of deflection cycles. For this case, however, the clamp is still part of the surroundings, but the surroundings could change in a very specific way due to processes occurring within the system.

Example 3: Electronic circuit

Consider the electronic circuitry of a common television set as a system. Assume the physical behavior of interest of the system is the current flow through all of the electrical components of the television circuitry when the TV is switched on. The initial state of the system is considered as that before it is switched on. In addition, assume that the TV is plugged into an electrical power outlet before it is switched on. That is, electrical power is applied to certain parts of the circuitry, but not all, in what is commonly called a *stand-by* or *ready* mode of the circuit. The final state of the system is considered to be the current flow in the circuitry after the TV is switched on for some time. One type of analysis would be to consider the functionality of all of the electrical components as elements of the system, and everything else as part of the surroundings. This type of problem would be purely an initial value problem, given by a system of ordinary differential equations (ODEs). One could also consider the electrical and magnetic characteristics of the components as a function of time, e.g., as they increased in temperature due to current flow and heating of nearby components. A more complex type of analysis would be to consider the thermo-physical properties and the physical geometric characteristics of each of the components as part of the system. For this type of analysis, the surroundings would be the air around each of the components, the physical connections of each of the electrical components to the various circuit boards, and the radiation heat transfer with other electrical components and the surroundings. This type of system would be represented mathematically as an initial-boundary value problem given by a system of partial differential equations (PDEs). An additional factor to consider in these examples is human intervention affecting the system, e.g., a human switched on the TV either by the physical switch on the television or by a remote control unit. A related factor that could be considered in the system is the mistreatment of the remote control unit by a child, such as rapid on/off switching of the unit. For these systems, the human would be considered as part of the surroundings.

3.1.2 Environments and scenarios

Scientific computing is often used to address the performance, safety or reliability of a system that is exposed to a wide variety of environments. We use the following definition.

Environment: the external condition or situation in which the system can be exposed to; specifically: normal, abnormal, or hostile conditions.

The three classes of environment (normal, abnormal, and hostile) were first formally defined as part of analysis of the safety, performance, and reliability of nuclear weapons in the US (AEC, 1966).

The *normal* system environment refers to either one of the following two conditions: (a) the operating environment in which the system is typically expected to operate or function and achieve its performance goals, or (b) an expected storage, shipping, or at-the-ready condition of the system. A normal operating environment for a system depends *entirely* on what should be the expected operating conditions of the system. For example, what may be considered a normal operating environment for one system may be considered an abnormal environment for another system. Examples of what could be considered a normal operating condition of some engineering systems are high temperature, pressure, or humidity; chemical or corrosive environments; vacuum conditions; a system covered or infiltrated with ice, snow, or sand; and a high intensity electromagnetic or radiation environment. Examples of typical storage, shipping, or at-the-ready conditions include a spacecraft either in ground storage before launch or in orbit in a non operational storage mode; a gas turbine engine being shipped from the manufacture or refurbishment facility to the user of the system; and safety or emergency systems for a nuclear power reactor that are at-the-ready. When a system is analyzed in a normal operating environment, the most common characteristics of interest are its performance and reliability. For systems in storage or shipping, the most common characteristics of interest are possible degradation of the system due to the environment, and safety of the system. For systems in at-the-ready environments, the most common characteristics of interest are such things as the response time of the system to full capability, and the degradation of the system performance or reliability as a function of time at-the-ready.

An *abnormal* environment of a system refers to either: (a) some type of accident or damaged-state environment, or (b) a very unusual condition that could put the system in jeopardy or cause it to be unsafe, even if the system is not operational. Examples of accident or damaged-state environments are: loss of primary coolant accident in a nuclear power plant, loss of electrical or hydraulic power during flight of an aircraft, exposure of the system to an accidental fire or explosive environment, flight control of a two-engine aircraft during one engine out conditions, and structural integrity of a hypersonic flight vehicle with damage to the thermal protection system. Some examples of systems in very unusual environments are: exposure of a nuclear power plant to an earthquake; lightning strike on a system during operation, shipping, or storage; operation of the system at temperatures or pressures outside of its normal operating conditions; and over-riding the safety control systems during a safety check or proof-testing of a system. When a system is analyzed in an abnormal environment, the most common characteristic of interest is the safety of the system.

A *hostile* environment is one in which the system is under any type of attack, in the sense that the intent of the attacker is to do harm to the system, defeat or disable the system, or render it unsafe. The hostile environment can expose the system to attack from either inside the system or by way of the surroundings of the system. Types of attack can be physical damage or destruction of the system, modifying or taking over computer control of the operation of the system, altering the security or safety of the system, or electromagnetic attack over any portion of the electromagnetic spectrum. Military systems have always been evaluated with respect to performance in hostile environments. Before the terrorist attacks on the US in September 2001, very few privately owned facilities or public works were analyzed with respect to effects of hostile environments. Some examples of hostile environments for military systems are: battle damage due to small-arms fire on the system, exposure of electronic equipment to high-power microwaves or millimeter waves, attack of the computer control system either by an insider or through a connection to the internet, and attack of a ground vehicle by an improvised explosive device. When military systems are analyzed for a hostile environment, the most common characteristics of interest are system performance and safety. When civilian facilities and public works are analyzed for a hostile environment, system safety is the most common concern.

Given any environment that the system could be exposed to, one can also consider various scenarios that could occur, given the context of the environment being considered. We use the following definition.

Scenario: a possible event, or event sequence, to which a system in a given environment could be exposed.

Given this definition, scenarios are typically identified at the conceptual modeling phase. This phase was discussed in Sections 2.1.4 and 2.2.3, and will be discussed in more detail in Section 3.4.1 below. It should be noted that a scenario does *not* mean a particular realization of the response of a system. A scenario usually refers to an ensemble of possible system responses, all resulting from a common situation or sequence of situations that are identified with a specific environment. An example of an ensemble of system responses would be one or more cumulative distribution functions characterizing the nondeterministic response of the system. A scenario can be specified as a particular event sequence, or an entire event tree or fault tree.

Figure 3.1 depicts a given environment of interest and M scenarios that might be considered for analysis of a system. One example would be the specification of all of the

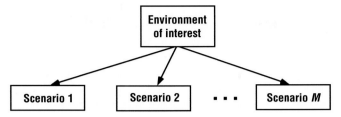

Figure 3.1 Environment-scenario tree.

extreme, or corner, conditions within the normal operating environment of the system; each identified as a scenario. For abnormal and hostile environments, it is especially important to identify multiple environments of interest within each category because there can be such a wide range of situations within each of the abnormal and hostile environments. As a result, there can be multiple environment-scenario trees like Figure 3.1 for a system in an abnormal environment. Identifying a number of scenarios for a given environment does not necessarily mean that each scenario will be analyzed. The environment-scenario tree only tries to identify possible conditions of the system that could be analyzed, for example, depending on the possible consequences or risk associated with each scenario. Examples of scenarios that could be considered for various environments of systems are (a) for a normal operating environment of a gas turbine engine on a transport aircraft in flight, consider the effect on engine performance of the scenarios of flight through rain, snow, freezing rain, and ice pellets (sleet), (b) for an accident environment of a hybrid automobile powered by both an internal combustion engine and a large battery unit, consider the scenarios of fire, explosion, and hazardous chemicals to the occupants of the automobile, bystanders or others involved in the accident, and emergency rescue personnel attending to the accident, and (c) for a hostile environment, consider the dispersion and transport of chemical or biological agents due to atmospheric winds, rain, storm drains, surface water, municipal water systems, surface vehicles, and people.

3.2 Fundamentals of models and simulations

3.2.1 Goals of scientific computing

The reasons for individuals, organizations, or governmental bodies to undertake activities in scientific computing are wide-ranging and diverse. However, these reasons can be grouped into the generation of new information or knowledge about systems or processes. This new information may then be used to influence the system or process analyzed, to design new and more capable systems, help avoid the detrimental and catastrophic effects of a possible situation, or it may be used to influence an individual's, organization's, or society's view of a system or process. The following is a general categorization of the motivations for scientific computing in engineering and the physical sciences (Bossel, 1994).

1 *Scientific knowledge*: scientific knowledge means knowledge generated solely for the improved understanding of the Universe and humankind's place in it. Probably the clearest example of the use of scientific computing for generation of scientific knowledge is in astrophysics. The knowledge generated in astrophysics improves human understanding of the Universe and their place in it, without any aspect of influence on the system or use of the knowledge toward other practical or earthly applications.

2 *Technological knowledge*: technological knowledge means the generation of knowledge used in some way for the creation of applied knowledge or the creation of new physical systems or processes. Technological knowledge is probably the most common type of knowledge generated from scientific computing in engineering and the applied physical sciences. In engineering simulations, the majority of this knowledge is used to design new engineering systems, improve the efficiency of existing systems, or assess the impact of existing or proposed systems. For systems not yet in existence, key drivers in scientific computing are issues such as: (a) creation and design of more capable systems than are presently on the market, particularly if they are a competitor's product; (b) creation of new materials and manufacturing processes to reduce costs and time to market; and (c) prediction of the potential environmental impact of new systems or manufacturing processes, not only at the present time, but in centuries to come. For the generation of new technological knowledge for systems already in existence, examples are (a) improvement of the performance, safety, or reliability of existing systems; (b) optimization of chemical processes for improved production output; (c) improvements in fuel consumption mileage of transportation vehicles; and (d) safety improvements to existing and future nuclear power plants, particularly improvements to address new threats.

Scientific computing is taking on increased public scrutiny, particularly for risk assessment of high consequence systems. The catastrophic failure of nuclear reactor number four at the Chernobyl nuclear power plant in Ukraine in 1986 riveted worldwide attention on the dangers of nuclear power as does the impact of environmental disasters beyond national borders. Although scientific computing primarily deals with technological issues, these issues commonly become convolved with public perceptions of risk, national responsibilities for the impact of technologies on the global climate, and organizational responsibilities for product and environmental liability. As is clear from these examples, the importance of scientific computing for the generation of technological knowledge is greatly expanding. Correspondingly, there is a compelling need to construct models that are technically sound, where the assumptions and uncertainties in the models are clearly revealed, and the modeling results are comprehensible to a wide range of audiences. The technical difficulties in achieving these goals in scientific computing are daunting in themselves; however, within the inevitable human, social, cultural, and political context, achieving them becomes nearly impossible.

The most obvious alternative method to the generation of new scientific and technological knowledge is the actual execution of the physical process or event that is of interest, i.e., conduct of a physical experiment. There are advantages and disadvantages to the physical experiment route, just as there are to the scientific computing approach. Some factors that should be considered in choosing scientific computing as compared to a physical experiment are the following (Neelamkavil, 1987; Bossel, 1994).

1 The cost and/or time schedule required to conduct a physical experiment may be considerably more than with scientific computing. Clear examples of this from recent history are in the simulation of electrical circuit functionality and performance as compared to the physical construction of an electrical circuit. Modern electrical circuits are designed almost entirely by scientific computing because of the speed and minimal cost of simulation. Another example is the simulation of large-scale structures, such as buildings and bridges. In the distant past, large-scale structures were built by trial and error, whereas during modern times there has been heavy reliance on scientific computing.

2 Because of the time scales involved in some physical process, it may be completely unrealistic to consider a physical experiment. For example, in disposal of radioactive nuclear wastes the time scales of decay of the wastes are on the order of thousands of years. An example with international environmental and economic dimensions is the long-term impact of burning of fossil fuels on global climate change.

3 Physical experiments with the actual system could possibly lead to unacceptable hazards or risks; cause large-scale disruptions in society, the economy, or the environment; be physically or financially infeasible; or not be allowed by international treaty. For example, consider the modification or repair of some large-scale structure such as a high-rise office building. Scientific computing would obviously be used to determine how the building structure might be modified for useful life extension or improved tolerance to physical attack. Scientific computing could be used to optimize the improvements to the structure with essentially no risk to the physical structure. An example that demonstrates the infeasible nature of a physical experiment is the response of a nuclear power plant to an earthquake. It is essentially impossible to generate a full-scale earthquake of proper amplitude and wavelength of ground motion for an experiment.

It should also be pointed out that there are limitations and weaknesses to using scientific computing in the generation of technological knowledge (Neelamkavil, 1987; Bossel, 1994). These are given in the following.

1 The cost and/or time required for construction of a mathematical model of a physical process may be excessive or impossible at the present time. For example, consider the detailed mathematical modeling of bolted joints between structural members in a structural dynamics problem. Even if one restricts the problem to the same two materials in contact at the joint, the physics and material science issues that must be addressed in the mathematical modeling are extraordinary. Some of the detailed aspects that must be addressed for an accurate mathematical model are (a) elastic and plastic deformation and irreversible changes of the material near the joint due to the compression of the bolt, (b) motion of the joint in six degrees of freedom (three translational plus three rotational), and (c) friction and heating between the two materials bolted together when they microscopically move and deform with respect to one another. In addition to these aspects of mathematical modeling, the model must take into account the uncertainty in each of these due to assembly, manufacturing, surface finish, oxidation, or corrosion of the material interfaces as a function of age and the surroundings, and deformation history.

2 The cost and/or time required to conduct the computational analysis may be excessive or economically unproductive. For example, consider the simulation of turbulent flow in fluid dynamics using as a model the time-dependent Navier–Stokes equations. If one attempts to solve these equations computationally, using what is referred to as direct numerical simulation, instead of using time-averaged models or turbulence models, one must have exceptionally powerful computer resources

available. Except for research interest into fluid dynamic turbulence, the costs of these types of simulation are prohibitive for high Reynolds number flows. Another example that may demonstrate inadequate schedule responsiveness of computational analyses is the time required to construct three-dimensional meshes for complex, multi-component assemblies.

3 Quantitative assessment of model accuracy may be difficult or impossible to attain because experimental measurements may be difficult or impossible to obtain, the cost may be prohibitively expensive, or the experiments may not be practical or allowed. Some examples are (a) obtaining detailed experimental measurements during hypervelocity impact of a particle on a spacecraft structure; (b) obtaining certain experimental data for the physiological response of humans to toxic chemicals; (c) conducting an experiment on the explosive failure of a full-scale reactor containment building; and (d) obtaining sufficient input and output data for the response of the global environment to a large-scale atmospheric event, such as a volcanic eruption or the impact of an sizeable asteroid.

3.2.2 Models and simulations

Diverse types of model are used in a wide range of disciplines. Neelamkavil (1987) gives a general and well-founded definition that covers many different types of models for physical systems.

Model: a representation of a physical system or process intended to enhance our ability to understand, predict, or control its behavior.

There are several variants of the definition of simulation in the literature, but we will use the following concise definition.

Simulation: the exercise or use of a model to produce a result.

Simulation of the behavior of systems can be achieved by two types of mathematical model (Bossel, 1994). The first type is referred to as an empirical or phenomenological model of the system. This type of mathematical model of the system is based on observations of how the system responds under different input, or stimulation, conditions. The representation commonly does not make an attempt to describe any of the detailed processes involved inside the system or determine why the system responds in the way it does. The system is considered to be a *black box* and the only issue is the global relationship between the inputs and outputs of the system. One relates the observed behavior of the system to the perceived influences on the system using some type of mathematical representation, such as statistical correlation or regression fit methods. An example of this type of model is the dynamic response of a structure to a bolted or riveted joint. If the system is only considered to be the joint, then an empirical model can be constructed of how the structure responds to the joint. The model would represent, say, the structural stiffness and torsional damping of the joint. The information to construct this type of model is usually obtained from experimental measurements of the dynamic response of the structure. Parameter identification methods are applied to the structural response to determine the input–output relationship over a range of conditions.

The second type of mathematical model is the physical law or explanatory model. For this type of model a great deal of information must be known about the actual processes occurring inside the system. In the physical sciences and engineering, this type of model is the one of principal interest. Past observations of the behavior of the system are primarily of value in determining what physical processes and laws must be considered and what can be ignored in the system, and secondarily, how physical modeling parameters can be adjusted to best represent the response of the system. Examples of this type of physical law model are Newton's second law, Fourier's law of heat conduction, the Navier–Stokes equations, Maxwell's equations, and Boltzman's equation. Many physical law models were devised more than a hundred years ago and they form the foundations of the modern analysis of physical systems. With the creation of extremely powerful computers, the technological impact of these fundamental laws is unprecedented in history.

The general strategy of model building that should be followed is to include *only* the elements and processes that are important to achieve the goals of the computational analysis. Often, preliminary simulations show that changes and improvements in the modeling approach are needed to achieve the goals of the analysis. Albert Einstein's classic advice in this matter was: "Make the model as simple as possible, but no simpler." This strategy of using the simplest possible theory to explain reality is also referred to as Occam's Razor. The predictive power of a model depends on its ability to correctly identify the dominant controlling factors and their influences, *not* upon its completeness. A model of limited, but known, applicability is generally more useful from a system design or decision-making perspective than a more complete model that requires more detailed information and computing resources.

Many fields of engineering and the physical sciences have largely ignored the argument for using moderate complexity models as opposed to higher complexity models. The argument is made that with continually increasing computing power, analysts should develop increasingly complex models, so as to include all the possible processes, effects, and interactions. One way in which the level of complexity of the model is constrained is to include the most physics complexity, while still seeking to obtain a solution within the time and computer resources available. There is some credence given to this constraint, but it is seldom realized in practice. Increasing physics modeling complexity is *always* at the expense of simulation result timeliness, nondeterministic simulations, investigation of possible environments and scenarios, sensitivity analyses, and investigation of the effect of alternative modeling approaches. Stated differently, most fields of engineering and the physical sciences are still entrenched in deterministic simulations, so they do not factor in the need for many simulations in order to conduct uncertainty quantification and sensitivity analysis. In many fields of engineering and the physical sciences, the vast increases in computer power have been consumed by increased modeling complexity, often leading to only limited improvement in risk-informed decision-making.

The construction of mathematical models of systems *always* involves simplifications of the physical reality. Modeling simplifications can usually be thought of as one of three types: omission, aggregation, and substitution (Pegden *et al.*, 1990). Omission simply means that certain physical characteristics, processes, features, or events of a system are ignored. For example, suppose one is interested in modeling the heat flux from the surface of a heated solid. If convective heat transfer is the dominant heat transfer mechanism, then the radiation heat transfer might be neglected in the model of the system. Simplification of a model by aggregation means that a characteristic is not ignored, but is combined or lumped together into a roughly equivalent characteristic. For example, in fluid dynamics if the mean free path of the atoms or molecules is much less than the characteristic length of the geometric features in the flow field, then a continuum fluid field is normally assumed. Simplification of a model by substitution means that some complex characteristics are replaced by a simpler characteristic. For example, in modeling of hydrocarbon fuel combustion the number of intermediate gas species that exist is typically in the hundreds. Depending on the needs of the simulation, a substitution combustion model for the number of gas species may only number 10 to 20.

The mathematical models of interest here are primarily given by PDEs or integro-differential equations. These equations result in initial value, boundary value, or initial-boundary value problems. The PDEs can be elliptic, parabolic, or hyperbolic in character, have two or more independent variables, and have one or more dependent variables. The PDEs describe the relationship between the dependent variables within the system, given the effect of the surroundings on the system. Information provided about the surroundings, by way of boundary conditions and system excitation conditions, is *independent* information needed for the solution of the PDEs. The differential equations can be solved by a wide variety of numerical methods, such as finite element, finite difference, or finite volume methods.

In addition to the primary PDEs of interest, there are commonly submodels, or auxiliary models, that can be stated in a variety of mathematical forms: algebraic, transcendental, table-lookup, matrix, differential, or integral equations. Examples of submodels are PDEs for modeling fluid dynamic turbulence, integro-differential equations for material constitutive properties in shock physics, and integral equations for linear viscoelasticity models in solid mechanics. The submodels can also be stated, all or in part, in tabular form so that numerical interpolation functions are used to construct the required functional relationship.

Figure 3.2 depicts a system of interest and its surroundings. For most systems of interest considered here, the key types of information describing the system are geometry, initial conditions, and physical modeling parameters. For simple systems, the geometry can be specified by engineering drawings and information concerning how the system is assembled. For most engineering systems, however, all the minute details in the geometry are specified in a computer aided design (CAD) software package. In addition, computer aided manufacturing (CAM) software may be used for more detail on the actual manufacturing and assembly process, such as deburring, riveting and bolting procedures, and electrical cable bending and pulling procedures. For systems that are modeled as an initial value problem, initial conditions (ICs) provide required information concerning (a) the initial state of all the dependent variables in the PDEs and (b) the initial state of all other physical

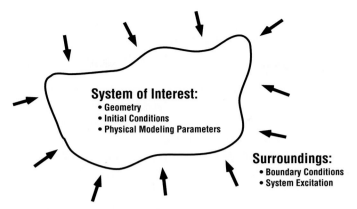

Figure 3.2 Types of information in the system and the surroundings.

modeling parameters, including geometric parameters, that could be dependent on time. As a result, the IC data could be a function of the remaining independent variables in the PDEs. The final element of information characterizing the model of the system is the physical modeling parameters. Examples of physical modeling parameters are Young's modulus, mass density, electrical conductivity, thermal conductivity, parameters in constitutive equations, damping and stiffness of assembled joints in a structure, effective chemical reaction rate, and thermal contact resistance in heat transfer. Some parameters can describe global characteristics of the system and some can vary as a function of both the independent and dependent variables in the PDEs. As will be discussed in Chapter 13, Predictive capability, some parameters can be measured independent of the system being modeled and some must be inferred based on the particular model being used and observations of the response of the system.

Two types of information must be provided concerning the surroundings: boundary conditions (BCs) and system excitation. BCs provide separate information concerning the dependent variables of the PDEs along the boundary of the domain. BCs can be dependent on one or more of the independent variables of the PDEs. These independent variables are typically other spatial dimensions and time, if the problem is formulated as an initial-boundary value problem. For example, in a structural dynamics problem the loading on the structure by way of the BCs can be time dependent. Examples of different types of BCs are: Dirichlet, Neumann, Robin, mixed, periodic, and Cauchy. System excitation refers to how the surroundings affect the system, *other than* through the BCs. System excitation always results in a change in the form of the PDEs being solved. Sometimes system excitation is referred to as a change in the right hand side of the PDEs to represent the effect of the surroundings on the system. Common examples of system excitation are (a) a force field acting on the system, such as due to gravity or an electric or magnetic field, and (b) energy deposition distributed through the system, such as by electrical heating or chemical reactions.

3.2.3 *Importance of nondeterministic simulations*

In many science and engineering communities, particularly for research activities, predictions are viewed strictly as deterministic predictions. Commonly, the purpose of these
investigations is to discover new physical phenomena or new characteristics of systems or
processes. Nondeterministic characteristics of the phenomena or system are of secondary
importance. Sometimes in these analyses, it is explicitly stated or implied that since the
investigator is only interested in *nominal* values of the output quantities, he/she can attempt
to compute these quantities using the nominal values for the input quantities. The nominal
values of the uncertain inputs may be specified as the mean value of each of the probability
distributions for the inputs. It is *rarely true*, however, that the statistical mean of the output
can be determined by performing a calculation for a single set of inputs chosen to be the
statistical mean of each of the uncertain inputs. Stated another way, the mean value of the
output cannot be computed by performing a simulation using the mean value of all input
parameters, except when the mapping of inputs to outputs is linear in the parameters. Linearity in the parameters essentially never occurs when the mapping of inputs to outputs is
given by a differential equation, *even a linear* differential equation. How much in error this
approximation is depends on the characteristics of the system, particularly the nonlinearity
in the input to output mapping of uncertain quantities.

In most engineering applications, as well as applications in the physical sciences, deterministic simulations are unacceptable approximations. The effort devoted to estimating
nondeterministic effects can vary widely depending on the goals of the computational
analysis, the expected performance, safety, and reliability of the system, and the possible
consequences of system failure or misuse. An example of a computational analysis that
might require little effort for nondeterministic effects is a system that is relatively simple,
the use of the system by the customer is well understood, and the risk of injury or misuse
of the system is minimal. For example, the computational analysis may only consider a
few important design parameters as aleatory uncertainties, i.e., precisely known random
variables, and not consider any epistemic uncertainties, i.e., uncertainties due to lack of
knowledge. The SRQs of interest computed by the computational analysis would then
be expressed as probability density functions (PDFs) or cumulative distribution functions
(CDFs).

Simulation of complex engineering systems, expensive commercial systems, and high-
consequence systems must include the nondeterministic features of the system and the
surroundings, in addition to the analysis of normal, abnormal, and hostile environments.
Several fields that regularly employ nondeterministic simulations are nuclear reactor safety
(Hora and Iman, 1989; Morgan and Henrion, 1990; NRC, 1990; Hauptmanns and Werner,
1991; Breeding *et al.*, 1992; Helton, 1994), underground contamination of toxic and radioactive waste materials (LeGore, 1990; Helton, 1993; Helton *et al.*, 1999; Stockman *et al.*,
2000), civil and structural engineering (Ayyub, 1994; Ayyub, 1998; Ben-Haim, 1999;
Melchers, 1999; Haldar and Mahadevan, 2000a, Moller and Beer, 2004; Ross, 2004; Fellin
et al., 2005; Tung and Yen, 2005; Ang and Tang, 2007; Choi *et al.*, 2007; Vinnem, 2007),

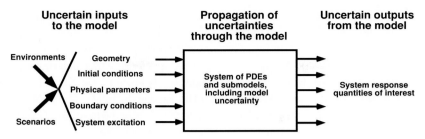

Figure 3.3 Propagation of input uncertainties to obtain output uncertainties.

environmental impact assessment (Beck, 1987; Bogen and Spear, 1987; Frank, 1999; Suter, 2007), and broader fields of risk assessment and reliability engineering (Kumamoto and Henley, 1996; Cullen and Frey, 1999; Melchers, 1999; Modarres *et al.*, 1999; Bedford and Cooke, 2001; Andrews and Moss, 2002; Bardossy and Fodor, 2004; Aven, 2005; Nikolaidis *et al.*, 2005; Ayyub and Klir, 2006; Singpurwalla, 2006; Singh *et al.*, 2007; Vose, 2008; Haimes, 2009). The emphasis in most of these fields has been directed toward representing and propagating parameter uncertainties through the mathematical model to obtain uncertain system responses. The majority of this work has used traditional probabilistic methods or Bayesian methods, where no real distinction is made between aleatory and epistemic uncertainties.

3.2.4 Analysis of nondeterministic systems

The key issue in nondeterministic simulations is that a single solution to the mathematical model is no longer sufficient. A set, or ensemble, of calculations must be performed to map the uncertain input space to the uncertain output space. Sometimes, this is referred to as *ensemble simulations* instead of nondeterministic simulations. Figure 3.3 depicts the propagation of input uncertainties through the model to obtain output uncertainties. The number of individual calculations needed to accurately accomplish the mapping depends on four key factors: (a) the nonlinearity of the PDEs; (b) the nonlinearity of the mapping in terms of the uncertain quantities; (c) the nature of the uncertainties, i.e., whether they are aleatory or epistemic uncertainties; and (d) the numerical methods used to compute the mapping. The number of mapping evaluations, i.e., individual numerical solutions of the mathematical model, can range from several to hundreds of thousands. Obviously, this latter value is shocking to those accustomed to a single solution to a set of PDEs.

With the descriptions given above, we can write the formal model structure that maps to the SRQs of interest as

$$\mathbb{M}(E, S; D, G, IC, MP, BC, SE) \rightarrow SRQ. \tag{3.1}$$

$\mathbb{M}$ is the specification of the mathematical model, E is the environment of the system, S is the scenario of the system, D is the differential or integro-differential equation describing the system, G is the geometry of the system, IC are the initial conditions of the system, MP

are the model parameters of the system, *BC* are the boundary conditions imposed by the surroundings, and *SE* is the system excitation imposed by the surroundings. *D*, *G*, *IC*, *MP*, *BC*, and *SE* are all conditional on the specified environment *E* and the scenario of interest *S*. If *D*, *G*, *IC*, *MP*, *BC*, and *SE* are all completely specified, either deterministically or nondeterministically, then the mathematical model $\mathbb{M}$, as given by Eq. (3.1), is referred to as the strong definition of a model (Leijnse and Hassanizadeh, 1994). The weak definition of a model, according to Leijnse and Hassanizadeh (1994), is one where only *D* is specified, given *E* and *S*. The weak definition of a model could then be written

$$\mathbb{M}(E, S; D) \to SRQ. \tag{3.2}$$

For a model given by Eq. (3.2), the SRQs can not be numerically computed because of the lack of specificity in the model. In addition, the weak definition of a model cannot be validated.

Many techniques exist for propagating input uncertainties through the mathematical model to obtain uncertainties in the SRQs. For a detailed discussion of many methods, see the following texts: (Kumamoto and Henley, 1996; Cullen and Frey, 1999; Melchers, 1999; Modarres *et al.*, 1999; Haldar and Mahadevan, 2000a; Bedford and Cooke, 2001; Ross, 2004; Aven, 2005; Ayyub and Klir, 2006; Singpurwalla, 2006; Ang and Tang, 2007; Kumamoto, 2007; Suter, 2007; Vose, 2008; Haimes, 2009). Sampling techniques are the most common approach because of a number of advantages: (a) they can be applied to essentially any type of mathematical model, regardless of the model's complexity or nonlinearity; (b) they can be applied to both aleatory and epistemic uncertainties, regardless of the magnitude of the uncertainties; and (c) they are not intrusive to the numerical solution of the mathematical model, i.e., sampling is done outside of numerical solution to the PDEs. Their key disadvantage is that they are computationally expensive because the number of mapping evaluations can be very large in order to obtain the statistics of interest for the SRQs. Sampling essentially solves the nondeterministic PDEs by segmenting the solution into multiple deterministic problems. If the nondeterministic PDEs are linear, it is well accepted that this segmented approach converges to the nondeterministic solution as the number of samples becomes large. If the PDEs are nonlinear, however, the correctness of this approach has not been proven, in general. See Taylor and Karlin (1998); Kloeden and Platen (2000); Serrano (2001); and Oksendal (2003) for detailed discussions of the numerical solution of stochastic PDEs.

The particular approach used in this text for nondeterministic simulations is *probability bounds analysis* (PBA) (Ferson, 1996; Ferson and Ginzburg, 1996; Ferson, 2002; Ferson *et al.*, 2003; Ferson and Hajagos, 2004; Ferson *et al.*, 2004; Kriegler and Held, 2005; Aughenbaugh and Paredis, 2006; Baudrit and Dubois, 2006). PBA is closely related to two more well-known approaches: (a) two-dimensional Monte Carlo sampling, also called nested Monte Carlo, and second order Monte Carlo (Bogen and Spear, 1987; Helton, 1994; Hoffman and Hammonds, 1994; Helton, 1997; Cullen and Frey, 1999; NASA, 2002; Kriegler and Held, 2005; Suter, 2007; Vose, 2008; NRC, 2009), and (b) evidence theory, also called Dempster–Shafer theory (Krause and Clark, 1993; Almond, 1995; Kohlas and

Monney, 1995; Klir and Wierman, 1998; Fetz *et al.*, 2000; Helton *et al.*, 2004, 2005; Oberkampf and Helton, 2005; Bae *et al.*, 2006). PBA is an approach that can be concisely described as a combination of interval analysis and traditional probability theory. PBA stresses the following perspectives: (a) mathematically characterize input uncertainty as either aleatory or epistemic; (b) characterize the model uncertainty as epistemic uncertainty; (c) map all input uncertainties through the model, typically using sampling techniques, while keeping each type of uncertainty separate; and (d) portray the uncertainty in the SRQs as a probability box, (p-box). A p-box is special type of cumulative distribution function that represents the set of all possible CDFs that fall within the prescribed bounds. As a result, probabilities can be interval-valued quantities as opposed to a single probability. A p-box expresses both epistemic and aleatory uncertainty in a way that does not confound the two. Two-dimensional Monte Carlo commonly retains some of the probabilistic nature in the sampling of the epistemic uncertainties, whereas PBA maintains a strict separation between aleatory and epistemic.

PBA typically uses standard sampling techniques, such as Monte Carlo and Latin Hypercube sampling (Cullen and Frey, 1999; Ross, 2006; Ang and Tang, 2007; Dimov, 2008; Rubinstein and Kroese, 2008). In the sampling process, however, the samples taken from the aleatory and epistemic input uncertainties are treated differently. The samples taken from aleatory uncertainties are treated as probabilistic realizations, i.e., a probability of occurrence is associated with each sample. The samples taken from the epistemic uncertainties are treated as *possible* realizations and, as a result, each sample is given a probability of *unity*. The reason epistemic uncertainties are treated this way is that they are samples drawn from interval-valued quantities. That is, all that can be claimed is that *all values* drawn from within the interval are possible, because the likelihood of one sample compared to another is unknown. This is a weaker statement of knowledge than claiming that all values within the interval are *equally* possible, i.e., a uniform PDF over the interval. As a result, the structure of a p-box for the SRQ is such that over the range where epistemic uncertainty exists, one will have an interval-valued range of probabilities. That is, over the range of epistemic uncertainty, the *most precise statement that can be made* about the SRQ is that the probability can be no larger than the computed value and no smaller than the computed value, given the epistemic uncertainty in the input. A distribution of this type is sometimes referred to as an *imprecise probability distribution*.

A simple example using PBA will be given in the next section. A more detailed discussion of PBA will be given in Chapter 13.

Types of uncertain quantities that can occur in a mathematical model are: parameters, event state specifications, independent variables, dependent variables, geometry, ICs, BCs, system excitation, and SRQs. Most parameters are viewed as continuous parameters, although it can be a simplification for mathematical convenience. For example, the number of mesh points in a numerical solution is considered continuous, even though it can only take on integer values. Uncertain parameters are usually specific values drawn from a population of a finite sample space. For example, consider a simple electrical circuit with an inductor, capacitor, and resistor. If the value of the resistance is considered to be uncertain due to manufacturing variability, then the resistance is usually treated as a continuous random variable. Some parameters are discrete, or quantized, values and they must be considered as such. For example, a switch on a control system may only have two settings (on or off), and in a safety analysis of a system with an access door, the door may be considered as only fully open or fully closed.

Event state specifications have some similarities to parameters that can take on discrete values, but event state specifications are primarily directed toward analyzing or finding specific system states that can severely impact the safety or reliability of a complex system (Kumamoto and Henley, 1996; Modarres *et al.*, 1999; Haimes, 2009). For example, fault-tree analyses are a deductive process to try and determine, given an undesirable event called the top event, all the system or component faults that could possibly happen to cause the top event. A similar technique is an event-tree analysis. If the successful operation of a system depends heavily on the chronological operation of units or subsystems, or the action of individuals, then possible events are considered to try and determine if undesirable events or states could occur.

SRQs can simply be the dependent variables in the PDEs in the mathematical model. They can also be more complex quantities such as derivatives of dependent variables, functionals of dependent variables, or complex mathematical relations between dependent variables and their frequency of occurrence. For example, an SRQ that is a functional of the dependent variables in the analysis of the plastic deformation of a structure would be the total strain energy absorbed by the structure as a function of time. If *any* input quantity to the model is nondeterministic, the SRQs are, in general, also nondeterministic.

When an uncertainty analysis is complete, it is commonly followed by a sensitivity analysis. A sensitivity analysis uses the nondeterministic results computed for the uncertainty analysis, but it attempts to answer somewhat different questions related to the system of interest. Sometimes sensitivity analyses are referred to as *what-if* or perturbation analyses of the system. The computational expense added by a sensitivity analysis is typically minimal compared to the uncertainty analysis because additional function evaluations are usually not needed. Two of the most common questions raised in a sensitivity analysis are the following.

First, what is the rate of change of SRQs of interest with respect to the uncertain input quantities? Here the focus is on local derivatives of SRQs with respect to uncertain inputs, all other input quantities remaining fixed at a specified value. This type of analysis is usually referred to as a *local sensitivity analysis*. When these derivatives are computed for a variety of input quantities, one can then rank the magnitude of the sensitivity of the output quantity with regard to the various input quantities. Note that these derivatives, and the resulting ranking of input quantities, can strongly depend on the values chosen for the input quantities. That is, the sensitivity derivatives typically vary widely over the range of uncertainty of the system design quantities and the range of operating conditions of the system.

Second, what uncertain inputs have the largest effect on SRQs of interest? Here the focus is *not* on the uncertainty of the SRQs, but on which input uncertainties have the largest

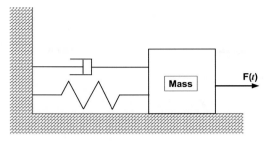

Figure 3.4 Example of a mass–spring–damper system.

global effect on SRQs of interest. This type of analysis is usually referred to as a *global sensitivity analysis*. Here *global* refers to a specific environmental condition and a specific scenario. For example, suppose there are ten uncertain parameters in a design study of the performance of some system under a normal environment and a given scenario. A global sensitivity analysis could rank order the uncertain design parameters according to which parameters produce the largest effect on a particular system performance measure, given the range of uncertainty of each design parameter. The answer to this question is of great value not only in optimization of design parameters of the system, but also for possibly restricting the operational parameters of the system that are imposed by the surroundings. For a detailed discussion of sensitivity analyses, see Kleijnen (1998); Helton (1999); Cacuci (2003); Saltelli *et al.* (2004); Helton *et al.* (2006); Saltelli *et al.* (2008); and Storlie and Helton (2008).

3.2.5 *Example problem: mechanical oscillation*

Consider the simulation of the oscillation of a mass–spring–damper system that is acted upon by a time dependent excitation force (Figure 3.4). The ordinary differential equation describing the oscillation of the system is given by

$$m\frac{\mathrm{d}^2x}{\mathrm{d}t^2} + c\frac{\mathrm{d}x}{\mathrm{d}t} + kx = F(t),$$

$$\text{Initial conditions: } x(0) = x_0 \quad \text{and} \quad \left(\frac{\mathrm{d}x}{\mathrm{d}t}\right)_{t=0} = \dot{x}_0, \tag{3.3}$$

where $x(t)$ is the displacement of the mass as a function of time, m is the mass of the system, c is the damping coefficient, k is the spring constant, and $F(t)$ is the external forcing function.

Consider two nondeterministic variants of this system.

3.2.5.1 *Aleatory uncertainty*

For the first system, assume that all features of the system, save one, are exactly known, i.e., deterministic. The damping coefficient, c, the spring constant, k, the initial state of the

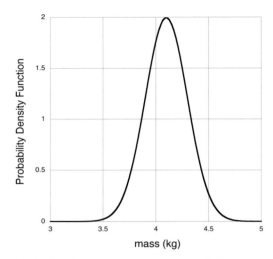

Figure 3.5 Probability density function of the system mass population.

system, x_0 and $\dot{x}_0$, and the forcing function, $F(t)$, are precisely known. These values are given as

$$c = 1 \quad \text{N/m/s}, \quad k = 100 \quad \text{N/m}, \quad x_0 = 10 \quad \text{m}, \quad \dot{x}_0 = 0 \quad \text{m/s}, \qquad (3.4)$$

and

$$F(t) = \begin{cases} 0 & \text{for } 0 \leq t < 2 \text{ s} \\ 1000 \ N & \text{for } 2 \text{ s} \leq t \leq 2.5 \text{ s} \\ 0 & \text{for } 2.5 \text{ s} < t. \end{cases} \qquad (3.5)$$

As can be seen from Eq. (3.4) and Eq. (3.5), the initial conditions are a displacement of 10 m and a velocity of zero. In addition, it is seen that the excitation function, $F(t)$, only comes into play during the time period of 2 to 2.5 s.

The mass of the system, m, is nondeterministic due to variability in its manufacturing. A large number of inspections have been made of the manufactured masses that are used in the system so that a precise probability density function (PDF) for the population can be generated. It was found that the PDF of the population could be accurately represented by a normal (Gaussian) distribution with a mean of 4.2 kg and a standard deviation of 0.2 kg, as shown in Figure 3.5.

Since Eq. (3.3) is linear, the solution to the mathematical model can be written analytically, i.e., in closed-form, or it can be solved numerically using a standard ODE solver. For our simulation, Eq. (3.3) was converted into two first-order ODEs and then solved numerically using MATLAB's Runge-Kutta 4(5) method, *ode45*. The numerical solution error for each time-step advancement was required to be less than 10^{-3} for the relative error, and less than 10^{-6} absolute error, for each dependent variable.

Since the nondeterministic nature of the system is purely aleatory, traditional sampling methods can be used to propagate the mass uncertainty into uncertainty of the SRQs of interest. We used Monte Carlo sampling incorporated in MATLAB's normal distribution sampler *randn* in order to obtain samples for the mass. The mean, μ, was set to 4.2 kg, and the standard deviation, σ, was set to 0.2 kg. In nondeterministic simulations using sampling, a random number seed is required so that one can reproduce precisely the same sequence of random numbers. This technique is referred to as pseudo-random number generation. In the MATLAB program *randn*, the default seed of 0 was used, with the number of samples, n, of 10, 100, and 1000.

Various SRQs can be computed, for example, position, velocity, and acceleration, $x(t)$, $\dot{x}(t)$, and $\ddot{x}(t)$, respectively. Figure 3.6, Figure 3.7, and Figure 3.8 show $x(t)$, $\dot{x}(t)$, and $\ddot{x}(t)$, respectively, for time up to 10 s, and $n = 10$, 100, and 1000. The expected oscillatory motion is seen in each of the SRQs. The effect of the excitation function during the time period of 2 to 2.5 s cannot be seen in the displacement plot, it is just barely noticeable in the velocity plot, and is clearly visible in the acceleration plot. In each plot, every Monte Carlo sample that is computed is shown. As a result, it is difficult to see any of the individual numerical solutions in the plots for $n = 100$ and 1000.

Since the nondeterministic simulation of the SRQs is a distribution of results, as opposed to an individual deterministic result, it is appropriate to interpret the results in terms of statistical measures of the SRQs. Table 3.1 and Table 3.2 show the estimated mean and standard deviation of $x(t)$, $\dot{x}(t)$, and $\ddot{x}(t)$, at $t = 1$ and 5 s, respectively, as a function of the number of samples computed, including 10 000 samples. The ˆ symbol indicates that the values for μ and σ are sample values for the mean and standard deviation as opposed to exact values of the population. As expected, both $\hat{\mu}$ and $\hat{\sigma}$ will change as a function of the number of samples computed because of relatively few samples. In the limit as the number of samples increases, $\hat{\mu} \rightarrow \mu$ and $\hat{\sigma} \rightarrow \sigma$. As expected in Monte Carlo sampling, there is relatively little change in μ and σ after 100 samples for most cases. The results in the tables are given to three significant figures for each set of samples.

Another traditional method of presenting the results of a nondeterministic system is to show a plot of the CDF of each of the SRQs. The CDF shows the fraction of the population that would have a value less than, or equal to, a particular value of the SRQ. A CDF shows the distributional information concerning a nondeterministic quantity, as opposed to some type of summary measure of the distribution, such as a mean or standard deviation. When a limited number of samples are computed, or measured in an experiment, the CDF is referred to as an empirical distribution function (EDF). The EDF shows the fraction of the *sampled* population that would have a value less than, or equal to, a particular value of the SRQ. Another traditional method of showing nondeterministic results is to show histograms of each of the SRQs. Although this can be helpful for certain situations, we do not generally use this method because it requires the analyst to pick a bin size for the histogram. Picking a bin size is actually an assumption that must be made in the analysis in order to show the statistical results. We are of the viewpoint that the fewer assumptions made in an analysis, particularly in a statistical analysis, the better.

Figure 3.9 and Figure 3.10 show the EDF of $x(t)$, $\dot{x}(t)$, and $\ddot{x}(t)$, at $t = 1$ and 5 s, respectively, for each of the number of samples computed. The most notable feature in each

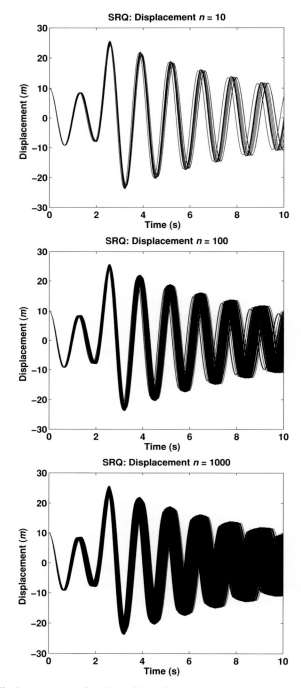

Figure 3.6 Mass displacement as a function of time for aleatory uncertainty.

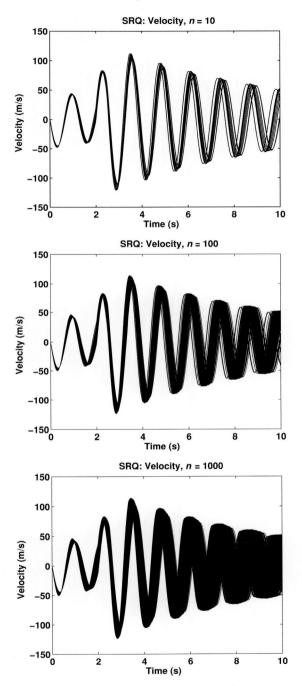

Figure 3.7 Mass velocity as a function of time for aleatory uncertainty.

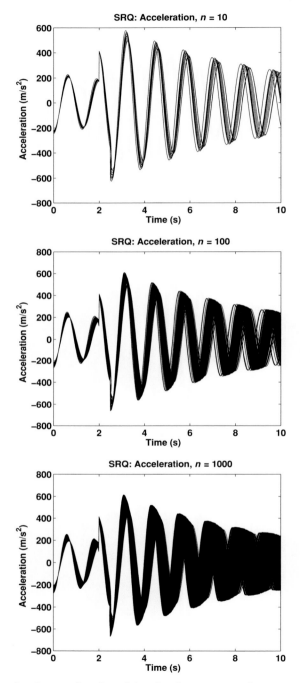

Figure 3.8 Mass acceleration as a function of time for aleatory uncertainty.

Table 3.1 *Statistics for displacement, velocity,*
and acceleration for t = 1 s.

	$\hat{\mu}$	$\hat{\sigma}$
Displacement x		
Samples (n)		
10	0.65	0.76
100	1.20	0.96
1000	1.29	1.03
10 000	1.29	1.01
Velocity $\dot{x}$		
Samples (n)		
10	42.5	0.286
100	42.4	0.462
1000	42.4	0.458
10 000	42.4	0.478
Acceleration $\ddot{x}$		
Samples (n)		
10	−25.5	18.5
100	−39.7	25.3
1000	−42.1	26.8
10 000	−42.0	26.2

graph, particularly to those not familiar with EDFs, is the stair-step nature of the curve for $n = 10$ samples. The reason for this characteristic is that there are so few samples to characterize the true distribution. It is seen in every plot with 10 or 100 samples that the EDF (a) is very rough and gives the appearance that it may be discontinuous, (b) apparently contains a bias error because it is commonly shifted to the left or right of the high fidelity EDF for $n = 1000$, and (c) is deficient in showing any of the tails of the high fidelity distribution. The rough, or stair-step, nature of the plot results from the fact that there is a jump in probability at each of the observed samples. With only 10 samples, each sample *must* represent a probability jump of 0.1. None of the EDFs are discontinuous, but each one is a stair-step where the height of each step is $1/n$. With few samples, there is commonly a bias error in the computed distribution. This tendency of a bias error due to a low number of samples can also be seen in computing μ and σ of the distributions, see Table 3.1 and Table 3.2. Since Monte Carlo sampling is an unbiased estimator of the statistics, the bias error approaches zero as the number of samples becomes very large. The inaccuracy in the computed tails of the distributions is usually referred to as the inaccuracy of computing low probability events with a small number of samples. This is a well-known deficiency in Monte Carlo sampling and it is discussed in Chapter 13. For a more detailed discussion, see Cullen and Frey (1999); Ang and Tang (2007); Dimov (2008); and Vose (2008).

Table 3.2 *Statistics for displacement, velocity,
and acceleration for t = 5 s.*

	$\hat{\mu}$	$\hat{\sigma}$
Displacement x		
Samples (n)		
10	10.4	4.33
100	12.7	4.10
1000	13.0	4.69
10 000	13.1	4.53
Velocity $\dot{x}$		
Samples (n)		
10	70.9	14.2
100	57.3	26.2
1000	54.0	26.9
10 000	54.4	26.5
Acceleration $\ddot{x}$		
Samples (n)		
10	−260	106
100	−320	105
1000	−329	118
10 000	−330	114

3.2.5.2 Epistemic uncertainty

All of the characteristics of this system are the same as the previous system, except for the nondeterministic character of the mass. For this case the system manufacturer concluded that the variability of the system response was unacceptably large due to the variability in the masses used. The primary concern was that, based on the characterization of the variability in the mass as a normal distribution, there could be masses with very low and very high values. Although there were very low probabilities associated with the very low and very high masses, these situations could cause the system to fail. Because the consequence of system failure was severe, project management became quite concerned with respect to legal liability.

As a result, the project manager found another supplier of masses for their system that claimed they could produce masses with a guaranteed bound on the variability of the masses they produced. The new supplier's procedure was to reject any masses produced during the production process that were either below or above a specification set by the customer. However, to cut costs, they did not weigh the production masses that pass their inspection process to determine what the variability is of their delivered product. Consequently, the new supplier could only guarantee that the uncertainty of the masses they delivered to the customer were within the specified interval. As a result, when the customer simulated their

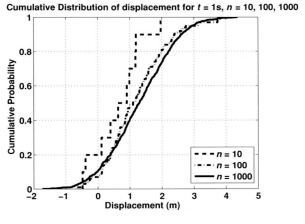

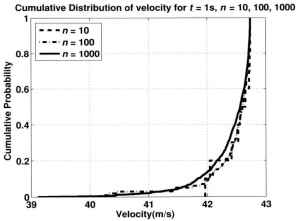

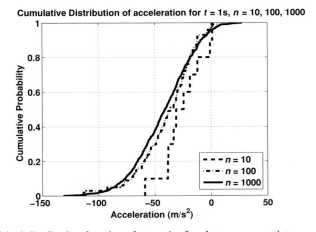

Figure 3.9 Empirical distribution functions for $t = 1$ s for aleatory uncertainty.

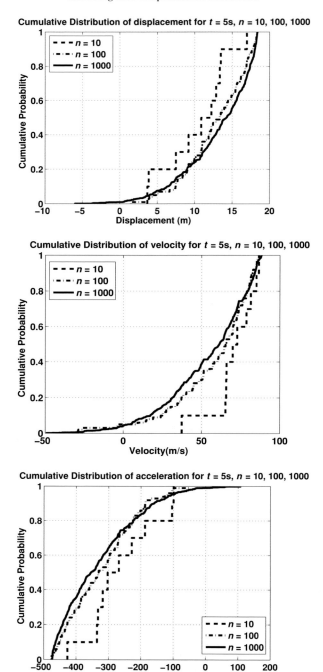

Figure 3.10 Empirical distribution functions for $t = 5$ s for aleatory uncertainty.

Table 3.3 *Maximum and minimum value of displacement, velocity, and acceleration for t = 1 s.*

	Max value	Min value
Displacement x		
Samples (n)		
10	3.69	−0.82
100	3.86	−1.01
1000	3.85	−1.11
10 000	3.87	−1.11
Velocity $\dot{x}$		
Samples (n)		
10	42.7	40.5
100	42.7	40.2
1000	42.7	40.2
10 000	42.7	40.2
Acceleration $\ddot{x}$		
Samples (n)		
10	8.7	−110
100	12.7	−115
1000	14.7	−115
10 000	14.8	−116

system with the masses provided by the new supplier, they could only justify an interval-valued quantity for the mass as [3.7, 4.7] kg. Stated differently, they had *no knowledge* to justify *any* PDF for the masses within the interval. Consequently, in the analysis of the system, the customer considered the uncertainty in the mass as a purely epistemic uncertainty.

With the epistemic uncertainty for the mass of the system, a probability bounds analysis (PBA) is required. Since there is no aleatory uncertainty in the system, the PBA reduces to an interval analysis. That is, if only interval-valued uncertainties exist on the inputs, then only interval-values can result for the SRQs. We used Monte Carlo sampling incorporated in MATLAB's random number generator *rand* to obtain samples over the interval-valued range of the mass. Since *rand* produces a random number scaled between 0 and 1, we shifted the output of *rand* so that it would produce a sequence of random numbers in the interval [3.7, 4.7]. The number of samples, n, was again set to 10, 100, and 1000. Note that we only used Monte Carlo sampling as a vehicle to sample over the interval-valued uncertainty. None of the samples are associated with a probability, i.e., each sample is simply considered as a *possible realization* that could occur in the system and no probability is assigned to it.

We will present the results for the interval-valued uncertainty in the mass in terms of tables of results, similar to Table 3.1 and Table 3.2, and in terms of plots of CDF,

Table 3.4 *Maximum and minimum value of
displacement, velocity, and acceleration for t = 5 s.*

	Max value	Min value
Displacement x		
Samples (n)		
10	18.3	0.51
100	18.4	−0.15
1000	18.4	−1.48
10 000	18.4	−1.50
Velocity $\dot{x}$		
Samples (n)		
10	87.5	−23.9
100	88.3	−31.4
1000	89.3	−30.3
10 000	89.3	−31.6
Acceleration $\ddot{x}$		
Samples (n)		
10	−29.9	−470
100	−15.2	−475
1000	13.0	−475
10 000	13.4	−475

similar to Figure 3.9 and Figure 3.10. Table 3.3 and Table 3.4 show the maximum and minimum value of $x(t)$, $\dot{x}(t)$, and $\ddot{x}(t)$ at $t = 1$ and 5 s, respectively, as a function of the number of samples computed, including 10 000 samples. Since we are only dealing with an interval-valued uncertain input, Table 3.3 and Table 3.4 show the maximum and minimum values of the various SRQs, based on the number of samples obtained. By comparing the results in Table 3.3 and Table 3.4 with the aleatory results shown in Table 3.1 and Table 3.2 (all for $n = 10\,000$), it is seen that the maximum and minimum values for $x(t)$, $\dot{x}(t)$, and $\ddot{x}(t)$ are bounded by the aleatory results using $\mu \pm 3\sigma$. However, depending on the nature of the system and the input uncertainties, the SRQ uncertainty due to aleatory input uncertainty can be quite different compared to epistemic input uncertainty.

An important computational point should be mentioned with regard to the sampling results shown in Table 3.3 and Table 3.4. For each of the three different numbers of samples shown, a *different* random number seed was used. For $n = 10$, 100, 1000, and 10 000, seed values of 0, 1, 2, and 3, respectively, were used in MATLAB. Using different seed values for the random number generator is referred to as *replicated Monte Carlo sampling*. Using different seeds will result in a different random number sequence for sampling the input. Consequently, each ensemble of output results will be different, i.e., each ensemble result, which is composed of n samples, is a different set of computed samples. Of course, in the limit as *n* becomes large, the interval-value bounds from each replicated Monte Carlo sample will become equivalent. For the case of sampling over an interval, replicated sampling is more important than for aleatory uncertainties because each sample over the interval is treated as a possible value instead of a value associated with a probability. In a probabilistic view, the probability of the sample is related to (a) the PDF characterizing the uncertainty, and (b) the number of samples obtained. As mentioned earlier in the chapter, what we mean by a *possible value* is to say that *every value* sampled can be considered to have a probability of *unity*. This feature of *n* sampled values, each with a probability of unity, is a source of disagreement with the Bayesian perspective.

Figure 3.11 shows the EDF of $x(t)$, $\dot{x}(t)$, and $\ddot{x}(t)$ at $t = 1$ for each of the number of samples computed. These graphs are strikingly different than those shown for aleatory uncertainty, Figure 3.9 and Figure 3.10. The reason, of course, is that the EDFs for epistemic uncertainty portray an interval-valued quantity for each SRQ. Even though Figure 3.11 presents the same information as given in Table 3.3, it is worthwhile to consider what an interval-valued quantity looks like in terms of an EDF. For an uncertainty that is characterized as an epistemic uncertainty, i.e., an interval-valued quantity, the EDF will be a p-box. The p-boxes shown in Figure 3.11 are a degenerate case of general p-boxes because there is only epistemic uncertainty and no aleatory uncertainty. The general case of p-boxes for mixed epistemic and aleatory uncertainty will be briefly addressed in Section 3.5.6, with a more detailed discussion given in Chapter 12, Model accuracy assessment, and Chapter 13.

Consider the interpretation of the p-boxes shown in Figure 3.11. For values of the SRQ less than the minimum value observed, the probability is considered to be zero, because no smaller values were computed. For values of the SRQ larger than the maximum value observed, the probability is considered to be unity, because no larger values were computed. For values of the SRQ between the minimum and maximum values observed, the probability can range from zero to unity. That is, given the epistemic uncertainty in the simulation, all that can be stated about the probability within the range of observed values is that the probability itself is an interval-valued quantity, i.e., [0, 1]. Stated another way, Figure 3.11 is simply the graphical depiction of an interval in terms of an empirical distribution function. When this interpretation is explained to a traditional frequency-based statistician or a Bayesian statistician, their reaction typically is "That's not saying *anything*!" Our response is: given the poor knowledge that is stated for the input, that is *all* that can be stated. Or equivalently: all values within the observed range of values are possible, but there is *no evidence* to claim any likelihood of outcomes within the range.

As a final comment on this example, if readers attempt to reproduce the results given in either the aleatory or epistemic uncertainty examples, they may not be able to reproduce exactly the same numerical results shown. If the reader uses MATLAB and all of the same numerical input values given here, one should be able to accurately repeat the results shown. However, if a different software package is used, particularly a different random number generator, then the results could vary noticeably because each random number generator will produce its own unique sequence of pseudo-random numbers. The differences in the present results and a reader's results will be most noticeable for a low numbers of samples.

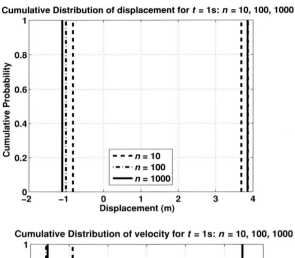

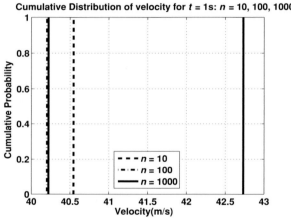

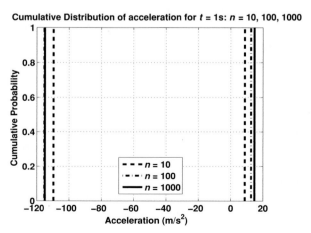

Figure 3.11 Empirical distribution functions for $t = 1$ s for epistemic uncertainty.

3.3 Risk and failure

We have referred to *risk* in various contexts, but the concept is so important, it must be defined more precisely. Essentially all modern quantitative risk analyses use the foundational concepts formulated by Kaplan and Garrick in their classic paper "On the quantitative definition of risk" (Kaplan and Garrick, 1981). They formulated the issue of quantitative risk in terms of asking three failure-related questions.

- What can go wrong?
- What is the likelihood that it will go wrong?
- If it does go wrong, what are the consequences?

They answer these questions in terms of the risk triplet

$$\langle s_i, p_i, x_i \rangle, \quad i = 1, 2, \ldots, n, \tag{3.6}$$

where s_i is the specific failure scenario being considered, p_i is the probability that the failure scenario occurs, x_i is the consequence or damage-measure from that failure scenario, and n is the number of failure scenarios being considered. s_i is simply an index for identifying a specific scenario, and x_i is a scalar that attempts to quantify in terms of dimensional units the magnitude of the consequence of a failure. For the remainder of the text we will simply use the term *failure* instead of failure scenario. The probability p_i could be stated in different ways; for example, for each use of the system, over a fixed period of a time, or over the lifetime of the system.

The conceptual framework of the risk triplet is very useful, but it is mathematically clumsy to deal with in a quantitative risk assessment (QRA) or probabilistic risk assessment (PRA) analysis. Many alternatives could be defined so that the risk could be computed by combining the three terms in Eq. (3.6). The most common method of defining risk is simply to take the product of the probability of failure occurring and the consequence of failure (Modarres *et al.*, 1999; Haimes, 2009). One has

$$\text{Risk} = p_i \bullet x_i, \quad i = 1, 2, \ldots, n. \tag{3.7}$$

The value of risk computed in Eq. (3.7) is a dimensional quantity, measured in terms of the units of the consequence of the failure x_i. The units most commonly used are monetary value, e.g., dollars or euros. For example, Eq. (3.7) could be used to estimate the total financial liability or expected total damages incurred over time as a result of a system failure. Consequences, however, can be very difficult to quantify because they can have a multitude of aspects; e.g., lost future business, environmental impact, societal impact, decrease in military security, or political impact. In addition, there are almost always unintended consequences; some of which have short-term and long-term negative effects (Tenner, 1996). The ability to identify short-term and long-term detrimental unintended consequences is extremely difficult for many reasons. High among them is that individuals, organizations, and governments tend to focus on the near-term benefits, as opposed to potential long-term risks or required changes in behavior.

Haimes (2009) and Lawson (2005) give an in-depth discussion of the three fundamental sources of failure in systems. They identify these as technical failure, individual human failure, and organizational failure. Technical failure occurs within the system, from either hardware or software, and commonly initiates some type of larger-scale system failure that has noticeable consequences. Hardware failures are commonly a result of inadequate system maintenance or inspection, or lack of needed repairs or improvements. Human failure can be of many types; e.g., system operator error, lack of proper safety training, human misuse of the system, or the system operator ignoring warning alarms. Organizational failure can occur due to gross negligence or malfeasance, but it is commonly caused by neglect or omission. As pointed out by Haimes (2009) and Lawson (2005), organizational failure is caused by humans in the organization, but the dominant feature of the failure is due to the culture and traditions within an organization. Some examples of organization failure are (a) overlooking system weaknesses or delaying maintenance because of competitive or schedule pressures; (b) poor or filtered communication between management and staff; (c) competition between groups within an organization such that a group remains silent concerning weaknesses in a competing group's design; (d) lack of incentives for a project group manager to identify weaknesses in his system's design; or (e) external political pressures on an organization causing impaired judgment of management. Each of these three fundamental sources of failure is interconnected to the others in direct and indirect ways. These connections can occur during the proposal preparation phase for a new system, design phase, testing, and operation and maintenance of the system.

A number of researchers and recent investigations of root causes of high-visibility system failures effectively argue that organizational failures are the dominant cause of most complex system failures (Dorner, 1989; Paté-Cornell, 1990; Petroski, 1994; Vaughan, 1996; Reason, 1997; Gehman *et al.*, 2003; Lawson, 2005; Mosey, 2006). Organizational failures are typically difficult to identify carefully and isolate, particularly for large organizations or the government. Organizational failure is usually connected to unintentional or intentional avoidance of an issue in some way, commonly brought on by competitive, schedule, budgetary, cultural, political, or face-saving pressures. News media coverage of failures tends to focus on the technical or human failure that initiated the event, such as "The captain of the ship was intoxicated while on duty." However, most complex systems require multiple contributing failures to occur before some type of disaster is precipitated. Many of these multiple contributors can be traced back to organizational failures.

3.4 Phases of computational simulation

The operations research (OR) and systems engineering (SE) communities have developed many of the general principles and procedures for M&S. Researchers in this field have made significant progress in defining and categorizing the various activities and phases of M&S. For recent texts in this field, see Bossel (1994); Zeigler *et al.* (2000); Severance (2001); Law (2006); and Raczynski (2006). The areas of emphasis in OR and SE include

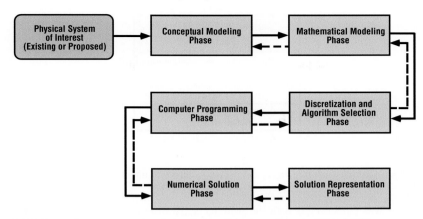

Figure 3.12 Phases for a computational simulation (Oberkampf *et al.*, 2000; 2002).

definition of the problem entity, definition of the conceptual model, assessment of data and information quality, discrete event simulation, and methods for using simulation results as an aid in decision making. From a computational simulation perspective, this work is not focused on models that are specified by PDEs. However, the OR and SE work is very helpful in providing a useful philosophical approach for identifying sources of uncertainty, as well as developing some of the basic terminology and model development procedures.

Based on the work of Jacoby and Kowalik (1980), Oberkampf *et al.* (2000, 2002) developed a comprehensive, new framework of the general phases of computational simulation. This structure is composed of six phases that represent a synthesis of the tasks recognized in the operations research, risk assessment, and numerical methods communities. Figure 3.12 depicts the phases of computational simulation appropriate to systems analyzed by the numerical solution of PDEs. The physical system can be an existing system or process, or it can be a system or process that is being proposed. The phases represent collections of activities required in a generic large-scale computational analysis. The ordering of the phases implies an information and data flow indicating which tasks are likely to impact analyses, decisions, and methodologies occurring in later phases. Each succeeding phase could be described as a *mapping of the preceding phase into a new phase* of activities. Any assumptions, approximations, aleatory uncertainties, recognized epistemic uncertainties, or blind epistemic uncertainties introduced in one phase are then propagated to *all* succeeding phases. Suppose, for example, it is discovered in some latter phase that an assumption or approximation was inappropriate, or a blind uncertainty (e.g., oversight or mistake) was introduced at some earlier phase. Then one must return to that phase and re-evaluate all subsequent phases to determine what changes must be made. This type of feedback interaction between the phases is shown by the dashed lines in Figure 3.12.

In the following sections, characteristics and activities of each of the phases are discussed. The emphasis in the discussion is on the identification and propagation of different types of uncertainty through the computational simulation process. In Section 2.3, taxonomy of

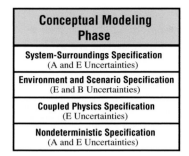

Figure 3.13 Conceptual modeling phase and primary sources of uncertainty.

uncertainties was constructed with the primary separation made between aleatory uncertainties and epistemic uncertainties. Epistemic uncertainties were further divided into (a) recognized uncertainty, i.e., uncertainty due to incomplete knowledge in which a conscious decision has been made to either characterize it in some way, or to ignore it with justification; and (b) blind uncertainty, i.e., uncertainty due to incomplete knowledge, but where it is *not* recognized that the knowledge is incomplete and relevant. The distinction between aleatory and epistemic uncertainty is important not only in assessing how each contributes to an estimate of total predictive uncertainty, but also how each should be mathematically represented and propagated through each phase.

3.4.1 Conceptual modeling phase

Activities conducted in the conceptual modeling phase are shown in Figure 3.13, along with the primary sources of uncertainty introduced in each activity. Note that in Figure 3.13, and all subsequent graphics of a similar nature, the text in brackets indicates the primary types of uncertainty that occur in that activity. *A Uncertainty* is aleatory uncertainty. *E Uncertainty* is recognized epistemic uncertainty. *B Uncertainty* is blind epistemic uncertainty, which is commonly referred to as unknown-unknowns.

The first activity is the specification of the physical system of interest and its surroundings. The primary conceptualization that must be specified in this activity is the demarcation between the system and the surroundings. As discussed in Section 3.1.1 above, the surroundings are not modeled as part of the system. The system responds to the surroundings. The uncertainties associated with the system and surroundings specification consist primarily of epistemic uncertainties that arise in defining the scope of the problem. For a complex engineered system, epistemic uncertainties commonly occur because of factors such as the following. Was the system incorrectly manufactured or assembled? How well was the system maintained? Was the system damaged in the past and not recorded? The system and surroundings specification would also contain aleatory uncertainties, such as variability due to manufacturing, systems exposed to weather conditions, and random excitation of a system by its surroundings. Unless a large number of empirical samples are available to characterize an aleatory uncertainty, then it is likely that the uncertainty would be a mixture of aleatory and epistemic uncertainty.

The second activity is the determination of the environments and the scenarios that will be considered in the computational simulation. As discussed earlier in this chapter, the three classes of environment are normal, abnormal, and hostile. Different conceptual models are almost always required if more than one class of environment is considered. Scenario specification identifies physical events or sequences of events that could *possibly* be considered for a given environment, see Figure 3.1. Identifying possible scenarios or event sequences is similar to developing an event-tree or fault-tree structure in the probabilistic risk assessment of high consequence systems, such as in nuclear reactor safety analyses. Event and fault trees include not only technical (hardware and software) failures, but also human actions that could be taken either within or outside the system, i.e., as part of the surroundings. Even if a certain sequence of events is considered extremely remote, it should still be included as a possible event sequence in the fault tree. Whether or not the event sequence will eventually be analyzed is not a factor that impacts its inclusion in the conceptual modeling phase. In this activity both epistemic and blind (epistemic) uncertainties are the most likely to occur. This is particularly true in identifying possible scenarios within abnormal and hostile environments. Creativity and imagination are especially useful qualities of individuals involved in analyzing abnormal and hostile environments.

The third activity is the specification of the possible types of coupling of different physical processes that will be incorporated in the modeling. During the coupled physics specification, no mathematical equations are written. After the system and surroundings are specified, options for various levels of possible physics couplings should be identified, even if it is considered unlikely that all such couplings will be considered subsequently in the analysis. If a physics coupling is not considered in this phase, it cannot be addressed later in the process.

The fourth activity is the specification of all aspects in the modeling that will be considered as nondeterministic. The nondeterministic specification applies to every aspect of the first three activities considered in conceptual modeling, assuming that the activity can be characterized as an aleatory uncertainty or a recognized epistemic uncertainty. Blind uncertainties, of course, are not characterized because they are not recognized as an uncertainty. These determinations must be based on the general requirements for the computational simulation effort. The question of what representation will be used for the uncertainty is deferred until later phases.

3.4.2 Mathematical modeling phase

The primary task in this phase is to develop a precisely stated mathematical model, i.e., analytical statements based on the conceptual model formulated in the previous phase. The four activities in mathematical modeling are shown in Figure 3.14. The number of analyses

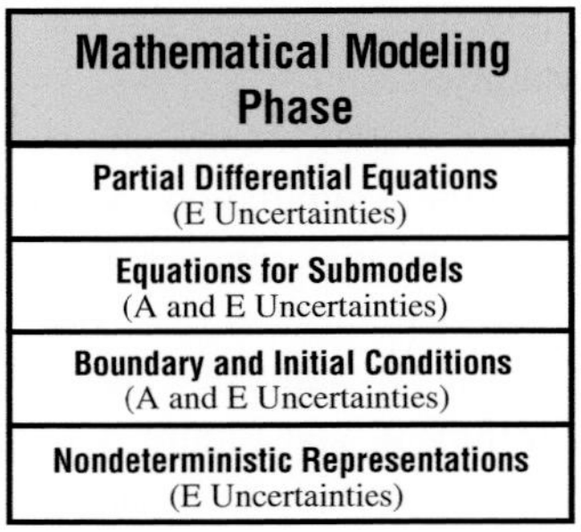

Mathematical Modeling Phase
Partial Differential Equations (E Uncertainties)
Equations for Submodels (A and E Uncertainties)
Boundary and Initial Conditions (A and E Uncertainties)
Nondeterministic Representations (E Uncertainties)

Figure 3.14 Mathematical modeling phase and primary sources of uncertainty.

to be conducted depends on how many combinations of environments and scenarios were identified in the conceptual model phase. For large-scale analyses, the number could be quite large and, as a result, prioritization of the more important analyses needs to be conducted. Typically, this prioritization is based on the risk (i.e., estimated probability multiplied by estimated consequence) that the environment–scenario pair represents to the success of the system of interest.

The complexity of the PDE models depends on the physical complexity of each phenomenon being considered, the number of physical phenomena being considered, and the level of coupling of different types of physics. The system-surroundings specification and the physics coupling specification should have been completed in the conceptual modeling phase. Some examples of epistemic uncertainties that occur in physics modeling are (a) fracture dynamics in any type of material; (b) coupling of the liquid, solid, and fluid phases in multiphase flow; (c) phase change of materials that are not in equilibrium; and (d) choosing to model a problem in 2-D instead of 3-D.

A complex mathematical model given by a set of PDEs is usually complemented by a number of mathematical submodels. Examples of submodels are (a) analytical equations or tabular data for mechanical, thermodynamic, electrical, and optical properties of materials; (b) ODEs and PDEs for constitutive properties of materials; and (c) PDEs for fluid dynamic turbulence modeling. The submodels, along with the boundary conditions, initial conditions, and any system excitation equations, complete the equation set for the system. BCs, ICs, and system excitation commonly exhibit aleatory and epistemic uncertainties. For abnormal and hostile environments, BCs, ICs, and system excitation are almost always dominated by epistemic uncertainties.

Any mathematical model, regardless of its physical level of detail, is *by definition* a simplification of reality. Any complex engineering system, or even an individual physical process, contains phenomena that are not represented in the model. As a result, specification of the mathematical models involves approximations and assumptions. These both result in epistemic uncertainties being introduced into the modeling process. Sometimes, in large-scale computational simulation projects, one can hear statements such as "The project will use such large-scale, massively parallel computers, that full physics simulations will be

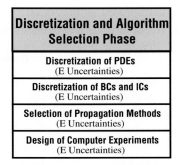

Figure 3.15 Discretization and algorithm selection phase and primary sources of uncertainty.

computed." These kinds of statements can only be considered as advertising hyperbole. The enduring truth of modeling was succinctly stated many years ago by George Box (1980): "All models are wrong, some are useful."

Another function addressed during this phase of analysis is selecting appropriate representations for the nondeterministic elements of the problem. Several considerations might drive these selections. Restrictions set forth in the conceptual modeling phase of the analyses may put constraints on the range of values or types of representations that might be used in the analysis. Within these constraints the quantity and/or limitations of available or obtainable data will play an important role. If sufficient sampling data is available for aleatory uncertainties, then a PDF or CDF can be constructed. In the absence of data, expert opinion or a similar type of information may be used. For this type of information, one could either represent the information as an interval, with no likelihood information claimed over the interval, or use a p-box. It would be highly suspect if an expert claimed that they could specify a precise probability distribution, i.e., a distribution with fixed values for the parameters of the distribution.

3.4.3 Discretization and algorithm selection phase

The discretization and algorithm selection phase maps the mathematical model developed in the previous phase into a fully discrete mathematical model. Figure 3.15 shows the four activities that are completed in this phase. These activities are grouped into two general tasks related to converting the mathematical model into a form that can be addressed through computational analysis. The first task involves conversion of the PDEs from the mathematical model into a discrete, or numerical, model. Simply stated, the mathematics is translated from a calculus problem into an arithmetic problem. In this phase, all of the spatial and temporal discretization methods are specified for discretization of the domain of the PDEs, including the geometric features, mathematical submodels, BCs, ICs, and system excitation. The discrete form of the PDEs is typically given by finite element, finite volume, or finite difference equations. In this task the discretization algorithms and methods are prescribed, but the spatial and temporal step sizes are simply given as quantities to be specified. The discretization phase focuses on the conversion of the mathematical model from continuum mathematics, i.e., derivatives and integrals, to discrete mathematics. The methods for the numerical solution of the discretized equations are discussed in a later phase.

Although we may not consciously specify all of the discretization methods in some computational analyses, such as when using commercial software packages, we strongly believe it is an important step because it can greatly assist in detecting certain types of numerical error. This conversion process is the root cause of certain difficulties in the numerical solution of PDEs. If the mathematical model contains singularities, or the solution is near or in a chaotic state, then much more care is required when choosing the numerical algorithms. Singularities commonly exist in the mathematical models, but they rarely exist in discrete mathematics. Yee and Sweby (1995; 1996; 1998); Yee *et al.* (1997) and others have investigated the numerical solution of nonlinear ODEs and PDEs that are near chaotic behavior. They have clearly shown that the numerical solution of these equations can be quite different from exact analytical solutions of the mathematical model even when using established methods that are well within their numerical stability limits, and using what is believed to be a mesh-resolved solution. Although it is beyond the scope of this book, much more research is needed in the simulation of chaotic solutions.

The third task of this phase of the analysis is the specification of uncertainty propagation methods and the design of computer experiments in order to accommodate the nondeterministic aspects of the problem. Both activities address conversion of the nondeterministic elements of the analysis into multiple runs, or solutions, of a deterministic computational simulation code. Selection of an uncertainty propagation method involves the determination of an approach, or approaches, to propagating uncertainties through the model. Examples of propagation methods include reliability methods (Melchers, 1999; Haldar and Mahadevan, 2000a; Ang and Tang, 2007; Choi *et al.*, 2007) and sampling methods such as Monte Carlo or Latin Hypercube (Cullen and Frey, 1999; Ross, 2006; Ang and Tang, 2007; Dimov, 2008; Rubinstein and Kroese, 2008). Traditional emphasis in uncertainty quantification and risk assessment is on propagation of parametric uncertainties, but in many complex physics simulations, model-form uncertainties tend to be the dominant contributor to uncertainty in SRQs. In this phase, methods for propagating model-form uncertainties are also specified. If any methods are used that approximate the propagation of input to output uncertainties, then they should also be specified in this phase. A very common approximation method is the use of response surface methods to reduce the number of numerical solutions of the discrete model that are needed to propagate uncertainties.

The design of computer experiments, i.e., statistical experiments, is driven to a large extent by the availability of computer resources and by the requirements of the analysis. Establishing an experimental design often involves more than just implementation of the propagation method specified above (Mason *et al.*, 2003; Box *et al.*, 2005). The problems associated with large analyses can often be decomposed in a way that permits some variables and parameters to be investigated using only portions of the code or, perhaps, simpler models

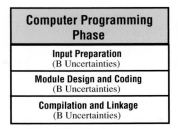

Figure 3.16 Computer programming phase and primary sources of uncertainty.

than are required for other variables and parameters. The decomposition of the problem and selection of appropriate models, together with the formal determination of inputs for the computer runs, can have a major effect on the estimate of uncertainty introduced into the analysis in this phase. This activity is performed here because the detailed specification of inputs and models will impact programming requirements, as well as the running of the computer model in the numerical solution phase.

As noted in Figure 3.15, the primary type of uncertainty introduced in this phase is epistemic uncertainty. These uncertainties are a specific type of epistemic uncertainty, i.e., they are due to the fidelity and accuracy of the numerical approximations. These numerical approximations are due to the *choice* of numerical methods to execute the mapping from continuum mathematics to discrete mathematics. As a result, they are analogous to choices for constructing mathematical models of physics processes. These numerical approximations are *not* analogous to numerical solution errors, such as mesh resolution errors, because numerical solution errors can usually be ordered in terms of accuracy. Choices of numerical methods and algorithms cannot always be ordered with respect to anticipated accuracy, reliability, and robustness.

3.4.4 Computer programming phase

The computer programming phase maps the discrete mathematical model formulated in the previous phase into software instructions executable on a digital computer. Figure 3.16 lists the activities conducted in this phase, as well as the primary sources of uncertainty introduced in this phase. These activities are divided into two groups: preparation of input for the computer code and computer programming activities. Preparation of input is part of this phase because it sets all of the numerical values of the input quantities that will be used in the actual computation, which occurs in the next phase. The dominant uncertainty that occurs in the preparation of input activity is the introduction of blind uncertainties, e.g., mistakes or blunders in the preparation of the input. Some researchers and analysts experienced only with relatively simple model problems do not appreciate the concern with input errors due to humans. This is, however, an important source of blind uncertainties when one is dealing with a complex and wide range of physical, modeling, and numerical details in a large code, multiple codes that are sequentially coupled, simulations that heavily rely

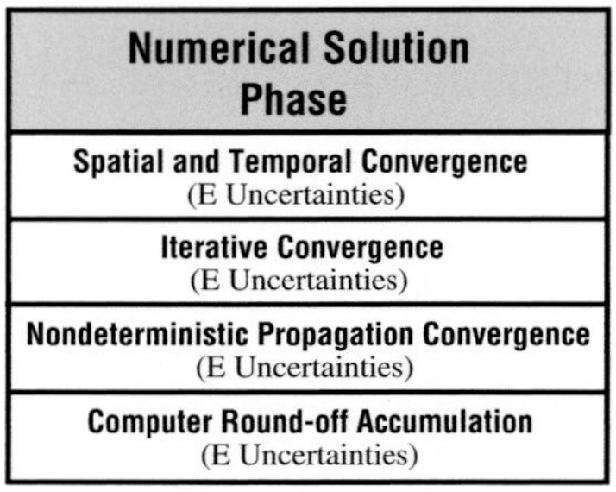

Numerical Solution Phase
Spatial and Temporal Convergence (E Uncertainties)
Iterative Convergence (E Uncertainties)
Nondeterministic Propagation Convergence (E Uncertainties)
Computer Round-off Accumulation (E Uncertainties)

Figure 3.17 Numerical solution phase and primary sources of uncertainty.

on geometries specified by sophisticated solid modeling software, and tens or hundreds of material models needed for input (Reason, 1997). The complexity of the input data and the resulting opportunity for error with such codes is extraordinary. The importance of input preparation has been recognized for some time in the thermal-hydraulics field concerned with the safety analyses for nuclear power reactors. Formal, structured, and rigorous procedures have been developed in this field to ensure the input data accurately reflects the intended input.

The second and third activities relate to all of the software elements used in the simulation, but here we concentrate on the application code itself. In the application code the computer program modules are designed and implemented through a high-level programming language. This high-level source code is then compiled into object code and linked to the operating system and libraries of additional object code to produce the final executable code. These activities are becoming more prone to blind uncertainties due to massively parallel computers, including elements such as (a) optimizing compilers, (b) message passing and memory sharing, and (c) the effect of individual processors or memory units failing during a computer simulation. The correctness of the computer-programming activities is most influenced by blind uncertainties. In addition to programming errors, there is the subtler problem of undefined variables. This occurs when particular code syntax is undefined within the programming language, leading to executable code whose behavior is compiler-dependent. Compilation and linkage introduce the potential for further errors unbeknownst to the developer. Primary among these are bugs and errors in the numerous libraries of object code linked to the application. Such libraries allow the developer to reuse previously developed data handling and numerical analysis algorithms. Unfortunately, the developer also inherits the undiscovered or undocumented errors in these libraries. There is also the possibility that the developer misunderstands how the library routines should be used, or he makes an error in the values that are needed by the library routines.

3.4.5 Numerical solution phase

This phase maps the software programmed in the previous phase into a set of numerical solutions using a digital computer. Figure 3.17 shows the various activities that are conducted during this phase. During the computation of the solution, *no* quantities are left arithmetically undefined or continuous; only discrete values of all quantities exist, all with finite precision. For example: (a) geometries only exist as a collection of points, (b) all independent and dependent variables that exist in the PDEs now only exist at discrete points, and (c) nondeterministic solutions only exist as an ensemble of individual discrete solutions. As stated by Raczynski (2006), "In the digital computer nothing is continuous, so continuous simulation using this hardware is an illusion."

The primary uncertainty introduced during this phase is epistemic uncertainty, specifically numerical solution errors. Roache categorizes these types of numerical solution errors as *ordered errors* (Roache, 1998). Most of the contributing errors in the four activities shown in Figure 3.17 can be ordered in terms of magnitude of their effect on the simulation outcomes; e.g., discretization size in terms of space or time, number of iterations in an implicit numerical procedure, number of computed samples in the propagation of input-to-out uncertainties, and word length of the computer system. The numerical solution errors introduced in the four activities shown in Figure 3.17 can be divided into three categories. The first category contains those that are due to the spatial and temporal discretization of the PDEs. The second category contains those that are due to the approximate solution of the discrete equations. Iterative convergence using an implicit method and computer round-off errors are of this type and they account for the difference between the exact solution to the discrete equations and the computed solution. Iterative solution errors can be due to, for example, iterative solution of a nonlinear matrix equation, or the iterative solution of a nonlinear time-dependent solution. The third category contains those that are due to the finite number of individual deterministic solutions obtained. The difference between using a finite number of solutions computed and the exact nondeterministic solution, for whatever probability distribution or statistic that is of interest, is the nondeterministic solution error. The most common example is the error due to a finite number of Monte Carlo samples used to approximate a nondeterministic solution. If stochastic expansion methods are used for uncertainty propagation, e.g., polynomial chaos expansions and the Karhunen–Loeve transform, then the nondeterministic solution error depends on the number of solutions computed to the discrete equations (Haldar and Mahadevan, 2000b; Ghanem and Spanos, 2003; Choi *et al.*, 2007). Multiple solutions can also be required if the mathematical modeling phase includes the nondeterministic effect of alternative mathematical model forms in order to estimate model-form uncertainty.

3.4.6 Solution representation phase

This final phase maps the raw numerical solutions, i.e., the numbers themselves, which are computed in the previous phase, into numerical results usable by humans. Figure 3.18 shows the activities and the primary source of uncertainty introduced in each activity. The solution representation phase is included in the six phases of computational simulation because of the sophisticated post-processing that is increasingly done to comprehend complex simulations, as well as the recognition that this phase can introduce unique types of uncertainties. Input

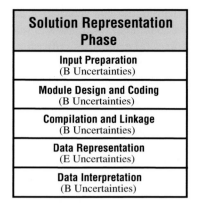

Figure 3.18 Solution representation phase and primary sources of uncertainty.

preparation, module design and coding, and compilation and linkage refer to the same types of activities listed in the computer programming phase, but here they refer to all of the post-processing software that is used. As before, all three of these activities have uncertainty contributions primarily from blind uncertainties.

Data representation is concerned with the construction of the functions that are intended to represent the dependent variables from the PDEs, as well as post-processing of the dependent variables to obtain other SRQs of interest. Post-processing includes three-dimensional graphical visualization of solutions, animation of solutions, use of sound for improved interpretation, and use of virtual reality tools that allow analysts to *go into the solution space*. Epistemic uncertainties are introduced in data representation, primarily ordered numerical errors, which can result in the inaccurate or inappropriate construction of either the dependent variables or other SRQs of interest. Some examples of numerical errors are (a) oscillations of the function in-between discrete solution points due to the use of a high-order polynomial function in the post-processor, (b) inappropriate interpolation of the discrete solution between multi-block grids, (c) inappropriate interpolation of the discrete solution when the solution to the PDEs is a discontinuous function, and (d) excessive amplification or damping of the interpolation function for the dependent variables that are used to compute other SRQs of interest. Concern for errors in data representation can be better understood by posing the question: what is the mathematically correct reconstruction of the functions using the discrete solution points, given that these point values are intended to represent a solution to a PDE? When viewed from this perspective, one recognizes the potential reconstruction errors better because this is *not* the perspective taken in modern data visualization packages. The view of these general-purpose packages is that the reconstruction is based on ease of use, speed, convenience, and robustness of the package. Stated differently, in data visualization packages there is no interest or concern with respect to insuring that the interpolation function conserves mass, momentum, or energy.

Data interpretation errors are made by the interpreter of the computational results, based on observations of the representation of the solution and the computed SRQs. The interpreter of the results could be, for example, the computational analysts using the code or a decision maker relying on the results. Data interpretation errors are blind uncertainties introduced by individuals or groups of individuals. Two examples of interpretation error are (a) concluding that a computed solution is chaotic when it is not (and vice versa); and (b) not recognizing the important frequency content in a complex SRQ. Importantly, our definition of data interpretation errors does *not* include poor decisions made by the user based on the simulation, such as incorrect design choices or inept policy decisions.

Individual deterministic solution results are typically used by researchers, physical scientists, and numerical analysts; whereas the collective nondeterministic results are more commonly used by system designers, decision makers, or policy makers. Each of these audiences usually has very different interests and requirements. The individual solutions provide detailed information on deterministic issues such as (a) the coupled physics occurring in the system; (b) the adequacy of the numerical methods and the mesh resolution needed to compute an accurate solution; and (c) how the SRQs vary as a function of the independent variables, the physical parameters in the model, and the boundary and initial conditions. The collective nondeterministic results are used, for example, to (a) understand the magnitude of the effect of aleatory and epistemic uncertainties on the SRQs of interest, particularly model form uncertainty; and (b) examine the results of a sensitivity analysis. A sensitivity analysis is commonly the most useful result to system designers and decision makers because it helps guide their thinking with regard to issues such as (a) changes needed to obtain a more robust design, (b) tradeoffs between design parameters or various operating conditions, and (c) allocation of resources to reduce the dominant uncertainties in system performance, safety, or reliability.

3.5 Example problem: missile flight dynamics

To demonstrate each of the phases of computational simulation, a system-level example is given of the flight dynamics of a rocket-boosted, aircraft-launched missile. This example is adapted from Oberkampf *et al.*, 2000; 2002. For a detailed discussion of this example, see these references. Figure 3.19 shows all six phases of computational simulation and the activities conducted in each. The missile is a short range, unguided, air-to-ground rocket. The missile is powered by a solid fuel rocket motor during the initial portion of its flight, and is unpowered during the remainder of its flight. The analysis considers the missile flight to be in the unspecified future. Thus, we are attempting to simulate future plausible flights, not analyze an event in the past (such as an accident investigation), or update models based on past observations of the system.

An additional example of a system in an abnormal, i.e., an accident, environment is given in Oberkampf *et al.* (2000).

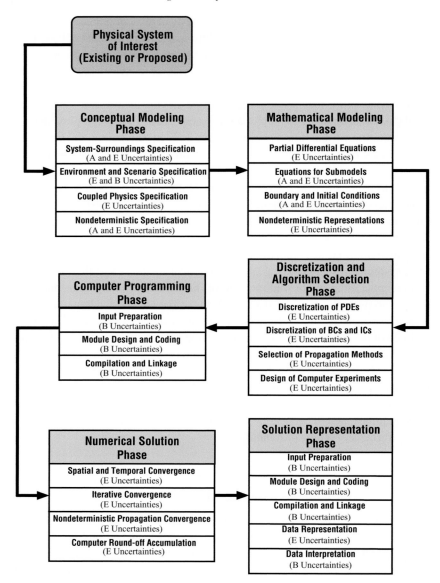

Figure 3.19 Phases and activities in computational simulation.

3.5.1 *Conceptual modeling phase*

Figure 3.20 shows three possible system-surroundings specifications for the missile flight example. Other specifications could be made, but these give a wide range of options that could be used for various types of simulation. The specifications are listed from the most physically inclusive, with regard to the system specification and the physics that

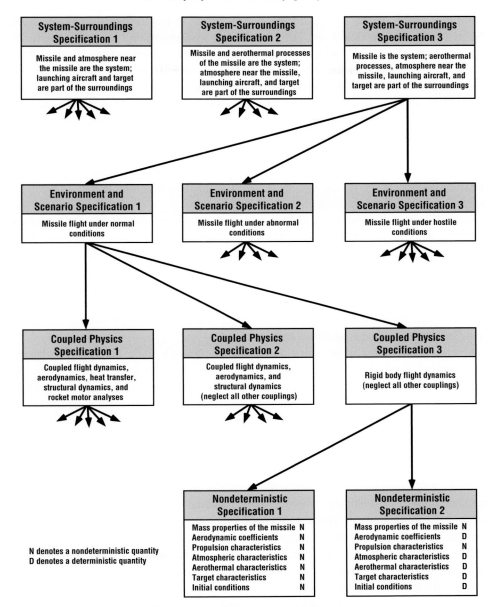

Figure 3.20 Conceptual modeling activities for the missile flight example.

could be coupled, to the least inclusive. For each row of blocks shown in Figure 3.20, the most physically inclusive are given on the left with decreasing physical complexity moving toward the right. System-surroundings specification 1 considers the missile and the atmosphere near the missile to be part of the system, whereas the launching aircraft and target are considered to be part of the surroundings. An example of an analysis that would be allowed with this specification is where the missile, the flow field of the missile, and the rocket exhaust are coupled to the flow field of the launching aircraft. Thus, the missile and the rocket exhaust could be influenced by the presence of the aircraft and its flow field, but the aircraft structure, for example, could not change its geometry or deform due to the rocket exhaust. Another example allowed by this specification would be the analysis of the missile flight inside a structure, e.g., launch from inside of a structure; or a flight inside of a tunnel, e.g., a target is inside a tunnel.

System-surroundings specification 2 considers the missile and the aerothermal processes occurring near the surface of the missile to be part of the system, whereas the atmosphere near the missile, the launching aircraft, and the target are considered part of the surroundings. This specification allows analyses that couple the missile and the aerothermal effects on the missile. For example, one could consider the structural deformation of the missile due to aerodynamic loading and thermal heating of the structure. Then one could couple the missile deformation and the flow field so that the aerodynamic loading and thermal heating could be simulated on the deformed structure.

System-surroundings specification 3 considers the missile to be the system, whereas the aerothermal processes external to the missile, the atmosphere near the missile, the launching aircraft, and the target are considered part of the surroundings. Even though this is the simplest specification considered here, it still allows for significant complexities in the analysis. Note that the missile flight example presented here will only pursue system-surroundings Specification 3.

The environment specification (Figure 3.20) identifies three general environments: normal, abnormal, and hostile. For each of these environments one then identifies all possible scenarios, physical events, or sequences of events that may affect the goals of the simulation. For relatively simple systems, isolated systems, or systems with very controlled surroundings or operational conditions, this activity can be straightforward. Complex engineered systems, however, are commonly exposed to a myriad of scenarios within each of the normal, abnormal, and hostile environments. Constructing environment and scenario specifications for these complex systems is a mammoth undertaking. A many-branched event tree and/or fault tree can be constructed with each scenario having a wide range of likelihoods and consequences. Even though the risk (probability times consequence) for many scenarios may be low, these scenarios should be identified at this phase. Often, when various scenarios are identified, other scenarios are discovered that would not have been discovered otherwise. The decision of which scenarios to pursue should be made *after* a very wide range of scenarios has been identified.

Normal environment conditions are those that can be reasonably expected during nominal operations of the aircraft and missile system. Some examples are (a) typical launch conditions from various types of aircraft that are expected to carry the missile, (b) nominal operation of the propulsion and electrical system, and (c) reasonably expected weather conditions while the missile is attached to the aircraft and during flight to the target. Examples of flight under abnormal conditions are (a) improperly assembled missile components or subsystems; (b) explosive failure of the propulsion system during operation, particularly while still attached or very near the aircraft; and (c) flight through adverse weather conditions, like hail or lightning. Examples of flight under hostile conditions are (a) detonation of nearby defensive weapon systems; (b) damage to missile components or subsystems resulting from small-arms fire; and (c) damage, either structural or electrical, from laser or microwave defensive systems. Note that the missile flight example will only pursue environment specification 1, normal environment. Furthermore, no unusual conditions will be considered within the realm of normal conditions.

Figure 3.20 identifies three levels of physics coupling, although more alternatives could be identified. Coupled physics specification 1 couples essentially all of the physics that could exist in this decision-thread of the analysis, i.e., system-surroundings specification 3 and environment and scenario specification 1. For example, this specification could couple the structural deformation and dynamics with the aerodynamic loading and thermal loading due to atmospheric heating. It could also couple the deformation of the solid-fuel rocket motor case due to combustion pressurization, the heat transfer from the motor case into the missile airframe, and the effect of nonrigid-body flight dynamics on the missile. Coupled physics specification 2 couples the missile flight dynamics, aerodynamics, and structural dynamics, neglecting all other couplings. This coupling permits the computation of the deformation of the missile structure due to inertial loading and aerodynamic loading. One could then, for example, recompute the aerodynamic loading and aerodynamic damping due to the deformed structure. Coupled physics specification 2 would result in a time-dependent, coupled fluid/structure interaction simulation. Coupled physics specification 3 assumes a rigid missile body; not only is physics coupling disallowed within the missile, but the missile structure is assumed rigid. The missile is allowed to respond only to inputs or forcing functions from the surroundings. Structural dynamics is removed from the analysis, i.e., only rigid-body dynamics is considered. Note that the missile flight example will only pursue coupled physics specification 3.

Before addressing the last activity of conceptual modeling, a few comments should be made concerning the possible sources of epistemic and blind uncertainty that could occur in the three activities discussed so far. Epistemic uncertainties arise primarily because of (a) situations, conditions, or physics that are poorly known or understood; (b) situations or conditions that are consciously excluded from the analysis; and (c) approximations made in situations or conditions considered. Blind uncertainties arise primarily because of situations or conditions that are *not* imagined or recognized, but are possible. The more complex the system, the more possibilities exist for blind uncertainties to occur.

Indeed, a common weakness of modern technological risk analyses is overlooking, either by oversight or negligence, unusual events, effects, possibilities, or unintended consequences. For example, automatic control systems designed to ensure safe operation of complex systems can fail (either hardware or software failures) in unexpected ways, or the safety systems are overridden during safety testing or maintenance. For systems in abnormal or hostile environments, the likelihood of blind uncertainties increases greatly compared to normal environments.

For the missile flight example we list only two alternative nondeterministic specifications, as shown in Figure 3.20. Nondeterministic Specification 1 includes the following (indicated by an N at the bottom of Figure 3.20): mass properties of the missile, aerodynamic force and moment coefficients, propulsion characteristics, atmospheric characteristics, aerothermal heating characteristics, target characteristics, and initial conditions at missile launch. Nondeterministic Specification 2 considers only two parameters as uncertain; the mass properties of the missile and the propulsion characteristics of the motor. All other parameters are considered as deterministic (indicated by a D in Figure 3.20). The missile flight example will only pursue nondeterministic specification 2.

3.5.2 *Mathematical modeling phase*

In the mathematical modeling phase, the PDEs, equations and data for submodels, BCs, ICs, and forcing functions are specified. Even with the specifications made in the conceptual model phase, there is always a wide range of mathematical models that one can choose from. Typically, the range of modeling choices can be arranged in order of increasing fidelity of the physics being considered.

For the missile flight example, two mathematical models are chosen; a six-degree-of-freedom (6-DOF) model and a three-degree-of-freedom (3-DOF) model (Figure 3.21). Both models are consistent with the conceptual model being analyzed: system–surroundings specification 3, environment specification 1, coupled physics specification 3, and nondeterministic specification 2 (Figure 3.20). For the 3-DOF and 6-DOF mathematical models of flight dynamics, one can unequivocally order these two models in terms of physics fidelity. The ability to clearly order the physics fidelity of multiple models can be used to great advantage in the following situations. First, there are often conditions where multiple models of physics should give very similar results for certain SRQs. By comparing the results from multiple models one can use this as an informal check between the models. Second, there are sometimes conditions where we expect multiple models of physics to compare well, but they don't. If we conclude that both models are correct, given their assumptions, these conditions can lead to a deeper understanding of the physics, particularly coupled physics. And third, by exercising multiple models of physics we can develop confidence in where and why the lower fidelity model gives essentially the same results as the higher fidelity model. If the higher fidelity model is much more computationally demanding, we can use the lower fidelity model for nondeterministic simulations over the range of conditions where we have developed trust in the model.

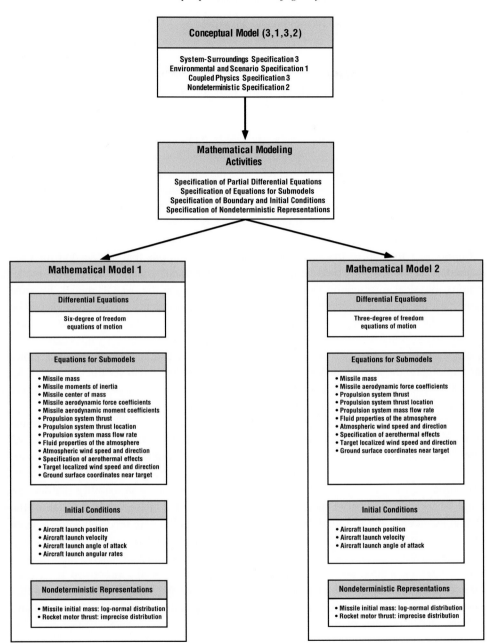

Figure 3.21 Mathematical modeling activities for the missile flight example.

The translational equations of motion can be written as

$$m\frac{\mathrm{d}\vec{V}}{\mathrm{d}t} = \sum \vec{F},\qquad(3.8)$$

where m is the mass of the vehicle, $\vec{V}$ is the velocity, and $\sum \vec{F}$ is the sum of all forces acting on the vehicle. The rotational equations of motion can be written as

$$[I]\frac{\mathrm{d}\vec{\omega}}{\mathrm{d}t} = \sum \vec{M} + \vec{\omega} \times \{[I] \bullet \vec{\omega}\},\qquad(3.9)$$

where $[I]$ is the inertia tensor of the vehicle, $\vec{\omega}$ is the angular velocity, and $\sum \vec{M}$ is the sum of all moments acting on the vehicle. Eq. (3.8) represents the 3-DOF equations of motion, and the coupling of Eq. (3.8) and Eq. (3.9) represent the 6-DOF equations of motion. Although the 3-DOF and 6-DOF equations are ODE models instead of the PDE models stressed in the present work, key aspects of the present framework can still be exercised.

Figure 3.21 lists all of the submodels and initial conditions that are needed for each mathematical model. As would be expected of higher-fidelity models, the 6-DOF model requires physical information well beyond that required by the 3-DOF model. In some situations, the increase in predictive capability from higher fidelity physics models can be offset by the increase in information that is needed to characterize the uncertainties required as input to the high fidelity model. That is, unless the additional uncertainty information that is needed in higher fidelity models is available, the poorer characterization of uncertainty can overwhelm the increase in physics fidelity as compared to the lower fidelity model. As a result, higher fidelity physics models *may yield poorer predictive capability* than lower fidelity models, a seemingly counterintuitive conclusion.

The two nondeterministic parameters considered in the missile flight example are the initial mass of the missile and the rocket motor thrust characteristics (Figure 3.21). Both parameters appear in each of the mathematical models chosen so that direct comparisons of their effect on each model can be made. For the initial mass, it is assumed that sufficient inspection data of manufactured missiles is available so that a probability distribution could be computed. Suppose that, after constructing either a histogram or an EDF of the measurement data, it was found that a log-normal distribution with precisely known mean and standard deviation could be used (Bury, 1999; Krishnamoorthy, 2006).

For the thrust of the solid rocket motor, suppose that a number of newly manufactured motors have been fired so that variability in thrust can be well represented by a two-parameter Gamma distribution (Bury, 1999; Krishnamoorthy, 2006). It is well known that the propulsion characteristics can vary substantially with the age of the solid propellant. Suppose that a number of motors with various ages have also been fired. For each age grouping of motors, it is found that a Gamma distribution can be used, but each group has a different set of distribution parameters. As a result, the uncertainty in thrust characteristics could be represented as a mixture of aleatory and epistemic uncertainty. The aleatory portion of the uncertainty is due to manufacturing variability of the motor and the epistemic uncertainty is due to the age of the motor. The representation of the thrust characteristics is given by a two-parameter gamma distribution, where the parameters of the distribution are given as interval-valued quantities. In the flight dynamics simulation, it is clear that the epistemic uncertainty in thrust can be reduced if information is added concerning the age of the motors of interest. For example, if all of the missiles that may be launched are known to be from a single production lot, then the epistemic uncertainty could be eliminated because it would be known when the production lot was manufactured. The two parameters of the gamma distribution would then become precisely known values.

3.5.3 *Discretization and algorithm selection phase*

The discretization method chosen to solve the ODEs of both mathematical models was a Runge-Kutta 4(5) method (Press *et al.*, 2007). The RK method is fifth-order accurate at each time step, and the integrator coefficients of Cash and Karp (1990) were used. The method provides an estimate of the local truncation error, i.e., truncation error at each step, so that adjusting the step size as the solution progresses can directly control the estimated numerical solution error. The local truncation error is computed by comparing the fourth-order accurate solution with the fifth-order accurate solution.

The method chosen for propagation of the uncertainties through the model was probability bounds analysis (PBA). As previously discussed in the mass–spring–damper example, a sampling procedure was used in which the aleatory and epistemic uncertainties are separated during the sampling. The particular sampling procedure used was Latin Hypercube Sampling (LHS) (Ross, 2006; Dimov, 2008; Rubinstein and Kroese, 2008). LHS employs stratified random sampling for choosing discrete values from the probability distribution specified for the aleatory uncertainties. For propagation of the epistemic uncertainty, samples are chosen from the two parameters of the gamma distribution characterizing the uncertainty in thrust of the solid rocket motor. Samples chosen over the two intervals are assigned a probability of unity. The method of obtaining samples over the two intervals can, in principle, be any method that obtains samples over the entire interval. The usual procedure used is to assign a uniform probability distribution over the interval and then use the same sampling procedure that is used for the aleatory uncertainties. It should be noted that the seeds for sampling the two interval-valued parameters were assigned different values so that there is no correlation between the random draws from each interval. The experimental design calls for performing the same number of LHS calculations for both the 3-DOF and 6-DOF models. An alternative procedure commonly used in complex analyses is to include a method to mix computer runs between the two models to maximize the accuracy and efficiency of the computations.

3.5.4 *Computer programming phase*

A computer code (TAOS) developed at Sandia National Laboratories was used to compute the trajectories of the missile flight example (Salguero, 1999). This general-purpose flight dynamics code has been used for a wide variety of guidance, control, navigation, and optimization problems for flight vehicles. We used only the ballistic flight option to solve both the 3-DOF and 6-DOF equations of motion.

3.5.5 Numerical solution phase

For the missile flight example, the numerical solution method used a variable time step so that the local truncation error could be directly controlled at each step. The local truncation error is estimated at each step for each state variable for each system of differential equations. For the 6-DOF model there are 12 state variables, and for the 3-DOF model there are six state variables. Before a new time step can be accepted in the numerical solution, a relative error criterion must be met for each state variable. In the TAOS code, if the largest local truncation error of all the state variables is less than 0.6 of the error criterion, then the step size is increased for the next time step.

The LHS method often provides an advantage in sampling convergence rate over traditional Monte Carlo sampling. However, that advantage is somewhat degraded because estimates of sampling error cannot be computed without replicating the LHS runs.

3.5.6 Solution representation phase

For this relatively simple example, the representation of solution results is rather straightforward. The primary SRQ of interest for the example was the range of the missile. The most common method of showing nondeterministic results is to plot the CDF for the SRQ of interest. If only aleatory uncertainties exist in a nondeterministic analysis, then only one CDF exists for any given SRQ. If epistemic uncertainty also exists, as it does in this simulation, then an ensemble of CDFs must be computed. One CDF results from *each sample* of all of the epistemic uncertainties. To compute the p-box of the SRQ, one determines the minimum and maximum probability from all of the CDFs that were computed at each value of the SRQ. If alternative mathematical models are used, as in the present case, then a p-box is shown for each model.

Figure 3.22 shows a representative result for the CDF of the range of the missile given as a p-box resulting from one of the mathematical models. The p-box shows that epistemic uncertainty due to the age of the solid propellant rocket motor is a major contributor to the uncertainty in the range of the missile. For example, at the median of the range (probability $= 0.5$), the range can vary by about 1 km depending on the age of the motor. A different way of interpreting the p-box is to pick a value of range, and then read the interval-valued probability. For example, the probability of attaining a range of 34 km, or less, can vary from 0.12 to 0.52, depending on the age of the motor.

Recall that the Gamma distribution represents the variability in thrust due to manufacturing processes and the epistemic uncertainty due to the age of the motor is represented by the two interval-valued parameters in the distribution. Some analysts would argue that

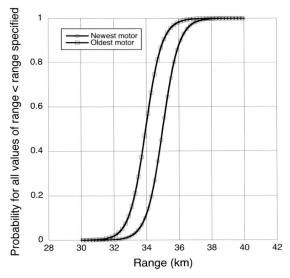

Figure 3.22 Representative p-box for range of the missile as a function of rocket motor age.

an alternative method of representing the uncertainty due to age is to replace the characterization of the parameters with two uniform PDFs over the same range of the intervals. They would argue that, if the age of the motors is uniformly distributed over time, then a uniform distribution should represent the age. The fallacy of this argument is that once a motor is selected for firing, the age of motor is fixed, but the variability of the thrust still exists, which is characterized by the gamma distribution. That is, once a motor is selected, the previously unknown age of the motor is now a number that identifies a single, precise gamma distribution. If this were done, then a *single* CDF would replace the p-box shown in Figure 3.22. If the uniform PDF approach were taken, the representation of the uncertainty in range would present a very different picture to the decision maker than what is shown in Figure 3.22. There would be *one* CDF that was within the p-box, disguising the true uncertainty in the range.

3.6 References

AEC (1966). *AEC Atomic Weapon Safety Program.* Memorandum No. 0560, Washington, DC, US Atomic Energy Commission.

Almond, R. G. (1995). *Graphical Belief Modeling.* 1st edn., London, Chapman & Hall.

Andrews, J. D. and T. R. Moss (2002). *Reliability and Risk Assessment.* 2nd edn., New York, NY, ASME Press.

Ang, A. H.-S. and W. H. Tang (2007). *Probability Concepts in Engineering: Emphasis on Applications to Civil and Environmental Engineering.* 2nd edn., New York, John Wiley.

Aughenbaugh, J. M. and C. J. J. Paredis (2006). The value of using imprecise probabilities in engineering design. *Journal of Mechanical Design.* **128**, 969–979.

Aven, T. (2005). *Foundations of Risk Analysis: a Knowledge and Decision-Oriented Perspective*, New York, John Wiley.

Ayyub, B. M. (1994). The nature of uncertainty in structural engineering. In *Uncertainty Modelling and Analysis: Theory and Applications*. B. M. Ayyub and M. M. Gupta, eds. New York, Elsevier: 195–210.

Ayyub, B. M., ed. (1998). *Uncertainty Modeling and Analysis in Civil Engineering*. Boca Raton, FL, CRC Press.

Ayyub, B. M. and G. J. Klir (2006). *Uncertainty Modeling and Analysis in Engineering and the Sciences*, Boca Raton, FL, Chapman & Hall.

Bae, H.-R., R. V. Grandhi, and R. A. Canfield (2006). Sensitivity analysis of structural response uncertainty propagation using evidence theory. *Structural and Multidisciplinary Optimization*. **31**(4), 270–279.

Bardossy, G. and J. Fodor (2004). *Evaluation of Uncertainties and Risks in Geology: New Mathematical Approaches for their Handling*, Berlin, Springer-Verlag.

Baudrit, C. and D. Dubois (2006). Practical representations of incomplete probabilistic knowledge. *Computational Statistics and Data Analysis*. **51**, 86–108.

Beck, M. B. (1987). Water quality modeling: a review of the analysis of uncertainty. *Water Resources Research*. **23**(8), 1393–1442.

Bedford, T. and R. Cooke (2001). *Probabilistic Risk Analysis: Foundations and Methods*, Cambridge, UK, Cambridge University Press.

Ben-Haim, Y. (1999). Robust reliability of structures with severely uncertain loads. *AIAA/ASME/ASCE/AHS/ASC Structures, Structural Dynamics, and Materials Conference and Exhibit, AIAA Paper 99-1605*, St. Louis, MO, American Institute of Aeronautics and Astronautics, 3035–3039.

Bogen, K. T. and R. C. Spear (1987). Integrating uncertainty and interindividual variability in environmental risk assessment. *Risk Analysis*. **7**(4), 427–436.

Bossel, H. (1994). *Modeling and Simulation*. 1st edn., Wellesley, MA, A. K. Peters.

Box, G. E. P. (1980). Sampling and Bayes' inference in scientific modeling and robustness. *Journal of the Royal Statistical Society: Series A*. **143**(A), 383–430.

Box, G. E. P., J. S. Hunter, and W. G. Hunter (2005). *Statistics for Experimenters: Design, Innovation, and Discovery*. 2nd edn., New York, John Wiley.

Breeding, R. J., J. C. Helton, E. D. Gorham, and F. T. Harper (1992). Summary description of the methods used in the probabilistic risk assessments for NUREG-1150. *Nuclear Engineering and Design*. **135**, 1–27.

Bury, K. (1999). *Statistical Distributions in Engineering*, Cambridge, UK, Cambridge University Press.

Cacuci, D. G. (2003). *Sensitivity and Uncertainty Analysis: Theory*, Boca Raton, FL, Chapman & Hall/CRC.

Cash, J. R. and A. H. Karp (1990). A variable order Runge-Kutta method for initial-value problems with rapidly varying right-hand sides. *ACM Transactions on Mathematical Software*. **16**(3), 201–222.

Choi, S.-K., R. V. Grandhi, and R. A. Canfield (2007). *Reliability-based Structural Design*, London, Springer-Verlag.

Cullen, A. C. and H. C. Frey (1999). *Probabilistic Techniques in Exposure Assessment: a Handbook for Dealing with Variability and Uncertainty in Models and Inputs*, New York, Plenum Press.

Dimov, I. T. (2008). *Monte Carlo Methods for Applied Scientists*. 2nd edn., Singapore, World Scientific Publishing.

Dorner, D. (1989). *The Logic of Failure, Recognizing and Avoiding Error in Complex Situations*, Cambridge, MA, Perseus Books.

Fellin, W., H. Lessmann, M. Oberguggenberger, and R. Vieider, eds. (2005). *Analyzing Uncertainty in Civil Engineering*. New York, Springer.

Ferson, S. (1996). What Monte Carlo methods cannot do. *Human and Ecological Risk Assessment*. **2**(4), 990–1007.

Ferson, S. (2002). *RAMAS Risk Calc 4.0 Software: Risk Assessment with Uncertain Numbers*. Setauket, NY, Applied Biomathematics Corp.

Ferson, S. and L. R. Ginzburg (1996). Different methods are needed to propagate ignorance and variability. *Reliability Engineering and System Safety*. **54**, 133–144.

Ferson, S. and J. G. Hajagos (2004). Arithmetic with uncertain numbers: rigorous and (often) best possible answers. *Reliability Engineering and System Safety*. **85**(1–3), 135–152.

Ferson, S., V. Kreinovich, L. Ginzburg, D. S. Myers, and K. Sentz (2003). *Constructing Probability Boxes and Dempster–Shafer Structures*. SAND2003-4015, Albuquerque, NM, Sandia National Laboratories.

Ferson, S., R. B. Nelsen, J. Hajagos, D. J. Berleant, J. Zhang, W. T. Tucker, L. R. Ginzburg, and W. L. Oberkampf (2004). *Dependence in Probabilistic Modeling, Dempster–Shafer Theory, and Probability Bounds Analysis*. SAND2004-3072, Albuquerque, NM, Sandia National Laboratories.

Fetz, T., M. Oberguggenberger, and S. Pittschmann (2000). Applications of possibility and evidence theory in civil engineering. *International Journal of Uncertainty*. **8**(3), 295–309.

Frank, M. V. (1999). Treatment of uncertainties in space: nuclear risk assessment with examples from Cassini Mission applications. *Reliability Engineering and System Safety*. **66**, 203–221.

Gehman, H. W., J. L. Barry, D. W. Deal, J. N. Hallock, K. W. Hess, G. S. Hubbard, J. M. Logsdon, D. D. Osheroff, S. K. Ride, R. E. Tetrault, S. A. Turcotte, S. B. Wallace, and S. E. Widnall (2003). *Columbia Accident Investigation Board Report Volume I*. Washington, DC, National Aeronautics and Space Administration Government Printing Office.

Ghanem, R. G. and P. D. Spanos (2003). *Stochastic Finite Elements: a Spectral Approach*. Revised edn., Mineda, NY, Dover Publications.

Haimes, Y. Y. (2009). *Risk Modeling, Assessment, and Management*. 3rd edn., New York, John Wiley.

Haldar, A. and S. Mahadevan (2000a). *Probability, Reliability, and Statistical Methods in Engineering Design*, New York, John Wiley.

Haldar, A. and S. Mahadevan (2000b). *Reliability Assessment Using Stochastic Finite Element Analysis*, New York, John Wiley.

Hauptmanns, U. and W. Werner (1991). *Engineering Risks Evaluation and Valuation*. 1st edn., Berlin, Springer-Verlag.

Helton, J. C. (1993). Uncertainty and sensitivity analysis techniques for use in performance assessment for radioactive waste disposal. *Reliability Engineering and System Safety*. **42**(2–3), 327–367.

Helton, J. C. (1994). Treatment of uncertainty in performance assessments for complex systems. *Risk Analysis*. **14**(4), 483–511.

Helton, J. C. (1997). Uncertainty and sensitivity analysis in the presence of stochastic and subjective uncertainty. *Journal of Statistical Computation and Simulation*. **57**, 3–76.

Helton, J. C. (1999). Uncertainty and sensitivity analysis in performance assessment for the waste isolation pilot plant. *Computer Physics Communications.* **117**(1–2), 156–180.

Helton, J. C., D. R. Anderson, H.-N. Jow, M. G. Marietta, and G. Basabilvazo (1999). Performance assessment in support of the 1996 compliance certification application for the Waste Isolation Pilot Plant. *Risk Analysis.* **19**(5), 959–986.

Helton, J. C., J. D. Johnson, and W. L. Oberkampf (2004). An exploration of alternative approaches to the representation of uncertainty in model predictions. *Reliability Engineering and System Safety.* **85**(1–3), 39–71.

Helton, J. C., W. L. Oberkampf, and J. D. Johnson (2005). Competing failure risk analysis using evidence theory. *Risk Analysis.* **25**(4), 973–995.

Helton, J. C., J. D. Johnson, C. J. Sallaberry, and C. B. Storlie (2006). Survey of sampling-based methods for uncertainty and sensitivity analysis. *Reliability Engineering and System Safety.* **91**(10–11), 1175–1209.

Hoffman, F. O. and J. S. Hammonds (1994). Propagation of uncertainty in risk assessments: the need to distinguish between uncertainty due to lack of knowledge and uncertainty due to variability. *Risk Analysis.* **14**(5), 707–712.

Hora, S. C. and R. L. Iman (1989). Expert opinion in risk analysis: the NUREG-1150 methodology. *Nuclear Science and Engineering.* **102**, 323–331.

Jacoby, S. L. S. and J. S. Kowalik (1980). *Mathematical Modeling with Computers*, Englewood Cliffs, NJ, Prentice-Hall.

Kaplan, S. and B. J. Garrick (1981). On the quantitative definition of risk. *Risk Analysis.* **1**(1), 11–27.

Kleijnen, J. P. C. (1998). Chapter 6: Experimental design for sensitivity analysis, optimization, and validation of simulation models. In *Handbook of Simulation: Principles, Methodology, Advances, Application, and Practice.* J. Banks, ed. New York, John Wiley: 173–223.

Klir, G. J. and M. J. Wierman (1998). *Uncertainty-Based Information: Elements of Generalized Information Theory*, Heidelberg, Physica-Verlag.

Kloeden, P. E. and E. Platen (2000). *Numerical Solution of Stochastic Differential Equations*, New York, Springer.

Kohlas, J. and P.-A. Monney (1995). *A Mathematical Theory of Hints – an Approach to the Dempster–Shafer Theory of Evidence*, Berlin, Springer-Verlag.

Krause, P. and D. Clark (1993). *Representing Uncertain Knowledge: an Artificial Intelligence Approach*, Dordrecht, The Netherlands, Kluwer Academic Publishers.

Kriegler, E. and H. Held (2005). Utilizing belief functions for the estimation of future climate change. *International Journal for Approximate Reasoning.* **39**, 185–209.

Krishnamoorthy, K. (2006). *Handbook of Statistical Distribution with Applications*, Boca Raton, FL, Chapman and Hall.

Kumamoto, H. (2007). *Satisfying Safety Goals by Probabilistic Risk Assessment*, Berlin, Springer-Verlag.

Kumamoto, H. and E. J. Henley (1996). *Probabilistic Risk Assessment and Management for Engineers and Scientists.* 2nd edn., New York, IEEE Press.

Law, A. M. (2006). *Simulation Modeling and Analysis.* 4th edn., New York, McGraw-Hill.

Lawson, D. (2005). *Engineering Disasters – Lessons to be Learned*, New York, ASME Press.

LeGore, T. (1990). Predictive software validation methodology for use with experiments having limited replicability. In *Benchmark Test Cases for Computational Fluid*

Dynamics. I. Celik and C. J. Freitas, eds. New York, American Society of Mechanical Engineers. FED-Vol. 93: 21–27.

Leijnse, A. and S. M. Hassanizadeh (1994). Model definition and model validation. *Advances in Water Resources*. **17**, 197–200.

Mason, R. L., R. F. Gunst, and J. L. Hess (2003). *Statistical Design and Analysis of Experiments, with Applications to Engineering and Science*. 2nd edn., Hoboken, NJ, Wiley Interscience.

Melchers, R. E. (1999). *Structural Reliability Analysis and Prediction*. 2nd edn., New York, John Wiley.

Modarres, M., M. Kaminskiy, and V. Krivtsov (1999). *Reliability Engineering and Risk Analysis; a Practical Guide*, Boca Raton, FL, CRC Press.

Moller, B. and M. Beer (2004). *Fuzz Randomness: Uncertainty in Civil Engineering and Computational Mechanics*, Berlin, Springer-Verlag.

Morgan, M. G. and M. Henrion (1990). *Uncertainty: a Guide to Dealing with Uncertainty in Quantitative Risk and Policy Analysis*. 1st edn., Cambridge, UK, Cambridge University Press.

Mosey, D. (2006). *Reactor Accidents: Institutional Failure in the Nuclear Industry*. 2nd edn., Sidcup, Kent, UK, Nuclear Engineering International.

NASA (2002). *Probabilistic Risk Assessment Procedures Guide for NASA Managers and Practitioners*. Washington, DC, NASA.

Neelamkavil, F. (1987). *Computer Simulation and Modelling*. 1st edn., New York, John Wiley.

Nikolaidis, E., D. M. Ghiocel, and S. Singhal, eds. (2005). *Engineering Design Reliability Handbook*. Boca Raton, FL, CRC Press.

NRC (1990). *Severe Accident Risks: an Assessment for Five U.S. Nuclear Power Plants*. NUREG-1150, Washington, DC, US Nuclear Regulatory Commission, Office of Nuclear Regulatory Research, Division of Systems Research.

NRC (2009). *Guidance on the Treatment of Uncertainties Assoicated with PRAs in Risk-Informed Decision Making*. Washington, DC, Nuclear Regulator Commission.

Oberkampf, W. L. and J. C. Helton (2005). Evidence theory for engineering applications. In *Engineering Design Reliability Handbook*. E. Nikolaidis, D. M. Ghiocel and S. Singhal, eds. New York, NY, CRC Press: 29.

Oberkampf, W. L., S. M. DeLand, B. M. Rutherford, K. V. Diegert, and K. F. Alvin (2000). *Estimation of Total Uncertainty in Computational Simulation*. SAND2000-0824, Albuquerque, NM, Sandia National Laboratories.

Oberkampf, W. L., S. M. DeLand, B. M. Rutherford, K. V. Diegert, and K. F. Alvin (2002). Error and uncertainty in modeling and simulation. *Reliability Engineering and System Safety*. **75**(3), 333–357.

Oksendal, B. (2003). *Stochastic Differential Equations: an Introduction with Applications*. 6th edn., Berlin, Springer-Verlag.

Paté-Cornell, M. E. (1990). Organizational aspects of engineering system failures: the case of offshore platforms. *Science*. **250**, 1210–1217.

Pegden, C. D., R. E. Shannon, and R. P. Sadowski (1990). *Introduction to Simulation Using SIMAN*. 1st edn., New York, McGraw-Hill.

Petroski, H. (1994). *Design Paradigms: Case Histories of Error and Judgment in Engineering*, Cambridge, UK, Cambridge University Press.

Press, W. H., S. A. Teukolsky, W. T. Vetterling, and B. P. Flannery (2007). *Numerical Recipes in FORTRAN*. 3rd edn., New York, Cambridge University Press.

Raczynski, S. (2006). *Modeling and Simulation: the Computer Science of Illusion*, New York, Wiley.

Reason, J. (1997). *Managing the Risks of Organizational Accidents*, Burlington, VT, Ashgate Publishing Limited.

Roache, P. J. (1998). *Verification and Validation in Computational Science and Engineering*, Albuquerque, NM, Hermosa Publishers.

Ross, S. M. (2006). *Simulation*. 4th edn., Burlington, MA, Academic Press.

Ross, T. J. (2004). *Fuzzy Logic with Engineering Applications*. 2nd edn., New York, Wiley.

Rubinstein, R. Y. and D. P. Kroese (2008). *Simulation and the Monte Carlo Method*. 2nd edn., Hoboken, NJ, John Wiley.

Salguero, D. E. (1999). *Trajectory Analysis and Optimization Software (TAOS)*. SAND99-0811, Albuquerque, NM, Sandia National Laboratories.

Saltelli, A., S. Tarantola, F. Campolongo, and M. Ratto (2004). *Sensitivity Analysis in Practice: a Guide to Assessing Scientific Models*, Chichester, England, John Wiley.

Saltelli, A., M. Ratto, T. Andres, F. Campolongo, J. Cariboni, D. Gatelli, M. Saisana, and S. Tarantola (2008). *Global Sensitivity Analysis: the Primer*, Hoboken, NJ, Wiley.

Schrage, M. (1999). *Serious Play: How the World's Best Companies Simulate to Innovate*, Boston, MA, Harvard Business School Press.

Serrano, S. E. (2001). *Engineering Uncertainty and Risk Analysis: a Balanced Approach to Probability, Statistics, Stochastic Modeling, and Stochastic Differential Equations*, Lexington, KY, HydroScience Inc.

Severance, F. L. (2001). *System Modeling and Simulation: an Introduction*, New York, Wiley.

Singh, V. P., S. K. Jain, and A. Tyagi (2007). *Risk and Reliability Analysis: a Handbook for Civil and Environmental Engineers*, New York, American Society of Civil Engineers.

Singpurwalla, N. D. (2006). *Reliability and Risk: a Bayesian Perspective*, New York, NY, Wiley.

Stockman, C. T., J. W. Garner, J. C. Helton, J. D. Johnson, A. Shinta, and L. N. Smith (2000). Radionuclide transport in the vicinity of the repository and associated complementary cumulative distribution functions in the 1996 performance assessment for the Waste Isolation Pilot Plant. *Reliability Engineering and System Safety*. **69**(1–3), 369–396.

Storlie, C. B. and J. C. Helton (2008). Multiple predictor smoothing methods for sensitivity analysis: description of techniques. *Reliability Engineering and System Safety*. **93**(1), 28–54.

Suter, G. W. (2007). *Ecological Risk Assessment*. 2nd edn., Boca Raton, FL, CRC Press.

Taylor, H. M. and S. Karlin (1998). *An Introduction to Stochastic Modeling*. 3rd edn., Boston, Academic Press.

Tenner, E. (1996). *Why Things Bite Back*, New York, Alfred A. Knopf.

Tung, Y.-K. and B.-C. Yen (2005). *Hydrosystems Engineering Uncertainty Analysis*, New York, McGraw-Hill.

Vaughan, D. (1996). *The Challenger Launch Decision: Risky Technology, Culture, and Deviance at NASA*, Chicago, IL, The University of Chicago Press.

Vinnem, J. E. (2007). *Offshore Risk Assessment: Principles, Modelling and Applications of QRA Studies*, Berlin, Springer-Verlag.

Vose, D. (2008). *Risk Analysis: a Quantitative Guide*. 3rd edn., New York, Wiley.

Yee, H. C. and P. K. Sweby (1995). Dynamical approach study of spurious steady-state numerical solutions of nonlinear differential equations II. Global asymptotic behavior of time discretizations. *Computational Fluid Dynamics*. **4**, 219–283.

Yee, H. C. and P. K. Sweby (1996). *Nonlinear Dynamics & Numerical Uncertainties in CFD*. Rept. No. 110398, Moffett Field, CA, NASA/Ames Research Center.

Yee, H. C. and P. K. Sweby (1998). Aspects of numerical uncertainties in time marching to steady-state numerical solutions. *AIAA Journal*. **36**(5), 712–724.

Yee, H. C., J. R. Torczynski, S. A. Morton, M. R. Visbal, and P. K. Sweby (1997). On spurious behavior of CFD simulations. *13th AIAA Computational Fluid Dynamics Conference, AIAA Paper 97-1869*, Snowmass, CO, American Institute of Aeronautics and Astronautics.

Zeigler, B. P., H. Praehofer, and T. G. Kim (2000). *Theory of Modeling and Simulation: Integrating Discrete Event and Continuous Complex Dynamic Systems*. 2nd edn., San Diego, CA, Academic Press.

Part II
Code verification

As we begin to address issues of validation in Part IV: Model validation and prediction (Chapters 10–13), the focus will be on whether the proper mathematical model has been chosen, where mathematical model refers to the governing partial differential or integral equations along with any auxiliary algebraic relations. Since the exact solutions to complex mathematical models are extremely rare, we generally use numerical solutions to the discretized equations as a surrogate for the exact solutions. Verification provides a framework for quantifying the numerical approximation errors in the discrete solution relative to the exact solution to the mathematical model. Since verification deals purely with issues of mathematics, no references to the actual behavior of real-world systems or experimental data will be found in Chapters 4 through 9.

Code verification ensures that the computer program (alternatively referred to as the computer code) is a faithful representation of the original mathematical model. It is accomplished by employing appropriate software engineering practices (Chapter 4), and by using order verification (Chapter 5) to ensure that there are no mistakes in the computer code or inconsistencies in the discrete algorithm. This part of the book dealing with code verification is completed by a discussion of exact solutions to mathematical models in Chapter 6. A key part of Chapter 6 is the Method of Manufactured Solutions (MMS), which is a powerful method for performing order verification studies on complex, nonlinear, coupled sets of partial differential or integral equations.

4

Software engineering

Software engineering encompasses the tools and methods for defining requirements for, designing, programming, testing, and managing software. It consists of monitoring and controlling both the software processes and the software products to ensure reliability. Software engineering was developed primarily from within the computer science community, and its use is essential for large software development projects and for high-assurance software systems such as those for aircraft control systems, nuclear power plants, and medical devices (e.g., pacemakers).

The reader may wonder at this point why a book on verification and validation in scientific computing includes a chapter on software engineering. The reason is that software engineering is critical for the efficient and reliable development of scientific computing software. Failure to perform good software engineering throughout the life cycle of a scientific computing code can result in much more additional code verification testing and debugging. Furthermore, it is extremely difficult to estimate the effect of *unknown* software defects on a scientific computing prediction (e.g., see Knupp *et al.*, 2007). Since this effect is so difficult to quantify, it is prudent to minimize the introduction of software defects through good software engineering practices.

Software engineers will no doubt argue that we have it backwards: *code verification* is really just a part of the software engineering process known as *software verification and validation*. While this is technically true, the argument for instead including software engineering as a part of code verification can be made as follows. Recall that we have defined scientific computing as the approximate solution to mathematical models consisting of partial differential or integral equations. The "correct" answer that should result from running a scientific computing code on any given problem is therefore not known: it will depend on the chosen discretization scheme, the chosen mesh (both its resolution and quality), the iterative convergence tolerance, the machine round-off error, etc. Thus special procedures must be used to test scientific computing software for coding mistakes and other problems that do not need to be considered for more general software. The central role of code verification in establishing the correctness of scientific computing software justifies our inclusion of software engineering as part of the code verification process. Regardless of the relation between software engineering and code verification, they are both important factors in developing and maintaining reliable scientific computing codes.

Computational scientists and engineers generally receive no formal training in modern software engineering practices. Our own search of the software engineering literature found a large number of contributions in various textbooks, on the web, and in scientific articles – mostly dominated by software engineering practices and processes that do not consider some of the unique aspects of scientific software. For example, most software engineering practices are driven by the fact that data organization and access is the primary factor in the performance efficiency of the software, whereas in scientific computing the speed of performing floating point operations is often the overriding factor. The goal of this chapter is to provide a brief overview of recommended software engineering practices for scientific computing. The bulk of this chapter can be applied to all scientific computing software projects, large or small, whereas the final section addresses additional software engineering practices that are recommended for large software projects.

Software engineering is an enormously broad subject which has been addressed by numerous books (e.g., Sommerville, 2004; McConnell, 2004; Pressman, 2005) as well as a broad array of content on the World Wide Web (e.g., SWEBOK, 2004; Eddins, 2006; Wilson, 2009). In 1993, a comprehensive effort was initiated by the Institute of Electrical and Electronics Engineers (IEEE) Computer Society to "establish the appropriate set(s) of criteria and norms for professional practice of software engineering upon which industrial decisions, professional certification, and educational curricula can be based" (SWEBOK, 2004). The resulting book was published in 2004 and divides software engineering into ten knowledge areas which comprise the Software Engineering Body of Knowledge (SWEBOK). In addition, there have been several recent workshops which address software engineering issues specifically for scientific computing (SE-CSE 2008, 2009) and high-performance computing (e.g., SE-HPC, 2004). In this chapter we will cover in detail the following software engineering topics: software development, version control, software testing, software quality and reliability, software requirements, and software management. An abbreviated discussion of many of the topics presented in this chapter can be found in Roy (2009).

4.1 Software development

Software development encompasses the design, construction, and maintenance of software. While software testing should also be an integral part of the software development process, we will defer a detailed discussion of software testing until a later section.

4.1.1 Software process models

A software process is an activity that leads to the creation or modification of software products. There are three main software process models: the waterfall model, the iterative and incremental development model, and component-based software engineering (Sommerville, 2004). In the traditional *waterfall model*, the various aspects of the software development process (requirements specification, architectural design, programming, testing, etc.) are decomposed into separate phases, with each phase beginning only after the previous phase is completed. In response to criticisms of the waterfall software development model, a competing approach called *iterative and incremental development* (also called the spiral model) was proposed. This iterative, or evolutionary, development model is based on the idea of interweaving each of the steps in the software development process, thus allowing customer feedback early in the development process through software prototypes which may initially have only limited capabilities. These software prototypes are then refined based on the customer input, resulting in software with increasing capability. A third model, *component-based software engineering*, can be used when a large number of reusable components are available, but often has only limited applicability to scientific computing (e.g., for linear solver libraries or parallel message passing libraries). Most modern software development models, such as the rational unified process (Sommerville, 2004) and agile software development (discussed later in this section), are based on the iterative and incremental development model.

4.1.2 Architectural design

Software architectural design is the process of identifying software sub-systems and their interfaces before any programming is done (Sommerville, 2004). The primary products of architectural design are usually documents (flowcharts, pseudocode, etc.) which describe the software subsystems and their structure. A software subsystem is defined as a subset of the full software system that does not interact with other subsystems. Each software subsystem is made up of components, which are subsets of the full system which interact with other components. Components may be based on a procedural design (subroutines, functions, etc.) or an object-oriented design, and both approaches are discussed in more detail in the next section.

4.1.3 Programming languages

There are a variety of factors to consider when choosing a programming language. The two main programming paradigms used in scientific computing are procedural programming and object-oriented programming. *Procedural programming* relies on calls to different procedures (routines, subroutines, methods, or functions) to execute a series of sequential steps in a given programming task. A significant advantage of procedural programming is that it is modular, i.e., it allows for reuse of procedures when tasks must be performed multiple times. In *object-oriented programming*, the program is decomposed into objects which interact with each other through the sending and receiving of messages. Objects typically make use of private data which can only be accessed through that object, thus providing a level of independence to the objects. This independence makes it easier to modify a given object without impacting other parts of the code. Object-oriented programming also allows for the reusability of components across the software system.

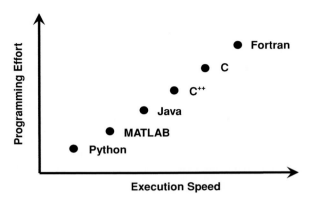

Figure 4.1 *Qualitative* example of programming effort versus execution speed (adapted from Wilson, 2009).

Most modern, higher-level programming languages used for scientific computing support both procedural and object-oriented programming. Programming languages that are primarily procedural in nature include BASIC, C, Fortran, MATLAB, Pascal, and Perl, while those that are primarily object-oriented include C^{++}, Java, and Python. Procedural programming is often used when mathematical computations drive the design, whereas object-oriented programming is preferred when the problem is driven by complex data relationships.

Low level computing languages such as machine language and assembly language (often found in simple electronic devices) execute extremely fast, but require additional time and effort during the programming and debugging phases. One factor to consider is that high-level languages, which often make use of more natural language syntax and varying levels of programming abstraction, have the advantage of making programming complex software projects easier, but generally will not execute as fast as a lower-level programming language. A qualitative comparison of selected programming languages is shown in Figure 4.1 which compares programming effort to execution speed. In scientific computing, the higher-level programming languages such as Python, MATLAB, and Java are ideal for small projects and prototyping, while production-level codes are usually programmed in C, C^{++}, or Fortran due to the faster execution speeds.

Another factor to consider when choosing a programming language is the impact on the software defect rate and the subsequent maintenance costs (Fenton and Pfleeger, 1997). Here we define a *software defect* as an error in the software that could potentially lead to software failure (e.g., incorrect result produced, premature program termination) and the *software defect rate* as the number of defects per 1000 lines of executable code. Evidence suggests that the software defect rate is at best weakly dependent on the choice of programming language (Hatton, 1997a). However, Hatton (1996) found that defects in object-oriented languages can be more expensive to find and fix, possibly by as much as a factor of three. The choice of compiler and diagnostic/debugging tool can also have a significant impact on the software defect rate as well as the overall code development productivity.

Standards for programming languages are generally developed by a costly and complex process. However, most programming language standards still contain coding constructs that are prone to producing software failures. These failure-prone constructs can arise in a number of different ways (Hatton, 1997a) including simple oversight by the standards process, lack of agreement on the content of the standards, because the decision was explicitly made to retain the functionality provided by the construct, or because of errors in the programming language standards documentation. In some cases, less fault-prone subsets of a programming language exist which reduce or eliminate the presence of the dangerous coding constructs. One example of a safe subset for the C programming language is Safer C (Hatton, 1995).

4.1.4 Agile programming

Most software development processes call for the requirements specification, design, implementation, and testing of the software to be performed sequentially. In this approach, changes to requirements can be costly and lead to extensive delays since they will impact the entire software development process. One notable exception is *agile programming* (also referred to as rapid software development, see agilemanifesto.org/), where requirements specification, design, implementation, and testing occur simultaneously (Sommerville, 2004).

Agile programming is iterative in nature, and the main goal is to develop useful software quickly. Some features of agile programming methods include:

* concurrency of development activities,
* minimal or automatic design documentation,
* only high-priority user requirements specified up front,
* significant user involvement in the development process, and
* incremental software development.

One of the intended advantages of agile programming is to provide software delivery (although initially with reduced capability) that allows for user involvement and feedback during the software design process and not just after the final software product has been delivered. Agile programming methods are good for small and medium-size software development efforts, but their efficiency for larger software development efforts which generally require more coordination and planning is questionable (Sommerville, 2004). Agile programming appears to be particularly suited for small to moderate size scientific computing software projects (Allen, 2009).

A popular form of the agile programming approach is extreme programming, or XP (Beck, 2000), and is so-called because it takes the standard software engineering practices to their extreme. In XP, requirements are expressed as potential scenarios that lead to software development tasks, which are then programmed by a pair of developers working as a team. Evidence suggests that pair programming productivity is similar to that of solo programmers (Williams and Kessler, 2003), but results in fewer errors since any code produced has necessarily undergone an informal software inspection process (Pressman, 2005). Unit tests (Section 4.3.3.1) must be developed for each task before the code is written, and all such tests must be successfully executed before integration into the software system, a process known as continuous integration testing (Duvall *et al.*, 2007). This type of test-first procedure also provides an implicit definition of the interface as well as proper usage examples of the component being developed. Software development projects employing XP usually have frequent releases and undergo frequent refactoring (Section 4.1.6) to improve quality and maintain simplicity. For an example of XP applied to scientific computing, see Wood and Kleb (2003).

4.1.5 Software reuse

Software reuse has become an important part of large software development projects (Sommerville, 2004). While its use in scientific computing is not as extensive, there are a number of areas in scientific computing where reuse is commonly found. Some examples of software reuse in scientific computing are: mathematical function and subroutine libraries (e.g., Press *et al.*, 2007), parallel message passing libraries (e.g., MPI), pre-packaged linear solvers such as the Linear Algebra Package (LAPACK) or the Portable Extensible Toolkit for Scientific Computation (PETSc), and graphics libraries.

4.1.6 Refactoring

Often, at the end of a software development effort, the developer realizes that choices made early in the software design phase have led to computationally inefficient or cumbersome programming. Refactoring is the act of modifying software such that the internal software structure is changed, but the outward behavior is not. Refactoring can reduce the complexity, computational time, and/or memory requirements for scientific software. However, refactoring should not be undertaken until a comprehensive test suite (Section 4.3.4) is in place to ensure that the external behavior is not modified and that programming errors are not introduced.

4.2 Version control

Version control tracks changes to source code or other software products. A good version control system can tell you what was changed, who made the change, and when the change was made. It allows a software developer to undo any changes to the code, going back to any prior version. This can be particularly helpful when you would like to reproduce results from an earlier paper, report, or project, and merely requires documentation of the version number or the date the results were generated. Version control also provides a mechanism for incorporating changes from multiple developers, an essential feature for large software projects or projects with geographically remote developers. All source code should be maintained in a version control system, regardless of how large or small the software project (Eddins, 2006).

Some key concepts pertaining to version control are discussed below (Collins-Sussman *et al.*, 2009). Note that the generic descriptor "file" is used, which could represent not only source code and other software products, but also any other type of file stored on a computer.

Repository   single location where the current and all prior versions of the files are stored. The repository can only be accessed through check-in and check-out procedures (see below).

Working copy   the local copy of a file from the repository which can be modified and then checked in to the repository.

Check-out   the process of creating a working copy from the repository, either from the current version or an earlier version.

Check-in   a check-in (or commit) occurs when changes made to a working copy are merged into the repository, resulting in a new version.

Diff   a summary of the differences between a working copy and a file in the repository, often taking the form of the two files shown side-by-side with differences highlighted.

Conflict   occurs when two or more developers attempt to make changes to the same file and the system is unable to reconcile the changes. Conflicts generally must be resolved by either choosing one version over the other or by integrating the changes from both into the repository by hand.

Update   merges recent changes to the repository from other developers into a working copy.

Version   a unique identifier assigned to each version of the file held in the repository which is generated by the check-in process.

The basic steps that one would use to get started with a version control tool are as follows. First, a *repository* is created, ideally on a network server which is backed up frequently. Then a software project (directory structure and/or files) is *imported* to the repository. This initial version can then be *checked-out* as a *working copy*. The project can then be modified in the working copy, with the differences between the edited working copy and the original repository version examined using a *diff* procedure. Before checking the working copy into the repository, two steps should be performed. First, an *update* should be performed to integrate changes that others have made in the code and to identify *conflicts*. Next, a set of predefined tests should be run to ensure that the modifications do not unexpectedly change the code's behavior. Finally, the *working copy* of the project can be *checked-in* to the repository, generating a new *version* of the software project.

There is a wide array of version control systems available to the software developer. These systems range from free, open-source systems such as Concurrent Versions Systems

(CVS) and Subversion (SVN) (Collins-Sussman *et al.*, 2009) to commercially available systems. A short tutorial showing the basic steps for implementing version control with a Windows-based tool can be found at www.aoe.vt.edu/~cjroy/MISC/TortoiseSVN-Tutorial. pdf.

4.3 Software verification and validation

4.3.1 Definitions

The definitions accepted by AIAA (1998) and ASME (2006) for verification and validation as applied to scientific computing address the mathematical accuracy of a numerical solution (verification) and the physical accuracy of a given model (validation); however, the definitions used by the software engineering community (e.g., ISO, 1991; IEEE, 1991) are different. In software engineering, verification is defined as ensuring that software conforms to it specifications (i.e., requirements) and validation is defined as ensuring that software actually meets the customer's needs. Some argue that these definitions are really the same; however, upon closer examination, they are in fact different.

The key differences in these definitions for verification and validation are due to the fact that, in scientific computing, we begin with a governing partial differential or integral equation, which we will refer to as our mathematical model. For problems that we are interested in solving, there is generally no known exact solution to this model. It is for this reason that we must develop numerical approximations to the model (i.e., the numerical algorithm) and then implement that numerical algorithm within scientific computing software. Thus the two striking differences between how the scientific computing community and the software engineering community define verification and validation are as follows. First, in scientific computing, validation requires a comparison to experimental data. The software engineering community defines validation of the software as meeting the customer's needs, which is, in our opinion, too vague to tie it back to experimental observations. Second, in scientific computing, there is generally *no true system-level software test* (i.e., a test for correct code output given some code inputs) for real problems of interest. The "correct" output from the scientific software depends on the number of significant figures used in the computation, the computational mesh resolution and quality, the time step (for unsteady problems), and the level of iterative convergence. Chapters 5 and 6 of this book address the issue of system-level tests for scientific software.

In this section, we will distinguish between the two definitions of verification and validation by inserting the word "software" when referring to the definitions from software engineering. Three additional definitions that will be used throughout this section are those for software defects, faults, and failures (Hatton, 1997b). A *software defect* is a coding mistake (bug) or the misuse of a coding construct that could potentially lead to a software failure. A *software fault* is a defect which can be detected without running the code, i.e., through static analysis. Examples of defects that can lead to software faults include dependence on uninitialized variables, mismatches in parameter arguments, and unassigned pointers. A *software failure* occurs when the software returns an incorrect result or when it terminates prematurely due to a run-time error (overflow, underflow, division by zero, etc.). Some examples of catastrophic software failures are given by Hatton (1997a).

4.3.2 Static analysis

Static analysis is any type of assessment of software correctness that does not require program execution. Examples of static analysis methods include software inspection, peer review, compiling of the code, and the use of automatic static analyzers. Hatton (1997a) estimates that approximately 40% of software failures are due to static faults. Some examples of static faults are:

- dependency on uninitialized or undeclared variables,
- interface faults: too few, too many, or wrong type of arguments passed to a function/subroutine,
- casting a pointer to a narrower integer type (C), and
- use of non-local variables in functions/subroutines (Fortran).

All of these static faults, as well as others that have their origins in ambiguities in the programming language standards, can be prevented by using static analysis.

4.3.2.1 Software inspection

Software inspection (or review) refers to the act of reading through the source code and other software products to find defects. Although software inspections are time intensive, they are surprisingly effective at finding software defects (Sommerville, 2004). Other advantages of software inspections are that they are not subject to interactions between different software defects (i.e., one defect will not hide the presence of another one), incomplete and nonfunctional source code can be inspected, and they can find other issues besides defects such as coding inefficiencies or lack of compliance with coding standards. The rigor of the software inspection depends on the technical qualifications of the reviewer as well as their level of independence from the software developers.

4.3.2.2 Compiling the code

Any time the code is compiled it goes through some level of static analysis. The level of rigor of the static analysis often depends on the options used during compilation, but there is a trade-off between the level of static analysis performed by the compiler and the execution speed. Many modern compilers provide different modes of compilation such as a release mode, a debug mode, and a check mode that perform increasing levels of static analysis. Due to differences in compilers and operating systems, many software developers make it standard practice to compile the source code with different compilers and on different platforms.

4.3.2.3 Automatic static analyzers

Automatic static analyzers are external tools that are meant to complement the checking of the code by the compiler. They are designed to find inconsistent or undefined use of a programming language that the compiler will likely overlook, as well as coding constructs that are generally considered as unsafe. Some static analyzers available for C/C^{++} include the Safer C Toolset, CodeWizard, CMT^{++}, Cleanscape LintPlus, PC-lint/FlexeLint, and QA C. Static analyzers for Fortran include floppy/fflow and ftnchek. There is also a recently-developed static analyzer for MATLAB called M-Lint (MATLAB, 2008). For a more complete list, or for references to each of these static analyzers, see www.testingfaqs. org/t-static.html.

4.3.3 Dynamic testing

Dynamic software testing can be defined as the "dynamic verification of the behavior of a program on a finite set of test cases . . . against the expected behavior" (SWEBOK, 2004). Dynamic testing includes any type of testing activity which involves running the code, thus run-time compiler checks (e.g., array bounds checking, pointer checking) fall under the heading of dynamic testing. The types of dynamic testing discussed in this section include defect testing (at the unit, component, and complete system level), regression testing, and software validation testing.

4.3.3.1 Defect testing

Defect testing is a type of dynamic testing performed to uncover the presence of a software defect; however, defect testing cannot be used to prove that no errors are present. Once a defect is discovered, the process of finding and fixing the defect is usually referred to as debugging. In scientific computing, it is convenient to decompose defect testing into three levels: unit testing which occurs at the smallest level in the code, component testing which occurs at the submodel or algorithm level, and system testing where the desired output from the software is evaluated. While unit testing is generally performed by the code developer, component and system-level testing is more reliable when performed by someone outside of the software development team.

Unit testing

Unit testing is used to verify the execution of a single routine (e.g., function, subroutine, object class) of the code (Eddins, 2006). Unit tests are designed to check for the correctness of routine output based on a given input. They should also be easy to write and run, and should execute quickly. Properly designed unit tests also provide examples of proper routine use such as how the routine should be called, what type of inputs should be provided, what type of outputs can be expected.

While it does take additional time to develop unit tests, this extra time in code development generally pays off later in reduced time debugging. The authors' experience with even

Table 4.1 *Example of a component-level test fixture for Sutherland's viscosity law (adapted from Kleb and Wood, 2006).*

Input: T (K)	Output: μ (kg/s-m)
$200 \leq T \leq 3000$	$B * \frac{T^{1.5}}{T+110.4}$
199	error
200	1.3285589×10^{-5}
2000	6.1792781×10^{-5}
3000	7.7023485×10^{-5}
3001	error

* where $B = 1.458 \times 10^{-6}$

small scientific computing code development in university settings suggests that the typical ratio of debugging time to programming time for students who do not employ unit tests is at least five to one. The wider the unit testing coverage (i.e., percentage of routines that have unit tests), the more reliable the code is likely to be. In fact, some software development strategies such as Extreme Programming (XP) require tests to be written before the actual routine to be tested is created. Such strategies require the programmer to clearly define the interfaces (inputs and outputs) of the routine up front.

Component testing

Kleb and Wood (2006) make an appeal to the scientific computing community to implement the scientific method in the development of scientific software. Recall that, in the scientific method, a theory must be supported with a corresponding experiment that tests the theory, and must be described in enough detail that the experiment can be reproduced by independent sources. For application to scientific computing, they recommend testing at the component level, where a component is considered to be a submodel or algorithm. Furthermore, they strongly suggest that model and algorithm developers publish *test fixtures* with any newly proposed model or algorithm. These test fixtures are designed to clearly define the proper usage of the component, give examples of proper usage, and give sample inputs along with correct outputs that can be used for testing the implementation in a scientific computing code. An example of such a test fixture for Sutherland's viscosity law is presented in Table 4.1.

Component-level testing can be performed when the submodel or algorithm are algebraic since the expected (i.e., correct) solution can be computed directly. However, for cases where the submodel involves numerical approximations (e.g., many models for fluid turbulence involve differential equations), then the expected solution will necessarily be a function of the chosen discretization parameters, and the more sophisticated code verification methods discussed in Chapters 5 and 6 should be used. For models that are difficult to test at the system level (e.g., the `min` and `max` functions significantly complicate the code verification process discussed in Chapter 5), component-level testing of the models (or different parts of the model) can be used. Finally, even when all components have been successfully tested individually, one should not get a false sense of security about how the software will behave at the system level. Complex interactions between components can only be tested at the system level.

System testing

System-level testing addresses code as a whole. For a given set of inputs to the code, what is the correct code output? In software engineering, system level testing is the primary means by which one determines if the software requirements have been met (i.e., software verification). For nonscientific software, it is often possible to *a priori* determine what the correct output of the code should be. However, for scientific computing software where partial differential or integral equations are solved, the "correct" output is generally not known ahead of time. Furthermore, the code output will depend on the grid and time step chosen, the iterative convergence level, the machine precision, etc. For scientific computing software, system-level testing is generally addressed through *order of accuracy verification*, which is the main subject of Chapter 5.

4.3.3.2 Regression testing

Regression testing involves the comparison of code or software routine output to the output from earlier versions of the code. Regression tests are designed to prevent the introduction of coding mistakes by detecting unintended consequences of changes in the code. Regression tests can be implemented at the unit, component, and system level. In fact, all of the defect tests described above can also be implemented as regression tests. The main difference between regression testing and defect testing is that regression tests do not compare code output to the correct expected value, but instead to the output from previous versions of the code. Careful regression testing combined with defect testing can minimize the chances of introducing new software defects during code development and maintenance.

4.3.3.3 Software validation testing

As discussed earlier, software validation is performed to ensure that the software actually meets the customer's needs in terms of software function, behavior, and performance (Pressman, 2005). Software validation (or acceptance) testing occurs at the system level and usually involves data supplied by the customer. Software validation testing for scientific computing software inherits all of the issues discussed earlier for system-level testing, and thus special considerations must be made when determining what the expected, correct output of the code should be.

4.3.4 *Test harness and test suites*

Many different types of dynamic software tests have been discussed in this section. For larger software development projects, it would be extremely tedious if the developer had to run each of the tests separately and then examine the results. Especially in the case of larger development efforts, automation of software testing is a must.

A *test harness* is the combination of software and test data used to test the correctness of a program or component by automatically running it under various conditions (Eddins, 2006). A test harness is usually composed of a test manager, test input data, test output data, a file comparator, and an automatic report generator. While it is certainly possible to create your own test harness, there are a variety of test harnesses that have been developed for a wide range of programming languages. For a detailed list, see en.wikipedia.org/wiki/List_of_unit_testing_frameworks.

Once a suite of tests has been set up to run within a test harness, it is recommended that these tests be run automatically at specified intervals. Shorter tests can be run in a nightly test suite, while larger tests which require more computer time and memory may be set up in weekly or monthly test suites. In addition, an approach called *continuous integration testing* (Duvall *et al.*, 2007) requires that specified test suites be run before any new code modifications are checked in.

4.3.5 *Code coverage*

Regardless of how software testing is done, one important aspect is the coverage of the tests. *Code coverage* can be defined as the percentage of code components (and possibly their interactions) for which tests exist. While testing at the unit and component levels is relatively straightforward, system-level testing must also address interactions between different components. Large, complex scientific computing codes generally have a very large number of options for models, submodels, numerical algorithms, boundary conditions, etc. Assume for the moment that there are 100 different options in the code to be tested, a conservative estimate for most production-level scientific computing codes. Testing each option independently (although generally not possible) would require 100 different system-level tests. Testing pair-wise combinations for interactions between these different options would require 4950 system level tests. Testing the interactions between groups of three would require 161 700 tests. While this is clearly an upper bound since many options may be mutually exclusive, it does provide a sense of the magnitude of the task of achieving complete code coverage of model/algorithm interactions. Table 4.2 provides a comparison of the number of system-level tests required to ensure code coverage with different degrees of option interactions for codes with 10, 100, and 1000 different code options. Clearly, testing the three-way interactions for our example of 100 coding options is impossible, as would be testing all pair-wise interactions when 1000 coding options are available, a number not uncommon for commercial scientific computing codes. One possible approach for addressing this combinatorial explosion of tests for component interactions is

Table 4.2 *Number of system-level tests required for complete code coverage for codes with different numbers of options and option combinations to be tested.*

Number of options	Option combinations to be tested	System-level tests required
10	1	10
10	2	45
10	3	720
100	1	100
100	2	4950
100	3	161 700
1000	1	1000
1000	2	499 500
1000	3	$\sim 1.7 \times 10^8$

application-centric testing (Knupp and Ober, 2008), where only those components and component interactions which impact a specific code application are tested.

4.3.6 Formal methods

Formal methods use mathematically-based techniques for requirements specification, development, and/or verification testing of software systems. Formal methods arise from discrete mathematics and involve set theory, logic, and algebra (Sommerville, 2004). Such a rigorous mathematical framework is expensive to implement, thus it is mainly used for high-assurance (i.e., critical) software systems such as those found in aircraft controls systems, nuclear power plants, and medical devices such as pacemakers (Heitmeyer, 2004). Some of the drawbacks to using formal methods are that they do not handle user interfaces well and they do not scale well for larger software projects. Due to the effort and expense required, as well as their poor scalability, we do not recommend formal methods for scientific computing software.

4.4 Software quality and reliability

There are many different definitions of quality applied to software. The definition that we will use is: *conformance to customer requirements and needs*. This definition implies not only adherence to the formally documented requirements for the software, but also those requirements that are not explicitly stated by the customer that need to be met. However, this definition of quality can often only be applied after the complete software product is delivered to the customer. Another aspect of software quality that we will find useful is software reliability. One definition of *software reliability* is the probability of failure-free operation of software in a given environment for a specified time (Musa, 1999). In this section we present some explicit and implicit methods for measuring software reliability. A discussion of recommended programming practices as well as error-prone coding constructs that should be avoided when possible, both of which can affect software reliability, can be found in the Appendix.

4.4.1 Reliability metrics

Two quantitative approaches for measuring code quality are *defect density analysis*, which provides an explicit measure of reliability, and *complexity analysis*, which provides an implicit measure of reliability. Additional information on software reliability can be found in Beizer (1990), Fenton and Pfleeger (1997), and Kaner *et al.* (1999).

4.4.1.1 Defect density analysis

The most direct method for assessing the reliability of software is in terms of the number of defects in the software. Defects can lead to static errors (faults) and dynamic errors (failures). The *defect density* is usually reported as the number of defects per executable source lines of code (SLOC). Hatton (1997a) argues that it is only by measuring the defect density of software, through both static analysis and dynamic testing, that an objective assessment of software reliability can be made. Hatton's T Experiments (Hatton, 1997b) are discussed in detail in the next section and represent the largest known defect density study of scientific software.

   A significant limitation of defect density analysis is that the defect rate is a function of both the number of defects in the software and the specific testing procedure used to find the defects (Fenton and Pfleeger, 1997). For example, a poor testing procedure might uncover only a few defects, whereas a more comprehensive testing procedure applied to the same software might uncover significantly more defects. This sensitivity to the specific approach used for defect testing represents a major limitation of defect density analysis.

4.4.1.2 Complexity analysis

Complexity analysis is an indirect way of measuring reliability because it requires a model to convert internal code quality attributes into code reliability (Sommerville, 2004). The most frequently used model is to assume that a high degree of complexity in a component (function, subroutine, object class, etc.) is bad while a low degree of complexity is good. In this case, components which are identified as being too complex can be decomposed into smaller components. However, Hatton (1997a) used defect density analysis to show that the defect density in components follows a U-shaped curve, with the minimum occurring at 150–250 lines of source code per component, independent of both programming language and application area. He surmised that the increase in defect density for smaller components may be related to the inadvertent adverse effects of component reuse (see Hatton (1996) for more details). Some different internal code attributes that can be used to indirectly assess code reliability are discussed in this subsection, and in some cases, tools exist for automatically evaluating these complexity metrics.

Lines of source code

The simplest measure of complexity can be found by counting the number of executable source lines of code (SLOC) for each component. Hatton (1997a) recommends keeping components between 150 and 250 SLOC.

NPATH metric

The NPATH metric simply counts the number of possible execution paths through a component (Nejmeh, 1988). Nejmeh (1988) recommends keeping this value below 200 for each component.

Cyclomatic complexity

The cyclomatic, or McCabe, complexity (McCabe, 1976) is defined as one plus the number of decision points in a component, where a decision point is defined as any loop or logical statement (if, elseif, while, repeat, do, for, or, etc.). The maximum recommended value for cyclomatic complexity of a component is ten (Eddins, 2006).

Depth of conditional nesting

This complexity metric provides a measure of the depth of nesting of if-statements, where larger degrees of nesting are assumed to be more difficult to understand and track, and therefore are more error prone (Sommerville, 2004).

Depth of inheritance tree

Applicable to object-oriented programming languages, this complexity metric measures the number of levels in the inheritance tree where sub-classes inherit attributes from super-classes (Sommerville, 2004). The more levels that exist in the inheritance tree, the more classes one needs to understand to be able to develop or modify a given object class.

4.5 Case study in reliability: the T experiments

In the early 1990s, Les Hatton undertook a broad study of scientific software reliability known collectively as the "T Experiments" (Hatton, 1997b). This study was broken into two parts: the first (T1) examined codes from a wide range of scientific disciplines using static analysis, while the second (T2) examined codes in a single discipline using dynamic testing.

The T1 study used static deep-flow analyzers to examine more than 100 different codes in 40 different application areas. All codes were written in C, FORTRAN 66, or FORTRAN 77, and the static analyzers used were QA C (for the C codes) and QA Fortran (for the

FORTRAN codes). The main conclusion of the T1 study was that the C codes contained approximately eight serious static faults per 1000 lines of executable code, while the FORTRAN codes contained approximately 12 faults per 1000 lines. A serious static fault is defined as a statically-detectable defect that is likely to cause the software to fail. For more details on the T1 study, see Hatton (1995).

The T2 study examined a subset of the codes from the T1 study in the area of seismic data processing which is used in the field of oil and gas exploration. This study examined nine independent, mature, commercial codes which employed the same algorithms, the same programming language (FORTRAN), the same user-defined parameters, and the same input data. Hatton refers to such a study as N-version programming since each code was developed independently by a different company. Each of the codes consisted of approximately 30 sequential steps, 14 of which used unambiguously defined algorithms, referred to in the study as primary calibration points. Agreement between the codes after the first primary calibration point was within 0.001% (i.e., approximately machine precision for single-precision computations); however, agreement after primary calibration point 14 was only within a factor of two. It is interesting to note that distribution of results from the various codes was found to be non-Gaussian with distinct groups and outliers, suggesting that the output from an N-version programming test should not be analyzed with Bayesian statistics. Hatton concluded that the disagreements between the different codes are due primarily to software errors. Such dismal results from the T2 study prompted Hatton to conclude that *"the results of scientific calculations carried out by many software packages should be treated with the same measure of disbelief researchers have traditionally attached to the results of unconfirmed physical experiments."* For more details on the T2 study, see Hatton and Roberts (1994).

These alarming results from Hatton's "T Experiments" highlight the need for employing good software engineering practices in scientific computing. At a minimum, the simple techniques presented in this chapter such as version control, static analysis, dynamic testing, and reliability metrics should be employed for all scientific computing software projects to improve quality and reliability.

4.6 Software engineering for large software projects

Up to this point, the software engineering practices discussed have been applicable to all scientific computing project whether large or small. In this section, we specifically address software engineering practices for large scientific computing projects that may be less effective for smaller projects. The two broad topics addressed here include software requirements and software management.

4.6.1 Software requirements

A software requirement is a "property that must be exhibited in order to solve some real-world problem" (SWEBOK, 2004). Uncertainty in requirements is a leading cause of failure in software projects (Post and Kendall, 2004). While it is certainly ideal to have all requirements rigorously and unambiguously specified at the beginning of a software project, this can be difficult to achieve for scientific software. Especially in the case of large scientific software development projects, complete requirements can be difficult to specify due to rapid changes in models, algorithms, and even in the specialized computer architectures used to run the software. While lack of requirements definition can adversely affect the development of scientific software, these negative effects can be mitigated somewhat if close communication is maintained between the developer of the software and the user (Post and Kendall, 2004) or if the developer is also an expert in the scientific computing discipline.

4.6.1.1 Types of software requirements

There are two main types of software requirements. User requirements are formulated at a high level of abstraction, usually in general terms which are easily understood by the user. An example of a user requirement might be: *this software should produce approximate numerical solutions to the Navier–Stokes equations.* Software system requirements, on the other hand, are a precise and formal definition of a software system's functions and constraints. The software system requirements are further decomposed as follows:

1. functional requirements – rigorous specifications of required outputs for a given set of inputs,
2. nonfunctional requirements – additional nonfunctional constraints such as programming standards, reliability, and computational speed, and
3. domain requirements – those requirements that come from the application domain such as a discussion of the partial differential or integral equations to be solved numerically for a given scientific computing application.

The domain requirements are crucial in scientific computing since these will be used to define the specific governing equations, models, and numerical algorithms to be implemented. Finally, if the software is to be integrated with existing software, then additional specifications may be needed for the procedure interfaces (application programming interfaces, or APIs), data structures, or data representation (e.g., bit ordering) (Sommerville, 2004).

4.6.1.2 Requirements engineering process

The process for determining software requirements contains four phases: elicitation, analysis, specification, and validation. *Elicitation* involves the identification of the sources for requirements, which includes the code customers, users, and developers. For larger software projects these sources could also include managers, regulatory authorities, third-party software providers, and other stakeholders. Once the sources for the requirements have been identified, the requirements are then collected either individually from those sources or by bringing the sources together for discussion.

In the *analysis* phase, the requirements are analyzed for clarity, conflicts, and the need for possible requirements negotiation between the software users and developers. In scientific computing, while the users typically want a code with a very broad range of capabilities, the developers must weigh trade-offs between capability and the required computational infrastructure, all while operating under manpower and budgetary constraints. Thus negotiation and compromise between the users and the developers is critical for developing computational tools that balance capability with feasibility and available resources.

Specification deals with the documentation of the established user and system requirements in a formal software requirements document. This requirements document should be considered a living document since requirements often change during the software's life cycle. Requirements *validation* is the final confirmation that the software meets the customer's needs, and typically comes in the form of full software system tests using data supplied by the customer. One challenge specific to scientific computing software is the difficulty in determining the correct code output due to the presence of numerical approximation errors.

4.6.1.3 Requirements management

Requirements management is the process of understanding, controlling, and tracking changes to the system requirements. It is important because software requirements are usually incomplete and tend to undergo frequent changes. Things that can cause the requirements to change include installing the software on a new hardware system, identification of new desired functionality based on user experience with the software, and, for scientific computing, improvements in existing models or numerical algorithms.

4.6.2 Software management

Software management is a broad topic which includes the management of the software project, cost, configuration, and quality. In addition, effective software management strategies must include approaches for improvement of the software development process itself.

4.6.2.1 Project management

Software project management addresses the planning, scheduling, oversight, and risk management of a software project. For larger projects, planning activities encompass a wide range of different areas, and separate planning documents should be developed for quality, software verification and validation, configuration management, maintenance, staff development, milestones, and deliverables. Another important aspect of software project management is determining the level of formality required in applying the software engineering practices. Ultimately, this decision should be made by performing a risk-based assessment of the intended use, mission, complexity, budget, and schedule (Demarco and Lister, 2003).

Managing software projects is generally more difficult than managing standard engineering projects because the product is intangible, there are usually no standard software management practices, and large software projects are usually one-of-a-kind endeavors

(Sommerville, 2004). According to Post and Kendall (2004), ensuring consistency between the software schedule, resources, and requirements is the key to successfully managing a large scientific computing software project.

4.6.2.2 Cost estimation

While estimating the required resources for a software project can be challenging, semi-empirical models are available. These models are called algorithmic cost models, and in their simplest form (Sommerville, 2004) can be expressed as:

$$Effort = A \times (Size)^b \times M. \tag{4.1}$$

In this simple algorithmic cost model, A is a constant which depends on the type of organization developing the software, their software development practices, and the specific type of software being developed. *Size* is some measure of the size of the software project (estimated lines of code, software functionality, etc.). The exponent b typically varies between 1 and 1.5, with larger values indicative of the fact that software complexity increases nonlinearly with the size of the project. M is a multiplier that accounts for various factors including risks associated with software failures, experience of the code development team, and the dependability of the requirements. *Effort* is generally in man-months, and the cost is usually assumed to be proportional to the effort. Most of these parameters are subjective and difficult to evaluate, thus they should be determined empirically using historical data for the organization developing the software whenever possible. When such data are not available, historical data from similar organizations may be used.

For larger software projects where more accurate cost estimates are required, Sommerville (2004) recommends the more detailed Constructive Cost Model (COCOMO). When software is developed using imperative programming languages such as Fortran or C using a waterfall model, the original COCOMO model, now referred to as COCOMO 81, can be used (Boehm, 1981). This algorithmic cost model was developed by Boehm while he was at the aerospace firm TRW Inc., and drew upon the historical software development data from 63 different software projects ranging from 2000 to 10000 lines of code. An updated model, COCOMO II, has been developed which accounts for object-oriented programming languages, software reuse, off-the-shelf software components, and a spiral software development model (Boehm *et al.*, 2000).

4.6.2.3 Configuration management

Configuration management deals with the control and management of the software products during all phases of the software product's lifecycle including planning, development, production, maintenance, and retirement. Here software products include not only the source code, but also user and theory manuals, software tests, test results, design documents, web pages, and any other items produced during the software development process. Configuration management tracks the way software is configured over time and is used for controlling changes to, and for maintaining integrity and traceability of, the software products

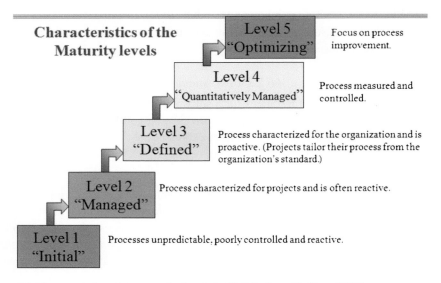

Figure 4.2 Characteristics of the maturity levels in CMMI (from Godfrey, 2009).

(Sommerville, 2004). The key aspects of configuration management include using *version control* (discussed in Section 4.2) for source code and other important software products, identification of the software products to be managed, recording, approving, and tracking issues with the software, managing software releases, and ensuring frequent backups are made.

4.6.2.4 Quality management

Software quality management is usually separated into three parts: quality assurance, quality planning, and quality control (Sommerville, 2004). *Quality assurance* is the definition of a set of procedures and standards for developing high-quality software. *Quality planning* is the process of selecting from the above procedures and standards for a given software project. *Quality control* is a set of processes that ensure the quality plan was actually implemented. It is important to maintain independence between the quality management team and the code development team (Sommerville, 2004).

4.6.2.5 Process improvement

Another way to improve the quality of software is to improve the processes which are used to develop it. Perhaps the most well-known software process improvement model is the Capability Maturity Model, or CMM (Humphrey, 1989). The successor to CMM, the Capability Maturity Model Integration (CMMI) integrates various process improvement models and is more broadly applicable to the related areas of systems engineering and integrated product development (SEI, 2009). The five maturity levels in CMMI are shown in Figure 4.2, and empirical evidence suggests that both software quality and developer productivity will improve as higher levels of process maturity are reached (Gibson *et al.*, 2006).

Post and Kendall (2004) found that not all software engineering practices are helpful for developing scientific software. They cautioned against blindly applying rigorous software standards such as CMM/CMMI without first performing a cost-benefit analysis. Neely (2004) suggests a risk-based approach to applying quality assurance practices to scientific computing projects. High-risk projects are defined as those that could potentially involve "great loss of money, reputation, or human life," while a low risk project would involve at most inconvenience to the user. High-risk projects would be expected to conform to more formal software quality standards, whereas low-risk projects would allow more informal, ad-hoc implementation of the standards.

4.7 References

AIAA (1998). *Guide for the Verification and Validation of Computational Fluid Dynamics Simulations*. AIAA-G-077–1998, Reston, VA, American Institute of Aeronautics and Astronautics.

Allen, E. B. (2009). Private communication, February 11, 2009.

ASME (2006). *Guide for Verification and Validation in Computational Solid Mechanics*. ASME V&V 10–2006, New York, NY, American Society of Mechanical Engineers.

Beck, K. (2000). *Extreme Programming Explained: Embrace Change*, Reading, PA, Addison-Wesley.

Beizer, B. (1990). *Software Testing Techniques*, 2nd edn., New York, Van Nostrand Reinhold.

Boehm, B. W. (1981). *Software Engineering Economics*, Englewood Cliffs, NJ, Prentice-Hall.

Boehm, B. W., C. Abts, A. W. Brown, S. Chulani, B. K. Clark, E. Horowitz, R. Madachy, D. J. Reifer, and B. Steece (2000). *Software Cost Estimation with Cocomo II*, Englewood Cliffs, NJ, Prentice-Hall.

Collins-Sussman, B., B. W. Fitzpatrick, and C. M. Pilato (2009). *Version Control with Subversion: For Subversion 1.5: (Compiled from r3305)* (see svnbook.red-bean.com/en/1.5/svn-book.pdf).

Demarco, T. and T. Lister (2003). *Waltzing with Bears: Managing Risk on Software Projects*, New York, Dorset House.

Duvall, P. F., S. M. Matyas, and A. Glover (2007). *Continuous Integration: Improving Software Quality and Reducing Risk*, Upper Saddle River, NJ, Harlow: Addison-Wesley.

Eddins, S. (2006). Taking control of your code: essential software development tools for engineers, *International Conference on Image Processing*, Atlanta, GA, Oct. 9 (see blogs.mathworks.com/images/steve/92/handout_final_icip2006.pdf).

Fenton, N. E. and S. L. Pfleeger (1997). *Software Metrics: a Rigorous and Practical Approach*, 2nd edn., London, PWS Publishing.

Gibson, D. L., D. R. Goldenson, and K. Kost (2006). *Performance Results of CMMI®-Based Process Improvement*, Technical Report CMU/SEI-2006-TR-004, ESC-TR-2006–004, August 2006 (see www.sei.cmu.edu/publications/documents/06.reports/06tr004.html).

Godfrey, S. (2009). *What is CMMI?* NASA Presentation (see software.gsfc.nasa.gov/docs/What%20is%20CMMI.ppt).

Hatton, L. (1995). *Safer C: Developing Software for High-Integrity and Safety-Critical Systems*, New York, McGraw-Hill International Ltd.

Hatton, L. (1996). Software faults: the avoidable and the unavoidable: lessons from real systems, *Proceedings of the Product Assurance Workshop, ESA SP-377*, Noordwijk, The Netherlands.

Hatton, L. (1997a). Software failures: follies and fallacies, *IEEE Review*, March, 49–52.

Hatton, L. (1997b). The T Experiments: errors in scientific software, *IEEE Computational Science and Engineering*, **4**(2), 27–38.

Hatton, L., and A. Roberts (1994). How accurate is scientific software? *IEEE Transactions on Software Engineering*, **20**(10), 785–797.

Heitmeyer, C. (2004). Managing complexity in software development with formally based tools, *Electronic Notes in Theoretical Computer Science*, **108**, 11–19.

Humphrey, W. (1989). *Managing the Software Process*. Reading, MA, Addison-Wesley Professional.

IEEE (1991). *IEEE Standard Glossary of Software Engineering Terminology*. IEEE Std 610.12–1990, New York, IEEE.

ISO (1991). *ISO 9000–3: Quality Management and Quality Assurance Standards – Part 3: Guidelines for the Application of ISO 9001 to the Development, Supply and Maintenance of Software*. Geneva, Switzerland, International Organization for Standardization.

Kaner, C., J. Falk, and H. Q. Nguyen (1999). *Testing Computer Software*, 2nd edn., New York, Wiley.

Kleb, B., and B. Wood (2006). Computational simulations and the scientific method, *Journal of Aerospace Computing, Information, and Communication*, **3**(6), 244–250.

Knupp, P. M. and C. C. Ober (2008). *A Code-Verification Evidence-Generation Process Model and Checklist*, Sandia National Laboratories Report SAND2008–4832.

Knupp, P. M., C. C., Ober, and R. B. Bond (2007). *Impact of Coding Mistakes on Numerical Error and Uncertainty in Solutions to PDEs*, Sandia National Laboratories Report SAND2007–5341.

MATLAB (2008). *MATLAB® Desktop Tools and Development Environment*, Natick, MA, The Mathworks, Inc. (see www.mathworks.com/access/helpdesk/help/pdf_doc/matlab/matlab_env.pdf).

McCabe, T. J. (1976). A complexity measure, *IEEE Transactions on Software Engineering*, **2**(4), 308–320.

McConnell, S. (2004). *Code Complete: a Practical Handbook of Software Construction*, 2nd edn., Redmond, WA, Microsoft Press.

Musa, J. D. (1999). *Software Reliability Engineering: More Reliable Software, Faster Development and Testing*, New York, McGraw-Hill.

Neely, R. (2004). Practical software quality engineering on a large multi-disciplinary HPC development team, *Proceedings of the First International Workshop on Software Engineering for High Performance Computing System Applications*, Edinburgh, Scotland, May 24, 2004.

Nejmeh, B. A. (1988). Npath: a measure of execution path complexity and its applications, *Communications of the Association for Computing Machinery*, **31**(2), 188–200.

Post, D. E., and R. P. Kendall (2004). Software project management and quality engineering practices for complex, coupled multiphysics, massively parallel computational simulations: lessons learned from ASCI, *International Journal of High Performance Computing Applications*, **18**(4), 399–416.

Press, W. H., S. A. Teukolsky, W. T. Vetterling, and B. P. Flannery (2007). *Numerical Recipes: the Art of Scientific Computing*, 3rd edn., Cambridge, Cambridge University Press.

Pressman, R. S. (2005). *Software Engineering: a Practitioner's Approach*, 6th edn., Boston, MA, McGraw-Hill.

Roy, C. J. (2009). Practical software engineering strategies for scientific computing, AIAA Paper 2009–3997, *19th AIAA Computational Fluid Dynamics, San Antonio, TX*, June 22–25, 2009.

SE-CSE (2008). *Proceedings of the First International Workshop on Software Engineering for Computational Science and Engineering*, Leipzig, Germany, May 13, 2008 (see cs.ua.edu/~SECSE08/).

SE-CSE (2009). *Proceedings of the Second International Workshop on Software Engineering for Computational Science and Engineering*, Vancouver, Canada, May 23, 2009 (see cs.ua.edu/~SECSE09/).

SE-HPC (2004). *Proceedings of the First International Workshop On Software Engineering for High Performance Computing System Applications*, Edinburgh, Scotland, May 24, 2004.

SEI (2009). CMMI Main Page, Software Engineering Institute, Carnegie Mellon University (see www.sei.cmu.edu/cmmi/index.html).

Sommerville, I. (2004). *Software Engineering*, 7th edn., Harlow, Essex, England, Pearson Education Ltd.

SWEBOK (2004), *Guide to the Software Engineering Body of Knowledge: 2004 Edition*, P. Borque and R. Dupuis (eds.), Los Alamitos, CA, IEEE Computer Society (www.swebok.org).

Williams, L. and R. Kessler (2003). *Pair Programming Illuminated*, Boston, MA, Addison-Wesley.

Wilson, G. (2009). *Software Carpentry*, www.swc.scipy.org/.

Wood, W. A. and W. L. Kleb (2003). Exploring XP for scientific research, *IEEE Software*, **20**(3), 30–36.

5

Code verification

In scientific computing, the goal of code verification is to ensure that the code is a faithful representation of the underlying mathematical model. This mathematical model generally takes the form of partial differential or integral equations along with associated initial condition, boundary conditions, and auxiliary relationships. Code verification thus addresses both the correctness of the chosen numerical algorithm and the correctness of the instantiation of that algorithm into written source code, i.e., ensuring there are no coding mistakes or "bugs."

A computer program, referred to here simply as a code, is a collection of instructions for a computer written in a programming language. As discussed in Chapter 4, in the software engineering community code verification is called software verification and is comprised of software tests which ensure that the software meets the stated requirements. When conducting system-level testing of non-scientific software, in many cases it is possible to exactly determine the correct code output for a set of given code inputs. However, in scientific computing, the code output depends on the numerical algorithm, the spatial mesh, the time step, the iterative tolerance, and the number of digits of precision used in the computations. Due to these factors, it is not possible to know the correct code output (i.e., numerical solution) *a priori*. The developer of scientific computing software is thus faced with the difficult challenge of determining appropriate system-level software tests.

This chapter discusses various procedures for verifying scientific computing codes. Although a formal proof of the "correctness" of a complex scientific computing code is probably not possible (Roache, 1998), code testing using the order verification procedures discussed in this chapter can provide a high degree of confidence that the code will produce the correct solution. An integral part of these procedures is the use of systematic mesh and time step refinement. For rigorous code verification, an exact solution to the underlying governing equations (i.e., the mathematical model) is required. We defer the difficult issue of how to obtain these exact solutions until Chapter 6, and for now simply assume that an exact solution to the mathematical model is available. Finally, unless otherwise noted, the code verification procedures discussed in this chapter do not depend on the discretization approach, thus we will defer our discussion of the different discretization methods (finite difference, finite volume, finite element, etc.) until Chapter 8.

5.1 Code verification criteria

Before choosing a criterion for code verification, one must first select the code outputs to be tested. The first code outputs to be considered are the dependent variables in the mathematical model. For all but the simplest code verification criteria, we will compare the solution to a reference solution, ideally an exact solution to the mathematical model. In this case, we can convert the difference between the code output and the reference solution over the entire domain into a single, scalar error measure using a norm.

If a continuous representation of the numerical solution is available (e.g., from the finite element method), then a continuous norm can be used. For example, the L_1 norm of the solution error over the domain is given by

$$\|u - u_{\text{ref}}\|_1 = \frac{1}{\Omega} \int_{\Omega} |u - u_{\text{ref}}| \, d\omega, \tag{5.1}$$

where u is the numerical solution, u_{ref} the reference solution, and Ω is the domain of interest. The L_1 norm is the most appropriate norm to use when discontinuities or singularities exist in the solution (Rider, 2009). If instead a discrete representation of the numerical solution is available (e.g., from a finite difference or finite volume method), then a discrete norm of the error can be used. The discrete L_1 norm provides a measure of the average absolute error over the domain and can be defined as

$$\|u - u_{\text{ref}}\|_1 = \frac{1}{\Omega} \sum_{n=1}^{N} \omega_n |u_n - u_{\text{ref},n}|, \tag{5.2}$$

where the subscript n refers to a summation over all N cells of size ω_n in both space and time. Note that for uniform meshes (i.e., those with constant cell spacing in all directions), the cell sizes cancel resulting in simply:

$$\|u - u_{\text{ref}}\|_1 = \frac{1}{N} \sum_{n=1}^{N} |u_n - u_{\text{ref},n}|. \tag{5.3}$$

Another commonly used norm for evaluating the discretization error is the L_2 (or Euclidean) norm, which effectively provides the root mean square of the error. For a uniform mesh, the discrete L_2 norm is given by

$$\|u - u_{\text{ref}}\|_2 = \left(\frac{1}{N} \sum_{n=1}^{N} |u_n - u_{\text{ref},n}|^2 \right)^{1/2}. \tag{5.4}$$

The max (or infinity) norm returns the maximum absolute error over the entire domain, and is generally the most sensitive measure of error:

$$\|u - u_{\text{ref}}\|_\infty = \max |u_n - u_{\text{ref},n}|, \quad n = 1 \text{ to } N. \tag{5.5}$$

In addition to the dependent variables, one should also examine any system response quantities that may be of interest to the code user. These quantities can take the form of derivatives (e.g., local heat flux, local material stress), integrals (e.g., drag on an object, net heat flux through a surface), or other functionals of the solution variables (e.g., natural frequency, maximum deflection, maximum temperature). All system response quantities that may potentially be of interest to the user should be included as part of the code verification process to ensure that both the dependent variables and the procedures for obtaining the system response quantities are verified. For example, a numerical solution for the dependent variables may be verified, but if the subsequent numerical integration used for a system response quantity contains a mistake, then incorrect values of that quantity will be produced.

There are a number of different criteria that can be used for verifying a scientific computing code. In order of increasing rigor, these criteria are:

1 simple tests,
2 code-to-code comparisons,
3 discretization error quantification,
4 convergence tests, and
5 order-of-accuracy tests.

The first two, simple tests and code-to-code comparisons, are the least rigorous but have the advantage that they can be performed for cases where an exact solution to the mathematical model is not available. The remaining criteria require that an exact solution to the mathematical model be available, or at the very least a demonstrably accurate surrogate solution. These five criteria are discussed in more detail below.

5.1.1 Simple tests

The following simple tests, while not a replacement for rigorous code verification studies, can be used as part of the code verification process. They have the advantage that they can be applied even when an exact solution to the mathematical model is not available since they are applied directly to the numerical solution.

5.1.1.1 Symmetry tests

In most cases, when a code is provided with a symmetric geometry, initial conditions, and boundary conditions, it will produce a symmetric solution. In some cases, physical instabilities can lead to solutions that are asymmetric at any given point in time, but may still be symmetric in a statistical sense. One example is the laminar, viscous flow past a circular cylinder, which will be symmetric for Reynolds numbers below 40, but will generate a von Karman vortex street at higher Reynolds numbers (Panton, 2005). Note that this test should not be used near a bifurcation point (i.e., near a set of conditions where the solution can rapidly change its basic character).

5.1.1.2 Conservation tests

In many scientific computing applications, the mathematical model will be based on the conservation of certain properties such as mass, momentum, and energy. In a discrete sense, different numerical approaches will handle conservation differently. In the finite-difference method, conservation is only assured in the limit as the mesh and/or time step are refined. In the finite element method, conservation is strictly enforced over the global domain boundaries, but locally only in the limiting sense. For finite volume discretizations, conservation is explicitly enforced at each cell face, and thus this approach should satisfy the conservation requirement even on very coarse meshes. An example conservation test for steady-state heat conduction is to ensure that the net energy flux into the domain minus the net energy flux out of the domain equals zero, either within round-off error (finite element and finite volume methods) or in the limit as the mesh is refined (finite difference method). See Chapter 8 for a more detailed discussion of the differences between these discretization approaches.

5.1.1.3 Galilean invariance tests

Most scientific computing disciplines have their foundations in Newtonian (or classical) mechanics. As such, solutions to both the mathematical model and the discrete equations should obey the principle of Galilean invariance, which states that the laws of physics are valid for all inertial reference frames. Inertial reference frames are allowed to undergo linear translation, but not acceleration or rotation. Two common Galilean invariance tests are to allow the coordinate system to move at a fixed linear velocity or to simply exchange the direction of the coordinate axes (e.g., instead of having a 2-D cantilevered beam extend in the x-direction and deflect in the y-direction, have it extend in the y-direction and deflect in the x-direction). In addition, for structured grid codes that employ a global transformation from physical space (x, y, z) to computational space (ξ, η, ζ), certain mistakes in the global mesh transformations can be found by simply re-running a problem with the computational coordinates reoriented in different directions; again this procedure should have no effect on the final numerical solution.

5.1.2 Code-to-code comparisons

Code-to-code comparisons are among the most common approaches used to assess code correctness. A *code-to-code comparison* occurs when the output (numerical solution or system response quantity) from one code is compared to the output from another code. Following Trucano *et al.* (2003), code-to-code comparisons are only useful when (1) the two codes employ the same mathematical models and (2) the "reference" code has undergone rigorous code verification assessment or some other acceptable type of code verification. Even when these two conditions are met, code-to-code comparisons should be used with caution.

If the same models are not used in the two codes, then differences in the code output could be due to model differences and not coding mistakes. Likewise, agreement between the two codes could occur due to the serendipitous cancellation of errors due to coding mistakes and differences due to the model. A common mistake made while performing code-to-code comparisons with codes that employ different numerical schemes (i.e., discrete equations) is to assume that the codes should produce the same (or very similar) output for the same problem with the same spatial mesh and/or time step. On the contrary, the code outputs will only be the same if exactly the same algorithm is employed, and even subtle algorithm differences can produce different outputs for the same mesh and time step.

For the case where the reference code has not itself been verified, agreement between the two codes *does not* imply correctness for either code. The fortuitous agreement (i.e., a false positive for the test) can occur due to the same algorithm deficiency being present in both codes. Even when the above two requirements have been met, "code comparisons do not provide substantive evidence that software is functioning correctly" (Trucano *et al.*, 2003). Thus code-to-code comparisons should not be used as a substitute for rigorous code verification assessments. See Trucano *et al.* (2003) for a more detailed discussion of the proper usage of code-to-code comparisons.

5.1.3 Discretization error evaluation

Discretization error evaluation is the traditional method for code verification that can be used when an exact solution to the mathematical model is available. This test involves the quantitative assessment of the error between the numerical solution (i.e., the code output) and an exact solution to the mathematical model using a single mesh and/or time step. The main drawback to this test is that once the discretization error has been evaluated, it requires a subjective judgment of whether or not the error is sufficiently small. See Chapter 6 for an extensive discussion of methods for obtaining exact solutions to the mathematical model.

5.1.4 Convergence tests

A *convergence test* is performed to assess whether the error in the discrete solution relative to the exact solution to the mathematical model (i.e., the discretization error) reduces as the mesh and time step are refined. (The formal definition of convergence will be given in Section 5.2.3.) As was the case for discretization error evaluation, the convergence test also requires an exact solution to the mathematical model. However, in this case, it is not just the magnitude of the discretization error that is assessed, but whether or not that error reduces with increasing mesh and time step refinement. The convergence test is the minimum criterion that should be used for rigorous code verification.

5.1.5 Order-of-accuracy tests

The most rigorous code verification criterion is the *order-of-accuracy test*, which examines not only the convergence of the numerical solution, but also whether or not the discretization error is reduced at the theoretical rate as the mesh and/or time step are refined. This theoretical rate is called the *formal order of accuracy* and it is usually found by performing a truncation error analysis of the numerical scheme (see Section 5.3.1). The actual rate at which the discretization error is reduced is called the *observed order of accuracy*, and its calculation requires two systematically refined meshes and/or time steps when the exact solution to the mathematical model is available. The procedures for computing the observed order of accuracy in such cases are presented in Section 5.3.2.

The order-of-accuracy test is the most difficult test to satisfy; therefore it is the most rigorous of the code verification criteria. It is extremely sensitive to even small mistakes in the code and deficiencies in the numerical algorithm. The order-of-accuracy test is the most reliable code verification criterion for finding coding mistakes and algorithm deficiencies which affect the order of accuracy of the computed solutions. Such order-of-accuracy problems can arise from many common coding mistakes including implementation of boundary conditions, transformations, operator splitting, etc. For these reasons, the order-of-accuracy test is the recommended criterion for code verification.

5.2 Definitions

The definitions presented in this section follow the standard definitions from the numerical analysis of partial differential and integral equations (e.g., Richtmyer and Morton, 1967). A firm grasp of these definitions is needed before moving on to the concepts behind the formal and observed order of accuracy used in the order-verification procedures.

5.2.1 Truncation error

The *truncation error* is the difference between the discretized equations and the original partial differential (or integral) equations. It is *not* the difference between a real number and its finite representation for storage in computer memory; this "digit truncation" is called *round-off error* and is discussed in Chapter 7. Truncation error necessarily occurs whenever a mathematical model is approximated by a discretization method. The form of the truncation error can usually be found by performing Taylor series expansions of the dependent variables and then inserting these expansions into the discrete equations. Recall the general Taylor series representation for the smooth function $u(x)$ expanded about the point x_0:

$$u(x) = u(x_0) + \frac{\partial u}{\partial x}\bigg|_{x_0} (x - x_0) + \frac{\partial^2 u}{\partial x^2}\bigg|_{x_0} \frac{(x - x_0)^2}{2} + \frac{\partial^3 u}{\partial x^3}\bigg|_{x_0} \frac{(x - x_0)^3}{6} + O\left[(x - x_0)^4\right],$$

where the $O[(x - x_0)^4]$ term denotes that the leading term that is omitted is on the order of $(x - x_0)$ to the fourth power. This expansion can be represented more compactly as:

$$u(x) = \sum_{k=0}^{\infty} \frac{\partial^k u}{\partial x^k}\bigg|_{x_0} \frac{(x - x_0)^k}{k!}.$$

5.2.1.1 Example: truncation error analysis

For a simple example of truncation error analysis, consider the following mathematical model for the 1-D unsteady heat equation:

$$\frac{\partial T}{\partial t} - \alpha \frac{\partial^2 T}{\partial x^2} = 0, \tag{5.6}$$

where the first term is the unsteady contribution and the second term represents thermal diffusion with a constant diffusivity α. Let $L(T)$ represent this partial differential operator and let $\tilde{T}$ be the exact solution to this mathematical model assuming appropriate initial and boundary conditions. Thus we have

$$L(\tilde{T}) = 0. \tag{5.7}$$

For completeness, this mathematical model operator $L(\cdot)$ should be formulated as a vector containing the partial differential equation along with appropriate initial and boundary conditions. For simplicity, we will omit the initial and boundary conditions from the following discussion.

Equation (5.6) can be discretized with a finite difference method using a forward difference in time and a centered second difference in space, resulting in the simple explicit numerical scheme

$$\frac{T_i^{n+1} - T_i^n}{\Delta t} - \alpha \frac{T_{i+1}^n - 2T_i^n + T_{i-1}^n}{(\Delta x)^2} = 0, \tag{5.8}$$

where the i subscripts denote spatial location, the n superscripts denote the temporal step, Δx is the constant spatial distance between nodes, and Δt is the time step. We can represent this discrete equation compactly using the discrete operator $L_h(T)$ which is solved exactly by the numerical solution T_h, i.e., we have

$$L_h(T_h) = 0. \tag{5.9}$$

The variable h is a single parameter that is used to denote systematic mesh refinement, i.e., refinement over the entire spatial domain, in all spatial coordinate directions, and in time (for unsteady problems). For the current example, this parameter is given by

$$h = \frac{\Delta x}{\Delta x_{\text{ref}}} = \frac{\Delta t}{\Delta t_{\text{ref}}}, \tag{5.10}$$

where Δx_{ref} and Δt_{ref} refer to some arbitrary reference spatial node spacing and time step, respectively. Later, the h parameter will be extended to consider different refinement ratios in time and even in the different coordinate directions. For the current purposes, the important point is that when h goes to zero, it implies that Δx and Δt also go to zero at the same rate. Note that, for this finite difference discretization, T_h represents a vector of temperature values defined at each node and time step.

In order to find the truncation error for the numerical scheme given in Eq. (5.8), we can expand the above temperature values in a Taylor series about the temperature at spatial location i and time step n (assuming sufficient differentiability of T):

$$T_i^{n+1} = T_i^n + \left.\frac{\partial T}{\partial t}\right|_i^n \frac{\Delta t}{1!} + \left.\frac{\partial^2 T}{\partial t^2}\right|_i^n \frac{(\Delta t)^2}{2!} + \left.\frac{\partial^3 T}{\partial t^3}\right|_i^n \frac{(\Delta t)^3}{3!} + O\left(\Delta t^4\right),$$

$$T_{i+1}^n = T_i^n + \left.\frac{\partial T}{\partial x}\right|_i^n \frac{\Delta x}{1!} + \left.\frac{\partial^2 T}{\partial x^2}\right|_i^n \frac{(\Delta x)^2}{2!} + \left.\frac{\partial^3 T}{\partial x^3}\right|_i^n \frac{(\Delta x)^3}{3!} + O\left(\Delta x^4\right),$$

$$T_{i-1}^n = T_i^n + \left.\frac{\partial T}{\partial x}\right|_i^n \frac{(-\Delta x)}{1!} + \left.\frac{\partial^2 T}{\partial x^2}\right|_i^n \frac{(-\Delta x)^2}{2!} + \left.\frac{\partial^3 T}{\partial x^3}\right|_i^n \frac{(-\Delta x)^3}{3!} + O\left(\Delta x^4\right).$$

Substituting these expressions into the discrete equation and rearranging yields

$$\underbrace{\frac{T_i^{n+1} - T_i^n}{\Delta t} - \alpha \frac{T_{i+1}^n - 2T_i^n + T_{i-1}^n}{(\Delta x)^2}}_{L_h(T)}$$

$$= \underbrace{\frac{\partial T}{\partial t} - \alpha \frac{\partial^2 T}{\partial x^2}}_{L(T)} + \underbrace{\left[\frac{1}{2}\frac{\partial^2 T}{\partial t^2}\right]\Delta t + \left[-\frac{\alpha}{12}\frac{\partial^4 T}{\partial x^4}\right](\Delta x)^2 + O\left(\Delta t^2, \Delta x^4\right)}_{\text{truncation error: } TE_h(T)}. \quad (5.11)$$

Thus we have the general relationship that the discrete equation equals the mathematical model plus the truncation error. In order for this equality to make sense, it is implied that either (1) the continuous derivatives in $L(T)$ and $TE_h(T)$ are restricted to the nodal points or (2) the discrete operator $L_h(T)$ is mapped onto a continuous space.

5.2.1.2 Generalized truncation error expression (GTEE)

Using the operator notation discussed earlier and substituting in the generic (sufficiently smooth) dependent variable u into Eq. (5.11) yields

$$L_h(u) = L(u) + TE_h(u), \quad (5.12)$$

where we again assume an appropriate mapping of the operators onto either a continuous or discrete space. We refer to Eq. (5.12) as the *generalized truncation error expression (GTEE)* and it is used extensively in this chapter as well as in Chapters 8 and 9. It relates the discrete equations to the mathematical model in a very general manner and is one of the most important equations in the evaluation, estimation, and reduction of discretization errors in scientific computing. When set to zero, the right hand side of the GTEE can be thought of as the actual mathematical model that is solved by the discretization scheme $L_h(u_h) = 0$. The GTEE is the starting point for determining the *consistency* and the *formal order of accuracy* of the numerical method. While the GTEE can be derived even for nonlinear mathematical models, for linear (or linearized) mathematical models, it also explicitly shows the relationship between the truncation error and the discretization error. As will be shown in Chapter 8, the GTEE can also be used to provide estimates of the truncation error. Finally, this equation provides a general relationship between the discrete equation and the (possibly nonlinear) mathematical model since we have not specified what the function u is, only that it satisfies certain differentiability constraints. It is relatively straightforward (although somewhat tedious) to show that the general polynomial function

$$u(x, t) = \sum_{i=0}^{N_x} a_i x^i + \sum_{j=0}^{N_t} b_j t^j$$

will satisfy Eq. (5.12) exactly for the example problem of 1-D unsteady heat conduction given above (hint: choose N_x and N_t small enough such that the higher-order terms are zero).

Most authors (e.g., Richtmyer and Morton, 1967; Ferziger and Peric, 2002) formally define the truncation error only when the exact solution to the mathematical model is inserted into Eq. (5.12), thus resulting in

$$L_h(\tilde{u}) = TE_h(\tilde{u}) \tag{5.13}$$

since $L(\tilde{u}) = 0$. For our specific finite difference example for the 1D unsteady heat equation given above, we have

$$\frac{\tilde{T}_i^{n+1} - \tilde{T}_i^n}{\Delta t} - \alpha \frac{\tilde{T}_{i+1}^n - 2\tilde{T}_i^n + \tilde{T}_{i-1}^n}{(\Delta x)^2}$$

$$= \left[\frac{1}{2} \frac{\partial^2 \tilde{T}}{\partial t^2} \right] \Delta t + \left[-\frac{\alpha}{12} \frac{\partial^4 \tilde{T}}{\partial x^4} \right] (\Delta x)^2 + O\left(\Delta t^2, \Delta x^4 \right) = TE_h\left(\tilde{T} \right), \tag{5.14}$$

where the notation $\tilde{T}_i^n$ implies that the exact solution is restricted to spatial location i and temporal location n. For the purposes of this book, we will employ the GTEE found from Eq. (5.12) since it will provide more flexibility in how the truncation error is used.

5.2.2 Discretization error

Discretization error is formally defined as the difference between the exact solution to the discrete equations and the exact solution to the mathematical model. Using our earlier notation, we can thus write the discretization error for the general dependent variable u as

$$\varepsilon_h = u_h - \tilde{u}, \tag{5.15}$$

where again the h subscript denotes the exact solution to the discrete equations and the overtilde denotes the exact solution to the mathematical model.

5.2.3 Consistency

For a numerical scheme to be *consistent*, the discretized equations $L_h(\cdot)$ must approach the mathematical model equations $L(\cdot)$ in the limit as the discretization parameters (Δx, Δy, Δz, Δt, denoted collectively by the parameter h) approach zero. In terms of the truncation error discussion above, a consistent numerical scheme can be defined as one in which the truncation error vanishes in the limit as $h \to 0$. Not all numerical schemes are consistent, and one notable example is the DuFort–Frankel finite difference method applied to the unsteady heat conduction equation, which has a leading truncation error term proportional to $(\Delta t/\Delta x)^2$ (Tannehill *et al.*, 1997). This scheme is only consistent under the restriction that Δt approach zero at a faster rate than Δx.

5.2.4 Stability

For initial value (i.e., hyperbolic and parabolic) problems, a discretization scheme is said to be *stable* if numerical errors do not grow unbounded in the marching direction. The numerical errors are typically considered to come from computer round-off (Ferziger and Peric, 2002), but in fact can come from any source. The idea of numerical stability originally derives from initial value problems for hyperbolic and parabolic partial differential equations (Crank and Nicolson, 1947), but the concepts can also be applied to relaxation methods for elliptic problems (e.g., see Hirsch, 2007). It is important to note that the concept of numerical stability applies only to the discrete equations (Hirsch, 2007), and should not be confused with natural instabilities that can arise in the mathematical model itself.

Most approaches for analyzing numerical stability apply only to linear partial differential equations with constant coefficients. The most popular approach for determining stability is von Neumann stability analysis (Hirsch, 2007). Also referred to as Fourier stability analysis, von Neumann's method employs a Fourier decomposition of the numerical error and neglects the boundary conditions by assuming these error components are periodic. The fact that von Neumann's method neglects the boundary conditions is not overly restrictive in practice and results in a fairly straightforward stability analysis (e.g., see Richtmyer and Morton, 1967; Hirsch, 2007). However, the restriction to linear differential equations with constant coefficients is significant. Time and time again, we will find that many of our tools for analyzing the behavior of numerical schemes are only applicable to linear equations. We are thus left in the uncomfortable situation of hoping that we can simply extend the results of these methods to the complicated, nonlinear mathematical models of interest, and this fact should not be forgotten. As a practical matter when dealing with nonlinear problems, a stability analysis should be performed for the linearized problem to provide initial guidance on the stability limits; then numerical tests should be performed to confirm the stability restrictions for the nonlinear problem.

5.2.5 Convergence

Convergence addresses whether or not the exact solution to the discrete equations approaches the exact solution to the mathematical model in the limit of decreasing mesh spacing and time step size. Whereas convergence and consistency both address the limiting behavior of the discrete method relative to the mathematical model, convergence deals with the solution while consistency deals with the equations. This definition of convergence should not be confused with convergence of an iterative method (see Chapter 7), which we will refer to as iterative convergence.

For marching problems, convergence is determined by Lax's equivalence theorem, which is again valid only for linear equations. Lax's theorem states that, given a well-posed initial value problem and a consistent numerical scheme, stability is the necessary and sufficient condition for convergence (Richtmyer and Morton, 1967). When used for code verification purposes, convergence is demonstrated by examining the actual behavior of the discretization error ε_h as $h \to 0$.

Recent work with finite volume methods (Despres, 2004) suggests that some modifications to (or perhaps clarifications of) Lax's equivalence theorem may be needed. In his work, Despres claims that the finite volume method is formally inconsistent for 2-D triangular meshes, but found it to be convergent assuming certain solution regularity constraints. It is interesting to note that while Despres does provide theoretical developments, numerical examples are not included. Given the work of Despres (2004) and the references cited therein, it is possible that Lax's theorem should be augmented with the additional assumption of systematic mesh refinement (discussed in Section 5.4) along with mesh topology restrictions. Additional work is required to understand these mesh quality and topology issues as they relate to the consistency and convergence of discretization schemes.

5.3 Order of accuracy

The term *order of accuracy* refers to the rate at which the discrete solution approaches the exact solution to the mathematical model in the limit as the discretization parameters go to zero. The order of accuracy can be addressed in either a theoretical sense (i.e., the order of accuracy of a given numerical scheme assuming it has been implemented correctly) or in a more empirical manner (i.e., the actual order of accuracy of discrete solutions). The former is called the *formal order of accuracy*, while the latter is the *observed order of accuracy*. These two terms are discussed in detail below.

5.3.1 Formal order of accuracy

The *formal order of accuracy* is the theoretical rate of convergence of the discrete solution u_h to the exact solution to the mathematical model $\tilde{u}$. This theoretical rate is defined only in an asymptotic sense as the discretization parameters (Δx, Δy, Δt, etc., currently represented by the single parameter h) go to zero in a systematic manner. It will be shown next that the formal order of accuracy can be related back to the truncation error; however, we are limited to linear (or linearized) equations to show this relationship.

The key relationship between the discrete equation and the mathematical model is the GTEE given by Eq. (5.12), which is repeated here for convenience:

$$L_h(u) = L(u) + TE_h(u). \qquad (5.12)$$

Inserting the exact solution to the discrete equation u_h into Eq. (5.12), then subtracting the original mathematical model equation $L(\tilde{u}) = 0$, yields

$$L(u_h) - L(\tilde{u}) + TE_h(u_h) = 0.$$

If the mathematical operator $L(\cdot)$ is linear (or linearized), then $L(u_h) - L(\tilde{u}) = L(u_h - \tilde{u})$. The difference between the discrete solution u_h and the exact solution to the mathematical model $\tilde{u}$ is simply the discretization error ε_h defined by Eq. (5.15), thus we find that the discretization error and the truncation error are related by

$$L(\varepsilon_h) = -TE_h(u_h). \tag{5.16}$$

Equation (5.16) governs the transport of the discretization error and is called the *continuous discretization error transport equation* since it employs the continuous mathematical operator (Roy, 2009). According to this equation, the discretization error is propagated in the same manner as the original solution u. For example, if the original mathematical model contains terms governing the convection and diffusion of u, then the discretization error ε_h will also be convected and diffused. More importantly in the context of our present discussion, Eq. (5.16) also shows that the truncation error serves as the local source for the discretization error (Ferziger and Peric, 2002); thus the rate of reduction of the local truncation error with mesh refinement will produce corresponding reductions in the discretization error. Applying this continuous error transport equation to the 1-D unsteady heat conduction example from Section 5.2.1 results in:

$$\frac{\partial \varepsilon_h}{\partial t} - \alpha \frac{\partial^2 \varepsilon_h}{\partial x^2} = -\left[\frac{1}{2} \frac{\partial^2 T_h}{\partial t^2} \right] \Delta t - \left[-\frac{\alpha}{12} \frac{\partial^4 T_h}{\partial x^4} \right] (\Delta x)^2 + O\left(\Delta t^2, \Delta x^4 \right).$$

Having tied the rate of reduction of the discretization error to the truncation error, we are now in the position to define the formal order of accuracy of a numerical scheme as the smallest exponent which acts upon a discretization parameter in the truncation error, since this will dominate the limiting behavior as $h \to 0$. For problems in space and time, it is sometimes helpful to refer to the formal order of accuracy in time separately from the formal order of accuracy in space. For the 1-D unsteady heat conduction example above, the simple explicit finite difference discretization is formally first-order accurate in time and second-order accurate in space. While it is not uncommon to use different order-of-accuracy discretizations for different terms in the equations (e.g., third-order convection and second-order diffusion), the formal order of accuracy of such a mixed-order scheme is simply equal to the lowest order accurate discretization employed.

The truncation error can usually be derived for even complicated, nonlinear discretization methods (e.g., see Grinstein *et al.*, 2007). For cases where the formal order of accuracy has not been determined from a truncation error analysis, there are three approaches that can be used to estimate the formal order of accuracy (note that Knupp (2009) refers to this as the "expected" order of accuracy). The first approach is to approximate the truncation error by inserting the exact solution to the mathematical model into the discrete equations.

Since the exact solution to the mathematical model will not satisfy the discrete equation, the remainder (i.e., the discrete residual) will approximate the truncation error as shown in Eq. (5.13). By evaluating the discrete residual on successively finer meshes (i.e., as $h \to 0$), the rate of reduction of the truncation error can be estimated, thus producing the formal order of accuracy of the discretization scheme (assuming no coding mistakes are present). This first approach is called the residual method and is discussed in detail in Section 5.5.6.1. The second approach is to compute the observed order of accuracy for a series of meshes as $h \to 0$, and this approach is addressed in the next section. In this case, if the observed order of accuracy is found to be two, then one is safe to assume that the formal order of accuracy is *at least* second order. The final approach is to simply assume the expected order of accuracy from the quadrature employed in the discretization. For example, a linear basis function used with the finite element method generally results in a second-order accurate scheme for the dependent variables, as does linear interpolation/extrapolation when used to determine the interfacial fluxes in the finite volume method (a process sometimes referred to as flux quadrature).

In the development of the truncation error, a certain degree of solution smoothness was assumed. As such, the formal order of accuracy can be reduced in the presence of discontinuities and singularities in the solution. For example, the observed order of accuracy for inviscid gas dynamics problems containing shock waves has been shown to reduce to first order for a wide range of numerical discretization approaches (e.g., Engquist and Sjogreen, 1998; Carpenter and Casper, 1999; Roy, 2003; Banks *et al.*, 2008), regardless of the formal order of accuracy of the scheme on smooth problems. Furthermore, for linear discontinuities (e.g., contact discontinuities and slip lines in inviscid gas dynamics), the formal order generally reduces to $p/(p + 1)$ (i.e., below one) for methods which have a formal order p for smooth problems (Banks *et al.*, 2008). In some situations, the formal order of accuracy of a numerical method may be difficult to determine since it depends on the nature and strength of the discontinuities/singularities present in the solution.

5.3.2 Observed order of accuracy

As discussed above, the *observed order of accuracy* is the actual order of accuracy obtained on a series of systematically-refined meshes. For now, we only consider the case where the exact solution to the mathematical model is known. For this case, the discretization error can be evaluated exactly (or at least within round-off and iterative error) and only two mesh levels are required to compute the observed order of accuracy. The more difficult case of computing the observed order of accuracy when the exact solution to the mathematical model is not known is deferred to Chapter 8.

Consider a series expansion of the solution to the discrete equations u_h in terms of the mesh spacing h in the limit as $h \to 0$:

$$u_h = u_{h=0} + \left.\frac{\partial u}{\partial h}\right|_{h=0} h + \left.\frac{\partial^2 u}{\partial h^2}\right|_{h=0} \frac{h^2}{2} + \left.\frac{\partial^3 u}{\partial h^3}\right|_{h=0} \frac{h^3}{6} + O(h^4). \qquad (5.17)$$

If a convergent numerical scheme is employed (i.e., if it is consistent and stable), then we have $u_{h=0} = \tilde{u}$. Furthermore, for a formally second-order accurate scheme, by definition we will have $\frac{\partial u}{\partial h}\big|_{h=0} = 0$ since terms of order h do not appear in the truncation error (recall Eq. (5.16)). Employing the definition of the discretization error from Eq. (5.15) we find that for a general second-order accurate numerical scheme

$$\varepsilon_h = g_2 h^2 + O(h^3), \tag{5.18}$$

where the coefficient $g_2 = g_2(x, y, z, t)$ only and is thus independent of h (Ferziger and Peric, 2002). Note that for discretizations that exclusively employ second-order accurate central-type differencing, the truncation error only contains even powers of h, and thus the higher order terms in Eq. (5.18) would be $O(h^4)$. For a more general pth-order accurate scheme, we have

$$\varepsilon_h = g_p h^p + O(h^{p+1}) \tag{5.19}$$

unless again central-type differencing is used, whereupon the higher order terms will be $O(h^{p+2})$.

Equation (5.19) provides an appropriate theoretical starting point for computing the observed order of accuracy. In the limit as $h \to 0$, the higher-order terms in Eq. (5.19) will become small relative to the leading term and can be neglected. Consider now two discrete solutions, one computed on a fine mesh with spacing h and another computed on a coarse mesh with spacing $2h$ found by eliminating every other cell or node from the fine mesh. Neglecting the higher-order terms (whether they are small or not), Eq. (5.19) can be written for the two solutions as

$$\varepsilon_{2h} = g_p (2h)^{\hat{p}},$$

$$\varepsilon_h = g_p h^{\hat{p}}.$$

Dividing the first equation by the second one, then taking the natural log, we can solve for the observed order of accuracy to give

$$\hat{p} = \frac{\ln\left(\frac{\varepsilon_{2h}}{\varepsilon_h}\right)}{\ln(2)}. \tag{5.20}$$

Here the "^" is used to differentiate this *observed order of accuracy* from the formal order of accuracy of the method. The observed order can be computed regardless of whether or not the higher-order terms in Eq. (5.19) are small; however, this observed order of accuracy $\hat{p}$ will only match the formal order of accuracy when the higher-order terms are in fact small, i.e., in the limiting sense as $h \to 0$.

A more general expression for the observed order of accuracy can be found that applies to meshes that are systematically refined by an arbitrary factor. Introducing the grid refinement factor r which is defined as the ratio of coarse to fine grid mesh spacing,

$$r \equiv \frac{h_{\text{coarse}}}{h_{\text{fine}}}, \tag{5.21}$$

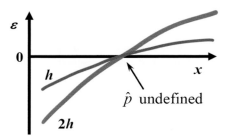

Figure 5.1 Qualitative plot of local discretization error on a coarse mesh (*2h*) and a fine mesh (*h*) showing that the observed order of accuracy from Eq. (5.20) can be undefined when examined locally.

where we require $r > 1$, the discretization error expansion for the two mesh levels becomes

$$\varepsilon_{rh} = g_p \, (rh)^{\hat{p}} \, ,$$

$$\varepsilon_h = g_p h^{\hat{p}}.$$

Again dividing the first equation by the second and taking the natural log, we find the more general expression for the observed order of accuracy

$$\hat{p} = \frac{\ln\left(\frac{\varepsilon_{rh}}{\varepsilon_h}\right)}{\ln(r)}. \tag{5.22}$$

At this point, it is important to mention that the exact solution to the discretized equations u_h is generally unknown due to the presence of round-off and iterative convergence errors in the numerical solutions. While round-off and iterative errors are discussed in detail in Chapter 7, their impact on the observed order of accuracy will be addressed in Section 5.3.2.2.

   The observed order of accuracy can be evaluated using the discretization error in the dependent variables, norms of those errors, or the discretization error in any quantities that can be derived from the solution. When applied to norms of the discretization error, the relationship for the observed order of accuracy becomes

$$\hat{p} = \frac{\ln\left(\frac{\|\varepsilon_{rh}\|}{\|\varepsilon_h\|}\right)}{\ln(r),} \tag{5.23}$$

where any of the norms discussed in Section 5.1 can be used. Care must be taken when computing the observed order of accuracy locally since unrealistic orders can be produced. For example, when the discrete solutions approach the exact solution to the mathematical model from below in some region and from above in another, the observed order of accuracy will be undefined at the crossover point. Figure 5.1 gives an example of just such a case and shows the discretization error versus a spatial coordinate *x*. Applying Eq. (5.22) would likely produce $\hat{p} \approx 1$ almost everywhere except at the crossover point, where if $\varepsilon_h = \varepsilon_{2h} = 0$, the observed order of accuracy from Eq. (5.22) is undefined (Potter *et al.*,

2005). For this reason, global quantities are recommended rather than local quantities for code verification purposes.

The observed order of accuracy can fail to match the nominal formal order due to mistakes in the computer code, discrete solutions which are not in the asymptotic range (i.e., when the higher-order terms in the truncation error are not small), and the presence of round-off and iterative error. The latter two issues are discussed in the following sections.

5.3.2.1 Asymptotic range

The *asymptotic range* is defined as the range of discretization sizes (Δx, Δy, Δt, etc., denoted here collectively by the parameter h) where the lowest-order terms in the truncation error and discretization error expansions dominate. It is only in the asymptotic range that the limiting behavior of these errors can be observed. For code verification purposes, the order of accuracy test will only be successful when the solutions are in this asymptotic range. In our experience, the *asymptotic range is surprisingly difficult to identify and achieve* for all but the simplest scientific computing applications. Even an experienced code user with a good intuition on the mesh resolution required to obtain a "good" solution will generally underestimate the resolution required to obtain the asymptotic range. As we shall see later in Chapter 8, all approaches for estimating discretization error also rely on the solution(s) being asymptotic.

5.3.2.2 Effects of iterative and round-off error

Recall that the underlying theory used to develop the general observed order-of-accuracy expression given in Eq. (5.22) made use of the exact solution to the discrete equation u_h. In practice, u_h is only known within some tolerance determined by the number of digits used in the computations (i.e., round-off error) and the criterion used for iterative convergence. The discrete equations can generally be iteratively solved to within machine round-off error; however, in practice, the iterative procedure is usually terminated earlier to reduce computational effort. Round-off and iterative error are discussed in detail in Chapter 7. To ensure that the computed solutions are accurate approximations of the exact solution to the discrete equations u_h, both round-off and iterative error should be at least 100 times smaller than the discretization error on the finest mesh employed (i.e., $\leq 0.01 \times \varepsilon_h$) (Roy, 2005).

5.4 Systematic mesh refinement

Up to this point, the asymptotic behavior of the truncation and discretization error (and thus the formal and observed orders of accuracy) has been addressed by the somewhat vague notion of taking the limit as the discretization parameters (Δx, Δy, Δt, etc.) go to zero. For time-dependent problems, refinement in time is straightforward since the time step is fixed over the spatial domain and can be coarsened or refined by an arbitrary factor, subject of course to stability constraints. For problems involving the discretization of a spatial domain, the refinement process is more challenging since the spatial mesh resolution and quality can vary significantly over the domain depending on the geometric complexity. In this section, we introduce the concept of systematic mesh refinement which requires uniformity of the refinement over the spatial domain and consistency of the refinement as $h \to 0$. These two requirements are discussed in detail, as well as additional issues related to the use of local and/or global mesh transformations and mesh topology.

5.4.1 Uniform mesh refinement

Local refinement of the mesh in selected regions of interest, while often useful for reducing the discretization error, is not appropriate for assessing the asymptotic behavior of discrete solutions. The reason is that the series expansion for the discretization error given in Eq. (5.17) is in terms of a single parameter h which is assumed to apply over the entire domain. When the mesh is refined locally in one region but not in another, then the refinement can no longer be described by a single parameter. This same concept holds for mesh refinement in only one coordinate direction, which requires special procedures when used for evaluating the observed order of accuracy (see Section 5.5.3) or for estimating the discretization error. The requirement that the mesh refinement be uniform is not the same as requiring that the mesh itself be uniform, only that it be refined in a uniform manner. Note that this requirement of uniform refinement is not restricted to integer refinement factors between meshes. Assuming that a coarse and fine mesh are related through *uniform refinement*, the grid refinement factor can be computed as

$$r_{12} = \left(\frac{N_1}{N_2} \right)^{1/d}, \tag{5.24}$$

where N_1 and N_2 are the number of nodes/cells/elements on the fine and coarse meshes, respectively, and d is the number of spatial dimensions.

An example of uniform and nonuniform mesh refinement is presented in Figure 5.2. The initial coarse mesh (Figure 5.2a) has 4×4 cells, and when this mesh is refined by a factor of two in each direction, the resulting uniformly refined mesh (Figure 5.2b) has 8×8 cells. The mesh shown in Figure 5.2c also has 8×8 cells, but has selectively refined to the x-axis and in the middle of the two bounding arcs. While the average cell length scale is refined by a factor of two, the local cell length scale varies over the domain, thus this mesh has not been uniformly refined.

5.4.2 Consistent mesh refinement

In general, one should not expect to obtain convergent solutions with mesh refinement when poor quality meshes are used. This is certainly true for the extreme example of a mesh with degenerate cells, such as those involving mesh crossover (see Figure 5.3), that persist with uniform refinement. We now introduce the concept of *consistent mesh refinement* which requires that mesh quality must either stay constant or improve in the limit as $h \to 0$.

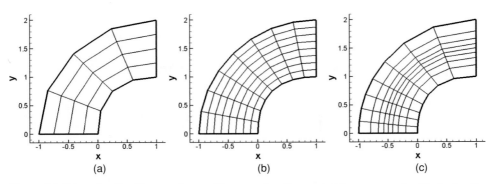

Figure 5.2 Example of uniform and nonuniform mesh refinement: (a) coarse mesh with 4×4 cells, (b) uniformly refined mesh with 8×8 cells, and (c) nonuniformly refined mesh with 8×8 cells.

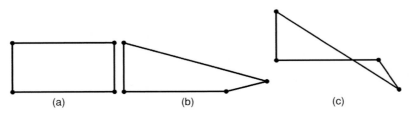

Figure 5.3 Example of a degenerate cell due to mesh crossover: (a) initial quadrilateral cell, (b) intermediate skewing of the cell, and (c) final skewing resulting in mesh crossover.

Examples of mesh quality metrics include cell aspect ratio, skewness, and stretching rate (i.e., the rate at which the mesh transitions from coarse to fine spacing).

To further illustrate the concept of consistent mesh refinement, consider the simple 2-D triangular mesh over the square domain given in Figure 5.4a. While this initial coarse mesh certainly has poor quality, it is the approach used for refining this mesh that will determine the consistency. Consider now three cases where this initial coarse mesh is uniformly refined. In the first case, the midpoints of each edge are connected so that each coarse mesh cell is decomposed into four finer cells with similar shape, as shown in Figure 5.4b. Clearly, if this refinement procedure is performed repeatedly, then in the limit as $h \to 0$ even very fine meshes will retain the same mesh qualities related to cell skewness, cell volume variation, and cell stretching (i.e., the change in cell size from one region to another). Another refinement approach might allow for different connectivity of the cells and also provide more flexibility in choosing new node locations (i.e., not necessarily at edge midpoints) as shown in Figure 5.4c. As this refinement approach is applied in the limit as $h \to 0$, the mesh quality will generally improve. A third refinement strategy might employ arbitrary edge node placement while not allowing changes in the cell-to-cell connectivity (Figure 5.4d). Considering Figure 5.4, refinement strategy (b) employs fixed quality meshes and strategy (c) employs meshes with improving quality as $h \to 0$, thus both are considered

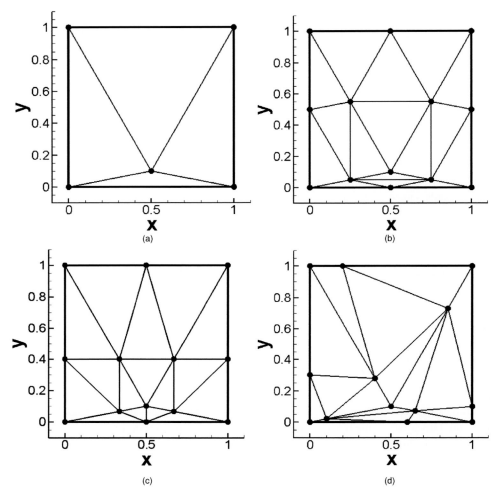

Figure 5.4 Example showing consistent and inconsistent mesh refinement: (a) poor quality coarse mesh with four unstructured triangular cells, (b) uniformly refined mesh that retains a fixed mesh quality, (c) uniformly refined mesh with improved mesh quality, and (d) uniformly refined mesh with inconsistent refinement.

consistent. Strategy (d) is an inconsistent mesh refinement approach since the quality of the mesh degrades with refinement.

Borrowing concepts from Knupp (2003), we assume the existence of a global mesh quality metric σ which varies between 0 and 1, with $\sigma = 1$ denoting an isotropic mesh, i.e., one with "ideal" mesh quality (square quadrilaterals, cubic hexahedrals, equilateral triangles, etc.). Smaller values of σ would denote anisotropic meshes with lower quality (skewness, stretching, curvature, etc). Consistent mesh refinement can thus be defined by requiring that $\sigma_{\text{fine}} \geq \sigma_{\text{coarse}}$ during refinement. Consistent refinement with $\sigma \to 1$ as $h \to 0$

can place significant burdens on the mesh generation and refinement procedure (especially for unstructured meshes), but provides the easiest criteria for discretization schemes to satisfy since meshes become more isotropic with refinement (e.g., they become Cartesian for quadrilateral and hexahedral meshes). A more difficult mesh quality requirement to satisfy from the code verification point of view is to require convergence of the numerical solutions for meshes with a fixed quality measure σ as $h \to 0$. Such nuances relating the numerical scheme behavior to the mesh quality fall under the heading of solution verification and are addressed in more detail in Chapters 8 and 9. For code verification purposes, it is important to document the asymptotic behavior of the quality of the meshes used for the code verification study.

5.4.3 Mesh transformations

Inherent in some discretization methods is an assumption that the mesh employs uniform spacing (i.e., Δx, Δy, and Δz are constant). When applied blindly to the cases with nonuniform meshes, schemes that are formally second-order accurate on uniform meshes will often reduce to first-order accuracy on nonuniform meshes. While Ferziger and Peric (1996) argue that these first-order errors will either be limited to small fractions of the domain or even vanish as the mesh is refined, this may result in extremely fine meshes to obtain the asymptotic range. The key point is that additional discretization errors will be introduced by nonuniform meshes.

In order to mitigate these additional errors, mesh transformations are sometimes used to handle complex geometries and to allow local mesh refinement. For discretization methods employing body-fitted structured (i.e., curvilinear) meshes, these transformations often take the form of global transformations of the governing equations. For finite-volume and finite-element methods on structured or unstructured meshes, these transformations usually take the form of local mesh transformations centered about each cell or element. An example of a global transformation for a body-fitted structured grid in 2-D is presented in Figure 5.5. The transformation must ensure a one-to-one mapping between the grid line intersections in physical space (a) and those in computational coordinates (b).

Consider the 2-D steady transformation from physical space (x, y) to a uniform computational space (ξ, η) given by:

$$\xi = \xi(x, y),$$
$$\eta = \eta(x, y). \tag{5.25}$$

Using the chain rule, it can be shown that derivatives in physical space can be converted to derivatives in the uniform computational space (Thompson *et al.*, 1985), e.g.,

$$\frac{\partial u}{\partial x} = \frac{y_\eta}{J} \frac{\partial u}{\partial \xi} - \frac{y_\xi}{J} \frac{\partial u}{\partial \eta}, \tag{5.26}$$

where y_η and y_ξ are metrics of the transformation and J is the Jacobian of the transformation defined as $J = x_\xi y_\eta - x_\eta y_\xi$. The accuracy of the discrete approximation of the solution

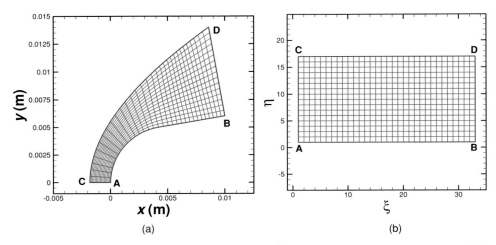

Figure 5.5 Example of a global transformation of a 2-D body-fitted structured mesh: (a) mesh in physical (x, y) coordinates and (b) mesh in the transformed computational (ξ, η) coordinates.

derivatives will depend on the chosen discretization scheme, the mesh resolution, the mesh quality, and the solution behavior (Roy, 2009).

The transformation itself can either be analytic or discrete in nature. Thompson *et al.* (1985) point out that using the same discrete approximation for the metrics that is used for solution derivatives can often result in smaller numerical errors compared to the case where purely analytic metrics are used. This surprising result occurs due to error cancellation and can be easily shown by examining the truncation error of the first derivative in one dimension (Mastin, 1999). As an example of a discrete approximation of the metrics, consider the metric term x_ξ which can be approximated using central differences to second-order accuracy as

$$x_\xi = \frac{x_{i+1} - x_{i-1}}{2\Delta\xi} + O(\Delta\xi^2).$$

When discrete transformations are used, they should be of the same order as, or possibly higher-order than, the underlying discretization scheme to ensure that the formal order of accuracy is not reduced. While mistakes in the discrete transformations can adversely impact the numerical solutions, these mistakes can be detected during the code verification process assuming sufficiently general mesh topologies are employed.

5.4.4 Mesh topology issues

There are many different mesh topologies that can be used in scientific computing. When conducting code verification studies, it is recommended that the most general mesh topology that will be employed for solving the problems of interest be used for the code verification studies. For example, if simulations will only be performed on Cartesian meshes, then

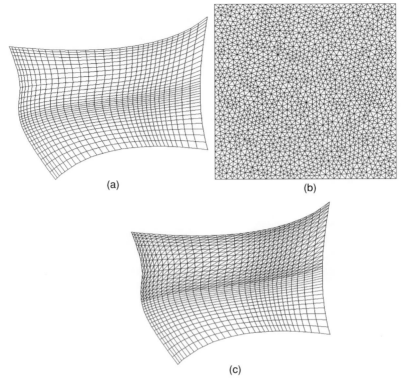

Figure 5.6 Example mesh topologies in 2-D: (a) structured curvilinear, (b) unstructured triangles, and (c) hybrid structured/unstructured curvilinear (adapted from Veluri *et al.*, 2008).

it is sufficient to conduct the code verification studies on Cartesian meshes. However, if simulations will be performed on non-isotropic (i.e., nonideal) meshes consisting of a combination of hexahedral, prismatic, and tetrahedral cells, then those mesh topologies should be used during code verification.

Meshes in 1-D consist of an order set of nodes or cells that may either be uniformly or nonuniformly distributed. For 2-D meshes, the nodes/cells may either be structured quadrilaterals, unstructured triangles, unstructured polygons with an arbitrary number of sides, or some hybrid combination of these. Examples of a hierarchy of 2-D mesh topologies appropriate for code verification are given in Figure 5.6 (Veluri *et al.*, 2008).

In 3-D, structured meshes can either be Cartesian, stretched Cartesian, or curvilinear (i.e., body fitted). 3-D unstructured meshes can contain cells that are tetrahedral (four-side pyramids), pyramidal (five-sided pyramids), prismatic (any 2-D cell type extruded in the third direction), hexahedral, polyhedral, or hybrid combinations of these. An example of a general 3-D hybrid mesh topology that has been employed for performing code verification on a scientific computing code with general unstructured mesh capabilities is given in Figure 5.7. This mesh consists of hexahedral and prismatic triangular cells extruded from

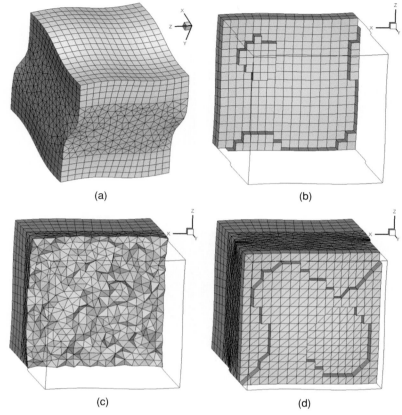

Figure 5.7 A general hybrid mesh topology in 3-D: (a) full 3-D mesh, (b) internal view showing hexahedral cells, (c) internal view showing tetrahedral cells, and (d) internal view showing prismatic cells.

the curved y_{min} and y_{max} boundaries joined together with a region of tetrahedral cells in the middle.

5.5 Order verification procedures

There are two books which deal with the subject of order-of-accuracy verification. Roache (1998) provides an overview of the subject, with emphasis on order verification using the method of manufactured solutions (discussed in Chapter 6). The book by Knupp and Salari (2003) is entirely dedicated to code order verification and is one of the most comprehensive references on the subject. Although Knupp and Salari prefer the terminology "code order verification," here we will simply use "order verification" to refer to order-of-accuracy verification of a scientific computing code. More recent reviews of order verification procedures are provided by Roy (2005) and Knupp *et al.* (2007).

Order verification entails a comparison between the limiting behavior of the observed order of accuracy and the formal order. Once an order verification test has been passed, then the code is considered verified for the code options (submodels, numerical algorithms, boundary conditions, etc.) exercised in the verification test. Any further order verification performed for those code options is simply considered confirmation of code correctness (Roache, 1998).

This section addresses the order verification procedures applicable for discretizations in space and/or time. These procedures can be invaluable for identifying the presence of coding mistakes (i.e., bugs) and problems with the numerical algorithms. Techniques are also discussed to aid in the debugging process once a coding mistake is found to exist. Limitations of the order verification procedure are then described, as well as different variants of the standard order verification procedure. This section concludes with a discussion of who bears the responsibility for code verification.

5.5.1 Spatial discretization

This section describes the order verification procedure for steady-state problems, i.e., those that do not have time as an independent variable. The order verification procedure discussed here is adapted from the procedure recommended by Knupp and Salari (2003). In brief, this procedure is used to determine whether or not the code output (numerical solution and other system response quantities) converges to the exact solution to the mathematical model at the formal rate with systematic mesh refinement. If the formal order of accuracy is observed in an asymptotic sense, then the code is considered verified for the coding options exercised. Failure to achieve the formal order of accuracy indicates the presence of a coding mistake or a problem with the numerical algorithm. The steps in the order verification procedure for steady-state problems are presented in Figure 5.8, and these steps are discussed in detail below.

1 Define mathematical model

The governing equations (i.e., the mathematical model) generally occur in partial differential or integral form and must be specified unambiguously along with any initial conditions, boundary conditions, and auxiliary equations. Small errors in defining the mathematical model can easily cause the order verification test to fail. For example, an error in the fourth significant digit of the thermal conductivity caused an order verification test to fail for a computational fluid dynamics code used to solve the Navier–Stokes equations (Roy *et al.*, 2007).

2 Choose numerical algorithm

A discretization scheme, or numerical algorithm, must be chosen. This includes both the general discretization approach (finite difference, finite volume, finite element, etc.) and the specific approaches to spatial quadrature. Discretization of any boundary or initial conditions involving spatial derivatives (e.g., Neumann-type boundary conditions) must

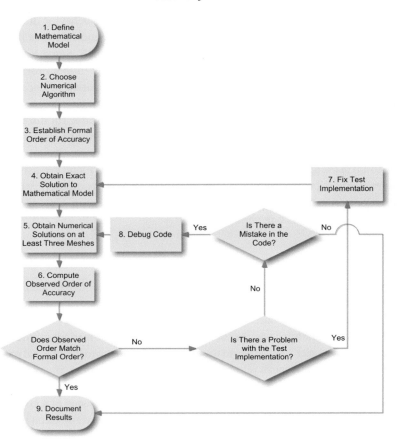

Figure 5.8 Flowchart showing the order verification procedure (adapted from Knupp and Salari, 2003).

also be considered. Note that different iterative solvers can be tested by simply starting the iterations with the final solution values from an iterative solver that has been used in the verification test, thus testing alternative iterative solvers does not require additional code verification tests (Roache, 1998).

3 Establish formal order of accuracy

The formal order of accuracy of the numerical scheme should be established, ideally by an analysis of the truncation error. As discussed in Section 5.3.1, for cases where a truncation error analysis is not available, either the residual method (Section 5.5.6.1), the order verification procedure itself (i.e., the observed order of accuracy), or the expected order of accuracy can be substituted.

4 Obtain exact solution to mathematical model

The exact solution to the mathematical model must be obtained, including both the solution (i.e., the dependent variables) and the system response quantities. New exact solutions are needed any time the governing equations are changed (e.g., when a new model is examined). The same exact solution can be reused if the only changes in the code relate to the numerical scheme (e.g., a different flux function is employed). A key point is that actual numerical values for this exact solution must be computed, which may reduce the utility of series solution as they are no longer exact once the series is truncated. See Chapter 6 for a description of various methods for obtaining exact solutions to mathematical models for scientific computing applications.

5 Obtain numerical solutions on at least four meshes

While only two mesh levels are required to compute the observed order of accuracy when the exact solution to the mathematical model is known, it is strongly recommended that at least four mesh levels be used to demonstrate that the observed order of accuracy is asymptotically approaching the formal order as the mesh discretization parameters (e.g., Δx, Δy, Δz) approach zero. The mesh refinement must be performed in a systematic manner as discussed in Section 5.4. If only one grid topology is to be tested, then the most general type of grid that will be run with the code should be used.

6 Compute observed order of accuracy

With numerical values from both the numerical solution and the exact solution to the mathematical model now available, the discretization error can be evaluated. Global norms of the solution discretization error should be computed as opposed to examining local values. In addition to the error norms for the solution, discretization errors in all system response quantities of interest should also be examined. Recall that the iterative and round-off errors must be small in order to use the numerical solution as a surrogate for the exact solution to the discrete equations when computing the discretization error. For highly-refined spatial meshes and/or small time steps, the discretization error can be small and thus round-off error can adversely impact the order-of-accuracy test. The observed order of accuracy can be computed from Eq. (5.22) for the system response quantities and from Eq. (5.23) for the norms of the discretization error in the solution.

Note that only for the simplest scientific computing cases (e.g., linear elliptic problems) will the observed order of accuracy match the formal order to more than approximately two significant figures during a successful order verification test. For complex scientific computing codes, it is more common that the observed order of accuracy will approach the formal order with increasing mesh refinement. Thus, it is the asymptotic behavior of the observed order of accuracy that is of interest. In addition, observed orders of accuracy that converge to a value higher than the formal order can either indicate the presence of unforeseen error cancellation (which should not be cause for concern) or mistakes in establishing the formal order of accuracy.

If the observed order of accuracy does not match the formal order in an asymptotic sense, then one should first troubleshoot the test implementation (see Step 7) and then debug the code (Step 8) if necessary. If the observed order does match the formal order, then the verification test is considered successful, and one should proceed to Step 9 to document the test results.

7 Fix test implementation

When the observed order of accuracy does not match the formal order of accuracy, the first step is to make sure that the test was implemented correctly. Common examples of incorrect test implementations include mistakes in constructing or evaluating the exact solution to the mathematical model and mistakes made during the comparison between the numerical and exact solutions. If the test implementation is found to be flawed, then the test should be fixed and then repeated. If the test was correctly implemented, then a coding mistake or algorithm inconsistency is likely present and one should proceed to Step 8 to debug the code.

8 Debug the code

When an order-of-accuracy test fails, it indicates either a mistake in the programming of the discrete algorithm, or worse, an inconsistency in the discrete algorithm itself. See Section 5.5.4 for a discussion of approaches to aid in debugging the scientific computing code.

9 Document results

All code verification results should be documented so that a subsequent user understands the code's verification status and does not duplicate the effort. In addition to documenting the observed order of accuracy, the magnitude of the discretization error should also be reported for both system response quantities and the numerical solution (i.e., the norms of the discretization error). It is further recommended that the meshes and solutions used in the code verification test be added to one of the less-frequently run dynamic software test suites (e.g., a monthly test suite), thus allowing the order-of-accuracy verification test to be repeated on a regular basis. Coarse grid cases, which can typically be executed rapidly, can be added as system-level regression tests to a test suite that is run more frequently, as discussed in Chapter 4.

5.5.2 Temporal discretization

The order verification procedure for temporal problems with no spatial dependency is essentially the same as for spatial problems described above. The only difference is that the time step Δt is refined rather than a spatial mesh, thus mesh quality is not a concern. For unsteady problems, the temporal discretization error can sometimes be quite small.

Therefore the round-off error should be examined carefully to ensure that it does not adversely impact the observed order-of-accuracy computation.

5.5.3 Spatial and temporal discretization

It is more difficult to apply the order verification procedure to problems that involve both spatial and temporal discretization, especially for the case where the spatial order of accuracy is different from the temporal order. In addition, temporal discretization errors can in some cases be much smaller than spatial errors (especially when explicit time marching schemes are used), thus making it more difficult to verify the temporal order of accuracy.

For numerical schemes involving spatial and temporal discretization, it is helpful to rewrite the discretization error expansion given in Eq. (5.19) by separating out the spatial and temporal terms as

$$\varepsilon_{h_x}^{h_t} = g_x h_x^p + g_t h_t^q + O(h_x^{p+1}) + O(h_t^{q+1}), \tag{5.27}$$

where h_x denotes the spatial discretization (i.e., $h_x = \Delta x/\Delta x_{\text{ref}} = \Delta y/\Delta y_{\text{ref}}$, etc.), h_t the temporal discretization (i.e., $h_t = \Delta t/\Delta t_{\text{ref}}$), p is the spatial order of accuracy, and q is the temporal order of accuracy. If adaptive time-stepping algorithms are employed, the adaptive algorithm should be disabled to provide explicit control over the size of the time step. Procedures similar to those described in this section can be used for independent refinement in the spatial coordinates, e.g., by introducing $h_x = \frac{\Delta x}{\Delta x_{\text{ref}}}$ and $h_y = \frac{\Delta y}{\Delta y_{\text{ref}}}$, etc. This section will discuss different spatial and temporal order verification procedures that can be either conducted separately or in a combined manner.

5.5.3.1 Separate order analysis

The simplest approach for performing order verification on a code with both spatial and temporal discretization is to first verify the spatial discretization on a steady-state problem. Once the spatial order of accuracy has been verified, then the temporal order can be investigated separately. The temporal order verification can employ a problem with no spatial discretization such as an unsteady zero-dimensional case or a case with linear spatial variations which can generally be resolved by second-order methods to within round-off error. Alternatively, a problem can be chosen which includes spatial discretization errors, but on a highly-refined spatial mesh (Knupp and Salari, 2003). In the latter approach, the use of a highly-refined spatial mesh is often required to reduce the spatial errors to negligible levels, thus allowing the spatial discretization error term $g_x h_x^p$ term to be neglected in Eq. (5.27) relative to the temporal error term $g_t h_t^q$. In practice, this can be difficult to achieve due to stability constraints (especially for explicit methods) or the expense of computing solutions on the highly-refined spatial meshes. An alternative is to reduce the spatial dimensionality of the problem in order to allow a highly-refined spatial mesh to be used. The drawback to using separate order analysis is that it will not uncover issues related to the interaction between the spatial and temporal discretization.

Table 5.1 *Mesh levels used in the
spatial and temporal code verification
study of Kamm* et al. *(2003).*

Spatial step, h_x	Temporal step, h_t
Δx	Δt
$\Delta x / r_x$	Δt
$\Delta x / r_x^2$	Δt
Δx	$\Delta t / r_t$
Δx	$\Delta t / r_t^2$
$\Delta x / r_x$	$\Delta t / r_t$
$\Delta x / r_x$	$\Delta t / r_t^2$

5.5.3.2 Combined order analysis

A combined spatial and temporal order verification method has been developed by Kamm *et al.* (2003). Their procedure begins with a general formulation of the discretization error, which for a global system response quantity can be written in the form

$$\varepsilon_{h_x}^{h_t} = g_x h_x^{\hat{p}} + g_t h_t^{\hat{q}} + g_{xt} h_x^{\hat{r}} h_t^{\hat{s}}, \tag{5.28}$$

where the observed orders of accuracy $\hat{p}$, $\hat{q}$, $\hat{r}$, and $\hat{s}$ are to be solved for along with the three coefficients g_x, g_t, and g_{xt}. In addition, for the norms of the discretization error, a similar expansion is employed,

$$\left\| \varepsilon_{h_x}^{h_t} \right\| = g_x h_x^{\hat{p}} + g_t h_t^{\hat{q}} + g_{xt} h_x^{\hat{r}} h_t^{\hat{s}}, \tag{5.29}$$

where of course the observed orders and coefficients may be different. In order to solve for these seven unknowns, seven independent levels of spatial and/or temporal refinement are required. Beginning with an initial mesh with Δx and Δt Kamm *et al.* (2003) alternately refined in space (by r_x) and time (by r_t) to obtain the seven mesh levels shown in Table 5.1. By computing these seven different numerical solutions, the discretization error expressions for all seven mesh levels result in a coupled, nonlinear set of algebraic equations. The authors solved this nonlinear system of equations using a Newton-type iterative procedure. An advantage of this approach is that it does not require that the three terms in the discretization error expression be the same order of magnitude. The main drawback is the computational expense since a single calculation of the observed orders of accuracy requires seven different numerical solutions. Additional solutions should also be computed to ensure the asymptotic behavior of the observed order of accuracy has been achieved.

Kamm *et al.* (2003) included the mixed spatial/temporal term because their application employed the explicit Lax–Wendroff temporal integration scheme combined with a Godunov-type spatial discretization, which has formal orders of accuracy of $p = 2$, $q = 2$,

Table 5.2 *Mesh levels recommended for the simpler error expansion of Eqs. (5.30) and (5.31) which omit the mixed spatial/ temporal term.*

Spatial step, h_x	Temporal step, h_t
Δx	Δt
$\Delta x / r_x$	Δt
Δx	$\Delta t / r_t$
$\Delta x / r_x$	$\Delta t / r_t$

and $r = s = 1$ (i.e., it is formally second-order accurate). For many spatial/temporal discretization approaches, the mixed spatial/temporal term can be omitted because it does not appear in the truncation error, thereby reducing the unknowns and the required number of independent mesh levels down to four. The resulting error expansion for global system response quantities becomes

$$\varepsilon_{h_x}^{h_t} = g_x h_x^{\hat{p}} + g_t h_t^{\hat{q}}, \tag{5.30}$$

while the expansion for discretization error norms becomes

$$\left\| \varepsilon_{h_x}^{h_t} \right\| = g_x h_x^{\hat{p}} + g_t h_t^{\hat{q}}. \tag{5.31}$$

Although not unique, recommended mesh levels to employ for the simpler error expansions given by Eqs. (5.30) and (5.31) are given in Table 5.2. The resulting four nonlinear algebraic equations have no closed form solution and thus must be solved numerically (e.g., using Newton's method) for the orders of accuracy $\hat{p}$ and $\hat{q}$ and the coefficients g_x and g_t.

An alternative based on the discretization error expansions of Eqs. (5.30) and (5.31) that does not require the solution to a system of nonlinear algebraic equations can be summarized briefly as follows. First, a spatial mesh refinement study using three meshes is performed with a fixed time step to obtain $\hat{p}$ and g_x. Then a temporal refinement study is performed using three different time steps to obtain $\hat{q}$ and g_t. Once these four unknowns have been estimated, the spatial step size h_x and the temporal step size h_t can be chosen such that the spatial discretization error term $(g_x h_x^p)$ has the same order of magnitude as the temporal error term $(g_t h_t^q)$. Once these two terms are approximately the same order of magnitude, a combined spatial and temporal order verification is conducted by choosing the temporal refinement factor such that the temporal error term drops by the same factor as the spatial term with refinement. This procedure is explained in detail below.

In order to estimate $\hat{p}$ and g_x, a spatial mesh refinement study is performed with a fixed time step. Note that this will introduce a fixed temporal discretization error (i.e., $g_t h_t^q$) for all computations, thus the standard observed order-of-accuracy relationship from Eq. (5.22) cannot be used. Considering only the discretization error norms for now (the same analysis will also apply to the discretization error of the system response quantities), Eq. (5.31) can be rewritten as

$$\left\| \varepsilon_{h_x}^{h_t} \right\| = \phi + g_x h_x^{\hat{p}}, \tag{5.32}$$

where $\phi = g_t h_t^{\hat{q}}$ is the fixed temporal error term. For this case, the observed order-of-accuracy expression from Chapter 8 given by Eq. (8.70) can be used, which requires three mesh solutions, e.g., coarse $(r_x^2 h_x)$, medium $(r_x h_x)$, and fine (h_x):

$$\hat{p} = \frac{\ln \left(\frac{\left\| \varepsilon_{r_x^2 h_x}^{h_t} \right\| - \left\| \varepsilon_{r_x h_x}^{h_t} \right\|}{\left\| \varepsilon_{r_x h_x}^{h_t} \right\| - \left\| \varepsilon_{h_x}^{h_t} \right\|} \right)}{\ln (r_x)} \tag{5.33}$$

By calculating $\hat{p}$ in this manner, the constant temporal error term ϕ will cancel out. The spatial discretization error coefficient g_x can then be found from

$$g_x = \frac{\left\| \varepsilon_{r_x h_x}^{h_t} \right\| - \left\| \varepsilon_{h_x}^{h_t} \right\|}{h_x^{\hat{p}} \left(r_x^{\hat{p}} - 1 \right)}. \tag{5.34}$$

A similar analysis is then performed by refining the time step with a fixed spatial mesh to obtain $\hat{q}$ and g_t. Once these orders of accuracy and coefficients have been estimated, then the leading spatial and temporal discretization error terms can be adjusted to approximately the same order of magnitude by coarsening or refining in time and/or space (subject to numerical stability restrictions). If the discretization error terms are of drastically different magnitude, then extremely refined meshes and/or time steps may be needed to detect coding mistakes.

At this point, if the formal spatial and temporal orders of accuracy are the same (i.e., if $p = q$), then the standard order verification procedure with only two mesh levels can be applied using Eqs. (5.22) or (5.23) since $r_x = r_t$. For the more complicated case when $p \neq q$, temporal refinement can be conducted by choosing the temporal refinement factor r_t according to Eq. (5.35) following Richards (1997):

$$r_t = (r_x)^{p/q} . \tag{5.35}$$

This choice for r_t will ensure that the spatial and temporal discretization error terms are reduced by the same factor with refinement when the solutions are in the asymptotic range. Some recommended values of r_t for $r_x = 2$ are given in Table 5.3 for various formal spatial and temporal orders of accuracy. The observed orders of accuracy in space and time are then computed using two mesh levels according to

$$\hat{p} = \frac{\ln \left(\frac{\left\| \varepsilon_{r_x h_x}^{r_t h_t} \right\|}{\left\| \varepsilon_{h_x}^{h_t} \right\|} \right)}{\ln (r_x)} \quad \text{and} \quad \hat{q} = \frac{\ln \left(\frac{\left\| \varepsilon_{r_x h_x}^{r_t h_t} \right\|}{\left\| \varepsilon_{h_x}^{h_t} \right\|} \right)}{\ln (r_t)}. \tag{5.36}$$

Table 5.3 *Temporal refinement factors required to conduct combined spatial and temporal order verification using only two numerical solutions.*

Spatial order, p	Temporal order, q	Spatial refinement factor, r_x	Temporal refinement factor, r_t	Expected error reduction ratio (coarse/fine)
1	1	2	2	2
1	2	2	$\sqrt{2}$	2
1	3	2	$\sqrt[3]{2}$	2
1	4	2	$\sqrt[4]{2}$	2
2	1	2	4	4
2	2	2	2	4
2	3	2	$\sqrt[3]{4}$	4
2	4	2	$\sqrt[4]{4}$	4
3	1	2	8	8
3	2	2	$\sqrt{8}$	8
3	3	2	2	8
3	4	2	$\sqrt[4]{8}$	8

The analysis using system response quantities from Eq. (5.30) is exactly the same as given above in Eq. (5.36), only with the norm notation omitted.

5.5.4 Recommendations for debugging

Order verification provides a highly-sensitive test as to whether there are mistakes in the computer code and/or inconsistencies in the discrete algorithm. In addition, aspects of the order verification procedure can be extremely useful for tracking down the mistakes (i.e., debugging the code) once they have been found to exist. Once an order verification test fails, and assuming the test was properly implemented, the local variation of discretization error in the domain should be examined. Accumulation of error near a boundary or a corner cell generally indicates that the errors are in the boundary conditions. Errors in regions of mild grid clustering or skewness can indicate mistakes in the mesh transformations or spatial quadratures. Mesh quality problems could be due to the use of a poor quality mesh, or worse, due to a discrete algorithm that is overly-sensitive to mesh irregularities. The effects of mesh quality on the discretization error are examined in detail in Chapter 9.

5.5.5 Limitations of order verification

A significant limitation of the order verification process is that the formal order of accuracy can change due to the level of smoothness of the solution, as discussed in Section 5.3.1. In addition, since order verification can only detect problems in the solution itself, it generally cannot be used to detect coding mistakes affecting the efficiency of the code. For example, a mistake that causes an iterative scheme to converge in 500 iterations when it should converge in ten iterations will not be detected by order verification. Note that this type of mistake would be found with an appropriate component-level test fixture for the iterative scheme (as discussed in Chapter 4). Similarly, mistakes which affect the robustness of the numerical algorithm will not be detected, since these mistakes also do not affect the final numerical solution.

Finally, the standard order verification procedure does not verify individual terms in the discretization. Thus a numerical scheme which is formally first-order accurate for convection and second-order accurate for diffusion results in a numerical scheme with first-order accuracy. Mistakes reducing the order of accuracy of the diffusion term to first order would therefore not be detected. This limitation can be addressed by selectively turning terms on and off, which is most easily accomplished when the method of manufactured solutions is employed (see Chapter 6).

5.5.6 *Alternative approaches for order verification*

In recent years, a number of variants of the order verification procedure have been proposed. Most of these alternative approaches were developed in order to avoid the high cost of generating and computing numerical solutions on highly-refined 3-D meshes. All of the approaches discussed here do indeed reduce the cost of conducting the order verification test relative to the standard approach of systematic mesh refinement; however, each approach is also accompanied by drawbacks which are also discussed. These alternative approaches are presented in order of increasing reliability, with a summary of the strengths and weaknesses of each approach presented at the end of this section.

5.5.6.1 *Residual method*

In general, when the discrete operator $L_h(\cdot)$ operates on anything but the exact solution to the discrete equations u_h, the nonzero result is referred to as the *discrete residual*, or simply the *residual*. This discrete residual is not to be confused with the iterative residual which is found by inserting an approximate iterative solution into the discrete equations (see Chapter 7). Recall that the truncation error can be evaluated by inserting the exact solution to the mathematical model $\tilde{u}$ into the discrete operator as given previously in Eq. (5.13). Assuming an exact solution to the mathematical model is available, the truncation error (i.e., the discrete residual) can be evaluated directly on a given mesh without actually solving for the numerical solution on this grid. Since no iterations are needed, this truncation error evaluation is usually very inexpensive. The truncation error found by inserting the exact solution to the mathematical model into the discrete operator can be evaluated on a series of systematically-refined meshes. The observed order of accuracy is then computed by Eq. (5.23), but using norms of the truncation error rather than the discretization error.

There are a number of drawbacks to the residual form of order verification that are related to the fact that the residual does not incorporate all aspects of the code (Ober, 2004). Specifically, the residual method does not test:

- boundary conditions that do not contribute to the residual (e.g., Dirichlet boundary conditions),
- system response quantities such as lift, drag, combustion efficiency, maximum heat flux, maximum stress, oscillation frequency, etc.,
- numerical algorithms where the governing equations are solved in a segregated or decoupled manner (e.g., the SIMPLE algorithm (Patankar, 1980) for incompressible fluids problems where the momentum equations are solved, followed by a pressure projection step to satisfy the mass conservation equation), and
- explicit multi-stage schemes such as Runge-Kutta.

In addition, it has been observed that the truncation error can converge at a lower rate than the discretization error for finite-volume schemes on certain unstructured mesh topologies (Despres, 2004; Thomas *et al.*, 2008). In these cases, it is possible that the residual method might exhibit a lower order of accuracy than a traditional order-of-accuracy test applied to the discretization error. For examples of the residual method applied for code verification see Burg and Murali (2004) and Thomas *et al.* (2008).

5.5.6.2 Statistical method

The *statistical form of order verification* was proposed by Hebert and Luke (2005) and uses only a single mesh, which is successively scaled down and used to sample over the chosen domain. The sampling is performed randomly, and norms of the volume-weighted discretization error are examined. The main advantage of the statistical method is that it is relatively inexpensive because it does not require refinement of the mesh. There are, however, a number of disadvantages. First, since the domain is sampled statistically, convergence of the statistical method must be ensured. Second, it tends to weight the boundary points more heavily as the grids are shrunk relative to traditional order verification since the ratio of boundary points to interior points is fixed rather than reducing with mesh refinement. Finally, this approach assumes that the discretization errors are independent random variables, thus neglecting the transported component of error into the refined domains. (See Chapter 8 for a discussion of the difference between transported and locally-generated components of the discretization error.) Due to these issues, it is possible to pass a statistical order verification test for a case that would fail a traditional order verification test based on systematic mesh refinement.

5.5.6.3 Downscaling method

The *downscaling approach* to order verification (Diskin and Thomas, 2007; Thomas *et al.*, 2008) shares a number of attributes with the statistical method described above. The major difference is that instead of statistically sampling the smaller meshes in the domain, the mesh is scaled down about a single point in the domain, which eliminates the statistical convergence issues associated with statistical order verification. The focal point to which

Table 5.4 *Comparison of different order verification approaches showing the cost and the type of order-of-accuracy estimate produced (adapted from Thomas* et al.*, 2008).*

Verification method	Cost	Type of order estimate
Standard order verification with systematic mesh refinement	High	Precise order of accuracy
Downscaling method	Moderate to low	Admits false positives
Statistical method	Moderate (due to sampling)	Admits false positives
Residual method	Very low	Admits false positives and false negatives

the grids are scaled can be chosen to emphasize the internal discretization, the boundary discretization, or singularities (Thomas *et al.*, 2008). A major benefit of the downscaling method is that it allows for boundary condition verification in the presence of complex geometries. The mesh scaling can be performed in a very simple manner when examining the interior discretization or straight boundaries, but must be modified to ensure the proper scaling of a mesh around a curved boundary. The downscaling method also neglects the possibility of discretization error transport into the scaled-down domain, and thus can provide overly optimistic estimates of the actual convergence rate.

5.5.6.4 Summary of order verification approaches

In order to summarize the characteristics of the different order verification approaches, it is first helpful to categorize the results of an order verification test. Here we will define a positive result as one in which the observed order of accuracy is found to match the formal order in an asymptotic sense, while a negative result is one where the observed order is less than the formal order. We now define a false positive as a case where a less-rigorous order verification test achieves a positive result, but the more rigorous order verification procedure with systematic mesh refinement produces a negative result. Similarly, a false negative occurs when the test result is negative, but standard order verification with systematic mesh refinement is positive. The characteristics of the four approaches for order-of-accuracy verification are given in Table 5.4. As one might expect, the cost of conducting and order verification study varies proportionately with the reliability of the observed order of accuracy estimate.

5.6 Responsibility for code verification

The ultimate responsibility for ensuring that rigorous code verification has been performed lies with the user of the scientific computing code. This holds true whether the code was developed by the user, by someone else in the user's organization, or by an independent organization (government laboratory, commercial software company, etc.). It is not sufficient for the code user to simply assume that code verification studies have been successfully performed.

In the ideal case, code verification should be performed during, and as an integrated part of, the software development process. While code verification studies are most often conducted by the code developers, a higher level of independence can be achieved when they are conducted by a separate group, by the code customer, or even by an independent regulatory agency (recall the discussion of independence of the verification and validation process in Chapter 2). While there are often fewer coding mistakes to find in a scientific computing code that has a prior usage history, performing code verification studies for a mature code can be expensive and challenging if the code was not designed with code verification testing in mind.

Commercial companies that produce scientific computing software rarely perform rigorous code verification studies, or if they do, they do not make the results public. Most code verification efforts that are documented for commercial codes seem to be limited to simple benchmark examples that demonstrate "engineering accuracy" rather than verifying the order of accuracy of the code (Oberkampf and Trucano, 2008). Recently, Abanto *et al.* (2005) performed order verification studies on three different commercial computational fluid dynamics codes which were formally at least second-order accurate. Most tests resulted in either first-order accuracy or nonconvergent behavior with mesh refinement. It is our opinion that code users should be aware that commercial software companies are unlikely to perform rigorous code verification studies unless users request it.

In the absence of rigorous, documented code verification evidence, there are code verification activities that can be performed by the user. In addition to the simple code verification activities discussed in Section 5.1, order verification tests can also be conducted when an exact solution (or a verifiably accurate surrogate solution) to the mathematical model is available. While the traditional approach for finding exact solutions can be used, the more general method of manufactured solutions procedure requires the ability to employ user-defined boundary conditions, initial conditions, and source terms, and thus can be difficult to implement for a user who does not have access to source code. The next chapter focuses on different approaches for obtaining exact solutions to the mathematical model including the method of manufactured solutions.

5.7 References

Abanto, J., D. Pelletier, A. Garon, J-Y. Trepanier, and M. Reggio (2005). *Verication of some Commercial CFD Codes on Atypical CFD Problems*, AIAA Paper 2005–682.
Banks, J. W., T. Aslam, and W. J. Rider (2008). On sub-linear convergence for linearly degenerate waves in capturing schemes, *Journal of Computational Physics.* **227**, 6985–7002.
Burg, C. and V. Murali (2004). *Efficient Code Verification Using the Residual Formulation of the Method of Manufactured Solutions*, AIAA Paper 2004–2628.

Carpenter, M. H. and J. H. Casper (1999). Accuracy of shock capturing in two spatial dimensions, *AIAA Journal.* **37**(9), 1072–1079.

Crank, J. and P. A. Nicolson (1947). Practical method for numerical evaluation of solutions of partial differential equations of the heat-conduction type, *Proceedings of the Cambridge Philosophical Society.* **43**, 50–67.

Despres, B. (2004). Lax theorem and finite volume schemes, *Mathematics of Computation.* **73**(247), 1203–1234.

Diskin, B. and J. L. Thomas (2007). *Accuracy Analysis for Mixed-Element Finite Volume Discretization Schemes*, Technical Report TR 2007–8, Hampton, VA, National Institute of Aerospace.

Engquist, B. and B. Sjogreen (1998). The convergence rate of finite difference schemes in the presence of shocks, *SIAM Journal of Numerical Analysis.* **35**(6), 2464–2485.

Ferziger, J. H. and M. Peric (1996). Further discussion of numerical errors in CFD, *International Journal for Numerical Methods in Fluids.* **23**(12), 1263–1274.

Ferziger, J. H. and M. Peric (2002). *Computational Methods for Fluid Dynamics*, 3rd edn., Berlin, Springer-Verlag.

Grinstein, F. F., L. G. Margolin, and W. J. Rider (2007). *Implicit Large Eddy Simulation: Computing Turbulent Fluid Dynamics*, Cambridge, UK, Cambridge University Press.

Hebert, S. and E. A. Luke (2005). *Honey, I Shrunk the Grids! A New Approach to CFD Verification Studies*, AIAA Paper 2005–685.

Hirsch, C. (2007). *Numerical Computation of Internal and External Flows (Vol. 1)*, 2nd edn., Burlington, MA, Elsevier.

Kamm, J. R., W. J. Rider, and J. S. Brock (2003). *Combined Space and Time Convergence Analyses of a Compressible Flow Algorithm*, AIAA Paper 2003–4241.

Knupp, P. M. (2003). Algebraic mesh quality metrics for unstructured initial meshes, *Finite Elements in Analysis and Design.* **39**(3), 217–241.

Knupp, P. M. (2009). Private communication, March 9, 2009.

Knupp, P. M. and K. Salari (2003). *Verification of Computer Codes in Computational Science and Engineering*, K. H. Rosen (ed.), Boca Raton, FL, Chapman and Hall/CRC.

Knupp, P., C. Ober, and R. Bond (2007). Measuring progress in order-verification within software development projects, *Engineering with Computers.* **23**, 271–282.

Mastin, C. W. (1999). Truncation Error on Structured Grids, in *Handbook of Grid Generation*, J. F. Thompson, B. K. Soni, and N. P. Weatherill, (eds.), Boca Raton, CRC Press.

Ober, C. C. (2004). Private communication, August 19, 2004.

Oberkampf, W. L. and T. G. Trucano (2008). Verification and validation benchmarks, *Nuclear Engineering and Design.* **238**(3), 716–743.

Panton, R. L. (2005). *Incompressible Flow*, 3rd edn., Hoboken, NJ, John Wiley and Sons.

Patankar, S. V. (1980). *Numerical Heat Transfer and Fluid Flow*, New York, Hemisphere Publishing Corp.

Potter, D. L., F. G. Blottner, A. R. Black, C. J. Roy, and B. L. Bainbridge (2005). *Visualization of Instrumental Verification Information Details (VIVID): Code Development, Description, and Usage*, SAND2005–1485, Albuquerque, NM, Sandia National Laboratories.

Richards, S. A. (1997). Completed Richardson extrapolation in space and time, *Communications in Numerical Methods in Engineering.* **13**, 573–582.

Richtmyer, R. D. and K. W. Morton (1967). *Difference Methods for Initial-value Problems*, 2nd edn., New York, John Wiley and Sons.

Rider, W. J. (2009). Private communication, March 27, 2009.

Roache, P. J. (1998). *Verification and Validation in Computational Science and Engineering*, Albuquerque, NM, Hermosa Publishers.

Roy, C. J. (2003). Grid convergence error analysis for mixed-order numerical schemes, *AIAA Journal*. **41**(4), 595–604.

Roy, C. J. (2005). Review of code and solution verification procedures for computational simulation, *Journal of Computational Physics*. **205**(1), 131–156.

Roy, C. J. (2009). *Strategies for Driving Mesh Adaptation in CFD*, AIAA Paper 2009–1302.

Roy, C. J., E. Tendean, S. P. Veluri, R. Rifki, E. A. Luke, and S. Hebert (2007). *Verification of RANS Turbulence Models in Loci-CHEM using the Method of Manufactured Solutions*, AIAA Paper 2007–4203.

Tannehill, J. C., D. A. Anderson, and R. H. Pletcher (1997). *Computational Fluid Mechanics and Heat Transfer*, 2nd edn., Philadelphia, PA, Taylor and Francis.

Thomas, J. L., B. Diskin, and C. L. Rumsey (2008). Toward verification of unstructured-grid solvers, *AIAA Journal*. **46**(12), 3070–3079.

Thompson, J. F., Z. U. A. Warsi, and C. W. Mastin (1985). *Numerical Grid Generation: Foundations and Applications*, New York, Elsevier. (www.erc.msstate.edu/publications/gridbook).

Trucano, T. G., M. M. Pilch, and W. L. Oberkampf (2003). *On the Role of Code Comparisons in Verification and Validation*, SAND 2003–2752, Albuquerque, NM, Sandia National Laboratories.

Veluri, S., C. J. Roy, S. Hebert, and E. A. Luke (2008). *Verification of the Loci-CHEM CFD Code Using the Method of Manufactured Solutions*, AIAA Paper 2008–661.

6

Exact solutions

The primary focus of this chapter is on the use of exact solutions to mathematical models for code verification. Recall that, in some cases, software testing can be performed by simply running the code and comparing the results to the correct code output. However, in scientific computing, "correct" code output depends on the chosen spatial mesh, time step, iterative convergence tolerance, machine precision, etc. We are thus forced to rely on other less definitive methods for assessing code correctness. In Chapter 5, the order of accuracy test was argued to be the most rigorous approach for code verification. When the order of accuracy test fails, or when the formal order of accuracy has not been determined, then the less rigorous convergence test may be used. In either case, an exact solution to the underlying mathematical model is required. When used for code verification, the ability of this exact solution to exercise all terms in the mathematical model is more important than any physical realism of the solution. In fact, realistic exact solutions are often avoided for code verification due to the presence of singularities and/or discontinuities. Numerous examples will be given in this chapter of exact solutions and their use with the order verification test. The final example given in this chapter employs the less rigorous convergence test with benchmark numerical solutions. In addition to code verification applications, exact solutions to mathematical models are extremely valuable for evaluating the accuracy of numerical schemes, determining solution sensitivity to mesh quality and topology, evaluating the reliability of discretization error estimators, and evaluating solution adaptation schemes. For these secondary applications, physically realistic exact solutions are preferred (see Section 6.4).

This chapter discusses methods for obtaining exact solutions to mathematical models used in scientific computing. These mathematical models typically take the form of either integral or differential equations. Because we will have to compute actual numerical values for these exact solutions, we will use a different definition for an exact solution than found in standard mathematics textbooks. The definition used here for an exact solution is a solution to the mathematical model that is in closed form, i.e., in terms of elementary functions (trigonometric functions, exponentials, logarithms, powers, etc.) or readily-computed special functions (e.g., gamma, beta, error, Bessel functions) of the independent variables. Solutions involving infinite series or a reduction of a partial differential equation to a system of ordinary differential equations which do not have exact solutions will be considered as approximate solutions and are addressed at the end of the chapter.

In scientific computing, the mathematical models can take different forms. When a set of physical laws such as conservation of mass, momentum, or energy (i.e., the conceptual model) are formulated for an infinitesimally small region of space, then the resulting mathematical model generally takes the form of differential equations. When applied to a region of space with finite size, the mathematical model takes the form of integral (or integro-differential) equations. The differential form is called the *strong form* of the equations, whereas the integral form, after application of the divergence theorem (which converts the volume integral of the gradient of a quantity to fluxes through the boundary), is called the *weak form*. The finite difference method employs the strong form of the equations, while the finite element and finite volume methods employ the weak form.

The strong form explicitly requires solutions that are differentiable, whereas the weak form admits solutions that can contain discontinuities while still satisfying the underlying physical laws, and these discontinuous solutions are called *weak solutions*. Weak solutions satisfy the differential equation only in a restricted sense. While exact solutions to the weak form of the equations exist that do contain discontinuities (e.g., the Riemann or shock tube problem in gas dynamics), the more general approaches for generating exact solutions such as the method of manufactured solutions discussed in Section 6.3 have not to our knowledge encompassed nondifferentiable weak solutions (although this extension is needed). This chapter will assume the strong (i.e., differential) form of the mathematical models unless otherwise noted. Since strong solutions also satisfy the weak form of the equations, the finite element and finite volume methods will not be excluded by this assumption, and we are simply restricting ourselves to smooth solutions.

Because scientific computing often involves complex systems of coupled partial differential equations (PDEs) which have relatively few exact solutions, the organization of this chapter is very different from that of standard mathematics texts. After a short introduction to differential equations in Section 6.1, a discussion of "traditional" exact solutions and solution methods is presented in Section 6.2. The method of manufactured solutions (MMS) is a more general approach for obtaining exact solutions to complicated mathematical models and is discussed in detail in Section 6.3. When physically realistic manufactured solutions are desired, the approaches discussed in Section 6.4 can be used. As discussed above, solutions involving infinite series, reduction of PDEs to ordinary differential equations, or numerical solutions of the underlying mathematical model with established numerical accuracy are relegated to Section 6.5.

6.1 Introduction to differential equations

Differential equations are ubiquitous in the study of physical processes in science and engineering (O'Neil, 2003). A differential equation is a relation between a variable and its derivatives. When only one independent variable is present, the equation is called an *ordinary differential equation*. A differential equation involving derivatives with respect to two or more independent variables (e.g., x and t, or x, y, and z) is called a *partial differential equation* (PDE). A differential equation can be a single equation with a single dependent variable or a system of equations with multiple dependent variables. The *order* of a differential equation is the largest number of derivatives applied to any dependent variable. The *degree* of a differential equation is the highest power of the highest derivative found in the equation.

A differential equation is considered to be *linear* when the dependent variables and all of their derivatives occur with powers less than or equal to one and there are no products involving derivatives and/or functions of the dependent variables. Solutions to linear differential equations can be combined to form new solutions using the linear superposition principle. A *quasi-linear* differential equation is one that is linear in the highest derivative, i.e., the highest derivative appears to the power one.

General solutions to PDEs are solutions that that satisfy the PDE but involve arbitrary constants and/or functions and thus are not unique. To find *particular solutions* to PDEs, additional conditions must be supplied on the boundary of the domain of interest, i.e., *boundary conditions*, at an initial data location i.e., *initial conditions*, or some combination of the two. Boundary conditions generally come in the form of *Dirichlet* boundary conditions which specify values of the dependent variables or *Neumann* boundary conditions which specify the values of derivatives of the dependent variables normal to the boundary. When both Dirichlet and Neumann conditions are applied at a boundary it is called a *Cauchy* boundary condition, whereas a linear combination of a dependent variable and its normal derivative is called a *Robin* boundary condition. The latter is often confused with *mixed* boundary conditions, which occur when different boundary condition types (Dirichlet, Neumann, or Robin) are applied at different boundaries in a given problem.

Another source of confusion is related to the order of the boundary conditions. The maximum order of the boundary conditions is at least one less than the order of the differential equation. Here *order* refers to the highest number of derivatives applied to any dependent variable as discussed above. This requirement on the order of the boundary condition is sometimes erroneously stated as a requirement on the order of accuracy of the discretization of a derivative boundary condition when the PDE is solved numerically. On the contrary, a reduction in the formal order of accuracy of a discretized boundary condition often leads to a reduction in the observed order of accuracy of the entire solution.

Partial differential equations can be classified as *elliptic*, *parabolic*, *hyperbolic*, or a combination of these types. For scalar equations, this classification is fairly straightforward in a manner analogous to determining the character of algebraic equations. For systems of PDEs written in quasi-linear form, the eigenvalues of the coefficient matrices can be used to determine the mathematical character (Hirsch, 2007).

6.2 Traditional exact solutions

The standard approach to obtaining an exact solution to a mathematical model can be summarized as follows. Given the governing partial differential (or integral) equations on some domain with appropriately specified initial and/or boundary conditions, find the exact solution. The main disadvantage of this approach is that there are only a limited number of exact solutions known for complex equations. Here the complexity of the equations could be due to geometry, nonlinearity, physical models, and/or coupling between multiple physical phenomena such as fluid–structure interaction.

When exact solutions are found for complex equations, they often depend on significant simplifications in dimensionality, geometry, physics, etc. For example, the flow between infinite parallel plates separated by a small gap with one plate moving at a constant speed is called Couette flow and is described by the Navier–Stokes equations, a nonlinear, second-order system of PDEs. In Couette flow, the velocity profile is linear across the gap, and this linearity causes the diffusion term, a second derivative of velocity, to be identically zero. In addition, there are no solution variations in the direction that the plate is moving. Thus the exact solution to Couette flow does not exercise many of the terms in the Navier–Stokes equations.

There are many books available that catalogue a vast number of exact solutions for differential equations found in science and engineering. These texts address ordinary differential equations (e.g., Polyanin and Zaitsev, 2003), linear PDEs (Kevorkian, 2000; Polyanin, 2002; Meleshko, 2005), and nonlinear PDEs (Kevorkian, 2000; Polyanin and Zaitsev, 2004; Meleshko, 2005). In addition, many exact solutions can be found in discipline-specific references such as those for heat conduction (Carslaw and Jaeger, 1959), fluid dynamics (Panton, 2005; White, 2006), linear elasticity (Timoshenko and Goodier, 1969; Slaughter, 2002), elastodynamics (Kausel, 2006), and vibration and buckling (Elishakoff, 2004). The general Riemann problem involves an exact weak (i.e., discontinuous) solution to the 1-D unsteady inviscid equations for gas dynamics (Gottlieb and Groth, 1988).

6.2.1 Procedures

In contrast to the method of manufactured solutions discussed in Section 6.3, the traditional method for finding exact solutions solves the forward problem: given a partial differential equation, a domain, and boundary and/or initial conditions, find the exact solution. In this section, we present some of the simpler classical methods for obtaining exact solutions and make a brief mention of more advanced (nonclassical) techniques. Further details on the classical techniques for PDEs can be found in Ames (1965) and Kevorkian (2000).

6.2.1.1 Separation of variables

Separation of variables is the most common approach for solving linear PDEs, although it can also be used to solve certain nonlinear PDEs. Consider a scalar PDE with dependent variable u and independent variables t and x. There are two forms for separation of variables, multiplicative and additive, and these approaches can be summarized as:

$$\text{multiplicative: } u(t, x) = \phi(t)\psi(x),$$

$$\text{additive: } u(t, x) = \phi(t) + \psi(x).$$

The multiplicative form of separation of variables is the most common.

For an example of separation of variables, consider the 1-D unsteady heat equation with constant thermal diffusivity α,

$$\frac{\partial T}{\partial t} = \alpha \frac{\partial^2 T}{\partial x^2}, \tag{6.1}$$

where $T(t, x)$ is the temperature. Let us first simplify this equation by employing the simple transformations $t = \alpha \bar{t}$ and $x = \alpha \bar{x}$. With these transformations, the heat equation can be rewritten in simpler form as:

$$\frac{\partial T}{\partial \bar{t}} = \frac{\partial^2 T}{\partial \bar{x}^2}. \tag{6.2}$$

Using the multiplicative form of separation of variables $T(\bar{x}, \bar{t}) = \phi(\bar{t})\psi(\bar{x})$, the differential equation can be rewritten as

$$\frac{\phi_t(\bar{t})}{\phi(\bar{t})} = \frac{\psi_{xx}(\bar{x})}{\psi(\bar{x})}, \tag{6.3}$$

where the subscript denotes differentiation with respect to the subscripted variable. Since the left hand side of Eq. (6.3) is independent of $\bar{x}$ and the right hand side is independent of $\bar{t}$, both sides must be equal to a constant a, i.e.,

$$\frac{\phi_t(\bar{t})}{\phi(\bar{t})} = \frac{\psi_{xx}(\bar{x})}{\psi(\bar{x})} = a. \tag{6.4}$$

Each side of Eq. (6.3) can thus be written as

$$\frac{d\phi}{d\bar{t}} - a\phi = 0,$$

$$\frac{d^2\psi}{d\bar{x}^2} - a\psi = 0. \tag{6.5}$$

Equations (6.5) can be integrated using standard methods for ordinary differential equations. After substituting back in for x and t, we finally arrive at two general solutions (Meleshko, 2005) depending on the sign of a:

$$a = \lambda^2 : u(t, x) = \exp\left(\frac{\lambda^2 t}{\alpha}\right) \left[c_1 \exp\left(\frac{-\lambda x}{\alpha}\right) + c_2 \exp\left(\frac{\lambda x}{\alpha}\right)\right],$$

$$a = -\lambda^2 : u(t, x) = \exp\left(\frac{-\lambda^2 t}{\alpha}\right) \left[c_1 \sin\left(\frac{\lambda x}{\alpha}\right) + c_2 \cos\left(\frac{\lambda x}{\alpha}\right)\right], \tag{6.6}$$

where c_1, c_2, and λ are constants that can be determined from the initial and boundary conditions.

6.2.1.2 *Transformations*

Transformations can sometimes be used to convert a differential equation into a simpler form that has a known solution. Transformations that do not involve derivatives are called point transformations (Polyanin and Zaitsev, 2004), while transformations that involve derivatives are called tangent transformations (Meleshko, 2005). An example of a point transformation is the hodograph transformation, which exchanges the roles between the independent and the dependent variables. Examples of tangent transformations include Legendre, Hopf–Cole, and Laplace transformations.

A well-known example of a tangent transformation is the Hopf–Cole transformation (Polyanin and Zaitsev, 2004). Consider the nonlinear Burgers' equation

$$\frac{\partial u}{\partial t} + u\frac{\partial u}{\partial x} = \nu\frac{\partial^2 u}{\partial x^2}, \tag{6.7}$$

where the viscosity ν is assumed to be constant. Burgers' equation serves as a scalar model equation for the Navier–Stokes equations since it includes an unsteady term $\left(\frac{\partial u}{\partial t}\right)$, a nonlinear convection term $\left(u\frac{\partial u}{\partial x}\right)$, and a diffusion term $\left(\nu\frac{\partial^2 u}{\partial x^2}\right)$. The Hopf–Cole transformation is given by

$$u = \frac{-2\nu}{\phi}\phi_x, \tag{6.8}$$

where again ϕ_x denotes partial differentiation of ϕ with respect to x. Substituting the Hopf–Cole transformation into Burgers' equation, applying the product rule, and simplifying results in

$$\frac{\phi_{tx}}{\phi} - \frac{\phi_t\phi_x}{\phi^2} - \nu\left(\frac{\phi_{xxx}}{\phi} - \frac{\phi_{xx}\phi_x}{\phi^2}\right) = 0, \tag{6.9}$$

which can be rewritten as

$$\frac{\partial}{\partial x}\left[\frac{1}{\phi}\left(\frac{\partial\phi}{\partial t} - \nu\frac{\partial^2\phi}{\partial x^2}\right)\right] = 0. \tag{6.10}$$

The terms in parenthesis in Eq. (6.10) are simply the 1-D unsteady heat equation (6.1) written with $\phi(t, x)$ as the dependent variable. Thus any nonzero solution to the heat equation $\phi(t, x)$ can be transformed into a solution to Burgers' equation (6.7) using the Hopf–Cole transformation given by Eq. (6.8).

6.2.1.3 Method of characteristics

An approach for finding exact solutions to hyperbolic PDEs is the *method of characteristics*. The goal is to identify characteristic curves/surfaces along which certain solution properties will be constant. Along these characteristics, the PDE can be converted into a system of ordinary differential equations which can be integrated by starting at an initial data location. When the resulting ordinary differential equations can be solved analytically in closed form, then we will consider the solution to be an exact solution, whereas solutions requiring numerical integration or series solutions will be considered approximate (see Section 6.5).

Table 6.1 *Exact solutions to the 1-D unsteady heat*
conduction equation.

Solutions to $\dfrac{\partial T}{\partial t} = \alpha \dfrac{\partial^2 T}{\partial x^2}$

$T(t, x) = A\left(x^3 + 6\alpha t x\right) + B$

$T(t, x) = A\left(x^4 + 12\alpha t x^2 + 12\alpha^2 t^2\right) + B$

$T(t, x) = x^{2n} + \displaystyle\sum_{k=1}^{n} \frac{(2n)(2n-1)\cdots(2n-2k+1)}{k!}(\alpha t)^k x^{2n-2k}$

$T(t, x) = A\exp\left(\alpha\mu^2 t \pm \mu x\right) + B$

$T(t, x) = A\dfrac{1}{\sqrt{t}}\exp\left(\frac{-x^2}{4\alpha t}\right) + B$

$T(t, x) = A\exp\left(-\mu x\right)\cos\left(\mu x - 2\alpha\mu^2 t + B\right) + C$

$T(t, x) = A\mathrm{erf}\left(\frac{x}{2\sqrt{\alpha t}}\right) + B$

6.2.1.4 Advanced approaches

Additional approaches for obtaining exact solutions to PDEs were developed in the latter half of the twentieth century. One example is the method of differential constraints developed by Yanenko (1964). Another example is the application of group theory, which has found extensive applications in algebra and geometry, for finding solutions to differential equations. While a discussion of these nonclassical analytic solutions techniques is beyond the scope of this book, additional information on the application of these methods for PDEs can be found in Polyanin (2002), Polyanin and Zaitsev (2004), and Meleshko (2005).

6.2.2 Example exact solution: 1-D unsteady heat conduction

Some general solutions to the 1-D unsteady heat conduction equation given by Eq. (6.1) are presented in Table 6.1 above, where A, B, C, and μ are arbitrary constants and n is a positive integer. These solutions, as well as many others, can be found in Polyanin (2002). Employing Eq. (6.8), these solutions can also be transformed into solutions to Burgers' equation.

6.2.3 Example with order verification: steady Burgers' equation

This section describes an exact solution for the steady Burgers' equation, which is then employed in an order verification test for a finite difference discretization. Benton and Platzmann (1972) describe 35 exact solutions to Burgers' equation, which is given above in Eq. (6.7). The steady-state form of Burgers' equation is found by restricting the solution u to be a function of x only, thus reducing Eq. (6.7) to the following ordinary differential equation

$$u\frac{du}{dx} = v\frac{d^2u}{dx^2},$$ (6.11)

where u is a velocity and v is the viscosity. The exact solution to Burgers' equation for a steady, viscous shock (Benton and Platzmann, 1972) is given in dimensionless form, denoted by primes, as

$$u'(x') = -2\tanh(x').$$ (6.12)

This dimensionless solution for Burgers' equation can be converted to dimensional quantities via transformations given by $x' = x/L$ and $u' = uL/v$ where L is a reference length scale. This solution for Burgers' equation is also invariant to scaling by a factor α as follows: $\bar{x} = x/\alpha$ and $\bar{u} = \alpha u$. Finally, one can define a Reynolds number in terms of L, a reference velocity u_{ref}, and the viscosity v as

$$\text{Re} = \frac{u_{\text{ref}}L}{v},$$ (6.13)

where the domain is generally chosen as $-L \leq x \leq L$ and u_{ref} the maximum value of u on the domain.

For this example, the steady Burgers' equation is discretized using the simple implicit finite difference scheme given by

$$\bar{u}_i\left(\frac{u_{i+1}^{k+1} - u_{i-1}^{k+1}}{2\Delta x}\right) - v\left(\frac{u_{i+1}^{k+1} - 2u_i^{k+1} + u_{i-1}^{k+1}}{\Delta x^2}\right) = 0,$$ (6.14)

where a uniform mesh with spacing Δx is used between the spatial nodes which are indexed by i. The formal order of accuracy of this discretization scheme is two and can be found from a truncation error analysis. The above discretization scheme is linearized by setting $\bar{u}_i = u_i^k$ and then iterated until the solution at iteration k satisfies Eq. (6.14) within round-off error using double precision computations. This results in the iterative residuals, found by substituting $\bar{u}_i = u_i^{k+1}$ into Eq. (6.14), being reduced by approximately fourteen orders of magnitude. Thus, iterative convergence and round-off errors can be neglected (see Chapter 7), and the numerical solutions effectively contain only discretization error.

The solution to Burgers' equation for a Reynolds number of eight is given in Figure 6.1, which includes both the exact solution (in scaled dimensional variables) and a numerical solution obtained using 17 evenly-spaced points (i.e., nodes). The low value for the Reynolds number was chosen for this code verification exercise to ensure that both the convection and the diffusion terms are exercised. Note that choosing a large Reynolds number effectively scales down the diffusion term since it is multiplied by 1/Re when written in dimensionless form. For higher Reynolds numbers, extremely fine meshes would be needed to detect coding mistakes in the diffusion term.

Numerical solutions for the steady Burgers' equation were obtained on seven uniform meshes from the finest mesh of 513 nodes ($h = 1$) to the coarsest mesh of nine nodes

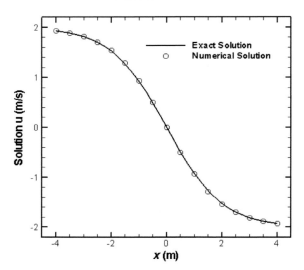

Figure 6.1 Comparison of the numerical solution using 17 nodes with exact solution for the steady Burgers equation with Reynolds number Re = 8.

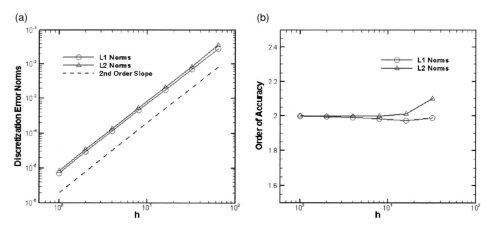

Figure 6.2 Discretization error (a) and observed orders of accuracy (b) for steady Burger's equation with Reynolds number Re = 8.

($h = 64$). Discrete L_1 and L_2 norms of the discretization error are given in Figure 6.2a and both norms appear to reduce with mesh refinement at a second-order rate. The order of accuracy, as computed from Eq. (5.23), is given in Figure 6.2b. Both norms rapidly approach the scheme's formal order of accuracy of two with mesh refinement for this simple problem. The code used to compute the numerical solutions to Burgers' equation is thus considered to be verified for the options exercised, namely steady-state solutions on a uniform mesh.

Figure 6.3 2-D linear elasticity problem for plane stress in a cantilevered beam loaded at the tip; an unstructured mesh with 64 triangular elements is also shown.

6.2.4 Example with order verification: linear elasticity

This section describes an exact solution for linear elasticity and includes an example of order verification for a finite element code. The problem of interest is a cantilevered beam that is loaded at the tip, as shown in Figure 6.3. The equations governing the displacements u and v in the x and y directions, respectively, arise from the static equilibrium linear momentum equations for plane stress. An isotropic linear elastic material is assumed along with small strain (i.e., small deformation gradient) assumptions. The equations governing the displacements can be written as

$$\left(1 + \frac{1-\alpha}{2\alpha-1}\right)\frac{\partial^2 u}{\partial x^2} + \frac{1}{2}\frac{\partial^2 u}{\partial y^2} + \left(\frac{1}{2} + \frac{1-\alpha}{2\alpha-1}\right)\frac{\partial^2 v}{\partial x \partial y} = 0,$$

$$\left(1 + \frac{1-\alpha}{2\alpha-1}\right)\frac{\partial^2 v}{\partial y^2} + \frac{1}{2}\frac{\partial^2 v}{\partial x^2} + \left(\frac{1}{2} + \frac{1-\alpha}{2\alpha-1}\right)\frac{\partial^2 u}{\partial x \partial y} = 0, \qquad (6.15)$$

where for plane stress

$$\alpha = \frac{1}{1+\nu}$$

and ν is Poisson's ratio.

For a beam of length L, height h, and width (in the z direction) of w, an exact solution can be found for the displacements (Slaughter, 2002). This solution has been modified (Seidel, 2009) using the above coordinate system resulting in an Airy stress function of

$$\Phi = -2\frac{xPy^3}{h^3 w} + 2\frac{LPy^3}{h^3 w} + 3/2\frac{xyP}{hw}, \qquad (6.16)$$

which exactly satisfies the equilibrium and compatibility conditions. The stresses can then be easily obtained by

$$\sigma_{xx} = \frac{\partial^2 \Phi}{\partial y^2} = -12\frac{xyP}{h^3 w} + 12\frac{LPy}{h^3 w},$$

$$\sigma_{yy} = \frac{\partial^2 \Phi}{\partial x^2} = 0,$$

$$\sigma_{xy} = \frac{\partial^2 \Phi}{\partial x \partial y} = 6\frac{Py^2}{h^3 w} - 3/2\frac{P}{hw}. \qquad (6.17)$$

The stress–strain relationship is given by

$$\sigma_{xx} = \frac{E}{1 - \nu^2} \left(\varepsilon_{xx} + \nu \varepsilon_{yy} \right),$$

$$\sigma_{yy} = \frac{E}{1 - \nu^2} \left(\nu \varepsilon_{xx} + \varepsilon_{yy} \right),$$

$$\sigma_{xy} = \frac{E}{1 + \nu} \varepsilon_{xy},$$

and the strain is related to the displacements by

$$\varepsilon_{xx} = \frac{\partial u}{\partial x},$$

$$\varepsilon_{yy} = \frac{\partial v}{\partial y},$$

$$\varepsilon_{xy} = \frac{1}{2} \left(\frac{\partial u}{\partial y} + \frac{\partial v}{\partial x} \right).$$

This solution results in traction-free conditions on the upper and lower surfaces, i.e.,

$$\sigma_{yy}(x, h/2) = \sigma_{xy}(x, h/2) = \sigma_{yy}(x, -h/2) = \sigma_{xy}(x, -h/2) = 0,$$

and static equivalent tip loads of zero net axial force, zero bending moment, and the applied shear force at the tip of $-P$:

$$\int_{-h/2}^{h/2} \sigma_{xx}(L, y) \mathrm{d}y = 0,$$

$$\int_{-h/2}^{h/2} y \sigma_{xx}(L, y) \mathrm{d}y = 0,$$

$$\int_{-h/2}^{h/2} \sigma_{xy}(L, y) \mathrm{d}y = -P/w.$$

The conditions at the wall are fully constrained at the neutral axis ($y = 0$) and no rotation at the top corner ($y = h/2$):

$$u(0, 0) = 0,$$

$$v(0, 0) = 0,$$

$$u(0, h/2) = 0.$$

The displacement in the x and y directions thus become

$$u = 1/2 \left(2 \frac{P y^3}{h^3 w} - 3/2 \frac{y P}{h w} + \alpha \left(-6 \frac{x^2 P y}{h^3 w} + 12 \frac{L P y x}{h^3 w} + 2 \frac{P y^3}{h^3 w} \right. \right.$$
$$\left. \left. - 1/2 \frac{(-2P + \alpha P)y}{w \alpha h} \right) \right) \mu^{-1},$$

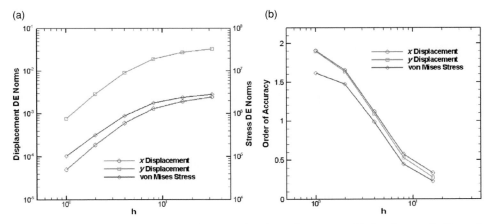

Figure 6.4 Discretization error (a) and observed orders of accuracy (b) for the steady Burger's equation with Reynolds number $Re = 8$.

$$v = 1/2 \left(6\frac{xPy^2}{h^3w} - 6\frac{xPLy^2}{h^3w} - 3/2\frac{xP}{hw} + \alpha \left(-6\frac{xPy^2}{h^3w} + 6\frac{PLy^2}{h^3w} \right. \right.$$
$$\left. \left. + 2\frac{x^3P}{h^3w} - 6\frac{PLx^2}{h^3w} + 1/2\frac{(-2P + \alpha P)x}{w\alpha h} \right) \right) \mu^{-1}, \tag{6.18}$$

where μ is the shear modulus.

Finite element solutions were obtained for the weak form of Eq. (6.15) using linear basis functions, which gives a formally second-order accurate scheme for the displacements (Seidel, 2009). The maximum von Mises stress J_2 was also computed according to

$$J_2 = \frac{1}{6} \left[\left(\sigma_{xx} - \sigma_{yy} \right)^2 + \sigma_{xx}^2 + \sigma_{yy}^2 + 6\sigma_{xy}^2 \right].$$

Simulations were run using six systematically-refined mesh levels from a coarse mesh of eight elements to a fine mesh of 8192 elements. Figure 6.4a shows the L_2 norms of the discretization error in the displacements and the discretization error in maximum von Mises stress, with all three quantities displaying convergent behavior. The orders of accuracy for these three quantities are given in Figure 6.4b and show that the displacements asymptote to second-order accuracy while the maximum von Mises stress appears to converge to somewhat less than second order.

6.3 Method of manufactured solutions (MMS)

This section addresses the difficult question of how to create an exact solution for complex PDEs, where complexity refers to characteristics such as nonlinearity, nonconstant coefficients, irregular domain shape, higher dimensions, multiple submodels, and coupled systems of equations. The traditional methods for obtaining exact solutions discussed

earlier generally cannot handle this level of complexity. The primary need for exact solutions
to complex PDEs is for order of accuracy testing during code verification.

The *method of manufactured solutions* (MMS) is a general and very powerful approach
for creating exact solutions. Rather than trying to find an exact solution to a PDE with given
initial and boundary conditions, the goal is to "manufacture" an exact solution to a slightly
modified equation. For code verification purposes, it is not required that the manufactured
solution be related to a physically realistic problem; recall that code verification deals only
with the mathematics of a given problem. The general concept behind MMS is to choose
a solution *a priori*, then operate the governing PDEs onto the chosen solution, thereby
generating additional analytic source terms that require no discretization. The chosen
(manufactured) solution is then the exact solution to the modified governing equations
made up of the original equations plus the additional analytic source terms. Thus, MMS
involves the solution to the backward problem: given an original set of equations and a
chosen solution, find a modified set of equations that the chosen solution will satisfy.

While the MMS approach for generating exact solutions was not new (e.g., see
Zadunaisky, 1976; Stetter, 1978), Roache and Steinberg (1984) and Steinberg and Roache
(1985) appear to be the first to employ these exact solutions for the purposes of code
verification. Their original work looked at the asymptotic rate of convergence of the discretization errors with systematic mesh refinement. Shih (1985) independently developed a
similar procedure for debugging scientific computing codes, but without employing mesh
refinement to assess convergence or order of accuracy.

The concepts behind MMS for the purpose of code verification were later refined by
Roache *et al.* (1990) and Roache (1998). The term "manufactured solution" was coined by
Oberkampf *et al.* (1995) and refers to the fact that the method generates (or manufactures)
a related set of governing equations for a chosen analytic solution. An extensive discussion
of manufactured solutions for code verification is presented by Knupp and Salari (2003)
and includes details of the method as well as application to a variety of different PDEs.
Recent reviews of the MMS procedure are presented by Roache (2002) and Roy (2005).
While it is not uncommon for MMS to be used for verifying computational fluid dynamics
codes (e.g., Roache *et al.*, 1990; Pelletier *et al.*, 2004; Roy *et al.*, 2004; Eca *et al.*, 2007),
it has also begun to appear in other disciplines, for example, fluid–structure interaction
(Tremblay *et al.*, 2006).

MMS allows the generation of exact solutions to PDEs of nearly arbitrary complexity, with notable exceptions discussed in Section 6.3.3. When combined with the order
verification procedure described in Chapter 5, MMS provides a powerful tool for code
verification. When physically realistic manufactured solutions are desired, the modified
MMS approaches discussed in Section 6.4 can be used.

6.3.1 Procedure

The procedure for creating an exact solution using MMS is fairly straightforward. For a
scalar mathematical model, this procedure can be summarized as follows.

Step 1 Establish the mathematical model in the form $L(u) = 0$, where $L(\bullet)$ is the differential operator and u the dependent variable.

Step 2 Choose the analytic form of the manufactured solution $\hat{u}$.

Step 3 Operate the mathematical model $L(\bullet)$ onto the manufactured solution $\hat{u}$. to obtain the analytic source term $s = L(\hat{u})$.

Step 4 Obtain the modified form of the mathematical model by including the analytic source term $L(u) = s$.

Because of the manner in which the analytic source term is obtained, it is a function of the independent variables only and does not depend on u. The initial and boundary conditions can be obtained directly from the manufactured solution $\hat{u}$. For a system of equations, the manufactured solution $\hat{u}$ and the source term s are simply considered to be vectors, but otherwise the process is unchanged.

An advantage of using MMS to generate exact solutions to general mathematical models is that the procedure is not affected by nonlinearities or coupled sets of equations. However, the approach is conceptually different from the standard training scientists and engineers receive in problem solving. Thus it is helpful to examine a simple example which highlights the subtle nature of MMS.

Consider again the unsteady 1-D heat conduction equation that was examined in Section 6.2.1.1. The governing partial differential equation written in the form $L(T) = 0$ is

$$\frac{\partial T}{\partial t} - \alpha \frac{\partial^2 T}{\partial x^2} = 0. \tag{6.19}$$

Once the governing equation has been specified, the next step is to choose the analytic manufactured solution. A detailed discussion on how to choose the solution will follow in Section 6.3.1.1, but for now, consider a combination of exponential and sinusoidal functions:

$$\hat{T}(x, t) = T_o \exp\left(t/t_o\right) \sin\left(\pi x/L\right). \tag{6.20}$$

Due to the analytic nature of this chosen solution, the derivatives that appear in the governing equation can be evaluated exactly as

$$\frac{\partial \hat{T}}{\partial t} = T_o \sin\left(\pi x/L\right) \frac{1}{t_o} \exp\left(t/t_o\right)$$

$$\frac{\partial^2 \hat{T}}{\partial x^2} = -T_o \exp\left(t/t_o\right) \left(\pi/L\right)^2 \sin\left(\pi x/L\right).$$

We now modify the mathematical model by including the above derivatives, along with the thermal diffusivity α, on the right hand side of the equation. The modified governing equation that results is

$$\frac{\partial T}{\partial t} - \alpha \frac{\partial^2 T}{\partial x^2} = \left[\frac{1}{t_0} + \alpha \left(\frac{\pi}{L}\right)^2\right] T_o \exp\left(t/t_o\right) \sin\left(\pi x/L\right). \tag{6.21}$$

The left hand side of Eq. (6.21) is the same as in the original mathematical model given by Eq. (6.19), thus no modifications to the underlying numerical discretization in the code under consideration need to be made. The right hand side could be thought of in physical terms as a distributed source term, but in fact it is simply a convenient mathematical construct that will allow straightforward code verification testing. The key concept behind MMS is that the exact solution to Eq. (6.21) is known and is given by Eq. (6.20), the manufactured solution $\hat{T}(x, t)$ that was chosen in the beginning.

As the governing equations become more complex, symbolic manipulation tools such as Mathematica™, Maple™, or MuPAD should be used. These tools have matured greatly over the last two decades and can produce rapid symbolic differentiation and simplification of expressions. Most symbolic manipulation software packages have built-in capabilities to output the solution and the source terms directly as computer source code in both Fortran and C/C++ programming languages.

6.3.1.1 Manufactured solution guidelines for code verification

When used for code verification studies, manufactured solutions should be chosen to be analytic functions with smooth derivatives. It is important to ensure that no derivatives vanish, including cross-derivatives if these show up in the governing equations. Trigonometric and exponential functions are recommended since they are smooth and infinitely differentiable. Recall that the order verification procedures involve systematically refining the spatial mesh and/or time step, thus obtaining numerical solutions can be expensive for complex 3-D applications. In some cases, the high cost of performing order verification studies in multiple dimensions using MMS can be significantly reduced simply by reducing the frequency content of the manufactured solution over the selected domain. In other words, it is not important to have a full period of a sinusoidal manufactured solution in the domain, often only a fraction (one-third, one-fifth, etc.) of a period is sufficient to exercise the terms in the code.

Although the manufactured solutions do not need to be physically realistic when used for code verification, they should be chosen to obey certain physical constraints. For example, if the code requires the temperature to be positive (e.g., in the evaluation of the speed of sound which involves the square root of the temperature), then the manufactured solution should be chosen to give temperature values significantly larger than zero.

Care should be taken that one term in the governing equations does not dominate the other terms. For example, even if the actual application area for a Navier–Stokes code will be for high-Reynolds number flows, when performing code verification studies, the manufactured solution should be chosen to give Reynolds numbers near unity so that convective and diffusive terms are of the same order of magnitude. For terms that have small relative magnitudes (e.g., if the term is scaled by a small parameter such as 1/Re), mistakes can still be found through order verification, but possibly only on extremely fine meshes.

A more rigorous approach to ensuring that all of the terms in the governing equations are roughly the same order of magnitude over some significant region of the domain is to examine ratios of those terms. This process has been used by Roy *et al.* (2007b) as part of the order of accuracy verification of a computational fluid dynamics code including

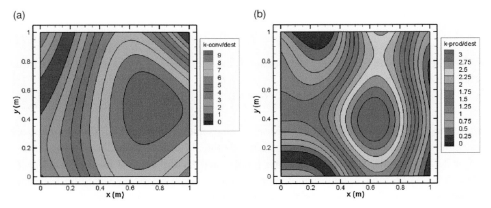

Figure 6.5 Ratios of (a) the convection terms and (b) the production terms to the destruction terms for a turbulent kinetic energy transport equation (from Roy *et al.*, 2007b).

a complicated two-equation turbulence model. Example ratios for different terms in the equation governing the transport of turbulent kinetic energy are given in Figure 6.5. These plots show that the convection, production, and destruction terms in this transport equation are of roughly the same order of magnitude over most of the domain.

6.3.1.2 Boundary and initial conditions

The discretization schemes for the PDE and the various submodels comprise a significant fraction of the possible options in most scientific computing codes. When performing code verification studies on these options, there are two approaches for handling boundary and initial conditions. The first approach is to impose the mathematically consistent boundary and initial conditions that are required according to the mathematical character of the differential equations. For example, if Dirichlet (fixed-value) or Neumann (fixed-gradient) boundary conditions are required, these can be determined directly from the analytic manufactured solution (although these will generally not be constant along the boundary). The second option is to simply specify all boundary values with Dirichlet or Neumann values from the manufactured solution. This latter approach, although mathematically ill-posed, often does not adversely affect the order of accuracy test. In any case, over-specification of boundary conditions will not lead to a false positive for order of accuracy testing (i.e., a case where the order of accuracy is verified but there is a mistake in the code or inconsistency in the discrete algorithm).

In order to verify the implementation of the boundary conditions, the manufactured solution should be tailored to exactly satisfy a given boundary condition on a domain boundary. Bond *et al.* (2007) present a general approach for tailoring manufactured solutions to ensure that a given boundary condition is satisfied along a general boundary. The method involves multiplying any standard manufactured solution by a function which has values and/or derivatives which are zero over a specified boundary. To modify the standard form of the manufactured solution for a 2-D steady-state solution for temperature, one may simply write the manufactured solution as follows:

$$\hat{T}(x, y) = T_0 + \hat{T}_1(x, y), \tag{6.22}$$

where $\hat{T}_1(x, y)$ is any baseline manufactured solution. For example, this manufactured solution could take the form

$$\hat{T}_1(x, y) = T_x f_s\left(\frac{a_x \pi x}{L}\right) + T_y f_s\left(\frac{a_y \pi y}{L}\right), \tag{6.23}$$

where the $f_s(\cdot)$ functions represent a mixture of sines and cosines and T_x, T_y, a_x, and a_y are constants (note the subscripts used here do not denote differentiation).

For 2-D problems, a boundary can be represented by the general curve $F(x, y) = C$, where C is a constant. A new manufactured solution appropriate for verifying boundary conditions can be found by multiplying the spatially-varying portion of $\hat{T}(x, y)$ by the function $[C - F(x, y)]^m$, i.e.,

$$\hat{T}_{BC}(x, y) = T_0 + \hat{T}_1(x, y)[C - F(x, y)]^m. \tag{6.24}$$

This procedure will ensure that the manufactured solution is equal to the constant T_0 along the specified boundary for $m = 1$. Setting $m = 2$, in addition to enforcing the above Dirichlet BC for temperature, will ensure that the gradient of temperature normal to the boundary is equal to zero, i.e., the adiabatic boundary condition for this 2-D steady heat conduction example. In practice, the curve $F(x, y) = C$ is used to define the domain boundary where the boundary conditions will be tested.

To illustrate this procedure, we will choose the following simple manufactured solution for temperature:

$$\hat{T}(x, y) = 300 + 25 \cos\left(\frac{7}{4} \frac{\pi x}{L}\right) + 40 \sin\left(\frac{4}{3} \frac{\pi y}{L}\right), \tag{6.25}$$

where the temperature is assumed to be in units of Kelvin. For the surface where the Dirichlet or Neumann boundary condition will be applied, choose:

$$F(x, y) = \frac{1}{2} \cos\left(\frac{0.4\pi x}{L}\right) - \frac{y}{L} = 0. \tag{6.26}$$

A mesh bounded on the left by $x/L = 0$, on the right by $x/L = 1$, on the top by $y/L = 1$, and on the bottom by the above defined surface $F(x, y) = 0$ is shown in Figure 6.6a. The standard manufactured solution given by Eq. (6.25) is also shown in Figure 6.6b, where clearly the constant value and gradient boundary conditions are not satisfied.

Combining the baseline manufactured solution with the boundary specification yields

$$\hat{T}_{BC}(x, y) = 300 + \left[25 \cos\left(\frac{7}{4} \frac{\pi x}{L}\right) + 40 \sin\left(\frac{4}{3} \frac{\pi y}{L}\right)\right]\left[-\frac{1}{2} \cos\left(\frac{0.4\pi x}{L}\right) + \frac{y}{L}\right]^m. \tag{6.27}$$

When $m = 1$, the curved lower boundary will satisfy the constant temperature condition of 300 K as shown in the manufactured solutions of Figure 6.7a. When $m = 2$ (Figure 6.7b),

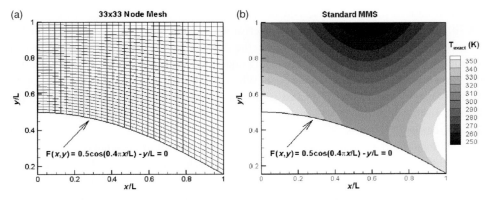

Figure 6.6 Grid (a) and baseline manufactured solution (b) for the MMS boundary condition example.

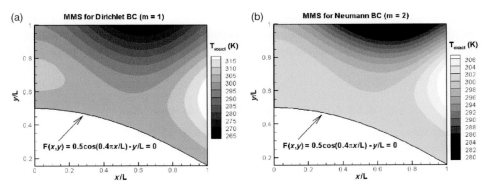

Figure 6.7 Manufactured solutions given by Eq. (6.27): (a) fixed temperature boundary condition ($m = 1$) and (b) fixed temperature and zero gradient (adiabatic) boundary condition ($m = 2$).

the zero gradient (i.e., adiabatic) boundary condition is also satisfied. For more details on this approach as well as extensions to 3-D, see Bond *et al.* (2007).

6.3.2 Benefits of MMS for code verification

There are a number of benefits to using the MMS procedure for code verification. Perhaps the most important benefit is that it handles complex mathematical models without additional difficulty since the procedures described above are readily extendible to nonlinear, coupled systems of equations. In addition, MMS can be used to verify most of the coding options available in scientific computing codes, including the consistency/convergence of numerical algorithms. The procedure is not tied to a specific discretization scheme, but works equally well for finite-difference, finite-volume, and finite-element methods.

The use of MMS for code verification has been shown to be remarkably sensitive to mistakes in the discretization (see for example Chapter 3.11 of Roache (1998)). In one particular case of a compressible Navier–Stokes code for unstructured grids (Roy *et al.*, 2007b), global norms of the discretization error were found to be non-convergent. Further investigation found a small discrepancy (in the fourth significant figure!) for the constant thermal conductivity between the governing equations used to generate the source terms and the model implementation in the code. When this discrepancy was corrected, the order verification test was passed. The same study uncovered an algorithm inconsistency in the discrete formulation of the diffusion operator that resulted in non-ordered behavior on skewed meshes. This same formulation had been implemented in at least one commercial computational fluid dynamics code (see Roy *et al.* (2007b) for more details).

In addition to its ability to indicate the presence of coding mistakes (i.e., bugs), the MMS procedure combined with order verification is also a powerful tool for finding and removing those mistakes (i.e., debugging). After a failed order of accuracy test, individual terms in the mathematical model and the numerical discretization can be omitted, allowing the user to quickly isolate the terms with the coding mistake. When combined with the approach for verifying boundary conditions discussed in the previous section and a suite of meshes with different topologies (e.g., hexahedral, prismatic, tetrahedral, and hybrid meshes, as discussed in Chapter 5), the user has a comprehensive set of tools to aid in code debugging.

6.3.3 *Limitations of MMS for code verification*

There are some limitations to using the MMS procedure for code verification. The principal disadvantage is that it requires the user to incorporate arbitrary source terms, initial conditions, and boundary conditions in a code. Even when the code provides a framework for including these additional interfaces, their specific form changes for each different manufactured solution. The MMS procedure is thus code-intrusive and generally cannot be performed as a black-box testing procedure where the code simply returns some outputs based on a given set of inputs. In addition, each code option which changes the mathematical model requires new source terms to be generated. Thus order verification with MMS can be time consuming when many code options must be verified.

Since the MMS procedure for code verification relies on having smooth solutions, the analysis of discontinuous weak solutions (e.g., solutions with shock-waves) is still an open research issue. Some traditional exact solutions exist for discontinuous problems such as the generalized Riemann problem (Gottlieb and Groth, 1988) and more complicated solutions involving shock waves and detonations have been developed that involve infinite series (Powers and Stewart, 1992) or a change of dependent variable (Powers and Aslam, 2006). However, to our knowledge, discontinuous manufactured solutions have not been created. Such "weak" exact solutions are needed for verifying codes used to solve problems with discontinuities.

Difficulties also arise when applying MMS to mathematical models where the governing equations themselves contain `min`, `max`, or other nonsmooth switching functions. These functions generally do not result in continuous manufactured solution source terms. These

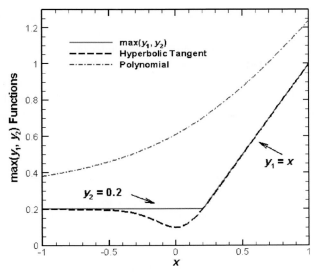

Figure 6.8 Examples of smooth approximations for max(y_1, y_2) using the hyperbolic tangent from Eq. (6.28) and the polynomial from Eq. (6.29).

switching functions can be dealt with by simply turning off different branches of the switching functions (Eca *et al.*, 2007) or by tailoring the manufactured solution so that only one switching branch will be used for a given verification test (Roy *et al.*, 2007b). The former is simpler but more code intrusive than the latter approach. We recommend that model developers employ smooth blending functions such as the hyperbolic tangent both to simplify the code verification testing and to possibly make the numerical solution process more robust. For example, consider the function max(y_1, y_2), where y_1 and y_2 are given by

$$y_1(x) = x,$$
$$y_2 = 0.2.$$

One approach for smoothing this max function in the region of $x = 0.2$ is the hyperbolic tangent smoothing function given by

$$\max(y_1, y_2) \approx F y_1 + (1 - F) y_2,$$
$$\text{where } F = \frac{1}{2} \left[\tanh \left(y_1 / y_2 \right) + 1 \right]. \tag{6.28}$$

Another approach is to use the following polynomial expression:

$$\max(y_1, y_2) \approx \frac{\sqrt{(y_1 - y_2)^2 + 1} + y_1 + y_2}{2}. \tag{6.29}$$

The two approximations of max(y_1, y_2) are shown graphically in Figure 6.8. The hyperbolic tangent approximation provides less error relative to the original max(y_1, y_2) function, but creates an inflection point where the first derivative (slope) of this function will change sign. The polynomial function is monotone, but gives a larger error magnitude. Models that rely on tabulated data (i.e., look-up tables) suffer from similar problems, and smooth approximations of such data should be considered. MMS is also limited when the mathematical model contains complex algebraic submodels which do not have closed-form solutions and thus must be solved numerically (e.g., by a root-finding algorithm). Such complex submodels are best addressed separately through unit and/or component level software testing discussed in Chapter 4.

6.3.4 Examples of MMS with order verification

Two examples are now presented which use MMS to generate exact solutions. These manufactured solutions are then employed for code verification using the order of accuracy test.

6.3.4.1 2-D steady heat conduction

Order verification using MMS has been applied to steady-state heat conduction with a constant thermal diffusivity. The governing equation simply reduces to Poisson's equation for temperature:

$$\frac{\partial^2 T}{\partial x^2} + \frac{\partial^2 T}{\partial y^2} = s(x, y), \tag{6.30}$$

where $s(x, y)$ is the manufactured solution source term. Coordinate transformations of the form

$$(x, y) \rightarrow (\xi, \eta)$$

are used to globally transform the governing equation into a Cartesian computational space with $\Delta \xi = \Delta \eta = 1$ (Thompson *et al.*, 1985). The transformed governing equation thus becomes

$$\frac{\partial F_1}{\partial \xi} + \frac{\partial G_1}{\partial \eta} = \frac{s(x, y)}{J}, \tag{6.31}$$

where J is the Jacobian of the mesh transformation. The fluxes F_1 and G_1 are defined as

$$F_1 = \frac{\xi_x}{J} F + \frac{\xi_y}{J} G,$$
$$G_1 = \frac{\eta_x}{J} F + \frac{\eta_y}{J} G,$$

where

$$F = \xi_x \frac{\partial T}{\partial \xi} + \eta_x \frac{\partial T}{\partial \eta},$$
$$G = \xi_y \frac{\partial T}{\partial \xi} + \eta_y \frac{\partial T}{\partial \eta}.$$

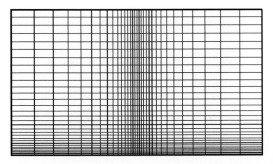

Figure 6.9 Stretched Cartesian mesh with 33×33 nodes for the 2-D steady heat conduction problem.

An explicit point Jacobi method (Tannehill *et al.*, 1997) is used to advance the discrete equations towards the steady-state solution. Standard, three-point, centered finite differences are used in the transformed coordinates and central differences are also employed for the grid transformation metric terms (x_ξ, x_η, y_ξ, etc.), thus resulting in a discretization scheme that is formally second-order accurate in space. The numerical solutions were iteratively converged to machine zero, i.e., the iterative residuals were reduced by approximately 14 orders of magnitude for the double precision computations employed. Thus iterative and round-off error are assumed to be negligible and the numerical solutions are effectively the exact solution to the discrete equation.

The following manufactured solution was chosen

$$\hat{T}(x, y) = T_0 + T_x \cos\left(\frac{a_x \pi x}{L}\right) + T_y \sin\left(\frac{a_y \pi y}{L}\right) + T_{xy} \sin\left(\frac{a_{xy} \pi x y}{L^2}\right), \quad (6.32)$$

where

$$T_0 = 400 \text{ K}, \quad T_x = 45 \text{ K}, \quad T_y = 35 \text{ K}, \quad T_{xy} = 27.5 \text{ K},$$
$$a_x = 1/3, \quad a_y = 1/4, \quad a_{xy} = 1/2, \quad L = 5 \text{ m},$$

and Dirichlet (fixed-value) boundary conditions were applied on all four boundaries as determined by Eq. (6.32). A family of stretched Cartesian meshes was created by first generating the finest mesh (129×129 nodes), and then successively eliminating every other gridline to create the coarser meshes. Thus systematic refinement (or coarsening in this case) is ensured. The 33×33 node mesh is presented in Figure 6.9, showing significant stretching in the x-direction in the center of the domain and in the y-direction near the bottom boundary. The manufactured solution from Eq. (6.32) is shown graphically in Figure 6.10. The temperature varies smoothly over the domain and the manufactured solution gives variations in both coordinate directions.

Discrete L_2 norms of the discretization error (i.e., the difference between the numerical solution and the manufactured solution) were computed for grid levels from 129×129 nodes ($h = 1$) to 9×9 nodes ($h = 16$). These norms are given in Figure 6.11a and closely follow the expected second order slope. The observed order of accuracy of the L_2 norms of the discretization error was computed from Eq. (5.23) for successive mesh levels, and the

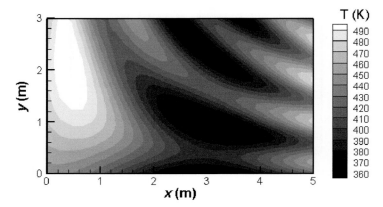

Figure 6.10 Manufactured solution for temperature for the 2-D steady heat conduction problem.

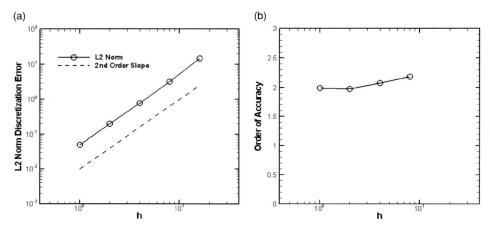

Figure 6.11 Code verification for the 2-D steady heat conduction problem: (a) discrete L2 norms of the discretization error and (b) observed order of accuracy.

results are shown in Figure 6.11b. The observed order of accuracy is shown to converge to the formal order of two as the meshes are refined, thus the code is considered to be verified for the options tested. Note that while the discrete transformations were tested with respect to the clustering of the mesh, this choice of grid topologies would not test the implementation of the grid metric terms dealing with cell skewness or coordinate rotation (e.g., ξ_y, η_x).

6.3.4.2 2D Steady Euler equations

This MMS example deals with the Euler equations, which govern the flow of an inviscid fluid. This example is adapted from Roy *et al.* (2004) and we will demonstrate the steps of both generating the exact solution with MMS and the order verification procedure. The two-dimensional, steady-state form of the Euler equations is given by

$$\frac{\partial(\rho u)}{\partial x} + \frac{\partial(\rho v)}{\partial y} = s_m(x, y),$$

$$\frac{\partial(\rho u^2 + p)}{\partial x} + \frac{\partial(\rho u v)}{\partial y} = s_x(x, y),$$

$$\frac{\partial(\rho v u)}{\partial x} + \frac{\partial(\rho v^2 + p)}{\partial y} = s_y(x, y),$$

$$\frac{\partial(\rho u e_t + p u)}{\partial x} + \frac{\partial(\rho v e_t + p v)}{\partial y} = s_e(x, y), \tag{6.33}$$

where arbitrary source terms $s(x, y)$ are included on the right hand side for use with MMS. In these equations, u and v are the Cartesian components of velocity in the x- and y-directions, ρ the density, p the pressure, and e_t is the specific total energy, which for a calorically perfect gas is given by

$$e_t = \frac{1}{\gamma - 1} RT + \frac{u^2 + v^2}{2}, \tag{6.34}$$

where R is the specific gas constant, T the temperature, and γ the ratio of specific heats. The final relation used to close the set of equations is the perfect gas equation of state:

$$p = \rho RT. \tag{6.35}$$

The manufactured solutions for this case are chosen as simple sinusoidal functions given by

$$\rho(x, y) = \rho_0 + \rho_x \sin\left(\frac{a_{\rho x} \pi x}{L}\right) + \rho_y \cos\left(\frac{a_{\rho y} \pi y}{L}\right),$$

$$u(x, y) = u_0 + u_x \sin\left(\frac{a_{ux} \pi x}{L}\right) + u_y \cos\left(\frac{a_{uy} \pi y}{L}\right),$$

$$v(x, y) = v_0 + v_x \cos\left(\frac{a_{vx} \pi x}{L}\right) + v_y \sin\left(\frac{a_{vy} \pi y}{L}\right),$$

$$p(x, y) = p_0 + p_x \cos\left(\frac{a_{px} \pi x}{L}\right) + p_y \sin\left(\frac{a_{py} \pi y}{L}\right). \tag{6.36}$$

The subscripts here refer to constants (not differentiation) with the same units as the variable, and the dimensionless constants a generally vary between 0.5 and 1.5 to provide low frequency solutions over an $L \times L$ square domain. For this example, the constants were chosen to give supersonic flow in both the positive x and positive y directions. While not necessary, this choice simplifies the inflow boundary conditions to Dirichlet (specified) values at the inflow boundaries, whereas outflow boundary values are simply extrapolated from the interior. The inflow boundary conditions are specified directly from the manufactured solution. The specific constants chosen for this example are shown in Table 6.2, and a plot of the manufactured solution for the density is given in Figure 6.12. The density varies smoothly in both coordinate directions between 0.92 and 1.13 kg/m³.

Table 6.2 *Constants for the supersonic Euler manufactured solution*

Equation, ϕ	ϕ_0	ϕ_x	ϕ_y	$a_{\phi x}$	$a_{\phi y}$
$\rho(\text{kg/m}^3)$	1	0.15	-0.1	1	0.5
$u(\text{m/s})$	800	50	-30	1.5	0.6
$v(\text{m/s})$	800	-75	40	0.5	2./3.
$p(\text{N/m}^2)$	1×10^5	0.2×10^5	0.5×10^5	2	1

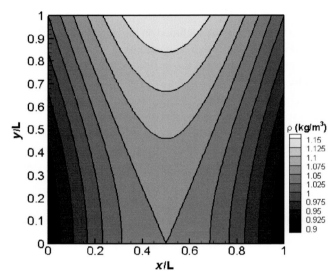

Figure 6.12 Manufactured solution for density for the Euler equations.

Substitution of the chosen manufactured solutions into the governing equations allows the analytic determination of the source terms. For example, the source term for the mass conservation equation is given by:

$$s_m(x, y) = \frac{a_{ux}\pi u_x}{L} \cos\left(\frac{a_{ux}\pi x}{L}\right) \left[\rho_0 + \rho_x \sin\left(\frac{a_{\rho x}\pi x}{L}\right) + \rho_y \cos\left(\frac{a_{\rho y}\pi y}{L}\right)\right]$$
$$+ \frac{a_{vy}\pi v_y}{L} \cos\left(\frac{a_{vy}\pi y}{L}\right) \left[\rho_0 + \rho_x \sin\left(\frac{a_{\rho x}\pi x}{L}\right) + \rho_y \cos\left(\frac{a_{\rho y}\pi y}{L}\right)\right]$$
$$+ \frac{a_{\rho x}\pi \rho_x}{L} \cos\left(\frac{a_{\rho x}\pi x}{L}\right) \left[u_0 + u_x \sin\left(\frac{a_{ux}\pi x}{L}\right) + u_y \cos\left(\frac{a_{uy}\pi y}{L}\right)\right]$$
$$+ \frac{a_{\rho y}\pi \rho_y}{L} \sin\left(\frac{a_{\rho y}\pi y}{L}\right) \left[v_0 + v_x \cos\left(\frac{a_{vx}\pi x}{L}\right) + v_y \sin\left(\frac{a_{vy}\pi y}{L}\right)\right].$$

The source terms for the momentum and energy equations are significantly more complex, and all source terms were obtained using Mathematica™. A plot of the source term for the energy conservation equation is given in Figure 6.13. Note the smooth variations of the source term in both coordinate directions.

Table 6.3 *Cartesian meshes employed
in the Euler manufactured solution*

Mesh name	Mesh nodes	Mesh spacing, h
Mesh 1	129×129	1
Mesh 2	65×65	2
Mesh 3	33×33	4
Mesh 4	17×17	8
Mesh 5	9×9	16

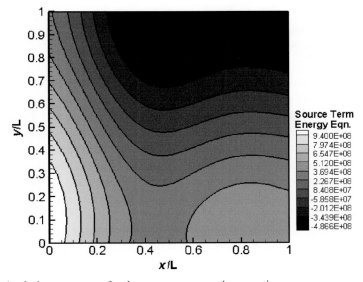

Figure 6.13 Analytic source term for the energy conservation equation.

The governing equations are discretized and solved on multiple meshes. In this case, two different finite-volume computational fluid dynamics codes were employed: Premo, an unstructured grid code, and Wind, a structured grid code (see Roy *et al.* (2004) for more details). Both codes utilized the second-order Roe upwind scheme for the convective terms (Roe, 1981). The formal order of accuracy of both codes is thus second order for smooth problems.

The five Cartesian meshes employed are summarized in Table 6.3. The coarser meshes were found by successively eliminating every other grid line from the fine mesh (i.e., a grid refinement factor of $r = 2$). It is important to note that while the current example was performed on Cartesian meshes for simplicity, a more general code verification analysis would employ the most general meshes which will be used by the code (e.g., unstructured

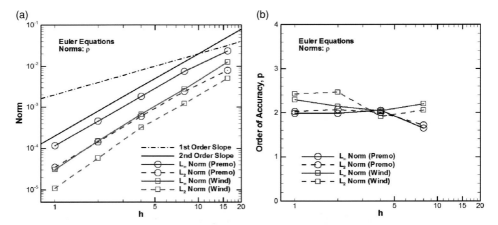

Figure 6.14 Code verification results for the 2-D steady Euler equations: (a) norms of the discretization error and (b) observed order of accuracy.

meshes with significant stretching, skewness, boundary orientations). See Section 5.4 for additional discussion of mesh topology issues.

The global discretization error is measured using discrete L_∞ and L_2 norms of the discretization error, where the exact solution comes directly from the chosen manufactured solution given by Eqs. (6.36). The behavior of these two discretization error norms for the density ρ as a function of the cell size h is given in Figure 6.14a. On the logarithmic scale, a first-order scheme will display a slope of unity, while a second-order scheme will give a slope of two. The discretization error norms for the density appear to converge with second-order accuracy.

A more quantitative method for assessing the observed order of accuracy is to calculate it using the norms of the discretization error. Since the exact solution is known, the relation for the observed order of accuracy of the discretization error norms comes from Eq. (5.23). A plot of the observed order of accuracy as a function of the element size h is presented in Figure 6.14b. The Premo code clearly asymptotes to second-order accuracy, while the Wind code appears to asymptote to an order of accuracy that is slightly higher than two. In general, an observed order of accuracy higher than the formal order can occur due to error cancellation and should not be considered as a failure of the order verification test (although it may indicate mistakes is determining the formal order of accuracy of the method). Further grid refinement would possibly provide more definitive results for the Wind code. In this case, the observed order of accuracy for both codes is near two, thus the formal order of accuracy is recovered, and the two codes are considered verified for the options examined.

6.4 Physically realistic manufactured solutions

The MMS procedure discussed in the previous section is the most general method for obtaining exact solutions to mathematical models for use in code verification studies. Since physical realism of the solutions is not required during code verification, the solutions are somewhat arbitrary and can be tailored to exercise all terms in the mathematical model. However, there are many cases in which physically realistic exact solutions are desired, such as assessing sensitivity of a numerical scheme to mesh quality, evaluating the reliability of discretization error estimators, and judging the overall effectiveness of solution adaptation schemes. There are two main approaches for obtaining physically realistic manufactured solutions to complex equations, and these two approached are discussed below.

6.4.1 Theory-based solutions

One approach to obtaining physically realistic manufactured solutions is to use a simplified theoretical model of the physical phenomenon as a basis for the manufactured solution. For example, if a physical process is known to exhibit an exponential decay in the solution with time, then a manufactured solution of the form

$$\alpha \exp\left(-\beta t\right)$$

could be employed, where α and β could be chosen to provide physically meaningful solutions.

There are two examples of this approach applied to the modeling of fluid turbulence. Pelletier *et al.* (2004) have verified a 2-D incompressible finite element code that employs a k-ε two-equation turbulence model. They constructed manufactured solutions which mimic turbulent shear flows, with the turbulent kinetic energy and the turbulent eddy viscosity as the two quantities specified in the manufactured solution. More recently, Eca and Hoekstra (2006) and Eca *et al.* (2007) developed physically realistic manufactured solutions mimicking steady, wall-bounded turbulence for 2-D incompressible Navier–Stokes codes. They examined both one- and two-equation turbulence models and noted challenges in generating physically realistic solutions in the near-wall region.

6.4.2 Method of nearby problems (MNP)

The second approach for generating physically realistic manufactured solutions is called the *method of nearby problems* (MNP) and was proposed by Roy and Hopkins (2003). This approach involves first computing a highly-refined numerical solution for the problem of interest, then generating an accurate curve fit of that numerical solution. If both the underlying numerical solution and the curve fit are "sufficiently" accurate, then it will result in a manufactured solution which has small source terms. The sufficiency conditions for the "nearness" of the problem have been explored for first-order quasi-linear ordinary differential equations (Hopkins and Roy, 2004) but rigorous bounds on this nearness requirement for PDEs have not yet been developed.

MNP has been successfully demonstrated for one-dimensional problems by Roy *et al.* (2007a) who used the procedure to create a nearby solution to the steady-state Burgers'

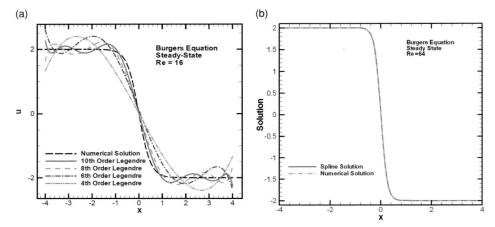

Figure 6.15 Examples of curve fitting for the viscous shock wave solution to Burgers' equation: (a) global Legendre polynomial fits for Re = 16 and (b) fifth-order Hermite splines for Re = 64 (from Roy *et al.*, 2007a).

equation for a viscous shock wave. They used fifth-order Hermite splines to generate the exact solutions for Reynolds numbers of 8, 64, and 512. To explain why spline fits must be used, rather than global curve fits, consider Figure 6.15. Global Legendre polynomial fits for the steady-state Burgers' equation for a viscous shock at a Reynolds number of 16 are given in Figure 6.15a. Not only is the viscous shock wave not adequately resolved, but the global fits also exhibit significant oscillations at the boundaries. Hermite spline fits for an even higher Reynolds number of 64 are given in Figure 6.15b, with the spline fit in very good qualitative agreement with the underlying numerical solution. MNP has been extended to 2-D problems by Roy and Sinclair (2009) and the further extension to higher dimensions is straightforward. A 2-D example of MNP used to generate an exact solution to the incompressible Navier–Stokes equations will be given in Section 6.4.2.2.

6.4.2.1 Procedure

The steps for generating physically realistic manufactured solutions using the MNP approach are:

1 compute the original numerical solution on a highly refined grid,
2 generate an accurate spline or curve fit to this numerical solution, thereby providing an analytic representation of the numerical solution,
3 operate the governing partial differential equations on the curve fit to generate analytic source terms (which ideally will be small), and
4 create the nearby problem by appending the analytic source terms to the original mathematical model.

If the source terms are indeed small, then the new problem will be "near" the original one, hence the name "method of nearby problems." The key point to this approach is that, by

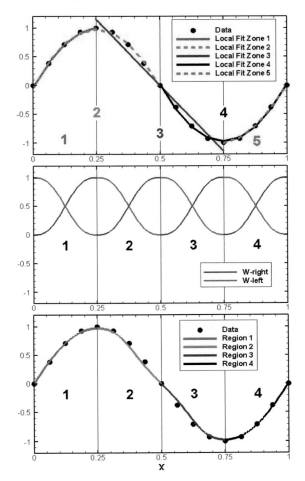

Figure 6.16 Simple one-dimensional example of the weighting function approach for combining local quadratic least squares fits to generate a C^2 continuous spline fit: local fits (top), weighting functions (middle), and resulting C^2 continuous spline fit (bottom) (from Roy and Sinclair, 2009). (See color plate section.)

definition, the curve fit generated in step 2 is the exact solution to the nearby problem. While the approach is very similar to MMS, in MNP the addition of the curve fitting step is designed to provide a physically realistic exact solution.

To demonstrate the MNP procedure, a simple 1-D example is presented in Figure 6.16, where the original data used to generate the curve fit are 17 points sampled at equal intervals from the function $\sin(2\pi x)$. The goal of this example is to create a spline fit made up of four spline regions that exhibits C^2 continuity at the spline zone interfaces (i.e., continuity up to the second derivative). The spline fitting is performed in a manner that allows arbitrary levels of continuity at spline boundaries and is readily extendible to multiple dimensions following Junkins *et al.* (1973).

The first step is to generate five overlapping local fits Z_1 through Z_5, with each of the interior fits spanning two spline regions (see top of Figure 6.16). A least squares method is used to find a best-fit quadratic function in each of the five regions:

$$Z_n(\bar{x}) = a_n + b_n\bar{x} + c_n\bar{x}^2. \tag{6.37}$$

The overbars in Eq. (6.37) specify that the spatial coordinate x is locally transformed to satisfy $0 \leq \bar{x} \leq 1$ in each of the interior spline zones. Since each spline zone now has two different local fits, one from the left and the other from the right, these two local fits are combined together with the left and right weighting functions shown in Figure 6.16 (middle). The form of the 1-D weighting function used here for C^2 continuity is

$$W_{\text{right}}(\bar{x}) = \bar{x}^3 \left(10 - 15\bar{x} + 6\bar{x}^2\right)$$

and the corresponding left weighting function is defined simply as

$$W_{\text{left}}(\bar{x}) = W_{\text{right}}(1 - \bar{x}).$$

Thus the final fit in each region can be written as

$$F(x, y) = W_{\text{left}}Z_{\text{left}} + W_{\text{right}}Z_{\text{right}}.$$

For example, for region 2, one would have $Z_{\text{left}} = Z_2$ and $Z_{\text{right}} = Z_3$. Note that, in addition to providing the desired level of continuity at spline boundaries, the weighting functions are also useful in reducing the dependence near the boundaries of the local fits where they often exhibit the poorest agreement with the original data. When these final fits are plotted (bottom of Figure 6.16), we see that they are indeed C^2 continuous, maintaining continuity of the function value, slope, and curvature at all three interior spline boundaries.

6.4.2.2 Example exact solution: 2-D steady Navier–Stokes equations

An example of the use of MNP to generate physically realistic manufactured solutions is now given for the case of viscous, incompressible flow in a lid-driven cavity at a Reynolds number of 100 (Roy and Sinclair, 2009). This flow is governed by the incompressible Navier–Stokes equations, which for constant transport properties are given by

$$\frac{\partial u}{\partial x} + \frac{\partial v}{\partial y} = s_{\text{m}}(x, y),$$

$$\rho u \frac{\partial u}{\partial x} + \rho v \frac{\partial u}{\partial y} + \frac{\partial p}{\partial x} - \mu \frac{\partial^2 u}{\partial x^2} - \mu \frac{\partial^2 u}{\partial y^2} = s_x(x, y),$$

$$\rho u \frac{\partial v}{\partial x} + \rho v \frac{\partial v}{\partial y} + \frac{\partial p}{\partial y} - \mu \frac{\partial^2 v}{\partial x^2} - \mu \frac{\partial^2 v}{\partial y^2} = s_y(x, y),$$

where $s(x, y)$ are the manufactured solution source terms. These equations are solved in finite-difference form on a standard Cartesian mesh by integrating in pseudo-time using Chorin's artificial compressibility method (Chorin, 1967). In addition, second- and fourth-derivative damping (Jameson *et al.*, 1981) was employed to prevent odd–even decoupling (i.e., oscillations) in the solution. Dirichlet boundary conditions are used for velocity, with

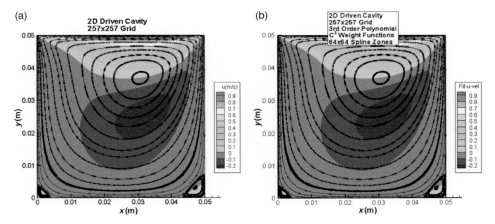

Figure 6.17 Contours of u-velocity and streamlines for a lid-driven cavity at Reynolds number 100: (a) 257×257 node numerical solution and (b) C^3 continuous spline fit using 64×64 spline zones (from Roy and Sinclair, 2009). (See color plate section.)

all boundary velocities equal to zero except for the u-velocity on the top wall which is set to 1 m/s.

A contour plot of the u-velocity (i.e., the velocity in the x-direction) from a numerical solution on a 257×257 grid is given in Figure 6.17a. Also shown in the figure are streamlines which denote the overall clockwise circulation induced by the upper wall velocity (the upper wall moves from left to right) as well as the two counter-clockwise rotating vortices in the bottom corners. A spline fit was generated using third order (i.e., bi-cubic) polynomials in x and y with C^3 continuous weighting functions and 64×64 spline zones. Note that while no additional boundary constraints are placed on the velocity components for the spline fit, the maximum deviations from the original boundary conditions are on the order of 1×10^{-7} m/s and are thus quite small. The u-velocity contours and streamlines for the spline fit are presented in Figure 6.17b. The fit solution is qualitatively the same as the underlying numerical solution. The streamlines were injected at exactly the same locations in both figures and are indistinguishable from each other. Furthermore, in both cases the streamlines near the center of the cavity follow the same path for multiple revolutions.

A more quantitative comparison between the underlying numerical solution and the spline fits is presented in Figure 6.18, which shows discrete norms of the spline fitting error in u-velocity relative to the underlying numerical solution as a function of the number of spline zones in each direction. The average error magnitude (L_1 norm) decreases from 1×10^{-3} m/s to 3×10^{-6} m/s with increasing number of spline zones from 8×8 to 64×64, while the maximum error (infinity norm) decreases from 0.7 m/s to 0.01 m/s.

6.5 Approximate solution methods

This section describes three methods for approximating exact solutions to mathematical models. The first two, series and similarity solutions, are often considered to be exact, but are

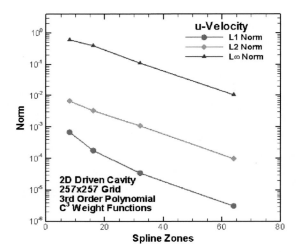

Figure 6.18 Variation of the error in *u*-velocity between the spline fits and the underlying 257×257 numerical solution as a function of the number of spline zones in each direction for the lid-driven cavity at Reynolds number 100 (from Roy and Sinclair, 2009).

treated as approximate here since we assume that numerical values for the solution must be computed. Furthermore, infinite series and similarity solutions are usually only available for simple PDEs. The third method involves computing a highly-accurate numerical solution to a given problem and is called a numerical benchmark solution.

6.5.1 Infinite series solutions

Solutions involving infinite series are sometimes used to solve differential equations with general boundary and initial conditions. The primary application of series solutions has been for linear differential equations, but they are also a useful tool for obtaining solutions to certain nonlinear differential equations. While these solutions are "analytic," they are not closed form solutions since they involve infinite series. When using infinite series as an approximation of an exact solution to the mathematical model, care must be taken to ensure that the series is in fact convergent and the numerical approximation error created by truncating the series is sufficiently small for the intended application. As Roache (1998) points out, there are many cases where subtle issues arise with the numerical evaluation of infinite series solutions, so they should be used with caution.

6.5.2 Reduction to ordinary differential equations

In some cases, a suitable transformation can be found which reduces a system of PDEs to a system of ordinary differential equations. Methods are available to compute highly-accurate numerical or series solutions for ordinary differential equations. One example is the well-known Blasius solution to the laminar boundary layer equations in fluid dynamics (Schetz, 1993). This solution employs similarity transformations to reduce the incompressible boundary layer equations for conservation of mass and momentum to a single, nonlinear ordinary differential equation, which can then be accurately solved using series solution (the original approach of Blasius) or by numerical approximation. Consider the situation where a code based on the full Navier–Stokes equation is used to solve for the laminar boundary layer flow over a flat plate. In this case, the solution from the Navier–Stokes code would not converge to the Blasius solution since these are two different mathematical models; the Navier–Stokes equations contain terms omitted from the boundary layer equations which are expected to become important near the leading edge singularity.

6.5.3 Benchmark numerical solutions

Another approximate solution method is to compute a *benchmark numerical solution* with a high-degree of numerical accuracy. In order for a numerical solution to a complex PDE to qualify as a benchmark solution, the problem statement, numerical scheme, and numerical solution accuracy should be documented (Oberkampf and Trucano, 2008). Quantifying the numerical accuracy of benchmark numerical solutions is often difficult, and at a minimum should include evidence that (1) the asymptotic convergence range has been achieved for the benchmark problem and (2) the code used to generate the benchmark solution has passed the order of accuracy code verification test for the options exercised in the benchmark problem. Extensive benchmark numerical solutions for solid mechanics applications are discussed in Oberkampf and Trucano (2008).

6.5.4 Example series solution: 2-D steady heat conduction

The problem of interest in this example is steady-state heat conduction in an infinitely long bar with a rectangular cross section of width L and height H (Dowding, 2008). A schematic of the problem is given in Figure 6.19. If constant thermal conductivity is assumed, then the conservation of energy equation reduces to a Poisson equation for temperature,

$$\frac{\partial^2 T}{\partial x^2} + \frac{\partial^2 T}{\partial y^2} = \frac{-\dot{g}'''}{k}, \tag{6.38}$$

where T is the temperature, k is the thermal conductivity, and $\dot{g}'''$ is an energy source term. The bottom and left boundaries employ zero heat flux (Neumann) boundary conditions, the right boundary a fixed temperature (Dirichlet) boundary condition, and the top boundary is a convective heat transfer (Robin) boundary condition. These boundary conditions are also given in Figure 6.19 and can be summarized as

$$\frac{\partial T}{\partial x}(0, y) = 0,$$
$$\frac{\partial T}{\partial y}(x, 0) = 0,$$
$$T(L, y) = T_\infty,$$
$$-k\frac{\partial T}{\partial y}(x, H) = h\left[T(x, H) - T_\infty\right], \tag{6.39}$$

where h is the film coefficient from convective cooling.

$$-k\frac{\partial T}{\partial y} = h(T - T_\infty)$$

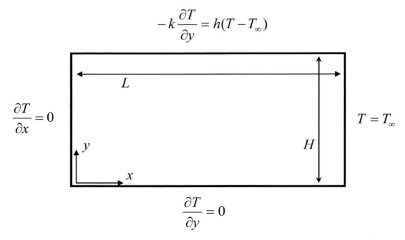

$$\frac{\partial T}{\partial x} = 0$$

$$T = T_\infty$$

$$\frac{\partial T}{\partial y} = 0$$

Figure 6.19 Schematic of heat conduction problem in an infinitely long bar of rectangular cross section (Dowding, 2008).

In order to make the Dirichlet boundary condition homogeneous (i.e., equal to zero), the following simple transformation is used:

$$\omega(x, y) = T(x, y) - T_\infty. \tag{6.40}$$

Note that the use of this transformation does not change the form of the governing equation, which can be rewritten in terms of ω as

$$\frac{\partial^2 \omega}{\partial x^2} + \frac{\partial^2 \omega}{\partial y^2} = \frac{-\dot{g}'''}{k}. \tag{6.41}$$

The problem statement in terms of $\omega(x, y)$ is shown in Figure 6.20.

The solution to the transformed problem in terms of ω can be found using separation of variables and is

$$\frac{\omega(x, y)}{\frac{\dot{g}''' L^2}{k}} = \frac{1}{2}\left(1 - \frac{x^2}{L^2}\right) + 2\sum_{n=1}^{\infty} \frac{(-1)^n}{\mu_n^3} \frac{\cosh\left(\frac{\mu_n y}{aH}\right) \cos\left(\mu_n \frac{x}{L}\right)}{\frac{1}{Bi}\frac{\mu_n}{a}\sinh\left(\frac{\mu_n}{a}\right) + \cosh\left(\frac{\mu_n}{a}\right)}, \tag{6.42}$$

where the eigenvalues μ_n are given by

$$\mu_n = (2n - 1)\frac{\pi}{2}, \quad n = 1, 2, 3, \ldots \quad \text{and} \cos(\mu_n) = 0,$$

and the constant a and the Biot number Bi are defined as:

$$a = \frac{L}{H}, \quad Bi = \frac{hH}{k}.$$

The infinite series is found to converge rapidly everywhere except near the top wall, where over 100 terms are needed to obtain accuracies of approximately seven significant figures (Dowding, 2008). The following parameters have been used to generate the exact solution given in Figure 6.21, which is presented in terms of the temperature by using the simple

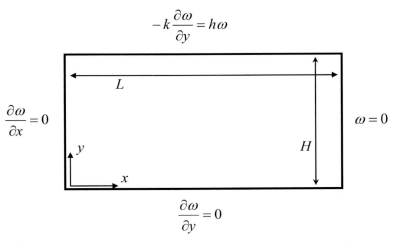

Figure 6.20 Schematic of heat conduction problem in terms of ω (Dowding, 2008).

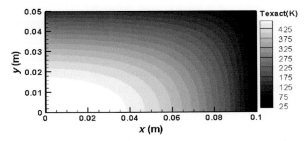

Figure 6.21 Infinite series solution for 2-D steady-state heat conduction.

transformation from Eq. (6.40):

$$\dot{g}''' = 135\,300 \text{ W/m}^3,$$
$$k = 0.4 \text{ W/(m} \cdot \text{K)},$$
$$L = 0.1 \text{ m},$$
$$H = 0.05 \text{ m},$$
$$T_\infty = 25 \text{ K}.$$

These parameters correspond to an aspect ratio of 2, a Biot number of 7.5, and a dimensionless heat source $\dot{g}''' L^2 / k$ of 3 382.5.

6.5.5 Example benchmark convergence test: 2-D hypersonic flow

An example of benchmark numerical solutions used with the convergence test for code verification is given by Roy *et al.* (2003). They considered the Mach 8 inviscid flow

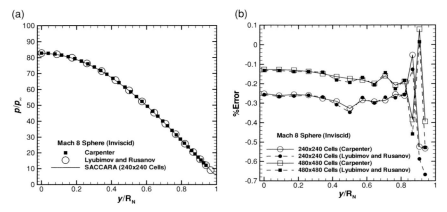

Figure 6.22 Compressible computational fluid dynamics predictions for the Mach 8 flow over a sphere: (a) surface pressure distributions and (b) discretization error in the surface pressure from the SACCARA code relative to the two benchmark solutions (from Roy *et al.*, 2003).

of a calorically perfect gas over a sphere-cone geometry. This flow is governed by the Euler equations in axisymmetric coordinates. Two benchmark numerical solutions were employed: a higher-order spectral solution (Carpenter *et al.*, 1994) and an accurate finite-difference solution (Lyubimov and Rusanov, 1973). Numerical solutions for surface pressure were computed using the compressible computational fluid dynamics code SACCARA (see Roy *et al.*, 2003 for details) and are compared to these two benchmark solutions on the spherical nose region in Figure 6.22. While the pressure distributions appear identical in Figure 6.22a, examination of the discretization error in the SACCARA solution relative to the benchmark solutions in Figure 6.22b shows that the discretization error is small (less than 0.7%) and that it decreases by approximately a factor of two with mesh refinement (i.e., the numerical solutions are convergent). Variations are seen in the discretization error near the sphere-cone tangency point due to the presence of the geometric singularity in the computational fluid dynamics solution (a discontinuity in surface curvature). While these results do demonstrate that the SACCARA code has passed the convergence test, it is generally difficult to assess the order of accuracy using benchmark numerical solutions. A similar benchmark solution for the Navier–Stokes equations involving viscous laminar flow can also be found in Roy *et al.* (2003).

6.6 References

Ames, W. F. (1965). *Nonlinear Partial Differential Equations in Engineering*, New York, Academic Press Inc.

Benton, E. R. and G. W. Platzman (1972). A table of solutions of the one-dimensional Burgers' equation, *Quarterly of Applied Mathematics*. **30**(2), 195–212.

Bond, R. B., C. C. Ober, P. M. Knupp, and S. W. Bova (2007). Manufactured solution for computational fluid dynamics boundary condition verification, *AIAA Journal*. **45**(9), 2224–2236.

Carpenter, M. H., H. L. Atkins, and D. J. Singh (1994). Characteristic and finite-wave shock-fitting boundary conditions for Chebyshev methods, In *Transition, Turbulence, and Combustion*, eds. M. Y. Hussaini, T. B. Gatski, and T. L. Jackson, Vol. 2, Norwell, MA, Kluwer Academic, pp. 301–312.

Carslaw, H. S. and J. C. Jaeger (1959). *Conduction of Heat in Solids*, 2nd edn., Oxford, Clarendon Press.

Chorin, A. J. (1967). A numerical method for solving incompressible viscous flow problems, *Journal of Computational Physics*. **2**(1), 12–26.

Dowding, K. (2008). Private communication, January 8, 2008.

Eca, L. and M. Hoekstra (2006). Verification of turbulence models with a manufactured solution, *European Conference on Computational Fluid Dynamics, ECCOMAS CFD 2006*, Wesseling, P., Onate, E., and Periaux, J. (eds.), Egmond ann Zee, The Netherlands, ECCOMAS.

Eca, L., M. Hoekstra, A. Hay, and D. Pelletier (2007). On the construction of manufactured solutions for one and two-equation eddy-viscosity models, *International Journal for Numerical Methods in Fluids*. **54**(2), 119–154.

Elishakoff, I. (2004). *Eigenvalues of Inhomogeneous Structures: Unusual Closed-Form Solutions*, Boca Raton, FL, CRC Press.

Gottlieb, J. J. and C. P. T. Groth (1988). Assessment of Riemann solvers for unsteady one-dimensional inviscid flows of perfect gases, *Journal of Computational Physics*. **78**(2), 437–458.

Hirsch, C. (2007). *Numerical Computation of Internal and External Flows: Fundamentals of Computational Fluid Dynamics*, 2nd edn., Oxford, Butterworth-Heinemann.

Hopkins, M. M. and C. J. Roy (2004) Introducing the method of nearby problems, *European Congress on Computational Methods in Applied Sciences and Engineering, ECCOMAS 2004*, P. Neittaanmaki, T. Rossi, S. Korotov, E. Onate, J. Periaux, and D. Knorzer (eds.), University of Jyväskylä (Jyvaskyla), Jyväskylä, Finland, July 2004.

Jameson, A., W. Schmidt, and E. Turkel (1981). *Numerical Solutions of the Euler Equations by Finite Volume Methods Using Runge-Kutta Time-Stepping Schemes*, AIAA Paper 81–1259.

Junkins, J. L., G. W. Miller, and J. R. Jancaitis (1973). A weighting function approach to modeling of irregular surfaces, *Journal of Geophysical Research*. **78**(11), 1794–1803.

Kausel, E. (2006). *Fundamental Solutions in Elastodynamics: a Compendium*, New York, Cambridge University Press.

Kevorkian, J. (2000). *Partial Differential Equations: Analytical Solution Techniques*, 2nd edn., Texts in Applied Mathematics, 35, New York, Springer.

Knupp, P. and K. Salari (2003). *Verification of Computer Codes in Computational Science and Engineering*, K. H. Rosen (ed.), Boca Raton, Chapman and Hall/CRC.

Lyubimov, A. N. and V. V. Rusanov (1973). *Gas Flows Past Blunt Bodies, Part II: Tables of the Gasdynamic Functions*, NASA TT F-715.

Meleshko, S. V. (2005). *Methods of Constructing Exact Solutions of Partial Differential Equations: Mathematical and Analytic Techniques with Applications to Engineering*, New York, Springer.

Oberkampf, W. L. and T. G. Trucano (2008). Verification and validation benchmarks, *Nuclear Engineering and Design*. **238**(3), 716–743.

Oberkampf, W. L., F. G. Blottner, and D. P. Aeschliman (1995). *Methodology for Computational Fluid Dynamics Code Verification/Validation*, AIAA Paper 95–2226 (see also Oberkampf, W. L. and Blottner, F. G. (1998). Issues in computational fluid dynamics code verification and validation, *AIAA Journal*. **36**(5), 687–695).

O'Neil, P. V. (2003). *Advanced Engineering Mathematics*, 5th edn., Pacific Grove, CA, Thomson Brooks/Cole.

Panton, R. L. (2005). *Incompressible Flow*, Hoboken, NJ, Wiley.

Pelletier, D., E. Turgeon, and D. Tremblay (2004). Verification and validation of impinging round jet simulations using an adaptive FEM, *International Journal for Numerical Methods in Fluids*. **44**, 737–763.

Polyanin, A. D. (2002). *Handbook of Linear Partial Differential Equations for Engineers and Scientists*, Boca Raton, FL, Chapman and Hall/CRC.

Polyanin, A. D. and V. F. Zaitsev (2003). *Handbook of Exact Solutions for Ordinary Differential Equations*, 2nd edn., Boca Raton, FL, Chapman and Hall/CRC.

Polyanin, A. D. and V. F. Zaitsev (2004). *Handbook of Nonlinear Partial Differential Equations*, Boca Raton, FL, Chapman and Hall/CRC.

Powers, J. M. and T. D. Aslam (2006). Exact solution for multidimensional compressible reactive flow for verifying numerical algorithms, *AIAA Journal*. **44**(2), 337–344.

Powers, J. M. and D. S. Stewart (1992). Approximate solutions for oblique detonations in the hypersonic limit, *AIAA Journal*. **30**(3), 726–736.

Roache, P. J. (1998). *Verification and Validation in Computational Science and Engineering*, Albuquerque, NM, Hermosa Publishers.

Roache, P. J. (2002). Code verification by the method of manufactured solutions, *Journal of Fluids Engineering*. **124**(1), 4–10.

Roache, P. J. and S. Steinberg (1984). Symbolic manipulation and computational fluid dynamics, *AIAA Journal*. **22**(10), 1390–1394.

Roache, P. J., P. M. Knupp, S. Steinberg, and R. L. Blaine (1990). Experience with benchmark test cases for groundwater flow. In *Benchmark Test Cases for Computational Fluid Dynamics*, I. Celik and C. J. Freitas (eds.), New York, American Society of Mechanical Engineers, Fluids Engineering Division, Vol. **93**, Book No. H00598, pp. 49–56.

Roe, P. L. (1981). Approximate Riemann solvers, parameter vectors, and difference schemes, *Journal of Computational Physics*. **43**, 357–372.

Roy, C. J. (2005). Review of code and solution verification procedures for computational simulation, *Journal of Computational Physics*. **205**(1), 131–156.

Roy, C. J. and M. M. Hopkins (2003). *Discretization Error Estimates using Exact Solutions to Nearby Problems*, AIAA Paper 2003–0629.

Roy, C. J. and A. J. Sinclair (2009). On the generation of exact solutions for evaluating numerical schemes and estimating discretization error, *Journal of Computational Physics*. **228**(5), 1790–1802.

Roy, C. J., M. A. McWherter-Payne, and W. L. Oberkampf (2003). Verification and validation for laminar hypersonic flowfields Part 1: verification, *AIAA Journal*. **41**(10), 1934–1943.

Roy, C. J., C. C. Nelson, T. M. Smith, and C.C. Ober (2004). Verification of Euler/Navier–Stokes codes using the method of manufactured solutions, *International Journal for Numerical Methods in Fluids*. **44**(6), 599–620.

Roy, C. J., A. Raju, and M. M. Hopkins (2007a). Estimation of discretization errors using the method of nearby problems, *AIAA Journal*. **45**(6), 1232–1243.

Roy, C. J., E. Tendean, S. P. Veluri, R. Rifki, E. A. Luke, and S. Hebert (2007b). *Verification of RANS Turbulence Models in Loci-CHEM using the Method of Manufactured Solutions*, AIAA Paper 2007–4203.

Schetz, J. A. (1993). *Boundary Layer Analysis*, Upper Saddle River, NJ, Prentice-Hall.

Seidel, G. D. (2009). Private communication, November 6, 2009.

Shih, T. M. (1985). Procedure to debug computer programs, *International Journal for Numerical Methods in Engineering*. **21**(6), 1027–1037.

Slaughter, W. S. (2002). *The Linearized Theory of Elasticity*, Boston, MA, Birkhauser.

Steinberg, S. and P. J. Roache (1985). Symbolic manipulation and computational fluid dynamics, *Journal of Computational Physics*. **57**(2), 251–284.

Stetter, H. J. (1978). The defect correction principle and discretization methods, *Numerische Mathematik*. **29**(4), 425–443.

Tannehill, J. C., D. A. Anderson, and R. H. Pletcher (1997). *Computational Fluid Mechanics and Heat Transfer*, 2nd edn., Philadelphia, PA, Taylor and Francis.

Thompson, J. F., Z. U. A. Warsi, and C. W. Mastin (1985). *Numerical Grid Generation: Foundations and Applications*, New York, Elsevier. (www.erc.msstate.edu/publications/gridbook)

Timoshenko, S. P. and J. N. Goodier (1969). *Theory of Elasticity*, 3rd edn., New York, McGraw-Hill.

Tremblay, D., S. Etienne, and D. Pelletier (2006). *Code Verification and the Method of Manufactured Solutions for Fluid–Structure Interaction Problems*, AIAA Paper 2006–3218.

White, F. M. (2006) *Viscous Fluid Flow*, New York, McGraw-Hill.

Yanenko, N. N. (1964). Compatibility theory and methods of integrating systems of nonlinear partial differential equations, *Proceedings of the Fourth All-Union Mathematics Congress*, Vol. **2**, Leningrad, Nauka, pp. 613–621.

Zadunaisky, P. E. (1976). On the estimation of errors propagated in the numerical integration of ordinary differential equations, *Numerische Mathematik*. **27**(1), 21–39.

Part III
Solution verification

Solution verification is an important aspect of ensuring that a given simulation of a mathematical model is sufficiently accurate for the intended use. It relies on the use of consistent and convergent numerical algorithms as well as mistake-free codes; the two key items addressed in Part II of this book. If code verification studies have not been conducted, then even the most rigorous solution verification activities are not sufficient since there is no guarantee that the simulations will converge to the exact solution to the mathematical model. Just as code verification is a necessary prelude to solution verification, meaningful model validation assessments (Part IV) cannot be conducted until solution verification has been completed.

The main focus of solution verification is the estimation of the numerical errors that occur when a mathematical model is discretized and solved on a digital computer. While some of the strategies employed will be similar to those used for code verification, there is an important difference. In solution verification, the exact solution to the mathematical model is not known, and thus the numerical errors must now be estimated and not simply evaluated. In some cases, when these numerical errors can be estimated with a high degree of confidence, then they can be removed from the numerical solution (a process similar to that used for well-characterized bias errors in an experiment). More often, however, the numerical errors are estimated with significantly less certainty, and thus they will be classified as numerical uncertainties.

Numerical errors can arise in scientific computing due to computer round-off, statistical sampling, iteration, and discretization. The first three sources are discussed in Chapter 7. Discretization error, discussed in detail in Chapter 8, is often the largest numerical error source and also the most difficult to estimate. For complex scientific computing problems (e.g., those involving nonlinearities, geometric complexity, multi-physics, multiple scales), generating an appropriate mesh to resolve the physics before any solutions are computed is often inadequate. Chapter 9 discusses approaches to solution adaptation wherein either the mesh or the numerical algorithm itself is modified during the solution process in order to reliably control the discretization error. In our opinion, solution adaptation is required for reliable numerical error estimates in complex scientific computing applications.

7

Solution verification

Solution verification addresses the question of whether a given simulation (i.e., numerical approximation) of a mathematical model is sufficiently accurate for its intended use. It includes not only the accuracy of the simulation for the case of interest, but also the accuracy of inputs to the code and any post-processing of the code results. Quantifying the numerical accuracy of scientific computing simulations is important for two primary reasons: as part of the quantification of the total uncertainty in a simulation prediction (Chapter 13) and for establishing the numerical accuracy of a simulation for model validation purposes (Chapter 12).

Most solution verification activities are focused on estimating the numerical errors in the simulation. This chapter addresses in detail round-off error, statistical sampling error, and iterative convergence error. These three numerical error sources should be sufficiently small so as not to impact the estimation of discretization error, which is discussed at length in Chapter 8. Discretization errors are those associated with the mesh resolution and quality as well as the time step chosen for unsteady problems. Round-off and discretization errors are always present in scientific computing simulations, while the presence of iterative and statistical sampling errors will depend on the application and the chosen numerical algorithms. This chapter concludes with a discussion of numerical errors and their relationship to uncertainties.

7.1 Elements of solution verification

Solution verification begins after the mathematical model has been embodied in a verified code, the initial and boundary conditions have been specified, and any other auxiliary relations have been determined. It includes the running of the code on a mesh, or series of meshes, possibly to a specified iterative convergence tolerance. Solution verification ends after all post-processing of the simulation results are completed to provide the final simulation predictions. There are thus three aspects of solution verification:

1 verification of input data,
2 verification of post-processing tools, and
3 numerical error estimation.

Verification of input and output data is particularly important when a large number of simulations are performed, such as for a matrix of simulations that vary different input conditions. Issues associated with the verification of input and output data are discussed in this section. The third aspect of solution verification, numerical error estimation, is discussed in detail in the remainder of this chapter as well as in Chapter 8.

Input data is any required information for running a scientific computing code. Common forms of input data include:

- input files describing models, submodels, and numerical algorithms,
- domain grids,
- boundary and initial conditions,
- data used for submodels (e.g., chemical species properties, reaction rates),
- information on material properties, and
- computer-aided drawing (CAD) surface geometry information.

There are various techniques that can aid in the verification of the input data. Checks for consistency between model choices should be made at the beginning of code execution. For example, the code should not allow a no-slip (viscous) wall boundary condition to be used for an inviscid simulation involving the Euler equations. For more subtle modeling issues, an expert knowledge database could be used to provide the user with warnings when a model is being used outside of its range of applicability (e.g., Stremel *et al.*, 2007). In addition, all input data used for a given simulation should be archived in an output file so that the correctness of the input data can be confirmed by post-simulation inspection if needed. Verification of input data also includes the verification of any pre-processing software that is used to generate the input data and thus the standard software engineering practices discussed in Chapter 4 should be used.

Post-processing tools are defined as any software that operates on the output from a scientific computing code. If this post-processing involves any type of numerical approximation such as discretization, integration, interpolation, etc., then the order of accuracy of these tools should be verified (e.g., by order verification), otherwise the standard software engineering practices should be followed. If possible, the post-processing steps should be automated, and then verified, to prevent common human errors such as picking the wrong solution for post-processing. If the user of the code is to perform the post-processing, then a checklist should be developed to ensure this process is done correctly.

Numerical errors occur in *every* scientific computing simulation, and thus need to be estimated in order to build confidence in the mathematical accuracy of the solution. In other words, numerical error estimation is performed to ensure that the solution produced by running the code is a sufficiently accurate approximation of the exact solution to the mathematical model. When numerical errors are found to be unacceptably large, then they should either be accounted for in the total uncertainty due to the modeling and simulation prediction (see Chapter 13) or reduced to an acceptable level by refining the mesh, reducing the iterative tolerance, etc. The four types of numerical error are:

1 round-off error,
2 statistical sampling error,
3 iterative error, and
4 discretization error.

This chapter discusses the first three numerical error sources in detail, while discretization error is addressed separately in Chapter 8.

7.2 Round-off error

Round-off errors arise due to the use of finite arithmetic on digital computers. For example, in a single-precision digital computation the following result is often obtained:

$$3.0^*(1.0/3.0) = 0.999\,9999,$$

while the true answer using infinite precision is 1.0. Round-off error can be significant for both ill-conditioned systems of equations (see Section 7.4) and time-accurate simulations. Repeated arithmetic operations will degrade the accuracy of a scientific computing simulation, and generally not just in the last significant figure of the solution. Round-off error can be reduced by using more significant digits in the computation. Although round-off error can be thought of as the truncation of a real number to fit it into computer memory, it should not be confused with truncation error which is a measure of the difference between a partial differential equation and its discrete approximation as defined in Chapter 5.

7.2.1 Floating point representation

Scientific computing applications require the processing of real numbers. Even when limiting these real numbers to lie within a certain range, say from -1 million to $+1$ million, there are infinitely many real numbers to be considered. This poses a problem for digital computers, which must store real numbers in a finite amount of computer memory. In order to fit these numbers into memory, both the precision (the number of significant figures) and the range of the exponent must be limited (Goldberg, 1991). An efficient way to do this is through an analogy with scientific notation, where both large and small numbers can be represented compactly. For example, $14\,000\,000$ can be represented as 1.4×10^7 and $0.000\,0014$ represented by 1.4×10^{-6}. In digital computers, floating point numbers are more generally represented as

$$S \times B^E,$$

where S is the significand (or mantissa), B is the base (usually 2 for binary or 10 for decimal), and E is the exponent. The term floating point number comes from the fact that in this notation, the decimal point is allowed to move to represent the significand S more efficiently.

Table 7.1 *Summary of floating point number formats in IEEE Standard 754 (IEEE, 2008).*

Precision format	Total # of bits used	Bits used for significand	Bits used for exponent	Approximate number of significant digits	Exponent range (base 10)
Single	32	24	8	7	±38
Double	64	53	11	15	±308
Half[a]	16	11	5	3	±5
Extended[a]	80	64	16	18	±9864
Quadruple[a]	128	113	15	34	±4932

[a] not available in some programming languages and/or compilers

For digital computer hardware and software, the most widely-used standard for floating point numbers is the IEEE Standard 754 (IEEE, 2008). This standard addresses number format, rounding algorithms, arithmetic operations, and exception handling (division by zero, numerical overflow, numerical underflow, etc.). While the IEEE standard addresses both binary and decimal formats, nearly all software and hardware used for scientific computing employ binary storage of floating point numbers. The most commonly used formats are single precision and double precision. Additional standard formats that may or may not be available on a given computer hardware or software system are half precision, extended precision, and quadruple precision.

Single precision employs 32 bits, or four bytes, of computer memory. The significand is stored using 24 bits, one of which is used to determine the sign of the number (positive or negative). The exponent is then stored in the remaining eight bits of memory, with one bit generally used to store the sign of the exponent. The significand determines the precision of the floating point number, while the exponent determines the range of numbers that can be represented. Single precision provides approximately seven significant decimal digits and can represent positive or negative numbers with magnitudes as large as $\sim 3.4 \times 10^{38}$ and as small as $\sim 1.1 \times 10^{-38}$. For double precision numbers, 64 bits (8 bytes) of memory are used, with 53 bits assigned to the significand and 11 bits to the exponent, thus providing approximately 15 significant decimal digits. The five standard binary formats are summarized in Table 7.1. The last two columns of Table 7.1 give the maximum and minimum precision and range where, for example, single precision numbers will be represented in base 10 as:

$$1.234567 \times 10^{\pm 38}.$$

The use of single (32 bit) and double (64 bit) precision for representing floating point numbers should not be confused with 32-bit and 64-bit computer architectures. The wide availability of 64-bit processors in desktop computers beginning in 2003 was initially

Table 7.2 *Data types used to specify the different precision formats in C/C^{++}, Fortran, and MATLAB$^®$.*

Precision format	C/C^{++}	Fortran 95/2003	MATLAB$^®$
Single	float	real, real*4 (default)^{a,b}	single
Double	double (default)	double precision, real*8^{a,b}	double (default)
Half	n/a	^{a,b}	n/a
Extended	long double^a	^{a,b}	n/a
Quadruple	long double^a	^{a,b}	n/a
Arbitrary	^{c}	^{c}	vpa^d

^{a} compiler dependent; ^{b} accessible via the "kind" attribute; ^{c} accessible via third-party libraries; ^{d} variable precision arithmetic (see Section 7.2.2.3)

driven by the fact that the amount of random access memory (RAM) addressable by a 32-bit integer is only 4 GB (2^{32} bytes or approximately 4.29×10^9 bytes). The 64-bit processors were developed for large databases and applications requiring more than 4 GB of addressable memory, providing a theoretical upper bound of approximately 17 billion GB (17×10^{18} bytes), although in practice the maximum addressable memory is much smaller. In addition to providing more addressable memory, 64-bit processors also may perform arithmetic faster on double precision (64 bit) floating point numbers, the most common floating point data type used in scientific computing applications. This speed-up occurs because the data path between memory and the processor is more likely to be 64 bits wide rather than 32 bits, so only one memory read instruction is needed to move a double precision floating point number from memory to the processor.

7.2.2 *Specifying precision in a code*

The approach for specifying the precision for floating point numbers generally depends on the programming language, the compiler, and the hardware. The data types used for specifying the precision of real numbers (variables, constants, and functions) in C/C^{++}, Fortran, and MATLAB$^®$ are summarized in Table 7.2. In addition, the C/C^{++} and Fortran programming languages have the capability to employ arbitrary precision floating point numbers through the use of third-party software libraries such as the GNU Multiple Precision (GMP) arithmetic library for C/C^{++} (GNU, 2009) and FMLIB for Fortran (Smith, 2009). In general, when more digits of precision are employed, program execution will be slower. A more detailed discussion of procedures for specifying the floating point precision for each programming language follows.

7.2.2.1 C/C++ programming languages

The C and C++ family of programming languages requires that variable types be explicitly declared at the beginning of each routine. The available floating point types are "`float`" (single precision) and "`double`" (double precision). In addition, some compilers support the "`long double`" data type, which can refer to extended precision, quadruple precision, or simply revert back to double precision depending on the compiler. The number of bytes used for storing a floating point number can be determined in C/C++ using the "`sizeof()`" function. In addition, the number of digits of precision for floating point output can be specified using the "`cout.precision(X)`" function where X is an integer determining the number of significant digits to output. A short C++ code segment which provides an example of single, double, and extended precision is given below.

```
float a;
double b;
long double c;
a = 1.F/3.F;
b = 1./3.;
c = 1.L/3.L;
cout.precision(25);
cout <<''a = '';cout << a; cout << ''\n'';
cout <<''b = '';cout << b; cout << ''\n'';
cout <<''c = '';cout << c; cout << ''\n'';
cout <<''Size of a = ''; cout << sizeof(a); cout << ''\n'';
cout <<''Size of b = ''; cout << sizeof(b); cout << ''\n'';
cout <<''Size of c = ''; cout << sizeof(c); cout << ''\n'';
```

When this code is compiled with the GNU C++ compiler (available on most Linux platforms) and executed, it produces the following output:

```
a = 0.3333333432674407958984375
b = 0.3333333333333333148296163
c = 0.3333333333333333333423684
Size of a = 4
Size of b = 8
Size of c = 16
```

which indicates the expected seven digits of precision for the single precision float, 16 digits of precision for the default double precision, and 19 digits of precision for long double. Note that omitting the ".L" in the definition of c will instead produce

```
c = 0.3333333333333333148296163
Size of c = 16
```

since the initial computation of 1./3. will by default produce a double precision number (only 16 digits of precision) which is then stored in the long double variable c.

7.2.2.2 *Fortran 95/2003 programming languages*

The standards documents for modern variants of Fortran such as Fortran 95 and Fortran 2003 require that two different floating point types be supported, but do not specify what those two types must be (Chapman, 2008). While this flexibility in the standard does complicate the type specification of real numbers, it also can have some advantages in scientific computing applications that required additional precision. For most Fortran compilers, the default data type for real numbers is single precision (32 bit). To complicate matters further, some Fortran compilers use the term "single precision" to refer to 64-bit floating point numbers and "double precision" to refer to 128-bit floating point numbers.

To specify the precision for floating point numbers in an unambiguous way, Fortran 95/2003 uses the "Kind" attribute, where Kind is an integer. For single precision real numbers, Kind is usually equal to 1 or 4, while for double precision real number, Kind is usually equal to 2 or 8, depending on the compiler and platform. In order to specify the level of precision in a platform- and compiler-independent manner, the Fortran programming language provides the "Selected_Real_Kind" function. This function has arguments that allow the specification of the desired decimal precision p and the decimal exponent range r, and returns an integer equal to the smallest floating point Kind type that matches the requirements. If none of the available types will meet the requirements, then the function will return -1. For example, to print the Kind number for the real data type that has at least 13 decimal digits of precision and maximum exponent of ± 200, one would use:

```
write(*,*) 'Kind = ',Selected_Real_Kind(p=13,r=200)
```

Following Chapman (2008), the selection of the desired floating point precision can be placed in a Fortran module to be used in every procedure of the code. An example of such a module is presented below.

```
Module Select_Precision
Implicit None
Save
Integer, Parameter :: hlf = Selected_Real_Kind(p=2)
Integer, Parameter :: sgl = Selected_Real_Kind(p=6)
Integer, Parameter :: dbl = Selected_Real_Kind(p=14)
Integer, Parameter :: ext = Selected_Real_Kind(p=17)
Integer, Parameter :: quad = Selected_Real_Kind(p=26)
! Default precision is set on the next line
Integer, Parameter :: Prec = dbl
End Module
```

The integer parameter "Prec" now contains the desired Kind number; in this case, the kind number for double precision. Examples of variable declarations using this chosen precision are as follows:

```
Real(kind=Prec) :: x = 0.1_Prec
Real(kind=Prec) :: y
Real(kind=Prec) :: Pi = acos(-1.0_Prec)
y = 1.0_Prec/3.0_Prec
```

Note that double precision variables and constants should be initialized with and operated on using double precision values as shown above. When double precision is desired (i.e., `Prec = dbl`), omitting the `_Prec` suffix from the argument of the arccosine function "`acos`" in the definition of `Pi` above will cause a loss of precision when the default is single precision. The desired double precision result is

```
Pi = 3.141592653589793
```

while omitting the `_Prec` results in

```
Pi = 3.141592741012573
```

because the arccosine function operating on a single precision argument will return a single precision result. Also, the `_Prec` is needed in the assignment for y to give

```
y = 0.333333333333333
```

whereas omitting the `_Prec` from the numbers 1.0 and 3.0 results in:

```
y = 0.3333333432674408
```

7.2.2.3 *MATLAB® Programming Language*

In MATLAB®, the default data type is double precision, but it supports the standard single (32 bit) and double (64 bit) floating point precision. One can convert any data type to single precision using the "`single()`" function and to double precision using the "`double()`" function. Arithmetic operations involving both single and double precision numbers will default to the single precision data type. In addition, the Symbolic Math Toolbox™ allows the specification of arbitrary levels of precision for variables using the Variable Precision Arithmetic (`vpa`) function (MATLAB, 2009), although it may result in significantly slower execution times. Scientific computing codes in MATLAB® can be written in such a way as to take advantage of all three floating point precision capabilities using function handles (MATLAB, 2009), which allow a variable to operate in the same manner as the function it is assigned to. For example, at the beginning of a code, one could simply insert the following:

```
digits(32); % Specify # of digits of precision for vpa

Prec = @vpa; % Set to use variable precision arithmetic

% Prec = @double; % Set to use double precision

% Prec = @single; % Set to use single precision

x = Prec(1)/Prec(3) % Precision of x defined by variable Prec
```

To ensure that variables do indeed employ the desired precision, all variables should be explicitly declared at the beginning of each routine. Although variable declarations are not required in MATLAB®, as discussed in the appendix, it is a recommended programming practice. Operations involving single or double precision numbers and variable precision numbers will inherit the variable precision type; however, any loss of precision that has occurred during the initial single or double precision computations is lost.

7.2.3 Practical guidelines for estimating round-off error

While the precision of a number is determined by the number of bits used for the significand (mantissa), the precision of a simulation also depends on all of the arithmetic and functional operations used to obtain the solution. Some scientific computing applications are prone to round-off errors. Examples include explicit time marching solutions which require small time steps but that simulate a long period of time. Another example is a "stiff" system where both large and small temporal and/or spatial scales are present. In both cases, the addition or subtraction of both large and small numbers will significantly reduce the precision of the computed solution. An extreme example of when such a loss of precision can occur is for the computation

$$x = (1.E - 9 + 1.0) - 1.0$$

which will return x = 0.0 for single precision computations and the correct x = 1.E-9 for double precision computations. In this case, simply rearranging the parenthesis will produce the correct result. Thus the expected magnitude of variables should be considered during the programming of arithmetic operations.

A practical approach for assessing the effects of round-off error on a simulation prediction is to run the simulation with the desired precision, then re-run the simulation with higher precision and compare the solutions. The same mesh and/or time step should be employed in both cases, and when iterative methods are used then both simulations should be iteratively converged to within machine precision, i.e., until the iterative residuals can no longer be reduced due to round-off error (see Section 7.4). This assessment will be complicated in cases where statistical sampling error is present since extremely large samples may be needed to reduce the statistical error to the point where the sensitivity to round-off error is discernable.

7.3 Statistical sampling error

In most cases, system response quantities in scientific computing are averaged quantities such as average lift and drag coefficient from an aerodynamics simulation or the vibrational modes from a structural dynamics simulation. If the simulations are steady and deterministic, then there will be no statistical sampling error. Statistical sampling error can occur in scientific computing predictions for many reasons. Certain scientific computing approaches are inherently stochastic in nature (e.g., stochastic differential equations, direct simulation Monte Carlo, lattice Boltzmann) and require time or ensemble averaging to determine mean system response quantities. If a submodel used in a scientific computing prediction is stochastic (e.g., a random walk model for Brownian motion), then a number of realizations may be needed to determine mean values. In addition, many unsteady simulations require

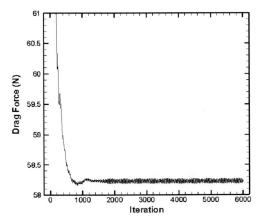

Figure 7.1 Instantaneous drag force on a simplified truck model (adapted from Veluri *et al.*, 2009).

averaging over time to determine mean properties. In some cases, steady simulations which employ iterative techniques can display unsteadiness due to strong physical instabilities in the problem (Ferziger and Peric, 2002). Solution unsteadiness can also occur due to numerical sources, even when stable numerical schemes are employed. Finally, the use of non-deterministic simulations (e.g., to propagate input uncertainties to the outputs) must also deal with statistical sampling error.

7.3.1 Estimation of statistical sampling error

Statistical sampling errors can be estimated by assessing the convergence of the desired system response quantities with increased number of realizations, iterations, or time steps. Consider Figure 7.1 which gives the instantaneous drag force on a simple, reduced-scale tractor trailer geometry as a function of iteration number (Veluri *et al.*, 2009). In this case, the steady-state Navier–Stokes equations are being solved with a submodel for turbulence. However, due to a small amount of vortex shedding that occurs behind the six support posts, the drag force oscillates about a steady-state value.

A number of approaches could be used to find the mean drag value. Perhaps the simplest approach is to simply inspect the instantaneous drag force plot and estimate the mean value. A slightly more sophisticated approach is to plot the running mean of the instantaneous drag force f_n at iteration n,

$$\bar{f} = \frac{1}{N} \sum_{n=1}^{N} f_n, \tag{7.1}$$

beginning at an iteration number where the large initial transients appear to have died out (approximately iteration 500 in the above example). The running average from this point could then be compared to the long time average (between iterations 2000 and 6000 and referred to as the "true mean") to estimate the statistical error, and the results of applying

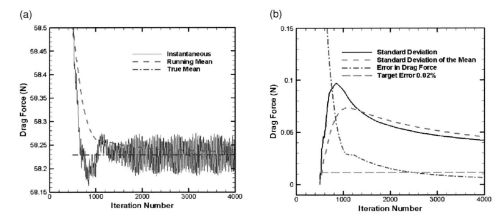

Figure 7.2 Statistical analysis of the drag force on a simplified tractor trailer: (a) instantaneous and mean values and (b) standard deviations and drag force error.

this procedure are shown in Figure 7.2a. The problem with this approach is that it requires the long time average to estimate the statistical error. Thus it is only after running for 6000 iterations that one can determine that the statistical errors in the mean value are sufficiently small (in this case 0.02% of the mean) at iteration 2500. An even better approach would be to determine a stopping criterion for the iterations (or samples) based on convergence of the standard deviation σ of the instantaneous drag force,

$$\sigma = \left[\left(\frac{1}{N} \sum_{n=1}^{N} f_n^2 \right) - (\bar{f})^2 \right]^{1/2}, \tag{7.2}$$

or even the standard deviation of the running mean drag values. These approaches are applied in Figure 7.2b. While these approaches are problem dependent and also depend on the beginning point for the statistical analysis (in this case iteration 500), when a large number of parametric runs are to be performed they can provide a heuristic stopping criterion. For example, for a desired 0.02% statistical error in the mean value, Figure 7.2b shows that the standard deviation of the running mean values should be reduced to 0.056 N. Note that as the running mean converges, the standard deviation of the running mean will go to zero.

7.4 Iterative error

Iterative error is the difference between the current approximate solution to an equation or system of equations and the exact solution. It occurs any time an iterative (or relaxation) method is used to solve algebraic equations. In scientific computing, the most common use of iterative methods is for solving the system of algebraic equations resulting from the discretization of a mathematical model. When this system of equations is nonlinear, then a linearization step must first be used. In most cases, each of these coupled algebraic equations contains only a few of the unknowns, and this type of system is referred to as a sparse system. For cases where the discretized equations are linear, direct solution methods may be used where the algebraic equations are solved exactly in a finite number of steps, which will recover the exact solution to the discrete equations (within round-off error). However, for nonlinear discretizations employing implicit algorithms iterative methods are required. Even in the case of linear systems, for a large number of unknowns (which generally occurs for 3-D scientific computing applications) the resulting system of algebraic equations can be solved to a sufficient level of iterative error much more efficiently using iterative methods than for direct methods.

The first iterative method for systems of equations was developed by Gauss nearly 200 years ago to handle the relatively large number of unknowns arising from his newly-developed least squares method (Hackbush, 1994). The advent of digital computers led to an explosion in the interest in iterative methods for solving the systems that arise from scientific computing applications. There are two main types of iterative method: stationary and Krylov subspace methods. Stationary iterative methods garnered much attention in the mid-1900s, whereas Krylov subspace methods were developed around the same time but were not applied to scientific computing applications until the 1970s. Current research focuses not only on developing new iterative methods, but also on combining stationary iterative methods with Krylov subspace methods, either through acceleration of the former (Hageman and Young, 1981) or preconditioning of the latter (Saad, 2003).

This section provides a broad overview of iterative methods for both single equations and systems of equations. The subject of iterative methods for systems of equations, especially those arising from the discretization of mathematical models, is an extremely broad subject. Here we provide only a limited overview of this topic, with some additional details provided for the simpler stationary iterative methods. Further information on iterative methods can be found in the textbooks by Hageman and Young (1981), Hackbush (1994), and Saad (2003) as well as on the World Wide Web by Barrett *et al.* (1994) and Saad (1996). A review of basic linear algebra and matrix analysis can be found in Golub and Van Loan (1996) and Meyer (2000).

7.4.1 Iterative methods

Iterative methods can be used to solve both single equations and systems of equations. The iteration process itself seeks to find a series of approximate solutions to the equations by starting with an initial guess. The difference between these approximate solutions and the exact solution to the equations is the iterative error. This section begins by first discussing iterative methods applicable to a single equation with a single unknown, which sometimes occurs in scientific computing. Linear systems of algebraic equations are then considered, which can arise from either linear mathematical models or from a linearization of a nonlinear mathematical model. The techniques discussed for solving these linear systems include direct solution methods, stationary methods, Krylov-subspace methods, and hybrid methods. Examples of simple iterative methods arising from simple scientific computing applications are then given, including both linear and nonlinear cases.

7.4.1.1 Equations with a single unknown

For single equations, iterative methods are often used to find solutions (i.e., roots) when the equation cannot be solved algebraically. This situation commonly occurs for transcendental equations (i.e., those involving transcendental functions such as exponentials, logarithms, or trigonometric functions) and most polynomials of fifth order (quintic) and higher. For such equations, the simplest iterative solution approach is the direct substitution method (e.g., Chandra, 2003). Consider the equation $F(x) = 0$ which we will assume cannot be solved algebraically. This equation is rearranged, possibly by adding x to both sides, to obtain

$$x = g(x), \tag{7.3}$$

where $g(x)$ is some new function of x. Given a suitable initial guess, Eq. (7.3) can be applied in an iterative fashion as

$$x^{k+1} = g(x^k), \quad k = 1, 2, 3, \ldots, \tag{7.4}$$

where k is called the iteration number. The nonzero result obtained by inserting the approximate solution x^k into the function

$$F(x^k) = \Re^k$$

is called the *iterative residual*, not to be confused with the discrete residual discussed in Chapter 5. While extremely simple, the drawback to the direct substitution approach is that it will only converge when $|\mathrm{d}g/\mathrm{d}x| < 1$.

More sophisticated methods for iteratively solving a single algebraic equation are based on either bracketing a solution (i.e., a root of the equation) or employing information on the function gradient $\mathrm{d}F/\mathrm{d}x$. The most basic bracketing approach is the bisection method, whereupon one starts with two initial guesses x_1 and x_2 for which $F(x_1) \cdot F(x_2) < 0$. This inequality ensures a solution will be within the interval; if the product is equal to zero then one of the endpoints itself is a solution. The interval is then repeatedly subdivided using $x_3 = (x_1 + x_2)/2$, with the new interval containing the solution being the one for which the product is again less than or equal to zero. This process is repeated (i.e., iterated) until a solution is found which provides for $F(x)$ sufficiently close to zero, i.e., until convergence of the iterative residual. Convergence of this method is linear, meaning that the iterative error will reduce by a constant factor (in this case 0.5) each iteration. While this convergence rate is quite slow, the bisection method is guaranteed to converge to a solution.

There are more advanced iterative methods that incorporate function gradient information to allow faster convergence, but at the cost of a decrease in the robustness of the iteration (i.e., convergence is no longer guaranteed) (Süli and Mayers, 2006). In order of increasing efficiency, and therefore decreasing robustness, these methods can be summarized as:

1 the *false position method* – similar to bisection but employing gradient information to aid in bracketing the solution,

2 the *secant method* $x^{k+1} = x^k - \dfrac{x^k - x^{k-1}}{F(x^k) - F(x^{k-1})} F(x^k)$, and

3 *Newton's method* $x^{k+1} = x^k - \dfrac{F(x^k)}{\frac{dF}{dx}(x^k)}$.

The secant method is preferred for cases where the analytic gradient dF/dx is not well-behaved or is undefined. When sufficiently close to a solution, Newton's method (also called Newton–Raphson) converges quadratically (see Section 7.4.2) while the secant method converges somewhat slower. However, far from a solution these two methods may not converge at all. For all of the above methods, convergence of the iterative procedure is usually monitored with the iterative residual

$$\Re^k = F(x^k). \tag{7.5}$$

For a more detailed discussion on the convergence of iterative methods, see Section 7.4.2.

7.4.1.2 Systems of equations

Systems of equations often arise from the discretization of mathematical models in scientific computing applications. Iterative methods are often, but not always, used when such systems of equations are large and/or nonlinear. For moderate size scientific computing applications in one or two spatial dimensions, the number of unknowns is usually between a thousand and a million. For larger 3-D applications, computations are routinely performed on spatial grids with 10–20 million cells/elements. For mathematical models that employ multiple, coupled differential equations, it is not uncommon to have five or more unknowns per grid point, resulting in around 100 million total unknowns. The largest scientific computing applications today often have up to 1 billion total unknowns.

Scientific computing applications do not always employ iterative methods. In some cases direct solution methods can be used; in addition, when explicit methods are used to solve marching problems then no iterations are involved. To understand when iterative methods may be used, and therefore where iterative error may occur, one must first have an understanding of the linearity of the mathematical model (discussed in Chapter 6), the type of numerical algorithm employed (explicit or implicit), and the mathematical character of the discrete algorithm. For explicit algorithms (e.g., Euler explicit, Runge–Kutta, Adams–Bashforth), each unknown can be computed as a function of known values, either from initial conditions or from a previous iteration/time step. Implicit algorithms require the solution of a simultaneous set of algebraic equations. While the mathematical character of the discrete algorithm often matches that of the underlying mathematical model (see Section 6.1), in some cases steady elliptic or mixed elliptic-hyperbolic problems are solved by marching in time to the steady-state solution, thus converting them into a hyperbolic system in time.

Table 7.3 *Use of iterative and direct solution methods in scientific computing based on the characteristics of the discrete model: mathematical character, linearity, and algorithm type.*

Mathematical character	Linearity	Explicit algorithm	Implicit algorithm
Initial-boundary value problem	Linear	No iteration	Iteration or direct
(hyperbolic/parabolic)	Nonlinear	No iteration	Iteration
Boundary-value problem	Linear	Iteration	Iteration or direct
(elliptic and mixed)	Nonlinear	Iteration	Iteration

Mathematical models that are elliptic in nature are called boundary-value problems. Regardless of whether the algorithms involved are explicit or implicit, boundary-value problems are usually solved using iterative methods. The only exception is when linear elliptic problems are solved implicitly, in which case direct solution methods may be used, although these tend to be expensive for large systems. Hyperbolic and parabolic mathematical models are called initial-boundary value problems and are solved via marching techniques. When explicit algorithms are used to solve initial-boundary value problems, then no iteration is needed. Initial-boundary value problems solved with implicit algorithms require iterative methods unless the problem is linear, in which case a direct solution approach can also be used. The situations where iterative methods can be used, and thus where iterative error will be present, are summarized in Table 7.3.

The remainder of this section will provide an overview of the different methods for solving linear systems of algebraic equations. The linear systems can arise from either linear or nonlinear mathematical models, with the latter requiring an additional linearization step (e.g., from a Picard iteration or Newton's method). A basic understanding of linear algebra is assumed (e.g., see Meyer, 2000).

Consider a linear system of algebraic equations of the form

$$A\vec{x} = \vec{b}, \tag{7.6}$$

where A is an $N \times N$ matrix of scalars, $\vec{b}$ a column vector of length N, $\vec{x}$ the desired solution vector of length N, and N is the total number of unknowns. In general, linear systems arising from the discretization of mathematical models will be sparse, meaning that most of the entries in the A matrix are zero. When the total number of unknowns N is sufficiently small, then direct solution techniques can be used (see Section 7.4.1.2). For large linear systems, iterative methods are much more efficient. The basic concept behind iterative methods is to first make an initial guess at the solution to Eq. (7.6) and then make successive approximations to improve the solution until satisfactory iterative convergence is reached. Because the approximate solutions will not exactly satisfy Eq. (7.6), convergence of these iterative methods is generally determined by monitoring the difference between the right and left hand sides of the equation. The iterative residual associated with the approximate solution at iteration k is thus defined as:

$$\vec{\Re}^k = \vec{b} - A\vec{x}^k. \tag{7.7}$$

Stationary iterative methods are discussed in some detail below, whereas only a broad overview of the more advanced Krylov subspace methods is given later. In addition, hybrid approaches that combine the stationary and Krylov subspace methods are also mentioned. This section concludes with examples of some stationary iterative methods applied to both linear and nonlinear mathematical models.

Direct solution methods

Direct solution methods are those which, neglecting round-off error, will produce the exact solution to the linear system given by Eq. (7.6) in a finite number of steps. In general, direct methods require on the order of N^3 operations (additions, subtractions, multiplications, and divisions) to find the solution, where N is the total number of equations to be solved. Unless the sparse structure of the linear system can be used to reduce this operation count, direct solution methods are prohibitively expensive for large scientific computing applications and iterative methods should be employed instead. The use of iterative methods is further supported by the fact that one is generally not required to drive the iterative error to zero, but only down to an acceptably small level.

An example of a direct solution method which makes efficient use of the sparse matrix structure is the *Thomas algorithm*. When the matrix A contains non-zero entries only along the three diagonals L_T, D, and U_T, e.g.,

$$A = \begin{bmatrix} D & U_T & 0 & \cdots & \cdots & \cdots & 0 \\ L_T & D & U_T & \ddots & & & \vdots \\ 0 & L_T & D & U_T & \ddots & & \vdots \\ \vdots & \ddots & \ddots & \ddots & \ddots & \ddots & \vdots \\ \vdots & & \ddots & L_T & D & U_T & 0 \\ \vdots & & & \ddots & L_T & D & U_T \\ 0 & \cdots & \cdots & \cdots & 0 & L_T & D \end{bmatrix}, \tag{7.8}$$

then a simplification of the standard direct solution technique of Gaussian elimination followed by back substitution can be used which only requires on the order of N operations. This tridiagonal matrix structure commonly arises during the discretization of 1-D mathematical models using second-order accurate methods. A similar approach called the block tridiagonal solver can be used when the L_T, D, and U_T entries themselves are square matrices. The approximate number of arithmetic operations (i.e., the operation count) for some common direct solution techniques is given in Table 7.4. Note that in Table 7.4, only the Thomas algorithm makes use of a sparse matrix structure. To get an idea of the computational time for these direct solution methods, today's modern desktop processors can perform computations at the gigaflops rate, meaning roughly 10^9 floating point operations per second. Thus, with 1 million unknowns, the Thomas algorithm would require approximately 0.008 seconds while Gaussian elimination would require 22.2 years. It is

Table 7.4 *Operation count for some direct solution techniques.*

Direct solution technique	Approximate operation count	Approximate operations for $N = 1000$	Approximate operations for $N = 1$ million
Thomas algorithm[a]	$8N$	8×10^3	8×10^6
Gaussian elimination	$\frac{2}{3}N^3$	7×10^8	7×10^{17}
LU decomposition	$\frac{2}{3}N^3$	7×10^8	7×10^{17}
	N^3	1×10^9	1×10^{18}
Gauss–Jordan			
Matrix inversion	$2N^3$	2×10^9	2×10^{18}
Cramer's rule	$(N + 1)!$	4.0×10^{2570}	8.3×10^{5565714}

[a] for tridiagonal systems only.

clear that as the total number of unknowns N becomes large, the direct solution techniques are no longer feasible unless a sparse matrix structure can be exploited.

Stationary iterative methods

Stationary iterative methods use approximations of the full linear matrix operator A to successively improve the solution. By splitting the matrix as $A = M - N$, these methods can be written in the form

$$M\vec{x}^{k+1} = N\vec{x}^k + \vec{b}, \tag{7.9}$$

where k refers to the iteration number and the matrices M and N and the vector $\vec{b}$ are generally constant (i.e., they do not depend on the iteration number). In the limit as the iterations converge, $\vec{x}^k = \vec{x}^{k+1}$ and thus the original linear system given in Eq. (7.6) is recovered. Note that for some approximations to nonlinear systems, the matrices M and N and the vector $\vec{b}$ may in fact be updated during the iteration process. Examples of stationary iterative methods include Newton's method, Jacobi iteration, Gauss–Seidel iteration, and algebraic multigrid methods.

Left-multiplying Eq. (7.9) by the inverse of M results in

$$\vec{x}^{k+1} = M^{-1}N\vec{x}^k + M^{-1}\vec{b} \tag{7.10}$$

or simply

$$\vec{x}^{k+1} = G\vec{x}^k + M^{-1}\vec{b}, \tag{7.11}$$

where $G = M^{-1}N$ is called the iteration matrix. As will be discussed in Section 7.4.2, the convergence rate of stationary iterative methods depends on the properties of this iteration matrix.

Some of the simpler stationary iterative methods can be developed by splitting the matrix A into its diagonal D, a lower-triangular matrix L, and an upper triangular matrix U:

$$
A = \begin{bmatrix} D & U & \cdots & \cdots & U \\ L & D & \ddots & & \vdots \\ \vdots & \ddots & \ddots & \ddots & \vdots \\ \vdots & & \ddots & D & U \\ L & \cdots & \cdots & L & D \end{bmatrix} = \begin{bmatrix} D & 0 & \cdots & \cdots & 0 \\ 0 & D & \ddots & & \vdots \\ \vdots & \ddots & \ddots & \ddots & \vdots \\ \vdots & & \ddots & D & 0 \\ 0 & \cdots & \cdots & 0 & D \end{bmatrix}
$$

$$
+ \begin{bmatrix} 0 & 0 & \cdots & \cdots & 0 \\ L & 0 & \ddots & & \vdots \\ \vdots & \ddots & \ddots & \ddots & \vdots \\ \vdots & & \ddots & 0 & 0 \\ L & \cdots & \cdots & L & 0 \end{bmatrix} + \begin{bmatrix} 0 & U & \cdots & \cdots & U \\ 0 & 0 & \ddots & & \vdots \\ \vdots & \ddots & \ddots & \ddots & \vdots \\ \vdots & & \ddots & 0 & U \\ 0 & \cdots & \cdots & 0 & 0 \end{bmatrix}. \tag{7.12}
$$

With this splitting, the Jacobi method can be defined with $M = D$ and $N = -L - U$, resulting in the following iterative scheme:

$$
D\vec{x}^{k+1} = -(L + U)\vec{x}^k + \vec{b}. \tag{7.13}
$$

The choice of $M = D$ decouples the equations at each iteration, thus resulting in an explicit iterative scheme where each component of the solution vector x_i^{k+1} depends only on known values from the previous iteration $\vec{x}$.

The Gauss–Seidel method is similar; however it uses the most recently updated information available during the solution. For a forward sweep through the unknowns, the Gauss–Seidel method uses the splitting $M = D + L$ and $N = -U$ to give

$$
(D + L)\vec{x}^{k+1} = -U\vec{x}^k + \vec{b}. \tag{7.14}
$$

A symmetric Gauss–Seidel method would employ a forward sweep with

$$
(D + L)\vec{x}^{k+1/2} = -U\vec{x}^k + \vec{b} \tag{7.15}
$$

followed by a backward sweep with

$$
(D + U)\vec{x}^{k+1} = -L\vec{x}^{k+1/2} + \vec{b}, \tag{7.16}
$$

where $k = 1/2$ indicates an intermediate iteration step. All three of these Gauss–Seidel iteration methods can be performed explicitly, i.e., without solving for multiple unknowns at the same time.

Another technique that should be mentioned since it has an impact on the convergence of stationary iterative methods is over/under-relaxation. Rather than employing the stationary iterative methods as discussed previously, one instead replaces the solution components found by applying the standard iterative method x_i^{k+1} with the following:

$$\hat{x}_i^{k+1} = x_i^k + \omega \left(x_i^{k+1} - x_i^k \right), \tag{7.17}$$

where $0 < \omega < 2$. Setting the relaxation parameter to one recovers the baseline iterative methods, whereas values greater than one or less than one result in over-relaxation or under-relaxation, respectively. When implemented with the forward Gauss–Seidel approach and with $\omega > 1$, this approach is called successive over-relaxation (SOR). The splitting for the SOR method is $M = D + \omega L$ and $N = -\omega U + (1 - \omega)D$ which can be written in matrix form as:

$$(D + \omega L)\vec{x}^{k+1} = [\omega U + (1 - \omega D)]\vec{x}^k + \omega\vec{b}. \tag{7.18}$$

In certain cases, the optimal relaxation factor can be estimated from properties of the iteration matrix (Saad, 1996).

Krylov subspace methods

In order to understand the basic ideas behind Krylov subspace methods, a quick review of matrix theory (Meyer, 2000) is first required. A vector space is a mathematical construct which includes definitions of vector addition and scalar multiplication. A vector subspace is any non-empty subset of a vector space. A basis for a subspace is a linearly independent set of vectors that can be linearly combined to form any vector in the subspace. The span of a set of vectors is the subspace formed by all linear combinations of those vectors, and when a set of spanning vectors are linearly independent then they also form a basis for that subspace.

Krylov subspace methods, also called nonstationary iterative methods, are popular for large sparse systems (Saad, 2003). They work by minimizing the iterative residual defined by Eq. (7.7) over the Krylov subspace. This subspace is the vector space spanned by the set of vectors formed by premultiplying an initial iterative residual vector by the matrix A to various powers. For any positive integer $m < N$ (where N is the number of unknowns), this space is defined as

$$K_m\left(A, \vec{\Re}^{k=0}\right) = \text{span}\left\{ \vec{\Re}^{k=0}, A\vec{\Re}^{k=0}, A^2\vec{\Re}^{k=0}, \ldots, A^{m-1}\vec{\Re}^{k=0}\right\}. \tag{7.19}$$

An advantage of the Krylov subspace methods is that they can be implemented such that they only require matrix–vector multiplication and avoid expensive matrix–matrix multiplication.

The most commonly used Krylov subspace methods are the conjugate gradient method (for symmetric matrices only), the biconjugate gradient method, the stabilized biconjugate gradient method, and the generalized minimum residual method (GMRES) (Saad, 2003). Because the sequence of vectors given in Eq. (7.19) tends to become nearly linearly dependent, Krylov subspace methods generally employ an orthogonalization procedure such as Arnoldi orthogonalization (for the conjugate gradient and GMRES methods) or a Lanczos biorthogonalization (for the biconjugate gradient and stabilized biconjugate gradient methods) (Saad, 2003). Krylov subspace methods are technically direct solution methods since they form a basis in the vector space which contains the solution vector $\vec{x}$ and will thus converge (within round-off error) in N steps. However, since the number of unknowns N is usually large for scientific computing applications, the process is almost always terminated early when the iterative residuals are sufficiently small, resulting in an iterative method.

Hybrid methods

Stationary and nonstationary iterative methods are often combined to take advantage of the strengths of each method. Preconditioned Krylov subspace methods premultiply the standard linear system given in Eq. (7.6) by an approximate inverse of the A matrix. For example, a Jacobi preconditioner is $P = D$ (the diagonal of matrix A), and the preconditioned system becomes

$$P^{-1}A\vec{x} = P^{-1}\vec{b}. \tag{7.20}$$

The preconditioner should be chosen such that P^{-1} is inexpensive to evaluate and the resulting system is easier to solve (Saad, 2003). Alternatively, the basic concepts behind Krylov subspace methods can be applied to the vector basis formed by linearly combining the sequence of iterative solutions $\vec{x}^{k}$ produced by a stationary iterative method. Hageman and Young (1981) refer to this process as polynomial acceleration.

Examples of iterative methods in scientific computing

This section provides some simple examples of linear systems that arise from the discretization of mathematical models. Various discretization approaches are applied to linear steady and unsteady 2-D heat conduction mathematical models. Explicit and implicit discretizations of unsteady Burgers equation are also examined, with the latter requiring a linearization step. In all cases, the types of linear systems arising from the discretization are discussed.

Linear equations While it is possible to employ direct solution techniques on linear equations, for a desired iterative error tolerance it is often more efficient to employ an iterative method, especially for large linear systems. Let us first consider the case of 2-D unsteady heat conduction with constant thermal diffusivity α:

$$\frac{\partial T}{\partial t} - \alpha \left(\frac{\partial^2 T}{\partial x^2} + \frac{\partial^2 T}{\partial y^2} \right) = 0. \tag{7.21}$$

This linear partial differential equation is parabolic in time and is thus an initial-boundary value problem which must be solved by a temporal marching procedure. A simple explicit finite difference discretization in Cartesian coordinates results in

$$\frac{T_{i,j}^{n+1} - T_{i,j}^{n}}{\Delta t} - \alpha \left(\frac{T_{i+1,j}^{n} - 2T_{i,j}^{n} + T_{i-1,j}^{n}}{\Delta x^2} + \frac{T_{i,j+1}^{n} - 2T_{i,j}^{n} + T_{i,j-1}^{n}}{\Delta y^2} \right) = 0, \tag{7.22}$$

where the n superscript denotes the temporal level and the i and j subscripts denote nodal points in the x and y directions, respectively. Applying this discrete equation over all of the interior grid nodes would result in the presence of temporal and spatial discretization error, but since no iterative method is employed, there would be no iterative error. In other words, this approach falls under the heading of a linear initial-boundary value problem discretized with an explicit algorithm in Table 7.3.

An implicit discretization could instead be chosen for Eq. (7.21), such as the Euler implicit method, which evaluates the spatial derivative terms at time level $n + 1$:

$$\frac{T_{i,j}^{n+1} - T_{i,j}^{n}}{\Delta t} - \alpha \left(\frac{T_{i+1,j}^{n+1} - 2T_{i,j}^{n+1} + T_{i-1,j}^{n+1}}{\Delta x^2} + \frac{T_{i,j+1}^{n+1} - 2T_{i,j}^{n+1} + T_{i,j-1}^{n+1}}{\Delta y^2} \right) = 0. \quad (7.23)$$

When this discrete equation is applied over each of the grid nodes, a linear matrix system results with a pentadiagonal structure, i.e.,

$$A = \begin{bmatrix}
D & U_T & 0 & \cdots & 0 & U_P & 0 & \cdots & 0 \\
L_T & D & U_T & \ddots & & \ddots & U_P & \ddots & \vdots \\
0 & L_T & D & U_T & \ddots & & \ddots & \ddots & 0 \\
\vdots & \ddots & \ddots & \ddots & \ddots & \ddots & & \ddots & U_P \\
0 & & \ddots & \ddots & \ddots & \ddots & \ddots & & 0 \\
L_P & \ddots & & \ddots & \ddots & \ddots & \ddots & \ddots & \vdots \\
0 & \ddots & \ddots & & \ddots & L_T & D & U_T & 0 \\
\vdots & \ddots & L_P & \ddots & & \ddots & L_T & D & U_T \\
0 & \cdots & 0 & L_P & 0 & \cdots & 0 & L_T & D
\end{bmatrix}. \quad (7.24)$$

While this pentadiagonal matrix could be solved directly and therefore with no iterative error, it is usually more efficient to use an iterative technique, especially for large systems. Introducing the superscript k to denote the iteration number, a line implicit discretization can be defined in the i direction such that

$$\frac{T_{i,j}^{n+1,k+1} - T_{i,j}^{n}}{\Delta t}$$
$$- \alpha \left(\frac{T_{i+1,j}^{n+1,k+1} - 2T_{i,j}^{n+1,k+1} + T_{i-1,j}^{n+1,k+1}}{\Delta x^2} + \frac{T_{i,j+1}^{n+1,k} - 2T_{i,j}^{n+1,k+1} + T_{i,j-1}^{n+1,k}}{\Delta y^2} \right) = 0,$$
$$\quad (7.25)$$

where the pentadiagonal contributions to the matrix structure (at $j \pm 1$) are evaluated at the known iteration level k. This discretization results in a tridiagonal system of equations for the unknowns at iteration level $k + 1$ with the same structure as the matrix given in Eq. (7.8), which can again be solved efficiently with the Thomas algorithm. This discretization scheme thus requires an iterative solution to a linear system to be performed at each time step.

This line implicit iterative scheme can be written in matrix form as follows. Consider a splitting of the full matrix A from Eq. (7.23) as

$$A = L_P + L_T + D + U_T + U_P, \tag{7.26}$$

where D represents the diagonal terms (i, j), L_T the $(i - 1, j)$ terms, L_P the $(i, j - 1)$ terms, U_T the $(i + 1, j)$ terms, and U_P the $(i, j + 1)$ terms. Equation (7.25) is thus equivalent to splitting the A matrix by separating out the pentadiagonal terms, i.e.,

$$M = (L_T + D + U_T), \quad N = -(L_P + U_P). \tag{7.27}$$

The iteration scheme can then be written as

$$(L_T + D + U_T) \vec{T}^{n+1,k+1} = -(L_P + U_P) \vec{T}^{n+1,k} + \vec{b} \tag{7.28}$$

or simply

$$\vec{T}^{n+1,k+1} = (L_T + D + U_T)^{-1} \left[-(L_P + U_P) \vec{T}^{n+1,k} + \vec{b} \right] = M^{-1} \left[N \vec{T}^{n+1,k} + \vec{b} \right]. \tag{7.29}$$

As discussed in Section 7.4.2, the convergence of this iterative scheme is governed by the eigenvalues of the iteration matrix $G = M^{-1}N$.

If we instead consider the steady-state form of the 2-D heat conduction equation, then the temporal derivative drops out, resulting in the following elliptic boundary value problem:

$$\frac{\partial^2 T}{\partial x^2} + \frac{\partial^2 T}{\partial y^2} = 0. \tag{7.30}$$

Discretizing with second-order accurate spatial finite differences on a Cartesian mesh results in

$$\frac{T_{i+1,j} - 2T_{i,j} + T_{i-1,j}}{\Delta x^2} + \frac{T_{i,j+1} - 2T_{i,j} + T_{i,j-1}}{\Delta y^2} = 0, \tag{7.31}$$

which is again a pentadiagonal system of equations. This system could be solved with a direct method without producing any iterative error; however, this approach is impractical for large systems. If instead an iterative scheme such as the line-implicit approach in the i direction is employed, then the following linear system results:

$$\frac{T_{i+1,j}^{k+1} - 2T_{i,j}^{k+1} + T_{i-1,j}^{k+1}}{\Delta x^2} + \frac{T_{i,j+1}^{k} - 2T_{i,j}^{k+1} + T_{i,j-1}^{k}}{\Delta y^2} = 0. \tag{7.32}$$

This choice for the iterative scheme is called the line relaxation method and again results in a tridiagonal system of equations which can be easily solved.

Even when steady-state solutions are desired, it is common in many scientific computing disciplines to include a temporal discretization term in order to stabilize the iteration process. This occurs because the temporal terms tend to increase the diagonal dominance of the resulting iteration matrix. These temporal terms effectively serve as an under-relaxation technique, with the under-relaxation factor approaching unity as the time step is increased. When temporal terms are included for steady-state problems, one must keep in mind that it is only the steady-state portion of the iterative residuals that should be monitored for iterative convergence.

Nonlinear equations   Nonlinear systems of equations often employ the same iterative methods used for linear systems, but they first require a linearization procedure such as a Picard iteration or a Newton's method. Consider the 1-D unsteady Burgers' equation

$$\frac{\partial u}{\partial t} + u\frac{\partial u}{\partial x} - v\frac{\partial^2 u}{\partial x^2} = 0, \tag{7.33}$$

which is parabolic in time and thus solved by temporal marching (i.e., an initial value problem). Applying a first-order accurate forward difference in time and second order accurate central differences for the spatial terms results in the following simple explicit scheme:

$$\frac{u_i^{n+1} - u_i^n}{\Delta t} + u_i^n \frac{u_{i+1}^n - u_{i-1}^n}{2\Delta x} - v\frac{u_{i+1}^n - 2u_i^n + u_{i-1}^n}{\Delta x^2} = 0. \tag{7.34}$$

While this explicit solution scheme is generally not used due to the severe stability restrictions and the presence of numerical oscillations in the solution, it requires no iterations and thus there is no accompanying iterative error.

If instead each of the dependent variables in the spatial terms were evaluated at time level $n + 1$, the resulting implicit method would be:

$$\frac{u_i^{n+1} - u_i^n}{\Delta t} + u_i^{n+1} \frac{u_{i+1}^{n+1} - u_{i-1}^{n+1}}{2\Delta x} - v\frac{u_{i+1}^{n+1} - 2u_i^{n+1} + u_{i-1}^{n+1}}{\Delta x^2} = 0. \tag{7.35}$$

Due to the nonlinearity in the convection term, this approach results in a *nonlinear* system of algebraic equations which is not in the form of Eq. (7.6) and thus cannot be readily solved by a digital computer. For nonlinear equations, we are required to perform a linearization step and then solve the resulting tridiagonal system of equations in an iterative manner. In this example, we will use a simple Picard iteration where the u_i^{n+1} in the convective term is evaluated at the known iterative solution location k:

$$\frac{u_i^{n+1,k+1} - u_i^n}{\Delta t} + u_i^{n+1,k} \frac{u_{i+1}^{n+1,k+1} - u_{i-1}^{n+1,k+1}}{2\Delta x} - v\frac{u_{i+1}^{n+1,k+1} - 2u_i^{n+1,k+1} + u_{i-1}^{n+1,k+1}}{\Delta x^2} = 0. \tag{7.36}$$

The solution procedure would be as follows:

1 provide an initial guess for all u values at the first iteration ($k = 1$),
2 solve the tridiagonal system of equations for the solution at iteration $k + 1$,
3 update the nonlinear term based on the new iterative solution, and
4 repeat the process until iterative residual convergence is achieved.

Thus for nonlinear equations, even when direct methods are used to solve the resulting linear system, the solution approach will still be iterative due to the linearization step (recall Table 7.3).

7.4.2 Iterative convergence

This section provides a brief discussion of the convergence of stationary iterative methods. See Saad (2003) for a discussion of the convergence of Krylov subspace methods. As mentioned previously, the iterative error is defined as the difference between the current numerical solution at iteration k and the exact solution to the discrete equations. For some global solution property f, we can thus define the iterative error at iteration k as

$$\varepsilon_h^k = f_h^k - f_h \tag{7.37}$$

where h refers to the discrete equation on a mesh with discretization parameters (Δx, Δy, Δt, etc.) represented by h, f_h^k is the current iterative solution, and f_h is the exact solution to the discrete equations, not to be confused with the exact solution to the mathematical model. In some cases, we might instead be concerned with the iterative error in the entire solution over the domain (i.e., the dependent variables in the mathematical model). In this case, the iterative error for *each* dependent variable u should be measured as a norm over the domain, e.g.,

$$\varepsilon_h^k = \left\| \vec{u}_h^k - \vec{u}_h \right\|, \tag{7.38}$$

where the vector signs denote a column vector composed of a single dependent variable at each discrete location in the domain. When multiple dependent variables are included (e.g., x-velocity, y-velocity, and pressure in a fluid dynamics simulation), then these should be monitored separately. The common norms employed include discrete L_1, L_2, and L_∞ norms (see Chapter 5 for norm definitions). Note that the standard texts on iterative methods do not differentiate between the different dependent variables, and thus lump all dependent variables at all domain locations into the unknown variable vector $\vec{x}$. We will switch between the scientific computing notation $\vec{u}$ and the linear systems notation $\vec{x}$ as necessary.

For stationary iterative methods applied to linear systems, iterative convergence is governed by the eigenvalues of the iteration matrix. Recall that M and N come from the splitting of the full matrix A in Eq. (7.6). The iteration matrix G comes from left-multiplying Eq. (7.9) by M^{-1}, i.e.,

$$\vec{x}^{k+1} = M^{-1} N \vec{x}^k + M^{-1} \vec{b}, \tag{7.39}$$

and can thus be expressed as $G = M^{-1}N$. Specifically, convergence is related to the eigenvalue of largest magnitude λ_G for the iteration matrix G. The absolute value of this eigenvalue is also called the *spectral radius* of the matrix,

$$\rho(G) = |\lambda_G|. \tag{7.40}$$

Convergence of the iterative method requires that the spectral radius be less than one, and the closer to unity the slower the convergence rate of the method (Golub and Van Loan, 1996). A crude approximation of the spectral radius of a matrix (Meyer, 2000) can be found by using the fact that the spectral radius is bounded from above by any valid matrix norm, i.e.,

$$\rho(G) \leq \|G\|. \tag{7.41}$$

For the Jacobi and Gauss–Seidel methods, convergence is guaranteed if the matrix A is strictly diagonally dominant, meaning that the magnitude of the diagonal entry of each row is larger than the sum of the magnitudes of other entries in the row, i.e.,

$$|A_{ii}| > \sum_{i \neq j} |A_{ij}|. \tag{7.42}$$

For linear problems, when the maximum eigenvalue λ_G of the iteration matrix G is real, then the limiting iterative convergence behavior will be monotone. When λ_G is complex, however, the limiting iterative convergence behavior will generally be oscillatory (Ferziger and Peric, 1996). For nonlinear problems, the linearized system is often not solved to convergence, but only solved for a few iterations (sometimes as few as one) before the nonlinear terms are updated. Iterative convergence of the nonlinear system is much more difficult to assess and, like equations with a single unknown, is often related to proximity of the initial guess to the converged solution. See Kelley (1995) for a discussion of iterative methods for nonlinear systems.

7.4.2.1 Types of iterative convergence

This section describes the different types of iterative convergence that may be observed. For simple scientific computing applications, iterative convergence is often found to be monotone or oscillatory. For more complex applications, a more general iterative convergence behavior is often found.

Monotone convergence

Monotone iterative convergence occurs when subsequent iterative solutions approach the exact solution to the discrete equations in a monotone fashion with no local minima or maxima in the iterative error plotted as a function of the iteration number. Monotone convergence is usually either linear or quadratic. Linear convergence occurs when the ratio of iterative error from one iteration to the next is constant, i.e.,

$$\varepsilon_h^{k+1} = C\varepsilon_h^k, \quad \text{where } C < 1, \tag{7.43}$$

thus the iterative error is reduced by the same fraction C for every iteration. Many scientific computing codes converge at best at a linear rate. Quadratic convergence occurs when the iterative errors drop with the square of the iterative errors from the previous iterations

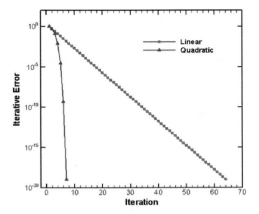

Figure 7.3 Example of monotone iterative convergence showing both linear and quadratic behavior.

(Süli and Mayers, 2006), i.e.,

$$\left|\varepsilon_h^{k+1}\right| = C \left(\varepsilon_h^k\right)^2, \quad \text{where } C < 1, \tag{7.44}$$

For nonlinear governing equations, quadratic convergence can be achieved for advanced iterative techniques (e.g., full Newton's method) as long as the current iterative solution is in the vicinity of the exact solution to the discrete equations (Kelley, 1995). Examples of linear and quadratic convergence are given in Figure 7.3, which shows the iterative error on a logarithmic scale as a function of the number of iterations. Although clearly desirable, quadratic convergence is difficult to obtain for practical scientific computing problems. In some cases, monotone iterative convergence can be accelerated by using over-relaxation ($\omega > 1$).

Oscillatory convergence

Oscillatory iterative convergence occurs when the iterative solution converges in an oscillatory manner to the exact solution to the discrete equations. An example of oscillatory iterative convergence is given in Figure 7.4, which shows the iterative convergence error in a general solution functional reducing in an oscillatory but convergent manner. Oscillatory convergence occurs when the largest eigenvalues of the iteration matrix $G = M^{-1}N$ are complex (Ferziger and Peric, 1996). In some cases, oscillatory iterative convergence can be accelerated by using under-relaxation ($\omega < 1$).

General convergence

General iterative convergence occurs when the iterative solutions converge in a complicated manner and exhibit a mixture of monotone and oscillatory convergence. An example of general convergence is given in Figure 7.5, which shows the iteration history for the yaw force on a missile geometry from an inviscid computational fluid dynamics simulation. This complex type of iterative convergence history is commonplace in practical scientific

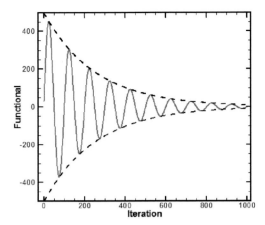

Figure 7.4 Example of oscillatory iterative convergence of a solution functional versus iteration number.

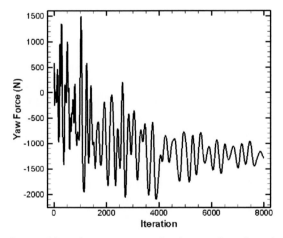

Figure 7.5 Example of general iterative convergence for the yaw force in an inviscid computational fluid dynamics simulation of the flow over a missile (adapted from Roy *et al.*, 2007).

computing simulations. The source of the oscillations for general convergence may be physical (e.g., strong physical instabilities or unsteadiness in a problem) or numerical.

7.4.2.2 *Iterative convergence criteria*

Two common methods for assessing iterative convergence are discussed in this section. The first examines the difference in solutions between successive iterates and can be misleading. The second approach is to examine the iterative residual and provides a direct measure of how well the discrete equations are solved by the current iterative solution.

Difference between iterates

One method commonly used to report the convergence of iterative methods is in terms of the difference (either absolute or relative) between successive iterates, e.g.,

$$f_h^{k+1} - f_h^k \quad \text{or} \quad \frac{f_h^{k+1} - f_h^k}{f_h^k}.$$

However, these approaches can be extremely misleading when convergence is slow or stalled (Ferziger and Peric, 2002). It is strongly recommended that these convergence criteria not be used.

Iterative residuals

A much better approach is to evaluate the iterative residuals of the discrete equations at each step in the iteration process. For linear systems, this iterative residual is given by Eq. (7.7). For scientific computing applications, this iterative residual is found by plugging the current iterative solution into the discretized form of the equations. Recall from Chapter 5 that the discrete equations can be written in the form

$$L_h(u_h) = 0, \tag{7.45}$$

where L_h is the linear or nonlinear discrete operator and u_h is the exact solution to the discrete equations. The iterative residual is found by plugging the current iterative solution u_h^{k+1} into Eq. (7.45), i.e.,

$$\mathfrak{R}_h^{k+1} = L_h(u_h^{k+1}), \tag{7.46}$$

where $\mathfrak{R}_h^{k+1} \to 0$ as $u_h^{k+1} \to u_h$. Note that although it appears to be evaluated in a similar fashion, this iterative residual is completely different from the discrete and continuous residuals discussed in Chapter 5, and this is a source of much confusion in scientific computing.

The form of the iterative residuals for the examples presented in Section 7.4.1.2 will now be given. For the 2-D steady-state heat conduction example using line relaxation given in Eq. (7.32), one would simple evaluate the iterative residual $\mathfrak{R}$ as:

$$\mathfrak{R}_{i,j}^{k+1} = \frac{T_{i+1,j}^{k+1} - 2T_{i,j}^{k+1} + T_{i-1,j}^{k+1}}{\Delta x^2} + \frac{T_{i,j+1}^{k+1} - 2T_{i,j}^{k+1} + T_{i,j-1}^{k+1}}{\Delta y^2}. \tag{7.47}$$

The residuals are generally monitored using discrete norms over the mesh points, as discussed in Chapter 5. The residual norms will approach zero as the iterations converge, thus ensuring that the numerical solution satisfies the discrete equations within round-off error; however, in practice, the iterations are generally terminated when the iterative error is considered sufficiently small (see Section 7.4.3). For the unsteady 2-D heat conduction example given by Eq. (7.25), the unsteady iterative residual must be used:

$$
\mathfrak{R}_{i,j}^{n+1,k+1} = \frac{T_{i,j}^{n+1,k+1} - T_{i,j}^{n}}{\Delta t}
$$
$$
- \alpha \left(\frac{T_{i+1,j}^{n+1,k+1} - 2T_{i,j}^{n+1,k+1} + T_{i-1,j}^{n+1,k+1}}{\Delta x^2} + \frac{T_{i,j+1}^{n+1,k+1} - 2T_{i,j}^{n+1,k+1} + T_{i,j-1}^{n+1,k+1}}{\Delta y^2} \right).
$$

(7.48)

However, in cases where the unsteady form of the governing equations is used to obtain solutions to the steady-state governing equations, the steady-state iterative residual (given by Eq. (7.47) in this case, either with or without the diffusivity α) must be used.

For the implicit discretization of the unsteady Burgers equation given by Eq. (7.36), the form of the iterative residual to be converged at each time step n is

$$
\mathfrak{R}_i^{n+1,k+1} = \frac{u_i^{n+1,k+1} - u_i^{n}}{\Delta t} + u_i^{n+1,k+1} \frac{u_{i+1}^{n+1,k+1} - u_{i-1}^{n+1,k+1}}{2\Delta x}
$$
$$
- \nu \frac{u_{i+1}^{n+1,k+1} - 2u_i^{n+1,k+1} + u_{i-1}^{n+1,k+1}}{\Delta x^2},
$$

(7.49)

where the velocity modifying the convective term must be evaluated at iteration $k + 1$. Again, when the unsteady formulation is used to obtain steady-state solutions, then the iterative residual that needs to be monitored is simply the steady-state residual given by

$$
\mathfrak{R}_i^{k+1} = u_i^{k+1} \frac{u_{i+1}^{k+1} - u_{i-1}^{k+1}}{2\Delta x} - \nu \frac{u_{i+1}^{k+1} - 2u_i^{k+1} + u_{i-1}^{k+1}}{\Delta x^2}.
$$

(7.50)

7.4.3 Iterative error estimation

While monitoring the iterative residuals often serves as an adequate indication as to whether iterative convergence has been achieved, it does not by itself provide any guidance as to the size of the iterative error in the solution quantities of interest. In this section, we discuss approaches for estimating the iterative error in general solution quantities. These approaches can be used to obtain a quantitative estimate of the iterative error. If the numerical solution is to be used in a code order verification study (Chapter 5) or a discretization error study (Chapter 8), the recommended iterative error levels are 100 times smaller than the discretization error levels so as not to adversely impact the discretization error evaluation/estimation process. For cases where the solution will not be used for discretization error evaluation/estimation (e.g., parametric studies where a large number of simulations are required), then larger iterative error levels can often be tolerated.

7.4.3.1 Machine zero method

Recall that the iterative error is defined as the difference between the current iterative solution and the exact solution to the discrete equations. We can get a very good estimate of the iterative error by first converging the solution down to machine zero. The iterative error in a solution function f at iteration k is then approximated as

$$\varepsilon_h^k = f_h^k - f_h \cong f_h^k - f_h^{k \to \infty}. \tag{7.51}$$

where $f_h^{k \to \infty}$ is the machine zero solution, i.e., the iterative solution found in the limit as the number of iterations goes to infinity. This location can be identified as the point in the iteration history where the residuals no longer reduce but instead display seemingly random oscillations about some value. This leveling off generally occurs near residual reductions of approximately seven orders of magnitude for single precision computations and 15 orders of magnitude for double precision computations (see Section 7.2). Due to the expense of converging complex scientific computing codes to machine zero, this approach is usually only practical when applied to a small subset of cases in a large parametric study.

7.4.3.2 Local convergence rate

Rather than converging the iterative residuals to machine zero, a more efficient approach is to use the current iterative solution and its neighboring iterates to estimate the iterative error during the solution process. This approach requires some knowledge of the type of iterative convergence displayed by the numerical solution. These iterative error estimates are most useful for larger scientific computing applications where the convergence is slow.

Monotone iterative convergence

Eigenvalue method For scientific computing analyses where iterative convergence is monotone, the convergence rate is often linear. For linear monotone convergence, the maximum eigenvalue λ_G of the iteration matrix $G = M^{-1}N$ is real. It can be shown (Ferziger, 1988; Golub and Van Loan, 1996) that the iterative error in any general solution quantity f can be approximated by

$$\varepsilon_h^k \cong \frac{f_h^{k+1} - f_h^k}{\lambda_G - 1}, \tag{7.52}$$

where λ_G can be approximated by

$$\lambda_G \cong \frac{|f_h^{k+1} - f_h^k|}{|f_h^k - f_h^{k-1}|}. \tag{7.53}$$

Solving instead for the *estimate* of the exact solution to the discrete equations $\hat{f}_h$, one obtains:

$$\hat{f}_h = \frac{f^{k+1} - \lambda_G f^k}{1 - \lambda_G}. \tag{7.54}$$

See Ferziger (1988) or Golub and Van Loan (1996) for additional details.

Blottner's method   A similar approach was developed by Blottner for cases where linear monotone convergence is observed in the iterative residuals and/or the iterative error (Roy and Blottner, 2001). When linear monotone convergence occurs, iterative solutions at three different iteration levels can be used to estimate the iterative error. Blottner's approach can be summarized as follows. Recall the iterative error in any quantity f from Eq. (7.37),

$$\varepsilon_h^k = f_h^k - f_h, \tag{7.55}$$

where f_h is the exact solution to the discrete equations. If convergence is linear monotonic, then the error will decrease exponentially as a function of iteration number,

$$\varepsilon_h^k = \alpha e^{-\beta k}, \tag{7.56}$$

where α and β are constants which are independent of the iteration number. Equations (7.55) and (7.56) can be combined and rewritten as

$$\beta k = \ln \alpha - \ln\left(f_h^k - f_h\right). \tag{7.57}$$

Equation (7.57) is then evaluated at three different iteration levels, for example, $(k-1)$, k, and $(k+1)$, and these relationships are then used to eliminate α and obtain

$$\beta \left(k - (k-1)\right) = \ln\left[\left(f_h^{k-1} - f_h\right)\big/\left(f_h^k - f_h\right)\right],$$
$$\beta \left(k+1 - (k)\right) = \ln\left[\left(f_h^k - f_h\right)\big/\left(f_h^{k+1} - f_h\right)\right]. \tag{7.58}$$

Assuming the increments between iterations are equal (as in the current example), then the left hand sides of Eq. (7.58) are equivalent. Equating the right hand sides gives

$$\ln\left[\left(f_h^{k-1} - f_h\right)\big/\left(f_h^k - f_h\right)\right] = \ln\left[\left(f_h^k - f_h\right)\big/\left(f_h^{k+1} - f_h\right)\right]$$

or simply

$$\left(f_h^{k-1} - f_h\right)\big/\left(f_h^k - f_h\right) = \left(f_h^k - f_h\right)\big/\left(f_h^{k+1} - f_h\right). \tag{7.59}$$

An estimate of the exact solution to the discretized equations $\hat{f}_h$ is then given by

$$\hat{f}_h = \frac{f_h^k - \Lambda^k f_h^{k-1}}{1 - \Lambda^k}, \quad \text{where } \Lambda^k = \frac{f_h^{k+1} - f_h^k}{f_h^k - f_h^{k-1}}. \tag{7.60}$$

This final result is closely related to the eigenvalue approach given above in Eq. (7.54), where here Λ^k plays the role of the estimated eigenvalues with the largest magnitude λ_G. When convergence is slow, it is often advantageous to use nonconsecutive iterations (e.g., $k - 10$, k, and $k + 10$) due to the relative importance of round-off error when the iterative solutions change very little from iteration to iteration.

   Blottner's method has been used to estimate the iterative error for a Navier–Stokes fluids simulation by Roy and Blottner (2003). They examined the iterative error in the surface shear stress for the hypersonic flow over flat plate aligned with the flow. Figure 7.6a shows

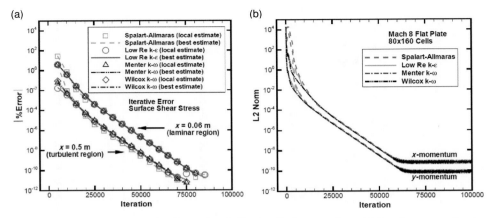

Figure 7.6 Mach 8 flow over a flat plate using the Navier–Stokes equations: (a) iterative error estimates from Blottner's method (local estimate) along with the machine zero method (best estimate) and (b) L_2 norms of the iterative residuals for the x- and y-momentum equations (reproduced from Roy and Blottner, 2003).

the above iterative error estimator applied to two different regions of the plate: one with laminar flow and the other with turbulent flow. The symbols labeled "local estimate" are from Blottner's iterative error estimation procedure, while the lines labeled "best estimate" were found from the machine zero method discussed in Section 7.4.3.1. Machine zero is reached at an iterative residual reduction of approximately 14 orders of magnitude for these double precision computations, as shown in Figure 7.6b. Blottner's method agrees quite well with the machine zero method and has the advantage of allowing early termination of the iterations once the iterative error is sufficiently small. However, Blottner's method should only be applied for cases where the iterative convergence is known (or demonstrated) to be monotone and linear.

Oscillatory iterative convergence

Ferziger and Peric (1996) have developed an iterative error estimator which addresses oscillatory iterative convergence. Recall that in the eigenvalue approach for monotone solutions (discussed in the last section), the eigenvalue of the iteration matrix with the largest magnitude λ_G is used to estimate the iterative error. For oscillatory convergence, the eigenvalues with the largest magnitude are complex (and occur as conjugate pairs) and can also be used to estimate the iterative error. See Ferziger and Peric (1996) and the cited references therein for details.

7.4.4 Relation between iterative residuals and iterative error

A number of studies have shown that the iterative residual reduction tracks extremely well with actual iterative error for a wide range of linear and nonlinear problems in scientific

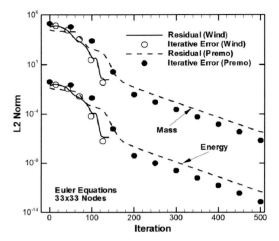

Figure 7.7 Discrete L_2 norms of the iterative convergence error and iterative residuals for manufactured solutions of the Euler equations (reproduced from Roy *et al.*, 2004).

computing (e.g., Ferziger and Peric, 2002; Roy and Blottner, 2003). This was demonstrated earlier in Figure 7.6 for a compressible Navier–Stokes example, which shows that the slope of the iterative error (Figure 7.6a) corresponds to the slope of the iterative residuals (Figure 7.6b), and thus they converge at the same rate. This observation supports the common practice of assessing iterative convergence indirectly by examining the iterative residuals. The key is then to find the appropriate scaling factor for a given class of problems to relate the norms of the iterative residuals to the iterative error in the quantity of interest.

Another example showing the relationship between iterative error and iterative residuals for the Euler equations is presented in Figure 7.7. These solutions were obtained for a manufactured solution computation with both a double precision code (Premo) and a single precision code (Wind) (Roy *et al.*, 2004). The system response quantity of interest is the full flowfield solution, so L2 norms of the iterative error over the domain for the mass and total energy per unit volume are found from the machine zero method (Section 7.4.3.1). These iterative error norms are then compared with L2 norms of the iterative residuals of the mass and total energy conservation equations. For both codes, the iterative residual norms closely follow the actual iterative error norms from the machine zero method. Note that, for these cases, the iterative residuals were scaled by a constant factor so as to line up more closely with the iterative errors, which will not affect the slopes. This scaling is required because the iterative residuals have the same general behavior, but not the same magnitude, as the iterative error.

7.4.5 *Practical approach for estimating iterative error*

For practical scientific computing problems, it may be difficult to apply the iterative error estimators discussed in the Section 7.4.3. This is particularly true when a large number

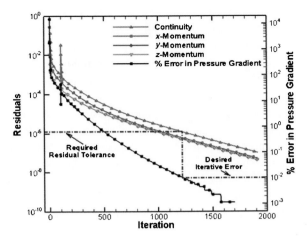

Figure 7.8 Norms of the iterative residuals (left axis) and percentage error in pressure gradient (right axis) for laminar flow through a packed bed (reproduced from Duggirala *et al.*, 2008).

of computational predictions must be made (e.g., for a parametric study or for conducting nondeterministic simulations). Most scientific codes monitor iterative convergence by examining norms of the iterative residuals. Since the iterative residual norms have been shown to follow closely with actual iterative errors for many problems, a small number of computations should be sufficient to determine how the iterative errors in the system response quantity scale with the iterative residuals for the cases of interest.

An example of this procedure is given in Figure 7.8 for laminar viscous flow through a packed bed of spherical particles (Duggirala *et al.*, 2008). The quantity of interest is the average pressure gradient across the bed, and the desired iterative error level in the pressure gradient is 0.01%. The iterative residuals in the conservation of mass (continuity) and conservation of momentum equations are first converged to 10^{-7}, then the value of the pressure gradient at this point is taken as an approximation to the exact solution to the discrete equations $\hat{f}_h$. The iterative error for all previous iterations is then approximated using this estimate of f_h. Figure 7.8 shows that for the desired iterative error level in the pressure gradient of 0.01%, the iterative residual norms should be converged down to approximately 10^{-6}. Simulations for similar problems can be expected to require approximately the same level of iterative residual convergence in order to achieve the desired iterative error tolerance in the pressure gradient.

7.5 Numerical error versus numerical uncertainty

All of the sources of numerical error that have been discussed in this chapter are correctly classified as errors. If the value (including the sign) of these errors is known with a high degree of certainty, then these errors can either be removed from the numerical solutions (a process similar to the removal of well-characterized bias errors from an experimental measurement) or, if sufficiently small, simply neglected. In cases where numerical errors cannot be estimated with a great deal of reliability (as is often the case in scientific computing), while they are still truly errors, our knowledge of these errors is uncertain. Thus when numerical error estimates are not reliable, they can correctly be treated as epistemic uncertainties. That is, they are uncertainties due to a lack of knowledge of the true value of the error.

When the errors and uncertainties due to all numerical error sources have been estimated, a quantitative assessment of the total numerical uncertainty budget can provide guidance as to the efficient allocation of resources. For example, if the total numerical uncertainty budget is estimated for a given class of problems, and the largest contributor to the total uncertainty is the spatial discretization error, then this suggests that an efficient use of resources is to focus on refining the spatial mesh. Just as important, this analysis will also suggest areas where resources should not be focused (e.g., in reducing round-off errors).

7.6 References

Barrett, R., M. Berry, T. F. Chan, J. Demmel, J. M. Donato, J. Dongarra, V. Eijkhout, R. Pozo, C. Romine, and H. Van Der Vorst (1994). *Templates for the Solution of Linear Systems: Building Blocks for Iterative Methods*, SIAM, Philadelphia, PA, (www.netlib.org/linalg/html_templates/Templates.html).

Chandra, S. (2003). *Computer Applications in Physics: with Fortran and Basic*, Pangbourne, UK, Alpha Science International, Ltd.

Chapman, S. J. (2008). *Fortran 95/2003 for Scientists and Engineers*, 3rd edn., McGraw-Hill, New York.

Duggirala, R., C. J. Roy, S. M. Saeidi, J. Khodadadi, D. Cahela, and B. Tatarchuck (2008). Pressure drop predictions for microfibrous flows using CFD, *Journal of Fluids Engineering*. **130**(DOI: 10.1115/1.2948363).

Ferziger, J. H. (1988). A note on numerical accuracy, *International Journal for Numerical Methods in Fluids*. **8**, 995–996.

Ferziger, J. H. and M. Peric (1996). Further discussion of numerical errors in CFD, *International Journal for Numerical Methods in Fluids*. **23**(12), 1263–1274.

Ferziger, J. H. and M. Peric (2002). *Computational Methods for Fluid Dynamics*, 3rd edn., Berlin, Springer-Verlag.

GNU (2009). GNU Multiple Precision Arithmetic Library, gmplib.org/.

Goldberg, D. (1991). What every computer scientist should know about floating-point arithmetic, *Computing Surveys*. **23**(1), 91–124 (docs.sun.com/source/806–3568/ncg_goldberg.html).

Golub, G. H. and C. F. Van Loan (1996). *Matrix Computations*, 3rd edn., Baltimore, The Johns Hopkins University Press.

Hackbush, W. (1994). *Iterative Solution of Large Sparse Systems of Equations*, New York, Springer-Verlag.

Hageman, L. A. and D. M. Young (1981). *Applied Iterative Methods*, London, Academic Press.

IEEE (2008). *IEEE Standard for Floating-Point Arithmetic*, New York, Microprocessor Standards Committee, Institute of Electrical and Electronics Engineers Computer Society.

Kelley, C. T. (1995). *Iterative Methods for Linear and Nonlinear Equations*, SIAM Frontiers in Applied Mathematics Series, Philadelphia, Society for Industrial and Applied Mathematics.

MATLAB (2009). *MATLAB® 7 Programming Fundamentals*, Revised for Version 7.8 (Release 2009a), Natick, The MathWorks, Inc.

Meyer, C. D. (2000). *Matrix Analysis and Applied Linear Algebra*, Philadelphia, Society for Industrial and Applied Mathematics.

Roy, C. J. and F. G. Blottner (2001). Assessment of one- and two-equation turbulence models for hypersonic transitional flows, *Journal of Spacecraft and Rockets*. **38**(5), 699–710 (see also Roy, C. J. and F. G. Blottner (2000). *Assessment of One- and Two-Equation Turbulence Models for Hypersonic Transitional Flows*, AIAA Paper 2000–0132).

Roy, C. J. and F. G. Blottner (2003). Methodology for turbulence model validation: application to hypersonic flows, *Journal of Spacecraft and Rockets*. **40**(3), 313–325.

Roy, C. J., C. C. Nelson, T. M. Smith, and C. C. Ober (2004). Verification of Euler/Navier–Stokes codes using the method of manufactured solutions, *International Journal for Numerical Methods in Fluids*. **44**(6), 599–620.

Roy, C. J., C. J. Heintzelman, and S. J. Roberts (2007). *Estimation of Numerical Error for 3D Inviscid Flows on Cartesian Grids*, AIAA Paper 2007–0102.

Saad, Y. (1996). *Iterative Methods for Sparse Linear Systems*, 1st edn., Boston, PWS Publishing (updated manuscript www-users.cs.umn.edu/~saad/books.html).

Saad, Y. (2003). *Iterative Methods for Sparse Linear Systems*, 2nd edn., Philadelphia, PA, Society for Industrial and Applied Mathematics.

Smith, D. M. (2009). FMLIB, Fortran Library, myweb.lmu.edu/dmsmith/FMLIB.html.

Stremel, P. M., M. R. Mendenhall, and M. C. Hegedus (2007). *BPX – A Best Practices Expert System for CFD*, AIAA Paper 2007–974.

Süli, E. and D. F. Mayers (2006). *An Introduction to Numerical Analysis*. Cambridge, Cambridge University Press.

Veluri, S. P., C. J. Roy, A. Ahmed, R. Rifki, J. C. Worley, and B. Recktenwald (2009). Joint computational/experimental aerodynamic study of a simplified tractor/trailer geometry, *Journal of Fluids Engineering*. **131**(8) (DOI: 10.1115/1.3155995).

8

Discretization error

Recall that our definition of a mathematical model is a governing partial differential or integral equation along with its associate initial and boundary conditions. In scientific computing, one is concerned with finding approximate solutions to this mathematical model, a process that involves the discretization of both the mathematical model and the domain. The approximation errors associated with this discretization process are called discretization errors, and they occur in nearly every scientific computing simulation. The *discretization error* can be formally defined as the difference between the exact solution to the discrete equations and the exact solution to the mathematical model:

$$\varepsilon_h = u_h - \tilde{u}. \tag{8.1}$$

In the next chapter, it will be shown that the discretization error arises out of the interplay between the chosen discretization scheme for the mathematical model, the mesh resolution, the mesh quality, and the solution behavior. Discretization error is the most difficult type of numerical error to estimate reliably (i.e., accurately) and is usually the largest of the four numerical error sources discussed in Chapter 7.

The discretization error has two components: one that is locally-generated and one that is transported from other parts of the domain. The transported component is also called pollution error in the finite element literature (e.g., Babuska *et al.*, 1997). The existence of these two components was shown mathematically in Chapter 5 using the continuous error transport equation which relates the convergence of the numerical solution (i.e., the discretization error) to the consistency of the discretization scheme (i.e., the truncation error). It was showed that the discretization error is transported in the same manner as the underlying solution properties (e.g., it can be convected and diffused) and that it is locally generated by the truncation error.

An example of discretization error transport for the Euler equations is shown in Figure 8.1, which gives the discretization error in the density for the inviscid, Mach 8 flow over an axisymmetric sphere-cone (Roy, 2003). The flow is from left to right, and large discretization errors are generated at the bow shock wave where the shock and the grid lines are misaligned. In the subsonic (i.e., elliptic) region of the flow immediately behind the normal shock, these errors are convected along the local streamlines. In the supersonic (hyperbolic) regions these errors propagate along characteristic Mach lines and

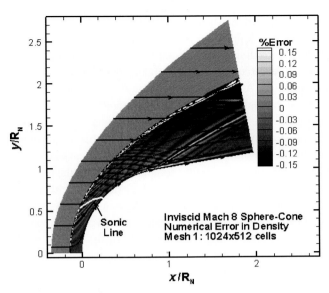

Figure 8.1 Contours of total estimated discretization error in density for the flow over an inviscid hypersonic sphere cone (from Roy, 2003). (See color plate section.)

reflect off the surface. Additional discretization error is generated at the sphere-cone tangency point (i.e., the point where the spherical nose joins the conical body), which represents a singularity due to the discontinuity in the surface curvature. Errors from this region also propagate downstream along the characteristic Mach line. An adaptation process which is driven by the global error levels would adapt to the characteristic line emanating from the sphere-cone tangency point, which is not desired. An adaptation process driven by the local contribution to the error should adapt to the sphere-cone tangency point, thus obviating the need for adaption to the characteristic line that emanates from it. Targeted mesh adaptation is discussed in detail in the next chapter.

This chapter contains an overview and classification of several approaches for estimating the discretization error, a summary of which is given by Roy (2010). Many of these approaches have arisen out of the finite element method, which due to its nature provides for a rigorous mathematical analysis. Other approaches to discretization error estimation seek to find an estimate of the exact solution to the mathematical model which is of a higher formal order of accuracy than the underlying discrete solution. Once this higher-order estimate is found, it can be used to estimate the discretization error in the solution.

While a wide range of approaches are discussed for estimating discretization error, particular attention is focused on Richardson extrapolation which relies on discrete solutions on two meshes to estimate the discretization error. The reason for this choice is straightforward: Richardson extrapolation is the only discretization error estimator that can be applied as a post-processing step to both local solutions and system response quantities from any discretization approach. The main drawback is the expense of generating and then computing another discrete solution on a systematically-refined mesh.

Regardless of the approach used for estimating the discretization error, the reliability of the resulting error estimate requires that the underlying numerical solution (or solutions) be in the asymptotic range. Achieving this asymptotic range can be surprisingly difficult, and confirming that it has indeed been achieved generally requires at least three discrete solutions. For complex scientific computing applications involving coupled, nonlinear, multi-dimensional, multi-physics equations, it is unlikely that the asymptotic range will be achieved without the use of solution adaptive procedures discussed in the next chapter.

The most common situation in scientific computing is when the discretization error estimate has been computed, but the reliability of that estimate is either (1) low because the asymptotic range has not been achieved or (2) unknown because three discrete solutions are not available. In these cases, the discretization error is more appropriately characterized as an epistemic uncertainty since the true value of the error is not known. Roache's grid convergence index converts the error estimate from Richardson extrapolation into an uncertainty by providing error bands.

Another important topic addressed in this chapter is the role of systematic mesh refinement for Richardson extrapolation-based discretization error estimators as well as for assessing the reliability of all discretization error estimators. The importance of systematic mesh refinement over the entire domain is discussed, along with approaches for assessing the systematic nature of the refinement. Issues with refinement in space and time, unidirectional refinement, fractional (or noninteger) refinement, and recommendations for refinement versus coarsening are also discussed. This chapter concludes with a discussion of some issues related to discretization error estimation that have not yet been adequately addressed by the research community.

8.1 Elements of the discretization process

The goal of the discretization process is to convert the mathematical model into a set of algebraic equations which can be readily solved on a digital computer. There are two distinct steps in this process: discretization of the mathematical model and discretization of the domain. While most applied scientific computing codes employ both aspects of discretization, some discretization schemes do not. For example, the method of weighted residuals does not include a domain discretization step (Huebner, 2001).

8.1.1 Discretization of the mathematical model

Throughout this book, we have made numerous references to the mathematical model being composed of partial differential equations. However, this is not the only form that the governing equations can take in scientific computing. The partial differential equation form arises when the conceptual model (e.g., the conservation of energy principle) is applied to an infinitesimal element. If instead a control volume of finite size is used, then the divergence theorem can be used to convert the volume integral of the gradient of a quantity to fluxes of that quantity through the boundary. The resulting integral (or integro-differential) form of the governing equations is called the weak form of the equations since it admits solutions with discontinuities (i.e., weak solutions) that satisfy the differential equation only in a restricted sense. The weak form is more fundamental since it admits discontinuous (weak) solutions, whereas the differential form relies on the dependent variables being differentiable and therefore continuous (i.e., strong solutions).

In order to find the solution to a mathematical model, initial and/or boundary conditions must be supplied. In some cases, these initial and boundary conditions also take the form of differential equations, such as the Neumann (or gradient) boundary condition, where the gradient of a property normal to a boundary is specified. For example, the adiabatic (or zero heat flux) boundary condition for a heat conduction problem has the form

$$\frac{\partial T}{\partial n}\bigg|_{\Gamma} = 0 \tag{8.2}$$

on the boundary Γ, where n is defined to be normal to the boundary. To ensure that the boundary condition discretization does not have an adverse impact on the overall order of accuracy of the code, the formal order of accuracy of the boundary condition discretization must be the same as (or higher than) that of the interior discretization scheme. This is not to be confused with the order of the boundary condition itself (i.e., the highest derivative in the boundary condition), which must be at most one order less than the governing equation.

While there are a number of different discretization approaches, the approaches discussed in this section are the primary ones found in scientific computing software. The finite difference method (Section 8.1.1.1) employs the strong form of mathematical model, whereas the finite volume method (Section 8.1.1.2) and the finite element method (Section 8.1.1.3) employ the weak form of the equations. Other approaches not discussed here but which can also result in consistent and convergent discretizations include boundary element methods, spectral element methods, and pseudo-spectral methods.

8.1.1.1 The finite difference method

Consider a general scalar partial differential equation in two spatial dimensions and time:

$$\frac{\partial u}{\partial t} + \frac{\partial f}{\partial x} + \frac{\partial g}{\partial y} = Q, \tag{8.3}$$

where f, g, and Q are all considered to be functions of u. In the finite difference method, the derivatives in Eq. (8.3) are replaced by finite differences which, for example, can be found using Taylor series expansions. If a first-order accurate forward difference in time is used, along with second-order accurate central differences in space, the finite difference discretization of Eq. (8.3) becomes:

$$\frac{u_{i,j}^{n+1} - u_{i,j}^{n}}{\Delta t} + \frac{f_{i+1,j}^{n} - f_{i-1,j}^{n}}{2\Delta x} + \frac{g_{i,j+1}^{n} - g_{i,j-1}^{n}}{2\Delta y} = Q_{i,j}^{n}. \tag{8.4}$$

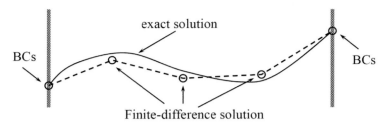

Figure 8.2 Simple example of a 1-D finite difference solution.

The superscripts denote discrete time location separated by the temporal step Δt, while the i and j subscripts denote discrete spatial locations separated by Δx in the x coordinate direction and Δy in the y coordinate direction, respectively. Due to the required ordering of spatial points, finite difference methods are generally implemented on structured grids. The above example employs a simple Cartesian mesh with constant spacing in the x and y directions and time. Finite difference methods can be applied to more general geometries with the use of transformations between physical space and a Cartesian computational space (e.g., see Chapter 9). See Richtmyer and Morton (1967), Tannehill *et al.* (1997), and Morton and Mayers (2005) for more details on finite difference methods.

A simple 1-D example of a typical finite difference solution is presented in Figure 8.2. While the exact solution exists for all points in the domain, the finite difference solution exists only at the discrete grid nodes. Interpolation between nodal values can be used to obtain the numerical solution between grid nodes, and the figure displays simple linear interpolation. Higher-order interpolations can be used to improve the accuracy between grid nodes, but care must be taken in interpreting any new extrema that arise. In any case, the interpolation will not produce values that are higher-order accurate than the underlying finite difference discretization.

8.1.1.2 The finite volume method

In contrast to the finite element and finite difference methods, the finite volume method requires the governing equations in integro-differential form. One approach for obtaining the equations in this form is to start with a finite control volume when deriving the governing equations. However, if the equations are already available in differential form, then the integro-differential form can be found by integrating the differential equations over the finite control volume δV, as

$$\int_{\Omega} \left(\frac{\partial u}{\partial t} + \frac{\partial f}{\partial x} + \frac{\partial g}{\partial y} - Q \right) d\Omega = 0, \qquad (8.5)$$

where Ω is the domain.

Applying the divergence theorem to the terms involving f and g gives

$$\int_{\Omega} \frac{\partial u}{\partial t} dV + \int_{\Gamma} \vec{\phi} \cdot \hat{n} d\Gamma = \int_{\Omega} Q dV, \qquad (8.6)$$

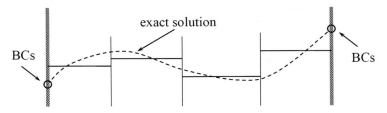

Figure 8.3 Simple example of a 1-D finite volume solution.

where Γ is the surface of the control volume, $\hat{n}$ is the outward-pointing unit normal vector, and $\vec{\phi}$ is the vector composed of the flux components, which in 2-D Cartesian coordinates is:

$$\vec{\phi} = f\hat{i} + g\hat{j}. \tag{8.7}$$

If the volume integrals are replaced by their exact averages over the cell, e.g.,

$$\bar{Q}_{i,j} = \frac{\int_\Omega Q d\Omega}{\delta\Omega}, \tag{8.8}$$

and the area integrals replaced by their exact averages over the face, e.g.,

$$\bar{f}_{i+1/2,j} = \frac{\int_{\Gamma_{i+1/2,j}} f d\Gamma}{\Gamma_{i+1/2,j}}, \tag{8.9}$$

then, assuming a 2-D Cartesian mesh, the integral equation can be rewritten as

$$\left.\overline{\frac{\partial u}{\partial t}}\right|_{i,j} + \frac{\bar{f}_{i+1/2,j} - \bar{f}_{i-1/2,j}}{\Delta x} + \frac{\bar{g}_{i,j+1/2} - \bar{g}_{i,j-1/2}}{\Delta y} = \bar{Q}_{i,j}. \tag{8.10}$$

For finite volume methods, the formal order of accuracy is related to the approximations used to represent cell averages (often simply by the cell-center value) and face averages. The face average fluxes are generally found by either interpolating neighboring cell center values (equivalent to a central differencing scheme on uniform meshes) or extrapolating in an appropriate upwind manner from neighboring cells, and these two procedures are collectively referred to as flux quadrature. Finite differences are usually used to discretize the unsteady term with respect to time (Δt). Additional information on the finite volume method can be found in Knight (2006) and Hirsch (2007).

An example of a finite volume solution in 1-D is presented in Figure 8.3. The discrete version of the integro-differential equation is applied in each of the regions shown. While the solution in each cell is generally considered to be a constant value, different order accurate quadratures can be used to determine interface flux values, resulting in higher-order schemes. Due to the manner in which these interface fluxes are calculated, the finite volume method satisfies local conservation of quantities from cell to cell.

8.1.1.3 The finite element method

Consider the 2-D steady heat conduction equation with a volumetric source term Q as given by

$$\frac{\partial}{\partial x}\left(k\frac{\partial T}{\partial x}\right) + \frac{\partial}{\partial y}\left(k\frac{\partial T}{\partial y}\right) - Q = 0, \tag{8.11}$$

where k is the thermal conductivity. Following closely the development of Zienkiewicz *et al.* (2005), we will apply the finite element method to Eq. (8.11), although we will omit the boundary conditions for simplicity. In the finite element method, approximate solutions are sought within a limited function space

$$T \approx \hat{T} = \sum_{i=1}^{n} N_i a_i, \tag{8.12}$$

where the N_i are shape (or basis) functions that are functions of the independent variables only and the a_i are unknown coefficients. Once the shape functions are chosen, then the finite element method involves solving for these a_i coefficients on domain subvolumes (i.e., elements). In solving for these coefficients, the finite element method employs the weak form of the governing equation. This weak form can generally be obtained in one of two ways: using the method of weighted residuals (i.e., the Galerkin procedure) or by a variational formulation which requires that a variational principle exist for the problem of interest. Since variational principles do not exist for all scientific computing applications, we will employ the method of weighted residuals in this example.

If Eq. (8.11) is equal to zero everywhere in the domain, then we are free to integrate this equation over the domain volume Ω using an arbitrary function v,

$$\int_{\Omega} v\left[\frac{\partial}{\partial x}\left(k\frac{\partial T}{\partial x}\right) + \frac{\partial}{\partial y}\left(k\frac{\partial T}{\partial y}\right) - Q\right] dxdy = 0, \tag{8.13}$$

where the functions v are called test (or trial) functions. In the finite element approximation, these test functions are also limited to some subspace of functions as

$$v = \sum_{j=1}^{n} w_j b_j, \tag{8.14}$$

where the w_j are functions of the independent variables and the b_j are coefficients. Note that performing the integration in Eq. (8.13) requires that the solution $T(x, y)$ be C^1 continuous, meaning that both the temperature and its slope are continuous. Applying integration by parts (i.e., using Green's identities) results in the weak form

$$\int_{\Omega}\left(\frac{\partial v}{\partial x}k\frac{\partial T}{\partial x} + \frac{\partial v}{\partial y}k\frac{\partial T}{\partial y} - vQ\right)dxdy - \int_{\Gamma} vk\left(\frac{\partial T}{\partial x}n_x + \frac{\partial T}{\partial y}n_y\right)d\Gamma = 0, \tag{8.15}$$

where

$$\frac{\partial T}{\partial n} = \frac{\partial T}{\partial x}n_x + \frac{\partial T}{\partial y}n_y \qquad (8.16)$$

is the derivative normal to the domain boundary Γ. Since only first derivatives appear in Eq. (8.15), this weak form thus requires only C^0 continuity (i.e., allowing discontinuous slopes) to be integrable. It is convenient to choose the test functions v such that they are zero on the boundary Γ, thus allowing Eq. (8.15) to be rewritten as simply

$$\int_\Omega \left(\frac{\partial v}{\partial x}k\frac{\partial T}{\partial x} + \frac{\partial v}{\partial y}k\frac{\partial T}{\partial y} \right) \mathrm{d}x\mathrm{d}y = \int_\Omega v Q \mathrm{d}x\mathrm{d}y. \qquad (8.17)$$

The choice of $w_j = N_j$ results in the Galerkin method (also called the Bubnov–Galerkin method). Any other choice for w_j is considered a Petrov–Galerkin scheme, and it can be shown that both the finite difference method and the finite volume method can be written as specific cases of Petrov–Galerkin schemes called point collocation and subdomain collocation, respectively (Zienkiewicz *et al.*, 2005).

Decomposing the domain into elements and using the Galerkin method (i.e., $w_j = N_j$), we can then write, for any given element Ω_k,

$$b_j \left[\int_{\Omega_k} \left(\frac{\partial N_j}{\partial x}k\frac{\partial \hat{T}}{\partial x} + \frac{\partial N_j}{\partial y}k\frac{\partial \hat{T}}{\partial y} \right) \mathrm{d}x\mathrm{d}y - \int_{\Omega_k} N_j Q \, \mathrm{d}x\mathrm{d}y \right] = 0, \quad j = 1, \ldots, n; \qquad (8.18)$$

therefore we are free to omit the b_j coefficients. Equation (8.18) represents n different equations since there are n terms in the summation for the test functions. Substituting the finite element approximation from Eq. (8.12) gives

$$\int_{\Omega_k} \left[\frac{\partial N_j}{\partial x}k\left(\sum_{i=1}^n \frac{\partial N_i}{\partial x}a_i \right) + \frac{\partial N_j}{\partial y}k\left(\sum_{i=1}^n \frac{\partial N_i}{\partial y}a_i \right) \right] \mathrm{d}x\mathrm{d}y$$

$$= \int_{\Omega_k} N_j Q \mathrm{d}x\mathrm{d}y, \quad j = 1, \ldots, n. \qquad (8.19)$$

Equations (8.19) form a system of n equations on each element with the n unknowns being the coefficients a_i. If the thermal conductivity k and the heat source Q are functions of x and y only, then Eqs. (8.19) are a linear system. If they are functions of the temperature, then this system of equations is nonlinear and requires linearization before solving in an iterative manner. The form of the shape functions will dictate the number of unknowns n (i.e., degrees of freedom) on each element as well as the formal order of accuracy of the method. For more information on the finite element method, see Oden and Reddy (1976), Szabo and Babuska (1991), Hughes (2000), and Zienkiewicz *et al.* (2005).

A notional representation of a 1-D finite element solution is presented in Figure 8.4. This solution shows interfaces that are discontinuous (left interface), C^0 or value continuous

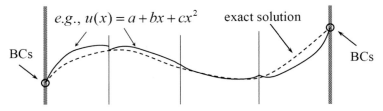

Figure 8.4 Simple example of a 1-D finite element solution.

(right interface), and C^1 or slope continuous (center interface). It is important to note that finite element methods enforce global conservation over the entire domain, but generally do not enforce conservation locally.

8.1.2 Discretization of the domain

For steady problems, discretization of the domain involves decomposing the spatial domain into nodes, cells, or elements where the discrete equations will be applied. For unsteady problems, the temporal domain must also be discretized by selecting an appropriate time step Δt to advance the simulations. This time step must be chosen to resolve the physical phenomena in question, to satisfy any stability criteria in the problem (recall the discussion of numerical stability in Chapter 5), and to achieve the desired level of temporal accuracy. The terms "mesh" and "grid" are often used to refer to the partitioned domain in space; however, for unsteady simulations the term "mesh" will also refer to the discretized temporal domain.

   For complex, 3-D geometries, the generation of an appropriate spatial mesh can require significant time and effort. Two mesh-related issues that have a significant impact on the discretization error are mesh resolution and mesh quality. The effects of mesh resolution on the discretization error are clear when one considers that the truncation error serves as the local source for generating discretization error. (This relationship was initially shown in Chapter 5 and is further developed in this chapter during the discussion of error transport equations in Section 8.2.2.1.) The truncation error contains the discretization parameters (Δx, Δy, etc.) to various powers, with the lowest power determining the formal order of accuracy of the discretization scheme. Thus the discretization error can be reduced by simply refining the mesh. Mesh quality addresses factors such as cell aspect ratio, cell stretching ratio, cell skewness, and orthogonality of mesh lines at a boundary. Poor quality spatial meshes can result in a reduction in the order of accuracy and even non-convergence of the discrete solution in extreme cases. The relationship between mesh quality and the discretization error is investigated further in Chapter 9.

8.1.2.1 Structured meshes

There are two basic types of spatial mesh: structured and unstructured. In 3-D structured meshes, each node or element is uniquely defined by an ordered set of indices (i, j, and k).

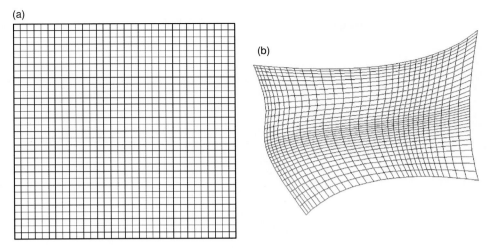

Figure 8.5 Structured mesh examples in 2-D: (a) Cartesian and (b) curvilinear.

Structured grids can either be Cartesian, stretched Cartesian, skewed Cartesian, or curvilinear. Cartesian grids have fixed spacing (Δx, Δy, and Δz) between orthogonal grid lines, whereas stretched Cartesian and skewed Cartesian relax the requirements for fixed spacing and orthogonality, respectively. Curvilinear structured grids allow the mesh to wrap around a surface and the spacing can vary over the domain. Examples of structured Cartesian and curvilinear meshes in 2-D are shown in Figure 8.5a and Figure 8.5b, respectively. The regular ordering of the structured grid generally makes it more efficient for computing numerical solutions than unstructured meshes, but at the cost of increased difficulty during mesh generation for complicated geometries.

8.1.2.2 Unstructured meshes

Unstructured meshes do not employ regular ordering of the nodes or elements. They can be composed of triangles, quadrilaterals, or arbitrary elements in 2-D, and pyramids, tetrahedrons, hexahedrons, prisms, and arbitrary elements in 3-D. There is no equivalent unstructured element type in 1-D as the nodes/elements in a 1-D mesh can always be indexed in an ordered manner. Two examples of unstructured meshes in 2-D are given in Figure 8.6. A general unstructured triangular mesh is shown in Figure 8.6a, while a hybrid mesh containing structured quadrilateral and triangular elements is shown in Figure 8.6b.

8.1.2.3 Cartesian meshes

Cartesian meshes can also be used for general geometries. For Cartesian grid methods, curved boundaries are usually handled with special boundary cells called cut-cells. An example of a Cartesian grid where the underlying mesh is structured is given in Figure 8.7a. This type of mesh could be handled by a structured grid code with special treatment of the curved boundaries. The more common example of a Cartesian grid

(a)

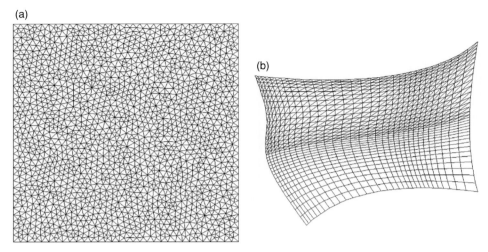

Figure 8.6 Unstructured meshes in 2-D: (a) general triangular and (b) hybrid structured/unstructured.

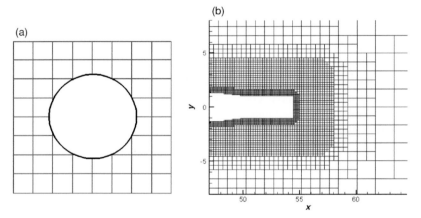

Figure 8.7 Cartesian grids in 2-D: (a) structured Cartesian and (b) unstructured Cartesian (Figure 8.7b is reproduced from Roy *et al.*, 2007).

where the underlying mesh is unstructured is given in Figure 8.7b. The unstructured nature of the grid allows clustering by subdividing selected cells, thus allowing more resolution of the surface geometry and/or solution features.

8.1.2.4 Mesh-free methods

There are a number of mesh-free methods in the area of fluid mechanics which generally do not require a volume mesh in the domain, but may require surface meshes. These approaches thus have the advantage of greatly simplifying the grid generation process by reducing the dimensionality of the mesh to be generated by one. These methods take a Lagrangian approach, thus allowing individual vortices or fluid particles to travel through the domain and interact with each other. Some examples of grid-free methods include vortex methods, smoothed particle hydrodynamics, and lattice Boltzmann. The actual form of the underlying governing equations and the consistency/convergence of these methods with increasing number of vortices, particles, etc. has generally not been adequately addressed.

8.2 Approaches for estimating discretization error

There are many approaches available for estimating discretization error. These methods can be broadly categorized as *a priori* methods and *a posteriori* methods. The *a priori* methods are those that allow a bound to be placed on the discretization error before any numerical solution is even computed. In general, one looks to bound the discretization error by an equation of the form

$$\varepsilon_h \leq C(u)h^p, \tag{8.20}$$

where ε_h is the discretization error, the function $C(u)$ usually depends on various derivatives of the exact solution, h is a measure of the element size (e.g., Δx), and p is the formal order of accuracy of the method. One approach to developing an *a priori* discretization error estimator is to perform a truncation error analysis for the scheme, relate the truncation error to the discretization error (as in Chapter 5), then develop some approximate bounds on the solution derivatives that comprise $C(u)$. The main failing of *a priori* error estimators is that $C(u)$ is extremely difficult to bound and, even when this is possible for simple problems, the resulting error estimate greatly over-estimates the true discretization error. *A priori* methods are generally only useful for assessing the formal order of accuracy of a discretization scheme. Current efforts in estimating the discretization error are focused on *a posteriori* methods. These methods provide an error estimate only after the numerical solution has been computed. They use the computed solution to the discrete equations (possibly including information from the problem being solved) to estimate the discretization error relative to the exact solution to the mathematical model.

The mathematical formalism that underlies the finite element method makes it fertile ground for the rigorous estimation of discretization error. Beginning with the pioneering work of Babuska and Rheinboldt (1978a), a tremendous amount of work has been done over the last 30 years on *a posteriori* estimation of discretization error by the finite element community (Ainsworth and Oden, 2000). The initial developments up to the early 1990s were concentrated on linear, elliptic, scalar mathematical models and focused on the *h*-version of finite elements. Early extensions of the *a posteriori* methods to parabolic and hyperbolic mathematical models were done by Eriksson and Johnson (1987) and Johnson and Hansbo (1992), respectively. Up to this point, *a posteriori* error estimation in finite elements was limited to analysis of the energy norm of the discretization error, which for

Poisson's equation can be written on element k as:

$$\||\varepsilon_h\||_k = \left[\int_{\Omega_k} \left| \vec{\nabla} u_h - \vec{\nabla} \tilde{u} \right|^2 \mathrm{d}\Omega \right]^{1/2}. \tag{8.21}$$

The finite element method produces the numerical solution from the chosen set of basis functions that minimizes the energy norm of the discretization error (Szabo and Babuska, 1991). Taken locally, the energy norm can provide guidance on where adaptive refinement should occur. Taken globally, the energy norm provides a global measure of the overall optimality of the finite element solution. In the early 1990s, important extensions of *a posteriori* error estimators to system response quantities were found that require the solution to an adjoint, or dual, problem (e.g., Johnson and Hansbo, 1992). For additional information on *a posteriori* error estimation in finite element methods, see Babuska *et al.* (1986), Whiteman (1994), Ainsworth and Oden (1997, 2000), and Estep *et al.* (2000). A more introductory discussion of error estimation in finite element analysis is presented by Akin (2005).

In general, the level of reliability of *a posteriori* error estimation methods is strongly problem dependent. All of the discretization error estimators to be discussed here were originally developed for elliptic problems. As a result, they tend to work well for elliptic problems, but are not as well-developed for mathematical models that are parabolic or hyperbolic in nature. The level of complexity of the problem is also an important issue. The error estimators work well for smooth, linear problems with simple physics and geometries; however, strong nonlinearities, discontinuities, singularities, and physical and geometric complexity can significantly reduce the reliability and applicability of *a posteriori* discretization error estimation methods.

One approach for measuring the accuracy and reliability of a discretization error estimator is through the effectivity index θ. Here we will define the *effectivity index* as a general norm of the estimated discretization error $\bar{\varepsilon}_h$ divided by the norm of the true error ε_h. The effectivity index can be computed locally by evaluating it on element or cell k,

$$\theta_k = \frac{\|\bar{\varepsilon}_h\|_k}{\|\varepsilon_h\|_k}, \tag{8.22}$$

or globally over the entire domain Ω,

$$\theta = \frac{\|\bar{\varepsilon}_h\|_\Omega}{\|\varepsilon_h\|_\Omega}. \tag{8.23}$$

One important property that is desired in a discretization error estimator is consistency (i.e., asymptotic exactness) of the estimate, which means the estimated error must approach the true error (i.e., $\theta \to 1$) as the mesh is refined ($h \to 0$) or as the order of the scheme is increased ($p \to \infty$). The practical utility of a given error estimator can also be gauged by examining its effectivity index on coarse meshes. Finally, if asymptotic exactness of the discretization error estimator cannot be shown, then we prefer to have error estimates that are conservative (i.e., they over-estimate the error). Thus a discretization error estimator that over-estimates the error is more desirable than one which under-estimates it.

There are two types of discretization error estimator discussed in this section. In the first type, an estimate of the exact solution to the mathematical model (or possibly its gradient) is obtained that is of higher formal order of accuracy than the underlying solution. This higher-order estimate relies only on information from the discrete solution itself, and thus can often be applied in a post-processing manner. For mesh and order refinement methods, higher-order estimates can be easily obtained for system response quantities as well. Residual-based methods, by contrast, also incorporate information on the specific problem being solved into the error estimate. While their implementation in a scientific computing code is generally more difficult and code-intrusive, they have the potential to provide more detailed information on the discretization error and its various sources. The extension of residual-based methods to provide discretization error estimates in system response quantities generally requires the solution to an adjoint (or dual) problem.

8.2.1 Type I: Higher-order estimates

One approach to error estimation is to compare the discrete solution to a higher-order estimate of the exact solution to the mathematical model. While this approach uses only information from the discrete solution itself, in some cases, more than one discrete solution is needed, with the additional solutions being obtained either on systematically-refined/coarsened meshes or with different formal orders of accuracy.

8.2.1.1 Mesh refinement methods

Mesh refinement methods are based on the general concept of Richardson extrapolation (Richardson 1911, 1927). Recall that in Chapter 5 we used a power series expansion to relate the discretization error in a system response quantity $\varepsilon_h = f_h - \tilde{f}$ to the mesh spacing parameter h, which for a convergent, pth-order discretization can be written as

$$f_h - \tilde{f} = g_p h^p + O(h^{p+1}), \tag{8.24}$$

where f_h is the discrete solution and $\tilde{f}$ the exact solution to the mathematical model. The basic premise behind mesh refinement methods is to compute two discrete solutions on systematically-refined meshes, then use Eq. (8.24) to solve for an estimate of the exact solution to the mathematical model $\bar{f}$. As with all discretization error estimators, the estimate will only be reliable in the asymptotic range where the terms of order h^{p+1} and higher can be neglected. In the asymptotic range, the estimate $\bar{f}$ is generally accurate to within order $p + 1$. This higher-order estimate of $\bar{f}$ can then be used to estimate the error in the discrete solutions. The main advantages of mesh refinement-based error estimators are that they can be applied as a post-processing step to any type of discretization and that they can be applied both to the solution and to any system response quantities. A more detailed discussion of Richardson extrapolation and its use as a discretization error estimator is presented in Section 8.3.

8.2.1.2 Order refinement methods

Order refinement methods are those which employ two or more discretizations on the same mesh but with differing formal orders of accuracy. The results from the two numerical solutions are then combined to produce a discretization error estimate. An early example of order refinement methods for error estimation is the Runge-Kutta–Fehlberg method (Fehlberg, 1969) for adaptive step size control in the solution of ordinary differential equations. This approach combines a basic fourth-order Runge-Kutta integration of the differential equations with an inexpensive fifth-order estimate of the error. Order refinement can be difficult to implement in finite difference and finite volume discretizations due to difficulties formulating higher-order accurate gradients and boundary conditions. Order refinement methods have been implemented within the context of finite elements under the name hierarchical bases (e.g., see Bank, 1996).

8.2.1.3 Finite element recovery methods

Recovery methods for estimating the discretization error were developed by the finite element community (e.g., Zienkiewicz and Zhu, 1987, 1992). For the standard *h*-version of finite elements with linear basis functions the solution is piece-wise linear; therefore, the gradients are only piece-wise constant and are discontinuous across the element faces. The user of a finite element code is often more interested in gradient quantities such as stresses than the solution itself, so most finite element codes provide for post-processing of these discontinuous gradients into piece-wise linear gradients using existing finite element infrastructure.

In some cases (see the discussion of superconvergence below), this reconstructed gradient is of a higher order of accuracy than the gradient found in the underlying finite element solution. Recall the definition of the energy norm of the discretization error given in Eq. (8.21). If the true gradient from the mathematical model is available, then this important error measure can be computed exactly. For the case where a reconstructed gradient is higher-order accurate than the finite element gradient, it can be used to approximate the true gradient in the energy norm. In addition to providing estimates of the discretization error in the solution gradients, due to their local nature, recovery methods are also often used as indicators of where solution refinement is needed in adaptive solutions (see Chapter 9).

In order to justify the use of the recovered gradient in the energy norm, it must in fact be higher-order accurate than the gradient from the finite element solution. This so-called *superconvergence property* can occur when certain regularity conditions on the mesh and the solution are met (Wahlbin, 1995) and results in gradients that are up to one order higher in accuracy than the underlying finite element gradients. For linear finite elements, the superconvergence points occur at the element centroids, whereas for quadratic finite elements, the location of the superconvergence points depends on the element topology. If the reconstructed gradient is superconvergent, and if certain consistency conditions are met by the gradient reconstruction operator itself, then error estimators based on this recovered gradient can be shown to be asymptotically exact with effectivity indices approaching unity (Ainsworth and Oden, 2000). While the superconvergence property appears to be a difficult one to attain for complex scientific computing applications, the discretization error estimates from some recovery methods tend to be "astonishingly good" for reasons that are not well-understood (Ainsworth and Oden, 2000).

Recovery methods have been shown to be most effective when the reconstruction step employs solution gradients rather than solution values. The *superconvergent patch recovery* (SPR) method (Zienkiewicz and Zhu, 1992) is the most widely-used recovery method in finite element analysis. Assuming the underlying finite element method is of order p, the SPR approach is based on a local least squares fitting of the solution gradient values at the superconvergence points using polynomials of degree p. The SPR recovery method was found to perform extremely well in an extensive comparison of *a posteriori* finite element error estimators (Babuska *et al.*, 1994). A more recent approach called *polynomial preserving recovery* (PPR) was proposed by Zhang and Naga (2005). In their approach, they use polynomials of degree $p + 1$ to fit the solution values at the superconvergence points, then take derivatives of this fit to recover the gradient. Both the SPR and PPR gradient reconstruction methods can be used to obtain error estimates in the global energy norm and in the local solution gradients. Extensions to system response quantities must be done heuristically. For example, a 5% error in the global energy norm may be found to correspond to a 10% error in a system response quantity for a given class of problems.

8.2.2 Type II: Residual-based methods

Residual-based methods use the discrete solution along with additional information from the problem being solved such as the mathematical model, the discrete equations, or the sources of discretization error. Examples of residual-based methods are error transport equations (both continuous and discrete) and finite element residual methods. As is shown in the next section, all of these residual-based methods are related through the truncation error. The truncation error can be approximated either by inserting the exact solution to the mathematical model (or an approximation thereof) into the discrete equation or by inserting the discrete solution into the continuous mathematical model. The former is the discrete residual which is used in most discretization error transport equations. The latter is simply the definition of the finite element residual. The use of adjoint methods to extend Type II (residual-based) discretization error estimation methods to provide error estimates in system response quantities is also discussed.

8.2.2.1 Error transport equations

Discretization error is transported through the domain in a similar fashion as the solution to the underlying mathematical model (Ferziger and Peric, 2002). For example, if a mathematical model governs the convection and diffusion of a scalar variable, then a discrete solution to the mathematical model will contain discretization error that is also convected and diffused. Babuska and Rheinboldt (1978a) appear to be the first to develop such a discretization error transport equation within the context of the finite element method. However, rather than solve this transport equation directly for the discretization error, the typical approach used in finite elements is to use this equation to either indirectly bound the error (explicit residual methods) or approximate its solution (implicit residual methods). Examples of the use of error transport equations for finite volume schemes can be found in Zhang *et al.* (2000), Cavallo and Sinha (2007), and Shih and Williams (2009).

Continuous discretization error transport equation

The following development from Roy (2009) is applicable to any discretization approach and is based on the *generalized truncation error expression* developed in Chapter 5 as Eq. (5.12). Recall that the original (possibly nonlinear) governing equation operator $L(\cdot)$ and the discrete equation operator $L_h(\cdot)$ are exactly solved by $\tilde{u}$ (the exact solution to the original mathematical model) and u_h (the exact solution to the discrete equations), respectively. Thus we can write:

$$L(\tilde{u}) = 0 \tag{8.25}$$

and

$$L_h(u_h) = 0. \tag{8.26}$$

Furthermore, the partial differential equation and the discretized equation are related through the *generalized truncation error expression* (Eq. (5.12), repeated here for convenience) as

$$L_h(u) = L(u) + TE_h(u), \tag{8.27}$$

which assumes some suitable mapping of the operators onto either a continuous or discrete space. Substituting u_h into Eq. (8.27) and then subtracting Eq. (8.25) gives

$$L(u_h) - L(\tilde{u}) + TE_h(u_h) = 0. \tag{8.28}$$

If the equations are linear, or if they are linearized, then we have $L(u_h) - L(\tilde{u}) = L(u_h - \tilde{u})$. With the definition of the discretization error

$$\varepsilon_h = u_h - \tilde{u} \tag{8.29}$$

we can thus rewrite Eq. (8.28) as

$$L(\varepsilon_h) = -TE_h(u_h). \tag{8.30}$$

Equation (8.30) is the mathematical model that governs the transport of the discretization error ε_h through the domain. Furthermore, the truncation error acting upon the discrete solution serves as a source term which governs the local generation or removal of discretization error and is a function of the local discretization parameters (Δx, Δy, etc.). Equation (8.30) is called the *continuous discretization error transport equation*. This equation can be discretized and solved for the discretization error in the solution variables assuming that the truncation error is known or can be estimated.

Discrete discretization error transport equation

A discrete version of the discretization error transport equation can be derived as follows. First the exact solution to the mathematical model $\tilde{u}$ is substituted into Eq. (8.27) and then Eq. (8.26) is subtracted to obtain

$$L_h(u_h) - L_h(\tilde{u}) + TE_h(\tilde{u}) = 0. \tag{8.31}$$

If the equations are again linear (or linearized), then this equation can be rewritten as

$$L_h(\varepsilon_h) = -TE_h(\tilde{u}). \tag{8.32}$$

Equation (8.32) is the discrete equation that governs the transport of the discretization error ε_h through the domain and is therefore called the *discrete discretization error transport equation*. This equation can be solved for the discretization error if the truncation error and the exact solution to the original partial differential equation (or a suitable approximation of it) are known.

Approximating the truncation error

While the development of discretization error transport equations is relatively straightforward, questions remain as to the treatment of the truncation error, which acts as the local source term. The truncation error can be difficult to derive for complex, nonlinear discretization schemes such as those used for the solution to the compressible Euler equations in fluid dynamics. However, if the truncation error can be reliably approximated, then this approximation can be used as the source term for the error transport equation.

Here we present three approaches for approximating the truncation error, with the first two approaches beginning with the *generalized truncation error expression* given by Eq. (8.27) (Roy, 2009). In the first approach, the exact solution to the mathematical model $\tilde{u}$ is inserted into Eq. (8.27). Since this exact solution will exactly solve the mathematical model, the term $L(\tilde{u}) = 0$, thus allowing the truncation error to be approximated as

$$TE_h(\tilde{u}) = L_h(\tilde{u}). \tag{8.33}$$

Since this exact solution is generally not known, it could be approximated by plugging an estimate of the exact solution, for example from Richardson extrapolation or any other discretization error estimator, into the discrete operator:

$$TE_h(u_{\mathrm{RE}}) \approx L_h(u_{\mathrm{RE}}). \tag{8.34}$$

Alternatively, the solution from a fine grid solution u_h could be inserted into the discrete operator for a coarse grid $L_{rh}(\cdot)$:

$$TE_h(\tilde{u}) = \frac{1}{r^p} TE_{rh}(\tilde{u}) \approx \frac{1}{r^p} TE_{rh}(u_h) = \frac{1}{r^p} L_{rh}(u_h). \tag{8.35}$$

Note that the subscript rh denotes the discrete operator on a grid that is a factor of r coarser in each direction than the fine grid. For example, $r = 2$ when the coarse mesh is formed by eliminating every other point in each direction of a structured mesh. This approach was used by Shih and Qin (2007) to estimate the truncation error for use with a discrete discretization error transport equation.

A second approach for estimating the truncation error is to insert the exact solution to the discrete equations u_h into Eq. (8.27). Since this solution exactly solves the discrete equations $L_h(u_h) = 0$, we have

$$TE_h(u_h) = -L(u_h). \qquad (8.36)$$

If a continuous representation of the solution is available then this evaluation is straightforward. In fact, the right hand side of Eq. (8.36) is the definition of the finite element residual that is given in the next section. For other numerical methods (e.g., finite difference and finite volume), a continuous projection of the numerical solution must be made in order to estimate the truncation error. For example, Sonar (1993) formed this residual by projecting a finite volume solution onto a finite element subspace with piece-wise linear shape functions.

A third approach that is popular for hyperbolic problems (e.g., compressible flows) is based on the fact that central-type differencing schemes often require additional numerical (artificial) dissipation to maintain stability and to prevent numerical oscillations. This numerical dissipation can either be explicitly added to a central differencing scheme (e.g., see Jameson *et al.*, 1981) or incorporated as part of an upwind differencing scheme. In fact, it can be shown that any upwind scheme can be written as a central scheme plus a numerical dissipation term (e.g., Hirsch, 1990). These two approaches can thus be viewed in the context of central schemes with the numerical dissipation contributions serving as the leading terms in the truncation error. While this approach may only be a loose approximation of the true truncation error, it merits discussion due to the fact that it can be readily computed with little additional effort.

System response quantities

A drawback to the error transport equation approach is that it provides for discretization error estimates in the local solution variables, but not in system response quantities. While adjoint methods can be used to provide error estimates in the system response quantities (see Section 8.2.2.3), Cavallo and Sinha (2007) have developed a simpler approach that uses an analogy with experimental uncertainty propagation to relate the local solution errors to the error in the system response quantity. However, their approach appears to provide overly-conservative error bounds for integrated quantities since it does not allow for the cancellation of competing errors. An alternative approach would be to use the local error estimates to correct the local quantities, then compute the integrated quantity with these corrected values. This "corrected" integrated quantity could then be used to provide the desired discretization error estimate.

8.2.2.2 *Finite element residual methods*

In a broad mathematical sense, a residual refers to what is left over when an approximate solution is inserted into an equation. In Chapter 5 we discussed the residual method for code order of accuracy verification where the residual was found by substituting the exact solution to the mathematical model into the discrete equations. In Chapter 7 we discussed iterative convergence in terms of the iterative residuals which are found by substituting an approximate iterative solution into the discrete equations. Consider now the general mathematical operator $L(\tilde{u}) = 0$ which is solved exactly by $\tilde{u}$. Because the finite element method provides for a continuous representation of the numerical solution u_h, it is natural to define the finite element residual in a continuous sense over the domain as

$$\Re(u_h) = L(u_h). \tag{8.37}$$

In a manner analogous to the development of the previous section, a continuous discretization error transport equation can be derived within the finite element framework (Babuska and Rheinboldt, 1978a). This so-called residual equation has three different types of term: (1) interior residuals that determine how well the finite element solution satisfies the mathematical model in the domain, (2) terms associated with any discretized boundary conditions on the domain boundary (e.g., Neumann boundary conditions), and (3) interelement residuals which are functions of the discontinuities in normal fluxes across element–element boundaries (Ainsworth and Oden, 2000). It is the treatment of these three terms that differentiates between explicit and implicit residual methods.

Explicit residual methods

Explicit residual methods are those which employ information available from the finite element solution along with the finite element residuals to directly compute the error estimate. First developed by Babuska and Rheinboldt (1978b), explicit residual methods lump all three types of residual terms under a single, unknown constant. The analysis requires the use of the triangle inequality, which does not allow for cancellation between the different residual types. Due both to the use of the triangle inequality and the methods for estimating the unknown constant, explicit residual methods tend to be conservative estimates of the discretization error. They provide an element-wise estimate of the *local contribution* to the bound for the global energy norm of the error, but not a local estimate of the true error, which would include both local and transported components. Since explicit residual methods deal only with local contributions to the error, they can also be used for solution adaptation procedures. Stewart and Hughes (1998) have provided a tutorial on explicit residual methods and also discuss their relationship to *a priori* error estimation.

Implicit residual methods

Implicit residual methods avoid the approximations required in explicit residual methods by seeking solutions to the residual equation which govern the transport and generation of the discretization error. In order to achieve nontrivial solutions to the global residual equation, either the mesh would have to be refined or the order of the finite element basis functions increased. Both of these approaches would be significantly more expensive than obtaining the original finite element solution and therefore are not considered practical. Instead, the global residual equation is decomposed into a series of uncoupled, local boundary value problems approximating the global equation. These local problems can be solved over a single element using the element residual method (Demkowicz *et al.*, 1984; Bank and Weiser, 1985) or over a small patch of elements using the subdomain residual method (Babuska and Rheinboldt, 1978a,b). The solution to the local boundary value problems provides the local discretization error estimate, while the global error estimate is simply summed over the domain. By directly treating all three types of terms that show up in the residual equation, implicit residual methods retain more of the structure of the residual equation than do the explicit methods, and thus should in theory provide tighter discretization error bounds.

8.2.2.3 Adjoint methods for system response quantities

Both error transport equations and finite element residual methods give localized estimates of the discretization error, which can then be combined through an appropriate norm to provide quantitative measures of the overall "goodness" of the discrete solutions. However, the scientific computing practitioner is often instead interested in system response quantities that can be post-processed from the solution. These system response quantities can take the form of integrated quantities (e.g., net flux through or force acting on a boundary), local solution quantities (e.g., maximum stress or maximum temperature), or even an average of the solution over some region.

Adjoint methods in scientific computing were initially used for design optimization problems (e.g., Jameson, 1988). In the optimization setting, the adjoint (or dual) problem can be solved for sensitivities of a solution functional (e.g., a system response quantity) that one wishes to optimize relative to some chosen design parameters. The strength of the adjoint method is that it is efficient even when a large number of design parameters are involved. In the context of optimization in scientific computing, adjoint methods can be thought of as constrained optimization problems where a chosen solution functional is to be optimized subject to the constraint that the solution must also satisfy the mathematical model (or possibly the discrete equations).

Adjoint methods can also be used for estimating the discretization error in a system response quantity in scientific computing applications. Consider a scalar solution functional $f_h(u_h)$ evaluated on mesh h. An approximation of the discretization error in this functional is given by

$$\varepsilon_h = f_h(u_h) - f_h(\tilde{u}). \tag{8.38}$$

Performing a Taylor series expansion of $f_h(\tilde{u})$ about the discrete solution gives

$$f_h(\tilde{u}) \cong f_h(u_h) + \left.\frac{\partial f_h}{\partial u}\right|_{u_h} (\tilde{u} - u_h), \tag{8.39}$$

where higher order terms have been neglected. Next, an expansion of the discrete operator $L_h(\cdot)$ is performed at $\tilde{u}$ about u_h:

$$L_h(\tilde{u}) \cong L_h(u_h) + \left.\frac{\partial L_h}{\partial u}\right|_{u_h} (\tilde{u} - u_h), \qquad (8.40)$$

where $L_h(\tilde{u})$ is the discrete residual, an approximation of the truncation error from Eq. (8.33), and $\left.\frac{\partial L_h}{\partial u}\right|_{u_h}$ is the Jacobian which linearizes the discrete equations with respect to the solution. This Jacobian may already be computed since it can also be used to formulate implicit solutions to the discrete equations and for design optimization. Since $L_h(u_h) = 0$, Eq. (8.40) can be rearranged to obtain

$$(\tilde{u} - u_h) = \left[\left.\frac{\partial L_h}{\partial u}\right|_{u_h} \right]^{-1} L_h(\tilde{u}). \qquad (8.41)$$

Substituting this equation into Eq. (8.39) gives

$$f_h(\tilde{u}) \cong f_h(u_h) + \left.\frac{\partial f_h}{\partial u}\right|_{u_h} \left[\left.\frac{\partial L_h}{\partial u}\right|_{u_h} \right]^{-1} L_h(\tilde{u}) \qquad (8.42)$$

or

$$f_h(\tilde{u}) \cong f_h(u_h) + \Psi^T L_h(\tilde{u}), \qquad (8.43)$$

where Ψ^T is the row vector of discrete adjoint sensitivities. The adjoint sensitivities are found by solving

$$\Psi^T = \left.\frac{\partial f_h}{\partial u}\right|_{u_h} \left[\left.\frac{\partial L_h}{\partial u}\right|_{u_h} \right]^{-1}, \qquad (8.44)$$

which can be put into the standard linear equation form by transposing both sides of Eq. (8.44)

$$\left[\left.\frac{\partial L_h}{\partial u}\right|_{u_h} \right]^T \Psi = \left[\left.\frac{\partial f_h}{\partial u}\right|_{u_h} \right]^T. \qquad (8.45)$$

The adjoint solution provides the linearized sensitivities of the solution functional f_h to perturbations in the discrete operator $L_h(\cdot)$. As such, the adjoint solution vector components are often referred to as the adjoint sensitivities. Equation (8.43) shows that the adjoint solution provides the sensitivity of the discretization error in the solution functional $f(\cdot)$ to the local sources of discretization error (i.e., the truncation error) in the domain. This observation will be used in Chapter 9 as the basis for providing solution adaptation targeted for solution functionals. Because the discrete operator $L_h(\cdot)$ is used above, this approach is called the *discrete adjoint method*. A similar analysis using expansions of the continuous mathematical operator $L(\cdot)$ and functional $f(\cdot)$ can be performed to obtain discretization error estimates using the *continuous adjoint method*. Both continuous and discrete adjoint methods also require appropriate formulations of initial and boundary conditions.

Adjoint methods in the finite element method

While the use of explicit and implicit residual methods for finite elements has reached a certain level of maturity for elliptic problems (Ainsworth and Oden, 2000), the drawback to these methods is that they only provide error estimates in the energy norm of the discretization error. While the energy norm is a natural quantity by which to judge the overall goodness of a finite element solution, in many cases scientific computing is used to make an engineering decision with regards to a specific system response quantity (called "quantities of interest" by the finite element community). Extension of both the explicit and implicit residual methods to provide error estimates in a system response quantity generally requires the solution to the adjoint system.

In one approach (Ainsworth and Oden, 2000), the discretization error in system response quantity is bounded by the product of the energy norm of the adjoint solution and the energy norm of the error in the original solution. Assuming the solutions are asymptotic, the use of the Cauchy–Schwarz inequality produces a conservative bound. In this case, the discretization error in the system response quantity will be reduced at twice the rate of the solution error. In another approach (Estep *et al.*, 2000), the error estimate in the system response quantity for a class of reaction–diffusion problems is found as an inner product between the adjoint solution and the residual. This approach results in a more accurate (i.e., less conservative) error estimate at the expense of losing the rigorous error bound. For more information on error estimation using adjoint methods in finite elements, see Johnson and Hansbo (1992), Paraschivoiu *et al.* (1997), Rannacher and Suttmeier (1997), Estep *et al.* (2000), and Cheng and Paraschivoiu (2004).

Adjoint methods in the finite volume method

Pierce and Giles (2000) have proposed a continuous adjoint approach that focuses on system response quantities (e.g., lift and drag in aerodynamics problems) and is not tied to a specific discretization scheme. They use the adjoint solution to relate the residual error in the mathematical model to the resulting error in the integral quantity of interest. Their approach also includes a defect correction step that increases the order of accuracy of the integral quantity. For example, if the original solution and the adjoint solution are both second-order accurate, then the corrected integral quantity will have an order of accuracy equal to the product of the orders of the original and adjoint solutions, or fourth order. Their approach effectively extends the superconvergence property of finite elements to other discretization schemes, and can also be used to further increase the order of accuracy of the integral quantities for the finite element method.

Venditti and Darmofal (2000) have extended the adjoint approach of Pierce and Giles (2000) to allow for the estimation of local mesh size contributions to the integral quantity of interest. Their approach is similar to that described earlier in this section, but expands the functional and discrete operator on a fine grid solution u_h about a coarse grid solution u_{rh}. The solution is not required on the fine grid, only residual evaluations. Their approach is thus a discrete adjoint method rather than continuous adjoint. In addition, their focus is on developing techniques for driving a mesh adaptation process (see Chapter 9). Their initial formulation was applied to 1-D inviscid flow problems, but they have also extended their approach to 2-D inviscid and viscous flows (Venditti and Darmofal, 2002, 2003). While adjoint methods hold significant promise as discretization error estimators for solution functionals, they currently require significant code modifications to compute the Jacobian and other sensitivity derivatives and have not yet seen widespread use in commercial scientific computing software.

8.3 Richardson extrapolation

The basic concept behind Richardson extrapolation (Richardson, 1911, 1927) is as follows. If one knows the formal rate of convergence of a discretization method with mesh refinement, and if discrete solutions on two systematically refined meshes are available, then one can use this information to obtain an estimate of the exact solution to the mathematical model. Depending on the level of confidence one has in this estimate, it can be used either to correct the fine mesh solution or to provide a discretization error estimate for it. While Richardson's original work applied the approach locally over the domain to the dependent variables in the mathematical model, it can be readily applied to any system response quantity. There is, however, the additional requirement that the numerical approximations (integration, differentiation, etc.) used to obtain the system response quantity be at least of the same order of accuracy as the underlying discrete solutions.

Recall the definition of the discretization error in some general local or global solution variable f on a mesh with spacing h,

$$\varepsilon_h = f_h - \tilde{f}, \tag{8.46}$$

where f_h is the exact solution to the discrete equations and $\tilde{f}$ is the exact solution to the original partial differential equations. We can expand the numerical solution f_h in either a Taylor series about the exact solution,

$$f_h = \tilde{f} + \frac{\partial \tilde{f}}{\partial h} h + \frac{\partial^2 \tilde{f}}{\partial h^2} \frac{h^2}{2} + \frac{\partial^3 \tilde{f}}{\partial h^3} \frac{h^3}{6} + O(h^4), \tag{8.47}$$

or simply a power series in h,

$$f_h = \tilde{f} + g_1 h + g_2 h^2 + g_3 h^3 + O(h^4), \tag{8.48}$$

where $O(h^4)$ denotes a leading error term on the order of h to the fourth power. Moving $\tilde{f}$ to the left hand side allows us to write the discretization error for a mesh with spacing h as

$$\varepsilon_h = f_h - \tilde{f} = g_1 h + g_2 h^2 + g_3 h^3 + O(h^4), \tag{8.49}$$

where the g coefficients can take the form of derivatives of the exact solution to the mathematical model $\tilde{f}$ with respect to either the mesh size h (as shown in Eq. (8.47)) or to the independent variables through the relationship with the truncation error (see Section 5.3.1). In general, we require numerical methods that are higher than first-order accurate, and thus discretization methods are chosen which cancel out selected lower-order terms. For example, if a formally second-order accurate numerical scheme is chosen, then the general discretization error expansion becomes

$$\varepsilon_h = f_h - \tilde{f} = g_2 h^2 + g_3 h^3 + O(h^4). \tag{8.50}$$

Equation (8.50) forms the basis for standard Richardson extrapolation, which is described next.

8.3.1 Standard Richardson extrapolation

The *standard Richardson extrapolation* procedure, as originally formulated by Richardson (1911), applies exclusively to cases where the numerical scheme is formally second-order accurate and the mesh is systematically refined (or coarsened) by a factor of two. Consider a second-order discretization scheme that is used to produce numerical solutions on two meshes: a fine mesh with spacing h and a coarse mesh with spacing $2h$. Since the scheme is second-order accurate, the g_1 coefficient is zero and the discretization error equation (Eq. (8.50)) can be rewritten as

$$f_h = \tilde{f} + g_2 h^2 + g_3 h^3 + O(h^4). \tag{8.51}$$

Applying this equation on two mesh levels h and $2h$ gives

$$\begin{aligned} f_h &= \tilde{f} + g_2 h^2 + g_3 h^3 + O(h^4), \\ f_{2h} &= \tilde{f} + g_2 (2h)^2 + g_3 (2h)^3 + O(h^4). \end{aligned} \tag{8.52}$$

Eliminating $\tilde{f}$ from these equations and solving for g_2 yields

$$g_2 = \frac{f_{2h} - f_h}{3h^2} - \frac{7}{3} g_3 h + O(h^2). \tag{8.53}$$

Substituting Eq. (8.53) into the fine grid expansion of Eq. (8.52) and solving for $\tilde{f}$ gives

$$\tilde{f} = f_h + \frac{f_h - f_{2h}}{3} + \frac{4}{3} g_3 h^3 + O(h^4). \tag{8.54}$$

Combining the terms of order h^3 and higher in Eq. (8.54) with the exact solution yields

$$\bar{f} = \tilde{f} - \frac{4}{3} g_3 h^3 + O(h^4). \tag{8.55}$$

The Richardson extrapolated estimate can thus be found by inserting Eq. (8.55) in Eq. (8.54) to give

$$\bar{f} = f_h + \frac{f_h - f_{2h}}{3}. \tag{8.56}$$

Equation (8.56) is the standard Richardson extrapolation relationship, and provides an estimate $\bar{f}$ of the exact solution $\tilde{f}$ which is higher-order accurate than the underlying numerical scheme. This estimate will therefore converge to the exact solution faster than the numerical solutions themselves as the mesh is refined. A discretization error estimate derived from the Richardson extrapolation procedure will therefore be asymptotically consistent.

There is often confusion as to the order of accuracy of the Richardson extrapolation estimate. As shown in Eq. (8.55), the estimates from standard Richardson extrapolation are generally third-order accurate. In Richardson's original work (Richardson, 1911), he used this extrapolation procedure to obtain a higher-order accurate solution for the stresses in a masonry dam based on two second-order accurate numerical solutions. The original partial differential equation was Poisson's equation and he employed central differences which cancelled out the odd powers in the truncation error (i.e., $g_3 = 0$). His estimate for the exact solution was thus fourth-order accurate, as is clearly shown in Eq. (8.55) when $g_3 = 0$.

8.3.2 Generalized Richardson extrapolation

Richardson extrapolation can be generalized to pth-order accurate schemes and for two meshes systematically refined by an arbitrary factor. First consider the general discretization error expansion for a pth-order scheme:

$$\varepsilon_h = f_h - \tilde{f} = g_p h^p + g_{p+1} h^{p+1} + g_{p+2} h^{p+2} + \cdots. \tag{8.57}$$

Introducing the grid refinement factor as the ratio of the coarse to fine grid spacing, we have

$$r = \frac{h_{\text{coarse}}}{h_{\text{fine}}} > 1 \tag{8.58}$$

and the coarse grid spacing can thus be written as $h_{\text{coarse}} = rh_{\text{fine}}$. Choosing $h_{\text{fine}} = h$, the discretization error equations on the two meshes can be written as

$$f_h = \tilde{f} + g_p h^p + g_{p+1} h^{p+1} + O(h^{p+2}),$$
$$f_{rh} = \tilde{f} + g_p (rh)^p + g_{p+1} (rh)^{p+1} + O(h^{p+2}). \tag{8.59}$$

As before, these equations can be used to eliminate the g_p coefficient and solve for $\tilde{f}$ to give

$$\tilde{f} = f_h + \frac{f_h - f_{rh}}{r^p - 1} + g_{p+1} h^{p+1} \frac{r^p(r-1)}{r^p - 1} + O(h^{p+2}). \tag{8.60}$$

Again, combining terms of order h^{p+1} and higher with the exact solution $\tilde{f}$ gives

$$\bar{f} = \tilde{f} - g_{p+1} \frac{r^p(r-1)}{r^p - 1} h^{p+1} + O(h^{p+2}). \tag{8.61}$$

Substituting this expression into Eq. (8.60) results in the generalized Richardson extrapolation estimate $\bar{f}$:

$$\bar{f} = f_h + \frac{f_h - f_{rh}}{r^p - 1}. \tag{8.62}$$

As is shown clearly by Eq. (8.61), this estimate of the exact solution is generally $(p + 1)$-order accurate estimate of the exact solution to the mathematical model $\tilde{f}$ unless additional error cancellation occurs in the higher-order terms (e.g., if the g_{p+1} coefficient is zero).

8.3.3 Assumptions

There are five basic assumptions required for Richardson extrapolation to provide reliable estimates of the exact solution to the mathematical model: (1) that *both* discrete solutions are in the asymptotic range, (2) that the meshes have a uniform (Cartesian) spacing over the domain, (3) that the coarse and fine meshes are related through systematic refinement, (4) that the solutions are smooth, and (5) that the other sources of numerical error are small. These five assumptions are each discussed in detail below.

8.3.3.1 Asymptotic range

The formal order of accuracy of a discretization scheme is the theoretical rate at which the discretization error is reduced as the mesh is systematically refined. Recall that in Chapter 5 we used a continuous discretization error transport equation to relate the formal order of accuracy to the lowest order term in the truncation error. This lowest order term will necessarily dominate the higher-order terms in the limit as the mesh spacing parameter h goes to zero. The dependent solution variables generally converge at the formal order of accuracy in the asymptotic range, as do any system response quantities of interest (unless of course lower-order numerical approximations are used in their evaluation). One should keep in mind that this asymptotic requirement applies not just to the fine mesh solution but to the coarse mesh solution as well. Procedures for confirming that the asymptotic range has been reached will be given in Section 8.4.2.

8.3.3.2 Uniform mesh spacing

The discretization error expansion is in terms of a single mesh spacing parameter h. This parameter is a measure of the size of the discretization, and thus has units of length for spatial discretizations and time for temporal discretizations. This could be strictly interpreted as allowing only Cartesian meshes with spacing h in each of the spatial coordinate directions. While this restriction seemingly prohibits the use of Richardson extrapolation for practical scientific computing applications, this is in fact not the case. Recall our previous discussions on the use of local or global mesh transformations and their impact on the order of accuracy in Section 5.4. Those findings also apply to the use of Richardson extrapolation. The spatial mesh quality can affect the formal order of accuracy of the method through interactions with the mesh resolution and the local solution behavior; this relationship is explored in detail in Chapter 9. Discrete transformations will not adversely impact the Richardson extrapolation procedure as long as they are of the same order of accuracy as the discretization scheme or higher. Thompson *et al.* (1985) note that there may be accuracy advantages to evaluating the discrete transformation metrics with the same underlying discretization used for the solution derivatives.

8.3.3.3 Systematic mesh refinement

An often overlooked requirement for the use of Richardson extrapolation is that the two mesh levels be systematically refined. Recall the definition of systematic mesh refinement given in Section 5.4, which requires that the mesh refinement be both uniform and consistent. Uniform refinement means that the mesh is refined by the same factor over the entire domain, which precludes the use of local refinement or adaptation during the Richardson extrapolation procedure. Consistent refinement requires that the mesh quality must either remain constant or improve with mesh refinement. Examples of mesh quality metrics include cell aspect ratio, cell skewness, and cell-to-cell stretching factor. Techniques for evaluating the uniformity and consistency of the mesh refinement are discussed in Section 8.7. For an example of how Richardson extrapolation can fail in the presence of nonuniform mesh refinement even in the asymptotic range, see Eca and Hoekstra (2009a).

8.3.3.4 Smooth solutions

As discussed earlier, the coefficients g in the discretization expansion given by Eq. (8.57) are generally functions of the solution derivatives. As such, the Richardson extrapolation procedure will break down in the presence of discontinuities in any of the dependent variables or their derivatives. This is further complicated by the fact that the observed order of accuracy often reduces to first order or lower in the presence of certain discontinuities and singularities, regardless of the formal order of accuracy of the method for smooth problems (see Section 8.8.1).

8.3.3.5 Other numerical errors sources

Recall that the discretization error is defined as the difference between the exact solution to the discrete equations and the exact solution to the mathematical model. The exact solution to the discrete equations is never known due to round-off error, iterative error, and statistical sampling errors (when present). In practice, the available numerical solutions are used as surrogates for the exact solution to the discretized equations. If the other numerical error sources are too large, then they will adversely impact the Richardson extrapolation procedure since any extrapolation procedure will tend to amplify "noise" (Roache, 1998). A good rule of thumb is to ensure that all other sources of numerical error are at least two orders of magnitude smaller than the discretization error in the fine grid numerical solution (Roy, 2005; Eca and Hoekstra, 2009b).

8.3.4 Extensions

This section describes three extensions of Richardson extrapolation when it is applied locally throughout the domain. The first addresses a method for obtaining the Richardson extrapolation estimate on all fine grid spatial points, while the second extends it to all fine mesh points in space and time. The third extension combines an extrapolation procedure with a discrete residual minimization and could be considered a hybrid extrapolation/residual method.

8.3.4.1 Completed Richardson extrapolation in space

If the Richardson extrapolation procedure is to be applied to the solution point-wise in the domain, then it requires that one obtain fine mesh solution values at the coarse grid points. For systematic mesh refinement with integer values for the refinement factor on structured grids, this is automatically the case. However, applying Richardson extrapolation to cases with integer refinement will result in estimates of the exact solution only at the coarse grid points. In order to obtain exact solution estimates at the fine grid points, Roache and Knupp (1993) developed the *completed Richardson extrapolation* procedure. Their approach requires interpolation of the fine grid correction (rather than the Richardson extrapolation estimate or the coarse grid solution) from the coarse grid to the fine grid. This interpolation should be performed with an order of accuracy at least as high as the underlying discretization scheme. When this fine grid correction is combined with the discrete solution on the fine grid, an estimate of the exact solution to the mathematical model is obtained that has the same order of accuracy as the Richardson extrapolation estimates on the coarse grid points.

8.3.4.2 Completed Richardson extrapolation in space and time

Richards (1997) further extended the completed Richardson extrapolation procedure of Roache and Knupp (1993). The first modification provides the higher-order estimate of the exact solution to be obtained on all the fine grid spatial points for integer refinement factors other than two. The second, more significant modification provides higher-order accurate estimates of the exact solution after a chosen number of coarse grid time steps. The approach allows for different formal orders of accuracy in space and time by choosing the temporal refinement factor in such a way as to obtain the same order of error reduction found in the spatial discretization. For a discretization that is formally pth-order accurate in space and qth-order accurate in time, the temporal refinement factor r_t should be chosen such that

$$r_t = (r_x)^{p/q} , \tag{8.63}$$

where r_x is the refinement factor in space. This procedure is closely related to the combined order verification procedure discussed in Section 5.5.

8.3.4.3 Least squares extrapolation

Garbey and Shyy (2003) have developed a hybrid extrapolation/residual method for estimating the exact solution to the mathematical model. Their approach involves forming a more accurate solution by taking linear combinations of discrete solutions on multiple mesh levels using a set of spatially-varying coefficients. Spline interpolation is employed to obtain a smooth representation of this solution on a yet finer grid. The coefficients are then determined by a least squares minimization of the discrete residual formulated on this finer mesh. Their approach thus requires only residual evaluations on this finer mesh, which are significantly less expensive than computing a discrete solution on this mesh. This least squares extrapolated solution is demonstrated to be order $(p + 1)$ accurate, where p is the formal order of accuracy of the method. The higher-order estimate of the exact solution to the mathematical model can be used as a local error estimator or to provide solution initialization within a multigrid-type iterative procedure.

8.3.5 Discretization error estimation

While it may be tempting to use the Richardson extrapolated value as a more accurate solution than the fine grid numerical solution, this should only be done when there is a high degree of confidence that the five assumptions underlying Richardson extrapolation have indeed been met. In particular, the observed order of accuracy (which requires discrete solutions on three systematically-refined meshes, as discussed in Section 8.4.2) must first be shown to match the formal order of accuracy of the discretization scheme. In any case, when only two mesh levels are available, the asymptotic nature of the solutions cannot be confirmed, thus one is limited to simply using the Richardson extrapolated value to estimate the discretization error in the fine grid numerical solution.

Substituting the estimated exact solution from the generalized Richardson extrapolation expression (Eq. (8.62)) into the definition of the discretization error on the fine mesh (Eq. (8.46)) gives the estimated discretization error for the fine mesh (with spacing h),

$$\bar{\varepsilon}_h = f_h - \bar{f} = f_h - \left(f_h + \frac{f_h - f_{rh}}{r^p - 1} \right)$$

or simply

$$\bar{\varepsilon}_h = -\frac{f_h - f_{rh}}{r^p - 1}. \tag{8.64}$$

While this does provide for a consistent discretization error estimate as the mesh is systematically refined, there is no guarantee that the estimate will be reliable for any given fine mesh (h) and coarse mesh (rh) discrete solutions. Therefore, if only two discrete solutions are available then this numerical error estimate should be converted into a numerical uncertainty, as discussed in Section 8.5.

8.3.5.1 Example: Richardson extrapolation-based error estimation

An example of using the Richardson extrapolation procedure as an error estimator was presented by Roy and Blottner (2003). They examined the hypersonic, transitional flow over a sharp cone. The system response quantity was the heat flux distribution along the surface. The surface heat flux is shown versus the axial coordinate in Figure 8.8a for three

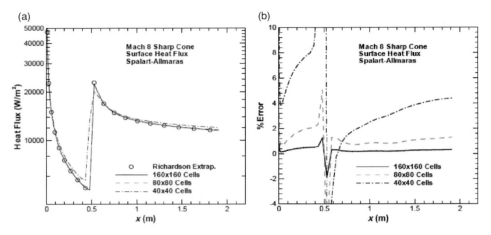

Figure 8.8 (a) Surface heat flux and (b) relative discretization error for the transitional flow over a sharp cone (Roy and Blottner, 2003).

systematically-refined mesh levels: fine (160×160 cells), medium (80×80 cells), and coarse (40×40 cells). Also shown are Richardson extrapolation results found from the fine and medium mesh solutions. The sharp rise in heat flux at $x = 0.5$ m is due to the specification of the location for transition from laminar to turbulent flow.

In Figure 8.8b, the Richardson extrapolation results are used to estimate the discretization error in each of the numerical solutions. Neglecting the immediate vicinity of the transition location, the maximum estimated discretization errors are approximately 8%, 2%, and 0.5% for the coarse, medium, and fine meshes, respectively. The solutions thus appear to be converging as $h \to 0$. Furthermore, these estimated errors display the expected h^p reduction for these formally second-order accurate computations. In the turbulent region, the maximum errors are also converging at the expected rate giving error estimates of approximately 4%, 1% and 0.25%. More rigorous methods for assessing the reliability of discretization error estimates are addressed in Section 8.4.

8.3.6 Advantages and disadvantages

The primary advantage that Richardson extrapolation holds over other discretization error estimation methods is that it can be used as a post-processing technique applied to any discretization scheme (finite difference, finite volume, finite element, etc.). In addition, it gives estimates in the total error, which includes both locally generated errors and those transported from other regions of the domain. Finally, it can be used for any quantity of interest including both local solution quantities and derived system response quantities (assuming that any numerical approximations have been made with sufficient accuracy).

There are, however, some disadvantages to using discretization error estimators based on Richardson extrapolation. First and foremost, they rely on having multiple numerical solutions in the asymptotic grid convergence range. This can place significant burdens on the grid generation process, which is already a bottleneck in many scientific computing applications. Furthermore, these additional solutions can be extremely expensive to compute. Consider the case where one starts with a 3-D mesh consisting of 1 million elements. Performing a mesh refinement with a refinement factor of two thus requires a solution on a mesh with 8 million elements. When one also accounts for the additional time steps or iterations required for this finer mesh, the solution cost easily increases by an order of magnitude with each refinement (note that integer refinement is not necessarily required, as discussed in Section 8.7.3).

The underlying theory of Richardson extrapolation requires smooth solutions, thus reducing the reliability of these error estimators for problems with discontinuities or singularities. In addition, the extrapolation procedure tends to amplify other sources of error such as round-off and iterative convergence error (Roache, 1998). Finally, the extrapolated quantities will not satisfy the same governing and auxiliary equations as either the numerical solutions or the exact solution. For example, if an equation of state is used to relate the density, pressure, and temperature in a gas, there is no guarantee that extrapolated values for density, pressure, and temperature will also satisfy this equation.

8.4 Reliability of discretization error estimators

One of the key requirements for reliability (i.e., accuracy) of any of the discretization error estimators discussed in this chapter is that the solution (or solutions) must be in the asymptotic range. This section provides a discussion of just what this asymptotic range means for discretization approaches involving both mesh (h) refinement and order (p) refinement. Regardless of whether h- or p-refinement is used, the *demonstration* that the asymptotic range has been achieved generally requires that at least three discrete solutions be computed. Demonstrating that the asymptotic range has been reached can be surprisingly difficult for complex scientific computing applications involving nonlinear, hyperbolic, coupled systems of equations. It is unlikely that the asymptotic range will be reached in such cases without the use of solution adaptation (see Chapter 9).

8.4.1 Asymptotic range

The asymptotic range is defined differently depending on whether one is varying the mesh resolution or the formal order of accuracy of the discretization scheme. When mesh refinement is employed, then the asymptotic range is defined as the sequence of systematically-refined meshes over which the discretization error reduces at the formal order of accuracy of the discretization scheme. Examining the discretization error expansion for a pth-order accurate scheme given by Eq. (8.57), the asymptotic range is achieved when h is sufficiently small that the h^p term is much larger than any of the higher-order terms. Due to possible differences in the signs for the higher-order terms, the behavior of the discretization error outside of the asymptotic range is unpredictable. Demonstrating that the asymptotic range has been reached using systematic mesh refinement is achieved by evaluating the observed order of accuracy. The observed order assesses the behavior of the discrete solutions over a range of meshes and its evaluation is discussed in the next section.

For discretization methods involving order refinement, the asymptotic range is determined by examining the behavior of the numerical solutions with successively refined basis functions, all on the same mesh. As the basis functions are refined and the physical phenomena in the problem are resolved, the discrete solutions will eventually become better approximations of the exact solution to the mathematical model. Convergence is best monitored with error norms since convergence can be oscillatory with increased basis order. An example of hierarchical basis functions used within the finite element method is given by Bank (1996).

8.4.2 Observed order of accuracy

The observed order of accuracy is the measure that is used to assess the confidence in a discretization error estimate. When the observed order of accuracy is shown to match the formal order, then one can have a high degree of confidence that the error estimate is reliable. In the discussion of the observed order of accuracy from Chapter 5, only two numerical solutions were required for its calculation because the exact solution was known. When the exact solution is not known, which is the case for solution verification, three numerical solutions on systematically-refined meshes are required to calculate the observed order of accuracy. For this observed order of accuracy to match the formal order of the discretization scheme, the requirements are the same as those given in Section 8.3.3 for Richardson extrapolation. When any of these requirements fail to be met, inaccurate values for the observed order of accuracy can be obtained (e.g., see Roy, 2003; Salas, 2006; and Eca and Hoekstra, 2009a).

8.4.2.1 Constant grid refinement factor

Consider a pth-order accurate scheme with numerical solutions on a fine mesh (h_1), a medium mesh (h_2), and a coarse mesh (h_3). For the case of a constant grid refinement factor, i.e.,

$$r = \frac{h_2}{h_1} = \frac{h_3}{h_2} > 1,$$

we can thus write

$$h_1 = h, \quad h_2 = rh, \quad h_3 = r^2h.$$

Using the discretization error expansion from Eq. (8.57), we can now write for the three discrete solutions:

$$
\begin{aligned}
f_1 &= \tilde{f} + g_p h^p + g_{p+1} h^{p+1} + O(h^{p+2}), \\
f_2 &= \tilde{f} + g_p (rh)^p + g_{p+1} (rh)^{p+1} + O(h^{p+2}), \\
f_3 &= \tilde{f} + g_p (r^2h)^p + g_{p+1} (r^2h)^{p+1} + O(h^{p+2}).
\end{aligned}
\tag{8.65}
$$

Neglecting terms of order h^{p+1} and higher allows us to recast these three equations in terms of a locally-observed order of accuracy $\hat{p}$:

$$f_1 = \bar{f} + g_p h^{\hat{p}},$$
$$f_2 = \bar{f} + g_p (rh)^{\hat{p}},$$
$$f_3 = \bar{f} + g_p (r^2 h)^{\hat{p}}, \tag{8.66}$$

which will only match the formal order of accuracy if the higher order terms are indeed small. Subtracting f_2 from f_3 and f_1 from f_2 yields

$$f_3 - f_2 = g_p \left(r^2 h \right)^{\hat{p}} - g_p \left(rh \right)^{\hat{p}} = g_p r^{\hat{p}} h^{\hat{p}} \left(r^{\hat{p}} - 1 \right) \tag{8.67}$$

and

$$f_2 - f_1 = g_p \left(rh \right)^{\hat{p}} - g_p h^{\hat{p}} = g_p h^{\hat{p}} \left(r^{\hat{p}} - 1 \right). \tag{8.68}$$

Dividing Eq. (8.67) by (8.68) gives

$$\frac{f_3 - f_2}{f_2 - f_1} = r^{\hat{p}}. \tag{8.69}$$

Taking the natural log of both sides and solving for the observed order of accuracy $\hat{p}$ gives

$$\hat{p} = \frac{\ln \left(\frac{f_3 - f_2}{f_2 - f_1} \right)}{\ln (r)}. \tag{8.70}$$

Consistent with the development of generalized Richardson extrapolation in Section 8.3.2, the Richardson extrapolated estimate of the exact solution $\bar{f}$ and the leading error term coefficient g_p are now given in terms of the observed order of accuracy $\hat{p}$ by

$$\bar{f} = f_1 + \frac{f_1 - f_2}{r^{\hat{p}} - 1} \tag{8.71}$$

and

$$g_p = \frac{f_1 - \bar{f}}{h^{\hat{p}}}. \tag{8.72}$$

Note that it is only when the observed order of accuracy matches the formal order of the numerical scheme that we can expect the discretization error estimate given by Eq. (8.71) to be accurate. This is equivalent to saying that the solutions on all three meshes are in the asymptotic range and the higher-order terms in Eqs. (8.65) are small for all three meshes. In practice, when this locally observed order of accuracy is used for the extrapolation estimate, it is often limited to be in the range

$$0.5 \leq \hat{p} \leq p_f,$$

where p_f is the formal order of accuracy of the discretization scheme. Allowing the observed order of accuracy to increase above the formal order can result in discretization error estimates that are not conservative (i.e., they underestimate the error). Furthermore, as $\hat{p}$ approaches zero, the magnitude of the extrapolated estimate grows without bound.

8.4.2.2 Non-constant grid refinement factor

For the case of non-constant grid refinement factors

$$r_{12} = \frac{h_2}{h_1} > 1, \quad r_{23} = \frac{h_3}{h_2} > 1,$$

where $r_{12} \neq r_{23}$, the determination of the observed order of accuracy $\hat{p}$ is more complicated. For this case, the following transcendental equation (Roache, 1998) must be solved for $\hat{p}$:

$$\frac{f_3 - f_2}{r_{23}^{\hat{p}} - 1} = r_{12}^{\hat{p}} \left(\frac{f_2 - f_1}{r_{12}^{\hat{p}} - 1} \right), \tag{8.73}$$

This equation can usually be solved with a simple direct substitution iterative procedure as discussed in Chapter 7 to give

$$\hat{p}^{k+1} = \frac{\ln \left[\left(r_{12}^{\hat{p}^k} - 1 \right) \left(\frac{f_3 - f_2}{f_2 - f_1} \right) + r_{12}^{\hat{p}^k} \right]}{\ln (r_{12} r_{23})}, \tag{8.74}$$

where an initial guess of $\hat{p}^k = p_f$ (the formal order of the scheme) can be used. Once the observed order of accuracy is found, the estimate of the exact solution $\bar{f}$ and the leading error term coefficient g_p are given by Eqs. (8.71) and (8.72) by replacing the constant grid refinement factor with $r = r_{12}$.

8.4.2.3 Application to system response quantities

Recall that system response quantities are defined as any solution property derived from the solution to the mathematical model or its discrete approximation. Examples of common system response quantities in scientific computing are lift and drag in aerodynamics, heat flux through a surface in heat transfer analysis, and maximum stress in a structural mechanics problem. The observed order of accuracy for system response quantities can be evaluated by the approaches described earlier in this section. For this observed order of accuracy to match the formal order of the discretization scheme, there is an additional requirement beyond those described in Section 8.3.3 for Richardson extrapolation. This additional requirement pertains to the order of accuracy of any numerical approximations used to compute the system response quantity. When the system response quantity is an integral, a derivative, or an average, then the numerical approximations used in its evaluation must be of at least the same order of accuracy as the underlying discretization scheme. In most cases, integrated quantities and averages are better behaved and converge more rapidly with mesh refinement than local quantities. However, in some cases the errors due to the numerical quadrature can interact with the numerical errors in the discrete solution and adversely impact the observed order of accuracy computation. An example of

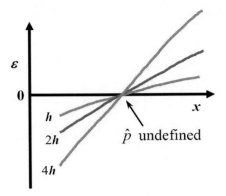

Figure 8.9 Simple example of how the observed order of accuracy computation will fail when applied locally over the domain: the observed order will be undefined at the crossover point.

these interactions for the computation of drag on an inviscid supersonic blunt body (mixed elliptic/hyperbolic) problem is given by Salas and Atkins (2009).

8.4.2.4 Application to local quantities

Problems often arise when the observed order of accuracy is evaluated on a point-by-point basis in the domain. A simple example of a case where this local evaluation of the order of accuracy will fail is given in Figure 8.9 which shows the discretization error on three different 1-D meshes. If the meshes are refined by a factor of two and the formal order of the scheme is first-order accurate, then we expect the discretization error to drop by a factor of two for each refinement. However, as can commonly occur in practical applications, the numerical solutions in one part of the domain can approach the exact solution from above while the numerical solutions in another part can approach it from below (Potter *et al.*, 2005). Even if we neglect any other sources of numerical error (such as round-off error), the observed order of accuracy at this crossover point will be undefined, even though the discretization error on all three meshes is exactly zero. When the observed order of accuracy is computed *near* this crossover point, the effects of other numerical error sources (e.g., round-off and iterative error) can become important. Such problems can be addressed by employing a globally evaluated observed order of accuracy (e.g., see Section 8.6.3.2).

Another example of the problems that can occur when examining the observed order of accuracy on a point-by-point basis through the domain was given by Roy (2003). The problem of interest is inviscid, hypersonic flow over a sphere-cone geometry. The mathematical character of this problem is elliptic immediately behind the normal shock wave that forms upstream of the sphere, but hyperbolic over the rest of the solution domain. The observed order of accuracy for the surface pressure is plotted versus the normalized axial distance based on three uniformly refined meshes in Figure 8.10. The finest mesh was 1024×512 cells and a refinement factor of two was used to create the coarse meshes. While a formally second-order accurate finite volume discretization was used, flux limiters were

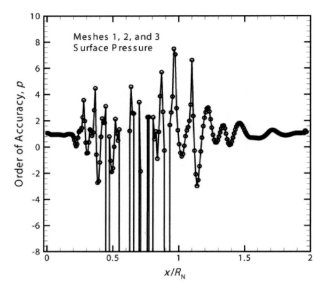

Figure 8.10 Observed order of accuracy in surface pressure for inviscid hypersonic flow over a sphere-cone geometry (from Roy, 2003).

employed in the region of the shock wave discontinuity to capture the shock in a monotone fashion by locally reducing the formal order of accuracy to one. The observed order of accuracy is indeed first order and well-behaved in the elliptic region (up to x/R_N of 0.2). However, in the hyperbolic region, the observed order of accuracy is found to undergo large oscillations between -4 and $+8$, with a few locations being undefined. Farther downstream, the observed order again becomes well-behaved with values near unity. The source of these oscillations is likely the local characteristic waves generated when the shock moves from one grid line to another. (This is the same example that is given in Figure 8.1 showing the local and transported components of the discretization error.) Clearly extrapolation-based error estimates using the local order of accuracy would not be reliable in this region. As mentioned above, a globally-evaluated observed order of accuracy could be used in this case. Alternatively, the formal order of accuracy (here $p = 1$) could be used.

8.5 Discretization error and uncertainty

As discussed previously, when it has been demonstrated that the solutions are in the asymptotic range, then one can have confidence that the error estimate is reliable and therefore use the error estimate to correct the solution. While the calculation of the observed order of accuracy requires three systematically refined meshes, a fourth mesh level is recommended to confirm that the asymptotic range has indeed been reached. However, the much more common case is when the formal order does not match the observed order. In this case, the error estimate is much less reliable and should generally be converted into a numerical uncertainty. While the difference between the discrete solution and the (unknown) exact solution to the mathematical model is still truly a numerical error, because we do not know the true value of this error it should be represented as an uncertainty. Uncertainties due to such a lack of knowledge are called epistemic uncertainties and are distinct from aleatory (or random) uncertainties. They can be reduced by providing more information, in this case, additional computations on more refined meshes. The treatment of these numerical uncertainties is discussed in Chapter 13. In the next section we address some approaches for converting Richardson extrapolation estimates of the discretization error into epistemic uncertainties.

8.6 Roache's grid convergence index (GCI)

Before proceeding with a discussion of the grid convergence index (Roache, 1994), we first provide some motivation by considering the state of affairs in the early 1990s regarding the reporting of mesh refinement studies. This time period is before the appearance of numerical accuracy policies for journals dealing with scientific computing simulations. In some cases, authors mistakenly reported discretization error estimates by giving the relative difference between two discrete solutions computed on different meshes, i.e.,

$$\frac{f_2 - f_1}{f_1},$$

where f_1 is a fine mesh solution and f_2 a coarse mesh solution. This relative difference can be extremely misleading when used as an error estimate. To see why, consider the estimate of the relative discretization error (RDE) found from generalized Richardson extrapolation, which for the fine grid can be written as

$$\mathrm{RDE}_1 = \frac{f_1 - \bar{f}}{\bar{f}}. \tag{8.75}$$

Substituting the generalized Richardson extrapolation result from Eq. (8.62) into the above equation gives

$$\mathrm{RDE}_1 = \frac{f_1 - \left(f_1 + \frac{f_1 - f_2}{r^{p-1}}\right)}{f_1 + \frac{f_1 - f_2}{r^{p-1}}} = \frac{f_2 - f_1}{f_1 r^p - f_2}. \tag{8.76}$$

As an example, consider two numerical solutions where some quantity of interest f has fine and coarse grid values of 20 and 21, respectively, for a relative difference between solutions of 5%. For a third-order accurate scheme with refinement factor $r = 2$, the error estimate based on Richardson extrapolation from Eq. (8.76) is 0.71%. However, for a first-order accurate numerical scheme with a grid refinement factor of 1.5, the error estimate based on Richardson extrapolation is 9.1%. Thus, a 5% relative difference in the two solutions can mean very different values for the relative discretization error, depending on the order of accuracy of the scheme and the grid refinement factor. This example illustrates the importance of accounting for the grid refinement factor r and the order of accuracy p when using extrapolation to estimate the discretization error. The desire to prevent misuse of this relative difference between discrete solutions as an error estimator led to the development of Roache's grid convergence index.

8.6.1 Definition

Roache (1994) proposed the *grid convergence index*, or GCI, as a method for uniform reporting of grid refinement studies. Roache's stated goal in formulating the GCI is to achieve a 95% certainty (i.e., that it provide conservative uncertainty estimates in 19 out of 20 cases) over a wide range of applications. The original GCI is based on the often reported relative difference between two discrete solutions, but also properly accounts for the amount of grid refinement and the order of accuracy. The GCI takes the further step of converting the discretization error estimate into an uncertainty estimate using absolute values. The GCI for the fine grid numerical solution is defined as

$$\text{GCI} = \frac{F_s}{r^p - 1} \left| \frac{f_2 - f_1}{f_1} \right|, \tag{8.77}$$

where F_s is a factor of safety. When only two discrete solutions are available, then the formal order of accuracy of the discretization scheme is used in the definition of the GCI along with a factor of safety of $F_s = 3$. However, when three discrete solutions are available then the observed order of accuracy can be computed. When the observed order matches the formal order of accuracy, then a less conservative factor of safety of $F_s = 1.25$ can be used (Roache, 1998). If the GCI is re-derived in terms of the Richardson extrapolation estimate (as in Eq. (8.76)), then f_1 in the denominator will be replaced with the Richardson extrapolation estimate $\bar{f}$; however, this modification will only significantly affect the uncertainty estimate when the uncertainties themselves are large (Roy, 2001). When the implementation of Eq. (8.77) is used, the GCI returns a fractional estimate of the relative uncertainty in the fine grid solution. For example, a GCI value of 0.15 indicates an uncertainty due to the discretization process of 15% in the fine grid solution. As with all extrapolation-based approaches, systematic mesh refinement must be used.

It is important to include the factor of safety in the GCI. The GCI is based on the Richardson extrapolated value, which is itself an ordered estimate of the exact solution to the mathematical model (recall Eq. (8.61)). Thus we do not know *a priori* whether the estimated exact solution is above or below the true exact solution to the mathematical model. Consider Figure 8.11, which shows two numerical solutions (f_1 and f_2), the estimated exact solution from Richardson extrapolation $\bar{f}$, and the true exact solution $\tilde{f}$. In general, there is an equal chance that the true exact solution is above or below the estimated value. Thus a factor of safety of $F_s = 1$ centered about the fine grid numerical solution f_1 will only provide 50% chance that the true error $\tilde{f}$ is within the uncertainty band. Increasing the factor of safety should increase the possibility that the true error will fall within the band. This argument is made simply to argue for the use of a factor of safety in converting the discretization error estimate into an epistemic uncertainty. It in no way implies that the

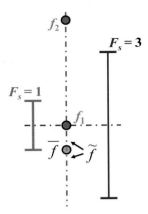

Figure 8.11 Factor of safety for extrapolation-based error bands (from Roy, 2005).

resulting uncertainty is a randomly distributed variable (i.e., an aleatory uncertainty). To reiterate the main point made in Section 8.4, the reliability of any discretization error or uncertainty estimate can only be determined by assessing the asymptotic nature of the discrete solutions. When the solutions are found to be far outside the asymptotic range, the reliability of the error/uncertainty estimate will likely be poor and its behavior erratic. In this case, no value for the factor of safety is guaranteed to be conservative.

8.6.2 Implementation

In order to avoid problems when the solution values are near zero, most recent implementations of the GCI omit the normalization by the fine grid solution in the denominator, i.e., the GCI is redefined as

$$\text{GCI} = \frac{F_s}{r^p - 1} |f_2 - f_1| . \tag{8.78}$$

This implementation thus provides an uncertainty estimate for the fine grid solution in the same units as the solution itself. Roache (1998) provides clear guidelines for choosing the factor of safety when:

1 solutions on only two grids are available ($F_s = 3$), or
2 solutions on three grids are available and the observed order of accuracy is calculated and shown to match the formal order of the scheme ($F_s = 1.25$).

In the first case, when only two grid levels are available, GCI estimates should be used with caution since one has no information on whether the solutions are in (or even near) the asymptotic range. Far from the asymptotic range, all approaches for estimating discretization error or uncertainty will be unreliable (see Section 8.4). For the second case, when three solutions are available, if the observed order of accuracy matches the formal order, then $F_s = 1.25$ is used and either the formal or observed order of accuracy can be employed

Table 8.1 *Proposed implementation of the GCI for solutions on three or more systematically refined grids using Eq. (8.78).*

$\left\lvert \frac{\hat{p} - p_f}{p_f} \right\rvert$	F_s	p
≤ 0.1	1.25	p_f
> 0.1	3.0	$\min(\max(0.5, \hat{p}), p_f)$

(since they match, this choice will have little effect on the estimate). Difficulties arise when the observed and formal orders of accuracy do not agree. Furthermore, exactly how does one define agreement? Ideally, one would simply continue to systematically refine the mesh until the solutions are demonstrably asymptotic, possibly incorporating local mesh refinement to achieve the asymptotic range faster (see Chapter 9). When no additional solutions are possible due to resource limitations, then Roache (1998) provides anecdotal examples of how to apply the GCI for a wide range of situations.

We propose the following procedure for calculating the GCI when solutions on three or more systematically-refined meshes are available. In all cases, the nonnormalized GCI given by Eq. (8.78) is used. When the observed order of accuracy $\hat{p}$ agrees with the formal order p_f within 10%, then the formal order of accuracy along with a factor of safety of 1.25 is used in the GCI calculation. When the observed order of accuracy does not agree within 10%, then a factor of safety of three ($F_s = 3.0$) is used. Furthermore, the order of accuracy is limited between 0.5 and the formal order. Allowing the order of accuracy to be much larger than the formal order causes the uncertainty estimates to be unreasonably small since the GCI goes to zero as $p \rightarrow \infty$, while allowing the order of accuracy to go to zero causes the uncertainty estimate to approach infinity. These recommendations are summarized in Table 8.1. While these recommendations are "reasonable" (Roache, 2009), they require testing to see if they produce the desired 95% uncertainty bands on a wide range of problems.

8.6.3 Variants of the GCI

There are a number of different variants of the GCI that have been developed in recent years. These variations address different ways of computing the factor of safety and/or the order of accuracy used in the GCI calculation. In addition, special cases are often addressed depending on the behavior of the observed order of accuracy.

8.6.3.1 Least squares method

The local calculation of the observed order of accuracy often exhibits large departures from the formal order of the discretization scheme. These variations can be due to a number of sources, including the discrete solutions not being asymptotic, errors transported from other regions (especially for hyperbolic problems), iterative error, round-off error, interpolation of solutions onto a common grid, and nonuniformity of the mesh refinement. Eca and Hoekstra (2002) developed a method for filtering out the "noise" from the observed order of accuracy calculation using a least squares fitting approach over four or more mesh levels. Recall the series expansion from generalized Richardson extrapolation from Eq. (8.57), which can be written for a general mesh level k as

$$f_k = \bar{f} + g_p h_k^{\hat{p}}.$$

In their approach, they minimize the function

$$S(\bar{f}, g_p, \hat{p}) = \left\{ \sum_{k=1}^{NG} \left[f_k - \left(\bar{f} + g_p h_k^{\hat{p}} \right) \right]^2 \right\}^{1/2}, \tag{8.79}$$

where k refers to a mesh level and NG is the total number of mesh levels ($NG > 3$). This is accomplished by setting the derivatives of S with respect to $\bar{f}$, g_p, and $\hat{p}$ to zero, which results in the following expressions:

$$\bar{f} = \frac{\sum_{k=1}^{NG} f_k - g_p \sum_{k=1}^{NG} h_k^{\hat{p}}}{NG}, \tag{8.80}$$

$$g_p = \frac{NG \sum_{k=1}^{NG} f_k h_k^{\hat{p}} - \left(\sum_{k=1}^{NG} f_k \right) \left(\sum_{k=1}^{NG} h_k^{\hat{p}} \right)}{NG \sum_{k=1}^{NG} h_k^{2\hat{p}} - \left(\sum_{k=1}^{NG} h_k^{\hat{p}} \right) \left(\sum_{k=1}^{NG} h_k^{\hat{p}} \right)}, \tag{8.81}$$

$$\sum_{k=1}^{NG} f_k h_k^{\hat{p}} \ln(h_k) - \bar{f} \sum_{k=1}^{NG} h_k^{\hat{p}} \ln(h_k) - g_p \sum_{k=1}^{NG} h_k^{2\hat{p}} \ln(h_k) = 0. \tag{8.82}$$

Eca and Hoekstra (2002) employed a false position method to iteratively solve Eq. (8.82) for $\hat{p}$. The main drawback to the least squares method is that it requires solutions on four or more systematically refined grids. While their original approach actually applies the uncertainty estimate to the extrapolated value $\bar{f}$ (Eca and Hoekstra, 2002), subsequent studies have all applied the uncertainty estimate to the fine grid solution by using the order of accuracy found by solving Eq. (8.82) directly in the GCI calculation of Eq. (8.78) (e.g., see Eca *et al.*, 2005).

8.6.3.2 *Global averaging method*

Cadafalch *et al.* (2002) employed a globally averaged value for the observed order of accuracy to provide local GCI estimates. Their approach can be summarized in the following five steps.

1. Interpolate the solutions from three systematically-refined meshes onto a common post-processing grid with a higher-order interpolation method.
2. Classify the nodes in the common mesh as either monotone $(f_3 - f_2)(f_2 - f_1) > 0$ or nonmonotone $(f_3 - f_2)(f_2 - f_1) < 0$ (they also treated a third case where the magnitude of this product was less than a tolerance of 10^{-30}).
3. Compute the local observed order of accuracy for all of the monotone converging nodes.

4 Compute a global observed order of accuracy by simply averaging all of the local observed orders computed in step 3.
5 Compute the local GCI values at the monotone converging nodes using a factor of safety of $F_s = 1.25$ and with the global observed order of accuracy from step 4.

A significant limitation of this approach is that it does not provide uncertainty estimates at any nodes in the common mesh where the solutions converge in a nonmonotone fashion with mesh refinement. This case could be easily treated by simply computing the GCI at these non-monotone nodes using larger factor of safety ($F_s = 3$) along with the global observed order of accuracy.

8.6.3.3 Factor of safety method

One of the drawbacks to the GCI is that the factor of safety only recognizes two cases: when the solutions are asymptotic ($F_s = 1.25$) and when they are not ($F_s = 3$). For solutions that are on the border of the asymptotic range (regardless of how it is defined), the uncertainty estimates will therefore differ by a factor of 2.4. It is natural to desire a smoother variation in the factor of safety, with increasing values as the solutions move further from the asymptotic range. In order to provide for such a smooth transition, Xing and Stern (2009) have developed the factor of safety method. Their approach is designed to address deficiencies (e.g., see Roache, 2003b) in an earlier version of their method (Stern *et al.*, 2001).

In their factor of safety method, Xing and Stern (2009) measure the distance to the asymptotic range in terms of a correction factor defined as

$$\mathrm{CF} = \frac{r^{\hat{p}} - 1}{r^{p_f} - 1},\tag{8.83}$$

where $\hat{p}$ is the observed order of accuracy and p_f the formal order. In the asymptotic range, CF will approach unity. The uncertainty estimate U is then found from

$$U = \begin{cases} [\mathrm{FS}_1\mathrm{CF} + \mathrm{FS}_0(1 - \mathrm{CF})]\,|\delta_{\mathrm{RE}}|, & 0 < \mathrm{CF} \le 1, \\ \frac{\mathrm{CF}}{2-\mathrm{CF}}[\mathrm{FS}_1(2 - \mathrm{CF}) + \mathrm{FS}_0(\mathrm{CF} - 1)]\,|\delta_{\mathrm{RE}}|, & 1 < \mathrm{CF} < 2, \end{cases}\tag{8.84}$$

where FS_0 and FS_1 are constants. The values for these constants are $\mathrm{FS}_0 = 2$ and $\mathrm{FS}_1 = 1.25$ and were determined by performing a statistical analysis for a wide range of problems and considering only the cases where $0 < \mathrm{CF} < 2$. The term δ_{RE} is the discretization error estimate found from generalized Richardson extrapolation using the observed order of accuracy, i.e.,

$$\delta_{\mathrm{RE}} = \frac{f_2 - f_1}{r^{\hat{p}} - 1}.\tag{8.85}$$

The main limitations of this approach are that it only applies to $0 < \mathrm{CF} < 2$ and the uncertainty estimates approach infinity as $\mathrm{CF} \to 2$. For a formally second-order accurate method with a grid refinement factor of $r = 2$, the infinite uncertainty estimate occurs when $\hat{p} \approx 2.81$, a situation that can certainly occur in complex scientific computing applications.

8.6.4 Reliability of the GCI

Three recent studies have carefully examined the reliability of the GCI. Eca and Hoekstra (2002) examined a wide range of fluid flow problems using a large number of noninteger refined meshes (at least sixteen different grids for each case). They employed a locally evaluated observed order of accuracy and found that the GCI with a factor of safety of $F_s = 1.25$ worked well on the finer meshes. Cadafalch *et al.* (2002) examined five test cases for fluid flow (some with heat transfer) using four to seven meshes for each case with a grid refinement factor of two. In their case, they employed the global averaging method given in Section 8.6.3.2. They also found good results for the GCI with a factor of safety of 1.25 on finer meshes. Finally, Eca *et al.* (2004) looked at potential flow solutions around 2-D airfoils where exact solutions were available. They achieved good uncertainty estimates using the GCI when the locally evaluated observed order of accuracy was not significantly larger than the formal order of the method. See Pelletier and Roache (2006) for additional discussion of the effectiveness of the GCI.

8.7 Mesh refinement issues

Second only to the inability to achieve the asymptotic grid convergence range, the failure of extrapolation-based methods for estimating discretization error can often be tied to problems achieving systematic mesh refinement on the meshes in question (e.g., Baker, 2005; Salas, 2006). The use of locally-refined meshes, meshes refined in only one coordinate direction, and refinement where the refinement factor varies locally over the domain are all examples of improper approaches to mesh refinement. When combined with the extrapolation-based methods discussed earlier for error or uncertainty estimation, these approaches are virtually guaranteed to fail.

8.7.1 Measuring systematic mesh refinement

Recall the definition of *systematic mesh refinement* given in Section 5.4, which requires that the mesh refinement be both uniform and consistent. Uniform refinement requires that the mesh be refined by the same factor over the entire domain. This does not mean that the mesh itself must be uniform over the domain, only that the ratio of grid refinement from one mesh to another must not vary over the domain. Consistent refinement requires that the meshes should maintain the same grid quality (skewness, aspect ratio, stretching factor, etc.) or possibly provide for improved grid quality with mesh refinement.

A simple technique to ensure that two meshes retain the same volume ratio over the domain was developed by Roy *et al.* (2007) and applied to 3-D unstructured Cartesian meshes used for aerodynamic force and moment computations. The level of uniformity of the mesh refinement was evaluated by comparing cell volume ratios between the two successive mesh levels as follows. First, the local cell volumes were calculated and stored at the nodes. Next, the fine grid volume distribution was interpolated onto the coarse grid

(a)   (b)

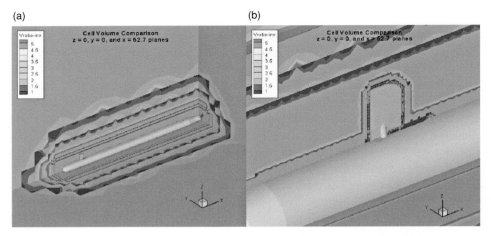

Figure 8.12 Contour plots of the cell volume ratio between the two unstructured Cartesian mesh levels for (a) the entire missile geometry and (b) a close-up of the canard (from Roy *et al.*, 2007). (See color plate section.)

with using an inverse distance function. Now that the coarse grid contains both fine and coarse grid cell volume information, the coarse to fine grid volume ratios can be calculated and examined. An example of the Cartesian mesh used here was given earlier in Figure 8.7b showing different layers of resolution. The volume ratios between two mesh levels are shown in Figure 8.12 and are fairly constant in the domain around a value of 1.6, with the exception of the regions where the Cartesian grid layers transition from one cell size to another. This approach could be easily extended to other mesh quality parameters such as skewness, aspect ratio, stretching factor, etc.

8.7.2 Grid refinement factor

As discussed earlier, the *grid refinement factor* is a measure of the ratio of mesh length or time scales in each of the coordinate directions. The refinement factor is simple to compute for structured grids, while for unstructured grids the refinement factor can be computed as follows. Assuming that the mesh has been refined uniformly (see Section 8.7.1), the refinement factor can be computed as a function of the total number of cells or elements in the mesh by

$$r = \left(\frac{N_1}{N_2}\right)^{1/d}, \tag{8.86}$$

where N_k is the number of cells/elements on mesh k and d is the dimensionality of the problem ($d = 1$ for 1-D, $d = 2$ for 2-D, etc.). Note that in the case where local mesh refinement is applied from one mesh to another, the grid refinement factor will vary over the domain and the numerical solutions should no longer be used in an extrapolation procedure or for the computation of the observed order of accuracy.

8.7.3 Fractional uniform refinement

It is not necessary to use grid refinement factors of two, a process referred to as grid doubling or grid halving, depending on whether one starts with the fine mesh or the coarse mesh. For simple mesh topologies (e.g., Cartesian meshes), grid refinement factors as small as $r = 1.1$ can be employed (Roache, 1998). Since the refinement must always be uniform, we will herein refer to this procedure as *fractional uniform refinement*. When refinement factors near one are used, one should take special care to ensure that round-off error does not become large relative to the difference between the two solutions. For example, solving a 2-D problem on two meshes of size 100×100 and 101×101 elements (i.e, $r = 1.01$) could easily result in solutions that differed by less than 0.01%. Single precision computations generally provide solution errors due to round-off of approximately 0.001%, so the expected round-off errors will be only one order of magnitude smaller than the discretization errors.

Using fractional uniform refinement has the added benefit that it increases the chances of getting discrete solutions on multiple meshes into the asymptotic grid convergence range. For example, consider a 3-D coarse mesh with 1 million elements which is in the asymptotic range. For three levels of mesh refinement with a factor of two, the fine mesh would require 64 million elements. If a refinement factor of 1.26 was used instead, then the fine mesh would have only 4 million cells and would thus be significantly less expensive to compute. However, non-integer grid refinement factors are difficult to apply to complex mesh topologies, especially those involving significant mesh stretching. For simulations using complex, structured meshes, the grid generation can sometimes make up the majority of the overall user's time to perform a given simulation. Thus, relying on the original grid generation procedure for grid refinement can be expensive; furthermore, it is difficult to enforce a constant grid refinement factor over the entire domain. Higher-order interpolation can be used for noninteger grid refinement. Here it is again better to start with the fine mesh and then coarsen (at least for structured meshes); however, this approach may not preserve the underlying surface geometry, especially in regions of high curvature.

When a grid refinement factor of two is employed on structured meshes, there is only significant effort involved in generating the fine mesh; the coarser meshes are found by simply removing every other point. The drawback is not only that the fine mesh may be unnecessarily expensive, but there is also an increased chance that the coarse mesh will be outside the asymptotic grid convergence range. Recall that all three meshes must be in the asymptotic range to demonstrate the reliability of the discretization error and uncertainty estimates.

Ideally, one would like the ability to simply create a grid and then have a grid generation tool generate a family of uniformly-refined meshes based on specified (possibly fractional) refinement factors. Such a capability would greatly improve the reliability of extrapolation-based error and uncertainty estimation procedures. To our knowledge, this automatic fractional uniform refinement capability does not exist in any commercially-available grid generators.

Finally, if the extrapolation (or error/uncertainty) estimation method is to be applied to the solution point-wise through the domain, then it is necessary to get fine grid information onto the coarse grid. This procedure is simple for integer refinement since the coarse grid is simply a subset of the fine grid. However, for fractional uniform refinement, fine mesh information must be interpolated to the coarse mesh points, possibly with an interpolation scheme that has a higher order of accuracy than the underlying numerical solutions (Roache and Knupp, 1993).

8.7.4 *Refinement vs. coarsening*

In theory, it should not make a difference whether we start with the coarse mesh or the fine mesh. However, in practice, grid coarsening on structured meshes is often easier than grid refinement, especially for complex meshes. Here complex meshes are defined as those with complex geometries and/or significant grid clustering. For uniform meshes, refinement can be performed by simply averaging neighboring spatial location. For stretched meshes, this type of refinement will lead to discontinuities in the ratio of neighboring element sizes near the original coarse grid nodes. (Although, as Ferziger and Peric (1996) point out, the fraction of locations with discontinuous stretching factors will decrease with increasing mesh refinement.) A better strategy for stretched meshes is to use higher-order interpolation to obtain smooth stretching distributions; however, this process can be challenging on highly complex grids. The primary problems that arise during mesh refinement are due to a loss of geometric definition at object surfaces, especially at sharp corners. Furthermore, for structured grid approaches requiring point-to-point match-up at subdomain boundaries, the refinement strategy must ensure that these points are co-located. Thus for complex, structured meshes, it is often easier to simply start with the fine mesh and successively remove every other point in each of the coordinate directions.

For unstructured meshes, it is generally easier to start with the coarse mesh, then refine by subdividing the elements. This is due to the difficulties of merging elements in a manner that preserves the element type while enforcing the requirement of a constant grid refinement factor over the entire domain. While refinement on unstructured grids inherits all of the drawbacks of refinement for structured grids discussed above, there are currently efforts underway to make surface geometry information directly available to mesh refinement routines (e.g., see King *et al.*, 2006).

The choice of methods for refining the elements will determine the effective grid refinement factor. In two dimensions, triangular elements can easily be refined by connecting the midpoints of the edges as shown in Figure 8.13, thereby creating four new triangular elements of similar shape. This figure also shows the corresponding refinement strategy for three-dimensional tetrahedra, where the midpoints of each edge are connected, eventually resulting in eight smaller tetrahedra. In this case, the four new outer tetrahedra will be geometrically similar to the original tetrahedron, but the four interior tetrahedral will not. In both cases shown in Figure 8.13, the grid refinement factor is two. Refinement of quadrilateral and hexahedral cells is straightforward to perform by simple edge bisection.

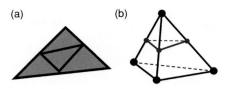

Figure 8.13 Refinement strategy for unstructured meshes: (a) 2-D triangles and (b) 3-D tetrahedra (from Roy, 2005).

8.7.5 Unidirectional refinement

It is sometimes the case that the discretization errors come primarily from just one of the coordinate directions. In such cases, it can be helpful to perform independent refinement in the coordinate directions to determine which one is the primary contributor to the overall discretization error. The approach discussed here is similar to the combined space-time method for code order of accuracy verification discussed in Section 5.5.3.2. For independent refinement in x and y, we can write the expansion of the numerical solution on mesh k about the exact solution to the original partial differential equation as

$$f_k = \tilde{f} + g_x(\Delta x_k)^p + g_y(\Delta y_k)^q + \cdots, \tag{8.87}$$

where the error terms for each coordinate direction are included. In order to keep the analysis general, the formal order of accuracy in the x direction is assumed to be p and the order of accuracy in the y direction to be q, where the two may or may not be equal. Note that for some numerical schemes (e.g., the Lax–Wendroff scheme), a cross term $g_{xy}(\Delta x)^s(\Delta y)^t$ may also be present.

Consider the case of solutions on two meshes levels (fine: $k = 1$ and coarse: $k = 2$) with refinement only in the x direction by a factor of r_x. As the Δx element size is refined, the term $g_y(\Delta y_k)^q$ will be constant. We are now unable to solve for an estimate of the exact solution $\tilde{f}$, but instead must solve for the quantity

$$\tilde{f}_x = \tilde{f} + g_y(\Delta y_k)^q, \tag{8.88}$$

which includes the error term due to the Δy discretization. This term will simply be constant on the two meshes since the Δy spacing does not change. Neglecting the higher-order terms into the estimated solution $\bar{f}$ results in the following two equations:

$$\begin{aligned} f_1 &= \bar{f}_x + g_x(\Delta x)^p, \\ f_2 &= \bar{f}_x + g_x(r_x\Delta x)^p, \end{aligned} \tag{8.89}$$

which can be solved for $\bar{f}_x$,

$$\bar{f}_x = f_1 + \frac{f_1 - f_2}{r_x^p - 1}, \tag{8.90}$$

and the leading x-direction error term,

$$g_x (\Delta x)^p = \frac{f_2 - f_1}{r_x^p - 1}. \tag{8.91}$$

Similarly, introducing a third solution ($k = 3$) with coarsening only in the y direction allows us to solve for the y-direction error term,

$$g_y (\Delta y)^q = \frac{f_3 - f_1}{r_y^q - 1}. \tag{8.92}$$

The size of the two error terms from Eqs. (8.91) and (8.92) can then be compared to determine the appropriate direction for further mesh refinement. In addition, since g_x and g_y have been estimated, Eq. (8.87) can be used to obtain an estimate of $\tilde{f}$.

8.8 Open research issues

There are a number of issues which are currently active areas of research. These include the presence of singularities and discontinuities (especially in hyperbolic problems), oscillatory grid convergence, multi-scale models, and approaches for estimating discretization errors on coarse grids which are not in the asymptotic range.

8.8.1 Singularities and discontinuities

Practical scientific computing applications are fraught with singularities and discontinuities. In some cases, they may take the form of relatively weak singularities/discontinuities such as discontinuous surface curvature in a linear elasticity analysis. Examples of strong singularities/discontinuities include shock waves in inviscid flow, the leading edge region in the flow over a sharp-nosed body, and the interface between two different materials in thermal or structural analysis problems. Nature tends to "smooth out" singularities such as the sharp leading edge that takes a more rounded appearance under high magnification or the shock wave that actually transports mass, momentum, and energy in the upstream direction via molecular motion. However, singularities and discontinuities in mathematical models are much more common than is often recognized, especially in idealized geometries and simplified mathematical models. Some examples include flow over a surface with discontinuous slope or curvature, loading of a structure with point loads, and loading of a plate with angled holes.

The presence of singularities and discontinuities can adversely impact our ability to obtain reliable estimates of the discretization error as well as our ability to compute the numerical solutions themselves. This is because all of the discretization error estimators (and most discretization schemes) require that the solutions be continuous and differentiable. Nevertheless, we still must compute numerical solutions to these problems and then estimate the discretization error in those solutions.

Work by Carpenter and Casper (1999) suggests that, for the Euler equations on sufficiently refined meshes, the simulation of flows containing shock waves will reduce to first-order accuracy, regardless of the formal order of the numerical scheme employed. This reduction to first-order accuracy in the presence of shock waves has also been observed by Roy (2001, 2003) for laminar and inviscid hypersonic flows. In these latter cases, flux limiters were employed to reduce a formally second-order accurate scheme to first order at a shock wave to prevent numerical oscillations.

Banks *et al.* (2008) provide an excellent explanation of why the formal order of accuracy of any discretization scheme will reduce to first-order accuracy or lower in the presence of discontinuities. They consider the inviscid Euler equations for compressible flows. The Euler equations admit discontinuous solutions such as shock waves, contact discontinuities, and slip lines. However, in the absence of viscosity which enforces the entropy condition in viscous flows, these discontinuous solutions are not unique (i.e., the Euler equations will admit infinitely many jump conditions). It is only in the limit of a vanishing viscosity that the correct Rankine–Hugoniot jump conditions are met. Note that this nonuniqueness generally does not pose a problem for numerical solutions to the Euler equations due to the presence of numerical viscosity in the form of even spatial derivatives in the truncation error. For nonlinear discontinuities such as shock waves, numerical schemes reduce down to first-order accuracy. For linear discontinuities (i.e., linearly degenerate waves) such as contact discontinuities and slip lines, Banks *et al.* (2008) perform a truncation error analysis to show that most discretization schemes reduce their formal order of accuracy to $p/(p+1)$, where p is the formal order of the method for smooth problems. They also provide numerical examples to confirm their theoretical analysis.

Regardless of the discretization scheme employed, the reduction of the order of accuracy to first order in the presence of discontinuities results in a numerical scheme that is of mixed order. In this case, the scheme will be second-order accurate (or higher) in the smooth regions, but locally first-order accurate at the shock wave. While technically this scheme is formally first-order accurate for flows with shocks, there may be a significant range of mesh resolutions where the solutions exhibit second-order accuracy. This mixed order behavior can lead to non-monotone convergence of the solutions with grid refinement, as is demonstrated below. In order to analyze mixed first- and second-order schemes, Roy (2001, 2003) proposed the following expansion for the discretization error:

$$f_k = \bar{f} + g_1 h_k + g_2 h_k^2. \tag{8.93}$$

In this approach, terms accounting for the formal order of accuracy in both smooth regions ($p = 2$) and nonsmooth regions ($p = 1$) are included. If three mesh levels are available, then Eq. (8.93) can be solved for the two unknown coefficients g_1 and g_2 as well as the estimated exact solution $\bar{f}$. Consider the case where three discrete solutions f_k are available on fine ($k = 1$), medium ($k = 2$), and coarse ($k = 3$) meshes, where the grid refinement factor is held constant between mesh levels (i.e., $r_{12} = r_{23} = r$). If we further arbitrarily set $h_1 = 1$ (this will simply require the absorbing of constants in the g_k coefficients), then the

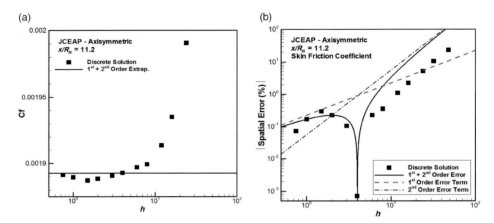

Figure 8.14 Dimensionless frictional resistance at one location on the body as a function of mesh spacing: (a) skin friction coefficient and (b) discretization error (from Roy, 2001).

expressions for the three unknowns become

$$g_1 = \frac{r^2(f_2 - f_1) - (f_3 - f_2)}{r(r-1)^2},$$
$$g_2 = \frac{(f_3 - f_2) - r(f_2 - f_1)}{r(r+1)(r-1)^2},$$
$$\bar{f} = f_1 + \frac{(f_3 - f_2) - (r^2 + r - 1)(f_2 - f_1)}{(r+1)(r-1)^2}. \tag{8.94}$$

These three expressions can be used not only to estimate the discretization error in the numerical solutions, but also to examine the behavior of the two different error terms in the discretization error expansion given by Eq. (8.93).

   This mixed-order analysis method has been applied to the dimensionless frictional resistance (i.e., skin friction coefficient) at points along the surface of a sphere-cone geometry in laminar, hypersonic flow (Roy, 2001). The results are shown below in Figure 8.14a for the behavior of the skin friction coefficient at one location with mesh refinement. The solution displays nonmonotone behavior as the skin friction first decreases with mesh refinement and then begins to increase. Insight into why this nonmonotone behavior occurs can be found by examining the discretization error given in Figure 8.14b, which also shows the first- and second-order error terms from Eq. (8.93). In this case, both error terms have the same magnitude near $h = 4$, but they have opposite signs. This leads to error cancellation at $h = 4$ which manifests as a crossing of the estimated exact solution in Figure 8.14a. Since the two terms have opposite signs, when the mesh is sufficiently refined such that the first order term dominates, the skin friction coefficient displays a local minimum when plotted versus the mesh spacing h.

8.8.2 Oscillatory convergence with mesh refinement

There has been much discussion in recent years on the presence of oscillatory convergence of numerical solutions with mesh refinement (e.g., see Coleman *et al.*, 2001; Celik *et al.*, 2005; and Brock, 2007). However, examination of the Taylor series expansion of the numerical solution about the exact solution the governing partial differential equations in terms of the mesh spacing parameter as given in Eq. (8.47), or even the more general series expansion from Eq. (8.48), shows that there can be only a single term that dominates the expansion *in the limit* as $h \to 0$. While this debate may not yet be settled, our opinion is that there can be no oscillatory convergence with mesh refinement in the asymptotic grid convergence range. The solution behavior being interpreted as oscillatory convergence is mostly likely due to a failure to achieve the asymptotic range (as discussed in Section 8.8.1), nonuniform refinement of the mesh (Eca and Hoekstra, 2002), or the presence of nonnegligible iterative and/or round-off errors. In the case of the former, we do not dispute the fact that the asymptotic range may be extremely difficult to achieve for complex scientific computing problems.

8.8.3 Multi-scale models

A multi-scale model is one that resolves different physical phenomena at different length and/or time scales. For some multi-scale models, the governing equations actually change as the mesh is refined, thus making it difficult to separate out issues of verification (mathematics) from those of validation (physics). A classic example of a multi-scale model is the large eddy simulation (LES) of turbulent flows, which generally involves a spatial filtering operation to remove small-scale turbulent structures. The length scale used in this spatial filtering thus explicitly appears in the mathematical model. In most LES computations, this length scale is tied to the mesh spacing. Thus as one refines the mesh, it is equivalent to filtering the Navier–Stokes equations with a different filter length scale (i.e., a different mathematical model). The rigorous assessment of numerical errors and physical modeling errors thus becomes extremely difficult since both are tied to the mesh spacing. One possible remedy for this problem is to fix the filter width at the coarse grid spacing while performing mesh refinement to assess numerical errors (e.g., see Moin, 2007).

8.8.4 Coarse grid error estimators

For scientific computing simulations where the physics and/or geometry are complex, the meshes are often under-resolved due to computational resource limitations. This is especially true for 3-D time-dependent problems. The ideal discretization error estimator is one that not only provides consistent error estimates as the mesh is refined, but also provides reliable error estimates on under-resolved coarse grids which are outside of the asymptotic grid convergence range. Although often buried deep within the details, all of the discretization error estimation methods discussed in this chapter require the solution (or solutions) to be within the asymptotic range. The reliability of discretization error estimators when the discrete solutions are not in (and possibly far from) the asymptotic range is an area for further investigation.

8.9 References

Ainsworth, M. and J. T. Oden (1997). A posteriori error estimation in finite element analysis, *Computer Methods in Applied Mechanics and Engineering*. **142**(1–2), 1–88.

Ainsworth, M. and J. T. Oden (2000). *A Posteriori Error Estimation in Finite Element Analysis*, New York, Wiley Interscience.

Akin, J. E. (2005). *Finite Element Analysis with Error Estimators*, Burlington, Elsevier.

Babuska, I. and A. Miller (1984). Post-processing approach in the finite element method – Part 3: A posteriori error estimates and adaptive mesh selection, *International Journal for Numerical Methods in Engineering*. **20**(12), 2311–2324.

Babuska, I. and W. C. Rheinboldt (1978a). A posteriori error estimates for the finite element method, *International Journal for Numerical Methods in Engineering*. **12**, 1597–1615.

Babuska, I. and W. C. Rheinboldt (1978b). Error estimates for adaptive finite element computations, *SIAM Journal of Numerical Analysis*. **15**(4), 736–754.

Babuska, I., O. C. Zienkiewicz, J. Gago, E. R. Oliveira (1986). *Accuracy Estimates and Adaptive Refinements in Finite Element Computations*, Chichester, Wiley.

Babuska, I., T. Strouboulis, and C. S. Upadhyay (1994). A model study of the quality of a posteriori error estimators for linear elliptic problems. Error estimation in the interior of patchwise uniform grids of triangles, *Computer Methods in Applied Mechanics and Engineering*. **114**(3–4), 307–378.

Babuska, I., T. Strouboulis, T. Gangaraj, and C. S. Upadhyay (1997). Pollution error in the h-version of the finite element method and local quality of the recovered derivative, *Computer Methods in Applied Mechanics and Engineering*. **140**(1–2), 1–37.

Baker, T. J. (2005). *On the Relationship between Mesh Refinement and Solution Accuracy*, AIAA Paper 2005–4875.

Bank, R. E. (1996). Hierarchical bases and the finite element method, *Acta Numerica*. **5**, 1–45.

Bank, R. R. and A. Weiser (1985). Some a posteriori error estimators for elliptic partial differential equations, *Mathematics of Computation*. **44**, 283–301.

Banks, J. W., T. Aslam, and W. J. Rider (2008). On sub-linear convergence for linearly degenerate waves in capturing schemes, *Journal of Computational Physics*. **227**, 6985–7002.

Barth, T. J. and M. G. Larson (2002). A-posteriori error estimation for higher order Godunov finite volume methods on unstructured meshes, In *Finite Volumes for Complex Applications III*, R. Herbin and D. Kroner (eds.), London, HERMES Science Publishing Ltd., 41–63.

Brock, J. S. (2007). *Bounded Numerical Error Estimates for Oscillatory Convergence of Simulation Data*, AIAA Paper 2007–4091.

Cadafalch, J., C. D. Perez-Segarra, R. Consul, and A. Oliva (2002). Verification of finite volume computations on steady-state fluid flow and heat transfer, *Journal of Fluids Engineering*. **24**, 11–21.

Carpenter, M. H. and J. H. Casper (1999). Accuracy of shock capturing in two spatial dimensions, *AIAA Journal.* **37**(9), 1072–1079.

Cavallo, P. A. and N. Sinha (2007). Error quantification for computational aerodynamics using an error transport equation, *Journal of Aircraft.* **44**(6), 1954–1963.

Celik, I., J. Li, G. Hu, and C. Shaffer (2005). Limitations of Richardson extrapolation and some possible remedies, *Journal of Fluids Engineering.* **127**, 795–805.

Cheng, Z. and M. Paraschivoiu (2004). A posteriori finite element bounds to linear functional outputs of the three-dimensional Navier–Stokes equations, *International Journal for Numerical Methods in Engineering.* **61**(11), 1835–1859.

Coleman, H. W., F. Stern, A. Di Mascio, and E. Campana (2001). The problem with oscillatory behavior in grid convergence studies, *Journal of Fluids Engineering.* **123**, 438–439.

Demkowicz, L., J. T. Oden, and T. Strouboulis (1984). Adaptive finite elements for flow problems with moving boundaries. Part I: Variational principles and a posteriori estimates, *Computer Methods in Applied Mechanics and Engineering.* **46**(2), 217–251.

Eca, L. and M. Hoekstra (2002). An evaluation of verification procedures for CFD applications, *24th Symposium on Naval Hydrodynamics*, Fukuoka, Japan, July 8–13, 2002.

Eca, L. and M. Hoekstra (2009a). Error estimation based on grid refinement studies: a challenge for grid generation, *Congress on Numerical Methods in Engineering*, Barcelona, Spain, June 29–July 2, 2009.

Eca, L. and M. Hoekstra (2009b). Evaluation of numerical error estimation based on grid refinement studies with the method of the manufactured solutions, *Computers and Fluids.* **38**, 1580–1591.

Eca, L., G. B. Vaz, J. A. C. Falcao de Campos, and M. Hoekstra (2004). Verification of calculations of the potential flow around two-dimensional foils, *AIAA Journal.* **42**(12), 2401–2407.

Eca, L., M. Hoekstra, and P. Roache (2005). *Verification of Calculations: an Overview of the Lisbon Workshop*, AIAA Paper 2005–4728.

Eriksson, K. and C. Johnson (1987). Error-estimates and automatic time step control for nonlinear parabolic problems. Part 1, *SIAM Journal of Numerical Analysis.* **24**(1), 12–23.

Estep, D., M. Larson, and R. Williams (2000). *Estimating the Error of Numerical Solutions of Systems of Nonlinear Reaction-Diffusion Equations*, Memoirs of the American Mathematical Society, Vol. **146**, No. 696, Providence, American Mathematical Society.

Fehlberg, E. (1969). *Low-Order Classical Runge-Kutta Formulas with Step Size Control and their Application to some Heat Transfer Problems*, NASA Technical Report 315, National Aeronautics and Space Administration, July 1969.

Ferziger, J. H. and M. Peric (1996). Further discussion of numerical errors in CFD, *International Journal for Numerical Methods in Fluids.* **23**(12), 1263–1274.

Ferziger, J. H. and M. Peric (2002). *Computational Methods for Fluid Dynamics*, 3rd edn., Berlin, Springer-Verlag.

Garbey, M. and W. Shyy (2003). A least square extrapolation method for improving solution accuracy of PDE computations, *Journal of Computational Physics.* **186**(1), 1–23.

Hirsch, C. (1990). *Numerical Computation of Internal and External Flows: Volume 2, Computational Methods for Inviscid and Viscous Flows*, Chichester, Wiley.

Hirsch, C. (2007). *Numerical Computation of Internal and External Flows: the Fundamentals of Computational Fluid Dynamics*, 2nd edn., Oxford, Butterworth-Heinemann.

Huebner, K. H. (2001). *The Finite Element Method for Engineers*, New York, Wiley.

Huebner, K. H., D. L. Dewhirst, D. E. Smith, and T. G. Byrom (2001). *The Finite Element Method of Engineers*, 4th edn., New York, John Wiley and Sons.

Hughes, T. J. R. (2000). *The Finite Element Method: Linear Static and Dynamic Finite Element Analysis*, 2nd edn., Mineola, Dover.

Jameson, A. (1988). Aerodynamic design via control theory, *Journal of Scientific Computing*. **3**(3), 233–260.

Jameson, A., W. Schmidt, and E. Turkel (1981). *Numerical Solutions of the Euler Equations by Finite Volume Methods Using Runge-Kutta Time-Stepping Schemes*, AIAA Paper 81–1259.

Johnson, C. and P. Hansbo (1992). Adaptive finite element methods in computational mechanics, *Computer Methods in Applied Mechanics and Engineering*. **101**(1–3), 143–181.

Kamm, J. R., W. J. Rider, and J. S. Brock (2003). *Combined Space and Time Convergence Analyses of a Compressible Flow Algorithm*, AIAA Paper 2003–4241.

King, M. L., M. J. Fisher, and C. G. Jensen (2006). A CAD-centric approach to CFD analysis with discrete features, *Computer-Aided Design & Applications*. **3**(1–4), 279–288.

Knight, D. D. (2006). *Elements of Numerical Methods for Compressible Flows*, New York, Cambridge University Press.

Moin, P. (2007). Application of high fidelity numerical simulations for vehicle aerodynamics, *The Aerodynamics of Heavy Vehicles II: Trucks, Buses and Trains*, Tahoe City, California, August 26–31, 2007.

Morton, K. W. and D. F. Mayers (2005). *Numerical Solution of Partial Differential Equations: an Introduction*, 2nd edn., New York, Cambridge University Press.

Oden, J. T. and J. N. Reddy (1976). *An Introduction to the Mathematical Theory of Finite Elements*, New York, Wiley.

Paraschivoiu, M., J. Peraire, and A. T. Patera (1997). A posteriori finite element bounds for linear functional outputs of elliptic partial differential equations, *Computer Methods in Applied Mechanics and Engineering*. **150**(1–4), 289–312.

Pelletier, D. and P. J. Roache (2006). Chapter 13: Verification and validation of computational heat transfer, in *Handbook of Numerical Heat Transfer*, 2nd edn., W. J. Minkowycz, E. M. Sparrow, and J. Y. Murthy, eds., Hoboken, NJ, Wiley.

Pierce, N. A. and M. B. Giles (2000). Adjoint recovery of superconvergent functionals from PDE approximations, *SIAM Review*. **42**(2), 247–264.

Potter, D. L., F. G. Blottner, A. R. Black, C. J. Roy, and B. L. Bainbridge (2005). *Visualization of Instrumental Verification Information Details (VIVID): Code Development, Description, and Usage*, SAND2005–1485, Albuquerque, NM, Sandia National Laboratories.

Rannacher, R. and F. T. Suttmeier (1997). A feed-back approach to error control in finite element methods: application to linear elasticity, *Computational Mechanics*. **19**(5), 434–446.

Richards, S. A. (1997). Completed Richardson extrapolation in space and time, *Communications in Numerical Methods in Engineering*. **13**, 1997, 573–582.

Richardson, L. F. (1911). The approximate arithmetical solution by finite differences of physical problems involving differential equations, with an application to the stresses in a masonry dam, *Philosophical Transactions of the Royal Society of London*. Series A, Containing Papers of a Mathematical or Physical Character. **210**, 307–357.

Richardson, L. F. (1927). The deferred approach to the limit. Part I. Single lattice, *Philosophical Transaction of the Royal Society of London*. Series A, Containing Papers of a Mathematical or Physical Character. **226**, 299–349.

Richtmyer, R. and K. Morton (1967). *Difference Methods for Initial-Value Problems*, 2nd edn., New York, Interscience Publishers.

Roache, P. J. (1994). Perspective: a method for uniform reporting of grid refinement studies, *Journal of Fluids Engineering*. **116**, 405–413.

Roache, P. J. (1998). *Verification and Validation in Computational Science and Engineering*, Albuquerque, NM, Hermosa Publishers.

Roache, P. J. (2003a). Conservatism of the grid convergence index in finite volume computations on steady-state fluid flow and heat transfer, *Journal of Fluids Engineering*. **125**(4), 731–732.

Roache, P. J. (2003b). Criticisms of the ''correction factor'' verification method, *Journal of Fluids Engineering*. **125**(4), 732–733.

Roache, P. J. (2009). Private communication, July 13, 2009.

Roache, P. J. and P. M. Knupp (1993). Completed Richardson extrapolation, *Communications in Numerical Methods in Engineering*. **9**(5), 365–374.

Roy, C. J. (2001). *Grid Convergence Error Analysis for Mixed-Order Numerical Schemes*, AIAA Paper 2001–2606.

Roy, C. J. (2003). Grid convergence error analysis for mixed-order numerical schemes, *AIAA Journal*. **41**(4), 595–604.

Roy, C. J. (2005). Review of code and solution verification procedures for computational simulation, *Journal of Computational Physics*. **205**(1), 131–156.

Roy, C. J. (2009). *Strategies for Driving Mesh Adaptation in CFD*, AIAA Paper 2009–1302.

Roy, C. J. (2010). *Review of Discretization Error Estimators in Scientific Computing*, AIAA Paper 2010–126.

Roy, C. J. and F. G. Blottner (2003). Methodology for turbulence model validation: application to hypersonic transitional flows, *Journal of Spacecraft and Rockets*. **40**(3), 313–325.

Roy, C. J., C. J. Heintzelman, and S. J. Roberts (2007). *Estimation of Numerical Error for 3D Inviscid Flows on Cartesian Grids*, AIAA Paper 2007–0102.

Salas, M. D. (2006). Some observations on grid convergence, *Computers and Fluids*. **35**, 688–692.

Salas, M. D. and H. L. Atkins (2009). On problems associated with grid convergence of functionals, *Computers and Fluids*. **38**, 1445–1454.

Shih, T. I.-P. and Y. C. Qin (2007). *A Posteriori Method for Estimating and Correcting Grid-Induced Errors in CFD Solutions Part 1: Theory and Method*, AIAA Paper 2007–100.

Shih, T. I.-P., and B. R. Williams (2009). *Development and Evaluation of an A Posteriori Method for Estimating and Correcting Grid-Induced Errors in Solutions of the Navier-Stokes Equations*, AIAA Paper 2009–1499.

Sonar, T. (1993). Strong and weak norm refinement indicators based on the finite element residual for compressible flow computation: I. The steady case, *Impact of Computing in Science and Engineering*. **5**(2), 111–127.

Stewart, J. R. and T. J. R. Hughes (1998). A tutorial in elementary finite element error analysis: a systematic presentation of a priori and a posteriori error estimates,

Computer Methods in Applied Mechanics and Engineering. **158**(1–2),
  1–22.
Stern, F., R. V. Wilson, H. W. Coleman, and E. G. Paterson (2001). Comprehensive
  approach to verification and validation of CFD simulations – Part I: Methodology
  and procedures, *ASME Journal of Fluids Engineering.* **123**(4), 793–802.
Szabo, B. A. and I. Babuska (1991). *Finite Element Analysis*, New York, Wiley.
Tannehill, J. C., D. A. Anderson, and R. H. Pletcher (1997). *Computational Fluid
  Mechanics and Heat Transfer*, 2nd edn., Philadelphia, Taylor and Francis.
Thompson, J. F., Z. U. A. Warsi, and C. W. Mastin (1985). *Numerical Grid Generation:
  Foundations and Applications*, New York, Elsevier. (www.erc.msstate.edu/
  publications/gridbook)
Venditti, D. A. and D. L. Darmofal (2000). Adjoint error estimation and grid adaptation
  for functional outputs: application to quasi-one dimensional flow, *Journal of
  Computational Physics.* **164**, 204–227.
Venditti, D. A. and D. L. Darmofal (2002). Grid adaptation for functional outputs:
  application to two-dimensional inviscid flows, *Journal of Computational Physics.*
  176, 40–69.
Venditti, D. A. and D. L. Darmofal (2003). Anisotropic grid adaptation for functional
  outputs: application to two-dimensional viscous flows, *Journal of Computational
  Physics.* **187**, 22–46.
Wahlbin, L. B. (1995). *Superconvergence in Galerkin Finite Element Methods*, Volume
  1605 of Lecture Notes in Mathematics, Springer-Verlag, Berlin.
Whiteman, J. R. (1994). *The Mathematics of Finite Element and Applications: Highlights
  1993*, New York, Wiley.
Xing, T. and F. Stern (2009). *Factors of Safety for Richardson Extrapolation*, IIHR
  Hydroscience and Engineering Technical Report No. 469, March 2009.
Zhang, X. D., J.-Y. Trepanier, and R. Camarero (2000). A posteriori error estimation for
  finite-volume solutions of hyperbolic conservation laws, *Computer Methods in
  Applied Mechanics and Engineering.* **185**(1), 1–19.
Zhang, Z. and A. Naga (2005). A new finite element gradient recovery method:
  superconvergence property, *SIAM Journal of Scientific Computing.* **26**(4),
  1192–1213.
Zienkiewicz, O. C., R. L. Taylor, and J. Z. Zhu (2005). *The Finite Element Method : Its
  Basis and Fundamentals*, 6th edn., Oxford, Elsevier.
Zienkiewicz, O. C. and J. Z. Zhu (1987). A simple error estimator and adaptive procedure
  for practical engineering analysis, *International Journal for Numerical Methods in
  Engineering.* **24**, 337–357.
Zienkiewicz, O. C. and J. Z. Zhu (1992). The superconvergent patch recovery and a
  posteriori error estimates, Part 2: Error estimates and adaptivity, *International
  Journal for Numerical Methods in Engineering.* **33**, 1365–1382.

9

Solution adaptation

The previous chapter focused on the estimation of numerical errors and uncertainties due to the discretization. In addition to estimating the discretization error, we also desire methods for reducing it when either it is found to be too large or when the solutions are not yet in the asymptotic range and therefore the error estimates are not reliable. Applying systematic mesh refinement, although required for assessing the reliability of all discretization error estimation approaches, is not the most efficient method for reducing the discretization error. Since systematic refinement, by definition, refines by the same factor over the entire domain, it generally results in meshes with highly-refined cells or elements in regions where they are not needed. Recall that for 3-D scientific computing applications, each time the mesh is refined using grid halving (a refinement factor of two), the number of cells/elements increases by a factor of eight. Thus systematic refinement for reducing discretization error can be prohibitively expensive.

Targeted, local solution adaptation is a much better strategy for *reducing* the discretization error. After a discussion of factors affecting the discretization error, this chapter then addresses the two main aspects of solution adaptation:

(1) methods for determining which regions should be adapted and
(2) methods for accomplishing the adaption.

This chapter concludes with a comparison of different approaches for driving mesh adaptation for a simple 1-D scalar problem.

9.1 Factors affecting the discretization error

There are three factors that affect the discretization error for uniform meshes: the chosen discretization scheme, the mesh resolution, and the local solution behavior (including solution derivatives). For nonuniform meshes, the mesh quality also plays a role. This section begins with a review of the relationship between the discretization error and the truncation error that was initially developed in Chapter 5. Then the truncation error is examined for a simple finite difference numerical scheme applied to the 1-D Burgers' equation; first on a uniform mesh and then on a nonuniform mesh using a global transformation. The truncation error developed in transformed coordinates clearly shows the interplay between mesh

343

resolution, mesh quality, and the solution behavior for the chosen discretization scheme. Implications for anisotropic mesh adaption are also discussed.

9.1.1 Relating discretization error to truncation error

Recall that in Chapter 8 we derived both the continuous discretization error transport equation (Eq. (8.30)) and the discrete discretization error transport equation (Eq. (8.32)). These equations are repeated here for convenience

$$L(\varepsilon_h) = -TE_h(u_h), \tag{9.1}$$

$$L_h(\varepsilon_h) = -TE_h(\tilde{u}), \tag{9.2}$$

where $L(\cdot)$ is the original (continuous) mathematical operator and $L_h(\cdot)$ is the discrete operator. These error transport equations can only be derived if the operators are linear or have been linearized. These two equations show that the discretization error can be both locally generated by the truncation error and also transported from other regions of the domain. Transport error is often called pollution error by the finite element community. Since the truncation error serves as the local source in the discretization error transport equations, reducing the truncation error should result in a commensurate reduction in the discretization error. Furthermore, any solution adaptation scheme should adapt only on the locally-generated error and not on the error transported from other regions in the domain.

9.1.2 1-D truncation error analysis on uniform meshes

The process of examining the truncation error first requires that a mathematical model be defined along with its discrete approximation. Consider the steady-state form of Burgers' equation given by

$$L(\tilde{u}) = \tilde{u}\frac{d\tilde{u}}{dx} - v\frac{d^2\tilde{u}}{dx^2} = 0, \tag{9.3}$$

where the first term is a nonlinear convection term, the second term is a diffusion term (multiplied by the constant viscosity v), and $\tilde{u}$ is the exact solution to this differential equation.

A simple second-order accurate finite difference discretization for the steady-state Burgers' equation is

$$L_h(u_h) = u_i\left(\frac{u_{i+1} - u_{i-1}}{2\Delta x}\right) - v\left(\frac{u_{i+1} - 2u_i + u_{i-1}}{\Delta x^2}\right) = 0, \tag{9.4}$$

where u_h denotes the exact solution to this discrete equation where we have assumed a Cartesian mesh with constant node spacing $h = \Delta x$. To find the truncation error associated with this discretization method, we first find the Taylor series expansions of u_{i+1} and u_{i-1}

expanded about u_i:

$$u_{i+1} = u_i + \frac{du}{dx}\bigg|_i \Delta x + \frac{d^2 u}{dx^2}\bigg|_i \frac{\Delta x^2}{2} + \frac{d^3 u}{dx^3}\bigg|_i \frac{\Delta x^3}{6} + \frac{d^4 u}{dx^4}\bigg|_i \frac{\Delta x^4}{24} + O\left[\Delta x^5\right], \qquad (9.5)$$

$$u_{i-1} = u_i - \frac{du}{dx}\bigg|_i \Delta x + \frac{d^2 u}{dx^2}\bigg|_i \frac{\Delta x^2}{2} - \frac{d^3 u}{dx^3}\bigg|_i \frac{\Delta x^3}{6} + \frac{d^4 u}{dx^4}\bigg|_i \frac{\Delta x^4}{24} + O\left[\Delta x^5\right]. \qquad (9.6)$$

Plugging these expansions into the discrete operator $L_h(\cdot)$ and rearranging gives

$$L_h(u) = \underbrace{u_i \frac{du}{dx}\bigg|_i - \nu \frac{d^2 u}{dx^2}\bigg|_i}_{L(u)} + \underbrace{u_i \frac{d^3 u}{dx^3}\bigg|_i \frac{\Delta x^2}{6} - \nu \frac{d^4 u}{dx^4}\bigg|_i \frac{\Delta x^2}{12} + O\left[\Delta x^4\right]}_{TE_h(u)}. \qquad (9.7)$$

The right hand side of Eq. (9.7) can be thought of as the actual differential equation that is represented by the discretization scheme. It contains the original partial differential equation, higher-order derivatives of the solution, and coefficients which are functions of the grid spacing to different powers. Since the leading terms are on the order of Δx^2, we find that the formal order of accuracy of this method is second order. Equation (9.7) also tells us that this discretization is consistent since the discrete equations approach the partial differential equation in the limit as Δx goes to zero. Equation (9.7) can be rewritten as the *generalized truncation error expression* (developed in Chapter 5) by employing our operator notation:

$$L_h(u) = L(u) + TE_h(u). \qquad (9.8)$$

Equation (9.8) states that the discretized equation is equal to the continuous mathematical model (in this case Burgers' equation) plus the truncation error (TE) associated with the discretization $h = \Delta x$. Note that in this form of the equation we have not specified the form that u will take. We will make extensive use of Eq. (9.8) in the following discussion.

9.1.3 1-D truncation error analysis on nonuniform meshes

One approach for examining the truncation error on nonuniform (anisotropic) meshes is to first perform a global transformation of the governing equation. An additional motivation for performing such a global transformation is that it will provide insight into the role of mesh quality on the solution discretization and truncation errors. Following Thompson *et al.* (1985) and Roy (2009), the first derivative in physical space can be transformed into a uniform computational space using the transformation $\xi = \xi(x)$ and the truncation error for the centered central difference method can be found as follows:

$$\frac{du}{dx} = \frac{1}{x_\xi}\frac{du}{d\xi} = \underbrace{\frac{1}{x_\xi}\left(\frac{u_{i+1} - u_{i-1}}{2\Delta\xi}\right)}_{L_h(u)} - \underbrace{\frac{1}{6}\frac{x_{\xi\xi\xi}}{x_\xi}\frac{du}{dx}\Delta\xi^2}_{Small} - \underbrace{\frac{1}{2}x_{\xi\xi}\frac{d^2 u}{dx^2}\Delta\xi^2}_{Stretching}$$

where the $L(u)$ underbrace corresponds to $\frac{1}{x_\xi}\frac{du}{d\xi}$.

$$\qquad\qquad - \underbrace{\frac{1}{6}x_\xi^2\frac{d^3 u}{dx^3}\Delta\xi^2}_{Standard\ TE} + O(\Delta\xi^4). \qquad (9.9)$$

Here we have assumed a fixed transformation $\xi = \xi(x)$ and thus $\Delta\xi \to 0$ with systematic mesh refinement. The derivatives of x with respect to ξ (e.g., x_ξ, $x_{\xi\xi}$) are called metrics of the transformation and are functions only of the mesh transformation itself. On the right hand side of this equation, the first term is the finite difference equation in transformed coordinates, the second term involving $x_{\xi\xi\xi}$ is zero when the discrete form of the metrics is used with the same central difference approximation (Mastin, 1999), the third term involving $x_{\xi\xi}$ is a grid stretching term, and the fourth term involving the square of x_ξ is the standard leading truncation error term that appears when the equations are discretized on a uniform mesh. The higher order terms (order $\Delta\xi^4$ and higher) can be neglected in the limit as the mesh spacing goes to zero. The grid stretching term is zero for a uniformly spaced mesh, but gets large as the mesh is stretched (e.g., from coarse to fine spacing).

This approach for examining the truncation error of the transformed equation illustrates some important features of the truncation error for anisotropic meshes. First, the truncation error is affected by the mesh resolution ($\Delta\xi$), the mesh quality ($x_{\xi\xi}$), and the local solution derivatives. Second, the quality of a mesh can only be assessed in the context of the local solution behavior and the mesh resolution since the grid stretching term $x_{\xi\xi}$ is multiplied by the second derivative of the solution and $\Delta\xi^2$.

In a similar manner, the truncation error for the second-order accurate centered second derivative in non-conservative form is:

$$
\frac{d^2u}{dx^2} = \overbrace{\frac{1}{x_\xi^2}\frac{d^2u}{d\xi^2} - \frac{x_{\xi\xi}}{x_\xi^3}\frac{du}{d\xi}}^{L(u)} = \overbrace{\frac{1}{x_\xi^2}\left(\frac{u_{i+1} - 2u_i + u_{i-1}}{\Delta\xi^2}\right) - \frac{x_{\xi\xi}}{x_\xi^3}\left(\frac{u_{i+1} - u_{i-1}}{2\Delta\xi}\right)}^{L_h(u)}
$$

$$
+ \frac{1}{12}\overbrace{\left(\frac{2x_{\xi\xi}x_{\xi\xi\xi} - x_\xi x_{\xi\xi\xi\xi}}{x_\xi^3}\right)}^{\text{Small}}\frac{du}{dx}\Delta\xi^2 + \frac{1}{12}\overbrace{\left(\frac{3x_{\xi\xi}^2 - 4x_\xi x_{\xi\xi\xi}}{x_\xi^2}\right)}^{\text{Small}}\frac{d^2u}{dx^2}\Delta\xi^2
$$

$$
- \underbrace{\frac{1}{3}x_{\xi\xi}\frac{d^3u}{dx^3}\Delta\xi^2}_{\text{Stretching}} - \underbrace{\frac{1}{12}x_\xi^2\frac{d^4u}{dx^4}\Delta\xi^2}_{\text{Standard TE}} + O(\Delta\xi^4). \tag{9.10}
$$

The third and fourth terms on the right hand side will usually be small when the discrete form of the metrics and smooth transformations are used. The fifth term involving $x_{\xi\xi}$ is a grid stretching term and the sixth term is the standard leading truncation error term that appears when the equations are discretized in physical space on a uniform grid.

Combining these two truncation error expressions and neglecting the small terms results in the following truncation error expression for the transformed Burgers' equation:

$$
u\frac{du}{dx} - v\frac{d^2u}{dx^2} = \overbrace{\left(\frac{u}{x_\xi} + \frac{vx_{\xi\xi}}{x_\xi^3}\right)\frac{du}{d\xi} - \frac{v}{x_\xi^2}\frac{d^2u}{d\xi^2}}^{L(u)}
$$

$$
= \overbrace{\left(\frac{u_i}{x_\xi} + \frac{vx_{\xi\xi}}{x_\xi^3}\right)\left(\frac{u_{i+1}-u_{i-1}}{2\Delta\xi}\right) - \frac{v}{x_\xi^2}\left(\frac{u_{i+1}-2u_i+u_{i-1}}{\Delta\xi^2}\right)}^{L_h(u)}
$$

$$
+ \underbrace{x_{\xi\xi}\left(\frac{v}{3}\frac{d^3u}{dx^3} - \frac{u_i}{2}\frac{d^2u}{dx^2}\right)\Delta\xi^2}_{\text{Stretching}} + \underbrace{x_\xi^2\left(\frac{v}{12}\frac{d^4u}{dx^4} - \frac{u_i}{6}\frac{d^3u}{dx^3}\right)\Delta\xi^2}_{\text{Standard TE}} + O(\Delta\xi^4).
$$

$$(9.11)$$

Thus the truncation error for second-order accurate central differences applied to Burgers' equation contains two types of term. The first is due to mesh quality (stretching in 1-D) and the second is due to the mesh resolution. For a uniform grid, the mesh stretching term is zero and the standard truncation error terms are exactly equal to the truncation error for Burgers' equation discretized in physical space on a uniform grid as given in Eq. (9.7).

Extending these mesh transformation procedures to higher dimensions results in additional truncation error terms related to the mesh quality such as mesh skewness, aspect ratio, etc. (Mastin, 1999). While the above procedures rely on a global transformation of the mathematical model, similar procedures could be developed for unstructured grid methods which rely on local transformations centered about each cell or element.

9.1.4 Isotropic versus anisotropic mesh adaptation

As shown above, the mesh quality plays a role in the truncation error which acts as the local source term for the discretization error. Some argue that isotropic (i.e., uniform or nearly uniform) meshes should be used in order to minimize the impact of the mesh quality on the solution. However, examination of Eq. (9.11), developed for the steady Burgers' equation, shows that the mesh quality (mesh stretching in this case) appears in the truncation error multiplied by second and third derivatives of the solution. Therefore, in regions where these solution derivatives are small, large variations in mesh stretching can be tolerated. Alternatively, the magnitude of the mesh stretching term can be reduced by increasing the mesh resolution. In our opinion, these two observations provide a sound argument for allowing significant mesh anisotropy in regions where the solution is well behaved or there is significant mesh clustering.

Two examples are now given for hyperbolic problems that employ mesh adaptation with large anisotropy. The first example is from Laflin (1997) who examined laminar hypersonic flow over a compression corner using structured grids. Figure 9.1a shows the adapted mesh and Figure 9.1b the Mach number contours. The hyperbolic free-stream region, where no

(a)

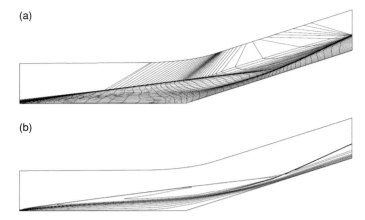

(b)

Figure 9.1 Example of anisotropic mesh adaption using structured grids for the laminar hypersonic flow over a compression corner: (a) r-adapted mesh and (b) Mach number contours (reproduced from Laflin, 1997).

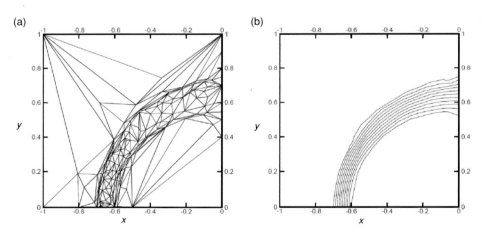

Figure 9.2 Example of anisotropic mesh adaption using unstructured grids for a 2-D linear advection equation: (a) r-adapted mesh and (b) velocity contours (reproduced from Wood and Kleb, 1999).

solution gradients occur, is contained by a single layer of large, high-aspect ratio, skewed cells. While these cells have very poor mesh quality, the fact that there are no gradients in this region means that no discretization errors are introduced. The second example is from Wood and Kleb (1999) who examined the 2-D linear wave equation using unstructured mesh adaptation. The adapted mesh is given in Figure 9.2a and the corresponding solution in Figure 9.2b. Again the mesh is extremely anisotropic away from the gradient regions and clustered only in the regions of the solution variation.

9.2 Adaptation criteria

One of the most difficult aspects of solution adaptation is finding a good criterion for driving the adaptation process. The least defensible methods for adaptation are based on either solution features or estimates of the discretization error. Another approach based on higher-order reconstructions of solution values or gradients (e.g., finite element recovery methods) is also commonly used. The most rigorous methods are based on evaluating or estimating the local truncation error, or equivalently the residual (e.g., from finite elements). We refer to these latter approaches as residual-based methods, and they account for the local cell/element contributions to the discretization error. In their basic form, residual-based methods, and to a lesser extent, the reconstruction methods, can provide for only globally "good" discrete solutions. For adaptation targeted to a specific system response quantity, an adjoint problem must also be solved in order to find the sensitivity of the discretization error in the system response quantity to the local errors generated at each cell/element.

9.2.1 Solution features

A commonly-used method for driving the solution adaptation process is to use solution features such as solution gradients, solution curvature, or even specific solution features to drive the adaptation process. When there is only one dominant feature to be resolved in a problem, then feature-based adaptation can often improve the solution. However, when multiple features are present (e.g., shock waves, expansion fans, contact discontinuities, and boundary layers in a compressible flow problem), feature-based adaptation often results in some features being over-refined while other features are not refined enough. In such cases, feature-based adaptation can fail "disastrously" (Ainsworth and Oden, 2000). An example of the failure of solution gradient-based adaptation is given in Section 9.2.5.

9.2.2 Discretization error

Since it is the discretization error that one wishes to reduce with solution adaptation, on the surface it might appear the discretization error, or perhaps its estimate, would serve as an appropriate driver for the adaption process. However, as will be shown later, the total discretization error is not an appropriate solution adaption criterion. One should instead adapt based on the *local contributions* to the discretization error, i.e., the truncation error. Due to the fact that the discretization error is also transported (i.e., convected and diffused) from other regions of the domain, it is possible that the total discretization error may be large in a region where the local contributions to the discretization error are small (e.g., near, but not at, a singularity). Similarly, it is possible for the total discretization error to be small even when the local contribution to the discretization error is large. For these reasons, adaptation based on the total discretization error is not recommended.

An example of the failure of mesh adaptation based on the total discretization error was given by Gu and Shih (2001) who examined the flow in an incompressible lid-driven cavity.

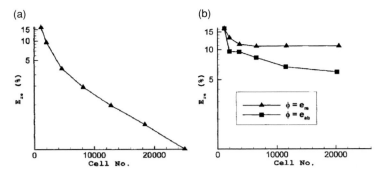

Figure 9.3 Example of Cartesian grid-based *h*-adaptation for a lid-driven cavity: (a) uniform refinement and (b) refinement based on the total discretization error (reproduced from Gu and Shih, 2001).

The cavity aspect ratio (width to height) was two, and the Reynolds number based on the cavity width was 2000. Figure 9.3 shows the changes in the L1 norm of the discretization error in velocity with the total number of cells. For the case of uniform refinement (Figure 9.3a), the error was reduced at the expected formal order of accuracy of two with refinement. In the case of mesh adaptation (Figure 9.3b), the solutions were nonconvergent when the relative discretization error was used, whereas only a small error reduction occurred when the absolute discretization error was used. This example highlights the dangers of adapting based on total discretization error which also includes error transported from other regions.

9.2.3 Recovery methods

An error indicator that is frequently used for solution adaptation for finite element methods is gradient recovery or reconstruction. In this approach, gradients of the finite element solution are compared to the gradients found from post-processing patches of neighboring elements. Larger mismatches between these two gradient computations serve as an indicator of larger local errors. Recall from Chapter 8 that recovery-based methods in finite elements such as the superconvergent patch recovery (SPR) method (Zienkiewicz and Zhu, 1992a) can provide higher-order accurate estimates of the solution gradients when the superconvergence property is attained. In this case, the SPR error estimator will act like an estimator of the total discretization error in the solution gradients. One would thus expect the SPR method to be a poor criterion on which to base a solution adaptation strategy; however, as was the case for discretization error estimation, the SPR method has been shown to be effective for driving solution adaptation, at least for elliptic problems (Ainsworth and Oden, 2000).

An example of mesh adaptation based on the SPR method in a linear elasticity problem was given by Zienkiewicz and Zhu (1992b). They examined an L-shaped domain in a plane stress condition as shown in Figure 9.4a. For this problem, the SPR method will provide local estimates of the discretization error in the stresses. By using adaptive remeshing with

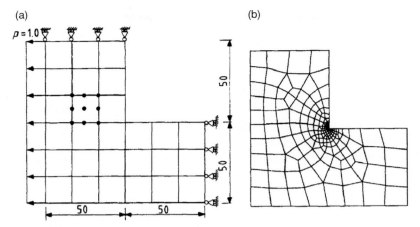

Figure 9.4 Application of the SPR recovery-based error estimator for estimating plane stress in an L-shaped linear elastic domain: (a) problem set up and initial mesh and (b) final adapted mesh with 229 elements (reproduced from Zienkiewicz and Zhu, 1992b).

h-refinement (discussed in Section 9.3), an adapted mesh with 229 elements is shown in Figure 9.4b with maximum discretization errors in the stress of under 1%. For an application of the SPR method to compressible turbulent flows with adaptive remeshing, see Ilinca *et al.* (1998).

Laflin (1997) and McRae and Laflin (1999) have developed a similar driver for adaptation based on solution interpolation error. The implementation along with *r*-adaptation (see Section 9.3.2.2) on structured meshes has been successful for a wide range of 2-D problems. The basic idea behind the approach is that the solution values are compared to values interpolated from a patch of neighboring cells. One difference between their approach and finite element-based recovery methods described above is that they deal with solution values rather than solution gradients. Examples of meshes and solutions found using their solution interpolation error approach along with *r*-adaptation were given in Figure 9.1; an additional example will be presented later in Figure 9.12. Both examples show a significant amount of anisotropic mesh adaptation.

9.2.4 Truncation error/residuals

The formal relationship between the discretization error and the truncation error comes from the discretization error transport equations discussed earlier. It was shown that the truncation error provides the local element's contribution to the discretization error. As such, the truncation error is a good indicator of where mesh adaptation should occur. The general concept behind truncation error-based adaptation is to reduce the truncation error where its magnitude is large in order to reduce the total discretization error. Baker (1997) notes that although the idea of truncation error-based adaptation is fundamentally sound, it has "surprisingly" seen little use. The factors affecting the truncation error for a given discretization scheme include the element size, mesh quality, and the local solution behavior.

9.2.4.1 General truncation error/residual-based methods

For simple discretization schemes, the truncation error can be computed directly. For more complex schemes where direct evaluation of the truncation error is difficult, an approach for its estimation is needed. Three approaches for estimating the truncation error were discussed in the last chapter in the context of error transport equations for estimating the discretization error. In the first approach, the exact solution to the mathematical model (or an approximation thereof) is substituted into the discretized equations, with the nonzero remainder (i.e., the discrete residual) approximating the truncation error. This approach has been used by Berger and Jameson (1985) for the Euler equations in fluid dynamics by approximating the exact solution to the mathematical model using Richardson extrapolation. In the second approach for estimating the truncation error, the exact solution to the discrete equations is inserted into the continuous mathematical model equations. This continuous residual can be easily evaluated if a continuous representation of the discrete solution is available, for example, in the finite element method. In fact, this is exactly the residual used in the finite element method, which measures how well the finite element solution satisfies the weak form of the mathematical model. The final approach for estimating the truncation error is to approximate it with any extra numerical dissipation used to stabilize the computations. The upwind schemes used for compressible flow problems fall into this category since any upwind scheme can be written as a central difference scheme plus a numerical diffusion term (e.g., see Hirsch, 1990).

9.2.4.2 Finite element residual-based methods

The residual-based methods for estimating discretization error in finite element solutions discussed in the last chapter also provide estimates of the local contributions to the total discretization error. The initial formulation of residual-based methods, including their use for mesh adaptation, was given by Babuska and Rheinboldt (1978a,b). Since explicit residual methods neglect the transported component of the error, their local behavior makes them suitable for solution adaptation. Implicit residual methods directly treat both the local and the transported components of the discretization error that appear in the residual equation. When applied in the context of solution adaptation, only the local component should be used. A review of explicit and implicit residual methods for solution adaption is given by Verfurth (1999), who also addresses recovery-based methods and hierarchical bases.

Stewart and Hughes (1996) provide an example of an explicit residual method applied to the Helmholtz equation for acoustic applications. The specific case examined is nonuniform acoustic radiation in an infinite rigid cylinder. They note that when used for mesh adaptation, the global constant in the explicit residual-based error estimates need not be computed, thus saving computational effort. Adaption is performed using adaptive remeshing (see

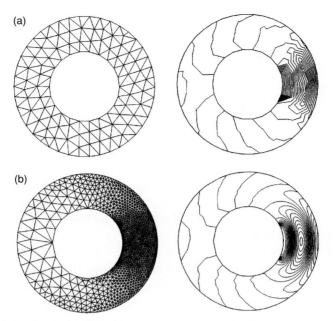

Figure 9.5 Nonuniform acoustic radiation in an infinite rigid cylinder: (a) initial uniform mesh and solution and (b) adapted mesh and solution (reproduced from Stewart and Hughes, 1996).

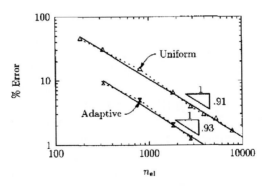

Figure 9.6 Global energy norms of the discretization error with increasing number of elements for both uniform and adaptive mesh refinement for acoustic radiation in an infinite rigid cylinder (reproduced from Stewart and Hughes, 1996).

Section 9.3.1). The initial uniform mesh and solution are presented in Figure 9.5a, while an adapted mesh and solution using five levels of refinement are given in Figure 9.5b. It is clear that the solution is significantly better resolved with adaptation. Figure 9.6 shows the behavior of the global energy norm of the discretization error with both uniform and adaptive mesh refinement, and both approaches appear to converge at close to the formal order of accuracy of two. To achieve global energy norms of 1%, the adaptive procedure requires fewer than 4000 elements, whereas approximately 13 000 elements are required for uniform mesh refinement.

9.2.5 *Adjoint-based adaptation*

A promising approach for solution adaptation to reduce the discretization error in a system response quantity is the adjoint method. Most adjoint methods for mesh adaptation use the truncation error/residual weighted by the adjoint sensitivities as indicators of where mesh adaptation should occur (see Section 8.2.2.3). Adjoint methods thus provide targeted mesh adaption for the chosen system response quantity. The main drawback to adjoint methods is their complexity and code intrusiveness, as evidenced by the fact that adjoint-based adaption has not yet found its way into commercial scientific computing codes. This section provides examples of adjoint-based adaptation methods based on the truncation error/residual or approximations thereof.

An example of a truncation error approximation method combined with an adjoint method for system response quantities is given by Dwight (2008), who considered the inviscid transonic flow over an airfoil using an unstructured finite-volume discretization. The discretization scheme employed a central-type flux quadrature combined with an artificial viscosity method for numerical stability. The adjoint method was formulated to provide the sensitivities of the total drag force to the numerical parameters used in the artificial viscosity stabilization technique. The underlying assumption is that these sensitivities will be large where the artificial viscosity is large and thus dominates the standard central-type truncation error terms.

Figure 9.7 shows the discretization error in the drag coefficient as a function of the number of nodes. Uniform refinement (squares) shows second-order convergence on the coarser grids, then a reduction to first order on the finer grids, likely due to the presence of the shock discontinuities (e.g., see Banks *et al.*, 2008). Feature-based adaptation using solution gradients (triangles) initially shows a reduction in the discretization error for the drag coefficient, but then subsequent adaptation steps show an increase in the error. The adjoint-based artificial dissipation estimators give the best results, especially when the drag coefficient is corrected by its discretization error estimate (circles).

The adapted grids for the gradient-based and adjoint-based adaption strategies are given in Figure 9.8a and b, respectively. The gradient-based adaptation refines the shock waves on the upper and lower surface as well as the region downstream of the trailing edge. The adjoint-based method also refines the mesh near the surface and in the region above the airfoil containing the two acoustic waves that emanate from the leading edge region and impinge on the trailing edge. In many cases, the mesh resulting from adjoint-based adaptation can be used to provide insight into the physical mechanisms that impact a given system response quantity, in this case the importance of the acoustic waves in determining the airfoil drag.

Another example of adjoint-based adaptation used to reduce discretization errors in a viscous, compressible flow problem was given by Venditti and Darmofal (2003). They used

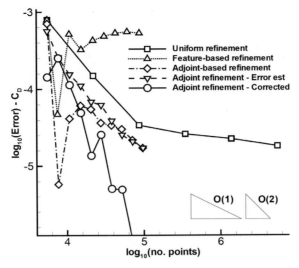

Figure 9.7 Discretization error in the drag coefficient for transonic flow over an airfoil comparing uniform refinement, local gradient-based adaptation, and adjoint, artificial dissipation-based adaptation (reproduced from Dwight, 2008).

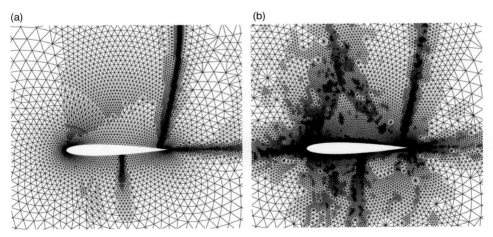

Figure 9.8 Adapted grids for transonic flow over an airfoil: (a) solution gradient-based adaptation and (b) adaptation with an adjoint-based artificial dissipation estimator for the drag force (reproduced from Dwight, 2008).

an unstructured grid finite volume scheme, and examined both the laminar and turbulent viscous flow over an airfoil. Their study also included a comparison to feature-based adaptation using the solution curvature (Hessian). A plot of the drag versus the number of mesh nodes is presented in Figure 9.9. The adjoint- (output-) based adaption converges much faster with mesh adaptation than the solution curvature-based (Hessian) method.

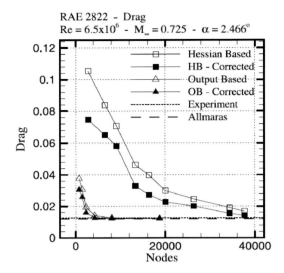

Figure 9.9 Drag for viscous transonic flow over an airfoil using solution curvature-based (Hessian) and adjoint-based adaptation (reproduced from Venditti and Darmofal, 2003).

The adapted grids for this case are presented in Figure 9.10 and show that adjoint-based adaptation results in significantly different final adapted meshes.

Rannacher and Suttmeier (1997) examined the case of a square elastic disk with a crack subjected to a constant boundary traction acting along a portion of the upper boundary as shown in Figure 9.11a. They then employed an explicit residual method both alone and combined with an adjoint method to drive a mesh adaptation routine. The system response quantity for the example shown here was the average normal stress over the clamped bottom and right boundaries. Final adapted meshes for the residual-based adaption and the adjoint method are given in Figure 9.11b and c, respectively. While both approaches adapted to the crack tip (near the center), the adjoint method also adapted to the lower boundary. The adjoint-based adaption was found to provide much lower discretization error levels in the average normal stress than the residual-based adaption. In fact, the adjoint-based method achieved similar error levels as the 65 000 elements residual-based method using under 9000 elements.

9.3 Adaptation approaches

Once the approach for driving the adaptation process has been implemented, the end result is typically a weighting function that varies over the spatial domain. In some cases, the weighting function may be a vector quantity indicating directionality preferences for the adaptation. With the weighting function in hand, local solution adaptation can be achieved in a variety of different ways. Adaptive remeshing generally starts with a coarse mesh, then

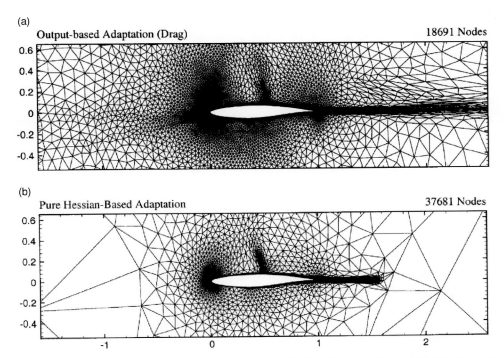

Figure 9.10 Adapted grids for subsonic flow over an airfoil: (a) adjoint-based adaptation for drag and (b) solution curvature-based (Hessian) adaptation (reproduced from Venditti and Darmofal, 2003).

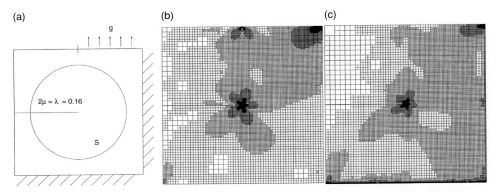

Figure 9.11 Linear elasticity considering the average normal stress over the clamped boundaries: (a) problem set up showing the crack emanating from the center and extending to the left boundary, (b) final mesh for residual-based adaption, and (c) final mesh for adjoint-based adaption (reproduced from Rannacher and Suttmeier, 1997).

employs a mesh generation tool in a recursive manner to improve the mesh. Alternatively, one could seek to adapt the mesh by adding additional cells/elements (*h*-adaptation) or moving them from one region to another while maintaining the original mesh connectivity (*r*-adaptation). Order refinement (*p*-adaptation) increases the formal order of accuracy of the discretization scheme in regions of high weighting function. Hybrid combinations of these approaches are also used such as mixed *h* and *r* adaption (mesh movement and refinement) and mixed *h* and *p* adaption (e.g., the *hp*-version of finite elements). For general unstructured grid methods, adaptive remeshing and *h*-adaptation are the most popular. For structured grid methods, the *r*-adaption approach is the most common since *h*-adaptation cannot be performed locally due to the required i, j, k ordering of the mesh. In addition to mesh refinement, other issues that should be considered when adapting a mesh are mesh quality, local solution behavior, and the alignment of the element faces.

9.3.1 *Adaptive remeshing*

Initial approaches to adaptation were based on adaptive remeshing, where a grid generation tool (often the same one used to create the initial mesh) is employed to adaptively improve the mesh. The weighting functions are usually accounted for as constraints in the remeshing process. An early example of adaptive remeshing for compressible fluid flow problems was given by Peraire *et al.* (1987), while a more recent application for solid mechanics is given by Bugeda (2006).

9.3.2 *Mesh adaptation*

There are two approaches for adapting a mesh that are not based on remeshing. Mesh refinement (*h*-adaptation) selectively sub-divides cells where the weighting function is large, and possibly coarsening cells where it is small. Mesh movement (*r*-adaptation) maintains the same number of nodes and node-to-node connectivity, but moves elements towards regions targeted for adaptation. In some cases, both procedures are used together in a mixed *h*- and *r*-adaptation process. These approaches to mesh adaptation are discussed below.

9.3.2.1 *Local mesh refinement/coarsening (h-adaptation)*

Local mesh refinement, or *h*-adaptation, is achieved by sub-dividing cells that have been targeted for refinement. One usually starts with an initial coarse mesh, and then begins refining, and possibly coarsening (a process known as agglomeration) the mesh in an iterative manner. The total number of local mesh refinement levels is usually specified, for example, by allowing a coarse grid cell to be refined up to a maximum of six times. Another constraint that is often used is that neighboring cells should be within one level of refinement of each other. This prevents the possibility of having a highly-refined cell adjacent to an extremely coarse cell. In some cases, *h*-adaptation employs edge swapping

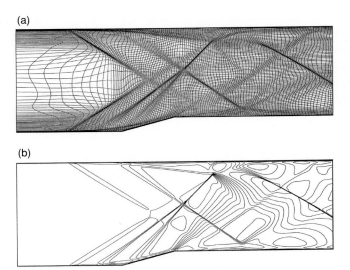

Figure 9.12 Structured grid adaptation for laminar flow through a supersonic inlet: (a) *r*-adapted mesh and (b) density contours (reproduced from McRae, 2000).

where the edge connecting two cells is moved to either improve mesh quality or to better align the faces with the solution features. One drawback of using pure *h*-adaptation is that the mesh quality is adversely affected at the interface between adapted and unadapted regions since the ratio of adjacent cell length scales (i.e., stretching factor) approaches two.

9.3.2.2 *Mesh movement (r-adaptation)*

Mesh movement, or *r*-adaptation, is more common in structured grids since local mesh refinement (*h*-adaptation) by sub-dividing cells results in an unstructured mesh. When mesh movement is used, the current number of cells and the mesh connectivity is retained, but cells/elements are moved in space according to the weighting function. The most common approaches for achieving mesh movement (Burg, 2006) are:

(1) the Laplacian and modified Laplacian (i.e., elliptic adaptation),
(2) the linear elasticity equations,
(3) the linear spring analogy,
(4) the torsional spring analogy, and
(5) variational methods.

An example of mesh movement is given in Figure 9.12 for laminar flow in a supersonic inlet (McRae, 2000). An elliptic adaption scheme is used based on the solution interpolation error, which is then modified to include grid quality measures. The figure shows both the solution adapted mesh and the density contours. The shock wave formed by the compression ramp separates the laminar boundary layer, leading to another shock forming upstream.

The impingement of these combined shocks on the upper wall also causes the upper-wall boundary layer to separate, producing another shock that emanates from the top wall. It is interesting to note that the shock waves and the boundary layers are clearly evident simply by examining the mesh. The mesh used in this example consists of only 121×91 nodes and the solution was found to provide similar solution quality to one computed on a mesh with approximately 700×900 evenly spaced (i.e., nearly isotropic) cells.

9.3.2.3 Mixed mesh refinement (r- and h-adaptation)

A number of researchers have found that a combination of different solution adaptation strategies provides the best approach for reducing discretization error. For example, Baker (2005) found a combination of local mesh refinement/coarsening and mesh movement to be effective for temporally varying (i.e., unsteady) problems on unstructured meshes.

9.3.3 Order refinement (p-adaptation)

Order refinement (or p-adaptation) can also be used to adaptively improve the solution. Order refinement consists of increasing the formal order of accuracy of the discretization scheme in regions targeted for refinement. While this approach is natural to implement with the p-version of finite elements, applying it to finite difference and finite volume discretizations is more difficult due to the difficulties of formulating higher-order discretizations for both the governing equations and the boundary conditions. In the finite element method, p-adaption and h-adaption are often combined in what is known as hp-adaptive finite elements. For a review of hp-adaptive finite elements, see Patra and Oden (1997).

9.4 Comparison of methods for driving mesh adaptation

The following example compares four different strategies for driving mesh adaption for the 1-D steady Burgers' equation (Roy, 2009). The approach used for adapting the mesh is an r-adaptation procedure where the nodal points are assumed to be connected by linear springs (e.g., see Gnoffo, 1982). The strength of these springs is specified by the weighting function, which is in turn determined by the chosen strategy for driving the adaptation. Four different strategies are examined:

- solution gradients,
- solution curvature,
- discretization error, and
- truncation error.

The first two approaches are both feature-based methods. The discretization error-based adaption is implemented in an exact manner since the exact solution to the mathematical model is available. The truncation error for this case was developed in Section 9.1.3 for the nonuniform mesh encountered during the r-adaptation process. The derivatives appearing in the truncation error are evaluated using finite-difference expressions formulated in transformed coordinates. The availability of an exact solution to the mathematical model is crucial for the unambiguous assessment of different adaptation strategies.

9.4.1 Mathematical model

The steady Burgers' equation is a quasi-linear ordinary differential equation of the form

$$u\frac{\mathrm{d}u}{\mathrm{d}x} = \nu\frac{\mathrm{d}^2 u}{\mathrm{d}x^2}, \tag{9.12}$$

where $u(x)$ is a scalar velocity field, x is the position, and ν is the viscosity. Since mesh adaptation will be used, we employ a global transformation $\xi = \xi(x)$ onto uniformly spaced computational coordinates. The steady-state form of Burgers' equation in transformed coordinates is thus

$$\left(\frac{u}{x_\xi} + \frac{\nu x_{\xi\xi}}{x_\xi^3}\right)\frac{\mathrm{d}u}{\mathrm{d}\xi} - \frac{\nu}{x_\xi^2}\frac{\mathrm{d}^2 u}{\mathrm{d}\xi^2} = 0, \tag{9.13}$$

where x_ξ and $x_{\xi\xi}$ are metrics of the mesh transformation. Since Burgers' equation in transformed coordinates is mathematically equivalent to the equation in physical coordinates, the exact solution discussed below will solve both forms of Burgers' equation.

9.4.2 Exact solution

We employ the steady-state viscous shock wave exact solution for the results presented here (Benton and Platzman, 1972). Dirichlet boundary conditions are used as found from the exact solution, which is given by

$$u'(x) = \frac{-2\sinh(x')}{\cosh(x')}, \tag{9.14}$$

where the prime denotes a non-dimensional variable. The Reynolds number for Burgers' equation can be defined as

$$\mathrm{Re} = \frac{u_{\mathrm{ref}} L_{\mathrm{ref}}}{\nu}, \tag{9.15}$$

where u_{ref} is taken as the maximum value for $u(x, t)$ in the domain (here $u_{\mathrm{ref}} = 2$ m/s), L_{ref} is the domain width (here $L_{\mathrm{ref}} = 8$ m), and the choice for ν specifies the Reynolds number.

This exact solution can be related to dimensional quantities by the following transformations:

$$x' = x/L_{\mathrm{ref}} \quad \text{and} \quad u' = uL_{\mathrm{ref}}/\nu. \tag{9.16}$$

Furthermore, the exact solution is invariant to scaling by a constant α:

$$\bar{x} = x/\alpha \quad \text{and} \quad \bar{u} = \alpha u. \tag{9.17}$$

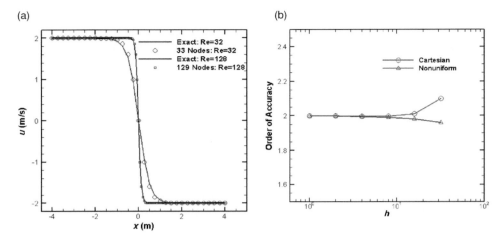

Figure 9.13 (a) Numerical and exact solutions for Burgers' equation in Cartesian coordinates for Reynolds numbers 32 and 128 and (b) order of accuracy of the L_2 norms of the discretization error for Reynolds number 8 (from Roy, 2009).

For simplicity, we find it convenient to solve Burgers' equation in dimensional coordinates on the physical domain -4 m $\leq x \leq 4$ m, choosing α such that the limiting u values vary between -2 m/s and 2 m/s.

9.4.3 Discretization approach

A fully implicit finite-difference code was developed to solve the steady-state form of Burgers' equation using the following discretization:

$$\left(\frac{u_i^n}{x_\xi} + \frac{\nu x_{\xi\xi}}{x_\xi^3}\right)\left(\frac{u_{i+1}^{n+1} - u_{i-1}^{n+1}}{2\Delta\xi}\right) - \frac{\nu}{x_\xi^2}\left(\frac{u_{i+1}^{n+1} - 2u_i^{n+1} + u_{i-1}^{n+1}}{\Delta\xi^2}\right) = 0. \qquad (9.18)$$

The nonlinear term is linearized and the resulting linear tridiagonal system is solved directly using the Thomas algorithm. This fully implicit method is formally second-order accurate in space for both the convection and diffusion terms, as was shown in Eq. (9.11). The resulting equations are iterated until the nonlinear system is converged to machine zero, an approximately 12 order of magnitude reduction in the iterative residual since double precision computations are used. Thus round-off and iterative error are neglected.

Numerical and exact solutions for Reynolds numbers of 32 and 128 are given in Figure 9.13a. These numerical solutions were computed on uniform meshes with 33 and 129 nodes for Re $= 32$ and 128, respectively. In order to verify the Burgers' equation code (see Chapter 5), numerical solutions were run for a Reynolds number of 8 using both uniform and nonuniform meshes. The choice of a lower Reynolds number for this code verification study was made to ensure that the convection and diffusion terms were of similar magnitude. The order of accuracy of the discrete L_2 norms of the discretization

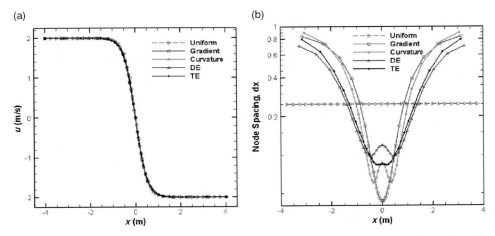

Figure 9.14 Different adaption schemes applied to Burgers' equation for Reynolds number 32: (a) numerical solutions and (b) local nodal spacing Δx (from Roy, 2009).

error is given in Figure 9.13b for increasingly refined meshes up to 513 nodes ($h = 1$). The numerical solutions quickly approach an observed order of accuracy of two with mesh refinement, thus providing evidence that there are no mistakes in the code which will affect the discretization error.

9.4.4 Results

In this section, different methods for driving the mesh adaption are analyzed and compared to the case without adaption (i.e., a uniform mesh). The four different methods for driving the mesh adaptation are: adaption based on solution gradients, adaption based on solution curvature, adaption based on the discretization error (DE), and adaption based on the truncation error (TE). Numerical solutions to the steady-state Burgers' equation for Reynolds number 32 are given in Figure 9.14a for the uniform mesh and the four mesh adaption approaches, all using 33 nodes. The final local node spacing is given in Figure 9.14b for each method and shows significant variations in the vicinity of the viscous shock ($x = 0$).

The discretization error is evaluated by subtracting the exact solution from the numerical solution. Figure 9.15a gives the discretization error for all five cases over the entire domain. The uniform mesh has the largest discretization error, while all mesh adaption approaches give discretization errors that are at least one-third of that from the uniform mesh. The different mesh adaption approaches are compared to each other in Figure 9.15b which shows an enlargement of the region $-2.5 \leq x \leq 0$. Note that the solutions and the discretization errors are all skew-symmetric about the origin, so we may concentrate on only one half of the domain. Truncation error-based adaption gives discretization errors that are less than half of that found from gradient-based adaption, while the other approaches fall in between the two.

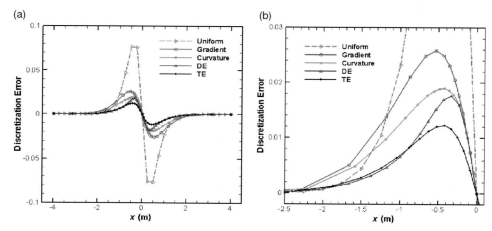

Figure 9.15 Discretization error for different adaptation schemes applied to Burgers' equation for Reynolds number 32: (a) entire domain and (b) enlargement of the region $-2.5 \leq x \leq 0$ (from Roy, 2009).

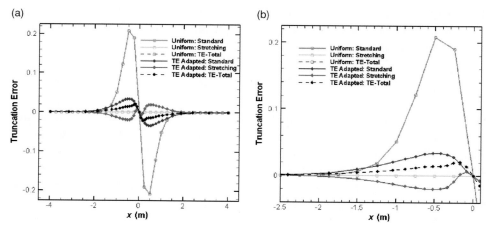

Figure 9.16 Truncation error for a uniform mesh and truncation error-based adaptation (TE) applied to Burgers' equation for Reynolds number 32: (a) entire domain and (b) enlargement of the region $-2.5 \leq x \leq 0$ (from Roy, 2009).

As discussed previously, the truncation error acts as a local source term for the discretization error. Thus it is also instructive to examine the truncation error and its components. The truncation error for the uniform mesh case and the case of truncation error-based adaption is given in Figure 9.16a. The truncation error terms shown are the standard truncation error term, the stretching term, and their sum (TE-Total) as defined by Eq. (9.11). For the uniform mesh, the stretching truncation error term is exactly zero, but the standard truncation error term is large. For the adapted case, the standard and stretching terms are much smaller,

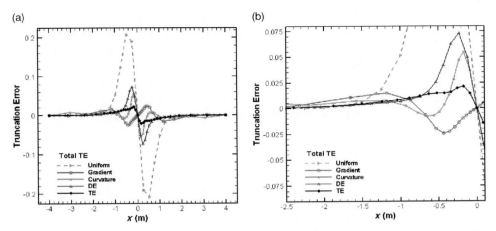

Figure 9.17 Total truncation error for various adaptation approaches applied to Burgers' equation for Reynolds number 32: (a) entire domain and (b) enlargement of the region $-2.5 \leq x \leq 0$ (from Roy, 2009).

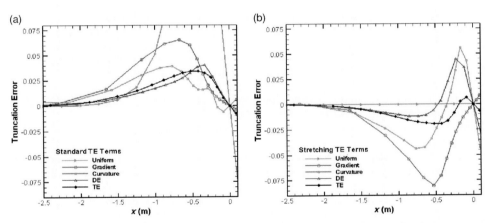

Figure 9.18 Truncation error terms for various adaptation approaches applied to Burgers' equation for Reynolds number 32: (a) standard terms and (b) stretching terms (from Roy, 2009).

and are generally of opposite sign, thus providing some truncation error cancellation. An enlarged view is presented in Figure 9.16b, which shows that the total truncation error (i.e., the sum of the standard and stretching terms) is an order of magnitude smaller for the adapted case than for the uniform mesh.

The total truncation error for all cases is shown in Figure 9.17a, with an enlargement showing only the adaption cases given in Figure 9.17b. The magnitude of the total truncation error is smallest and shows the smoothest variations for the truncation error-based adaption case, while the other three cases show spikes at either $x = -0.4$ m (gradient) or $x = -0.2$ m (DE and curvature).

The two components of the truncation error, the standard terms and the stretching terms, are given in Figure 9.18a and b, respectively. The standard truncation error terms are actually quite similar for all mesh adaption cases, with the gradient-based adaption showing a slightly larger magnitude than the other cases. The biggest differences are seen in the stretching truncation error terms (Figure 9.18b), where the feature-based adaption cases (gradient and curvature) show large mesh stretching contributions. The truncation error-based adaption approach provides the smallest magnitude of the truncation error due to mesh stretching.

9.5 References

Ainsworth, M. and J. T. Oden (2000). *A Posteriori Error Estimation in Finite Element Analysis*, New York, Wiley Interscience.

Babuska, I. (1986). *Accuracy Estimates and Adaptive Refinements in Finite Element Computations*, New York, Wiley.

Babuska, I. and W. C. Rheinboldt (1978a). A posteriori error estimates for the finite element method, *International Journal for Numerical Methods in Engineering.* **12**, 1597–1615.

Babuska, I. and W. C. Rheinboldt (1978b). Error estimates for adaptive finite element computations, *SIAM Journal of Numerical Analysis.* **15**(4), 736–754.

Babuska, I., T. Strouboulis, S. K. Gangaraj, and C. S. Upadhyay (1997). Pollution error in the h-version of the finite element method and local quality of the recovered derivatives, *Computer Methods in Applied Mechanics and Engineering.* **140**, 1–37.

Baker, T. J. (1997). Mesh adaptation strategies for problems in fluid dynamics, *Finite Elements in Analysis and Design*, **25**, 243–273.

Baker, T. J. (2005). Adaptive modification of time evolving meshes, *Computer Methods in Applied Mechanics and Engineering.* **194**, 4977–5001.

Bank, R. E. (1996). Hierarchical bases and the finite element method, *Acta Numerica.* **5**, 1–45.

Banks, J. W., T. Aslam, and W. J. Rider (2008). On sub-linear convergence for linearly degenerate waves in capturing schemes, *Journal of Computational Physics.* **227**, 6985–7002.

Benton, E. R. and G. W. Platzman (1972). A table of solutions of the one-dimensional Burgers' equation, *Quarterly of Applied Mathematics.* **30**, 195–212.

Berger, M. J. and A. Jameson (1985). Automatic adaptive grid refinement for the Euler equations. *AIAA Journal*, **23**(4), 561–568.

Bugeda, G. (2006). A new adaptive remeshing scheme based on the sensitivity analysis of the SPR point wise error estimation, *Computer Methods in Applied Mechanics and Engineering.* **195**(4–6), 462–478.

Burg, C. (2006). Analytic study of 2D and 3D grid motion using modified Laplacian, *International Journal for Numerical Methods in Fluids.* **52**, 163–197.

Dwight, R. P. (2008). Heuristic a posteriori estimation of error due to dissipation in finite volume schemes and application to mesh adaptation, *Journal of Computational Physics.* **227**(5), 2845–2863.

Gnoffo, P. (1982). *A Vectorized, Finite-Volume, Adaptive Grid Algorithm Applied to Planetary Entry Problems*, AIAA Paper 1982–1018.

Gu, X. and T. I.-P. Shih (2001). *Differentiating between Source and Location of Error for Solution-Adaptive Mesh Refinement*, AIAA Paper 2001–2660.

Hirsch, C. (1990). *Numerical Computation of Internal and External Flows: Volume 2, Computational Methods for Inviscid and Viscous Flows*, Chichester, Wiley.

Ilinca, F., D. Pelletier, and L. Ignat (1998). Adaptive finite element solution of compressible turbulent flows, *AIAA Journal*. **36**(12), 2187–2194.

Johnson, C. and P. Hansbo (1992). Adaptive finite element methods in computational mechanics, *Computer Methods in Applied Mechanics and Engineering*. **101**(1–3), 143–181.

Laflin, K. R. (1997). *Solver-Independent r-Refinement Adaptation for Dynamic Numerical Simulations*, Doctoral Thesis, North Carolina State University.

Mastin, C. W. (1999). Truncation error on structured grids, in *Handbook of Grid Generation*, J. F. Thompson, B. K. Soni, and N. P. Weatherill, eds., Boca Raton, CRC Press.

McRae, D. S. (2000). r-refinement grid adaptation algorithms and issues, *Computer Methods in Applied Mechanics and Engineering*. **189**, 1161–1182.

McRae, D. and K. R. Laflin (1999). Dynamic grid adaption and grid quality, in *Handbook of Grid Generation*, J. F. Thompson, B. K. Soni, and N. P. Wetherill, eds., Boca Raton, FL, CRC Press, 34-1–34-33.

Patra, A. and J. T. Oden (1997). Computational techniques for adaptive hp finite element methods, *Finite Elements in Analysis and Design*. **25**(1–2), 27–39.

Peraire, J., M. Vahdati, K. Morgan, and O. Zienkiewicz (1987). Adaptive remeshing for compressible flow computations, *Journal of Computational Physics*. **72**(2), 449–466.

Rannacher, R. and F. T. Suttmeier (1997). A feed-back approach to error control in finite element methods: application to linear elasticity, *Computational Mechanics*. **19**(5), 434–446.

Roy, C. J. (2003). Grid convergence error analysis for mixed-order numerical schemes, *AIAA Journal*. **41**(4), 595–604.

Roy, C. J. (2009). *Strategies for Driving Mesh Adaptation in CFD*, AIAA Paper 2009–1302.

Stewart, J. R. and T. J. R. Hughes (1996). A posteriori error estimation and adaptive finite element computation of the Helmholtz equation in exterior domains, *Finite Elements in Analysis and Design*. **22**(1), 15–24.

Thompson, J. F., Z. U. A. Warsi, and C. W. Mastin (1985). *Numerical Grid Generation: Foundations and Applications*, New York, Elsevier (www.erc.msstate.edu/publications/gridbook/).

Venditti, D. A. and D. L. Darmofal (2003). Anisotropic grid adaptation for functional outputs: application to two-dimensional viscous flows, *Journal of Computational Physics*. **187**, 22–46.

Verfurth, R. (1999). A review of a posteriori error estimation techniques for elasticity problems, *Computer Methods in Applied Mechanics and Engineering*. **176**(1–4), 419–440.

Wood, W. A. and W. L. Kleb (1999). *On Multi-dimensional Unstructured Mesh Adaption*, AIAA Paper 1999–3254.

Zienkiewicz, O. C. and J. Z. Zhu (1992a). The superconvergent patch recovery and a posteriori error estimates, Part 2: Error estimates and adaptivity, *International Journal for Numerical Methods in Engineering*. **33**, 1365–1382.

Zienkiewicz, O. C. and J. Z. Zhu (1992b). Superconvergent patch recovery (SPR) and adaptive finite element refinement, *Computer Methods in Applied Mechanics and Engineering*. **101**(1–3), 207–224.

Part IV

Model validation and prediction

This section of the book presents an in-depth discussion of the topic of model validation and prediction. As discussed in Part I, this book uses the restricted meaning of model validation, i.e., assessment of model accuracy as determined by comparison of model outputs with experimental measurements. Stated differently, if you are not comparing model predictions of system response quantities (SRQs) with experimental measurements of the SRQs for the purpose of assessing the accuracy of the model, you are not conducting model validation. Prediction, as discussed in Part I, deals with the use of the model and all information that is available concerning the system of interest, as well has how well the model has performed in model validation activities, to predict the response of the system of interest for which no experimental data is presently available. That is, we use the model to foretell the response of the system of interest given our knowledge of the system, and how well the model has compared with available experimental measurements, including our estimates of all of the uncertainties involved in every element of the simulation.

Model validation can be viewed from three perspectives. First, we have the perspective of the mathematical model builder or computational analysts involved in the activity. This perspective is primarily discussed in Chapter 10, Model validation fundamentals. This perspective addresses issues such as the goals and strategy of validation and how model accuracy assessment can be conducted at different levels of physics and system complexity. Second, we have the perspective of the experimentalist involved in the activity. This perspective is discussed in Chapter 11, Design and execution of validation experiments. This perspective deals with the technical issues and practical concerns of experimentalists, such as how are validation experiments different from traditional experiments and tests of systems, what has been learned from experimentalists who have conducted high-quality validation experiments, and why validation experiments are difficult to conduct from both a technical perspective and a business perspective of experimental facility operators. Third, we have the perspective of how one quantitatively compares model and experimental results? This perspective is discussed in Chapter 12, Model accuracy assessment. The task of model accuracy assessment, which we refer to as the construction and evaluation of a validation metric, might, at first, seem fairly simple. We discuss how the task is complicated due to aleatory and epistemic uncertainty in both the model predictions and the experimental measurements. In this chapter we also discuss how model accuracy assessment differs from the common practices of model calibration and model updating. We also point out that there are widely varying perspectives on validation metrics and model calibration (updating).

Model prediction is discussed in Chapter 13, Predictive capability. This chapter will synthesize the key results of verification, validation, and uncertainty quantification from the previous chapters and incorporate them into an approach for nondeterministic predictions. This chapter, in contrast to all other chapters, does not stress the theme of assessment, but deals with the more complex issue of model extrapolation. The accuracy of the prediction is based on the fidelity of the physics, the soundness of the assumptions incorporated into the model, and the accuracy of the following at the application conditions of interest: (a) the extrapolation of the previously observed model accuracy, (b) the knowledge of all of the input data to the model, and (c) the estimation of the numerical solution error. We stress that one must be careful in the interpretation of the concept of *accuracy* in the prediction of a nondeterministic system for which one has limited knowledge. Two newly developed methods are discussed for estimating the uncertainty in model predictions. This chapter is not meant to be a comprehensive coverage of the topic of uncertainty estimation in predictions, but only give the reader an introduction to the topic and present the basic steps in nondeterministic predictions. Predictive capability is an active area of research and a number of references are given for further study.

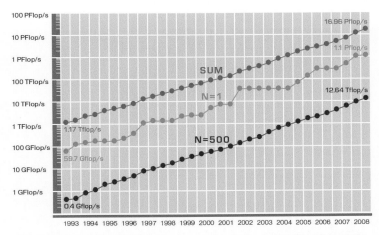

Figure 1.1 Computing speed of the 500 fastest computers in the world (Top500, 2008).

(a)

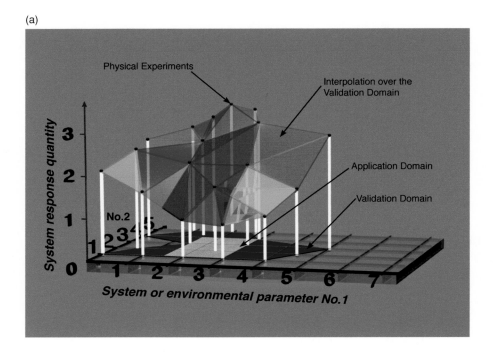

(b)

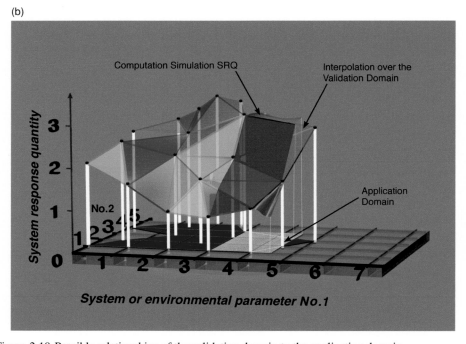

Figure 2.10 Possible relationships of the validation domain to the application domain.

(c)

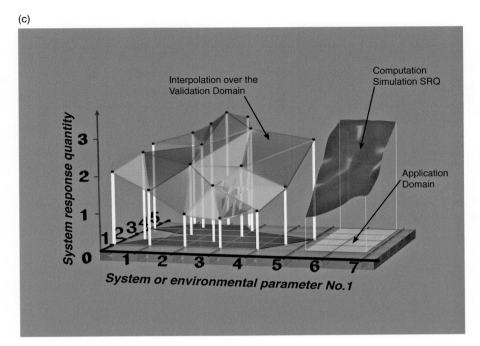

Figure 2.10 (*cont.*)

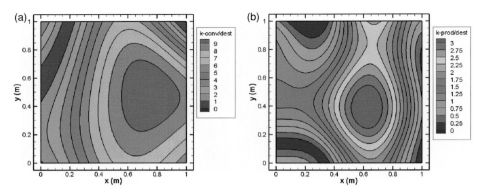

Figure 6.5 Ratios of (a) the convection terms and (b) the production terms to the destruction terms for a turbulent kinetic energy transport equation (from Roy *et al.*, 2007b).

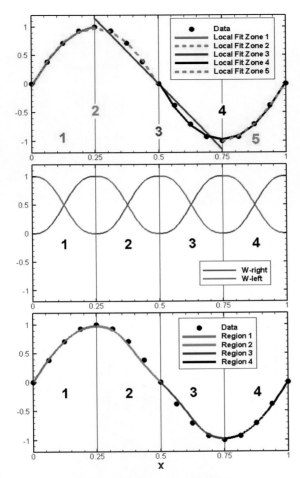

Figure 6.16 Simple one-dimensional example of the weighting function approach for combining local quadratic least squares fits to generate a C^2 continuous spline fit: local fits (top), weighting functions (middle), and resulting C^2 continuous spline fit (bottom) (from Roy and Sinclair, 2009).

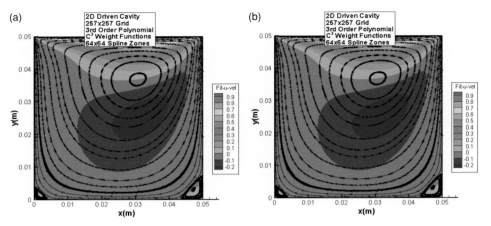

Figure 6.17 Contours of *u*-velocity and streamlines for a lid-driven cavity at Reynolds number 100: (a) 257×257 node numerical solution and (b) C³ continuous spline fit using 64×64 spline zones (from Roy and Sinclair, 2009).

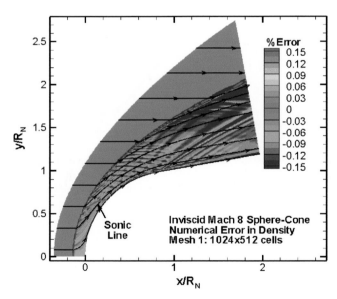

Figure 8.1 Contours of total estimated discretization error in density for the flow over an inviscid hypersonic sphere cone (from Roy, 2003).

(a) 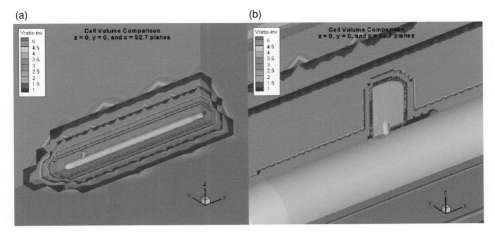 (b)

Figure 8.12 Contour plots of the cell volume ratio between the two unstructured Cartesian mesh levels for (a) the entire missile geometry and (b) a close-up of the canard (from Roy *et al.*, 2007).

Figure 11.2 Sandia hypersonic wind tunnel with the aft section retracted from the test section (flow is from left to right). The model is visible in the open section and the yellow support is part of the rear-mounting fixture to hold the model (Oberkampf *et al.*, 1993).

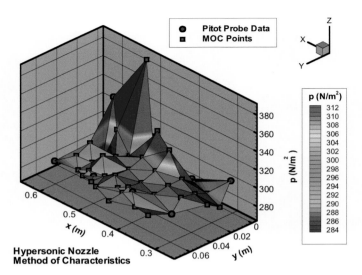

Figure 11.14 Free-stream static pressures from a combination of flowfield calibration data and MOC generated data (Roy *et al.*, 2003).

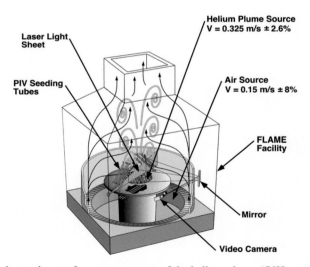

Figure 12.7 Experimental setup for measurements of the helium plume (O'Hern *et al.*, 2005).

10

Model validation fundamentals

Because of the well-developed methodologies and techniques developed in metrology, experimental measurements are usually viewed as the best way to estimate a true value, if one exists. This level of trust and credibility in experimental measurements has been built over at least four millennia of learning, both from mistakes and successes. This is not meant to imply that experimental measurements *always* yield an accurate estimate of the true value. Experimental measurements can be inaccurate, or downright wrong, for many reasons. What is meant by the trustworthiness of an experimental measurement is that techniques for investigating its limitations, weaknesses, and uncertainties are generally well understood. When new experimental diagnostic techniques are developed they must be carefully investigated and understood. Where possible, comparisons need to be made with measurements from existing, better understood, techniques so that measurement uncertainty can be better quantified. As science and technology progresses, new measurement techniques can increase the confidence in measurement accuracy and also begin to measure physical quantities that were previously immeasurable.

An enlightening way of thinking about the trustworthiness of experimental measurements is to think of an experimental measurement as "asking a question of nature" (Hornung and Perry, 1998). When a measurement result is obtained, the result can be thought of as nature's answer to a question we have asked. We tend to believe that the answer obtained is the answer to the question we think we asked. However, this is not actually the case because there are always assumptions involved on our part. For example, when we measure the fluid velocity in a flow field, we believe we asked the question: given the flow field of interest, what is the velocity of the fluid at a certain point? Our intent is to ask nature the question that excludes or minimizes the effect of random or systematic errors in the measurement. If, however, there is significant random measurement error or if there is an unknown systematic error either in the measurement itself or in the data reduction procedure, then the question asked of nature is different from what we thought we asked. That is, nature answered the question that *includes* the random and systematic errors, whether large or small.

In addition, nature can use any vagueness or ambiguity in our question to deceive us. The deceit is not in any sense trickery or maliciousness on the part of nature. It is the questioner who can easily deceive him/herself because either it is not recognized that the question is vague, or because our preconceived notions or agendas led us astray. The goal of science, whether discoveries are through experiment, theory, or simulation, is to refine our understanding and description of nature, regardless of our present confusion or beliefs. Consider the following example. Suppose we are interested in measuring some local quantity in a physical domain, e.g., the local strain in a solid, the local velocity in a flow field, or the total energy at a point. We frame our question of nature within a certain mindset, such as the strain is elastic, the flow field is steady, or certain components of energy are unimportant. Then we make our measurements and interpret the results within our mindset. Often the interpretation makes perfect sense and is fully consistent within our framework, but our interpretation could be *completely* wrong. Our mindset most often involves assumptions concerning the relevant physics and the measurement technique, but it also includes our presumption that the theory or the simulation is correct. Any disagreements or oddities in the measurements that don't quite fit our theory or simulation are relegated to experimental error or dissolved into our model using calibration of parameters. Human nature places great value on success, but nature has no agenda.

From a validation perspective, we could think about asking our simulation the same question that is asked of nature. The philosophical foundation of validation experiments is to ask precisely the *same* question of our model that we ask of nature. From our discussion above, we see that this presents a dichotomy. From an experimental measurement viewpoint, we strive for precision in the question of nature while minimizing (a) the constraints of our measurement assumptions, and (b) the uncertainty of our measurements. From a simulation viewpoint, we are fundamentally constrained by the assumptions embedded in the model. To bridge this gulf, we must steadfastly seek to ensure that the experiment provides all the input information needed for the simulation. In this way, we can critically test the accuracy of the assumptions in our model. For example, the experimentalist should provide all the boundary conditions (BCs), initial conditions (ICs), system excitation, geometric features, and other input data needed for the simulation. If our knowledge of the needed conditions is poor or pieces of information are missing, then our simulation is answering a somewhat different question than was asked of nature. Or, if there is a systematic uncertainty in the measurements, then the question asked of nature is different from what was asked of our simulation.

10.1 Philosophy of validation experiments

10.1.1 Validation experiments vs. traditional experiments

Experimentalists, computational analysts, and project managers ask: what is a validation experiment? Or: how is a validation experiment different from other experiments? These are appropriate questions. Traditional experiments could be grouped into three general categories (Oberkampf and Trucano, 2002; Trucano *et al.*, 2002; Oberkampf *et al.*, 2004). The first category comprises experiments that are conducted primarily to improve the fundamental understanding of some physical process. Sometimes these are referred to as physical discovery or phenomena discovery experiments. Examples are (a) experiments that measure fundamental fluid turbulence characteristics; (b) experiments that investigate crack propagation in solids; (c) experiments in high-energy density physics; and (d) experiments probing the onset and stability of phase changes in solids, liquids, and gases.

The second category of traditional experiments consists of those conducted primarily for constructing, improving, or determining parameters in mathematical models of fairly-well understood physical processes. Sometimes these are referred to as model calibration or model updating experiments. Examples are (a) experiments to measure reaction rate parameters in reacting or detonating flows, (b) experiments to measure thermal emissivity of material surfaces, (c) experiments to calibrate parameters in a model for predicting large plastic deformation of a structure, and (d) experiments to calibrate mass diffusion rate parameters in a mass transport chemistry model.

The third category of traditional experiments includes those that determine the reliability, performance, or safety of components, subsystems, or complete systems. These experiments are sometimes referred to as acceptance tests or qualification tests of engineered components, subsystems, or systems. Examples are (a) tests of a new combustor design in gas turbine engines, (b) pressurization tests of a new design of a filament-wound composite pressure vessel, (c) safety test of the emergency cooling system in a nuclear power reactor, and (d) a limit load test of an aircraft wing structure.

Validation experiments constitute a new type of experiment. (See Oberkampf and Aeschliman, 1992; Marvin, 1995; Oberkampf *et al.*, 1995; Aeschliman and Oberkampf, 1998, for a discussion of the early concepts of a validation experiment.) A validation experiment is conducted for the primary purpose of determining the predictive capability of a mathematical model of a physical process. In other words, a validation experiment is designed, executed, and analyzed for the purpose of quantitatively determining the ability of the model and its embodiment in a computer code to simulate a well-characterized physical process. In a validation experiment *the model builder is the customer* or similarly *the computational analyst is the customer*. Only during the last two decades has scientific computing matured to the point where it could even be considered as a separate customer in experimental activities. As modern technology increasingly moves toward engineering systems that are designed, certified, and even fielded based primarily on scientific computing, then scientific computing itself will increasingly become the customer of experiments.

One other aspect of validation experiments that is different from traditional experiments is that traditional experiments place a great deal of emphasis on measurements of processes in a controlled environment. Only with a controlled environment can measurements of physical processes be reliably repeated by other experimentalists; models carefully calibrated; and the reliability, performance, and safety of systems assessed. In validation experiments, however, *characterization* of the experiment is the more important goal. By *characterization* we mean measuring all of the important characteristics of the experiment that are needed for the simulation, both within the system and in the surroundings. Stated differently, control and repeatability of the experiment are less important in a validation experiment than precisely *measuring* the conditions of an uncontrolled experiment. Variability in the surroundings of a validation experiment, for example due to weather conditions, is

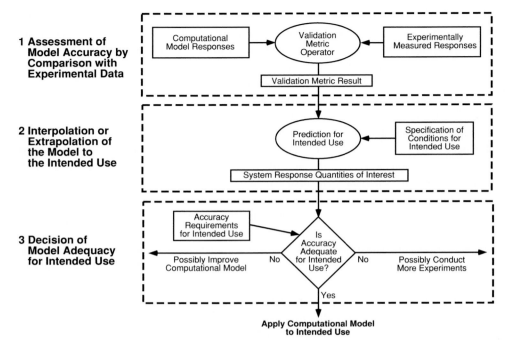

Figure 10.1 Three aspects of the encompassing view of model validation (Oberkampf and Trucano, 2007; Oberkampf and Trucano, 2008).

not critical, as long as the conditions of the surroundings are precisely measured. For experiments with uncontrolled conditions, however, a number of experimental realizations are necessary to carefully characterize the variability of the system and surroundings so that this information can be provided to the computational analyst.

10.1.2 Goals and strategy of validation

In Chapter 2, Fundamental concepts and terminology, the fundamental concepts of validation were introduced. In Section 2.2.3, three aspects of the encompassing view of model validation were discussed with regard to Figure 10.1. Aspect 1 involves the quantitative comparison of computational responses and experimentally measured responses. The mathematical operator used to make the comparisons is a *validation metric operator*. The operator is usually formulated as a difference operator so that the validation metric result is a measure of the disagreement between the computational and experimental responses. Aspect 2 deals with the use of the model to make predictions, in the sense of interpolation or extrapolation, for the conditions of the intended use of the model. Aspect 3 deals with (a) the comparison of the estimated accuracy of the model relative to the accuracy requirements of the model for the domain of the model's intended use, and (b) the decision of adequacy/inadequacy of the model over the domain of the model's intended use.

Aspect 1 can be thought of in two ways: scientific validation and project-oriented valida-tion. *Scientific validation* is a quantitative assessment of model accuracy without regard to any specific accuracy requirements or engineering project needs. This is the most common type of validation activity that is published in the literature. *Project-oriented validation* is a quantitative assessment of model accuracy with the needs of the project taking priority. The following sections will discuss each type of validation activity in detail. We remind the reader that this book uses the restricted view of the term *validation*, meaning model accuracy assessment as depicted in Aspect 1.

10.1.2.1 Scientific validation

A number of authors have written papers and articles concerning the general strategy of conducting model validation. Some of the key contributors were Marvin (1995); Rykiel (1996); Aeschliman and Oberkampf (1998); Barber (1998); Benek *et al.* (1998); Kleijnen (1998); Kleindorfer *et al.* (1998); Murray-Smith (1998); Roache (1998); Sargent (1998); Balci *et al.* (2000); Refsgaard (2000); Anderson and Bates (2001); Oberkampf and Trucano (2002); Trucano *et al.* (2002); Oberkampf *et al.* (2004); and Oberkampf and Barone (2006). Most published work dealing with comparing model and experimental results is directed toward what is referred to here as *scientific validation*. By using this term, we are *not* contrasting validation in scientific endeavors versus engineering endeavors. We are using the term in the broad sense to mean any type of quantitative comparison between computational results and experimental measurements for the purpose of accuracy assessment of a physics-based model. Discussed here are some of the important strategies for improved accuracy assessment that have been learned through the years.

Descriptions and documentation of experiments that are subsequently used for model validation seldom provide all of the important input information needed for the model. For documentation of experiments that appear in journal articles, there is considerable pressure to limit the length of the article and avoid including detailed information. The biggest reason, however, for the lack of documented information is that many experimentalists do not understand or care about the input information needs of an analyst who wants to use the experiment for model validation. In addition, the experimentalists are at a disadvantage because they can only guess at all of the types of information that might be needed for different modeling approaches. Given this lack of information, computational analysts almost always choose to adjust unknown parameters or conditions so that the best agreement is obtained between their results and the experimental measurements. Any type of adjustment of parameters, conditions, or modeling approaches degrades the primary goal of validation: assessment of predictive accuracy of a model. Sometimes the adjustment of parameters or conditions is explicit, for example, using calibration or parameter estimation procedures. This, of course, significantly decreases critical assessment of model predictive accuracy. Sometimes, the adjustment procedures are not explicitly mentioned or explained, either intentionally or unintentionally. For example, certain modeling approaches were attempted, gave poor agreement with the experimental data, and were abandoned. The experience, however, was used to guide new modeling assumptions that yielded modeling results with improved agreement with the data.

For experiments that are designed and conducted in the future, a much more constructive procedure is for both the computational analysts and the experimentalists to jointly design the experiment. Many of the difficulties just mentioned can be eliminated in a joint effort. This topic will be discussed in depth in Chapter 11, Design and execution of validation experiments, but here, two aspects of a joint effort will be mentioned. First, in a joint effort, the analyst must inform the experimentalist of the input information required by the model. In addition, the analyst must communicate to the experimentalist what system response quantities (SRQs) are of particular interest so that they can be measured. Second, the experimental measurements of the SRQs should be withheld from the analysts so that a blind-test computational prediction can be made. Although the value of blind predictions in scientific computing is not uniformly accepted, we believe it is crucial to withhold the measured SRQs so as to critically assess the predictive accuracy of a model. Some fields of science, such as drug testing in medicine, have long recognized that without blind or double-blind testing, conclusions are commonly distorted and misleading.

In comparing computational and experimental results, emphasis should be placed on quantitative comparison methods. Color contour levels of a SRQ over a two-dimensional region, one for a computational result and one for an experimental result, can be qualitatively useful. However, little quantitative information can be gained, especially if the quantitative values of the color scale are not given. The most common comparison method is a graph where computationally predicted and experimentally measured SRQs are shown over a range of an input, or control, parameter. Two quantitative shortcomings of this method are the following. First, agreement or disagreement between computational and experimental results is not quantified, sometimes not even stated. The focus is on the trends in the SRQ, not quantifying the computation-experiment disagreement. Observations and conclusions are commonly made about the claimed agreement, such as "good" or "excellent" or "the model is validated," but all of these are in the eye of the beholder in this approach.

Second, these types of graph rarely have any type of information concerning the effect of the uncertainties on the results. For example, the computational results are commonly deterministic results. Additionally, no information is shown concerning the influence of the numerical solution errors on the results. For the experimental results, it is still common to see experimental results without any experimental uncertainty estimates shown. Significant improvement in quantitative comparisons is made if the effects of the uncertainties on both the computational and experimental results are shown. One method is to show the mean value and the uncertainty bars with plus or minus two standard deviations for both the computational results and experimental measurements. The topic of quantitative comparison of computational and experimental results will be discussed in detail in Chapter 12, Model accuracy assessment.

Computational results and experimental results produce many different SRQs. Validation is concerned with the comparison of the same SRQ under the same conditions from both the computation and experiment. There is a range of difficulty in predicting and experimentally

Spectrum of system response quantities

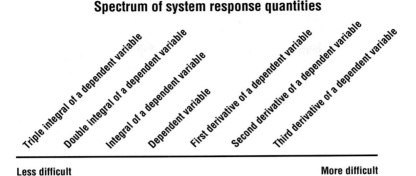

Figure 10.2 Spectrum of various types of SRQs and the difficulty to predict and measure each.

measuring different SRQs. By *prediction difficulty* we mean aspects such as (a) the fidelity of the physics model that is required to accurately predict an SRQ; (b) the range of spatial and/or temporal scales exhibited by an SRQ; and (c) the spatial, temporal, and iterative convergence characteristics required to computationally resolve multiple physical scales and physical phenomena. By *experimental difficulty* we mean that there is a wide range of difficulty in measuring different SRQs. In experiments, this range of difficulty is primarily due to large differences in spatial and/or temporal scales either within an SRQ or across various SRQs. With modern digital electronic equipment, temporal scales do not generate as great a degree of difficulty as measurement of a wide range of spatial scales. Difficulty in experimental measurements commonly translates to increased experimental uncertainty for smaller spatial and temporal scales, both in bias and random uncertainty.

Figure 10.2 depicts the range of difficulty in predicting and measuring different SRQs. The spectrum could have a different type of ordering for some complex physics cases, but the conceptual ordering of interest here is shown in the figure. The scale of difficulty is ordered in terms of derivatives and integrals of the dependent variables in the partial differential equations (PDEs) of interest. For example, consider steady-state heat conduction through a homogenous solid with constant thermal conductivity. The PDE for the temperature distribution through a two-dimensional solid is given by Laplace's equations,

$$\frac{\partial^2 T}{\partial x^2} + \frac{\partial^2 T}{\partial y^2} = 0. \tag{10.1}$$

The dependent variable in the PDE is the temperature $T(x, y)$. This quantity is represented in the middle of the range in Figure 10.2. If one is interested in predicting and measuring the heat flux through a vertical line at $x = $ constant, the heat flux q as a function of y is given by

$$q(y) = -k \left(\frac{\partial T}{\partial x} \right)_{x=\text{constant}}. \tag{10.2}$$

From this equation it is seen that the heat flux is an SRQ that is dependent of the first derivative of the dependent variable in the PDE. This quantity is represented just to the right of the dependent variable in Figure 10.2. Various types of integral of dependent variables are also of interest as SRQs. These are referred to as functionals because they operate on a function and produce a real number. These are shown to the left of the middle in Figure 10.2 and they are ordered in terms of the number of integrals of the dependent variable of the PDE.

In validation activities, computational analysts will commonly compare their computational results with experimental measurements at one level of difficulty shown in the spectrum in Figure 10.2 and then claim the model accurate at all levels in the spectrum. Because there exists a spectrum of difficulty in prediction, a validation claim at one level of difficulty does *not necessarily* translate into accuracy at higher levels of difficulty. For example, if one were to show good agreement for the temperature distribution through a solid, it is more demanding of the model to accurately predict the heat flux because of the derivative operator. However, demonstrated accuracy at high levels of difficulty *does imply* accuracy at lower levels of predictive difficulty because of the integral operator. For example, if heat flux can be accurately predicted over the entire domain of the PDE, then the temperature distribution would be expected to be at least as accurate as the heat flux prediction.

10.1.2.2 Project-oriented validation

Project-oriented validation is similar to scientific validation in that one is still interested in a quantitative assessment of model accuracy as measured with respect to experimental data. However, in project-oriented validation, the focus shifts to how validation activities contribute to assessing the predictive accuracy of the model when the model is applied to the specific system of interest. Project-oriented validation is interested in evaluating the model accuracy with project-relevant experimental data, in addition to where predictions are needed in the application domain. As discussed in Chapter 2, the validation domain may or may not overlap with the application domain. For regions of overlap, interpolation is required to estimate the model accuracy for points away from the experimental data. For nonoverlapping regions, extrapolation of model accuracy is required for the application domain. (See Figure 2.10 for a discussion of overlapping and nonoverlapping regions of the validation and application domains.) Chapter 13, Predictive capability, will deal with the issue of extrapolation of model accuracy using validation metrics and alternative plausible models.

During the last decade, large scientific computing projects, such as the US National Nuclear Security Administration (NNSA) Advanced Simulation and Computing (ASC) program, have developed methods to improve the planning and prioritization of project-oriented validation experiments (Pilch *et al.*, 2001; Trucano *et al.*, 2002; Oberkampf *et al.*, 2004; Pilch *et al.*, 2004). Improved planning and prioritization were found to be critical for managing the allocation of time, money, facilities, and talent resources to optimally advance

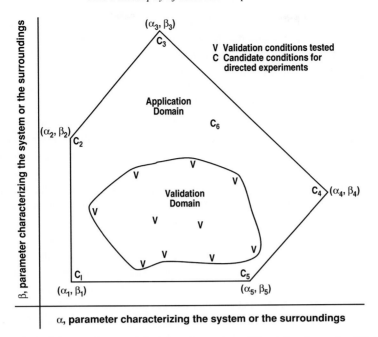

β, parameter characterizing the system or the surroundings

α, **parameter characterizing the system or the surroundings**

Figure 10.3 Application domain, validation domain, and candidates for directed validation experiments (adapted from Trucano *et al.*, 2002).

the predictive capability of a project-oriented computational effort. Project-oriented validation experiments, referred to here simply as *directed experiments*, are those designed purposefully with specific goals linked to the project or the objectives of the system of interest. Occasionally, experimental data directly relevant to the system of interest can be found in the published technical literature or proprietary company reports, but this is rare because of the specificity of project needs. Because directed experiments are required to allow quantitative comparisons of computations with experimental data, important requirements are placed on directed experiments to create the greatest opportunities for performing these comparisons. In addition, directed experiments should be designed to assist, if needed, computational analysts and model builders to understand why the model may have performed poorly.

Figure 10.3 shows a two-dimensional space defined by the two parameters α and β, each one characterizing some feature of the system or the conditions imposed by the surroundings. The validation domain is shown as the region in which various validation experiments have been conducted, denoted by V. The application domain shows the region of interest, from a project perspective, in which the predictive capability is needed. As is typical of operating conditions of a system, the corners of the operating envelope are specified in terms of pairs of coordinates (α_i, β_i), $i = 1, 2, \ldots, 5$. The relationship between the application domain and the validation domain shown in Figure 10.3 is part of the class of relationships shown in Figure 2.10b in Chapter 2. That is, the application domain is *not* a subset of the validation domain, but there is overlap between them.

Presume that a validation metric result has been computed at each of the conditions marked with a V. The boundary of the validation domain would represent the apparent limit where the model accuracy has been assessed. The validation metric result can be thought of as the model error E interpolated over the validation domain, $E(\alpha, \beta)$. The application domain for the system of interest is shown as the polygon. Let the conditions C_i, $i = 1$, $2, \ldots, 6$, denote the points in the parameter space that are candidates for future directed experiments. The coordinates of C_i, $i = 1, 2, \ldots, 5$ usually correspond to the corners of the operating envelope of the system, (α_i, β_i), $i = 1, 2, \ldots, 5$. For each of these five conditions, an estimate should be made of the accuracy of the model. In addition, an estimate of the model accuracy should be made over the entire application domain. Estimation of model accuracy over the validation and application domains requires interpolation and extrapolation of the model and its observed accuracy, which will be discussed in Chapter 13. The condition corresponding to C_6 is shown to suggest that this condition was found to have the largest estimated model error over the application domain. The largest inaccuracies usually occur on the boundaries of the application domain, but this need not be the case because of complex physics interactions that can occur.

As is typical of project-oriented validation, system designers and project managers usually try to jump from the question of model accuracy assessment to the question of required accuracy of the model for their system. This is understandable because they are usually focused on their system, but the distinction between model accuracy assessment and accuracy requirements should always be kept in mind. Comparing the estimated model accuracy with the accuracy requirements of the project will help guide where future validation experiments may be needed. If there are multiple conditions for potential validation experiments, then these must be prioritized in some way. Chapter 14, Planning and prioritization in modeling and simulation, provides a detailed discussion of various methods for planning and prioritization of not only directed experiments, but also other activities of scientific computing.

The mathematical model should not only be applied in the decision of what conditions should be used in possible directed experiments, but also in other key factors in the design of these experiments. Some examples are (a) determination of key geometric features of the component or system to be tested, (b) guidance in determining the BCs and ICs, (c) guidance about where to locate diagnostic instrumentation, and (d) estimation of what magnitudes of SRQs could be expected for different sensors so that the proper sensors can be employed. The overarching theme of the design of the experiment is achieving system characteristics and responses that are of interest to the application driver. For example, if the successful operation of the system required that a certain design feature not fail, then special instrumentation would be designed to be certain this feature was captured during the experiment.

In a directed experiment, there must be a balance between the project needs and the needs of a high-quality validation experiment. As mentioned above, the primary purpose of

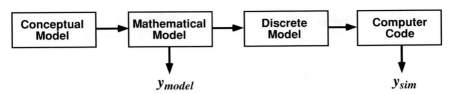

Figure 10.4 Sequence of model mappings to produce a simulation result.

a validation experiment is determining the predictive accuracy of a model. In engineering applications, there is usually some level of conflict between the goals of the project and the goals of a validation experiment. This tension is exacerbated if the project is funding the design, execution, and analysis of the directed experiment. For example, in the design of the directed experiment, the project leader typically would like the system geometry and functionality of the hardware to be similar to the actual system being designed. The computational analysts, however, would like the experiment to be as focused as much as possible on the physics processes that are of concern in the modeling. The viewpoint of the experimentalists also enters the discussion because their goals are to obtain the highest accuracy measurements possible, given the time and resource available. There are no straightforward cures to this three-way tension. The only general recommendation that can be made is to openly discuss the logic and priorities of each perspective so that a reasonable compromise can be attained. Our experience is that the project perspective commonly dominates any debate concerning design trade-offs of the validation experiment to the detriment of the validation goals of the experiment. Project managers who have personal experience with scientific computing, as well as an understanding of the role of scientific computing in helping the system achieve its performance goals, can provide enlightened decision-making on needed compromises. Chapter 11 will discuss these types of issue in more detail.

10.1.3 Sources of error in experiments and simulations

We now describe the fundamental sources of error in experimental measurements and scientific computing. For this discussion it is more useful to consider errors instead of uncertainties because we begin by using the definition of error in a quantity, either experimental or computational. This discussion expands on the development in Oberkampf *et al.* (2004). Let y_{sim} be an SRQ that results from a computational simulation. As discussed in Section 3.4, y_{sim} is a final result of the various mappings shown in Figure 10.4. Let y_{nature} be the true value of the SRQ from nature that, of course, can never be known exactly. Using the common definition of error discussed in Section 2.4, we define the error in the simulation, E_{sim}, as

$$E_{\text{sim}} = y_{\text{sim}} - y_{\text{nature}}. \tag{10.3}$$

Both terms on the right side of Eq. (10.3) can be separated into additional terms in order to explicitly identify various contributors to error. We rewrite Eq. (10.3) as

$$E_{\text{sim}} = (y_{\text{sim}} - y_{\text{Pcomputer}}) + (y_{\text{Pcomputer}} - y_{\text{model}}) + (y_{\text{model}} - y_{\text{exp}}) + (y_{\text{exp}} - y_{\text{nature}}).$$

$$(10.4)$$

$y_{\text{Pcomputer}}$ is the SRQ that could be theoretically computed on a perfect computer with infinite speed, precision, and memory such that we are able to take the limit as the discretization error and iterative error approach zero. Note that the same mathematical model, the same algorithms, and the same computer code used in y_{sim} are also used in $y_{\text{Pcomputer}}$. y_{model} is the SRQ resulting from the exact solution to the mathematical model; i.e., the model given by the PDEs, BCs, ICs, system excitation, geometric features, and all other input data needed for the simulation (Figure 10.4). y_{exp} is the value of the SRQ that is measured in an experiment.

A more compact form of Eq. (10.4) can be written as

$$E_{\text{sim}} = E_1 + E_2 + E_3 + E_4, \qquad (10.5)$$

where

$$E_1 = (y_{\text{sim}} - y_{\text{Pcomputer}}),$$
$$E_2 = (y_{\text{Pcomputer}} - y_{\text{model}}),$$
$$E_3 = (y_{\text{model}} - y_{\text{exp}}),$$
$$E_4 = (y_{\text{exp}} - y_{\text{nature}}). \qquad (10.6)$$

E_1 through E_4 represent all of the fundamental sources of error in a comparison of a computational result and an experimental measurement. The only two quantities in Eq. (10.5) that are always known are y_{sim} and y_{exp}. Writing the simulation error in this way clearly demonstrates the possibility of error cancellation in the sum of the errors resulting in $E_{\text{sim}} = 0$. When model calibration is introduced, it is seen that error cancellation becomes the *goal*. For special cases where y_{model} is known, it is seen that y_{model} provides an important benchmark in the midst of this featureless landscape. The processes of verification and validation attempt to estimate each error contributor so that increased confidence can be gained concerning the magnitude of the sum. These processes are depicted in Figure 10.5 with respect to each of the error terms identified in Eq. (10.5). These terms will now be discussed.

E_1 represents all numerical errors resulting from the difference between the discrete solution, y_{sim}, (obtained using a finite discretization size, finite iterative convergence, and finite precision computer) and the exact solution to the discrete equations obtained on a perfect computer as the discretization size approaches zero, $y_{\text{Pcomputer}}$. E_1 is referred to as the solution or calculation error and is estimated by solution verification procedures. Chapters 7 and 8 discussed a number of methods for estimating the magnitude of the solution error. In the limit as the discretization size approaches zero, we still use the same numerical algorithms and computer code for $y_{\text{Pcomputer}}$ as is used for y_{sim}. If the numerical algorithm is deficient in some way, or the computer code contains programming errors,

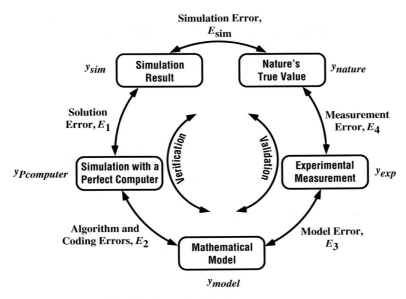

Figure 10.5 Error sources and verification and validation.

E_1 would be contingent on these errors but they would not technically be present in E_1. For example, suppose an algorithm error or a coding mistake was present in the computer code. Further, suppose that these errors caused the numerical solution to converge to an incorrect solution. E_1 would still represent the solution error due to a finite discretization size, finite iterative convergence, and a finite precision computer, exclusive of the algorithm and coding errors.

E_2 represents all errors resulting from the difference between the exact solution to the discrete equations as the discretization size approaches zero, $y_{\text{Pcomputer}}$, and the exact solution of the mathematical model, y_{model}. These errors are due to algorithm and coding errors and they are addressed by code verification procedures. Chapters 4 through 6 discussed a number of methods for detecting and removing these errors. Since we are not typically able to compute the exact solution of the discrete equations in the limit, we must rely on a systematic mesh and time-step convergence study with highly converged iterative solutions. To briefly summarize, the strategy is to compute the observed order of accuracy in the asymptotic region obtained during the convergence study. If an algorithm error (or deficiency) or a coding error causes an unexpected observed order of accuracy, we can be assured something is amiss. However, the reverse is not true, i.e., if the observed order of error matches the expected order of error it is not a proof that the algorithms are perfect and the coding is without error. The key to computing the observed order of accuracy is the availability of an exact solution to the mathematical model. The most demanding exact solutions have been found to be manufactured solutions, i.e., solutions obtained by picking y_{sim} and manufacturing the mathematical model that reproduces y_{sim}.

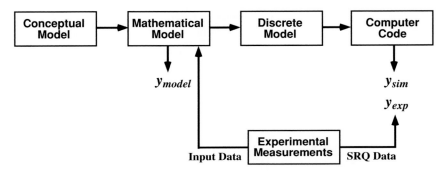

Figure 10.6 Model mappings with experimental data.

E_3 represents all errors resulting from the difference between the exact solution to the mathematical model, $y_{\text{Pcomputer}}$, and the experimental measurement, y_{exp}. E_3 is referred to as the model error or model form error although, as we will discuss, it is convolved with experimental measurement error. Estimating model error is conceptually and mathematically more difficult that estimating E_1 and E_2 for two reasons. First, experimental measurements always contain both random and systematic uncertainty since the true value from nature, y_{nature}, is never known. Examples of random and systematic experimental measurement uncertainties are multiple measurements of a quantity when the same experiment is repeated and improper calibration of a measurement instrument, respectively. Second, the experimental measurement provides not only y_{exp}, but also the necessary input data for the mathematical model; e.g., BCs, ICs, system excitation, and geometric features (see Figure 10.6). As a result, the mathematical model now depends on uncertain experimental data. It can be seen from Figure 10.6 that if unknown or poorly known parameters in the model are considered as adjustable parameters, then model calibration can be seen as a closed feedback loop. If one is also interested in quantifying model error during the model calibration process, model error has become inextricably convolved with calibration.

There are two different extremes when convolving model error and experimental error. First, suppose the experimental uncertainty is perfectly characterized and assume the systematic uncertainty is zero. This means that both the input data needed for the mathematical model from the experiment and y_{exp} are perfectly characterized as purely aleatory uncertainties. Then the uncertainty in y_{sim} can be characterized as a purely aleatory uncertainty, for example using Monte Carlo sampling of the mathematical model. Then one can quantitatively compare y_{sim} and y_{exp} using a validation metric operator that computes the difference between two probability distributions. Even though the experimental uncertainty is convolved with the model error, the model error can still be separately quantified in the validation metric result.

Second, suppose the experimental uncertainty is not perfectly characterized. For example, suppose very few experimental samples are obtained for an uncertain input quantity, or the experimentalist simply did not measure some of the needed input quantities. One can either characterize this lack of knowledge as a probability box (p-box) or one can use the poor characterization as flexibility in the mathematical model to calibrate model parameters. When using a validation metric operator, the first route will result in epistemic uncertainty in quantifying model error, while the second route will inextricably convolve model error and experimental uncertainty. Chapters 12 and 13 will provide an in-depth discussion of these issues.

E_4 represents all errors due to the difference between the true, but unknown value of nature, y_{nature}, and the measurement of a physical quantity, y_{exp}. The true value from nature can be viewed as either a deterministic quantity or a nondeterministic quantity. If y_{nature} is considered as a deterministic quantity, then we are saying that a fixed set of physical conditions is exactly reproduced in an experiment, resulting in the same physical quantity from nature. Only in very simple experiments, such as measurement of the mass of a fixed object, can y_{nature} be considered as an unknown deterministic quantity. In general, this viewpoint is not very constructive because in most experiments there are uncontrollable factors that change the measured quantity of interest. It is more useful to consider y_{nature} as a nondeterministic quantity because exactly the same physical conditions cannot be reproduced from one physical realization to the next. For example, even in a very well-controlled experiment using the same physical system, it is common to have slightly different BCs, ICs, or system excitation. y_{exp} is always nondeterministic because of random and systematic uncertainties in the experimental measurement. As a result, only in special situations is E_4 considered a fixed but unknown error, as opposed to an uncertain quantity composed of both aleatory and epistemic uncertainties.

10.1.4 Validation using data from traditional experiments

Most researchers in the field of validation methodology have learned, often the hard way, why the various goals, strategies, and procedures discussed here are fundamentally constructive and necessary for assessment of model accuracy. However, there is commonly significant resistance to implementing these strategies and procedures in practice. Often the resistance is simply due to the inertia of human nature to respond to change. Sometimes, technical or practical arguments are presented as to why validation experiments, as described here, should not be embarked on. Practical arguments against conducting new validation experiments typically center on schedule and money constraints of the underlying project. The resistance is usually voiced, in its most low-key form, as: "We have been collecting experimental data for decades on similar systems, why can't you use existing data to validate your models?" A technically sound and defensible answer to this recurring question is so important that we will provide a detailed discussion of possible responses. These responses are a compilation of experiences from several researchers (Marvin, 1995; Porter, 1996; Aeschliman and Oberkampf, 1998; Barber, 1998; Rizzi and Vos, 1998; Oberkampf and Trucano, 2002; Trucano *et al.*, 2002; Oberkampf *et al.*, 2004; Oberkampf and Trucano, 2008). Although these responses do not apply in some situations, they give the reader an idea of typical difficulties in using traditional experiments for validation.

The most common reason for not being able to use existing experimental data for validation is that important information needed for defining input for the simulation is not available or documented as part of the description of the experiment. The general types of information not documented, or poorly quantified, are system characteristics, BCs, ICs, and system excitation. Examples of system characteristics not documented are (a) mechanical, electrical, thermal, chemical, magnetic, optical, acoustical, radiological, and atomic properties of materials or components; (b) spatial distribution of these characteristics throughout the system, if this is needed as input data; (c) detailed geometric features of the system, such as material gaps and as-tested geometric inspection data; and (d) system assembly details, such as the preload torque on bolts and information of friction-fit assemblies. Examples of BCs are (a) Dirichlet, Neumann, Robin, mixed, periodic, and Cauchy, and (b) any information needed by the PDEs concerning how the surroundings affect the domain of the PDEs, including possible time dependence of the BCs. Examples of ICs are (a) knowledge of the spatial distribution of all dependent variables of the PDEs over the domain of interest, and (b) knowledge of all the required temporal derivatives of the dependent variables over the domain of the PDE. And finally, examples of system excitation are (a) knowledge of the excitation over the spatial and/or temporal domain of the PDEs, (b) knowledge of how the excitation may change over time, and (c) knowledge of the excitation when the system is deformed or in a damaged state due to response to the excitation.

The level of characterization of the input information can range from: (a) a precisely known (deterministic) value or function; (b) a precisely known random variable, i.e., a pure aleatory uncertainty; (c) a random variable characterized by a family of probability distributions, but the parameters of the distribution are imprecisely known; (d) expert opinion that characterizes the uncertain quantity by an interval, i.e., a pure epistemic uncertainty; or (e) an opinion of the form "my best recollection is." The causes of the poor information conditions can range from (a) quantitative information was recorded, documented, and archived, but no one can find it now; to (b) the person who knew all about the experiment has retired and is skiing in Idaho. Of course, not all needed input information is important to the prediction of the SRQs of interest. The poorer the knowledge of important input information, the poorer the ability to quantitatively assess the accuracy of the model.

As an example, suppose a traditional experiment was conducted and all details of the experiment were well documented, including all input data needed for a simulation. As part of the documentation of the experiment, suppose all input data needed for the solution of the PDEs was deterministic and it was exactly known, save one parameter. That parameter was only known to be in a specified interval with no likelihood information known. Further, suppose that there is only one SRQ of interest, and that in the experiment it was perfectly measured, i.e., the experimental measurement uncertainty was zero. Using all of the information from the experiment, a nondeterministic simulation was computed because of the one interval-valued parameter. Then, the single SRQ of interest from the model would also be an interval-valued quantity. When a quantitative comparison is made between the computational and experimental results, one is comparing an interval from the computation with an exactly measured quantity from the experiment. If the interval is large, for example, because the input interval is very important in predicting the SRQ, then what can be concluded from the comparison? If the measurement value falls anywhere within the computational interval, one could say "That's good." However, very little can be quantitatively concluded concerning model accuracy, particularly if the interval is large.

The example just described is the *best result* that could occur in a validation exercise. What more commonly happens is that the computational analyst determines the value of the parameter within the interval that gives the best agreement with the experimental measurement, and then he/she declares the model validated. Nothing substantive is usually said concerning what was uncertain in the input data, nor how uncertain parameters were chosen. Our observation, and that of many other researchers in validation methodology, is that either: (a) the uncertainties in the simulation are so large because of missing information that nothing quantitative can be learned, or (b) uncertainties in the simulation due to missing input information are used as free parameters to optimize agreement between computation and experiment. The first result contributes little to assessing predictive accuracy, and the second result is misleading at best and fraudulent at worst.

The second most common deficiency in attempting to use data from traditional experiments for validation is that very few measurements of the SRQs of interest are made in experiments. With limited experimental data, only a limited number of statements can be made concerning quantitative accuracy of the model. Two types of situation commonly occur. First, experimental measurements of a local SRQ are made over a very limited portion of the domain of the PDE. For example: (a) flow field velocity measurements are made only over a very small region near a vehicle geometry of interest, (b) temperature measurements are made for a small number of points on the surface of an component in a heat transfer simulation, and (c) a small number of vibrational modes of a structure are measured over a portion of the structure. Second, experimental measurements are made of some SRQs of interest, but not the most important SRQs; for example: (a) surface pressure measurements are made on a vehicle, but the SRQ of interest is the predicted region of separated flow; (b) the strain is measured at various locations on the internal and external surface of a composite structure, but the SRQ of interest is delamination between layers of the structure; and (c) the material recession rate is measured on an ablating heat shield of a high-speed vehicle, but the SRQ of interest is the heat transfer rate to the heat shield. When little experimental data are available, the inferences concerning validation are weak. This deficiency can be magnified when the SRQ of interest is one or two derivatives removed from the experimentally measured quantity. (See the discussion in Section 10.1.2.1 concerning the spectrum shown in Figure 10.2.)

The third most common deficiency in trying to use traditional experiments in validation is that little or no estimation of experimental uncertainty is given for the SRQs measured. Even though uncertainty estimation has been a long tradition in experimental measurements, it is surprising how often measurements are reported without an uncertainty estimate. If an estimate of measurement uncertainty is provided, many times it underestimates the true uncertainty. Some reasons for a possible underestimate are (a) the uncertainty estimate provided is an estimate of the repeatability of the measurement, not an estimate of a broader class of random and systematic uncertainties in the experiment; (b) the estimate is simply a guess based on experience or what *appears* to look right; (c) systematic uncertainties due to particular diagnostic techniques, specific experimental procedures, or experimental facilities have not been quantified by conducting experiments using different diagnostics, procedures, or experimental facilities; and (d) only one experimental realization is conducted so that any estimate of uncertainty is based primarily on optimistic conjecture.

The common situation of underestimation of experimental measurement uncertainty was highlighted in a famous article by metrologist William Youden, "Enduring Values" (Youden, 1972), as well as by (Morgan and Henrion, 1990). In his paper Youden states: "Why do results obtained by different investigators characteristically disagree by more than would be expected by their estimates of uncertainty?" Youden notes that everything gets changed in another laboratory, whereas the investigator can (or does) make only minor changes within his/her laboratory. Youden gives two examples of systematic uncertainties in measurements of fundamental physical constants. He shows 15 values of the Astronomical Unit measured by investigators over the period 1895 to 1961. He points out that each investigator's reported value of uncertainty is *outside the limits* reported by his immediate predecessor. Youden also references the article by McNish (1962) concerning measurements of the speed of light. McNish (and Youden) show 24 measurements of the speed of light along with each investigator's estimate of their experimental uncertainty. The graph of the measurements shows that the estimated value (the experimenter's best estimate for the speed of light) is changing at a rate of about 1 km/s for every seven investigators who measure it! For the 24 investigators, the estimated value has changed 3.5 km/s, and half of the investigators estimated their experimental uncertainty as *under* 0.5 km/s. Youden points out that the problem is that the experimenters significantly underestimated unknown systematic uncertainties in their measurements. Even though Youden and other metrologists have called attention to the problem of underestimation of measurement uncertainty, human nature, saving face among investigators, and competition between commercial laboratories never change.

10.2 Validation experiment hierarchy

During the 1980s and 1990s, a number of researchers in fluid dynamics were struggling with the fundamental issue of: how should validation be undertaken for complex engineering systems? The *building block approach* that is used today was developed by Lin *et al.* (1992); Cosner (1995); Marvin (1995); Sindir *et al.* (1996); Sindir and Lynch (1997); and AIAA (1998). A similar hierarchical structure was developed in the nuclear reactor safety community during the same time frame for the purpose improving the understanding of

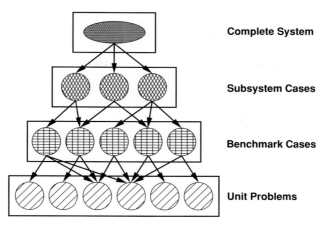

Figure 10.7 Validation hierarchy tiers (AIAA, 1998).

mass, momentum, and energy exchange in an accident environment (Zuber *et al.*, 1998). The building block or hierarchical approach is shown in Figure 10.7, as depicted in the AIAA Guide (AIAA, 1998). This approach divides the complex engineering system of interest into an arbitrary number of progressively simpler tiers. If the complex system is divided into three tiers, they are usually referred to as *subsystem*, *benchmark*, and *unit*. The strategy of the tiered approach encourages assessment of the accuracy of the model at multiple levels of complexity and physics coupling. The approach is clearly constructive in that it: (a) recognizes there is a hierarchy of complexity in real systems and simulations, and (b) recognizes that the quantity and accuracy of information that is obtained from experiments vary radically over the range of the hierarchy. The arrows from a higher tier to a lower tier indicate the primary impact of that element on a lower tier element.

The hierarchical view of validation is distinctly a system-oriented perspective. The system of interest is placed at the pinnacle of the validation hierarchy. The purpose of the validation hierarchy is to help identify a range of lower level tiers where experiments can be conducted for assessment of model accuracy for simpler systems and physics. A validation hierarchy is typically constructed by large-scale projects, with their system of interest as the focus. As one passes from the top tiers to the lower tiers of the hierarchy, the emphasis moves from system-oriented engineering to a physics-assessment orientation. Scientific validation, as discussed earlier, typically occurs at the lowest tier of the hierarchy. It should be pointed out that most validation hierarchies differ at the top tiers because the system or subsystems of interest are different, but they share many common elements at the lower tiers. For the common elements at the lower tiers, scientific validation can have a widespread impact on many projects.

Characteristics of each of the four tiers are discussed below. Additional tiers could be added to the validation hierarchy, but it would not significantly alter the discussion or the recommended methodology.

Complete System Tier	
Physical Characteristics	**Measured Data for Validation**
Actual system hardware Actual geometry, materials, and features Complete physics and chemistry Actual BCs, ICs, and system excitation	Very limited measurement of model inputs Very limited measurement of model outputs Very few experimental realizations Little or no estimate of experimental uncertainty

Figure 10.8 Characteristics of validation at the system tier (adapted from AIAA, 1998).

10.2.1 Characteristics of the complete system tier

The *complete system tier* consists of the actual engineering hardware or system of interest (Figure 10.8). Thus, by definition, it is functioning hardware with all the geometric characteristics, materials, and features associated with manufacturing and assembly of the system. For typical complex engineering systems such as a gas turbine engine, multi-disciplinary, coupled physical phenomena occur in the system. The BCs, ICs, and system excitation would commonly correspond to those that are of interest for realistic operating conditions of the system. One may also be interested in poorly defined or poorly controlled abnormal or hostile environments.

Experimental data are measured on the engineering hardware under operating conditions. The quantity and quality of these measurements, however, are always very limited because: (a) the diagnostic and instrumentation systems must have minimal impact on operational systems, and (b) the test programs are typically conducted on a rigid schedule and with a tightly constrained budget. It is difficult, and sometimes impossible, for complex systems' tests to quantify even a small percentage of the input conditions required for computational simulation. As a result, little or no information is available for most of the input needed for simulation, including the uncertainty of the input quantities. Such tests generally provide only data that are related to engineering parameters of clear design interest, system functionality, and high-level system performance measures. Referring to Figure 10.2, these high-level measures would correspond to multiple integrals of dependent variables appearing in the PDEs of the model. Sometimes, the performance measures of a complete system test are simply: Did it work? Did it meet contract specifications? Did it fail safely?

Experimental data from complete systems are always specific to existing operational hardware and are available mainly through large-scale test programs. Existing data from these tests have traditionally focused on issues such as the functionality, performance, safety, or reliability of the system. Often, competition between alternative system designs underlies large-scale tests. If the competition is between outside organizations or suppliers of hardware, then the ability to obtain complete and unbiased information for validation becomes essentially impossible. The test programs typically require expensive ground-test facilities, full-scale flight testing, or testing under dangerous conditions, such as unpredictable weather, or abnormal or hostile environments. Also, there are certain situations where it is not possible to conduct a validation experiment of the complete system. Such

Subsystem Tier	
Physical Characteristics	**Measured Data for Validation**
Functional subsystem hardware Most geometry, materials, and features Some physics and chemistry coupled Simplified BCs, ICs, and system excitation	Some measurement of model inputs Some measurement of model outputs Few experimental realizations Experimental uncertainty given on some quantities

Figure 10.9 Characteristics of validation at the subsystem tier (adapted from AIAA, 1998).

situations could involve public safety or environmental safety hazards, unattainable experimental testing requirements, or international treaty restrictions.

10.2.2 Characteristics of the subsystem tier

The *subsystem tier* represents the first decomposition of the actual system hardware into subsystems or subassemblies (Figure 10.9). Each of the subsystems or subassemblies is composed of actual functional hardware from the complete system. Subsystems usually exhibit three or more types of physics that are coupled. The physical processes of the complete system are partially represented by the subsystem tier, but the degree of coupling between various physical phenomena in the subsystem tier is typically reduced. For example, there is reduced coupling between subsystems as compared to the complete system. Most geometric characteristics are restricted to the particular subsystem and its attachment or simplified connection to the complete system. Essentially all of the materials, features, and capabilities of the subsystems are present. During subsystem testing, the BCs, ICs, and excitation are usually simplified compared to the operation of the complete system.

In subsystem tests there is commonly a significantly increased opportunity for all types of experimental measurement. There is usually much more willingness of test managers for installation of instrumentation and there is more interest in better understanding the details and operating conditions of the subsystem. In addition, there is usually less pressure from the project schedule, cost constraints, and high-level management attention. A much wider range of test facilities are possible for subsystems, with an accompanying improvement in control of the test conditions. There is an increased percentage of measured inputs and outputs for simulation, relative to complete system tests. There are commonly more experimental realizations than complete system tests. Experimental uncertainty estimates are given on some of the measured outputs, but few uncertainty estimates are commonly provided on measured input quantities.

10.2.3 Characteristics of the benchmark tier

The *benchmark tier*, sometimes referred to as the component tier, represents the next level of decomposition and simplification beyond the subsystem tier (Figure 10.10). For the benchmark tier, special hardware is fabricated to represent the main features of each subsystem.

Benchmark Tier	
Physical Characteristics	**Measured Data for Validation**
Special, nonfunctional, hardware fabricated Simplified geometry, materials, and features Little coupling of physics and chemistry Very simple BCs, ICs, and system excitation	Most model inputs measured Many model outputs measured Several experimental realizations Experimental uncertainty given on most quantities

Figure 10.10 Characteristics of validation at the benchmark tier (adapted from AIAA, 1998).

By special hardware, we mean hardware that is specially fabricated with simplified materials, properties, and features. For example, benchmark hardware is normally *not* functional or production hardware, nor is it fabricated with the same materials as actual subsystems. For benchmark cases, typically only two or three types of physical phenomenon are considered. The benchmark cases are normally simpler geometrically than those cases at the subsystem level. The only geometric features that are retained from the subsystem tier are those critical to the types of physical phenomenon that are considered at the benchmark tier. In addition, at this tier there is a distinct shift from project focused goals and schedules to those that are aimed at improved understanding of the physics involved and also the accuracy of the mathematical models that are used.

For this tier, most of the inputs needed for simulation are measured, or at least most of the important inputs are measured. Many of the model outputs that are measured correspond to dependent variables in the PDEs, or possibly one integral removed from the dependent variables. Since the benchmark tier uses nonfunctional hardware and special materials, the ability to instrument the hardware is significantly improved. Most of the experimental data obtained have associated estimates of measurement uncertainties. The experimental data, both model input data and output data, are usually documented with moderate detail. Examples of important experimental data that are documented include (a) detailed inspection of all hardware, (b) characterization of the variability of materials used in the experiment, (c) detailed information concerning assembly of the hardware, and (d) detailed measurement of BCs and excitation that were produced by the experimental apparatus or testing equipment.

10.2.4 Characteristics of the unit problem tier

Unit problems represent the total decomposition of the complete system into isolated physical processes that are amenable to high-quality validation experiments (Figure 10.11). At this level, high precision, special-purpose hardware is fabricated and inspected. This hardware may only vaguely resemble some features of the subsystem or benchmark tier, especially in the view of the system project manager. Unit problems are characterized by very simple geometries that are accurately characterized. The geometry features are commonly two-dimensional, either planar or axisymmetric, or they can be very simple three-dimensional geometries with important geometric symmetry features. One element

Unit Problem Tier	
Physical Characteristics	**Measured Data for Validation**
Very simple, nonfunctional, hardware fabricated Very simple geometry and features No coupled physics Very simple BCs, ICs, and system excitation	All model inputs measured Most model outputs measured Many experimental realizations Experimental uncertainty given on all quantities

Figure 10.11 Characteristics of validation at the unit problem tier (adapted from AIAA, 1998).

of complex physics is allowed to occur in each of the unit cases that are examined. The purpose of these cases is to isolate elements of complex physics so that critical evaluations of mathematical models or submodels can be evaluated. In fluid dynamics, for example, unit problems could individually involve (a) fluid turbulence for single phase flow, (b) fluid turbulence for two phase flow, (c) unsteady laminar flows, or (d) laminar diffusion flames. If one were interested in turbulent reacting flow, which combines turbulence and chemical reactions, it is recommended to consider this as one tier above the unit problem tier since it combines two aspects of complex physics.

For this tier, all of the important model inputs needed for simulation must be measured or well characterized. This, of course, is a highly demanding requirement for an experiment; a requirement that may not be attainable in many complex physics modeling situations. The following is a procedure that can be used to address this situation. First, experiments are conducted for the purpose of calibrating those parameters in the model that cannot be directly measured independently of the model. Second, follow-on experiments are conducted in which a few deterministic input parameters, i.e., accurately measured parameters with very small aleatory and epistemic uncertainty, are changed and the SRQs are remeasured. Third, new simulations are computed with the new values for the deterministic input parameters that were changed. And fourth, a validation metric result is computed by comparing the new computational and experimental results.

By changing a few deterministic input parameters, and *not* conducting any new calibrations, one can critically test the predictive capability of the model for new, well-defined conditions. This procedure is basically a two-step process; calibration and then validation on a closely related system. It requires a fairly large number of experiments for both steps of the process. A large number of experiments is needed in the calibration step so that very well characterized probability distributions can be determined for the calibrated parameters. In the second step, a large number of experiments is needed to precisely characterize the SRQs measured in the new experiment. With a correspondingly large number of nondeterministic simulations for both steps, a critical comparison can be made between the predicted and measured probability distributions for the SRQs.

As an example of this procedure, consider the prediction of the vibrational modes in a production lot of bolted-frame structures. First, a large number of bolted-frame structures are assembled using a fixed specification for the pre-load torque on all of the bolts in the structure. Experimental measurements are made on all of the structures to determine all of the vibrational modes of interest. Using a parameter optimization procedure, the estimated stiffness and damping in each of the bolted joints for all of the structures is determined using the mathematical model. Well-characterized probability distributions can then be computed for the stiffness and damping in all of the joints. The probability distributions represent the effect of variability in manufactured parts, the assembly of the structures, and the experimental measurement uncertainty.

Second, a large number of new structures are assembled such that the pre-load torque on all the bolts is changed. Suppose the torque on half of the bolts was doubled and half of the torques were decreased by a factor of two. The new structures are assembled using the same production lot of frame components and the same technicians assembling the structures. Experiments are conducted on the new structures to measure the vibrational modes of interest. A sufficient number of structures must be tested in order to construct a well-characterized probability distribution for the SRQs of interest. In addition, the new measurements are *not* shown to the computational analysts.

Third, simulations are computed using the new preload information on the bolt torques for the new structures. It is presumed that a submodel is included that can predict the change in stiffness and damping in joints due to bolt torque. Presuming a Monte Carlo sampling procedure is used, a sufficient number of simulations must be computed so that a well-characterized probability distribution can be computed for the SRQs of interest.

Fourth, using the new simulations and the new experimental data, a validation metric result is computed for SRQs of interest. The validation metric operator must be able to accept probability distributions as input from the simulation and the experiment. The validation metric operator computes the difference between the probability distribution from the simulation and the experiment for the SRQs of interest. The validation metric result is a quantitative measure of the predictive accuracy of the model. For example, if the metric result was small, then the predictive accuracy is high. Chapters 12 and 13 discuss combined calibration and validation procedures in more detail.

In the unit problem tier, highly instrumented, highly accurate experimental data are obtained and an extensive uncertainty analysis of the experimental data is conducted. If possible, experiments on unit problems should be repeated using different diagnostic techniques, and possibly in separate experimental facilities, to ensure that systematic uncertainties (bias) in the experimental data are quantified. These types of experiment could be conducted in any organization that has the experimental facilities, the technical expertise, *and* the willingness to embrace this type of critical evaluation of both the experiment and the computation. Commonly, these experiments are conducted at universities or research laboratories.

10.2.5 Construction of a validation hierarchy

The underlying concept of system engineering in the validation hierarchy is not new. What is new is the consistent theme of model accuracy assessment over the spectrum from full-scale engineering systems to experiments focusing on physics models at the lower levels of the hierarchy. Stated differently, hierarchical model validation is application driven, *not* physics driven. The construction of a hierarchical validation structure and the identification of the types of experiments that could be conducted at each tier are formidable challenges. There are many ways of constructing the tiers; no single construction is best for all cases. In addition, one validation hierarchy would not be appropriate for systems in different environments; for example, normal, abnormal, and hostile. In fact, there could be different validation hierarchies for different scenarios *within* each environment condition.

A good hierarchical tier construction is one that accomplishes two tasks. First, the construction carefully disassembles the complete system into tiers in which each lower-level tier has one fewer level of physical complexity. For complex engineered systems, this will require more than the four tiers shown in Figure 10.7. The types of physical complexity that could be uncoupled from one tier to the next are spatial dimensionality, temporal nature, geometric complexity, and physical process coupling, including multi-scale coupling. The most important of these types of physical complexity to decouple or segregate into separate effects experiments, from one tier to the next, is physical process coupling. The reason is that physical process coupling generally produces the highest nonlinear response due to the various contributors. It is important to recognize the nonlinear nature of all of the contributors in the construction of the tiers because the philosophy of the tier construction rests heavily on linear system thinking. That is, it is assumed that confidence in predictive capability for the complete system can be built from assessment of predictive accuracy of each of its parts. The complete system of interest clearly does not have to be linear, but the philosophy of the hierarchical validation approach loses some of its utility and strength when strong nonlinear coupling occurs from one tier to the next.

The second task accomplished by a good hierarchical tier construction is the selection of individual experiments in a tier that are practically attainable and able to produce validation-quality data. In other words, the individual experiments should be (a) practically achievable given the experimental test facilities, budget, and schedule, and (b) capable of producing quantitative experimental measurements of all the important input quantities and multiple SRQs that can critically assess the model. As discussed earlier, the ability to conduct a true validation experiment at the complete system tier is extremely difficult, if not impossible, for complex systems. At the subsystem tier, it is feasible to conduct validation experiments, but it is still quite difficult and expensive. One usually chooses a single hardware subsystem or group of subsystems that are closely related in terms of physical processes or functionality. For complex subsystems, one might want to add a new tier below subsystems called *subassemblies*. As with subsystems, this tier would consist of actual operational hardware.

When one defines the individual experiments at the benchmark-tier level, then special hardware, i.e., nonoperational, nonfunctional hardware would be fabricated. The benchmark tier is probably the most difficult to formulate because it represents the transition from a hardware focus in the two top tiers to a physics-based focus in the bottom tiers of the hierarchy. At the bottom tier, unit problems, one should identify simple geometry experiments that have a single element of physical process complexity. For high-quality

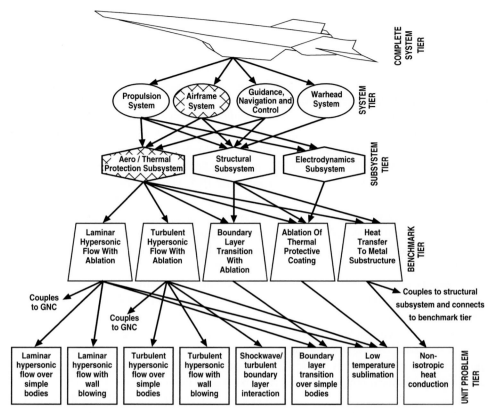

Figure 10.12 Example of a validation hierarchy for a hypersonic cruise missile (Oberkampf and Trucano, 2000).

validation experiments (a) one must be able to provide the necessary, highly characterized, input data to the simulation and (b) the experiments must be designed and conducted so that experimental uncertainty can be estimated in both inputs and outputs. High-quality validation experiments are practically attainable at the benchmark and unit-problem tiers, but they are not simple to conduct, nor inexpensive.

10.3 Example problem: hypersonic cruise missile

Here, we consider an example of a validation hierarchy for a hypersonic cruise missile (Oberkampf and Trucano, 2000). Assume the following characteristics of the missile system: (a) it is launched by an aircraft toward a ground target; (b) it is powered by a conventional gas turbine propulsion system, without a ducted fan; (c) it has an autonomous guidance, navigation, and control (GNC) system with an on-board millimeter-wave target seeker; and (d) it is functioning in a normal operating environment. Figure 10.12 shows a five-tier validation hierarchy for the hypersonic cruise missile that forms the basis of this discussion.

10.3.1 System tier

The entire missile is referred to as the *complete system* and the following as systems: propulsion, airframe, GNC, and warhead. These systems are as expected in the engineering design of such a vehicle. Additional elements could be added, however, depending on the perspective of the system engineer or the potential customer for the vehicle. The launch aircraft is not included at the system tier because its location in the hierarchy would be at the next higher tier, i.e., above the cruise missile. The hierarchical structure shown is not unique and it is not necessarily optimum for every system aspect that may be of interest, e.g., with regard to performance, reliability, or safety. In addition, the hierarchy shown emphasizes the airframe and aero/thermal protection subsystem (with cross-hatching), as will be discussed shortly.

10.3.2 Subsystem tier

At the subsystem tier, we have identified the following elements: aerodynamic performance and thermal protection, structural, and electrodynamics. The electrodynamics subsystem deals with the aspects of electromagnetic detectability of the cruise missile. This would range from radio frequencies used to detect the missile by radar, to detection in the visible spectrum. Only three elements are identified at the subsystem tier because they are the primary engineering design features that deal with the airframe system. Arrows drawn from the system-tier elements to the subsystem-tier elements indicate the primary elements that influence the subsystem tier. Recall at the subsystem tier that each element should be identified with functional hardware of the cruise missile. Consider how one would begin to conduct validation experiments at the subsystem tier depending on the computational discipline of interest. For example, the aero/thermal protection subsystem would contain subsystem hardware that is functionally related to the aerodynamic performance and heat transfer protection of any portion of the cruise missile. Some examples are (a) the as-manufactured thermal protective coating over the metal skin of the missile; (b) the as-manufactured metallic skin of the vehicle; (c) the metal or composite substructure under the skin of the vehicle; (d) all lifting surfaces, such as the vertical tail, and any control surfaces with their actuators; and (e) internal flow paths through the propulsion system, particularly the inlet and the exhaust ducts. However, the aero/thermal subsystem probably would not contain any other hardware inside the vehicle, unless some particular fluid flow path or heat conduction path was important. Note that there is commonly hardware that is in multiple subsystem-tier elements. For example, essentially all of the aero/thermal protection and the electrodynamics subsystem elements are also in the structural subsystem. The types of validation experiment and measurement, however, would be very different for each subsystem.

Suppose one were interested in validation experiments for the structural subsystem. If one were interested in the static deflection and stress of the various structural components, one would need to consider the mechanical coupling with nearby components and the aerodynamic loading, thermally induced loads, and any high-intensity acoustic excitation. For example, if one were interested in the deflection of the horizontal tail, the vertical tail and the nearby mechanical components of the fuselage would need to be included. If one were interested in the structural dynamic response of the various components, one would need to include essentially every piece of hardware from the missile because every part of the structure is dynamically coupled to every other part of the structure. Certain simplifications of the hardware, however, would be appropriate. For example, one could substitute mass-mockups for certain components, such as the completely functional propulsion system and the warhead, with little loss in fidelity. However, the structural dynamic and acoustic excitation caused by the propulsion system would be quite important in the validation of the structural subsystem.

10.3.3 Benchmark tier

At the benchmark tier, Figure 10.12 shows only the elements that would be functionally related to the aero/thermal protection subsystem. Although additional benchmark-tier elements could be shown, only the following elements are identified: (a) laminar hypersonic flow with ablation, (b) turbulent hypersonic flow with ablation, (c) boundary-layer transition with ablation, (d) ablation of the thermal protective coating, and (e) heat transfer to the metal substructure. The arrows drawn from the structural and electrodynamics subsystems to the benchmark tier only show coupling from these two subsystems to elements depicted at the benchmark tier.

At the benchmark tier one fabricates specialized, nonfunctional hardware. For example, the laminar, turbulent, and boundary-layer-transition elements may not contain the as-manufactured ablative coating of the missile. Instead, a simpler material might be used – one that would produce wall blowing and possibly gases or particles that may react within the boundary layer, yet simpler than the typically complex gas and particle chemistry that results from actual ablative materials. The element for ablation of the thermal protective coating may use the actual material on the missile, but the validation experiment may be conducted, for example, at conditions that are attainable in arc-jet tunnels. The arrow from the structural subsystem to the boundary-layer-transition element is drawn to show that structural vibration modes of the vehicle surface can influence transition. An arrow is drawn from each of the elements for hypersonic flow with ablation that are marked "Couples to GNC." These arrows indicate a coupling of the boundary layer flow field to the millimeter-wave seeker in the GNC hierarchy (not shown here). The element for the heat-transfer-to-metal substructure shows an arrow that would connect to elements at the benchmark tier in the structural subsystem hierarchical tree. This arrow indicates the coupling that will result in thermally induced stresses and cause temperature-dependent material properties to be considered in the structural simulation.

10.3.4 Unit-problem tier

The following elements are identified at the unit-problem tier: (a) laminar hypersonic flow over simple bodies, (b) laminar hypersonic flow with wall blowing, (c) turbulent hypersonic flow over simple bodies, (d) turbulent hypersonic flow with wall blowing, (e) shock wave/turbulent boundary layer interaction, (f) boundary layer transition over simple bodies, (g) low temperature sublimation, and (h) non-isotropic heat conduction. Many other elements could be identified at this tier, but these are representative of the types of validation experiment that should be conducted at the unit-problem tier. The identification of elements at this tier is easier than at the benchmark tier because unit-problem elements are more closely related to traditional mathematical model building experiments and model calibration experiments in fluid dynamics and heat transfer.

A point of clarification should be made concerning experiments at the lower tiers of the hierarchy, particularly at the unit-problem tier. Some researchers and system designers refer to experiments at the lower tiers, such as laminar hypersonic flow in a wind tunnel, as a *simulation* of the flight vehicle in the atmosphere. From the perspective of a project engineer interested in performance of the *real* vehicle, this view about experimentation is appropriate. From the perspective of conducting a validation experiment, however, this view only confuses the issue. That is, an experiment conducted at any tier is a physical realization of a process whose results can be used to assess the accuracy of a simulation. The relationship of the physical experiment to the performance of some engineering system is not the critical issue with regard to the *reality* of the validation experiment. *Any* experiment is reality. However, the project engineer who is interested in performance of the *real* vehicle may not appreciate how certain experiments relate to goals of his/her project.

10.3.5 Validation pyramid

To explain better how the validation hierarchy of the airframe system is related to the validation hierarchy of the propulsion, GNC, and warhead systems, see Figure 10.13. The validation hierarchy of each of these four systems could be viewed as the primary facets of a four-sided pyramid. In the earlier discussion, the airframe facet was divided into three additional facets, each representing the three subsystems: aero/thermal protection, structural, and electrodynamics. The propulsion system could be divided into four additional facets to represent its subsystems: compressor, combustor, turbine, and thermal signature. Similarly, the GNC and the warhead systems could be divided into subsystems appropriate to each. On the surface of this multifaceted pyramid, one could more clearly and easily indicate the coupling from one facet to another. For example, we discussed the coupling of laminar and hypersonic flow with ablation to the millimeter-wave seeker of the GNC system. This coupling would be shown by an arrow connecting these hypersonic flow elements to appropriate elements on the GNC facet of the pyramid.

The validation pyramid stresses the system engineering viewpoint, as opposed to a scientific discipline viewpoint sometimes used in simulation-based design. Each facet of the

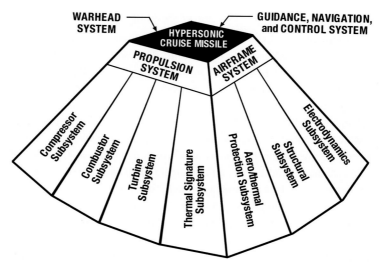

Figure 10.13 Example of a validation pyramid for a hypersonic cruise missile (Oberkampf and Trucano, 2000).

pyramid can then be devoted to identifying validation experiments for each computational model responsible for part of the design of the system. As one traverses around the top of the pyramid, the number of facets is equal to the number of systems that are identified. For example, in the hypersonic cruise missile, this would total four. As one traverses around the bottom of the pyramid, the number of facets is equal to the total number of elements that have been identified around the entire pyramid at the unit-problem tier. For a complex system, the total number of facets would likely be larger than a hundred. For example, in the hypersonic cruise missile, we identified eight elements at the unit-problem tier that were primarily due to the aero/thermal protection subsystem. However, several additional elements could be identified at the unit problem tier; all primarily related to the aero/thermal protection subsystem. We strongly believe this type of system engineering thinking is necessary to increase the confidence in complex systems that are designed, manufactured, certified, and deployed with higher reliance on scientific computing and reduced levels of testing.

10.3.6 Final comments

Two comments are in order concerning the construction of a validation hierarchy. First, the location of a particular validation experiment within the hierarchy must be determined relative to all of the surrounding elements in the hierarchy; i.e., it must be appropriately related to all of the experiments above it, below it, and in the same tier. Stated differently, the same validation experiment can be at different tiers for validation hierarchies that are constructed for different complex systems of interest. For example, the same turbulent-separated-flow experiment could be at the unit-problem tier in a complex system and at the benchmark tier in a simpler engineering system.

Second, a validation hierarchy is constructed for a particular engineered system operating under a particular class of operating conditions; for example, normal operating conditions. A new validation hierarchy would be constructed if one were interested in computationally analyzing other classes of system operating conditions or environments. Suppose one was interested in abnormal or hostile environments and the particular scenario of interest is that certain subsystems failed. Two examples are (a) certain weather environments or battle damage caused loss of a portion of the thermal protection system, and (b) certain electrical components of the GNC system failed or were damaged due to a microwave pulse of energy from defensive weapon systems. For these types of scenario, one would construct a different pyramid because different mathematical models would come into play.

10.4 Conceptual, technical, and practical difficulties of validation

10.4.1 Conceptual difficulties

In Chapter 2, the philosophical issues underlying the concept of validation of models were touched on. It was pointed out that philosophers of science generally agree that theories and laws of nature can only be *disproved* or *failed to be disproved*. But, it was also stated that this perspective is unproductive and even debilitating for assessing the credibility of models in engineering and some natural science fields. The greatest debate over model validation seems to come from the field of hydrology, specifically surface water flow and subsurface water transport (Oreskes *et al.*, 1994; Chiles and Delfiner, 1999; Anderson and Bates, 2001; Morton and Suarez, 2001; Oreskes and Belitz, 2001). Hydrologists have well-justified concerns of validation concepts because of the nature of their models. Their models are dominated by parameters that are calibrated based on measurements of system responses. The calibrated parameters typically are not just a few scalar quantities, but also scalar fields in two and three dimensions, as well as tensor fields. As a result, there is astounding flexibility in hydrological models to match observations. From a conceptual viewpoint, one is still left with the question: can calibrated models be validated? We give two answers to the question, depending on the definition of validation one chooses.

First, suppose we use the restricted view of the term *model validation* as we have done throughout this book. That is, model validation refers to Aspect 1 in Figure 10.1 shown earlier in this chapter: assessment of model accuracy by comparison with experimental data. The unequivocal answer to the question would be *yes*. The accuracy of a model can be assessed regardless of whether the model has been calibrated or not. If the model uses very closely related experimental data (from a physics perspective) for accuracy assessment as used for calibration, however, the test of accuracy adds little value in the sense of new knowledge about the shortcomings of the model.

Second, we refer back to the discussion in Section 2.2.3 of Chapter 2 concerning the *encompassing view* of model validation. This view of validation includes all three aspects of validation as shown in Figure 10.1, above. First, assessment of model accuracy by comparison with experimental data; second, interpolation or extrapolation of the model to the intended use; and third, decision of model adequacy for the intended use. If one uses this view, as is done by the ASME Guide, one would also answer the question *yes*. Each of the three aspects of validation can be accomplished regardless of whether the model had been calibrated or not. That is, the restricted view and the encompassing view of the validation make *no presumptions* concerning *how* the model was built.

We argue that the more important question to be asked is: how can the predictive capability of a calibrated model be assessed? This question intuitively reflects the science-based perspective that is our foundation. Zeigler *et al.* (2000) discusses validation in terms of a sequence of more demanding requirements for the model. They define *replicative validity* to mean "for all of the experiments possible within the experimental frame, the behavior of the model and system agree within acceptable tolerance." By *predictive validation* they require "not only replicative validity, but also the ability to predict as yet unseen system behavior." By *structural validity* they require "that the model not only is capable of replicating the data observed from the system, but also mimics in step-by-step, component-by-component fashion the way in which the system does it transitions." Bossel (1994) touches on the same issues by defining two types of model: descriptive models and explanatory models. *Descriptive models* are those that can imitate the behavior of the system based on previous observations of the system. *Explanatory models* are those that represent a system's structure and its components, and their connections so that one can understand the future system behavior even under conditions never before experienced.

As discussed in Section 3.2.2, examples of descriptive models are regression and empirical models that relate the inputs to outputs. They can also be very sophisticated stochastic Markov chain Monte Carlo models to deal with nondeterministic features of not only the inputs and outputs, but also some presumed internal features of the system. Descriptive models require a great deal of data to gain confidence that the mathematical mapping of inputs to outputs is properly characterized. Explanatory models require a great deal of knowledge concerning the fundamental relationships and interactions occurring within the system. Input data are only needed to make specific predictions of outputs. The goal of science is clearly explanatory models because the strength of the model inference is built on detailed knowledge. Computational simulation of complex physical systems must live in the world between descriptive and explanatory models. We prefer to think of our models as scientific, but many times the reality is that they are more descriptive than we would like to admit.

We suggest a framework for providing a graded answer to the question of predictive capability, depending on the degree of calibration of the model. Figure 10.14 depicts the notional ability to assess the predictive capability of a model as a function of the number of free parameters in the model. *Free* parameters are those that *cannot* be independently measured separate from the model being assessed. As suggested in Figure 10.14, the ability to

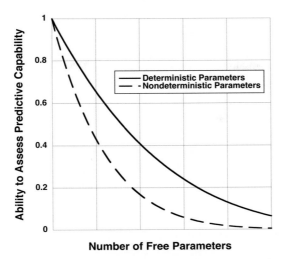

Figure 10.14 Ability to assess predictive capability as a function of the number of free parameters.

assess the model's predictive capability depends on whether the free parameters are deterministic (scalars) or nondeterministic (functions). If one is dealing with nondeterministic parameters, there is much greater flexibility in calibrating because one has probability distributions as opposed to just being numbers. The free parameters may have some physical justification based on knowledge of the processes occurring within the system, for example, they may be effective physical properties. However, their quantification is fundamentally dependent on the assumptions and mental constructs of the model, as well as the observed responses of the system. The numbers on the ordinate of the graph (Figure 10.14) are only notional in the following sense. First, the ability to assess a model is simply represented as a scale based on unity as a crisp *yes*, and zero as a crisp *no*. Second, the ability to assess a model does not only depend on the number of free parameters, but also on how sensitive the model is to the various parameters. For example, a model may have a hundred free parameters, but only five are important in the prediction of a given SRQ.

By answering the predictive capability question in this way, we suggest the following framework. First, the ability to assess a model's predictive capability rapidly decreases as the number of free parameters increases. For a model with a large number of free parameters, the calibrated parameters *become* the essence of the model, as opposed to the posited knowledge in the assumptions of the model. Hydrological models, for example, are clearly in this domain. The number of free parameters in a two- or three-dimensional scalar field typically depends on the spatial discretization that is chosen in the computational simulation. This number can total into the millions on modern supercomputers. Additionally, the free parameters are usually given by probability distributions, which gives additional flexibility to the model.

Second, most models in scientific computing are physics-based models. These models conserve mass, momentum, and energy so the associated conservation equations (which are typically PDEs) can be viewed as constraints on the calibration process. As a result, calibration of parameters in these models can be viewed as a PDE constrained optimization problem. When the number of free parameters becomes large, even in a physics-based model, the effect of the physics constraints becomes imperceptible. That is, a physics-based model becomes equivalent to a descriptive model that has little internal structure and is adapted to fit experimental observations of the system.

And third, our postulated framework gives no credit or loss for models that approach model accuracy assessment as a two-step process: calibration then validation. For example, suppose a deterministic model contained a handful of free parameters that were calibrated based on ten or twenty observations of the system. The parameters could be estimated using an optimization procedure to minimize some type of error measure based on the difference between model output and the observations. The two-step process is very useful, and often necessary, in complex physics modeling. But the framework argues that the ability to assess a model's predictive capability depends primarily on how many free parameters are available, not on the degree of independence between the calibration data and the validation data. Depending on the closeness of the calibration and validation data, as argued above and in Chapter 12, the ability to assess a model's predictive capability is additionally diminished.

As a result, the suggested framework does not address the issue of how demanding is the test of model accuracy assessment. For example, suppose a model has been calibrated with one set of observed system responses, and then the model accuracy is assessed with a very closely related set of observations. This test of model accuracy is very weak compared to a test where the model is asked to predict the system response for a substantially different set of conditions. The issue of rigorously understanding *how demanding* is a model accuracy test, or *how dissimilar* are new conditions from calibration conditions, is an open research topic. Section 14.5 discusses this issue in more detail.

10.4.2 *Technical and practical difficulties*

There are situations where technical and practical difficulties in obtaining experimental measurements either hinder or eliminate the possibility of model validation. These difficulties can be generally grouped into (a) the technology is presently unavailable to make the measurements needed, (b) it is technically impossible to obtain the data regardless of the technology, and (c) it is impractical or not cost effective to obtain the measurements. Some examples where the technology is unavailable at the present time are the following. First, experimental data on hypervelocity impact is extremely limited in terms of spatial detail or the measurement of a variety of SRQs. Typical experimental results are photographs of the impact crater or hole through a specimen after the impact. In some facilities, high speed imaging of the penetration event is available. These data are useful in validation, but they greatly limit the ability to quantitatively assess the accuracy of various SRQs from the model. Second, the measurement of underground transport of substances, primarily due to water flow through porous media, is very limited. The typical procedure is to inject tracer substances at locations where wells have been drilled, then monitor the tracer concentration at nearby wells as a function of depth and time. The porosity and permeability of the surrounding subsurface material that appear in the PDEs are then adjusted so that the observed tracer concentration record is matched. As can be seen, this results in the solution of an inverse (calibration) problem. That is, given the observed output, what field characteristics should the system have for the assumed model to produce the observed output. Third, the ability of measuring both simulation input quantities and SRQs at the micrometer scale and smaller is very limited. As mathematical models continue to develop for spatial scales in these ranges, the ability to validate these models will be a pacing item. As a result, confidence in predictions at these spatial scales for materials science, biochemistry, and biophysics will be significantly impeded.

An example of a situation where it is conceptually impossible to obtain the needed experimental data for validation is in modeling physical phenomena with very long time scales, on the order of centuries or tens of centuries, or very large physical scales. Some examples are (a) long-term prediction of the underground storage of toxic or nuclear wastes; (b) long-term prediction of the effect of various contributors to global warming; and (c) response of the global environment to a large-scale atmospheric event, such as a volcanic eruption or the impact of a sizeable asteroid.

There are also situations where it is not cost effective, impractical, or not allowed to obtain experimental data for validation, even though experiments are technically feasible. Some of these are (a) conducting an experiment on the explosive failure of a full-scale reactor containment building, (b) conducting an experiment on the earthquake or explosive failure of a large-scale dam, (c) obtaining certain experimental data for the physiological response of humans to toxic chemicals or substances, and (d) hazardous or environmentally damaging tests that are banned by international treaties.

10.5 References

Aeschliman, D. P. and W. L. Oberkampf (1998). Experimental methodology for computational fluid dynamics code validation. *AIAA Journal*. **36**(5), 733–741.

AIAA (1998). *Guide for the Verification and Validation of Computational Fluid Dynamics Simulations*. AIAA-G-077–1998, Reston, VA, American Institute of Aeronautics and Astronautics.

Anderson, M. G. and P. D. Bates (2001). Hydrological science: model credibility and scientific integrity. In *Model Validation: Perspectives in Hydrological Science*. M. G. Anderson and P. D. Bates (eds.). New York, John Wiley.

Anderson, M. G. and P. D. Bates, eds (2001). *Model Validation: Perspectives in Hydrological Science*. New York, NY, John Wiley.

Balci, O., W. F. Ormsby, J. T. Carr, and S. D. Saadi (2000). Planning for verification, validation, and accreditation of modeling and simulation applications. *2000 Winter Simulation Conference*, Orlando FL, 829–839.

Barber, T. J. (1998). Role of code validation and certification in the design environment. *AIAA Journal*. **36**(5), 752–758.

Benek, J. A., E. M. Kraft, and R. F. Lauer (1998). Validation issues for engine–airframe integration. *AIAA Journal*. **36**(5), 759–764.

Bossel, H. (1994). *Modeling and Simulation*. 1st edn., Wellesley, MA, A. K. Peters.

Chiles, J.-P. and P. Delfiner (1999). *Geostatistics: Modeling Spatial Uncertainty*, New York, John Wiley.

Cosner, R. R. (1995). CFD validation requirements for technology transition. *26th AIAA Fluid Dynamics Conference*, AIAA Paper 95–2227, San Diego, CA, American Institute of Aeronautics and Astronautics.

Hornung, H. G. and A. E. Perry (1998). Personal communication.

Kleijnen, J. P. C. (1998). Experimental design for sensitivity analysis, optimization, and validation of simulation models. In *Handbook of Simulation: Principles, Methodology, Advances, Application, and Practice*. J. Banks (ed.). New York, John Wiley: 173–223.

Kleindorfer, G. B., L. O'Neill, and R. Ganeshan (1998). Validation in simulation: various positions in the philosophy of science. *Management Science*. **44**(8), 1087–1099.

Lin, S. J., S. L. Barson, and M. M. Sindir (1992). Development of evaluation criteria and a procedure for assessing predictive capability and code performance. *Advanced Earth-to-Orbit Propulsion Technology Conference*, Marshall Space Flight Center, Huntsville, AL.

Marvin, J. G. (1995). Perspective on computational fluid dynamics validation. *AIAA Journal*. **33**(10), 1778–1787.

McNish, A. G. (1962). The speed of light. *Institute of Radio Engineers, Transactions on Instrumentation*. **I-11**(3–4), 138–148.

Morgan, M. G. and M. Henrion (1990). *Uncertainty: a Guide to Dealing with Uncertainty in Quantitative Risk and Policy Analysis*. 1st edn., Cambridge, UK, Cambridge University Press.

Morton, A. and M. Suarez (2001). Kinds of models. In *Model Validation: Perspectives in Hydrological Science*. M. G. Anderson and P. D. Bates (eds.). New York, John Wiley.

Murray-Smith, D. J. (1998). Methods for the external validation of continuous systems simulation models: a review. *Mathematical and Computer Modelling of Dynamics Systems*. **4**, 5–31.

Oberkampf, W. L. and D. P. Aeschliman (1992). Joint computational/experimental aerodynamics research on a hypersonic vehicle: Part 1, Experimental results. *AIAA Journal*. **30**(8), 2000–2009.

Oberkampf, W. L. and M. F. Barone (2006). Measures of agreement between computation and experiment: validation metrics. *Journal of Computational Physics*. **217**(1), 5–36.

Oberkampf, W. L. and T. G. Trucano (2000). Validation methodology in computational fluid dynamics. *Fluids 2000 Conference*, AIAA Paper 2000–2549, Denver, CO, American Institute of Aeronautics and Astronautics.

Oberkampf, W. L. and T. G. Trucano (2002). Verification and validation in computational fluid dynamics. *Progress in Aerospace Sciences*. **38**(3), 209–272.

Oberkampf, W. L. and T. G. Trucano (2007). *Verification and Validation Benchmarks*. SAND2007–0853, Albuquerque, NM, Sandia National Laboratories.

Oberkampf, W. L. and T. G. Trucano (2008). Verification and validation benchmarks. *Nuclear Engineering and Design*. **238**(3), 716–743.

Oberkampf, W. L., D. P. Aeschliman, J. F. Henfling, and D. E. Larson (1995). Surface pressure measurements for CFD code validation in hypersonic flow. *26th AIAA Fluid Dynamics Conference*, AIAA Paper 95–2273, San Diego, CA, American Institute of Aeronautics and Astronautics.

Oberkampf, W. L., T. G. Trucano, and C. Hirsch (2004). Verification, validation, and predictive capability in computational engineering and physics. *Applied Mechanics Reviews*. **57**(5), 345–384.

Oreskes, N. and K. Belitz (2001). Philosophical issues in model assessment. In *Model Validation: Perspectives in Hydrological Science*. M. G. Anderson and P. D. Bates (eds.). New York, John Wiley.

Oreskes, N., K. Shrader-Frechette, and K. Belitz (1994). Verification, validation, and confirmation of numerical models in the earth sciences. *Science*. **263**, 641–646.

Pilch, M., T. G. Trucano, J. L. Moya, G. K. Froehlich, A. L. Hodges and D. E. Peercy (2001). *Guidelines for Sandia ASCI Verification and Validation Plans – Content and Format: Version 2*. SAND2000–3101, Albuquerque, NM, Sandia National Laboratories.

Pilch, M., T. G. Trucano, D. E. Peercy, A. L. Hodges, and G. K. Froehlich (2004). *Concepts for Stockpile Computing (OUO)*. SAND2004–2479 (Restricted Distribution, Official Use Only), Albuquerque, NM, Sandia National Laboratories.

Porter, J. L. (1996). A summary/overview of selected computational fluid dynamics (CFD) code validation/calibration activities. *27th AIAA Fluid Dynamics Conference*, AIAA Paper 96–2053, New Orleans, LA, American Institute of Aeronautics and Astronautics.

Refsgaard, J. C. (2000). Towards a formal approach to calibration and validation of models using spatial data. In *Spatial Patterns in Catchment Hydrology: Observations and Modelling*. R. Grayson and G. Bloschl (eds.). Cambridge, Cambridge University Press: 329–354.

Rizzi, A. and J. Vos (1998). Toward establishing credibility in computational fluid dynamics simulations. *AIAA Journal*. **36**(5), 668–675.

Roache, P. J. (1998). *Verification and Validation in Computational Science and Engineering*, Albuquerque, NM, Hermosa Publishers.

Rykiel, E. J. (1996). Testing ecological models: the meaning of validation. *Ecological Modelling*. **90**(3), 229–244.

Sargent, R. G. (1998). Verification and validation of simulation models. *1998 Winter Simulation Conference*, Washington, DC, 121–130.

Sindir, M. M., S. L. Barson, D. C. Chan, and W. H. Lin (1996). On the development and demonstration of a code validation process for industrial applications. *27th AIAA Fluid Dynamics Conference*, AIAA Paper 96–2032, New Orleans, LA, American Institute of Aeronautics and Astronautics.

Sindir, M. M. and E. D. Lynch (1997). Overview of the state-of-practice of computational fluid dynamics in advanced propulsion system design. *28th AIAA Fluid Dynamics Conference*, AIAA Paper 97–2124, Snowmass, CO, American Institute of Aeronautics and Astronautics.

Trucano, T. G., M. Pilch, and W. L. Oberkampf (2002). *General Concepts for Experimental Validation of ASCI Code Applications*. SAND2002–0341, Albuquerque, NM, Sandia National Laboratories.

Youden, W. J. (1972). Enduring values. *Technometrics*. **14**(1), 1–11.

Zeigler, B. P., H. Praehofer and T. G. Kim (2000). *Theory of Modeling and Simulation: Integrating Discrete Event and Continuous Complex Dynamic Systems*. 2nd edn., San Diego, CA, Academic Press.

Zuber, N., G. E. Wilson, M. Ishii, W. Wulff, B. E. Boyack, A. E. Dukler, P. Griffith, J. M. Healzer, R. E. Henry, J. R. Lehner, S. Levy, and F. J. Moody (1998). An integrated structure and scaling methodology for severe accident technical issue resolution: development of methodology. *Nuclear Engineering and Design*. **186**(1–2), 1–21.

11

Design and execution of validation experiments

Chapter 10, Model validation fundamentals, discussed the philosophy of validation experiments and how they differ from traditional experiments as well as calibration experiments. A validation experiment is conducted for the primary purpose of determining the predictive accuracy of a mathematical model. In other words, a validation experiment is designed, executed, and analyzed for the purpose of quantitatively determining the ability of a mathematical model and its embodiment in a computer code to simulate a well-characterized physical process. In this chapter we describe six primary guidelines for the design and execution of validation experiments. Our discussion will also deal with how these guidelines can be carried out and why they are sometimes difficult to execute in practice.

We will then discuss a high-quality validation experiment that the authors, as well as several others, designed and executed. The experiment is referred to as the Joint Computational/Experimental Aerodynamics Program (JCEAP). From the beginning of the project, it was designed to synergistically couple computational fluid dynamics development and an experimental research in a hypersonic wind tunnel. The program was initiated in 1990 at Sandia National Laboratories and came to a successful close in 1997. The program helped develop the six fundamental guidelines for the design and execution of high-quality validation experiments. We use JCEAP to exemplify these six guidelines and make recommendations for how they can be applied to validation experiments in general.

11.1 Guidelines for validation experiments

These guidelines were developed over a period of several years and were originally reported in Aeschliman and Oberkampf (1998); Oberkampf and Blottner (1998); and Oberkampf and Trucano (2002). Although JCEAP greatly assisted in refining these ideas, most of these ideas had been presented individually by computational and experimental researchers in the past. Some of the key contributors to developing these ideas were Cosner (1995); Marvin (1995); Porter (1996); Barber (1998); Benek *et al.* (1998); and Roache (1998).

In each of the guidelines we refer to *a validation experiment*. We want to stress that this term is simply for convenience. A high quality validation experiment is always a *suite* or *ensemble* of many experiments, sometimes numbering into the hundreds, that all share a common goal: critical evaluation of the predictive accuracy of a model.

11.1.1 Joint effort between analysts and experimentalists

Guideline 1: A validation experiment should be jointly designed by experimentalists, model developers, code developers, and code users working closely together throughout the program, from inception to documentation, with complete candor about the strengths and weaknesses of each approach.

By *model developers* we mean applied researchers who build the mathematical models that are incorporated into computer codes. By *code developers* we mean those who write the computer software or implement the mathematical models into the software. By *code users* we mean those who use the code for analysis of engineering systems or processes. For our purposes here, we will group these various types of people into the term *analysts*.

To some, Guideline 1 may sound relatively easy to accomplish. Our experience has shown, however, that it is extraordinarily difficult to accomplish in practice. There are several reasons why this is true: some practical and some human nature. The first requirement to form a team of experimentalists and analysts for the design and execution of a validation experiment is that funding is available for both at the same time. Experimentalists and analysts have traditionally sought funding from separate sources. If these two groups wanted to design and conduct a validation experiment, they would each go their own way to seek funding. It would be rare for both to obtain support for their work during the same time frame, if at all. Contributing to this is the long held tradition, both in industry and in government, that one source is not responsible for funding both experiments and computations. It is certainly understandable why these traditions are in place, but if they continue, high quality validation experiments will remain rare.

If funding does become available for both experimentalists and analysts at the same time, then one must deal with the technical synchronization of both activities. The experimental facility and diagnostic instrumentation needed for the validation experiment must be available and ready for use; not in the construction or development phase. Similarly, the code and the options needed for validation must be operational and have been adequately tested through code verification activities. Some analysts will question this last requirement. They feel that code debugging and testing can be conducted in parallel with validation. This is a gross misjudgment that was discussed in Chapter 2, Fundamental concepts and terminology, and Chapter 10, Model validation fundamentals. Having both the experimental and computational capabilities fully prepared and the needed personnel available at the same time requires careful planning.

Another practical reason why it is very difficult to form a unified team of experimentalists and analysts is that team members are commonly from different organizations. For example, suppose a group of analysts is from a company that does not have the needed experimental facilities. If the analysts' company obtains funding for validation activities related to their models and codes, then the analysts' company would seek bids for the work and subcontract with a company that could conduct the experiments. Although technical qualifications of potential bidders for the experimental work are important, there are two business issues that come into play. First, when the analysts' company is seeking a facility in which to conduct the experiment, this is clearly a competitive situation for potential bidders. The potential bidders will be reluctant to expose any weakness, limitations, or deficiencies within their facility. Not only would they risk losing the potential contract, they would also fear that the information could be used against them in the future by their competitors. Second, the analysts' company, once the contract is placed, is in control of funding and the direction of the project. From the perspective of the experimentalists' company, they are the supplier and the analysts' company is the customer. As a result, the experimentalists are the subordinate team members.

Suppose the experimentalists and the analysts are from two different organizations in the same corporation, government organization, or university. As is very commonly the case, the experimentalists and the analysts may be familiar with each other, but they have not developed a close working relationship. In fact, their history may be that they have been competitors for funding or recognition of achievement in the past. For example, the "computers versus wind tunnels" mentality (Chapman *et al.*, 1975) that has existed in the past in some areas of the computational fluid dynamics (CFD) community is a perfect example of competition, not collaboration. Also, because of the nature of their technical training and professional work, there is typically a gulf separating computationalists' and experimentalists' technical interests and possibly backgrounds. These factors, both obvious and insidious, will deter the candor and openness needed to forthrightly discuss the strengths and weaknesses in the computational and experimental approaches, during both the design and the execution of the validation experiment. These can be overcome in time, but it requires patience, respect, and understanding. In the fast-paced modern, competitive environment, these can be in short supply.

Some changes are obvious concerning how to overcome these substantive difficulties, but some are not. Funding organizations need to recognize the importance of funding both experimental and computational activities together. Even if it were recognized, there would probably be structural changes needed within the funding organization to actually accomplish funding of joint experimental and computational activities.

Organizations that contract for experimental services to provide validation data need to understand the new requirements in high quality validation experiments. Valuing candor and forthrightness in subcontracting for these types of services will be a difficult change to make for both sides of the business enterprise.

Finally, within organizations that conduct validation experiments and simulations, a change in management perspective is needed. Funding groups within an organization must understand that experimental and computational activities need to be funded at the same time. For applied research groups, it is reasonable to imagine this change. For project groups that are focused on building and delivering hardware and staying on budget and schedule, this is extremely difficult to achieve. Some farsighted project managers may devote project funds to core competency development such as validation, but our experience is that these are rare individuals. For organizations that *are* able to fund both experimental and computational groups in a validation experiment project, management must understand that it is the success or failure of the joint activity that should be openly recognized and rewarded.

A common viewpoint of scientific computing managers is that if the joint project shows that the model performed poorly, then the project is considered a failure. Stated differently, many scientific computing managers feel that the goal of a validation activity is to make the model look good. It is difficult for more enlightened managers to change this viewpoint.

11.1.2 Measurement of all needed input data

Guideline 2: A validation experiment should be designed to capture the essential physics of interest, and measure all relevant physical modeling data, initial and boundary conditions, and system excitation information required by the model.

The validation experiment should be designed to address the physics of interest with regard to its spatial dimensionality, temporal nature, and geometric complexity. For example, one may be interested in conducting a two-dimensional (2-D), either planar or axisymmetric, experiment. The question is: are the three-dimensional (3-D) effects in the experiment negligibly small so that a 2-D simulation can be appropriately compared with the experimental data? Since the ability of the experimentalist to detect 3-D effects is very limited, the analyst should attempt to answer this question. Both 2-D and 3-D simulations of the experiment should be computed to predict the spatial dimensionality effect on the system response quantities (SRQs) of interest. If the change in the SRQs between the 2-D and 3-D simulations is comparable to the expected experimental measurement uncertainty, and the 3-D simulations are credible, then a 3-D simulation should be used in model validation. Note that both solutions must be mesh resolved and iteratively converged to the same level so that a proper comparison of results can be made. If the 3-D simulations are not computed, then the difficulty is what to conclude if poor agreement is obtained between the experimental measurements and the 2-D simulations. Is the disagreement due to the 2-D assumption in the model, or other weaknesses in the model? Recent experience by several researchers in fluid dynamics has shown that some experiments that were thought to be essentially planar 2-D were found to have significant 3-D effects. An analogous question arises with regard to temporal assumptions in the model. Can a steady-state assumption be made in the model, or is an unsteady simulation required?

Guideline 2 points out that the goal-directed activities of the validation experiment must be understood by both the computational and experimental members of the team. From the computational side, the analysts must understand what spatial dimensionality, temporal nature, and geometric simplifications are appropriate in modeling a specific experiment. From the experimental side, the experimentalists must decide what design and operational features should exist in the experimentally tested system, in the experimental facility, and in the instrumentation so that the specified modeling assumptions are properly tested. If the parameters that are initially requested by the analyst for the simulation cannot be satisfied in the proposed experimental facility, it may be feasible to alter the model inputs and still satisfy the primary validation goals. Or it may be necessary to look for another facility. For example, in a fluid dynamics experiment, can a laminar boundary layer on a surface be ensured and can it be accurately characterized? Is the type and quantity of instrumentation appropriate to provide the required data in sufficient quantity and at the required accuracy and spatial resolution? Conversely, analysts must understand, or be informed by the experimentalists, concerning the limitations of the experimental equipment, the instrumentation, and the facility.

As part of the requirement for Guideline 2, the experimentalists should measure all important physical modeling data, initial conditions (ICs), boundary conditions (BCs), and system excitation information needed as input for the simulation. Any important experimental conditions needed by the code, but not measured, will significantly undermine the value of the validation experiment. If key input data are not measured, as discussed in Chapter 10, the best result that can be obtained is that the simulation will yield imprecise results, e.g., either SRQ intervals or probability-boxes (p-boxes), which must be compared with the measurements. (p-boxes were introduced in Chapter 3, Modeling and computational simulation, and will be discussed in more detail in Chapter 12, Model accuracy assessment.) The much more likely result is that the analyst will use the unmeasured quantities as adjustable parameters to calibrate their models to obtain the best agreement with the measured system responses. This, of course, destroys the fundamental goal of validation: assessment of model predictive accuracy.

The input quantities that should be used in the computational simulation are those that are *actually measured* in the validation experiment. Some of these input quantities from the experiment may not be known or even knowable for various reasons. Two different reasons for not precisely knowing input quantities can arise. First, a quantity can be epistemically uncertain, for example: (a) a quantity was not measured because of poor communication between the analyst and the experimentalist, but was characterized by the experimentalist as an interval; (b) a quantity was not measured and the experimentalist simply estimated the quantity based on experience, or took the value from an engineering handbook, as opposed to actual measurement; or (c) the geometric description of the test article is taken from the fabrication drawings of the hardware, as opposed to determining the deflection of the article due to mechanical and thermal loading in the actual experiment.

Second, a quantity is known to be a random variable, *and* it is not independently measurable before, during, or after the validation experiment. Some examples are (a) a quantity cannot be measured independently from the validation experiment because the measurement alters the quantity, such as a destructive test; (b) a quantity cannot be measured independently from the experiment because its characterization changes during the experiment; and (c) a quantity in the experiment is not controllable from one experiment to the next, and it is not independently measurable. If the input quantity is uncertain because of both a lack of knowledge (epistemic uncertainty) and a random process (aleatory uncertainty), then the quantity should be characterized as a p-box.

Input quantities that are aleatory uncertainties and, in addition, are *not* independently measurable as part of the validation experiment, should be characterized in terms of a probability density function or a cumulative distribution function. For example, suppose a material property is an input quantity in a validation experiment, but it has inherent variability due to manufacturing. The property can be measured, but the measurement alters the specimen, rendering it useless for the validation experiment. The proper procedure is to characterize the variability of the property by drawing samples from the parent population, e.g., a given production lot. After a number of samples are obtained, a probability distribution is constructed for the population and it is used as the input to the model. This probability distribution is propagated through the model to obtain a probability distribution for the SRQ of interest. A quantitative comparison can then be made between a probability distribution of experimental measurements and the probability distribution from the simulation. This procedure is discussed in more detail in Chapter 12.

To give an indication of the level of detail that is needed in characterizing a validation experiment, various fluid dynamics experiments will be discussed. The following are examples of the level of detail that may be needed for physical modeling and boundary conditions for a vehicle tested in a wind tunnel:

- accurate measurements of the actual model dimensions, as opposed to nominal or as requested specifications;
- surface roughness condition, including imperfections or mismatches in body components or attachments;
- location of boundary layer transition over the surface of the vehicle for all free-stream conditions, angles of attack, and control surface deflections;
- measurement of free-stream turbulence quantities in the wind tunnel;
- accurate measurement of locations and geometric detail of all instrumentation, as opposed to requested locations or installations stated in the fabrication drawings;
- location of where the free-stream conditions were measured in the wind tunnel, especially for a subsonic free-stream;
- for a subsonic free-stream, pressure measurements on the tunnel walls inside the test section near the beginning and end of the computational domain;
- detailed dimensions and geometric detail of all hardware for mounting the model in the wind tunnel.

For aircraft configurations, wings, and deformable bodies, an additional important detail is the measurement of the actual deformed geometry under the experimental load. A much less desirable approach is to calculate of the shape of the deformed structure. The measurements or calculations of the deformed structure may involve time-dependent histories. In long duration hypersonic wind tunnels, the deformation of the vehicle due to aerodynamic heating should be measured or, if necessary, estimated. For hypersonic and supersonic tunnels, the model's surface temperature should be measured at an appropriate number of locations over the surface of the model during the run-time of the wind tunnel.

In wind tunnels, the free-stream flow provides the inflow boundary conditions for the simulation. This information comes from measurements of flowfield quantities in the test section of the tunnel, such as the free-stream Mach number; total pressure and static pressure; and total temperature and static temperature. These data are measured at a number of points in the test section during the calibration of the wind tunnel. Commonly, these data are spatially averaged over the test section and these averages are used in simulations. For boundary layer transition experiments, the calibration measurements should also include free-stream turbulence intensity and Reynolds stresses. Some facility managers may be reluctant to share such detailed flow quality data with users (and competitors). However, for experimental data that will be compared with CFD simulations that use sophisticated turbulence models or transition models, these data are critical.

For supersonic wind tunnels, the flowfield calibration measurements at the beginning of the test section could be used to set the flow properties as location dependent boundary conditions upstream of the bow shock wave of the vehicle. Such an approach, although conceptually feasible, is just now being attempted in simulations for validation experiments. Some might consider this approach excessive and unnecessary for wind tunnels with high quality, i.e., very uniform, flowfields. However, in Section 11.4.2 we show that flowfield nonuniformity is the largest contributor to experimental measurement uncertainty in three high quality supersonic wind tunnels that have been used for validation experiments. We contend this is true for most wind tunnels.

For subsonic wind tunnels, the question of boundary conditions becomes much more complex because of the elliptic character of the PDEs describing the flowfield. For low-speed wind tunnels, even with low levels of model blockage, one of the first issues that must be addressed by the CFD analyst is: should I model the flow in the entire test section of the tunnel, or assume an infinite-size tunnel? This question could be restated as: for the system response quantities that will be measured in the tunnel and compared with the CFD simulations, what are the changes in these quantities if I compute the simulation of the wind tunnel used in the experiment, versus an infinite-sized tunnel? Although, to our knowledge, no detailed analyses addressing this question have been published, we believe that the sensitivity to tunnel blockage will be significant even at low to moderate blockage. Wind tunnel experimentalists use correction factors to try to eliminate blockage effects on various measured quantities, but these can be of questionable accuracy. For transonic flow tunnels these correction factors are much more in doubt.

11.1.3 Synergism between computation and experiment

Guideline 3: A validation experiment should strive to emphasize the inherent synergism that is attainable between computational and experimental approaches.

By *synergism* we mean a joint computational and experimental activity that generates improvements in the capability, understanding, or accuracy in both approaches. The improvements in each approach can be immediate, for example, during the present activity, or they can be improvements that will benefit future projects. Those discovering the benefits of joint computational/experimental efforts sometimes claim that synergism is the primary benefit of the effort. Discovering the strong positive reinforcement of analysts and experimentalists working closely together can be pleasantly surprising, but validation experiments contribute much more than this. We give two examples from fluid dynamics of how this synergism can be exemplified.

First, the strength of one approach can be used to offset a weakness of the other approach. Consider the example of perfect-gas, laminar flow in a supersonic wind tunnel. Assume that a wind tunnel model is designed so that it can be easily reconfigured from simple to complex geometries. For the simple geometry at a low angle of attack with no separated flow, one should be able to compute flowfield solutions with very high confidence, exclusive of the separated flow in the base region of the vehicle. This may require independent CFD codes and analysis teams, but it is certainly possible with present CFD technology. High-accuracy solutions can then be compared with wind tunnel measurements to detect a wide variety of shortcomings and weaknesses in the facility, the instrumentation, and the data recording system. An example of this synergism will be discussed in Sections 11.2 and 11.4. If the high accuracy solution is for the flowfield of the probe geometry used in the calibration of the test section, then the calibration measurements can be more accurately interpreted to improve the calibration of the test section flowfield. If the wind tunnel model is reconfigured into a complex vehicle geometry, then the situation reverses from the simple geometry case because this geometry would have strongly 3-D flows, separated flows, and shock wave/boundary layer separation. For this complex flow case, highly accurate CFD models do not yet exist. The experimental measurements would be expected to be more accurate than the CFD simulation, and the complex geometry case would then be viewed as a validation experiment to test the physics models in the code.

Second, one can use CFD simulations in the planning stages of a validation experiment to dramatically improve the design, instrumentation, and execution of the experiment. For example, one can compute shock wave locations and their impingement on a surface, separated flow and reattachment locations, regions of high heat flux, and vortical flows near a surface. Such computations allow the experimentalist to improve the design of the experiment, especially the type, sensitivity, and location of the instrumentation. This strategy can also be taken a step further by optimizing the design of the experiment to most directly stress the models in the code, i.e., design the experiment to *break the model*. Optimizing the experimental design to break the model can be done by (a) optimizing the physical modeling parameters, such as the Reynolds number and the Mach number; (b) modifying the boundary conditions, such as model geometry and wall surface conditions; and (c) changing the initial conditions for an initial value problem, such as a blast wave problem. We should point out that analysts commonly do not find it appealing to pursue a strategy of optimizing the experiment to break their models.

11.1.4 Independence and dependence between computation and experiment

Guideline 4: Although the experimental design should be developed cooperatively, independence must be maintained in obtaining the computational and experimental system response results.

The goal of this guideline is to achieve a blind test prediction for comparison with the experimentally measured results. There are varying opinions as to the value added of blind test predictions contrasted to comparisons made with measurements known to the analysts. Guideline 4 makes clear our view of the importance of blind test predictions. Most experimentalists and experienced project managers who have relied on computational predictions in the past share this view. Guideline 4 can be viewed as the essence of what predictive accuracy should be and how it should be experimentally evaluated.

Analysts often view Guideline 4 as a personal affront to their integrity. This is clearly *not* the intention. The intention is to learn from the experiences of many individuals and projects as to the impact of knowing the correct (experimental) result when a computation–experiment comparison is to be made. It should also be noted that very rarely are blind test predictions openly conducted and published in the literature. If a blind test prediction exercise is conducted within an industrial organization, then the results are sometimes considered proprietary, whether the comparisons are good or bad. Analysts, or more precisely their organizations, see very little benefit to be gained in a blind test prediction, and a great deal of risk if poor comparison results are to become public knowledge. It is not unheard of for organizations that have produced poor results to resort to devious means to conceal or limit the distribution of the results of a blind prediction. There must be an extraordinary incentive for organizations to participate in these blind test prediction activities. The most common motivator is that if the organization does not participate, then they will be barred from certain future bidding opportunities or government certification of their codes.

It is difficult to accomplish the close cooperation of the analysts and the experimentalists promoted in Guideline 1 and, at the same time, retain the appropriate independence of computational and experimental results. However, this challenge can be met by careful attention to the procedural and management details, outlined in the following. When the experimental measurements are processed and analyzed, the analysts should *not* be given the system response results initially. The analysts should be given the complete details of all of the input data needed for their modeling approach, e.g., the physical modeling parameters, ICs, BCs, and system excitation, *exactly* as it was conducted. That is, everything that is needed for the analysts to compute solutions must be provided – but no more. The analysts should not be shown the experimental measurements of the SRQs. In addition, the analysts must be required to quantify the numerical solution errors and propagate any aleatory or epistemic uncertainties in the input so as to obtain uncertainties in the quantities that will be compared with experimental measurements. Then the comparisons between the computational and experimental results are made, preferably by the experimentalists or organizers of the effort. Even if the agreement is poorer than hoped for, investigating the causes of differences invariably leads to a deeper understanding of the experiments and the simulations.

As a final procedural comment, we recommend that management *not* be involved in the initial comparisons and discussions. The discussions should just involve analysts and experimental staff. Often it is found in the initial discussions that miscommunications or misinterpretations between team members will be exposed and appropriate changes are made in the results of one or both team members. If management is involved before these necessary discussions or corrections are made, over zealousness on one side of the team can sometimes occur, possibly leading to behavior that is destructive of teamwork.

Guideline 4 stresses the independence of the computational and experimental validation activities for an engineering environment, not a research code or a mathematical model-building environment. For example, one may have the situation where experiments are being conducted for the purpose of building mathematical models of physical processes, e.g., turbulence models. As was pointed out in Chapter 10, experiments to better understand physical processes are not validation experiments, but are model building experiments. Model building experiments require very close cooperation and communication between the model builder and the experimentalist; sometimes they are the same person.

It is also recommended that validation experiments should not produce data that fundamentally depend on closely related model calculations for critical data reduction tasks. By *closely related model calculations* we mean calculations from a data reduction code that shares many of the same physical assumptions as the model that is being validated. Data from such validation experiments do not properly address the need for independence of experimental data and simulations. Experimental data that require closely related model calculations for data processing can never be a desirable outcome for a validation experiment, although this exact situation may arise in other kinds of experiments. For an example of what we mean, consider the problem of determining the material temperature from experimentally acquired shock hydrodynamic data (density, pressure, and velocity fields) using simulations of shock wave physics rather than some type of diagnostic that directly measures the temperature. The only possible validation data that will emerge from shock hydrodynamics experiments without temperature diagnostics are the shock hydrodynamic data. This problem is relevant, since it arises in investigations of temperature dependence in high-pressure, shock-driven, material response. Such experiments often need simulations to estimate the associated thermal conditions under shock loading. For purposes of scientific discovery, this is permissible though speculative. Such experiments, however, cannot be claimed to provide validation data for the high-pressure thermomechanical response of the material because of the lack of independence of calculations and experiment.

11.1.5 Hierarchy of experimental measurements

Guideline 5: Experimental measurements should be made of a hierarchy of system response quantities, for example, from globally integrated quantities to local quantities.

A discussion was given in Chapter 10 concerning the concept of a hierarchy of difficulty to predict and measure various SRQs. The spectrum of difficulty was ordered in terms of integrals and derivatives of the dependent variables appearing in the mathematical model. Here we repeat the figure discussed in Chapter 10 as Figure 11.1. Measurements in a validation experiment should be made, if possible, over multiple levels of the hierarchy. That is, design the experiment with the strategy such that measurements of the SRQs are made over at least two or three levels of the hierarchy. Experience has shown that a strategy of concentrating on measuring one or two SRQs at the same level can produce inconclusive

Spectrum of system response quantities

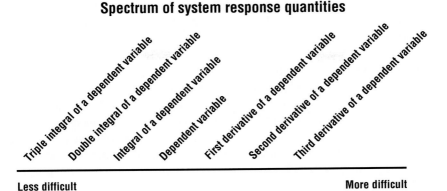

Less difficult   **More difficult**

Spectrum of difficulty to predict and/or measure

Figure 11.1 Spectrum of SRQs and the difficulty to predict and measure each.

and misleading validation results. A model with substantive predictive capability should yield robust predictions over at least two, if not more, levels of the hierarchy.

An important practical advantage also comes into play by taking measurements over a range of difficulty. There are occasions where the model performs much more poorly than expected. If measurements are only taken at one level of difficulty, or only a few SRQs are measured at the same level, then it can be very difficult for the model builders to discover the root causes of the weaknesses in the model. In addition, multiple levels of measurement could also help determine if there are inconsistencies, flaws, or mistakes in the experimental results. If, on the other hand, measurements were made over a range of difficulty, and a range of different types of SRQs, then this is much more helpful to the model builders in uncovering the weaknesses. This is especially important if there is a wide range of spatial and temporal scales occurring in the physics, such as multi-scale modeling, or there is strong coupling of different types of physics.

There is another advantage in conducting measurements over multiple levels of difficulty. Suppose that measurements were only made at one level of difficulty, but it was a very demanding level for predictive capability. Also, suppose that the model agreed well, maybe surprisingly well, with the measurements. Sometime afterwards, however, a similar validation experiment is conducted but it is found that there is a surprisingly large *disagreement* between the model and the measurements. Further investigation shows that the good agreement on the first set of experiments was entirely fortuitous. It was discovered that cancellation of modeling errors, or the fortuitous benefit of numerical solution errors, was the reason for the good agreement; not the high fidelity physics of the model. If measurements are made at different levels of difficulty and different types of SRQs, fortuitous good agreement can usually be spotted. For example, suppose one observes that very good agreement is obtained for fine spatial or temporal detail in the physics, but the model is not able to predict larger scale features of the physics. Something is seriously amiss in either the model or the experiment. Our recommendation is that whether the agreement between computation and experiment is good or bad, computation and experiment each should be subjected to critical examination.

Two pragmatic realities that must be factored into the strategy of measurements at multiple levels of difficulty are the following. First, a wider range of experimental diagnostic capability must be available. This is an expense not only for the additional diagnostics and possibly modifications to the experimental facility, but also in the wider range of technical staff capabilities that must be supported. Second, the experimental measurement uncertainty typically increases as one moves to higher levels of difficulty in the spectrum shown in Figure 11.1. The rate of increase of measurement uncertainty can be substantial as one moves to higher levels in the spectrum, particularly if new diagnostic measurement techniques must be developed and perfected.

One diagnostic method to cover two, and possibly three, levels on the measurement hierarchy is the use of modern optical techniques. With the wide range in framing speeds and pixel resolutions available in digital recording cameras, one can record many time-dependent features of a system's response over a large two- or three-dimensional field. This breadth of spatial and temporal scales allows quantitative data to be obtained over multiple levels of the measurement hierarchy. For example, in certain types of experiment it is very difficult, or impossible, to place sensors in locations of interest. Some examples are (a) flight motion of small objects such as bullets, birds, or insects; (b) impact and penetration of high-speed objects; (c) interaction of a fluid and a very thin flexible structure; (d) in situ shock wave dynamics in both fluids and solids; and (e) various types of free surface flow. In some situations where the sensors influence the physical phenomena of interest one can include the physical and geometric characteristics of the sensors directly in the simulations.

In fluid dynamics, for example, modern techniques, such as particle image velocimetry (PIV) and planar laser-induced fluorescence (PLIF), can measure local fluid velocity, mass concentration, temperature, and pressure over a plane of data. This is an extraordinary increase in the quantity of data compared to local or point measurements in a field. Experimental data from video recording systems can commonly be compared directly with computed SRQs. Alternatively, computational solutions could be post-processed by solving an additional set of physics equations for modeling optical responses through the domain of interest. For example, in fluid dynamics the computed flowfield solution, including the mass density field, can be used to compute a Schlieren or interferometer photograph that can then be compared with the experimental image. Obtaining quantitative experimental data over a plane and comparing it with computational results is much more demanding of a model's predictive capability than local measurements in a field.

Video and audio recording of an experiment or setup of the experiment has proven to be very helpful in detecting experimental setup problems, improving the understanding of the physics, and documenting the experiment. Depending on the time scales in the experiment, one could use inexpensive standard framing rate digital AV equipment or use high-speed digital video recordings. Some examples where standard AV equipment can prove very beneficial are (a) unexpected interactions of sensors with the phenomenon that is being sensed, (b) unexpected flowfield interactions either within the facility in which the experiment is conducted or between various elements of the geometry being tested, (c) discovering that modeling assumptions concerning BCs or ICs were inappropriate, and (d) discovering that surface characteristics or assembly of test articles were not what was intended or what was modeled. High-speed video recordings can now be coupled with automatic feature recognition algorithms to produce quantitative data for position, velocity, and acceleration. In addition, with the large amount of AV records that can now be stored, new technologies are becoming available that can search AV records for certain classes of objects or words.

11.1.6 Estimation of experimental uncertainty

Guideline 6:   The experimental design should be constructed to analyze and estimate the components of random (precision) and systematic (bias) experimental uncertainties.

This guideline is, of course, recommended in any type of experimental measurement, but in validation experiments its importance is crucial. One could ask: why is it so important? Since the primary goal of a validation experiment is to assess the accuracy of a model, the *core issue is uncertainty estimation.* By contrast, in the field of metrology the focus is on estimating the *true value* of a quantity along with the estimated uncertainty. Granted, these two perspectives are closely related, but the emphasis is different. In validation experiments, it is more important to quantitatively and rigorously estimate the uncertainty of all needed quantities than to infer what the true value might be based on those measurements. We are *not* suggesting that high accuracy measurements are unimportant. We are stressing that accurate estimation of uncertainty of (a) experimental conditions needed for a simulation, and (b) measured SRQs are of the utmost importance in validation experiments.

The standard technique for estimating experimental measurement uncertainty is the International Organization of Standardization (ISO) technique described in the *Guide to the Expression of Uncertainty in Measurement* (GUM) (ISO, 1995; ISO, 2008). The same procedure is codified in the *US Guide to the Expression of Uncertainty in Measurement* published by the American National Standards Institute (ANSI, 1997). The ISO/ANSI technique has also been described in detail in certain disciplines, such as wind tunnel testing (AIAA, 1999, 2003). This technique is the minimum level of effort that should be required for uncertainty estimation in validation experiments. The technique is primarily concerned with the expression of uncertainty in the measurement of a fixed quantity that is referred to as the true value. Uncertainties are not categorized according to the usual terms random and systematic, but according to the *method* which is used to characterize an uncertainty. The ISO/ANSI technique divides uncertainties into

Type A: uncertainties that are evaluated using a statistical analysis of a collection or ensemble of observations;

Type B: uncertainties that are evaluated by means other than a statistical analysis of a collection or ensemble of observations.

The combined standard uncertainty of a quantity (the result of a number of other measured quantities) is the positive square root of a sum of terms. The terms are the variances or covariances of the other measured quantities weighted according to how the measurement result varies with changes in these quantities. The fact that Type B uncertainties are supposed to come from "non-statistical means" does not deter the ISO/ANSI approach from using statistical concepts anyway.

A different approach has been used by the statistical sampling community for at least the last four decades (Montgomery, 2000; Box *et al.*, 2005; Hinkelmann and Kempthorne, 2008). This is an entirely statistical approach that is based on analyzing comparisons of multiple measurements of quantities of interest. It is usually referred to as statistical design of experiments (DOE) because it analyzes the final measured result of the quantities of interest, based on specially designed sampling techniques. In the DOE approach one identifies various classes of source that are believed to contribute to the combined uncertainty in the final quantities of interest. Then experimental strategies are designed to quantify the statistical contribution that each of these sources contributes to the final quantities of interest. The strategy of the DOE is quite different from the ISO/ANSI approach mentioned above. The approach uses replication, randomization, and blocking techniques in the design of the sample data collected in an experiment. This approach has been widely used in analyzing data from many fields, for example, production process control, system and component reliability, environmental statistics, biostatistics, medication testing, epidemiology, etc. This approach, however, has seen limited use in experiments in engineering and physics. Oberkampf, Aeschliman, and colleagues have used this technique extensively in wind tunnel validation experiments and compared it with the results obtained from the ISO/ANSI approach (Oberkampf *et al.*, 1985; Oberkampf and Aeschliman, 1992; Oberkampf *et al.*, 1993, 1995; Aeschliman and Oberkampf, 1998). Both the ISO/ANSI and DOE approaches will be discussed in detail in Section 11.3.

11.2 Validation experiment example: Joint Computational/Experimental Aerodynamics Program (JCEAP)

11.2.1 Basic goals and description of JCEAP

In 1990, Sandia National Laboratories initiated a long-term, coupled CFD/experimental research effort, referred to as the Joint Computational/Experimental Aerodynamics Program (JCEAP). The goal of the program was twofold: (a) improve Sandia's hypersonic wind tunnel experimentation and CFD simulation capabilities, and (b) improve the understanding of how CFD and experiments could synergistically work together for a more rapid development of each. The research program came to a successful close in 1997 and a number of reports, conference papers, and journal articles were produced describing the effort (Oberkampf and Aeschliman, 1992; Walker and Oberkampf, 1992; Oberkampf *et al.*, 1993; Aeschliman *et al.*, 1994, 1995; Oberkampf *et al.*, 1995, 1996; Aeschliman and Oberkampf, 1998; Oberkampf and Blottner, 1998). The program produced an extensive database of force and moment, and surface pressure measurements on a hypersonic vehicle configuration. More importantly, the program developed the fundamental concepts for the design and execution of high quality validation experiments. The six guidelines discussed above evolved from the experiences of JCEAP, and not all were learned easily. The discussion that follows excludes many details that would be needed to use the experimental data as a validation database for assessing CFD codes in hypersonic flow. See the references just given for the details. Here we will concentrate on using JCEAP to exemplify the six guidelines discussed.

The first phase of the program involved the computational and experimental study of the aerodynamic forces and moments on a flight vehicle configuration in a hypersonic flowfield. During this phase of the program, the geometry of the vehicle was determined, the force and moment (F&M) wind tunnel model was fabricated, the experimental conditions were determined, and the F&M data were obtained. The second phase of the program addressed the next level of difficulty in prediction and experimentation; surface pressures on an identically sized and shaped geometry at the same flow conditions. As part of both the F&M and pressure experiments, an experimental uncertainty estimation procedure was developed. The procedure was based on a statistical DOE procedure that had been used in a previous wind tunnel experiment, unrelated to JCEAP (Oberkampf *et al.*, 1985).

All of the experimental measurements were obtained in the Sandia National Laboratories long-duration, blowdown, hypersonic wind tunnel (HWT). The tunnel is a blowdown-to-vacuum facility that can operate up to a minute, depending on operating conditions. The nozzle and test section consist of three contoured axisymmetric nozzles, arranged as a large fixture that can revolve around a common hub. Figure 11.2 shows an overall view of the wind tunnel with the test section open. Depending on which nozzle is used, the test section Mach number is nominally 5, 8, or 14. The diameter of the circular test section of each nozzle is roughly the same, about 0.35 m. Each nozzle is provided with its own electric resistance heater to prevent flow condensation in the test section. The total pressure and temperature of the flow is controlled during a run so that a chosen Reynolds number can be obtained within the operating envelope of the facility. During a run the total pressure is manually controlled, but all other operating parameters are computer controlled. Usable run times are typically 30–60 s, depending on the flow Reynolds number, and the turnaround time between runs is one hour or less. Model pitch angle (angle of attack) is varied during a run using a computer-controlled, arc sector drive mounted far aft of the model. Model roll angle and configuration changes are made between runs by retracting the aft portion of the wind tunnel and manually making the needed changes to the mounting of the model on the sting support.

11.2.2 Joint planning and design of the experiment

11.2.2.1 Wind tunnel conditions

From the very beginning of the effort, JCEAP was designed to be a validation experiment. What that meant, however, was not fully recognized. The first design decision that needed to be made was: what Mach number condition should be used in the HWT? The primary

Figure 11.2 Sandia hypersonic wind tunnel with the aft section retracted from the test section (flow is from left to right). The model is visible in the open section and the yellow support is part of the rear-mounting fixture to hold the model (Oberkampf *et al.*, 1993). (See color plate section.)

CFD requirement was that the flow over the model should be entirely laminar flow. This was a very unusual request in wind tunnel testing because the normal desire is to have turbulent flow over the vehicle that matches the flowfield of the vehicle in flight. The reason laminar flow was the critical driver was that only with laminar flow was it conceivable that the CFD simulations could *possibly* compute some flow conditions more accurately than experimental measurements could be made. With turbulent flow, no such claim could be made; and this is still true two decades after the initiation of JCEAP.

The Reynolds number of the flow over the vehicle is the primary factor in determining if the flow is laminar or turbulent over a vehicle. The Reynolds number is a dimensionless ratio defined as $R_L = \rho V L / \mu$, where ρ is the free-stream density, V is the free-stream velocity, L is a characteristic length scale (usually the total length of the vehicle), and

μ is the absolute fluid viscosity in the free-stream. The lower the Reynolds number, the more likely the flow will remain laminar over the entire vehicle. As the Reynolds number increases, the flow will transition to turbulent flow over different portions of the vehicle (Wilcox, 2006).

The operating conditions of the HWT facility for the Mach 5 nozzle were examined, given a reasonable estimate on the length of the model that could be used in the test section. It was found that at the lowest Reynolds number conditions that were producible for Mach 5, it was unavoidable that a mixture of laminar and turbulent flow would occur over the geometry. For the Mach 14 nozzle, the range of Reynolds numbers attainable is much lower because of the larger expansion of the flow into the test section. As a result, laminar flow could be assured over the model at any operating condition of the facility. The primary argument against using the Mach 14 nozzle was that the pressures in the test section were so low that very accurate measurement of surface pressure would become questionable.

For the range of operating conditions available for the Mach 8 nozzle, Reynolds numbers could be produced that balanced the needs of the experiment. Operating at the higher-pressure conditions of the operating envelope would produce a mixture of laminar and turbulent flow. Operating at the lower end of the envelope would produce the all-laminar flow desired, and the pressure in the test section is sufficiently large to measure surface pressures accurately. The Mach 8 test section has a diameter of 0.350 m and is provided with 0.2×0.38 m Schlieren-grade windows on the top, bottom, and sides. The high-grade windows provide excellent access for optical diagnostics.

11.2.2.2 Model geometry

We were interested in designing a vehicle geometry that could produce a range of flow features. It was required that the simplest flowfield would have the possibility of being computed more accurately than it could be measured. This could be attained with a simple geometry and using low angles of attack. Complex flowfields could be attained by modifying the geometry and using higher angles of attack. Also factored into our thinking was the desire to produce a geometry that could be of interest to the Sandia project group that flight-tested re-entry vehicles. They were interested in maneuvering re-entry vehicles, that is, vehicles that could maneuver during hypersonic flight by deflecting control surfaces on the vehicle.

After a number of design iterations for the geometry using CFD, we settled on a spherically blunted cone with a half-angle of $10°$ with a sliced region on the aft portion of the cone. We did not choose a sharp-nosed vehicle for three reasons. First, no matter how sharp a machinist fabricates a nose tip, there is always finite nose bluntness. If a sharp tip were used, then a very precise inspection would be required to accurately characterize exactly what the geometry was for the CFD simulations. Second, a very small radius nose tip would change the flow regime from continuum fluid dynamics that exists over the rest of the geometry to rarified flow over the minute nose tip. Stated differently, one of the key assumptions in the mathematical model would be violated, damaging the high confidence

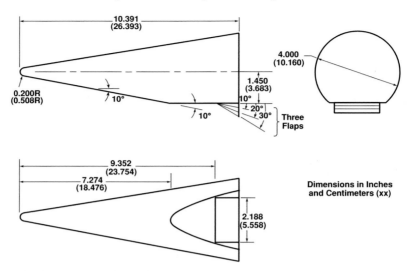

Figure 11.3 JCEAP geometry (Aeschliman and Oberkampf, 1998).

that is desired for certain flowfield solutions. Third, a sharp tip can be easily damaged over a long period of usage in a wind tunnel test. The damage could be from slight erosion due to impact from minute particles in the free-stream, or it could be due to accidental damage due to handling the model. As a result, the nose tip would have to be re-inspected regularly during the course of the experiment to determine if any changes occurred. Based on CFD simulations, 10% nose bluntness was chosen. That is, the nose had a radius equal to 0.1 of the base radius of the cone. This nose radius provided a good balance between the having an entropy gradient approaching the slice on the vehicle, but not an excessively large region of subsonic flow near the nose of the vehicle.

Based on CFD simulations, it was decided to begin the slice, which was parallel to the axis of the cone, at 0.7 of the length of the vehicle. See Figure 11.3 for the final vehicle design. Given that the test section diameter of the Mach 8 nozzle was 0.355 m, a base diameter of 0.1016 m was chosen. With this base diameter and the 10° cone half-angle, the resulting length of the model was 0.2639 m. To increase the difficulty of the CFD simulation for certain geometries, and to make the geometry more appealing to the flight test project group, the model was designed so that different flaps could be attached to the aft portion of the slice. Flap deflection angles of 0, 10, 20, and 30° were chosen, and all of the flaps extended to the baseplane. By designing the flaps to extend to the model baseplane for all flap deflections, a substantial simplification became possible in constructing the computational mesh for the body geometry and for the base flow. This also simplifies setting the outflow boundary conditions across the baseplane in the numerical simulation. Note that, in an actual flight vehicle, this would not be the case. In a flight vehicle, the flap would be hinged near the leading edge of the flap, and as the flap was deflected, the trailing edge of the flap would not extend to the baseplane of the vehicle.

After the vehicle geometry was finalized, we discussed the geometry of JCEAP with the flight test project group. They were interested in the maneuvering re-entry vehicle geometry and its potential advantages from their perspective. However, when we explained to them that we were only going to test in laminar flow, their interest flagged considerably. As a result, they were not interested in providing funding for the project. Fortunately, there was strong support for the project from internal research and development (IR&D) funding. As was briefly discussed in Section 10.1.2, there is commonly conflict between project needs for a validation experiment and the needs for a high quality validation experiment. If funding for the experiment comes from the project group, their requirements usually take precedent.

11.2.2.3 Model fabrication and instrumentation

Two different physical models were fabricated, but both had the same geometry (Figure 11.3). The F&M model was used in conjunction with a precision six-component strain gauge balance. The balance was installed internal to the model geometry, as is typically done to improve the accuracy of the measurements of the aerodynamically induced forces and moments. The pressure model was significantly more complicated in design and fabrication because of the additional instrumentation required. A total of 96 pressure ports were machined in the model surface. The orifices were connected to either the 2482 N/m^2 or the 6895 N/m^2 electronically scanned pressure module, both of which were located inside the model. The choice of which ports were attached to which module was based on CFD predictions of the pressure level expected. The model also incorporated nine semiconductor bridge Kulite gauges to detect high-frequency surface pressure fluctuations at certain locations along the surface. The model incorporated four thermocouples mounted in the model wall at two different axial locations along the model. The thermocouples provided model surface temperature for input boundary conditions required for the final CFD calculations.

The pressure model was constructed in four sections (plus detachable nose tips) to permit machining operations and the installation of steel pressure port inserts during fabrication. Figure 11.4 shows a longitudinal cross section of the model, the adjacent portion of the base cover and sting, and the sting cover. This design approach also greatly facilitated tubing connections between ports and internally mounted pressure modules during subsequent model assembly. A base cover extension, slightly smaller in diameter than the base diameter of the model, was fabricated as part of the sting and provided the attachment point to the model. It also provided a hollow recess with additional volume for the pressure modules, pressure tubing, and electrical wiring. The base cover extension had a flat section on one side to conform to the slice on the model. The model was supported in the tunnel by a stiff, thick-walled sting to reduce the deflection of the model due to aerodynamic loading during a run. The sting connects the model to the arc sector drive located downstream of the test section that pitches the model to angle of attack. The sting length is designed so that the center of rotation of the arc sector is at about the mid-length of the model. In this way,

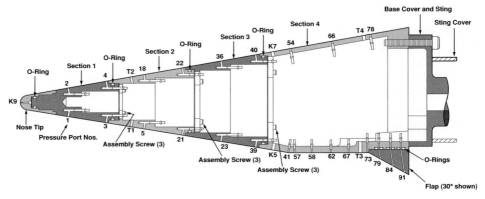

Figure 11.4 Longitudinal cross section of the pressure model showing some of the surface pressure ports denoted by a number, Kulite gauges denoted by K*n*, and thermocouples denoted by T*n* (Oberkampf *et al.*, 1995).

when the model is moved to a non-zero angle of attack, it remains in the center portion of the test section flowfield.

In preliminary tests of the pressure model, an amalgamation of pressure reference tubing, pressure module electrical cables, wires from the Kulite gauges, and thermocouple wires were taped to the outside of the sting. All of these tubes and cables needed to go from the base of the model to the aft portion of the tunnel where they could exit the downstream flowfield of the tunnel. In a project review of the preliminary JCEAP tests, it was pointed out by CFD analysts that this taped bundle of tubing and cables would cause a complex surface geometry for modeling in a CFD analysis. If a CFD analyst chose to simulate the flow in the base region of the model, near the model sting, then the CFD analysis would need to know the surface geometry of the bundle. After this was pointed out, we recognized that modeling the bundle was of *no interest* to the goals of the validation experiment. As a result, a cylindrical section that covered the bundle and sting was fabricated and attached to the sting, as shown in Figure 11.4. The cover provided an easily definable and repeatable geometry that could be much more easily meshed in a CFD solution. This simplification in base flowfield geometry exemplifies the principle: exclude any complex geometric features that *do not* provide value to the goals of the validation experiment.

The overriding consideration in the development of the surface pressure measurement system was the pressure lag time (commonly referred to as settling time) in the small diameter tubing connecting the model surface pressure ports to the two pressure transducer modules. If a pressure lag error existed, this could introduce a significant systematic uncertainty in the surface pressure measurements. To determine the actual lag characteristic of each port for the tunnel flow conditions of interest, the model was pitched from $0°$ angle of attack to $10°$ angle of attack in one continuous sweep, while pressure data were recorded for each of the 96 ports. The same type of sweep was made from $0°$ to $-10°$ angle of attack. Typical pressure lags were 0.05–0.10 s to achieve a stable pressure within 0.1% of

Figure 11.5 Assembly of the pressure model (Oberkampf *et al.*, 1995).

the final value. The largest lag time observed was 0.3 s, which occurred at one of the ports on the slice. To be conservative, a delay time of 0.5 s was used prior to recording pressure data following each change to a new angle of attack during data acquisition runs. The key to achieving this response frequency was mounting both pressure modules and the tubing, along with everything else inside the model. Figure 11.5 suggests the challenge of forcing everything inside the model during assembly, without kinking any of the pressure tubing or breaking any electrical connections.

11.2.3 Characterize boundary conditions and system data

After each model was fabricated, a detailed inspection of the surface geometry of the model was conducted. Although the model was precision made, the actual inspected dimensions of the model were used in future CFD simulations. For the pressure model, the location of the pressure orifices, the Kulite gauges, and the thermocouples were all inspected with regard to the quality of the sensor installation and the precise location of each. As stressed in Guideline 2, the geometry data that should be used in the simulation are the *as-tested* geometry. For the F&M model and the pressure model, they were built with very thick walls so that no deflection due to aerodynamic loads was possible. In addition, for the total temperature conditions available in the HWT, there was no change in geometry due to aerothermal heating of the model.

Preliminary wind tunnel tests were conducted to determine precisely what Reynolds number conditions would be used to attain laminar flow over the model. To aid in this determination, shear-stress-sensitive liquid crystals were employed. With this technique, the liquid crystals are painted over the surface of the model before a wind tunnel run. The crystals change color, depending on the local surface shear stress applied to them. For the preliminary tests at moderate Reynolds numbers, the technique worked moderately well, but it was not definitive. For the lowest Reynolds number condition tested, however, the shear stress level was lower than the sensitivity range of the crystals that were available. The liquid crystals also provided streak visualization of flow on the surface of the model. By examining photographs of these surface flows, boundary layer transition waves due to cross-flow at angle of attack could be seen at the moderate Reynolds numbers tested. The existence of laminar boundary layer instabilities due to cross-flow had been computationally investigated as precursors to turbulent flow (Spall and Malik, 1991, 1992) At $R_L = 1.8 \times 10^6$ ($R = 6.82 \times 10^6$/m), however, no transition waves could be seen. As a result, all further experiments and computational simulations were conducted at this Reynolds number.

The wind tunnel flowfield had been calibrated on multiple occasions not only for the Reynolds number and total temperature of interest in JCEAP, but also for many other conditions in the operating envelope. Based on these calibrations, the spatially averaged free-stream Mach number across the central region of the test section was found to be 7.84. As in all wind tunnels, there is a slight variation in free-stream flow characteristics across the central portion of the test section. The spatially averaged conditions from the wind tunnel calibration were used as the inflow boundary conditions in the CFD simulations. It should be noted that the only time this Reynolds number and Mach number condition had been run before was during calibration of the wind tunnel. This exemplifies the common situation that experimental facilities are commonly used at unusual conditions for validation experiments, relative to the needs of project groups.

The run schedule for the combinations of angle of attack, model roll angle, and flap deflection angle was devised very differently from typical wind tunnel tests for project groups. For project groups, the goal is to obtain information at a wide range of operating conditions that are of interest for their system's performance. For validation experiments, the goal is to obtain information at a restricted set of conditions so that experimental uncertainty can be rigorously estimated for all input quantities needed for the simulation, as well as all SRQs that are measured. For JCEAP, the run schedule was constructed so that a number of replications were conducted, runs were randomized, and blocking techniques were incorporated. During each run the angle of attack was varied from -9 to $18°$. The sequence of nominal angle of attack, α, during a run was 0, -9, -6, -3, 0, 3, 6, 9, 12, 15, 18, and $0°$. For each of these αs, the roll angle was set at 0 (slice on the windward side), 90, 180, and $270°$. In addition, measurements were made with the model at two different axial locations in the test section by changing the length of the model sting. The forward axial location places the model essentially at the center of rotation of the arc sector drive. As a result, the model stays near the center region of the test section as it rotates. At the aft axial station, the model rotates and translates downward in the test section for positive αs; conversely, it rotates and translates upward for negative αs. Table 11.1 and Table 11.2

Table 11.1 *Run number schedule for the F&M experiment (Oberkampf and Aeschliman, 1992).*

Roll angle (deg.)	$\delta = 0°$	$\delta = 10°$	$\delta = 20°$	$\delta = 30°$
Model at forward tunnel station				
0	34, 36, 37, 73	63, 72	64, 71	65, 70
90	39	66, 67	69	68
180	40	55	56, 57	58
270	41	62	61	59, 60
Model at aft tunnel station				
0	74, 75	83	82	81
180	76, 77	78	79	80

Table 11.2 *Run number schedule for the pressure experiment (Oberkampf et al., 1995).*

Roll angle (deg.)	$\delta = 0°$	$\delta = 10°$	$\delta = 20°$	$\delta = 30°$
Model at forward tunnel station				
0	20, 22, 62	42, 43	48, 49	56, 57
90	24, 26, 59, 61	37, 39	46	54
180	30, 32, 58	35, 36	44, 45	50, 53
270	28, 29	40, 41	47	55
Model at aft tunnel station				
0	101, 102	118, 119	124, 126	131, 133
180	103, 112	115, 116	122, 123	127, 129

give the complete run schedule for the F&M experiment and the pressure experiment, respectively.

During the F&M experiment, the aerodynamic load on the model was measured. This measured load was then used to calibrate the change in angle of attack due to deflection of the mounting sting. While the tunnel was open, the model was loaded over the same range of aerodynamic loads and the change in angle of attack was measured. This angular deflection was then used to correct the indicated angle of attack from the arc sector mechanism. For the pressure experiment, the same procedure was used, except, because of the stiff sting, the deflections were much smaller than the sting used in the F&M experiment.

Finally, thermocouples were used to measure the surface temperature of the model during a run. The largest differences in the surface temperatures occur between the windward and leeward sides of the model at angle of attack. Consequently, the thermocouple measurements were made 180° apart around the model. The measured temperature was then used as the surface temperature boundary condition in the CFD simulations.

11.2.4 Synergism between computation and experiment

Examples have been given of the synergistic interaction of computation and experiment in the design of the JCEAP experiment. Here a more detailed discussion will be given of an interaction that could not have happened without the real-time synergism of the computational and experimental team members. Stated differently, if the computational and experimental team members are diverted from a validation experiment for significant portions of their time, or worse, they do not even work on it at the same time, the extraordinary synergism that is possible will not be realized. In addition, it may not even be realized that it was lost.

After the F&M wind tunnel tests were completed, a detailed experimental uncertainty analysis (to be discussed) was conducted. This analysis revealed an anomaly that was most notable in the experimental data for the pitch moment at zero angle of attack for a flap deflection of 0°. The anomaly could also be seen for other flap angles and it could be seen in the normal force for zero angle of attack, but it was not as obvious. Based on the assumption of a uniform free-stream flowfield, it must be true that at zero angle of attack the pitch moment for $\phi = 0°$ and $\phi = 180°$ should be the same mean value (based on many statistical samples), after the appropriate sign reversal was made for symmetry. It was observed that the difference in pitch moment coefficient between $\phi = 0°$ and 180° was 0.008. Although this may seem small, if this error is converted into an error in measuring the angle of attack, it would convert to an error of 0.6°. This was much larger than what the measurement error in angle of attack was demonstrated to be.

To resolve this issue, several possible sources of error were investigated. An analysis was conducted to determine if the nonuniform spatial distribution of base pressure could contribute to pitch moment. Based on five pressure measurements distributed over the base of the model, this effect was found to be negligible. Another possibility investigated was the misalignment of the strain gauge balance mounting taper with respect to the model centerline, which would result in an angle of attack error. Precision model inspection showed misalignment to be less than one minute; therefore, this was not a significant contribution to the discrepancy.

In parallel with the experimental investigation, a CFD effort was initiated to try and assist in understanding the situation. A number of additional CFD solutions were generated with very refined meshes for the zero angle of attack case. These solutions had the highest confidence in simulation accuracy because they were for $\alpha = 0°$ and $\delta = 0°$, where the flowfield is the simplest case of the entire experiment. The computed results for the pitch moment produced a value that did not match experimental results that were in question. The computational results were essentially halfway between each of the experimental results for $\phi = 0°$ and 180°, respectively. Different members of the team, however, had different levels of confidence in the CFD results.

It was also suggested that this anomaly could be caused by operating the wind tunnel at a Reynolds number much lower than the designed Reynolds number of the nozzle. The nozzle contour was designed taking into account a boundary layer displacement thickness corresponding to operating the tunnel at a Reynolds number of $R = 19.7 \times 10^6$/m. At the low Reynolds number used in JCEAP, the displacement thickness would be larger and, consequently, this could produce slight flow non-uniformity in the test section. Therefore, it was decided to conduct another tunnel entry to reproduce the anomaly at the JCEAP Reynolds number and also to conduct F&M measurements at the designed Reynolds number of the nozzle. During this second tunnel entry at the JCEAP Reynolds number the pitch moment anomaly could *not* be reproduced. The mean value of the zero angle of attack pitch moment coefficient for $\phi = 0°$ and $\phi = 180°$ matched within 0.001, which was the expected level of uncertainty in the data. Then began an even more intensive investigation to discover what had changed since the first tunnel entry.

It was suggested that the test section of the tunnel might have moved slightly from the horizontal since the last tunnel entry. This was possible because all of the different Mach number test sections are on a large revolver-type mechanism. The test section was moved, reassembled, and checked several times. It was always found to be horizontal within one minute. During this checking of angles, however, it was found that the model pitched nose down when the tunnel is closed and locked in place using hydraulic cylinders. Repeated closures and measurements showed this movement to be a constant $-0.08°$. This consistent systematic error due to tunnel closure had, to our knowledge, existed in the facility since it was built. This constant $-0.08°$ error correction in angle of attack was made to all of the data. The correction, however, was not sufficient in magnitude to explain the anomaly previously identified.

During the second tunnel entry, it was observed that our attempt at reproducing the anomaly did not include the base pressure instrumentation. When the base pressure transducers were installed and the pitch moment measured, the anomaly *was* precisely reproduced. Each of the five base pressures was connected to a transducer that had a full scale of 0.007 atmospheres; therefore, these transducers were grossly off-scale when the tunnel was opened to atmospheric pressure before and after a run. When all the strain gauge instrumentation was connected into the data system and the base pressure transducers were off-scale, in response to atmospheric pressure, those analog data channels were saturated. This introduced a systematic error to all data channels through the common signal return line. This systematic error was easily circumvented and eliminated from the data by using the second air-off zero taken after the tunnel was evacuated just before a run.

Two final observations were made. First, this systematic error due to an electrical ground loop had existed in the past any time base pressures were measured on a test item. It could not be classified as a major experimental error, but the error was definitely detectable by careful statistical checks of the data. These kinds of error are rarely reported anywhere, but good organizations learn from them. Second, the CFD results were exactly correct in predicting the final measured result after the ground loop bias error was removed from the data. Members of the team who had not believed CFD could calculate some flowfield cases more accurately than they could be measured were stunned.

11.2.5 Independence and dependence between computation and experiment

The nature of the physics modeling for JCEAP lent itself to natural independence between computation and experiment. That is, for laminar flow of an ideal gas, there are essentially no other major modeling issues. Some of the assumptions in the submodels could be challenged, as will be discussed in Section 11.4.1, but these were not expected to produce significant changes in the simulation results.

As discussed in Guideline 4, the simulation must be provided with the input data measured during the experiments. After each of the models was geometrically inspected, these geometry measurements were used in all of the simulations. After the experiments were completed, the *as-tested* model input data from the experiments were used to compute new CFD simulations. For example, the measured average values for the entire run schedule for free-stream conditions and wall temperature boundary conditions were used in the new simulations. Since these data were very similar to what had been assumed in the initial simulations, there was very little change in the computational results.

Before these final simulations were computed, however, a formal mesh convergence analysis was completed. Richardson's extrapolation was used to estimate the mesh convergence error for the 3-D flowfield, as discussed in Chapter 8, Discretization error. This analysis was only done for the primary CFD code used, a parabolized Navier–Stokes code (Walker and Oberkampf, 1992). This code could accurately simulate all of the $\delta = 0°$ cases at angles of attack up to about 16°. For the flap deflection cases, separated flow ahead of the flap did not permit this modeling approach to be used. For the separate flow cases, a full Navier–Stokes code was used. For this code, however, no mesh convergence analysis was conducted because of the computational resources required.

11.2.6 Hierarchy of experimental measurements

JCEAP was designed from the beginning to span two levels of the spectrum of difficulty (see Figure 11.1). Measurements and predictions were made of a dependent variable in the PDEs (pressure), as well as measurements and predictions of integrated quantities (F&Ms). In addition to these measurements, liquid crystal and Schlieren photographs were taken. The liquid crystals not only provided excellent information in the determination of laminar flow conditions, but they were also very valuable in surface flow visualization of separated flows over the geometry. Figure 11.6 is an example of one of these visualizations of the streak pattern on the surface of the geometry. Figure 11.6 is for $\alpha = 0°$ and a flap deflection of 10°. The deflected flap causes a shock wave to form just ahead of the flap, generating an adverse pressure gradient along the slice portion of the geometry. The laminar boundary layer cannot tolerate the adverse pressure gradient, so the boundary layer separates on the slice region. Near the plane of symmetry through the slice the flow reattaches midway up the

Figure 11.6 Surface flow visualization on JCEAP for $\alpha = 0°$ and $\delta = 10°$ (Oberkampf and Aeschliman, 1992).

length of the flap, but the reattachment point moves toward the front along the flap edges. Visualization photographs, such as these, can provide excellent qualitative information for determining if the physics modeling assumptions are appropriate for the particular conditions of the experiment.

Schlieren photographs show the shadow pattern due to the deflection of light by a refractive index gradient through the flowfield. Schlieren photographs were taken at every angle of attack on every wind tunnel run. These photographs were helpful and instructive in understanding the flowfield, particularly the shock waves in the field.

At one point during the F&M testing it was noticed that for certain model geometries at large angles of attack ($15°$ to $18°$) the normal force and pitch moment measurements deviated from the expected trend with α. The situations where this trend was particularly evident were large flap deflections for $\phi = 0°$, large angles of attack, and when the model was at the aft tunnel station. It was suspected that wall interference could be causing the anomaly, so the Schlieren photographs were examined. In addition, a high-speed Schlieren video was taken of these suspect situations. Figure 11.7 is a Schlieren photograph of the model at $\alpha = 17.9°$, $\phi = 0°$, $\delta = 20°$, at the aft tunnel station (Run 82). This figure graphically shows upstream interference in the form of a shock wave from the lower wall of the test section impinging on the underside of the model.

After various analyses and tests, it was concluded that the flow mechanism for wall interference upstream of the model was by way of the window cavity. The window cavity

Figure 11.7 Schlieren photograph showing the shock wave from the window cavity impinging on the lower side of the model (Oberkampf *et al.*, 1993).

is the volume formed between the inside surface of the flat windows and the circular cross section of the wind tunnel. At large angle of attack and large flap deflection, the strong shock wave from the flap merged with the bow shock wave and impinged on the window cavity. The high pressure from the shock wave was fed forward in the subsonic separated flow of the window cavity. This, in turn, increased the angle of the free shear layer over the open cavity, which caused a shock wave to be generated at the *front* of the cavity. This shock wave then impinged on the bottom of the model, as seen in Figure 11.7. This phenomenon was exacerbated at aft tunnel stations because the model was significantly aft of the center of rotation of the arc sector mechanism. This caused the model to translate farther downward as the angle of attack increased, bringing it closer to the window cavity.

Methods were investigated to determine at what angle of attack wall interference began to affect the F&M data for any configuration and tunnel station. Using the Schlieren photographs for each angle of attack, we were able to identify most of the cases of when interference occurred. The most sensitive measure was found to be the trend of base pressure with angle of attack. When the wall interference shock wave began to impinge on the separated flow in the base of the model, the base pressure would begin to rise uncharacteristically. The base pressure for each orifice was plotted versus angle of attack for every wind tunnel run. When the base pressure began to abruptly increase with angle of attack, it was concluded that the shock wave was near the base of the model. Although this in itself does not contaminate the data because the base pressure was eliminated from the data regardless of its value, it was decided not to use any F&M data for higher angle of attack for that particular run. Once this wall interference was recognized, the windows were removed and metal blanks were inserted that conformed to the circular inner surface of the test section. This removed any feature of the window with regard to the flow inside the test section. For the pressure experiment, the window blanks were installed for the entire experiment.

11.3 Example of estimation of experimental measurement uncertainties in JCEAP

Techniques for estimating experimental measurement uncertainty can be grouped into (a) the ISO/ANSI approach described in the ISO *Guide to the Expression of Uncertainty in Measurement* (GUM) (ISO, 1995, 2008) and the *US Guide to the Expression of Uncertainty in Measurement* published by the American National Standards Institute (ANSI, 1997), and (b) the statistical design of experiment (DOE) method (Montgomery, 2000; Box *et al.*, 2005; Hinkelmann and Kempthorne, 2008). Each method has strengths and weaknesses and situations where one has advantages over the other. Given the centuries that measurement uncertainty has been studied, one would think that the foundational issues have been established. Not so! There has been a major international debate within the metrology community for at least the last three decades concerning fundamental terminology and concepts. Although the ISO/ANSI technique is internationally sanctioned, there are a number of well-founded criticisms of the terminology and procedures. Four recent monographs have captured most of the criticisms of the ISO/ANSI approach (Grabe, 2005; Rabinovich, 2005; Drosg, 2007; Salicone, 2007). It is beyond our scope to discuss these criticisms, other than to say we agree with most of them. Our goal here is to discuss in some detail the DOE method and how it was effectively used in the JCEAP validation experiment. Our experience clearly demonstrated that the DOE method gave a much more representative estimate of experimental measurement uncertainty than the ISO/ANSI method. Given the focus on accurate estimation of measurement uncertainty in validation experiments, this is a major finding.

11.3.1 Random and systematic uncertainties

As discussed in Chapter 2, Fundamental concepts and terminology, we will use the terminology of Grabe (2005); Rabinovich (2005); and Drosg (2007):

Error in a quantity: a deviation from the true value of the quantity.

Referring to Eq. (2.2), we have

$$\varepsilon_m = y_m - y_T, \tag{11.1}$$

where (for our interest here) ε_m is the error in the measured quantity y, y_m is the measured value of the quantity, and y_T is the true value of the measured quantity. Here we assume y_T is a scalar quantity as opposed to a random variable. For a measured quantity, y_T is *never* known; it is only estimated (unless a reference standard is available). Similarly, ε_m is *never* known for a measured quantity, only estimated. Any estimate of ε_m is referred to as an *uncertainty estimate*, as opposed to an error estimate. Let the estimation of ε_m be given as ε. The estimation ε is always considered a positive quantity, since the sign of ε_m cannot be known. As a result, ε_m is estimated by the interval $[-\varepsilon, +\varepsilon]$. Whether the estimate is accurate or not, does not change the fundamental concepts or notation. For example, ε_m may or may not be in the interval $[-\varepsilon, +\varepsilon]$, depending on the accuracy of the estimate.

The traditional concept in metrology is to segregate contributors to uncertainty into two types according to their property: random and systematic (Grabe, 2005; Rabinovich, 2005; Drosg, 2007). The following definitions are central to metrology.

Random uncertainties: inaccuracies of a measurement that, in the course of multiple measurements of the same quantity under the same conditions, vary in an unpredictable way.

Systematic uncertainties: inaccuracies of a measurement that, in the course of multiple measurements of the same quantity under the same conditions, remain constant or vary in a predictable way.

Random and systematic uncertainties are *always* present in any measurement. Whether they are large relative to the magnitude of the true value, y_T, or which one dominates in magnitude, depend on many details of the measurement process.

The characterization of the random uncertainty requires that multiple measurements be made. This is usually referred to as *replication* of the experimental measurement. For example, suppose a fixed mass is being weighed on a mechanical scale with a dial indicator. Each time the mass is weighed, there is a random component to the measurement uncertainty due to the mechanical mechanism, laboratory environment conditions, as well as to the person reading the indicator. If one only weighed the mass once, but had several people read the indicator, this is not actually a replication of the experiment. If one person made multiple measurements using the same instrument, using the same procedure, in the same environment, this is sometimes referred to as a 0th order replication (Moffat, 1988; Coleman and Steele, 1999). These references suggest higher orders of replication are possible.

To quantitatively deal with these issues, certain definitions and concepts from probability and statistics need to be introduced. Let y_i, $i = 1, 2, \ldots, n$, be the individual values obtained in a measurement process. There is no assumption made concerning how these individual measurements were made, e.g., they could be made using the same instrument or different instruments, by the same laboratory or different laboratories, or over a short period of time or a long period of time. Let $\bar{y}$ be defined as the sample mean of these measurements,

$$\bar{y} = \frac{1}{n} \sum_{i=1}^{n} y_i. \tag{11.2}$$

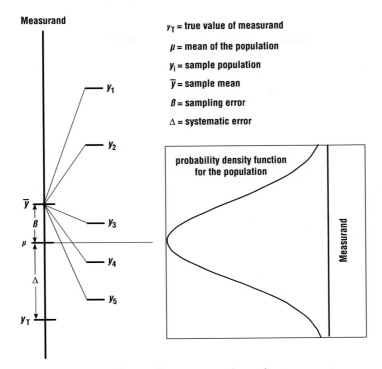

Figure 11.8 Random and systematic contributors to experimental measurement error.

The individual y_is are assumed to be independent draws from the parent population. The mean of the parent population, μ, is defined as

$$\mu = \frac{1}{N} \sum_{i=1}^{N} y_i, \quad \text{where } N \text{ is countably infinite.} \qquad (11.3)$$

Figure 11.8 depicts the various contributors to measurement error. Let β be defined as the error in $\bar{y}$, so that we have

$$\beta = \bar{y} - \mu. \qquad (11.4)$$

Note that here we can refer to the contributors as *errors* because we are defining the quantities with respect to their true, but unknown, values. β is the error in $\bar{y}$ due to taking a finite number of samples from the parent population. β is a random variable and we will refer to it as the *sampling error* for any set of n measurements.

Let Δ be defined as the *systematic error* in the experimental measurement, so that we have

$$\Delta = \mu - y_{\mathrm{T}}. \qquad (11.5)$$

The fundamental error equation can be written as

$$\beta + \Delta = \bar{y} - y_T. \tag{11.6}$$

The only quantity in Eq. (11.6) that is known is $\bar{y}$. Using DOE techniques we attempt to estimate β and Δ so that we can estimate y_T. Even though β and Δ are convolved in every measurement made, we know that $\beta \rightarrow 0$ as $n \rightarrow \infty$. Estimating Δ is much more difficult because we generally have poor knowledge of its possible causes. The exception to this, of course, is when we have a reference standard so that we know y_T. It should be noted that the ISO/ANSI technique does *not* make a distinction between the true value, y_T, and μ (Grabe, 2005). Quoting the ISO/ANSI Guide "the terms 'value of a measurand' (or a quantity) and 'true value of a measurand' (for a quantity) are viewed as equivalent."

If the probability distribution for the random uncertainty is given by, or assumed to be, a normal distribution, then it is well known that a statistical confidence interval can be derived for β (Devore, 2007).

$$|\beta| \leq t_{\alpha/2,\nu} \frac{s}{\sqrt{n}}, \tag{11.7}$$

where $t_{\alpha/2,n-1}$ is the $1 - \alpha/2$ quantile of the t distribution for $n - 1$ degrees of freedom, and s is the sample standard deviation. s is given by

$$s = \left[\frac{1}{n-1} \sum_{i=1}^{n} (y_i - \bar{y})^2 \right]^{1/2}. \tag{11.8}$$

Any level of confidence can be chosen, which is given by $100(1 - \alpha)\%$. The higher the confidence level chosen, the wider the bounds on $|\beta|$ because $t_{\alpha/2,n-1}$ increases for a fixed n. For n greater than 16, the cumulative t distribution and the cumulative standard normal distribution differ by less than 0.01 for all quantiles. In the limit as $n \rightarrow \infty$, the t distribution approaches the standard normal distribution.

The real difficulty in experimental measurement uncertainty is estimating the systematic (bias) uncertainty, Δ. The two strategies for dealing with systematic uncertainties are (a) to identify and attempt to reduce them, and (b) to estimate their magnitude. Systematic uncertainty is an epistemic uncertainty because it is due to lack of knowledge. Depending on the situation, it could be viewed as either a recognized epistemic uncertainty or a blind epistemic uncertainty. Recalling the definitions given in Section 2.3.2, we have

Recognized epistemic uncertainty: an epistemic uncertainty for which a conscious decision has been made to either characterize or deal with it in some way, or to ignore it for practical reasons.

Blind epistemic uncertainty: an epistemic uncertainty for which it is not recognized that the knowledge is incomplete and that the knowledge is relevant to modeling the system of interest.

In either case, adding knowledge to the measurement process (e.g., by using higher accuracy equipment or using different high quality measurement laboratories) can decrease or better quantify their magnitude.

The traditional emphasis and belief are that with very accurate reference standards and with careful calibration and laboratory procedures, systematic uncertainties would become insignificant. For simple measurement processes of the basic physical characteristics of a manufactured product, this is generally the case. However, for most measurements in engineering and the physical sciences, systematic uncertainties are *not* insignificant. In fact, they are commonly the *dominant* contributor to uncertainty because no reference standards are directly applicable. This situation is disconcerting to many experimentalists and not believed by some. However, it has been found in many situations to be the case and only rarely is it openly discussed (Youden, 1972; Morgan and Henrion, 1990). One of the reasons is that more creative designs for sampling must be devised in order to use the power of classical statistics in dealing with systematic uncertainties.

The sampling concepts in DOE methods can be employed to attack systematic uncertainties (Montgomery, 2000; Box *et al.*, 2005; Hinkelmann and Kempthorne, 2008). This is done by using randomization and blocking techniques in the design of the samples taken in an experiment. *Randomization* is designing the samples so that all factors that could possibly affect the measurement result are randomly included in the samples. *Blocking* is a design technique used to either: (a) improve the precision with which comparisons among the factors of interest can be made, or (b) identify the individual factors that contribute to uncertainty. In essence, these techniques use specially designed sampling to convert systematic uncertainties into random uncertainties. Then they can be estimated with traditional statistical techniques. As a result, when systematic uncertainties are quantified in this way they are referred to as *correlated systematic, or bias, uncertainties*, meaning that they are uncertainties that are correlated with specific sources identified through random sampling. Note that in attempting to identify systematic uncertainty sources, the random, or background, uncertainty is also present. The random uncertainty can be segregated from the systematic sources using blocking.

Using randomization to help quantify systematic uncertainties means devising different experiments so that one can expose the factors that could contribute to systematic uncertainty. There are many different kinds of factors that come into play in a complex experiment. Here we list a number of different types of factors and several examples.

- *Experimental instrumentation*: unknown bias in a sensor, measuring device, or transducer; hysteresis in a strain-gauge; shift in zero-reading due to thermal, pressure, acceleration, or radiation sensitivity; frequency response of a complete measuring system; unknown electrical ground loop; misalignment or miscalibration of optical equipment; drifting time reference; drifting frequency reference.
- *Experimental procedures*: calibration procedure; preparation procedure; measuring procedure.
- *Experimental hardware*: imperfections or asymmetry in test hardware; assembly of test hardware; installation of test hardware in the facility.
- *Facility characteristics*: preparation of the facility for a test; calibration of the facility; nonuniformity or asymmetry in facility hardware or characteristics.
- *Data recording and reduction*: analog measurement; analog-to-digital conversion; data reduction procedure such as a programming error in the software.

- *Experimental personnel*: individual technique in human controlled instruments or piece of equipment, such as individual operators of the equipment; individual technique in assembly of the test hardware or facility preparation.
- *Time of experiment*: dependence on time of day, day of week, week of month, or month of year.
- *Weather conditions*: dependence on atmospheric conditions including temperature, pressure, winds, humidity, dust, sunshine, and clouds.

As can be seen from the types of factors and examples shown above, the list of possible sources of systematic uncertainty is surprisingly long. After an experimentalist compiles a list of all of the possible sources for their experiment, he/she must attempt to determine which ones may be important and which ones can be varied so that their effect can be randomly sampled. When considering which ones may be important, one must resolutely keep an open mind. The common attitude that must be overcome is "We've checked all of these before and everything is fine." The proper attitude is "What can possibly be changed so that we can compare our existing results with a new technique or procedure?" These ideas must, of course, be balanced with (a) the options that are possible within a facility; (b) whether qualified personnel needed to implement a new technique are available; (c) costs for new equipment, personnel, and their training; and (d) time needed for the additional experiments to be conducted.

Sometimes it may be impossible to make any significant changes in techniques or procedures within a facility. For this situation, one should consider using a different experimental facility. There is no better sampling technique than to conduct blind test comparisons using different facilities. Using different facilities, particularly if they have entirely different instrumentation techniques, addresses most of the types of factor discussed above, thereby assessing many of the most troublesome systematic uncertainties. If one is conducting relatively standard tests in commercial facilities, then there is typically a wide range of options for conducting the experiment. If one is using specialized facilities or one-of-a kind facilities, then one has few options available.

11.3.2 Example of DOE procedure for JCEAP force and moment experiment

The following discussion is taken from Oberkampf and Aeschliman (1992); Oberkampf *et al.* (1993); and Aeschliman and Oberkampf (1998) dealing with the force and moment (F&M) measurement portion of the JCEAP experiment. The F&M quantities that were measured on the configuration were the normal force, the pitch moment, the axial center of pressure, and the forebody axial force. The forebody axial force is the total axial force measured on the model using the six-component strain-gauge balance, minus the axial force due to pressure on the base of the model. See these references for more details.

11.3.2.1 DOE principles

In the F&M experiment it was decided to identify only two blocks of measurements over which randomization of experimental runs would take place. The first block contains a mixture of random uncertainties and systematic uncertainties. The random uncertainties are those that would normally be considered to contribute to variability in the measurement of F&M. The systematic uncertainties are those that would only be found through deliberate intent to sample their effect. Here we simply list them together because, depending on your perspective, they could be segregated differently:

- run-to-run variation in the F&M strain gauge output;
- hysteresis, nonlinearity, thermal sensitivity shift, and thermal zero shift in the F&M strain gauge output;
- run-to-run variation in base pressure transducers and instrumentation for eliminating the base drag;
- analog data-reduction system and analog-to-digital conversion;
- digital data recording system;
- model pitch, roll, and yaw alignment in the test section using different qualified technicians to make the measurements;
- imperfections and nonsymmetric features in the model geometry;
- assembly and reassembly of the model using different qualified technicians;
- run-to-run variation due to facility operating conditions over days, weeks, and months;
- run-to-run variation due to atmospheric condition effects on the facility;
- run-to-run variation in the wind tunnel operator setting free-stream conditions in the test section using different qualified operators.

The combination of all of these uncertainties is commonly referred to as end-to-end random uncertainty in the experimental result. Here we will refer to them simply as *random*.

The second block of samples was directed at identifying the systematic uncertainty due to nonuniformity of the flowfield in the test section of the wind tunnel. It has been long recognized that flowfield nonuniformity, or flowfield quality, is a significant contributor to uncertainty in wind tunnel measurements, but there has been only limited success to quantify this contributor (AGARD, 1994; AIAA, 1999). Flowfield nonuniformity in the test section of any type of wind tunnel can be caused by many sources. Here we list a few sources that are primarily associated with supersonic wind tunnels:

- poorly designed wall contours ahead of the test section, including the contraction section ahead of the nozzle throat, the nozzle expansion region, and the test section region;
- turbulence generated from the heater section of the wind tunnel ahead of the contraction section and the nozzle throat;
- poorly manufactured wind tunnel sections and their assembly for an experiment;
- operation of a fixed nozzle wall wind tunnel at a Reynolds number different from the design condition;
- slight changes in the location of boundary layer transition on the walls upstream or downstream of the nozzle throat due to slight variability in the wall temperature, acoustic environment, upstream flow control valves, and vibration of the walls.

All of the systematic uncertainties associated with the flowfield nonuniformity component will be referred to simply as *flowfield*.

The approach used in JCEAP was to devise a sampling procedure to test the presumption of a perfectly uniform free-stream flowfield in the test section. The fundamental idea is the following: what is the increase in uncertainty, beyond the random uncertainty in F&M measurements, due to testing the model at different locations within the test section? Stated differently, by placing the model at different locations in the test section and comparing this uncertainty to the uncertainty obtained from just testing at one location, what is the increase in uncertainty on the final measured quantities of interest? The number of possible locations for comparisons is greatly expanded by recognizing that the F&M measured at a positive angle of attack and $\phi = 0°$ should be the same for a negative angle of attack of the same magnitude and $\phi = 180°$, *if* the flowfield is perfectly uniform. Because of physical and mechanical limitations of the test section hardware, there were a limited number of locations that could be attained. All of these locations are within regions of the test section where the flowfield is considered *acceptable* for testing.

11.3.2.2 DOE analysis and results

Using the technique of blocking, comparisons are made between different wind tunnel runs and portions of different runs to segregate random and flowfield uncertainty contributors. To calculate the random uncertainty, one compares all possible combinations of F&M measurements that were made for the same physical location in the test section. In this way one can estimate the complete end-to-end random measurement uncertainty. By examining the run number schedule (Table 11.1) one can choose run pairs that have the same roll angle ϕ, the same flap deflection angle δ, and the same location in the test section. Then comparisons can be made between the same F&M quantities for the same angles of attack. The total number of run pairs that can be formed for quantifying the random uncertainty is 14. All of these run pairs are shown in the second column of Table 11.3. The number of angle of attack pairs for each run pair is shown in the third column of the table. The total number of angle of attack pairs constructed in this way is 160 for each F&M quantity.

To calculate the additional uncertainty contribution due to the flowfield, one examines Table 11.1 to determine which run pairs place the model at different locations in the test section. One finds two ways of attaining different locations. The first method forms run pairs that have the same ϕ and δ, but are at different axial stations in the test section. All of the run pairs that can be constructed in this way are shown in the fourth column in Table 11.3. The total number of run pairs that can be formed in this way is 20. Also shown in the fifth column of the table is the number of angles of attack that are in common for each run pair. The total number of angle of attack pairs constructed in this way is 220 for each F&M quantity.

The second method forms run pairs based on mirror symmetry between the model at a roll angle of 0° and pitched to a positive α, and the model at $\phi = 180°$ and pitched to negative α, both conditions for the same δ. The mirror symmetry pairs are formed for both runs at the same axial station. As the maximum negative angle of attack was $-10°$, the residuals for individual angles of attack can only be calculated over the range $-10°$ to

Table 11.3 *Run pairs for F&M uncertainty analysis (Oberkampf et al., 1993).*

Pair number	Random		Axial location		Mirror symmetry	
	Run pair	No. of αs	Run pair	No. of αs	Run pair	No. of αs
1	(34, 36)	12	(34, 74)	12	(34, 40)	8
2	(34, 37)	12	(34, 75)	12	(36, 40)	8
3	(34, 73)	12	(36, 74)	12	(37, 40)	8
4	(36, 37)	12	(36, 75)	12	(73, 40)	8
5	(36, 73)	12	(37, 74)	12	(63, 55)	8
6	(37, 73)	12	(37, 75)	12	(72, 55)	8
7	(63, 72)	12	(73, 45)	12	(64, 56)	8
8	(64, 71)	11	(73, 75)	12	(64, 57)	8
9	(65, 70)	10	(63, 83)	11	(71, 56)	8
10	(66, 67)	11	(72, 83)	11	(71, 57)	8
11	(56, 57)	11	(64, 82)	10	(65, 58)	8
12	(59, 60)	11	(71, 82)	12	(70, 58)	8
13	(74, 75)	12	(65, 81)	10	(74, 76)	8
14	(76, 77)	10	(70, 81)	10	(74, 77)	8
15	–	–	(40, 76)	10	(75, 76)	8
16	–	–	(40, 77)	10	(75, 77)	8
17	–	–	(55, 78)	10	(83, 78)	8
18	–	–	(56, 79)	10	(82, 79)	8
19	–	–	(57, 79)	10	(81, 80)	8
20	–	–	(58, 80)	10	–	–

$+10°$. All run pairs that can be constructed for estimation of this uncertainty component are shown in sixth column of Table 11.3. The total number of run pairs that can be formed in this way is 19. Using interpolation for the angle of attack range to obtain four positive and four negative angles of attack, the seventh column in the table shows the total number of angles of attack that are in common for each run pair. The total number of angle of attack pairs constructed in this way is 152 for each F&M quantity.

Now that it is seen what types of different run pairs are needed for the comparisons shown in Table 11.3, some comments are needed concerning how the run schedule (Table 11.1) was constructed before the experiment. First, replicate runs are *not* afterthoughts in the design of randomization and blocking techniques. Careful thought must be devoted to the construction of the run schedule before the experiment begins to achieve the needed samples. Second, replicate runs should be done as far apart in the run schedule as possible so as to incorporate the most changes of all of the factors discussed above. For example, replicate runs for conditions associated with runs 63 and 72 are better than replicate runs for conditions associated with runs 66 and 67. Runs 66 and 67 were conducted on the same day, whereas runs 63 and 72 were conducted weeks apart.

For each run pair an average value, $(\bar{\ })$, of the measured F&M quantity can be defined as

$$
\begin{aligned}
\left(\bar{C}_{\mathrm{n}}\right)_{\alpha_i} &= \left\{\left[(C_{\mathrm{n}})_p + (C_{\mathrm{n}})_q\right]_{\alpha_i}\right\}\Big/2, \quad i = 1, 2, \ldots, I, \\
\left(\bar{C}_{\mathrm{m}}\right)_{\alpha_i} &= \left\{\left[(C_{\mathrm{m}})_p + (C_{\mathrm{m}})_q\right]_{\alpha_i}\right\}\Big/2, \quad i = 1, 2, \ldots, I, \\
\left(\bar{x}_{\mathrm{cp}}\right)_{\alpha_i} &= \left\{\left[(x_{\mathrm{cp}})_p + (x_{\mathrm{cp}})_q\right]_{\alpha_i}\right\}\Big/2, \quad i = 1, 2, \ldots, I, \\
\left(\bar{C}_{\mathrm{a}}\right)_{\alpha_i} &= \left\{\left[(C_{\mathrm{a}})_p + (C_{\mathrm{a}})_q\right]_{\alpha_i}\right\}\Big/2, \quad i = 1, 2, \ldots, I.
\end{aligned}
\tag{11.9}
$$

C_{n}, C_{m}, x_{cp} and C_{a} are the normal force coefficient, pitch moment coefficient, axial center of pressure, and forebody axial force coefficient, respectively. p and q represent the run numbers from which measurements are taken, α_i refers to the angle of attack at which each F&M measurement was made, and I is the maximum number of angles of attack which are in common for both run pairs.

The pitch sector mechanism in the wind tunnel is programmed to yield a specified pitch angle according to the digital counter, given an initial starting angle. It lacks, however, a feedback control system for the pitch angle desired. As a result, the pitch increments programmed are not accurately repeatable from run to run because of slight variability in friction in the mechanism. As a result, the nonrepeatability in pitch angles ranges up to 0.5°. The actual pitch angle attained, however, is known to within ±0.02° based on the digital counter output. Therefore, in the average quantities calculated for each run pair in Eq. (11.9), it would be inappropriate to assign to measurement uncertainty the fact that identical pitch angles were not obtained from run to run. That is, the inaccuracy is not in the data itself, but caused by a requirement of the uncertainty analysis procedure. This inaccuracy can be eliminated by using a least squares fit of each F&M quantity for each pitch sequence for each run. Using these data fits, it is then possible to calculate the F&M measurements at precisely the same angle of attack for each run pair.

Let the difference between an individual F&M quantity and the average measurement at each angle of attack be defined as a local residual, so that

$$
\begin{aligned}
(\Delta C_{\mathrm{n}})_{\alpha_i} &= (C_{\mathrm{n}})_{\alpha_i} - \left(\bar{C}_{\mathrm{n}}\right)_{\alpha_i}, \quad i = 1, 2, \ldots, I, \\
(\Delta C_{\mathrm{m}})_{\alpha_i} &= (C_{\mathrm{m}})_{\alpha_i} - \left(\bar{C}_{\mathrm{m}}\right)_{\alpha_i}, \quad i = 1, 2, \ldots, I, \\
(\Delta x_{\mathrm{cp}})_{\alpha_i} &= (x_{\mathrm{cp}})_{\alpha_i} - \left(\bar{x}_{\mathrm{cp}}\right)_{\alpha_i}, \quad i = 1, 2, \ldots, I, \\
(\Delta C_{\mathrm{a}})_{\alpha_i} &= (C_{\mathrm{a}})_{\alpha_i} - \left(\bar{C}_{\mathrm{a}}\right)_{\alpha_i}, \quad i = 1, 2 \ldots, I.
\end{aligned}
\tag{11.10}
$$

The total number of random residuals, i.e., measurements at each pitch angle (based on the second and third columns in Table 11.3) is 320 for each F&M quantity. Because of the definition for the run pair average given in Eq. (11.9), 160 of the residuals are positive and 160 are negative, i.e., mirror images. Based on the fourth and fifth columns in Table 11.3, the total number of axial location residuals was 440. Based on the sixth and seventh columns in Table 11.3, the total number of mirror symmetry residuals was 304. The total number of residuals for the F&M experiment was 1064.

Table 11.4 *Summary of results for F&M uncertainty analysis (Oberkampf and Aeschliman, 1992).*

Uncertainty component	C_n		C_m		x_{cp}/L		C_a	
	$\hat{\sigma}$	%	$\hat{\sigma}$	%	$\hat{\sigma}$	%	$\hat{\sigma}$	%
Random	0.474×10^{-3}	20	0.406×10^{-3}	19	0.413×10^{-3}	9	0.426×10^{-3}	63
Flowfield	0.941×10^{-3}	80	0.851×10^{-3}	81	1.322×10^{-3}	91	0.324×10^{-3}	37
Total	1.054×10^{-3}	100	0.943×10^{-3}	100	1.385×10^{-3}	100	0.535×10^{-3}	100

The sample variance for the random component and also for the total experiment (random and flowfield components combined) is calculated using the equation

$$\hat{\sigma}^2 = \frac{1}{2m} \sum_{j=1}^{m} \left(\Delta_1^2 + \Delta_2^2 \right)_j, \qquad (11.11)$$

where m is the number of local residuals and Δ_1 and Δ_2 are the residuals for each run pair from Eq. (11.10). (Note that the sample variance is an estimate of a population variance and is indicated by ^.) Because of the independence between random uncertainty and flowfield uncertainty, the sum of the variances can be written

$$\hat{\sigma}_{total}^2 = \hat{\sigma}_{random}^2 + \hat{\sigma}_{flowfield}^2. \qquad (11.12)$$

The sample variance due to the random component and that for the total experiment can each be computed separately. As a result, the component due to the flowfield can be found from

$$\hat{\sigma}_{flowfield} = \sqrt{\hat{\sigma}_{total}^2 - \hat{\sigma}_{random}^2}. \qquad (11.13)$$

Table 11.4 gives the estimated standard deviation $\hat{\sigma}$ (square root of the variance estimate) due to random uncertainty, flowfield uncertainty, and the total for each F&M quantity in the experiment. Also shown in the table is the percent contribution due to each of the components identified. In the calculation for the standard deviation for x_{cp}/L, all residuals for angle of attack $0°$ were excluded. This was done because it is well known that the uncertainty in x_{cp} becomes indefinite as the normal force approaches zero. If the model geometry were axisymmetric, then the standard wind tunnel procedure of computing the ratio of $C_{m_\alpha}/C_{n_\alpha}$ for x_{cp} would be appropriate. For the present nonsymmetric geometry, however, this method is not applicable because it is not known at what angle of attack, if any, both C_m and C_n attain zero. Except for the case of calculating x_{cp} for $\alpha = 0$, all experimental F&M measurements were included in the results shown in Table 11.4, i.e., *no measurement outliers were discarded in the entire uncertainty analysis.*

From Table 11.4 it can be seen that the random uncertainty in C_n, C_m, and x_{cp} due to the entire wind tunnel system ranges from 9 to 20%, whereas that due to the flowfield nonuniformity is 80 to 91%. The random component of uncertainty in C_a is 63% and that due to the flowfield is 37%. This reversal of uncertainty contributions compared to the other quantities is believed to be due to (a) the axial force being very *insensitive* to flowfield nonuniformity because it is the sum of the normal stress and shear stress acting along the axis of the body and (b) the difficulty in removing the base pressure component from the total axial force.

Although this type of uncertainty analysis is new to wind tunnel uncertainty estimation, the JCEAP F&M experiment clearly demonstrates that, for most measured quantities, the dominant contributor is the systematic uncertainty due to the flowfield nonuniformity; *not* the random uncertainty. The long established procedure for wind tunnel uncertainty estimation is based on the ISO/ANSI practice, which, as is well known, is focused on estimating the random component of uncertainty, *not* the flowfield uncertainty. Some will quickly jump to the conclusion that the obvious problem is the poor quality flow in the Sandia hypersonic wind tunnel. As will be seen in the discussion of the JCEAP pressure experiment in the next section, this is *not* the case.

11.3.3 *Example of DOE procedure for JCEAP surface pressure experiment*

The following discussion is taken from Oberkampf *et al.* (1995) and Aeschliman and Oberkampf (1998), dealing with surface pressure measurements in the JCEAP experiment. See these references for more details. The DOE technique was applied to the surface pressures measured by the two pressure modules, but not the high frequency measurements from the Kulite gauges.

11.3.3.1 *DOE principles*

In the JCEAP pressure experiment we quantified three contributors to measurement uncertainty. Two of the three contributors were discussed earlier in the F&M experiment: end-to-end random uncertainty and flowfield nonuniformity. The random component for the pressure experiment is nearly the same, except now it includes uncertainties associated with the surface pressure measurement system instead of those associated with the F&M measurement system. The flowfield component for the pressure experiment is the same as discussed earlier. Some examples of the pressure measurement contributors that will be grouped into random uncertainty are:

- run-to-run variation in the individual pressure transducers within each pressure module;
- hysteresis, nonlinearity, thermal sensitivity shift, and thermal zero shift in the pressure modules;
- run-to-run variation in the reference pressure that is fed to the pressure modules;
- analog data reduction system and analog-to-digital conversion;
- digital data recording system;
- model pitch, roll, and yaw alignment in the test section using different qualified technicians to make the measurements;
- run-to-run variation due to facility operating conditions over days, weeks, and months;

- run-to-run variation due to atmospheric condition effects on the facility;
- run-to-run variation in the wind tunnel operator setting free-stream conditions in the test section using different qualified operators.

In addition to the random and flowfield components, local measurements (such as surface pressure and shear stress) allow an additional component of systematic uncertainty to be identified. This component is the uncertainty due to (a) imperfections or asymmetry in the wind tunnel model, and (b) imperfections due to the individual pressure sensor in each module, their connecting tubing, and the associated orifice on the surface of the model. For model and pressure sensor imperfections to be identified, however, the model must have at least two planes of mirror symmetry. All of the systematic uncertainties associated with the model and pressure sensor imperfections will be referred to simply as *model*.

Examples of some of the sources that fall into the model component are:

- model fabrication deficiencies that cause the loss of mirror symmetry of the surface contour of the wind tunnel model;
- accidental damage to the model, for example during wind tunnel testing or handling, that causes the loss of mirror symmetry of the surface contour of the model;
- any deflection or distortion of the axis of the model, such as due to fabrication or aerodynamic or aerothermal heating of the model;
- any deflection or distortion of the model surface or lifting surfaces that causes the loss of mirror symmetry of the surface contour of the model, such as due to fabrication or aerodynamic or aerothermal heating of the model;
- a poorly fabricated pressure orifice, such as one containing a burr from machining;
- accidental damage to a pressure orifice, such as a damaged edge near the model surface that occurred any time after the model was fabricated;
- a pressure leak occurring anywhere between the pressure orifice and the connection of the tubing to the pressure module;
- any blockage or a kink in the connecting tubing anywhere between the pressure orifice and the pressure module.

Using blocking techniques, we are able to identify three components contributing to measurement uncertainty: random, flowfield, and model. We will briefly summarize the blocking strategy and discuss each one in more detail.

- Random: compare pairs of measurements that have the same physical location in the test section, the same pressure port on the model, and exposure to the same induced flowfield of the model.
- Flowfield: compare pairs of measurements that have the same pressure port on the model, exposure to the same induced flowfield of the model, but are at different physical locations in the test section.
- Model: compare pairs of measurements that have same physical location in the test section, exposure to the same induced flowfield of the model, but are different pressure ports on the model.

To calculate the random uncertainty, one compares pressure measurements from different runs for the same: location in the test section, pressure port, angle of attack, roll angle, and flap deflection angle. With these restrictions, each pair of ports compared will have the same location in the vehicle-induced flowfield. When differences in pressure port measurements are computed, the uncertainty due to flowfield and model cancels out in computing the residual.

To calculate the flowfield uncertainty, a two-step process is needed. First, one compares pressure measurements from the same pressure port and exposure to the same induced flowfield, but at different locations in the test section. The same induced flowfield can be generated by having the same angle of attack, roll angle, and flap deflection angle, but it can also be generated by using mirror symmetry features as discussed with regard to the F&M uncertainty analysis. When the differences in pressure port measurements are computed, they will be a combination of the random and flowfield components, but the component due to the model cancels out in computing the residual. The second step is to subtract the variance due to the random component from the combined variance due to the random and flowfield components, leaving only the contribution due to the flowfield.

To calculate the model uncertainty, a similar two-step process is needed. First, one compares pressure measurements from the same physical location in the test section and exposure to the same induced flowfield, but using different pressure ports. Given these constraints, the only possibility for comparisons is to have two or more planes of mirror symmetry of the model geometry. For the JCEAP geometry, it only has one plane of symmetry aft of the beginning of the slice. As a result, comparisons of ports on JCEAP can only be made for ports on the conical portion of the geometry. This symmetry feature is also common with most aircraft geometries. For four-finned missile geometries, however, there are four planes of symmetry over the fin region so more comparisons could be made.

For JCEAP, we can only compare pressure ports that are sufficiently upstream of the slice on the geometry. In addition, we should only use data from deflected flap cases where we are confident there is no influence of the deflected flap upstream of the beginning of the slice. The case of $\delta = 0°$ produces no axially separated flow on the model, so there is no concern that there is any influence upstream on the cone surface. For $\delta = 10°$ and $20°$, liquid crystal surface flow visualization showed that no axially separated flow progressed ahead of the beginning of the slice. A flap deflection of $30°$, however, showed a separated flow influence over the entire slice region so this flap deflection was not used in these comparisons. Therefore, only run pairs with 0, 10, and $20°$ flap deflections were used. To further reduce the possibility of any upstream influence of the slice or flap on the ports used only axial stations up to 15.75 cm were considered. This is 2.73 cm ahead of the slice, or about 10 to 20 boundary layer thicknesses. The second step in the calculation process is to subtract the variance due to the random component from the combined variance due to the random and model components, leaving only the model component.

11.3.3.2 DOE analysis and results

To calculate the random uncertainty, one examines the run schedule (Table 11.2) and chooses run pairs that have the same roll and flap angles and have the same tunnel location. In addition, the run pairs chosen must allow comparison only between the same pressure ports on the model. Examples of run pairs that meet these conditions are (20,22), (24,61), (103,112), (42,43), (124, 126), and (131,133). It can be shown that a total of 29 run pairs meet the required conditions. Pressure measurements were obtained for a total of 12 angles of attack for each run; nine distinct angles of attack and three measurements at $\alpha = 0$. As a result, there are a total of 18 combinations of α where pressure comparisons can be made (nine distinct α comparisons plus nine permutations of $\alpha = 0$ measurements). Therefore, the total number of pressure port comparisons is

$$(96 \text{ ports}) \times (29 \text{ run pairs}) \times (18 \ \alpha \text{ pairs}) = 50\,112 \text{ comparisons}.$$

The actual number of comparisons is slightly less than this estimate because some pressure ports were outside the calibrated range for certain conditions. As a result, the total number of pressure port comparisons for random uncertainty was found to be 48 164.

To make these pressure port comparisons, it is required that the α for each of the two runs is identical. If they are not the same, then part of the difference in the two measurements will be due to non-repeatability of α caused by the model pitch mechanism. As mentioned earlier, the pitch control mechanism does not have a feedback control system, so the repeatability of α from one pitch sweep of the mechanism to another can be as large as $\pm 0.5°$. Since it was known that very similar angles of attack were needed for the pressure comparisons, roughly 10 to 20 runs had to be repeated because the resulting α deviated by more than $\pm 0.3°$ from the nominal values. For the final run numbers shown in Table 11.2, α did not deviate from the nominal value by more than $\pm 0.28°$. The average deviation from the nominal value of α for all runs listed in Table 11.2 was $0.057°$.

Deviations in α of up to $0.28°$ from run to run would introduce an unacceptably large error in the estimated surface pressure uncertainty. To minimize this uncertainty in the analysis, all of the pressure measurements were interpolated to the nominal angles of attack. To accomplish this, a cubic spline interpolation with adjustable knot locations was computed for each pressure port as a function of α for each run.

Differences in pressure port measurements were computed with the following technique. Let the pressure measurement for port i and angle of attack j be denoted as $\left(\frac{p_i}{p_\infty}\right)_j^r$, where the superscript denotes the run number r. Then the average pressure of the port for the two runs being compared is given by

$$\left(\frac{\bar{p}_i}{p_\infty}\right)_j^{r,s} = \frac{1}{2}\left[\left(\frac{p_i}{p_\infty}\right)_j^r + \left(\frac{p_i}{p_\infty}\right)_j^s\right], \tag{11.14}$$

where $i = 1, 2, \ldots, 96$ and $j = 1, 2, \ldots, 18$, where 18 is the total number of αs. Let the absolute value of the difference between a pressure measurement and the average pressure be defined as the residual. Then the residual is given by

$$\left(\frac{\Delta p_i}{p_\infty}\right)_j^{r,s} = \left|\left(\frac{p_i}{p_\infty}\right)_j^r - \left(\frac{\bar{p}_i}{p_\infty}\right)_j^{r,s}\right|. \tag{11.15}$$

Note that the residual can be computed using either the pressure measurement from run r or s.

To calculate the flowfield uncertainty, one examines Table 11.2 and chooses run pair that have the same induced flowfield and the same flap deflection angle, but the model

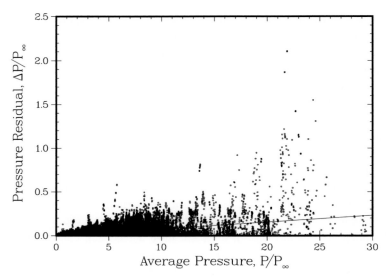

Figure 11.9 All pressure residuals for random, flowfield nonuniformity, and model geometry uncertainty (Oberkampf *et al.*, 1995).

has different locations in the test section. In addition, the run pairs chosen must allow a comparison only between the same pressure ports on the model. One finds four types of run pairs that will produce the types of comparisons desired. These are (a) comparisons between measurements made at different axial locations in the test section, (b) comparisons between different roll angles at $\alpha = 0$ at the same tunnel station, (c) comparisons between positive α with a roll angle of $0°$ and negative α with a roll angle of $180°$, and (d) comparisons between positive α with a roll angle of $90°$ and negative α with a roll angle of $270°$. Examples of run pairs for each of these types of comparison are, respectively, (20,101), (24,32), (35,43), and (46,47).

The total number of pressure port comparisons for these four types, minus the number of comparisons lost due to over-ranged ports, is 101 838 residuals. The residuals for flowfield and random uncertainty are computed by the same equations given above, but the number of angles of attack, j, for each of the types is different.

To calculate the model uncertainty, one examines Table 11.2 for combinations of roll angle, flap deflection angle, both runs at the same tunnel station, the same induced flow field, but different pressure ports are compared. One finds six types of run pairs that meet the required conditions. All of these pairs are formed by comparing different roll angles, the same flap angle, and the same tunnel location. The total number of pressure port comparisons for these six types, minus the number of comparisons lost due to over-ranged ports, is 24 196. The residuals for model and random uncertainty are computed using the same equations given above.

Plotted in Figure 11.9 are all of the residuals computed for random, flowfield, and model uncertainty. In the entire pressure uncertainty analysis no pressure measurement outliers were discarded. It can be seen from this figure that the magnitude of the uncertainty steadily increases with the magnitude of the pressure measured. This characteristic is typical of nearly all experimental measurements. This trend is accounted for in the residuals by scaling the residuals with the magnitude of measured pressure. A least squares fit of the residuals was computed using a linear function constrained to pass through zero. The resulting fit was computed to be

$$\frac{\Delta p_{\text{ls}}}{p_\infty} = 0.00875 \frac{p_\text{s}}{p_\infty}, \tag{11.16}$$

where p_s is the surface pressure measured. This linear fit is also shown in Figure 11.9.

The sample variance is now calculated with each local sample scaled according to the least squares fit given above. The equation for estimating each type of variance, normalized by the least squares fit of the residuals, is given by

$$\hat{\sigma}^2 = \frac{1}{N} \sum_{k=1}^{N} \left[\frac{(\Delta p / p_\infty)}{(\Delta p_{\text{ls}} / p_\infty)} \right]_k^2, \tag{11.17}$$

where N is the total number of residuals (i.e., pressure comparisons) and the subscript k indicates the kth residual. The sample standard deviation due to the flowfield and the model can then be calculated from

$$\hat{\sigma}_{\text{flow}} = \sqrt{\hat{\sigma}^2_{\text{flow+instrumentation}} - \hat{\sigma}^2_{\text{instrumentation}}}, \tag{11.18}$$

$$\hat{\sigma}_{\text{model}} = \sqrt{\hat{\sigma}^2_{\text{model+instrumentation}} - \hat{\sigma}^2_{\text{instrumentation}}}, \tag{11.19}$$

respectively. The sample standard deviation due to all of the uncertainty sources is given by

$$\hat{\sigma}_{\text{total}} = \sqrt{\hat{\sigma}^2_{\text{instrumentation}} + \hat{\sigma}^2_{\text{flow}} + \hat{\sigma}^2_{\text{model}}}. \tag{11.20}$$

Table 11.5 gives the summary statistics for the uncertainty estimates for the pressure measurements. It is seen from the table that the dominant contributor to uncertainty of pressure measurements, as was seen in the F&M measurements, is due to the nonuniformity of the flowfield in the test section. The second most important contributor was the model; the least important was the end-to-end random contribution due to the entire instrumentation system and wind tunnel facility.

The dominant contribution of non-uniform flow to uncertainty suggests the question: is this just characteristic of the present wind tunnel or is it characteristic of other hypersonic wind tunnels? An earlier application of the DOE uncertainty estimation procedure was applied to a similar surface pressure experiment in Tunnels A and B of the von Karman Gas Dynamics Facility at the US Air Force Arnold Engineering Development Center, Tullahoma, Tennessee (Oberkampf *et al.*, 1985). Tunnel A is a variable Mach number facility in the supersonic range and Tunnel B can be operated at Mach 6 and 8. The absolute magnitude (no normalization using the free-stream static pressure) of the present results

Table 11.5 *Summary of results for the surface pressure uncertainty analysis (Oberkampf et al., 1995).*

Component of uncertainty	Number of residuals	Normalized $\hat{\sigma}$	% of total RMS uncertainty
Random	48 164	0.56	12
Flowfield	101 838	1.28	64
Model	24 196	0.79	24
Total	174 198	1.60	100

for flowfield uncertainty was compared to those for Mach 8 in Tunnel B of the von Karman Gas Dynamics Facility (Oberkampf *et al.*, 1995). Hypersonic Tunnel B is recognized world wide for the quality of its flowfield. This comparison showed that the Sandia HWT and Tunnel B are *comparable* in terms of the effect of the flowfield non-uniformity on surface pressure measurements. As an independent check on the results of DOE procedure, it was also found that the random uncertainty computed using the DOE technique compared very closely to that computed by the traditional ISO/ANSI technique by the von Karman Gas Dynamics Facility staff (Oberkampf *et al.*, 1985).

In summary, the DOE approach using randomization and blocking techniques has been used on four different wind tunnel experiments: three of the data sets were for surface pressure measurements and one was for body forces and moments. The method has been applied to three wind tunnels: (a) two hypersonic wind tunnels, Tunnel B of the von Karman Gas Dynamics Facility and the HWT Facility at Sandia National Laboratories; and (b) one supersonic wind tunnel, Tunnel A operating at Mach 3. The method showed that, even in these high-quality flowfield facilities, the largest contributor was systematic uncertainty due to nonuniformity of the flowfield. It was shown that the flowfield nonuniformity was typically four to five times larger than the end-to-end random uncertainty of the facility. We strongly suspect that the largest contribution to experimental uncertainty in most, if not all, hypersonic wind tunnels is due to flowfield nonuniformity. Although this technique has not been applied, to our knowledge, to any other wind tunnel, we suggest the flowfield nonuniformity may also dominate in other facilities. A similar DOE technique has been applied recently to wind tunnel testing, but no quantitative assessments have been made with regard to the magnitude of flowfield nonuniformity to other contributors (DeLoach, 2002, 2003).

The natural question is: why hasn't this procedure been investigated by wind tunnel facilities over the past 14 years when it was published in the open literature? There are number of possible answers, some of which are: (a) natural resistance to new procedures and technology in organizations; (b) users of wind tunnels, i.e., paying customers, are more interested in quantity of data obtained during the experiment than careful uncertainty estimation of data; and (c) facility owners would rather not deal with this risky topic.

We argue that the experimental uncertainty issue, just as issues with code verification, solution verification, and uncertainty quantification, must be faced in the future if increased credibility is to be earned in both experimental measurements and computational simulations. We believe the customers and decision makers using these products must provide the long-term motivation for moving ahead because they are the ones most at risk. They are the ones with the most skin in the game.

11.4 Example of further computational–experimental synergism in JCEAP

Roughly five years after the completion of the JCEAP project, there was renewed interest at Sandia National Laboratories in the experiment (Roy *et al.*, 2000). The interest was primarily directed toward using the pressure data for validation activities related to the Sandia Advanced Code for Compressible Aerothermodynamics Research and Analysis (SACCARA) code (Payne and Walker, 1995; Wong *et al.*, 1995a,b). The SACCARA code evolved from a parallel-distributed memory version of the INCA code (Amtec, 1995), originally developed by Amtec Engineering. The SACCARA code employs a massively parallel-distributed memory architecture based on multi-block structured meshes. The Navier–Stokes equations are solved for conservation of mass, momentum, global energy, and vibrational energy (where applicable) in finite volume form. The viscous terms are discretized using central differences. The SACCARA code has two options for determining the inviscid interface fluxes, the Steger–Warming flux vector splitting scheme (Steger and Warming, 1981) and Yee's symmetric TVD scheme (Yee, 1987). Second-order spatial accuracy is obtained with the former via MUSCL extrapolation of the primitive variables, while the latter is nominally second order in smooth regions of the flow. Both schemes employ a flux limiter that reduces to first-order spatial accuracy in regions with shock waves.

Initial comparisons were made between the SACCARA code and the JCEAP pressure results for low angles of attack and zero flap deflection. For these attached flow cases, there was high confidence that the predictions should be very accurate. It was found, however, there was larger than expected disagreement. So, improved simulations were computed for a specialized case: flow over the conical portion of the vehicle at zero angle of attack case so that a 2-D axisymmetric flow could be accurately computed (Roy *et al.*, 2000; Roy *et al.*, 2003a,b). Figure 11.10 shows the surface pressure vs. the nondimensional axial length, x/R_N, where R_N is the nose radius of the vehicle. The experimental measurement shown at each axial station is the mean value of all measurements taken during the experiment, along with $\pm 2\sigma$ of the estimated total uncertainty (random, flowfield, and model). The number of individual measurements at each axial station ranged from 48 (on the side of the body opposite to the slice) to 768 (on the slice side of the body at $x/R_N = 16$ and 26). The large number of samples is the reason the $\pm 2\sigma$ values are extremely small, since the uncertainty band decreases as $1/\sqrt{n}$. As can be seen in Figure 11.10, the computed pressures fall consistently below the experimental data, with the poorest agreement occurring just

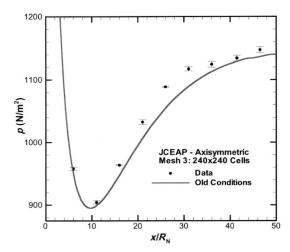

Figure 11.10 SACCARA simulation (curve) compared with the JCEAP pressure data for the surface pressure data on the cone, $\alpha = 0$ (Roy *et al.*, 2003).

upstream of the slice location, which begins at $x/R_N = 36.37$. The maximum difference, occurring at the $x/R_N = 26$ location, is 3.3%; well outside the estimated experimental 2σ uncertainty bounds.

As a result, an investigation was launched into trying to discover the cause of the unexpected disagreement. The first phase of the investigation was an extensive code verification and solution verification effort. These efforts were reported in Roy *et al.* (2000, 2003a), and discussed in Chapters 6–8. The results of the first phase showed no noticeable change in the results shown in Figure 11.10. The second phase of the investigation pursued a number of other possible sources for the disagreement (Roy *et al.*, 2000, 2003b). This second phase of the investigation is briefly reported here; focusing on the strategy that could be used when one is faced with the situation of unexplained disagreement between high confidence simulations and experimental results. This type of investigation almost always yields improved understanding of the simulation and experimental results, as well as unexpected synergism between each approach. See the cited references for the full details.

11.4.1 Assessment of computational submodels

In any modern scientific computing analysis there is a wide range of submodels that are combined to yield the complete physics model for the simulation. In an investigation such as this, it is important to critically examine (a) each submodel to try and determine if the assumptions in the submodel are appropriate for the experiment of interest and (b) evaluate important modeling assumptions of the flowfield to determine their effect. Stated differently, one conducts a quantitative sensitivity analysis with respect to the submodels and numerical approximations to determine if they might explain the disagreement between computation and experiment. The following submodels and numerical approximations were evaluated and the result is summarized.

11.4.1.1 Transport property submodels

A study of the transport properties of nitrogen was undertaken in order to insure accuracy over the temperature range of interest (50 K to 650 K). Three different models for absolute viscosity were evaluated: Keyes' model, Sutherland's law, and a power law model. Each was evaluated using available experimental data. In critical evaluations, it is highly recommended to plot the estimated *error* in the model as a function of the independent variable, and *not* just the quantity of interest vs. the independent variable. A much more critical perspective can be gained of the model accuracy. Keyes' model was found to be the most accurate over the temperature range with a maximum error of 5% found in the low temperature range.

Keyes' model for the thermal conductivity takes the same form as that for the absolute viscosity; however, the constants used are different. Using the usual constants in Keyes' model for thermal conductivity and comparing with experimental data showed that the model performed poorly at both low and high temperatures. Better agreement with the data is found by simply assuming a constant molecular Prandtl number along with Keyes' model for viscosity. Using this model showed significantly smaller errors of 10% and 40% in the higher and lower temperatures, respectively. While the choice of transport models can have a large impact on the skin friction and heat transfer, the choice of the model was found to have negligible effects on the surface pressure, as would be expected.

11.4.1.2 Equation of state submodel

To test the validity of the ideal gas equation of state, the densities and temperatures from an ideal gas solution were used in an *a posteriori* calculation of the pressure using the more accurate Beattie–Bridgeman equation of state. These pressures were then compared to the ideal gas solution results, with maximum differences found to be less than 0.05% for the entire flowfield. Thus, the ideal gas equation of state was used.

11.4.1.3 Thermodynamic submodel

In order to determine the thermal state of the flow, i.e., vibrational equilibrium versus nonequilibrium in each section of the wind tunnel, calculations were performed for the HWT Mach 8 nozzle. These calculations employed the SACCARA code and assumed fully turbulent boundary layers on the tunnel wall from the heater section, through the contraction section, through the expansion section, and into the test section. This is a reasonable assumption based on the community of operators of hypersonic wind tunnels. The design specifications (pre-fabrication) were used for the geometry definition, as opposed to post-fabrication inspection of the wind tunnel. One difference between the two was that an inspection of the nozzle throat diameter indicated a diameter of 23.01 mm as compared to 22.70 mm in the design specifications. This difference is probably due to slight erosion of the metal throat through the years of operation. Although this difference is small (1.37%), it could lead to Mach number overprediction by as much as 0.4% based on a simple isentropic analysis. Since a full inspection of the contour of the various sections was not feasible at the time, it was decided to use the design specifications for each section. Three axisymmetric mesh levels were employed in order to ensure mesh convergence of the solution, with the fine mesh having 280×120 cells in the axial and radial directions, respectively.

In order to determine the thermal state of the flow at the test section, the nozzle flow was simulated assuming thermal nonequilibrium using the standard Landau–Teller formulation for vibrational relaxation. Simulation results convincingly showed that the vibrational temperature freezes out very near the plenum stagnation temperature of 633 K, resulting in nonequilibrium flow through the contraction region, throat, and expansion region of the nozzle. This is significant because the nozzle flowfield was *calibrated* using the assumption of thermal equilibrium.

As a result, it was incumbent to investigate the effect of this inappropriate assumption in the calibration of the facility on the JCEAP results. To address this question, a one-dimensional analysis code was written for calculating the isentropic flow in the nozzle. This code integrates the adiabatic and isentropic relationships from the nozzle plenum conditions out to a specified static pressure, and assumes either (a) the gas is vibrationally frozen at a specified temperature, or (b) thermal equilibrium is modeled via a harmonic oscillator. Using this 1-D analysis, the effects of vibrational nonequilibrium on the free-stream conditions can be estimated. Relative to the thermal equilibrium case, the effects of vibrational nonequilibrium on Mach number, static pressure, static temperature, and velocity at the test section were found to be in error by +0.11%, −0.21%, −0.93%, and −0.35%, respectively. Since we were concerned with validation of the surface pressures, the effect on the free-stream pressure of only 0.21% was considered negligible.

11.4.1.4 Continuum flow assumption

In order to ensure that the assumption of continuum flow is valid for the wind tunnel nozzle in the low-pressure rapid expansion region, Bird's continuum breakdown parameter P was calculated. Continuum flow theory begins to break down for $P > 0.02$. The maximum values calculated in the Mach 8 nozzle simulations were approximately 2×10^{-5}. This result supports the use of the continuum flow assumption.

11.4.1.5 Outflow boundary condition assumption

The SACCARA simulations for the surface pressure on the conical portion of the vehicle used a zero gradient condition in the axial direction applied at the outflow boundary. The outflow boundary was specified as the baseplane of the vehicle, $x/R_N = 51.96$. This boundary condition is not appropriate in the subsonic portion of the boundary layer where pressure disturbances can travel upstream from the separated base flow of the vehicle.

In order to assess the effects of this boundary condition assumption on the pressure distributions, an axisymmetric case was computed, which included the base region. The computational domain (without a support sting) was extended roughly 2 m past the base-plane of the model. The computational region was extended for such a long distance beyond the baseplane to ensure that supersonic flow existed everywhere across the outflow boundary of the new computational region. The wake was assumed to remain laminar over the entire region. A highly clustered mesh near the baseplane was used to capture the shear layer separating near the circular edge of the base. In the simulation, it was observed that the pressure drops dramatically as the boundary layer nears the baseplane. The upstream influence (from the baseplane forward) was $2.5R_N$, which was approximately four boundary layer thicknesses. Thus, the presence of the base flow affects the surface pressure no further forward than an axial distance of $x/R_N = 49.5$ (see Figure 11.10). Given that the experimental data comparisons only extend to $x/R_N = 46.5$, it is concluded that the original outflow boundary condition in SACCARA was adequate.

11.4.1.6 Axisymmetric flow assumption

In critically questioning the strength of each physical modeling assumption, the question was raised: could the presence of the slice on the opposite side of the body from the pressure orifices affect the pressure readings by way of the subsonic region of the boundary layer? The validity of the axisymmetric flow assumption was addressed by conducting full three-dimensional calculations of the JCEAP geometry including the planar slice on the aft end of the model. A symmetry plane was assumed, thus only half of the model was simulated. The three-dimensional mesh was based on the 240×240 axisymmetric mesh and employed 105 azimuthal mesh cells from the cone-symmetry plane to the slice-symmetry plane (180 deg apart). The wall normal spacing from the 240×240 axisymmetric mesh was retained over the entire surface of the three-dimensional mesh.

With the exception of the planar slice region, essentially no effect was found on the cone-side of the vehicle compared to the axisymmetric solutions.

11.4.1.7 Re-evaluation of the experimental data

After all of this computational effort, it was time to start critically examining the experimental data again. The first, and easiest, thing to check in the experimental data was the calculation of the average free-stream conditions from all of the 48 wind tunnel runs shown in Table 11.2. Surprisingly, an arithmetic error was found in computing the free-stream static pressure originally reported in the experiment. When the free-stream static pressure values were re-averaged, the resulting static pressure was found to be 1.4% larger than the static pressure initially reported in the experiment.

The corrected free-stream conditions were then run with the SACCARA code. The results are shown in Figure 11.11, along with the old conditions. As expected, the effect of increasing the free-stream static pressure by 1.4% is to increase the surface pressure by approximately 1.4%. The computational results with the new free-stream static pressure are now in better agreement with the experimental data. Accounting for the estimated

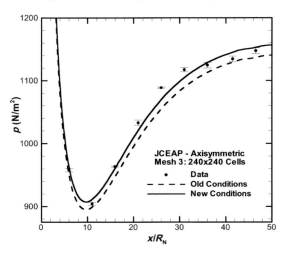

Figure 11.11 SACCARA simulation compared with the surface pressure data using both the old and corrected free-stream conditions, $\alpha = 0$ (Roy *et al.*, 2003).

experimental uncertainty bounds and an estimate of the numerical errors, the maximum error in surface pressure relative to the experimental data is now 1.5% at $x/R_N = 26$.

11.4.2 Simulation of the flowfield nonuniformities

Examining Figure 11.11, there appear to be two trends in the experimental data corrected for the error in free-stream static pressure that are not captured in the simulations. The first anomalous trend is that the experimental pressure is increasingly higher than the simulation as one moves from $x/R_N = 16$ to about $x/R_N = 30$. The second trend is that the experimental data has a marked decrease in slope beginning at $x/R_N = 30$. This latter feature is more disturbing because no such feature can occur on a blunted cone at zero angle of attack in a uniform, ideal gas, laminar hypersonic flow. In obtaining the experimental data for $\alpha = 0$, data were taken at various azimuthal angles around the model, various roll angles, and at two different axial locations in the tunnel. This type of data averaging procedure, however, will not account for the effects of axisymmetric nonuniformities, i.e., nonuniformities that are functions of the radial coordinate in the wind tunnel, because all the data were taken along the centerline of the test section. An attempt to quantify the axisymmetric nonuniformities in the test section was initiated.

11.4.2.1 Use of the flowfield calibration data

As part of the calibration procedure of the wind tunnel flowfield, the stagnation pressure is measured in the plenum, where the heaters are located. The stagnation temperature of the flowfield is determined from the measured plenum pressure and the mass flow rate that is measured upstream of the heaters. The local Mach number in the test section is calibrated

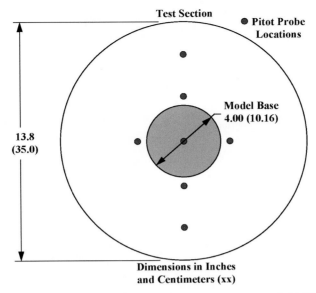

Figure 11.12 Pitot probe locations for calibration of the test section flowfield (JCEAP model base shown for reference) (Roy *et al.*, 2003).

using a seven-probe pitot pressure rake. The pitot probe locations are shown in Figure 11.12 along with the wind tunnel cross section (outer circle) in the test section. The JCEAP model base radius is shown (shaded circle) just for reference. The measured pressure points in the test section are at three radial coordinates: $y = 0$, 5.72, and 11.4 cm. The measurements from the four probes located 5.72 cm away from the centerline were averaged. Similarly, the measurements from the top and bottom probes, located 11.4 cm from the centerline, were averaged.

The pitot probe data of interest exist at seven axial stations in the test section. The pitot probe locations are presented in Figure 11.13 as the circular points. The flow direction is left to right, the zero axial station, $x = 0$, is located at the farthest upstream pitot probe location, and the radial coordinate is denoted by y. Only pitot data taken at Reynolds numbers within 15% of the JCEAP test Reynolds number were used, and these data were then corrected to the nominal Reynolds number. The corrections were considered reliable because flowfield calibrations were conducted at a range of Reynolds numbers.

The pitot probe data were then used in a newly written method of characteristics code to generate a complete flowfield in the vicinity of the JCEAP model locations. This complete flowfield, including axisymmetric nonuniformities, could then be used in a new simulation of the flow over the JCEAP geometry. The axisymmetric method of characteristics (MOC) scheme of Hartree was employed (Owczarek, 1964). This MOC implementation used an implicit integration scheme, that is, it determined the slope of the characteristic line as the average between the origination point and the destination point. For example, the C^- characteristic shown in Figure 11.13 uses the average slope found between points B and

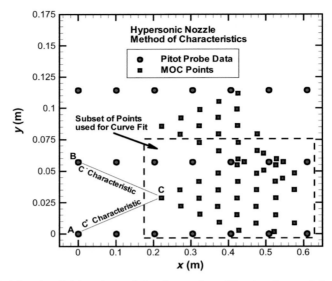

Figure 11.13 Axial and radial locations of the pitot probe calibration data and the data generated using the method of characteristics (Roy *et al.*, 2003).

C, and the C^+ characteristic uses the average of points A and C. In this manner, the characteristic network shown in Figure 11.13 is generated. The major assumption is that the radial velocity of the flow at the pitot probe locations is zero. This assumption must be made because the pitot probe data contain no information on the flow angularity.

Using the measured calibration points and the MOC generated data, an axisymmetric, nonuniform flowfield can be constructed. Figure 11.14 shows the three-dimensional surface of the computed free-stream pressure data as a function of axial and radial coordinates in the test section. A number of expansion and compression waves are evident, with a dominant axisymmetric wave-focusing effect occurring at $x = 0.52$ m at the centerline.

11.4.2.2 Simulation using the nonuniform flowfield

There is now sufficient data resolution to include the axisymmetric nonuniformities as a nonuniform inflow boundary condition for new simulations of the flow over the model. Since there were two different axial testing locations used for the vehicle, two different sets of inflow boundary conditions were used in the simulations. The simulation results accounting for axisymmetric flowfield nonuniformities at both the fore and aft model locations are presented in Figure 11.15. Up until the $x/R_N = 30$ axial location, the two simulations accounting for nonuniformities obtain even better agreement with the experimental data than the uniform flow free-stream conditions. However, for $x/R_N > 30$, the nonuniform boundary simulations over predict the pressure relative to the experimental data.

Although the computational construction of the nonuniform flowfield showed significant improvement with the measurements over most of the length of the model, the construction does have two weaknesses. First, there is very sparse radial resolution of the calibration data

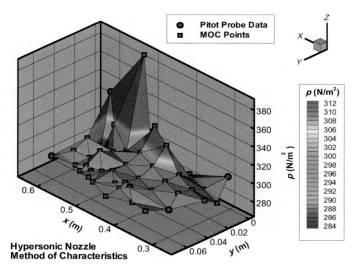

Figure 11.14 Free-stream static pressures from a combination of flowfield calibration data and MOC generated data (Roy *et al.*, 2003). See color plate section.

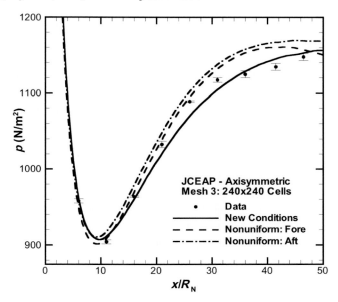

Figure 11.15 Comparison of the experimental data and SACCARA simulations accounting for axisymmetric nonuniformities, $\alpha = 0$ (Roy *et al.*, 2003).

over the test section of the wind tunnel. Second, the assumption of zero radial velocity at the calibration data points is only an approximation to the actual flowfield. A more spatially precise and definitive calibration of the test section, especially the beginning of the test section, would eliminate these weaknesses so that an accurate nonuniform flowfield could be used for future simulations.

11.4.3 Lessons learned for validation experiments

The JCEAP experiment and the subsequent computational analyses provided an exceptional opportunity to develop the fundamental ideas of what validation experiments should be. Not that the JCEAP experiment did everything correctly, but it was a valuable learning experience. Specific lessons were learned concerning validation experiments in wind tunnels, but many of these can be extended to validation experiments over a wide variety of physics. Here, we give a few summary comments for validation experiments applicable to essentially any technical field.

The value of joint planning and design in the JCEAP experiment was seen in almost every aspect of the project. There were two key features that allowed this joint activity to occur. First, there was the joint funding for both the experimental and the initial computational effort. The funding was from an internal research and development source, allowing much more of a research and discovery environment. Second, the experimental and computational team members were from the same organization and had worked together in the past. This was a luxury that is nearly impossible to achieve in large-scale validation activities, especially for projects of a national or international scale.

The level of characterization of an experimental facility that is needed for a validation experiment is remarkably higher than what is normally available from the facility. This high level of characterization is usually difficult and expensive to obtain. It requires research oriented personnel and those who question accepted assumptions concerning the facility, instead of more production-oriented personnel. In addition, this raises the question of the feasibility of conducting validation experiments in high-cost, high-volume data output facilities. These types of facility usually have testing capabilities well beyond small research facilities, but in these expensive facilities there is unrelenting pressure to keep data production high for the facility customer, instead of taking time to refine the facility characterization or investigate possible sources of uncertainty. As a result, to do validation experiments in high-cost facilities requires a much higher level of planning and preparation before the testing begins, as well as additional financial resources compared to traditional production testing in the facility. Finally, facility customers who want to conduct a high-quality validation experiment should clearly notify the facility operator during the planning stage that it desires personnel who have the appropriate experience and mindset for a validation experiment. Experimental facilities that embrace a more critical and comprehensive uncertainty estimation procedure could use this to their advantage with validation-type customers.

As commonly occurs in validation experiments, there are differences observed between computational results and experimental results. If there is an opportunity to pursue the possible causes of these differences, a great deal can be learned concerning both the simulation and the experimental measurements. For example in the follow-on computational work to JCEAP, even small differences between simulation and experiment were pursued. This resulted in a higher level of understanding of both the simulations and the experimental facility. Weaknesses in the facility were uncovered and specific recommendations were made concerning how the characterization of the facility could be improved for future testing. Indeed, the next higher level of validation activities will involve accounting for the known imperfections in a facility in the computational simulations.

The use of DOE with randomization and blocking conclusively showed that in three different wind tunnel facilities the systematic uncertainties dominate the experimental measurement uncertainty. This is not welcome news to most wind tunnel operators because the experimental uncertainty that is traditionally quoted is only the random component of uncertainty. Various esteemed metrologists, such as Youden (1972), have called attention to the importance of systematic uncertainties in experimental measurements. However, the change in perspective in the experimental measurement community occurs at a glacial pace. More that two decades ago, McCroskey (1987) tried to call attention to the problem of systematic errors in wind tunnel testing by stating:

Reliable determination and assessment of the accuracy of aerodynamic data generated in wind tunnels remains one of the most vexing problems in aeronautics. Aerodynamic results are seldom duplicated in different facilities to the level of accuracy that are required either for risk-free engineering development or for the true verification of theoretical and numerical methods. This shortcoming is particularly acute with regard to today's rapid proliferation of new Computational Fluid Dynamic (CFD) codes that lack adequate validation.

As we have tried to point out, this lack of interest in seeking out and quantifying systematic errors is not just in the wind tunnel community, but it is a systemic problem in experimental facilities. It is our view that only when experimental facilities see that it is to their advantage will they change their procedures.

11.5 References

Aeschliman, D. P. and W. L. Oberkampf (1998). Experimental methodology for computational fluid dynamics code validation. *AIAA Journal*. **36**(5), 733–741.

Aeschliman, D. P., W. L. Oberkampf, and H. F. Henfling (1994). Fast-response, electronically-scanned multi-port pressure system for low-pressure hypersonic wind tunnel applications. *AIAA Aerospace Ground Testing Conference*, AIAA Paper 94-2580, Colorado Springs, CO, American Institute of Aeronautics and Astronautics.

Aeschliman, D. P., W. L. Oberkampf, and F. G. Blottner (1995). A proposed methodology for CFD code verification, calibration, and validation. *16th International Congress on Instrumentation for Aerospace Simulation Facilities*, Paper 95-CH3482-7, Dayton, OH, ICIASF.

AGARD (1994). *Quality Assessment for Wind Tunnel Testing*. NATO Advisory Group for Aerospace Research & Development (AGARD), AGARD-AR-304.

AIAA (1999). *Assessment of Experimental Uncertainty with Application to Wind Tunnel Testing*. S-071A-1999, Reston, VA, American Institute of Aeronautics and Astronautics.

AIAA (2003). *Assessing Experimental Uncertainty – Supplement to AIAA S-071A-1999*, Reston, VA, American Institute of Aeronautics and Astronautics.

Amtec (1995). *INCA User's Manual*. Bellevue, WA, Amtec Engineering, Inc.

ANSI (1997). *U.S. Guide to the Expression of Uncertainty in Measurement*. Boulder, CO, American National Standards Institute.

Barber, T. J. (1998). Role of code validation and certification in the design environment. *AIAA Journal.* **36**(5), 752–758.

Benek, J. A., E. M. Kraft, and R. F. Lauer (1998). Validation issues for engine – airframe integration. *AIAA Journal.* **36**(5), 759–764.

Box, G. E. P., J. S. Hunter, and W. G. Hunter, (2005). *Statistics for Experimenters: Design, Innovation, and Discovery*. 2nd edn., New York, John Wiley.

Chapman, D. R., H. Mark, and M. W. Pirtle (1975). Computer vs. wind tunnels. *Astronautics & Aeronautics.* **13**(4), 22–30.

Coleman, H. W. and W. G. Steele, Jr. (1999). *Experimentation and Uncertainty Analysis for Engineers*. 2nd edn., New York, John Wiley.

Cosner, R. R. (1995). CFD validation requirements for technology transition. *26th AIAA Fluid Dynamics Conference*, AIAA Paper 95-2227, San Diego, CA, American Institute of Aeronautics and Astronautics.

DeLoach, R. (2002). Tactical defenses against systematic variation in wind tunnel testing. *40th AIAA Aerospace Sciences Meeting & Exhibit*, AIAA-2002-0885, Reno, NV, American Institute of Aeronautics and Astronautics.

DeLoach, R. (2003). Blocking: a defense against long-period unexplained variance in aerospace ground testing. *41st Aerospace Sciences Meeting and Exhibit*, AIAA-2003-0650, Reno, NV, American Institute of Aeronautics and Astronautics.

Devore, J. L. (2007). *Probability and Statistics for Engineers and the Sciences*. 7th edn., Pacific Grove, CA, Duxbury.

Drosg, M. (2007). *Dealing with Uncertainties: a Guide to Error Analysis*, Berlin, Springer-Verlag.

Grabe, M. (2005). *Measurement Uncertainties in Science and Technology*, Berlin, Springer-Verlag.

Hinkelmann, K. and O. Kempthorne (2008). *Design and Analysis of Experiments: Volume 1 – Introduction to Experimental Design*. 2nd edn., Hoboken, NJ, John Wiley.

ISO (1995). *Guide to the Expression of Uncertainty in Measurement*. Geneva, Switzerland, International Organization for Standardization.

ISO (2008). *Uncertainty of Measurement – Part 3: Guide to the Expression of Uncertainty in Measurement*. ISO/IEC Guide 98-3:2008, Geneva, Switzerland, International Organization for Standardization.

Marvin, J. G. (1995). Perspective on computational fluid dynamics validation. *AIAA Journal.* **33**(10), 1778–1787.

McCroskey, W. J. (1987). *A Critical Assessment of Wind Tunnel Results for the NACA 0012 Airfoil*. Washington, DC, National Aeronautics and Space Administration.

Moffat, R. J. (1988). Describing the uncertainties in experimental results. *Experimental Thermal and Fluid Science.* **1**(1), 3–17.

Montgomery, D. C. (2000). *Design and Analysis of Experiments*. 5th edn., Hoboken, NJ, John Wiley.

Morgan, M. G. and M. Henrion (1990). *Uncertainty: a Guide to Dealing with Uncertainty in Quantitative Risk and Policy Analysis*. 1st edn., Cambridge, UK, Cambridge University Press.

Oberkampf, W. L. and D. P. Aeschliman (1992). Joint Computational/Experimental Aerodynamics Research on a Hypersonic Vehicle: Part 1, Experimental Results. *AIAA Journal.* **30**(8), 2000–2009.

Oberkampf, W. L. and F. G. Blottner (1998). Issues in computational fluid dynamics code verification and validation. *AIAA Journal.* **36**(5), 687–695.

Oberkampf, W. L. and T. G. Trucano (2002). Verification and validation in computational fluid dynamics. *Progress in Aerospace Sciences.* **38**(3), 209–272.

Oberkampf, W. L., A. Martellucci, and P. C. Kaestner (1985). *SWERVE Surface Pressure Measurements at Mach Numbers 3 and 8.* SAND84-2149, SECRET Formerly Restricted Data, Albuquerque, NM, Sandia National Laboratories.

Oberkampf, W. L., D. P. Aeschliman R. E. Tate, and J. F. Henfling (1993). *Experimental Aerodynamics Research on a Hypersonic Vehicle.* SAND92-1411, Albuquerque, NM, Sandia National Laboratories.

Oberkampf, W. L., D. P. Aeschliman J. F. Henfling, and D. E. Larson (1995). Surface pressure measurements for CFD code validation in hypersonic flow. *26th AIAA Fluid Dynamics Conference*, AIAA Paper 95-2273, San Diego, CA, American Institute of Aeronautics and Astronautics.

Oberkampf, W. L., D. P. Aeschliman, J. F. Henfling, D. E. Larson, and J. L. Payne (1996). Surface pressure measurements on a hypersonic vehicle. *34th Aerospace Sciences Meeting*, AIAA Paper 96-0669, Reno, NV, American Institute of Aeronautics and Astronautics.

Owczarek, J. A. (1964). *Fundamentals of Gas Dynamics*, Scranton, PA, International Textbook.

Payne, J. L. and M. A. Walker (1995). Verification of computational aerodynamics predictions for complex hypersonic vehicles using the INCA code. *33rd Aerospace Sciences Meeting and Exhibit*, Reno, NV, American Institute of Aeronautics and Astronautics.

Porter, J. L. (1996). A summary/overview of selected computational fluid dynamics (CFD) code validation/calibration activities. *27th AIAA Fluid Dynamics Conference*, AIAA Paper 96-2053, New Orleans, LA, American Institute of Aeronautics and Astronautics.

Rabinovich, S. G. (2005). *Measurement Errors and Uncertainties: Theory and Practice.* 3rd edn., New York, Springer-Verlag.

Roache, P. J. (1998). *Verification and Validation in Computational Science and Engineering*, Albuquerque, NM, Hermosa Publishers.

Roy, C. J., M. A. McWherter-Payne, and W. L. Oberkampf (2000). Verification and validation for laminar hypersonic flowfields. *Fluids 2000 Conference*, AIAA Paper 2000-2550, Denver, CO, American Institute of Aeronautics and Astronautics.

Roy, C. J., M. A. McWherter-Payne, and W. L. Oberkampf (2003a). Verification and validation for laminar hypersonic flowfields, Part 1: Verification. *AIAA Journal.* **41**(10), 1934–1943.

Roy, C. J., W. L. Oberkampf, and M. A. McWherter-Payne (2003b). Verification and validation for laminar hypersonic flowfields, Part 2: Validation. *AIAA Journal.* **41**(10), 1944–1954.

Salicone, S. (2007). *Measurement Uncertainty: an Approach via the Mathematical Theory of Evidence*, Berlin, Springer-Verlag.

Spall, R. E. and M. R. Malik (1991). Effect of transverse curvature on the stability of compressible boundary layers. *AIAA Journal.* **29**(10), 1596–1602.

Spall, R. E. and M. R. Malik (1992). Linear stability of three-dimensional boundary layers over axisymmetric bodies at incidence. *AIAA Journal.* **30**(4), 905–913.

Steger, J. L. and R. F. Warming (1981). Flux vector splitting of the inviscid gasdynamic equations with applications to finite-difference methods. *Journal of Computational Physics*. **40**, 263–293.

Walker, M. A. and W. L. Oberkampf (1992). Joint computational/experimental aerodynamics research on a hypersonic vehicle: Part 2, Computational results. *AIAA Journal*. **30**(8), 2010–2016.

Wilcox, D. C. (2006). *Turbulence Modeling for CFD*. 3rd edn., La Canada, CA, DCW Industries.

Wong, C. C., F. G. Blottner, J. L. Payne, and M. Soetrisno (1995a). Implementation of a parallel algorithm for thermo-chemical nonequilibrium flow solutions. *AIAA 33rd Aerospace Sciences Meeting*, AIAA Paper 95-0152, Reno, NV, American Institute of Aeronautics and Astronautics.

Wong, C. C., M. Soetrisno, F. G. Blottner, S. T. Imlay, and J. L. Payne (1995b). *PINCA: A scalable Parallel Program for Compressible Gas Dynamics with Nonequilibrium Chemistry*. SAND94-2436, Albuquerque, NM, Sandia National Laboratories.

Yee, H. C. (1987). *Implicit and Symmetric Shock Capturing Schemes*. NASA, NASA-TM-89464.

Youden, W. J. (1972). Enduring values. *Technometrics*. **14**(1), 1–11.

12

Model accuracy assessment

As has been discussed in a number of chapters, particularly Chapter 10, Model validation fundamentals, and Chapter 11, Design and execution of validation experiments, model accuracy assessment is the core issue of model validation. Our intent in model accuracy assessment is to critically and quantitatively determine the ability of a mathematical model and its embodiment in a computer code to simulate a well-characterized physical process. We, of course, are only interested in well-characterized physical processes that are useful for model validation. How critical and quantitative the model accuracy assessment is will depend on (a) how extensive the experimental data set is in exploring the important model input quantities that affect the system response quantities (SRQs) of interest; (b) how well characterized the important model input quantities are, based on measurements in the experiments; (c) how well characterized the experimental measurements and the model predictions of the SRQs of interest are; (d) whether the experimental measurements of the SRQs were available to the computational analyst before the model accuracy assessment was conducted; and (e) if the SRQs were available to the computational analysts, whether they were used for model updating or model calibration. This chapter will explore these difficult issues both conceptually and quantitatively.

We begin the chapter by discussing the fundamental elements of model accuracy assessment. As part of this discussion, we review traditional and recent methods for comparing model results and experimental measurements, and we explore the relationship between model accuracy assessment, model calibration, and model prediction. Beginning with the engineering society definitions of terms given in Chapter 2, Fundamental concepts and terminology, the perspective of this book is to segregate, as well as possible, each of these activities. There is, however, an alternative perspective in the published literature that believes all of these activities should be combined. We briefly review this alternative perspective and the associated approaches, and contrast these with approaches that segregate these activities.

Whereas model calibration has a long history, primarily in the statistical literature, quantitative model accuracy assessment has had much less development. During the last decade, model accuracy assessment has focused on constructing mathematical operators that compute the difference between the experimentally measured results and simulation results. These operators are referred to as *validation metrics*. We review recommendations that have been proposed for the optimum construction of validation metrics. We then discuss in detail two validation metrics that have been developed. The first metric computes the difference between the estimated statistical mean of the measurements and the predictions. The second metric computes the area between the probability-boxes (p-boxes) resulting from the measurements and the predictions. Each metric is demonstrated with various examples.

12.1 Elements of model accuracy assessment

The task of model accuracy assessment might, at first, seem fairly simple: compare the prediction supplied by the modeler to the observation(s) made by the empiricist and see whether they match. They might match perfectly, or the model might be somewhat in error, or the model could be totally incorrect. However, in reality there are several issues that arise to complicate this comparison, as well as the model's ultimate use in predictions for which no experimental data is available. Some of the important questions are:

- How should one deal with experiment-to-experiment variability in the measured data?
- What should be done if the experimental data are given as a probability distribution or a sequence of intervals?
- What if there are statistical trends in the experimental data that do not appear in the simulation?
- What if the prediction is a probability distribution rather than a point, i.e., a deterministic, value?
- Do model accuracy requirements have any place in model accuracy assessment?
- Should the measure of model accuracy assessment represent evidence for agreement between experiment and simulation, or evidence for disagreement?
- What should be done in a comparison with experimental data if important information is not available to make the prediction?
- How should model accuracy assessment be influenced by limited experimental data obtained over a high-dimensional model input space?
- What could be done if there is only one experiment for comparison?
- What could be done to synthesize comparisons about different outputs from the model and experimental data?
- How should aleatory and epistemic uncertainty in either the simulation or the experiment be handled?
- How should an accuracy measure be constructed to penalize or reward a very precise model prediction versus a very imprecise prediction?
- What if the predictions from the model are extremely expensive to compute and only a few simulations can be computed?
- What should be done differently in model accuracy assessment if the parameters in the model are first calibrated using related experimental data?

Some of these questions were dealt with in previous chapters, but they will be revisited here in more detail.

In many research situations in traditional scientific procedures, the emphasis in validation is about deciding whether a model is right or wrong *per se*. In most engineering situations,

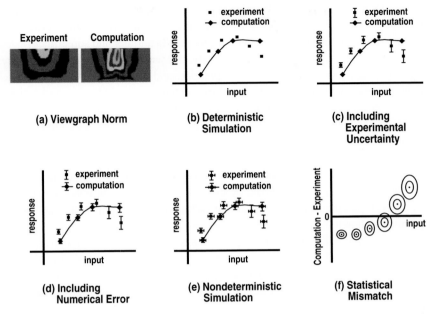

Figure 12.1 Increasing precision for comparing simulations and experiments (Oberkampf *et al.*, 2004).

however, this is *not* the case. In engineering, the emphasis is about estimating the accuracy of the model, based on comparisons with experimental data, and determining if the model is adequate for the intended use. As George Box famously asserted two decades ago, "All models are wrong. Some are useful" (Box and Draper, 1987). For a deterministic model prediction, validation can be a fairly straightforward affair. The model makes a point estimate for its prediction about some quantity. This prediction would be compared against one or more measurements about that quantity and the difference(s) would be understood as a measure of how accurate the model was. A model could be consistently inaccurate and yet close enough for its purpose. Likewise, even a highly accurate model might not be good enough if the accuracy requirements are more demanding for modeling some high-performance system.

12.1.1 Methods of comparing simulations and experiments

There are a wide variety of methods for comparing simulations and experimental measurements. Figure 12.1 summarizes the methods for comparisons and identifies the direction in which more quantitative methods need to progress. This figure illustrates the conceptual increase of quantification in performing validation comparisons as increased attention is paid to experimental uncertainty, numerical error, and nondeterministic simulations. Let us consider each panel of this figure in some detail.

Figure 12.1a depicts a qualitative comparison referred to as a *viewgraph norm* comparison (Rider, 1998) of computational and experimental data often seen in practice. This comparison is typically one picture or contour plot next to another and sometimes no legend is given showing the scales involved; or similarly, the scales are adjusted so as to present the most flattering agreement between computation and experiment. Clearly, in such as case no quantitative statement about the comparison between computation and experiment can be made, but it does provide some feel of comparison at an intuitive level. Feel and intuition about agreement between computation and experiment are, of course, in the eye of the beholder. These type comparisons are commonly seen in advertising and marketing material for scientific computing software, or in proposals for potential funding.

The plot in Figure 12.1b portrays the most common type of comparison between computational results and experimental data. It shows the system response as a function of the input, or control, parameter in the experiment. While discrete experimental and computational points are shown in this plot, the concept also encompasses the display of curves for experiment and computation without any points shown. The key problem with comparisons implemented at the level of Figure 12.1b is that there is no recognition of uncertainty in the experimental or computational results, or in the quantitative comparison of the two. Conclusions drawn from this type of comparison are really only qualitative, such as "fair agreement" or "generally good agreement."

Figure 12.1c suggests that the next step for improving the method of comparison is to place estimated uncertainty bars around the experimental data. Occasionally, the meaning of the uncertainty bars is carefully justified and clearly explained. The much more common situation is where the uncertainty bars are qualitative, in the sense that: (a) they are not rigorously justified concerning what is included in terms of random and systematic experimental uncertainty, (b) a statement is made such as "Essentially all of the experimental data fell within the uncertainty bars shown," or (c) the effect of experimental uncertainty in the input quantity is not addressed with regard to the response quantity. An increasing number of technical journals are requiring some type of statement of experimental uncertainty, such as Figure 12.1c.

Figure 12.1d represents the case where there is a more quantitative estimate of experimental uncertainty and there is an estimate of numerical solution error. For example, concerning the experimental uncertainty, multiple experimental realizations could have been obtained so the experimental data point shown would represent the mean of all of the samples. In addition, it might be clarified if any "outlier" measurements were discarded and that the uncertainty bar would represent two standard deviations of an assumed normal probability distribution. Concerning the numerical solution error, an *a posteriori* numerical error estimate from the computation would be given for the specific response quantity that was plotted in the graph, as opposed to some global error norm related to the quantity shown.

Figure 12.1e suggests a further improvement in the estimation of experimental uncertainty and now, at this level, nondeterministic simulations are included. The information concerning experimental uncertainty could be improved, for example, in two ways. First, one could use a statistical design of experiments (DOE) approach with randomization and blocking to better quantify certain systematic uncertainties. Also, one may have conducted the same experiment at separate facilities, possibly using different diagnostic techniques. Second, an estimate of the experimental uncertainty in the measured input quantity is also obtained and is shown as the lateral uncertainty bar. The uncertainty bars for the input quantity and the measured response, for instance, could represent two standard deviations for a normal probability distribution. Concerning the nondeterministic simulations, we are referring to an ensemble of computations at each of the experimental conditions. For example, multiple simulations would be made using the experimentally estimated probability distribution for the input quantity. As a result, the computational data point would be the mean of the nondeterministic simulations for both the input and the response quantity. Note that to use the experimental uncertainty distributions for the input quantity, computations would need to be made at the measured input conditions, or one must assume they could be used for other input conditions.

Figure 12.1f shows a genuine quantitative measure of the comparison between the simulations and the experimental measurements over the range of the input quantity. What is depicted in Figure 12.1f is the *mismatch* between the simulation and the experiment at each of the experimental data points. In terms of information content, one could have the same data as contained in Figure 12.1e, but now the statistical differences in the simulation and experiment are displayed. Assuming that probability distributions for both computational and experimental data are well characterized, as discussed in Figure 12.1e, comparing computations and experiments will require a difference, or more properly, a convolution of pairs of probability distributions. The elliptical symbols in Figure 12.1f are meant to signify one and two standard deviation contours of the convolutions of the simulation and experimental probability distributions. The "dot" in the center of each contour is the difference in the mean, or expected value, of the simulation and experimental distributions.

We will refer to quantitative comparisons between simulation and experiment, similar to Figure 12.1f, as a *validation metric operator*. We will formally use the definition:

Validation metric: a mathematical operator that measures the difference between a system response quantity (SRQ) obtained from a simulation result and one obtained from experimental measurements.

The validation metric should be an objective measure of the distance, in some sense, between simulation and experimental data. The distance measure should have the characteristic that any difference between the simulation and experimental data is a positive quantity. For example, whether the simulation is less than or greater than the experimental data, the metric is positive and additive. Objectiveness means that, given a collection of predictions and observations, a validation metric will produce the same assessment no matter what analyst uses the metric. This is a basic tenet of scientific and engineering practice; that the conclusion is reproducible and that it does not depend on the attitudes or predilections of the analysts. If some inescapable subjectivity must enter the evaluation of the metric, it would be good to keep this intrusion as small and as limited as possible so as to emphasize the objectiveness of the method and minimize the elements subject to dispute.

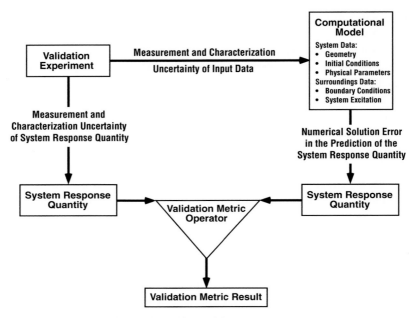

Figure 12.2 Sources of uncertainty and error in model accuracy assessment.

In general, the validation metric result is a function of all of the input parameters to the model. Commonly, however, the SRQ is primarily dependent on a handful of dominant input parameters. The validation metric should be viewed as a statistical operator because the simulation and experimental results are not single numbers but are functions; specifically they are commonly either a probability distribution or a *probability box* (p-box). A p-box is special type of cumulative distribution function (CDF) that represents the set of possible CDFs that fall within prescribed bounds (Ferson, 2002; Ferson *et al.*, 2003, 2004; Kriegler and Held, 2005; Aughenbaugh and Paredis, 2006; Baudrit and Dubois, 2006). p-boxes were first introduced in Chapter 3, Modeling and computational simulation. A p-box can express both epistemic and aleatory uncertainty in either the simulation, the experimental results, or both. p-boxes will be discussed in more detail later in this chapter.

12.1.2 Uncertainty and error in model accuracy assessment

Model accuracy assessment would be fairly straightforward if we did not have to deal with uncertainties and errors clouding the issue in the experiment and in the simulation. In earlier chapters, e.g., Chapters 10 and 11, we have discussed uncertainties and errors primarily from an estimation point of view. Here we discuss them with regard to where they occur, how they are propagated, and how they affect validation metrics results.

Figure 12.2 shows a validation experiment and the corresponding computational model, the sources of uncertainty and error in experimental measurements and numerical simulations, and the validation metric as a difference operator. First we will discuss the experimental sources of uncertainty. In Chapter 10, we discussed the two fundamental sources of experimental uncertainty: measurement uncertainty and characterization uncertainty. Measurement uncertainty is due to random and systematic (bias) uncertainties in every experimental measurement that is made. Measurement uncertainty is primarily dependent on the diagnostic techniques used, as well as the experimental measurement procedures used, e.g., replication, randomization, and blocking techniques to estimate random and systematic measurement uncertainties. Characterization uncertainty is due to a limited number of measurements of a quantity that is a random variable. Two examples are (a) an input quantity needed for the computational model was not measured in the experiment, so the experimentalists recommends an interval in which he/she believes the true value lies, and (b) a SRQ is known to be a random variable in the experiment, but too few samples of the quantity are measured because of time and cost constraints.

Also discussed in Chapter 10 were the three sources of error in the simulation: formulation of the mathematical model (i.e., model form error), mapping of the mathematical model to the discrete model (including the computer code), and numerical solution of the discrete model on a computer. The estimation of the model form error is, of course, the primary goal of model accuracy assessment. In Figure 12.2, we simply combine the second and third sources into "numerical solution error."

It is seen in Figure 12.2 that the experimental measurement and characterization uncertainties directly affect both the input data to the model and the SRQ from the experiment. Noting that the experimental measurement input uncertainties are statistically confounded with the inherent variability of the input quantities in the experiment, an important issue in model accuracy assessment is exposed. We are requiring that the model correctly map the experimental measurement input uncertainties to the SRQ, even though there is *no physics variability* that corresponds to these in the model. Stated differently, the experimental measurement uncertainties *do not* represent physics uncertainties in the input, but are purely an artifact of the measurements made in the experiment. Contrast these experimental uncertainties with true physics uncertainties in the experiment, such as (a) a parameter in the experiment that is a random variable, e.g., the material used in an experiment that is a random draw from a production-lot population, or (b) the boundary conditions are uncontrolled parameters in the experiment, e.g., weather conditions in multiple flight experiments. These later examples are *true physics uncertainties* that we expect the model to correctly propagate, whereas we are also requiring the model to correctly propagate nonphysics uncertainties, i.e., experimental measurement uncertainties. Although research needs to be dedicated to this issue, we believe it is a conceptually improper expectation of the model. If this is true, then the only route forward is to minimize the experimental measurement uncertainties relative to the input uncertainties due to physics variability.

To demonstrate this point, consider the following example. Suppose an experiment is repeated a large number of times and, in addition, every aspect of the physics is perfectly repeatable. That is, all conditions in the system and in the surroundings are precisely repeatable every time, so that the SRQ is also precisely repeatable. Further, suppose that

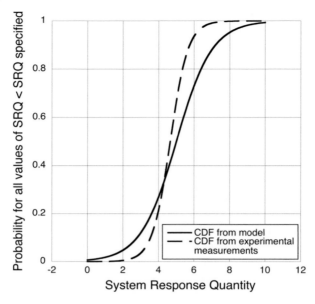

Figure 12.3 Example of cumulative distribution functions for a system response quantity from experimental measurements and from a model that is provided with apparent input physics variability.

all of the systematic (bias) errors in the experimental measurements are zero. As a result, the experimental measurement uncertainty would only consist of random error, and the experimental characterization error would be zero because all input quantities and the SRQ are perfectly characterized (i.e., known) random variables. In addition, suppose the model *perfectly* represents the relevant physics in the validation experiment. Also, suppose the numerical solution error is zero. Figure 12.3 depicts the cumulative distribution functions of the SRQ obtained from the experimental measurements and the model. They will be different because the CDF from the experiment represents the variability due to random measurement error, whereas the CDF from the model represents the variability in the SRQ due to the *apparent* physics variability in the input quantities. That is, the perfect physics model will propagate the experimental measurement uncertainty *as if* it were physics variability. When the validation metric operator measures the difference between the experimentally measured CDF and the predicted CDF from the model, the difference will *not* be zero. That is, the model will be judged to be "imperfect," when in fact it is *perfect*.

12.1.3 Relationship between model accuracy assessment, calibration, and prediction

Figure 12.4 depicts several important aspects of validation, as well as features of calibration and prediction of models. The left-center portion of Figure 12.4 shows the first step in validation. The figure illustrates that the same SRQ must be obtained from both the model

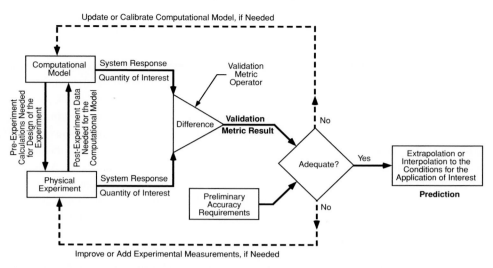

Figure 12.4 Validation, calibration, and prediction (Oberkampf and Barone, 2004).

and the physical experiment. The SRQ can be any type of physically measurable quantity, or it can be a quantity that is based on, or inferred from, measurements. For example, the SRQ can involve derivatives, integrals, or more complex data processing of computed or measured quantities such as the maximum or minimum of functionals over a domain. When significant data processing is required to obtain an SRQ, it is important to process both the computational results and the experimentally measured quantities in the same manner. The computational and experimental SRQs are input to the validation metric operator to compute a validation metric result. The SRQs are commonly one of three mathematical forms: (a) a deterministic quantity, i.e., a single value, such as a mean value or a maximum value over a domain; (b) a probability distribution; or (c) a p-box. Each of these forms can be functions of a parameter or multiple parameters in the model, such as a temperature or pressure; a function of spatial coordinates, such as Cartesian coordinates (x, y, z); or a function of both space and time. If both the computational and experimental SRQs are deterministic quantities, the validation metric will also be a deterministic quantity. If either of the SRQs is a probability distribution or p-box, the result of the validation metric could be a number, a probability distribution, or a p-box; depending on the construction of the validation metric operator.

As discussed in Chapters 10 and 11, Figure 12.4 suggests the appropriate interaction between computation and experimentation that should occur in a validation experiment. To achieve the most value from the validation experiment, there should be in-depth, forthright, and frequent communication between analysts and experimentalists during the planning, design, and execution of the experiment. Also, after the experiment has been completed, the experimentalists should provide to the analysts all the important input quantities needed to conduct the simulation. What should *not* be provided to the analysts in a rigorous validation activity is the measured SRQ. Stated differently, a blind-test prediction should be compared with experimental results so that a true measure of predictive capability can be assessed in the validation metric.

The right-center portion of Figure 12.4 shows the comparison of the validation metric result with the preliminary accuracy requirement for the application of interest. This is referred to as a *preliminary* requirement because the conditions of the application of interest, i.e., the application domain, may be different from the validation domain. If they are different, as is the usual case, then only preliminary accuracy requirements can be applied. If the model passes these preliminary accuracy requirements, then the model prediction would be made using extrapolation or interpolation of the model. Accuracy requirements for the application, i.e., final accuracy requirements, would be applied after the model has been extrapolated or interpolated to the conditions of the application of interest. Setting preliminary accuracy requirements is also useful if the preliminary model accuracy is inadequate. The following gives two examples. First, it may be concluded that the assumptions and approximations made in the conceptual model are inadequate to achieve the accuracy needed. This may necessitate a reformulation of the model, as opposed to calibration of model parameters at a later stage. Second, preliminary accuracy assessment provides a natural mechanism for adjusting and adapting the final accuracy requirements to the cost and schedule requirements of the engineering system of interest. For example, trade-offs can be made between required final accuracy, system design, and performance, in addition to cost and schedule.

If the preliminary accuracy requirements are not met, then one has two options, as shown in Figure 12.4. First, the dashed-line upper feedback loop provides for any of the activities referred to as model updating, model calibrating, or model tuning. Depending on the ability to determine parameters, either by direct measurement or by inference from a model, we have divided parameter updating into three categories: parameter measurement, parameter estimation, and parameter calibration. If the model parameters are updated, one could proceed again through the validation metric operator. It is now very likely that the validation metric result would be significantly reduced, implying much better agreement between the model and the experimental results. The parameter updating may be physically justifiable, or it may simply be expedient. How to determine the scientific soundness of the updating, and its impact on predictive capability, is a very difficult issue. This issue will be discussed in more detail in the next chapter. Second, the lower feedback loop could be taken if: (a) improvements or changes are needed in the experimental measurements, such as improved diagnostic techniques; (b) additional experiments are needed to reduce experimental uncertainty; or (c) additional experiments are needed that are more representative of the application of interest.

The right portion of the figure deals with the issue of use of the model to make a prediction for the conditions of the application of interest. It should be noted that Figure 12.4 is completely consistent with the diagram showing the three aspects of validation (Figure 2.8) in Chapter 2, Fundamental concepts and terminology. Also, Figure 12.4 is conceptually consistent with the ASME Guide diagram shown in Figure 2.5 of Chapter 2. The ASME diagram, however, does not explicitly show the extrapolation or interpolation of the model to conditions where no data are available. Each of these figures can be applied at *any* level of the validation hierarchy. Two examples of applications requiring different types of extrapolation are given. First, suppose the physical experiment conducted is on the complete system of interest, i.e., the actual operational system hardware. Suppose the experiment, however, is conducted at a set of conditions that do not correspond to the actual operational conditions of interest because of physical size constraints, safety concerns, or environmental restrictions. The SRQs are measured in the experiment, predicted by the model, and a validation metric result is computed. Suppose further that the model satisfies the preliminary accuracy requirements. Then an extrapolation is required, using the model, to predict the SRQs of interest corresponding to the actual operational conditions of interest. This type of extrapolation is the most common in engineering applications.

Second, suppose now that the experiments in Figure 12.4 are conducted on all of the subsystems of the complete system of interest and no experiments were conducted on the complete system. Suppose further that all of the validation metrics of all of the SRQs of interest for each subsystem meet the preliminary accuracy requirements. Even if the subsystems are tested at the same operational conditions as the complete system, any real engineering system functions as a closely coupled, highly interacting group of subsystems. As a result, one could characterize this as a large extrapolation because the model of the complete system is required to predict the interactions of each of the models for each of the subsystems. This extrapolation, of course, has no parameter associated with it and the ability of the model to predict the interactions has in no way been assessed.

12.2 Approaches to parameter estimation and validation metrics

During the last decade, model validation (in the broad sense of the term) and validation metrics have received increased attention. Model validation has been primarily pursued using traditional approaches, specifically: parameter estimation, hypothesis testing, and Bayesian updating. These approaches, particularly hypothesis testing, are related to the concepts embodied in validation metrics as discussed here. Although we refer to parameter estimation and Bayesian updating as model calibration, many researchers and practitioners in the field refer to these approaches as model validation. In this section, parameter estimation, hypothesis testing, Bayesian updating, and newer approaches to validation metrics will be briefly discussed. It should be stressed that the development of quantitative measures for validation is a new field of research and various perspectives are being vigorously debated. A special workshop was held in May 2006 to bring together a number of researchers in the field to discuss and debate various approaches to model validation. For this workshop, three challenge problems were proposed, each one in a different engineering field: heat transfer, solid mechanics, and solid dynamics. All of the contributions to the workshop were published in a special issue of *Computer Methods in Applied Mechanics and Engineering* (Dowding *et al.*, 2008; Pilch, 2008). The reader should consult this special issue for an excellent survey of the wide ranging approaches to model validation.

12.2.1 Parameter estimation

In the 1960s, the structural dynamics community began developing sophisticated techniques for comparing computational and experimental results, as well as techniques for improving agreement between the results using parameter estimation techniques (Wirsching *et al.*, 1995). In many analyses in structural dynamics, certain model input parameters are considered as deterministic (but poorly known) quantities that are estimated using modal data on the structures of interest. A numerical optimization procedure is used so that the best agreement between computational and experimental results can be obtained for a single SRQ, or a group of SRQs. Multiple solutions of the model are required to evaluate the effect of different values of the model parameters on the SRQ. Although these techniques are used to compare computational and experimental results, their primary goal is to improve agreement based on available experimental data. During the last decade, more sophisticated and reliable methods have been developed for optimizing parameters in a wider range of stochastic systems (Crassidis and Junkins, 2004; Raol *et al.*, 2004; Aster *et al.*, 2005; van den Bos, 2007). In this more recent work, the parameters are considered as random variables represented as probability distributions with unknown parameters, or nonparametric distributions. The experimental data can come from multiple experiments on the same structure but under different loading conditions, or from experiments on different structures. A similar, but more complex, optimization procedure is used to determine the probability distributions for each of the uncertain parameters that maximize agreement between the model and the experimental results.

Although the terminology used in this text clearly refers to this type of procedure as calibration, as opposed to validation, we mention it here because the process begins with measuring the difference between the model results and the experimental results.

12.2.2 Hypothesis testing

Statistical hypothesis testing, or significance testing, is used throughout the experimental sciences (Wellek, 2002; Lehmann and Romano, 2005; Law, 2006; Devore, 2007). Hypothesis testing is a highly developed statistical method of choosing between two competing models of an experimental outcome by using probability theory to minimize the risk of an incorrect decision. In hypothesis testing, the validation-quantification measure is formulated as a "decision problem" to determine whether or not the hypothesized model is consistent with the experimental data. This technique is regularly used in the operations research (OR) community for comparing mutually exclusive models, i.e., the model is either true or false. For example, suppose the hypothesis is made that a coin is fair, i.e., in the toss of the coin it is equally likely that "heads" will appear as often as "tails." The competing hypothesis is that the coin is unfair. Experimental data are then obtained by tossing the coin a given number of times, say N, and recording what percentage of the outcomes is heads and what percentage is tails. Hypothesis testing then allows one to statistically determine the confidence of a fair coin. The confidence in the determination will depend on N, that is, as N increases, the confidence in the conclusion increases.

Hypothesis testing has recently been employed in validation studies (Hills and Trucano, 2002; Paez and Urbina, 2002; Hills and Leslie, 2003; Rutherford and Dowding, 2003; Chen *et al.*, 2004; Dowding *et al.*, 2004; Hills, 2006). In this approach, the validation assessment is formulated as a decision problem of whether or not the model's predictions are consistent with the available empirical information. Typically, empirical observations are collectively compared to a distribution of realizations computed by the model, such as by Monte Carlo sampling, which together constitutes a prediction about some SRQ. The consistency between the model and the data is characterized as a probability value, with low probability values denoting a mismatch of such magnitude that it is unlikely to have occurred by chance. This probability is often considered meaningful only within the hypothesis-testing context and does not serve as a stand-alone validation metric that indicates the degree of agreement or disagreement between model and empirical results. Instead, the approach focuses on answering the yes-no question about whether a model is accurate to within a specified margin of error, or sometimes on the either-or question choosing between mutually exclusive models.

Despite its being pressed into service as a tool for validation, hypothesis testing is not ideally suited to the task. In general, the purpose of hypothesis testing is to identify statements for which there is compelling evidence of truth or falsehood. But this is a different goal from that of validation, which is more pragmatic and more focused on assessing the quantitative accuracy of a model. The model could be relatively "poor," but the question in validation could be stated as "How poor?" In hypothesis testing, an accuracy requirement could be stated, either as a preliminary or final accuracy statement, and then the result would be the probability that the model met the required accuracy. Two practical difficulties arise with this type of result. First, how should a builder of physics models or a project manager interpret the result? It is not intuitive how to interpret probability as an accuracy measure. The natural perspective of design engineers and project managers is to ask, "What is the absolute or relative error of the model?" Second, no matter what level of accuracy is specified, the model can be proven false at that level with more experimental data. That is, any model can be proven false, given enough data. As will be discussed shortly, a key difficulty with hypothesis testing is that the requirement of accuracy is built *directly into* the validation metric.

Even though the hypothesis-testing approach does not appear to be a constructive route forward for validation metrics, the approach has developed the concept of error types for incorrect conclusions drawn from hypothesis testing (Wellek, 2002; Lehmann and Romano, 2005; Law, 2006). The technique has identified two types of error in decisions that are useful and instructive for other types of validation metrics. It should be stressed that these two types of error are not limited to statistical analyses. They are actually types of error in logic. A type 1 error, also referred to as *model builder's risk*, is the error in rejecting the validity of a model when the model is actually valid. This can be caused by errors on both the computational side and the experimental side. On the computational side, for example, if a mesh is not sufficiently converged and the computational result is contaminated by numerical error, then an adverse comparison with experimental data is misleading. That is, a poor comparison leads one to conclude that a model needs to be improved or recalibrated when the source of the poor comparison is simply an under-resolved mesh. On the experimental side, the model builder's risk is most commonly caused by a poor comparison of computational results and experimental data that is due to an unknown bias error in the experimental data. We believe that unknown bias errors in experimental results are the *most damaging* in validation because if the experimental measurement is accepted as correct, then it is concluded that the computational result is consistently in error; whereas in reality, the experimental data is the culprit. If the error is believed to be in the computation, then a great deal of effort will be expended trying to find the source of the error. Or worse, a mathematical model will be recalibrated using the biased experimental data. This results in *transferring* the experimental bias into the mathematical model and then biasing all future computations with the model.

The type 2 error, also referred to as *model user's risk*, is the error in accepting the validity of a model when the model is actually invalid. As with the type 1 error, this can be caused by errors on both the computational side and the experimental side. On the computational side, the logical reverse of the type 1 error described above can occur. That is, if a mesh is not sufficiently converged and the computational result agrees well with the experiment, then the favorable comparison is also misleading. For example if a finer mesh is used, one can find that the favorable agreement can disappear. This shows that the original favorable agreement has compensating, or canceling, errors in the comparison. We believe that compensating errors in complex simulations is a common phenomenon. Only the tenacious user of the model may dig deep enough to uncover compensating errors. Similarly, a model developer may suspect that there is a code bug that may be the cause of unexpectedly good results. In a competitive, time-constrained, or commercial code-development environment, such users or model developers as these can be very unpopular, and even muffled by co-workers and management. On the experimental side, the logical reverse of the type 1 error described above can occur. That is, if an unknown bias error exists in the experiment, and a favorable comparison between computational results and experimental data is obtained, the implication of good model accuracy is incorrect. Similarly to the type 2 error on the computational side, only the self-critical and determined experimentalist will continue to examine the experiment in an attempt to find any experimental bias errors.

Type 1 and type 2 errors are two edges of the same sword. In the operations research literature, however, it is well known that model user's risk is potentially the more disastrous. The reason, of course, is that an apparently correct model (one that has experimental evidence that it produces accurate results) is used for predictions and decision making, when in fact it is incorrect. Type 2 errors produce a false sense of security. In addition to the potentially disastrous use of the model, we contend that the model user's risk is also the more likely to occur in practice than the model builder's risk. The reason is that with experimental evidence that the model is valid, there is little or no interest by analysts, experimentalists, managers, or funding sources to expend any more time or resources pursuing possible deficiencies in either the model or the experiments. Everyone is enthused by the agreement of results and "Victory" is easily and quickly declared. Anyone who questions the results can risk loss of personal advancement or recognition within his or her organization. Only with some possible future experimental data, or system failure, would the caution and wisdom of these individuals be recognized. But then, as is said, it's too late.

12.2.3 Bayesian updating

Bayesian updating, or Bayesian statistical inference, has received a great deal of attention during the last two decades from statisticians, risk analysts, and some physicists and structural dynamicists. For a modern treatment of the topic from a Bayesian perspective, see Bernardo and Smith (1994); Gelman *et al.* (1995); Leonard and Hsu (1999); Bedford and Cooke (2001); Ghosh *et al.* (2006); and Sivia and Skilling (2006). Although the process is quite involved, Bayesian analysis can be summarized in three steps. Step 1 is to construct, or assume, a probability distribution for each input quantity in the model that is chosen to be an adjustable, random variable. Step 2 involves conditioning or updating the previously chosen probability models for the input quantities based on comparison of the computational and experimental results. To update the probability models, one must first propagate input probability distributions through the model to obtain probability distributions for the SRQs commensurate with those measured in the experiment. The updating of the input probability distributions, using Bayes' Theorem to obtain posterior distributions, commonly assumes that the mathematical model is structurally correct. That is, the updating is done assuming that all of the disagreement between the model and the experimental data is due to deficient probability distributions of the parameters. Step 3 involves comparing new computational results with the existing experimental data and quantifying the changes in the updated probability distributions. The new computational results are obtained by propagating the updated probability distributions through the model. If any new experimental data becomes available, then the entire process is repeated. Much of the theoretical development in Bayesian estimation has been directed toward optimum methods for updating statistical models of uncertain parameters and in reducing the computational resources required for propagating the uncertainties through the model.

Bayesian methods have been offered as an alternative approach to validation (Anderson *et al.*, 1999; Hanson, 1999; Kennedy and O'Hagan, 2001; DeVolder *et al.*, 2002; Hasselman *et al.*, 2002; Zhang and Mahadevan, 2003; Chen *et al.*, 2006; O'Hagan, 2006; Trucano *et al.*, 2006; Bayarri *et al.*, 2007; Babuska *et al.*, 2008; Chen *et al.*, 2008). The Bayesian approach is sophisticated, comprehensive, and computationally demanding in terms of the number of model evaluations, i.e., solutions of the partial differential equations (PDEs), which are needed. In addition, it is associated with some controversy that may cause analysts to consider alternatives. One of the major criticisms, from a validation perspective, is that the updating usually assumes that the model is itself correct. Recent work has suggested Bayesian strategies to account for uncertainty in the structure of the model by way of a model bias error (Kennedy and O'Hagan, 2001; Higdon *et al.*, 2004, 2009; Rougier, 2007; Liu *et al.*, 2009; McFarland and Mahadevan, 2008; Wang *et al.*, 2009).

The Bayesian approach to validation is primarily interested in evaluating the subjective probability, i.e., a personal belief, that the model is correct. Yet, to our minds, this is not the proper focus of validation. We are not concerned about anyone's belief that the model is right; we're interested in *objectively measuring the conformance of data with predictions.* We disavow the subjectivity that is central in the Bayesian approach. Specifically, we argue that validation should not depend on the analyst's prior opinion about the correctness of the model in question. This is, after all, a large part of what is being assessed in validation, so it seems that it would be proper to refrain from assuming a key element of the consequence. While subjectivity is perfectly reasonable for making personal decisions, it can be problematic when the methods are (a) applied to high-consequence decision-making, for example, nuclear power plant safety or environmental impact studies, and (b) applied to public safety regulations that are stated in terms of frequency of events.

Bayesian claims of individual rationality do not generalize with respect to decisions made by groups. Some have asserted that predictive models cannot be validated objectively (Hazelrigg, 2003). We strongly believe that it is possible to objectively measure the performance of a model vis-à-vis the data that is relevant to the model's performance. We recognize that there are components that influence professional judgment or other subjective elements of how validation assessments should be carried out. For example, the selection of the experimental data to be applied in validation is arguably a subjective decision, as is choosing which validation metric is to be used from among the several possible metrics. Once these issues are defined, however, the application of the metric can be an objective characterization of the disagreement between predictions and data. Even in this limited context, objectiveness is valuable. The conclusion ought not to be that we should abandon the quest for objectivity because subjectivity cannot be escaped entirely. That would be like empiricists concluding from the Heisenberg Uncertainty Principle that it's useless to measure anything at all.

The Bayesian perspective always prefers to place any analytical question in the context of decision making. Model accuracy assessment *per se* need not be a part of decision making. Asking whether or to what degree a model is supported or contradicted by available evidence is surely a legitimate question by itself. Assessing the value of a metric that measures its conformity with observations should be recognized as a reasonable solution to this question. What one does with the knowledge that different models have different metrics is not formally part of the problem. Bayesians might argue that it should be because making good decisions requires such inclusive considerations. We agree that this may well be true, but it does not thereby de-legitimize model accuracy assessments that are not subsumed as a part of decision problems. For various practical and inescapable reasons, model accuracy assessments are sometimes needed before the decision context has even been specified; for example, national security concerns and comparison of competitive system performance when other portions of the decision context have not yet be formulated.

12.2.4 Comparison of mean values

A distinctly different approach, and one that is conceptually simpler, is to compare the estimated mean from both the experiment and the simulation. For the case where there is only one experiment and only a deterministic simulation, the comparison approach is equivalent. For this type of comparison, one would intuitively think of using traditional vector norms. Let $S(x_i)$ be the simulation result as a function of the control parameter x_i and let $\mathcal{E}(x_i)$ be the experimental measurement, where $i = 1, 2, 3, \ldots, N$. The parameter x_i could be an input parameter or it could be time in a time-dependent system. The L_1 and L_2 vector norms (normalized by N) have been used as validation metrics, which are given by

$$ \|S - \mathcal{E}\|_p = \left(\frac{1}{N} \sum_{i=1}^{N} |S(x_i) - \mathcal{E}(x_i)|^p \right)^{1/p}, \tag{12.1} $$

where $p = 1$ or 2. Several researchers have constructed validation metrics based on the L_1 and L_2 norms (Coleman and Stern, 1997; Easterling, 2001, 2003; Stern *et al.*, 2001; Oberkampf and Trucano, 2002; Oberkampf and Barone, 2004, 2006). For strongly time-dependent responses or system responses with a wide spectrum of frequencies, metrics have been constructed that summed the amplitude and phases differences between the simulation and the experiment (Geers, 1984; Russell, 1997a,b; Sprague and Geers, 1999, 2004). Although the vector norm metrics and those that combine amplitude and phase errors have different perspectives, their common theme is a more engineering-oriented, less statistical approach than those discussed above. They focus only on comparing a deterministic value of the SRQ from the model with the estimated statistical mean (or a single time history) of the experimental data. Most of these investigators do not propagate uncertain input parameters through the model to obtain a probability distribution for the SRQs of interest. Rather, it is commonly assumed that the mean of any uncertain input quantities maps to the mean of the SRQs of interest.

The primary perceived advantage in deterministic computational results, as opposed to propagating input uncertainties to determine output uncertainties, is the much lower computational costs involved in deterministic simulations. Many computational analysts argue that computational resources are not available to provide both spatially and temporally resolved solutions, as well as a large number of nondeterministic solutions, for complex simulations. Risk assessment of high-consequence systems, e.g., safety of nuclear power reactors and underground storage of nuclear waste, has shown that with an adequate, but not excessive, level of physical modeling detail, one *can* afford the computational costs of nondeterministic simulations. However, we recognize that there is substantial resistance in many fields to attain both mesh-resolved, nondeterministic simulations. Consequently, there is a need to construct validation metrics that can be computed with only deterministic computational results. The perspective of many in the fields that are resistant to change is that physics modeling fidelity is *much more* important than uncertainty quantification in engineering analyses. As a result, they construct models of such physical complexity that they consume essentially all of the computer resources available for a single solution, leaving no time for nondeterministic simulations. This tradition is deeply embedded in many scientific and engineering fields and it will be very slow and difficult to change this culture.

Later in this chapter, the approach of Oberkampf and Barone (2004, 2006) for comparing mean values from computation and experiment will be discussed in depth.

12.2.5 Comparison of probability distributions and p-boxes

The difference between the probability distributions of the experiment and the simulation can be characterized in many ways. Suppose X and Y are the CDFs from the experiment and the simulation, respectively. One could consider using the following types of differences between X and Y: the convolved distribution $X - Y$, some type of average of $X - Y$, or some type of difference between the shapes of X and Y. The characterization that seems to be the most useful and understandable in the context of validation of models is based on comparing the shape of the two CDFs. Random variables whose distribution functions are identical are said to be "equal in distribution." As discussed earlier, this cannot occur even with a perfect model of the physics. If the distributions are not quite identical in shape, the discrepancy can be measured with many possible measures that have been proposed in traditional statistics (D'Agostino and Stephens, 1986; Huber-Carol *et al.*, 2002; Mielke and Berry, 2007): statistical goodness of fit, probability scoring rules, and information theory.

The difficulty with these traditional measures is that they are only well developed for random variables, i.e., purely aleatory uncertainty. We are interested in determining the difference between experiment and simulation when either or both results are given by a p-box. None of the approaches discussed earlier are able to address a combination of aleatory and epistemic uncertainty in the simulation or experimental results. Later in this chapter, we will discuss an approach for computing a validation metric result using p–boxes as input (Oberkampf and Ferson, 2007; Ferson *et al.*, 2008; Ferson and Oberkampf, 2009).

12.3 Recommended features for validation metrics

A validation metric is a formal measure of the mismatch between predictions and experimental data. A low value of the metric means there is a good match and a higher value means that prediction and data disagree more. It should be possible to apply the validation metric when predictions are either deterministic or nondeterministic. The metric should be mathematically well behaved and intuitively understandable to engineers, project managers, and decision makers. In the following discussion we will recommend seven desirable properties of validation metrics that would be useful in assessing the accuracy of models used in science and engineering simulations (Oberkampf and Trucano, 2002; Oberkampf and Barone, 2004, 2006).

12.3.1 Influence of numerical solution error

A metric should either (a) explicitly include an estimate of the numerical error in the SRQ of interest resulting from the simulation, or (b) exclude the numerical error in the SRQ of interest only if the numerical error was previously estimated, by some reasonable means, to be negligible. The primary numerical error of concern here is the error due to lack of spatial and/or temporal resolution in the discrete solution, and secondarily the iterative solution error. Numerical error could be explicitly included in the predicted SRQ by including an upper and a lower estimated bound on the error, i.e., an epistemic uncertainty in the SRQ that would be represented by an interval. Recall that an interval is a special case of a p-box. An explicit inclusion of the numerical error in the simulation result would be appealing because it would clearly identify the numerical error contribution, exclusive of any other uncertainty, either in the experimental data or the simulation input data. However, it would add complexity to the theoretical derivation and calculation of the metric because it would require the metric to use p-boxes as input.

A simpler approach would be to quantitatively show that the numerical error is small before the metric is computed. The numerical error should be judged small in comparison to the estimated magnitude of the uncertainty in the experimental measurements and the simulation. For two-dimensional or three-dimensional unsteady PDEs, it is a formidable task to achieve mesh and time-step independence. If this can be done, however, one can eliminate the issue from the calculation and interpretation of the metric.

12.3.2 Assessment of the physics-modeling assumptions

A metric should be a quantitative evaluation of predictive accuracy of the SRQ of interest, including all of the combined modeling assumptions, physics approximations, and previously obtained physical parameters embodied in the model. Stated differently, the metric evaluates the aggregate accuracy of the model, including all of its submodels, and all of the physical parameters associated with the models. Consequently, there could be offsetting errors or widely ranging sensitivities in the model that could show very accurate results for one SRQ, but poor accuracy for a different SRQ. If there is interest in evaluating the accuracy of individual submodels or the effect of the accuracy of individual input parameters within the model, one should conduct a sensitivity analysis of the SRQ to these effects. However, sensitivity analysis is a separate issue from constructing a validation metric.

12.3.3 Inclusion of experimental data post-processing

A metric should include, either implicitly or explicitly, an estimate of the approximation error resulting from post-processing of the experimental and computational data to obtain the SRQ of interest. Examples of the types of post-processing of experimental data are as follows: (a) the construction of a regression function, e.g., least-squares fit, of the data to obtain a continuous function over a range of an input (or control) quantity; (b) the processing of experimental data obtained on a very different spatial or temporal scale than what is addressed, i.e., assumed, in the model; and (c) the use of complex mathematical models of the physically measured quantities to process the experimental data into a useable

SRQ. A case where the post-processing described in example (b) might be necessary is when there are localized underground measurements of a pollutant concentration and the model contains a large-scale, spatially averaged permeability model. One might require the type of post-processing defined in example (c) when additional mathematical models of the physical features measured are also needed to process and interpret the experimental data into a useable form for comparison with the computational results. Some examples of experimental data processing are (a) image processing, (b) processing the motion of markers in a sequence of images, (c) object recognition, and (d) pattern recognition.

It should be noted that this recommendation is completely separate from the features discussed in Section 12.3.1 above. Any numerical error associated with the post-processing of the numerical solution of PDEs should be considered as part of the error in the model. As discussed in Section 12.3.1, the numerical error should be either quantified using an interval or it should be demonstrated that it is small compared to the experimental and simulation uncertainty.

12.3.4 Inclusion of experimental uncertainty estimation

A metric should incorporate, or include in some explicit way, an estimate of the aleatory and epistemic measurement uncertainties in the experimental data for the SRQ. The possible sources for measurement uncertainties depend on a very wide range of factors, some of which were discussed in Chapter 11. For a comprehensive discussion of experimental measurement uncertainty, see Grabe (2005); Rabinovich (2005); and Drosg (2007). At a minimum, a validation metric should include an estimate of random uncertainties, i.e., uncertainties due to random measurement errors. To the extent possible, the metric should also include an estimate of the systematic uncertainties in the experiment.

The epistemic measurement uncertainties are usually segregated into two parts: (a) characterization uncertainty due to a limited number of measurements of the SRQ, and (b) epistemic uncertainty that can exist in the measurement itself. The characterization uncertainty is due to limited knowledge of the stochastic nature of the random error in the measurements and is usually referred to as the sampling error. Epistemic uncertainty in the measurements themselves can be due to (a) uncertainty in a measurement that is reported as a plus-or-minus value, (b) uncertainty implied by specifying a certain number of significant digits in a quantity, (c) uncertainty due to intermittent measurements of a process that is known to be periodic, (d) uncertainty in measurements when the quantity being measured is less than the detectable limit of the diagnostic method, i.e., non-detects, (e) uncertainty due to statistical censoring, e.g., when the data is only known with specified ranges or bins, and (f) uncertainty due to important data that is known to be missing from a random variable (Manski, 2003; Gioia and Lauro, 2005; Ferson *et al.*, 2007). When a collection of such intervals comprise a data set, one can think of the breadths of the intervals as representing epistemic uncertainty, while the scatter among the intervals represents aleatory uncertainty. The characterization uncertainty can be directly represented by using the individual measurements themselves, i.e., using an empirical distribution function (EDF). The epistemic uncertainty in the measurements would require a validation metric that could use a p-box as input to compute the difference between the experiment and the simulation.

If possible, the experimental uncertainty estimation method should use measurements from replications of experiments, as opposed to a propagation of uncertainty technique (ISO, 1995). If replications of the experiment are conducted, then the uncertainty in the metric should depend on the number of replicated measurements of a given SRQ of interest. Replications should be used, along with blocking and randomization, to vigorously attempt to quantify random and systematic uncertainties in measurements. In addition, if a SRQ is measured for different conditions of an input or control parameter, then techniques should be used to reduce the experimental uncertainty of the SRQ over the range of the input parameter.

12.3.5 Inclusion of aleatory and epistemic uncertainties

A metric should, in a mathematically rigorous way, be able to compute the difference between the computational and experimental results for the SRQ when these results exhibit aleatory and epistemic uncertainty. This uncertainty, for example, could be due to uncertain input quantities or an estimate of numerical solution error. If the computational and experimental results both exhibit aleatory and epistemic uncertainty, then they could both be characterized as p-boxes or some other imprecise probability structure, such as belief and plausibility functions in evidence theory (Krause and Clark, 1993; Almond, 1995; Kohlas and Monney, 1995; Klir and Wierman, 1998; Fetz *et al.*, 2000; Helton *et al.*, 2004, 2005; Oberkampf and Helton, 2005; Bae *et al.*, 2006).

Consider the case when the computational and experimental results are each characterized as precise probability distributions, i.e., only aleatory uncertainty is present. If the variance in each distribution approaches zero, then the difference between the distributions should approach the difference in the mean of each distribution. As another example, suppose the computational and experimental results are each characterized as p-boxes, i.e., a combination of aleatory and epistemic uncertainty. If the aleatory and epistemic uncertainty in each distribution approach zero, then the difference between the p-boxes should reduce to the difference in the two point values, i.e., the difference between two scalar quantities.

12.3.6 Exclusion of any type of adequacy implication

A metric should *exclude* any indications, either explicit or implicit, of the level of adequacy in agreement, or satisfaction of accuracy requirements, between computational and experimental results. That is, the metric should only measure the mismatch between the computational and experimental results, separate from *any* other features or characteristics of the computational or experimental results. If any other features or characteristics are combined in the mismatch measure, then one defeats the goal of independently setting accuracy requirements, as set by the intended use of the model (see Figure 12.4, as well as Figures 2.5 and 2.8). Some examples of inappropriately combining the mismatch feature of the comparison with other features, are the following: (a) comparisons of computational and experimental results that yield or imply value judgments, such as "adequate," "good," or "excellent"; (b) computational results judged to be adequate if they lie within some stated uncertainty band or observed range of the experimental measurements; (c) a comparison that combines the mismatch measure and the confidence or probability of the mismatch; and (d) a comparison that combines the mismatch measure and an estimate of the experimentally observed uncertainty.

This last example of constructing an inappropriate validation metric (combining the metric with the experimentally observed uncertainty) is hotly debated. The most common method of constructing an inappropriate metric such as this is to scale the mismatch between the computational and experimental results by the standard deviation of the experimental measurements. For example, suppose the L1 vector norm is used as the mismatch measure between computation and experiment and this norm is normalized by the sample standard deviation of the measurements, s. For the validation metric one would have $\| S - \mathcal{E} \|_1 / s$. We argue that this metric would be inappropriate because the metric has explicitly mixed two different types of measure; a difference measure between simulation and experiment SRQ, and a measure of the scatter of the experimental data. The scatter in the experimental data should not be mixed with the first measure because the experimental scatter is controlled by sources that have nothing to do with the ability of the model to predict the observed responses of the system. Two examples of these sources are uncertainty in the response due to uncertainty in input quantities and experimental measurement uncertainty. What would be acceptable, in our view, would be a validation metric that measures the mismatch between the predicted standard deviation and the measured standard deviation.

12.3.7 *Properties of a mathematical metric*

A validation metric should be a *true metric* in the mathematical sense, i.e., a true distance measure. The validation metric would then measure, by some means, the distance between the simulation and experimental results. By definition, a mathematical metric d has four properties (Giaquinta and Modica, 2007):

non-negativity,	$d(x, y) \geq 0$,
symmetry,	$d(x, y) = d(y, x)$,
triangle inequality,	$d(x, y) + d(y, z) \geq d(x, z)$, and
identity of indiscernibles,	$d(x, y) = 0$ if and only if $x = y$.

12.4 Introduction to the approach for comparing means

12.4.1 Perspectives of the present approach

The present approach computes a validation metric by comparing the estimated mean of the computational results with the estimated mean of the experimental measurements. A statistical confidence interval is computed that reflects the confidence in the estimation of model accuracy, given the uncertainty in the experimental data. Although a comparison of mean values gives only very limited information, it is typically the first quantity that is considered when the accuracy of a prediction is considered. This type of metric would be useful for situations in which a computational analyst, a model developer, or competing model developers are interested in quantifying which model among alternative models is most accurate for a given set of experimental data. In addition, this type of metric would be useful to a design engineer or a project engineer for specifying model accuracy requirements in a particular application domain of the model. It should be noted that if the application domain is outside the validation domain, one must account for the additional uncertainty due to extrapolation of the model to the application domain.

The validation metric developed in this section satisfies most, but not all of the recommendations given in the previous section. Here we summarize the seven recommendations and comment if the present metric does not satisfy a particular recommendation.

1. Influence of numerical solution error – yes.
2. Assessment of physics-modeling assumptions – yes.
3. Inclusion of experimental data post-processing – yes.
4. Inclusion of experimental uncertainty estimation – yes, except for epistemic uncertainty.
5. Inclusion of aleatory and epistemic uncertainties – no. Since the metric only makes a comparison between the mean values of the experimental and computational SRQs, aleatory uncertainty in the SRQs due to aleatory uncertainty in the input quantities is not addressed. In addition, the metric cannot deal with any epistemic uncertainties.
6. Exclusion of any type of adequacy implication – yes.
7. Properties of a mathematical metric – no. The metric does not satisfy the symmetry property because it takes into account whether the model result is greater than or less than the experimental measurement. The metric does not satisfy the triangle inequality property because it does not measure the distance between the computational result and the experimental measurement in two dimensions; it only measures in the dimension of the SRQ.

The validation metrics developed here are applicable to SRQs that do not have a periodic character and that do not have a complex mixture of many frequencies. For example, the present metrics would not be appropriate for analysis of standing or traveling waves in acoustics or modal analyses in structural dynamics. Another example of an inappropriate use would be the time-dependent fluid velocity at a point in turbulent flow. These types of SRQ require sophisticated time-series analysis and/or mapping to the frequency domain.

The input quantities that should be used, if possible, in the simulation of the SRQ of interest are those that are *actually measured* in the validation experiment. Some of these input quantities from the experiment may not be known for various reasons, for example, a quantity may be epistemically uncertain or it may be a random variable that is not independently measurable before the experiment. If an input quantity is a random variable and it is well characterized, then it should be propagated through the model to obtain a probability distribution for the SRQ. To avoid this computational cost, it is commonly assumed that propagating only the mean, i.e., the expected value, of all uncertain input parameters through the model can approximate the mean value of the SRQ. This approach is appropriate under two conditions. First, the response of the system is linear in the input random variables; or second, it is locally accurate in terms of the system response when (a) the coefficient of variation (COV) of the important input random variables is small, and (b) the model is not extremely nonlinear with respect to these random variables. The COV is defined as σ/μ, where σ and μ are the standard deviation and mean of the random variable, respectively. We will briefly discuss this assumption, however, it is addressed in many texts on propagation of uncertain inputs through a model. See, for example, Haldar and Mahadevan (2000).

A Taylor series can be written that clarifies the nature of the approximation. Let Y_m be the SRQ that is the random variable resulting from the model. Let $g(\bullet)$ represent the PDE with the associated initial conditions and boundary conditions that map uncertain inputs to the uncertain SRQ. And let χ_i, where $i = 1, 2, \ldots, n$, be the uncertain input random variables. Assuming appropriate smoothness in the solution to the PDE, a Taylor series for uncorrelated input random variables can be expanded about the mean of each of the input variables, μ_x, and written as (Haldar and Mahadevan, 2000)

$$E(Y_m) = g(\mu_{\chi_1}, \mu_{\chi_2}, \ldots, \mu_{\chi_n}) + \frac{1}{2} \sum_{i=1}^{n} \left(\frac{\partial^2 g}{\partial \chi_i^2}\right)_{\mu_{\chi_i}} \mathrm{Var}(\chi_i) + \cdots. \qquad (12.2)$$

$E(Y_m)$ is the expected value, i.e., the mean, of the SRQ and $\mathrm{Var}(\chi_i)$ is the variance of each of the input variables. It is seen from Eq. (12.2) that the first term of the expansion is simply g evaluated at the mean of the input variables. The second term is the second derivative of g with respect to the input variables. This term, in general, will be small with respect to the first term if either g is nearly linear in the input variables or the COV of all of the input variables is small. Linearity in the response of the system as a function of the input variables essentially never occurs when the mapping of inputs to outputs is given by a differential equation, even a *linear* differential equation.

In summary, the present validation metric requires the mean of the SRQ for comparison with the experimental data. The most accurate method of obtaining this mean is to propagate, usually through a sampling procedure, the uncertain inputs through the model and obtain the probability distribution of the SRQ. From a sufficiently sampled distribution, the mean can be easily computed. If the uncertainty propagation approach is not taken, then one can use the assumption discussed above. One must recognize, however, that there can be significant error in this procedure. Note that when using this approximation one could obtain poor agreement between computational and experimental results, and the cause is *not* the model *per se*, but the inaccuracy of the computational mean caused by the assumption of the propagation of the mean of the inputs.

12.4.2 Development of the fundamental equations

The fundamental ideas of the present validation metric are developed for the case where the SRQ of interest is defined for a single value of an input or operating condition variable. This will allow some discussion of how the present approach implements some of the recommended features discussed above, as well as giving an opportunity to review the classical development of statistical confidence intervals. Since it may be confusing why we begin the development of validation metrics with a discussion of statistical confidence intervals, we make the following point. We are interested in obtaining a difference measure between a computational result and the *mean of a population* of experimental measurements for which only a finite set of measurements has been obtained. Once this goal is understood, it is realized that the key issue is the statistical nature of the sample mean of the measured system response, *not* the level of mismatch between the computational result and the sample mean. With this perspective, it becomes clear that the point of departure should be a fundamental understanding of the statistical procedure for estimating a confidence interval for the true (population) mean. In traditional statistical testing procedures, specifically hypothesis testing, the point of departure is the derivation for the confidence interval of the difference between two hypotheses. As a result, hypothesis testing immediately embeds a stated level of agreement, or disagreement, in the difference operator, making it impossible to satisfy the recommendation discussed in Section 12.3.6.

A short review and discussion will be given for the construction of a statistical confidence interval. The development of confidence intervals is discussed in most texts on probability and statistics. The following development is based on the derivation by Devore (2007), Chapter 7.

Let X be a random variable characterizing a population having a mean μ and a standard deviation σ. Let $x_1, x_2, \ldots, x_n$ be actual sample observations from the population, which are assumed to be the result of a random sample $X_1, X_2, \ldots, X_n$ from the population. Let $\bar{X}$ be the sample mean, which is a random variable based on the random sample $X_1, X_2, \ldots, X_n$. Provided that n is large, the central limit theorem implies that $\bar{X}$ has approximately a normal distribution, *regardless* of the nature of the population distribution. Then it can be shown that the standardized random variable

$$Z = \frac{\bar{X} - \mu}{S/\sqrt{n}} \tag{12.3}$$

has an approximate normal distribution with zero mean and a standard deviation of unity. S is the sample standard deviation, which is a random variable, based on random samples $X_1, X_2, \ldots, X_n$. It can also be shown, provided n is large, that a probability interval for Z

can be written as

$$P(z_{-\alpha/2} < Z < z_{\alpha/2}) = 1 - \alpha. \tag{12.4}$$

$z_{\alpha/2}$ is the value of the random variable Z at which the integral of Z from $z_{-\alpha/2}$ to $+\infty$ is $\alpha/2$. Since Z is symmetrical and has its mean at zero, the integral of Z from $-\infty$ to $z_{-\alpha/2}$ is also equal to $\alpha/2$. The total area from both tail intervals of the distribution is α.

Equation (12.4) can be rearranged to show that the probability interval for μ, the mean of the population that is the unknown quantity of interest, is given by

$$P\left(\bar{X} - z_{\alpha/2} \cdot \frac{S}{\sqrt{n}} < \mu < \bar{X} + z_{\alpha/2} \cdot \frac{S}{\sqrt{n}}\right) = 1 - \alpha. \tag{12.5}$$

For sufficiently large n, Eq. (12.5) can be rewritten as a confidence interval for the population mean using sampled quantities for the mean and standard deviation,

$$\mu \sim \left(\bar{x} - z_{\alpha/2} \cdot \frac{s}{\sqrt{n}}, \bar{x} + z_{\alpha/2} \cdot \frac{s}{\sqrt{n}}\right). \tag{12.6}$$

$\bar{x}$ and s are the sample mean and standard deviation, respectively, based on n observations. Note that $\bar{x}$ and s are computed from the realizations $X_1 = x_1, X_2 = x_2, \ldots, X_n = x_n$. The term $s/\sqrt{n}$ is the standard error of the sample mean that measures how far the sample mean is likely to be from the population mean. The level of confidence that μ is in the interval given by Eq. (12.6) can be shown to be $100(1 - \alpha)\%$. The value of α is arbitrarily assigned and is typically chosen to be 0.1 or 0.05, corresponding to confidence levels of 90% or 95%, respectively.

The confidence interval for the population mean can be interpreted in a strict frequentist viewpoint or in a subjectivist, or Bayesian, viewpoint. Let C be the confidence level chosen, i.e., $C = 100(1 - \alpha)\%$, for stating that the true mean μ is in the interval given by Eq. (12.6). The frequentist would state, "μ is in the interval given by Eq. (12.6) with confidence C," which means that if the experiment on which μ is estimated is performed repeatedly; for a sufficiently large number of samples μ will fall in the interval given by Eq. (12.6) $C\%$ of the time. The subjectivist would state (Winkler, 1972), "Based on the observed data, it is my belief that μ is in the interval given by Eq. (12.6) with probability C." The reason that it *cannot* be strictly stated that C is the probability that μ is in the interval given by Eq. (12.6) is that the true probability is either zero or one. That is, the true mean μ is either in the interval or it is not; we simply *cannot know with certainty* for a finite number of samples from the population. Notwithstanding these fine points of interpretation, we will essentially use the subjectivist interpretation in a slightly different form than that presented above. We will use the interpretation: μ is in the interval given by Eq. (12.6) with confidence C.

Now consider the case of calculating a confidence interval for an arbitrary number of experimental observations n, with n as small as two. It can be shown (Devore, 2007) that if it is assumed that the samples are drawn from a normal distribution, the equation analogous to Eq. (12.6) is

$$\mu \sim \left(\bar{x} - t_{\alpha/2,\nu} \cdot \frac{s}{\sqrt{n}}, \bar{x} + t_{\alpha/2,\nu} \cdot \frac{s}{\sqrt{n}} \right). \tag{12.7}$$

The level of confidence is given by $100(1 - \alpha)\%$ and $t_{-\alpha/2,\nu}$ is the $1 - \alpha/2$ quantile of the t distribution for $\nu = n - 1$ degrees of freedom. For n greater than 16, the cumulative t distribution and the cumulative standard normal distribution differ by less than 0.01 for all quantiles. In the limit as $n \to \infty$, the t distribution approaches the standard normal distribution.

Equation (12.7) can be used for hypothesis testing in classical statistical analysis. However, our perspective in the construction of validation metrics is notably different. We wish to quantify the difference between the computational results and the true mean of the experimental results. Stated differently, we wish to measure shades of gray between a model and an experiment – not make a "yes" or "no" statement about the congruence of two hypotheses for a given accuracy level.

12.4.3 Construction of the validation metric for one condition

For the validation metric we wish to construct, we are interested in two quantities. First, we want to estimate an error in the SRQ of the model based on the difference between the model and the estimated mean of the population based on the experimentally measured samples of the SRQ. Let y_m be the SRQ from the model. Changing the notation used previously for the experimental measurements from $\bar{x}$ to $\bar{y}_e$, we define the estimated error in the model as

$$\tilde{E} = y_m - \bar{y}_e. \tag{12.8}$$

$\bar{y}_e$ is the estimated, or sample, mean based on n experiments conducted. $\bar{y}_e$ is given by

$$\bar{y}_e = \frac{1}{n} \sum_{i=1}^{n} y_e^i, \tag{12.9}$$

where $y_e^1, y_e^2, \ldots, y_e^n$ are the individually measured results of the SRQ from each experiment.

Second, we wish to compute an interval that contains the true error in the model, which we do not know, at a specified level of confidence. Let the true error in the model E be defined as

$$E = y_m - \mu, \tag{12.10}$$

where μ is the true mean of the population. Writing the confidence interval expression, Eq. (12.7), for μ as an inequality relation and changing the notation as just mentioned, we have

$$\bar{y}_e - t_{\alpha/2,\nu} \cdot \frac{s}{\sqrt{n}} < \mu < \bar{y}_e + t_{\alpha/2,\nu} \cdot \frac{s}{\sqrt{n}}. \tag{12.11}$$

s is the sample (not population) standard deviation given by

$$s = \left[\frac{1}{n-1} \sum_{i=1}^{n} \left(y_e^i - \bar{y}_e \right)^2 \right]^{1/2}.$$ (12.12)

Multiplying Eq. (12.11) by -1 and adding y_m to each term, we have

$$y_m - \bar{y}_e + t_{\alpha/2,\nu} \cdot \frac{s}{\sqrt{n}} > y_m - \mu > y_m - \bar{y}_e - t_{\alpha/2,\nu} \cdot \frac{s}{\sqrt{n}}.$$ (12.13)

Substituting the expression for the true error, Eq. (12.10), into Eq. (12.13) and rearranging, one obtains

$$y_m - \bar{y}_e - t_{\alpha/2,\nu} \cdot \frac{s}{\sqrt{n}} < E < y_m - \bar{y}_e + t_{\alpha/2,\nu} \cdot \frac{s}{\sqrt{n}}.$$ (12.14)

Substituting the expression for the estimated error, Eq. (12.8), into Eq. (12.14), we can write the inequality expression as an interval containing the true error where the level of confidence is given by $100\,(1 - \alpha)\,\%$:

$$\left(\tilde{E} - t_{\alpha/2,\nu} \cdot \frac{s}{\sqrt{n}}, \tilde{E} + t_{\alpha/2,\nu} \cdot \frac{s}{\sqrt{n}} \right).$$ (12.15)

Using the level of confidence of 90%, one can state the validation metric in the following way: the estimated error in the model is $\tilde{E} = y_m - \bar{y}_e$ with a confidence level of 90% that the true error is in the interval

$$\left(\tilde{E} - t_{0.05,\nu} \cdot \frac{s}{\sqrt{n}}, \tilde{E} + t_{0.05,\nu} \cdot \frac{s}{\sqrt{n}} \right).$$ (12.16)

Three characteristics of this validation metric should be mentioned. First, the statement of confidence is made concerning an interval in which the true error is believed to occur. The statement of confidence is *not* made concerning the magnitude of the estimated error, nor concerning an interval around the computational prediction. The reason such statements cannot be made is that the fundamental quantity that is uncertain is the *true* experimental mean. Stated differently, although we are asking how much error there is in the computational result, the actual uncertain quantity is the *referent*, i.e., the true experimental value, *not* the computational result.

Second, the interval believed to contain the true error is symmetric around the estimated error. We can also state that the rate of decrease of the magnitude of the interval is a factor of 2.6 when going from two experiments to three experiments, the sample standard deviation s remaining constant. For a large number of experiments, the rate of decrease of the magnitude of the interval is $1/\sqrt{n}$. Additionally, the size of the interval decreases linearly as the sample standard deviation decreases.

Third, for small numbers of experimental measurements it must be assumed that the measurement uncertainty is normally distributed. Although this is a very common assumption in experimental uncertainty estimation, and probably well justified, it is rarely *demonstrated* to be true. However, for a large number of experimental measurements, as discussed above, the confidence interval on the mean is valid regardless of the type of probability distribution representing measurement uncertainty.

Finally, we stress the primacy we give to the experimental data. As can be clearly seen from Eq. (12.10), the referent for the error measure is the experimental data, not the model or some type of weighted average between the model and the experiment. However, our trust in the accuracy of experimental measurements is not without some risk, specifically, if an undetected bias error exists in the experimental data.

12.4.4 Example problem: thermal decomposition of foam

As an example of the application of the validation metric just derived, consider the assessment of a model for the rate of decomposition of polyurethane foam due to thermal heating. The model solves the unsteady energy equation for the heating of the foam and is composed of three major components: (a) thermal diffusion through the materials involved, (b) chemistry models for the thermal response and decomposition of polymeric materials due to high temperature, and (c) radiation transport within the domain and between the boundaries of the physical system. The foam decomposition model predicts the mass and species evolution of the decomposing foam and was developed by Hobbs *et al.* (1999). Dowding *et al.* (2004) computed the results for this example using the computer code Coyote that solves the mathematical model using a finite element technique (Gartling *et al.*, 1994). Three-dimensional, unsteady solutions were computed until the foam decomposed, vaporized, and escaped from a vent in the container. The container was a cylinder with a diameter of 88 mm and a length of 146 mm. Solution verification for the computational results relied on the mesh refinement studies previously conducted by Hobbs *et al.* (1999). These earlier mesh refinement studies estimated that the mesh discretization error was less than 1% for the velocity of the foam decomposition front for mesh sizes less than 0.1 mm.

The experiment designed to evaluate the model was composed of polyurethane foam enclosed in a stainless steel cylinder that was heated using high-intensity lamps (Figure 12.5). The experiment was conducted by Bentz and Pantuso and is reported in Hobbs *et al.* (1999). The position of the foam–gas interface was measured as a function of time by X-rays passing through the cylinder. The steel cylinder was vented to the atmosphere to allow gas to escape, and it was heated from different directions during different experiments: top, bottom, and side. For some of the experiments, a solid stainless steel cylinder or hollow aluminum component was embedded in the foam.

The SRQ of interest is the steady-state velocity of the foam decomposition front when the front has moved between 1 and 2 cm. The steady-state velocity was typically achieved after 5 to 10 minutes, depending on the heating temperature. The SRQ was measured as a function of the imposed boundary condition temperature. Since we are only considering one operating condition for the present validation metric example, we pick the temperature condition of $T = 750\,°C$ because it had the largest number of experimental replications. Some of the replications, shown in Table 12.1, were the result of different orientations

Table 12.1 *Experimental data for foam decomposition*
(Hobbs et al., 1999).

Experiment no.	Temperature (°C)	Heat orientation	V (experiment) (cm/min)
2	750	bottom	0.2323
5	750	bottom	0.1958
10	750	top	0.2110
11	750	side	0.2582
13	750	side	0.2154
15	750	bottom	0.2755

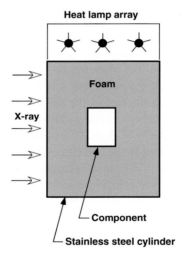

Figure 12.5 Schematic of foam decomposition experiment (Oberkampf and Barone, 2004).

of the heat lamps. No estimates of experimental measurement uncertainty were provided. Computational simulations by Dowding *et al.* (2004) showed that cylinder orientation had little effect on the velocity of the decomposition front. Since we are only interested in a single deterministic result from the model, we picked one of the Dowding *et al.* results for the computational SRQ. The computational prediction for the foam decomposition velocity was 0.2457 cm/min. With this approximation, we assigned the variability resulting from the heating orientation of the cylinder to uncertainty in the experimental measurements. In addition, there is variability in the material composition of the foam during the fabrication process resulting in variability of the decomposition front velocity for a fixed temperature. Consequently, the material variability effect is confounded with the experimental measurement uncertainty.

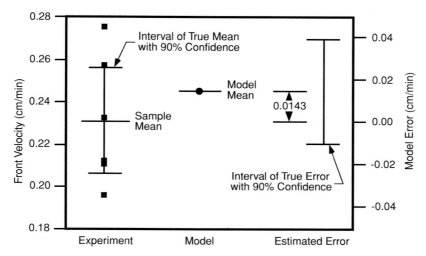

Figure 12.6 Statistical and validation metric results of foam decomposition (Oberkampf and Barone, 2006).

Using the data in Table 12.1 and Eqs. (12.7)–(12.9), (12.12), and (12.16), we obtain

number of samples $= n = 6$,
sample mean $= \bar{y}_e = 0.2314$ cm/min,
estimated error $= \tilde{E} = 0.2457 - 0.2314 = 0.0143$ cm/min,
sample standard deviation $= s = 0.0303$ cm/min,
degrees of freedom $= n - 1 = \nu = 5$,
t distribution for 90% confidence $(\nu = 5) = t_{0.05,\nu} = 2.015 \pm t_{0.05,\nu} \cdot \frac{s}{\sqrt{n}} = \pm 0.0249$ cm/min,
true mean with 90% confidence $= \mu \sim (0.2065, 0.2563)$ cm/min,
true error with 90% confidence $\sim (-0.0106, 0.0392)$ cm/min.

Figure 12.6 depicts the sample mean, the model mean, the estimated interval of the true mean, and the estimated error with 90% confidence. In summary form, the result of the validation metric is $\tilde{E} = 0.0143 \pm 0.0249$ cm/min with 90% confidence. Note that the validation metric result is given in the physical units of the SRQs being compared, *not* some sort of statistical measure or a probability. Since the magnitude of the uncertainty in the experimental data is roughly twice the estimated error in the model, one cannot make any more precise conclusions than ± 0.0249 cm/min (with 90% confidence) concerning the accuracy of the model.

Whether the estimated accuracy with its uncertainty is adequate for the intended use of the model is a separate step in the encompassing view of validation, as discussed earlier. If the estimated accuracy with its uncertainty is not adequate for a model use decision, then one has two options. The first option, which is the more reasonable option for this case, is to reduce the experimental uncertainty by obtaining additional experimental measurements, changing the experimental procedure, or improving the diagnostic method to reduce the experimental uncertainty. The second option would be to improve, or update, the model so that it gives more accurate results for this situation. However, in the present case, the error in the model is small with respect to the experimental uncertainty. As a result, this option would be uncalled for.

12.5 Comparison of means using interpolation of experimental data

12.5.1 *Construction of the validation metric over the range of the data*

We are now interested in the case where the SRQ is measured over a range of the input variable or the operating condition variable. For example, in the foam decomposition experiment just discussed, we would be interested in the velocity of the foam decomposition front as a function of the heating temperature of the cylinder. Another example would be the thrust of a rocket motor as a function of burn time. Here we consider the case of one input variable while all others are held constant. This is probably the most common type of comparison between computational and experimental results. The present ideas could be extended fairly easily to the case of multiple input variables as long as the input variables were independent.

The following assumption is made with regard to the computational results. The SRQ is computed at a sufficient number of values over the range of the input variable to allow an accurate construction of an interpolation function to represent the SRQ.

The following assumptions are made with regard to the experimental measurements.

(1) The input variable from the experiment is measured much more accurately than the SRQ. Quantitatively, this means that the coefficient of variation (COV) of the input variable is much smaller than the COV of the SRQ. The assumption must relate the COV of each quantity because the COV is a dimensionless statistic of the variability of a random variable. Note that this assumption allows for the case where the input variable is uncontrolled in the experiment, and could even be a random variable. However, the key is that it can be accurately measured for each replication of the experiment.
(2) Two or more experimental replications have been obtained, and each replication has multiple measurements of the SRQ over the range of the input variable. Using the terminology of Coleman and Steele (1999), it is desirable that Nth-order replications have been obtained, and possibly even replications by different experimentalists using different facilities and different diagnostic techniques.
(3) The measurement uncertainty in the SRQ from one experimental replication to the next, and from setup to setup, is given by a normal distribution.
(4) Each experimental replication is independent from other replications; that is, there is zero correlation or dependence between one replication and another.
(5) For each experimental replication, the SRQ is measured at a sufficient number of values over the range of the input variable so that a smooth and accurate interpolation function can be constructed to represent the SRQ. By *interpolation* we mean that the function constructed to represent the data must match each measured value of the SRQ.

With these assumptions, the equations developed above are easily extended to the case in which both the computational result and the experimental mean for the SRQ are functions of the input variable x. Rewriting Eq. (12.16), the true error as a function of x is in the interval

$$\left(\tilde{E}(x) - t_{0.05,\nu} \cdot \frac{s(x)}{\sqrt{n}}, \ \tilde{E}(x) + t_{0.05,\nu} \cdot \frac{s(x)}{\sqrt{n}} \right), \tag{12.17}$$

with a confidence level of 90%. The standard deviation as a function of x is given by

$$s(x) \sim \left[\frac{1}{n-1} \sum_{i=1}^{n} \left(y_e^i(x) - \bar{y}_e(x) \right)^2 \right]^{1/2}. \tag{12.18}$$

Note that $y_e^i(x)$ is interpolated using the experimental data from the ith experimental replication, i.e., the ensemble of measurements over the range of x from the ith experiment. Each experimental replication need not make measurements at the same values of x because a separate interpolation function is constructed for each ensemble of measurements, i.e., each ith experimental replication.

12.5.2 Global metrics

Although these equations provide the results of the validation metric as a function of x, there are some situations where it is desirable to construct a more compact, or global, statement of the model accuracy. For example, in a project management review it may be useful to quickly summarize the accuracy for a large number of models and experimental data. A convenient method to compute a global metric would be to use a vector norm of the estimated error over the range of the input variable. The L_1 norm is useful to interpret the estimated average absolute error of the model over the range of the data. Using the L_1 norm, one could form an average absolute error or a relative absolute error over the range of the data. We choose to use the relative absolute error by normalizing the absolute error by the estimated experimental mean and then integrating over the range of the data. We define the *average relative error metric* to be

$$\left| \frac{\tilde{E}}{\bar{y}_e} \right|_{\text{avg}} = \frac{1}{(x_u - x_l)} \int_{x_l}^{x_u} \left| \frac{y_m(x) - \bar{y}_e(x)}{\bar{y}_e(x)} \right| dx. \tag{12.19}$$

x_u is the largest value and x_l is the smallest value, respectively, of the input variable. As long as $|\bar{y}_e(x)|$ is not near zero for any x_l, the average relative error metric is a useful quantity.

The confidence interval that should be associated with this average relative error metric is the average confidence interval normalized by the absolute value of the estimated experimental mean over the range of the data. We define the *average relative confidence indicator* as the half-width of the confidence interval averaged over the range of the data:

$$\left| \frac{\text{CI}}{\bar{y}_e} \right|_{\text{avg}} = \frac{t_{0.05,\nu}}{(x_u - x_l)\sqrt{n}} \int_{x_l}^{x_u} \left| \frac{s(x)}{\bar{y}_e(x)} \right| dx. \tag{12.20}$$

We refer to $|\text{CI}/\bar{y}_e|_{\text{avg}}$ as an indicator, as opposed to an interval, because the uncertainty structure of $s(x)$ is not maintained through the integration operator. Although $|\text{CI}/\bar{y}_e|_{\text{avg}}$

is not an average relative confidence interval over the range of the data, it is a quantity useful for interpreting the significance of the magnitude of $|\tilde{E}/\bar{y}_e|_{avg}$. Stated differently, the magnitude of $|\tilde{E}/\bar{y}_e|_{avg}$ should be interpreted relative to the magnitude of the normalized uncertainty in the experimental data, $|CI/\bar{y}_e|_{avg}$.

There may be situations where the average relative error metric may not adequately represent the model accuracy because of the strong smoothing nature of the integration operator. For example, there may be a large error at some particular point over the range of the data that should be noted. It is useful to define a maximum value of the absolute relative error over the range of the data. Using the L_∞ norm to accomplish this, we define the *maximum relative error metric* as

$$\left|\frac{\tilde{E}}{\bar{y}_e}\right|_{max} = \max_{x_l \leq x \leq x_u} \left|\frac{y_m(x) - \bar{y}_e(x)}{\bar{y}_e(x)}\right|. \tag{12.21}$$

If one observes a significant difference between $|\tilde{E}/\bar{y}_e|_{avg}$ and $|\tilde{E}/\bar{y}_e|_{max}$, then one should more carefully examine the trend of the model with respect to the trend of the experimental data. For example, if $|\tilde{E}/\bar{y}_e|_{max}$ is much greater than $|\tilde{E}/\bar{y}_e|_{avg}$, the model is failing to predict either a local or global trend of the experimental data.

The confidence interval that should be associated with the maximum relative error metric is the confidence interval normalized by the estimated experimental mean. Both the confidence interval and the estimated experimental mean are evaluated at the point where the maximum relative error metric occurs. Let the x value where $|\tilde{E}/\bar{y}_e|_{max}$ occurs be defined as $\hat{x}$. Then the confidence interval half-width associated with the maximum relative error metric is

$$\left|\frac{CI}{\bar{y}_e}\right|_{max} = \frac{t_{0.05,\nu}}{\sqrt{n}}\left|\frac{s(\hat{x})}{\bar{y}_e(\hat{x})}\right|. \tag{12.22}$$

12.5.3 Example problem: turbulent buoyant plume

As an example of the validation metric just derived, consider the assessment of a model for a turbulent buoyant plume that is exiting vertically from a large nozzle. Turbulent buoyant plumes, typically originating from the combustion of fuel–air mixtures, have proven to be especially difficult to model in CFD. This is primarily because of the strong interaction between the density field and the momentum field dominated by large turbulent eddies. The slowest turbulent scales are on the order of seconds in large fires, and this large-scale unsteadiness is beyond the modeling capability of a Reynolds–average Navier–Stokes (RANS) formulation. The model to be evaluated here solves the continuity equation and the temporally filtered Navier–Stokes (TFNS) equations. The TFNS equations are similar to RANS equations, but a narrower filter width is used so that large-scale unsteadiness can be captured (Pruett *et al.*, 2003). Tieszen *et al.* (2005) computed the unsteady,

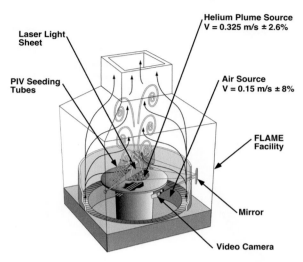

Figure 12.7 Experimental setup for measurements of the helium plume (O'Hern *et al.*, 2005). See color plate section.

three-dimensional simulations used here for a large-scale helium plume using the TFNS model and the standard k-ε turbulence model.

The experimental data for the validation metric were obtained in the Fire Laboratory for Accreditation of Models and Experiments (FLAME) facility at Sandia National Laboratories. The FLAME facility is a building designed for indoor fire experiments, as well as other buoyant plumes, so that the plumes are not influenced by atmospheric winds, and all other boundary conditions affecting the plume can be measured and controlled. For the present experiment, a large inflow jet of helium was used (Figure 12.7) (DesJardin *et al.*, 2004; O'Hern *et al.*, 2004). The helium source is 1 m in diameter and is surrounded by a 0.51-m wide horizontal surface to simulate the ground plane that is typical in a fuel-pool fire. Inlet air is allowed in from outside the building at the bottom of the facility and is drawn in by the vertically accelerating helium plume that exits the chimney of the building.

The experimental data consist of velocity field measurements using particle image velocimetry (PIV) and scalar concentration measurements using planar-induced fluorescence (PLIF). Here we are interested in only the PIV measurements, but details of all of the diagnostic procedures and uncertainty estimates can be found in O'Hern *et al.* (2005). The PIV data are obtained from photographing the flowfield, which has been seeded with glass microspheres, at 200 images/s. Flowfield velocities are obtained in a plane that is up to 1 m from the exit of the jet and illuminated by a laser light sheet. The flow velocity of interest here, i.e., the SRQ that is input to the validation metric, is the time-averaged vertical velocity component along the centerline of the helium jet. For unsteady flows such as this, there are a number of large-scale oscillatory modes that exist within the plume, as well as turbulence scales that range down to the micron level. The SRQ of interest is time

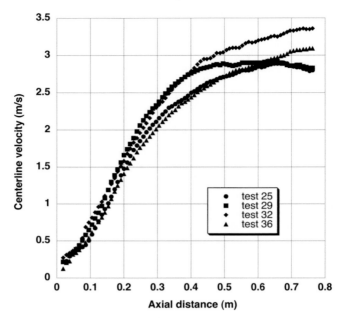

Figure 12.8 Experimental measurements of time-averaged vertical velocity along the centerline for the helium plume. Data from O'Hern *et al.* (2005).

averaged for roughly 10 s in the experiment, which is roughly seven cycles of the lowest oscillatory mode in the jet.

Shown in Figure 12.8 are four experimental measurements of time-averaged vertical velocity along the centerline as a function of axial distance from the exit of the helium jet. The experimental replications were obtained on different days, with different equipment setups, and with multiple recalibrations of the instrumentation. A large number of velocity measurements were obtained over the range of the input variable, the axial distance, so that an accurate interpolation function could be constructed.

Tieszen *et al.* (2005) investigated the sensitivity of their numerical solutions for the helium plume to both modeling parameters and numerical discretization on an unstructured mesh. The key modeling parameter affecting the TFNS solutions is the size of the temporal filter relative to the period of the largest turbulent mode in the simulation. Four spatial discretizations were investigated, resulting in the following total number of mesh points: 0.25M, 0.50M, 1M, and 2M elements ($1M = 10^6$). In order to process the vertical velocity solutions in the same way that the experimentalist processed the data, each of these solutions was time averaged over roughly seven puffing cycles. Using the method for computing the observed order of spatial convergence discussed in Chapter 8, Discretization error, and Tieszen *et al.* (2005) solutions for 0.50M, 1M, and 2M elements, it does not appear that the solutions are in the asymptotic region. A finer mesh, say, 4M elements, would greatly help in determining whether the computational results are actually converged. However,

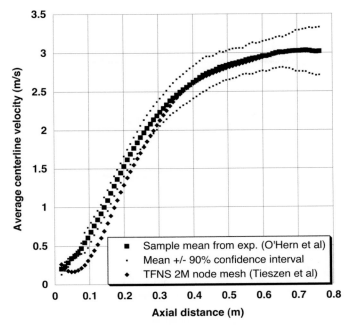

Figure 12.9 Experimental sample mean with 90% confidence interval and computational result for vertical velocity in the helium plume (Oberkampf and Barone, 2004).

computational resources were not available to compute the 4M-element solution. As a result, we will use their 2M-element solution as only representative data with which to demonstrate the present validation metric.

Using the experimental data shown in Figure 12.8, noting that $n = 4$, one obtains the sample mean of the measurements, $\bar{y}_e(x)$, shown in Figure 12.9. Also, using the interpolated function for the experimental sample mean and the confidence interval for the true mean, one obtains the interval around the estimated mean in which the true mean will occur with 90% confidence (Figure 12.9). The computational solution obtained from the 2M-element mesh is also shown in Figure 12.9.

The level of disagreement between computational and experimental results can be more critically seen by plotting the estimated error, $\tilde{E}(x) = y_m(x) - \bar{y}_e(x)$, instead of simply showing the SRQ as a function of the input variable. Figure 12.10 shows this type of plot, along with the 90% confidence interval from the experiment, as given by Eq. (12.17). Presentation of model accuracy assessment results such as Figure 12.10, even without the confidence interval, is rarely seen in practice. This type of plot very critically examines the differences between the model and the experimental results. Even though it presents the same information as Figure 12.9, the critical examination of the difference never flatters the model or the experiment. In Figure 12.10, the largest modeling (relative) error occurs very near the beginning of the plume. This error is noticeable in Figure 12.9, but it is not dominant as it is in Figure 12.10. We remind the reader that we are discussing the model

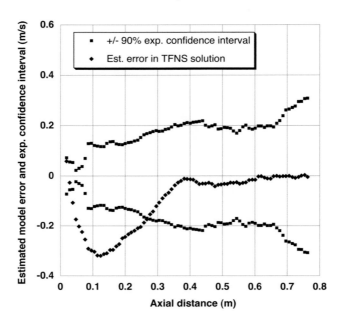

Figure 12.10 Validation metric result and 90% confidence interval for centerline velocity (Oberkampf and Barone, 2004).

error as if it were due to physics modeling, however, it may not be that at all. It may be simply due to the insufficiently mesh converged solution, but at this point one cannot be certain what the source of the error is.

The validation metric result shown in Figure 12.10 can be quantitatively summarized using the global metrics given in Eqs. (12.19)–(12.22). Over the range of the data, these results are as follows:

average relative error = 11% ± 9% with 90% confidence,
maximum relative error = 54% ± 9% with 90% confidence.

Thus, the average relative error could be as large as 20% and as small as 2% (on average) over the range of the data, with 90% confidence considering the uncertainty in the experimental data. The average relative error shows that the model accuracy (on average) is comparable to the average confidence indicator in the experimental data. Similarly, the maximum relative error could be as small as 45% and as large as 63%, with 90% confidence considering the uncertainty in the experimental data. The maximum relative error, 54%, which occurs at $x = 0.067$ m, is five times the average relative error, indicating a significant difference in the local character of the model and the experimental data. Note that, for these experimental data, the average relative confidence indicator, 9%, happens to be essentially equal to the relative confidence interval at the maximum relative error; however, this need not be the case in general. If one was using both the average relative error and the maximum relative error for a "first look" evaluation of the model, a large difference between these

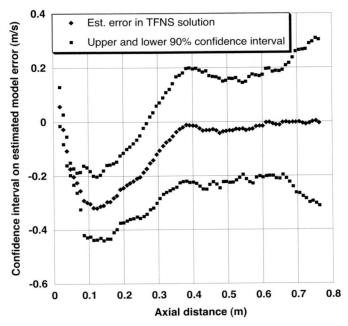

Figure 12.11 Estimated error and true error in the model with 90% confidence interval (Oberkampf and Barone, 2004).

values should prompt a more careful examination of the data, for example, examination of plots such as Figure 12.9 and Figure 12.10.

The final method of displaying the results of the validation metric is to plot the 90% confidence interval of the true error in velocity predicted by the model as a function of the axial distance from the exit of the jet. Using Eq. (12.17), one obtains the result shown in Figure 12.11. Our best approximation of the true error in the model is the estimated error. However, with 90% confidence we can state that the true error is in the interval shown in Figure 12.11.

Although Figure 12.11 displays essentially the same data as shown in Figure 12.10, Figure 12.11 allows us to consider slightly different perspectives for assessing the model. For example, we could view Figure 12.11 from the perspectives of those who might use the validation metric results to evaluate the predictive capability of the model. A model builder, for example, would likely investigate the cause of the largest error, i.e., near $x =$ 0.1 m, and explore ways to improve the model and/or compute a solution on a more highly resolved mesh. For an analyst, i.e., a person who is going to use the model for predictions of flowfields that are related to the present flowfield, the perspective is somewhat different from that of the model builder. The analyst might conclude that the accuracy of the model is satisfactory for its intended use and simply apply the model as it is. Alternatively, the analyst might decide to use Figure 12.11 to incorporate a bias-error correction directly on the SRQ, i.e., the vertical velocity on the centerline of the plume. However, this procedure for model correction would clearly involve high risk because it completely ignores the physical and/or numerical cause of the error. Stated differently, the analyst would be treating the estimated error *as if* it was physics, but this claim is very weak because of evidence of an unresolved mesh solution.

12.6 Comparison of means requiring linear regression of the experimental data

12.6.1 Construction of the validation metric over the range of the data

We are now interested in a case where the quantity of experimental data is not sufficient to construct an interpolation function over the range of the input variable. Consequently, a regression function (curve fit) must be constructed to represent the estimated mean over the range of the data. Some examples are lift (or drag) of a flight vehicle as a function of the Mach number, turbopump mass flow rate as a function of backpressure, and depth of penetration into a material during high-speed impact. Construction of a regression function is probably the most common situation that arises in comparing computational and experimental results when the input variable is *not* time. When time-dependent SRQs are recorded, the temporal resolution is typically high so that the construction of an interpolation function is commonly used. Time series analyses, however, must normally deal with both high-frequency characteristics in the SRQs *and* uncertainty in the experimental measurements.

Regression analysis procedures are well developed in classical statistics for addressing how two or more variables are related to each other when one or both contain random uncertainty. We are interested here in the restricted case of univariate regression, i.e., how one variable (the SRQ) relates to another variable (the input variable) when there is only uncertainty in the SRQ. The first four assumptions pertaining to the experimental measurements discussed in Section 12.5.1 are also made for the present case. In addition to these, the following assumption is made with regard to the experimental uncertainty: the standard deviation of the normal distribution that describes the measurement uncertainty is constant over the entire range of measurements of the input parameter. It should also be noted that this assumption is probably the most demanding of the experimental measurement assumptions listed.

In the present development, it was initially thought that traditional confidence intervals, as discussed above, could be applied when a regression analysis was involved. We realized, however, that commonly used confidence intervals only apply to the case of a specific, but arbitrary, value of the input parameter. That is, the traditional confidence interval is a statement of the accuracy of the estimated mean as expressed by the regression for *point values* of the input parameter x. The traditional confidence interval is written for μ conditional on a point value of x, say, x^*, i.e. $\mu[\bar{y}_e(x)|x^*]$, where (|) denotes that the preceding quantity is conditional on the following quantity. As a result, the traditional confidence interval analysis cannot be applied to the case of a validation metric over a range of the input variable where the determination of a regression is also involved.

A more general statistical analysis procedure was found that develops a confidence interval for the entire range of the input parameter (Miller, 1981; Draper and Smith, 1998;

Seber and Wild, 2003). That is, we wish to determine the confidence interval that results from uncertainty in the regression coefficients over the complete range of the regression function. The regression coefficients are all correlated with one another because they appear in the same regression function used to fit the range of the experimental data. This type of confidence interval is typically referred to as a *simultaneous confidence interval*, a *simultaneous inference*, or a *Scheffé confidence interval*, so that it can be distinguished from traditional (or single comparison) confidence intervals.

Let the set of n experimental measurements of the SRQ of interest be given by

$$\left(y_e^i, x_i\right) \quad \text{for} \quad i = 1, 2, \ldots, n. \tag{12.23}$$

Here we consider the simplest case of representing the estimated mean of the data, $\bar{y}_e(x)$, using a linear regression function over the range of the data. The linear regression function is written as

$$\bar{y}_e(x) = \theta_1 + x\theta_2 + \varepsilon, \tag{12.24}$$

where θ_1 and θ_2 are the unknown coefficients of the regression function; and ε is the random measurement error. For this case, the equations for the Scheffé confidence intervals can be analytically derived (Miller, 1981).

The estimate of the interval for the true mean $\mu(x)$ is given by

$$\mu(x) \sim (\bar{y}(x) - \text{SCI}(x), \bar{y}(x) + \text{SCI}(x)), \tag{12.25}$$

where $\text{SCI}(x)$ is the width of the Scheffé confidence interval as a function of x and is given by

$$\text{SCI}(x) = s\sqrt{[2F(2, n - 2, 1 - \alpha)]\left[\frac{1}{n} + \frac{(x - \bar{x})^2}{(n-1)s_x^2}\right]}, \tag{12.26}$$

where s is the standard deviation of the residuals for the entire curve fit, $F(\nu_1, \nu_2, 1 - a)$ is the F probability distribution, ν_1 is the first parameter specifying the number of degrees of freedom, ν_2 is the second parameter specifying the number of degrees of freedom, $1 - \alpha$ is the quantile for the confidence interval of interest, n is the number of experimental measurements, $\bar{x}$ is the mean of the input values of the experimental measurements, and s_x^2 is the variance of the input values of the experimental measurements. One has the definitions

$$s = \sqrt{\frac{1}{(n-1)}\sum_{i=1}^{n}\left[y_e^i - \bar{y}_e(x_i)\right]^2}, \tag{12.27}$$

$$\bar{x} = \frac{1}{n}\sum_{i=1}^{n} x_i, \tag{12.28}$$

$$s_x^2 = \frac{1}{(n-1)}\sum_{i=1}^{n}(x_i - \bar{x})^2. \tag{12.29}$$

Using the definition of the estimated error in the model, Eq. (12.8), one can write the estimated error as a function of x as

$$\tilde{E}(x) = y_{\mathrm{m}}(x) - \bar{y}_{\mathrm{e}}(x), \tag{12.30}$$

Using this equation, and Eq. (12.25), the interval containing the true error with confidence level $100(1 - \alpha)\%$ is given by

$$(\tilde{E}(x) - \mathrm{SCI}(x),\ \tilde{E}(x) + \mathrm{SCI}(x)). \tag{12.31}$$

One can compare Eq. (12.31) with the equation for the traditional confidence interval, Eq. (12.17). One finds that the equations are identical except for the coefficient

$$\sqrt{2F(2, n - 2, 1 - \alpha)}. \tag{12.32}$$

For the traditional confidence interval one has the coefficient $t_{\alpha/2,n-1}$. In general,

$$\sqrt{2F(2, n - 2, 1 - \alpha)} > t_{\alpha/2,n-1}. \tag{12.33}$$

As a result, the Scheffé confidence intervals are always larger, commonly by a factor of two, than traditional confidence intervals. This larger confidence interval reflects the experimental uncertainty on the entire regression function; not just uncertainty at a given value of x.

12.6.2 Global metrics

If we would like to make a quantitative assessment of the global modeling error, then we can use the global measures expressed earlier in Eqs. (12.19) and (12.21). However, the average relative confidence indicator, Eq. (12.20), and the confidence interval associated with the maximum relative error, Eq. (12.22), must be changed to take into account the simultaneous nature of the regression. Using Eq. (12.31), one can rewrite Eq. (12.20) as

$$\left| \frac{\mathrm{CI}}{\bar{y}_{\mathrm{e}}} \right|_{\mathrm{avg}} = \frac{1}{(x_{\mathrm{u}} - x_{\mathrm{l}})} \int_{x_{\mathrm{l}}}^{x_{\mathrm{u}}} \left| \frac{\mathrm{SCI}(x)}{\bar{y}_{\mathrm{e}}(x)} \right| \mathrm{d}x \tag{12.34}$$

for the average relative confidence indicator.

The confidence interval associated with the maximum relative error metric, Eq. (12.22), is

$$\left| \frac{\mathrm{CI}}{\bar{y}_{\mathrm{e}}} \right|_{\mathrm{max}} = \left| \frac{\mathrm{SCI}(\hat{x})}{\bar{y}_{\mathrm{e}}(\hat{x})} \right|, \tag{12.35}$$

where $\hat{x}$ is the x value where $|\tilde{E}/\bar{y}_{\mathrm{e}}|_{\mathrm{max}}$ occurs.

12.6.3 Example problem: thermal decomposition of foam

As an example of use of the validation metric using linear regression, consider again the model for the thermal decomposition of polyurethane foam described in Section 12.4.4.

Table 12.2 *Experimental and computational data for a range of operating conditions, (Hobbs* et al., *1999).*

Experiment no.	Temperature (°C)	Heat orientation	V (experiment) (cm/min)	V (computation) (cm/min)
1	600	bottom	0.1307	0.0913
2	750	bottom	0.2323	0.2457
5	750	bottom	0.1958	0.2457
10	750	top	0.2110	0.2457
11	750	side	0.2582	0.2457
13	750	side	0.2154	0.2457
15	750	bottom	0.2755	0.2457
14	900	bottom	0.3483	0.4498
16	1000	bottom	0.5578	0.7698

Now, however, a more complete set of data is considered for heating the foam over a range of temperatures. The experimental data for foam decomposition obtained by Bentz and Pantuso is shown in Table 12.2. The computational data given by Easterling (2001, 2003); and Dowding *et al.* (2004) were used for a range of temperature conditions from $T = 600\,°C$ to $T = 1000\,°C$. Table 12.2 shows the experimental and computational results used to compute the various elements of the validation metric.

Using the experimental data in Table 12.2, standard linear regression methods, and Eqs. (12.24)–(12.29), one obtains

number of samples $= n = 9$,
y intercept from the linear curve fit $= \theta_1 = -0.5406$,
slope from the linear curve fit $= \theta_2 = 0.001042$,
standard deviation of the residuals of the curve fit $= s = 0.04284$,
square of the regression coefficient $= R^2 = 0.895$,
0.9 quantile of the F probability distribution for $v_1 = 2$ and $v_2 = 7$, $F(2, 7, 0.9) = 3.26$,
mean of the x input values $= \bar{x} = 777.8$,
variance of the x input values $= s_x^2 = 12\,569$,
Scheffé confidence interval $= \text{SCI}(x) = \pm 0.044284\sqrt{1 + 8.9 \times 10^{-5}(x - 777.8)^2}$.

Note that here we use the generic variable x, as developed in the equations, to represent the temperature.

To obtain a continuous function for the model, a curve fit of the computational data in Table 12.2 was made. As discussed in Section 12.4.4, the computational analysis of Hobbs *et al.* (1999) showed that the discretization error was less than 1% of the front velocity. In addition to the four computational values listed in Table 12.2, it was recommended that the model is linear for the lower ranges of temperature (Hobbs, 2003). As a result, a cubic spline curve fit was used to represent the model over the range of data.

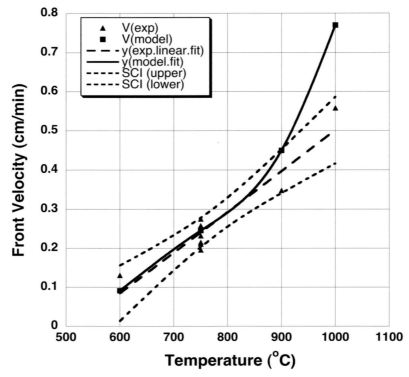

Figure 12.12 Estimated sample mean and simultaneous confidence intervals using linear regression for foam decomposition compared with the model prediction.

Figure 12.12 shows the comparison of the results for the linear regression of the experimental data, the Scheffé confidence intervals, and computational curve fit results. Two observations should be made from Figure 12.12. First, the linear regression of the experimental data seems to be a reasonably accurate representation of the data, noting that $R^2 = 0.895$. Second, the model falls within the confidence interval up to a temperature of roughly $850\,°C$ and then departs markedly from the experimental data.

Figure 12.13 shows the estimated model accuracy over the range of experimental data, as well as the simultaneous confidence intervals for the experimental data. As mentioned above, the calculation of a validation metric result focuses directly on the mismatch between computation and experiment. As a result, any weaknesses in the model or the experimental data are much more evident than the typical comparison, such as Figure 12.12. Also note in Figure 12.13 that the simultaneous confidence intervals are symmetric with respect to zero as a result of Eq. (12.31). The upper and lower simultaneous confidence intervals are a hyperbolic conic section centered on $\bar{x} = 0$ because of the form of Eq. (12.26). One can intuitively surmise that altering the values of temperature where data were obtained could significantly decrease the magnitude of the confidence intervals. It is left as an exercise to the reader to investigate an optimum set of temperatures that minimize the magnitude of

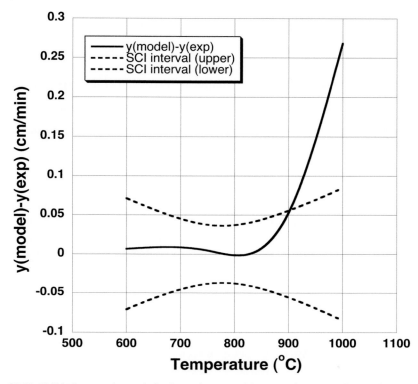

Figure 12.13 Validation metric result for foam decomposition over the range of operating conditions.

the confidence intervals, given the constraint of a fixed number of temperatures. This is the type of question that should be addressed early in the design of validation experiments.

Using Eqs. (12.19), (12.21), (12.34), and (12.35), the global validation metrics, along with their confidence indicators, can be computed as

average relative error $= 11.2\% \pm 22.7\%$ with 90% confidence,
maximum relative error $= 53.5\% \pm 16.9\%$ with 90% confidence.

Consider these global metrics as if viewing them from the perspective of not having examined the two previous graphs. For example, in a summary presentation to management, there might not be sufficient time to show the two previous graphs, so only the global metrics are given. The average relative error result is not particularly noteworthy, but it is seen that the average experimental uncertainty is roughly twice the average relative error. It is clear that the large experimental uncertainty prohibits any clear conclusions concerning the average model error. It is seen that the maximum relative error is a factor of 4.8 larger than the average relative error. When this occurs, it signals that there is a significant error in the trend of the model with respect to the trend in the experimental data. Since the relative experimental uncertainty is much smaller than the maximum relative error at that condition, one can be certain that there is an incorrect trend in the model. With this signal of a modeling problem, management may ask for more details concerning the issues involved.

12.7 Comparison of means requiring nonlinear regression of the experimental data

12.7.1 Construction of the nonlinear regression equation

Now consider the general case where we need to represent the estimated mean of the experimental data, $\bar{y}_e(x)$, as a general nonlinear regression function,

$$\bar{y}_e(x) = f(x; \vec{\theta}) + \varepsilon. \tag{12.36}$$

$f(x; \bullet)$ is the chosen form of the regression function over the range of the input parameter x; $\vec{\theta} = \theta_1, \theta_2, \ldots, \theta_p$ are the unknown coefficients of the regression function; and ε is the random measurement error. Using a least-squares fit of the experimental data, it can be shown (Draper and Smith, 1998; Seber and Wild, 2003) that the error sum of squares $S(\vec{\theta})$ in p-dimensional space is

$$S(\vec{\theta}) = \sum_{i=1}^{n} \left[y_e^i(x) - f(x_i; \vec{\theta}) \right]^2. \tag{12.37}$$

The vector that minimizes $S(\vec{\theta})$ is the solution vector, and it is written as $\vec{\hat{\theta}}$. This system of simultaneous, nonlinear equations can be solved by various software packages that compute solutions to the nonlinear least-squares problem. (See, for example, Press *et al.*, 2007.)

12.7.2 Computation of simultaneous confidence intervals for the metric

Draper and Smith (1998) and Seber and Wild (2003) discuss a number of methods for the computation of the confidence regions around the point $\vec{\hat{\theta}}$ in p-dimensional space. For any specified confidence level $100(1 - \alpha)\%$, a unique region envelops the point $\vec{\hat{\theta}}$. For two regression parameters, (θ_1, θ_2), we have a two-dimensional space, and these regions are contours that are similar to ellipses with a curved major axis. For three parameters, $(\theta_1, \theta_2, \theta_3)$, we have a three-dimensional space, and these regions are contours that are similar to bent ellipsoids, i.e., shaped like a banana. A procedure that appears to be the most robust to nonlinear features in the equations (Seber and Wild, 2003) and that is practical when p is not too large, is to solve an inequality for the set of $\vec{\theta}$:

$$\vec{\theta} \text{ such that } S(\vec{\theta}) \leq S(\vec{\hat{\theta}}) \left[1 + \frac{p}{n - p} F(p, n - p, 1 - \alpha) \right]. \tag{12.38}$$

In Eq. (12.38), $F(\nu_1, \nu_2, 1 - \alpha)$ is the F probability distribution; $\nu_1 = p, \nu_2 = n - p, 1 - \alpha$ is the quantile for the confidence interval of interest; and n is the number of experimental measurements.

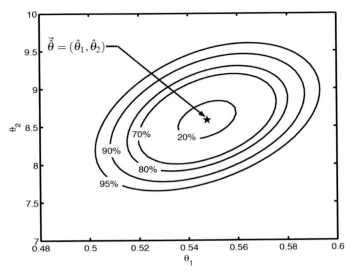

Figure 12.14 Example of various confidence regions for the case of two regression parameters (Oberkampf and Barone, 2004).

We consider a geometric interpretation of Eq. (12.38) to facilitate the numerical evaluation of the inequality. We seek the complete set of $\vec{\theta}$ values that satisfy the inequality. For a given confidence level α, the inequality describes the interior of a p-dimensional hyper-surface in $\vec{\theta}$ space. Thus, for $p = 2$, it describes a *confidence region* bounded by a closed contour in the parameter space (θ_1, θ_2). An example of a set of such contours is depicted in Figure 12.14. As the confidence level increases, the corresponding contours describe larger and larger regions about the least-squares parameter vector $\vec{\hat{\theta}}$.

The numerical algorithm recommended here discretizes the interior of the confidence region using several contour levels that lie within the highest confidence contour; for example, suppose we wish to calculate the 90% confidence interval given the confidence regions depicted in Figure 12.14. We would evaluate the regression equation at a number of points, say, 20, along the entire 90% contour. Then we would do the same along the 80% contour, the 70% contour, and so on down to the 10% contour. With all of these regression function evaluations, we would then be able to compute the maximum and minimum of the regression function over the range of the input parameter x. This would provide reasonably good coverage of the 90% confidence interval of the regression function. If more precision was needed, one could choose more function evaluations along each contour and compute each contour in 1% increments of the confidence level.

For a three-dimensional regression parameter space, slices can be taken along one dimension of the resulting three-dimensional surface, and each slice can be discretized in the manner described for the two-dimensional case. Generalizing to N dimensions, one may generate a recursive sequence of hypersurfaces of lower dimension until a series of two-dimensional regions are obtained and evaluation over all of the two-dimensional regions gives the desired envelope of regression curves.

To determine the upper and lower confidence intervals associated with the regression equation, Eq. (12.36), we use the solution to Eq. (12.38), i.e., all $\vec{\theta}$ lying within (and on) the desired contour. The confidence intervals are determined by computing the envelope of regression curves resulting from *all* $\vec{\theta}$ lying within the confidence region. If we think of the solution to Eq. (12.38) as given by a set of discrete vectors of $\vec{\theta}$, then we can substitute this set of parameter vectors into the regression equation, Eq. (12.36). For each element in this set of $\vec{\theta}$s, we obtain a specific regression function. If we evaluate the ensemble of all regression functions by using all of the $\vec{\theta}$s, we can compute the maximum value of the regression function, $y^+_{\text{CI}}(x)$, and the minimum value of the regression function, $y^-_{\text{CI}}(x)$, over the range of x. As a result, $y^+_{\text{CI}}(x)$ and $y^-_{\text{CI}}(x)$ define the upper and lower bounds on the confidence intervals, respectively, over the range of x. These confidence intervals need not be symmetric as they were for the interpolation and linear regression cases discussed earlier. One may ask why the regression function must be evaluated over the entire confidence region. This must be done because the nonlinear regression function can have maxima and minima *anywhere* within the confidence region.

12.7.3 Global metrics

If we would like to make a quantitative assessment of the global modeling error, the global metrics expressed in Eqs. (12.19) and (12.21) can still be used. However, the equations for the average relative confidence indicator and the maximum relative error metric, Eqs. (12.34) and (12.35), must be replaced because they are based on symmetric confidence intervals. Since we no longer have symmetric confidence intervals, we approximate these by computing the average half-width of the confidence interval over the range of the data and the half-width of the confidence interval at the maximum relative error, respectively. As a result, we now have

$$\left.\left|\frac{\text{CI}}{\bar{y}_e}\right|\right|_{\text{avg}} = \frac{1}{(x_u - x_l)} \int_{x_l}^{x_u} \left|\frac{y^+_{\text{CI}}(x) - y^-_{\text{CI}}(x)}{2\bar{y}_e(x)}\right| dx \qquad (12.39)$$

for the average relative confidence indicator. $y^+_{\text{CI}}(x)$ and $y^-_{\text{CI}}(x)$ are the upper and lower confidence intervals, respectively, as a function of x. As stated earlier, $|\text{CI}/\bar{y}_e|_{\text{avg}}$ provides a quantity with which to interpret the significance of the magnitude of $|\tilde{E}/\bar{y}_e|_{\text{avg}}$.

Also, we have

$$\left.\left|\frac{\text{CI}}{\bar{y}_e}\right|\right|_{\text{max}} = \left|\frac{y^+_{\text{CI}}(\hat{x}) - y^-_{\text{CI}}(\hat{x})}{2\bar{y}_e(\hat{x})}\right| \qquad (12.40)$$

for the half-width of the confidence interval associated with the maximum relative error metric $|\tilde{E}/\bar{y}_e|_{\text{max}}$. The maximum relative error point $\hat{x}$ is defined as the x value where

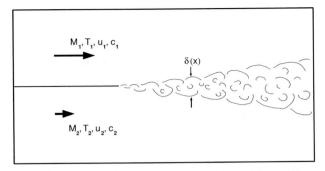

Figure 12.15 Flow configuration for the turbulent free shear layer (Oberkampf and Barone, 2004).

$|\tilde{E}/\bar{y}_e|$ achieves a maximum, that is,

$$\hat{x} = x \text{ such that } \left| \frac{y_m(x) - \bar{y}_e(x)}{\bar{y}_e(x)} \right| \text{ is a maximum for } x_l \le x \le x_u. \qquad (12.41)$$

12.7.4 Example problem: compressible turbulent mixing

The example chosen for the application of the nonlinear regression case is the prediction of compressibility effects on the growth rate of a turbulent free shear layer. An introduction to the problem is given, followed by a discussion of the available experimental data. Details of the model and verification of the numerical solutions are briefly described along with the validation metric results. Further details on this example can be found in Barone *et al.* (2006) and Oberkampf and Barone (2006).

12.7.4.1 Problem description

The planar free shear layer is a canonical turbulent flow and a good candidate for use in a unit-level validation study. Figure 12.15 shows the flowfield configuration in which a thin splitter plate separates two uniform streams (numbered 1 and 2) with different flow velocities and temperatures, but both at the same pressure. The two streams mix downstream of the splitter plate's trailing edge, forming the free shear layer within which momentum and energy are diffused. For a high-Reynolds-number flow, the boundary layers on both sides of the plate and the free shear layer are turbulent. In the absence of any applied pressure gradients or other external influences, the flowfield downstream of the trailing edge consists of a shear layer development region near the edge, followed by a similarity region. Within the development region, the shear layer adjusts from its initial velocity and temperature profiles inherited from the plate boundary layers. Further downstream in the similarity region, the shear layer thickness, $\delta(x)$, grows linearly with streamwise distance x, resulting in a constant value of $d\delta/dx$.

Of particular interest in high-speed vehicle applications is the behavior of the shear layer as the Mach number of one or both streams is increased. A widely accepted parameter correlating the shear layer growth rate with compressibility effects is the convective Mach number, M_c, for mixing two streams of the same gas (Bogdanoff, 1983). M_c is defined as

$$M_c = \frac{u_1 - u_2}{c_1 + c_2}, \qquad (12.42)$$

where u is the fluid velocity and c is the speed of sound. It has been found experimentally that an increase in the convective Mach number leads to a decrease in the shear layer growth rate for fixed velocity and temperature ratios of the streams. This is usually characterized by the compressibility factor Φ, which is defined as the ratio of the compressible growth rate to the incompressible growth rate at the same velocity and temperature ratios:

$$\Phi = \frac{(\mathrm{d}\delta/\mathrm{d}x)_c}{(\mathrm{d}\delta/\mathrm{d}x)_i}. \qquad (12.43)$$

12.7.4.2 Experimental data

Experimental data on high-speed shear layers are available from a number of independent sources. The total collection of experimental investigations employs a wide range of diagnostic techniques within many different facilities. Comparisons of data obtained over a range of convective Mach numbers from various experiments indicate significant scatter in the data. Recently, Barone *et al.* (2006) carefully re-examined the available data and produced a recommended data set that exhibits smaller scatter in the measurements.

The resulting ensemble of data from Bogdanoff (1983); Chinzei *et al.* (1986); Papamoschou and Roshko (1988); Dutton *et al.* (1990); Elliot and Samimy (1990); Samimy and Elliott (1990); Goebel and Dutton (1991); Debisschop and Bonnet (1993); Gruber *et al.* (1993); Debisschop *et al.* (1994); and Barre *et al.* (1997) is presented in Figure 12.16. The data are organized into groups of sources, some of which are themselves compilations of results from several experiments.

12.7.4.3 Mathematical model

The Favre-averaged compressible Navier–Stokes equations were solved using the standard $k - \varepsilon$ turbulence model (Wilcox, 2006). The low-Reynolds number modification to the $k - \varepsilon$ model of Nagano and Hishida (1987) was applied near the splitter plate. Most turbulence models in their original form do not correctly predict the significant decrease in shear layer growth rate with increasing convective Mach number, necessitating inclusion of a compressibility correction. Several compressibility corrections, derived from a variety of physical arguments, are widely used in contemporary computational fluid dynamics (CFD) codes. In this study, the dilatation-dissipation compressibility correction of Zeman (1990) was used.

The solutions were computed using the Sandia Advanced Code for Compressible Aerothermodynamics Research and Analysis (SACCARA) (Wong *et al.*, 1995a,b), which

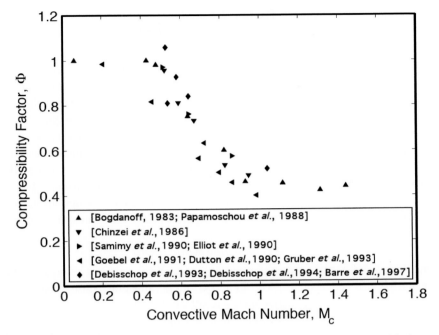

Figure 12.16 Experimental data for compressibility factor versus convective Mach number (Oberkampf and Barone, 2004).

employs a block-structured, finite volume discretization method. The numerical fluxes are constructed with the symmetric TVD scheme of Yee (1987), which gives a second-order convergence rate in smooth flow regions. The equations are advanced to a steady state using the LU-SGS scheme of Yoon and Jameson (1987). Solutions were considered iteratively converged when the L_2 norm of the momentum equation residuals had decreased by eight orders of magnitude. Numerical solutions were obtained over the convective Mach number range of the experimental data, from 0.1 to 1.5, in increments of 0.14.

For each convective Mach number, solutions were calculated on three meshes: coarse, medium, and fine. The meshes are uniform in the streamwise, or x, direction, and stretched in the cross-stream, or y, direction, so that mesh cells are clustered within the shear layer. The cells are highly clustered in the y direction near the trailing edge and become less clustered with increasing x to account for the shear layer growth. Richardson's extrapolation (Roache, 1998) was used to estimate the discretization error on $d\delta/dx$. The maximum error in the fine-mesh solution was estimated to be about 1% at $M_c = 0.1$ and about 0.1% at $M_c = 1.5$.

We defined δ using the velocity layer thickness definition. As mentioned previously, the thickness grows linearly with x only for large x due to the presence of the development region, which precedes the similarity region. Given that the growth rate approaches a constant value asymptotically, the thickness as a function of x is fitted with a curve that mimics this asymptotic character. The function used for the fit is

$$\delta(x) = \beta_0 + \beta_1 x + \beta_2 x^{-1}. \tag{12.44}$$

The coefficient β_1 is the fully developed shear layer growth rate as x becomes large.

Following extraction of the compressible growth rate, $(\mathrm{d}\delta/\mathrm{d}x)_{\mathrm{c}}$, the incompressible growth rate, $(\mathrm{d}\delta/\mathrm{d}x)_{\mathrm{i}}$, must be evaluated at the same velocity and temperature ratio. Incompressible or nearly incompressible results are difficult to obtain with a compressible CFD code. Therefore, the incompressible growth rate was obtained by computing a similarity solution for the given turbulence model and flow conditions. The similarity solution is derived by Wilcox (2006) in his turbulence modeling text and implemented in the MIXER code, which is distributed with the text. The similarity solution is computed using the same turbulence model as the Navier–Stokes calculations, but under the assumptions that (a) the effects of laminar viscosity are negligible, and (b) there exists a zero pressure gradient.

12.7.4.4 Validation metric results

The quantities δ and $\mathrm{d}\delta/\mathrm{d}x$ are post-processed from the finite-volume computational solution and the MIXER code, but the SRQ of interest for the validation metric is the compressibility factor Φ. Before the validation metric result can be computed, we must prescribe a form for the nonlinear regression function to represent the experimental data in Figure 12.16. It is important that the proper functional behavior of the data, established through theoretical derivation or experimental measurement, be reflected in the form of the regression function. For the compressible shear layer, we know that Φ must equal unity, by definition, in the incompressible limit $M_{\mathrm{c}} \to 0$. Experimental observations and physical arguments also suggest that $\Phi \to$ constant as M_{c} becomes large. These considerations lead to the following choice of the regression function, taken from Paciorri and Sabetta (2003):

$$\Phi = 1 + \hat{\theta}_1 \left(\frac{1}{1 + \hat{\theta}_2 M_{\mathrm{c}}^{\hat{\theta}_3}} - 1 \right). \tag{12.45}$$

Using Eq. (12.45) and the experimental data shown in Figure 12.16, we used the MATLAB (MathWorks, 2005) function *nlinfit* from the Statistics Toolbox, to calculate the following regression coefficients:

$$\hat{\theta}_1 = 0.5537, \qquad \hat{\theta}_2 = 31.79, \qquad \hat{\theta}_3 = 8.426. \tag{12.46}$$

We now compute the 90% confidence interval of the regression function in Eq. (12.45), with the $\vec{\theta}$ values given in Eq. (12.46) and the inequality constraint given by Eq. (12.38). We use the method outlined above to compute the 90% confidence region in the three-dimensional space described by θ_1, θ_2, and θ_3. The resulting confidence region, pictured in Figure 12.17, resembles a curved and flattened ellipsoid, especially for small values of θ_2. The elongated shape in the θ_2 direction indicates the low sensitivity of the curve fit to θ_2 relative to the other two regression parameters. Evaluation of the regression function Eq. (12.45) for all $\vec{\theta}$ lying within the 90% confidence region yields the desired simultaneous confidence intervals.

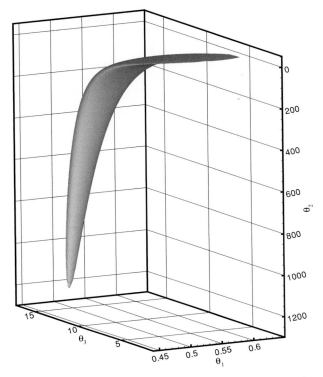

Figure 12.17 Three-dimensional 90% confidence region for the regression fit to the shear layer experimental data (Oberkampf and Barone, 2006).

Figure 12.18 shows the final result of the analysis in graphical form: a plot of the experimental data along with the regression fit, the 90% confidence intervals, and the computational simulation result. Concerning the error assessment of the $k - \varepsilon$ model, it is seen that the Zeman compressibility correction predicts a nearly linear dependence of the compressibility factor on M_c over the range $0.2 \leq M_c \leq 1.35$. One could claim that the trend is correct, i.e., the Zeman model predicts a significant decrease in the turbulent mixing as the convective Mach number increases; however, the Zeman model does not predict the nonlinear dependency on M_c. We did not compute any simulation results for $M_c > 1.5$ and, as a result, did not determine the asymptotic value of Φ for the Zeman compressibility correction. However, the solutions for $M_c = 1.36$ and $M_c = 1.50$ suggest that the asymptotic value is near $\Phi = 0.49$.

By noting the large width of the confidence intervals for large M_c in Figure 12.18, it is seen that the largest uncertainty in the experimental data occurs in this region. The parameter θ_1 in the regression function, Eq. (12.45), has the main influence on the size of the confidence intervals for large M_c. From the viewpoint of the design of needed validation experiments, one can conclude that future experiments should be conducted at higher convective Mach numbers to better determine the asymptotic value of Φ.

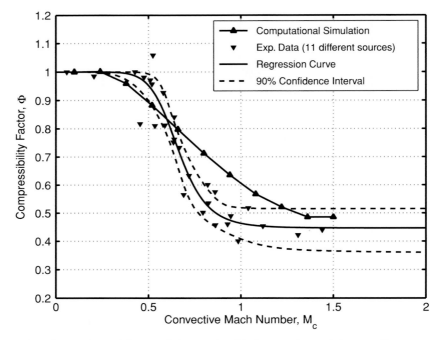

Figure 12.18 Comparison of the simulation result with the experimental data, nonlinear regression curve, and 90% simultaneous confidence interval (Oberkampf and Barone, 2006).

The estimated error, $\tilde{E}(x)$, of the model as a function of M_c is plotted in Figure 12.19 along with the 90% confidence interval from the experimental data. This plot presents the validation metric result, i.e., the difference between computation and the regression fit of the experimental data, along with the 90% confidence interval representing the uncertainty in the experimental data. As pointed out previously in the helium plume example, the validation metric critically examines both the model and the experimental data. With this plot, it is seen that there is a slight under-prediction of turbulent mixing in the range $0.3 \leq M_c \leq 0.6$ and a significant over-prediction of turbulent mixing in the range $0.7 \leq M_c \leq 1.3$. Examining an error plot such as this, one could conclude that the Zeman model does not capture the nonlinear trend of decreasing turbulent mixing with increasing convective Mach number. Whether the model accuracy is adequate for the requirements of the intended application is, of course, a completely separate issue.

Note that in Figure 12.19 the confidence intervals are not symmetric with respect to zero. In the case of nonlinear regression, Eq. (12.36), the nonlinear function need not possess any symmetry properties with respect to the regression parameters. Therefore, evaluation of the nonlinear function over the set of $\vec{\theta}$ satisfying Eq. (12.38) results in asymmetric confidence intervals over the range of the input parameter. For the shear layer example, Eq. (12.45) is evaluated over the volume of regression coefficients shown in Figure 12.17.

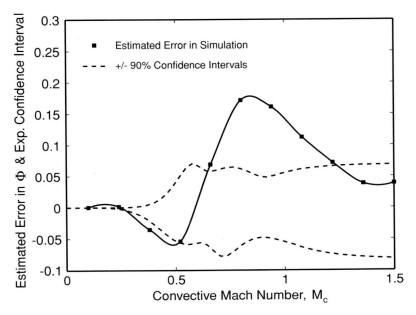

Figure 12.19 Validation metric result and 90% confidence interval for Φ (Oberkampf and Barone, 2006).

Using Eqs. (12.19), (12.21), (12.39), and (12.40), the global metric results for the $k - \varepsilon$ model with the Zeman compressibility correction over the range $0 \leq M_c \leq 1.5$ are as follows:

average relative error $= 13\% \pm 9\%$ with 90% confidence,
maximum relative error $= 35\% \pm 10\%$ with 90% confidence.

The average error of 13% seems reasonable, given Figure 12.18. As in the helium plume and the foam decomposition examples, we see a maximum error that is noticeably larger than the average error, i.e., roughly a factor of three. From Figure 12.19 it can be found that the maximum absolute error occurs at $M_c = 0.83$. The maximum relative error, however, occurs at $M_c = 0.88$. At this value of M_c, one determines that the 90% confidence interval is $\pm 10\%$.

12.7.5 Observations on the present approach

The validation metrics derived here are relatively easy to compute and interpret in practical engineering applications. When nonlinear regression functions are required for the metric, the nonlinear regression function requires a software package, such as Mathematica or MATLAB, to perform the computations. A software package called VALMET has recently been completed that computes the validation metrics described here for both the interpolation and regression case (Iuzzolino *et al.*, 2007). Experimental and computational data can be provided to VALMET in the form of Excel spreadsheets or text files. Either linear or spline interpolation can be used for both the experimental and computational data. For regression, fifteen different functional forms can be chosen, or user chosen functions can be programmed. The program can be run on a computer with an installed version of MATLAB, or as a stand-alone compiled code on a computer using Microsoft Windows® 2000/XP.

The interpretation of the present metrics in engineering decision making should be clear and understandable to a wide variety of technical staff (analysts, model builders, and experimentalists) and management. The metric result has the following form: estimated error of the model ± an interval that represents experimental uncertainty with specified confidence. The present metric only measures the mismatch between computational and experimental mean response of the system. The present metrics can be used to compare the modeling accuracy of different competing models, or they can help to assess the adequacy of the given model for an application of interest. It has been stressed that the manner in which the result of a validation metric relates to an application of interest is a separate and more complex issue, especially if there is significant extrapolation of the model.

The validation metrics presented here should apply to a wide variety of physical systems in engineering and science. If the SRQ is a complex time-varying quantity, then it may be possible to time average the quantity so that the present approach could be used. If the SRQ were a complex time series, such as modes in structural dynamics, then the present metrics would not be appropriate. If the response is mapped to the frequency domain, it may be possible to apply the method to the amplitudes and frequencies of the lower modes. In addition, the present metrics apply to single SRQs that are a function of a single input or control quantity. Extension of the method to multivariate analysis would require the incorporation of the correlation structure between the variables.

12.8 Validation metric for comparing p-boxes

When computational predictions are probability distributions, there is a great deal more information contained in how a system responds than compared to a simple deterministic response of a system. One can think of the model as a mapping of all uncertain inputs to produce a set of uncertain system responses. In this mapping, all of the uncertain inputs are convolved according to the physical processes described by the PDEs of interest. A validation metric could be viewed as asking the question: how well does the model map the inputs to the outputs, compared to the way that nature maps these?

The simplest method of comparing experimental data and predictions is in terms of their means, variances, covariances, and other distributional characteristics. The main limitation of approaches based on comparing summary statistics is that it considers only the central tendencies or other specific behaviors of data and predictions and not their entire distributions. When predictions are distributions, they contain a considerable amount of detail and it is not always easy to know what statistics are important for a particular application. While some statistical tests are certainly helpful in comparing experimental data and predictions, most do not directly address the validation metric perspective of interest here. In addition, traditional statistical tests, as well as the Bayesian approach to validation, do not address the issue of epistemic uncertainty in either, or both, the experimental data and the prediction. If epistemic uncertainty exists in either, we will consider the representation to be given by a p-box.

In the following section, we introduce the notion of comparing imprecise probabilistic quantities, including p-boxes; describe some of the desirable properties that a validation metric should have; and suggest a particular approach that has these properties. Several simple examples are given which display some of the features of this validation metric. This section is taken from Oberkampf and Ferson (2007); Ferson *et al.* (2008); and Ferson and Oberkampf (2009).

12.8.1 Traditional methods for comparing distributions

There are a variety of standard ways to compare random variables in probability theory. If random numbers X and Y always have the same value, the random variables are said to be "equal," or sometimes "surely equal." A much weaker notion of equality is useful in the construction of validation metrics because we are interested in comparing distributions, i.e., functions as opposed to numbers. If we can only say that the expectation, i.e., the mean, of the absolute values of the differences between X and Y is zero, the random variables are said to be "equal in mean." If X and Y are not quite equal in mean, we can measure their mismatch by defining the mean metric, d_{E}, as

$$d_{\mathrm{E}}(X, Y) = E(|X - Y|) \neq |E(X) - E(Y)|, \tag{12.47}$$

where E denotes the expectation operator. Note that this difference is not the same as the absolute value of the difference between the means. The idea can be generalized to higher-order moments, and equality in a higher-order moment implies equality in all lower-order moments.

The notion of equality for randomly varying quantities can be loosened further still by comparing only the *shapes* of the probability distributions of the random variables. Random variables whose distributions are identical are said to be "equal in distribution." This is often denoted as $X \sim Y$, or sometimes by $X =^{\mathrm{d}} Y$. This is really a rather loose kind of equality, because it does not require the individual values of X and Y to ever be equal, or even to ever be close. For instance, suppose X is normally distributed with mean zero and unit variance. If we let $Y = -X$, then X and Y are obviously equal in distribution, but are about as far from equality as can be imagined. Nevertheless, equality in distribution is an important concept because a distribution often represents all that is known about the values of a random variable.

If the distributions are not quite identical in shape, the discrepancy can be measured with many possible measures that have been proposed for various purposes. For instance, a very common such measure is the maximal probability, i.e., vertical, difference between the two cumulative distribution functions

$$d_S(X, Y) = \sup_z |\Pr(X \le z) - \Pr(Y \le z)|. \tag{12.48}$$

d_S is the *Smirnov metric*, and sup is the supremum over the sample space of X and Y. d_S
defines the Kolmogorov–Smirnov statistical test for comparing distributions (D'Agostino
and Stephens, 1986; Huber-Carol *et al.*, 2002; Mielke and Berry, 2007). One of the properties of the Smirnov distance is that it is symmetric, which is to say that $d_S(X, Y)$ always
equals $d_S(Y, X)$. The symmetry might be considered unnecessary or even counterintuitive as
a feature for validation. We do not view predictions and observations as exchangeable with
each other; in a validation metric it matters which is which. Suppose, for instance, that we
inadvertently switched the predicted distribution with the experimental data distribution.
One might expect to obtain a different result from having made such a mistake, but the
Smirnov distance does not change whether the prediction and data are exchanged or not.

The *Kullback–Leibler divergence* is another very widely used measure of the discrepancy
between distributions that is not symmetric (D'Agostino and Stephens, 1986; Huber-Carol
et al., 2002; Mielke and Berry, 2007). It is defined, in its discrete formulation, for a
probability mass function p for X and a probability mass function q for Y as

$$\sum_z p(z) \log_2 \frac{p(z)}{q(z)}, \tag{12.49}$$

where z takes on all values in the common range of X and Y. The p distribution summarizes
the observations and the q distribution summarizes the model prediction. The continuous
formulation is similar except that the summation is replaced by integration. The term
divergence in this metric may be misleading because this quantity has nothing to do with
notions of divergence familiar from calculus as the inner product of partial derivatives or
the flux per unit volume. Instead, the term is used here in its other meaning as deviation
from a standard. The Kullback–Leibler divergence is commonly used in information theory
and also in physics. It is interpreted as the relative entropy between p and q, i.e., the entropy
of the distribution p with respect to the distribution q.

As we have mentioned, there are, in fact, many other measures that could be used to
compare data and prediction distributions. But, given the broad acceptance and ubiquity
of the Smirnov and Kullback–Leibler measures in probability and physics, it is perhaps
necessary to explain why we simply don't use one of these as our validation metric. This
question is addressed in the next section.

12.8.2 *Method for comparing p-boxes*

12.8.2.1 *Discussion of p-boxes*

A validation metric was recently proposed by Oberkampf and Ferson (2007); Ferson *et al.*
(2008); and Ferson and Oberkampf (2009) to measure the mismatch between a prediction
and empirical observations. The prediction and the experimental measurements can both

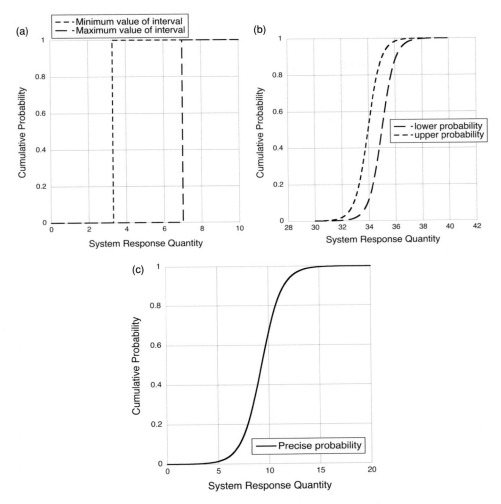

Figure 12.20 p-boxes for varying degrees of aleatory and epistemic uncertainty.
(a) p-box for purely epistemic uncertainty.
(b) p-box for a mixture of aleatory and epistemic uncertainty.
(c) Degenerate p-box for purely aleatory uncertainty.

be given by a p-box. A p-box expresses both epistemic and aleatory uncertainty in a way that does not confound the two. For a more complete discussion of p-boxes, see Ferson (2002); Ferson *et al.* (2003, 2004); Kriegler and Held (2005); Aughenbaugh and Paredis (2006); and Baudrit and Dubois (2006).

Figure 12.20 shows examples of three p-boxes with varying degrees of aleatory and epistemic uncertainty for a predicted SRQ. Figure 12.20a shows a p-box for an interval, i.e., there is no aleatory uncertainty and there is purely epistemic uncertainty. For values of the SRQ less than the minimum value of the interval, the cumulative probability is zero.

That is, there is certainty that all possible values of the SRQ are greater than the minimum value of the interval. For values of the SRQ over the range of the interval, the cumulative probability is in the interval [0, 1]. This interval-valued probability is, of course, a nearly vacuous statement in the sense that the SRQ probability could be *anything* over the range of zero to unity. For values of the SRQ greater than the maximum value of the interval, the cumulative probability is unity. That is, there is certainty that all possible values of the SRQ are less than or equal to the maximum value of the interval.

Figure 12.20b shows a p-box for a mixture of aleatory and epistemic uncertainty in the SRQ. The p-box shows the fraction, expressed as interval-valued quantity, of the sampled population that would have a value less than, or equal to, a particular value of the SRQ. Some examples are (a) for an SRQ = 32, the fraction of the population that would have a value of 32 or less would be in the range [0.0, 0.02], and (b) for an SRQ = 34, the fraction of the population that would have a value of 34 or less would be in the range [0.1, 0.5]. The interval-valued fraction is due to lack of knowledge from any source in the simulation. As is typical of a mixture of aleatory and epistemic uncertainty, the range of the interval-valued probability approaches zero for rare events of small values of the SRQ, and rare events of large values of the SRQ. It should also be noted that the horizontal breadth of the p-box expresses the magnitude of the epistemic uncertainty in terms of the SRQ, and the slope of the p-box expresses the magnitude of the aleatory uncertainty.

Figure 12.20c shows a degenerate p-box, i.e., a precise CDF, for the SRQ. The p-box is degenerate in the sense that the epistemic uncertainty is very small, or zero, compared to the aleatory uncertainty. Precise probabilities are, of course, the foundation of traditional probability theory and its application. p-boxes are also referred to as imprecise probabilities because the probability is not necessarily a unique quantity, but can be interval valued. During the last few decades, extensions of traditional probability theory have identified a number of types of imprecise probability; i.e., more complex than the p-box discussed here. For a discussion of these extensions, some recent texts are Walley (1991); Dubois and Prade (2000); Nguyen and Walker (2000); Molchanov (2005); and Klir (2006).

12.8.2.2 *Validation metric for p-boxes*

Any nondeterministic prediction from the model can always be characterized as a cumulative distribution function $F(x)$. In this notation, x is the predicted variable, i.e., the SRQ. The observation(s), on the other hand, are usually provided as a collection of point values in a data set. The distribution function for a data set, which is referred to as an empirical distribution function (EDF), summarizes the data set as a function suitable for graphical representation. It is a function that maps x to the probability scale on the interval [0, 1]. It is constructed as a non-decreasing step function with a constant vertical step size of $1/n$, where n is the sample size of the data set. The locations of the steps correspond to the values of the data points. Such a distribution for data $x_i, i = 1, \ldots, n$, is

$$S_n(x) = \frac{1}{n} \sum_{i=1}^{n} I(x_i, x),$$

(12.50)

where

$$I(x_i, x) = \begin{cases} 1, & x_i \leq x, \\ 0, & x_i > x. \end{cases} \tag{12.51}$$

$S_n(x)$ is simply the fraction of data values in the data set that are at or below each value of x.

An EDF is an advantageous representation, as opposed to a continuous CDF, because it is an exact representation of the distribution of the data, regardless of the amount of data. In addition, an EDF does not require any assumptions to represent the data, for example, as is required to construct a histogram of the data set. An EDF preserves the statistical information in the data set about its central tendency or location, its dispersion or scatter, and, in fact, all other statistical features of the distribution. The only information in the original data set that is not in the distribution is the order in which the values were originally given, which is meaningless whenever the data were sampled at random. When the data set consists of a single value, then the S_n function is a simple spike at the location along the x-axis given by that value; that is, it is zero for all x less than that value and one for all x larger than that value. For graphical clarity, however, it becomes convenient not to depict these flat portions at zero and one when the functions are plotted.

We propose the use of the Minkowski L_1 metric as a validation metric and we will refer to it as the *area metric*. It is defined as the *area* between the prediction distribution F and the data distribution S_n as the measure of the mismatch between them. Mathematically, the area between the curves is the integral of the absolute value of the difference between the functions

$$d(F, S_n) = \int_{-\infty}^{\infty} |F(x) - S_n(x)| \, dx. \tag{12.52}$$

It is clear geometrically that this quantity is also equal to the average horizontal difference between the two functions, $\int |F^{-1}(p) - S_n(p)^{-1}| dp$, but this is not the same as the average of the absolute differences between *random values* from these two distributions. (Such an average would not be zero if the distributions were coincident.) The area metric is thus a function of the shapes of the distributions, but is not readily interpretable as a function of the underlying random variables. The area measures the *disagreement* between theory and empirical evidence, as opposed to measuring the agreement. It is a metric so long as the integral exists.

It should be stressed that since this mismatch measure is always positive, it should *not* be interpreted in the same way as the common definition for error,

$$\varepsilon = y_{\text{obtained}} - y_T, \tag{12.53}$$

where ε is the error in the quantity y_{obtained} and y_T is the true value of y. For example, we contrast the mismatch measure defined in Eq. (12.52) with the error measure associated with the confidence interval approach, Eq. (12.8). In the confidence interval approach,

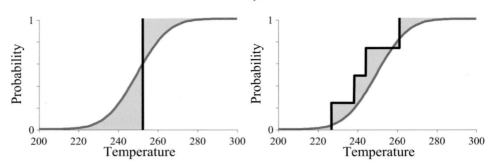

Figure 12.21 Example data sets, with $n = 1$ on the left and $n = 4$ on the right, shown as S_n distributions (black) against a prediction distribution (smooth). The validation metric is the areas (shaded) between the prediction distribution and the two data sets (Ferson *et al.*, 2008).

$\tilde{E} > 0$ meant the model prediction was greater than the experimental measurement. For the area metric there is no such indication of how the model differs from the measurement.

Figure 12.21 illustrates this area measure of mismatch for two data sets against a prediction distribution of temperature, which represents an arbitrary SRQ. The prediction distribution, shown as the smooth curve, is the same in both graphs. This prediction distribution might be obtained by propagating input uncertainties through a mathematical model by using a large number of samples from a Monte Carlo simulation. Superimposed on these graphs are distribution functions S_n for two hypothetical data sets. On the left graph, the data set consists of the single value $252\,°C$, and on the right, the data set consists of the values $\{226, 238, 244, 261\}$. In complex engineering systems it is not uncommon to have only one experimental test of the complete system. In such cases, the empirical distributions are not complex step functions, but instead single-step spikes representing point values (i.e., degenerate distributions). Note that the empirical distribution function is zero for all values smaller than the minimum of the data and unity for all values larger than the maximum of the data. Likewise, beyond the range (support) of the prediction distribution, the value of $F(x)$ is either zero or one extending to infinity in both directions. For graphical clarity, however, these flat portions at probability zero or unity are not depicted when the distributions are plotted.

The areas measuring the mismatches between the prediction and the two data sets in Figure 12.21 are shaded. In the left graph, the area consists of a region to the left of the datum at 252, and a region to right of it. In the right graph, there are four shaded regions composing the total area between the prediction distribution and the data distribution. The area metric is a generalization of the deterministic comparisons between scalar values that have no uncertainty. That is, if the prediction and the observation are both scalar point values, the area is simply equal to their difference. It is clear that the area metric reflects the difference between the full distribution of both the prediction and the observations. However, the area will tend not to be sensitive to minor discrepancies in the distribution tails because there is little probability mass in the tails of the distributions.

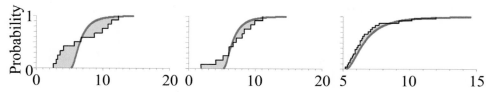

Figure 12.22 Examples of mismatch between a prediction distribution (smooth) and different empirical data sets (steps) (Ferson *et al.*, 2008).

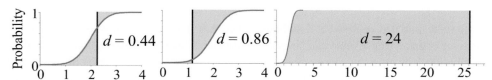

Figure 12.23 Comparisons of a prediction distribution (smooth) with three different data points (spikes) (Ferson *et al.*, 2008).

Figure 12.22 shows how the area metric differs from a validation metric based on merely matching in the mean or matching in both the mean and variance. In each of three cases, the prediction distribution is shown as a smooth curve. It is the same in all three graphs, although the scale in the third graph is a bit different from the other two. The step functions represent three different data sets as empirical distribution functions S_n. In the leftmost graph, the prediction distribution and the observed data have the same mean. But, otherwise, the data look rather different from the prediction; the data appear to be mostly in two clusters on either side of the mean. Indeed, so long as the average of the data balances at that mean, those data clusters could be arbitrarily far away from each other. Any validation measure based only on the mean would not detect any discrepancy between the theory and the data, even though the data might bear utterly no resemblance to the prediction, apart from their matching in the mean. In the middle graph, both the mean and the variance of the observed data and the theoretical prediction match. However, one would not claim the comparison between prediction and data were extremely good because of how the prediction deviates from the left tail of the empirical distribution. Smaller values are more prevalent in the real data than were predicted. In the third graph, the agreement between the prediction and the data is good overall. This is reflected in the smallness of the area between the prediction distribution and the data distribution. The only way for the area to be small is for the two distributions to match closely over the entire range of each. In each of these cases, the overall mismatch can be measured by the area between the two curves. It measures disagreements that the lower-order moments like the mean and variance cannot address.

Figure 12.23 shows how the area metric d varies with different values for a single datum matched against a prediction distribution. In these three examples, the prediction distribution

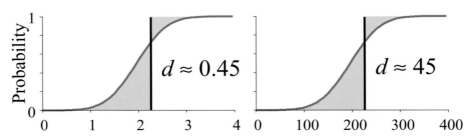

Figure 12.24 Further examples showing the metric's dependence on the scale (Ferson *et al.*, 2008).

is the same, and it is centered at 2 and ranges between 0 and 4. The most important thing to notice is that a single value can never perfectly match the entire distribution, unless that distribution is itself a degenerate point value. The first and second graphs of the figure compare the prediction distribution to a single observation at 2.25 and 1.18, respectively, yielding corresponding values for the area metric of 0.44 and 0.86. About the best possible match that a single datum could have occurs when the datum is located at the distribution's median, but, even there, the area metric will often be significant. In the case of the prediction distribution depicted in Figure 12.23, the area metric will be smallest when the observation is 2, which yields a value of 0.4 for the metric.

If, for example, the prediction distribution in Figure 12.23 were a uniform probability density function over the range $[a, b]$, a single observation can't be any "closer" to it than $(b - a)/4$, which is the value of the area metric if the point is at the median. That's the best match possible with a single data point. Stated differently, the mismatch between theory and experiment *could* be much better if more experimental measurements were available, but, due to sampling error in the experiment, it is the smallest mismatch that can exist. How *bad* could the match be? The match could be very bad; indeed, it can be bad to an arbitrarily large degree. The rightmost graph in Figure 12.23 shows another example of a single datum compared to the same prediction distribution. In this case, the data point is at 26, which means that it is about 24 units away from the distribution. The area metric can be arbitrarily large, and it reduces to the simple difference between the datum and the prediction when both are point values. Because probability is dimensionless, the units of the area are always the same as the units of the abscissa.

The area metric depends on the scale in which the prediction distribution and data are expressed. The two graphs in Figure 12.24 depict a pair of comparisons in which the corresponding shapes are identical but the scales are different, as though the left graph were expressed in meters and the right graph in centimeters. Although the shapes are the same, the area metric is different by 100 fold. It would, of course, be possible to normalize the area measure, perhaps by dividing it by the standard deviation of the prediction distribution, but we do not believe this would be a good idea because the result would no longer be expressed in the physical units of the abscissa. Such normalization would destroy the *physical meaning* of the metric.

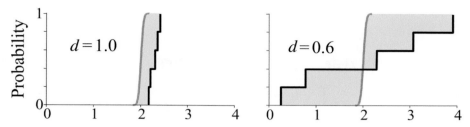

Figure 12.25 Why physical units are important for a validation metric (Ferson *et al.*, 2008).

Figure 12.25 illustrates why retaining the scale and physical units (degrees, meters, newtons, newtons/m², etc.) of the data is important for the intuitive appeal of a validation metric. The two graphs are drawn with the same *x*-axis, and they depict the same prediction distribution as a gray curve concentrated around 2. Two data sets are summarized as the S_n distributions shown as black step functions on the graphs. From a statistical perspective it might be argued that the comparison in the right graph reveals a better match between the theory and the data than the comparison in the left graph. In the left graph, the two distributions do not even overlap, whereas in the right graph the distributions at least overlap and are similar in their means. Using a traditional Kolmogorov–Smirnov test for differences between the two distributions, one would find statistically significant evidence that the distributions in the left graph are different ($d_S = 1.0$, $n = 5$, $p < 0.05$), but would *fail* to find such evidence for the distributions in the right graph ($d_S = 0.6$, $n = 5$, $p > 0.05$). But this is not at all how engineers and analysts would understand these two comparisons. For engineers and scientists, the main focus is on the difference between the two distributions, in units along the *x*-axis. In this sense, the comparison on the left is a much better match between theory and data than the comparison on the right. Engineers and scientists have a strong intuition that the data–theory comparison on the left might be attributed to a small bias error in the theory or the data, but the theory does a good job of capturing the variability of the physics. The discrepancy on the left is never larger than half a unit along the *x*-axis, whereas the discrepancy on the right could be larger than two units. It's this physical distance measuring the theory–data disagreement that really matters to engineers and analysts, not some arcane distance measured in terms of a probability. This is the reason why the validation metric should be expressed in the original units, as is the case for the area metric.

Finally, consider the behavior of the area metric as theory and evidence diverge further and further. Figure 12.26 shows two graphs, each with a prediction distribution drawn in gray and data distribution drawn in black. The traditional and commonly used Smirnov's distance (which is the maximum vertical distance between the two distributions) cannot distinguish between these two comparisons. The maximal vertical distance in both cases is just unity, so the distributions are both as far apart as they can be according to the Smirnov metric. Under this measure, each data distribution is simply "far" from its prediction distribution. The area metric, on the other hand, is about 2 for the left graph and about 40

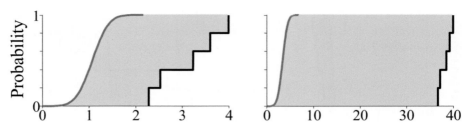

Figure 12.26 Distinguishing nonoverlapping data and prediction distributions (Ferson *et al.*, 2008).

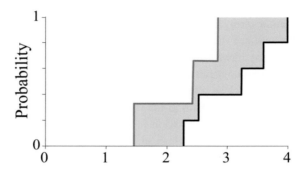

Figure 12.27 The area metric when the prediction distribution (gray) is characterized by only three simulations (Ferson *et al.*, 2008).

for the right graph. The area metric therefore identifies the left graph as having considerably more concordance between data and prediction than the right graph. If the criterion for an acceptably accurate prediction is that it is within 10 units of the actual data, then it might be that the prediction in the left graph is acceptable for the intended purpose, even though the prediction in this case does not overlap with the data. Likewise, given the same accuracy requirement, the prediction in the right graph is not acceptable for the intended use.

    The area metric proposed here is applicable even when the predictions are sparse. Suppose, for instance, that it is practical to compute only a small number of simulations of a complex model to produce a handful of quantitative predictions. Although these computed results cannot produce the smooth prediction distributions shown earlier, it may be reasonable to consider the values computed to be *samples* from that smooth distribution. If they are random samples (as they would be if inputs are selected randomly), then the "empirical" distribution function formed from these values is an unbiased nonparametric estimator of the true distribution that would emerge with asymptotically many runs.

    Figure 12.27 illustrates the idea of constructing S_n functions for both data and predictions, the latter being the values from the sample runs of the model. In this case, there were only three simulations of the model conducted, whose values are random samples from the underlying distributions of the input. They are to be compared against a data set consisting of five values. Having very few simulation runs really means that analysts can construct only a vague picture of what the model is actually predicting. This implies the prediction will have substantial epistemic uncertainty arising from sampling error. When only a few random samples are available from either the model or the measurements, the area metric could actually be *much smaller* if a larger number of samples were available. As a result, the present area metric should be viewed as the *evidence for the mismatch between the model and the measurements*, instead of the evidence for matching.

12.8.3 Pooling incomparable CDFs

12.8.3.1 u-pooling

The previous section described how several observations of a physical process can be collected into an empirical distribution S_n for comparison against a single prediction distribution. In practice, however, a model is often used to make several *different* predictions. For instance, a heating model might be used to predict the time-dependent temperature at a given location on an object. At one point in time, we have one predicted distribution of temperatures representing uncertainty about temperature then, and at another point in time, the predicted temperature distribution is different. Sometimes a model makes predictions about multiple SRQs. For instance, a single model might predict temperature, but also electrical resistivity and material stress. This would imply that we would have multiple values of the validation metric to compute. One could certainly compute all the areas separately for each pair of prediction distribution and its observation(s). Even if the data relate to a single SRQ, it would be improper to pool all of them into an empirical distribution function if they are to be compared against different prediction distributions. Each datum must be compared to the prediction distribution to which it corresponds.

A strategy was recently introduced, referred to as *u*-pooling, to deal with this situation (Oberkampf and Ferson, 2007; Ferson *et al.*, 2008). Multiple system response quantities, even if they are physically unrelated physical quantities, are combined by converting them to a universal scale via probability transformations. This strategy allows us to pool fundamentally incomparable data in terms of the relevance of each datum as evidence about the model's mismatch with experimental data. It also allows us to quantitatively answer questions like "Is the mismatch for temperature similar to the mismatch for material stress?"

To determine whether the data are generally drawn from distributions that are the same as their corresponding prediction distributions, a strategy must overcome the problem of incomparability among data and express the conformance of theory and data on some universal scale. Probability is an appropriate scale for this purpose for probabilistic models. Each datum x_i is transformed by the prediction distribution F_i with which it corresponds to obtain a variate $u_i = F_i(x_i)$ on the universal probability scale, which ranges on the unit interval [0, 1]. Figure 12.28 shows such transformations for three hypothetical cases. Each case is a pair of an observation depicted as a spike, i.e., single measurement, and its corresponding prediction distribution shown as a smooth curve. The prediction for the first graph is an exponential distribution on a temperature scale. In the middle graph, it is a roughly normal distribution on a scale measuring resistivity in ohms. The third graph

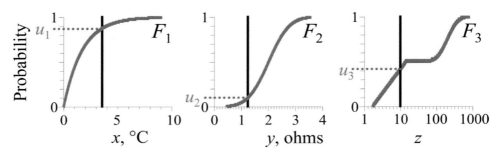

Figure 12.28 Translation of single observations (spikes) through prediction distributions (smooth) to a probability scale (ordinates) from three dimensionally inconsistent scales (abscissas) (Oberkampf and Ferson, 2007).

depicts an unusual distribution of a dimensionless quantity z. The intersections of the spikes and their respective distribution functions identify values on the probability scale for each u-value. The prediction distributions F_i can be any shape at all, and they need not be the same for different observations. The u-values are always defined because $F(x) = 1$ for any value of x larger than the largest value in the distribution, and $F(x) = 0$ for any value smaller than the smallest value in the distribution.

The various resulting u-values produced by these transformations can then be pooled to obtain an *overall* summary metric for the mismatch of the model's predictions to the data, even when the various individual comparisons are in different dimensions. Under the assumption that the x_i are distributed according to their respective distributions F_i, these u_i will have a uniform distribution on [0, 1]. This fact is called the *probability integral transform theorem* in statistics (Angus, 1994). This is what it means for a random variable to be "distributed according" to a distribution. The converse of this fact is perhaps more familiar to engineers and scientists because it is often used to generate random deviates from any specified probability distribution: given a distribution F and a uniform random value u between zero and one, the value $F^{-1}(u)$ will be a random variable distributed according to F. Conversely, as is needed here, if x is distributed according to F, then $u = F(x)$ is distributed according to a uniform distribution over [0, 1]. None of this changes if there happen to be multiple x- and u-values and, in fact, none of it changes if there are multiple distribution functions so long as the x-values are properly matched with their respective distributions. Each u-value tells how the datum from which it was derived compares to its prediction distribution. The x-values are made into compatible u-values by this transformation.

Because all the u-values are randomly and uniformly distributed over the same range, pooling them together yields a set of values that are randomly and uniformly distributed over that range. If, however, we find that the u_i are not distributed according to the uniform distribution over [0, 1], then we can infer that the x observations must *not* have been distributed according to their prediction distribution functions.

In principle, the area metric can be applied directly to a pooling of all of the u-values. They would be collected into an empirical distribution function S_n that would be compared

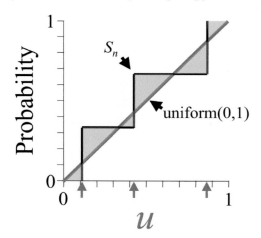

Figure 12.29 Comparison of three pooled u-values (black step function) against the standard uniform distribution (45° line).

against the standard uniform distribution, which is the prediction for all the u-values. Because both the standard uniform distribution and an empirical distribution function of the transformed values are constrained to the unit square (i.e., zero to one for cumulative probability and zero to one for the universal scale of the u-values), the largest possible value of the area metric is 0.5. This is the largest discrepancy between the 45° line of the uniform distribution and any distribution whose range is limited to the interval [0, 1]. The smallest possible discrepancy is zero, which would correspond to the empirical distribution function being identical to the standard uniform distribution. This would occur if and only if: (a) the data points are indeed distributed according to their respective predictions, and (b) there are sufficient data so that their step function S_n approaches the continuous uniform distribution. Such a value for the validation metric would be strong evidence that there is little mismatch between the model and the measurements.

Figure 12.29 shows an example application of the area metric comparing the u-values from Figure 12.28, which have been synthesized into the black three-step empirical distribution function S_n, against the standard uniform distribution depicted as the diagonal line. The shaded region between the two functions has an area of about 0.1. The distribution of pooled u-values can be studied to infer characteristics of the overall match between the x-values and their respective prediction distributions. For instance, the area metric can be applied directly to the u-values compared against the standard uniform distribution. Also, the model's mismatch for different predictions, generated from their particular observations, can also be compared to each other. This would allow one to conclude that, for example, a model predicts well for, say, high temperatures but not for low temperatures. The reason this is possible is that we have transformed all the observations into the same universal probability scale for the comparisons.

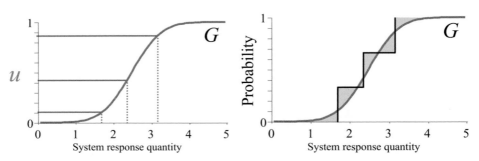

Figure 12.30 Back-transformation from the u-scale to an archetypical scale determined by a distribution G (left) and the area metric for the pooled back-transformed values against the G distribution (right) (Oberkampf and Ferson, 2007).

Transforming the observations into a universal probability scale is useful for aggregating incomparable data and comparing evidence collected in incommensurable dimensions, but, by itself, it has the disadvantage of abandoning the original physical units of the comparisons and retreating to a bounded metric constrained to the range [0, 0.5]. The deficiency can be repaired by back-transforming the u-values through a suitable distribution function G that restores the units, scale, and their interpretation to the u-values. The area metric can then be computed in the physically meaningful units after this back-transformation. The justification for this transformation back to SRQs can certainly be questioned for the case where the back-transform u-values were pooled from evidence expressed in different SRQs. However, back-transformation seems very defensible for pooling of the same SRQ that was predicted and measured for different times in a time-dependent simulation, or different spatial locations over the domain of the PDEs.

Figure 12.30 shows how this would work for the three u-values considered in the previous two figures. The result in the right graph is the area between the distribution G and a data distribution of back-transformed data values,

$$y_i = G^{-1}(u_i) = G^{-1}(F_i(x_i)). \tag{12.54}$$

All of these y_i have the same units, which are inherited from G. This back-transformation, and any physical meaning associated with the units it reattaches to the u-values, depends on the specification of the G distribution. The right graph in Figure 12.30 also shows, with shading, the area metric between the back-transformed y_i and the prediction distribution G. This metric is in the physically meaningful units as a result of the back-transformation.

What distribution should be used to define the back-transformation? In some cases, the scientific or application context of the model accuracy assessment will specify the distribution to use for the back-transformation. This is the distribution, after all, that spells out *where* we are specifically interested in the model's predictive capability. Using the specified prediction distribution as the G distribution allows all the available observations germane to *any* predictions made by the model to be used to characterize the uncertainty about this most important prediction. In general, one would want to use a distribution that expresses where the interest in the model's predictive capability lays. This might be the prediction distribution associated with the prediction that is most important in some sense. Specifying some *G* distribution to use as the back-transformation allows all the available observations germane to any predictions made by the model to be used to characterize the uncertainty about this most important prediction.

In validation activities for which there is no particular application requirement, there are many choices for the back-transformation distribution available to an analyst, and almost any choice one might make could yield reasonable results. For instance, the back-transformation *G* depicted in Figure 12.30 yields a value for the area metric of almost 0.3 units. Had we instead used a uniform distribution for *G* ranging, say, from 0 to 100 seconds, the corresponding shaded area would have the same shape as that shown in Figure 12.29, but it would have an area of about 10 units. If the *G* were an exponential distribution, the back-transformation would emphasize deviations in the right tail of the distribution. Naturally, different *G* distributions will express the mismatch of the data to the model in different units. But being able to express the error in different units is exactly what we want to be able to do whenever we extrapolate forecasts from models.

We note that *u*-pooling is not the only possible way to obtain an overall validation measure for data observations that address different prediction distributions. An obvious alternative is to use a multi-variate approach to the problem of validation. Such an approach could take account of any dependence information there might be in the data when different SRQs are measured simultaneously. If, for example, large deviations in temperature are typically associated with large deviations in resistivity, the correlation may be relevant to a multi-variate assessment of validation. Of course, any advantage would be at the cost of an increase in methodological complexity.

12.8.3.2 Statistical significance of a metric

As mentioned earlier, the proposed validation metric can be viewed as the evidence for mismatch between measurements and predictions. The question arises: "Is the magnitude of the metric primarily due to model error, or is it primarily due to limited samples of either or both the measurements or the predictions?" Consider, for instance, two situations. In the first, experimental observations have been exhaustively collected so that there is essentially no sampling uncertainty about the data distribution, and likewise the function evaluations are cheap so the prediction can also be specified without any sampling uncertainty. Suppose that we compute the validation metric in this situation to be $d = 1$. In the second situation, we compute the validation metric to be $d = 10$, but it is based on a very small sample size of empirical observations, or a small number of function evaluations, or both. In the first situation, the disparity between the predictions and the data is statistically significant in the sense that it cannot be explained by randomness arising from the sampling uncertainty (because there is none), but must rather be due to inaccuracies in the model. In the second situation, however, it is not clear that the disagreement between the predictions and the data is significant, even though it is ten times larger. The computed discrepancy might be entirely due to the vagaries of random chance that were at play when the observations and function evaluations were made. Some kind of statistical analysis is required to give a *context* for these two *d* values to understand when a value is statistically significant. Note that here we are only discussing statistical significance of the computed *d* values, *not* the model accuracy requirement for an intended use that was discussed in Figure 12.4.

We suggest that statistical methods to detect evidence of significant mismatch between a model and its validation data can be constructed by applying standard statistical tests to the *u*-values or the *y*-values derived in the previous section. These methods can be used by an analyst to formally justify an impression or conclusion that the experimental observations disagree with the model's predictions. Transforming the *x*-values to *u*-values and pooling all the *u*-values together can substantially increase the power of the statistical test because the sample size is larger in a single, synthetic analysis. That is, *u*-pooling is a powerful tool to reduce sampling uncertainty even if it is applied to multiple measurements of the *same* SRQ.

Standard statistical tests for departures from uniformity, such as the traditional Kolmogorov–Smirnov test (D'Agostino and Stephens, 1986; Mielke and Berry, 2007), applied to the *u*-values can identify significant overall failure of the model's predictive capability. This test assumes that the experimental data values are *independent* of one another, which is not always true in practice, especially when observations have been collected for a single SRQ as a function of time. There are other statistical tests that can be applied in this situation, including the traditional chi-squared test and Neyman's smooth tests (D'Agostino and Stephens, 1986; Rayner and Rayner, 2001). The test can also be applied to compare the y_i values against the predicted distribution *G* in the physically meaningful scale. One could also define statistical tests of whether the discrepancy between data and theory is larger than some threshold size. Providing a statistical significance indicator with the validation metric result would provide the analyst, and the decision maker using the results, more information concerning model accuracy assessment. This addition would be in the same vein as the information provided by the confidence interval associated with the comparison of means approach discussed earlier in this chapter.

12.8.4 Inconsistency between experimental and simulation CDFs

The technique of *u*-pooling to synthesize data corresponding to different prediction distributions has a technical limitation that is important to address (Oberkampf and Ferson, 2007). If a prediction distribution is bounded and a datum falls completely outside its range, the prediction is asserting that the datum is impossible. That is, the datum's value is in a region the prediction characterizes as having zero probability density. This is not a problem if all the data are in the same units because we can simply use the mixture S_n to pool the data as described above, but if we need *u*-pooling to transform them to a common scale, then all values outside the range of the prediction distribution are transformed to zero or one (depending on whether they are below or above the range). This means that values just outside the range are considered to be the same as those very far outside the range.

Consequently, we would not be penalizing the model enough for any experimental data values that are far afield from the prediction distribution.

There are two ways to react to the situation of a prediction saying some of the data are impossible. We could conclude that the model is patently false and not bother with trying to compute any validation metric to describe its performance with respect to the data. This would, in essence, remand the problem back to the modeler who would need to develop a more reasonable model. While this might be an entirely appropriate reaction in many cases, it is perhaps not the most helpful reaction. We think that a practically robust approach to validation would tolerate very large discrepancies, even when they amount to a logical contradiction between data and prediction. The whole point of validation is to assess the performance of a model's predictive accuracy. One obvious way in which it might be wrong is if it claims that some observations are impossible, when they are not. Such a failure should be duly cataloged and appropriately incorporated into the calculation of the validation metric. Of course, data are not immune from imperfection themselves. If perchance the contradiction arises because of outlier or otherwise erroneous measurements rather than flaws in the model, then the remedy would not be a better model. In either of these cases, it would be reasonable to have some way to finesse impossibility and still make the validation metric calculation in a reasonable way.

There are different possible cases of impossibility in an attempted comparison of a model and data. Is the datum outside the prediction's range, but just outside? Is it many units away from the largest or smallest values characterized as possible? Is it orders of magnitude away? Clearly, this degree of mismatch, whatever it is, could be quantified by a reasonably designed validation metric. This section describes a strategy for designing such a metric. Although it might at first seem ad hoc, it addresses the underlying problem of large disagreements in an effective way with minimal assumptions needed to resolve them.

The robust validation metric we seek will somehow preserve *how far away* the datum is from the prediction range. The computational problem that prevents this occurs in the mapping of the data to their u-values. If the distribution function is infinite in both directions, then the impossibility situation will never occur, and the mapping from the data to their u-values is always defined in a natural way. If, however, the predicted range is bounded, then there can be data values x for which $F(x)$ is not defined or is defined trivially to be zero or one. In such cases, we should like to define an *extended function* F^* to use to make u-values. There are many ways to form a suitable extended function F^* from a probability distribution. F^* should be a left-continuous (but not necessarily differentiable) and monotonically increasing combination of three functions:

$$F^*(x) = \begin{cases} F^<(x), & x < \max F^{-1}(0), \\ F(x), & \max F^{-1}(0) \leq x \leq \min F^{-1}(1), \\ F^>(x), & \min F^{-1}(1) < x, \end{cases} \quad (12.55)$$

where $F^<$ and $F^>$ are extrapolation mappings chosen in some way that captures how far away "impossible" data are.

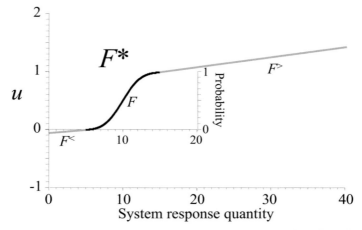

Figure 12.31 An extended function F^*, consisting of a distribution function F (black) and extensions $F^<$ and $F^>$ (gray) to the left and right respectively.

Figure 12.31 gives an example of an extended function for a triangular distribution ranging over the interval [5, 15]. The extension mappings might be chosen by the validation analyst, or perhaps by the modeler or by some agreement between them. They might be constructed as lines whose slopes are functions of the standard deviation or interquartile range of the prediction distribution, as exemplified in the figure, or they might be more complicated nonlinear functions. The sole purpose of these mappings is to quantify the degree of the mismatch between the data and the predicted distribution in regions where the distribution itself no longer quantifies that disagreement. It is proper that these extensions are defined in an ad hoc way for a particular application whenever analysts want to accommodate the influence of the impossibility on the validation metric.

Alternatively, the extensions can be simply defined as relocated 45° lines:

$$F^<(x) = x - \max F^{-1}(0) \tag{12.56}$$

and

$$F^>(x) = x - \min F^{-1}(1) + 1. \tag{12.57}$$

In addition to being objective, these definitions have the advantage of preserving the dimensional units of the x-axis.

We emphasize that the extended function F^* encodes a distribution function, but it is not a probability distribution itself. F^* can have values less than zero and larger than one, so it is certainly no distribution function. It is merely an artifice that will allow us to quantify the extreme disagreement between a prediction distribution and data that would be considered impossible by that distribution.

Extended functions allow arbitrary data values to be translated into extended u-values and pooled into a common scale. These extended u-values range on the reals rather than only on

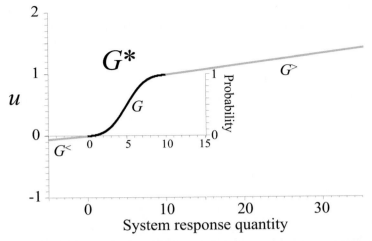

Figure 12.32 An extended back-transformation function G^*, consisting of a distribution function G (black) and extensions $G^<$ and $G^>$ (gray) on the left and right.

the unit interval [0, 1]. The back-transformation distribution can similarly be extended to a G^* function such as shown in Figure 12.32 to accept these u-values with values below zero or above one. This extension of the distribution function G in Figure 12.30 parallels the extension of F in Figure 12.31. This simple maneuver of extending the F and G distributions allows values considered impossible by a particular prediction to be represented, combined with other predictions and re-expressed on a common scale for calculation of a general validation metric. It can be used to combine comparisons made against bounded prediction distributions with comparisons made against prediction distributions that are infinite.

The impossibility issue does not arise when prediction distributions are infinite in both directions, like normal distributions. But of course, in practice, many prediction distributions are bounded. For instance, Weibull, exponential, and Poisson distributions cannot be negative; and beta, binomial, uniform, and triangular distributions are constrained to a range bounded above and below. If the prediction distribution is computed by Monte Carlo simulation, its range will be bounded in both directions. Even seemingly trivial bounds can lead to the problem identified here when data contain experimental uncertainties. For instance, slight leaks in a fluid transfer system composed of tubing can lead to a measurement of fluid mass that would appear to be impossible. Likewise, unsuspected addition or loss of heat in an assumed adiabatic system could lead to unrealistic measurements of thermal conductivity.

Clearly, the selection of the G distribution is subjective. Another significant limitation of the approach outlined in this section is that it does not seem applicable when the back-transformation is based on a G distribution that already has infinite tails such as a normal distribution. If any of the prediction distributions had to be extended, there will be some u-values outside the range [0, 1]. Back-transforming these values will require inverting an extended function G^* that can accept values outside [0, 1], otherwise, the back-transformed values will be undefined, or located at either plus or minus infinity. If any back-transformed values are placed at plus or minus infinity, the resulting value of the area metric will of course be infinite.

12.8.5 Dealing with epistemic uncertainty in the comparisons

12.8.5.1 Epistemic uncertainty in the prediction and measurements

As discussed in Chapters 10 and 11, high-quality validation experiments should minimize, if not eliminate, epistemic uncertainties in the input quantities for the model. There are a number of situations, however, in which it cannot be avoided. Some examples are (a) the experiment was not conducted as a high quality validation experiment so that several important inputs were not measured; (b) information concerning certain inputs was measured, but it was not documented; (c) certain input quantities were quantified as interval-valued quantities based on expert opinion; and (d) the experimentalist never expected that the fidelity of physics models would be developed to the point that extremely detailed information would be needed as input data in the future. For most of these situations, the unknown information should be treated as a lack of knowledge, i.e., as an epistemic uncertainty, in the prediction.

For many of these situations, the lack of knowledge of input data needed for simulations should be represented as an interval. Giving an interval as the representation of an estimated quantity is asserting that the value (or values) of the quantity lie somewhere within the interval. Note that the interval-valued quantity can be used to represent an uncertain input quantity, or it can be used to represent the uncertainty in a parameter in a parameterized family of probability distributions. In the latter case, the uncertain quantity would be a mixture of aleatory and epistemic uncertainty that would be represented as a p-box. As discussed earlier, when these intervals, precise probability distributions, and/or p-boxes, are propagated through the model, the model prediction is a p-box for the SRQ of interest. An example of such a p-box was shown in Figure 12.20b.

Empirical observations can also contain epistemic uncertainty. A number of examples of where these occur in experimental measurements were discussed in Section 12.3.4. Again, the simplest form of this is an interval. When a collection of such intervals comprise a data set, one can think of the breadth of each interval as representing epistemic uncertainty while the scatter among the intervals represents aleatory uncertainty. Recent reviews (Manski, 2003; Gioia and Lauro, 2005; Ferson *et al.*, 2007) have described how interval uncertainty in data sets also produce p-boxes. When empirical observations have uncertainty of this form that is too large to simply ignore, these elementary techniques can be used to characterize it in a straightforward way.

12.8.5.2 Epistemic and aleatory uncertainty in the metric

The comparison between two fixed real numbers reduces to the scalar difference between the two. Suppose that, instead of both being scalar numbers, at least one of them is an interval range representing an epistemic uncertainty. If the prediction and the observation overlap, then we should say that the prediction is *correct*, in a specific sense, relative to the

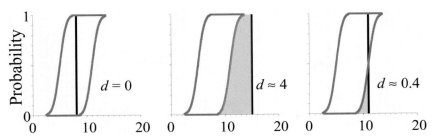

Figure 12.33 Comparison of a prediction characterized as p-boxes (smooth bounds) against three separate single observations (black spikes).

observation. If the prediction is an interval, this means that the model, for whatever reason, is making a weaker claim about what is being predicted. For example, the assertion that some system component will record a maximum operating temperature between 400 and 800 °C is a much weaker claim than saying it will be exactly 600 °C. It is also a stronger claim than saying the temperature will be between 200 and 1200 °C. In the extreme case, a prediction with extraordinarily large bounds, while not very useful, is certainly true, if just because it isn't claiming anything that might be false. For example, predicting that some probability will be between zero and one doesn't require any foresight, but at least it is free from contradiction. It is proper that a prediction's express uncertainty be counted toward reducing any measure of mismatch between theory and data in this way because the model is admitting doubt. If it were not so, an uncertainty analysis could otherwise have no epistemological value. From the perspective of validation, when the uncertainty of prediction encompasses the actual observation, there is *no evidence* of mismatch because *accuracy is distinct from precision*. Both are important in determining the usefulness of a model, but it is reasonable to distinguish them and give credit where it is due.

A reciprocal consideration applies, by the same token, if the datum is an interval to be compared against a prediction that's a real number. If the datum is an interval, and the prediction falls within the measured interval, there is no evidence of mismatch between the two. For instance, if the prediction is, say, 30% and the observation tells us that it was measured to be somewhere between 20% and 50%, then we would have to admit that the prediction might be perfectly correct. If on the other hand the evidence was that it was between 35% and 75%, then we would have to say that the disagreement between the prediction and the observation might be as low as 5%. We could also be interested in how bad the comparison might be, but a validation metric should not penalize the model for the empiricist's imprecision. In most conceptions of the word, the "distance" between two things is the length of the shortest path between them. Thus, the validation metric between a point prediction and an interval datum is the shortest difference between the characterizations of the quantities.

Figure 12.33 gives three examples of how a single point observation might compare with a prediction that is expressed as a p-box. The prediction is the same in all three graphs and is shown as smooth bounds representing the p-box for some SRQ. Against this prediction, a single observation is to be compared, and the area between this datum and the prediction

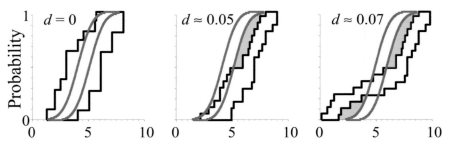

Figure 12.34 Three comparisons of predictions (smooth bounds) against empirical observations (black step function bounds), both containing aleatory and epistemic uncertainty.

is shaded. In the leftmost graph, the datum happens to fall entirely inside the bounds on the prediction. The comparison in this graph evidences no discrepancy at all between the datum and the uncertain prediction. At this value of x, the spike fits entirely inside the graph of the p-box, which tells us that a (degenerate) point distribution at 8 is perfectly consistent with the predictions made by the model. Thus, the area between the datum and the prediction is zero, i.e., there is no evidence for mismatch. In contrast, the data value at 15 in the middle graph is completely outside the range of either bounding distribution. The area between 15 and the prediction is about 4 units, which is the area between the spike and the right bound of the p-box. In the rightmost graph, the observation is located at the intermediate value of 11, which is within the range of the right bound of the prediction distribution. The area of mismatch in this case is only about 0.4 because the area only includes the small shaded region between 9 and 11. These comparisons are qualitatively unlike those between a scalar observation and a well-specified probability distribution. We see now that a single observation *can* perfectly match a prediction so long as the prediction has epistemic uncertainty.

Figure 12.34 illustrates three more examples, this time with epistemic uncertainty in both the prediction (shown as smooth lines) and the data (black step functions). The leftmost comparison has a distance of zero because there is at least one distribution from the prediction that can be drawn simultaneously inside both empirical distribution functions from the measurements. The area of mismatch exists only when there are no possible probability distributions that lie within both the bounds on the prediction distribution and the bounds on the data distribution. For instance, there is no such distribution consistent with both data and prediction in the middle or rightmost graph.

It should be noted that the area between the prediction and data no longer constitutes a true mathematical metric when at least one is an interval or a p-box. The reason is that the area can fall to zero without the prediction and data becoming identical (as in the leftmost graph of Figure 12.34), which violates the identity-of-indiscernibles property of a true metric. There may be ways to generalize the area metric from probability distributions to p-boxes that are mathematical metrics. However, these have not yet been developed.

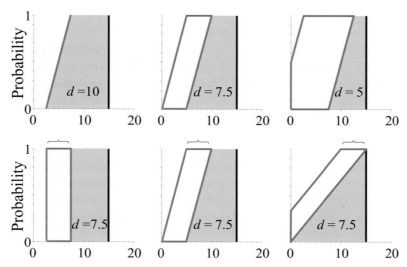

Figure 12.35 Increasing epistemic uncertainty (breadth) of predictions in the top panel and increasing variance (slant) of predictions in the lower panel.

In the cases just discussed in Figure 12.33 and Figure 12.34, the shaded regions indicate the mismatch. The validation metric now is defined by the integral

$$\int_{-\infty}^{\infty} \Delta([F_R(x),\, F_L(x)],\, [S_{nR}(x),\, S_{nL}(x)])\, dx, \qquad (12.58)$$

where F and S_n denote the prediction and the data distributions, respectively. The subscripts L and R denote the left and right bounds for those distributions, and

$$\Delta(A,\, B) = \min_{\substack{a \in A \\ b \in B}} |a - b| \qquad (12.59)$$

is the shortest distance between two intervals, or zero if the intervals touch or overlap. This measure integrates the regions of nonoverlap between the two sets of bounds, for every value along the probability axis. This validation metric accepting epistemic uncertainty in either, or both, the model and the measurements is still the measure of mismatch between the model and the measurements.

Figure 12.35 illustrates another feature of this approach to assessing mismatch between prediction and measurement. As before, predictions are shown in gray and the datum is a black spike. Increasing the *breadth* of an uncertain prediction so that it possesses larger epistemic uncertainty and wider bounds can result in lowering the mismatch between the theory and data, as illustrated in the upper panel of three graphs. This breadth is a measure of the epistemic uncertainty in the prediction. It is not the same as the dispersion or variance of a distribution, which measures aleatory uncertainty. In contrast, the lower panel of three graphs in the figure shows that increasing variance in the prediction – reflected in the *slant* of the p-box – does *not* by itself reduce the mismatch.

These behaviors of the area distinguish it from another commonly used measure of disagreement between a data value and a probability distribution expressed as the datum's displacement in standard deviation units. That measure would suggest that the three graphs in the lower panel of Figure 12.35 depict increasing agreement because the datum is progressively closer to the prediction in terms of standard deviation units. This contrast suggests that accounting for epistemic uncertainty of predictions and observations with p-boxes and measuring their mismatch as the area between those p-boxes is quite different from the common statistical idea of measuring the disagreement as displacement in standard deviation units. We think that our approach has the distinct advantage of distinguishing between aleatory and epistemic uncertainties. These uncertainties are confounded by the validation metric based on displacement in standard deviation units. For example, although the displacement decreases in the three lower graphs of Figure 12.35, the differences between small realizations from the prediction in the rightmost graph on the lower panel are necessarily larger than the corresponding difference in the graphs on the left.

12.9 References

Almond, R. G. (1995). *Graphical Belief Modeling*. 1st edn., London, Chapman & Hall.

Anderson, M. C., T. K. Hasselman, and T. G. Carne (1999). Model correlation and updating of a nonlinear finite element model using crush test data. *17th International Modal Analysis Conference (IMAC) on Modal Analysis*, Paper No. 376, Kissimmee, FL, Proceedings of the Society of Photo-Optical Instrumentation Engineers, 1511–1517.

Angus, J. E. (1994). The probability integral transform and related results. *SIAM Review*. **36**(4), 652–654.

Aster, R., B. Borchers, and C. Thurber (2005). *Parameter Estimation and Inverse Problems*, Burlington, MA, Elsevier Academic Press.

Aughenbaugh, J. M. and C. J. J. Paredis (2006). The value of using imprecise probabilities in engineering design. *Journal of Mechanical Design*. **128**, 969–979.

Babuska, I., F. Nobile, and R. Tempone (2008). A systematic approach to model validation based on bayesian updates and prediction related rejection criteria. *Computer Methods in Applied Mechanics and Engineering*. **197**(29–32), 2517–2539.

Bae, H.-R., R. V. Grandhi, and R. A. Canfield (2006). Sensitivity analysis of structural response uncertainty propagation using evidence theory. *Structural and Multidisciplinary Optimization*. **31**(4), 270–279.

Barone, M. F., W. L. Oberkampf, and F. G. Blottner (2006). Validation case study: prediction of compressible turbulent mixing layer growth rate. *AIAA Journal*. **44**(7), 1488–1497.

Barre, S., P. Braud, O. Chambres, and J. P. Bonnet (1997). Influence of inlet pressure conditions on supersonic turbulent mixing layers. *Experimental Thermal and Fluid Science*. **14**(1), 68–74.

Baudrit, C. and D. Dubois (2006). Practical representations of incomplete probabilistic knowledge. *Computational Statistics and Data Analysis*. **51**, 86–108.

Bayarri, M. J., J. O. Berger, R. Paulo, J. Sacks, J. A. Cafeo, J. Cavendish, C. H. Lin, and J. Tu (2007). A framework for validation of computer models. *Technometrics*. **49**(2), 138–154.

Bedford, T. and R. Cooke (2001). *Probabilistic Risk Analysis: Foundations and Methods*, Cambridge, UK, Cambridge University Press.

Bernardo, J. M. and A. F. M. Smith (1994). *Bayesian Theory*, New York, John Wiley.

Bogdanoff, D. W. (1983). Compressibility effects in turbulent shear layers. *AIAA Journal*. **21**(6), 926–927.

Box, E. P. and N. R. Draper (1987). *Empirical Model-Building and Response Surfaces*, New York, John Wiley.

Chen, W., L. Baghdasaryan, T. Buranathiti, and J. Cao (2004). Model validation via uncertainty propagation. *AIAA Journal*. **42**(7), 1406–1415.

Chen, W., Y. Xiong, K.-L. Tsui, and S. Wang (2006). Some metrics and a Bayesian procedure for validating predictive models in engineering design. *ASME 2006 International Design Engineering Technical Conferences and Computers and Information in Engineering Conference*, Philadelphia, PA.

Chen, W., Y. Xiong, K.-L. Tsui, and S. Wang (2008). A design-driven validation approach using bayesian prediction models. *Journal of Mechanical Design*. **130**(2).

Chinzei, N., G. Masuya, T. Komuro, A. Murakami, and K. Kudou (1986). Spreading of two-stream supersonic turbulent mixing layers. *Physics of Fluids*. **29**(5), 1345–1347.

Coleman, H. W. and W. G. Steele, Jr. (1999). *Experimentation and Uncertainty Analysis for Engineers*. 2nd edn., New York, John Wiley.

Coleman, H. W. and F. Stern (1997). Uncertainties and CFD code validation. *Journal of Fluids Engineering*. **119**, 795–803.

Crassidis, J. L. and J. L. Junkins (2004). *Optimal Estimation of Dynamics Systems*, Boca Raton, FL, Chapman & Hall/CRC Press.

D'Agostino, R. B. and M. A. Stephens, eds. (1986). *Goodness-of-Fit-Techniques*. New York, Marcel Dekker.

Debisschop, J. R. and J. P. Bonnet (1993). Mean and fluctuating velocity measurements in supersonic mixing layers. In *Engineering Turbulence Modeling and Experiments 2: Proceedings of the Second International Symposium on Engineering Turbulence Modeling and Measurement*. W. Rodi and F. Martelli (eds. New York, Elsevier.

Debisschop, J. R., O. Chambers, and J. P. Bonnet (1994). Velocity-field characteristics in supersonic mixing layers. *Experimental Thermal and Fluid Science*. **9**(2), 147–155.

DesJardin, P. E., T. J. O'Hern, and S. R. Tieszen (2004). Large eddy simulation of experimental measurements of the near-field of a large turbulent helium plume. *Physics of Fluids*. **16**(6), 1866–1883.

DeVolder, B., J. Glimm, J. W. Grove, Y. Kang, Y. Lee, K. Pao, D. H. Sharp, and K. Ye (2002). Uncertainty quantification for multiscale simulations. *Journal of Fluids Engineering*. **124**(1), 29–41.

Devore, J. L. (2007). *Probability and Statistics for Engineers and the Sciences*. 7th edn., Pacific Grove, CA, Duxbury.

Dowding, K. J., R. G. Hills, I. Leslie, M. Pilch, B. M. Rutherford, and M. L. Hobbs (2004). *Case Study for Model Validation: Assessing a Model for Thermal Decomposition of Polyurethane Foam*. SAND2004–3632, Albuquerque, NM, Sandia National Laboratories.

Dowding, K. J., J. R. Red-Horse, T. L. Paez, I. M. Babuska, R. G. Hills, and R. Tempone (2008). Editorial: Validation challenge workshop summary. *Computer Methods in Applied Mechanics and Engineering*. **197**(29–32), 2381–2384.

Draper, N. R. and H. Smith (1998). *Applied Regression Analysis*. 3rd edn., New York, John Wiley.

Drosg, M. (2007). *Dealing with Uncertainties: a Guide to Error Analysis*, Berlin, Springer-Verlag.

Dubois, D. and H. Prade, eds. (2000). *Fundamentals of Fuzzy Sets*. Boston, MA, Kluwer Academic Publishers.

Dutton, J. C., R. F. Burr, S. G. Goebel, and N. L. Messersmith (1990). Compressibility and mixing in turbulent free shear layers. *12th Symposium on Turbulence*, Rolla, MO, University of Missouri-Rolla, A22–1 to A22–12.

Easterling, R. G. (2001). *Measuring the Predictive Capability of Computational Models: Principles and Methods, Issues and Illustrations*. SAND2001–0243, Albuquerque, NM, Sandia National Laboratories.

Easterling, R. G. (2003). *Statistical Foundations for Model Validation: Two Papers*. SAND2003–0287, Albuquerque, NM, Sandia National Laboratories.

Elliot, G. S. and M. Samimy (1990). Compressibility effects in free shear layers. *Physics of Fluids A*. **2**(7), 1231–1240.

Ferson, S. (2002). *RAMAS Risk Calc 4.0 Software: Risk Assessment with Uncertain Numbers*. Setauket, NY, Applied Biomathematics.

Ferson, S. and W. L. Oberkampf (2009). Validation of imprecise probability models. *International Journal of Reliability and Safety*. **3**(1–3), 3–22.

Ferson, S., V. Kreinovich, L. Ginzburg, D. S. Myers, and K. Sentz (2003). *Constructing Probability Boxes and Dempster-Shafer Structures*. SAND2003–4015, Albuquerque, NM, Sandia National Laboratories.

Ferson, S., R. B. Nelsen, J. Hajagos, D. J. Berleant, J. Zhang, W. T. Tucker, L. R. Ginzburg, and W. L. Oberkampf (2004). *Dependence in Probabilistic Modeling, Dempster-Shafer Theory, and Probability Bounds Analysis*. SAND2004–3072, Albuquerque, NM, Sandia National Laboratories.

Ferson, S., V. Kreinovich, H. Hajagos, W. L. Oberkampf, and L. Ginzburg (2007). *Experimental Uncertainty Estimation and Statistics for Data Having Interval Uncertainty*. Albuquerque, Sandia National Laboratories.

Ferson, S., W. L. Oberkampf, and L. Ginzburg (2008). Model validation and predictive capability for the thermal challenge problem. *Computer Methods in Applied Mechanics and Engineering*. **197**, 2408–2430.

Fetz, T., M. Oberguggenberger, and S. Pittschmann (2000). Applications of possibility and evidence theory in civil engineering. *International Journal of Uncertainty*. **8**(3), 295–309.

Gartling, D. K., R. E. Hogan, and M. W. Glass (1994). *Coyote – a Finite Element Computer Program for Nonlinear Heat Conduction Problems, Part I – Theoretical Background*. SAND94–1173, Albuquerque, NM, Sandia National Laboratories.

Geers, T. L. (1984). An objective error measure for the comparison of calculated and measured transient response histories. *The Shock and Vibration Bulletin*. **54**(2), 99–107.

Gelman, A. B., J. S. Carlin, H. S. Stern, and D. B. Rubin (1995). *Bayesian Data Analysis*, London, Chapman & Hall.

Ghosh, J. K., M. Delampady, and T. Samanta (2006). *An Introduction to Bayesian Analysis: Theory and Methods*, Berlin, Springer-Verlag.

Giaquinta, M. and G. Modica (2007). *Mathematical Analysis: Linear and Metric Structures and Continuity*, Boston, Birkhauser.

Gioia, F. and C. N. Lauro (2005). Basic statistical methods for interval data. *Statistica Applicata.* **17**(1), 75–104.

Goebel, S. G. and J. C. Dutton (1991). Experimental study of compressible turbulent mixing layers. *AIAA Journal.* **29**(4), 538–546.

Grabe, M. (2005). *Measurement Uncertainties in Science and Technology*, Berlin, Springer-Verlag.

Gruber, M. R., N. L. Messersmith, and J. C. Dutton (1993). Three-dimensional velocity field in a compressible mixing layer. *AIAA Journal.* **31**(11), 2061–2067.

Haldar, A. and S. Mahadevan (2000). *Probability, Reliability, and Statistical Methods in Engineering Design*, New York, John Wiley.

Hanson, K. M. (1999). A framework for assessing uncertainties in simulation predictions. *Physica D.* **133**, 179–188.

Hasselman, T. K., G. W. Wathugala, and J. Crawford (2002). A hierarchical approach for model validation and uncertainty quantification. *Fifth World Congress on Computational Mechanics*, wccm.tuwien.ac.at, Vienna, Austria, Vienna University of Technology.

Hazelrigg, G. A. (2003). Thoughts on model validation for engineering design. *ASME 2003 Design Engineering Technical Conference and Computers and and Information in Engineering Conference*, DETC2003/DTM-48632, Chicago, IL, ASME.

Helton, J. C., J. D. Johnson, and W. L. Oberkampf (2004). An exploration of alternative approaches to the representation of uncertainty in model predictions. *Reliability Engineering and System Safety.* **85**(1–3), 39–71.

Helton, J. C., W. L. Oberkampf, and J. D. Johnson (2005). Competing failure risk analysis using evidence theory. *Risk Analysis.* **25**(4), 973–995.

Higdon, D., M. Kennedy, J. Cavendish, J. Cafeo and R. D. Ryne (2004). Combining field observations and simulations for calibration and prediction. *SIAM Journal of Scientific Computing.* **26**, 448–466.

Higdon, D., C. Nakhleh, J. Gattiker, and B. Williams (2009). A Bayesian calibration approach to the thermal problem. *Computer Methods in Applied Mechanics and Engineering.* In press.

Hills, R. G. (2006). Model validation: model parameter and measurement uncertainty. *Journal of Heat Transfer.* **128**(4), 339–351.

Hills, R. G. and I. Leslie (2003). *Statistical Validation of Engineering and Scientific Models: Validation Experiments to Application.* SAND2003–0706, Albuquerque, NM, Sandia National Laboratories.

Hills, R. G. and T. G. Trucano (2002). *Statistical Validation of Engineering and Scientific Models: a Maximum Likelihood Based Metric.* SAND2001–1783, Albuquerque, NM, Sandia National Laboratories.

Hobbs, M. L. (2003). Personal communication.

Hobbs, M. L., K. L. Erickson, and T. Y. Chu (1999). *Modeling Decomposition of Unconfined Rigid Polyurethane Foam.* SAND99–2758, Albuquerque, NM, Sandia National Laboratories.

Huber-Carol, C., N. Balakrishnan, M. Nikulin, and M. Mesbah, eds. (2002). *Goodness-of-Fit Tests and Model Validity.* Boston, Birkhauser.

ISO (1995). *Guide to the Expression of Uncertainty in Measurement.* Geneva, Switzerland, International Organization for Standardization.

Iuzzolino, H. J., W. L. Oberkampf, M. F. Barone, and A. P. Gilkey (2007). *User's Manual for VALMET: Validation Metric Estimator Program.* SAND2007–6641, Albuquerque, NM, Sandia National Laboratories.

Kennedy, M. C. and A. O'Hagan (2001). Bayesian calibration of computer models. *Journal of the Royal Statistical Society Series B – Statistical Methodology.* **63**(3), 425–450.

Klir, G. J. (2006). *Uncertainty and Information: Foundations of Generalized Information Theory*, Hoboken, NJ, Wiley Interscience.

Klir, G. J. and M. J. Wierman (1998). *Uncertainty-Based Information: Elements of Generalized Information Theory*, Heidelberg, Physica-Verlag.

Kohlas, J. and P.-A. Monney (1995). *A Mathematical Theory of Hints – an Approach to the Dempster-Shafer Theory of Evidence*, Berlin, Springer-Verlag.

Krause, P. and D. Clark (1993). *Representing Uncertain Knowledge: an Artificial Intelligence Approach*, Dordrecht, The Netherlands, Kluwer Academic Publishers.

Kriegler, E. and H. Held (2005). Utilizing belief functions for the estimation of future climate change. *International Journal for Approximate Reasoning.* **39**, 185–209.

Law, A. M. (2006). *Simulation Modeling and Analysis*. 4th edn., New York, McGraw-Hill.

Lehmann, E. L. and J. P. Romano (2005). *Testing Statistical Hypotheses*. 3rd edn., Berlin, Springer-Verlag.

Leonard, T. and J. S. J. Hsu (1999). *Bayesian Methods: an Analysis for Statisticians and Interdisciplinary Researchers*, Cambridge, UK, Cambridge University Press.

Liu, F., M. J. Bayarri, J. O. Berger, R. Paulo, and J. Sacks (2009). A Bayesian analysis of the thermal challenge problem. *Computer Methods in Applied Mechanics and Engineering.* **197**(29–32), 2457–2466.

Manski, C. F. (2003). *Partial Identification of Probability Distributions*, New York, Springer-Verlag.

MathWorks (2005). *MATLAB*. Natick, MA, The MathWorks, Inc.

McFarland, J. and S. Mahadevan (2008). Multivariate significance testing and model calibration under uncertainty. *Computer Methods in Applied Mechanics and Engineering.* **197**(29–32), 2467–2479.

Mielke, P. W. and K. J. Berry (2007). *Permutation Methods: a Distance Function Approach*. 2nd edn., Berlin, Springer-Verlag.

Miller, R. G. (1981). *Simultaneous Statistical Inference*. 2nd edn., New York, Springer-Verlag.

Molchanov, I. (2005). *Theory of Random Sets*, London, Springer-Verlag.

Nagano, Y. and M. Hishida (1987). Improved form of the k-epsilon model for wall turbulent shear flows. *Journal of Fluids Engineering.* **109**(2), 156–160.

Nguyen, H. T. and E. A. Walker (2000). *A First Course in Fuzzy Logic*. 2nd edn., Cleveland, OH, Chapman & Hall/CRC.

Oberkampf, W. L. and M. F. Barone (2004). Measures of agreement between computation and experiment: validation metrics. *34th AIAA Fluid Dynamics Conference*, AIAA Paper 2004–2626, Portland, OR, American Institute of Aeronautics and Astronautics.

Oberkampf, W. L. and M. F. Barone (2006). Measures of agreement between computation and experiment: validation metrics. *Journal of Computational Physics.* **217**(1), 5–36.

Oberkampf, W. L. and S. Ferson (2007). Model validation under both aleatory and epistemic uncertainty. *NATO/RTO Symposium on Computational Uncertainty in Military Vehicle Design*, AVT-147/RSY-022, Athens, Greece, NATO.

Oberkampf, W. L. and J. C. Helton (2005). Evidence theory for engineering applications. In *Engineering Design Reliability Handbook*. E. Nikolaidis, D. M. Ghiocel and S. Singhal (eds.). New York, NY, CRC Press: 29.

Oberkampf, W. L. and T. G. Trucano (2002). Verification and validation in computational fluid dynamics. *Progress in Aerospace Sciences.* **38**(3), 209–272.

Oberkampf, W. L., T. G. Trucano, and C. Hirsch (2004). Verification, validation, and predictive capability in computational engineering and physics. *Applied Mechanics Reviews*. **57**(5), 345–384.

O'Hagan, A. (2006). Bayesian analysis of computer code outputs: a tutorial. *Reliability Engineering and System Safety*. **91**(10–11), 1290–1300.

O'Hern, T. J., E. J. Weckman, A. L. Gerhart, S. R. Tieszen, and R. W. Schefer (2005). Experimental study of a turbulent buoyant helium plume. *Journal of Fluid Mechanics*. **544**, 143–171.

Paciorri, R. and F. Sabetta (2003). Compressibility correction for the Spalart-Allmaras model in free-shear flows. *Journal of Spacecraft and Rockets*. **40**(3), 326–331.

Paez, T. L. and A. Urbina (2002). Validation of mathematical models of complex structural dynamic systems. *Proceedings of the Ninth International Congress on Sound and Vibration*, Orlando, FL, International Institute of Acoustics and Vibration.

Papamoschou, D. and A. Roshko (1988). The compressible turbulent shear layer: an experimental study. *Journal of Fluid Mechanics*. **197**, 453–477.

Pilch, M. (2008). Preface: Sandia National Laboratories Validation Challenge Workshop. *Computer Methods in Applied Mechanics and Engineering*. **197**(29–32), 2373–2374.

Press, W. H., S. A. Teukolsky, W. T. Vetterling, and B. P. Flannery (2007). *Numerical Recipes in FORTRAN*. 3rd edn., New York, Cambridge University Press.

Pruett, C. D., T. B. Gatski, C. E. Grosch, and W. D. Thacker (2003). The temporally filtered Navier-Stokes equations: properties of the residual stress. *Physics of Fluids*. **15**(8), 2127–2140.

Rabinovich, S. G. (2005). *Measurement Errors and Uncertainties: Theory and Practice*. 3rd edn., New York, Springer-Verlag.

Raol, J. R., G. Girija and J. Singh (2004). *Modelling and Parameter Estimation of Dynamic Systems*, London, UK, Institution of Engineering and Technology.

Rayner, G. D. and J. C. W. Rayner (2001). Power of the Neyman smooth tests for the uniform distribution. *Journal of Applied Mathematics and Decision Sciences*. **5**(3), 181–191.

Rider, W. J. (1998). Personal communication.

Roache, P. J. (1998). *Verification and Validation in Computational Science and Engineering*, Albuquerque, NM, Hermosa Publishers.

Rougier, J. (2007). Probabilistic inference for future climate using an ensemble of climate model evaluations. *Climate Change*. **81**(3–4), 247–264.

Russell, D. M. (1997a). Error measures for comparing transient data: Part I, Development of a comprehensive error measure. *Proceedings of the 68th Shock and Vibration Symposium*, Hunt Valley, Maryland, Shock and Vibration Information Analysis Center.

Russell, D. M. (1997b). Error measures for comparing transient data: Part II, Error measures case study. *Proceedings of the 68th Shock and Vibration Symposium*, Hunt Valley, Maryland, Shock and Vibration Information Analysis Center.

Rutherford, B. M. and K. J. Dowding (2003). *An Approach to Model Validation and Model-Based Prediction – Polyurethane Foam Case Study*. Sandia National Laboratories, SAND2003–2336, Albuquerque, NM.

Samimy, M. and G. S. Elliott (1990). Effects of compressibility on the characteristics of free shear layers. *AIAA Journal*. **28**(3), 439–445.

Seber, G. A. F. and C. J. Wild (2003). *Nonlinear Regression*, New York, John Wiley.

Sivia, D. and J. Skilling (2006). *Data Analysis: a Bayesian Tutorial*. 2nd edn., Oxford, Oxford University Press.

Sprague, M. A. and T. L. Geers (1999). Response of empty and fluid-filled, submerged spherical shells to plane and spherical, step-exponential acoustic waves. *Shock and Vibration*. **6**(3), 147–157.

Sprague, M. A. and T. L. Geers (2004). A spectral-element method for modeling cavitation in transient fluid-structure interaction. *International Journal for Numerical Methods in Engineering*. **60**(15), 2467–2499.

Stern, F., R. V. Wilson, H. W. Coleman, and E. G. Paterson (2001). Comprehensive approach to verification and validation of CFD simulations – Part 1: Methodology and procedures. *Journal of Fluids Engineering*. **123**(4), 793–802.

Tieszen, S. R., S. P. Domino, and A. R. Black (2005). *Validation of a Simple Turbulence Model Suitable for Closure of Temporally-Filtered Navier Stokes Equations Using a Helium Plume*. SAND2005–3210, Albuquerque, NM, Sandia National Laboratories.

Trucano, T. G., L. P. Swiler, T. Igusa, W. L. Oberkampf, and M. Pilch (2006). Calibration, validation, and sensitivity analysis: what's what. *Reliability Engineering and System Safety*. **91**(10–11), 1331–1357.

van den Bos, A. (2007). *Parameter Estimation for Scientists and Engineers*, Hoboken, NJ, Wiley-Interscience.

Walley, P. (1991). *Statistical Reasoning with Imprecise Probabilities*, London, Chapman & Hall.

Wang, S., W. Chen and K.-L. Tsui (2009). Bayesian validation of computer models. *Technometrics*. **51**(4), 439–451.

Wellek, S. (2002). *Testing Statistical Hypotheses of Equivalence*, Boca Raton, FL, Chapman & Hall/CRC.

Wilcox, D. C. (2006). *Turbulence Modeling for CFD*. 3rd edn., La Canada, CA, DCW Industries.

Winkler, R. L. (1972). *An Introduction to Bayesian Inference and Decision*, New York, Holt, Rinehart, and Winston.

Wirsching, P., T. Paez and K. Ortiz (1995). *Random Vibrations: Theory and Practice*, New York, Wiley.

Wong, C. C., F. G. Blottner, J. L. Payne, and M. Soetrisno (1995a). Implementation of a parallel algorithm for thermo-chemical nonequilibrium flow solutions. *AIAA 33rd Aerospace Sciences Meeting*, AIAA Paper 95–0152, Reno, NV, American Institute of Aeronautics and Astronautics.

Wong, C. C., M. Soetrisno, F. G. Blottner, S. T. Imlay, and J. L. Payne (1995b). *PINCA: A Scalable Parallel Program for Compressible Gas Dynamics with Nonequilibrium Chemistry*. SAND94–2436, Albuquerque, NM, Sandia National Laboratories.

Yee, H. C. (1987). *Implicit and Symmetric Shock Capturing Schemes*. Washington, DC, NASA, NASA-TM-89464.

Yoon, S. and A. Jameson (1987). An LU-SSOR scheme for the Euler and Navier-Stokes equations. *25th AIAA Aerospace Sciences Meeting*, AIAA Paper 87–0600, Reno, NV, American Institute of Aeronautics and Astronautics.

Zeman, O. (1990). Dilatation dissipation: the concept and application in modeling compressible mixing layers. *Physics of Fluids A*. **2**(2), 178–188.

Zhang, R. and S. Mahadevan (2003). Bayesian methodology for reliability model acceptance. *Reliability Engineering and System Safety*. **80**(1), 95–103.

13

Predictive capability

This chapter will synthesize the key results from the previous chapters and incorporate them into modern predictive capability in scientific computing. This chapter, in contrast to all other chapters, does not stress the theme of assessment. Here we discuss the fundamental steps in conducting a nondeterministic analysis of a system of interest. With this discussion we show how verification and validation (V&V) can directly contribute to predictive capability.

The previously covered material and the new material are organized into six procedural steps to make a prediction:

1 identify all relevant sources of uncertainty,
2 characterize each source of uncertainty,
3 estimate numerical solution error in the system response quantities of interest,
4 estimate uncertainty in the system response quantities of interest,
5 conduct model updating,
6 conduct sensitivity analysis.

All of these steps, except step 3, are widely practiced in nondeterministic simulations and risk analysis. Step 3 is not commonly addressed for three reasons. First, in many simulations the numerical solution error is assumed to be small compared to other contributors to uncertainty. Sometimes this assumption is quantitatively justified, and sometimes it is simply posited with little or no evidence. Second, in some computationally intensive simulations, it is understood that the numerical solution error is important, and possibly even dominant, but it is argued that various modeling parameters can be adjusted to compensate for the numerical error. If the application of interest is sufficiently similar to the conditions for which experimental data are available, then it is claimed that the adjustable parameters can be used to match the existing data and thereby make reasonable predictions. Third, even if the numerical error is estimated, and it is not small relative to other uncertainties, there are no generally accepted procedures for including its effect on the system response quantities (SRQs) of interest.

It is the beyond the scope of this chapter to deal in depth with each of the steps. Many techniques in predictive capability are well summarized in the following texts (Cullen and Frey, 1999; Melchers, 1999; Modarres *et al.*, 1999; Haldar and Mahadevan, 2000a; Bedford and Cooke, 2001; Bardossy and Fodor, 2004; Nikolaidis *et al.*, 2005; Ayyub and Klir, 2006; Singpurwalla, 2006; Ang and Tang, 2007; Choi *et al.*, 2007; Kumamoto, 2007; Singh *et al.*, 2007; Suter, 2007; Vinnem, 2007; Vose, 2008; Haimes, 2009; EPA, 2009). Some of these texts should be consulted for a more in-depth understanding of uncertainty quantification (UQ) and risk assessment. Even though the classic text of Morgan and Henrion (1990) is rather dated, we believe it is still one of the most comprehensive discussions of the myriad aspects of UQ and risk assessment. It is highly recommended reading, not only for people new to the field, but also for experienced UQ analysts.

The three dominant approaches to UQ and risk assessment are: traditional probabilistic methods, Bayesian inference, and probability bounds analysis (PBA). As discussed in several earlier chapters, this text concentrates on PBA. Some of the key references in the development and use of PBA are Ferson (1996, 2002); Ferson and Ginzburg (1996); Ferson *et al.* (2003, 2004); Ferson and Hajagos (2004); Kriegler and Held (2005); Aughenbaugh and Paredis (2006); Baudrit and Dubois (2006) and Bernardini and Tonon (2010). PBA is closely related to two other approaches: (a) two-dimensional Monte Carlo sampling, also called nested Monte Carlo, and second-order Monte Carlo (Bogen and Spear, 1987; Helton, 1994, 1997; Hoffman and Hammonds, 1994; Cullen and Frey, 1999; NASA, 2002; Kriegler and Held, 2005; Suter, 2007; Vose, 2008; NRC, 2009), and (b) evidence theory, also called Dempster–Shafer theory (Krause and Clark, 1993; Almond, 1995; Kohlas and Monney, 1995; Klir and Wierman, 1998; Fetz *et al.*, 2000; Kyburg and Teng, 2001; Helton *et al.*, 2004, 2005a; Oberkampf and Helton, 2005; Bae *et al.*, 2006). The PBA approach stresses the following aspects in an analysis: (a) keep aleatory and epistemic uncertainties segregated throughout each step of the analysis; (b) mathematically characterize aleatory uncertainty as probability distributions; (c) characterize epistemic uncertainty as interval-valued quantities, i.e., all values over the range of the interval are possible, but no likelihood is associated with any value; (d) if independence between uncertainty quantities cannot be justified, then dependence should be considered as an epistemic uncertainty; (e) map all input uncertainties through the model; and (f) display SRQs as bounds of probability distributions, i.e., a p-box. A p-box is special type of cumulative distribution function that represents the set of all possible CDFs that fall within the prescribed bounds. As a result, probabilities can be interval-valued quantities as opposed to a single probability. A p-box expresses both epistemic and aleatory uncertainty in a way that does not confound the two.

Returning to the topic of the six steps for prediction, the six steps discussed here are similar to the six phases of computational simulation discussed in Chapter 3, Modeling and computational simulation. The phases in Chapter 3, however, stressed the modeling and computational aspects of simulation. In the six steps discussed here, more emphasis is given to the UQ aspects because we believe that V&V are supporting elements in nondeterministic predictions. It should also be stressed that we assume that before the six steps discussed here are initiated, the goals of the simulation analysis have been clearly identified and agreed upon by those conducting the analysis, as well as those who will use the results of the analysis. As discussed in Chapter 14, Planning and prioritization in modeling and simulation, this is a critical, but difficult, task.

In addition, the following aspects of modeling should be considered and specified *before* the analysis is begun:

- systems and surroundings,
- environments,
- scenarios,
- application domain of the system.

These aspects were discussed in Chapter 2, Fundamental concepts and terminology, Chapter 3, and Chapter 14.

For complex system analyses, there may be multiple possibilities considered for each of these aspects, resulting in multiple sets of simulations, each addressing a particular aspect of the system. For example, in an abnormal environment there may be many failure scenarios identified; however, only some may be analyzed in detail. If multiple environments and scenarios are identified, each one may have an estimated probability of occurrence associated with it. If some type of consequence can be quantified for each possibility identified, then one may only choose to analyze the highest risk possibilities. In the discussion that follows, however, we will not address these probabilities or consequences. For simplicity, we will only consider one set of conditions at a time, i.e., system, surroundings, environments, scenarios, and application domain. In most engineering analyses, multiple sets of conditions must be analyzed.

13.1 Step 1: identify all relevant sources of uncertainty

When the above mentioned aspects of formulating a model have been completed, then a process is conducted to identify all the aspects of the model that will be considered as uncertain and those that will be considered as deterministic. For example, in the analysis of the performance of an electrical automatic control system, the electrical properties of many of the components will be considered as uncertain due to manufacturing variability and assembly. Properties such as Planck's constant, the speed of light in a vacuum, and the elementary charge would normally be considered as deterministic. The *goals of the analysis* should be the primary determinant for what is considered as fixed versus what is considered as uncertain. The general philosophy that should be used is: consider an aspect as uncertain unless there is a strong and convincing argument that the uncertainty in the aspect will result in minimal uncertainty in *all* of the system response quantities of interest in the analysis. It should be convincing to the project leader, as well as all of the members of the team conducting the analysis. If the sensitivity analysis conducted in step 6 shows that the contribution to uncertainty from certain aspects is small, then these aspects can be considered as deterministic. If, however, an aspect is considered as deterministic, the model cannot provide any indication of how sensitive the results are to that assumed aspect.

In large-scale analyses, a *screening analysis* or *scoping study* is commonly conducted to obtain a better indication of what aspects may be important and what may be unimportant. A screening analysis is a preliminary modeling and UQ analysis, done with simplified

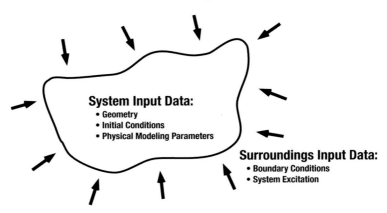

Figure 13.1 System and surroundings input data.

models, to assist in identifying the most important and the least important contributors to uncertainty. The screening analysis is intentionally biased toward being conservative toward the important outcomes of the analysis. That is, a screening analysis attempts to err on the side of identifying all possible changes in modeling and uncertainties that may result in detrimental outcomes of interest. For example, in a complex system there are many subsystems and components that can interact in several ways. Additionally, there would commonly be many different types of physics occurring, along with different types of interactions. A screening analysis attempts to identify what aspects of the system, subsystems, components, physics, and interacting physics should be included in the full analysis and what could safely be excluded. A proper screening analysis can aid analysts and decision makers in directing limited resources toward the more important aspects of the work. This also includes resources devoted to obtaining experimental measurements on needed model inputs.

13.1.1 Model inputs

Model inputs can be divided into two general groups: system input data and surroundings input data. Figure 13.1 depicts these groups, along with the subgroups of each. Quantities in each of the subgroups can be deterministic or uncertain, depending on the needs of the UQ analysis. Each subgroup will be briefly discussed in order to point out what type of uncertainty might need to be considered, and what kinds of difficulty commonly arise.

System geometry data can be specified in a number of ways. For example, it could be specified in detail in a computer aided design (CAD) software package. In addition, computer aided manufacturing (CAM) software may be used for more detail on the actual manufacturing and assembly process, such as final surface preparation, methods and specifications for installing rivets and bolts, welding procedures, installation, and assembly of hydraulic lines, and electrical sensor and wiring installation. If CAD/CAM software is used, however, the ability to consider uncertainties in the geometry in an automated way is rather very limited. By *automated*, we mean that the user of the CAD/CAM package can specify a subset of the geometry features as uncertain, assign values to that subset, and then have all of the remaining geometry features re-computed. Because of the many ways in which CAD/CAM packages are structured, and because of the multitude of ways the geometry within a package can be built, the ability to automate uncertainties in a system design can be quite problematic. As a result, one should be very cautious in choosing CAD/CAM packages so that they have the flexibility that is needed in specific UQ analyses.

A similar situation occurs when a user constructs a simplified geometry within a commercial software package that is designed for specific types of analysis, e.g., solid mechanics or fluid dynamics. The user usually specifies many of the geometry features as parameters. Then, if they want to consider some of them as uncertain, they must individually input many of the uncertain parameters in the geometry. However, one must be careful so as not to over-specify the geometry or cause inconsistencies in the geometry when certain features are considered as uncertain. As a simple example, suppose one is interested in computing the deflection of a triangular-shaped plate due to a load distribution over the surface of the plate. Because of manufacturing variability, the three internal angles of the plate are considered as continuous random variables. One can only choose two of the angles, because choosing three would over-specify the geometry. This example also points out that there is a correlation structure between the three angles. Correlation of input information will be discussed shortly.

Initial conditions (ICs) provide required information for a model of a system that is formulated as an initial value problem. ICs provide required information concerning: (a) the initial state of all of the dependent variables in the partial differential equations; and (b) the initial state of all other physical modeling parameters, including geometric parameters, that could be dependent on time. As a result, the IC data could be a function of the remaining independent variables in the PDEs. Typically, the most important aspect of the ICs is the state of all of the dependent variables over the domain of the PDE. In addition, the initial state of all of the dependent variables in all of the submodels, e.g., auxiliary PDEs, must be given. If the ICs are considered as uncertain, the uncertainty structure is clearly more complicated than input geometry data because one must deal with functions of one or more of the independent variables.

The most common inputs that are considered uncertain in analyses are data for parameters that appear in the model. There are a number of types of parameters that can occur in models. The following is a useful classification:

- geometry parameters,
- parameters that characterize features of the ICs,
- physical modeling parameters that characterize features of the system,
- parameters that characterize features of the boundary conditions,
- parameters that characterize the excitation of the system due to the surroundings,
- parameters occurring in the mathematical characterization of uncertainties,
- numerical solution parameters associated with the numerical algorithms used.

Depending on its role in the model, a parameter can be a scalar, a scalar field, a vector, or a tensor field. Although we will primarily discuss physical modeling parameters dealing with the system, ICs, and BCs, many of the concepts will apply to the other types of parameters listed.

Surroundings input data consists of two subgroups: boundary conditions and excitation of the system. BCs can be dependent on one or more of the independent variables of the PDEs. These independent variables are typically other spatial dimensions and time, if the problem is formulated as an initial-boundary value problem. For example, in a fluid-structure interaction problem, the boundary condition between the structure and the fluid is a compatibility condition. For the boundary condition of the structure there is a distributed pressure and shear stress loading imposed by the fluid. For the boundary conditions of the fluid, there is no flow through the surface, and the fluid on the boundary must be equal to the local velocity of the boundary. Examples of different types of BCs are Dirichlet, Neumann, Robin, mixed, periodic, and Cauchy. If the BCs are considered as uncertain, the effect on the solution procedure can range from minimal to a situation where the solution procedure must be completely changed. For example, if the uncertainty in the BCs does not cause a change in the coupling of the BCs to the solution procedure for the PDEs, then the uncertainty can usually be treated similarly to parametric uncertainty. For example, one could use a sampling procedure to propagate the effect of the uncertainty in the BCs onto the SRQs. If, on the other hand, the uncertainty in the BCs causes a change in the way the BCs must be coupled to the solution to the PDEs, then more sophisticated procedures must be used. For example, if the uncertainty in the BC deforms the boundary to such a degree that the deformation cannot be considered as small, then one must significantly change the numerical solution procedure, and possibly even the mathematical model, to deal with the uncertainty.

System excitation refers to how the surroundings affect the system, *other than* through the BCs. System excitation always results in a change in the PDEs that are being solved. Sometimes system excitation is referred to as a change in the right hand side of the PDEs to represent the effect of the surroundings on the system. Common examples of system excitation are (a) a force field acting on the system, such as that due to gravity or an electric or magnetic field; and (b) energy deposition distributed through the system, such as by electrical heating, chemical reactions, and ionizing or nonionizing radiation. System excitation uncertainties are usually treated as an uncertain parameter that is a scalar or tensor field. Similar to large uncertainties in BCs, however, if large uncertainties occur in system excitation, then the mathematical model and/or the numerical solution procedure may need to be changed.

13.1.2 Model uncertainty

By *model uncertainty*, we specifically mean uncertainty that is caused by the assumptions embedded in the formulation of the model, as opposed to uncertainty in inputs to the model. As discussed in Chapter 3, formulation of the model occurs in both the conceptual modeling and mathematical modeling phases. Sometimes model uncertainty is referred to as *model form uncertainty*, and we will use that term when the context is not clear as to what uncertainty we mean. It must be emphasized that model uncertainty is the uncertainty due to the *entire aggregation of all components of the formulation of the structure of the model*, exclusive of model input uncertainty. For example, this would include (a) the specification of the environment of interest, (b) the scenario of interest, (c) physical interactions or couplings that are included or ignored, (d) the PDEs of the primary model, and (e) the PDEs of all submodels that complete to the primary model. Stated differently, model uncertainty includes all assumptions, conceptualizations, abstractions, and mathematical formulations on which the model relies.

Model uncertainty is rarely analyzed in texts on UQ and risk analysis because it is difficult to deal with. It is much more difficult to deal with than input uncertainty, for two reasons. First, model uncertainty is *totally* an epistemic uncertainty, i.e., it is completely due to lack of knowledge as opposed to the inability to know the precise outcome of a random process. Recall from Chapter 2 that epistemic uncertainty was divided into two types: (a) *recognized uncertainty*, an epistemic uncertainty for which a conscious decision has been made to either characterize or deal with it in some way, or to ignore it for practical reasons; and (b) *blind uncertainty*, an epistemic uncertainty for which it is not recognized that the knowledge is incomplete and that the knowledge is relevant to modeling the system of interest. Model uncertainty can be either a recognized or blind epistemic uncertainty. Second, estimating any type of useful bound on model uncertainty is very difficult. These difficulties are, of course, rooted in the fact that model uncertainty necessarily deals with a property of, or choices made by, the modeler or observer. In a UQ analysis, one should not ignore model uncertainty simply because it is difficult to deal with and conceptualize. That would be equivalent to the idiom of ignoring the elephant in the room. In order to achieve reliable predictive capability, model uncertainty must commonly be dealt with, even though it is messy, controversial, and causes a great deal of discomfort. Section 13.2 will discuss some methods for addressing and characterizing model uncertainty.

13.1.3 Example problem: heat transfer through a plate

Consider the heat transfer analysis of a system that is coupled to a larger system solely through the boundary conditions. We are interested in simulating the heat transfer through a solid metal plate of size 1×1 m and thickness 1 cm (Figure 13.2). The SRQ of interest is the total heat flux through the west face of the plate. The key assumptions for modeling the heat transfer through the plate are the following:

- the plate is homogeneous and isotropic;
- the plate is in steady-state condition;
- thermal conductivity of the plate is not a function of temperature;
- heat transfer only occurs in the x-y plane, i.e., there is no heat loss or gain over the surface of the plate in the z-direction.

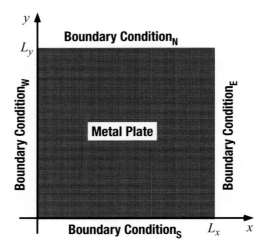

Figure 13.2 System geometry for heat transfer through a metal plate.

The PDE for the temperature distribution through the plate is given by Laplace's equation:

$$\frac{\partial^2 T}{\partial x^2} + \frac{\partial^2 T}{\partial y^2} = 0. \tag{13.1}$$

As shown in Figure 13.2, boundary conditions are given on the north, south, east, and west boundaries.

The dimensions of the plate, L_x, L_y, and the thickness, τ, are assumed to be well controlled in manufacturing, so that they are characterized as deterministic quantities. The plate is made of aluminum and the thermal conductivity, k, is considered to be uncertain due to manufacturing variability. That is, due to metal composition, forming, and rolling processes there is variability in k from one manufactured plate to the next, i.e., inter-individual variability. The BCs for the east and west faces are $T_E = 450$ K and $T_W = 300$ K, respectively, and they are considered as deterministic. The north face is exposed to air that freely circulates above the top edge of the plate. As a result, the BC on the north face is given as

$$q_N(x) = -k\left(\frac{\partial T}{\partial y}\right)_{y=L_y} = h(T_{y=L_y} - T_a), \tag{13.2}$$

where h is the convective heat transfer coefficient at the surface and $T_a = 300$ K is the ambient air temperature above the plate. h is an empirical coefficient that depends on several factors, such as the air pressure, the speed of air currents above the surface, and whether the plate may possibly have a small amount of moisture on its surface. These conditions are poorly known for the operational conditions of the system, so h is characterized as an epistemic uncertainty and represented as an interval.

The south face of the plate is well insulated so that the BC is given by

$$q_S(x) = -k \left(\frac{\partial T}{\partial y} \right)_{y=0} = 0. \tag{13.3}$$

The model will be used to predict the total heat flux through the west face of the plate, which is given by

$$(q_W)_{\text{total}} = \tau \int_0^{L_y} q_W(y)\, \mathrm{d}y, \tag{13.4}$$

where

$$q_W(y) = -k \left(\frac{\partial T}{\partial x} \right)_{x=0}. \tag{13.5}$$

$(q_W)_{\text{total}}$ is of interest because the adjacent system to the west of the system of interest could be damaged due to high heating levels.

To develop confidence in the model, a validation experiment is designed and conducted so that the measurements from the experiment can be compared to predictions from the model. As commonly occurs, the system cannot be tested in available experimental facilities because of its size. So the model will be evaluated using predictions on a scale-model; a plate of size 0.1 m × 0.1 m, but the same thickness, $\tau = 1$ cm. The validation experiment uses the same plate material as the system, and the facility is able to replicate two of the four BCs of the actual system. The BCs on the south and west faces can be duplicated, but the BCs on the east and north faces are modified from the system of interest. Because of facility limitations on heating capability, the maximum temperature that can be achieved in the facility is 390 K. To evaluate the model over a range of temperatures, experiments are conducted at east face temperatures of 330, 360, and 390 K. For each of these T_E conditions, multiple measurements of the SRQ, $(q_W)_{\text{total}}$, are measured in the validation experiment.

For the north face, a different kind of situation exists. The experimentalist, being familiar with the design of validation experiments, realizes that the model accuracy cannot be precisely assessed if significant epistemic uncertainty in the convective heat transfer coefficient, h, is allowed to occur in the validation experiment. The experimentalist recommends that in the validation experiment the north face of the plate be provided with a well controlled and carefully measured value of h. In consultation with the computational analyst, they agree to set the value of h at the middle of the interval range of h for the system of interest. Table 13.1 summarizes the system and surroundings input data for both the system of interest and the scale model used in the validation experiments.

In addition to the model input data uncertainties, one should also try to identify the potential weaknesses in the modeling, i.e., possible sources of uncertainty in the formulation of the model. As discussed in Chapter 3 and Chapter 12, Model accuracy assessment, identifying and quantifying model form uncertainty is always difficult. The task is made more challenging if the analyst does not have an open mind concerning the various sources of model uncertainty. One procedure is to try and identify some of the assumptions that may be questionable in the modeling. This aids in improved understanding of modeling

Table 13.1 *Model input data for the system of interest and the validation experiment for the heat transfer example.*

Model input data	System of interest	Validation experiment
System input data		
Geometry, L_x and L_y	$L_x = L_y = 1$ m, deterministic	$L_x = L_y = 0.1$ m, deterministic
Geometry, τ	$\tau = 1$ cm, deterministic	$\tau = 1$ cm, deterministic
Thermal conductivity, k	k, aleatory uncertainty	k, aleatory uncertainty
Surroundings input data		
BC east face	$T_E = 450$ K, deterministic	$T_E = 330, 360, 390$ K, deterministic
BC west face	$T_W = 300$ K, deterministic	$T_W = 300$ K, deterministic
BC north face	h, epistemic uncertainty	h, deterministic
	$T_a = 300$ K, deterministic	$T_a = 300$ K, deterministic
BC south face	$q_S = 0$, deterministic	$q_S = 0$, deterministic

uncertainties, not only in the actual system, but also in the validation experiment. The following describes some concerns with modeling assumptions, listed in order of decreasing concern.

- The assumption that thermal conductivity is independent of temperature is fairly well justified for the temperature range and metal considered here. However, it is believed to be the weakest assumption of those listed above in formulating the analysis.
- The assumption of no heat loss or gain over the front and back surfaces of the plate is well justified in the validation experiment because it is a well-controlled and well-characterized environment. In the actual system, however, it is a questionable assumption because of the design, manufacturing, and assembly of the complete system, i.e., the larger system in which the present system operates.
- The assumption of a homogeneous plate, i.e., k equal to a constant throughout the plate, was made for both the full-size system plates and the scale-model plates used in the validation experiments. In the validation experiment, multiple plates are cut from the actual production plates of the system. However, since the validation plates are 100th the size of the system plates, the homogeneity of k in the validation plates may be higher than in the system plates. Stated differently, the validation experiments may not fully test the assumption of homogeneity in the system plates.
- The steady-state heat transfer assumption is very good after the system has been operating for a period of time. During startup of the system, however, the assumption is erroneous. The purpose of the simulation discussed here is to predict the heat flux through the west face of the plate because of possible damage the heating might have on the adjacent system. During startup of the system most of the thermal energy goes into heating the plate, as opposed to being transferred to the adjacent system. As a result, the assumption of steady-state heat transfer will tend to produce a higher heating value into the adjacent system, requiring a design of the adjacent system that is more tolerant of higher temperatures.

In the following sections we will discuss this example in the context of the steps of prediction.

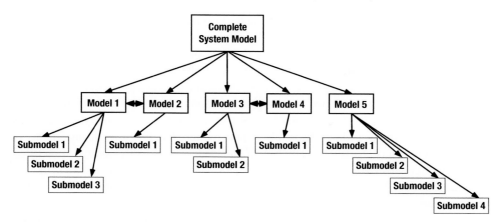

Figure 13.3 Tree structure for models and submodels.

13.1.4 Final comments on step 1

As part of the completion of step 1, a list should be compiled of all of the sources of uncertainty that will be considered in the model. For complex analyses, this list of uncertainty sources could number over a hundred. Some type of logical structure should be developed to help understand where all the sources of uncertainty appear in the analysis. This structure will not only aid the analysts involved in the project, but also the project managers and stakeholders in the analysis. If the project is exposed to an external review panel, it is critically important to devise a method for clearly and quickly displaying what is considered as uncertain, and what is considered as deterministic.

One method for summarizing the model input uncertainties and deterministic quantities is to begin with a tree-structured diagram of models and submodels that make up the complete system model. Figure 13.3 gives an example of a complete system model that is composed of five models, and each model has anywhere from one to four submodels. All five models interact in the complete system model, but only models 1 and 2, and models 3 and 4 directly interact. That is, models 1 and 2, and models 3 and 4 are strongly coupled, whereas the remaining models are only coupled in the complete system model. Once the tree-structured diagram of models is created, then the model input uncertainties and deterministic quantities can be summarized in a table for each model and each submodel. A simplified version of Table 13.1 for the heat transfer example could be used for each model and submodel. This summary information is time consuming to compile, but it is of great value not only to project managers, stakeholders, and external reviewers, but also to analysts because it can uncover inconsistencies and contradictions in a complex analysis.

13.2 Step 2: characterize each source of uncertainty

By *characterizing a source of uncertainty* we mean (a) assigning a mathematical structure to the uncertainty and (b) determining the numerical values of all of the needed elements of the structure. Stated differently, characterizing the uncertainty requires that a mathematical structure is given to the uncertainty and all parameters of the structure are numerically specified, such that the structure represents the state of knowledge of every uncertainty considered. The primary decision to be made concerning the mathematical structure for each source is: should it be represented as a purely aleatory uncertainty, a purely epistemic uncertainty, or a mixture of the two? As discussed in Chapter 2, a purely aleatory uncertainty is one that is completely characterized by inherent randomness, i.e., purely chance. The classic examples are the roll of a die and Brownian motion. Purely epistemic uncertainty is one that is completely characterized by lack of knowledge. Stated differently, if knowledge is added to the characterization of the uncertainty, the uncertainty will decrease. If sufficient knowledge is added, it is conceptually possible that the source will become deterministic, i.e., a number.

At first glance, it may seem rather easy to segregate uncertainties into aleatory or epistemic. In reality, it can be difficult. The difficulty commonly arises because of very different, yet pragmatic reasons. First, the risk assessment community has had a long tradition of *not* separating aleatory and epistemic uncertainties. Only during the last decade or so have a number of leading risk analysts begun to stress the importance of different mathematical representations for aleatory and epistemic uncertainty. See, for example, Morgan and Henrion (1990); Ayyub (1994); Helton (1994); Hoffman and Hammonds (1994); Rowe (1994); Ferson (1996); Ferson and Ginzburg (1996); Frey and Rhodes (1996); Hora (1996); Parry (1996); Paté-Cornell (1996); Rai *et al.* (1996); Helton (1997); Cullen and Frey (1999); and Frank (1999). Second, essentially all of the commercial risk assessment, UQ, and SA software available are completely focused on purely aleatory uncertainty. To deal with this, most of the large risk assessment projects build their own software to separate aleatory and epistemic uncertainty. Medium and small risk assessment projects, however, usually do not have the resources to develop the software tools. And third, a slight change in the perspective or the question that is asked concerning an input uncertainty can change its mathematical structure. For example, if one question were asked concerning the source, it could be characterized as an aleatory uncertainty. If a slightly different question were asked, it could be characterized as an epistemic uncertainty or as a mixed uncertainty. As a result, careful planning must go into what questions should be asked so that they are aligned with the goals of the system analysis. In addition, UQ analysts must be very careful and clear in explaining the question to experts providing opinions, or experimentalists providing empirical data.

Three different examples of an epistemic and aleatory uncertainty will be discussed. First, consider the case of guessing the number of marbles inside of a jar. Suppose that the jar is transparent so that a person could see a relatively large number of the marbles inside the jar. The number of marbles inside the jar is a pure epistemic uncertainty. It is *not* a random number, but a unique number that is simply unknown to the viewer. Depending on the motivation for guessing the right number of marbles, for example some type of wager, we may guess a single number. However, this type of situation is not what engineering is about: *adequacy is the issue, not perfection*. We may guess an interval in which we believe the actual number may lie, or we may guess an interval with some type of personal belief structure on the interval. For example, we may give a triangular belief structure over the range of the interval. As we study the jar, we may start estimating the number of marbles and possibly make some measurements of the marbles and the jar. With this time and effort, we are improving our knowledge. As a result, we may revise our interval estimate of the true value of the number of marbles. If we spend a significant amount of time, and maybe even modeling of the marbles in the jar, we may significantly reduce the size of our interval estimate. If we empty the jar and count the number of marbles, we have added sufficient knowledge so that the number is exactly known. In engineering, seldom do we know the exact value; we have to make decisions based on imprecise knowledge.

Second, consider the roll of a fair die. Before the die is rolled, the uncertainty in purely aleatory and the probability of each face of the die is 1/6. After the die is rolled, but *before* the die is observed, the uncertainty is purely epistemic. That is, after the die is rolled, there is a fixed outcome, whether we know it or not. In this example it is seen that whether we consider the uncertainty as aleatory or epistemic depends on what question is asked. Are we asking an uncertainty question before the die is rolled, or after the die is rolled? A similar example occurs in risk assessment. Suppose the safety of a certain design nuclear power plant is being analyzed. The question could be: what is the estimated safety of the set of plants of similar design, based on our knowledge as of today? Or, *after* an accident has occurred at one of the plants: what is our estimate of the safety after we have investigated the accident and studied related issues at the other plants? If our estimate of the safety has decreased after a plant accident, then we have either underestimated or underrepresented the safety of the plants before the accident.

Third, consider the case of pseudo-random number generation. Suppose a person observes a long sequence of numbers and asks the question: is this a random sequence of numbers? They may conduct various statistical tests and conclude that the sequence is indeed random, and that the next number is not knowable. Suppose now that the person was provided the algorithm that generated the sequence and the seed that started the sequence. With this knowledge, the person can determine, with perfect confidence, what the next number in the sequence will be. Without this knowledge, the sequence would be characterized as aleatory. With this knowledge, it would become completely deterministic.

Now consider the case of an uncertainty that is a mixture of aleatory and epistemic. This case will be discussed by way of two examples. First, consider the situation of a stranger approaching you in a casino and asking if you would like to place a wager on the roll of a die. You're feeling lucky, so you say Yes. He reaches in his pocket and pulls out a die. He says he will pick a number between 1 and 6, and then you will pick another number between 1 and 6. He will throw the die and whoever's number comes up first, wins the wager. How much do you want to bet? Before you answer, you start considering various ways to estimate the probability of winning or losing. If you were a Bayesian, you would assume a noninformative prior distribution, i.e., assume a uniform probability distribution that any number between 1 and 6 is equally likely.

Being cautious and skeptical, you note that you have essentially *no basis* for assuming a uniform distribution. You have not seen the die, and you have never seen this person before in your life. So you ask if you can see the die. You look at the die, it indeed has six unique faces, and it looks *normal*. With this step, you have added significant knowledge to the decision process. There is now *some* evidence that the uniform distribution is reasonable.

Being really cautious, and gambling with your own money, you seek to add more knowledge before you characterize the uncertainty. You ask if you can roll the die a number of times to see if it appears to be fair. He agrees, and you start rolling the die. Each roll of the die adds knowledge concerning the probability of each number of the die appearing. You continue to roll the die a large number of times and, finally, conclude that the die *is* fair. About this time, the stranger shakes his head in frustration, takes the die, and walks off.

This example shows that when the stranger initially asks you to bet, you can *only* defend a characterization of pure epistemic uncertainty; everything else is *presumption*. As you gather information, the uncertainty becomes a mixture of aleatory and epistemic uncertainty, and at the final stage, it becomes purely aleatory uncertainty. Without this knowledge, you cannot be assured that the stranger is not making a Dutch book against you. (See Leonard and Hsu, 1999; Kyburg and Teng, 2001; and Halpern, 2003 for a discussion of a Dutch book in statistics.)

The second example of mixed aleatory and epistemic uncertainty deals with characterizing an uncertainty based on samples from a population. Suppose you are interested in the variability of the mass of individual manufactured parts. Suppose you have just received the first shipment of parts from a new supplier. The contract with the supplier specifies the metal from which the parts are to be machined, the dimensional tolerance requirements for the part, as well as the material properties, but nothing specifically dealing with mass variability of the part. You have very little knowledge of their manufacturing process, their quality control processes, or their reputation for quality manufacturing. Suppose that all of the parts from the new supplier were dimensionally inspected and they were all found to satisfy the dimensional tolerances in the contract. Before any mass measurements were made of the parts, one could compute the maximum and minimum volume of the part based on the tolerances given for each dimension. A reasonably defensible characterization of the maximum and minimum mass of the part would be to assume a maximum and minimum density of the metal and use these values multiplied by the maximum and minimum volume, respectively. To assign a variability of mass over this range, it would be reasonable to assign a uniform probability distribution over this range. One could argue that there should be less variability of the mass than a uniform distribution, but there is little evidence to support that view.

If some of the parts were also measured for their mass, then one has a good deal more information concerning the variability. To decide what theoretical family of distributions might be used to represent the variability, one could use the PUMA technique, i.e., Pulled oUt of MidAir; then one would compute a best fit for the parameters of the chosen distribution. Or, one could conduct various statistical tests to determine which distribution appears reasonable to characterize the variability. (A wide variety of commercial software exists for analyses such as this; for example, JMP and STAT from SAS Inc., BestFit from Palisade Inc., Risk Solver from Frontline Systems, Inc., STATISTICA from StatSoft, Inc., and the statistical toolbox in MATLAB from The MathWorks, Inc.). Suppose that a two-parameter log-normal distribution looked sensible, so it is chosen to characterize the variability. Using the samples available, one could estimate the two parameters in the distribution using various methods. If this were done, one would be characterizing the variability as a purely aleatory uncertainty. Although this is common practice, it actually under-represents the true state of knowledge. If the number of mass measurements made is rather small, or the choice of the distribution is not all that convincing, then the strength of the argument for the mass as a purely aleatory uncertainty becomes embarrassing.

A more defensible approach would be to characterize each of the parameters of the log-normal distribution (i.e., the parent distribution) as having probability distributions themselves. A mathematical structure such as this is usually referred to as a *second-order distribution*. The parameters of the second-order distributions are usually referred to as second-order parameters. This mathematical structure directly displays the uncertainty due to sampling, or as it is sometimes referred to, the epistemic uncertainty of the variability. A detailed discussion of how the second order distributions can be calculated is beyond the scope of this book. See Vose (2008) for a more detailed discussion. The second-order distribution is actually a special type of p-box, referred to as a *statistical p-box*. The statistical p-box could be computed by sampling the second-order parameters. For each sample, a cumulative distribution function (CDF) of the parent distribution can be computed. After a number of samples are computed, one generates an ensemble of CDFs. For all samples within the outer envelope of the p-box constructed from sampling, there is a statistical structure within the p-box. One could contrast this structure with the p-box where the parameters are intervals. For the case of interval-valued parameters, there would be *no structure* within the p-box. Both types of p-box have epistemic uncertainty, but the statistical p-box contains structure because of the knowledge of sampling uncertainty, whereas the p-box resulting from intervals contains no knowledge of the inner structure.

In the discussion that follows concerning model input uncertainty, aleatory, epistemic, and mixed structures can be used, depending on whether we are dealing with a random variable or not and the amount of information available. For model uncertainty, only an epistemic uncertainty structure should be used.

13.2.1 Model input uncertainty

Characterizing the uncertainty in model inputs is commonly a major effort in any UQ analysis. For large-scale analyses, uncertainty characterization can take as much time and financial resources as the development of the model and the analysis of the results. Information obtained for the characterization of input quantities can come from one or more of the following three sources:

- experimentally measured data for quantities taken from the actual system or similar systems under relevant conditions;
- theoretically generated data for quantities appearing in the model of the system, but the data come from separate models that provide information to the larger analysis;
- opinions expressed by experts familiar with the system of interest and the models used in the analysis.

In using each of these sources, one is attempting to characterize the uncertainty in an input quantity. However, when any one of these is used, the uncertainty due to the source itself is convolved with the uncertainty in the quantity. Different procedures should be used to minimize the effect of the source uncertainty. For example, it is well known that in experimental measurements there are random measurement uncertainties and there are systematic, or bias, uncertainties. Within a UQ analysis, one usually employs a mixture of the above listed sources. These sources of information will be briefly discussed in this section.

For small-scale analyses of a relatively simple system, the analyst may be able to estimate the uncertainties in all of the input quantities. For most analyses, however, a wide range of expertise is required to gather the needed information. This expertise may have no association with the larger UQ analysis or the organization conducting the analysis. If systems similar to the one of interest have been operational and tested in the past, then significant information can be obtained from these sources. However, this route usually requires searching through old records, digging through data, and finding individuals who are familiar with the data in order to fill in gaps in the information and provide the proper interpretation. In many cases, separate laboratories or organizations are contracted by the organization conducting the larger UQ analysis so that needed data can be generated. The data can be either experimental measurements or theoretical studies using models that are specifically constructed so that their SRQs are the input quantities for the larger UQ analysis of interest.

Eliciting and analyzing expert opinion has received a great deal of attention recently (Cullen and Frey, 1999; Ayyub, 2001; Meyer and Booker, 2001; Vose, 2008). This is due to the recognition of how important it is in UQ analyses, as well as how often it must be done. The references cited list a number of procedures for eliciting, analyzing, and characterizing expert opinion. It is important to recognize that these elicited experts should have two kinds of expertise: substantive expertise on the issue at hand, i.e., in-depth technical knowledge of the issue; and normative expertise, i.e., understanding of the methods of quantification of the uncertainty in the elicited information. The references given discuss a number of pitfalls that can occur in expert elicitation, as well as methods for reducing or eliminating their impact. Two of the primary pitfalls are misinterpretation and misrepresentation of expert data. By *misinterpretation*, we mean that either the expert misinterpreted the question being asked by the elicitor or the elicitor misinterpreted the information provided by the expert. By *misrepresentation*, we mean that the elicitor misrepresents, unintentionally or intentionally, the information from the expert. This most commonly occurs when the elicitor converts the expert information into a mathematical structure that is used as input to the model.

In this regard, risk analysts using PBA have found that the most common difficulty is the lack of understanding of aleatory, epistemic, and mixed uncertainties by the experts. It is the responsibility of the *elicitor* to clearly explain and give a number of examples to the expert before the elicitation process is initiated. After it appears that the expert understands each type of uncertainty, then specific questions dealing with the model inputs can be queried. After the expert provides answers to the questions, it is highly advisable that the elicitor gives back to the expert his/her interpretation of what the expert seemed to have said. Often one finds that there is a miscommunication, primarily because of the subtle differences between aleatory, epistemic, and mixed uncertainties that are not fully grasped by the expert.

Cullen and Frey (1999) stress the importance of both the expert and elicitor understanding what kind of aleatory uncertainty is being captured in the elicitation. Here, we will refer to aleatory uncertainty as simply variability. Cullen and Frey (1999) point out that there are three types of variability: (a) temporal variability, (b) spatial variability, and (c) inter-individual variability. Temporal variability deals with the question of how a quantity varies as a function of the time scale of interest in the analysis. For example, suppose the variability of wind speed at a given location is needed in the analysis. Suppose the analysis requires, because of the assumptions in the model, the distribution of wind speed averaged over the period of a month, individually for each month of the year. All of these aspects should be made clear to the expert so that no confusion or miscommunication occurs. For example, the expert may have never dealt with the wind speed variability over such a long time period.

Spatial variability refers to how a quantity varies in space. If a quantity varies over space, ignoring time dependence for the present, then one must clarify for the expert what type of spatial averaging one is interested in for the model. For example, suppose the model is dealing with the dispersal of a contaminant in the atmosphere. Suppose the finest scale for the discretization of space in the computational model is 1 m^3 of air and this occurs near the surface of the Earth. As a result, the finest spatial scale of concentration of the mass of the contaminant is 1 m^3 of air. If an expert is questioned about his/her opinion of spatial scales of fluid dynamic turbulence, then it must be clarified that the smallest spatial scale of turbulence that exists in the model is 1 m^3.

Inter-individual variability refers to how an outcome can vary over the sample space of all possible outcomes, i.e., the population. Outcomes can be the result of physical measurements, a theoretical model, or a sequence of observations. When a model for the UQ analysis is constructed, a specific definition of a population is defined. For example, one may be interested in the population of all parts manufactured by a supplier during a particular month or a particular year. If this information is not experimentally available, it may be elicited from an expert knowledgeable about similar manufactured parts, but not necessarily from the same supplier. The elicitation process must be very clear to the expert concerning exactly what population is of interest for the model in the UQ analysis.

Depending on the perspective of the elicitor, they may require that the expert provide information in terms of very rigid mathematical structures, e.g., "We will not let the expert out of the room until they give us a probability distribution for the input." We, of course, do not subscribe to that type of interrogation technique. The expert should not be pressured into providing more information than they feel they can support. The following are examples of the types of mathematical structure that can be provided by an expert for an input quantity. The list is ordered in terms of the least information provided to the most information.

- A single (deterministic) value for the quantity is presumed to exist. The expert only claims that they know this value to within an interval.
- A single (deterministic) value for the quantity is presumed to exist. The expert claims that they know this value over an interval, but they have a higher level of confidence over certain regions of the interval than others. As a result, they can provide a belief structure over the interval.
- The quantity is a continuous random variable. The expert claims that the sample space cannot be less than a certain value and it cannot be greater than a certain value.
- The quantity is a continuous random variable. The expert claims that the probability distribution is a specific theoretical distribution, the sample space cannot be less than a certain value and it cannot be greater than a certain value.
- The quantity is a continuous random variable. The expert claims that the probability distribution is a specific theoretical distribution and that all the parameters in the distribution are known to be within specified intervals.
- The quantity is a continuous random variable. The expert claims that the probability distribution is a specific theoretical distribution and all the parameters are precisely known.

Mathematical characterization of certain types of information can be constructed by some of the software packages mentioned above. Another package that can deal with characterizing information with epistemic uncertainties is CONSTRUCTOR (Ferson *et al.*, 2005).

Whenever there is uncertainty, either aleatory or epistemic, in more than one input quantity, correlation or dependencies commonly exist between the quantities. There are two basic types of dependency, aleatory dependency and epistemic dependency. How to deal with aleatory dependence is fairly well understood. See, for example, Cullen and Frey (1999); Devore (2007); and Vose (2008). How to deal with epistemic or mixed dependence, however, is still is still a research topic. See, for example, Couso *et al.* (2000); Cozman and Walley (2001); and Ferson *et al.* (2004). Deducing dependency between model inputs can be aided by experimental data, theoretical modeling information, or expert opinion. The task of determining dependency increases rapidly as the number of uncertain inputs in the UQ analysis increases. As a result, the most common approach is to assume independence between all inputs and proceed with the UQ analysis. This assumption, although very expedient, can greatly underestimate the uncertainty in the outcomes of the UQ analysis. It is beyond the scope of this summary to deal with issues of characterization of dependency. For a detailed discussion, see the references just mentioned.

13.2.2 Model uncertainty

Here we are interested in characterizing the model form uncertainty, as discussed in Section 13.1.2, by estimating the model uncertainty over the domain where the model

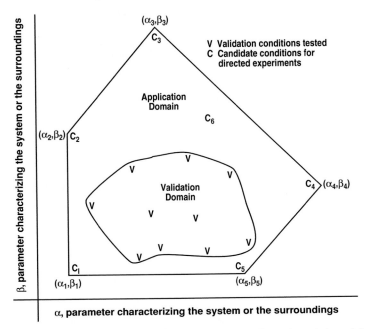

Figure 13.4 Validation domain and application domain in two dimensions (adapted from Trucano *et al.*, 2002).

will be used, i.e., the application domain. We have also referred to model uncertainty as model bias uncertainty, calling attention to the analogy with experimental bias, or systematic, uncertainty. If the application domain is completely enclosed in the validation domain, then model uncertainty can generally be well estimated based on validation metric results, as discussed in Chapter 12. When we compute a validation metric we ask two questions. First, how well do the predictions match the actual measurements that are available for the system? And second, what does the model uncertainty in the predictions tell us about what we should infer about other predictions? That is, when we make a new prediction, it is based on the physics in the model, how well the model has performed in the past, and the conditions for the new prediction. Model uncertainty is based directly on what has been observed in (preferably blind) *prediction performance* of the model. If any portion of the application domain is outside the validation domain, then some type of extrapolation procedure must be used for the estimation of model uncertainty. In practical engineering applications, some degree of extrapolation is commonly required.

Figure 13.4, from Chapter 10, Model validation fundamentals, captures the essence of the concept of interpolation and extrapolation of the model in two dimensions. Recall that α and β are parameters characterizing conditions of the system or the surroundings. The Vs denotes conditions where experimental data have been obtained and (α_i, β_i), $i = 1, 2, \ldots, 5$, denote the corners of the application domain for the engineering system, sometimes called the operating envelope of the system. A validation metric result can

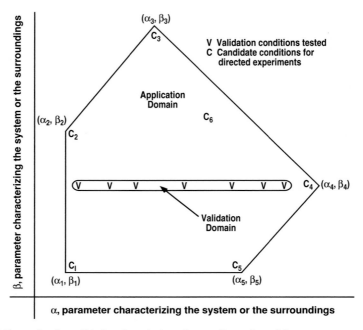

Figure 13.5 Example of a validation domain in only one dimension of the parameter space.

be computed at each of the Vs in Figure 13.4. One can imagine a surface above the $\alpha - \beta$ plane representing the estimated uncertainty in the model over the validation domain.

In Chapter 12, two approaches were discussed in detail for computing validation metrics: the confidence interval approach, and the method of comparing CDFs from the model and the experiment. The first approach estimated the model uncertainty in the mean of the SRQ of interest, and the CDF approach estimated the evidence for model mismatch of the SRQ. To estimate the model uncertainty over the validation domain, either an interpolation function or regression fit of the estimated uncertainty at each of the Vs can be computed. Whether one uses an interpolation function or a regression fit, one must include in the representation the scatter in the experimental data and the aleatory and epistemic uncertainty that may exist in the model prediction. If one uses a regression fit, one must also include the uncertainty due to the lack of fit because of the choice of the regression function.

More commonly, one of the following situations occurs: (a) the data are sparse over the validation domain, (b) the dimensionality of the parameter space characterizing the system or surroundings is very large and data are available only for a few of these dimensions, and (c) all of the data are for a fixed value of one of the dimensions of the parameter space. An example of this last case is shown in Figure 13.5. For the case where there is sparse data, one should use a low order polynomial regression fit of the model uncertainty estimates (the Vs) in the dimensions where data are available. A regression fit using a first- or second-degree polynomial would probably not capture all of the features of the model uncertainty over the validation domain, but it would be a much more robust and reliable estimate than the vagaries of an interpolation function. Robustness of the estimation of the model uncertainty is especially important if extrapolation of the uncertainty is required outside of the validation domain. For the case where data are available only along certain dimensions of the parameter space, one is forced to extrapolate the model uncertainty in all of the remaining dimensions. For example, in Figure 13.5, model uncertainty in the β dimension must be estimated either by extrapolation or by the use of alternative plausible models. For the case shown in the figure, the extrapolation is so weak that it would only support a model uncertainty function that does not change in the β direction. Both the extrapolation approach and the alternative models approach will be discussed in more detail in Section 13.4.2.

When the application domain is outside the validation domain, extrapolation must deal with two issues. First, there is extrapolation of the model itself, in the sense that the model is used to make a prediction in terms of the input data and parameters characterizing the system or surroundings. For physics-based models, this extrapolation can be viewed as constrained by the equations for conservation of mass, momentum, and energy, and any other physics-based principles embedded in the model or submodels. For nonphysics-based models, e.g., purely regression fits of data, extrapolation would be foolhardy. Second, one must also extrapolate the model uncertainty that has been observed over the validation domain. Extrapolating model uncertainty is a complex theoretical issue because it is extrapolating the error structure of a model, combined with the uncertainty in the experimental data, in a high dimensional space. However, it is *not as risky*, in our view, as extrapolating a regression fit of the measured SRQs themselves without the benefit of physics. For a system exposed to abnormal or hostile environments, the concept of interpolation or extrapolation of a validation metric result is questionable because of the complexity of the environment. These environments are usually not well characterized by parameters defining a validation domain because there are commonly strong interactions between subsystems, poorly known system geometries or surroundings, and strongly coupled physics.

13.2.3 Example problem: heat transfer through a solid

Here, we continue with the development of the heat transfer example begun in Section 13.1.3.

13.2.3.1 Model input uncertainty

Recalling Table 13.1, there are two uncertain model input parameters in the heat transfer example, k and h. The characterization of the uncertainty in k is based on experimental measurements conducted on small samples of aluminum cut from the actual plates used in the system. Samples were cut from multiple locations on multiple plates so that the measured variability in k is representative of both causal factors. The location of the samples was drawn randomly over the area of the plate, and the plates were drawn randomly from multiple production lots of plates. A total of 20 samples were cut from the various plates. Since there was a concern about the dependence of k on temperature, k was measured for

Table 13.2 *Experimentally measured values of k for the heat transfer example (W/m-K).*

Sample no.	$T = 300$ K	$T = 400$ K	$T = 500$ K
1	159.3	164.8	187.8
2	145.0	168.0	180.1
3	164.2	170.3	196.1
4	169.6	183.5	182.1
5	150.8	165.2	186.4
6	170.2	183.6	200.4
7	172.2	182.0	199.6
8	151.8	170.2	192.7
9	154.4	165.8	191.8
10	163.7	175.6	194.3
11	157.1	169.0	191.9
12	167.1	181.7	192.4
13	161.1	174.6	185.2
14	174.5	194.4	199.4
15	165.8	177.3	181.9
16	163.9	172.4	189.4
17	171.3	182.2	195.9
18	154.3	170.3	191.9
19	159.4	174.4	196.7
20	155.1	170.6	184.1

each sample at three temperatures; 300, 400, and 500 K. All of the measured values of k are shown in Table 13.2.

Figure 13.6 plots the measured k values for each of the 20 samples as a function of temperature. Scatter in the measurements is due not only to manufacturing variability, but also experimental measurement uncertainty. Here, we do not attempt to separate the two sources of uncertainty, although this could be done statistically using design of experiments (DOE) techniques (Montgomery, 2000; Box *et al.*, 2005) discussed in Chapter 11, Design and execution of validation experiments. Also shown in Figure 13.6 is a linear regression fit of the data using the method of least squares. Although the assumption has been made that k is independent of temperature, the data show an 18% increase in the mean value of k over the range of measured temperatures. The effect of this temperature dependence on the SRQ of interest should be detected in the validation experiments. The regression fit of k and the residual scatter is given by

$$k \sim 116.8 + 0.1473T + N(0, 7.36) \quad \text{W/m-K.} \tag{13.6}$$

The normal distribution indicates the residual standard error from the regression analysis results in a mean of zero and a standard deviation $\sigma = 7.36$. σ quantifies the vertical scatter

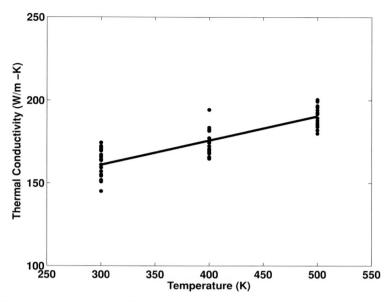

Figure 13.6 Measurements of k for 20 plate samples as a function of temperature.

of k at a given value of temperature. The R^2 value of the regression fit is 0.735. R^2 is referred to as the square of the multiple correlation coefficient, or the coefficient of multiple determination (Draper and Smith, 1998). R^2 is interpreted as the proportion of the observed variation in k that can be represented by the regression model.

Concerning various sources of uncertainty in k, one could ask the question: for a given temperature, how much of the variability in k is due to the variability from plate to plate, versus how much is due to location on the plate? If the information on each of the samples was recorded as to which plate it was cut from and where on each plate it was cut, then the question could be answered using design of experiment (DOE). As is common, however, the analyst may have only thought about this question after the experiments were conducted and after he starts to think about what could be the sources of uncertainty. In any type of experimental measurement program, it is not uncommon for the experimentalist to tell the analyst who requests measurements: "If you had only told me to measure it, I could have easily done it." We make this comment to stress Guideline 1 discussed in Section 12.1.1: *A validation experiment should be jointly designed by experimentalists, model developers, code developers, and code users working closely together throughout the program, from inception to documentation, with complete candor about the strengths and weaknesses of each approach.*

Figure 13.7 shows the empirical distribution function (EDF) (solid line) for all of the measurements of k. To characterize the possibility of more extreme values that were not seen among the limited samples, and to obtain a continuous approximation of the EDF for a large number of samples, it is common practice to fit a distribution to the data. We

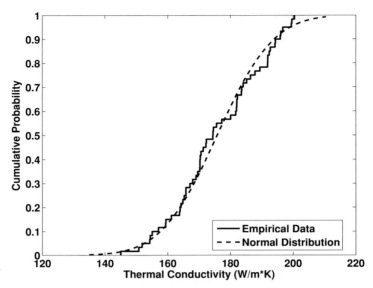

Figure 13.7 Empirical distribution function for k and the normal distribution obtained by the method of matching moments.

used a normal distribution to characterize the variability of k, such that the distribution had the same mean and standard deviation as the data set, according to the method of matching moments (Morgan and Henrion, 1990). It is easily computed that the sample mean, $\bar{k}$, is 175.8 W/m-K and the sample deviation is 14.15. Therefore, the computed normal distribution is given by

$$k \sim N(175.8, 14.15) \quad \text{W/m-K.} \tag{13.7}$$

The normal distribution is shown in Figure 13.7 as the dashed line.

A discrete representation of the PDE describing the heat transfer, the boundary conditions, and the heat flux through the west face will now be considered. Using a second order, central difference scheme for the PDE, Eq. (13.1), one obtains

$$\frac{T_{i+1,j} - 2T_{i,j} + T_{i-1,j}}{\Delta x^2} + \frac{T_{i,j+1} - 2T_{i,j} + T_{i,j-1}}{\Delta y^2} = 0,$$

$$i = 1, 2, \ldots, i_{\max} \quad \text{and} \quad j = 1, 2, \ldots, j_{\max}, \tag{13.8}$$

where $i_{\max}$ and $j_{\max}$ are the number of mesh points in the x and y directions, respectively.

Using a second-order, one-sided, finite-difference approximation for the BC on the north face, Eq. (13.2), one obtains

$$-k \left(\frac{3T_{i,j_{\max}} - 4T_{i,j_{\max}-1} + T_{i,j_{\max}-2}}{2\Delta y} \right) = h \left(T_{i,j_{\max}} - T_{\mathrm{a}} \right). \tag{13.9}$$

Solving for the boundary temperature, $T_{i,j_{\max}}$, one obtains the BC for the north face:

$$T_{i,j_{\max}} = \frac{(2\Delta yh/k)T_a + 4T_{i,j_{\max}-1} - T_{i,j_{\max}-2}}{3 + (2\Delta yh/k)}. \tag{13.10}$$

h is considered a fixed but unknown quantity over the north face of the plate for a given operating condition. However, the system can operate under many different conditions that can alter the value of h. Because of the variety of poorly known conditions, h is characterized as an interval-valued quantity. Both fluid dynamics simulations and expert opinion based on operating experience of similar systems are used to determine the interval

$$h = [150,\ 250]\ \text{W/m}^2\text{-K}. \tag{13.11}$$

For the validation experiments, the airflow over the north face is adjusted and calibrated to yield a value of $h = 200$ W/m^2-K.

Using a second-order, one-sided, finite difference approximation for the BC on the south face, Eq. (13.3), we have

$$-k\left(\frac{-3T_{i,1} + 4T_{i,2} - T_{i,3}}{2\Delta y}\right) = 0. \tag{13.12}$$

Solving this equation for the boundary temperature, $T_{i,1}$, we have the BC for the south face

$$T_{i,1} = \frac{4}{3}T_{i,2} - \frac{1}{3}T_{i,3}. \tag{13.13}$$

Using a second-order, one-sided, finite-difference approximation for the local heat flux through the west face, Eq. (13.5), we have

$$q_{\text{w}}(y) = -k\left(\frac{-3T_{1,j} + 4T_{2,j} - T_{3,j}}{2\Delta x}\right) + O(\Delta x^2). \tag{13.14}$$

$q_{\text{w}}(y)$ can be directly evaluated once the iterative solution for $T_{i,j}$ has converged. The mid-point rule of integration can be used for the total heat flux through the west face, Eq. (13.4), resulting in

$$(q_{\text{w}})_{\text{total}} = \frac{\tau}{2}\sum_{j=1}^{j_{\max}-1}\left[(q_{\text{w}})_j + (q_{\text{w}})_{j+1}\right]\Delta y. \tag{13.15}$$

The appropriate BCs for each of the four surfaces are coupled to the solution for the finite difference equation for the interior mesh points, Eq. (13.8). Solving Eq. (13.8) for the interior mesh point $T_{i,j}$, one has

$$T_{i,j} = \frac{T_{i+1,j} + T_{i-1,j} + (\Delta x^2/\Delta y^2)T_{i,j+1} + (\Delta x^2/\Delta y^2)T_{i,j-1}}{2 + (\Delta x^2/\Delta y^2)}. \tag{13.16}$$

This equation, coupled with the appropriate finite difference equations for the BCs, is solved iteratively. We use the Gauss–Seidel method discussed in Chapter 7, Solution verification. In Section 13.3 we discuss a method for estimating the discretization and iterative errors.

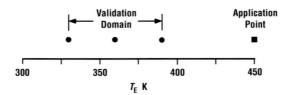

Figure 13.8 Validation domain and application point for the heat transfer example.

13.2.3.2 Model uncertainty

Examining Table 13.1, we can characterize the space of system and surroundings parameters as an eight-dimensional space; L_x, L_y, τ, k, T_E, T_W, h, and q_S. For this example, there is only one parameter, T_E, which is actually varied. All of the other parameters are either deterministic or an uncertain parameter. As a result, we have a 1-dimensional application and validation domain. This 1-dimensional space is depicted in Figure 13.8. Validation data are obtained at the three conditions shown in Figure 13.8, 330, 360, and 390 K, and a validation metric result is calculated for these conditions. The validation metric result, however, will need to be extrapolated to the application point of 450 K. Since we observed that k increases slightly with temperature, there will clearly be increased uncertainty in the prediction due to the extrapolation of the validation metric results.

As discussed in Section 13.1.3, the validation experiment used aluminum plates of size 0.1×0.1 m that were cut from the system plates. Similar to the material samples for measuring k, validation plates were cut from multiple locations on system plates, from multiple plates, and from multiple production lots. All of these samples were drawn randomly from their respective populations. As a result, the variability of k in the validation experiment plates should be similar to the variability in k shown above in Figure 13.6 and Figure 13.7.

Four sets of independent validation experiments were conducted. One experimental setup was used for each of the three temperatures tested, $T_E = 330$, 360, and 390 K. That is, for a given experimental setup, one measurement of q_W was made at each of the three temperatures. Then the experimental setup was disassembled, old diagnostic sensors were removed, new sensors installed, and the experimental setup was reassembled with a new plate. This procedure takes advantage of DOE principles to reduce systematic (bias) uncertainties in the experimental measurements. For all of the validation experiments the convective heat transfer coefficient on the north face was controlled so that $h = 200$ W/m²-K.

Table 13.3 gives the experimental data for q_W from the four sets of validation experiments. The negative sign for the heat flux indicates that the heat transfer is in the $-x$ direction, i.e., out of the west face of the plate. Just as with measurements of k, the experimental uncertainty in q_W includes both the experimental measurement uncertainty and the variability in k.

To characterize model uncertainty, we use the confidence interval approach that is based on comparing the mean response of the model and the mean of the measurements, as discussed in Sections 13.4 through 13.7. Using the experimental data in Table 13.3 and the appropriate equations from Section 13.6.1, we obtain

Table 13.3 *Experimental measurements of q_W from the validation experiments (W).*

Experimental setup	$T_E = 330$ K	$T_E = 360$ K	$T_E = 390$ K
1	−41.59	−100.35	−149.71
2	−49.65	−95.85	−159.96
3	−55.06	−99.45	−153.68
4	−49.36	−104.54	−155.44

number of samples $= n = 12$,
y intercept from the linear curve fit $= \theta_1 = 533.5$,
slope from the linear curve fit $= \theta_2 = -1.763$,
standard deviation of the residuals of the curve fit $= s = 4.391$,
coefficient of determination $= R^2 = 0.991$,
0.9 quantile of the F probability distribution for $v_1 = 2$ and $v_2 = 10$, yields $F(2,10,0.9) = 2.925$,
mean of the x input values $= \bar{x} = 360$,
variance of the x input values $= s_x^2 = 654.5$.

To keep this analysis simpler, we have made an approximation that should be pointed out. This confidence interval analysis assumes that the 12 experimental samples are independent samples. However, as described above in the description of the validation experiments, there were four independent experiments and each experiment made three measurements of q_W. As a result, this analysis could under-represent the uncertainty in the experimental measurements.

The linear regression equation for the experimental data is

$$[\bar{q}_W(T_E)]_{\exp} = 533.5 - 1.763 T_E, \tag{13.17}$$

and the Scheffeé confidence intervals are

$$\text{SCI}\,(x) = \pm 3.066\sqrt{1 + 0.001667(T_E - 360)^2}. \tag{13.18}$$

This validation metric approach only uses the mean of the model result to compare with the estimated mean of the experimental data. We could take the common approach of simply computing one solution for each of the three temperatures used in the experiment. Each of these solutions would use the sample mean of k determined from the material characterization experiments, $\bar{k} = 175.8$ W/m-K, to compute the three values of q_W. As discussed in Section 13.4.1, this approach is not recommended because the mean of an uncertain input quantity maps to the mean of the SRQ *only* for the case when the model is *linear* in the uncertain quantity. This situation rarely occurs, even for linear PDEs. If the coefficient of variation (COV) of the important input random variables is small and the model is not extremely nonlinear with respect to these random variables, then the

Table 13.4 *Values of $\bar{q}_W$ computed*
from Monte Carlo sampling for the
validation temperatures.

T_E, (K)	$\bar{q}_W$, (W/m^2)
330	-51.59
360	-103.93
390	-155.54

approximation of using the mean value of all of the uncertain input variables can give reasonably accurate results. The COV is defined as σ/μ, where σ and μ are the standard deviation and mean of the random variable, respectively.

Even though for the present example the $(COV)_k = 0.08$, we will still use Monte Carlo sampling to propagate the distribution of k through the model to obtain the mean of q_W, $\bar{q}_W$, for each value of T_E. Each distribution of q_W was calculated by computing 1000 Monte Carlo simulations using the variability of k given by $N(175.8, 14.15)$ W/m-K. (A more detailed discussion of Monte Carlo sampling will be given in Section 13.4.1.) With these three distributions for the SRQ, we have a great deal more information about the predicted uncertain response of the system. As a result, we could also use the validation metric approach based on comparing CDFs, but we reserve using this metric for the example problem discussed later in this chapter. Table 13.4 gives $\bar{q}_W$ computed from each set of 1000 Monte Carlo simulations for the three temperatures used in the validation experiment.

Figure 13.9 shows the linear regression of the experimental data, the Scheffé confidence intervals, and the $\bar{q}_W$ resulting from the model. The quadratic interpolation of the model is given by

$$(\bar{q}_W)_{\text{model}} = 572.3 - 2.025 \, T_E + 0.0004056 \, T_E^2. \tag{13.19}$$

Over this range in temperature the model is nearly linear. It is seen that the model slightly over-predicts (in absolute value) the measured heat flux over the temperature range measured. One may not expect this over-prediction because Figure 13.6 shows that the thermal conductivity increases with temperature. The explanation for the over-prediction is that the CDF of k (Figure 13.7) is derived from the *entire* set of material characterization data, resulting in a shift of $\bar{k}$ to a higher value that would be appropriate for higher temperatures. As the temperature increases, it can be seen in Figure 13.9 that the model gives a more accurate prediction of the data.

Figure 13.10 shows the estimated model error and the Scheffé confidence intervals of the experimental data as a function of temperature. This plot is much clearer than Figure 13.9 because we concentrate on the *difference* between the model and the mean of the experimental data; not on the magnitude of the SRQ itself. Since the mean of the

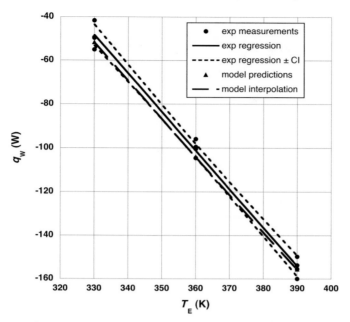

Figure 13.9 Comparison of experimental measurements and model predictions for heat flux over the range of validation data.

experimental data is expressed as a linear function, and the model prediction is nearly linear, it can be seen in Figure 13.10 that the estimated model error is nearly linear. Using a linear regression function to represent the experimental data, the Scheffé confidence intervals, Eq. (13.18), are seen to be symmetric hyperbolic functions. The confidence intervals shown represent the extent of the true mean of the experimental data for a confidence level of 90%, given the experimental data that has been observed. This shows that the estimated model error falls within the ±90% confidence intervals of the data.

Even though we are primarily interested in the model error, we must also include the uncertainty in the estimate. For the confidence interval approach to validation metrics, the uncertainty is *only* representative of the experimental uncertainty, i.e., it does not take into account any uncertainty in the model prediction. The validation metric function d is the characterization of the estimated model uncertainty and is written as

$$d(T_\mathrm{E}) = [\bar{q}_\mathrm{w}\,(T_\mathrm{E})]_\mathrm{model} - \left\{[\bar{q}_\mathrm{w}\,(T_\mathrm{E})]_\mathrm{exp} \pm \mathrm{SCI}(T_\mathrm{E})\right\}. \qquad (13.20)$$

Into this equation we substitute the linear fit of the experimental data, Eq. (13.17); the Scheffé confidence interval, Eq. (13.18); and the quadratic interpolation of the model prediction, Eq. (13.19), to obtain the final expression

$$d(T_\mathrm{E}) = 38.8 - 0.262\,T_\mathrm{E} + 0.0004056\,T_\mathrm{E}^2 \mp 3.0066\sqrt{1 + 0.001667(T_\mathrm{E} - 360)^2}. \quad (13.21)$$

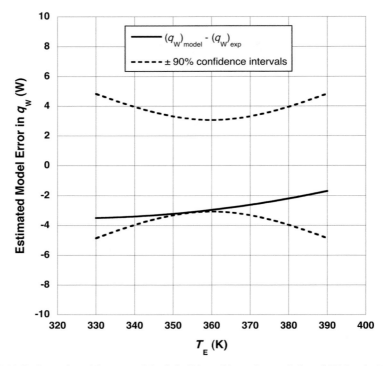

Figure 13.10 Estimated model error and the Scheffé confidence intervals for a 90% level of confidence over the validation domain.

Figure 13.11 shows a graph of Eq. (13.21) along with the estimated model error over the validation domain. This figure contains essentially the same information as Figure 13.10, but with Figure 13.11 certain interpretations are clearer. First, even though the model error is estimated to be small relative to the magnitude of the q_W, the uncertainty in the estimate is noticeably larger due to the uncertainty in the experimental measurements. For example, at $T_E = 330$ K, the estimated model error is only 3.5 W, but it may be as small as zero or as large as 8.3 W with a confidence level of 90%. Second, because the confidence intervals are a hyperbola, the uncertainty in the estimated model prediction will grow rapidly when the model is extrapolated beyond the validation domain.

13.3 Step 3: estimate numerical solution error

This step involves the estimation of two key sources of error in the numerical solution of PDEs: iterative and discretization error. As discussed in several earlier chapters, there are a number of other error sources that can occur in the numerical solution of PDEs, for example: (a) defective numerical solution algorithms, (b) data input

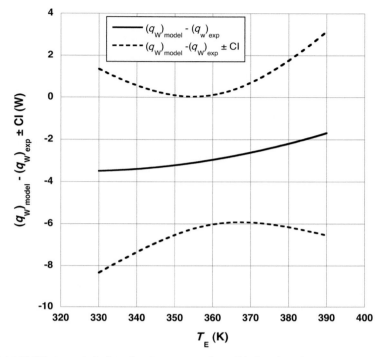

Figure 13.11 Validation metric function for q_W over the validation domain.

mistakes, (c) computer programming errors, (d) computer round-off errors, and (e) data post-processing mistakes. In this step, however, we will not deal with these sources.

It is stressed here that the estimation of iterative and discretization error must be conducted *on the SRQs of interest* in the analysis. It has been pointed out in various contexts that the sensitivity of SRQs to iterative and discretization error can vary drastically from one SRQ to another. Stated differently, for a fixed number of iterations and mesh points, some SRQs can be numerically converged orders of magnitude more (or less) than other SRQs. As discussed in Chapter 10, the discretization convergence rate is commonly related to the order of the derivatives and integrals of the dependent variables in the PDE. That is, the higher the order of the spatial or temporal derivative of one SRQ as compared to another SRQ, the slower the convergence rate. For example, in fluid dynamics the local shear stress at a point on a surface converges more slowly than the total shear stress integrated over an entire surface. As a result, the convergence of all of the SRQs of interest should be evaluated or checked in some way. If certain SRQs are known to be less sensitive to iterative and discretization error than others, and if the low sensitivity is observed over the entire domain of all conditions of interest in the analysis, then one can be more confident in the higher level of convergence of these SRQs.

13.3.1 Iterative error

13.3.1.1 Iterative methods

As discussed in Chapter 7, Solution verification, iterative convergence error arises due to incomplete convergence of the discrete equations. Iterative methods are usually required for the solution of nonlinear discrete equations (except for explicit marching methods), as well as for large linear systems. Various types of iterative error estimation technique were discussed for both stationary iterative methods and nonstationary (Krylov subspace) methods. Stationary methods tend to be more robust in applications compared to nonstationary methods. However, stationary methods tend to produce lower convergence rates than nonstationary methods.

Iterative methods are commonly applied in two different types of numerical solution: initial value problems (IVPs) and boundary value problems (BVPs). For IVPs where implicit methods are used, very few iterations are typically required for each step in the marching direction. This is because the initial guess for the iterative solution is based on the previously converged solution, and that the solution does not change much in the marching direction. For BVPs, typically a larger number of iterations are required to obtain a converged solution. As a result, for BVPs convergence characteristics should be closely monitored to determine if one has monotone, oscillatory, or mixed convergence characteristics. The most convenient method of tracking the iterative convergence is to compute the L_2 norm of the residuals of each of the PDEs as a function of iteration number. The most reliable method, however, is to estimate the iterative error as a function of the number of iterations. Depending on whether one has monotone, oscillatory, or mixed convergence, this can be cumbersome.

As discussed in Chapter 7, the iterative error should be driven at least as small as 1% of the discretization error when extrapolation-based discretization error estimators are used. However, it is advisable to reduce the error even smaller, e.g., 0.1%, because complex interactions can occur between iterative and discretization error. For example, if the iterative error is not driven small enough, it can result in a misleading or confusing trend in observed order of accuracy as the mesh resolution is changed. An alternative to estimating the iterative error is to monitor the discrete residuals, i.e., the nonzero remainder that occurs when the current iterative solution is substituted into the discrete equations. However, relating residual convergence to iterative error must be done heuristically for a given class of problems. As pointed out above, different SRQs typically converge at widely differing rates, so one should monitor the most slowly converging SRQs of interest. Monitoring the change between successive iterates is *not* reliable and should always be avoided.

13.3.1.2 Practical difficulties

To stress the variety of SRQs that can exist in an analysis, let the set of all SRQs of interest be written as a vector array $\vec{y}$. Let n be the number of elements in the array, each one being an SRQ of interest, so that one has

$$\vec{y} = \{y_1, y_2, \ldots, y_n\}. \tag{13.22}$$

Some of the elements of the array are typically the dependent variables in the PDEs. However, some of the array elements may be very different kinds of quantities, for example: (a) derivatives of dependent variables with respect to the independent variables, or derivatives with respect to input parameters to the model; (b) functionals such as integrals, time-averages, or min and max operators on the dependent variables; (c) cumulative distribution functions or a specific value of a CDF; and (d) indicator functions, for example, if the system is in a certain state, then a SRQ has the binary value of zero. If the system is in another state, the SRQ has a binary value of one.

Iterative convergence is normally thought of as dealing with the convergence of dependent variables of the PDEs. For example, one commonly monitors the convergence of a norm of the dependent variables over the domain of the PDE. However, one can also think of the mapping of the dependent variables to the elements of $\vec{y}$. Then one could ask the question: how do we quantify the iterative convergence of each of the elements of $\vec{y}$? If the quantity can be computed using the present solution that is being calculated, then one can monitor the iterative convergence of the quantity. For example, suppose one element of $\vec{y}$ is an integral of some dependent variable over the domain of the PDE. Then this quantity can be computed at each iteration and its convergence monitored. However, if the quantity *cannot* be computed from simply knowing the present solution, then iterative convergence of the quantity can be a difficult, or impossible, to monitor. For example, suppose one of the elements of $\vec{y}$ is a CDF. As will be discussed in Section 13.4, there are a number of methods for propagating input uncertainties to obtain uncertainties in $\vec{y}$. The most common method of propagating the uncertainties is to use sampling. When this is done, there will be an ensemble of hundreds or thousands of $\vec{y}$s, one for each sample of the uncertain input. As a result, the CDF cannot be computed until *after* an ensemble of solutions to the PDEs has been computed. For this latter case, one usually relies on stringent iterative convergence criteria for the dependent variables that are being monitored.

It should be stressed that the iterative convergence characteristics, as well as the mesh convergence characteristics to be discussed shortly, of the elements of $\vec{y}$ can change drastically over the sample space of the uncertain input quantities. Since the number of uncertain input quantities can be quite large for a complex analysis, this presents an additional complexity for monitoring iterative convergence. In addition, for unsteady simulations and hyperbolic PDEs, convergence rates of SRQs, particularly local SRQs, can change significantly over time and space. A good understanding of the dominant physical effects on the SRQs can greatly help in identifying the most troublesome convergence situations. If one is dealing with multi-physics simulations with large differences in temporal and spatial scales, one must be extremely cautious.

To try to deal with this, one should attempt to determine (a) what input quantities cause the most difficulties with regard to iterative convergence, (b) what range of values of these input quantities are the most troublesome, and (c) what SRQs converge at the slowest rate. Note that if one is dealing with an unsteady simulation or one has mixed or oscillatory convergence, this can be difficult. Even if one identifies the troublesome parameters and the problematic ranges, monitoring the convergence characteristics is still quite time consuming, and is highly prone to oversights. As a result, it is important to automate the monitoring of convergence as much as possible. Automatic tests should be programmed into the important iterative solvers so that if the iterative convergence of an element of $\vec{y}$ is suspect, then a special output warning flag is included in the output of the results. These *red flag* warning indictors should be checked on every sample that is computed for the ensemble.

13.3.2 Discretization error

13.3.2.1 Temporal discretization error

When temporal discretization errors are present in a problem, there are two basic approaches for controlling it: (a) the error is estimated at each time step, compared to some error criterion, and then adjustments are possibly made to the step size; and (b) an entire solution is computed with a fixed time step and then recomputed with either a larger or smaller fixed time step. The former approach is usually referred to as a variable or adaptive time step method and the latter as a fixed time step method. Note that for a variable time step method, the error criterion must be satisfied for *all* dependent variables and *all* spatial points in the domain of the PDE. In addition, since variable time step methods only estimate the per step temporal discretization error, they are susceptible to error accumulation when a large number of steps are taken. Both methods can be effective, but the former is typically more accurate, reliable, and efficient. It should be noted that although we refer to integration in time, the integration could be in any independent variable of a hyperbolic system. For example, in fluid dynamics, the boundary layer equations are integrated in a wall-tangent spatial direction (the downstream flow direction).

Practitioners of finite element methods typically use Runge-Kutta methods for time integration. Most Runge-Kutta methods are explicit methods of order 2, 3, or 4, and they are able to estimate the discretization error at each time step. Variable time step Runge-Kutta methods are known to be very reliable and robust, resulting in their widespread use. The primary shortcomings of Runge-Kutta methods, and all explicit methods, are that they require relatively small time steps because they are conditionally stable schemes and that they can suffer from error accumulation when a large number of steps is required.

Implicit time integration methods provide a significant increase in numerical stability. This allows very large time steps to be taken, while damping both temporal and spatial modes of instability. Of course, this trade-off is at the expense of temporal discretization accuracy. Implicit methods provide significant advantages in the solution of stiff differential equations. Since most implicit methods are only second order, there is a rapid increase in discretization error as the time step is increased. Implicit Runge-Kutta methods have recently been developed and these have advantageous properties. See Cellier and Kofman

(2006) and Butcher (2008) for a detailed discussion of numerical methods for ordinary differential equations. The choice of implicit versus explicit methods should depend on both the stability restrictions and the accuracy needed to resolve the time scales in the problem.

13.3.2.2 Finite-element-based methods for mesh convergence

The Zienkiewicz–Zhu (ZZ) error estimator combined with the super–convergent patch recovery (SPR) method is probably the most widely used discretization error estimator (Zienkiewicz and Zhu, 1992). The ZZ-SPR recovery method can obtain error estimates in terms of the global energy norm or in terms of local gradients, given two conditions: (a) finite element types are used that have the superconvergent property, and (b) the mesh is adequately resolved. The method has recently been extended to finite-difference and finite-volume schemes. However, accurate error estimates can only be made in the global energy norm, which is a significant disadvantage for addressing many SRQs of interest.

Residual-based methods also provide error estimates in terms of the global energy norm. Since the global energy norm is rarely an SRQ, the adjoint system for PDEs must be solved along with the primal error PDE. As discussed in Chapter 7, an extension of the residual methods, referred to here as adjoint methods, has recently been applied to various SRQs as well as to other discretization schemes (e.g., finite-volume and finite-difference methods). These approaches are very promising and are currently under investigation by a number of researchers.

13.3.2.3 Richardson extrapolation error estimators for mesh convergence

Richardson extrapolation based error estimators are quite popular, particularly in fluid dynamics, because they are extremely general in their applicability. These methods do not depend on the numerical algorithm used, whether it is an IVP or BVP, the nonlinearity of the PDEs, the submodels that may be used, or whether the mesh is structured or unstructured. One disadvantage is that they require multiple solutions of the PDEs using different mesh resolutions. Standard Richardson extrapolation can be used if the numerical algorithm is second-order accurate and if the mesh is refined by a factor of two in each coordinate direction. Generalized Richardson extrapolation can be used for any order accuracy algorithm and with arbitrary refinement factors. Richardson extrapolation requires uniform mesh refinement or coarsening as one changes from one mesh solution to another. That is, the refinement or coarsening ratio must be nearly constant over the entire mesh from one mesh to the other. This type of refinement or coarsening requires significant capability of the mesh generator, particularly if an unstructured mesh is used.

The primary difficulty with using Richardson extrapolation is that the meshes must be sufficiently resolved so that all numerical solutions are within the asymptotic convergence region for the SRQ of interest. The spatial resolution required to attain the asymptotic region depends on the following factors: (a) the nonlinearity of the PDEs; (b) the range of spatial scales across the domain of the PDEs, i.e., the stiffness of the equations; (c) how rapidly the spatial mesh resolution changes over the mesh, i.e., how nonuniform the mesh is; (d) the presence of singularities or discontinuities in the solution e.g., shock waves, flame fronts, or discontinuities in the first or second derivatives of the boundary geometry; and (e) lack of iterative convergence.

If only two mesh solutions are computed, the grid convergence index (GCI) method (Roache, 1998) can be used with a safety factor of three to indicate spatial discretization error. However, if one has no empirical evidence that the meshes are in the asymptotic region, then the GCI estimate is not reliable. Computational analysts, even experienced analysts, commonly misjudge what spatial resolution is required to attain the asymptotic region. A more reliable procedure is to obtain three mesh solutions and then compute the observed order of convergence based on the three solutions. If the observed order is relatively near the formal order of the numerical method, then one has direct empirical evidence that the three meshes are in, or near, the asymptotic region for the SRQ of interest. A factor of safety of 1.25 or 1.5 would then be justified to yield a reliable uncertainty indication for the discretization error.

13.3.2.4 Practical difficulties

Three practical difficulties were mentioned with regard to iterative convergence: (a) the wide range of types of SRQ in $\vec{y}$, (b) dealing with hundreds or thousands of samples of $\vec{y}$, and (c) the sensitivity of certain elements of $\vec{y}$ to certain ranges of input quantities that are sampled. Temporal and mesh convergence methods suffer from these same difficulties. In addition, there is a difference in the mathematical structure between iterative convergence and temporal/spatial convergence. Iterative convergence characteristics are typically monitored by examining the magnitude of the residuals during the iterations of each solution to the discrete equations. This, of course, is monitored by tracking the norm of various quantities computed over the domain of the PDEs. With temporal/spatial convergence characteristics, however, one must monitor the change in local quantities in the domain of the PDEs as the mesh is resolved. This presumes that at least one of the elements of $\vec{y}$ is a local quantity over the domain. Local quantities could include not only dependent variables, but also spatial or temporal derivatives of dependent variables. As discussed in Chapter 10, derivatives, particularly higher order derivatives, converge much more slowly with respect to discretization error than dependent variables.

If one retreats to dealing with the L_2 norm of the error for the SRQs, then the risk is identical to those methods discussed earlier that only yield error norms of the spatial discretization error. Monitoring the L_∞ norm provides a much more sensitive indicator of temporal/spatial convergence error for each solution. The disadvantage, however, is that a great deal more *noise* will exist in the L_∞ norm. The noise results from this norm's ability to jump from any point in the domain for one level of spatial or temporal resolution to any other point in the domain for another level of spatial or temporal resolution. Stated differently, noise in the L_∞ norm is expected because of the nature of the mathematical operator, whereas noise in the L_2 norm is a clear sign of lack of convergence. Even though more noise exists with the L_∞ norm, it is a recommended quantity to monitor because it keeps a direct indication of the magnitude of the largest local error in a quantity over the domain of the PDEs.

A final recommendation is made to deal with some of the practical difficulties of temporal/spatial convergence, as well as iterative convergence. In an analysis that must deal with a wide range of values of the input quantities, it is advisable to try to identify what combinations of input quantities produce the slowest temporal, spatial, and iterative convergence rates for the most sensitive elements of $\vec{y}$. Sometimes the troublesome combinations of inputs can be deduced based on the physics occurring within the domain of the PDEs. Sometimes the troublesome combinations simply need to be found by experimentation with multiple solutions with different time steps, spatial discretizations, and iterative convergence criteria. Whatever method is used, it can greatly improve the efficiency and reliability of monitoring the temporal, spatial, and iterative error if the troublesome combinations of input are identified. That is, if the solution errors are estimated for the troublesome combinations, then these estimates can be used as bounds for the solution errors over the entire range of input quantities. These bounds may be extremely large for certain combinations of inputs, but this limited number of bounds is much easier to keep track of than estimates over a high-dimensional space of inputs.

13.3.3 *Estimate of total numerical solution error*

The risk assessment community has, in general, taken the view that the numerical solution error should be reduced to the point that its contribution to uncertainty is much less than the aleatory and epistemic uncertainties in the analysis. This is a very prudent approach because then one can be certain that the predicted outcomes are truly a result of the assumptions and physics in the model and the characterized uncertainties, as opposed to some unknown numerical distortion of the two. There are a number of science and engineering communities, however, that continue to develop models of such complexity that available computer resources do not allow the numerical solution error to be demonstrably neglected. Faced with this situation, one has two options for proceeding. First, calibrate the adjustable parameters so that computed results agree, or nearly agree, with available experimental measurements. Sometimes researchers are unaware they have even chosen this option because they have not quantified the magnitude of the numerical solution error on the SRQs of interest. Second, explicitly quantify the numerical solution error and characterize it in some way as an uncertainty in the prediction. Essentially all researchers choose the first option.

To our knowledge, the only researchers who have made an attempt to characterize numerical solution error and then explicitly include it in the uncertainty analysis were Coleman and Stern (1997); Stern *et al.* (2001); and Wilson *et al.* (2001). They define the uncertainty due to numerical solution error, U'_N, to be the square root of the sum of the squares of the following contributors: U_I is the estimated iterative solution error; U_S

is the estimated spatial discretization error; U_T is the estimated time discretization error; and U_P is the estimated solution error caused by adjustable parameters in the numerical algorithms. U_N' can be written as

$$U_N' = \sqrt{U_I^2 + U_S^2 + U_T^2 + U_P^2}. \tag{13.23}$$

Although they represent the solution error as an interval, it is clear from Eq. (13.23) that they characterize the solution error as a random variable. That is, if U_I, U_S, U_T, and U_P are independent random variables, then the sum of their variances is equal to the variance of U_N'. It is clear from the previous chapters that none of these quantities is a random variable. In addition, there is a dependency structure between these four quantities of which little is usually known or quantified. One could argue that far from the region of smooth iterative convergence, or far from the asymptotic range of spatial or temporal convergence, these quantities would display a random character. However, in this random region none of the methods for error estimation would be applicable, specifically Richardson extrapolation.

Our approach for explicitly including the estimated numerical solution error is to consider each contributor as an epistemic uncertainty for each of the SRQs of interest. Even though some numerical error estimators will provide a sign for the error, we will not take advantage of this knowledge because it may not be reliable. For example, if Richardson extrapolation is used to estimate the spatial discretization error, but we are not confident we are in the asymptotic region, the estimate could be significantly in error and even the sign may be incorrect. As a result, we will always take the absolute value of the estimate of each contributing quantity. Without assuming any dependence structure between the contributors, we can write

$$(U_N)_{y_i} = |U_I|_{y_i} + |U_S|_{y_i} + |U_T|_{y_i} \quad \text{for } i = 1, 2, \ldots, n. \tag{13.24}$$

We stress again, as discussed above, that the combination of input quantities that produce a maximum value of U_N for one y_i is commonly different than the combination of input quantities that produce a maximum for a different y_i.

We do not include the uncertainty due to the adjustable parameters in the numerical algorithms because this contribution is already included in the three terms shown in Eq. (13.24). That is, adjustable parameters such as relaxation factors in iterative algorithms, numerical damping parameters, and limiters in algorithms are already reflected in the terms shown in Eq. (13.24). It can be easily shown that

$$U_N' \leq U_N \quad \text{for all } U_I, U_S, \quad \text{and} \quad U_T. \tag{13.25}$$

It is clear from Eq. (13.24) that $U_N' = U_N$ only when two of the three contributors to uncertainty are negligible relative to the third.

13.3.4 Example problem: heat transfer through a solid

Here we continue with the development of the example problem discussed in Sections 13.1.3 and 13.2.3. We will discuss the iterative and discretization error related to the numerical solution of Eq. (13.16) in combination because they are always intertwined in computational analyses.

13.3.4.1 Iterative and discretization error estimation

As mentioned above, an analyst should attempt to identify what range of input parameters cause the SRQ of interest to converge the slowest. From a physical understanding of the heat transfer example, the slowest iterative and discretization convergence rates will occur when: (a) T_E is the highest; and (b) the thermal conductivity of the plate, k, is the highest. Referring to Table 13.1, the highest value of T_E, 450 K, occurs for the system of interest, so we will only address that case. Since k is given as a normal distribution without any stated bounds, i.e., the distribution has infinite support, some reasonable cumulative probability from the distribution must be chosen. We choose a cumulative probability of 0.99. Using Eq. (13.7), which is graphed in Figure 13.7, we find that $k = 209.7$ W/m-K for $P = 0.99$.

The largest temperature gradients in the plate will occur along the north face of the plate because heat is being lost along the north face and it is adjacent to the highest temperature surface, the east face. It can be seen from Eq. (13.9) that the highest heat flux through the north face will occur when h is a maximum. Since the highest value of h occurs in the system of interest, as opposed to the validation experiment, we use the interval-valued characterization of h, given by Eq. (13.11), to find that $h_{max} = 250$ W/m-K.

Chapter 7, Solution verification, and Chapter 8, Discretization error, discuss a number of different methods for estimating iterative and discretization error, respectively. For the heat transfer example, we will use the iterative error estimation technique developed by Duggirala *et al.* (2008) and we will use Richardson extrapolation to estimate the discretization error. Since these errors commonly interact in a simulation, the proper procedure is to evaluate each error component in a stepwise fashion and then conduct tests to determine if the interaction has been eliminated. Figure 13.12 depicts the 11 steps in the form of a flowchart for the estimation of iterative and discretization error.

1 Pick a sequence of three mesh resolutions such that the finest mesh resolution is believed to be adequate to satisfy the discretization error criterion. During either the preparation of a V&V plan or the conceptual modeling phase, one should decide on the maximum allowed discretization error. A discretization error criterion should be picked for each of the SRQs of interest. For the heat transfer example, we only have one SRQ, q_w. It is usually best to pick a relative error criterion, since this automatically scales the absolute error with the magnitude of the quantity. One should choose a demanding error criterion relative to the accuracy needs of the analysis because one should be certain that any disagreement between the model predictions and the experimental measurements is due to the physics assumptions in the model and *not* due to numerical errors. Here we pick a relative discretization error criterion for q_w of 0.1%.

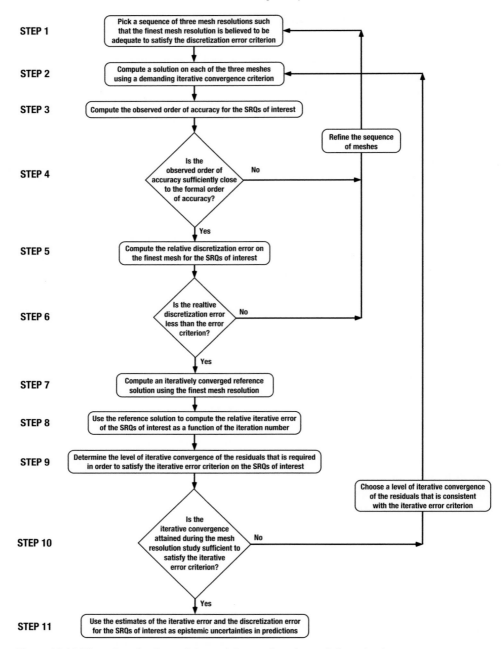

Figure 13.12 Flow chart for determining satisfactory iterative and discretization convergence.

The estimation of what mesh resolution will satisfy the error criterion is commonly based on experience with the numerical solution of similar problems with similar numerical methods. The mesh resolution required also depends on the effectiveness of the mesh clustering structure. Our experience, along with many others, is that numerically accurate solutions almost always require finer meshes than one would expect. Here we pick the three mesh resolutions, 21×21, 31×31, and 46×46, yielding a constant mesh refinement factor of 1.5 for both refinements. As discussed in Chapter 8, when one chooses a noninteger refinement factor and one of the SRQs of interest is a local quantity over the domain of the PDE, one must resort to an interpolation procedure to make the needed calculations for Richardson extrapolation. Since q_W is not a local quantity, we avoid this difficulty.

2 Compute a solution on each of the three meshes using a demanding iterative convergence criterion. Eq. (13.16) is solved for the interior mesh points and the BCs are given by $T_E = 450$ K, $T_W = 300$ K, Eq. (13.10) for the north face with $k = 209.7$ W/m-K and $h = 250$ W/m-K, and Eq. (13.13) for the south face. The initial guess for temperature over the solution domain is simply taken as the average temperature between the east and west faces, $T_{\text{initial}} = 375$ K. The iterative method used is the well-known Gauss–Seidel relaxation method. The iterative convergence criterion chosen here is based on the L_2 norm of the residuals of the dependent variable in the PDE, i.e., T, being solved. The convergence criterion chosen at this point is rather arbitrary because the definitive criterion will be set later in Step 9. One attempts to pick a criterion that is sufficiently demanding so that it is expected to satisfy the criterion evaluated in Step 10. Here we require that the norm of the residuals decrease by nine orders of magnitude compared to the first L_2 norm computed.

3 Compute the observed order of accuracy for the SRQs of interest. As discussed in Chapter 8, the observed order of discretization accuracy, p_O, can be computed using Richardson's method and three solutions. We have

$$p_O = \frac{\ln\left(\frac{f_3 - f_2}{f_2 - f_1}\right)}{\ln(r)}, \tag{13.26}$$

where f_1, f_2, and f_3 are the solutions for the SRQ on the fine, medium, and coarse meshes, respectively, and r in the mesh refinement factor.

4 Test if the observed order of accuracy of the SRQs of interest is sufficiently close to the formal order of accuracy. To use Richardson's method, one must have some evidence that the three mesh solutions are in or near the asymptotic region of spatial convergence. Computing p_O and comparing it with the formal order of accuracy, p_F, which is 2 for the present case, can provide the evidence. There is no strict requirement on how close p_O must be to p_F, but a typical requirement is

$$|p_O - p_F| < 0.5. \tag{13.27}$$

If p_O is not sufficiently close to p_F, then the mesh resolutions are not sufficiently in the asymptotic region and we must refine the sequence of meshes, and return to Step 1. If p_O and p_F are sufficiently close, then we can proceed to Step 5.

5 Compute the relative discretization error on the finest mesh for the SRQs of interest. The relative discretization error, normalized by the extrapolated estimate of the exact solution, $\bar{f}$, is given by

$$\frac{f_1 - \bar{f}}{\bar{f}} = \frac{f_2 - f_1}{f_1 r^{p_O} - f_2}. \tag{13.28}$$

This equation can also be solved for $\bar{f}$ to give

$$\bar{f} = f_1 + \frac{f_1 - f_2}{r^{p_o} - 1}. \tag{13.29}$$

6 Test if the relative discretization error is less than the error criterion. Using Eq. (13.28), we can compute the relative discretization error in q_{W} and determine if it is less than the relative error criterion of 0.1%. If the computed error is not less than the error criterion, then we must refine the sequence of meshes and return to Step 1. If the computed error is less than the error criterion, then we can proceed to Step 7.

7 Compute an iteratively converged reference solution using the finest mesh resolution. The technique we use for estimating the iterative error is based on generating a reference solution and then developing a mapping between the reference solution and the L_2 norm of the residuals for the PDE being solved. The norm of the residuals for the reference solution should be converged at least ten orders of magnitude; possibly even to machine precision. This solution will be used as the fully converged or reference solution to the discrete equations. When this reference solution is being iteratively converged, the L_2 norm of the residuals as well as the SRQs of interest should be saved every 50 or 100 iterations. The saved results will be used to construct the mapping between the reference solution and the L_2 norm of the residuals for the PDE. If any of the SRQs are quantities defined over the domain of the PDEs, e.g., dependent variables, then the L_2 norm of the quantity should be used.

8 Use the reference solution, $f_{\mathrm{reference}}$, to compute the relative iterative error as a function of the iteration number for the SRQs of interest. Using the reference solution as the exact solution, one can compute the relative iterative error as a function of the iteration number using

$$\% \text{ error in } f_{i\text{th iteration}} = \left| \frac{f_{\mathrm{reference}} - f_{i\text{th iteration}}}{f_{\mathrm{reference}}} \right| \times 100\%, \tag{13.30}$$

where $f_{i\text{th iteration}}$ is the value of the SRQ, or the L_2 norm of the quantity if it is a dependent variable in the PDE, at the ith iteration.

9 Determine the level of iterative convergence of the residuals that is required in order to satisfy the iterative convergence criterion on the SRQs of interest. The iterative convergence criterion should be specified during the preparation of the V&V plan or during the conceptual modeling phase. It is recommended to be 1/100th of the relative discretization error criterion specified for any SRQs of interest. This much smaller value for the relative iterative error criterion is chosen so that we can be certain that there is little or no interaction between iterative convergence and discretization convergence. Here we pick a relative iterative convergence criterion of 0.001% for q_{W}.

Using the quantities saved in Step 7, one can plot the iterative convergence history of the residuals along with the relative iterative error in the SRQs as a function of the iteration number. Using the relative iterative error criterion as the requirement, one can then determine the level of iterative convergence of the residuals that is needed in order to satisfy the iterative error criterion. That is, the combined plot provides a mapping between the desired iterative error in the SRQs and the iterative convergence of the residuals. When other numerical solutions are computed, such as varying the input parameters in a design study or in Monte Carlo sampling of the uncertain inputs, the iterative convergence rate of most SRQs will change. However, as long as the mapping relationship between the iterative error in the SRQs and the iterative convergence of the residuals remains the same, then this iterative error estimation procedure will be reliable.

10 Test if the iterative convergence attained in the L_2 residuals during the mesh resolution study is sufficient to satisfy the iterative error criterion in the SRQs of interest. The purpose of this test is to determine if the level of convergence of the L_2 residuals used in Step 2 is smaller than the level of convergence of the L_2 residuals determined in Step 9. If the convergence of the residuals in Step 2 was inadequate, then we must use the residual convergence level determined in Step 9 and return to Step 2. If the convergence of the residuals in Step 2 is satisfactory, we can proceed to Step 11.

11 Use the estimates of the iterative error and the discretization error for the SRQs of interest as epistemic uncertainties in predictions. The values computed for the relative iterative error and the relative discretization error for the SRQs of interest are converted to absolute errors so that they can be substituted into Eq. (13.24). Since these errors are, hopefully, for the case(s) of slowest iterative and discretization convergence, they should be conservative bounds on the errors for all other conditions computed in the analysis.

13.3.4.2 Iterative and discretization error results

Now, we give the key results for the heat transfer example from various steps discussed above.

From Step 2: The L_2 norm of T on the first iteration was computed to be 1.469×10^4 K. Using the preliminary relative iterative convergence criterion of nine orders of magnitude decrease in the L_2 norm, we have $10^{-9} \bullet 1.469 \times 10^4 = 1.469 \times 10^{-5}$ K as the preliminary L_2 norm criterion.

From Step 3: The observed order of accuracy in q_w is computed from the solutions on the three meshes 21×21, 31×31, and 46×46. The values of q_w from these three solutions are $-270.260\,295\,374$, $-270.477\,983\,330$, $-270.575\,754\,310$ W, respectively. Using these values and Eq. (13.26), the result is $p_O = 1.974$.

From Step 4: Since $p_O = 1.974$ satisfies Eq. (13.27), the test in Step 4 is satisfied.

From Step 5: The relative discretization error in q_w is computed on the 46×46 mesh using Eq. (13.28), the solutions on the 31×31 and 46×46 meshes, and the observed order of accuracy of 1.974. The relative discretization error is computed to be -3.1214×10^{-4}. Using Eq. (13.29), the estimate of the converged solution obtained from Richardson extrapolation is computed to be $-270.660\,237\,711$ W. This results in an estimated discretization error in the 46×46 mesh solution of 0.08448 W.

From Step 6: Since this relative discretization error is less than the error criterion of 1×10^{-3}, the test in Step 6 is satisfied.

From Steps 7–10: Figure 13.13 shows the iterative convergence of the L_2 residuals of temperature on the left axis and the relative iterative error in q_w on the right axis. The reference solution was converged 12 orders of magnitude compared to the magnitude of the L_2 norm computed on the first iteration. The L_2 norm on the first iteration is 1.469×10^4 K. The relative iterative error in q_w was computed using the reference solution and Eq. (13.30). Using Figure 13.13 one can map from right to left the relative iterative error criterion of 1×10^{-5} to the L_2 norm of the residuals resulting in a value of 2.2×10^{-5} K. Since this value of the L_2 norm is larger than the criterion imposed on the L_2 norm in Step 2 (1.469×10^{-5} K), the test in Step 10 is satisfied. The value of 1.469×10^{-5} K in the L_2 norm can then be mapped back to 0.64×10^{-5} for the relative iterative error in q_w.

Table 13.5 *Levels of iterative convergence of the q_W for the 46 × 46 mesh*

Order of magnitude drop in the L_2 norm	L_2 norm at convergence (K)	Number of iterations at convergence	Calculated relative discretization error	Observed order of accuracy, p_O
4	1.469×10^0	1250	1.266×10^{-2}	−0.592
5	1.469×10^{-1}	2135	-1.049×10^{-3}	1.136
6	1.469×10^{-2}	3021	-3.595×10^{-3}	1.864
7	1.469×10^{-3}	3907	-3.166×10^{-3}	1.963
8	1.469×10^{-4}	4793	-3.125×10^{-3}	1.973
9	1.469×10^{-5}	5679	-3.121×10^{-3}	1.974
10	1.469×10^{-6}	6565	-3.121×10^{-3}	1.974

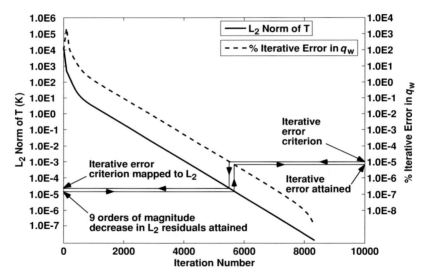

Figure 13.13 Iterative convergence history of the L_2 norm of temperature and the relative iterative error in q_W.

As an independent check on the adequacy of the iterative convergence, the following procedure is commonly done. When Step 7 is satisfactorily attained, one can compute a series of solutions that are iteratively converged to increasingly higher degrees. Table 13.5 shows varying levels of iterative convergence for q_W on the 46 × 46 mesh. The solutions are converged by four orders of magnitude up to ten orders of magnitude compared to the initial value of the L_2 norm. It can be seen from the fourth and fifth columns of the table that the calculated relative discretization error and the observed order of accuracy do not stabilize at the correct value until the solution has been converged at least eight orders

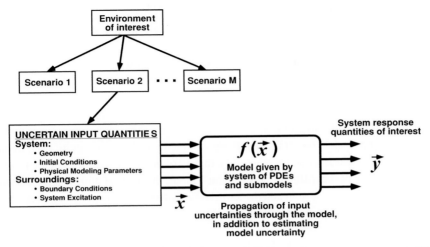

Figure 13.14 Example of sources of uncertainties that yield uncertain system response quantities.

of magnitude. Stated differently, until the solution is converged at least eight orders of magnitude there is an interaction of the iterative error and the discretization error, which results in erroneous results for the computed discretization error and the observed order of accuracy. This type of pollution of observed order of accuracy has certainly occurred in the published literature.

Referring back to the stepwise procedure described above and the results shown in Figure 13.13, it is seen that the procedure yields results that are consistent with the convergence results show in Table 13.5. For example, the requirement that the relative iterative error criterion should be set at 1/100th of the relative discretization error criterion is justified by noting the results in Table 13.5. An iterative error criterion of 1/10th of the relative discretization error criterion could have been used for this example, but it would have been right at the edge of noticeable interaction of the iterative and discretization errors.

From Step 11: Summarizing, from Step 5, we use the estimated discretization error on the 46×46 mesh to give $U_S = 0.08448$ W. From Step 10 we use the value of 0.8×10^{-5} for the relative iterative error in q_W to compute $U_I = -0.00173$ W. Although these values are very small compared to the estimated model uncertainty discussed in Section 13.2.3, they will be included in the next section to estimate the total predictive uncertainty of the simulation.

13.4 Step 4: estimate output uncertainty

Figure 13.14 shows an overview of the procedure for estimating output uncertainty. Here we start with the specification of the environment of interest, identify the scenarios of interest, characterize the uncertain inputs, propagate these through the model, and produce a vector of SRQs of interest, $\vec{y}$. Although there may be probabilities associated with a particular environment and a particular scenario, for our present purposes we will ignore those probabilities. Here we are focused on how the input, model, and numerical solution uncertainties combine to affect $\vec{y}$. Let $\vec{x}$ be the vector of all uncertain input quantities. Let m be the number of uncertain elements in the vector, so that we have

$$\vec{x} = \{x_1, x_2, \ldots, x_m\}. \tag{13.31}$$

Let $f(\vec{x})$ represent the dependence of the model on the uncertain input quantities. $f(\vec{x})$ can also be thought of as the function that maps input uncertainties to output uncertainties. If there are multiple models for $f(\vec{x})$, then there will be multiple mappings of input to output uncertainties. Here we assume, for generality, that all of the input quantities of the model are uncertain. Because of the different way in which input, model, and numerical uncertainties occur in the model of the system and the surroundings, they are normally treated separately. Determining the affect of the input uncertainties, $\vec{x}$, on the response vector $\vec{y}$ is termed *propagation of input uncertainties.*

There is a wide range of methods to propagate input to output uncertainties. It is beyond the scope of this book to discuss all of them and when each is appropriate in a UQ analysis. For a detailed discussion of various methods, see Morgan and Henrion (1990); Cullen and Frey (1999); Melchers (1999); Haldar and Mahadevan (2000a); Ang and Tang (2007); Choi *et al.* (2007); Suter (2007); Rubinstein and Kroese (2008); and Vose (2008). As discussed earlier, probability bounds analysis (PBA) is used in the characterization of the input uncertainties, $\vec{x}$, the model uncertainty, and the characterization of the uncertainties in the SRQs, $\vec{y}$. To our knowledge, the only methods that are able to propagate aleatory and epistemic uncertainties through an arbitrary, i.e., black box, model are Monte Carlo sampling methods. For very simple models that are not black box, one could program each of the arithmetic operations in the model and propagate the input uncertainties to obtain the output uncertainties (Ferson, 2002). Because this approach is very limited in applicability, we will only discuss Monte Carlo sampling methods.

13.4.1 Monte Carlo sampling of input uncertainties

Monte Carlo methods were first used about a century ago, but they have only become popular during the last half-century. They are used in a wide range of calculations in mathematics and physics. There are a number of variants of Monte Carlo sampling (MCS), each serving particular goals with improved efficiency (Cullen and Frey, 1999; Ross, 2006; Ang and Tang, 2007; Dimov, 2008; Rubinstein and Kroese, 2008; Vose, 2008). The key feature of all Monte Carlo methods is that the mathematical operator f of interest is evaluated repeatedly using some type of random sampling of the input. As indicated in Figure 13.14 above, we write

$$\vec{y} = f(\vec{x}). \tag{13.32}$$

Let $\vec{x}^k$ denote a random sample drawn from all of the components of the input vector $\vec{x}$. Let $\vec{y}^k$ be the response vector after evaluation of the model using the random sample $\vec{x}^k$. Then

Eq. (13.32) can be written for the number of samples N as

$$\vec{y}^k = f(\vec{x}^k), \quad k = 1, 2, 3, \ldots, N. \tag{13.33}$$

The key underlying assumption of *simple* or *basic* MCS can be stated as: given a set of N random samples drawn from all of the aleatory and epistemic input uncertainties, one can make strong statistical statements concerning the nondeterministic response of the model. There are *no assumptions* concerning: (a) the characteristics of the uncertainty structure of the input to the model, e.g., parametric versus nonparametric, epistemic versus aleatory, correlated versus uncorrelated; or (b) the characteristics of the model, e.g., whether there is any required smoothness or regularity in the model. The only critical issue in MCS is that the strength of the statistical statements about the system response depends on the number of samples obtained. If $f(\vec{x}^k)$ is computationally expensive to evaluate, then one may have to deal with less precise statistical conclusions concerning the response of the system. Alternatively, one may have to simplify the model or neglect unimportant submodels in order to afford the needed number of samples. However, with the power of highly parallel computing, this computational disadvantage of MCS is mitigated. This is also true with the latest desktop computer systems being designed with multiple compute cores on a single chip. Each of the function evaluations, $f(\vec{x}^k)$, can be done in parallel.

Some academic researchers developing new techniques for propagating input to output uncertainties are harshly critical of any form of MCS because of the computational expense involved in evaluating $f(\vec{x}^k)$. Other methods have been proposed, such as the use of stochastic expansions, i.e., polynomial chaos expansions and the Karhunen–Loeve transform (Haldar and Mahadevan, 2000b; Ghanem and Spanos, 2003; Choi *et al.*, 2007). These methods converge rapidly and are most promising. However, many of these methods require that the computer code that solves for $f(\vec{x}^k)$ be substantially modified before they can be used, i.e., they are intrusive to the code. For academic exercises or specialized applications, this is quite doable. However, for complex analyses of real systems, where the codes can have hundreds of thousands of lines, have possibly been used for decades, and where multiple codes are executed in sequence, this route is completely impractical. In addition, and just as important, the new methods have not been able to deal with epistemic uncertainty. Generality with regard to models chosen, robustness of the method, and ability to deal with both aleatory and epistemic uncertainty has sustained the use of MCS for decades in UQ analyses.

13.4.1.1 Monte Carlo sampling for aleatory uncertainties

The initial discussion of MCS will only deal with uncertain inputs that are aleatory, i.e., they are given by precise probability density functions or CDFs. Figure 13.15 depicts the basic concepts in MCS for a system of three uncertain inputs (x_1, x_2, x_3) resulting in one uncertain output, y. The first step is to draw uniformly sampled random deviates between zero and one. Figure 13.15 shows how these samples applied to the probability axis will generate the random deviates $(x_1, x_2, x_3)^k$, based on the particular CDF characterizing each input quantity. Each of these random deviates is used to evaluate the function f to compute

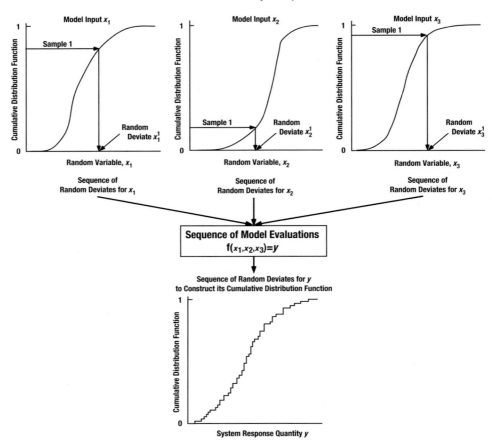

Figure 13.15 Schematic of MCS for three uncertain inputs and one output.

one y. After many function evaluations using many random deviates, $k = 1, 2, 3, \ldots, N$, one can construct an empirical CDF as shown in the bottom panel of Figure 13.15.

Figure 13.16 shows a flowchart and gives more of the details for the activities in the various steps in the process for uncorrelated uncertain inputs. Let the number of uncertain aleatory inputs be α and the remainder of the uncertain inputs, $m - \alpha$, be epistemic. Sampling of the epistemic uncertainties will be discussed in the next section. The following explains each of the steps for basic MCS.

1 Generate α sequences of N pseudo-random numbers, one for each of the uncertain aleatory inputs. Since each sequence must be independent of the other, each sequence must use a different seed for the pseudo-random number (PRN) generator or be a continuation of a sequence. As is common with most PRN generators, the numbers range between zero and unity.
2 Picking an individual number from each of the sequences of PRNs, create an array of numbers of length α. That is, take one number from the first sequence of PRNs, take one number from the

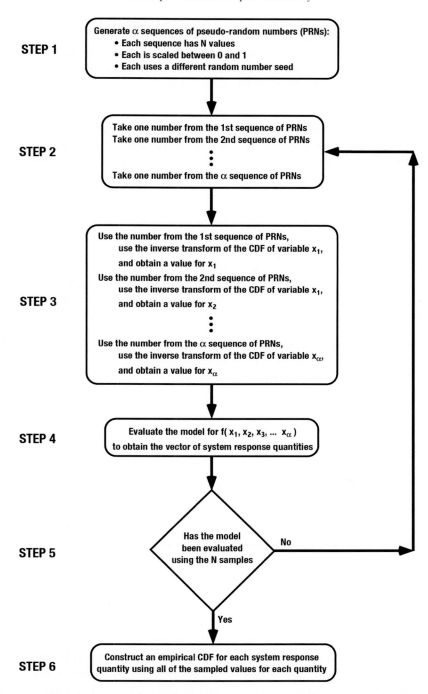

Figure 13.16 Flow chart for simple MCS with only aleatory uncertainties and no correlated input quantities.

second sequence, etc., until the array of length α is created. Once a number from the sequence has been used, it is not used again.

3 Each number in the array generated in Step 2 can be viewed as drawn from a uniform distribution over the range of (0,1). The probability integral transform theorem in statistics is used to map the uniform distribution, using the CDF for each uncertain aleatory input, to obtain a value of the uncertain input (Angus, 1994; Ang and Tang, 2007; Dimov, 2008; Rubinstein and Kroese, 2008). That is: given a distribution F and a uniform random value u between zero and one, the value $F^{-1}(u)$ will be a random variable distributed according to F. This is what it means for a random variable to be "distributed according" to a distribution. The result of this step is an array of α model input quantities, $(x_1, x_2, \ldots x_\alpha)$, that are distributed according to the given distribution for input 1, 2, 3, $\ldots$, α, respectively. The process in this step is what is depicted in the top panel of Figure 13.15.

4 Use the array $(x_1, x_2, \ldots, x_\alpha)$ as input to evaluate the mathematical model. By solving the PDEs, along with all of the ICs, BCs, and system excitation, compute the array, $(y_1, y_2, \ldots, y_n)$, of SRQs.

5 Test if all N PRNs have been used to evaluate the mathematical model. If No, return to Step 2. If Yes, go to Step 6.

6 Construct an empirical CDF for each element of the SRQ array, $(y_1, y_2, \ldots, y_n)$. The empirical CDF is constructed using each of the samples from the Monte Carlo simulation. The abscissa of the empirical CDF is the observed (sampled) values of an SRQ, y_i, and the ordinate of the empirical CDF is the observed cumulative probability for all of the sampled values less than or equal to y_i. The y_i are ordered from the smallest to the largest. The empirical CDF is constructed as a nondecreasing step function with a constant vertical step size of $1/N$, where N is the sample size from the MCS. The locations of the steps correspond to the observed values of y_i. Such a distribution for the samples y^k, $k = 1, 2, 3 \ldots, N$ is

$$S_N(y) = \frac{1}{N} \sum_{k=1}^{N} I(y^k, y), \qquad (13.34)$$

where

$$I(y^k, y) = \begin{cases} 1, & y^k \le y, \\ 0, & y^k > y. \end{cases} \qquad (13.35)$$

$S_n(y)$ is simply the fraction of data values in the data set that are at or below each y^k. From Eq. (13.34) it is clear that the total probability mass accumulated from the total of N empirical samples is unity. An example of an empirical CDF is shown in the bottom panel of Figure 13.15.

There are a number of additional topics concerning MCS that are important in practical analyses and are not addressed in Figure 13.15 and Figure 13.16. Two of these will be briefly mentioned here, but the reader should consult the following references for details (Cullen and Frey, 1999; Ross, 2006; Ang and Tang, 2007; Dimov, 2008; Rubinstein and Kroese, 2008; Vose, 2008). First, some type of correlation or dependence structure may exist between various uncertain inputs. If a correlation structure exists between two (or more) inputs, then it means that one is statistically related to the other(s). For example, suppose one considers uncertainty in both thermal and electrical conductivity. For most materials there is a strong correlation between thermal and electrical conductivity. If a correlation structure exists between two (or more) inputs then one is claiming that one has a *causal* relationship with the other(s), e.g., there is a high dependence between how much rest time an equipment operator has and the likelihood of errors made during the operation of the equipment. Determining a correlation or dependence structure is usually an involved task that is based primarily on large amounts of experimental data, as well as an understanding of the physical relationship between the quantities. If correlation or dependence structures are quantified, it is accounted for in Step 3.

Second, how many Monte Carlo samples are needed for calculating various statistical quantities of the response depends on different factors. The most important of these is the probability value of interest. Ang and Tang (2007) give an estimate of the sampling error in MCS as

$$\% \text{ error in } P = 200\sqrt{\frac{1-P}{NP}}, \tag{13.36}$$

where P is the probability value of interest. It can be seen that the mean converges most rapidly, while low probability events converge very slowly. For example, if a probability of 0.01 is needed, then 100 000 samples are typically required to assure an error of less than 6%. It should be stressed, however, that one of the important advantages of a Monte Carlo sample is that the convergence rate does *not* depend on the number of uncertain quantities or their variance.

To improve the convergence rate of MCS, variance reduction techniques can be used (Cullen and Frey, 1999; Helton and Davis, 2003; Ross, 2006; Dimov, 2008; Rubinstein and Kroese, 2008). These techniques adjust the random samples of the inputs so that certain features of the output distribution converge more rapidly. The most well known is stratified Monte Carlo sampling or Latin Hypercube sampling (LHS). LHS stratifies the uniform distribution that is used with the inverse transform procedure into equal intervals of probability. The most common procedure is to let the number of intervals be equal to the number of samples that will be computed. Across all of these intervals a PRN generator is used to obtain a separate random number for each interval so that a random sample is obtained from each interval. LHS almost always converges faster than simple MCS, so it is the most commonly used sampling technique. For a small number of uncertain quantities, e.g., less than five, LHS converges much faster than simple MCS. For one uncertain quantity, Dimov (2008) shows that

$$\% \text{ error in } P \sim N^{-3/2}. \tag{13.37}$$

All of the modern risk assessment software packages contain a number of sophisticated features, such as dealing with correlations, dependencies, and different methods for variance reduction in the sampling. Examples of some of the packages are JMP and STAT from SAS Inc., Risk Solver from Frontline Systems, Inc., STATISTICA from StatSoft, Inc., @Risk from Palisade Software, and Crystal Ball from Oracle, Inc.

13.4.1.2 Monte Carlo sampling for combined aleatory and epistemic uncertainties

Modifying the simple Monte Carlo procedure to deal with the epistemic uncertainties is rather straightforward. Recall that the epistemically uncertain inputs are $(x_{\alpha+1}, x_{\alpha+2}, \ldots, x_m)$. We presume that each of these quantities is given by an interval, i.e., there is no belief or knowledge structure within the interval. There are generally two types of epistemic uncertainty occurring in the modeling process. First, there are those that occur in the modeling of the physical characteristics of the system and the surroundings. Some examples are geometry characteristics, physical modeling parameters (such as material properties), and boundary conditions (such as pressure loading on a system). Second, there are those that occur in the uncertainty characterization of aleatory uncertainties. The most common example is specifying the parameters of a family of distributions as intervals. For example, suppose one is modeling the manufacturing variability of a material property using a three-parameter gamma distribution, where each parameter is specified as an interval. Then each of the three parameters of the distribution would be an element of the array $(x_{\alpha+1}, x_{\alpha+2}, \ldots, x_m)$. The uncertainty structure of this gamma distribution would be the set of all possible gamma distributions whose parameters lie within each of the specified intervals of the parameters.

Since the epistemic uncertainties have no structure within the interval, one could use basic MCS over the range of each interval-valued quantity. This would be the same procedure as described above for aleatory uncertainties. However, it must be stressed that the sampling of the intervals is *fundamentally different* in terms how these samples are processed and interpreted. Each of these samples represents *possible realizations* that could occur in these epistemically uncertain quantities. There is *no likelihood or probability associated with these samples*, which is in contrast to the samples taken from the aleatory uncertainties. As a result, the key to sampling when epistemic and aleatory uncertainties are present is to separate the sampling for the epistemic uncertainties from the sampling of the aleatory uncertainties. This procedure is the essence of a PBA.

To accomplish this, one constructs a double-loop sampling structure. The outer loop is for sampling of the epistemic uncertainties, and the inner loop is for sampling the aleatory uncertainties. It has been found that LHS is more efficient for sampling the epistemic uncertainties (outer loop) than simple MCS because LHS forces the samples into partitions across the interval-valued quantities (Helton and Davis, 2003; Helton *et al.*, 2005b, 2006; Helton and Sallaberry, 2007). Figure 13.17 shows a flow chart for the double-loop sampling strategy. The flow chart is described as if there is only one SRQ, but the same procedure would be used for any number of SRQs. The following gives a brief explanation of each step of the procedure.

1 Choose the number of samples, *M*, that will be used for sampling of the epistemic uncertainties. Because of the interval nature of the epistemic uncertainties, an appropriate structure for sampling would be a combinatorial design. If LHS is used, *M* must be sufficiently large to insure satisfactory coverage of the combinations of all of the epistemic uncertainties in the mapping to the SRQs. Based on the work of Ferson and Tucker (2006); Kreinovich *et al.* (2007); and Kleb and Johnston

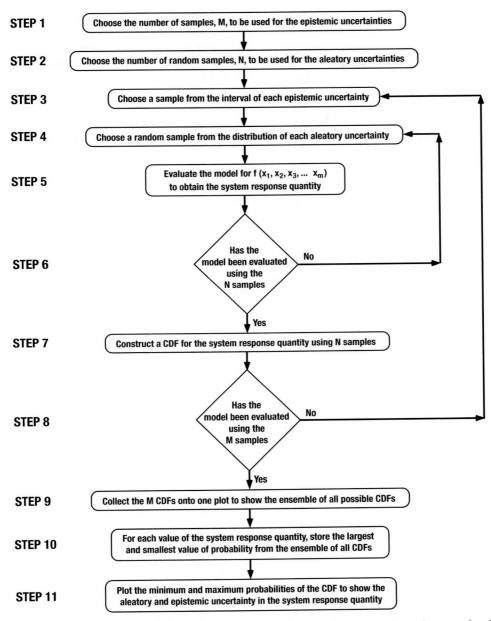

STEP 1 Choose the number of samples, M, to be used for the epistemic uncertainties

STEP 2 Choose the number of random samples, N, to be used for the aleatory uncertainties

STEP 3 Choose a sample from the interval of each epistemic uncertainty

STEP 4 Choose a random sample from the distribution of each aleatory uncertainty

STEP 5 Evaluate the model for f (x_1, x_2, x_3, ... x_m) to obtain the system response quantity

STEP 6 Has the model been evaluated using the N samples   No
Yes

STEP 7 Construct a CDF for the system response quantity using N samples

STEP 8 Has the model been evaluated using the M samples   No
Yes

STEP 9 Collect the M CDFs onto one plot to show the ensemble of all possible CDFs

STEP 10 For each value of the system response quantity, store the largest and smallest value of probability from the ensemble of all CDFs

STEP 11 Plot the minimum and maximum probabilities of the CDF to show the aleatory and epistemic uncertainty in the system response quantity

Figure 13.17 Flow chart for MCS with both aleatory and epistemic uncertainties and no correlated input quantities.

(2008), we suggests that a minimum of three LHS samples be taken for each epistemic uncertainty, in combination with all of the remaining epistemic uncertainties. An approximation to this suggestion for the minimum number of samples is given by $(m - \alpha)^3 + 2$, where $(m - \alpha)$ is the number of epistemic uncertainties. If $(m - \alpha)$ is not very large, the suggested minimum number of samples should be computationally affordable. Sallaberry *et al.* (2008) suggest that replicated LHS sampling be used in order to detect if there is sensitivity of the results to the number of samples. Replicated sampling is the procedure where multiple sets of samples are computed, each set having a different seed for the pseudo-random number (PRN) generator. Instead of using LHS sampling, Kreinovich *et al.* (2007) suggest a sampling method based on Cauchy deviates. Although LHS sampling is shown in Figure 13.17, the methods of Sallaberry *et al.* (2008) and Kreinovich *et al.* (2007) could also be incorporated.

2 Choose the number of samples, *N*, that will be used for the random sampling of the aleatory uncertainties. Depending on what quantile is of interest for the SRQ, the number of samples may need to be very large, as discussed earlier.

3 Choose a sample from the interval of each epistemic uncertainty. If LHS sampling is used, the number of strata for each epistemic uncertainty should be set equal to *M*. In addition, it is recommended to use a uniform distribution for each of the strata to map the random samples on the probability axis to obtain the random deviates of the epistemic uncertainties. An additional technique that has proven effective is to require that the end points of each epistemic uncertainty be sampled. That is, for each of the strata on the ends of the interval, one ignores the uniform sampling and chooses the end point of the interval. This technique ensures that the full range of the interval for each epistemic uncertainty is sampled, regardless of the number of LHS samples.

4 Choose a random sample from each distribution of each aleatory uncertainty. LHS is also recommended for sampling the aleatory uncertainties, particularly if there are a small number of aleatory uncertainties. The number of strata of each aleatory uncertainty should be set equal to *N*.

5 Use the complete array of sampled values $(x_1, x_2, \ldots, x_m)$ to evaluate the mathematical model and compute the SRQ.

6 Test if all *N* samples of the aleatory uncertainties have been used to evaluate the mathematical model. If No, return to Step 4. If Yes, go to Step 7.

7 Construct a CDF based on the *N* observed (sampled) values of the aleatory uncertainties.

8 Test if all *M* samples of the epistemic uncertainties have been used to evaluate the mathematical model. If No, return to Step 3. If Yes, go to Step 9.

9 Collect the *M* CDFs onto one plot to show the ensemble of all CDFs. Each CDF shows a possible distribution of realizations of the SRQ.

10 For each observed value of the SRQ, store the largest and smallest value of probability from the ensemble of all CDFs.

11 Plot the minimum and maximum CDFs over the range of the observed SRQs. This plot shows the possible range in probabilities for all of the observed SRQs. This is referred to as a p-box because it shows interval-valued probabilities for the SRQ. That is, given the information characterized in the uncertain input quantities, no tighter range of probabilities can be claimed for the response of the system.

Figure 13.18 is a sample of a p-box with large epistemic uncertainty in the system response quantity. For any value of the SRQ, only an interval-valued probability can be determined. Likewise, for any value of probability, only an interval-valued response can be determined.

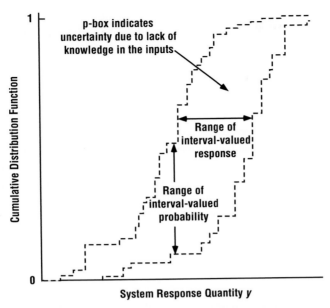

Figure 13.18 Example of p-box obtained for a system response quantity with large epistemic uncertainty.

As a result, this type of mathematical structure is sometimes called an *imprecise probability function*. However, that term suggests the probabilities are vague or *fuzzy* in some sense; this would give the wrong interpretation. The probabilities shown in a p-box are *as precise, and the bounds are as small, as can be stated given the information that is claimed for the input quantities.*

When a decision maker is presented with information that segregates aleatory and epistemic uncertainty, as in Figure 13.18, more enlightened and better decisions or actions can be taken. For example, if the system response is dominated by epistemic uncertainty, then the decision maker must add more knowledge, or make restrictions on the bounds of epistemic uncertainties, in order to reduce the response uncertainty. If one had conducted the same Monte Carlo analysis, but assumed each of the epistemic uncertainties were represented as a uniform distribution, then one would have obtained a plot that would have had *one* CDF near the center of the p-box shown in Figure 13.18. This would have presented a *very* different picture of uncertainty to the decision maker. The representation of the interval as a uniform distribution would have had two unjustified changes in a statement of knowledge: (a) the quantity is a random variable instead of a quantity that has a unique, but unknown value; and (b) all possible values of the unknown quantity are *equally likely*.

In Figure 13.18 one should note the relatively distinct changes in trends that can occur in both the upper and lower probability curves. These trend changes are common in the boundaries of the p-boxes because the boundaries represent the minimum and maximum of the ensemble of *all possible CDFs* for the system. For example, in one region of the system response a particular CDF could represent the maximum, but then at a slightly different response, a different CDF could become the maximum. Stated differently, the p-box boundaries typically have several trade-offs between individually realizable, or possible, CDFs. If one or two epistemically uncertain input quantities dominate the epistemic uncertainty in the response, then there is less chance for these types of trade-off.

A final comment should be made concerning an unintended benefit of MCS or LHS. When random samples are drawn over a wide range of each $\{x_1, x_2, \ldots, x_m\}$, there will be a number of unusual combinations of the $\{x_1, x_2, \ldots, x_m\}$. That is, there will be combinations of $\{x_1, x_2, \ldots, x_m\}$ that no one would ever think about using in a simulation of a system because they would not normally occur together, or they may even be physically impossible. What a number of UQ analysts have found is that when these unusual combinations on inputs are attempted in the code, the code will "crash." When these crashes are investigated, it is commonly found that they were caused by bugs in the code that had not been found in any of the SQE testing. This, of course, is similar to many code developers' experience: "If you want to find bugs in your code, let a new user run it."

13.4.2 Combination of input, model, and numerical uncertainty

How to combine input, model, and numerical solution uncertainties is an open research topic subject to considerable debate. In fact, many researchers and risk analysts either: (a) ignore the quantification of model and numerical uncertainties; (b) ignore the issue of how to combine input, model, and numerical uncertainties because it is such a difficult and controversial issue; or (c) avoid directly dealing with the issue because they use model updating of input and model parameters to attain good agreement between the model and measurements, regardless of model and numerical uncertainties. We, on the other hand, have continually stressed the importance of directly dealing with each of these uncertainties in the prediction of a system response.

Although model and numerical uncertainty are very different kinds of beast, they are both frustrating because we always believe that with more sophisticated physics models and bigger computers we can eliminate them. Often, project leaders and decision makers do not have the luxury of waiting for model and numerical improvements to be made, but must make decisions and move on. The fact of the matter is that in the simulation of complex systems model uncertainty is commonly the *dominant* uncertainty in risk-informed decision-making.

We present two methods for combining model and input uncertainty. The first method uses validation metrics, discussed in Chapter 12, to estimate model uncertainty. The estimate of model uncertainty is then combined with input uncertainty using a method based on recent work by Oberkampf and Ferson (2007) and Ferson *et al.* (2008). The second method is based on using alternative plausible models for the system of interest to try to quantify the combination of model and input uncertainty (Morgan and Henrion, 1990; Cullen and Frey, 1999; Helton *et al.*, 2000; Helton, 2003; NRC, 2009). This method has, of course, been around for decades, but risk analysts rarely use it because it is expensive and time consuming to develop multiple models of the system of interest, as well as computing the additional simulations from these models. Only in large-scale risk assessments of high-consequence systems are alternative plausible models seriously investigated.

A method for including numerical solution uncertainty will be discussed in the final subsection. It can be applied to either of the methods for combining model and input uncertainty.

13.4.2.1 Combination of input and model uncertainty

Model uncertainty is fundamentally due to lack of predictive knowledge in the model, so it should be represented as an epistemic uncertainty. If the validation metric is characterized in terms of the physical units of the SRQ of interest, we argue that the most defensible way to combine model and input uncertainty is to add the model uncertainty to the p-box representing the output uncertainty. By *add*, we mean increase the lateral extent of the output p-box (resulting from mapping the aleatory and epistemic input uncertainties to the output) by the amount of the estimated model uncertainty. That is, for every value of cumulative probability, the model uncertainty would be subtracted from the left side of the p-box, and/or added to the right side of the p-box, depending on the sign of the estimated model uncertainty. If the input uncertainty is only aleatory, then the output uncertainty will be a single CDF, i.e., the degenerate case of a p-box. The subtraction from the left side and addition to the right side can only be made if the validation metric is given in terms of the SRQ.

By expanding the p-box on the left and right, we are treating model uncertainty as an interval-valued quantity. The approach is directly equivalent to the addition of simple intervals, and *no assumption* is made concerning dependence between the various sources producing the intervals. Both validation metric approaches developed in Chapter 12, the confidence interval approach and the area metric, can be used in this way because they are both error measures in terms of the dimensional units of the SRQ. If hypothesis testing is used for validation, then one does not have an error measure in terms of the SRQs, but a probability measure indicating a likelihood of agreement between computation and experiment. If Bayesian updating is used for validation, the model form uncertainty is either assumed to be zero, or it is estimated in combination with updating the distributions for the input and model parameters. Even if the latter option is used, updating parameter distributions becomes inextricably convolved with estimating model uncertainty because they are computed jointly.

To apply either the confidence interval approach or the area metric, we need to quantify the model uncertainty at the conditions where the model is applied, i.e., the application condition of interest. That condition, or set of conditions, may be inside or outside the validation domain. If the application condition is inside the validation domain, one can think of the validation metric function as an interpolating function. If the application condition is outside the validation domain, one is extrapolating the validation metric function to the condition of interest. In this section, we will only consider the combination of input and model uncertainty where the model uncertainty is estimated using the confidence interval approach. In Section 13.7.3.1, we will consider the approach for combining input and model uncertainty where model uncertainty is estimated by the area metric.

The confidence interval approach is rather simple for three reasons. First, it only assesses model uncertainty over a single input or control parameter. If there are additional inputs to the model, the model uncertainty is assumed constant with respect to all other inputs. Second, the model uncertainty is based on taking the difference between the mean value of the experimental measurements and the simulation results. And third, it automatically constructs a validation metric function as part of the approach. These simplifications, particularly the first and second, also restrict the applicability of the approach.

Referring to Sections 12.4 through 12.7 of Chapter 12, we have

$$d(x) = \tilde{E}(x) \pm \text{CI}(x). \tag{13.38}$$

$d(x)$ is the validation metric function, $\tilde{E}(x) = \bar{y}_\text{m}(x) - \bar{y}_\text{e}(x)$ is the estimated mean of the model error, $\bar{y}_\text{m}(x)$ is the mean of the model prediction, $\bar{y}_\text{e}(x)$ is the mean of the experimental measurements, and $\text{CI}(x)$ is the confidence interval of the experimental data. $\text{CI}(x)$ is defined with respect to the mean of the experimental data, $\bar{y}_\text{e}(x)$. Equation (13.38) can written as an interval at the application point of interest x^*.

$$\left(\tilde{E}(x^*) - \text{CI}(x^*), \tilde{E}(x^*) + \text{CI}(x^*) \right). \tag{13.39}$$

Note that even if the model matches the experimental data perfectly, that is, $\bar{y}_\text{m}(x^*) = \bar{y}_\text{e}(x^*)$, $d(x)$ is given by the interval $(-\text{CI}(x^*), +\text{CI}(x^*))$.

For the nonlinear regression case, Section 12.7, it was found that the confidence intervals are not symmetric with respect to $\bar{y}_\text{m}(x)$. For this case we would simply average the upper and lower confidence intervals to obtain an average value so that it could be used in Eq. (13.39). The confidence level used in computing the confidence interval would be chosen at the discretion of the analysts and/or the needs of the customer using the simulation results. Typically, 90% or 95% confidence levels are chosen. Note that the magnitude of $\text{CI}(x)$ grows rapidly as the confidence level increases beyond 90%.

The confidence interval approach has a great deal of flexibility concerning the regression function one wishes to use to represent the mean of the experimental data, $\bar{y}_\text{e}(x)$. The model prediction, $\bar{y}_\text{m}(x^*)$, can either be interpolated, if sufficient data are available, or computed from the model. Let x_l be the lowest value of the validation data and let x_u be the upper value of the data. If $x_\text{l} \le x^* \le x_\text{u}$, we can interpolate the experimental data using the regression function for $\bar{y}_\text{e}(x^*)$ and compute $\text{CI}(x^*)$. We will consider this case first.

Consider how Eq. (13.39) is combined with the p-box representing the uncertainty in the predicted SRQ, where the uncertainty is only due to uncertain inputs. To explain the concept, we will simplify the p-box to a continuous CDF for the SRQ. The concept, however, applies equally well to (a) a p-box that is due to epistemic uncertainty in the input,

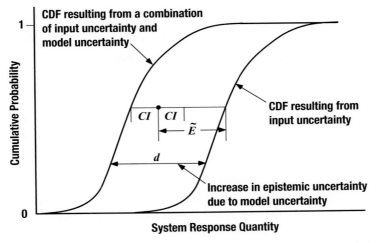

Figure 13.19 Method of increasing the uncertainty on the left of the SRQ distribution due to model uncertainty.

and (b) an empirical distribution function (EDF) that is constructed from a limited number of model evaluation samples.

Figure 13.19 shows how Eq. (13.39) is used to expand the uncertainty to the left of the CDF for the case of $\tilde{E}(x^*) > 0$. The increase due to model uncertainty is not only due to estimated model error, but also due to uncertainty in the experimental data. As a result, the total left displacement of the CDF is

$$\tilde{E}(x^*) + \text{CI}(x^*). \tag{13.40}$$

If

$$\tilde{E}(x^*) + \text{CI}(x) < 0, \tag{13.41}$$

then the left displacement is zero because epistemic uncertainty cannot be negative. The magnitude of the displacement is a constant over the complete range of the CDF, i.e., for all responses of the system at x^*. As can be seen from Figure 13.19, even if the response of the system is purely aleatory, due to purely aleatory input uncertainties, the response from the combined input and model uncertainty is a p-box. The p-box can be correctly interpreted in two different ways. First, for a fixed system response anywhere along the distribution, the combined uncertainty is now an interval-valued probability. Second, for a fixed cumulative probability, the combined uncertainty is now an interval-valued response.

A similar development can be shown for the right displacement of the CDF. The equations for the left and right displacement of the CDF, or a p-box if the input uncertainty contains both aleatory and epistemic uncertainties, can be shown to be

$$d_{\text{left}} = \begin{cases} [\bar{y}_m\,(x^*)]_{\text{left}} - \bar{y}_e\,(x^*) + \text{CI}(x^*) & \text{if} \quad [\bar{y}_m\,(x^*)]_{\text{left}} - \bar{y}_e\,(x^*) + \text{CI}(x^*) \geq 0, \\ 0 & \text{if} \quad [\bar{y}_m\,(x^*)]_{\text{left}} - \bar{y}_e\,(x^*) + \text{CI}(x^*) < 0, \end{cases}$$

$$(13.42)$$

$$d_{\text{right}} = \begin{cases} \left| [\bar{y}_m\,(x^*)]_{\text{right}} - \bar{y}_e\,(x^*) - \text{CI}(x^*) \right| & \text{if} \quad [\bar{y}_m\,(x^*)]_{\text{right}} - \bar{y}_e\,(x^*) - \text{CI}(x^*) \leq 0, \\ 0 & \text{if} \quad [\bar{y}_m\,(x^*)]_{\text{right}} - \bar{y}_e\,(x^*) - \text{CI}(x^*) > 0. \end{cases}$$

$$(13.43)$$

$[\bar{y}_m\,(x^*)]_{\text{left}}$ is the mean of the predicted SRQ from the left boundary of the p-box and $[\bar{y}_m\,(x^*)]_{\text{right}}$ is the mean from the right boundary of the p-box. If the model is over-predicting the experiment, then the p-box is increased more on the left than the right. If the model is under-predicting the experiment, then the p-box is increased more on the right than the left. It can be seen from these equations that the increase in the lateral extent of the system response p-box is only symmetric left to right when both of the following equations are true:

$$\left[\bar{y}_m\,(x^*) \right]_{\text{left}} = \left[\bar{y}_m\,(x^*) \right]_{\text{right}}$$
$$\text{and} \quad \left[\bar{y}_m\,(x^*) \right]_{\text{left}} = \bar{y}_e\,(x^*). \qquad (13.44)$$

In this case, the increase on the left and right are equal to the magnitude of the confidence interval of the experimental data.

If one must extrapolate $d(x)$ outside of the validation domain to attain the application condition of interest, one should generally not extrapolate the function $d(x)$ itself. It is not recommended because $d(x)$ will display more complex features than the three individual functions $\bar{y}_m(x)$, $\bar{y}_e(x)$, and $\text{CI}(x)$. It is recommended that a first or second degree polynomial be used in a least squares fit for $\bar{y}_e(x)$ and $\text{CI}(x)$. Low-degree polynomials may not capture the detailed features of $\bar{y}_e(x)$ and $\text{CI}(x)$, but they should be more reliable in extrapolation because they would, in general, have fewer degrees of freedom than $\bar{y}_e(x)$ and $\text{CI}(x)$. Note that the extrapolation of $\text{CI}(x)$ only involves the extrapolation of one function, since the confidence intervals are symmetric around $\bar{y}_e(x)$. One method of improving the least squares fit of the low degree polynomials and capturing a trend that is important for extrapolation is to fit only a portion of the range of the experimental data. One should not use a regression function for extrapolating the model prediction $\bar{y}_m(x^*)$, but simply calculate the value using the model. After the low-order polynomials are computed for extrapolating $\bar{y}_e(x)$ and $\text{CI}(x)$, and $\bar{y}_m(x^*)$ is evaluated, Eqs. (13.42) and (13.43) can be used to calculate d_{left} and d_{right}.

It should be pointed out that when extrapolation of the model is required, as is commonly the case, the estimate for the *model uncertainty* as presented here is a regression-based extrapolation. That is, the accuracy of the extrapolation of the model uncertainty does *not* depend on the accuracy of the model, but on the accuracy of the extrapolation of the observed uncertainty in the model. The accuracy of the prediction from the model, however, *is* based on the fidelity of the physics and the soundness of the assumptions incorporated into the model, i.e., its predictive capability.

An uncertainty extrapolation procedure that is not regression based has recently been proposed by Rutherford (2008). The procedure uses the concept of a non-Euclidean space for the input quantities in order to predict the uncertainty in the system responses. The method is intriguing because it does not rely on the concept that the input quantities are simply parameters, i.e., continuous variables, in the extrapolation of the uncertainty structure of the model.

13.4.2.2 Estimation of model uncertainty using alternative plausible models

When experimental data is sparse over the validation domain, or no data exists for closely related systems under similar conditions, large extrapolations of the model are required. The second approach for estimating model uncertainty is to compare predictions from alternative plausible models. This method is also referred to as the *method of competing models*. The approach is simple, but it is not commonly used because of the time and expense of developing multiple models for a system. There are two important cases where large extrapolations of the model are required, and this method should be used instead of the method for extrapolating the validation metric result. First, models that must predict complex processes far into the future must deal with extraordinary extrapolations. Two timely examples are underground storage of nuclear waste and global climate-change modeling. Models for these systems attempt to make predictions for hundreds and thousands of years into the future for physical processes that are very poorly understood, and the surrounds (e.g., BCs) are even less known. Second, there are model predictions that are needed for systems, particularly failure modes of systems or event trees, which cannot be tested. Some examples are large-scale failure scenarios of nuclear power plants, aging and failure of a full-scale dam, explosive eruption and surrounding damage from a volcano, and a chemical or radiological terrorist attack. Extrapolation of models for these situations can be thought of in terms of the validation hierarchy, but it is of limited quantitative value. For example, certain relevant experiments can be conducted on subsystems, scale models of systems, or surrogate systems in the validation hierarchy. However, the complete system cannot be tested at all, or cannot be tested under relevant conditions. As a result, it is inappropriate and misleading to use the mental model of extrapolation in terms of parameters describing the system or the surroundings.

To use the approach of alternative plausible models, one should have at least two independently developed models of the system and then a comparison is made of the prediction of the same SRQs of interest from each model. In this approach, *none* of the models are presumed to be correct; each one is simply a postulated representation of reality. The only presumption is that each of the models is reasonable and scientifically defensible for the task at hand. Some models may present strong arguments that they are more reliable than others. For example, there has been recent work in the area referred to as hierarchical, or multiscale, physics modeling (Berendsen, 2007; Bucalem and Bathe, 2008; Steinhauser,

2008). If strongly convincing arguments can be made for having higher confidence in the results of some models over others, then the higher confidence models might be used to calibrate the lower level models over some range of conditions. However, if such arguments cannot be decisively made for each aspect of the higher confidence model (physics fidelity, system input data, surroundings input data, and VV&UQ), then each of the models should be treated as having equal confidence. Predictive accuracy assessment of each model may have been done with different sets of experimental data, or possibly even the same set of data. Each model may have used parameter estimation or calibration of model parameters. These details are not critically important.

The most important issue in using alternate models is the *independence* of the teams and the formulations of the models, including assumptions dealing with the surroundings, scenarios, event trees, fault trees, and possible human interaction with the system. In comparing results from each team, it is very often found that each team will have thought of important aspects affecting the modeling and the results that the other team did not think of. Then analyses can be reformulated, improved, and possibly corrected for further comparisons. For example, investigating why two models do not predict similar results for a simplified scenario can help identify blind epistemic uncertainties such as user input and output errors, and coding errors.

This approach does not actually provide an estimate of model uncertainty. It only provides an indication of the similar or dissimilar nature of each model prediction. In the prediction of hurricane or typhoon paths it is a very welcome sight for the news media to show the multiple paths predicted by the various hurricane models. Sometimes these are call *spaghetti plots* of hurricane paths. The results of each of the models should be considered by the decision maker; not averaged or combined in any way. Some argue that the results from each of the models should be considered as equally likely, and treated as a random variable. This would be treating model uncertainty as an aleatory uncertainty, as if physics modeling error is a random process. This forces the square peg of physics modeling into the round hole of probability theory.

Comparing alternative models should be thought of as a sensitivity analysis with respect to model uncertainty, as opposed to an estimation of model uncertainty. Our experience, and the experience of others who have used it, have found it is extremely revealing; often distressing. When results from alternative models are shown together for the first time, particularly from analysts who have been working independently, there is usually a significant *surprise index* (Morgan and Henrion, 1990; Cullen and Frey, 1999). This always generates a great deal of discussion and debate concerning model assumptions, experimental data used for comparisons, and model calibration procedures. This interaction is beneficial and constructive to improving all of the models. On the second iteration of comparing alternative models, there is typically more agreement between models, but not always. Regardless of the level of agreement, we argue that all the results should be presented to the decision makers for their consideration. Given the uncertainty from all sources, the decision makers and managers are responsible for deciding future activities. These activities could be, for example: (a) making system design changes so that the system can successfully tolerate large uncertainties, (b) restricting the operating envelope of the application domain so that the system will not be exposed to unacceptable uncertainties, or (c) deciding to obtain more experimental data or improve the physics modeling fidelity to reduce the predicted uncertainty.

13.4.2.3 Inclusion of numerical solution uncertainty

As discussed earlier in this chapter, we will represent the estimated numerical solution error as an epistemic uncertainty, U_N. Repeating Eq. (13.24) here,

$$(U_N)_{y_i} = |U_I|_{y_i} + |U_S|_{y_i} + |U_T|_{y_i} \quad \text{for } i = 1, 2, \ldots, n, \tag{13.45}$$

where U_I is the iterative solution uncertainty, U_S is the spatial discretization uncertainty, and U_T is the temporal discretization uncertainty. Analogous to the method for increasing the p-box due to model uncertainty, we use each $(U_N)_{y_i}$ computed to expand the width of the p-box for the particular y_i under consideration. Since there is no reference condition, such as experimental measurements in model validation, U_N equally expands the left and right boundaries of the SRQ p-box. That is, the left boundary is shifted to the left by U_N, and the right boundary is shifted to the right by U_N. This procedure for including numerical solution uncertainty can be applied to both procedures for estimating model uncertainty: the method using validation metrics and the method using alternative plausible models.

Some would argue that the increase in uncertainty due to U_N is generally so small compared to model uncertainty that it should be neglected. If one properly quantifies U_N, and it is indeed much smaller than d, then this can certainly be done. Our experience is that U_N is not quantified in most simulations, but it is dismissed with claims like "We only use high order accuracy methods, so the numerical error is small." Or "We have computed this solution with many more finite elements than is usually done, so this is much more accurate than past simulations." Or "The agreement with experimental data is excellent, why are you being difficult?" For a simulation to be scientifically defensible, the numerical solution error must be quantified for a number of representative solutions of all the SRQs of interest; preferably solutions that are judged to be the most numerically challenging.

13.4.3 Example problem: heat transfer through a solid

Here, we continue with the development of the example problem discussed in Sections 13.1.3, 13.2.3, and 13.3.4. We are now interested in predicting the heat transfer through the west face for the system of interest. As described in Section 13.1.3, the two differences between the validation experiment and the system are (a) in the validation experiment T_E never exceeded 390 K, while in the system of interest attains an east face temperature of 450 K, and (b) in the validation experiment the north face was cooled such that the convective heat transfer coefficient h was set at the middle of the possible range that could exist for the system of interest. The prediction discussed here will include the increase in uncertainty due to these two differences.

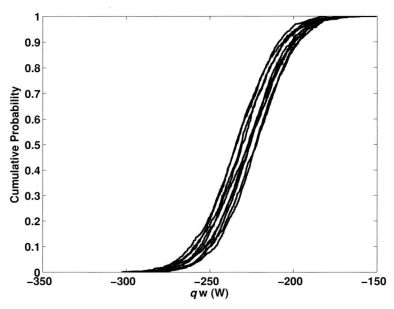

Figure 13.20 Input uncertainty in q_W as represented by ten CDFs from sampling h, where each CDF is composed of 1000 MC samples from k.

13.4.3.1 Input uncertainties

The two input uncertainties are the thermal conductivity in the plate k and the convective heat transfer coefficient on the north face of the plate h. The uncertainty in k is a pure aleatory uncertainty and is given by Eq. (13.7), and the uncertainty in h is a pure epistemic uncertainty and is given by Eq. (13.11). We propagate the uncertainty in k using MCS and the uncertainty in h using LHS, according to the method described in Section 13.4.1. We use ten samples and ten subintervals for h, and 1000 samples of k for each sample of h. Although the resulting 10 000 samples may be excessive for many analyses, we use this number here to give well-converged results. According to Table 13.1, the remaining BCs for the system are $T_E = 450$ K, $T_W = 300$ K, $q_S = 0$.

Figure 13.20 shows the ten individual CDFs for q_W from the outer loop sampling of h. Each CDF results from 1000 MC samples and represents the aleatory uncertainty in k, given a sampled realization of the epistemically uncertain h. It should be stressed that each one of the CDFs represent the variability in q_W that could occur, given the poor state of knowledge of the epistemic uncertainty h. Stated differently, admitting that we only can give an interval for h, there is *no more precise statement of uncertainty* that can be made concerning q_W than is represented by the ensemble of all of the CDFs. All of the heat flux predictions shown in Figure 13.20 are negative, meaning that the heat flux is out of the west face of the system being analyzed and into the adjacent system. Note that some of the CDFs cross one another. The likelihood of CDFs crossing depends on the nonlinearity of the SRQ as a function of the epistemic uncertainties in the input.

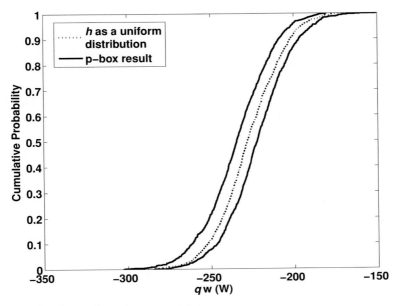

Figure 13.21 p-box for q_W due to input uncertainty.

The p-box for q_W is found by computing the envelope of all of the CDFs shown in Figure 13.20. That is, for each value of q_W computed from both inner and outer sampling, the minimum and maximum of all of the CDFs is found. These minima and maxima form the p-box of the SRQ. Figure 13.21 shows the p-box for q_W, due to input uncertainty, as the solid lines. From a system design perspective, the area of interest in the figure is the region of large negative values of heat flux because this flux could possibly damage the system adjacent to the west face of the system of interest. As expected, these heat fluxes have low values of probability. By noting the width of the p-box, one can assess the magnitude of the uncertain response that is due to the epistemic uncertainty in h. For example, if one were interested in the range of heat flux that could occur for the cumulative probability of 0.1, one would have the interval $[-247, -262]$ W. Similarly, if one were interested in the range of probabilities that could occur if $q_W = -250$ W, one would have an uncertainty given by the probability interval $[0.08, 0.22]$.

Also plotted in Figure 13.21 is the CDF that would be obtained if h were treated as an aleatory uncertainty instead of an epistemic uncertainty. That is, if the interval-valued characterization of h were replaced by a uniform distribution over the interval, one would obtain the dotted CDF shown inside the p-box. It is clear that the characterization of the uncertainty in q_W would be greatly reduced as compared to the p-box representation. For example, the dotted curve shows that the probability of attaining a heat flux of -250 W (or greater in the absolute sense) is 0.12. This interpretation underestimates the uncertainty in q_W due to h and would be misleading to project managers, decision makers, and any other customers of the analysis.

13.4.3.2 Combination of input, model, and numerical uncertainties

We first compute the increase in the width of the input uncertainty p-box that is due to model uncertainty. Because the condition of interest, $T_E = 450$ K, is beyond the highest temperature in the validation experiments, 390 K, extrapolation of $\bar{y}_e(x)$, $CI(x)$, and $\bar{y}_m(x)$ is required. As discussed in Section 13.4.2.1, we use low-order polynomials for the extrapolation of $\bar{y}_e(x)$ and $CI(x)$. We use a linear regression for $\bar{y}_e(x)$, as given by Eq. (13.17). We could directly use the Scheffé confidence interval as given by Eq. (13.18) for the extrapolation. However, here we use the more general procedure of computing a low degree polynomial fit of the confidence interval. Using Eq. (13.18) to generate the data for the regression fit over the range of $330 \leq T_E \leq 390$ K, we compute the following quadratic fit:

$$CI(x) = 264.6 - 1.452T_E + 0.002017T_E^2. \tag{13.46}$$

The sampling results discussed above yield $[\bar{y}_m (450)]_{\text{left}} = -234.7$ W and $[\bar{y}_m (450)]_{\text{right}} = -222.1$ W for the left and right median values, respectively, of the p-box shown in Figure 13.21. Substituting the appropriate values into Eqs. (13.42) and (13.43), we have

since $-234.7 - (-259.9) + 19.5 = 25.2 + 19.5 = 44.7 \geq 0$,

we obtain $d_{\text{left}}(450) = 44.7$ W, $\tag{13.47}$

and

since $-222.1 - (-259.9) - 19.5 = 37.8 - 19.5 = 18.3 > 0$,

we obtain $d_{\text{right}}(450) = 0$ W, $\tag{13.48}$

respectively. From these equations we see that the model is over-predicting the extrapolated experimental mean (although the model result is smaller in absolute value) by 25.2 and 37.8 W for the left and right bound of the p-box, respectively. For the left bound, the model bias error combines with the extrapolated experimental uncertainty of 19.5 W to yield a total model uncertainty shift to the left of 44.7 W. It can be seen that 44% of the leftward shift of the CDF is due to uncertainty in the experimental measurements. If one required a model prediction for a higher temperature, say $T_E = 500$ K, the percentage of the model uncertainty due to measurement uncertainty would increase to roughly 63%. For the right bound, it is seen that the over prediction of the model is larger than the extrapolated experimental uncertainty, resulting in no rightward shift of the CDF due to model uncertainty.

Now consider the additional increase of width of the p-box due to numerical solution error. As discussed earlier, we treat these estimates of error as epistemic uncertainties. In Section 13.3.4.2, we computed $U_I = -0.00173$ W and $U_S = 0.08448$ W for the iterative and discretization uncertainty, respectively. Substituting these results into Eq. (13.45), we have

$$U_N = |-0.00173| + |0.08448| = 0.08621 \text{ W}. \tag{13.49}$$

It is seen that U_N is two orders of magnitude smaller than $d_{\text{left}} (450)$. As a result, it will be neglected in the final estimate of predictive uncertainty for the heat transfer simulation.

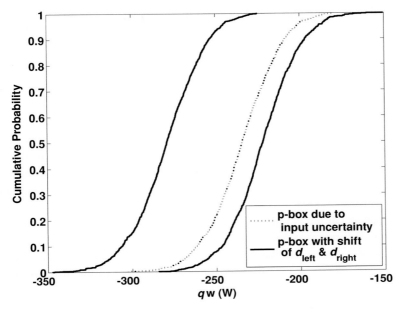

Figure 13.22 p-box for q_w due to the combined input and model uncertainty.

Figure 13.22 shows the final p-box for the combination of input and model uncertainty for q_w. The total uncertainty was obtained by combining the input uncertainty shown in Figure 13.21 and the model uncertainty given by $d_{left}(450) = 44.7$ W and $d_{right}(450) = 0$ W. It is obvious that the estimated model uncertainty contributes significant additional uncertainty to the predicted response. This increase is due solely to the leftward shift of the input p-box and it is considered a constant over the entire distribution. The magnitude of the increase is due to a nearly equal combination of model bias error and experimental measurement uncertainty. The question could be raised whether the experimental uncertainty should be separately accounted for in the estimate of model bias error. We strongly argue that it should be included because ignoring it would deny the stochastic nature of experimental measurements, as well as the epistemic uncertainty due to obtaining limited experimental samples. In addition, the experimental uncertainty contribution should increase as a function of the magnitude of the extrapolation.

The impact of including model uncertainty can be viewed in two ways. First, for any value of cumulative probability the uncertainty in the system response is increased by a constant amount; $d_{left}(450) + d_{right}(450)$. Second, the predicted probability interval for a fixed system response can significantly increase depending on what level of system response is of interest. The following two examples capture this impact. First, consider the increase in uncertainty for a heat flux in the mid-range of the predicted response. From Figure 13.21 it can be seen that for $q_w = -230$ W the interval-valued probability is [0.34, 0.59]. However, when model uncertainty is included (see Figure 13.22) the interval-valued probability increases to [0.34, 0.995]. Second, consider the increase in uncertainty for a large absolute value heat flux that is of concern to over-all system safety, reliability, and performance, say $q_W = -300$ W. The probability interval has increased to $[\sim0., 0.153]$ when model uncertainty is included, as compared to $[\sim0., 0.0025]$ for input uncertainty alone. Both of these examples are a striking demonstration of the increase in uncertainty when model uncertainty is included.

13.5 Step 5: conduct model updating

Model updating can take many different forms. For example, model updating could involve significant reformulation in scenarios, event trees, failure modes, changes in how the system interacts with the surroundings, modeling assumptions, replacement of certain submodels that are performing poorly, and updating of model parameters. Although it is common practice to conduct different types of model updating, here we will only deal with updating of parameters that occur *within* models. That is, the model form or mathematical model structure does not change, but the parameters that occur in the model are altered based on various types of information. These parameters could be part of the mathematical model for the surroundings (such as boundary conditions and system excitation) or the system (such as geometry, initial conditions, and material properties). The parameter can be either a deterministic value, such as a scalar determined by some optimization process, or a nondeterministic value, such as a quantity given by a probability distribution. In addition, the parameter can be, in some circumstances, a scalar field, a vector, or a tensor field.

Updating of parameters in models, and submodels, is often a necessary activity in essentially any simulation. Some readers may feel we have been unfairly harsh on the activity of parameter updating in Chapter 12. Our criticisms have been primarily directed at the detrimental, and dangerous, concept of thinking that updating (or estimating or calibrating) parameters in models is fundamentally the same as model validation. Similarly, we are concerned with the erroneous belief that all types of parameter updating have a similar effect on predictive capability. In this section, we fully recognize the importance and necessity of updating parameters in models. However, we will argue that it is important to keep the concepts of parameter updating and model validation separate. As discussed in Section 13.2, the goal of parameter updating is to improve the agreement between simulation and experiment, whereas the goal of model validation is model accuracy assessment. As will be pointed out in this section, we agree there are shades of gray, or overlap, between parameter updating and validation of a model. We will discuss the extremes of updating and validation and the areas in between to try and clarify the varying effects of updating on predictive capability.

13.5.1 Types of model parameter

To better understand the various approaches to parameter updating, it is appropriate to first discuss the various classes of parameters that occur in simulation activities, a topic that has not been well studied. One would think that theorists in modeling and simulation would have more carefully examined the issue of parameter classes, but, to our knowledge, this is not the case. Morgan and Henrion (1990) discuss several classes of parameter that are quite helpful for risk assessment and uncertainty quantification. We use their basic classification and we segregate certain important classes into additional classes. For simulation activities, we divide model parameters into the following six classes:

- measurable properties of the system or the surroundings,
- physical modeling parameters,
- ad hoc model parameters,
- numerical algorithm parameters,
- decision parameters,
- uncertainty modeling parameters.

Each of these will be briefly discussed, along with the type of information that is commonly available for updating each class of parameters.

Measurable properties of the system or surroundings are physical quantities or characteristics that are directly measurable, at least in principle, either now or at some time in the past or future. Specifically, these are quantities that are measured separately from complex models associated with the system of interest. Metrologists point out that empirical quantities always have some type of conceptual or mathematical model associated with the quantity to be measured (Rabinovich, 2005). Measurable properties of the system or surrounding generally rely on either (a) a simple, well accepted, model of the physical nature of the quantity; or (b) some type of well-understood performance or reliability characteristic of the system or the surroundings. Several examples of system properties in this class are: Young's modulus, tensile strength, mass density, electrical conductivity, dielectric constant, thermal conductivity, specific heat, melting point, surface energy, chemical reaction rate, thrust of an engine, thermal efficiency of a power plant, the failure rate of a valve, and age distribution of subsystems within a system. Examples of properties of surroundings that are in this class are: wind loading on a structure, external heating on a flight vehicle, atmospheric characteristics surrounding a nuclear power plant that could exist after a serious accident, electrical and magnetic characteristics of a lightning strike on a system, and physical or electronic attack on a system.

Physical modeling parameters are those that are *not* measurable outside of the context of the mathematical model of the system under consideration. These quantities are physically meaningful in the sense that they are associated with some type of well-accepted physical process occurring in the system. However, because of the complexity of the process, no separate mathematical model exists for the process. Stated differently, some type of basic physical process is known to occur in the system, but because of the coupling of the process, the physical effect of the process is combined into a simple model that only exists within the framework of the complex model. Quantifying these parameters relies on inference within the context of the assumptions and formulation of the complex model. Examples of these types of parameter are (a) internal dynamic damping in a material, (b) aerodynamic damping of a structure, (c) damping and stiffness of assembled joints in a multi-element structure, (d) effective chemical reaction rate in turbulent reacting flow, (e) effective surface roughness in turbulent flow along a surface, and (f) thermal and electrical contact resistance between material interfaces.

Ad hoc model parameters are those that are introduced in models, or submodels, simply to provide a method for adjusting the results of a model to obtain better agreement with experimental data. These parameters have little or no physical justification in the sense that they do not characterize some feature of a physical process. They exist solely within the context of the model or submodel in which they are used. Some examples are (a) most parameters in fluid dynamic turbulence models, (b) most parameters in models for strain hardening in plastic deformation of materials, (c) most parameters in models for material fatigue, and (d) parameters inserted into a complex model that are used solely to adjust model predictions to obtain agreement with experimental data.

Numerical algorithm parameters are those that exist within the context of a numerical solution method that can be adjusted to meet the needs of a particular solution. These parameters typically have a recommended range of values, but they can be changed to give better performance or reliability of the numerical method. Here, we *do not mean* discretization levels or iterative convergence levels, but quantities that typically appear in the formulation or execution of a numerical algorithm. Some examples are (a) the relaxation factor in the successive over-relaxation method for the iterative solution of algebraic equations, (b) the number of iterations used on each level of a multi-grid method, (c) artificial damping or dissipation parameters in numerical methods, and (d) parameters to control the hour-glassing phenomena in finite element models for solids.

Decision parameters are those that exist within an analysis whose value is determined or controlled by the analyst, designer, or decision maker. Sometime these are referred to as design variables, control variables, or policy decision parameters. The question of whether a quantity is considered as a decision parameter or, say, a measurable property of the system, depends on the context and intent of the analysis. Decision parameters are commonly used in design to optimize the performance, safety, or reliability of a system. In the analysis of abnormal or hostile environments, these parameters can be varied to determine the most vulnerable conditions that could affect the safety or security of the system. These parameters are also used, for example, in models constructed for aiding in public policy decisions, public health regulations, or environmental impact analyses.

Uncertainty modeling parameters are those that are defined only in the context of characterizing the uncertainty of a quantity or a model. Uncertainty modeling parameters, simply referred to as *uncertainty parameters* from here on, are typically parameters of a family of distributions, e.g., the four parameters defined as part of a beta distribution. Uncertainty parameters can be a point value, an interval, or a random variable. As a result, an uncertainty parameter can be either a number or an aleatory or epistemic uncertainty itself. Uncertainty parameters can be used to characterize the uncertainty of any of the foregoing parameters.

Of the six classes of parameters just discussed, numerical algorithm and decision parameters are not normally viewed as being updated. They can certainly can be changed and optimized during an analysis so as to better achieve the goals of the analysis. For example, numerical algorithm parameters are usually adjusted to obtain better numerical

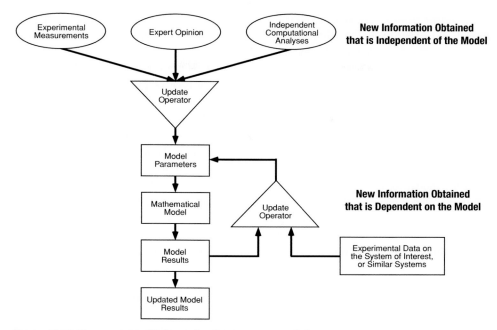

Figure 13.23 Two sources of information for parameter updating.

performance or stability for the various types of physics occurring within the system of interest. However, this type of adjustment of parameters is not normally considered as updating because it does not fundamentally deal with the mathematical model itself. The remaining four classes of parameters are fundamental to the model and they should be updated as new information becomes available.

13.5.2 Sources of new information

New information upon which to update a parameter can come in various forms. Some of the most common sources of new information are (a) newly available experimental measurements of parameters, (b) additions or improvements in expert opinion concerning parameters, (c) separate computational analyses or theoretical studies that add information concerning parameters used in the present analysis, and (d) new experimental results for the system of interest or from systems similar to the present system. From our perspective of calibration and validation, it is clear that the type of information obtained from the system of interest provides fundamentally different inferential information than the other three sources listed. That is, the first three sources of information provide independent information for updating model parameters. The last source, however, provides information that can *only* be interpreted within the context of the mathematical model of the complete system.

Figure 13.23 shows how information for updating parameters falls into two categories. First, information obtained directly on parameters, either from experimental measurements, expert opinion, or independent computational analyses. This information is fundamentally *independent* from the model of interest. Second, information obtained from comparing model and experimental results on the system or similar systems. This information is fundamentally *dependent* on the model. That is, the updated scalar value or probability distribution for a given parameter is *conditional* on the model of the system. Statisticians refer to any type of updating of parameters from any type of information as *statistical inference*. They do not make a distinction between the two fundamentally different types of information. To them, data are data and all data should be used to update the model. Their traditions, however, are deeply rooted in updating statistical models, i.e., models built on regression fits of data with no causality between input and output. In these models, the parameters have *no physical significance*; they are just *knobs* to be adjusted to obtain a best fit of the model to the experimental data. In physics-based models, however, these knobs are quite often physical modeling parameters with a *clear meaning independent from the present model*. Herein lies the conflict between viewpoints on the scientific justification of updating parameters in models.

With this perspective in mind, some of the key questions in parameter updating are:

- Should the source of new information affect the choice of the method used in updating?
- Should the type of new information, e.g., whether it contains aleatory and/or epistemic uncertainty, affect the choice of the method used in updating?
- How does the source of the new information affect the estimation of uncertainty in the updated model predictions, i.e., how does the source of the information affect the predictive capability of the model?

Some of the issues surrounding these questions will be addressed in the following sections.

13.5.3 *Approaches to parameter updating*

Approaches to parameter updating are generally divided into methods for estimating scalar quantities and methods for estimating probability distributions for a parameter that is considered a random variable (Crassidis and Junkins, 2004; Raol *et al.*, 2004; Aster *et al.*, 2005; van den Bos, 2007). Here, we will focus on methods for estimating parameters that are given by probability distributions. This type of estimation can be considered as part of the broad field of statistical inference. In fact, most of statistics is devoted to statistical inference. The general problem of statistical inference is, given some information on uncertain quantities, how can the information be used to characterize uncertainty about the quantity. The vast majority of traditional statistical inference is focused on the characterization of random variables, i.e., aleatory uncertainty. Because of the breadth and depth of the development of statistical inference, we will only touch on some of the approaches and issues involved. For an in-depth discussion of the topic of statistical inference, see, for example, Bernardo and Smith (1994); Gelman *et al.* (1995); Leonard and Hsu (1999); Mukhopadhyay (2000); Casella and Berger (2002); Wasserman (2004); Young and Smith (2005); Cox (2006); Ghosh *et al.* (2006); and Sivia and Skilling (2006).

Unfortunately, statisticians are not in agreement about the way in which statistical inference should be accomplished. There are a wide variety of methods available that give rise to different estimates and different interpretations of the same estimate. In addition, statisticians do not agree on the principles that should be used to judge the quality and accuracy of estimation techniques. The two major camps of statistical inference are Frequentists and Bayesians. Both approaches are regularly used, often with much discussion of successes and little discussion of failure or erroneous inferential interpretations. Failure can be the most instructive and beneficial to the continued development of an approach and the development of improved guidance concerning when one approach is more appropriate than another.

The Frequentist approach is also commonly called the classical approach and it involves a number of methods. Two primary features of the Frequentist approach are particularly important with respect to parameter updating. First, probability is *strictly* interpreted as the relative frequency of an event occurring in the limit of a large number of random trials or observations from an experiment. The set of all possible outcomes of a random trial is called the sample space of the experiment. An event is defined as a particular subset, or realization, of the sample space. Second, updating can *only be done* when the new information is derived from experimental measurements obtained directly on the parameters of interest. Some of the more common classes of methods are: point-estimation of a scalar, interval-estimation of a scalar, hypothesis testing, and regression and correlation analyses. Here we are mainly interested in methods for estimating uncertainty parameters, e.g., parameters of a probability distribution that is chosen to represent the random variable of interest. In the estimation of a point value for an uncertainty parameter, it is assumed that the parameter is constant, but imprecisely known because only a sample of the population is available. Various types of best estimate method are available to estimate the point value. There are also methods available for interval-estimates for the parameters of the distribution. When this is done, the uncertain quantity of interest becomes a mixture of aleatory and epistemic uncertainty. The two most commonly used methods are the method of moments and the method of maximum likelihood. Because of the restriction on the type of information that can be used and the quantity of information that is required, Frequentist methods are generally considered less applicable for the type of parameter updating shown in Figure 13.23. The primary advantage of Frequentist methods is that they are widely viewed as simpler and easier to use than Bayesian methods.

Bayesian methods take a different and broader perspective concerning statistical inference. They consider the distribution characterizing the uncertainty in the physical parameter as a function that is (a) initially unknown, and (b) should be updated as more information becomes available concerning the distribution. The initial postulated distribution for the uncertainty parameter can come from any source or mixture of sources, for example, experimental measurements, expert opinion, or computational analyses. More importantly, the distribution for the uncertainty parameter can be updated when any type of new information becomes available. Before updating, the distribution is referred to as the *prior distribution*, and after updating it becomes the *posterior distribution*. It is well accepted that the proper method of updating distributions is Bayes' theorem.

When no information is available for the prior distribution, the analyst can simply choose as prior his/her personal probability. The Bayesian paradigm uses the notion of subjective probability, or personal degree of belief, defined in the theory of rational decision making. In this theory, every rational individual is a free agent and is not constrained to choose the same prior as another individual. This, of course, leads to vehement criticisms from the Frequentists to the Bayesian paradigm. The Frequentists commonly raise the question, how can such subjectivity in choosing probability distributions lead to trustworthy inference? In the present context of simulation, how can personal beliefs expressed in the input parameters to a model lead to trustworthy decision making based on the model outputs? This question is especially critical if the resulting output probabilities are interpreted as a frequency of occurrence, for example, in terms of regulatory requirements on safety or reliability of a system. These are serious criticisms if little or no justification for prior distributions is available. The primary defense of Bayesian inference is based on the argument that continually adding new information from all available sources minimizes the impact of the subjectivity in the initial choice of prior distributions. And, as a result, the initial choice of prior distributions will have little affect on the final model outputs needed for decision making.

In this discussion, we have focused on the updating of uncertainty parameters for characterizing aleatory uncertainty in measurable parameters, physical modeling parameters, and ad hoc parameters. A related question is: if the uncertainty parameters are epistemic uncertainties, e.g., intervals, how can they be updated? For example, suppose that an expert gives the uncertainty characterization for a measurable system parameter as an interval. How should the parameter be updated or modified if a new, equally credible, expert provides a non-overlapping interval? Neither Frequentist nor Bayesian approaches recognize epistemic uncertainty as a separate type of uncertainty, and as a result, they cannot address this question. Over the last decade, the topic of updating epistemic uncertainties, usually referred to as information aggregation or data fusion, has received increasing attention. The practical need for this type of updating is obvious, if one accepts the separation of aleatory and epistemic uncertainty. The emphasis in this field has concentrated on dealing with contradictions or conflict in information from various sources because the information content in epistemic uncertainty can be minimal and it can represent different types of epistemic uncertainty. For example, one may also have to deal with differences in linguistic interpretation of knowledge and, as a result, use fuzzy set theory or a combination of fuzzy set theory and classical probability theory. For an in-depth discussion of aggregation methods for various types of uncertainties, see Yager *et al.* (1994); Bouchon-Meunier (1998); Sentz and Ferson (2002); Ferson *et al.* (2003); Beliakov *et al.* (2007); and Torra and Narukawa (2007).

13.5.4 *Parameter updating, validation, and predictive uncertainty*

Whether one uses the Frequentist or Bayesian approach for updating parameters, from our perspective there are two serious difficulties that are caused by convolving parameter

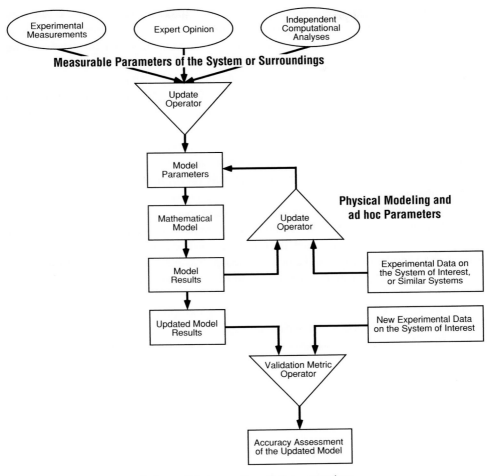

Figure 13.24 Parameter updating, validation, and predictive uncertainty.

updating with the model of the system. We are not the first, of coarse, to raise these concerns (Beck, 1987). These concerns will be discussed in the following two sections.

13.5.4.1 Parameter updating

In Figure 13.23 discussed above, we segregated the various sources of new information into two groups: information obtained that is independent from the model and information obtained that is dependent on the model. Figure 13.24 maps three types of physical parameters discussed in Section 13.5.1 onto the concepts shown in Figure 13.23. Measurable physical parameters of the system or surroundings (simply measurable parameters) can be determined, at least in principle, through measurements that are independent of the system of interest. Physical modeling parameters and ad hoc parameters can *only be determined* by using the model of the system of interest in concert with the experimental data for the system. As a result, measurable parameters are shown at the top of the figure where they could be independently updated. Physical modeling and ad hoc parameters are shown on the right of the figure because they can only be updated in the feedback loop shown using the mathematical model of the system.

We believe the proper approach to updating the measurable parameters of the system or surroundings is to do so separately from the model for the system of interest. If they are updated with the model of the system, using experimental data for the system, then our concern is the same as with updating physical modeling and ad hoc parameters. That is, our concern is that the updated parameters were determined by convolving parameter updating while using the model of the system. Suppose one used either a Frequentist or a Bayesian approach for model updating and the question was asked: how would you conceptually describe the updating approach to parameters in a physics-based model? There would certainly be a wide range of responses. We suggest that two extremes would cover the range of opinions. Respondent A: The approach attempts to optimally use the information available for the inputs to the model, the physics embodied in the model, and the available experimental results to produce the best prediction possible from the model. Respondent B: The approach is a constrained regression fit of the experimental data in the sense that the physics-based model represents the constraint on the parameters. We would agree more with Respondent B than A. We present the following thought experiment to suggest that B is the more accurate conceptual description.

Recalling the discussion in Chapter 10, the total error in a simulation result can be written as the sum of four sources,

$$E_{\text{sim}} = E_1 + E_2 + E_3 + E_4, \qquad (13.50)$$

where the sources are

$$
\begin{aligned}
E_1 &= (y_{\text{sim}} - y_{\text{Pcomputer}}), \\
E_2 &= (y_{\text{Pcomputer}} - y_{\text{model}}), \\
E_3 &= (y_{\text{model}} - y_{\text{exp}}), \\
E_4 &= (y_{\text{exp}} - y_{\text{nature}}).
\end{aligned}
\qquad (13.51)
$$

E_1 represents all numerical errors resulting from the difference between the discrete solution, y_{sim} (obtained using a finite discretization size, finite iterative convergence, and finite precision computer), and the exact solution to the discrete equations obtained on a perfect computer as the discretization size approaches zero, $y_{\text{Pcomputer}}$. E_1 is referred to as the solution error and the most important contributor to this error is an inadequately resolved mesh or time step.

E_2 represents all errors resulting from the difference between the exact solution to the discrete equations as the discretization size approaches zero, $y_{\text{Pcomputer}}$, and the exact solution of the mathematical model, y_{model}. The most important contributor to this error is coding errors in the software computing the model result.

E_3 represents all errors resulting from the difference between the exact solution to the mathematical model, $y_{Pcomputer}$, and the experimental measurement, y_{exp}. E_3 is referred to as the model error or model form error and the most important contributors to this error are model bias error, i.e., $d(x)$, and errors made by the analyst in preparation of the input data.

E_4 represents all errors due to the difference between the true, but unknown value of nature, y_{nature}, and the measurement of a physical quantity, y_{exp}. The most important contributors to this error are systematic and random errors in experimentally measured quantities.

Suppose that at a given point in the conduct of an analysis of a system there have been a number of updates on all adjustable parameters using the model and the experimental measurements from a number of systems. Suppose that any one of the following situations occurred that caused a large change in the predicated SRQ of interest: (a) a finer mesh resolution or a smaller time step was used, (b) a coding error was discovered and then corrected in one of the computer codes of the model, (c) an input error was discovered and corrected in one of the computer codes, and (d) an error was discovered and corrected in the data reduction procedure processing the experimental sets of data used in the updating. Each one of these situations would have caused a large increase in the magnitude of at least one of the E_i components discussed above, and a large increase in the newly-calculated total simulation error, E_{sim}.

Whether it is Respondent A or B discussed above, a new effort would be initiated to update all of the adjustable parameters in the model. Given the presumption that there would be a large increase in E_{sim}, there would presumably be large changes in at least some of the three types of updated parameters: measurable, physical, and ad hoc. This is because updating attempts to *achieve error cancellation among the various sources* by adjusting all of the available parameters in the model in order to minimize E_{sim}. There has been, of course, *no change at all* in the physics of the system. Large changes in the measurable parameters are the most embarrassing because there should be *no changes* in these quantities since they are independently measurable quantities. In addition, if large changes occur in the physical modeling parameters, it is also troubling because they have a clear physical meaning associated with well-accepted physical processes. Large changes in both types of parameter demonstrate that updating is conceptually aligned with regression fitting of experimental data, constrained by the physics model structure.

13.5.4.2 Validation after parameter updating

In the lower portion of Figure 13.24, we show the validation metric operator along with its two inputs and the output of model accuracy assessment of the updated model. Our concern deals with the important question: how should one interpret the validation metric result when an updated model is assessed for accuracy? The answer to this question is critically important to understand because this information is used, for example, by decision makers in assessing the predicted safety, reliability, and performance of systems; and government regulators in determining public safety and potential environmental impact. We give two situations: the first where the model can be appropriately assessed for accuracy, and the second where the assessment would be erroneous and misleading.

Suppose that new experimental data became available on the system of interest. Presume the data were for input conditions that were substantially different from previous experimental data used in updating the model. For this case, we believe a comparison of model results and the new experimental data would properly constitute an assessment of model accuracy. Consider the following example. Suppose one were interested in several vibrational modes of a built-up structure. The structure is composed of multiple structural elements that are bolted together at a number of connection points of the elements. The experimental data used for updating the model were obtained on the structure with the torsional preload on each bolt specified at a certain value. The stiffness and damping of all of the joints were determined using either Frequentist or Bayesian updating applied to the results from the model and the experimental data from several prototype structures that were tested.

Then, because of some design considerations, the assembly requirements were changed such that the preload on all of the bolts was doubled. The model included a submodel for how the stiffness and damping of the joints of the structure would depend on preload of the bolts. Several of the existing structures were modified and retested as a result of this bolt–preload doubling. We argue that when the new results from the model are compared in a blind-test prediction with the new experimental data, an appropriate assessment of model predictive capability can be made. If so desired, one could compute a validation metric to quantitatively assess model accuracy using the new predictions and measurements. An even more demanding test of the predictive capability of the model would be if the new assembly requirements included changing some of the bolted joints to riveted joints, presuming that a submodel was available for riveted joints.

Now, consider the case where new experimental data became available on the system of interest, and that the model had been updated using previously available data on the same system. For this case, we argue that one could *not* claim that the predictive accuracy of the model was being assessed by comparison with the new experimental data because the new data were obtained for the same system, except for random variability in the system. For example, suppose that in the structural vibration example just described, additional data were obtained on newly assembled structures. However, the structures were assembled using exactly the same specifications for all of the structural elements and the same preload on all of the bolts in the structure as those used earlier to update the model. That is, no new physics was exercised in the model for the new predictions. Even though one would be obtaining new experimental data that has never been used in updating the model, the experimental samples were drawn from the same parent population as the previous samples. The new data would provide additional sampling information concerning manufacturing variability in structural elements and bolt fastening, but it would *not* provide any new test of the physics embedded in the model. Specifically, it would not represent an estimate of the model form error, $d(x)$. As a result, it could *not* be claimed that the accuracy of the model was being assessed by comparison with the new data.

As can be seen from these two examples there is a very wide range of how comparisons with experimental data should be interpreted when model updating is involved. Understanding that the philosophical root of V&V is skepticism, claims of good agreement with data should always be questioned.

13.6 Step 6: conduct sensitivity analysis

Morgan and Henrion (1990) provide the broadest definition of sensitivity analysis: the determination of how a change in any aspect of the model changes any predicted response of the model. The following are some examples of elements of the model that could change, thereby producing a change in the response of the model: (a) specification of the system and the surroundings; (b) specification of the normal, abnormal, or hostile environments; (c) assumptions in the formulation of the conceptual or mathematical model; (c) assumptions concerning coupling of various types of physics between submodels; (d) assumptions concerning which model inputs are considered deterministic and which are considered uncertain; (e) a change in variance of an aleatory uncertainty or a change in the magnitude of an epistemic uncertainty of model inputs; and (f) assumptions concerning independence and dependence between uncertain inputs. As can be seen from these examples, changes in the model can be viewed as either what-if analyses, or analyses determining how the outputs change as a function of changes in the inputs, whether the inputs are deterministic, epistemic uncertainty, aleatory uncertainty, or a combination of the two. Uncertainty analysis, on the other hand, is the quantitative determination of the uncertainty in any SRQ as a function of any uncertainty in the model.

Although uncertainty analysis and sensitivity analysis (SA) are closely related, SA is concerned with the characterization of the relative importance of how various changes in the model will change the model predictions. Recalling Eq. (13.32), we have

$$\vec{y} = f(\vec{x}), \tag{13.52}$$

where $\vec{x} = \{x_1, x_2, \ldots, x_m\}$ and $\vec{y} = \{y_1, y_2, \ldots, y_n\}$. SA is a more complex mathematical task than UQ because it explores the mapping of $\vec{x} \rightarrow \vec{y}$ in order to assess the effects of individual elements of $\vec{x}$ on elements of $\vec{y}$. In addition, SA also deals with how changes in the mapping, f, changes elements of $\vec{y}$. SA is usually done after a UQ analysis, or at least after a preliminary UQ analysis has been completed. In this way the SA can take advantage of a great deal of information that has been generated as part of a UQ analysis.

Results from an SA are typically used in two ways. First, if an SA is conducted on the elements dealing with the formulation of the model or the choice of the submodels, then one can use the results as a planning tool for improved allocation of resources on a project. For example, suppose that a number of submodels are used and they are coupled through the model for the system. An SA could be conducted to determine the ranking of which submodels have the most impact on each of the elements of $\vec{y}$. For simplicity, suppose that each submodel resulted in one output quantity that was then used in the model of the system.

The output quantity from each submodel could be artificially changed, say by 10%, before the quantity was used as input to the system model. This would be done one submodel at a time. One could then rank in order from largest to smallest, which models produced the largest change on each of the elements of $\vec{y}$. The rank order for each element of $\vec{y}$ would normally be different than another element. If it was found that certain submodels had essentially no effect on any of the elements of $\vec{y}$, then the lead analyst or project manager could alter the allocation of resources within the project. He/she could move funding and resources from the less important submodels to the most important submodels. This can be a difficult adjustment for some involved in a scientific computing project.

Second, it is more common that an SA is used to determine how changes in input uncertainties affect the uncertainty in the elements of $\vec{y}$. Some examples of how this information can be used are (a) reducing the manufacturing variability in key input quantities to improve the reliability of the system, (b) altering the operating envelope of the system in order to improve system performance, and (c) altering the system design to improve system safety when it is discovered that an important input uncertainty cannot be reduced. When used in this way, one usually conducts either a local or global SA. Local and global SAs will be briefly discussed below. For a detailed discussion of SA, see Helton *et al.* (2006) and Saltelli *et al.* (2008).

13.6.1 Local sensitivity analysis

In a local SA, one is interested in determining how outputs locally change as a function of inputs. This is equivalent to computing the partial derivatives of the SRQs with respect to each of the input quantities. Although a local SA can be conducted without the assumption of the existence and continuity of partial derivates of the SRQs, it is a simpler approach to introduce the concepts. Here we will focus on the input quantities that are uncertain, although one could certainly considered all input quantities. A local SA computes $m \times n$ derivatives of the random variable y_j with respect to the random variable x_i:

$$\left(\frac{\partial y_j}{\partial x_i}\right)_{\vec{x}=\vec{c}}, \quad i = 1, 2, 3, \ldots m \quad \text{and} \quad j = 1, 2, 3, \ldots, n, \quad (13.53)$$

$x_i = \{x_1, x_2, \ldots, x_m\}$, $y_j = \{y_1, y_2, \ldots, y_n\}$, and $\vec{c}$ is a vector of constants that specifies a statistic of the input quantities at which the derivatives are evaluated. The vector $\vec{c}$ can specify any input condition over which the system can operate. The most common condition of interest is the mean of each of the input parameters, $\bar{x}_i$. In most engineering systems, one can usually consider the input quantities as continuous variables, as opposed to discrete quantities. Since we have focused on sampling techniques, one must compute a sufficient number of samples in order to construct a smooth function so that the partial derivative in Eq. (13.53) can be computed.

As an example, suppose that $\vec{x} = \{x_1, x_2, x_3\}$ and $\vec{y} = \{y_1, y_2\}$. Figure 13.25 depicts y_1 and y_2 as a function of x_2, given that $x_1 = c_1$ and $x_3 = c_3$. Since $\vec{x}$ exists in a three-dimensional space, and y_1 and y_2 each exist in a four-dimensional space, Figure 13.25 can

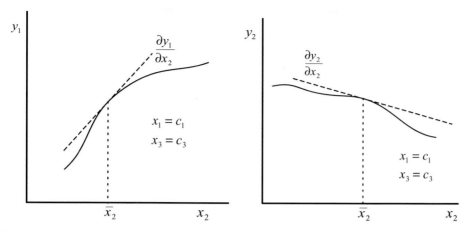

Figure 13.25 Example of system responses and derivatives in a local sensitivity analysis.

be viewed as y_1 and y_2 as a function of x_2, in the plane of $x_1 = c_1$ and $x_3 = c_3$. Also shown in the figure are the derivatives $\left(\frac{\partial y_1}{\partial x_2}\right)_{x_1=c_1, x_3=c_3}$ and $\left(\frac{\partial y_2}{\partial x_2}\right)_{x_1=c_1, x_3=c_3}$ evaluated at the mean of x_2, $\bar{x}_2$. Note that $\{y_1, y_2\}$ and the derivatives can be computed without assuming any uncertainty structure of the inputs. y_1 and y_2 are simply evaluated at a sufficient number of samples over the needed range of each x_i. If the mean of any of the input quantities is needed, then a sufficient number of samples of $\{x_1, x_2, x_3\}$ must be computed so that the mean can be satisfactorily estimated.

Results from local SAs are most commonly used in system design and optimization studies. For example, one could consider how all the input parameters affect the performance, reliability or safety of the system. Some of the input parameters the designer has control over; some are fixed by design constraints on the system, such as the operating envelope, size, and weight. For those that can be controlled, a local SA can greatly aid in optimizing the design, including any flexibility in the operating envelope, so that improved performance, reliability, and safety can be obtained.

13.6.2 Global sensitivity analysis

A global SA is conducted when information is needed concerning how the uncertainty structure of all of the inputs maps to the uncertainty structure of each of the outputs. A global SA is appropriate when a project manager and decision maker needs information on what are the most important uncertain inputs driving specific uncertain outputs. This is especially needed, for example, when the outputs fall outside system performance requirements, or exceed governmental regulatory requirements. With the information from a global SA, a project manager can determine what are the most important contributors forcing the outputs of interest into unwanted ranges of response. The information concerning the ordering of

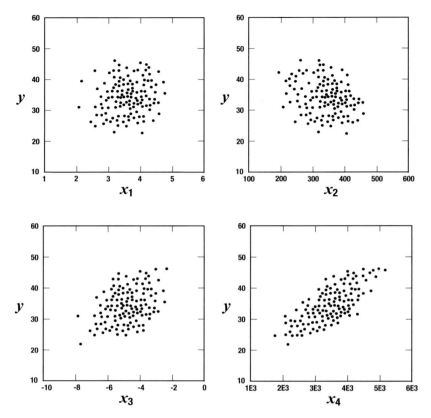

Figure 13.26 Scatter plots for one output quantity as a function of four input quantities.

these input contributors based on their effect on the individual outputs will also include the effects of the uncertainties from all of the other input quantities in the simulation.

A common first step in a global SA is to construct a scatter plot for each of the y_j as a function of each x_i. This would result in a total of $m \times n$ plots. The data points in the scatter plots can come from the MCS or LHS that are computed as part of the UQ analysis. The purpose of the scatter plots is to determine if any trend exists in each output quantity y_j as a function of each x_i. For example, suppose we have one output quantity, y, and four input quantities, $\{x_1, x_2, x_3, x_4\}$. Figure 13.26 shows the four scatter plots that would be generated, given a total of 100 LHS samples. The scatter plots are a projection from a five-dimensional uncertainty space, $\{y, x_1, x_2, x_3, x_4\}$, onto the $y - x_1$ plane, the $y - x_2$ plane, the $y - x_3$ plane, and the $y - x_4$ plane, respectively. The shape of the uncertainty clouds indicate that: (a) there is no discernable trend of y with x_1, (b) there is a slightly decreasing trend of y with x_2, (c) there is a clear trend of y increasing with x_3, and (d) there is a strong trend of y increasing with x_4. Note that there could be nonlinear trends buried within the clouds shown in Figure 13.26. One could attempt to rank order the x_i to determine which one has the strongest influence on y by computing a linear regression of each scatter plot. Using the slope of the linear regression, one could compare the magnitude of

$$\left|\frac{\partial y}{\partial x_1}\right|, \quad \left|\frac{\partial y}{\partial x_2}\right|, \quad \left|\frac{\partial y}{\partial x_3}\right|, \quad \text{and} \quad \left|\frac{\partial y}{\partial x_4}\right|. \tag{13.54}$$

This result, however, would be of limited value in a global SA because the magnitude of each derivative would depend on the dimensional units of each x_i. In addition, each derivative has no information concerning the nature of the uncertainty in each x_i.

It is standard practice to reformulate the scatter plots so that all the x_i are rescaled by their respective estimated means, $\bar{x}_i$, and y is rescaled by its estimated mean, $\bar{y}$. In this way one can then properly compare the regression slopes given in Eq. (13.54). We then have

$$\left|\frac{\partial(y/\bar{y})}{\partial(x_1/\bar{x}_1)}\right|, \quad \left|\frac{\partial(y/\bar{y})}{\partial(x_2/\bar{x}_2)}\right|, \quad \left|\frac{\partial(y/\bar{y})}{\partial(x_3/\bar{x}_3)}\right|, \quad \text{and} \quad \left|\frac{\partial(y/\bar{y})}{\partial(x_4/\bar{x}_4)}\right|. \tag{13.55}$$

The terms in Eq. (13.55) are either referred to as the sigma-normalized derivatives, or the standardized regression coefficients (SRCs) (Helton *et al.*, 2006; Saltelli *et al.*, 2008). If the response y is nearly linear in all of the x_i, and the x_i are independent random variables, then the SRCs listed in Eq. (13.55) can be rank ordered from largest to smallest to express the most important to least important effects of input quantities on the output quantity. In most SAs it is found that even if there are a large number of uncertain inputs x_i, there are only several inputs that dominate the effect on a given output quantity. As a final point, it should be clear that the rank ordering of the SRCs for one output quantity need not be the same, or even similar, to the rank ordering for a different output quantity. If there are multiple output quantities of high importance to a system's performance, safety, or reliability, then the list of important input quantities (considering all of the important output quantities) can grow significantly.

The most common method of determining if y is linear with each of the x_i, and determining if the x_i are independent, is to examine the sum of the R^2 values from each of the linear regression fits. R^2 is interpreted as the proportion of the observed y variation with x_i that can be represented by the regression model. For the four input quantities in the present example, these are written as R_1^2, R_2^2, R_3^2, R_4^2, respectively. If the sum of the R^2 values is near unity, then there is reasonable evidence that a linear regression model can be used to rank order the SRCs. If one finds that the sum of the R^2 values is much less than unity, there could be (a) nonlinear trends of y with some of the x_i; (b) statistical dependencies or correlations between the x_i; or (c) strong interactions between the x_i within the mapping of $x_i \to y$, e.g., in the physics represented in the model. Applying a linear regression to each of the graphs shown in Figure 13.26, one finds

$$R_1^2 = 0.01, \quad R_2^2 = 0.11, \quad R_1^2 = 0.27, \quad \text{and} \quad R_1^2 = 0.55. \tag{13.56}$$

The sum of the R^2 values is 0.94, indicating there is evidence that the SRCs computed from the regression fits can properly estimate the relative importance of each of the input quantities in the global SA. If the sum of the R^2 values is significantly less than unity, then more sophisticated techniques such as rank regression, nonparametric regression, and variance decomposition must be used (Helton *et al.*, 2006; Saltelli *et al.*, 2008; Storlie and Helton, 2008a,b).

13.7 Example problem: thermal heating of a safety component

This example is taken from a recent workshop dealing with investigating methods for model validation and predictive capability (Hills *et al.*, 2008; Pilch, 2008). The organizers of the workshop constructed three example problems, each one dealing with different physical phenomena: thermal heating of a safety component, static deflection of a frame structure, and dynamic deflection of a structural element. Each mathematical model constructed was purposefully designed with some model weaknesses and vagaries in order to realistically reflect common situations analysts encounter. For example, there are modeling assumptions that seem questionable, including assertions that certain parameters are constants, that interacting variables are mutually independent, and that there are no experimental data on the system of interest at operational conditions.

Each of the three problems constructed for the workshop had a similar formulation: a mathematical model was specified along with an analytical solution, experimental data were given for the system or closely related systems, and a prediction was required concerning the probability that the system satisfy a regulatory safety criterion. The thermal heating challenge problem is described in Dowding *et al.* (2008). For the thermal heating problem, the regulatory criterion specified that the temperature at a specific location and time not exceed a temperature of 900 °C with a probability of larger than 0.01. This criterion can be written as

$$P\{T(x = 0, t = 1000) > 900\} < 0.01, \tag{13.57}$$

where T is the temperature of the component, $x = 0$ is the face of the component, and the time is 1000 s. In this section, we describe an analysis approach to the thermal heating problem that is based on Ferson *et al.* (2008). For a complete description of each challenge problem and the analyses presented by a number of researchers, see Hills *et al.* (2008).

The model for the thermal problem is one-dimensional, unsteady, heat conduction through a slab of material (Dowding *et al.*, 2008). A heat flux, q_W, is specified at $x = 0$ and an adiabatic condition ($q_W = 0$) is specified at $x = L$ (see Figure 13.27). The initial temperature of the slab is uniform at a value of T_i. The thermal conductivity, k, and the volumetric heat capacity, ρC_p, of the material in the slab are considered as independent of temperature. k and ρC_p, however, are uncertain parameters due to manufacturing variability of the slab material. That is, k and ρC_p can vary from one manufactured slab to the next, but within a given slab, k and ρC_p are constant. For this simple model, an analytical solution

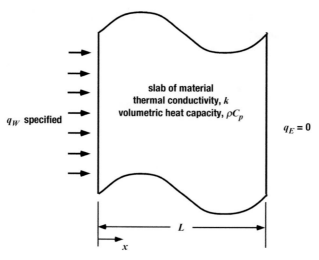

Figure 13.27 Schematic for the thermal heating problem.

to the PDE can be written as

$$T(x,t) = T_i + \frac{q_w L}{k} \left\{ \frac{1}{3} - \frac{x}{L} + \frac{1}{2}\left(\frac{x}{L}\right)^2 + \frac{kt}{\rho C_p L^2} \right.$$
$$\left. - \frac{2}{\pi^2} \sum_{n=1}^{\infty} \frac{1}{n^2} \exp\left[-\frac{n^2 \pi^2 k t}{\rho C_p L^2} \cos\left(n\pi \frac{x}{L}\right) \right] \right\}. \quad (13.58)$$

$T(x, t)$ is the temperature at any point in the slab, x, and at any value of time, t.

In comparing this example with the previously discussed example in this chapter it is seen there are some similarities, but there are four significant differences. First, an analytical solution is available to the PDE describing the system response, as opposed to the need to compute a numerical solution. Second, this example deals with a time dependent system response, as opposed to a steady state problem. Third, the validation metric is computed using the mismatch between CDFs of the model prediction and the experimental measurements, as opposed to the confidence interval approach. And fourth, the SRQ of interest depends on four coordinate dimensions q_W, L, x, and t, that will be used in computing the validation metric and in the extrapolation of the model, as opposed to one for the earlier example problem.

This example will discuss steps 1, 2, and 4 of the prediction procedure. Step 3 is omitted because an analytical solution is give for the mathematical model, resulting in negligible numerical solution error. Steps 5 and 6 are omitted because they were not part of the analysis of Ferson *et al.* (2008).

Table 13.6 *Model input data for the system of interest and the validation experiments for the thermal heating example.*

Model input data	System of interest	Validation experiments
System input data		
Slab thickness, L	$L = 1.9$ cm, deterministic	$L = 1.27, 2.54, 1.9$ cm, deterministic
Initial temperature, T_i	$T_i = 25\ °C$, deterministic	$T_i = 25\ °C$, deterministic
Thermal conductivity, k	k, aleatory uncertainty	k, aleatory uncertainty
Volumetric heat capacity, ρC_p	ρC_p, aleatory uncertainty	ρC_p, aleatory uncertainty
Surroundings input data		
Heat flux, q_W	$q_W = 3500$ W/m^2, deterministic	$q_W = 1000, 2000, 3000$ W/m^2, deterministic
Heat flux, q_E	$q_E = 0$, deterministic	$q_E = 0$, deterministic

13.7.1 Step 1: identify all relevant sources of uncertainty

Segregating the model input data into system data and surroundings data, we can construct Table 13.6 for the thermal heating problem. The system of interest, the one for which Eq. (13.57) needs to be evaluated, has the characteristics shown in the middle column of Table 13.6. Various validation experiments were conducted with differing characteristics shown in the right hand column of Table 13.6. k and ρC_p are considered aleatory uncertainties due to manufacturing variability.

13.7.2 Step 2: characterize each source of uncertainty

13.7.2.1 Model input uncertainty

The characterization of the uncertainty in k and ρC_p is based on three sets of experimental data for the material in the slab. The tabular data for each of the sets of data, referred to as low, medium, and high in reference to the quantity of data obtained. Table 13.7 and Table 13.8 give the material characterization data for k and ρC_p, respectively.

Figure 13.28 shows the empirical CDFs for k and ρC_p for the medium materials characterization data. These observed patterns likely understate the true variability in these parameters because they represent only 20 observations for each one. (For the formulation of the workshop problems, experimental measurement uncertainty was assumed to be zero.) To model this possibility of more extreme values than were seen among the limited samples, it is common to fit a distribution to data to model the variability of the underlying population. We used normal distributions for this purpose, configured so that they had the same mean and standard deviation as the data themselves, according to the method of matching moments (Morgan and Henrion, 1990). The fitted normal distributions are shown in Figure 13.28 as the smooth cumulative distributions. Fitting of distributions for the material characterization is not model calibration, as discussed earlier, because the distributions

Table 13.7 *Thermal conductivity data for low, medium and high data sets (W/m-C)* *(Dowding et al., 2008).*

$k(20\,^\circ C)$	$k(250\,^\circ C)$	$k(500\,^\circ C)$	$k(750\,^\circ C)$	$k(1000\,^\circ C)$
Low data set, $n = 6$				
0.0496	–	0.0602	–	0.0631
0.053	–	0.0546	–	0.0796
Medium data set, $n = 20$				
0.0496	0.0628	0.0602	0.0657	0.0631
0.053	0.062	0.0546	0.0713	0.0796
0.0493	0.0537	0.0638	0.0694	0.0692
0.0455	0.0561	0.0614	0.0732	0.0739
High data set, $n = 30$				
0.0496	0.0628	0.0602	0.0657	0.0631
0.053	0.062	0.0546	0.0713	0.0796
0.0493	0.0537	0.0638	0.0694	0.0692
0.0455	0.0561	0.0614	0.0732	0.0739
0.0483	0.0563	0.0643	0.0684	0.0806
0.049	0.0622	0.0714	0.0662	0.0811

Table 13.8 *Volumetric heat capacity for low, medium and high data sets (J/m^3-C)* *(Dowding et al., 2008).*

$\rho C_p(20\,^\circ C)$	$\rho C_p(250\,^\circ C)$	$\rho C_p(500\,^\circ C)$	$\rho C_p(750\,^\circ C)$	$\rho C_p(1000\,^\circ C)$
Low data set, $n = 6$				
3.76E + 05	–	4.52E + 05	–	4.19E + 05
3.38E + 05	–	4.10E + 05	–	4.38E + 05
Medium data set, $n = 20$				
3.76E + 05	3.87E + 05	4.52E + 05	4.68E + 05	4.19E + 05
3.38E + 05	4.69E + 05	4.10E + 05	4.24E + 05	4.38E + 05
3.50E + 05	4.19E + 05	4.02E + 05	3.72E + 05	3.45E + 05
4.13E + 05	4.28E + 05	3.94E + 05	3.46E + 05	3.95E + 05
High data set, $n = 30$				
3.76E + 05	3.87E + 05	4.52E + 05	4.68E + 05	4.19E + 05
3.38E + 05	4.69E + 05	4.10E + 05	4.24E + 05	4.38E + 05
3.50E + 05	4.19E + 05	4.02E + 05	3.72E + 05	3.45E + 05
4.13E + 05	4.28E + 05	3.94E + 05	3.46E + 05	3.95E + 05
4.02E + 05	3.37E + 05	3.73E + 05	4.07E + 05	3.78E + 05
3.53E + 05	3.77E + 05	3.69E + 05	3.99E + 05	3.77E + 05

Table 13.9 *Characterization of the uncertainty in k and ρC_p using a normal distribution for the low, medium, and high data sets (Ferson et al., 2008).*

	Low data set ($n = 6$)	Medium data set ($n = 20$)	High data set ($n = 30$)
Thermal conductivity k, (W/m-C)			
Mean	0.06002	0.06187	0.06284
Standard deviation	0.01077	0.00923	0.00991
Volumetric heat capacity, ρC_p (J/m^3-C)			
Mean	405 500	402 250	393 900
Standard deviation	42 065	39 511	36 251

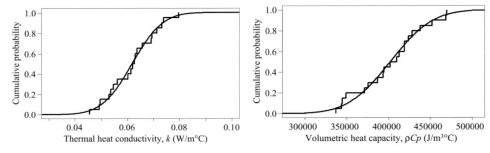

Figure 13.28 Empirical CDF (step functions) and a continuous normal distribution for k and ρC_p using the medium data for materials characterization (Ferson *et al.*, 2008).

are not selected with reference to the model of the system nor the SRQ of interest. Instead, the distributions merely summarize the material characterization data based on independent measurements of a measurable property of the system.

We fitted normal distributions to the low and high data sets as well. The computed moments for the three data sets for each parameter are given in Table 13.9.

The experimental data were examined for possible dependence between k and ρC_p in the data collected during materials characterization. Figure 13.29 shows the scatter plot of these two variables for the medium data set, which reveals no apparent trends or evidence of statistical dependence between the two input quantities. For each value of k measured, the corresponding measured value of ρC_p is plotted, based on the medium set of materials characterization data. When more than two statistical quantities exist, then the scatter plot is shown for two-dimensional planes through the higher-dimensional space. The Pearson correlation coefficient between these twenty points is 0.0595, which is not remotely statistically significant ($P \gg 0.5$, df $= 18$, where df is the number of degrees of freedom). Because there are no physical reasons to expect correlations or other dependencies between these variables, it is reasonable to assume that these quantities are

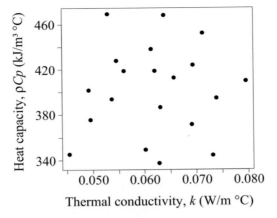

Figure 13.29 Scatter plot of ρC_p and k obtained from the medium data set for materials characterization (Ferson *et al.*, 2008).

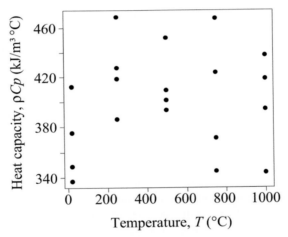

Figure 13.30 Scatter plot of ρC_p as a function of temperature from the medium data set for materials characterization (Ferson *et al.*, 2008).

statistically independent of one another. Plotting and correlation analysis for the high and low data sets gave qualitatively similar results (Ferson *et al.*, 2008).

13.7.2.2 Model uncertainty

Possible temperature dependence of material properties

In the description of the mathematical model for thermal heating k and ρC_p are assumed to be independent of temperature T. It is reasonable to ask whether this assumption is tenable, given the available materials characterization data. Figure 13.30 is the scatter plot for the medium data set for heat capacity, ρC_p, as a function of temperature. Linear and quadratic

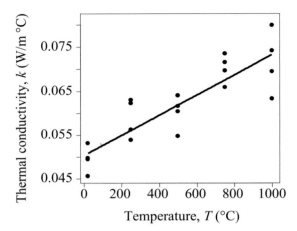

Figure 13.31 Scatter plot of k as a function of temperature from the medium data set for materials characterization (Ferson *et al.*, 2008).

regression analyses reveal no statistically significant trend among these points. The pictures are qualitatively the same for the low and high data sets for ρC_{p} in that no trend or other stochastic dependence is evident. Thus, the experimental data for heat capacity support the assumption in the mathematical model.

A similar analysis was conducted for the thermal conductivity data. Figure 13.31 shows the scatter plot of thermal conductivity as a function of temperature for the medium data. The data clearly show a dependence of k on temperature. A linear regression fit was computed using the least squares criterion, yielding

$$k \sim 0.0505 + 2.25 \times 10^{-5}T + N(0, 0.0047) \text{ (W/m-C)}. \qquad (13.59)$$

The normal function denotes a normal distribution with mean zero and standard deviation σ. $\sigma = 0.0047$ is the residual standard error from the regression analysis. This σ is the standard deviation of the Gaussian distributions that, under the linear regression model, represent the vertical scatter of k at a given value of the temperature variable. There is no evidence that this trend is other than linear; quadratic regression does not provide a significant improvement in the regression fit.

The medium materials characterization data (Figure 13.31) as well as the low and high data sets, clearly show a dependence of k on T. This empirical data show that the model assumption of independence is not appropriate. Weaknesses in models, sometimes severe, are the norm, not the exception, in scientific computing analyses. The important pragmatic question is: what should be done to inform the decision maker of options for possible paths forward? Weaknesses in the modeling assumptions should be clearly explained to the decision maker. He/she may decide to devote time and resources to improve the deficient models before proceeding further with a design or with certain elements of the project. Commonly, however, the decision maker does not have that luxury, so the design and the project must proceed with the uncertainties identified. As a result, the constructive path forward is to forthrightly deal with the uncertainties and not resort to adjusting the many parameters that are commonly available to the mathematical modeler, the computational analyst, or the UQ analyst.

For the thermal heating problem one option that was explored was to use the dependence of k on T from the materials characterization data directly in the model provided, Eq. (13.58). This, of course, is an ad hoc attempt at repairing the model because Eq. (13.58) would *not* be the solution to the unsteady heat conduction PDE with k dependent on temperature. Even though it is an ad hoc repair of the model, it is *not* a calibration of the model or its parameters to the experimental data for the system, but a use of independent auxiliary data available for a component of the system. A regression fit for the dependence of k on T was computed for each data set, low, medium (Figure 13.31), and high. $k(T)$ from the regression fits and $T(x, t; k)$ in Eq. (13.58) create a system of two equations that can be solved iteratively for each model evaluation as a function of space and time. In this iterative approach, we start with the distribution of k observed in the materials characterization data, and compute from it the resulting temperature distribution through the slab. We then project this distribution of T through the regression function to compute another distribution of k. That is, we compute the new distribution $k \sim 0.0505 + 2.25 \times 10^{-5} T + N(0, 0.0047)$, where T is the just computed temperature distribution through the slab, and the normal function generates normally distributed random deviates centered at zero with standard deviation 0.0047. As is seen in Figure 13.31, and the low and high materials characterization data sets, the parameters in the normal distribution are independent of the temperature. The resulting distribution of k values conditional on temperature is then used to reseed the iterative process, which is repeated until the distribution of T through the slab converges. We found that only two or three iterations were needed for convergence.

This ad hoc attempt at repair of the model is offered as an alternative model, not as our belief that it is the best approach. We are just exploring this as a simple attempt to see whether it could possibly reduce the model uncertainty. As mentioned above, once the dependence of k on T is found in the materials characterization data, the better physics-based approach is to reformulate the model into a nonlinear PDE with k dependent on T, and compute a numerical solution. In the analysis that follows, we present both the results of the specified model, Eq. (13.58), and the ad hoc model for k dependent on T. As will be seen next, the weakness in the model due to the assumption of k independent of T will be exposed as model uncertainty.

Characterization of model uncertainty

The approach used in the present analysis to characterizing model uncertainty is the validation metric operator that is based on estimating the mismatch between the p-box predicted by the model and the p-box from the experimental measurements (see Section 12.8). This metric measures the integral of the absolute value of the difference between the simulation p-box and the experimental p-box. The integral is taken over the entire range of predicted

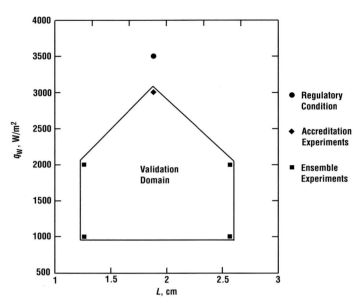

Figure 13.32 Two dimensions of the parameter space for the validation domain and the application condition.

and measured system responses. When no epistemic uncertainty exists in either the simulation or the experiment, such as the thermal heating problem, each p-box reduces to a CDF. Using this metric, we seek the answer to two questions: how well do the predictions match the actual measurements that are available for the system? and what does the mismatch between empirical data and the model's predictions tell us about what we should infer about predictions for which we have no experimental data?

The validation data were divided in the heating problem into ensemble and accreditation data. Figure 13.32 shows these data conditions, along with the regulatory condition where the safety requirement for the system is stated, Eq. (13.57). Only two of the coordinates for the validation domain and the regulatory condition are shown in Figure 13.32, the thickness of the slab, L, and the heat flux to the slab, q_W. The remaining two coordinates are x and t. Validation data for the ensemble and accreditation conditions were taken over the range $0 \le x \le L$ and $0 \le t \le 1000$ s. The ensemble and accreditation measurements are considered to define the validation domain in the four dimensional space, q_W, L, x, and t. As can be seen from Figure 13.32, an extrapolation of the model in the heat flux dimension will be required in order to address the question of the safety requirement at the regulatory condition.

For the ensemble data, temperatures were measured at ten points in time, up to 1000 seconds, and one x position, $x = 0$. The ensemble data are shown in Table 13.10. The conditions for each of the configurations in the ensemble data are shown in Table 13.11.

Table 13.10 *Ensemble data for temperature (°C) at x = 0 (Dowding et al., 2008).*

Time (s)	Exp. 1	Exp. 2	Exp. 3	Exp. 4	Exp. 1	Exp. 2	Exp. 3	Exp. 4
		Configuration 1				**Configuration 2**		
100.0	105.5	109.0	96.3	111.2	99.5	106.6	96.2	101.3
200.0	139.3	143.9	126.0	146.9	130.7	140.4	126.1	133.1
300.0	165.5	170.5	148.7	174.1	154.4	165.9	148.7	157.2
400.0	188.7	193.5	168.5	197.5	174.3	187.2	167.7	177.2
500.0	210.6	214.6	186.9	219.0	191.7	205.8	184.3	194.8
600.0	231.9	234.8	204.6	239.7	207.3	222.4	199.3	210.6
700.0	253.0	254.6	222.0	259.9	221.7	237.6	213.0	225.0
800.0	273.9	274.2	239.2	279.9	235.0	251.7	225.7	238.4
900.0	294.9	293.6	256.4	299.9	247.6	264.9	237.6	251.0
1000.0	315.8	313.1	273.5	319.8	259.5	277.4	248.9	262.9
		Configuration 3				**Configuration 4**		
100.0	183.1	177.8	187.2	171.3	173.4	178.9	179.3	188.2
200.0	247.4	240.2	254.2	231.6	234.2	241.9	242.6	254.6
300.0	296.3	287.4	306.1	277.6	279.7	289.1	290.1	304.2
400.0	338.7	327.8	351.9	317.4	317.4	328.4	329.6	345.4
500.0	378.0	364.8	395.4	354.2	350.2	362.6	363.9	381.1
600.0	416.0	400.2	437.9	389.7	379.5	393.2	394.7	413.1
700.0	453.5	434.8	480.0	424.5	406.3	421.1	422.8	442.1
800.0	490.8	469.1	522.1	459.1	430.9	446.9	448.8	469.0
900.0	528.2	503.3	564.1	493.7	454.0	471.1	473.3	494.0
1000.0	565.6	537.6	606.2	528.2	475.6	493.9	496.4	517.6

Table 13.11 *Conditions for the ensemble data (Dowding et al., 2008).*

Experimental configuration	Data set	Heat flux, q_W (W/m^2)	Slab thickness, L (cm)
1	low, medium, and high	1000	1.27
2	medium and high	1000	2.54
3	high	2000	1.27
4	high	2000	2.54

For the accreditation data, temperatures were measured at 20 points in time, up to 1000 s, at three x positions, $x = 0$, $L/2$, and L. The accreditation data are shown in Table 13.12. All of the accreditation data were obtained at $q_W = 3000$ W/m^2 and $L = 1.9$ cm. Table 13.13 shows how the accreditation data were segregated into low, medium, and high data sets.

Table 13.12 *Accreditation data for temperature (°C) (Dowding et al., 2008).*

Time (s)	Experiment 1			Experiment 2		
	$x = 0$	$x = L/2$	$x = L$	$x = 0$	$x = L/2$	$x = L$
50.0	183.8	26.3	25.0	179.2	25.9	25.0
100.0	251.3	34.0	25.1	243.9	32.2	25.1
150.0	302.2	47.7	26.0	292.2	44.2	25.6
200.0	344.6	64.9	28.3	332.3	59.9	27.3
250.0	381.7	83.9	32.7	367.1	77.5	30.6
300.0	414.9	103.7	39.3	398.3	96.2	35.8
350.0	445.4	124.0	48.1	426.7	115.3	42.9
400.0	473.6	144.4	58.7	452.9	134.7	52.0
450.0	500.0	164.9	71.1	477.4	154.2	62.7
500.0	525.0	185.4	84.9	500.5	173.6	74.9
550.0	548.8	205.9	100.0	522.4	193.1	88.4
600.0	571.7	226.3	116.1	543.4	212.5	103.1
650.0	593.8	246.8	133.0	563.5	231.8	118.7
700.0	615.2	267.2	150.7	583.0	251.1	135.0
750.0	636.1	287.6	169.0	602.0	270.3	152.1
800.0	656.6	307.9	187.8	620.4	289.5	169.7
850.0	676.7	328.3	207.0	638.5	308.7	187.8
900.0	696.4	348.6	226.5	656.3	327.8	206.3
950.0	716.0	369.0	246.3	673.9	346.9	225.1
1000.0	735.4	389.3	266.3	691.2	366.0	244.2

Table 13.13 *Conditions for the accreditation data (Dowding et al., 2008).*

Experiment	Data set	Heat flux, q_W (W/m^2)	Slab thickness, L (cm)
1	low, medium, and high	3000	1.9
2	high	3000	1.9

The type of data obtained in the ensemble and accreditation experiments is typical of more complex systems in the sense that data are obtained for a variety of conditions and different values of the dependent variables in the PDEs, but there is insufficient data to adequately assess the accuracy of the model. Stated differently, there are usually very few replicated experiments of the system, if any, at the various operating conditions tested so that system variability can be more accurately separated from assessing model accuracy. Project management on real engineering systems tends to place much more emphasis on better understanding system performance than assessing the predictive capability of the model. Using the validation metric approach of comparing CDFs from prediction and experiment, we could compute a validation metric result, d, for every paired comparison of prediction and experiment. If we computed a large number of simulations for each condition of the experiment, we could compute a smooth CDF for the simulation. The difficulty, however, is that for the vast majority of experimental conditions, we have only one experimental measurement so that we only have a single-step function for the empirical CDF. For the ensemble and accreditation data there are a few exceptions where replicate experiments are available. For example, in the ensemble data for the medium data, there are 20 conditions where four replications are available (see Table 13.10 – Table 13.11). These occur for configurations 1 and 2. For the accreditation data, no replications occur for the medium data (see Table 13.12 and Table 13.13). Only using data where several experimental replicates are available would be waste of valuable data.

For the cases where we only have one experimental measurement, we will obtain an inflated estimate of the true value of d (obtained from a large number of experiments) because the metric measures the *evidence for mismatch* between the simulation and the experiment. As discussed in Section 12.8.2, the inflation of the metric is a direct result of the very poor representation of the true CDF (with a large number of experiments) compared to the empirical CDF with only one experimental measurement. This poor representation is due to sampling uncertainty, which is an epistemic uncertainty. To reduce this perpetual problem of conflicting experimental goals of understanding how a system responds to various inputs versus assessing the predictive capability of a model, the concept of u-pooling was developed by Ferson *et al.* (2008). This concept was discussed in Section 12.8.3 and it can be used for two different situations: (a) when we have a single measurement of an SRQ at a wide variety of experimental conditions; and (b) when we have a single experimental measurement of *different* SRQs, all of which are predicted by the model. As an example of this last case, suppose the thermal heating model was coupled with a thermal stress model so that both temperature and stress were predicted by the coupled model. If both temperatures and stresses were measured in the slab during the same experiment, then we could combine these different SRQs into a common SRQ so that the accuracy of the models could be better assessed.

The u-pooling transforms the experimental measurement and the model prediction for each comparison to probability space, and then uses an inverse transform to return to a transformed measurement coordinate. The inverse transform is based on the model prediction at the application condition of interest so that all of the measurements are transformed in the same way to conditions directly relevant to the application.

We will briefly explain the u-pooling concept before applying it to the thermal heating problem. Figure 13.33 shows a comparison of a single experimental measurement, y_j, with a distribution for the model prediction for the physical conditions of the experiment and the value of the dependent variables of the PDE appropriate to location of the measurement. The model prediction is shown here as a smooth CDF with no epistemic uncertainty, but it could be a p-box if epistemic uncertainty existed in the model. To obtain a smooth model prediction, one needs to compute a significant number of samples using MCS or LHS. If a set of measurements is made and only the independent variables of the PDE are

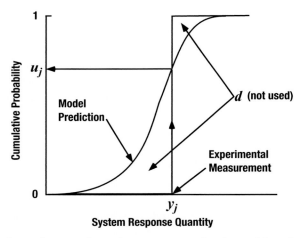

Figure 13.33 Transform of an experimental measurement using the model to obtain a probability.

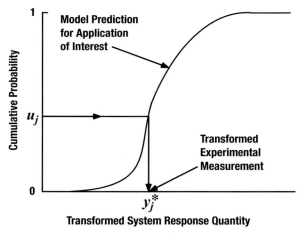

Figure 13.34 Inverse transform using the model for the conditions of the application of interest to obtain a transformed experimental measurement.

different for the individual measurements, then the same simulation can be used for the measurements. If, however, the conditions of the experiment are different, e.g., the input data are different, then each condition requires that a separate CDF be computed for each condition. As shown in the figure, a d can be computed directly from this comparison, but the d value would be inflated, as discussed earlier. Using the concept of u-pooling, we transform the physical measurement, y_j, into a probability, u_j, using the CDF predicted by the model.

   Figure 13.34 depicts how the inverse transform takes the probability from Figure 13.33 and maps it into a transformed measurement of the SRQ of interest. For this inverse

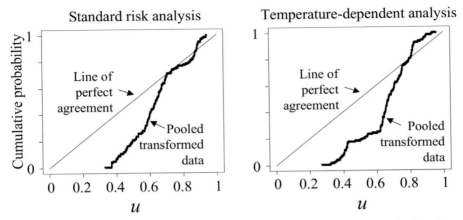

Figure 13.35 Model performance for the medium data set for two analyses as summarized by observed distribution functions of u-values (step functions) compared to uniform distributions for perfect agreement (straight lines) (Ferson *et al.*, 2008).

transform, we use the model prediction for the conditions of the application of interest. The same inverse transform is used for all of the probabilities resulting from individual measurements and individual conditions. The inverse transform is simply a consistent monotone rescaling of all of the probabilities. One may criticize the use of the model in the rescaling because the accuracy of the model is what we are trying to assess. This criticism is ineffective because, whether the model is accurate or not, the model is simply used to rescale the measurements in a consistent manner. With all of the original experimental measurements transformed in this way, one can then compute a smoother empirical CDF representing the measurements as if they were mapped to the application condition of interest. One can then compute a d by comparing the CDF from the prediction and the empirical CDF.

We now assess the performance of the thermal heating model over the validation domain by using the method of u-pooling. We compute a summary assessment of the overall mismatch between the model and the data by using all the ensemble and accreditation data. Although the ensemble and accreditation data were segregated in the formulation of the validation challenge problem, our analysis dealt with both types of data in the same way. Every observation in the validation domain is associated with values of the control parameters q_w, L, x and t. These four parameters, along with the distributions characterizing the variability of k and ρC_p, were used in 10 000 Monte Carlo samples to compute the prediction distribution of temperatures using Eq. (13.58). Every temperature observation in the validation domain is thereby paired with a prediction distribution of temperature. There are 140 of these pairs in the medium data set. The pairs define the u-values $u_j = F_j\,(T_j)$, where T_j is the observed temperature and F denotes the associated prediction distribution and $j = 1,2,\ldots,140$.

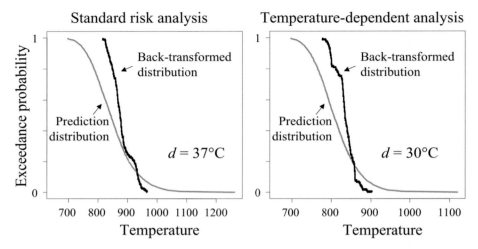

Figure 13.36 Distributions for the medium data set of back-transformed *u*-values (step functions) compared to predicted temperature distributions (smooth lines) for the two analyses (Ferson *et al.*, 2008).

Figure 13.35 shows empirical distributions of these *u*-values using the medium data set. These empirical distributions constitute summaries of the performances of the standard model, Eq. (13.58), and the model for *k* dependent on temperature. The small step function in each graph represents all 140 observations of temperature in the medium data set compared to their respective prediction distributions generated under that analysis. The step functions are the empirical distributions of the *u*-values produced by these comparisons. These distributions are to be compared against the uniform distribution over [0, 1], whose graph appears in each graph as the 45° line. These 45° lines are lines of perfect agreement. If the observed temperatures were sampled from distributions matching those that were predicted by the model under an analysis, then the step function would match the uniform distribution to within fluctuations due to random chance.

Figure 13.36 shows the back-transformations of these distributions to the physically meaningful scale of temperature. The figure is shown in terms of the exceedance proba-bility, which is the complementary CDF, versus temperature for both *k* independent and *k* dependent on temperature. Exceedance probability is commonly used in risk assessment studies to obtain clearer information about the probability of exceeding specified thresholds. The smooth curves in the graphs are the prediction distributions under the two analyses for the conditions of the regulatory requirement. Also displayed in Figure 13.36, as step functions, are the corresponding pooled distributions of *u*-values *back-transformed onto the same temperature scale* via the inverse probability integral transforms specified by the respective prediction distributions. That is, they are the distributions of the quantity $G^{-1}(u_j)$, where *G* is the prediction distribution on which the regulatory requirement is stated.

The graphs in Figure 13.36 are simply nonlinear rescalings of the graphs in Figure 13.35. Under these rescalings, the straight lines become the smooth curves, and the tails of the

Table 13.14 *Validation metric results over the validation domain using the medium data set ($^{\circ}C$) (Ferson et al., 2008).*

Analysis	d, validation metric result	95% confidence interval
Model with temperature independent k	37.2	[34.0, 42.7]
Model with temperature dependent k	30.4	[27.4, 33.7]

step functions are stretched relative to central values of the distributions. For each graph, the transformation of the abscissa is exactly the one that changes the standard uniform distribution into the prediction distribution. The result translates the evidence embodied in all 140 observations in the ensemble and accreditation data sets onto the scale defined by the prediction distribution for the regulatory requirement, Eq. (13.57). These distributions should not be interpreted as though they were themselves actual data collected on this transformed temperature scale. They were, after all, collected for a variety of heat fluxes, various slab thicknesses, different time values, and different locations in the slab. They are pooled for the sake of estimating the predictive accuracy of the model, where data are available. Thus, they do not represent direct evidence about what the temperatures will be under the conditions of the regulatory requirement, but only how well the prediction distributions produced by the model have matched temperatures for all of the data in the medium data set validation domain.

The temperature-dependent analysis, illustrated in the right graph of Figure 13.36, has a somewhat better match with the available empirical data than the standard analysis, illustrated in the left graph. The distribution of back-transformed u-values is closer in this analysis to its prediction distribution shown as the smooth curve. The superiority of this match is reflected by the area metric d in Table 13.14.

Recall that the area metric d measures the area between the empirical distribution of back-transformed pooled u-values and the prediction distribution, which is our expectation about them. The 95% confidence intervals were computed by a nonparametric bootstrap method based on resampling from the 140 u-values. (For a discussion of the bootstrap technique, see Efron and Tibshirani, 1993; Draper and Smith, 1998; and Vose, 2008). That is, we took a random sample of size 140 from the distribution of u-values (with replacement) and recomputed the value of d by comparing the distribution of these randomly selected u values to the prediction distribution. We repeated this process 10 000 times and sorted the resulting array of d-values. The 95% confidence interval was estimated as $[d_{(2.5N/100)}, d_{(N-(2.5/100)N)}] = [d_{(250)}, d_{(9750)}]$, i.e., the interval between the 250th and 9750th values from the sorted list of 10 000 d values. Each confidence interval estimates the sampling uncertainty associated with the actual value of d arising from having computed it from only 140 observations.

Table 13.15 *Validation metric results and the 95% confidence interval over the validation domain for the low, medium, and high data sets (°C) (Ferson* et al., *2008).*

Analysis	Low data set ($n = 100$)	Medium data set ($n = 140$)	High data set ($n = 280$)
Model with temperature independent k	52.6, [49.4, 55.9]	37.2, [34.0, 42.7]	18.5, [15.3, 23.9]
Model with temperature dependent k	34.1, [30.0, 38.1]	30.4, [27.4, 33.7]	11.6, [9.5, 15.0]

Both of the graphs in Figure 13.36 suggest that the standard model, Eq. (13.58), is somewhat better at predicting temperatures close to 900 °C than it is at predicting lower temperatures. The temperature-dependent analysis used regression and an iterative convergence scheme to represent the dependence evident in the materials characterization data between temperature and thermal conductivity. The reward for the extra iterative calculation is a modest improvement in the model's assessed performance vis-à-vis the total amount of data. The match for this analysis was quantitatively better than that of the standard risk analysis, Table 13.14.

Calculations were also done with the low and high data sets, which yielded qualitatively similar results. The performances of the model, in terms of the validation metric, under the two analyses for all three data sets are shown in Table 13.15. Also shown in the table is the interval of the metric *d* using the bootstrap technique and a 95% confidence level. The temperature-dependent analysis was somewhat better than the standard risk analysis for both data sets in the area metric. It should be stressed that validation metrics shown are measures of the mismatch, i.e. inaccuracy, for each of the two models, for different quantities of data, and for *all experimental measurements* made in the validation domain of the indicated data set. This kind of data is valuable for quantitatively comparing the performance of various competing models with the same experimental data.

Figure 13.37 summarizes the validation metric performance results graphically for the low and high materials characterization data. Distributions are shown of the back-transformed *u*-values compared to the respective prediction distributions for the two analyses.

Table 13.15 and Figure 13.37 reveal that the area metric *d* as used in the validation assessment is strongly sensitive to the sample size of the observations on which it is based. This is not because the model is getting more accurate with more data. Rather, it is the result of there being *less evidence of a mismatch* between the model and the data. Of course, this might not have been true if the model were making very inaccurate predictions. Insofar as assessing model accuracy is concerned, increasing the sample size tends to decrease *d* to its lower limit of mismatch. The dependence of *d* on the number of observations means that we should only compare performances of models that are based on the same sample size. In this case, the temperature-dependent analysis has a consistently better (smaller) overall *d* than the standard analysis at all three sample sizes described in the challenge problem.

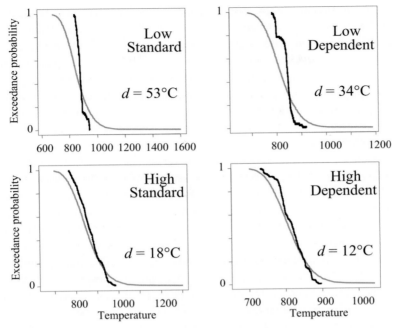

Figure 13.37 Model performances as distributions of back-transformed u-values (step functions) compared to prediction distributions (smooth curves) for low and high data sets and the standard and temperature-dependent analyses (Ferson *et al.*, 2008).

13.7.3 Step 4: estimate output uncertainty

Since there is no numerical solution error for the thermal heating problem, output uncertainty need only combine input and model uncertainty. We first discuss the general approach for combining input and model uncertainty using the validation metric based on the mismatch in p-boxes (or CDFs) from prediction and experimental CDFs. Then we apply this approach to the thermal heating problem.

13.7.3.1 General discussion of combining input and model uncertainty

Since the validation metric approach using the mismatch of p-boxes is directly applicable to a higher dimensional space of input parameters than the confidence interval approach, we begin our discussion in this vein. A function representing the model uncertainty must be constructed over the m-dimensional input space of the model. Let ξ be the number of input parameters over which experimental data has been obtained at different conditions during validation activities. Assume the subset of parameters for which experimental data were obtained is listed as the first ξ elements of the array of input quantities, so that we have $(x_1, \ldots, x_\xi, x_{\xi+1}, \ldots, x_m)$. Let $d(x_1, \ldots, x_\xi)$ be the validation metric result that quantifies the model uncertainty over the dimensions where there are experimental data, $(x_1, \ldots, x_\xi)$. Let ν be the total number of experimental measurements of any of the SRQs made during the validation experiments.

As discussed in Section 12.8, the number of individual d values that can be computed can range from 1 to ν. This is an advantage over the confidence interval approach, but a more important advantage is that when multiple measurements are available, they need not have *any* relationship to one another in the space of $(x_1, \ldots, x_\xi)$. For example, in a particular analysis we could have (x_1, x_2, x_3, x_4) represent the independent variables in the PDE (three spatial coordinates and time), x_5 represent a BC, and (x_6, x_7, x_8, x_9) represent four design parameters of the system. We could have one or more experimental measurements from validation experiments in all nine dimensions; none having a commonality or relationship to any of the other measurements.

Since there is no restriction on how many d values can be evaluated, other than that the number is no larger than ν, we consider here the two different ways the available experimental measurements could be used. One could maximize the total number of d values computed by treating each paired experimental measurement and simulation separately. The advantage is that we maximize the number of d values over the space of $(x_1, \ldots, x_\xi)$ with which to construct some type of interpolation or regression function for $d(x_1, \ldots, x_\xi)$. The disadvantage is that by treating each experimental measurement separately, we inflate the validation metric d due to sampling (epistemic) uncertainty. That is, the evidence for mismatch will tend to be greater using fewer experimental measurements compared to using a larger number of measurements. Note that even if the model is *perfect*, in the sense that the model can exactly predict the measured CDFs of the system responses from the experiment, there is still inflation of the validation metric due to limited sampling.

On the other end of the spectrum, if we use u-pooling to combine all of the measurements and their respective comparisons with the model, we can end up with one d. The advantage of this computed d is that it is a combined or summary d over the entire set of data forming the validation domain. This was the method used in Section 13.7.2.2. This approach is the best representation of the evidence for mismatch between the model and the measurements that can be obtained with the available amount of empirical data. For example, suppose the model is perfect in the sense just mentioned. As a result, when an increasing number of measurements are used to assess the accuracy of the perfect model, we will have $d \to 0$. The disadvantage is that as we combine more data into the evaluation of d, we have *less* data with which to construct the function $d(x_1, \ldots, x_\xi)$. That is, an empirical measurement can be used either to better assess the accuracy of the model by contributing to an estimate of d, or it can be used in the construction of the hypersurface $d(x_1, \ldots, x_\xi)$; but not both. One could investigate the question of the optimum use of the experimental data so as to have the maximum decrease in d with the minimum effect on the inaccuracy in the construction of $d(x_1, \ldots, x_\xi)$. This question, however, has not been investigated.

Now consider the question of how to construct $d(x_1, \ldots, x_\xi)$, whatever balance one chooses between the precision of the model accuracy assessment and the ability to construct $d(x_1, \ldots, x_\xi)$. A reasonable method of constructing this function is to compute a least squares regression fit of the computed d values using a low-degree polynomial. Let η be the number of data points available to compute the regression function, where $\eta \leq \nu$. Note that if we use a first-degree polynomial, we must have at least two data points in each dimension x_i. The following situations suggest that a first-degree polynomial should be used instead of a higher-degree polynomial: (a) if η is not much greater than 2ξ, and (b) if a large extrapolation of the regression function beyond the validation domain is needed in order to evaluate $d(x_1, \ldots, x_\xi)$ at the application conditions of interest.

Let the polynomial regression fit for $d(x_1, \ldots, x_\xi)$ be given by

$$d(x_1, x_2, \ldots, x_\xi) \sim \mathcal{P}(x_1, x_2, \ldots, x_\xi) + N(0, \sigma). \tag{13.60}$$

$\mathcal{P}(x_1, x_2, \ldots, x_\xi)$ is the polynomial regression function and $N(0, \sigma)$ is the normally distributed residual error arising from the scatter in the fit to the individual d values. This regression fit, of course, has no knowledge of how the model uncertainty might behave in the remaining $m - \xi$ dimensions of the input space. As a result, d is assumed independent of these remaining parameters. The polynomial portion of Eq. (13.60) will result in a single value of d at each condition of interest. The uncertainty in the value of d should be expressed by using the *statistical prediction interval* based on $N(0, \sigma)$. A prediction interval should be used to represent: (a) the scatter in the experimental data and/or model data, and (b) the scatter of the model uncertainty not captured by the choice of the regression function. A prediction interval should be used instead of a confidence interval because here we are interested in estimating the uncertainty in a *single future value of the uncertainty*. A confidence interval, however, is an estimate of the uncertainty in the mean of a collection of data. Prediction intervals are always larger than confidence intervals, and they do not approach zero as the number of samples becomes larger (Devore, 2007). A reasonable confidence level for the prediction interval would be either 90% or 95%. Because we are trying to capture the epistemic uncertainty in the model as compared to the experimental data, as well as the aleatory uncertainty due to measurement uncertainty, we should always use the upper bound from the prediction interval.

Once the regression function $\mathcal{P}(x_1, x_2, \ldots, x_\xi)$ is computed for the conditions of interest, we can use a procedure similar to that discussed in Section 13.4.2.1 to combine input and model uncertainty. One of the important differences between the metric based on the mismatch of p-boxes and the confidence interval approach for estimating model uncertainty is that the mismatch approach measures the absolute value of the difference between the p-boxes. As a result, there is *no* sign associated with the mismatch measure, leaving no indication whether the model prediction is higher or lower than the empirical measurements. Consequently, when model uncertainty is combined with the p-box due to input uncertainty, the contribution due to model uncertainty expands the left and right sides of the p-box equally. Let $\text{PI}^u(x_1^*, x_2^*, \ldots, x_\xi^*)$ denote the upper bound of the prediction interval evaluated at the conditions of the application of interest, $(x_1^*, x_2^*, \ldots, x_\xi^*)$. We then have for the magnitude of the displacement on the left and right of the input uncertainty p-box

$$d(x_1^* x_1^*, x_2^*, \ldots, x_\xi^*) \sim \text{PI}^u(x_1^*, x_2^*, \ldots, x_\xi^*). \tag{13.61}$$

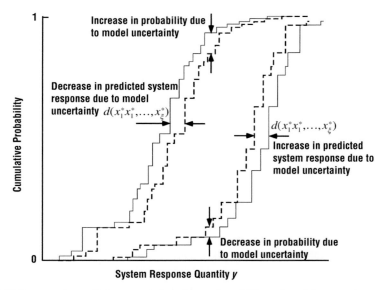

Figure 13.38 Increase in predictive uncertainty due to the addition of model uncertainty.

Figure 13.38 gives an example of how a p-box due to a combination of aleatory and epistemic input uncertainty is expanded due to model uncertainty. As can be seen in the figure, the $d(x_1^*, x_2^*, \ldots, x_\xi^*)$ value that is added to and subtracted from the SRQ p-box is a constant over the entire response. However, the increase and decrease in the probability of various responses will depend on the shape of the p-box. It may appear that the primary effect of accounting for model uncertainty is near the median, $P = 0.5$. This simply occurs because of the probability-constrained shape of CDFs; probability must be bounded by zero and one. Model uncertainty also has a large effect on low and high cumulative probabilities. For example, an undesirable system response can easily change from one in a thousand to one in fifty, as suggested in the left tail of the distribution shown in Figure 13.38.

13.7.3.2 *Combining input and model uncertainty for the thermal heating problem*

The regulatory condition, Eq. (13.57), is outside the validation domain, defined by the ensemble and accreditation data. As a result, extrapolation of the validation metric, as well as model, is required to determine if the regulatory condition is satisfied. We employed linear regression to extrapolate in the four dimensional space, q_W, L, x, and t, to estimate the model uncertainty at the regulatory condition. Here we describe this extrapolation for the temperature-dependent risk analysis under the medium data set (140 measurements). Entirely analogous calculations are possible for the constant conductivity model and the other data sets.

Figure 13.39 shows the model prediction at the regulatory condition for both the temperature-dependent model and the constant conductivity model only accounting for input uncertainty. The figure shows the uncertainty in terms of the exceedance probability,

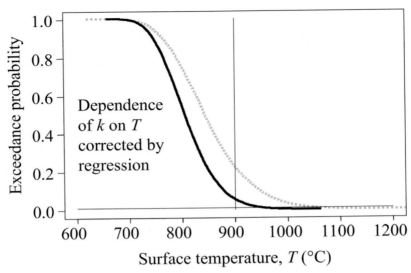

Figure 13.39 Model prediction for exceedance probability at the regulatory condition for the temperature-dependent model (solid line) and the conductivity independent of temperature model (dotted line) (Ferson *et al.*, 2008).

i.e., the complimentary cumulative distribution function (CCDF). The CCDF shows the fraction of the population that would have a response greater than a particular value of the response. Since the regulatory criterion, Eq. (13.57), for the thermal heating analysis is written in terms of an exceedance probability, it is appropriate to show analysis results in this way. Given that the input uncertainties in k and ρC_p are only aleatory, both model predictions are only aleatory. Note that the predicted exceedance probability for the constant conductivity and the temperature-dependent model, 0.22 and 0.05, respectively, both exceed the safety criterion of 0.01. When the model uncertainty is combined with the input uncertainty, only more uncertainty will be included in the predicted result.

There are various ways to construct the regression function for model uncertainty based on the validation data. As discussed in the previous section, one approach is to compute the metric at the conditions where each of the 140 measures were made. Each of these metrics would be based on single measurements, so they would be inflated estimates of the mismatch of the model vis-à-vis the experiment. With these 140 values spread over the q_w, L, x, and t space, one could compute a linear regression hypersurface. Then one could compute the 95% upper prediction interval at the regulatory condition, $q_w = 3500$ W/m^2, $L = 1.9$ cm, $x = 0$, $t = 1000$ s. Using $PI^u(x_1^*, x_2^*, \ldots, x_\xi^*)$ and the computed CDF resulting from the temperature dependent model, one could estimate the combination of input uncertainty, shown in Figure 13.39, and the model uncertainty using the procedure discussed in Figure 13.38. This would be a reasonable and defensible approach.

Another approach is used because it improves the relevancy of the individual d values to the regulatory condition (Ferson *et al.*, 2008). Instead of pooling these 140 u-values, as we did in the calculation of the summary d in Section 13.7.2.2, we back-transform each u-value directly to the temperature scale using the prediction distribution associated with the conditions of the regulatory requirement. That is, we compute the back-transformed temperature $T_j^* = G^{-1}(F_j(T_j))$, where T denotes observed temperature, F denotes the associated prediction distribution, G is the distribution from the model with only variability of the input parameters, and $j = 1, 2, \ldots, 140$ indexes the observations. We then compute the area metric $d(T_j^*, G)$ between the back-transformed temperature and the prediction distribution of regulatory interest for each observation–prediction pair. These comparisons of scalar values and the prediction distribution for temperature at the conditions for the regulatory requirement thus yielded 140 values of the area metric. The mean of these areas was 69, with values ranging between 56 and 129. The primary reason for the large increase in the mean and the scatter, compared to the values listed in Table 13.14, is that this mean is based on individual d values for all of the 140 points, as opposed to pooling all of the d values.

The 140 d values were regressed against the input variables q_{W}, L, x, t with a linear model for extrapolation. The best fitting linear model for the expected value of the area metric for a single (new) observation as a function of heat flux, thickness, position and time is

$$d \sim 126 - 0.016 q_{\mathrm{W}} - 914 L + 201 x - 0.0124 t + N(0, 10.8) \quad {}^{\circ}\mathrm{C}. \qquad (13.62)$$

The last term is the normally distributed residual error arising from random scatter in the area values. At the regulatory requirement, this becomes

$$d^* \sim 40.2 + N(0, 10.8) \quad {}^{\circ}\mathrm{C}. \qquad (13.63)$$

Because we are extrapolating to conditions specified in the regulatory requirement for which there is no experimental data, it is especially important to account for sampling uncertainty in predicting the magnitude of the area metric under those conditions. The 95% prediction interval for the value of the area metric at the regulatory conditions is computed to be

$$d^* \sim [17, 63] \quad {}^{\circ}\mathrm{C}. \qquad (13.64)$$

Because we are trying to capture the epistemic uncertainty of the model's predictions vis-à-vis the data, we use the *upper* bound from the prediction interval as our estimate of the upper bound on the uncertainty of the model, 63 °C.

Figure 13.40 shows the model prediction after combining the input uncertainty and the estimate of model uncertainty. The graph shows a prediction distribution as the inner curve, representing only the input uncertainty, with a parallel distribution on either side of it displaced by 63 °C. The central prediction distribution uses the medium data set for the material characterization and the temperature dependent model. In our view, the p-box prediction represents a reasonable estimate of the combined input and model uncertainty associated with the predictive capability of the model as evidenced by the validation assessment on available data. The expectation is that future data, if it became available, would form a distribution

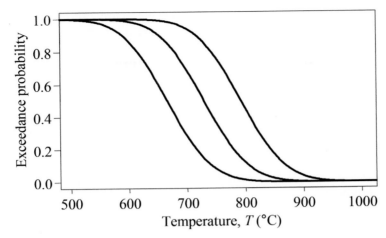

Figure 13.40 P-box prediction after combining input and model uncertainty for the temperature-dependent model using the medium data (Ferson *et al.*, 2008).

within these bounds. In the mid temperature ranges, e.g., 700 to 800 °C, the increase in uncertainty due to model uncertainty is stunning. To many analysts, this method of increasing the predictive uncertainty would appear to be excessive. However, we argue that it is a highly defensible representation of predictive capability that is based directly on the observed accuracy of the model. If data became available at the regulatory condition it could be outside of the p-box shown in Figure 13.40. The p-box *does not guarantee* that the actual result will be inside the p-box. It is a statistical inference based on the model and observations that are available.

An argument can be made for a simpler method for estimating the model uncertainty at the regulatory condition. In Section 13.7.2.2, model uncertainty was estimated using the ensemble and accreditation data and the method of u-pooling. In the u-pooling process, all of the measurements were transformed to the regulatory condition to compute a summary d. One can then argue that the upper bound on the 95% confidence interval can be used as the estimated model uncertainty at the regulatory condition. Referring to Table 13.15, we see that the summary d and the 95% confidence interval for the temperature-dependent model at the regulatory condition are 30.4°C and [27.4, 33.7]°C, respectively. One could then treat the 33.7 °C as the model uncertainty at the regulatory condition, d^*. This would be about half of the model uncertainty estimated by using the 95% upper bound on the prediction interval from extrapolating the linear regression. 33.7 °C may seem unrealistically low compared to the 63 °C value but we know that this latter value is inflated due to using single experimental measurements to compute d. Recall from Table 13.15 that the 95% upper bound on the confidence interval for the temperature-dependent model decreased from 38.1 °C to 15.0 °C as the quantity of data changed from the low data set to the high data set. As a result, the change in the d from 63 °C to 33.7 °C between the two different approaches is consistent. Since the concept of u-pooling has only recently been published,

Table 13.16 *Probability of failure of the safety component using various heating models and different quantities of experimental data (Ferson* et al., *2008).*

Analysis	Low data set	Medium data set	High data set
Input uncertainty only, temperature independent k	0.28	0.22	0.24
Input uncertainty only, temperature dependent k	0.09	0.05	0.05
Input and model uncertainty, temperature independent k	[0.13, 0.52]	[0.17, 0.29]	[0.17, 0.32]
Input and model uncertainty, temperature dependent k	[0.04, 0.18]	[0.03, 0.09]	[0.03, 0.09]

additional research is needed to investigate the reliability of using a summary d on a wide range of problems.

13.7.3.3 Predicted probabilities for the regulatory condition

The regulatory criterion was defined in Eq. (13.57) as

$$P\{T(x=0, t=1000) > 900\} < 0.01. \tag{13.65}$$

Table 13.16 gives the summary of results for the failure probabilities, i.e., exceedance probabilities, from the various analyses that were conducted. The first two rows are the results of an analysis that would only consider input uncertainty, i.e., variability in k and ρC_p. This procedure is the standard risk assessment approach that is practiced today. It does not take into account an estimate of the uncertainty in the model that could be inferred from experiments on systems that are similar to the actual system of interest. The standard risk assessment approach predicts that the system safety would be inadequate, but there is a wide difference in results depending on whether k is considered independent or dependent on temperature. If an analyst were to perform both of these analyses and observe the large difference in predicted safety, they would properly suspect that the weakness in the model was due the assumptions concerning k. Unless a new nonlinear heat transfer analysis was formulated and computed, however, they would be at a loss to estimate the uncertainty due to model form.

The last two rows of Table 13.16 are the results from the present approach that takes into account input and model uncertainty. The square brackets are the bounds on the failure probabilities from the model when the validation metric results are included in the analysis. The bounds were obtained from the displacement to the left and right of the response distribution due to input variability alone (see Figure 13.40). The predicted interval-valued bounds were assessed by extrapolating the observed uncertainty of the predicted temperature distributions to the regulatory condition. Comparing these probability intervals to

Table 13.17 *Probability of failure of the safety component reported by Liu* et al. *(2009) and Higdon* et al. *(2009).*

Analysis	Low data set	Medium data set	High data set
Liu *et al.* (2009), temperature independent k	–	0.02	0.04
Higdon *et al.* (2009), temperature independent k	0.07	0.03	0.03

the standard risk assessment procedures, which do not assess model accuracy; one sees a striking increase in uncertainty. These bounds on the probabilities should be interpreted as the range of failure probabilities that are expected, given the present state of knowledge concerning model uncertainty. Stated differently, given the observed input variability, the observed model uncertainty over the validation domain, and the extrapolation of this uncertainty to the regulatory condition, there is no evidence that the failure probabilities will be outside this range. Noting that all six of the lower failure probabilities are greater than 0.01, one can state that there is *no evidence* that the safety requirement can be met given the present state of knowledge. If any of the lower bounds on the failure probabilities had been *less than* 0.01, then one could conclude that it is possible, i.e., there is some evidence, that the criterion *could* be satisfied. However, this would certainly be insufficient evidence to certify the safety component. If the upper value of the predicted interval is less than 0.01, then one can state that, given the estimated aleatory and epistemic uncertainty, the safety component satisfies the criterion.

The present approach to validation is unlike the more common approaches based on hypothesis testing or Bayesian methods. With its focus on updating, the Bayesian approach convolves calibration and validation, which we believe ought to be rigorously separated. Bayesian methods attempt to use whatever data is available to improve the model as much as possible. Our approach reserves the first use of any validation data for assessing the performance of the model so as to reveal to decision makers and other would-be users of the model an unambiguous characterization of its predictive abilities.

One of the many valuable lessons learned from the Model Validation Challenge Workshop was that many different risk assessment approaches were applied to the three challenge problems. For the thermal challenge problem, two Bayesian analyses were applied by Liu *et al.* (2009) and Higdon *et al.* (2009). Their results are shown in Table 13.17. Comparing their values of failure probability with the present approach shown in Table 13.16, there is a striking difference in the predicted safety. Since the organizers of the Workshop have not released the underlying model that produced the results, it is unknown which analyses more properly represented the "true" failure probability of the safety component.

13.8 Bayesian approach as opposed to PBA

The PBA perspective is markedly different from a Bayesian perspective (Bernardo and Smith, 1994; Gelman *et al.*, 1995; Leonard and Hsu, 1999; Ghosh *et al.*, 2006; Sivia and Skilling, 2006). Three central Bayesian principles are (a) all uncertainties are fundamentally dependent on individual subjective belief and they should be interpreted as subjective belief, (b) all uncertainties are represented by subjective probability distributions, and (c) subjective probability distributions are viewed as flexible functions that should be adjusted as new information becomes available. Bayesians reason that the uncertainty results obtained with the PBA approach will commonly yield such large uncertainties that the analysis results are of little value to decision makers. Stated differently, the Bayesians reason that the resources spent on a PBA are wasted because the analysis provides such large ranges of uncertainty with no likelihood information that the decision maker cannot make an informed decision. They further emphasize that the time, resources, and effort spent on a PBA would be better spent on providing a *best estimated prediction* for the system of interest. Since the strategy of PBA is to represent lack of knowledge uncertainty as an interval, as opposed to representing the uncertainty as a probability distribution, it is evident that the uncertainty of the outcomes will be significantly greater with PBA than what a Bayesian approach would yield. We believe the Bayesian criticism of PBA summarized above is without merit and we give the following counter-arguments.

First, PBA lucidly shows the decision maker how poorly the SRQs are predicted because of lack of knowledge. Stated differently, PBA does not bury or disguise any assumptions; if something is not known, it is simply included in the analysis as bounds on possible outcomes. Large uncertainty bounds in PBA usually cause a great deal of angst and frustration in the decision maker. It may even provoke them to the point of saying, "Why did we spend all of this money on modeling and simulation when you can't predict something any better than that?" One might give two responses: "That's the way it is, given our present state of knowledge" Or: "Would you prefer that we make a number of weakly defensible assumptions, mix frequency of occurrence with personal beliefs, and then show much smaller uncertainties?" Sometimes these responses don't seem to help the situation.

Second, because a sensitivity analysis (SA) *must* also be provided with the PBA, the results of the SA tell the decision maker what are the major contributors to the uncertainty in the SRQs of interest. For example, if the p-box of the SRQ is very broad due to epistemic uncertainty, then the SA can identify which contributors to epistemic uncertainty are the culprits. With this list of uncertainty contributors, the decision maker can determine which contributors they have control over, and which ones they do not. For example, they may have significant control over the design of the system, but very little control over the environment or surroundings of the system. For those contributors that are under some control, a well founded cost–benefit analysis can be conducted to determine the time and money needed to reduce certain contributors as compared to other large contributors. A follow-up UQ analysis can then be conducted with estimated reductions in the controllable epistemic uncertainties so that the decision maker can see the impact on reducing the uncertainty in the SRQs of interest.

13.9 References

Almond, R. G. (1995). *Graphical Belief Modeling*. 1st edn., London, Chapman & Hall.

Ang, A. H.-S. and W. H. Tang (2007). *Probability Concepts in Engineering: Emphasis on Applications to Civil and Environmental Engineering*. 2nd edn., New York, Wiley.

Angus, J. E. (1994). The probability integral transform and related results. *SIAM Review*. **36**(4), 652–654.

Aster, R., B. Borchers, and C. Thurber (2005). *Parameter Estimation and Inverse Problems*, Burlington, MA, Elsevier Academic Press.

Aughenbaugh, J. M. and C. J. J. Paredis (2006). The value of using imprecise probabilities in engineering design. *Journal of Mechanical Design*. **128**, 969–979.

Ayyub, B. M. (1994). The nature of uncertainty in structural engineering. In *Uncertainty Modelling and Analysis: Theory and Applications*. B. M. Ayyub and M. M. Gupta (eds.). New York, Elsevier: 195–210.

Ayyub, B. M. (2001). *Elicitation of Expert Opinions for Uncertainty and Risks*, Boca Raton, Florida, CRC Press.

Ayyub, B. M. and G. J. Klir (2006). *Uncertainty Modeling and Analysis in Engineering and the Sciences*, Boca Raton, FL, Chapman & Hall.

Bae, H.-R., R. V. Grandhi, and R. A. Canfield (2006). Sensitivity analysis of structural response uncertainty propagation using evidence theory. *Structural and Multidisciplinary Optimization*. **31**(4), 270–279.

Bardossy, G. and J. Fodor (2004). *Evaluation of Uncertainties and Risks in Geology: New Mathematical Approaches for their Handling*, Berlin, Springer.

Baudrit, C. and D. Dubois (2006). Practical representations of incomplete probabilistic knowledge. *Computational Statistics and Data Analysis*. **51**, 86–108.

Beck, M. B. (1987). Water quality modeling: a review of the analysis of uncertainty. *Water Resources Research*. **23**(8), 1393–1442.

Bedford, T. and R. Cooke (2001). *Probabilistic Risk Analysis: Foundations and Methods*, Cambridge, UK, Cambridge University Press.

Beliakov, G., A. Pradera, and T. Calvo (2007). *Aggregation Functions: a Guide for Practitioners*, Berlin, Springer-Verlag.

Berendsen, H. J. C. (2007). *Simulating the Physical World; Hierarchical Modeling from Quantum Mechanics to Fluid Dynamics*, Cambridge, UK, Cambridge University Press.

Bernardini, A. and F. Tonon (2010). *Bounding Uncertainty in Civil Engineering*, Berlin, Springer-Verlag.

Bernardo, J. M. and A. F. M. Smith (1994). *Bayesian Theory*, New York, John Wiley.

Bogen, K. T. and R. C. Spear (1987). Integrating uncertainty and interindividual variability in environmental risk assessment. *Risk Analysis*. **7**(4), 427–436.

Bouchon-Meunier, B., ed (1998). *Aggregation and Fusion of Imperfect Information*. Studies in Fuzziness and Soft Computing. New York, Springer-Verlag.

Box, G. E. P., J. S. Hunter, and W. G. Hunter (2005). *Statistics for Experimenters: Design, Innovation, and Discovery*. 2nd edn., New York, John Wiley.

Bucalem, M. L. and K. J. Bathe (2008). *The Mechanics of Solids and Structures: Hierarchical Modeling*, Berlin, Springer-Verlag.

Butcher, J. C. (2008). *Numerical Methods for Ordinary Differential Equations*. 2nd edn., Hoboken, NJ, Wiley.

Casella, G. and R. L. Berger (2002). *Statistical Inference*. 2nd edn., Pacific Grove, CA, Duxbury.

Cellier, F. E. and E. Kofman (2006). *Continuous System Simulation*, Berlin, Springer-Verlag.

Choi, S.-K., R. V. Grandhi, and R. A. Canfield (2007). *Reliability-based Structural Design*, London, Springer-Verlag.

Coleman, H. W. and F. Stern (1997). Uncertainties and CFD code validation. *Journal of Fluids Engineering*. **119**, 795–803.

Couso, I., S. Moral, and P. Walley (2000). A survey of concepts of independence for imprecise probabilities. *Risk Decision and Policy*. **5**, 165–181.

Cox, D. R. (2006). *Principles of Statistical Inference*, Cambridge, UK, Cambridge University Press.

Cozman, F. G. and P. Walley (2001). Graphoid properties of epistemic irrelevance and independence. *Proceedings of the Second International Symposium on Imprecise Probability and Their Applications*, Ithaca, NY, Shaker Publishing.

Crassidis, J. L. and J. L. Junkins (2004). *Optimal Estimation of Dynamics Systems*, Boca Raton, FL, Chapman & Hall/CRC Press.

Cullen, A. C. and H. C. Frey (1999). *Probabilistic Techniques in Exposure Assessment: a Handbook for Dealing with Variability and Uncertainty in Models and Inputs*, New York, Plenum Press.

Devore, J. L. (2007). *Probability and Statistics for Engineers and the Sciences*. 7th edn., Pacific Grove, CA, Duxbury.

Dimov, I. T. (2008). *Monte Carlo Methods for Applied Scientists*. 2nd edn., World Scientific Publishing.

Dowding, K. J., M. Pilch, and R. G. Hills (2008). Formulation of the thermal problem. *Computer Methods in Applied Mechanics and Engineering*. **197**(29–32), 2385–2389.

Draper, N. R. and H. Smith (1998). *Applied Regression Analysis*. 3rd edn., New York, John Wiley.

Duggirala, R. K., C. J. Roy, S. M. Saeidi, J. M. Khodadadi, D. R. Cahela, and B. J. Tatarchuk (2008). Pressure drop predictions in microfibrous materials using computational fluid dynamics. *Journal of Fluids Engineering*. **130**(7), 071302–1,071302–13.

Efron, B. and R. J. Tibshirani (1993). *An Introduction to the Bootstrap*, London, Chapman & Hall.

EPA (2009). *Guidance on the Development, Evaluation, and Application of Environmental Models*. EPA/100/K-09/003, Washington, DC, Environmental Protection Agency.

Ferson, S. (1996). What Monte Carlo methods cannot do. *Human and Ecological Risk Assessment*. **2**(4), 990–1007.

Ferson, S. (2002). *RAMAS Risk Calc 4.0 Software: Risk Assessment with Uncertain Numbers*. Setauket, NY, Applied Biomathematics.

Ferson, S. and L. R. Ginzburg (1996). Different methods are needed to propagate ignorance and variability. *Reliability Engineering and System Safety*. **54**, 133–144.

Ferson, S. and J. G. Hajagos (2004). Arithmetic with uncertain numbers: rigorous and (often) best possible answers. *Reliability Engineering and System Safety*. **85**(1–3), 135–152.

Ferson, S. and W. T. Tucker (2006). *Sensitivity in Risk Analyses with Uncertain Numbers*. SAND2006–2801, Albuquerque, NM, Sandia National Laboratories.

Ferson, S., V. Kreinovich, L. Ginzburg, D. S. Myers, and K. Sentz (2003). *Constructing Probability Boxes and Dempster-Shafer Structures*. SAND2003–4015, Albuquerque, NM, Sandia National Laboratories.

Ferson, S., R. B. Nelsen, J. Hajagos, D. J. Berleant, J. Zhang, W. T. Tucker, L. R. Ginzburg, and W. L. Oberkampf (2004). *Dependence in Probabilistic Modeling,*

Dempster-Shafer Theory, and Probability Bounds Analysis. SAND2004–3072, Albuquerque, NM, Sandia National Laboratories.

Ferson, S., J. Hajagos, D. S. Myers, and W. T. Tucker (2005). *CONSTRUCTOR: Synthesizing Information about Uncertain Variables.* SAND2005–3769, Albuquerque, NM, Sandia National Laboratories.

Ferson, S., W. L. Oberkampf, and L. Ginzburg (2008). Model validation and predictive capability for the thermal challenge problem. *Computer Methods in Applied Mechanics and Engineering.* **197**, 2408–2430.

Fetz, T., M. Oberguggenberger, and S. Pittschmann (2000). Applications of possibility and evidence theory in civil engineering. *International Journal of Uncertainty.* **8**(3), 295–309.

Frank, M. V. (1999). Treatment of uncertainties in space nuclear risk assessment with examples from Cassini Mission applications. *Reliability Engineering and System Safety.* **66**, 203–221.

Frey, H. C. and D. S. Rhodes (1996). Characterizing, simulating, and analyzing variability and uncertainty: an illustration of methods using an air toxics emissions example. *Human and Ecological Risk Assessment.* **2**(4), 762–797.

Gelman, A. B., J. S. Carlin, H. S. Stern, and D. B. Rubin (1995). *Bayesian Data Analysis,* London, Chapman & Hall.

Ghanem, R. G. and P. D. Spanos (2003). *Stochastic Finite Elements: a Spectral Approach.* Revised edn., Mineola, NY, Dover Publications.

Ghosh, J. K., M. Delampady, and T. Samanta (2006). *An Introduction to Bayesian Analysis: Theory and Methods,* Berlin, Springer-Verlag.

Haimes, Y. Y. (2009). *Risk Modeling, Assessment, and Management.* 3rd edn., New York, John Wiley.

Haldar, A. and S. Mahadevan (2000a). *Probability, Reliability, and Statistical Methods in Engineering Design,* New York, John Wiley.

Haldar, A. and S. Mahadevan (2000b). *Reliability Assessment Using Stochastic Finite Element Analysis,* New York, John Wiley.

Halpern, J. Y. (2003). *Reasoning About Uncertainty,* Cambridge, MA, The MIT Press.

Helton, J. C. (1994). Treatment of uncertainty in performance assessments for complex systems. *Risk Analysis.* **14**(4), 483–511.

Helton, J. C. (1997). Uncertainty and sensitivity analysis in the presence of stochastic and subjective uncertainty. *Journal of Statistical Computation and Simulation.* **57**, 3–76.

Helton, J. C. (2003). Mathematical and numerical approaches in performance assessment for radioactive waste disposal: dealing with uncertainty. In *Modelling Radioactivity in the Environment.* E. M. Scott (ed.). New York, NY, Elsevier Science Ltd.: 353–389.

Helton, J. C. and F. J. Davis (2003). Latin Hypercube sampling and the propagation of uncertainty in analyses of complex systems. *Reliability Engineering and System Safety.* **81**(1), 23–69.

Helton, J. C. and C. J. Sallaberry (2007). *Illustration of Sampling-Based Approaches to the Calculation of Expected Dose in Performance Assessments for the Proposed High Level Radioactive Waste Repository at Yucca Mountain, Nevada.* SAND2007–1353, Albuquerque, NM, Sandia National Laboratories.

Helton, J. C., D. R. Anderson, G. Basabilvazo, H.-N. Jow, and M. G. Marietta (2000). Conceptual structure of the 1996 performance assessment for the Waste Isolation Pilot Plant. *Reliability Engineering and System Safety.* **69**(1–3), 151–165.

Helton, J. C., J. D. Johnson, and W. L. Oberkampf (2004). An exploration of alternative approaches to the representation of uncertainty in model predictions. *Reliability Engineering and System Safety.* **85**(1–3), 39–71.

Helton, J. C., F. J. Davis, and J. D. Johnson (2005b). A comparison of uncertainty and sensitivity analysis results obtained with random and Latin Hypercube sampling. *Reliability Engineering and System Safety.* **89**(3), 305–330.

Helton, J. C., W. L. Oberkampf, and J. D. Johnson (2005a). Competing failure risk analysis using evidence theory. *Risk Analysis.* **25**(4), 973–995.

Helton, J. C., J. D. Johnson, C. J. Sallaberry, and C. B. Storlie (2006). Survey of sampling-based methods for uncertainty and sensitivity analysis. *Reliability Engineering and System Safety.* **91**(10–11), 1175–1209.

Higdon, D., C. Nakhleh, J. Battiker, and B. Williams (2009). A Bayesian calibration approach to the thermal problem. *Computer Methods in Applied Mechanics and Engineering.* **197**(29–32), 2431–2441.

Hills, R. G., M. Pilch, K. J. Dowding, J. Red-Horse, T. L. Paez, I. Babuska, and R. Tempone (2008). Validation Challenge Workshop. *Computer Methods in Applied Mechanics and Engineering.* **197**(29–32), 2375–2380.

Hoffman, F. O. and J. S. Hammonds (1994). Propagation of uncertainty in risk assessments: the need to distinguish between uncertainty due to lack of knowledge and uncertainty due to variability. *Risk Analysis.* **14**(5), 707–712.

Hora, S. C. (1996). Aleatory and epistemic uncertainty in probability elicitation with an example from hazardous waste management. *Reliability Engineering and System Safety.* **54**, 217–223.

Kleb, B. and C. O. Johnston (2008). Uncertainty analysis of air radiation for lunar return shock layers. *AIAA Atmospheric Flight Mechanics Conference*, AIAA 2008–6388, Honolulu, HI, American Institute of Aeronautics and Astronautics.

Klir, G. J. and M. J. Wierman (1998). *Uncertainty-Based Information: Elements of Generalized Information Theory*, Heidelberg, Physica-Verlag.

Kohlas, J. and P.-A. Monney (1995). *A Mathematical Theory of Hints – an Approach to the Dempster-Shafer Theory of Evidence*, Berlin, Springer-Verlag.

Krause, P. and D. Clark (1993). *Representing Uncertain Knowledge: an Artificial Intelligence Approach*, Dordrecht, The Netherlands, Kluwer Academic Publishers.

Kreinovich, V., J. Beck, C. Ferregut, A. Sanchez, G. R. Keller, M. Averill, and S. A. Starks (2007). Monte-Carlo-type techniques for processing interval uncertainty, and their potential engineering applications. *Reliable Computing.* **13**, 25–69.

Kriegler, E. and H. Held (2005). Utilizing belief functions for the estimation of future climate change. *International Journal for Approximate Reasoning.* **39**, 185–209.

Kumamoto, H. (2007). *Satisfying Safety Goals by Probabilistic Risk Assessment*, Berlin, Springer-Verlag.

Kyburg, H. E. and C. M. Teng (2001). *Uncertain Inference*, Cambridge, UK, Cambridge University Press.

Leonard, T. and J. S. J. Hsu (1999). *Bayesian Methods: an Analysis for Statisticians and Interdisciplinary Researchers*, Cambridge, UK, Cambridge University Press.

Liu, F., M. J. Bayarri, J. O. Berger, R. Paulo, and J. Sacks (2009). A Bayesian analysis of the thermal challenge problem. *Computer Methods in Applied Mechanics and Engineering.* **197**(29–32), 2457–2466.

Melchers, R. E. (1999). *Structural Reliability Analysis and Prediction.* 2nd edn., New York, John Wiley.

Meyer, M. A. and J. M. Booker (2001). *Eliciting and Analyzing Expert Judgment: a Practical Guide*, New York, Academic Press.

Modarres, M., M. Kaminskiy, and V. Krivtsov (1999). *Reliability Engineering and Risk Analysis; a Practical Guide*, Boca Raton, FL, CRC Press.

Montgomery, D. C. (2000). *Design and Analysis of Experiments*. 5th edn., Hoboken, NJ, John Wiley.

Morgan, M. G. and M. Henrion (1990). *Uncertainty: a Guide to Dealing with Uncertainty in Quantitative Risk and Policy Analysis*. 1st edn., Cambridge, UK, Cambridge University Press.

Mukhopadhyay, N. (2000). *Probability and Statistical Inference*, Boca Raton, FL, CRC Press.

NASA (2002). *Probabilistic Risk Assessment Procedures Guide for NASA Managers and Practitioners*. Washington, DC, NASA.

Nikolaidis, E., D. M. Ghiocel, and S. Singhal, eds (2005). *Engineering Design Reliability Handbook*. Boca Raton, FL, CRC Press.

NRC (2009). *Guidance on the Treatment of Uncertainties Assoicated with PRAs in Risk-Informed Decision Making*. Washington, DC, Nuclear Regulator Commission.

Oberkampf, W. L. and S. Ferson (2007). Model validation under both aleatory and epistemic uncertainty. *NATO/RTO Symposium on Computational Uncertainty in Military Vehicle Design*, AVT-147/RSY-022, Athens, Greece, NATO.

Oberkampf, W. L. and J. C. Helton (2005). Evidence theory for engineering applications. In *Engineering Design Reliability Handbook*. E. Nikolaidis, D. M. Ghiocel, and S. Singhal (eds.). New York, NY, CRC Press: 29.

Parry, G. W. (1996). The characterization of uncertainty in probabilistic risk assessments of complex systems. *Reliability Engineering and System Safety*. **54**, 119–126.

Paté-Cornell, M. E. (1996). Uncertainties in risk analysis: six levels of treatment. *Reliability Engineering and System Safety*. **54**, 95–111.

Pilch, M. (2008). Preface: Sandia National Laboratories Validation Challenge Workshop. *Computer Methods in Applied Mechanics and Engineering*. **197**(29–32), 2373–2374.

Rabinovich, S. G. (2005). *Measurement Errors and Uncertainties: Theory and Practice*. 3rd edn., New York, Springer-Verlag.

Rai, S. N., D. Krewski, and S. Bartlett (1996). A general framework for the analysis of uncertainty and variability in risk assessment. *Human and Ecological Risk Assessment*. **2**(4), 972–989.

Raol, J. R., G. Girija, and J. Singh (2004). *Modelling and Parameter Estimation of Dynamic Systems*, London, UK, Institution of Engineering and Technology.

Roache, P. J. (1998). *Verification and Validation in Computational Science and Engineering*, Albuquerque, NM, Hermosa Publishers.

Ross, S. M. (2006). *Simulation*. 4th edn., Burlington, MA, Academic Press.

Rowe, W. D. (1994). Understanding uncertainty. *Risk Analysis*. **14**(5), 743–750.

Rubinstein, R. Y. and D. P. Kroese (2008). *Simulation and the Monte Carlo Method*. 2nd edn., Hoboken, NJ, John Wiley.

Rutherford, B. M. (2008). Computational modeling issues and methods for the "Regulatory Problem" in engineering – solution to the thermal problem. *Computer Methods in Applied Mechanics and Engineering*. **197**(29–32), 2480–2489.

Sallaberry, C. J., J. C. Helton, and S. C. Hora (2008). Extension of Latin Hypercube samples with correlated variables. *Reliability Engineering and System Safety*. **93**, 1047–1059.

Saltelli, A., M. Ratto, T. Andres, F. Campolongo, J. Cariboni, D. Gatelli, M. Saisana, and S. Tarantola (2008). *Global Sensitivity Analysis: the Primer*, Hoboken, NJ, Wiley.

Sentz, K. and S. Ferson (2002). *Combination of Evidence in Dempster-Shafer Theory*. SAND2002–0835, Albuquerque, NM, Sandia National Laboratories.

Singh, V. P., S. K. Jain, and A. Tyagi (2007). *Risk and Reliability Analysis: a Handbook for Civil and Environmental Engineers*, New York, American Society of Civil Engineers.

Singpurwalla, N. D. (2006). *Reliability and Risk: a Bayesian Perspective*, New York, NY, Wiley.

Sivia, D. and J. Skilling (2006). *Data Analysis: a Bayesian Tutorial*. 2nd edn., Oxford, Oxford University Press.

Steinhauser, M. O. (2008). *Computational Multiscale Modeling of Fluids and Solids: Theory and Applications*, Berlin, Springer-Verlag.

Stern, F., R. V. Wilson, H. W. Coleman, and E. G. Paterson (2001). Comprehensive approach to verification and validation of CFD simulations – Part 1: Methodology and procedures. *Journal of Fluids Engineering*. **123**(4), 793–802.

Storlie, C. B. and J. C. Helton (2008a). Multiple predictor smoothing methods for sensitivity analysis: description of techniques. *Reliability Engineering and System Safety*. **93**(1), 28–54.

Storlie, C. B. and J. C. Helton (2008b). Multiple predictor smoothing methods for sensitivity analysis: example results. *Reliability Engineering and System Safety*. **93**(1), 55–77.

Suter, G. W. (2007). *Ecological Risk Assessment*. 2nd edn., Boca Raton, FL, CRC Press.

Torra, V. and Y. Narukawa (2007). *Modeling Decision: Information Fusion and Aggregation Operators*, Berlin, Springer-Verlag.

Trucano, T. G., M. Pilch, and W. L. Oberkampf (2002). *General Concepts for Experimental Validation of ASCI Code Applications*. SAND2002–0341, Albuquerque, NM, Sandia National Laboratories.

van den Bos, A (2007). *Parameter Estimation for Scientists and Engineers*, Hoboken, NJ, Wiley-Interscience.

Vinnem, J. E. (2007). *Offshore Risk Assessment: Principles, Modelling and Applications of QRA Studies*, Berlin, Springer-Verlag.

Vose, D. (2008). *Risk Analysis: a Quantitative Guide*. 3rd edn., New York, Wiley.

Wasserman, L. A. (2004). *All of Statistics: a Concise Course in Statistical Inference*, Berlin, Springer-Verlag.

Wilson, R. V., F. Stern, H. W. Coleman, and E. G. Paterson (2001). Comprehensive approach to verification and validation of CFD simulations – Part 2: Application for RANS simulation of a cargo/container ship. *Journal of Fluids Engineering*. **123**(4), 803–810.

Yager, R. R., J. Kacprzyk, and M. Fedrizzi, eds (1994). *Advances in the Dempster-Shafer Theory of Evidence*. New York, John Wiley.

Young, G. A. and R. L. Smith (2005). *Essentials of Statistical Inference*, Cambridge, UK, Cambridge University Press.

Zienkiewicz, O. C. and J. Z. Zhu (1992). The superconvergent patch recovery and a posteriori error estimates. *International Journal for Numerical Methods in Engineering*. **33**, 1365–1382.

Part V

Planning, management, and implementation issues

This final section of the book primarily deals with the topic of how managers – both line managers and project managers – plan, implement, develop, and sustain verification, validation, and uncertainty quantification (VV&UQ) capabilities in their organizations. Some readers may feel this topic is inappropriate in a book on scientific computing; however, our experience and the experience of others has convinced us that while technical issues and computing resources are important, they are not the limiting factor in improving the credibility and usefulness of scientific computing used in a decision-making environment. We point out that although computing speed has continued to increase by a factor of ten every four years for multiple decades, we do not believe there has been a comparable impact of the information produced in modeling and simulation (M&S). We believe that nontechnical issues have significantly constrained improvements in the credibility of the information produced in M&S. Examples of these issues are (a) poor allocation of resources relative to the simulation needs of a project, (b) inadequate and ambiguous characterization and understanding of uncertainties in simulations, and (c) the difficulty of management and staff to assess how the time and resources invested in VV&UQ produce a net benefit for the credibility of the simulation results produced.

Chapter 14, Planning and prioritization in modeling and simulation, deals with a process for allocating resources, given a wide range of M&S activities, to best achieve the goals of a project. We take the perspective of the management responsibilities for a large-scale, project-oriented activity as opposed to a research effort or general capability development of a commercial software package. Our discussion applies to both projects within industry and government. We emphasize engineering system projects, but the discussion also applies to the analysis of natural systems. The system of interest could be a new or proposed system in the design phase, an existing system that is being considered for modification or upgrade, or analysis of a system as it presently exists.

Chapter 15, Maturity assessment of modeling and simulation, reviews several approaches for assessing the maturity and, in some sense, the quality of a M&S effort. Given our perspective of scientific computing, we discuss the strengths and weaknesses of several well-developed approaches. We then present a detailed discussion of a recently developed technique that has been used at Sandia National Laboratories. The procedure gives a description of four levels of maturity for the following technical contributors to M&S: representation and geometric fidelity, physics and material model fidelity, code verification, solution verification, model validation, and uncertainty quantification and sensitivity analysis. The procedure has proven very beneficial in assessing progress in M&S activities, as well as helping identify activities where improvements are needed.

The concluding chapter of the book is Chapter 16, Development and responsibilities for verification, validation, and uncertainty quantification. We present a summary of some of the key research topics that we feel are needed to advance VV&UQ in scientific computing. This list is not meant to be comprehensive, but only suggestive. We then discuss our view of staff and management responsibilities in VV&UQ activities. Ours is primarily a business perspective of M&S, i.e., how M&S can produce credible information on which to make decisions. We then give a brief discussion of our ideas on how V&V databases might be developed in various technical communities. We close with a few final remarks on the role of engineering societies and the International Organization for Standardization (ISO) in the development of engineering standards in V&V.

14

Planning and prioritization in modeling and simulation

In Chapter 2, Fundamental concepts and terminology, a summary discussion was given concerning an integrated view of verification, validation, and prediction. This chapter will discuss in detail Element 2, Planning and prioritization of activities, as shown in Figure 14.1. The topic of this chapter could be summarized as: given the wide range of activities dealing with modeling and simulation, how does one allocate resources to best achieve the goals of the project? Here, we are interested in dealing with the perspective of the management responsibilities for a large-scale, project-oriented activity as opposed to a research effort or general capability development of a commercial software package. Our discussion applies to projects within both industry and government. We emphasize engineering system projects, but the discussion also applies to the analysis of natural systems, e.g., underground storage of radioactive wastes, global climate change, and transport of contaminants or chemical agents due to atmospheric winds. The system of interest could be a new or proposed system in the design phase, an existing system that is being considered for modification or upgrade, or analysis of a system as it presently exists.

14.1 Methodology for planning and prioritization

For large-scale projects, planning and prioritization (P&P) are major activities that require a significant investment in time, money, and specialized personnel talent. Although we are primarily concerned with P&P in V&V and prediction, we comment here on the importance of P&P in large-scale projects for the development of an M&S capability. Depending on the type of organization developing the capability, it can be challenging for management to assemble the personnel with the needed talent and interest in P&P. For example, if a large-scale M&S project arrives in the midst of ongoing computational development activities, it can be difficult for management and staff to change pre-existing viewpoints, traditions and ingrained habits that are no longer appropriate, and possibly even very detrimental, to the goals of the new project. Needed changes can be particularly onerous to affect in a research or government organization.

It is a widely held view that the crucial importance of P&P is commonly ignored, almost always with dire consequences (Dorner, 1989; Flowers, 1996; Stepanek, 2005; Vose, 2008).

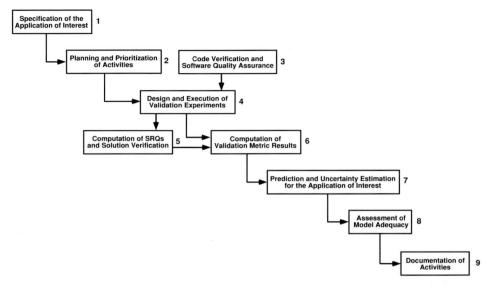

Figure 14.1 Integrated view of the elements of verification, validation, and prediction (adapted from Trucano *et al.*, 2002).

In an article in *IEEE Spectrum* in 2005, Charette (2005) states, "This year, organizations and governments will spend an estimated $1 trillion on IT hardware, software, and services worldwide. Of the IT projects that are initiated, from 5 to 15 percent will be abandoned before or shortly after delivery as hopelessly inadequate. Many others will arrive late and over budget or require massive reworking. Few IT projects, in other words, truly succeed." He lists a dozen of the most common reasons for massive software failures, but several of these can be grouped as a lack of P&P in the software project.

A number of very helpful texts are available that deal with P&P of software projects (Flowers, 1996; Karolak, 1996; Galin, 2003; Wiegers, 2003). Here, we concentrate on the broader aspects of projects that have been discussed, e.g., modeling and experimental activities, not just the software aspects. Another well-developed approach used in P&P and decision making in complex situations is the Analytical Hierarchy Process developed primarily by Saaty (2001). The method has been developed over the last three decades and has been used in a wide variety of applications in business, government, policy decisions, economic planning, military operations, service delivery, and environmental impact. The Analytical Hierarchy Process, however, has not yet been applied within the relatively new framework for V&V.

14.1.1 Planning for a modeling and simulation project

Planning in a large-scale M&S project begins by specifying the application of interest, the first element shown in Figure 14.1. Sometimes the activities in this element are referred to as development and specification of customer requirements. These activities should involve significant interaction between the customer and the development team. The following summarizes the most important topics to be addressed *before* prioritization of activities can begin.

- Specification of the application of interest. The key physical process, engineering system, or event of interest should be well defined. The expected informational-contributions or value added from the computational effort should also be specified.
- Specification of the application domain of the system that the computational effort is expected to address. The application domain could be restricted to the normal environment, e.g., the operating envelope of the system, but it could also include certain abnormal and hostile environments of the system.
- Identification of important scenarios for each of the specified environments. The scenarios correspond to conditions that the system could be exposed to within a specified environment, various event sequences, event trees, or fault trees.
- Specification of the system and it surroundings. Different specifications for the system and the surroundings could be given, depending on the environments and scenarios of interest.
- Specification of the system response quantities of interest. This should include all SRQs for each of the environments and scenarios of interest. For the normal environment, typical SRQs of interest are related to system performance and reliability; for abnormal and hostile environments, SRQs are usually related to some aspect of safety or security of the system.
- Specification of the accuracy requirements by the customer or stakeholder for each SRQ of interest. If the system specification is at an early stage, or the environments and scenarios are not well defined, then these requirements may be very poorly known. For example, accuracy requirements of some SRQs may only be known to within an order of magnitude, or just a qualitative feature of the SRQ may be specified. Even though the customer may poorly know the accuracy requirements, recognizing that they may be modified later because of the cost and schedule involved, it is of utmost importance that initial expectations be discussed.

Completing these tasks will require a significant effort by a diverse group of customer representatives and project managers and staff. It will require in-depth, and often difficult, discussions between the project managers, the customer, and stakeholders in the effort. By *customers* we mean both those who will use the software produced by the project and those who will directly use the results of the analyses, e.g., decision makers. By *stakeholders* we mean those who have any type of vested interest in the development of the simulation capability, those who use the simulation results as secondary information in their activities, and those whose success is dependent on the success of the simulation capability or the customer's success. The funding source for the simulation capability is usually the customer, but in certain situations, e.g., governmental funding, this is not always the case. When the funding source is *not* the customer, the likelihood of confusion, misunderstandings, delivering the wrong product, and failure increases dramatically.

The discussions between the project managers, customer, and stakeholders will involve a great deal of clarification of issues, negotiation of trade-offs, and compromise. Sometimes the customer only has a vague idea of needed requirements because either he has not carefully thought about his requirements, or because the application of interest has not yet been fully defined. Many times the customer will request more than what is realistic, given the time and money available for the effort. The manager of the effort must therefore be realistic in what can be delivered, given the resources available. The cause of many software project failures is that the project manager either (a) is initially unrealistic in what could be accomplished; or (b) allows significant changes or increases in requirements, features, or capabilities to be imposed during software development. During the negotiation of the specifications given in the bullet list above, there must be flexibility by the customer and the project management, an open exchange of information concerning costs for various capabilities desired, and the customer clearly expressing his value system concerning trade-offs of deliverables. For example, the project manager must try to assess the time and costs required to achieve certain customer accuracy requirements. On the other hand, the customer must be flexible in trading-off one requirement of lesser value for requirements that are more important to his goals for the performance of the system.

For some projects, it will already be specified which computer code, or group of codes, will be used in the various analyses of the system of interest. So that, in addition to the activities listed above, there will also be significant specificity of many of the additional elements listed for the verification, validation, and prediction shown in Figure 14.1, as well as the additional phases of project discussed in Chapter 3, Modeling and computational simulation. For example, if the project is using commercial software, then the planning phase will deal much more about comparing customer requirements with options available in the software. In commercial software there would typically be more detailed documentation available concerning available user options, compared to software written and supported by a corporate or government organization.

14.1.2 Value systems for prioritization

Here we are interested in value systems for prioritizing future work on activities such as physics modeling, software development, software quality assurance (SQA), code verification, solution verification, experiments associated with validation, construction of validation metrics, and uncertainty quantification (UQ) associated with predictions. Our interest is in attempting to best allocate resources between various activities to achieve the highest possible level of success of a project-oriented M&S effort, given the constraints on resources. It should be recognized that the success of the M&S effort is not synonymous with success of the engineering system project. The success of the engineering project typically depends on many other factors not of interest here. By *success of the M&S effort* we mean an effort that best contributes to assisting (a) the engineering system to attain its performance goals, or (b) the customer to attain his informational needs.

By *resources* we primarily mean the time, money, personnel expertise, and facilities required to complete an activity. These will be grouped together for convenience, because we will not deal with individual types of resource in any detail. It should be recognized throughout this discussion that there are strong dependencies between each of these resources. For example, there is typically a strong connection between the personnel that conduct SQA activities and those that conduct code verification activities, i.e., they may be the same people. Likewise, there is commonly overlapping expertise between physics model builders and software developers. Here, we will not deal with these types of dependency in resources types.

There are various value systems that can be used to prioritize project-oriented activities. In some projects, however, the prioritization of activities has little to do with project-oriented goals, but with the organizational power base of groups or the physics interests of groups within the organization conducting the M&S effort. Since there are many different types of activities that are conducted throughout the elements shown in Figure 14.1, one needs to map all of the activities back to one common feature that links all of the elements. The most logical feature to use is physics modeling, i.e., mathematical modeling of the various physical processes occurring in the system of interest. Without this common feature, the remainder of the activities would have little meaning or effect on the goals of the M&S effort.

Here we will discuss three of the more common value systems and where each may be appropriate in optimizing resource allocation.

1 Rank the modeling of individual physical processes occurring in the system according to the expected level of *inaccuracy*. In this approach, the highest rank would be given to those physical processes that are expected to be modeled the *least* accurately. This prioritization scheme is based on the anticipated level of understanding of the physics processes and their interactions within the system. This approach would be appropriate for improving the understanding of complex systems and multi-physics processes, as well as systems exposed to abnormal or hostile environments, such as severe accident conditions, highly damaged systems, electromagnetic pulse attack on a computer controlled system, and a terrorist attack on a public transportation system. This approach would *not* be appropriate for engineering systems in normal environments, such as well-understood operating conditions.
2 Rank according to the expected impact of individual physical processes on SRQs of interest. In this approach, the highest rank would be given to those physical processes that have the *largest expected effect* on specific SRQs related to system performance, safety, or reliability. This approach would also be appropriate for improving the understanding of complex physics processes in abnormal and hostile environments. Here, however, the focus is ranking the impact of the physics processes on specific system responses, not just their impact on understanding the physics of the system. The most well-developed method using this prioritization scheme is the phenomena identification and ranking table (PIRT). It was developed by several organizations for the US Nuclear Regulatory Commission (NRC) to improve assessment of nuclear reactor safety in abnormal, i.e., accident, environments. The PIRT approach will be discussed in Section 14.2.
3 Rank according to the expected ability to predict the impact of individual physical processes on SRQs of interest. This is a two-step method where one would first conduct approach 2 just mentioned, and then focus on the more important physical processes to determine if the modeling effort can adequately address these phenomena. This method concentrates on the *weaknesses* in the modeling effort to predict the important SRQs related to system performance, safety, or

reliability. As a result, this prioritization scheme is commonly referred to as the *gap analysis method*. Although this approach was initiated by several organizations for the NRC, it has recently been extended as part of the Advanced Simulation and Computing (ASC) Program (previously called the Accelerated Strategic Computing Initiative) sponsored by the US Department of Energy. It has been used for normal, abnormal, and hostile environments by Sandia National Laboratories. This method will be discussed in Section 14.3.

14.2 Phenomena identification and ranking table (PIRT)

The nuclear reactor safety community, as it has done in many areas of risk assessment, developed a new process for improving the understanding of nuclear plants in accident scenarios. In 1988, the NRC issued a revised emergency core cooling system rule for light water reactors that allows, as an option, the use of best estimate plus uncertainty (BE+U) methods in safety analyses (NRC, 1988). To support the licensing revision, the NRC and its contractors developed the code scaling, applicability, and uncertainty (CSAU) evaluation methodology to demonstrate the feasibility of the BE+U approach. The phenomena identification and ranking table was developed in support of the CSAU methodology. The PIRT process was initially developed by Shaw *et al.* (1988) to help analyze the safety of pressurized water nuclear reactors during a loss of coolant accident. Since its initial development, the process has been developed further and applied many times to various nuclear reactor designs. For a detailed discussion of PIRTs, see Boyack *et al.* (1990); Wilson *et al.* (1990); Wulff *et al.* (1990); Hanson *et al.* (1992); Rohatgi *et al.* (1997); Kroeger *et al.* (1998); and Wilson and Boyack (1998).

During the 1990s, it was found that the PIRT process was a much more powerful tool than originally conceived (Wilson and Boyack, 1998). It was found that it could also be used to aid in identifying needed future experiments, physics model development, and needed improvements in UQ. The additional objectives, however, were still focused on improving the physical understanding of the plant behavior and the interactions of systems and subsystems during a specific accident scenario. The generalized PIRT process, as described by Wilson and Boyack (1998), is a 15-step process that requires significant resources, if completed in detail.

As part of the ASC program, various researchers and projects at Sandia National Laboratories modified the PIRT process so that it was more oriented towards modeling activities (Pilch *et al.*, 2001; Tieszen *et al.*, 2002; Trucano *et al.*, 2002; Boughton *et al.*, 2003). In addition, they simplified the PIRT process to five steps so that it could be used by individual code development projects. The PIRT process has focused on abnormal and hostile environments because these environments typically involve large uncertainties in (a) knowing the condition, state, or geometry of the system; (b) the surroundings as they affect the system through the BCs or the excitation function; (c) strongly coupled physics that commonly occur; and (d) important human or computer controlled intervention that that could occur as part of the functioning of the system, the BCs, or the excitation function. For the design of systems in abnormal or hostile environments, the primary goal is typically *not* to analyze the performance of the system, but rather to seek system designs that will behave in predictable ways.

14.2.1 Steps in the PIRT process for modeling and simulation

The five steps for a simplified PIRT process are:

- assembly of the team,
- definition of the objectives of the PIRT process,
- specification of environments and scenarios,
- identification of plausible physical phenomena,
- construction of the PIRT.

The following description combines the work and recommendations of Wilson and Boyack (1998), the Sandia researchers referenced above, and the present authors.

14.2.1.1 Assembly of the team

PIRT development is best accomplished using a team that has a broad base of knowledge and expertise in a number of areas. The most important areas for individual knowledge and representation are (a) goals of the M&S effort, (b) needs of the customer, (c) operation of the system of interest or closely related systems, (d) environments and scenarios of interest, (e) different physical processes and phenomena occurring in the system as well as how they are modeled, and (f) analysts with experience in simulating the system of interest or closely related systems. Additional expertise should be included, depending on the nature of the system of interest and the modeling effort. The number of people on the team should be roughly five to ten. Teams any larger than this become inefficient, burdensome to keep on track, and meetings become difficult to arrange so that all team members can attend every meeting. The team members should have a demonstrated capability to work in a team environment, particularly the ability to control their individual agendas in the interest of the team effort. The assistance of technical and administrative support staff significantly improves the efficiency and productivity of the team. Finally, and most importantly, the team should have a clearly defined leader who has the recognized authority and is ultimately responsible for the effort and its documentation. This person should also have participated in previous PIRT efforts and be familiar with all aspects of the PIRT process.

14.2.1.2 Definition of the objectives of the PIRT process

The objectives of the PIRT process should be narrowly focused, as opposed to the objectives of the development of a M&S capability. Typically, the objectives of the PIRT process are oriented toward the performance, safety, or reliability of a system or subsystem. If the objectives are too broad, then the results of the process tend to be of limited value for prioritizing future efforts. For example, if the scenarios of interest are too broad or ill defined, then the prioritization result commonly is: everything needs work. Prioritization is fundamentally about ordering needs: some things will get done and some will not. As part of the definition of objectives, the team should specify what predictions are needed from the simulation capability. These can almost always be categorized as one or more SRQs. If multiple physics codes are coupled together to produce the SRQ of ultimate interest, there may be several SRQs from intermediate codes that are needed to predict the ultimate SRQ. Also, the SRQs of interest can be quantitative or qualitative in nature. For example, suppose one were interested in an accident scenario concerned with the separation or fracturing of a fan blade attached to the rotor disk on a gas turbine engine. One may be only interested in predicting if any fragments of the fan penetrate the engine cowling after the blade separates from the rotor; not in the detailed prediction of the deformation of the cowling.

It should be stressed that in the PIRT process there should be *no connection* to existing computer codes and needed simulation capabilities. The PIRT process is focused on discovering what are the most important physical phenomena that affect a system and its response, *not* on whether an existing computer code can simulate the phenomena or how well it can be simulated. These latter issues derail the discussion into expected performance or promotion of existing codes.

During formulation of the objectives of the PIRT process, the team must estimate the resources required to complete the identified objectives, compared with the resources available for the effort. The team should be fairly cautious and restrictive in its objectives, because of the time required to conduct the effort, as well as document the results.

14.2.1.3 Specification of environments and scenarios

Typically only one environment is specified for analyzing in the PIRT process; normal, abnormal, or hostile. For the environment chosen, one or more scenarios are usually specified, but they should be closely related. The scenarios specified should match the technical expertise and background of the team. If the scenarios are unrelated, then separate PIRT process teams should be formed. In the specification of the environment and scenarios, key parameters characterizing the system and surroundings should be specified, and, if possible, a range of parameter values should be specified. For example, these could be (a) the quantity and characteristics of coolant available in an emergency cooling system, (b) type and range of damage to a system or subsystem, (c) quantity of fuel available in a fuel fire, and (d) level of access to a computer control system by an attacker. In certain situations, the team may be given freedom to identify scenarios that have never been considered, but may also be pursued. The possibility of this approach should be specified in setting the objectives in Step 1 because, as will be seen in Section 14.2.1.5, a PIRT will be constructed for each scenario.

Figure 14.2 depicts the given environment chosen, the scenarios of interest, and the SRQs of interest for each scenario. As can be seen from this tree structure, the total number of quantities of interest that will be analyzed in the PIRT process can become quite large, if the scope of the effort is not limited. It should also be noted that, at the beginning of a PIRT process, not all of the scenarios of interest and the SRQs are necessarily recognized. For example, as the PIRT process evolves, new failure modes or coupled physics interactions are commonly discovered, that were not recognized initially.

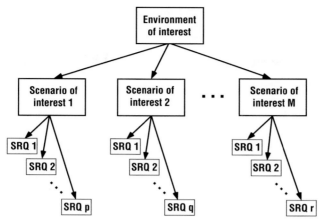

Figure 14.2 Environment–scenario–SRQ tree.

14.2.1.4 Identification of plausible physical phenomena

All plausible physical phenomena and interactions of phenomena should be considered for each scenario of interest, given that the phenomena could have an impact on the SRQs of interest. In many scenarios, it has proven beneficial to divide the scenario into time phases, since different physical phenomena tend to be important in different phases. For example, in loss of coolant accidents in nuclear reactors, the time phases could be divided into (a) initial rapid loss of coolant, (b) high heating of subsystems before emergency coolant is introduced, (c) initial introduction of emergency coolant onto high temperature subsystems, and (d) flooding of the system with emergency coolant. In some analyses, it is also useful to spatially divide the system or subsystem into regions where plausible phenomena can be better identified. For example, in a terrorist attack of a facility, it is useful to consider varying levels of physical access and control of a facility, as well as levels of armament and technical capability of the attackers.

Trying to discover all of the plausible phenomena that may occur in the system is a difficult task. The team can never be sure that they have discovered all of them; which is referred to as the problem of incompleteness. Creative, *thinking out of the box* type individuals on the team can significantly aid in this step. Different approaches can be used to generate ideas about plausible phenomena. Depending on the makeup of the team, one approach that has proven beneficial is to use some type of brainstorming. In this approach, many different, apparently unrelated, ideas are suggested. Sometimes these ideas are fruitful in themselves and sometimes they lead to other creative ideas that may be fruitful. Regardless of whether a team-brainstorming approach is used, or a more separate individual approach, the key is that no ideas are criticized or ridiculed. The key element in phenomena identification is *discovery, not* evaluation, appraisal, or ranking of importance of phenomena or ideas. The team leader plays an important role here to be certain that a proper and constructive atmosphere is maintained during the discussions of the team. Simplified simulations of the scenarios, or order of magnitude analyses, can be used to

Table 14.1 *Example of initial PIRT for a given environment and scenario.*

SRQ / Phenomena	SRQ 1	SRQ 2	•••	SRQ p
Physical phenomenon 1				
Physical phenomenon 2				
Physical phenomenon 3				
Physical phenomenon 4				
⋮				
Physical phenomenon n				

aid in the discussions. Use of more complex simulations is not recommended because they begin to focus the discussion on details of the analysis and existing modeling capabilities, instead of what is plausible. Most importantly, the M&S capability that will be evaluated later in the gap analysis, Section 11.3, should *never* be used during the PIRT process.

14.2.1.5 Construction of the PIRT

A PIRT is constructed for each scenario of interest by listing all of the plausible phenomena identified in the previous step (see Table 14.1). The phenomena can be listed in arbitrary order in the table, but it is recommended that they be grouped into general classes of phenomena or processes. For example in a heat transfer problem, they would be listed as conduction, convection, and radiation. All of the single-physics processes should be listed together. Physical processes that produce important effects because of strong coupling between single-physics processes should be listed as separate entries. If there are multiple SRQs for a scenario, then they can be listed across the top of the table. If a scenario were divided into multiple time phases or spatial regions, then a separate PIRT would be given for each phase or region.

   After the initial PIRT is constructed, then the heart of the PIRT process begins: the discussion and debate to rank order the list of physical phenomena in terms of their importance on a particular SRQ of interest. Various methods of ranking the phenomena can be used. The simplest, and usually the most effective, is to define three relative ranks of importance: high, moderate, and low. A five-level scale can also be used: very high, high,

Table 14.2 *Example of a completed PIRT for a given environment and scenario.*

Phenomena \ SRQ	SRQ 1	SRQ 2	...	SRQ p
Physical Phenomenon 1	(moderate)	(high)		(low)
Physical Phenomenon 2	(low)	(moderate)		(high)
Physical Phenomenon 3	(high)	(low)		(moderate)
Physical Phenomenon 4	(moderate)	(low)		(low)
⋮				
Physical Phenomenon n	(low)	(high)		(moderate)

■ High Importance	▬ Moderate Importance	☐ Low Importance

moderate, low, and very low. No more than a five-level scale should be used because a higher level of precision is not necessary for a qualitative effort such as this. In addition, the more levels of importance the more difficult it is to obtain agreement by a group of individuals.

Depending on the composition of the team and the resources set aside for the effort, the discussion and debate on ranking can be quite lengthy and energetic. The team leader should show a great deal of discretion and patience in the debates. Unless the team leader has a very strong opinion on a certain ranking, he should avoid taking sides in a debate concerning a particular ranking. Taking sides in a debate can lead team members to concluding he is aligning with certain factions within the team. The team leader should serve more in the role of an unbiased, rational observer and referee in the debate. After an appropriate amount of time debating the issues, the leader should call for a vote on the issue at hand. Any team member should be allowed *not* to vote, if they so choose.

After agreement has been reached on what level each phenomenon should be placed, the completed PIRT table would appear similar to that shown in Table 14.2. This table shows three levels: high is black, moderate is gray, and low is light-gray. Note that if a particular physical phenomenon is a combination of two other single-physics phenomena, it could be ranked at a higher level than the each of the single-physics phenomena. This could occur because of a strong nonlinear interaction of each of the contributing physical phenomena. One of the most common examples in fluid dynamics is the combination of chemical diffusion reaction and fluid dynamic turbulence. When multiple SRQs are listed in a PIRT table, it should be stressed that the ranking must be consistent across all of the SRQs. Stated differently, the level of ranking is a function of the individual phenomena, *not* the importance of one SRQ relative to another. If ranking of the importance of the individual SRQs is needed, based on the objectives of the PIRT process, this ranking should be done separately.

14.3 Gap analysis process

Because the ASC program was oriented toward developing new mathematical models and codes directed toward project needs, the Sandia researchers significantly extended the concept of a *gap analysis* (Pilch *et al.*, 2001; Tieszen *et al.*, 2002; Trucano *et al.*, 2002; Boughton *et al.*, 2003). In the gap analysis, the emphasis shifts from developing knowledge and prioritizing physical phenomena to an in-depth knowledge of the capabilities *available* in existing software. The key question that is answered in the gap analysis is: *Where does the existing capability presently stand, relative to the phenomena and SRQs that have been identified as important?* To answer this question, different expertise is needed on the team compared to the expertise needed in the construction of the PIRT. For the gap analysis, individuals are needed with knowledge of (a) physics models available in the code, (b) geometry and mesh generation options available in the code, (c) code and solution verification status of the code, (d) validation of the models for the system of interest or related systems, and (e) UQ of predictions for the system of interest or related systems. This is a wide range of expertise needed, but most of these areas could be filled by developers of the code in question, as well as analysts experienced with the system, or similar systems, of interest. New team members with the needed expertise should be added to the existing PIRT team, since the expertise now needed would probably not be represented on the original PIRT team. Some of the existing PIRT team members may choose to drop from the team for the gap analysis portion.

By having code developers or any other proponents of the existing code on the team, a formidable dilemma is posed. The code developers, or their proponents, have a very real vested interest in espousing the capabilities of the code, instead of critically assessing its capabilities. There is no single method of dealing with this situation, because it depends on the individuals and organization involved. The managers responsible for the formation of the gap analysis team, as well as the team leader, must be cognizant of the dilemma posed to the individuals involved. If the code developers or proponents are unrealistic in evaluating the existing capability, or are always on the defensive of criticisms of the code, it can greatly hinder or mislead the gap analysis process. If the code developers or proponents are critical of the existing capability, then they risk severe criticism from their peers or their management. If the existing code being evaluated is from an external organization, for example, commercial software, different issues come into play. These will be briefly discussed in a later section.

Table 14.3 *Example of an initial gap analysis table for a given environment, scenario, and SRQ of interest.*

Gap Areas / Phenomena	Physics Modeling	Code and Solution Verification	Model Validation	Uncertainty Quantification
Physical Phenomenon 1				
Physical Phenomenon 2				
Physical Phenomenon 3				
Physical Phenomenon 1				
Physical Phenomenon 2				
Physical Phenomenon 3				
Physical Phenomenon 4				

14.3.1 Construct the gap analysis table

The gap analysis begins with the information generated in the completed PIRT, Table 14.2. For each SRQ of interest, the most important one or two levels of physical phenomena are singled out for a gap analysis. The most common groups of activities for assessment of gaps are physics modeling, code verification, model validation, and uncertainty quantification. Table 14.3 shows the initial table for a gap analysis for these groups for the top two levels of physical phenomena identified in the PIRT process. In this table it is assumed that there are three phenomena in the top level (indicated by the dark stripe), and four in the second level (indicated by the gray stripe). The order of listing of the phenomena within a level is usually not important at this point.

The purpose of the assessment is to determine if each of the four activities listed across the top of the gap analysis table has been adequately addressed for the physical phenomena so that the SRQ of interest can be adequately predicted. The meaning of *adequacy* depends on the specific activity. In the following, the general question that should be addressed concerning adequacy is listed for each activity, as well as detailed examples of questions for each activity.

1 Physics modeling: does the code have the capability to adequately address the phenomena in question? Examples of detailed questions in this activity are
  • Does it have the ability to model the phenomena, and any physics coupling, over some or all of the physical parameter space of interest?

- Are all of the code options needed to compute the SRQ of interest operational?
- Does the code have alternative models that may be used to deal with the phenomena of interest?
- Are the models physics-based; or are they empirical, data-fit models?
- Does the model have the capability to address the needed spatial and temporal scales in the phenomena?
- Does the model have the flexibility to deal with the geometries of interest, as well as geometry details that may be needed?
- Does the code have all of the material models needed and are they operational over the needed range of parameters?

2 Code and solution verification: has the code undergone adequate code verification testing for the code options that would be used, and can it adequately estimate numerical solution error in the SRQs of interest? Examples of detailed questions in this activity are

- Is there a regression test suite that adequately tests the options that would be used and is it run routinely?
- Have adequate test problems, such as manufactured solutions, been successfully computed that test the software options and algorithms that would be used?
- Are there any outstanding code bugs that have been reported for the code options that would be used?
- Are adequate methods available in the code to estimate or control iterative solution error?
- Are adequate methods available in the code to estimate spatial discretization error in the SRQs of interest?
- Are methods available in the code for generating global mesh refinement with adequate user control e.g., refinement of the mesh uniformly?
- Does the code have the capability for adaptive re-meshing of the domain of interest and, if needed, re-meshing as a function of time?

3 Model validation: is the model validation domain adequate for the phenomena in question, and have adequate quantitative accuracy assessments of the model been made for the SRQ of interest? Examples of detailed questions in this activity are

- At what tiers in the validation hierarchy has the model been compared to experimental measurements for the phenomena in question?
- Has the model been compared to experimental measurements over the range of relevant parameters for the phenomena of interest?
- Was adequate spatial and temporal discretization attained for the comparisons that were made with experimental data to be certain that the physics of the model was evaluated, as opposed to a mixture of physics and numerical error?
- For the comparisons that have been made, is there adequate quantitative agreement between simulation and experiment for the SRQs for the phenomena of interest?
- Have the comparisons that were made adequately related to the phenomena of interest in terms of system geometry and material properties?

4 Uncertainty quantification: is the accuracy of the predicted SRQ of interest, including its estimated uncertainty, adequate for the phenomena of interest? Examples of detailed questions in this activity are

- Are small or large extrapolations of the model required from the validation domain to the conditions and phenomena of interest?

- Are extrapolations required in terms of the relevant parameters for the phenomena of interest, or are the extrapolations required in terms of higher tiers in the validation hierarchy?
- Are the extrapolations based on calibration of the model over the validation domain, or are they based on extrapolation of validation metrics computed over the validation domain?
- Will adequate spatial and temporal discretization be possible for the conditions and phenomena of interest, given the computer resources available?
- Are adequate UQ computational tools and expertise available for the task at hand?
- Are computer resources available to compute an adequate number of simulations to estimate the uncertainty in the SRQ of interest for the phenomena of interest?

Answering these questions requires a great deal of knowledge about the models and the code, forthright assessment of past performance of the models and codes, and a reasonable idea of what is required for the physical phenomena and system of interest. The discussion of these questions among the team should be frank and constructive. The questions should be answered given their status at the time of the gap analysis effort, not some anticipated or hoped for capability or completion date. Many of the issues related to physics modeling, code and solution verification, and model validation are more factual than speculative. For example, they are more of the variety *Does the code have this option?* or *Have we made this comparison with data?* Most of the issues related to uncertainty quantification are more speculative. For example, they are commonly of the type *Do we believe the models or code can do this?* or *How large do we think the uncertainty will be?* On the more speculative questions, expect a wide range of views and substantial debate.

After some level of consensus among the team has been achieved, the gap analysis table can be completed. Table 14.4 shows an example of a completed gap analysis table for a given environment, scenario, and SRQ of interest. This table only shows three levels of assessment: adequate, inadequate, and unknown. When the gap analysis approach was being developed only two levels were available, adequate and inadequate. It was found, however, that there were a number of situations where there was unavailable or conflicting information concerning the adequacy or inadequacy of an activity. As a result, the unknown level was created to keep the gap analysis process moving instead of prolonged debate on the adequacy. As will be discussed in Section 14.3.3, updates and new information can be added to a completed gap analysis table.

Two observations should be pointed out in Table 14.4. First, the most important activities that need to be pursued to close perceived gaps in needed capabilities are those that occur in the most important phenomena. These are denoted by the dark stripe on the left. Which ones to pursue is more than a technical issue, it is also a resource issue and an organizational responsibility issue. Although it is beyond the scope of this discussion to delve into these topics, one example is mentioned. One can have the situation where an important physical phenomenon is assessed *inadequate*, but the organization responsible for the activity either disagrees with this assessment or is unresponsive to the needs of the project sponsoring the gap analysis. Second, note that there is a clear directional nature to the table. Once an unknown or inadequate level occurs for a phenomenon, it only gets worse as one

Table 14.4 *Example of a completed gap analysis table for a given environment, scenario, and SRQ of interest.*

Gap Areas / Phenomena	Physics Modeling	Code and Solution Verification	Model Validation	Uncertainty Quantification
Physical Phenomenon 1	Adequate	? (Unknown)	Inadequate	Inadequate
Physical Phenomenon 2	Adequate	Adequate	Adequate	? (Unknown)
Physical Phenomenon 3	Adequate	Adequate	Inadequate	Inadequate
Physical Phenomenon 1	Adequate	Adequate	Adequate	Adequate
Physical Phenomenon 2	Adequate	Adequate	? (Unknown)	Inadequate
Physical Phenomenon 3	Inadequate	Inadequate	Inadequate	Inadequate
Physical Phenomenon 4	? (Unknown)	Inadequate	Inadequate	Inadequate

Legend: Adequate | Inadequate | ? Unknown

proceeds to the right in the table. For example, if code and solution verification or model validation is unknown or inadequate, uncertainty quantification has little chance of being adequate. It should also be noted that in model validation, if an unknown or inadequate is registered, it may *not* be a modeling deficiency with the code. It may simply be that the experimental data is not available for comparison in order to make the accuracy assessment needed.

14.3.2 Documenting the PIRT and gap analysis processes

Although it is seldom a welcomed task, documentation of the work of the team is an extremely important aspect of the project. The PIRT and gap analysis tables produced capture only the summary information from the processes. A report should be completed that also captures the objectives of the processes, specification of the environments, discovery and description of the scenarios and the SRQs of interest, identification of the plausible phenomena, ranking of the phenomena, and justification of the gap analysis table. The documentation should include the reasoning and arguments made for important decisions, as well as why certain aspects or issues were excluded from the processes.

As discussed earlier in this chapter, the purpose of the PIRT and gap analysis processes is to recommend how best to allocate resources between various activities to achieve success of a project-oriented effort. The PIRT and gap analysis processes should be viewed as a generation of information, which management should use for optimizing the allocation of resources. If the processes are not documented at some appropriate level of formality and detail, then experience has shown that the value and impact of the effort will be minimal. Not only will the resources expended during the processes be wasted, but, more importantly, there could be a major waste of resources in the M&S effort. This waste of information could possibly lead to the failure of the effort, as well as failure of the engineering system to which it is contributing.

14.3.3 Updating the PIRT and gap analysis

The results of the combined PIRT and gap analysis processes should not be viewed as cast in stone once the documentation is complete. It must be fully recognized that the information generated falls into the category of expert opinion. The quality of the expert opinion depends on the quality of the team members and team leadership, how the processes were conducted, and the level of effort expended. With reasonable effort, the information generated is always valuable, but there can be errors and misjudgments in certain aspects of the expert opinion. When new information becomes available, the gap analysis table can be updated, for example: (a) activities marked as unknown can be changed to adequate or inadequate, (b) capabilities are added to a code, or verification testing is completed, (c) experimental data is obtained and model validation activities are conducted, and (d) UQ activities are conducted on a similar system. If appropriate for a large-scale effort, a Gantt chart can be constructed and updated as new information becomes available, particularly when identified gaps in capability are eliminated.

It is to be expected that some surprises will be found in the follow-on efforts related to each activity. Examples of some surprises, most of them bad, which have been observed in practice, are the following.

- A combination of code options that was needed for the physical phenomena of interest was known to be available, but it was discovered that the code would not run the needed combination.
- It was discovered that when a manufactured solution was constructed to test the combination of options needed, the code was found to be 0th order accurate, i.e., it converged to the wrong answer.
- It was discovered that the numerical solution error estimator would not run on the physical phenomenon, i.e., it showed wild oscillations for the problems of interest.
- After an experiment or simulation was conducted, it was found that a physical phenomenon that had been ranked as high importance was changed to moderate importance.
- A model comparison with an experiment that had shown good agreement was recomputed and it was found that when the mesh resolution was improved, the agreement became unacceptable.
- When a new validation experiment was conducted, it was found that a major recalibration of the model parameters had to be conducted to obtain good agreement with the data.
- When an alternative plausible model for a physical phenomenon was used to compute the SRQ of interest, it was found that there was a large disagreement compared to the traditional model used.

14.4 Planning and prioritization with commercial codes

Our discussion on P&P has concentrated on large-scale M&S projects that are conducted primarily within an organization. Here we make several comments concerning how P&P would be conducted differently by an organization that is using, or is considering using, commercial software. The context of P&P when using commercial software must be understood as a business relationship between the organization doing the planning and the software company, *not* a technical relationship. Technical issues are certainly important, especially to staff members, but the dominant issue is: *can the organization build a strategic business relationship with a software company as a stakeholder?* If the organization only has relatively few software licenses from the software company, it is doubtful that a substantive relationship can be built. The software company may proclaim how important a stakeholder relationship is to them, but if few licenses are involved, there will be little genuineness in the claim. Only when the software company becomes a true stakeholder can the kind of P&P discussed here be accomplished.

An important aspect that management of the organization needs to consider before a stakeholder relationship is considered is the question of confidence that the software company can and will protect their proprietary information. The proprietary information would not only deal with existing products the organization sells, but also research information, proprietary experimental data, proposal information, and designs for new products. The mind set toward information within a software company is typically very different from a company that designs and sells hardware products. If the organization is dealing with a large software company, then another issue comes into play. The software company may also be working closely with a competitor of the organization. For example, the same software company may have information on, or be working on, two competing proposals from their clients.

To conduct the gap analysis discussed here, the software company would need to be an intimate part of the discussions and probably represented on the gap analysis team. The software company individuals on the team would need to be very candid and constructively critical of their own company's product. When explicitly discussing shortcomings in their software, they would be concerned about potentially losing the organization's business, as well as detrimental information being passed on to other potential new customers for their software. It is clear this is a delicate business as well as technical issue. On the one hand, the organization needs to be certain it will obtain forthright information from the software company. On the other hand, the software company needs to be certain it will not lose its client, nor have its skeletons in the closet exposed for public consumption.

As a final topic, consider the issue of ownership of software capabilities. Suppose that after a gap analysis has been completed, it is found that a new capability is needed in the commercial software. The software company may decide it would be in its best interest to fund the development and testing of the new capability. It may decide, however, that it has other priorities for new capability development. Suppose the new capability is of high importance to the company conducting the planning so that it will fund the development and testing of the new capability as an add-on, standalone feature, to the code. If so, then the planning issues will also include the level of support and information needed from the software company. It may even involve proprietary information from the software company, requiring negotiated contracts protecting the intellectual property of the software company.

Suppose, however, the organization did not have the expertise to develop and test the new capability, or the capability must be added directly in the source code. The organization may fund the software company to develop, test, and document the new capability. Then the question must be addressed: who will own the new capability? The organization would primarily view the issue as: what is the return on investment for funding the new capability? It may also want increase its return on investment by not allowing any competitor to use the capability. The software company would view the issue as: how can we increase our software license sales by advertising this new capability to existing or potential new customers? Various solutions to these differing perspectives would need to be carefully negotiated between the organization and the software company. One idea would be to allow the organization to have exclusive rights to use the new capability for a set period of time in the future. In addition, the software company could not advertise or discuss the capability until after that time period.

14.5 Example problem: aircraft fire spread during crash landing

The example discussed here is concerned with fire spreading on board a commercial transport aircraft during a crash landing. The abnormal environment is defined to be a survivable crash and the fuel fire initiates immediately after initial contact of the aircraft with the ground. The goal of the PIRT analysis is to identify and rank the importance of the physical phenomena with regard to the survivability of the passengers to the fire environment. The goal of the gap analysis is to identify the important gaps in an existing capability for predicting certain SRQs of interest. In our discussion, we will identify various scenarios and SRQs, but only one branch of the scenario-SRQ tree will be pursued.

The environment is specified as:

- the aircraft has a single aisle and carries 150 passengers and crew;
- the crash does minor damage to the aircraft cabin structure;
- the fuel carried on board is JET A-1, and the quantity can range from 1000 L to 25 000 L;
- the fire initiates in the undercarriage of the aircraft as it first impacts the ground.

The scenarios are specified as:

- Scenario 1: 1000 L of fuel are on board, the landing gear is extended and has minor damage during landing rollout on a runway, and fully equipped aircraft rescue and firefighting (ARFF) personnel arrive at the aircraft in 2 min.
- Scenario 2: 25 000 L of fuel are on board, the landing gear is extended, but it is destroyed during rollout on a runway, and fully equipped ARFF personnel arrive at the crash in 5 min.

Table 14.5 *Completed PIRT for the aircraft fire environment and scenario 3.*

Physical Phenomena \ SRQ	SRQ 1	SRQ 2	SRQ 3	SRQ 4	SRQ 5
Convective: Buoyant turbulent mixing	Moderate	Moderate	Moderate	Moderate	High
Convective: Combusting turbulent flow	High	High	High	High	High
Convective: Wind effects	Moderate	Moderate	Moderate	High	High
Mass transport: Fuel evaporation	Moderate	Moderate	Moderate	Moderate	Low
Chemistry: Fuel combustion	Moderate	Moderate	Moderate	High	Low
Chemistry: Soot production	Low	High	Moderate	Moderate	Moderate
Chemistry: Cabin material combustion	High	High	High	Moderate	Low
Chemistry: Carbon monoxide production	Low	Moderate	High	Moderate	Low
Radiation: Emissive flux soot formation	Moderate	High	Moderate	Moderate	Low
Radiation: Emissive flux combustion chemistry	Moderate	High	Moderate	Moderate	Low
Radiation: Mesoscale turbulent mixing	Moderate	High	Moderate	Moderate	Moderate
Radiation: Material properties in cabin	High	High	High	Moderate	Low
Radiation: Material properties of emergency slide	Low	Low	Low	High	Moderate
Conduction: Through aluminum structure	Low	Low	Low	Moderate	Moderate
Structure: Aluminum melting	Low	Low	Low	Moderate	Moderate
Structure: Emergency slide melting	Low	Low	Low	High	Moderate

High Importance   **Moderate Importance**   **Low Importance**

- Scenario 3: 1000 L of fuel are on board, the landing gear is not deployed before ground impact, there is considerable damage to the underbelly of the aircraft during impact and deceleration on an open field, and no ARFF personnel are available.

A team of experts with the needed expertise was formed to conduct the PIRT and gap analysis. The key modeling expertise needed for the PIRT are combustion modeling of a wide range of materials, toxicology, fluid dynamics, heat transfer, and solid dynamics. The team was not given the SRQs of interest as part of the goals of the analysis, so these had to be defined. A number of possible SRQs were considered by the team to try to determine what were appropriate quantities for gauging the survivability and escape of the passengers and crew from the burning aircraft. The following quantities were chosen for all three scenarios:

- SRQ 1: gas temperature at mid-height of the cabin, along the center of the aisle, as a function of time;
- SRQ 2: soot temperature at mid-height of the cabin, along the center of the aisle, as a function of time;
- SRQ 3: carbon monoxide concentration at mid-height of the cabin, along the center of the aisle, as a function of time;

Table 14.6 *Completed gap analysis table for the aircraft fire environment, scenario 3, and SRQ 1.*

Gap Areas / Phenomena	Physics Modeling	Code and Solution Verification	Model Validation	Uncertainty Quantification
Convective: Combusting turbulent flow			?	
Chemistry: Cabin material combustion				
Radiation: Material properties in cabin				
Convective: Buoyant turbulent mixing		?	?	
Convective: Wind effects				
Chemistry: Fuel combustion			?	
Radiation: Emissive Flux soot formation				

	Adequate		Inadequate	?	Unknown

- SRQ 4: time of collapse of the emergency exit slide due to melting;
- SRQ 5: gas temperature along a vertical line from the top of each cabin exit to the ground, as a function of time.

Plausible physical phenomena were considered that could affect each of the scenarios and the prediction of the SRQs of interest. The key difference between scenarios 1 and 2 and scenario 3 is the effect of the ARFF personnel in containing and controlling the fire. In addition to the fire-spread issues, scenarios 1 and 2 would also need to deal directly with physical phenomena related to various foams, fire fighting, and life-saving tactics. In scenario 3, these phenomena would not come into play. Table 14.5 lists all the physical phenomena considered by the team for scenario 3. The table also shows the results of the team's analysis yielding three levels of importance ranking of phenomena for each SRQ.

The team was then asked to conduct a gap analysis for the physical phenomena and the SRQs identified in Table 14.5. The code being assessed was an existing in-house code. Since some of the PIRT analysis team members were unfamiliar with the code, new team members were added that were part of the team that developed the code, as well as those that provide maintenance and support for the code.

The four areas of assessment of the existing code were physics modeling, code and solution verification, model validation, and uncertainty quantification. A gap analysis table was then constructed for each of the SRQs listed in Table 14.5, considering only the high and moderate importance levels. Table 14.6 shows the completed gap analysis table for SRQ 1.

As can be seen from the gap analysis, the existing code did not fare very well. In two of the three high importance phenomena it is missing modeling options for combustion chemistry of cabin material and properties for materials commonly occurring in cabin interiors. In addition, its existing validation domain had very little overlap with this application domain and/or its level of agreement with existing validation data was inadequate for the present application. This type of gap analysis result commonly occurs when existing codes are assessed for new applications. If one were to rely on the broad claims and advertising of code capabilities, a project or a proposal effort could be severely misled. Even though this experience is widely recognized, it is still very difficult to convince project managers, especially for proposal efforts, to set aside time and resources to make informed decisions concerning needed capabilities and existing deficiencies.

14.6 References

Boughton, B., V. J. Romero, S. R. Tieszen, and K. B. Sobolik (2003). *Integrated Modeling and Simulation Validation Plan for W80–3 Abnormal Thermal Environment Qualification – Version 1.0 (OUO)*. SAND2003–4152 (OUO), Albuquerque, NM, Sandia National Laboratories.

Boyack, B. E., I. Catton, R. B. Duffey, P. Griffith, K. R. Katsma, G. S. Lellouche, S. Levy, U. S. Rohatgi, G. E. Wilson, W. Wulff, and N. Zuber (1990). Quantifying reactor safety margins, Part 1: An overview of the code scaling, applicability, and uncertainty evaluation methodology. *Nuclear Engineering and Design*. **119**, 1–15.

Charette, R. N. (2005). Why software fails. *IEEE Spectrum*. September.

Dorner, D. (1989). *The Logic of Failure, Recognizing and Avoiding Error in Complex Situations*, Cambridge, MA, Perseus Books.

Flowers, S. (1996). *Software Failures: Management Failure: Amazing Stories and Cautionary Tales*, New York, John Wiley.

Galin, D. (2003). *Software Quality Assurance: From Theory to Implementation*, Upper Saddle River, NJ, Addison Wesley.

Hanson, R. G., G. E. Wilson, M. G. Ortiz, and D. P. Grigges (1992). Development of a phenomena identification and ranking table (PIRT) for a postulated double-ended guillotine break in a production reactor. *Nuclear Engineering and Design*. **136**, 335–346.

Karolak, D. W. (1996). *Software Engineering Risk Management*, Los Alamitos, CA, IEEE Computer Society Press.

Kroeger, P. G., U. S. Rohatgi, J. H. Jo, and G. C. Slovik (1998). *Preliminary Phenomena Identification and Ranking Tables for Simplified Boiling Water Reactor Loss-of-Coolant Accident Scenarios*. Upton, NY, Brookhaven National Laboratory.

NRC (1988). *Acceptance Criteria for Emergency Core Cooling Systems for Light Water Reactors*. U. S. N. R. Commission, U. S. Code of Federal Regulations. 10 CFR 50.

Pilch, M., T. G. Trucano, J. L. Moya, G. K. Froehlich, A. L. Hodges, and D. E. Peercy (2001). *Guidelines for Sandia ASCI Verification and Validation Plans – Content and*

Format: Version 2. SAND2000–3101, Albuquerque, NM, Sandia National Laboratories.

Rohatgi, U. S., H. S. Cheng, H. J. Khan, and W. Wulff (1997). *Preliminary Phenomena Identification and Ranking Tables (PIRT) for SBWR Start-Up Stability*. NUREG/CR-6474, Upton, NY, Brookhaven National Laboratory.

Saaty, T. L. (2001). *Decision Making for Leaders – the Analytic Hierarchy Process for Decisions in a Complex World*. 3rd edn., Pittsburgh, PA, RWS Publications.

Shaw, R. A., T. K. Larson, and R. K. Dimenna (1988). *Development of a Phenomena Identification and Ranking Table (PIRT) for Thermal-Hydraulic Phenomena during a PWR LBLOCA*. Idaho Falls, ID, EG&G.

Stepanek, G. (2005). *Software Project Secrets: Why Software Projects Fail*, Berkeley, CA, Apress.

Tieszen, S. R., T. Y. Chu, D. Dobranich, V. J. Romero, T. G. Trucano, J. T. Nakos, W. C. Moffatt, T. F. Hendrickson, K. B. Sobolik, S. N. Kempka, and M. Pilch (2002). *Integrated Modeling and Simulation Validation Plan for W76–1 Abnormal Thermal Environment Qualification – Version 1.0 (OUO)*. SAND2002–1740 (OUO), Albuquerque, Sandia National Laboratories.

Trucano, T. G., M. Pilch, and W. L. Oberkampf (2002). *General Concepts for Experimental Validation of ASCI Code Applications*. SAND2002–0341, Albuquerque, NM, Sandia National Laboratories.

Vose, D. (2008). *Risk Analysis: a Quantitative Guide*. 3rd edn., New York, Wiley.

Wiegers, K. E. (2003). *Software Requirements*. 2nd edn., Redmond, Microsoft Press.

Wilson, G. E. and B. E. Boyack (1998). The role of the PIRT in experiments, code development and code applications associated with reactor safety assessment. *Nuclear Engineering and Design*. **186**, 23–37.

Wilson, G. E., B. E. Boyack, I. Catton, R. B. Duffey, P. Griffith, K. R. Katsma, G. S. Lellouche, S. Levy, U. S. Rohatgi, W. Wulff, and N. Zuber (1990). Quantifying reactor safety margins, Part 2: Characterization of important contributors to uncertainty. *Nuclear Engineering and Design*. **119**, 17–31.

Wulff, W., B. E. Boyack, I. Catton, R. B. Duffey, P. Griffith, K. R. Katsma, G. S. Lellouche, S. Levy, U. S. Rohatgi, G. E. Wilson, and N. Zuber (1990). Quantifying reactor safety margins, Part 3: Assessment and ranging of parameters. *Nuclear Engineering and Design*. **119**, 33–65.

15

Maturity assessment of modeling and simulation

In Chapter 1, Introduction, we briefly discussed how credibility is built in modeling and simulation (M&S). The four elements mentioned in that chapter were: quality of the analysts conducting the analysis, quality of the physics modeling, verification and validation activities, and uncertainty quantification and sensitivity analysis. The latter three elements are technical elements that can be assessed for completeness or maturity. Assessment of maturity is important to the staff conducting the modeling and simulation effort, but it is critically important for project managers and decision makers who use computational results as an element in their decision making. It is also important for internal or external review committees who are asked to provide recommendations on the credibility and soundness of computational analyses. This chapter deals with reviewing methods that have been developed for assessing similar activities, and then presents a newly developed technique reported in Oberkampf *et al.* (2007). This chapter is taken in large part from this reference.

15.1 Survey of maturity assessment procedures

Over the last decade, a number of researchers have investigated how to measure the maturity and credibility of software and hardware development processes and products. Probably the best-known procedure for measuring the maturity of software product development and business processes is the Capability Maturity Model Integration (CMMI). The CMMI is a successor to the Capability Maturity Model (CMM). Development of the CMM was initiated in 1987 to improve software quality. For an extensive discussion of the framework and methods for the CMMI, see West (2004); Ahern *et al.* (2005); Garcia and Turner (2006); and Chrissis *et al.* (2007). The CMMI, and other approaches discussed here, respond to the need for measuring the maturity (i.e., some sense of quality, capability and completeness) of a process to do one or more of the following:

- improve identification and understanding of the elements of the process;
- determine the elements of the process that may need improvement so that the intended product of the process can be improved;
- determine how time and resources can best be invested in elements of the process to obtain the maximum return on the investment expended;

- better estimate the cost and schedule required to improve elements of the process;
- improve the methods of aggregating maturity information from diverse elements of the process to better summarize the overall maturity of the process;
- improve the methods of communicating to the decision maker the maturity of the process so that better risk-informed decisions can be made;
- measure the progress of improving the process so that managers of the process, stakeholders, and funding sources can determine the value added over time;
- compare elements of the process across competitive organizations so that a collection of best practices can be developed and used;
- measure the maturity of the process in relation to requirements imposed by the customer.

The CMMI was developed by the Software Engineering Institute, a Federally funded research and development center sponsored by the US Department of Defense (DoD) and operated by Carnegie Mellon University. The latest release of the CMMI is CMMI for Development, (CMMI-DEV version 1.2) (Garcia and Turner, 2006; SEI, 2006; Chrissis *et al.*, 2007). The CMMI-DEV is divided into four process areas: engineering, process management, project management, and support (Garcia and Turner, 2006). The engineering process area is further divided into six subareas: product integration, requirements development, requirements management, technical solution, verification, and validation. The meaning of V&V referred to in the CMMI-DEV relates to concepts developed by the Institute of Electrical and Electronics Engineers (IEEE) for software quality engineering (SQE) (IEEE, 1989). As discussed in Chapter 2, Fundamental concepts and terminology, these concepts of V&V are quite different from those used in this book.

A maturity measurement system that has its origins in risk management is the Technology Readiness Levels (TRLs) system pioneered by NASA in the late 1980s (Mankins, 1995). The intent of TRLs is to lower acquisition risks of high technology systems by more precisely and uniformly assessing the maturity of a technology. TRLs are used in both NASA and the DoD. We do not review TRLs in detail in this document, but the interested reader can consult GAO (1999) for more information. TRLs consider nine levels of maturity in the evolution of technological systems. These levels are described by the DoD in DoD (2005) as follows.

- *TRL Level 1: Basic principles observed and reported.* Lowest level of technology readiness. Scientific research begins to be translated into applied research and development. Examples might include paper studies of a technology's basic properties.
- *TRL Level 2: Technology concept and/or application formulated.* Invention begins. Once basic principles are observed, practical applications can be invented. The application is speculative and there is no proof or detailed analysis to support the assumption. Examples are still limited to paper studies.
- *TRL Level 3: Analytical and experimental critical function and/or characteristic proof of concept.* Active research and development is initiated. This includes analytical studies and laboratory studies to physically validate analytical predictions of separate elements of the technology. Examples include components that are not yet integrated or representative.

- *TRL Level 4: Component and/or breadboard validation in laboratory environment.* Basic technological components are integrated to establish that the pieces will work together. This is relatively low fidelity compared to the final system. Examples include integration of *ad hoc* hardware in a laboratory.
- *TRL Level 5: Component and/or breadboard validation in relevant environment.* Fidelity of breadboard technology, i.e. experimental electrical circuit prototype, increases significantly. The basic technological components are integrated with reasonably realistic supporting elements so that the technology can be tested in a simulated environment. An example is high-fidelity laboratory integration of components.
- *TRL Level 6: System/subsystem model or prototype demonstration in a relevant environment.* A representative model or prototype system, which is well beyond the breadboard tested for TRL 5, is tested in a relevant environment. This represents a major step up in a technology's demonstrated readiness. Examples include testing a prototype in a high-fidelity laboratory environment or in a simulated operational environment.
- *TRL Level 7: System prototype demonstration in an operational environment.* The prototype is near or at the planned operational system. This represents a major step up from TRL 6, requiring the demonstration of an actual system prototype in an operational environment with representatives of the intended user organization(s). Examples include testing the prototype in structured or actual field use.
- *TRL Level 8: Actual system completed and operationally qualified through test and demonstration.* The technology has been proven to work in its final form and under expected operational conditions. In almost all cases, this TRL represents the end of true system development. Examples include developmental test and evaluation of the system in its intended or pre-production configuration to determine if it meets design specifications and operational suitability.
- *TRL Level 9: Actual system, proven through successful mission operations.* The technology is applied in its production configuration under mission conditions, such as those encountered in operational test and evaluation. In almost all cases, this is the last *bug* fixing aspect of true system development. An example is operation of the system under operational mission conditions.

The nominal specifications of TRLs as presented above are clearly aimed at assessing the maturity of hardware products, *not* software products. Smith (2004) has examined the difficulties in using TRLs for nondevelopmental software, including commercial-off-the-shelf (COTS) and government-off-the-shelf (GOTS) software and open sources of software technology and products. Clay *et al.* (2007) have also studied the issue of using TRLs to assess the maturity of M&S software. Both studies concluded that significant changes in TRLs are needed before they would be useful for assessing the maturity of software. Stated more directly, TRLs are *not* useful for assessing the maturity of software of any kind. Whether they are useful in assessing the likelihood of the successful completion of a proposed hardware system (in the sense of attaining the planned cost, schedule, and performance), is clearly debatable.

A maturity assessment procedure that deals more directly with M&S processes than the CMMI and the TRLs has been developed by Balci *et al.* (2002) and Balci (2004). He argues that M&S quality can be assessed based on indicators of product, process, and project. By *product* he means either (a) the overall completed M&S application, or

(b) a work product created during the M&S development life cycle such as the conceptual model, M&S requirements specification, M&S design specification, and an executable M&S module. By *process* he refers to the process used to create a work product during the M&S development life cycle, such as conceptual modeling, requirements, engineering, design, implementation, integration, experimentation, and presentation. *Project* refers to the quality indicators of the project plan, the capabilities and experience of the organization conducting the M&S, and the technical quality of the people tasked to develop the M&S application. Some of the attributes of the assessment of quality of product, process, and project are: accuracy, verity, validity, clarity, completeness, acceptability, maintainability, timeliness, reliability, robustness, supportability, understandability, visibility, and maturity.

Harmon and Youngblood (2003, 2005) focus on assessing the maturity of the validation process for simulation models. Their work takes the encompassing view of validation, as is commonly taken by the DoD. As discussed in Section 2.2.3, the *encompassing view* means that the term "validated model" denotes that the following three related issues have been addressed with regard to the accuracy and adequacy of the M&S results.

- The system response quantities (SRQs) of interest produced by the model have been assessed for accuracy with respect to some referent.
- The model's domain of intended use is defined and the model can be applied over this domain.
- The model meets the accuracy requirements for the "representation of the real world" over the domain of its intended use.

It should be noted here that the perspective of validation taken by the AIAA and the ASME is that the referent can *only be experimentally measured data*. The DoD does not take this restrictive perspective. Thus, the DoD permits the referent to be, for example, results from other computer models, as well as expert opinion.

Harmon and Youngblood (2003, 2005) clearly state that validation is a process that generates information about the accuracy and adequacy of the simulation model as its sole product. They argue that the properties of information quality are defined by (a) correctness of the information, (b) completeness of the information, and (c) confidence that the information is correct for the intended use of the model. They view the validation process as using information from five contributing elements: (1) the conceptual model of the simulation, (2) verification results from intermediate development products, (3) the validation referent, (4) the validation criteria, and (5) the simulation results. The technique used by Harmon and Youngblood (2003, 2005) ranks each of these five elements into six levels of maturity. From lowest to highest the six levels of maturity are:

1 we have no idea of the maturity;
2 it works, trust me;
3 it represents the right entities and attributes;
4 it does the right things; its representations are complete enough;
5 for what it does, its representations are accurate enough;
6 I'm confident this simulation is valid.

Pilch *et al.* (2004) proposed a framework for how M&S can contribute to the nuclear weapons program of the US. They suggested that there are four key contributors to M&S: qualified computational practitioners, qualified codes, qualified computational infrastructure, and appropriate levels of formality. As part of qualified codes, Pilch *et al.* described nine elements:

1 request for service,
2 project plan development,
3 technical plan development,
4 technical plan review,
5 application-specific calculation assessment,
6 solution verification,
7 uncertainty quantification,
8 qualification and acceptance,
9 documentation and archiving.

For each of these elements, Pilch *et al.* (2004) described the key issues and the key evidence artifacts that should be produced. They also described four levels of formality that would generally apply over a wide range of M&S situations:

1 formality appropriate for research and development tasks, such as improving the scientific understanding of physical phenomena;
2 formality appropriate for nuclear weapon design support;
3 formality appropriate for nuclear weapon qualification support, i.e., confidence in component performance is supported by simulations;
4 formality appropriate for qualification of nuclear weapon components, i.e., confidence in component performance is heavily based on simulations.

Pilch *et al.* then constructed a table with rows corresponding to the nine elements and the columns corresponding to the four levels of formality. In each element of the table, the characteristics that should be achieved for a given element at a given level of maturity are listed. This table, or matrix, could then be used to assess the maturity of a M&S effort.

NASA recently released a technical standard that specifically deals with M&S as it contributes to decision making (NASA, 2008). The primary goal of this standard is to ensure that the credibility of the results from M&S is properly conveyed to those making critical decisions. Critical decisions are those related to design, development, manufacturing, ground or flight operations that may impact human safety or program/project-defined mission success criteria. The secondary goal is to assess whether the credibility of the results meets the project requirements. This standard is intended to ensure that sufficient details of the M&S process are available to support project requirements and to respond to in-depth queries by the decision maker. The standard applies to M&S used by NASA and its contractors for critical decisions in design, development, manufacturing, ground operations, and flight operations. The standard also applies to the use of legacy as well as COTS, GOTS, and modified-off-the-shelf (MOTS) M&S to support critical decisions. NASA staff developed the standard with an intensive effort over a period of three years.

The following references give a description of its development and examples of the use of the standard in various projects: (Bertch *et al.*, 2008; Blattnig *et al.*, 2008; Green *et al.*, 2008; Steele, 2008).

The NASA standard describes a credibility assessment scale for assessing the credibility of M&S results. The scale defines eight factors for assessing credibility (NASA, 2008).

1 *Verification*: Were the models implemented correctly, and what was the numerical error/uncertainty?
2 *Validation*: Did the M&S results compare favorably to the referent data, and how close is the referent to the real-world system?
3 *Input pedigree*: How confident are we of the current input data?
4 *Results uncertainty*: What is the uncertainty in the current M&S results?
5 *Results robustness*: How thoroughly are the sensitivities of the current M&S results known?
6 *Use history*: Have the current M&S been used successfully before?
7 *M&S management*: How well managed were the M&S processes?
8 *People qualifications*: How qualified were the personnel?

These eight factors are grouped into three categories: (a) M&S development (verification and validation), (b) M&S operations (input pedigree, results uncertainty, and results robustness), and (c) supporting evidence (use history, M&S management, and people qualifications). The M&S development and M&S operations categories have two subfactors for evaluation (evidence and technical review), whereas supporting evidence does not have subfactors.

Each of the eight factors given above has five levels of credibility or maturity that are numerically quantified as 0, 1, 2, 3, and 4. There is no uniform description or characterization of the requirements needed to attain a given level across each of the eight factors. That is, each factor has specific descriptors to characterize what is needed to achieve a specific level, except for level 0. Level 0 means either that no evidence exists for that factor, or that the evidence that does exist does not meet even the level 1 criteria. Although no uniform characterization is provided, increasing credibility levels must demonstrate increasing accuracy, formality, and recommended practice.

The final contribution to the literature reviewed comes from the field of information theory. If one agrees with the concept of Harmon and Youngblood (2003, 2005), as we do, that the product of M&S is information, then one must address the fundamental aspects of information quality. Wang and Strong (1996) conducted an extensive survey of information consumers to determine the important attributes of information quality. Stated differently, they went directly to a very wide range of customers that use, act on, and purchase information to determine what were the most important qualities of information. Wang and Strong (1996) analyzed the survey results and then categorized the attributes into four aspects.

- *intrinsic information quality*: believability, accuracy, objectivity, and reputation;
- *contextual information quality*: value added, relevancy, timeliness, completeness, and amount of information;

- *representational information quality*: interpretability, ease of understanding, consistent representation, and concise representation;
- *accessibility information quality*: accessibility and security aspects.

If the user of the information is not adequately satisfied with essentially all of these important attributes, then the user could (a) make minimal use of the information for the decision at hand; (b) completely ignore the information; or (c) misuse the information, either intentionally or unintentionally. These outcomes range from wasting information (and the time and resources expended to create it) to a potentially disastrous result caused by misuse of the information.

15.2 Predictive capability maturity model

Building on this previous work, we now describe the *predictive capability maturity model* (PCMM), also referred to as the predictive capability maturity matrix. The present version of the PCMM was first documented in Oberkampf *et al.* (2007) and has been tested in various forms at Sandia National Laboratories since 2005. During this time there was close collaboration with Thomas Zang of NASA and his team in the development of both the Interim NASA Standard (NASA, 2006) and the final NASA Standard (NASA, 2008).

The PCMM was developed to focus more on the computational aspects of M&S as compared to the broader class of models considered in the NASA Standard or the work of Harmon and Youngblood (2003, 2005). There is no single best method for assessing maturity in M&S. One should choose the method that is best suited for the type of M&S activity in question.

15.2.1 Structure of the PCMM

As can be seen in the literature review, a number of similar elements have been identified as contributors to the confidence one should place in the simulation activity itself and in the results of the activity. The PCMM identifies six elements that fundamentally contribute to the credibility of the simulation. These elements are as follows:

- representation and geometric fidelity,
- physics and material model fidelity,
- code verification,
- solution verification,
- model validation,
- uncertainty quantification and sensitivity analysis.

Each of these six elements is defined for minimal overlap or dependency between the elements; i.e., each element attempts to contribute a separate type of information to the simulation activity. The elements listed are some of the most important contributors to simulation credibility, as well as the conceptual issues related to the four aspects of information quality identified by Wang and Strong (1996). When researchers at Sandia attempted to use the approaches discussed in the literature review given above, it was concluded that the primary shortcoming was representational information quality, specifically interpretability. That is, previous work, in our view, lacked a clear and unambiguous specification of what the information meant and how it should be used. We discovered that the primary reason for the shortcoming was that previous work had not adequately segregated some of the underlying conceptual issues, particularly what was being assessed. Was it the quality of the simulation process or the quality of the simulation results that was being assessed? Without improved interpretability, decision makers cannot properly use and act on the information produced in an assessment. These issues will be discussed further in Section 15.2.2.

Of the six elements identified only two, representation and geometric fidelity and physics and material model fidelity, have not been discussed in detail earlier in this book. These will be briefly discussed below because they have been identified as important contributors to simulation maturity. In addition, all the approaches discussed in the literature review agree that some type of graded scale is needed to measure the maturity, or confidence, of each contributing element. This topic will also be discussed in the following.

15.2.1.1 Representation and geometric fidelity

Representational and geometric modeling fidelity refers to the level of detail included in the spatial and temporal definition of all constituent elements of the system being analyzed. Note that when we refer to a *system*, we mean *any* engineered system, e.g., a subsystem, a component, or a part of a component. In M&S, the representational and geometric definition of a system is commonly specified in a computer-aided design (CAD) software package. The traditional emphasis in CAD packages has been on manufacturing-related dimensional, fabrication, and assembly specifications. As M&S has matured, CAD vendors are now beginning to address issues that are specifically important to computational-analysis needs, e.g., mesh generation and feature definitions that are important to various types of physics modeling. Even though some progress has been made that eases the transition from traditional CAD files to the construction of a computational mesh, a great deal of work still needs to be done. Aside from geometry clean-up and simplification activities, which are directed at making CAD geometries more useful in simulation, there is no general process for verifying that the CAD geometries loaded into calculations are appropriate and consistent with the physics modeling assumptions. A key issue that complicates the mapping of CAD geometries to a geometry ready for construction of a computational mesh is that the mapping is dependent on the particular type of physics to be modeled and the specific assumptions in the modeling. For example, a change in strength of material properties along the surface of a flight vehicle would be important to a structural dynamics analysis, but it may not be important to an aerodynamic or electromagnetic analysis. As a result, the CAD vendors cannot provide a simple or algorithmic method to address the wide variety of feature definitions and nuances required for different types of physics model. The time-consuming task of addressing detailed representation and geometric fidelity issues becomes the responsibility of technically trained staff with different backgrounds, such as CAD package developers, computational scientists, and mesh-generation experts.

15.2.1.2 Physics and material model fidelity

It is well recognized that improvement in the fidelity of physics modeling has been the dominant theme pursued in most simulations directed toward engineering systems. The range of physics modeling fidelity can vary from empirical models that are based on the fitting of experimental data (empirical models) to what is typically called *first-principles physics*. The three types of model in this range are referred to here as fully empirical models, semi-empirical models, and physics-based models. Physical process models that are *completely* built on statistical fits of experimental data are referred to as *fully empirical models*. These fully empirical models typically have *no* relationship to physics-based principles. Consequently, the fully empirical models rest entirely on the calibration of responses to identified input parameters over a specified range and should not be used (extrapolated) beyond their calibration domain. A *semi-empirical model* is partially based on physical principles and is highly calibrated by experimental data for the system or process of interest. An example of a semi-empirical model that has been heavily used in nuclear reactor safety is the control volume, or lumped parameter, model. Semi-empirical models typically conserve mass, momentum, and energy, but at clearly finite physical scales compared to the system of interest. For example, a 3-D system may be divided into $10 \times 10 \times 10$ control volumes in an analysis. In addition, they rely heavily on fitting experimental data as a function of dimensional or nondimensional parameters, such as Reynolds or Nusselt numbers, to calibrate the models. By *physics-based models* we mean models that are heavily reliant on partial differential or integro-differential equations that represent conservation of mass, momentum, and energy at infinitesimal length and time scales relative to the physical scales in the system. Some physicists use the term first-principles, or *ab initio*, physics to mean modeling that starts at the atomic or molecular level. These models, however, are essentially never used in design and analysis of engineering systems.

Another important aspect of physics modeling fidelity is the degree to which various types of physics are coupled in the mathematical model of the system. For fully empirical and semi-empirical models, strong assumptions are made to greatly simplify the physics considered, and little or no coupling of different types of physics is included. For physics-based models, however, the modeling assumptions must include various types of physical phenomena, as well as certain types of physics coupling. As shown in Figure 15.1, two basic approaches are used to couple the physics involved in the physical process:

- one-way causal effect, i.e., one physical phenomenon affects other phenomena, but the other phenomena do not affect the originating phenomenon; and
- two-way interactions, i.e., all physical phenomena affect all other physical phenomena.

In physics-based modeling, each physical phenomenon is represented by a mathematical model with boundary conditions (BCs) and initial conditions (ICs). In one-way coupling (Figure 15.1a), the physics of phenomenon 1 affect phenomena 2 and 3, but there is no direct

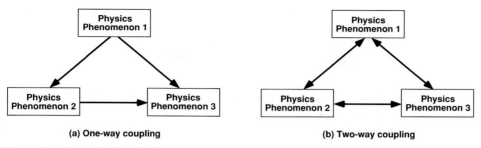

Figure 15.1 Example of two basic types of coupling of physical phenomena (Oberkampf *et al.*, 2007).

feedback from phenomena 2 and 3 to phenomenon 1. Phenomenon 1 affects phenomena 2 and 3 either by way of BCs or through some type of system excitation, e.g., the addition of a source term on the right side of the PDEs for phenomena 2 and 3. In addition, as shown in Figure 15.1a, the BCs or source terms of phenomenon 3 are determined by phenomenon 2. In two-way coupling (Figure 15.1b), all phenomena in the system affect all other phenomena. This two-way interaction can be modeled as strong coupling, where two or more phenomena are modeled within the same mathematical model, or as weak coupling, where the interactions between phenomena occur through BCs between separate sets of mathematical models. If one has a time-dependent mathematical model, this coupling can be either accounted for iteratively within each time step or accounted for in the next time step computed, i.e., time-lagged coupling.

15.2.1.3 Maturity assessment

In the review of the literature given above, three methods were described for ranking the maturity of the various simulation elements. The five-point maturity ranking scale of Harmon and Youngblood (2003, 2005) was dominated by the concepts of credibility, objectivity, and sufficiency of accuracy for the intended use. The four-point scale of Pilch *et al.* (2004) was dominated by the level of formality, the degree of risk in the decision based on the simulation effort, the importance of the decision to which the simulation effort contributes, and sufficiency of accuracy for the intended use. The five-point scale of NASA (2008) displays increasing accuracy, formality, and recommended practice, *excluding* the adequacy requirements of the simulation results. NASA clearly separated the ideas of credibility assessment of the simulation results from the requirements for a given application that use the simulation results.

Comparing each of these three maturity-ranking methods, we first note that the methods use scales of different magnitude for ranking maturity. We believe, however, that this difference is not fundamentally important. The key difference in our opinion between the three methods is that only the NASA scale *explicitly excludes* the issue pertaining to adequacy in the maturity assessment; adequacy is addressed *after* the assessment. We believe this was a major step forward in the interpretability of the assessment of a simulation effort because it segregates the assessed maturity of the results from the issue of required maturity (or credibility) of the results, as might be independently specified. We expect that some users of a maturity assessment would prefer to have the maturity scale include, or at least imply, the adequacy of the results for some intended use because it would seem to make their decisions easier. However, we strongly believe that the issues of maturity assessment and maturity assessment requirements should be dealt with independently as much as possible to reduce misunderstandings or misuse of a maturity assessment.

Pilch *et al.* (2004, 2006) discuss a method for assessing the maturity of each simulation element based on the risk tolerance of the decision maker. Stated differently, the maturity scale would be given an ordinal ranking based on the risk assumed by the decision maker who uses results generated by the simulation effort. This approach has some appealing features, but it also introduces additional complexities. We mention three difficulties in using a risk-based scale that have practical impact when constructing a maturity scale.

First, risk assessment is commonly defined as having two components: (a) likelihood of an occurrence and (b) magnitude of the adverse effects of an occurrence. We argue that the estimated likelihood of the occurrence, the identification of possible adverse occurrences, and the estimated magnitude of the adverse consequences are very difficult and costly to determine for complex systems. Consequently, complicated risk assessments commonly involve significant analysis efforts in their own right. Further, combining these complicated risk assessments with the maturity ranking of a simulation effort is difficult to achieve and certainly difficult for anyone to interpret.

Second, the risk tolerance of decision makers or groups of decision makers is a highly variable and a difficult attribute to quantify. The original discussion of Pilch *et al.* correlated the risk-tolerance scale with the increased risk perception of passing from exploratory research to qualification of weapon systems and subsystems. There are certainly other possibilities for quantifying risk aversion.

Third, the risk tolerance of decision makers inherently involves comparison of the apparent or assessed risk with the requirement of acceptable risk from the perspective of the decision makers. As discussed previously, we reject the concept of incorporating requirements into the maturity assessment. As a result, the maturity ranking scale proposed here will not be based on risk or on the risk tolerance of the person or decision maker who uses the information.

Because of these challenges, we take an alternative path. The PCMM levels discussed here are based on two fundamental information attributes discussed by Wang and Strong (1996):

- *intrinsic information quality*: accuracy, correctness, and objectivity;
- *contextual information quality*: completeness, amount of information, and level of detail.

The use of maturity levels is an attempt to objectively track intellectual artifacts or evidence obtained in an assessment of a simulation effort. Any piece of information about the simulation effort can be considered an artifact. As one moves to higher levels of maturity, both the quality and the quantity of intrinsic and contextual information artifacts must increase. We define four levels with the general characteristics of maturity that apply to all six elements as follows.

- *Level 0* – Little or no assessment of the accuracy and/or completeness has been made; little or no evidence of maturity; individual judgment and experience only; convenience and expediency are the primary motivators. This level of maturity is commonly appropriate for low-consequence systems, systems with little reliance on simulation, scoping studies, or conceptual design support.
- *Level 1* – Some informal assessment of the accuracy and/or completeness has been made; generalized characterization; some evidence of maturity. This level of maturity is commonly appropriate for moderate consequence systems, systems with some reliance on simulation, or preliminary design support.
- *Level 2* – Some formal assessment of the accuracy and/or completeness has been made; detailed characterization; significant evidence of maturity; some assessments have been made by an internal peer review group. This level of maturity is commonly appropriate for high-consequence systems, systems with high reliance on simulation, system qualification support, or final design support.
- *Level 3* – Formal assessment of the accuracy and/or completeness has been made; precise and accurate characterization; detailed and complete evidence of maturity; essentially all assessments have been made by independent peer-review groups. This level of maturity is commonly appropriate for high-consequence systems in which decision making is fundamentally based on simulation, e.g., where certification or qualification of a system's performance, safety, and reliability is primarily based on simulation as opposed to being primarily based on information obtained from complete system testing.

We have not mentioned the roles or importance of reproducibility, traceability, and documentation of the artifacts. We have excluded these attributes because they do not directly measure the quality of the information produced. Rather, these attributes fundamentally contribute to (a) *proof* of the existence of the artifacts, and (b) the details of the information that is available for each element. We believe that reproducibility, traceability, and documentation of the artifacts are important in any simulation effort, particularly those that support certification or qualification of the safety and reliability of high-consequence systems. For example, the roles of reproducibility, traceability, and documentation of all artifacts produced by computational analyses in risk assessments for nuclear reactor safety, as well as in performance assessments for the Waste Isolation Pilot Plant (WIPP) and the Yucca Mountain Project, are well recognized and mandated by regulatory policy. Not withstanding this experience, the PCMM will exclude reproducibility, traceability, and documentation of the artifacts. If appropriate for the M&S effort, one could add an element that assessed the level of reproducibility, traceability, and documentation of all of the other six elements in the PCMM.

15.2.2 Purpose and uses of the PCMM

For each of the six elements that are used in the PCMM, a maturity level is evaluated. The PCMM differs from NASA (2008) in that the NASA approach assesses the maturity level of the *results* from M&S. It is our view that assessing the maturity or credibility of

Table 15.1 *Table format for PCMM assessment (Oberkampf et al., 2007).*

Element \ Maturity	Maturity level 0	Maturity level 1	Maturity level 2	Maturity level 3
Representation and geometric fidelity				
Physics and material model fidelity				
Code verification				
Solution verification				
Model validation				
Uncertainty quantification and sensitivity analysis				

results is actually a step removed, and more difficult, than assessing the maturity of the processes that occur in each of the elements. We argue that the *representational information quality*, specifically the interpretability and ease of understanding, is significantly improved if one focuses on the maturity of the contributing elements, and not on the broader issue of maturity of results.

The contributing elements and the maturity of each element can be thought of as relatively independent measures, or attributes, of predictive capability. Accordingly, the PCMM can be summarized in a table or matrix format, where the elements form the rows of the table and the maturity levels (0 through 3) form the columns, as shown in Table 15.1.

A PCMM assessment consists of evaluating the maturity level of six individual elements and scoring the maturity level of each element. For each level of maturity, there is a set of predefined descriptors that are used to assess the maturity level of a particular element. If an element is characterized by an assessor (an individual who performs the actual assessment of the maturity level for an element) as attaining the entire set of descriptors at a given level of maturity, the element can be considered to be fully assessed at that level of maturity. An element that is fully assessed at a particular level of maturity will generally be assigned, by the assessor, a score that is equivalent to the maturity level. Thus, for example, if an element were assessed so that it fully met all of the predefined descriptors at maturity level 1, the element would have a score of 1. In preliminary testing of the PCMM table over a range of engineering applications, we have commonly found that some, but not all, of the descriptors at a given level have been achieved. For example, at maturity level 2, only half the descriptors for a given attribute may have been attained. For this common situation, it has proven useful to give a fractional score for the maturity level instead of strictly assigning an integer score at the lower level of maturity. As a result, noninteger maturity scores expressed in tenths, such as 1.5 for partially achieving level 2, should be considered in assessing the maturity level of each element. Upon completion of the assessment, the table would have six individual scores, one score per element.

Before presenting additional details about the table constructed for the PCMM, it is appropriate to discuss more clearly the purpose of this table, certain characteristics of the

Table 15.2 *Example of a PCMM table after maturity assessment (Oberkampf et al., 2007).*

Element	Maturity level 0	Maturity level 1	Maturity level 2	Maturity level 3	Element score
Representation and geometric fidelity		Assessed			1
Physics and material model fidelity			Assessed		2
Code verification		Assessed			1
Solution verification	Assessed				0
Model validation		Assessed			1
Uncertainty quantification and sensitivity analysis	Assessed				0

table, and how the results (i.e., scores) from completing this table can be used. Simply stated, the purpose of the table is to assess the level of maturity, at a given moment in time, of the key elements in a simulation effort that are directed at an application of interest. The assessment should be conducted, in principle, with little or no regard to any programmatic (or project) requirement for the maturity of the simulation effort. Objectivity, a key ingredient of intrinsic information quality, increases to the degree that maturity assessment is separated from maturity requirements specified by a project.

Table 15.2 gives an example of a PCMM table after a maturity assessment of a simulation effort has been completed.

For purposes of explanation, consider that all elements in Table 15.2 were assessed with the scores shown to the right of the table. The designator *Assessed* would then be placed in the appropriate row and column in the table. Once the assessment has been completed, the set of scores for each element can be compiled. In Table 15.2, the set of scores completed by the assessor(s) for the six elements is [1, 2, 1, 0, 1, 0].

We believe the type of summary information shown in Table 15.2 will prove very useful and informative in many programmatic and review committee situations. Following are some of the experiences derived in preliminary use of the PCMM table.

• In attempting to conduct a PCMM assessment, we found that the assessors are generally not familiar with many of the concepts in the table. By learning about these concepts, the assessors will greatly broaden and deepen their knowledge of many of the elements that contribute to confidence in simulation.
• Conducting a PCMM assessment and sharing it with interested parties, decision makers, and stakeholders engenders discussions that would *not* have occurred without such an assessment. This kind of communication is one of the most significant consequences of a simulation maturity assessment in general. An example of a beneficial interaction would be to initiate a conversation with a stakeholder who may not be familiar with any of the contributing elements to simulation

and help to educate that stakeholder about the importance of these elements and the results of the assessment.
- PCMM assessments made over a period of time can be used to track the progress of simulation efforts. This is useful for managers, stakeholders (decision makers using the results of the simulation effort), and funding sources to determine progress or value added over time.

A key practical issue in completion of the PCMM table is, *who* should provide the assessments in the table? We strongly believe that an individual, or a team, that has detailed knowledge of an element should complete that element of the table. These individuals should be very familiar with the elements of the simulation effort and the application of interest. Sometimes, depending on the magnitude of the simulation effort, a simulation project manager is sufficiently familiar with all elements of the table and can complete it in its entirety. The assessed levels in the completed table should represent the actual status of the simulation effort, not some anticipated or expected future status. In other words, the table should measure the maturity of the actual status at a given moment in time, not something that is *nearly* attained or a status that would *look good* in a program review or in a marketing activity.

With the PCMM, we are primarily interested in providing simulation maturity assessment information for an application of interest to program managers, relevant stakeholders, and decision makers. Some applications of interest that commonly involve simulation efforts are (a) design or optimization of new systems; (b) modification or optimization of existing systems; and (c) assessment of the performance, safety, or reliability of existing or proposed systems. In addition, the specification of a system includes the specification of the surroundings of the system and the environment in which the system must operate, e.g., normal, abnormal, or hostile environments. With the system, surroundings, and environment specified, one can then begin to identify particular aspects of each of the six elements that are important to the simulation effort.

An important aspect should be mentioned again concerning the interpretation of scores from a PCMM assessment. Although this aspect was discussed previously, it needs to be stressed and clarified further because it can cause great confusion, as we have seen in testing. We have observed that users of the PCMM commonly interpret an increase in maturity assessment over time to mean that the accuracy of the predictions has improved. This is *not necessarily* true. Stated differently, many people want to interpret the PCMM scores as a predictive accuracy assessment or, similarly, as a measure of the accuracy of the simulation results. As stressed earlier, the PCMM assesses the maturity of the simulation process elements, *not necessarily* the accuracy of the simulation results. The accuracy of the simulation results would commonly increase as the PCMM scores improve, but there is *not* a one-to-one correspondence.

To clarify why this is true, consider an example based on Table 15.2. As explained previously, the maturity level scores shown in Table 15.2 are written as the sequence [1, 2, 1, 0, 1, 0] for the six elements. Suppose that the element of uncertainty quantification and sensitivity analysis was improved from a 0 assessment (the last value in the maturity assessment above) to the condition where multiple simulations were obtained and resulted in capturing some of the uncertainties present in the system being analyzed. For example, suppose the uncertainty quantification analysis began to show a large effect due to variability in the strength of welded joints in a component. With this improved uncertainty quantification, suppose the maturity assessment of the PCMM then became [1, 2, 1, 0, 1, 1], i.e., the last value in the sequence changed from 0 to 1. The decision maker would then have more complete information about the system's uncertainty quantification. The decision maker would then have an estimate of the uncertainty of the SRQs of interest as a function of the variability in weld strength, whereas previously the decision maker may have had no idea of the uncertainty. While the accuracy of the predictions in these hypothetical cases has not changed at all, the decision maker would now be able to recognize some of the contributing uncertainties to the predicted performance of the system.

15.2.3 Characteristics of PCMM elements

A brief description of each element of the PCMM table is given in Table 15.3. This table can be used as summary statements of the basic descriptors of each element. Note that the requirements of the descriptors at each maturity level accumulate as one moves to higher maturity levels within an element. For example, to attain a given maturity level for a given element, the descriptors within the specific element of the table must be satisfied, in addition to all descriptors at the lower levels in that row.

A detailed discussion follows for each element of the table.

15.2.3.1 Representation and geometric fidelity

This element is directed primarily toward the level of physical or informational characterization of the system being analyzed or the specification of the geometrical features of the system. For fully empirical and semi-empirical models, there may be little geometric fidelity, e.g., lumped-mass representations or representations that simply deal with the functionality of system components. For physics-based models that solve PDEs or integral equations, significant geometric fidelity may be specified that is then used to prescribe the ICs and BCs for such equations. For other mathematical models, such as electrical circuit or agent-based models, other concepts of representation fidelity are needed. For example, in the case of electrical circuit models, characterization deals with the fidelity of the electrical circuit diagram and level of characterization of the electrical components in the system. For agent-based models, for example, modeling the movement and interaction of robots, representation fidelity might be the geography over which agents move. Geometric fidelity may increase proportionately as physical modeling fidelity increases because of the additional information that is required for the modeling. Thus, the lowest level of maturity assesses geometric fidelity based on convenience, simplicity, and the judgment of the computational practitioner. The higher levels of geometric maturity provide increasingly detailed information that may be more representative of the *as built* geometry; accordingly, levels of stylization of the system and environment decrease. For example, the geometry, material and surface characteristics, and mechanical assembly of the system are typically

Table 15.3 *General descriptions for elements of the PCMM table (Oberkampf* et al., *2007).*

Maturity / Element	Maturity level 0 Low consequence, minimal simulation impact, e.g. scoping studies	Maturity level 1 Moderate consequence, some simulation impact, e.g. design support	Maturity level 2 High consequence, high simulation impact, e.g. qualification support	Maturity level 3 High consequence, decision-making based on simulation, e.g. qualification or certification
Representation and geometric fidelity What features are neglected because of simplifications or stylizations?	• Judgment only • Little or no representational or geometric fidelity for the system and BCs	• Significant simplification or stylization of the system and BCs • Geometry or representation of major components is defined	• Limited simplification or stylization of major components and BCs • Geometry or representation is well defined for major components and some minor components • Some peer reviews conducted	• Essentially no simplification or stylization of components in the system and BCs • Geometry or representation of all components is at the detail of *as built*, e.g., gaps, material interfaces, fasteners • Independent peer review conducted
Physics and material model fidelity How fundamental are the physics and material models and what is the level of model calibration?	• Judgment only • Model forms are either unknown or fully empirical • Few, if any, physics-informed models • No coupling of models	• Some models are physics based and are calibrated using data from related systems • Minimal or ad hoc coupling of models	• Physics-based models for all important processes • Significant calibration needed using separate effects tests (SETs) and integral effects tests (IETs) • One-way coupling of models • Some peer reviews conducted	• All models are physics based • Minimal need for calibration using SETs and IETs • Sound physical basis for extrapolation and coupling of models • Full, two-way coupling of models • Independent peer review conducted
Code verification Are algorithm deficiencies, software errors, and poor SQE practices corrupting the simulation results?	• Judgment only • Minimal testing of any software elements • Little or no SQE procedures specified or followed	• Code is managed by SQE procedures • Unit and regression testing conducted • Some comparisons made with benchmarks	• Some algorithms are tested to determine the observed order of numerical convergence • Some features & capabilities (F&C) are tested with benchmark solutions • Some peer reviews conducted	• All important algorithms are tested to determine the observed order of numerical convergence • All important F&Cs are tested with rigorous benchmark solutions • Independent peer review conducted

Solution verification Are numerical solution errors and human procedural errors corrupting the simulation results?	• Judgment only • Numerical errors have an unknown or large effect on simulation results	• Numerical effects on relevant SRQs are qualitatively estimated • Input/output (I/O) verified only by the analysts	• Numerical effects are quantitatively estimated to be small on some SRQs • I/O independently verified • Some peer reviews conducted	• Numerical effects are determined to be small on all important SRQs • Important simulations are independently reproduced • Independent peer review conducted
Model validation How carefully is the accuracy of the simulation and experimental results assessed at various tiers in a validation hierarchy?	• Judgment only • Few, if any, comparisons with measurements from similar systems or applications	• Quantitative assessment of accuracy of SRQs not directly relevant to the application of interest • Large or unknown experimental uncertainties	• Quantitative assessment of predictive accuracy for some key SRQs from IETs and SETs • Experimental uncertainties are well characterized for most SETs, but poorly known for IETs • Some peer reviews conducted	• Quantitative assessment of predictive accuracy for all important SRQs from IETs and SETs at conditions/geometries directly relevant to the application • Experimental uncertainties are well characterized for all IETs and SETs • Independent peer review conducted
Uncertainty quantification and sensitivity analysis How thoroughly are uncertainties and sensitivities characterized and propagated?	• Judgment only • Only deterministic analyses are conducted • Uncertainties and sensitivities are not addressed	• Aleatory and epistemic (A&E) uncertainties propagated, but without distinction • Informal sensitivity studies conducted • Many strong UQ/SA assumptions made	• A&E uncertainties segregated, propagated and identified in SRQs • Quantitative sensitivity analyses conducted for most parameters • Numerical propagation errors are estimated and their effect known • Some strong assumptions made • Some peer reviews conducted	• A&E uncertainties comprehensively treated and properly interpreted • Comprehensive sensitivity analyses conducted for parameters and models • Numerical propagation errors are demonstrated to be small • No significant UQ/SA assumptions made • Independent peer review conducted

specified in a CAD file. For systems that may be in a dangerous state of excessive wear, a damaged condition, or crack propagation due to cyclic loading, the specification of the geometry and surface properties can become quite complex and uncertain.

General descriptions of the levels of physical representation and geometric fidelity follow.

- *Level 0*: Simplicity, convenience, and functional operation of the system dominate the fidelity of the representation and the geometry for the system being analyzed. There is heavy reliance on judgment and experience, with little or no expectation or quantification of representation and geometric fidelity.
- *Level 1*: Quantitative specifications are applied to describe the geometry of the major components of the system being analyzed. Much of the real system remains stylized or ignored, e.g., gaps between components, changes in materials, and surface finish.
- *Level 2*: Quantitative specifications are applied to replicate the geometric fidelity of most of the components of the real system. Little of the real system remains stylized or ignored. For example, important imperfections due to system assembly or defects due to wear or damage in the system are included. A level of peer review, such as informal or internal reviews, of the model representation and geometric fidelity has been conducted.
- *Level 3*: The geometric representation in the model is *as built* or *as existing*, meaning that no aspect of the geometry of the modeled real system is missing, down to scales that are determined to be relevant to the level of physical modeling chosen. An example is a complete CAD model for the real system as assembled and meshed for the discrete model with no significant approximations or simplifications included. Independent peer review of the model representation and geometric fidelity has been conducted, e.g., formal review by the simulation effort customer or by reviewers external to the organization conducting the simulation.

15.2.3.2 Physics and material model fidelity

This attribute primarily addresses the following:

- the degree that models are physics based, i.e., are they fully empirical, semi-empirical, or physics based;
- the degree to which the models are calibrated;
- the physics fidelity basis with which the models are being extrapolated from their validation and calibration database to the conditions of the application of interest;
- the quality and degree of coupling the multi-physics effects that exist in the application of interest.

Generally, as the physical fidelity of the model increases, and the needed input data is provided to the model for a simulation, the model is increasingly able to provide physics-based explanatory power for the particular physical phenomenon of interest. Within the broad class of physics-based models, there are important distinctions in the degree to which the model is calibrated. For example, does the model require recalibration (updating) even if there are relatively small changes in the system design or small changes in the BCs or ICs? Alternately, does the model require calibration only at lower levels in the validation hierarchy, i.e., separate effects tests (SETs), in order to yield accurate predictions? Or, does the model also require calibration or recalibration at higher levels of the validation hierarchy, i.e., integral effects tests (IETs), to attain accurate predictions? For two models yielding *the same* level of agreement with experimentally measured responses at the IET level, one model calibrated only at the SET level and one model calibrated at the IET level, the model that requires calibration at the SET level has more predictive capability than does the model that requires calibration at the IET level. This statement is understandable by noting that the model calibrated with SETs has demonstrated that it can yield the same prediction accuracy as the model calibrated with IETs, even though the SET-calibrated model must extrapolate further from its calibration domain than the IET-calibrated model.

General descriptions of the various levels of physics and material model fidelity follow.

- *Level 0*: The model is fully empirical, or the model form is not known. There is little or no coupling of models representing multiple functional elements of the system, and the coupling that does exist is not physics based. Confidence in the model is strictly based on the judgment and experience of the practitioner.
- *Level 1*: The model is semi-empirical in the sense that portions of the modeling are physics based; however, important features, capabilities, or parameters in the model are calibrated using data from very closely related physical systems. The coupling of functional elements or components is minimal or ad hoc, and not based on detailed physics.
- *Level 2*: All important physical process models and material models are physics based. Calibration of important model parameters is necessary, using data from SETs and IETs. All model calibration procedures are implemented on the model input parameters, not on the SRQs. Important physical processes are coupled using physics-based models with couplings in one direction. Some level of peer review, such as informal or internal reviews, of the physics and material models has been conducted.
- *Level 3*: All models are physics based with minimal need for calibration using SETs and IETs. Where extrapolation of these models is required, the extrapolation is based on well understood and well accepted physical principles. All physical processes are coupled in terms of physics-based models with two-way coupling and physical process effects on physical and material parameters, BCs, geometry, ICs, and forcing functions. Independent peer review of the physics and material models have been conducted, e.g., formal review by the simulation effort customer or by reviewers external to the organization conducting the simulation.

15.2.3.3 Code verification

This attribute focuses on the following:

- correctness and fidelity of the numerical algorithms used in the code relative to the mathematical model, e.g., the PDEs;
- correctness of source code;
- configuration management, control, and testing of the software through SQE practices.

The correctness and fidelity of the numerical algorithms and the correctness of the source code are primarily determined by conducting various types of tests on the code. The primary type of test we advocate compares the numerical solution results from the code with highly accurate solutions, which are usually referred to as benchmark numerical solutions (Oberkampf and Trucano, 2008). The most rigorous benchmark solutions are manufactured and analytical solutions discussed in detail in Chapter 6, Exact solutions.

Comparisons between the results of the code being tested and the benchmark solutions typically yield two types of numerical accuracy information. First, the error in the SRQs from the code being tested is evaluated by using the benchmark result as the exact solution. Although this is useful, it provides no information concerning the numerical convergence characteristics of the code being tested. Second, using two or more solutions with uniformly refined discretizations for the code being tested, and using the benchmark as the exact solution, one can compute the observed order of convergence of the numerical algorithms in the code being tested. Observed order of convergence is a much more definitive statement of code verification.

The maturity of the SQE practices should measure the scope and rigor of configuration management and software control. Chapter 4, Software engineering gave a detailed discussion of this topic.

General descriptions of the levels of code verification are as follows.

- *Level 0*: Code verification is based almost entirely on the judgment and experience of the computational practitioners involved. There is little or no formal verification testing of the software elements. Little or no SQE practices are defined and practiced in the implementation, management, and use of the code.
- *Level 1*: Most associated software is implemented and managed with formal SQE practices. Unit and regression testing of the software is conducted regularly with a high percentage of line coverage attained. Verification test suites using benchmark solutions are minimal and only error measures are obtained in some SRQs.
- *Level 2*: All associated software is implemented and managed with formal SQE practices. Verification test suites are formally defined and systematically applied using benchmark solutions to compute the observed order of convergence of some numerical algorithms. Some features and capabilities (F&Cs), such as complex geometries, mesh generation, physics, and material models, have been tested with benchmark solutions. Some level of peer review, such as informal or internal reviews, of the code verification has been conducted.
- *Level 3*: All important algorithms have been tested using rigorous benchmark solutions to compute the observed order of convergence. All important F&Cs, such as two-way coupling of multiphysics processes, have been tested with rigorous benchmark solutions. Independent peer review of code verification has been conducted, e.g., formal review by the simulation effort customer or by reviewers external to the organization conducting the simulation.

15.2.3.4 Solution verification

This attribute deals with assessment of the following:

- numerical solution errors in the computed results;
- confidence in the computational results as they may be affected by human error.

Rigor and numerical solution accuracy are the dominant components of the assessment of this element. Numerical solution errors are any errors due to mapping the mathematical model to the discretized model and any errors due to solution of the discretized model on a computer. Of concern in this element are numerical solution errors due to spatial and temporal discretization of the PDEs or integral equations, and the iterative solution error due to a linearized solution approach to a set of nonlinear discretized equations. Additional numerical solution errors that should be addressed are the potential detrimental effects of numerical parameters in solution algorithms; errors due to approximate techniques used to solve nondeterministic systems, e.g., error due to a small number of samples used in a Monte Carlo sampling method; and round-off error due to finite precision on a computer. Human errors, i.e., blind uncertainties, are also a concern in the assessment of this element, such as those made in (a) preparing and assembling the elements of the discrete model; (b) executing the computational solution; and (c) post-processing, preparing, or interpreting the computational results.

General descriptions of the levels of solution verification are as follows.

- *Level 0*: No formal attempt is made to assess any of the possible sources of numerical error. Any statement about the impact of numerical error is based purely on the judgment and experience of the computational practitioner. No assessment about the correctness of software inputs or outputs has been conducted.
- *Level 1*: Some kind of formal method is used to assess the influence of numerical errors on some SRQs. This could include *a posteriori* error estimation of global norms, iterative convergence studies, or sensitivity studies to determine how sensitive certain SRQs are to changes in mesh or temporal discretization. A formal effort is made by the computational practitioners to check the correctness of input/output (I/O) data.
- *Level 2*: Quantitative error estimation methods are used to estimate numerical errors on some SRQs, and these estimates show that the errors are small for some conditions of the application of interest. I/O quantities have been verified by knowledgeable computational practitioners who have some level of independence from the simulation effort. Some level of peer review, such as informal or internal reviews, of the solution verification activities has been conducted.
- *Level 3*: Quantitative error estimation methods are used to estimate numerical errors on all important SRQs, and these estimates show that the errors are small over the entire range of conditions for the application of interest. Important simulations are reproduced, using the same software, by independent computational practitioners. Independent peer review of solution verification activities has been conducted, e.g., formal review by the simulation effort customer or by reviewers external to the organization conducting the simulation.

A subtle, but important, point should be stressed regarding the maturity levels of solution verification. It was pointed out that higher levels of maturity do not *necessarily* imply higher levels of accuracy of the simulation results. However, in the descriptions of maturity levels just given it is apparent that higher levels of maturity *require* increased solution accuracy. This apparent dichotomy is resolved by understanding that increased numerical solution accuracy is necessary to gain more confidence in the fidelity of the mapping of the mathematical model to the solution of the discrete model. We are *not* necessarily gaining confidence in the comparison of the computational results with experimental data. In other words, we require increased correctness and accuracy of the numerical solution, including code verification, so that when we compare computational results and experimental results we are confident that we are indeed comparing the physics as simulated by the mathematical model with nature's reflection of reality in experimental measurements. High levels of maturity in code verification and solution verification are an indication of how well the numerical results represent the physics in the mathematical model, as opposed to a contaminated mixture of physics, numerical error, and possibly human error. If we cannot have confidence in what we believe we are comparing, then we are dealing with a convolved mixture of physics modeling, physics modeling approximations (error), and numerical error, in which no bases for confidence can be made. It will be seen below that more accurate comparisons between the computational results and the experimental measurements, although desired, are not *necessarily* required to achieve higher maturity levels in model validation.

15.2.3.5 Model validation

This attribute focuses on the following:

- thoroughness and precision of the accuracy assessment of the computational results relative to the experimental measurements;
- completeness and precision of the characterization of the experimental conditions and measurements;
- relevancy of the experimental conditions, physical hardware, and measurements in the validation experiments compared to the application of interest.

The focus of model validation in the PCMM is on the precision and completeness of the process of the model accuracy assessment, *not* on the accuracy of the mathematical model itself. By *precision* of validation we mean (a) how carefully and accurately are the experimental uncertainties estimated and (b) how well understood and quantified are all the conditions of the experiment that are required as inputs for the mathematical model? By *completeness* of validation we mean: how well do the conditions (geometry, BCs, ICs, and system excitation) and actual physical hardware of the validation experiments conducted relate to the actual conditions and hardware of the application of interest?

For SETs, it is expected that there will be many dissimilarities between the SET experiments and the actual application of interest because they occur at lower levels in the validation hierarchy. For IETs, however, there should be a close relationship between the IET experiments and the application of interest, particularly with respect to the experimental hardware and the coupled physical phenomena occurring in each. For a more complete discussion of the concepts behind and the construction of a validation hierarchy, see Chapter 10, Model validation fundamentals.

As discussed earlier, the correctness and credibility of model validation fundamentally relies on assumptions that the numerical algorithms are reliable, that the computer program is correct, that no human procedural errors have been made in the simulation, and that the numerical solution error is small. These are major assumptions that we, and many others, have discovered are commonly unfounded. Consequently, to properly inform the user of the information in the PCMM table about the veracity of these assumptions, we require that the maturity level of the elements model validation and uncertainty quantification and sensitivity analysis can be *no higher than two levels above* the maturity levels of the minimum of code verification and solution verification. This requirement places further restrictions on conducting the PCMM assessment and means that *the maturity levels of code verification and solution verification must be assessed before the maturity levels of model validation and of uncertainty quantification and sensitivity analysis are assessed.* As an example of the dependencies between elements, assume that, as discussed in Table 15.2, code verification and solution verification were at levels 1 and 0, respectively. Consequently, the maximum maturity level that the model validation element and the uncertainty quantification and sensitivity analysis element could be is level 2, even if the assessor(s) were to independently judge either or both of these elements at a level higher than 2.

General descriptions of the various levels of model validation are as follows.

- *Level 0*: Accuracy assessment of the model is based almost entirely on judgment and experience. Few, if any, comparisons have been made between computational results and experimental measurements of similar systems of interest.
- *Level 1*: Limited quantitative comparisons are made between computational results and experimental results. Either comparisons for SRQs have been made that are not directly relevant to the application of interest, or the experimental conditions are not directly relevant to the application of interest. Experimental uncertainties, either in the SRQs and/or in the characterization of the conditions of the experiment, are largely undetermined, unmeasured, or based on experience.
- *Level 2*: Quantitative comparisons between computational results and experimental results have been made for some key SRQs from SET experiments and limited IET experiments. Experimental uncertainties are well characterized (a) for most SRQs of interest and (b) for experimental conditions for the SETs conducted. However, the experimental uncertainties are not well characterized for the IETs. Some level of peer review, such as informal or internal reviews, of the model validation activities has been conducted.
- *Level 3*: Quantitative comparisons between computational and experimental results have been made for all important SRQs from an extensive database of both SET and IET experiments. The conditions of the SETs should be relevant to the application of interest; and the conditions, hardware, and coupled physics of the IETs should be similar to the application of interest. Some of the SET computational predictions and most of the IET predictions should be *blind*. Experimental uncertainties and conditions are well characterized for SRQs in both the SET and IET experiments. Independent peer review of the model validation activities has been conducted, e.g., formal review by the simulation effort customer or by reviewers external to the organization conducting the simulation.

15.2.3.6 Uncertainty quantification and sensitivity analysis

This attribute focuses on the following:

- thoroughness and soundness of the uncertainty quantification (UQ) effort, including identification and characterization of all plausible sources of uncertainty;
- accuracy and correctness of propagating uncertainties through a mathematical model and interpreting uncertainties in the SRQs of interest;
- thoroughness and precision of a sensitivity analysis to determine the most important contributors to uncertainty in system responses.

Recognition of uncertainties refers to the activity of identifying and understanding all possible uncertainties within the system of interest (e.g., physical parametric uncertainty and uncertainties in the geometry), in the surroundings (e.g., BCs and system excitation), and in the environment (e.g., normal, abnormal, and hostile). Characterization of model predictive uncertainty primarily deals with the proper estimation and representation of all uncertainties that could exist as part of the prediction for the system of interest. A key aspect of characterization is the segregation of uncertainties into aleatory and epistemic elements. This segregation has been discussed at length in this book.

A sensitivity analysis (SA) provides additional important information to the user of the computational simulation analysis beyond what is typically considered a part of an uncertainty quantification analysis. SA was briefly discussed in Chapter 13, Predictive capability, but for a detailed discussion, see Helton *et al.* (2006) and Saltelli *et al.* (2008). A SA is typically directed at two closely related goals. First, one may be interested in determining how outputs locally change as a function of inputs. This is usually referred to as a local SA. The information obtained from a local SA is commonly used for system design and optimization, as well as for determination of the most advantageous operational conditions for maximizing system performance. Second, one may be interested in determining how the uncertainty structure of all of the inputs maps to the uncertainty structure of each of the outputs. This is usually referred to as a global SA. The information from a global SA may be used, for example, to determine which manufacturing variabilities contribute most to variability in certain SRQs, or to determine what physical experiments should be conducted to most reduce the epistemic uncertainty that is due to poorly understood coupled-physics phenomena.

As discussed with regard to model validation, the maturity level of the UQ and SA elements can be *no higher than two levels above the maturity levels of the minimum of code verification and solution verification.*

General descriptions of the various levels of UQ and SA are as follows.

- *Level 0*: Judgment and experience are dominant forms of uncertainty assessment. Only deterministic analyses were conducted for the system of interest. Informal *spot checks* or *what-if* studies for various conditions were conducted to determine their effect.
- *Level 1*: Uncertainties in the system of interest are identified, represented, and propagated through the mathematical model, but they are not segregated with respect to whether the uncertainties are aleatory or epistemic. Sensitivity of some system responses to some system uncertainties and environmental condition uncertainties was investigated, but the sensitivity analysis was primarily informal or exploratory rather than systematic. Many strong assumptions are made with respect to the UQ and SA; for example, most probability density functions are characterized as Gaussian, and uncertain parameters are assumed to be independent of all other parameters.
- *Level 2*: Uncertainties in the system of interest are characterized as either aleatory or epistemic. The uncertainties are propagated through the computational model, while their character is kept segregated both in the input and in the SRQs. Quantitative SAs were conducted for most system parameters, while segregating aleatory and epistemic uncertainties. Numerical approximation or sampling errors due to propagation of uncertainties through the model are estimated, and the

effect of these errors on the UQ and SA results is understood and/or qualitatively estimated. Some strong UQ and SA assumptions were made, but qualitative results suggest that the effect of these assumptions is not significant. Some level of peer review, such as informal or internal reviews, of the uncertainty quantification and sensitivity analyses has been conducted.

- *Level 3*: Aleatory and epistemic uncertainties are comprehensively treated, and their segregation in the interpretation of the results is strictly maintained. Detailed investigations were conducted to determine the effect of uncertainty introduced due to model extrapolations (if required) to the conditions of the system of interest. A comprehensive SA was conducted for both parametric uncertainty and model uncertainty. Numerical approximation or sampling errors due to propagation of uncertainties through the model are carefully estimated, and their effect on the UQ and SA results is demonstrated to be small. No significant UQ and SA assumptions were made. Independent peer review of UQ and SA have been conducted, e.g., formal review by the simulation effort customer or by reviewers external to the organization conducting the simulation.

15.3 Additional uses of the PCMM

In this section, we suggest additional ways that the PCMM can be used and propose a method for the aggregation of scores in the PCMM table should that information be required. We also point out that the PCMM is only one of many factors that contribute to risk-informed decision making.

15.3.1 Requirements for modeling and simulation maturity

After an objective assessment of M&S maturity has been made using the PCMM table, one can introduce the *project maturity requirements* for each element in the table. Six project maturity requirements can be specified, one for each element in the table. Project maturity requirements may be a result of, for example, system qualification or regulatory requirements, or they may simply be progress requirements for the development of a simulation effort. For this exercise, the essential question to ask for each element is: what should the appropriate level of maturity be for my intended use of the simulation activity? For example, a given element in the table has been assessed at a maturity level of 2. Is that an appropriate level for which the simulation information will be used, or should it be at a higher level? Although we have not discussed this issue, it is obvious that the costs, both in terms of time and resources, increase significantly as higher levels of maturity are attained. To determine the project maturity requirements, one uses the same descriptors in Table 15.3 that were used to complete the PCMM table. For this use of Table 15.3, we consider the descriptors to be project maturity requirements.

Table 15.4 depicts the results of specifying project maturity requirements for each of the assessed elements discussed earlier. The designator *Required* is used to indicate the project maturity requirement for each element. The scores for the project maturity requirements in this example are [2, 2, 1, 2, 2, 3].

Table 15.4 *Example of PCMM table assessment and project maturity requirements (Oberkampf et al., 2007).*

Element \ Maturity	Maturity level 0	Maturity level 1	Maturity level 2	Maturity level 3
Representation and geometric fidelity		Assessed	Required	
Physics and material model fidelity			Assessed Required	
Code verification		Assessed Required		
Solution verification	Assessed		Required	
Model validation		Assessed	Required	
Uncertainty quantification and sensitivity analysis	Assessed			Required

In an assessment such as Table 15.4, the values would be color coded and have the following meanings:

- green – the assessment meets or exceeds the requirement (rows 2 and 3);
- yellow – the assessment does not meet the requirement by one level or less (rows 1 and 5);
- pink – the assessment does not meet the requirement by two levels or less (row 4);
- red – the assessment does not meet the requirement by three levels or less (row 6).

Some examples of the useful benefits of comparisons of simulation maturity and simulation project maturity requirements, as shown in Table 15.4, follow.

- To construct Table 15.4, one must have already addressed the question: what are the project requirements for simulation maturity? In our experience, we have found that either (a) this question may not have been asked or (b) answering this question has proven difficult, but quite useful in its own right. If this question is asked, we have found that it initiates conversations not only within the simulation customer's organization (typically engineering design groups or decision makers) but also between the simulation developer, the customer, and the stakeholders. We have found that this conversation is particularly important when the simulation customer is not the source of funding for the simulation effort.
- Table 15.4 can be used as a project management tool to adjust resources for elements that are lagging in their progress to meet project schedule requirements. Note that some elements do not depend solely on computational or software issues. For example, the model validation element depends very heavily on capabilities and progress in experimental activities. We have found that one of the most common and damaging difficulties is the technical, scheduling, and/or funding disconnection between the computational and experimental activities in validation.

15.3.2 *Aggregation of PCMM scores*

The description of the PCMM has focused on the use of simulation for a particular engineering application. Situations can exist where PCMM scores will need to be aggregated into one score, such as the following.

- Suppose one has obtained a set of scores for multiple subsystems within a system, each subsystem represented by six scores. The desire is to aggregate all of the scores for the multiple subsystems into a single score for all of the subsystems.
- Suppose one has obtained a set of scores for multiple systems of different design, and each system is represented by six scores. The desire is to aggregate all of the scores for the multiple systems into one score that would represent, in some sense, a single score for the collection of systems or the system of systems.

Although we recognize that arguments can be made to compute PCMM aggregate scores, we strongly recommend that this *not* be done. The score assessed for each of the six simulation elements is an ordinal scale – the four levels of maturity constitute a total order because each pair of levels can be simply ordered. However, the six elements *cannot be collectively ordered in any way*; they are apples and oranges. Each element is important and conceptually independent from each other element. If one argues that an average maturity of a simulation effort could be computed by simply taking the arithmetic mean of each of the six elements, the average value would have little meaning. The argument for using the average value would be analogous to someone claiming to compute the breaking strength of a chain by averaging the strength of each link in the chain. It is a fallacious argument.

Even though we argue against any type of aggregation method, our experience with using the PCMM has shown that pressure to condense information for decision makers can be irresistible. Given this reality, we recommend a simple procedure that would aid in maintaining some of the key information in the individual PCMM scores. We recommend that a set of three scores *always* be computed and presented to the user of the PCMM when *any* aggregation of PCMM scores is computed. The scores consist of the minimum over all of the elements being aggregated, the average of all the elements, and the maximum of all the elements. This aggregation triple can be written as:

$$\widehat{PCMM} = \left[\min_{i=1,2,\ldots,n} PCMM_i, \; \frac{1}{n}\sum_{i=1}^{n} PCMM_i, \; \max_{i=1,2,\ldots,n} PCMM_i \right], \quad (15.1)$$

where n is the total number of individual PCMM scores that are being aggregated. We believe that keeping the worst score of all aggregated scores will call attention to the situation so that the decision maker can pursue the issue in more depth if desired.

As an example, suppose that a system was made up of four subsystems. Assume each subsystem was assessed using the PCMM table discussed above, with the following result:

$$\text{PCMM}_{\text{subsystem1}} = \begin{bmatrix} 1 \\ 1.5 \\ 1 \\ 0 \\ 0.5 \\ 1 \end{bmatrix}, \quad \text{PCMM}_{\text{subsystem2}} = \begin{bmatrix} 1.5 \\ 1 \\ 0 \\ 0.5 \\ 1.5 \\ 0 \end{bmatrix},$$

$$\text{PCMM}_{\text{subsystem3}} = \begin{bmatrix} 2 \\ 1.5 \\ 0.5 \\ 1 \\ 1.5 \\ 1 \end{bmatrix}, \quad \text{PCMM}_{\text{subsystem4}} = \begin{bmatrix} 2 \\ 2 \\ 1 \\ 0.5 \\ 1.5 \\ 1.5 \end{bmatrix}. \qquad (15.2)$$

Using Eqs. (15.1) and (15.2), we compute the PCMM aggregate triple:

$$\widehat{\text{PCMM}} = [0.0, 1.1, 2.0]. \qquad (15.3)$$

This example demonstrates what we have observed in preliminary use of the PCMM: there is commonly a surprisingly wide range of scores uncovered in assessments. As an aside, it has also been found that sometimes there is resistance to conduct a PCMM assessment because it is suspected beforehand that the result will be similar to Eq. (15.3).

15.3.3 Use of the PCMM in risk-informed decision making

As we have discussed, the PCMM is carefully and narrowly focused so that it can be properly understood and correctly used by computational practitioners, experimentalists, project managers, decision makers, and policy makers. Earlier, we suggested some ways in which the PCMM could be used to assess progress, used as a project-planning tool for both simulation and experimental activities, and used by consumers of the simulation information. In the larger context, however, the PCMM is only one factor that contributes to risk-informed decision making for engineering systems. Figure 15.2 depicts a number of factors that could affect the risk-informed decision making for an engineering system.

Figure 15.2 divides the factors into two major groups: technical issues and programmatic issues. Although not all factors are shown, the figure demonstrates that a number of diverse and complex factors are important in decision making. Sometimes individual technical factors are characterized fairly well. For example, required system performance and predicted system performance, say, for system reliability in normal operating conditions, might be mathematically characterized as a precisely known probability distribution. However, most of the factors in Figure 15.2, particularly programmatic issues, are not characterized well, or at all. For example, it is commonly very difficult to estimate the consequences of poor system reliability on financial liability and future business opportunities. As depicted, there are interactions and trade-offs between the two groups of issues and within each group.

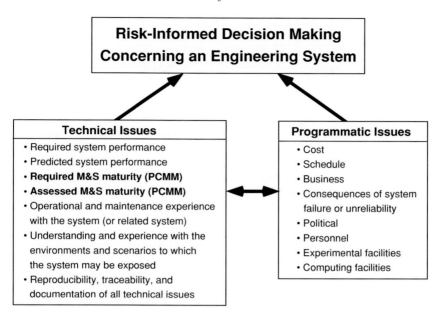

Figure 15.2 Factors influencing risk-informed decision making (Oberkampf *et al.*, 2007).

Managers and decision makers must weigh the importance of all factors, try to understand the complex interactions of factors, and decide on the trade-offs that must be made to optimize their view and their organization's view of success. Of course, success can mean widely varying things to the various participants and stakeholders involved.

Our purpose in constructing and discussing Figure 15.2 is to make it clear how the PCMM is but one factor in a complex set of factors. We have argued here that the assessment of simulation maturity is a relatively new factor that should be explicitly included in risk-informed decision making. In addition, we have argued that the assessment should be clearly separated from other important factors in decision making. If this is not done, there will be, at best, a convolution of factors causing confusion and miscommunication and, at worst, a contortion of factors intended to satisfy various agendas of individuals and organizations involved.

15.4 References

Ahern, D. M., A. Clouse, and R. Turner (2005). *CMMI Distilled: a Practical Introduction to Integrated Process Improvement*. 2nd edn., Boston, MA, Addison-Wesley.

Balci, O. (2004). Quality assessment, verification, and validation of modeling and simulation applications. *2004 Winter Simulation Conference*, 122–129.

Balci, O., R. J. Adams, D. S. Myers, and R. E. Nance (2002). A collaborative evaluation environment for credibility assessment of modeling and simulation applications. *2002 Winter Simulation Conference*, 214–220.

Bertch, W. J., T. A. Zang, and M. J. Steele (2008). Development of NASA's models and simulations standard. *2008 Spring Simulation Interoperability Workshop* Paper No. 08S-SIW-037, Providence, RI, Simulation Interoperability Standards Organization.

Blattnig, S. R., L. L. Green, J. M. Luckring, J. H. Morrison, R. K. Tripathi, and T. A. Zang (2008). Towards a credibility assessment of models and simulations. *49th AIAA/ASME/ASCE/AHS/ASC Structures, Structural Dynamics, and Materials Conference*, AIAA 2008–2156, Schaumburg, IL, American Institute of Aeronautics and Astronautics.

Chrissis, M. B., M. Konrad, and S. Shrum (2007). *CMMI: Guidelines for Process Integration and Product Improvement.* 2nd edn., Boston, MA, Addison-Wesley.

Clay, R. L., S. J. Marburger, M. S. Shneider, and T. G. Trucano (2007). *Modeling and Simulation Technology Readiness Levels.* SAND2007–0570, Albuquerque, NM, Sandia National Laboratories.

DoD (2005). *Technology Readiness Assessment (TRA) Deskbook.* Washington, DC, Department of Defense.

GAO (1999). *Best Practices: Better Management of Technology Development Can Improve Weapon System Outcomes.* GAO/NSIAD-99–162, Washington, DC, U. S. Government Accounting Office.

Garcia, S. and R. Turner (2006). *CMMI Survival Guide: Just Enough Process Improvement*, Boston, MA, Addison-Wesley.

Green, L. L., S. R. Blattnig, J. M. Luckring, and R. K. Tripathi (2008). An uncertainty structure matrix for models and simulations. *49th AIAA/ASME/ASCE/AHS/ASC Structures, Structural Dynamics, and Materials Conference*, AIAA 2008–2154, Schaumburg, IL, American Institute of Aeronautics and Astronautics.

Harmon, S. Y. and S. M. Youngblood (2003). A proposed model for simulation validation process maturity. *Simulation Interoperability Workshop*, Paper No. 03S-SIW-127, Orlando, FL, Simulation Interoperability Standards Organization.

Harmon, S. Y. and S. M. Youngblood (2005). A proposed model for simulation validation process maturity. *The Journal of Defense Modeling and Simulation.* **2**(4), 179–190.

Helton, J. C., J. D. Johnson, C. J. Sallaberry, and C. B. Storlie (2006). Survey of sampling-based methods for uncertainty and sensitivity analysis. *Reliability Engineering and System Safety.* **91**(10–11), 1175–1209.

IEEE (1989). *IEEE Standard Glossary of Modeling and Simulation Terminology.* Std 610.3–1989, New York, IEEE.

Mankins, J. C. (1995). *Technology Readiness Levels.* Washington, DC, National Aeronautics and Space Administration.

NASA (2006). *Interim Technical Standard for Models and Simulations.* NASA-STD-(I)-7009, Washington, DC, National Aeronautics and Space Administration.

NASA (2008). *Standard for Models and Simulations.* NASA-STD-7009, Washington, DC, National Aeronautics and Space Administration.

Oberkampf, W. L., M. Pilch, and T. G. Trucano. (2007). *Predictive Capability Maturity Model for Computational Modeling and Simulation.* SAND2007–5948, Albuquerque, NM, Sandia National Laboratories.

Oberkampf, W. L. and T. G. Trucano (2008). Verification and validation benchmarks. *Nuclear Engineering and Design.* **238**(3), 716–743.

Pilch, M., T. G. Trucano, D. E. Peercy, A. L. Hodges, and G. K. Froehlich (2004). *Concepts for Stockpile Computing (OUO).* SAND2004–2479 (Restricted Distribution, Official Use Only), Albuquerque, NM, Sandia National Laboratories.

Pilch, M., T. G. Trucano, and J. C. Helton (2006). *Ideas Underlying Quantification of Margins and Uncertainties (QMU): a White Paper*. SAND2006–5001, Albuquerque, NM, Sandia National Laboratories.

Saltelli, A., M. Ratto, T. Andres, F. Campolongo, J. Cariboni, D. Gatelli, M. Saisana, and S. Tarantola (2008). *Global Sensitivity Analysis: the Primer*, Hoboken, NJ, Wiley.

SEI (2006). *Software Engineering Institute: Capability Maturity Model Integration*. www.sei.cmu.edu/cmmi/.

Smith, J. (2004). *An Alternative to Technology Readiness Levels for Non-Developmental Item (NDI) Software*. CMU/SEI-2004-TR-013, ESC-TR-2004–013, Pittsburgh, PA, Carnegie Mellon, Software Engineering Institute.

Steele, M. J. (2008). Dimensions of credibility in models and simulations. *International Simulation Multi-Conference*, Paper No. 08E-SIW-076, Edinburgh, Scotland, Simulation Interoperability Standards Organization/The Society for Modeling and Simulation.

Wang, R. Y. and D. M. Strong (1996). Beyond accuracy: what data quality means to data consumers. *Journal of Management Information Systems*. **12**(4), 5–34.

West, M. (2004). *Real Process Improvement Using the CMMI*, Boca Raton, FL, CRC Press.

16

Development and responsibilities for verification, validation and uncertainty quantification

This chapter discusses some perspectives on the responsibilities for the development, conduct, delivery, and management of verification, validation, and uncertainty quantification (VV&UQ). The topics considered here deal with both technical and nontechnical issues, but all are focused on the strategic goals of improved credibility and proper use of simulations. Our experience, and the experience of others, has convinced us that while technical issues and computing resources are important, they are not the limiting factor in improving the credibility and usefulness of scientific computing used in a decision-making environment. We believe that nontechnical issues have significantly constrained the improvements in credibility that VV&UQ can provide.

Examples of the issues discussed in this chapter are (a) suggestions for needed technical developments in VV&UQ, (b) responsibilities for the various technical activities that encompass VV&UQ, (c) recommendations for management responsibilities and leadership in deploying VV&UQ practices, (d) development of V&V databases for general use, and (e) development of industrial and engineering standards for V&V.

There are diverse perspectives on many of these topics from different groups, such as companies that produce hardware products or commercial software, government organizations, organizations that sell simulation services, and special interest groups. We do not claim to have all of the answers, or even the correct answers, to some of the questions raised. We are simply attempting to provide perspectives on some important technical and nontechnical themes of responsibility and development of VV&UQ. As scientific computing continues to have an increasing impact on everyday life, economic competitiveness, environmental safety, global warming analyses, and national security, we believe these topics must involve a wider discussion and debate.

16.1 Needed technical developments

In most chapters we discuss various technical weaknesses and challenges related to the methods and techniques discussed in the chapter. Here we present a summary of some of the key research topics that we feel are needed to advance VV&UQ in scientific computing. This list is not meant to be comprehensive, but only suggestive. These topics are presented in the order that the topics appeared in the book:

- automated (in-situ) code verification, where a manufactured solution/source term is automatically generated and an order of accuracy test is automatically run based on chosen code options one desires to verify;
- construction of manufactured solutions for much wider range of technical fields in scientific computing;
- improved methods to measure coverage of code verification testing based on features and capabilities options in the code;
- reliable, i.e., demonstrably asymptotic, discretization error estimation for complex scientific computing problems, including hyperbolic partial differential equations and problems with discontinuities;
- reliable mesh adaptation for complex scientific computing problems, especially for anisotropic problems such a boundary layers and shock waves;
- further development and use of the validation hierarchy as it is focused on the system of interest;
- further development and use of the phenomena identification and ranking table (PIRT) and the gap analysis table;
- development of validation metrics for various types of system response quantities, particularly time dependent responses with a wide range of frequencies, and SRQs that depend on a large number of input parameters;
- development of methods for incorporating validation metric results into uncertainty estimation of predicted responses, e.g., extrapolation of model uncertainties as a function of input parameters and inclusion of epistemic uncertainty in predictions;
- improved understanding of the positive and negative effects of model calibration on model predictive capability.
- uncertainty estimation of SRQs at higher levels in the validation hierarchy, based on validation metric results where available, and multiple mathematical models at all levels in the validation hierarchy.

16.2 Staff responsibilities

By *staff* we mean individuals who are technically trained to conduct any part of the computational analysis related to VV&UQ. This includes engineers, scientists, mathematicians, statisticians, and computer scientists involved in the theoretical, computational, or experimental activities of the overall effort. Management responsibilities will be discussed in Section 16.3.

16.2.1 Software quality assurance and code verification

16.2.1.1 Who should conduct SQA and code verification?

Software quality assurance (SQA) and code verification are primarily the responsibility of code developers and commercial software suppliers. Most commercial software companies are subjected to demanding quality and reliability requirements from their customers. Yet, it is impossible to obtain public information concerning the percentage of resources devoted to SQA and code verification compared to total resources devoted to developing and selling commercial software. Factors that should be important for these companies as part of their business activities include the following.

1 The software company should put in place and practice a high level of SQA for every stage of the software life cycle. These stages range from a new research module, to preliminary release of modules, to bug-fixing patches of released software products. Each of these modules will require separate SQA tracking and different levels of code verification testing for its quality assurance.
2 The software company should educate its customers to understand that it is impossible to cover all possible combinations of physical, boundary, material, and geometrical conditions available in the code during the verification testing process. The software company should (a) carefully prioritize what combinations are important for its range of customers, and (b) inform the interested customers which combinations have been tested and which ones have not. If the customer is not satisfied with extent of the testing for their applications, they should express those views to the software company.
3 The software product should be compiled and ported to a wide variety of computer platforms (serial, multi-core, and parallel processor machines) that may be used by their customers. They should also be rigorously tested under different operating systems and a range of versions of operating systems.

The SQA and code verification procedures within a software company's development environment constitute an ongoing process. With every software release, the company should have SQA test procedures that are set up under the supervision of a software quality group. These procedures should include automatic reporting features for the results of the testing. In particular, the activities related to fixing, tracking, and managing software bugs should be a critical part of the global SQA procedures of the software company.

Code development within organizations, separate from software suppliers, usually falls into two groups: (a) groups within a large organization or a large project that develop either proprietary software or special purpose software, and (b) research groups within corporations, universities, or institutes. Within many research groups, there is considerable resistance to the implementation of formal SQA practices. The degree of formality, software development constraints, user restricted access, and costs of SQA are key factors in their resistance. For many research groups, there is also a well-established value system that new knowledge, as well as publishable results, is the crucial product, not reliable software, algorithms, reproducibility, and SQA and code verification documentation.

The notable exception to the generally low level of SQA and code verification procedures is a computational project involved in high-consequence systems. The two most important examples are nuclear power reactor safety and underground storage of nuclear wastes. These projects have intense government and public scrutiny not only in results of the analyses, but also in all of the steps leading up to the results. In the US, primary oversight of nuclear power reactor analyses resides with the Nuclear Regulatory Commission. Primary oversight of underground storage of nuclear wastes resides with the Department of Energy, the Nuclear Regulatory Commission, and the Environmental Protection Agency. These projects have extraordinarily rigorous SQA procedures, including detailed documentation of all of the software components. In fact, there is credence to the argument that the procedures are so demanding that they severely constrain the introduction of improved mathematical models and numerical algorithms. A proper balance must be struck between appropriate SQA procedures and improved numerical techniques.

16.2.1.2 *Who should require SQA and code verification?*

Code users are primarily responsible for requiring SQA and code verification from code developers and commercial software companies. Code users may also contribute to conducting SQA and code verification, but when doing so they are serving more in the role of code developers. When we refer to *code*, we are referring to the entire software package or any subset of the software used in a computational analysis. We believe the appropriate conceptual framework for understanding responsibilities in all of the VV&UQ activities discussed in Section 16.2 is that of supplier and customer. *Suppliers* are individuals or organizations that provide products or information used in the analysis. *Customers* are individuals and organizations that receive a product (such as a code) or information produced by the code or the analysis. An individual or an organization can serve as both a supplier and a customer during different activities or phases of the analysis.

The code developers and commercial software companies are clearly the suppliers of the code as a product. The final responsibility for the quality of the code used in the analysis, however, lies with the customer. The customer is the user of the product or the information produced by the product and he/she must provide the requirements, due diligence, and proper use of the product or information. As a result, we believe the value placed on SQA and code verification by the customer is the *driving factor* in quality. If the customer simply *assumes* that SQA and code verification are adequately done and does not require any documentation, details, or evidence of these activities, then the supplier appropriately considers the requirement void of content or bogus. For *any* item of importance to a customer, the customer should require demonstration of capability, proof of performance, inspection, or documentation of quality and reliability.

If the customer is dealing with a supplier that essentially has a monopoly on the software market, then this situation is very different and more complex. If the market is relatively small and the customer is important to the supplier, then the customer has some leverage with respect to specifying requirements. If on the other hand, the market is large, individual customers are at a distinct disadvantage and have few options to require improvements. They can either tolerate the product quality provided by the supplier, or they can pursue more strategic solutions. For example, the customer may seek to promote new competitors in the market, or if the situation warrants it, the customer may seek governmental or legal actions to break the monopoly. These solutions, or course, are very slow and costly.

Commercial software companies have long recognized the importance of documentation for their product's use and capabilities. Their documentation has mainly described the use of the graphical user interface (GUI), the capabilities of the code, mesh generation capabilities, numerical algorithm techniques, post-processing capabilities, and output graphics. Documentation of code verification procedures and results by commercial software companies, however, has generally been very limited, or nonexistent. Customers presume that the software company has satisfactorily conducted SQA and code verification, but there is a great deal of evidence to the contrary. We believe the old adage of quality processes applies here: if it isn't documented, it didn't happen.

Some large commercial code companies specializing in solid mechanics have developed an extensive set of verification benchmarks that can be exercised by licensed users of their codes (see, for example, (ANSYS, 2005; ABAQUS, 2006)). These documented benchmarks are intended to demonstrate the performance of the code on relatively simple benchmark problems, as well as serve as a training aid for users of the code. The primary weakness of essentially all of the documented verification testing is that it only demonstrates "engineering accuracy" of the code; but does not carefully quantify the order of convergence of the numerical methods (Oberkampf and Trucano, 2008). As stated in one set of documentation, "In some cases, an exact comparison with a finite-element solution would require an infinite number of elements and/or an infinite number of iterations separated by an infinitely small step size. Such a comparison is neither practical nor desirable" (ANSYS, 2005). This argument is without merit. As discussed by many authors, and at length in this book, the discretization order of convergence and iterative convergence characteristics of the numerical methods can be practically and rigorously tested. It is of great value to a customer to demonstrate what the code actually produces in terms of convergence rate characteristics on a variety of relevant test problems, versus what is claimed in glossy marketing material.

Computational fluid dynamics (CFD) software has, in general, not provided the same level of documentation of code verification as that provided by commercial solid mechanics codes. As an indication of the poor state of maturity of CFD software, a recent paper by Abanto *et al.* (2005) tested three unnamed commercial CFD codes on relatively simple verification test problems. The poor results of the codes were shocking to some people, but not to the authors of the paper, nor to us.

16.2.2 Solution verification

16.2.2.1 Who should conduct solution verification?

Solution verification is primarily the responsibility of the analyst conducting the simulation. If it is a simulation involving multiple analysts and software packages, there should be close communication between the analysts to ensure adequate monitoring of numerical solution error. As discussed in Chapter 7, Solution verification, and Chapter 8, Discretization error, the recommended procedure is to quantitatively estimate both the iterative and mesh discretization error for each SRQ of interest. If a sequence of codes is used where the output of one code provides the input to the next in order to produce a final set of SRQs, then the estimation procedure for solution error becomes convolved with the uncertainty estimation procedure.

The level of effort needed to ensure high quality solution verification can vary tremendously, depending on the complexity of the analysis. For large-scale analyses, the effort needed to carefully estimate and document numerical solution error is major. For example, with a hundred uncertain input quantities resulting in tens of uncertain SRQs, the solution error would need to be estimated for each SRQ over the 100-dimensional input space. For those SRQs where the estimated error is not negligible, then the error would need to be combined with other uncertainties estimated in the prediction. A new method for combining these uncertainties was presented in Chapter 13, Predictive capability. This is a time-consuming task in a large-scale analysis, especially if a sequence of codes is used where the output of one becomes the uncertain input for the next code. Our experience, and observations from the journal literature, indicates there is careful attention paid to solution verification only for high-consequence, high public visibility projects.

For a deterministic analysis with relatively few SRQs, the task of numerical error estima-tion is relatively straightforward. For those SRQs where the estimated error is not negligible, the SRQ should be represented as an interval in order to reflect the uncertainty in the SRQ. Even for this type of problem, it is still common to see little or no information concern-ing solution verification in conference papers or journal articles. For analyses documented in internal corporate or project reports, it is our experience that solution verification is addressed infrequently.

Probably the simplest technique for quantifying discretization error is to use the grid convergence index (GCI) method (Roache, 1998). To use the method, the analyst (a) must have a solution on two different mesh and/or temporal resolutions; (b) should have some type of evidence that the solution for the particular SRQ of interest is in the asymptotic region for each of the independent variables in the mathematical model; (c) should compute the observed order of convergence, or alternatively assume the formal order of convergence, of the discretization method; and (d) should pick an appropriate factor of safety for the error estimate.

Sometimes even the GCI is not used and the analyst resorts to qualitative methods. For example, the solution is computed on two different mesh resolutions and the difference between the solution values are examined for each of the SRQs of interest. If the differences are all considered "small," the mesh resolution is deemed acceptable and the analysis proceeds. This latter approach is unreliable and can be very misleading with respect to the inferred accuracy of the results of the analysis.

16.2.2.2 *Who should require solution verification?*

Users of the analysis results from the simulation are primarily responsible for requiring quantitative information concerning solution verification. We again apply the supplier–customer model discussed above. Here, the analyst is the supplier of information to the customer who uses the analysis results. The customer can be anyone who directly uses the results of the analyses; e.g., a designer, a project manager, or decision maker. Stakeholders, i.e., those who have an appropriate and legitimate interest in the analysis results, may also share some of the responsibility of solution verification, but this would normally be minimal. Stakeholders are typically secondary users of the information provided by the analysis, such as those who benefit or profit from the analysis, or those who must plan their future activities based on the analysis.

Some have argued that the complete responsibility for solution verification should rest with the analyst conducting the work, instead of a shared responsibility with the customer. They argue that "The analysts are the experts in error estimation, so they should be responsible." Or, "We are not trained in these matters, why should we be responsible?" This argument has little merit and we reject it. We argue that it would be delinquent, if not negligent, to *assume* that solution verification was adequately done in an analysis. The argument for shared responsibility for solution verification between the analyst and the customer is analogous to the previous discussion of shared responsibility for SQA and code verification between code developers and code users.

Commonly the situation arises where the customer may be inexperienced or completely ignorant of solution verification techniques. For example, the customer could be a project leader or decision maker who is experienced in other technical fields, such as systems engineering and testing, but *not* in aspects of scientific computing. A more problematic situation would be if the project leader or decision maker is not technically trained, for example, their background is in business, marketing, or law. For these situations, it would be useful to have advisory staff or consultants experienced in scientific computing.

16.2.3 Validation

16.2.3.1 Who should conduct validation?

Validation is the joint responsibility of the analysts conducting the simulation and the experimentalists conducting the experiment. As discussed in Chapter 11, Design and execution of validation experiments, validation experiments should be designed, executed, analyzed, and documented as a team effort. Various members of the team must be familiar with and decide on a wide range of technical details for the validation activity, such as (a) what predictive capabilities of the model are of primary importance to the application of interest? (b) can the available experimental facilities provide adequate conditions to assess the model's predictive capabilities? (c) what SRQs are of interest and can they be measured with adequate experimental accuracy? (d) what are the key input quantities to the model and how can these quantities, along with their uncertainties, be measured in the experiment? (e) can the numerical solution errors in the SRQs of interest be estimated and adequately reduced? and (f) does an appropriate validation metric exist that is relevant to the application of interest, or does one need to be developed? Assembly of a competent validation team is challenging, and joint funding and coordination can also be formidable.

If poor agreement between simulations and experiments occur, some may feel that the validation effort has been wasted. We believe this response reflects a misunderstanding of the primary goal of validation. Validation is conducted for the purpose of critically assessing the predictive capability of a mathematical model; *not* for the purpose of showing good agreement of model and experiment. Consider two very beneficial outcomes that can occur when agreement between simulation and experiment is found to be unexpectedly poor. The usual situation for these outcomes is when it is strongly believed that the model should be very accurate for the range of input conditions tested. First, it can be found that the cause of the disagreement with experiment is due to a previously undetected programming error in the software or an unexpected numerical algorithm deficiency. Although there is a definite penalty to be paid for this lack of sufficient code verification, it is a very valuable piece of information not only for the present analysis, but also for past and future analyses. Two examples of the penalty that may result are (a) past simulations may be affected by this code bug or algorithm deficiency and these will need to be revisited, and (b) all model parameters that have been calibrated and are affected by this code bug will need to be recalibrated. These kinds of repercussion can be very expensive, humiliating, and damaging to the confidence in the organization responsible for the simulations.

Second, it can be found that the cause of the disagreement is due to an unexpected systematic (bias) error in the experimental measurements. As just discussed, this can have negative repercussions to the experimentalist who conducted the experiment or the facility in which the experiment was conducted. On the positive side, it can also be beneficial in convincing staff and management to improve measurement techniques and experimental facilities in the future.

Code developers or commercial software providers are only secondarily responsible for validation. They commonly conduct various unit level validation activities, but these are usually generic in nature. For example, commercial software providers typically compare their simulations with classic experiments using publicly available experimental data. These cases are usually documented as part of marketing material for the software or user training cases. One procedure that can be very helpful to a potential new customer for a commercial software license is to request that the software company compute a blind prediction as a validation test case. Most potential customers have proprietary or restricted distribution experimental data on systems, subsystems, or components that they design, market, or use. All of the needed input data from the experiment can be given to the software supplier and then the software company computes the SRQs of interest to the software customer. The comparisons of the simulations with the data may, or may not, be shared with the software supplier, depending on the business or security sensitivity of the situation. In this type of blind prediction, the software customer must be extremely careful to provide to the software supplier all of the needed information that is appropriate for their modeling approach. If some input quantities are not available, then the software supplier will need to conduct a nondeterministic analysis for comparison with the experimentally measured SRQs.

16.2.3.2 Who should require validation?

The analysis results user, i.e., the customers for the information produced, is primarily responsible for requiring detailed information concerning validation activities. Customers of computational analyses have traditionally recognized this responsibility with regard to validation activities. We believe this tradition exists because most customers of computational analyses have intuitively expected critical comparisons of predictions and experimental measurements that are closely related to their system of interest.

Given the validation framework discussed in this book, there are four aspects of validation particularly important to a customer. (a) At what levels of the validation hierarchy were the experiments conducted, compared to the top-level system of interest in the hierarchy? (b) What is the relationship of the validation domain where the experiments were conducted, compared to the application domain of the system? (c) Were the validation metrics used in model accuracy assessment relevant to the application of interest? and (d) How accurate were the model predictions over the validation domain? Here, we comment on the first two areas of importance.

Occasionally, it has been observed that the validation conditions are inappropriately influenced by the needs of the model developers as opposed to the needs of the customer. For example, model developers (and sometimes analysts) can invent reasons why certain validation conditions that would test the model more critically are not possible, practical, affordable, or useful. This type of thinking reflects a cognitive bias and is usually referred to as *confirmation bias* (Pohl, 2004). That is, most people have a strong tendency to process and search for information in a way that confirms their preconceptions or existing viewpoints, and avoid information that might contradict, challenge, or threaten their present beliefs. This bias is the primary reason for lack of enthusiasm for blind-test experiments among many model developers. This bias, of course, is not restricted to model builders, but is even more dangerous when exhibited by the customers of computational analyses.

16.2.4 Nondeterministic predictions

16.2.4.1 Who should conduct nondeterministic predictions?

Analysts are primarily responsible for conducting nondeterministic predictions. The nondeterministic predictions referred to here are those focused on predictions of SRQs at the application conditions for the system of interest. These predictions are the culmination of all of the efforts devoted to V&V. This activity is commonly the most demanding in terms of time and resources because it brings together (a) the V&V efforts directed to the system of interest, (b) the modeling effort devoted to identifying and characterizing the environments and scenarios of the system of interest, and (c) the UQ for the system of interest. The level of effort devoted to the nondeterministic predictions can vary widely, depending on the needs of the analysis. As a result, the burden of responsibility on the analyst can vary considerably. We briefly describe two extremes of nondeterministic predictions to stress the range of responsibility.

For the first extreme, consider the emergency cooling of the core of a nuclear power reactor. This type of analysis involves a large team of people, commonly spread over several organizations, because it deals with a high-consequence system in an abnormal environment. For this environment, many possible scenarios are identified and several of the highest risk scenarios are analyzed in detail. The nondeterministic analysis includes many different types of mathematical models, codes that have gone through years of verification testing, experimental data from a wide variety of experiments, and an extensive range of uncertainties that are carefully characterized. As is appropriate, much is expected of the analysis in order to support risk-informed decision making related to the system. This type of nondeterministic analysis is highly demanding in terms of time, resources, and the variety of technical expertise needed on the team, but it is appropriate for high-consequence systems.

For the second extreme, consider the solid mechanics analysis of a non-safety-critical component of a gas turbine engine. Here, we presume the analysis is directed toward an incremental design change of the component, but the change is expected to have minimal impact on the performance or reliability of the system. As a result, one individual conducts the nondeterministic analysis. Although the analysis could take into account different environments, scenarios, and a wide range of uncertainties, the analyst decides that because of schedule and resource constraints, he is only able to conduct a meager nondeterministic analysis. This situation is very common in industrial settings where competition between manufacturers is intense and time scales are very short. This type of industrial environment for scientific computing was well summarized by Hutton and Casey (2001). Risks due to approximations and short cuts in the non-deterministic analysis are greatly mitigated because relatively little is required from the analysis. For this type of situation, the primary basis for decision-making is the extensive operating experience and developmental testing of the system.

16.2.4.2 Who should require nondeterministic predictions?

Consistent with our previous argument, the customer for the results should require nondeterministic predictions, if these are needed for the decisions at hand. It is now standard practice in the design of most engineered systems that some portions of the analysis of the performance, reliability, and safety of the system are nondeterministic. Some fields of engineering still rely on a factor of safety design procedure or some even declare the reliability of their system is so high that the reliability is unity. In preliminary design studies and physical phenomena research, however, nondeterministic analyses are rarely conducted. For these types of situations a deterministic analysis is appropriate, except for the following cases: (a) when there are large uncertainties in important input quantities to the analysis, and (b) when the SRQs of interest are highly sensitive to uncertainties in any input quantities. For risk-informed decision making on final designs that rely heavily on M&S, the appropriate level of effort that is devoted to nondeterministic analyses should depend on a wide range of technical, liability, and resource factors.

A summary of our views on primary responsibilities for the conduct of an activity and who should require confirmation of the activity is shown in Table 16.1. The table shows how the responsibilities can change between the various participants depending on how the participant is involved in a particular activity. The *supplier* designation in the table

Table 16.1 *Primary role of participants in VV&UQ activities.*

Activity	Code developer	Analyst (code user)	Analysis result user	Experimentalist
SQA and code verification	Supplier	Customer	Customer	–
Solution Verification	–	Supplier	Customer	–
Validation	–	Supplier	Customer	Supplier
Nondeterministic predictions	–	Supplier	Customer	–

indicates the participant who is primarily responsible for the conduct of the activity, and the *customer* designation indicates who is primarily responsible for confirmation that the activity is satisfactorily completed.

16.3 Management actions and responsibilities

This section discusses various actions that management can take to help or hinder the development, implementation, and effectiveness of good VV&UQ practices in an organization. Most of the discussion is directed toward private businesses and government organizations, while some discussion is also appropriate for research institutes and universities. The topics are discussed in the context of responsibilities of management of scientific computing projects whose results are either used in their organization or are provided as a service to other organizations. Some of the recommendations for management are for the purpose of leading and motivating staff toward more effective and efficient VV&UQ practices.

When we refer to *management*, we are primarily referring to line management of an organization. Line managers are those appointed to the relatively permanent structure needed for the coordination and functioning of an organization. In certain instances, the discussion of actions and responsibilities will also refer to project management. Project managers are those whose responsibilities are directly tied to the execution and completion of a project. Project managers in business are commonly under severe constraints related to scope, schedule, and cost of the project. We recognize and respect their perspective and project responsibilities.

16.3.1 Implementation issues

Many of the responsibilities discussed in Section 16.2, with regard to who should require a certain activity, are directed at staff and project management. Often the situation arises where the manager is not familiar with, or technically trained in, all of the VV&UQ activities in a project. As a result, the manager is placed in a difficult position with regard to assessing the adequacy of all of the activities needed to achieve the goals of the computational analysis. For example, there may be inadequate solution verification that could place the analysis results into question, or worse, the results are more influenced by solution error than physics modeling. The manager may also perceive a risk with regard to large uncertainties in predicted system performance and he/she may need to move resources from one activity to fund another activity that appears to be lacking. The predictive capability maturity model (PCMM), discussed in Chapter 15, Maturity assessment of modeling and simulation, can be helpful in this regard. The PCMM is a framework for assessing the maturity of each of the four activities discussed above, in addition to the activities of representation of geometric fidelity and physics and material model fidelity. The PCMM is focused on assessing M&S maturity for an application-focused project. The manager can require that the analysts involved in the six M&S activities complete the PCMM table and present their maturity assessment at progress reviews of the project. If appropriate, the manager may also wish to add an activity referred to as *reproducibility, traceability, and documentation* of the six previously mentioned activities. Even if the manager is not familiar with certain activities being assessed, he/she can learn a great deal not only from the maturity assessment presented, but also how the analyst justifies the assessment results. After the PCMM assessment is complete, the manager can then determine if the assessed levels of maturity are adequate for the requirements of the project.

It is our observation that in many organizations there is either a competitive relationship between computational analysts and experimentalists, or there is a major disjunction between the two. This type of relationship can be found at the individual level as well as between computational and experimental groups. It could be due to (a) competition over organizational resources, (b) a perception of unjustified recognition of one group over the other, (c) experimentalists feeling that increasing capability in scientific computing will reduce or eliminate the need for their expertise, or (d) simply due to the divisional structure of the organization. Management often does not recognize the problem, or if they do, they may consciously or subconsciously ignore it. Even without competitive or adversarial pressures, there is commonly a notable difference in technical and personal cultures between computational analysts and experimentalists. For validation activities to contribute to the greatest degree possible, it is imperative that management assesses the state of the relationship between analysts and experimentalists in their organizations. In addition, it is critical that management *creates opportunities* for bringing the different individuals, groups, and cultures together in cooperative and mutually beneficial efforts. For example, management must make it clear that the success of a validation team effort will benefit both groups equally, and that failure will be the responsibility of both groups. By *success* we mean high quality computational simulations, experimental measurements, model accuracy assessment, and timeliness of the effort; *not* whether the agreement between computation and experiment was good or bad.

Implementation of most of the approaches and procedures recommended in this book will be neither inexpensive nor easy. Furthermore, some of these approaches may even be technically or economically impractical in particular situations. In addition, some of the approaches and procedures have not been developed satisfactorily for implementation in a design-engineering environment. With each included step, however, the quality of the

VV&UQ processes will be improved, resulting in increased confidence in the simulation results. We firmly believe that VV&UQ is a process, *not* a product. In addition, VV&UQ are not processes that can be *inspected in* the simulation results. That is, the technical complexities of M&S and VV&UQ do not allow for a comprehensive set of rules to be laid down, and then simply followed. Good VV&UQ processes are akin to best practices in engineering and business. The development of good VV&UQ processes requires a change in the culture of scientific computing; a culture of healthy skepticism and disbelief. Even though technological change can occur at a stunning rate, changes in habits and traditions are exceedingly slow and painful.

Some individuals and managers will overtly or covertly thwart the implementation of VV&UQ activities because they believe that: (a) the costs of the activities exceed their value added, and (b) it unnecessarily delays the completion of a computational analysis. If the resistance to VV&UQ is done openly, then the management team must have frank discussions concerning the value added by VV&UQ, and the costs and schedule implications of implementing VV&UQ activities. If resistance is hidden or surreptitious, then it is much more difficult for management to address.

From a business perspective, the results from a computational analysis is considered as a *service*, because it involves the production of intangible goods; specifically, the generation of knowledge. As has been stressed throughout this book, VV&UQ add quality to the computational analysis, i.e., to the service. Business will evaluate the quality improvement due to VV&UQ in the same way as the introduction of any new technology or business process; what is the value added compared to the resources and time expended? Although many business sectors have devised innovative methods to measure quality of the service provided, we contend that the quality added by VV&UQ to the knowledge generated in a computational analysis is significantly more difficult to measure.

The following is a suggested framework useful for considering the business issue of cost versus benefit: what is the cost and time required for VV&UQ compared to the risk of incorrect or improper decisions made based on simulation. In probabilistic risk assessment, the risk is typically defined as the product of the probability of the occurrence of an adverse event and the consequence of the event. As the level of effort devoted to VV&UQ increases, it is reasonable to expect that the probability of incorrect or improper decisions based on simulation decreases. The decrease in the probability, however, is difficult to measure. One recommended guideline is that one must weigh how much of the decision is based on computational analysis versus other traditional factors, such as experimental testing and operational experience with the system. Stated differently, how far beyond our base of experience and experimental data are we relying on the predictions from the analysis? The consequence of an incorrect or improper decision can also be difficult to measure, primarily because there is such a variety of consequences that can be considered. The only guideline we can recommend is that the assessment of consequences should be broadly examined, as discussed above, not only in the short term, but also over the long term. For example, suppose an erroneous conclusion is made concerning the physics of some process simulated in an article in a research journal. The erroneous result would rightly be viewed as a low-consequence risk, if noticed at all. On the other hand, if erroneous conclusions based on simulation are made on important aspects of a system, decision makers could place at risk their corporation, their customers, the public, or the environment.

16.3.2 Personnel training

Individuals experienced and trained in V&V are relatively rare at the present time because V&V, as recognized fields of research and application, are actually quite new. There is much wider experience and training, however, in the foundational fields of V&V: SQA, numerical error estimation, experimental uncertainty estimation, and probability and statistics. University graduate courses in the foundational topics have been in existence for at least four decades. Some major universities in the US are now beginning to teach graduate courses specifically in the field of V&V. Consequently, it will be at least another decade or two before there will be a sizeable cadre of highly qualified individuals in the field of V&V.

We suggest that if there are at least several experienced individuals in the field of VV&UQ within an organization, then management should consider forming a group of these individuals. This group can provide training and mentoring for other staff members, as well as leading VV&UQ activities within a project. This option will be discussed more in Section 16.3.4.

During the near term, the best method for training staff and managers in V&V is through professional development short courses. These continuing education courses typically range from one to five days and are offered by professional societies, universities, and institutes. They are also taught at professional society conferences or, upon request, at the site of the interested organization. At the present time there are roughly five short courses taught in the field of V&V by different organizations.

16.3.3 Incorporation into business goals

The incorporation of computational analyses into the goals of a business, or any organization, is a broad topic. Here, we will focus on how VV&UQ contribute to the quality of the information generated in an analysis. In Chapter 15, we discussed the results of the comprehensive study by Wang and Strong (1996) concerning the most important qualities of information. They categorized the key attributes into four aspects:

- *intrinsic information quality*: believability, accuracy, objectivity, and reputation;
- *contextual information quality*: value added, relevancy, timeliness, completeness, and amount of information;
- *representational information quality*: interpretability, ease of understanding, consistent representation, and concise representation;
- *accessibility information quality*: accessibility and security aspects.

In the following sections, we will briefly discuss how VV&UQ contribute to the first three attributes of information quality.

16.3.3.1 Intrinsic information quality

Throughout this book, we have dealt with four intertwined issues of VV&UQ: (a) quality of simulation software, (b) accuracy of the numerical calculations, (c) uncertainty in the validation experiments, and (d) uncertainty in predictions. When we consider the intrinsic information quality of simulation in terms of how it is used, we must broaden our perspective away from the details of the analysis. The proper perspective should be: how is the information from an analysis properly used by management in a decision-making environment? We argue that the proper use of the information is, in large part, dependent on the accuracy and objectivity aspects of intrinsic information quality. To make this point, we contrast the broader and more comprehensive meaning of the term *accuracy*. Here, we stress the meaning of accuracy in sense of faithfulness, objectiveness, and completeness, as opposed to the implication of precision of the results. We make this point in two different contexts.

First, predictions for any real engineering system must deal with uncertainty in the response of the system. The uncertainty can be due to many sources, for example: (a) the environment in the sense of normal, abnormal, or hostile; (b) the possible scenarios that can occur in the system, (c) the uncertainty inherent in the system; (d) the uncertainty in the influence of the surroundings on the system; and (e) the uncertainty due to the mathematical model used in the analysis. The simulation result, therefore, must be characterized as an uncertain number; *not simply a number*. The uncertain number can be expressed in several ways, such as an interval, a precise probability distribution, or a p-box. Several fields of engineering and systems analysis moved to this paradigm decades ago; e.g., nuclear reactor safety, structural dynamics, and the broad field of risk assessment. Many fields of engineering and science, however, have not moved from the tradition of deterministic predictions. More importantly, many decision makers in business are not comfortable with the concept of simulation results presented as an uncertain number. It can be disconcerting to let go of the apparent precision of a deterministic prediction, but the precision is only a ruse for accuracy. Quoting a Chinese proverb, "To be uncertain is uncomfortable, but to be certain is ridiculous."

Second, when uncertainty is incorporated in the analysis, through whatever source, one must commonly deal with the issue of aleatory and epistemic uncertainty. As discussed in several chapters, including epistemic uncertainty in the analysis can result in a large increase in uncertainty in the response of the system, as compared to characterization of the uncertainty as a random variable. For example, if an input uncertainty is initially characterized as a uniform distribution over some interval, but then changed to an interval-valued quantity over the same interval, there can be a large increase in the uncertainty of a SRQ. The characterization of the SRQ changes from a single probability distribution associated with the uniform distribution to a p-box, i.e., an infinite ensemble of distributions. Some experienced risk analysts have commented that simply changing an input probability distribution to an interval will not yield a significant change in the characterization of the output. If the uncertain input quantity were a significant contributor to uncertainty in the output, then they would be stunned at the increase in uncertainty. With regard to simulation accuracy, the point can be made in the following way. If certain inputs to the simulation are known so poorly that the knowledge can only be represented as an interval, then the p-box result of the system responses is the *least uncertain result* that can be claimed. An assumption that characterizes the input as a random variable, such as assuming a uniform distribution over the interval, will actually *under-represent* the uncertainty of the responses to the decision maker. The result showing less uncertainty in the system response can be viewed as being more precise, but it is indeed less accurate and, at best, misleading to the decision maker.

16.3.3.2 Contextual information quality

The two attributes of contextual information quality that we will stress here, with regard to decision making, are value added and timeliness. Several chapters in this book have dealt with the added value of computational analyses in the sense of detailed knowledge generated for the decision maker. To better appreciate our stress on added value, consider the wisdom that can be learned from examining past failures. Here, we specifically refer to knowledge that can be learned by examining the root causes of past engineering system failures (Dorner, 1989; Petroski, 1994; Vaughan, 1996; Reason, 1997; Chiles, 2001; Gehman *et al.*, 2003; Lawson, 2005; Mosey, 2006). Most of these authors stress the importance of errors in judgment of the responsible decision makers. Sometimes the error is made by an individual decision maker, but in catastrophic failures of large systems the error is more commonly made by a group of decision makers, i.e., an organizational failure. Petroski (1994) bluntly states:

Human error in anticipating failure continues to be the single most important factor in keeping the reliability of engineering designs from achieving the theoretically high levels made possible by modern methods of analysis and materials. This is due in part to a de-emphasis on engineering experience and judgment in the light of increasingly sophisticated numerical and analytical techniques. (pp. 7–8)

His view, and that of many others who help us to learn from our past mistakes, is primarily directed at the lack of vigor that some project managers have toward investigating how their system can fail or could cause other associated systems to fail. Many managers tend to view VV&UQ with the same mind set. Instead of grasping how VV&UQ adds value to the quality of the information provided in the analysis, they see it as a potential risk to their project or personal agenda, or simply as a drain on resources. This is especially true if the VV&UQ activity is controlled and funded by a separate project or line manager who does not report to them, because then they have little or no control over the activities. This type of systemic failure in the attitude of a project toward a safety organization was scathingly criticized by Adm. Harold Gehman as part of his testimony to a US Senate Committee concerning the loss of the Space Shuttle Columbia and her crew: "The [NASA] safety organization sits right beside the person making the decisions. But behind the safety organization, there's nothing back there. There's no people, money, engineering expertise, analysis." (AWST, 2003).

A widespread difficulty encountered when using simulation results in a design-engineering environment is the lack of appreciation of timeliness among simulation analysts. The time scales required for making the multitude of design decisions on a system are generally very short. Some analysts, especially applied research analysts, are completely unaccustomed to these schedule requirements. For example, it is not uncommon for the design engineer to tell the analyst "If you get the analysis results to me by next week, I will use the results to make a design decision. If you don't, I will make the decision without your help." VV&UQ activities take time to complete, possibly resulting in a degradation of the prompt response times required. However, as discussed above, there must be an appropriate tradeoff between the time required to produce an adequately reliable result and the consequences of improper decisions based on an inaccurate or incomplete result.

16.3.3.3 Representational information quality

As part of the attribute of representational information quality, we will stress the importance of interpretability (and ease of understanding) and consistent representation of results and VV&UQ activities. Most people think about this attribute of information quality with regard to written documentation of a simulation. Although written documentation is certainly important for a permanent record of the details of an analysis, we believe representational information quality is a more important quality with regard to oral presentations to management. It is our view that much of the discussion and debate concerning significant decisions occurs when presentations to management are made. By the time detailed documentation is prepared and published, usually at the completion of the project, most decisions are cast in stone.

In any summary presentation of a mathematical modeling approach and computational results to management, the importance of interpretability and ease of understanding cannot be overstated. This is in no way a criticism of management's abilities or backgrounds. As part of human nature, technical staff who prepare the summary presentations tend to think that others have similar backgrounds; technically, experientially, and culturally. This is, in general, a gross misjudgment that can be devastating to the clarity and effectiveness of a presentation. Summary presentations must greatly condense the amount of information generated from developing, testing, analyzing, and understanding the models and the simulations, obtaining experimental data, and interpreting the results. For large team efforts, the condensation factor is even greater. Similarly, large condensations of information also occur when presentations are given to external review panels or governmental regulatory agencies. As a result, management must stress to their staff the crucial importance of interpretability and ease of understanding of an analysis in their presentations.

In this same regard, we urge that the presentations have a proper balance, explaining the strengths *and* weaknesses of not only the M&S effort, but also the VV&UQ activities. Presentations tend to overly stress the strengths of an analysis and minimize the weaknesses, if they are mentioned at all. A presentation or detailed documentation of an M&S effort that does not discuss the effects of important assumptions should be highly suspect by managers and external reviewers. Ignoring the justification and effects of important assumptions is, in our view, one of the single most damaging indicators of the quality of an M&S effort. Analyses that have not identified, or do not discuss, their primary weaknesses can expose decision makers and stakeholders to significant risks.

The importance of significant assumptions also carries over to the second aspect of representational information quality: consistent representation. It is common practice that summary presentations of a major M&S effort are repeated to different audiences, usually with a slightly different emphasis, depending on the nature and interest of the audience. Although it is appropriate to stress different aspects of the analysis in each presentation, it is important that the primary issues receive consistent representation. For example, consider the situation where presentations to lower level management are made by the staff who conducted the analysis. At this level, time is usually available for significant detail to be presented, along with the major assumptions made in the analysis. It is common in many organizations, especially in organizations that place heavy emphasis on a hierarchical management structure, that managers of the staff who conducted the analysis brief higher levels of management on the analysis. The presentations to upper management are usually accompanied by additional condensation of the information. We recommend that VV&UQ activities be included in these higher level presentations, and not eliminated from the presentations with the argument "Of course we conducted adequate VV&UQ measures." This can jeopardize the consistency of the representation of the information and it can put higher levels of management at increased risk of making poor decisions.

16.3.4 Organizational structures

There are two basic organizational approaches to the deployment of V&V practices in a business or government agency. One involves the formation of a small organization within the parent organization that is composed of experienced V&V staff. This organization is responsible for developing and deploying V&V practices and training of staff and management in other organizations within the parent company. The second is a dispersed approach where the experienced staff are placed in various organizations that are conducting computational analyses and experimental validation activities. Since there are a relatively small number of individuals trained and experienced in V&V at the present time, and since V&V serves in a support role to simulation, it is an open question as to which approach is best suited to the deployment of V&V. In fact, it is certainly reasonable that one approach may be optimum for one organization, while the other approach would be better in a different organization. There are many site-specific factors that managers should consider in deciding which approach would be best for their organization. Here, we will briefly discuss some of the features of each approach, as well as some of the advantages and disadvantages.

There are a number of advantages in forming a V&V group. With close interactions in the group, it can serve as a critical mass of ideas and expertise so that additional energy is generated around the topic. This approach was used at Sandia National Laboratories beginning in 1999 with a large degree of success. Included in this group were staff members who, although not familiar with V&V, were experienced in UQ. This combination of both activities in the same group proved to be an excellent approach. As V&V methodologies developed, the strong connection between validation and UQ, particularly model uncertainty, became better understood. Another benefit in the initial formation of the group was the inclusion of experienced individuals in nuclear reactor safety analyses. These individuals were experienced not only in each topic of VV&UQ, but also in risk analysis techniques, e.g., fault tree analyses and the phenomena identification and ranking table (PIRT).

The existence of a VV&UQ group in an organization is, even today, an anomaly. Since there is essentially no formal university training devoted exclusively to VV&UQ at the present time, the mixture of technical disciplines of the staff in a VV&UQ group is expected to be diverse. Although the principles of VV&UQ are the same regardless of the application area, there are noticeable differences in some of the techniques depending on the application area. For example, in fluid dynamics, heat transfer, and solid mechanics there are many applications that are steady state or involve slowly varying responses as a function of time. In structural dynamics, shock wave dynamics, and electrodynamics, however, the time series nature of the responses is a dominant factor that significantly complicates VV&UQ. Although the group would probably be focused on simulation, there should be some expertise included with a background in experimental methods. It has been our experience that individuals who have experience in both computational and experimental methods are the most adept at grasping the philosophy of validation and the principles for the design and execution of validation experiments. An individual who was entirely focused on experiments, however, would probably not fit well in a group such as this.

The responsibilities of the VV&UQ group should include three areas. First, the group should develop VV&UQ techniques that are useful not only for the needs within the group, but also for other organizations within the parent organization. Some examples of development areas are (a) manufactured solutions, (b) numerical solution error estimators, (c) validation metrics, and (d) propagation methods applicable to both aleatory and epistemic uncertainties. Second, the group should deploy VV&UQ practices to other computational and experimental groups. Deployment of practices can take several forms, such as (a) explain and promote the concepts, procedures, and benefits of VV&UQ; (b) apply VV&UQ techniques to various computational projects within the parent organization, i.e., become a practitioner instead of just a theorist; and (c) write and document software packages that are useful in various VV&UQ tasks. Concerning this last suggestion, it responds to the criticism that is sometimes posited by other organizations: "We don't have the expertise or the time to write the needed software packages to do what you are promoting." Third, the group should train staff and managers in other organizations concerning VV&UQ practices. Ideas for different types of training are (a) offer short courses or formal training on topics, (b) serve as consultants for computational and experimental projects in other organizations, and (c) serve as mentors to train and advise staff in VV&UQ. We should stress that significant training is usually needed with regard to UQ concepts and methods. Very few engineering and science educational disciplines involve courses in statistics and the analysis of uncertainty in systems.

The second approach to the deployment of V&V practices is to disperse experienced V&V staff into various computational and experimental project groups. For a small organization, this is a more appropriate method. The individuals could accomplish the suggestions given in the previous paragraph, but their focus would be more on tactical, near term issues of their parent project group. The success of this approach would depend in part on how much time the project manager would allow the staff member to devote to V&V activities. If the manager were to allow a significant portion of time to be devoted to both near-term and long-term V&V needs, then this arrangement could be effective. If project tasks, for example those directed toward building new mathematical models for the computational analysis, were to always take priority over V&V needs, then little would be accomplished in moving the group toward better V&V practices.

Whichever deployment method is used, one key factor is crucial to the success of V&V deployment in an organization: the strong and genuine support of management for VV&UQ practices throughout the organizations involved in computational analyses and validation experiments. If management, in all organizations involved and at multiples levels, does not genuinely support VV&UQ, then deployment will be spotty at best; or at worst, a failed effort. As has been discussed in this and several other chapters, the key to long-term success of VV&UQ is the understanding of the value added to the information quality of computational analyses. To comprehend this, management must embrace a commitment to change the culture of M&S in their organizations.

16.4 Development of databases

This section discusses the major V&V databases and gives recommendations for improvements in the quality and usability of databases in the future. We only discuss major databases that are either publicly available or available on a membership basis. There are, as one would suspect, major proprietary databases built and maintained by for-profit organizations. Some examples of these are the large commercial software companies and essentially every large manufacturer that uses scientific computing in the design, optimization, and evaluation of their products. These proprietary databases are not addressed here.

The suggested recommendations for future development of publicly available or membership-based databases are made because we believe that the influence of scientific computing in the world will continue to grow in depth and breadth. We also believe that V&V databases built around individual technical fields can be a very positive influence on the quality and reliability of scientific computing in these fields. For those industries where the competitive pressure between manufacturers is intense, we argue that simplified test cases, i.e., lower levels in the validation hierarchy, can be found where competitors can safely share data. For these simplified cases, it can be more cost effective and efficient to jointly build and share V&V data than using proprietary databases. Some corporations feel that their proprietary data is the lifeblood to their continued competitiveness. We agree that some of these data are, but not all. Unless these data are well documented, effectively catalogued, easily found, and efficiently retrieved, the data are of little value. The business model of having key senior staff be the keepers of the data jewels is no longer realistic and it can easily fail for various reasons.

16.4.1 Existing databases

During the last two decades, the National Agency for Finite Element Methods and Standards (NAFEMS) has developed some of the most widely known V&V benchmarks (NAFEMS, 2006). Roughly 30 verification benchmarks have been constructed by NAFEMS. The majority of these benchmarks have targeted solid mechanics simulations, though some of the more recent benchmarks have been in fluid dynamics. Most of the NAFEMS verification benchmarks consist of an analytical solution or an accurate numerical solution to a simplified physical process described by a partial differential equation. The NAFEMS benchmark set is carefully defined, numerically demanding, and well documented. However, these benchmarks are currently very restricted in their coverage of various mathematical and/or numerical challenges (such as discontinuities) and in their coverage of physical phenomena. Further, the performance of a given code on the benchmark is subject to interpretation by the user of the code. It is also likely that the performance of a code on the benchmark is dependent on the experience and skill of the user.

In the field of nuclear reactor engineering, the Nuclear Energy Agency, Committee on the Safety of Nuclear Installations (CSNI) devoted significant resources toward developing validation benchmarks, which they refer to as International Standard Problems (ISPs). This effort began in 1977 with recommendations for the design, construction, and use of ISPs for loss-of-coolant accidents (LOCAs) (NEA, 1977). The CSNI recognized the importance of issues such as (a) providing a detailed description of the actual operational conditions in the experimental facility, not simply those conditions that were requested or desired; (b) preparing careful estimates of the uncertainty in experimental measurements and informing the analyst of the estimates; (c) reporting the initial and boundary conditions that were realized in the experiment, not those conditions that were simply desired; and (d) conducting a sensitivity analysis to determine the most important factors that affect the predicted system responses of interest. The CSNI has continually refined the guidance for ISPs, such that the most recent recommendations for the ISPs address any type of experimental benchmark, not just benchmarks for LOCA accidents (CSNI, 2004). Thus, the primary goal of the ISPs remains the same for all types of benchmark: "to contribute to a better understanding of postulated and actual events" that could affect the safety of nuclear power plants.

A number of efforts have been undertaken in the development of validation databases that could mature into well-founded benchmarks. In the United States, the NPARC Alliance has developed a validation database that has roughly 20 different flows (NPARC, 2000). In Europe, starting in the early 1990s, there has been a much more organized effort to develop validation databases. These databases have primarily focused on aerospace applications. ERCOFTAC (the European Research Community on Flow, Turbulence and Combustion) has collected a number of experimental datasets for validation applications (ERCOFTAC, 2000). QNET-CFD is a thematic network on quality and trust for the industrial applications of CFD (QNET-CFD, 2001). This network has more than 40 participants from several countries who represent research establishments in many sectors of the industry, including commercial CFD software companies. For a history and review of the various efforts, see Rizzi and Vos (1998) and Vos *et al.* (2002).

We note that the validation databases described by Rizzi and Vos (1998) and Vos *et al.* (2002) contain many cases that are for complex flows, which are sometimes referred to as *industrial applications*. We have observed, both through our own experience and in the scientific literature, that attempts to validate models on complex physical processes are commonly unsuccessful for two reasons. First, inadequate information concerning detailed system features, boundary conditions, or initial conditions are provided by the experimentalists. Second, the computational results compare very poorly with the experimental measurements for difficult-to-predict SRQs. Then, the computational analysts often do one of the following: (1) they engage in a model calibration activity, adjusting both physical and numerical parameters in the model, to obtain better agreement; (2) they reformulate the assumptions in their model to obtain better agreement, thereby changing the model; or (3) they start pointing accusatory fingers at the experimentalists about either what is wrong with the experimental data or what the experimentalists should have measured to make the data more effective for validation. Our view of these responses by the analysts has been discussed in several chapters dealing with validation and prediction.

16.4.2 Recent activities

Oberkampf *et al.* (2004) introduced the concept of *strong-sense benchmarks* (SSBs) in V&V. They argued that SSBs should be of sufficiently high quality that they could be viewed as *engineering reference standards*. They stated that SSBs are test problems that have the following four characteristics: (1) the purpose of the benchmark is clearly understood, (2) the definition and description of the benchmark is precisely stated, (3) specific requirements are stated for how comparisons are to be made with the results of the benchmark, and (4) acceptance criteria for comparison with the benchmark are defined. In addition, they required that information on each of these characteristics be promulgated, i.e., the information is well documented and publicly available. Although a number of benchmarks are available, a few of which were discussed above, these authors asserted that SSBs do not presently exist in science or engineering. They suggested that professional societies, academic institutions, governmental or international organizations, and newly formed nonprofit organizations would be the most likely to construct SSBs.

Oberkampf and Trucano (2008) present an in-depth discussion of how SSBs should be constructed and describe the key features that are needed to qualify as an SSB for both verification and validation. Concerning verification benchmarks, the following elements are discussed that should be contained in the documentation of a verification benchmark: (a) conceptual description, (b) mathematical description, (c) accuracy assessment, and (d) additional user information. Examples are provided for applying these elements to the four types of benchmarks, namely, manufactured solutions, analytical solutions, numerical solutions to ordinary differential equations, and numerical solutions to PDE models. Oberkampf and Trucano (2008) recommend that when a candidate code is compared with a verification benchmark, the results of the comparisons with benchmarks should *not* be included in the benchmark documentation *per se*. They also discuss how formal comparison results could be used and identify the types of information that should be included in the comparisons.

Concerning validation benchmarks, Oberkampf and Trucano (2008) present four elements that should be contained in the documentation of a validation benchmark: (a) conceptual description; (b) experimental description; (c) uncertainty quantification of benchmark measurements; and (d) additional user information. They also discuss how candidate code results could be compared with the benchmark results, paying particular attention to issues related to the computation of nondeterministic results to determine the uncertainty of SRQs due to uncertainties in input quantities, the computation of validation metrics to quantitatively measure the difference between experimental and computational results, the minimization of model calibration in comparisons with validation benchmarks, and the constructive role of global sensitivity analyses in validation experiments.

They also discuss why validation benchmarks are much more difficult to construct and use than verification benchmarks. The primary difficulty in constructing validation benchmarks is that experimental measurements in the past have rarely been designed to provide true validation benchmark data. The validation benchmarks that have been compiled and documented by organized efforts, some of which were discussed above, are indeed instructive and useful to users of the codes and to developers of physics models. However, they argue that much more needs to be incorporated into the validation benchmarks, both experimentally and computationally, to achieve the next level of usefulness and critical assessment.

16.4.3 Implementation issues of Databases

If V&V SSBs and a database to house them were to become a reality, a number of complex and difficult implementation and organizational issues would need to be addressed. Some of these issues would be, for example,

- agreement on the primary and secondary goals of the database,
- initial construction of the database,
- review and approval procedures for entries into the database,
- open versus restricted use of the database,
- structure of the software framework for searching and retrieving information on SSBs in the database,

- organizational control of the database,
- relationship of the controlling organization to existing private and governmental organizations and engineering societies,
- initial and long-term funding of the database.

These issues are of major importance to the joint community of individuals, corporations, commercial software companies, nonprofit organizations, engineering societies, universities, and governmental organizations with serious interest in improving scientific computing.

Initial construction of the database would be technically and organizationally complex, as well as costly. Populating the database with relevant, high-quality benchmarks would require a wide-ranging effort that cuts across major communities of applied mathematics, model building, experimentation, computation, engineering applications, and business decision making. Putting this kind of collaborative effort together hinges on a careful plan that takes the long-term view for the database. The construction of SSBs is not feasible as a short-term task. Much of what we recommend clearly aims at a sustainable and long-term use of the database, with an implication that the quality and breadth of the database improves over a long period of time. The long-term success of the database requires a sound starting point, with broad consensus from all interested parties about goals, use, access, and funding over the long term.

Broad organizational issues must be addressed very early in the planning stage. For example, will a single organization (nonprofit, academic, or governmental) have responsibility for database maintenance, configuration management, and day-to-day operation? Will the database have a role beyond its immediate community? *Broad impact* then implies that there is the goal of open access to the database for the good of the simulation community, specifically the world community in each of the traditional scientific and engineering disciplines. But how is this goal compatible with the significant expense needed to create, maintain, and improve the database? Potential financial supporters and users of the database would need to be convinced of the value returned to them for their investment. This returned value could be in many forms, such as improvements in their software products, the ability to attract new customers to their software products, and use of the database as a quality assessment tool for organizations or government agencies to allow contractors to bid on new projects. If proprietary information is used in the database, we believe it would greatly diminish or possibly eliminate the ability to create and sustain the database. Some have argued that the database could be constructed so that proprietary information could be segregated from generally available information. We believe that private corporations would not be convinced such segregation could be accomplished with high confidence, and that the database manager would not be able to adequately protect the proprietary information.

It seems that V&V databases of the type we have discussed should be constructed along the lines of traditional engineering and science disciplines, e.g., fluid dynamics, solid dynamics, electrodynamics, neutron transport, plasma dynamics, and molecular dynamics.

How each of these disciplines might begin to construct databases certainly depends on the traditions, applications, and funding sources in each of these fields. The nuclear power industry, for example, has a deeply embedded, long-term tradition of international cooperation. On the other hand, the aerospace industry, both aircraft and spacecraft builders, has a fierce competitive nature. We envision that different implementations and database structures would be chosen in various communities.

We also suggest that a secondary purpose for the establishment and use of SSBs is for the development of best practices in scientific computing. As recognized by NAFEMS (NAFEMS, 2006) and ERCOFTAC (Casey and Wintergerste, 2000), there is a compelling need for improvements in the professional practice of scientific computing. In our opinion, a convincing argument could be made that the most common failures in industrial applications of scientific computing result from mistakes made by practitioners using the code. Corporate and governmental management, of course, shoulders the ultimate responsibility for mentoring and training these practitioners, as well as for monitoring their work products. Given the qualities of SSBs discussed previously, these benchmarks could be viewed as very carefully documented step-by-step sample problems from which practitioners, new and experienced, could learn a great deal.

Rizzi and Vos (1998) and Vos *et al.* (2002) discuss how validation databases could be built and used by a wide range of individuals and organizations. They stress the importance of close collaboration between corporations and universities in the construction, use, and refinement of a validation database. In this regard, they also stress the value of workshops that are focused on specialty topics to improve the modeling efforts and simulations that are compared to experimental data. They discuss a number of workshops and initiatives in Europe, primarily funded by the European Union. Often, these workshops provide dramatic evidence of the power of carefully defined and applied V&V benchmarks. One such effort organized in the United States, but with participants from around the world, is the series of Drag Prediction Workshops (Levy *et al.*, 2003; Hemsch, 2004; Hemsch and Morrison, 2004; Laflin *et al.*, 2005; Rumsey *et al.*, 2005). These workshops have been extraordinarily enlightening from two perspectives: (a) there was great variability in the drag predictions from computational analysts for a relatively simple aircraft geometry, and (b) there were surprisingly large differences between the computational results and the experimental measurements. The key factor in this exercise that resulted in a "surprising large range of results" is that this was a blind comparison. Results from these types of workshop could form the basis for initial submittals of new V&V benchmarks into the database.

We believe an Internet-based system would provide the best vehicle for the deployment of V&V databases for three reasons. First, the ability to build, quickly share, and collaborate with an Internet-based system is now blatantly obvious. A paper-based system would be completely unworkable, as well as decades behind the current state of information technology.

Second, descriptive terms for a particular application of interest could be input to a search engine that could find all of the benchmarks that would contain those terms. The search engine could operate much like that found in Google or Wikipedia. Functionality could be expanded to include a relevancy-ranking feature that would further improve the search-and-retrieval capability. The overall system design would include configuration-, document-, and content-management elements. Then the benchmarks that were retrieved could be sorted according to their relevance to the words input to the search. One could then select the hyperlinks embedded within any of the benchmarks found. When a particular benchmark is displayed, it could have links from important words in the benchmark description to more detailed information in the benchmark.

Third, the computer-based system could instantly provide much more detail about each benchmark. We recommend that the documentation of V&V benchmarks be produced in an electronic format that is widely usable and robust across many computer operating systems. Of the electronic formats available, Adobe Portable Document Format (PDF) is the most commonly used and has many desirable characteristics; however, we also recommend that this format be supplemented with additional file formats for specialized information. For example, tabular data could be stored in ASCI text files or in Microsoft Excel files; high-resolution digital photographs should be stored in easily usable formats such as TIFF, PDF, and JPEG; digital video files should be stored in formats such as QuickTime, MPEG, or AVI; and computer software should be written in common languages such as C++, Fortran, or Java. The computer software would be necessary for documenting the source terms in database entries submitted for the method of manufactured solutions.

In the long term, new validation experiments should be funded either by the organization controlling the database or by for-profit private, nonprofit, university, or governmental organizations. The organization controlling the database could receive its funding from subscribing members to the organization, and possibly from governmental funding. The funding could be directed to both operation and maintenance of the database and to constructing new V&V benchmarks. When new validation results are entered into the database, there would be a unique opportunity for blind comparisons. As we have stressed several times, blind comparisons are the real test of predictive-capability prowess. We believe that identification of new validation experiments should be the responsibility of both the application community and the database organization. The organizational role and facilitation of discussions regarding which experiments should be conducted is best served by the database organization. For example, the database organization could serve as an unbiased referee between for-profit corporations desiring more application-relevant experiments and model builders who are more knowledgeable of the weaknesses of modeling for complex systems.

16.5 Development of standards

The efficient maturation of V&V depends on concerted efforts by individuals and organizations throughout the world to develop international standards with regard to terminology, basic philosophy, and proven procedures. In the US, the American National Standards

Institute (ANSI) oversees the development and approval of voluntary consensus standards in products and services. Although ANSI does not develop standards itself, it sets the rules and procedures by which standards are developed by member organizations, e.g., engineering societies. ANSI is the official US representative to the two major international standards organizations, the International Organization for Standardization (ISO) and the International Electrotechnical Commission (IEC). In a new field, such as V&V, it is critically important to develop standards that (a) have broad participation from industry, government, and universities, (b) are thoroughly vetted both within the committee and to interested groups, and (c) are on sound technical and practical grounds. In a new field, there must be extraordinary caution in developing standards because they are much more than research ideas or seemingly good practices. Standards are more than guides for engineering practices or recommended practices; they are expected to establish the highest levels of reliability and permanence to industry.

Concerning terminology, the efforts of the US Department of Defense, the American Institute of Aeronautics and Astronautics, and the American Society of Mechanical Engineers have been extremely productive in providing understandable, useful, and workable definitions for critical terms in scientific computing. Their definitions are on solid rational and pragmatic grounds. There is still some debate and confusion, however, concerning the encompassing view and the restricted view of validation, as discussed in Chapter 2, Fundamental concepts and terminology. However, we do not feel this is a critical issue, as long as people make it clear which definition they are using. Our primary concern is with the significant difference in V&V terminology between the scientific computing community (the focus of this book) and the ISO/IEEE communities, as discussed in Chapter 2. We are adamant that a rejection and dismissal of the scientific computing definitions by the ISO/IEEE communities would be a *major step backwards* in the development and use of scientific computing around the world. How this dichotomy in definitions will be resolved, and if it will be resolved, is unknown.

In our view, the most appropriate organizations for developing new standards are the professional engineering societies that have ANSI-approved standards writing committees and procedures. At the present time, only ASME has standards committees that are actively producing V&V standards. The AIAA and the American Nuclear Society have standards committees, but they have not recently produced new V&V standards. When these two societies, and possibly others, become more active in developing new V&V standards there must be a concerted effort to promote consistent concepts and procedures. One possibility would be for ANSI to take a more active role in coordinating these activities.

A complementary approach, one that is appropriate at the worldwide level, is the involvement of ISO in writing V&V standards. If this were to occur, it would require close coordination between ISO and ANSI. We believe there is also a contribution to be made by organizations such as the US National Institute of Standards and Technology (NIST), and by similar organizations in the European Union, such as NAFEMS and ERCOFTAC. As more organizations become interested in V&V standards, however, there must be significantly improved coordination among the interested parties.

16.6 References

Abanto, J., D. Pelletier, A. Garon, J.-Y. Trepanier, and M. Reggio (2005). Verification of some commercial CFD codes on atypical CFD problems. *43rd AIAA Aerospace Sciences Meeting and Exhibit*, Paper 2005–0682, Reno, NV, AIAA.

ABAQUS (2006). *ABAQUS Benchmarks Manual.* Version 6.6, Providence, RI, ABAQUS Inc.

ANSYS (2005). *ANSYS Verification Manual.* Release 10.0, Canonsburg, PA, ANSYS, Inc.

AWST (2003). Slamming shuttle safety. *Aviation Week & Space Technology*, May 2003, 23.

Casey, M. and T. Wintergerste, eds. (2000). *ERCOFTAC Special Interest Group on Quality and Trust in Industrial CFD: Best Practices Guidelines*, Lausanne Switzerland, European Research Community on Flow, Turbulence, and Combustion.

Chiles, J. (2001). *Inviting Disaster-Lessons from the Edge of Technology.* 1st edn., New York, HarperCollins.

CSNI (2004). *CSNI International Standard Problem Procedures, CSNI Report No. 17 – Revision 4.* NEA/CSNI/R(2004)5, Paris, France, Nuclear Energy Agency, Committee on the Safety of Nuclear Installations.

Dorner, D. (1989). *The Logic of Failure, Recognizing and Avoiding Error in Complex Situations*, Cambridge, MA, Perseus Books.

ERCOFTAC (2000). *Portal to Fluid Dynamics Database Resources.* ercoftac.mech.surrey.ac.uk.

Gehman, H. W., J. L. Barry, D. W. Deal, J. N. Hallock, K. W. Hess, G. S. Hubbard, J. M. Logsdon, D. D. Osheroff, S. K. Ride, R. E. Tetrault, S. A. Turcotte, S. B. Wallace, and S. E. Widnall (2003). *Columbia Accident Investigation Board Report Volume I.* Washington, DC, National Aeronautics and Space Administration, Government Printing Office.

Hemsch, M. (2004). Statistical analysis of computational fluid dynamic solutions from the Drag Prediction Workshop. *Journal of Aircraft.* **41**(1), 95–103.

Hemsch, M. and J. H. Morrison (2004). Statistical analysis of CFD solutions from 2nd Drag Prediction Workshop. *42nd AIAA Aerospace Sciences Meeting and Exhibit*, Reno, NV, American Institute of Aeronautics and Astronautics, 4951–4981.

Hutton, A. G. and M. V. Casey (2001). Quality and trust in industrial CFD – a European perspective. *39th AIAA Aerospace Sciences Meeting*, AIAA Paper 2001–0656, Reno, NV, American Institute of Aeronautics and Astronautics.

Laflin, K. R., S. M. Klausmeyer, T. Zickuhr, J. C. Vassberg, R. A. Wahls, J. H. Morrison, O. P. Brodersen, M. E. Rakowitz, E. N. Tinoco, and J.-L. Godard (2005). Data summary from the second AIAA Computational Fluid Dynamics Drag Prediction Workshop. *Journal of Aircraft.* **42**(5), 1165–1178.

Lawson, D. (2005). *Engineering Disasters – Lessons to be Learned*, New York, ASME Press.

Levy, D. W., T. Zickuhr, R. A. Wahls, S. Pirzadeh, and M. J. Hemsch (2003). Data summary from the first AIAA Computational Fluid Dynamics Drag Prediction Workshop. *Journal of Aircraft.* **40**(5), 875–882.

Mosey, D. (2006). *Reactor Accidents: Institutional Failure in the Nuclear Industry.* 2nd edn., Sidcup, Kent, UK, Nuclear Engineering International.

NAFEMS (2006). NAFEMS Website. www.NAFEMS.org.

NEA (1977). *Loss of Coolant Accident Standard Problems.* Committee on the Safety of Nuclear Installations, Report No. 17, Paris, France, Nuclear Energy Agency.

NPARC (2000). *CFD Verification and Validation: NPARC Alliance*. www.grc.nasa. gov/WWW/wind/valid/homepage.html.

Oberkampf, W. L. and T. G. Trucano (2008). Verification and validation benchmarks. *Nuclear Engineering and Design*. **238**(3), 716–743.

Oberkampf, W. L., T. G. Trucano, and C. Hirsch (2004). Verification, validation, and predictive capability in computational engineering and physics. *Applied Mechanics Reviews*. **57**(5), 345–384.

Petroski, H. (1994). *Design Paradigms: Case Histories of Error and Judgment in Engineering*, Cambridge, UK, Cambridge University Press.

Pohl, R., ed. (2004). *Cognitive Illusion: a Handbook on Fallacies and Biases in Thinking, Judgement and Memory*. New York, Psychology Press.

QNET-CFD (2001). *Thematic Network on Quality and Trust for the Industrial Applications of CFD*. www.qnet-cfd.net.

Reason, J. (1997). *Managing the Risks of Organizational Accidents*, Burlington, VT, Ashgate Publishing Limited.

Rizzi, A. and J. Vos (1998). Toward establishing credibility in computational fluid dynamics simulations. *AIAA Journal*. **36**(5), 668–675.

Roache, P. J. (1998). *Verification and Validation in Computational Science and Engineering*, Albuquerque, NM, Hermosa Publishers.

Rumsey, C. L., S. M. Rivers, and J. H. Morrison (2005). Study of CFD variation on transport configurations for the second Drag-Prediction Workshop. *Computers & Fluids*. **34**(7), 785–816.

Vaughan, D. (1996). *The Challenger Launch Decision: Risky Technology, Culture, and Deviance at NASA*, Chicago, IL, The University of Chicago Press.

Vos, J. B., A. Rizzi, D. Darracq, and E. H. Hirschel (2002). Navier–Stokes solvers in European aircraft design. *Progress in Aerospace Sciences*. **38**(8), 601–697.

Wang, R. Y. and D. M. Strong (1996). Beyond accuracy: what data quality means to data consumers. *Journal of Management Information Systems*. **12**(4), 5–34.

Appendix
Programming practices

Recommended programming practices

The following is a list of recommended programming practices designed to increase the reliability of scientific computing software, along with a brief description of each practice.

Use strongly-typed programming languages

Although there is some ambiguity in the definition, here we refer to a strongly-typed programming language as one which (1) requires that a variable or object maintain the same type (e.g., integer, floating point number, character) during program execution and (2) has strict rules as to which types can be used during operations (i.e., implicit type conversions are not allowed). Common examples of the latter are the use of integer division on floating point numbers and the use real functions (e.g., **cos, log**) on integers. BASIC and C are considered weakly-typed languages, while C^{++}, Java, Fortran, Pascal, and Python are considered strongly-typed. For type information on other programming languages, see en.wikipedia.org/wiki/Template:Type_system_cross_reference_list. A type-safe program can be written in a weakly-typed language by using explicit type conversions (to convert integers to real numbers, real numbers to integers, etc.). In other words, explicit type conversions should be used, even when not required by the programming language.

Use safe programming language subsets

In order to avoid error-prone coding constructs, safe programming language subsets are recommended. An example of a safe subset for the C programming language is Safer C (Hatton, 1995).

Use static analyzers

Hatton (1997) estimates that approximately 40% of all software failures are due to static faults which are readily found with the use of static analyzers (see Chapter 4).

Use long, descriptive identifiers

Most modern programming languages allow long, descriptive names to be used for variables, objects, functions, subroutines, etc. The extra time spent typing in these longer names will be more than made up by the reduction in time spent figuring out what a variable contains or what a routine does.

Write self-commenting code

The good software developer will endeavor to write code in such a way that the coding itself clearly explains its purpose (Eddins, 2006). This is certainly aided by the use of descriptive identifiers as discussed above. While the use of comments is still a subject of debate, an extreme example where 100 lines of comments are needed to explain the workings of 10 lines of executable source code suggest that the code is not well written.

Use private data

Accidental over-writing of data can be minimized through the use of private data, where data is made available only to those objects and routines that need to process it. Both C++ and Fortran 90/95 allow for the use of private data, the latter through the use of `Public` and `Private` attributes within modules.

Use exception handling

Exceptions can occur due to internal conditions (e.g., division by zero, overflow) or external factors (e.g., insufficient memory available, input file does not exist). Exception handling can be as simple as letting the user know the local state of the system and the location where the exception occurred, or it could transfer control to a separate exception-handling code. Some programming languages such as Java and C++ have built-in exception-handling constructs.

Use indentation for readability

Indent the coding blocks to denote different levels of looping structures and logical constructs to make them more readable. An example of an indented Fortran 95 code construct is given below.

```
if(mms == 0) then
  !Set standard boundary conditions
  Call Set_Boundary_Conditions
elseif(mms == 1) then
  !Calculate exact solution for temperature
```

```
do j = 1, jmax
do i = 1, imax
Temperature_MMS(i,j) = MMS_Exact_Solution(x,y)
enddo
enddo
!Set MMS boundary conditions
Call Set_MMS_Boundary_Conditions
else
!Check for invalid values of variable mms
write(*,*) 'Error: mms must equal 0 or 1 !!!'
Error_Flag = 1
endif
```

Use module procedures (Fortran only)

The use of module procedures (functions and subroutines) in Fortran rather than standard procedures provides an explicit interface between the procedure and its calling program. Thus interface consistency can be checked and interface errors can be found during code compilation rather than at run time.

Error-prone programming constructs

Although allowed in certain programming languages, the following programming constructs are known to be error prone and should be avoided when possible.

Implicit type definitions

Implicit variable type definitions, where new variables can be introduced in a program without a corresponding type specification, should be avoided. For the Fortran programming language, this means that `'Implicit None'` should appear at the beginning of every routine.

Mixed-mode arithmetic

With the exception of exponentiation, integer and real variables should not be used in a single expression. When they do occur together, explicit type conversions (e.g., real to integer or integer to real) should be used.

Duplicate code

When the same coding construct appears multiple times in a program, it is a good indication that the piece of coding should be replaced with a function or subroutine. Duplicate code can make software development tedious since a modification to one instance requires the developer to also search out all other instances of the repeated code. Eddins (2006) cautions that "anything repeated in two or more places will eventually be wrong in at least one."

Equality checks for floating point numbers

Since floating point (real) numbers are subject to machine round-off errors, equality comparisons between them should be avoided. For example, instead of checking for equality between the floating point numbers A and B, one could instead check to see if the absolute value of $(A - B)$ is less than a specified tolerance.

Recursion

Recursion occurs when a component calls itself, either directly or indirectly. A recursive programming construct can be difficult to analyze, and errors in a recursive program can lead to the allocation of a system's entire available memory (Sommerville, 2004).

Pointers

A pointer is a programming construct that contains the address of a direct location in machine memory (Sommerville, 2004). The use of pointers should be avoided since pointer errors can cause unexpected program behavior (e.g., see aliasing below), can be extremely difficult to find and correct, and can be inefficient for scientific computing codes.

Aliasing

Aliasing "occurs when more than one name is used to refer to the same entity in a program" (Sommerville, 2004) and should be avoided.

Inheritance

Inheritance occurs when an object "inherits" some characteristics from another object. Objects that employ inheritance are more difficult to understand since their defining characteristics are located in multiple locations in the program.

GOTO statements

GOTO statements should be avoided as they make the program difficult to follow, often resulting in a complex and tangled control structure (i.e., "spaghetti" code).

Parallelism

Although the use of parallel processing in large scientific computing applications is usually unavoidable, the developer should be aware of the potential for unexpected behavior due to timing interactions between processes. Accounting for parallelism during the initial architectural design can result in more reliable software as compared to the case where parallelism is added after the serial version of the software is developed. In general, these issues cannot be detected with static analysis and may be platform dependent.

References

Eddins, S. (2006). Taking control of your code: essential software development tools for engineers, *International Conference on Image Processing*, Atlanta, GA, Oct. 9, (see blogs.mathworks.com/images/steve/92/handout_final_icip2006.pdf).

Hatton, L. (1995). *Safer C: Developing Software for High-Integrity and Safety-Critical Systems*, McGraw-Hill International Ltd., UK.

Hatton, L. (1997). Software failures: follies and fallacies, *IEEE Review*, March, 49–52.

Sommerville, I. (2004). *Software Engineering*, 7th edn., Harlow, Essex, England, Pearson Education Ltd.

Index

Printed in the United States
By Bookmasters